THE COLLECTED LETTERS OF
C. S. LEWIS

VOLUME I

BOOKS BY C. S. LEWIS

AVAILABLE FROM HARPERSANFRANCISCO
Mere Christianity
Mere Christianity Journal
The Screwtape Letters (with "Screwtape Proposes a Toast")
Miracles
The Abolition of Man
The Great Divorce
The Problem of Pain
The Weight of Glory
A Grief Observed
George MacDonald: An Anthology
A Year With C. S. Lewis
The Collected Letters of C. S. Lewis Volume II

ALSO AVAILABLE FROM HARPERCOLLINS
The Chronicles of Narnia:
The Magician's Nephew
The Lion, the Witch and the Wardrobe
The Horse and His Boy
Prince Caspian
The Voyage of the Dawn Treader
The Silver Chair
The Last Battle

THE COLLECTED LETTERS OF
C. S. LEWIS

—————— VOLUME I ——————

Family Letters 1905–1931

EDITED BY WALTER HOOPER

HarperSanFrancisco

A Division of HarperCollins*Publishers*

On the cover: Background C. S. Lewis handwriting image supplied by the Marion E. Wade Center, Wheaton College, Wheaton, IL.

THE COLLECTED LETTERS OF C. S. LEWIS, VOLUME I: *Family Letters 1905–1931*. Copyright © 2004 by C. S. Lewis Pte Ltd. All rights reserved. Printed in the United States of America. No part of this book may be used or reproduced in any manner whatsoever without written permission except in the case of brief quotations embodied in critical articles and reviews. For information address HarperCollins Publishers, Inc., 10 East 53rd Street, New York, NY 10022.

HarperCollins books may be purchased for educational, business, or sales promotional use. For information please write: Special Markets Department, HarperCollins Publishers, Inc., 10 East 53rd Street, New York, NY 10022.

HarperCollins Web site: http://www.harpercollins.com

HarperCollins®, 📖 ®, and HarperSanFrancisco™ are trademarks of Harper-Collins Publishers, Inc.

FIRST EDITION

Library of Congress Cataloging-in-Publication Data is available upon request.

ISBN 0–06–072763–2

04 05 06 07 08 RRD(H) 10 9 8 7 6 5 4 3 2 1

CONTENTS

PREFACE

'A heavy responsibility rests on those who forage through a dead man's correspondence and publish it indiscriminately.' Thus C. S. Lewis wrote to his father, Albert Lewis, on 5 June 1926 about *The Letters of Sir Walter Raleigh* which both were reading. Sir Walter Raleigh (1861–1922), whom Lewis had known, was the first Professor of English at Oxford (1904).

'The funny thing,' Lewis went on to say, is that Raleigh's 'views on the things of the spirit ... are not really in opposition to the atmosphere of Christianity. Whatever he thought about the historical side of it, he must have known...that the religious view, whether literally true or not, was at any rate much more *like* the reality than the views of the scientists and rationalists.'

It is surprising to find C. S. Lewis – the *clearest* of writers – attempting to create vagueness by his use of the phrases 'not really', 'the religious view' and 'the historical side'. He was 28 and had been a Fellow of Magdalen College for nine months. But since he ceased to believe in Christianity at the age of 14, he had been hiding his atheism from his father. In trying to make Raleigh's beliefs appear more orthodox than they were, 'Jack', as he was known to his friends, may have expressed the anxiety he felt about his father discovering *his* unbelief.

Only three years later, 1929, Albert Lewis died. Shortly before his father's death Jack converted to theism, a change that did much to unite his private beliefs with his public face. Then two years after this came the step which did away with the need for subterfuge altogether. On 28 September 1931 Jack was taken to Whipsnade Zoo in his brother's sidecar. 'When we set out,' he later said in *Surprised by Joy*, 'I did not believe that Jesus Christ is the Son of God, and when we reached the zoo I did. Yet I had not exactly spent the journey in thought. Nor in great emotion. "Emotional" is perhaps the last word we can apply to some of the most important events. It was more like when a man, after long sleep, still lying motionless in bed, becomes aware that he is now awake.'

Family Letters is the first of what is to be a three-volume collection of C. S. Lewis's letters. It covers the period November 1905 to 18 October

1931, from the first letter we have of Lewis's, written when he was seven, up to his acceptance of Christianity as true. To prevent the book from being too long it was necessary to leave out a few letters, but the volume contains about 95 per cent of the letters from that period. Many of the letters I have omitted were weekly 'regulation' letters from Jack to his father from his various schools. I have also left out certain letters to Owen Barfield and Cecil Harwood. In these Lewis was primarily arguing philosophical points or criticizing his correspondents' poetry. It was thought these letters would be of comparatively marginal interest to most people or of relatively small significance in the larger story.

When Albert Lewis died, Jack and his brother Warren, or 'Warnie', found their father had preserved masses of family papers going back to 1850. The papers were moved to Oxford, and Warnie spent much of 1933 to 1935 copying them. He undertook this enormous task using the hunt-and-peck system on his little Royal typewriter. Both brothers added valuable editorial notes along the way, and the papers were bound into 11 volumes entitled 'Memoirs of the Lewis Family: 1850–1930', now widely referred to as the 'Lewis Papers'. The original of the Lewis Papers is in the Marion E. Wade Center at Wheaton College in Illinois, with microfilms in the Bodleian Library, Oxford, and the Southern Historical Collection at the University of North Carolina at Chapel Hill. Any dubious spelling or dating in the Lewis Papers is impossible to check against the original manuscripts. When Roger Lancelyn Green and I borrowed the Lewis Papers for help in writing *C. S. Lewis: A Biography*, Warnie urged us (letter of 1 April 1967) to 'take the greatest care of them – for there is only this one copy in existence, and the originals from which all material was drawn were burnt by Jack in 1936'. It is unlikely that Lewis would have thought publishing letters from this collection an 'indiscriminate' use because he helped to assemble them.

The Lewis Papers came into use when Warnie wished to commemorate his brother after Jack's death in 1963. 'I intend to see what sort of a hand I make at a "Life and Letters" of dear Jack,' he wrote to me on 8 February 1964. 'Not exactly a L. & L. in the usual sense, for of course I shall not use anything he has himself told us in *Surprised by Joy*. It will be more what the French 17th Cent. writers used to call *Mémoires pour servir* etc.' That book eventually became *Letters of C. S. Lewis*, edited, with a Memoir by W. H. Lewis (1964). However, because Warnie originally set out to write a biography, not edit a volume of letters, he restricted his brother's letters to what are, in effect, quotations. None of the family letters quoted in *Letters of C. S. Lewis* is complete. I hope those who enjoyed reading fragments of Lewis's letters to his father and brother in the 1966 *Letters* and the Enlarged Edition of 1988 will be pleased to find them here in their entirety.

While the volume includes letters to Owen Barfield and other friends he met at Oxford, most were written to Albert Lewis, Warnie and his boyhood friend Arthur Greeves. Some of the best of those he wrote to Warnie arose out of Warnie's long stay in South Africa with the Army Service Corps. He knew Warnie would be lonely so far away and that he found letters companionable. 'As we talk a good deal of odd fragments out of books when we are together,' Jack wrote to him in March 1921, 'there's no reason why we should not reproduce the same sort of tittle-tattle. Perhaps one of the reasons why letters are so hard to write and so much harder to read is that people confine themselves to news – in other words think nothing worth writing except that which would not be worth saying.'

The letters to his father are by no means all *news*, but they differ from the ones to Warnie and Arthur in being more or less obligatory reports from his various schools. There are times when news is very interesting too, and on occasions we find Jack begging his father for precisely that, *news*. One of the turning points in this volume comes soon after 1925 when his ideas *are* the news. Jack, now a don at Magdalen College, writes to his father as an independent young man and we see that seminal work of literary history, *The Allegory of Love*, taking shape before our eyes.

Jack Lewis was later to regret that he was so cavalier about dating his early correspondence, and my guess is that it was Albert Lewis who preserved the postmarks of many of his son's letters. This helped Warnie when arranging them in the Lewis Papers. Sometimes he did not even have a postmark to guide him, and in some instances where he failed I had the advantage of comparing the family letters to those written to Arthur Greeves, and vice versa. In one of the many undated letters to his father (2? April 1919), Jack said, 'Did you see the "very insolent" review of me on the back page of the Times Literary Supplement last week?' I found the review in *The Times Literary Supplement* of 27 March 1919, and we are able to see almost exactly where the letter fits.

The letters to Arthur Greeves were published in 1979 as *They Stand Together: The Letters of C. S. Lewis to Arthur Greeves (1914–1963)*, a book which has been out of print many years. The originals of all the Greeves letters in *Family Letters* are in Wheaton College, with copies in the Bodleian. Jack described Arthur as his 'First Friend'. 'I had been so far from thinking such a friend possible,' he said of him in *Surprised by Joy*, 'that I had never even longed for one; no more than I longed to be King of England.' The letters to Arthur are exactly the balance needed for those Jack wrote to his father, not merely because they were young men of the same age with similar interests, but because Arthur was his confidant. The only clear statement we have about Lewis's religious beliefs as a teenager was made to Arthur in October 1916. 'All religions, that is, all mythologies to give them their proper name,' he wrote on 12 October 1916, 'are merely man's own invention.' And when, following the death of his father, he began to look at Christianity, and himself, in a new light, he confided in Arthur. 'You are my only real Father Confessor', he said.

And it was to Arthur that Jack confided his teenage sexual fantasies beginning with the letter of 28 January 1917. Years later, when he re-read the letters in which this subject is mentioned, he told Arthur (1 October 1931): 'I am now inclined to agree with you in *not* regretting that we confided in each other even on this subject, because it has done no harm in the long run – and how could young adolescents really be friends without it?' Before his death, Arthur, as an old man, sought to make his friend's letters more respectable by scribbling over those passages in which this particular excess of youth had appeared. In deciding what to do about this, I came to the conclusion that if I omitted these passages, but retained the letter of 30 January 1930 in which Lewis accuses himself of the deadly sin of Pride, I would be treating the teenage lusts of the flesh with a seriousness they don't deserve. My solution in this volume is the same one I used when the letters were first published in 1979. The passages which Arthur, for whatever reason, scribbled through are found in brackets shaped like this – < >.

I should include an Editorial Note at this point. We have none of the letters Arthur wrote to Jack during the years covered in this book, but it is clear Arthur was always pleading with Jack to put dates on his letters. Jack rarely complied, and as a result the letters to Arthur were harder to date than the ones to his father. As I explained in the Editor's Note I wrote for *They Stand Together*, I used various methods of dating, including comparing the various nibs Jack used in composing the letters. Lewis almost always wrote with an old-fashioned nib pen that is dipped into an inkwell as one writes. Each nib writes slightly differently and it is possible to see which letters were written with which nib. It is not a method to condemn. When Lewis dictated letters to me, he always had me read them aloud afterwards. He told me that in writing letters, as well as books, he always 'whispered the words aloud'. Pausing to dip the pen in an inkwell provided exactly the rhythm needed. 'It's as important to please the *ear*,' he said, 'as it is the eye.'

What Lewis was not concerned with was how the page looked. He preferred to save paper, and most of his letters were not divided into paragraphs. I have taken the liberty of introducing paragraphs, with the result, I hope, that Lewis's clearly ordered ideas stand out and are more enjoyable to read. I have tried throughout to preserve Lewis's spelling. This was easy when transcribing from the original letters to Arthur, but I suspect that Warnie silently corrected some of his brother's frequent misspellings.

Following the name of every person to whom a letter is addressed I have indicated where the reader might consult the original letter, if there is one, or where in the Lewis Papers he will find the copy used in this book. Thus 'To his Father (LP III: 82)' means 'Lewis Papers, Volume III, page 82'. In the case of the letters to Arthur Greeves the reader will notice that sometimes I refer to letters being in both Wheaton and the Lewis Papers (e.g. W/LP). This means that the original, from which the Lewis Papers version was copied, is now in Wheaton. Jack borrowed many of his letters from Arthur so Warnie could include them in the Lewis Papers. I am not sure what happened, but those dated 1 and 8 February 1916 and those which run from 7 March 1916 to 27 September 1916 seem to have got lost because these only exist as copies in the Lewis Papers. The initial 'B' means the original is in the Bodleian, and 'P' means it is in a private collection. It should not be difficult to consult the letters on either side of the Atlantic because the Bodleian and the Wade Center have a reciprocal arrangement which means each has copies of what the other has. Thus, those letters cited as in 'W' (Wade Center), such as the Barfield letters, may also be consulted in 'B' (Bodleian).

Nearly all the letters in this volume were written to people so important in Lewis's life that I did not feel it would be enough to identify them with a mere footnote. The solution was to include short biographies in a Biographical Appendix.

I hope my friends will be as satisfied as I am by the appearance of this volume for I have been tireless in seeking their knowledge and advice. I wish to thank in particular Dr A. T. Reyes, Professor James Como, Father Seán Finnegan, Professor Emrys Jones, Dr Barbara Everett, Madame Eliane Tixier, Professor G. B. Tennyson, Dr Stephen Logan, Miss Priscilla Tolkien, The Rt Hon. David Bleakley MP, Michael Ward, Andrew Cuneo, Edward Nelson, Jonathan Brewer, Paul Tankard, Edward De Rivera, Fr Jerome Bertram, Brother Alexander Master and the Fathers and Brothers of the Oxford Oratory.

No editor could have been served so well by his publishers as I have been. I am very grateful to Kathy Dyke, managing editor of

HarperCollins*Religious*, for guiding the book through to press, and to many others. My thanks to all concerned.

Walter Hooper
27 March 1999
Oxford

ABBREVIATIONS

AMR = *All My Road Before Me: The Diary of C. S. Lewis 1922–1927*, edited by Walter Hooper (1991).

BF = *Brothers and Friends: The Diaries of Major Warren Hamilton Lewis*, edited by Clyde S. Kilby and Marjorie Lamp Mead (1982).

CG = Walter Hooper, *C. S. Lewis: A Companion and Guide* (1996).

LP = unpublished 'Lewis Papers' or 'Memoirs of the Lewis Family: 1850–1930' in 11 volumes.

'Memoir' = Memoir by W. H. Lewis contained in *Letters of C. S. Lewis*, edited with a Memoir by W. H. Lewis (1966), and reprinted in *Letters of C. S. Lewis*, edited with a Memoir by W. H. Lewis, revised and enlarged edition, edited by Walter Hooper (1988).

SBJ = C. S. Lewis, *Surprised by Joy: The Shape of My Early Life* (1955).

1905–1910

―――――― ❧ ――――――

*T*he Lewises were a happy family. Albert Lewis[1] had prospered as a
police court solicitor, and on 18 April 1905 the family moved from the
semi-detached Dundela Villas, where Warnie and Jack were born, into a
house Albert had specially built for his wife, Flora.[2] This was 'Little Lea', one
of the new 'big houses' of Strandtown, a lovely area of Belfast. Outside, the
family looked over wide fields to Belfast Lough, and across the Lough to the
mountains of the Antrim shore.

Albert and Flora, like most Anglo-Irish parents, wanted their children
to be educated in English public schools, and on 10 May 1905 Flora took
Warnie,[3] who was eight, across the water to Wynyard School in Watford,
Hertfordshire. In complete innocence she was delivering her son into the
hands of a madman. The headmaster, Robert Capron or 'Oldie' as the boys
called him,[4] 'lived in a solitude of power,' Jack was later to write, 'like a sea-
captain in the days of sail' (SBJ II). In two years' time he would have a
High Court action taken against him for cruelty. For the time being Warnie
joined the dwindling band of some dozen boys who lived in the pair of
semi-detached houses which made up Wynyard School.

Meanwhile, Jack was tutored at home, his mother teaching him French
and Latin and his governess, Annie Harper,[5] teaching him everything else.
He was almost eight when he wrote this first letter to Warnie:

---

1 See **Albert James Lewis** in the Biographical Appendix.
2 See **Florence Augusta 'Flora' Lewis** in the Biographical Appendix.
3 See **Warren Hamilton 'Warnie' Lewis** in the Biographical Appendix.
4 See **Robert Capron** in the Biographical Appendix.
5 Miss Annie Harper was governess to the Lewis boys from 1898 to 1908.

TO HIS BROTHER (LP III: 63):

Little Lea.
Strandtown.
[c. November 1905]

My dear Warnie

Peter[6] has had two un-fortunate aventures since I last wrote, however they came out all right in the end. No. 1, Maude[7] was in her room (*up there* remember) heard *Peter howling*. When she came down, what do you think? sitting on the floor ready to spring on Peter was a big *black cat*. Maude chased it for a long way. I was not able to help matters because I was out on my bych.

The next adventure was not so starling, never the-less it is worth while relating that a mouse got into his cage.

Tim[8] got the *head staggers* the other day while running on the lawn, he suddenly lay down and began to kick and foam at the mouth and shudder.

On Halow-een we had great [fun?] and had fireworks; rockets, and catterine wheels, squbes, and a kind of thing that you lit and twirled and then they made *stars*. We hung up an apple and bit at it we got Grand-father[9] down to watch and he tried to bite. Maud got the ring out of the barn-brach and we had apple dumpling with in it a button a ring and a 3 penny bit. Martha got the button, Maude got nothing, and I got the ring and the 3 pence all in one bite. We got some leaves off the road the other day, that is to say the roadmen gave us some that they had got off the road, in fact they wanted them because they make good manure. I am doing french as well as latin now, and I think I like the latin better. Tomorrow I decline that old 'Bonus,' 'Bona,' 'Bonum' thing, but I think it is very hard (not now of course but it was).

Diabolos are all the go here, evrrey body has one except us, I don't

---

6 Jack's canary.

7 Maude and Martha were housemaids at Little Lea.

8 Tim was the family dog of whom Lewis said in *SBJ* X: 'He may hold a record for longevity among Irish terriers since he was already with us when I was at Oldie's [1908–10] and did not die till 1922...Poor Tim, though I loved him, was the most undisciplined, unaccomplished, and dissipated-looking creature that ever went on four legs. He never exactly obeyed you; he sometimes agreed with you.'

9 Grandfather was Richard Lewis (1832–1908), the father of Albert. See **The Lewis Family** in the Biographical Appendix.

think the Lewis temper would hold out do you? Jackie Calwell has one and can do it beautifully (wish I could)

your loving
brother Jacks

TO HIS BROTHER (LP III: 75–6):

Little Lea.
Strandtown.
[c. 1906]

My dear Warnie

I am sorry that I did not write to you before. At present Boxen is *slightly* convulsed.[10] The news has just reached her that King Bunny is a prisoner. The colonists (who are of course the war party) are in a bad way: they dare scarcely leave their houses because of the mobs. In Tararo the Prussians and Boxonians are at fearful odds against each other and the natives.

Such were the states of affairs recently: but the able general Quicksteppe is taking steps for the rescue of King Bunny. (the news somewhat pacified the rioters.)

your loving
brother Jacks.

TO HIS BROTHER (LP III: 79):

Little Lea.
Strandtown.
18 May 1907

My dear Warnie,

Tommy is very well thank you. We have got the telephone in to our house. Is Bennett beter again, as he has been ill you see that you are not the onley boy who stayes at home.

We have nearly seteld that we are going to france this summer, all though I do not like that country I think I shall like the trip, wont you. I liked the card you sent me, I have put it in the album. I was talking to the

---

10 Boxen was a world invented by Jack and Warnie a year or so before this time, and about which Jack was to write many stories and histories involving the characters mentioned here – King Bunny, General Quicksteppe and others. Much of this juvenilia has been published as *Boxen: The Imaginary World of the Young C.S. Lewis*, ed. Walter Hooper (1985).

Greaves through the telephone I wanted Arthur but he was out and I onley got Thom.[11]

I am sorry I can't give you any news about Nearo, but I have not got anny to give. The grass in the front is coming up nicely. It is fearfully hot here. I have got an adia, you know the play I was writing. I think we will try and act it with new stage don't say annything about it not being dark we will have it up stairs and draw the thick curtains and the wight ones, the scenery is rather hard, but still I think we shall do it.

your loving
brother Jacks

TO HIS BROTHER (LP III: 80):

Little Lea.
Strandtown.
[August 1907?]

My dear Warnie
Thank you very much for the post-cards I liked them, the herald was the nicest I think, dont you. Now that I have finished the play I am thinking of writeing a History of Mouse-land and I have even gon so far as to make up some of it, this is what I have made up.

Mouse-land had a very long stone-age during which time no great things tooke place it lasted from 55 BC to 1212 and then king Bublich I began to reign, he was not a good king but he fought gainest yellow land. Bub II his son fought indai about the lantern act, died 1377 king Bunny came next.[12]

Your loving
brother Jacks

---

11 See the Biographical Appendix for **Joseph Arthur Greeves**, a boy who lived across the road from the Lewises.
12 This 'History of Mouse-Land' is found in *Boxen*, op. cit., pp. 39–41.

TO HIS FATHER (LP III: 82):

[Pension Petit-Vallon,
Berneval,
Près Dieppe]
4th Sept. '07.[13]

My dear Papy,

excuse this post-card being so dirty, but in our rooms everything is so dusty. It is still lovely weather still. I was sick and had to go to bed but am quite beter now. I hope you are all right. Are Tommy and Peter all right?

your loving son,
Jacks.

TO HIS BROTHER (LP III: 105):

Tigh-na-mara,
Larne Harbour,
Co. Antrim.
[May 1908][14]

My dear Warnie

how are you geting on. Mamy is doing very well indeed. I am sending you a picture of the 'Lord Big',[15] I forgot until it was too late that she was screw not paddle, but of course there might be 2 boats in the same line that have one name. Did I tell you about going to chains memorial?[16] It is a funny old place, one thing that struck me was the thickness of the walls. The light (as I suppose you know) is worked by gas, while I was there the man broct two mantles. Did you get my letters? one of them had a home drawn post card on it, I got yours and now I had beter stop, as there is nothing to say.

your loving brother,
Jacks

---

13 This was to be the last holiday Jack and Warnie took with their mother. They travelled to London, and from there they went on to Berneval in France, where they were on holiday from 20 August until 18 September.

14 Jack was here on holiday with his mother.

15 Lord Big, a frog, is the most memorable of the Boxen characters.

16 Warnie Lewis wrote: '"chains memorial" is a lighthouse at the entrance to Larne Harbour, erected to the memory of James Chaine, a prominent local landowner; he is buried in an upright position, in unconsecrated ground, overlooking the harbour' (LP III: 105).

Flora Lewis had been ill for months and an operation on 15 February revealed she had cancer. The following month she seemed better, but during this period of uncertainty Albert Lewis's father died on 24 March. The last letter from Flora Lewis in the Lewis Papers was written to Warnie on 15 June 1908. 'I am sorry not to have been able to write to you regularly this term,' she said, 'but I find I am really not well enough to do so. I have been feeling very poorly lately and writing tires me very much. But I must write today to wish you a happy birthday' (LP III: 106). Flora was very ill, and the impending tragedy at Little Lea resulted in Warnie being brought home at the end of June. Following another operation, she died at home on Albert's forty-fifth birthday, 23 August 1908. The following month Jack accompanied his brother to Wynyard School in Watford, and the next letter is the first Jack wrote to his father after his arrival there.

TO HIS FATHER (LP III: 140):

> [Wynyard School,
> Watford,
> Hertfordshire
> 19? September 1908]

My dear Papy,

I suppose you got our telgy-graph to say that we were all right.

It was rather rough crossing, poor Warnie was very sea sick, I was sick once. Unfortunately Warnie was sick again in the train, also the breakfast car was so full that we could not get anything to eat till a long way after Crewe, we were both very hungry but when at last it came Warnie could not eat any worth talking about. When we arrived at Euston we saw both our trunks and plaboxs, the side of mine was dinged in. When we got to Watford the play-boxs were missing, evedently (though Warnie gave him 3d.) the porter had omitted to put them in at Euston. The railways officials think they can find them.

I cannot of course tell you yet but I think I shall like this place. Misis Capron and the Miss Caprons are very nice and I think I will be able to get on with Mr. Capron though to tell the truth he is rather eccentric.[17]

---

17 Robert Capron was assisted in his teaching by all the members of the family, his wife Ellen Barnes Capron (1849–1909), his son Wynyard Capron (1883–1959), and his three daughters, Norah, Dorothy and Eva. See **Robert Capron** in the Biographical Appendix.

Anything we want Warnie is telling you about in his letter.

your loving son,

Jacksie

TO HIS FATHER (LP III: 147):

[Wynyard School]
Postmark: 29 September 1908

My dear Papy

Mr. Capron said some-thing I am not likely to forget 'curse the boy' (behind Warnie's back) because Warnie did not bring his jam in to tea, no one ever heard such a rule before.

Please may we not leave on Saturday? We simply *cannot* wait in this hole till the end of term.

your loving
son Jack

TO HIS FATHER (LP III: 149):

[Wynyard School]
Postmark: 3 October 1908

My dear Papy

We are getting on much better since Aunt Any's visit.[18] We went up to the Franco-British exhibition and enjoyed it very much, but I suppose Aunt Any has told you all about it.

Warnie was just a little sick last night and had to go to bed early and take 2 pills, he is quite well today but did not go to church. I do not like church here at all because it is so frightfully high church that it might as well be Roman Catholic.

You must excuse me writing a long letter as I have a lot of people to write.

your loving
son Jacks

---

18 Annie Sargent Harley Hamilton (1866–1930) was the wife of Flora's brother, Augustus 'Gussie' Hamilton, who undertook much of the care of Jack and Warnie following their mother's death. A Canadian by birth, she married Augustus Hamilton in 1897, and was thereafter Flora's best friend. Lewis said of her in *SBJ* III: 'In her I found what I liked best – an unfailing, kindly welcome without a hint of sentimentality, unruffled good sense, the unobtrusive talent for making all things at all times as cheerful and comfortable as circumstances allowed. What one could not have one did without and made the best of it. The tendency of the Lewises to reopen wounds and to rouse sleeping dogs was unknown to her as to her husband.'

The contrast between what was said of the church the boys of Wynyard attended – St John's Church, Watford – and what it meant in retrospect is very great. In a little diary kept at Wynyard and dated November 1909, Jack said:

> *We...marched to church in a dismal column. We were obliged to go to St John's, a church which wanted to be Roman Catholic, but was afraid to say so. A kind of church abhorred by respectful Irish Protestants. Here Wyn Capron, the son of our Head Master, preached a sermon better than his usual ones. In this abominable place of Romish hypocrites and English liars, the people cross themselves, bow to the Lord's Table (which they have the vanity to call an altar), and pray to the Virgin. (LP III: 194)*

Recalling it some years later in SBJ II, he said:

> *I have not yet mentioned the most important thing that befell me at [Wynyard]. There first I became an effective believer. As far as I know, the instrument was the church to which we were taken twice every Sunday. This was high 'Anglo-Catholic.' On the conscious level I reacted strongly against its peculiarities – was I not an Ulster Protestant, and were not these unfamiliar rituals an essential part of the hated English atmosphere? Unconsciously, I suspect, the candles and incense, the vestments and the hymns sung on our knees, may have had a considerable, and opposite, effect on me...What really mattered was that here I heard the doctrines of Christianity (as distinct from general 'uplift') taught by men who obviously believed them.*

TO HIS FATHER (LP III: 151):

[Wynyard School]
Postmark: 25 October 1908

My dear Papy,

Did you get my letter? Is Maud still with you, I hope so. How is your back?

I am very sorry you are so much annoyed at Mr. Capron's letter, but it is quite untrue, Warnie is not lazy.[19] How is Ant Any? And now you must excuse me writing such a short letter, but as every day is the same as the last I have little or nothing to say.

your loving

son

Jacks

TO HIS FATHER (LP III: 154):

[Wynyard School]
Postmark: 22 November 1908

My dear Papy,

There are only 3 more Sundays this term, next one is my birthday. The term brakes up on 17th Thursday. How is your back? We have thought of a splendid new idea; a book club, it is going to be started next term, Warnie is going to get the Pearson's, and I the Strand. Field is getting the Captain.[20]

I find school very nice but it is frightfully monotenis.

with love

from

Jacks

TO HIS FATHER (LP III: 155):

[Wynyard School
27? November 1908]

My dear Papy,

How are you feeling? As to what you say about leaving I cannot know quite what to say, Warnie does not particularly want to, he says it look like being beaten in the fight.

---

19 On 22 October, Mr Capron wrote to Albert Lewis saying: 'Not only is Clive an exceptionally bright, intelligent, and most lovable little boy, but he is also very keen and eager to learn. Would that I could write to you in the same strain of Warren! Ever averse to effort, physical and mental, he grows worse, and I am almost driven to regard his indolence in the light of a disease' (LP III: 150).

20 These were three magazines for boys. *Pearsons Magazine* ran from 1903 to 1936; *The Strand Magazine* was an illustrated monthly which aimed at 'cheap, healthful literature' in the form of stories and articles – Arthur Conan Doyle's *Adventures of Sherlock Holmes* was among its first serials – and ran from 1891 to 1950; *The Captain*, another magazine for boys, ran from 1899 to 1924.

In spight of all that has happened I like Mr. Capron very much indeed. Have you still got Maud? How are they all down at Sandycroft? Give Joey my love and tell him I will write to him as soon as I have time.[21]

Your loving
son Jacks

TO HIS FATHER (LP III: 173):

[Wynyard School]
Postmark: 21 February 1909

My dear Papy,

According to certain authorities this is half term Sunday, others are inclined to think it will fall sometime during the week. But almost everyone is unanimous on the fact that next Sunday will be well over half term.

This week many things of interest are happening here, according to rumour, Peckover, Reis, and a few others are going soon. Peckover we know is for certain, we being in close privy confidence with him. Between us and the other boys great changes are taking place; a secret society got up by 'Squivy' included everyone but us. However Peckover (who has up till now been Squivy's chum) does not seem to think that Squivy is the best of friends, so he more or less sided with us in preference. He contrived to make Jeyes and Bowser assume an aspect of friendship towards us, and enmity towards Squivy. So Squivy and his toady Mears remain together, under the blissful delusion that they are still popular, and in the case of a row would be staunchly supported by every boarder but us. I am delighted to observe Squivy's popularity and power gradually disappearing. Peckover is leaving because Mr. Capron gives him such a bad time of it here (assisted by Wyn), and in reality, Peckover has been shamefully handled. John Burnett is leaving for a similar reason. Reis (being a day boy, and a nasty one at that), I have not bothered to look into his case.

---

21 'Sandycroft' was the Belfast home of Albert's brother, Joseph Lewis (1856–1908) who died on 3 September 1908. He was a marine consulting engineer. In 1880 he married Mary Tegart, and they had five children, of which Joseph or 'Joey' (1898–1969) was at this time Jack's best friend. See **The Lewis Family** in the Biographical Appendix.

I may mention that the day boys have taken no part in what I am telling about Squivy.

Thanks for the '1st men in the moon',[22] I have already finished it and enjoyed it very much. Is Aunt Annie any better, please tell me all about her, and *your* back in the next letter you write.

your loving
son Jacks

P.S. Peckover begs me to tell you not to tell anything about what I've told you.

J.

TO HIS FATHER (LP III: 175):

[Wynyard School
28 February 1909]

My dear Papy,

Thank you very much for the note paper. Did you get the letter I wrote on Friday (at least I think it was Friday) night? A rather amusing incident occurred yesterday afternoon. We went for a walk in the afternoon and those day boys who wished, came with us too. And it so happened that Poppy, the brother of John, and Boivie (the sociable Swede) came with us. Now Boivie is a Swede, and therefore a good old northerner, and like us, hates anything that savours of the south of England: so I mentioned in the course of our conversation how intensely I hated the churches down here: 'There're so high' said I. 'Oh, yes', replied Boivie 'the ones in Denmark are much nicer, look there (pointing to a church across the road) look how high the steeple is'. And he didn't mean it as a joke either.

Now as there is not much news I must stop.

your loving
son Jacks

On 28 July 1909 Warnie won his release from Wynyard School, and on 16 September he arrived in Malvern, Worcestershire, to begin his first term at Malvern College.

---

22 H.G. Wells, *The First Men in the Moon* (1901).

TO HIS FATHER (LP III: 185–6):

[Wynyard School]
Postmark: 19 September 1909

My dear Papy,

I arrived safely (as you heard in the telegraph), after a pleasant journey. Oldy met me at Euston as you said, but as his train was late, he was not at my platform. However, I got my luggage attended to all right, and met him on the Watford platform. Euston is not nearly so muddling as I thought, and coming back to here next term I don't think Oldy need meet me here.

I am sorry to say that there are no new boys this term, but there is a rumour that Oldy is going to have a private pupil (whatever that may mean) later on. He is over sixteen and stands 6 ft. 2., according to Oldy, but then I don't believe that.

There are thirteen weeks this term, which sounds a lot, but it will soon go past, at least I hope so.

Have you heard any more from Warnie, and if so how is the old chap getting on? I hope to send an epistle to him today. I have not seen the day boys yet, as school does not begin in earnest until tomorrow morning. 'And now as the time alloted for correspondance is drawing to a close' etc. But now I must stop, with love and good wishes,

yours loving son,
Jack

P.S. Don't forget to write very plainly in your letter which I am expecting tomorrow.

TO HIS FATHER (LP III: 195–6):

[Wynyard School
16? December 1909]

My dear Papy,

This time next week I will be at home with you. Isn't it just splendid? One of the causes of writing this letter to you is to remind you to send the journey-money (not that I think you would ever forget); but last time it came *just in the nick of time*, which made Warnie rather anxious.

I don't think I will have the microscope for Christmas. In order to study entomological specimens, it would of course be needful to kill them: and to go about exterminating harmless insects, with no other motive in view than the gratification of one's own whimsical tastes does not seem to me very nice, when I look at it in that light. Of course it must be said that death to the insect is painless and quick; and that certain kinds of beetles (and other insects as well), when turned on their backs, cannot move. One could study these species through the microscope without killing them. However, the arguments against *practical* entomology are, I think, much stronger than those for it. Consequently I have decided not to have the microscope for Christmas, and it would be nicer not to know what I am going to get.[23]

Yesterday (Wednesday) we went for a paper chase. Mears and I were the hares, which was rather absurd, seeing that we are the two worst runners in the school, and know less about the country than the others. Both you and I know that I have got hardly any 'puff', and so you will be surprised to read as I was to find, that I kept up all right. We ran for a good long way, and however got caught in the end. I can tell you I slept well afterwards. Today we are all very, very stiff.

As the end of term draws nearer and nearer, we must soon decide all about the journey home. I think I had better go by Liverpool; for if I could arrange to meet Warnie at Lime St. Station, it would no longer be necessary for you to come over.

Now I must stop: with much love,

your son,

Jacks

TO HIS FATHER (LP III: 209–10):

[Wynyard School]
Postmark: 21 May 1910

My dear Papy,

I am writing to you today (Saturday) because we are going to St. Alban's to see Wyn ordained tomorrow.

We have quite settled down to the term here, and the time is beginning to fly: I hope it will go quickly with you too.

I have been thinking about the school question, but the more I think the more difficult it seems to arrive at any *definite* conclusion. Of course half formed, nebulous, impossible ideas will bubble up spontaneously.

---

23 Jack apparently got over his scruples about the microscope, for he received one for Christmas.

Yesterday (Friday) we went to church in the morning and afternoon; in the afternoon a great many boy scouts were present. Somehow I don't think 'Wee Georgie' (minus the Wood) will be *very* popular at first: but what is this to Shakespearian students like you and I who know what happens –

'After a well graced actor leaves the stage.'[24]

The other day we had a general knowledge examination: it was very exciting. I got 62 marks out of 100, and was second, Bowser was first. Thank goodness Squiffy came out miles below Bowser and I. If I cannot triumph over Squiffy in games and out of school, I will do my level best to triumph over him in work (which I *can* do), and which is perhaps a far better way of getting my own.

If you are 'thinking long' because this is a long term, remember that the holidays are long in proportion.

your loving
son Jacks

P.S. Have you seen the comet? We have not.

---

24 William Shakespeare, *Richard II* (1595), V, ii, 24.

1911–1912

*T*hat was Jack's last term at Wynyard. The school had been foundering for a long time, and now with too few pupils to provide him with a livelihood, it sank beneath the headmaster's feet. Mr Capron wrote to Albert on 27 April 1910 to say he was 'giving up school work'. After the boys left in July, Mr Capron was inducted into the little church at Radwell on 13 June 1910. It did not last. He began beating the choirboys, and had to be put under restraint. He died in the Camberwell House Asylum on 18 November 1911.

Jack spent one term, between September and December 1910, at Campbell College, Belfast. Then in January 1911 he and Warnie travelled together to Malvern, Warnie to Malvern College and Jack to the little preparatory school, Cherbourg School, which lay only yards from the College. It was made up of about twenty boys between the ages of 8 and 12, and had been founded in 1907 under the headmastership of Arthur Clement Allen (1868–1957). After the stultifying effects of Capron's teaching, with its 'sea of arithmetic' and a 'jungle of dates, battles, exports, imports and the like, forgotten as soon as learned' (SBJ II), Jack experienced something like a renaissance at Cherbourg, which in Surprised by Joy he calls 'Chartres' after the most glorious cathedral in France. 'Here indeed my education really began. The Headmaster, whom we called Tubbs, was a clever and patient teacher; under him I rapidly found my feet in Latin and English' (SBJ IV).

TO HIS FATHER (LP III: 226–7):

[Cherbourg School,
Malvern
January 1911]

My dear Papy,

Warnie and I arrived safely at Malvern after a splendid journey. Cherbourge is quite a nice place. There are 17 chaps here. There are three masters, Mr. Allen,[1] Mr. Palmer, and Mr. Jones, who is *very* fat.

It is only going to be a ten week term I think, so there are 79 more days.

Luckily we escaped all Pinguis's Malvern friends and were able to travel alone.

Malvern is one of the nicest English towns I have seen yet. The hills are beautiful, but of course not so nice as ours.

Two or three chaps here remember Mears.

Are you sure you have packed my Prayer Book? I cannot find it anywhere. If you find it at home, please send it on as soon as possible, and some stamps.

The weather here is miserably cold, and the air is thin and rarified: one can see ones breath all the time. One good thing is that we have hot water in the mornings, which we didnt have either at Campbell or Wynyard.

I haven't discovered the 'small museum' yet, and I am inclined to think it is a minus quantity.

Now I must stop.

yours affectionate

son,

Jacks

---

1 Arthur Clement Allen (1868–1957), the headmaster, was educated at Repton and New College, Oxford, where he read Classics. After taking a BA in 1891 he was a teacher at Silloth School from 1902 until 1907 when he founded Cherbourg School. In 1925 he moved the school to Woodnorton, Evesham, and the school closed officially when he retired in 1931.

TO HIS FATHER (LP III: 228):

[Cherbourg School]
Postmark: 5 February 1911

My dear Papy,

Sunday come round again – hurray! We had great fun this week, we went to the 'Messiah'.[2] It was only an amateur performance, but still it was simply lovely. I heard our old friends 'Comfort ye', and 'I know that my Redeemer liveth'. The former was specially well sung by a stout and hideous gentleman with an excellent voice.

On Wednesday we went for a walk across the flat side of Malvern and a funny thing happened. We were going through some fields when some one said 'look out', and we cleared off the path to make way for a college run which was coming. First came some big chaps with blue shields on their shirts, some distinction, I don't know what. Then came a motley crowd, and then!: A familiar voice said 'Hullo Jack', and looking round, I saw Pinguis himself. There he was. Its rather a comfort to know that he likes running.

That reminds me, the College breaks up on the 4th of April, and we do not [leave] till some days later. I suppose however you will arrange that I always go home on the same day as Pinguis. Be sure and tell me in your next letter what you think about this: I am positive you will agree. So when it gets near April 4th, just write to Mr. Allen and tell him about my coming home early. If you don't do this I don't know how we shall manage, for I couldn't face this complicated Malvern journey alone.

Last week we had some very bitter weather, but we did not feel it much as we wore our sweaters under our greatcoats. The other day we went off for a ripping walk over the hills, right across into Wales, a good step on the other side, and home through a sort of cutting.

Only nine more weeks if I come home on the 4th.

Yours loving

son,

J.

---

2 *Messiah*, an oratorio by George Frideric Handel, was first performed in 1752.

TO HIS FATHER (LP III: 239):

[Cherbourg School]
May 14th [1911]

My dear P.,

Thanks very much indeed for the money. I certainly did have a great fright, I could not think what had become of it. However I realised that it must have got left behind. I am glad to hear that Warnie has got his shove, where is he in his new form? I was pained and surprised to hear that you were not producing 'an old soldier and his wife', they would have been a novelty if nothing else.

We have found this time that it is much more comfortable to have lunch at Shrewsbury and go on by a later train.

Thank goodness that old pig Jonah has left, so I shall be able to enjoy myself this term. In his place we have got a chap named Turner, he is quite decent. In fact he is a very queer fellow indeed, I do not understand him and I think there is a good deal more to find out about him than anyone guesses. He is very quiet. Next week we are going to see Benson[3] in 'The Merchant of Venice'.[4] Of course Malvern has a rotten theatre, but it always gets very good things, I can't think why.

I enclose a photo of the characters in our play (that we had last term), in their stage costumes. The people from left to right are back row, Clutterbuck,[5] Nadin, front row, Me, Maxwell, Bowen.

your loving son
Jack

---

3 Sir Frank Robert Benson (1858–1939), English actor-manager, founded his own Shakespearean company. Beginning in 1883 he took his company on tours, producing all Shakespeare's plays with the exception of *Titus Andronicus* and *Troilus and Cressida*.

4 William Shakespeare, *The Merchant of Venice* (1600).

5 Jack Ernest Clutterbuck (1898–1975) went from Cherbourg School to Malvern College where he was a pupil from 1912 to 1915. After training at the Royal Military Academy, Woolwich, he received a commission in the Royal Engineers and served in the First World War. He went to Trinity Hall, Cambridge, and took a BA in 1922. After more than twenty years in the army, during which he reached the rank of brigadier, he was Chief Engineer of the G.I.P. Railway in Bombay, 1946–47. He retired in 1950. The photograph is reproduced in Walter Hooper, *Through Joy and Beyond: A Pictorial Biography of C.S. Lewis* (1982), p. 31.

TO HIS FATHER (LP III: 284–5):

Cherbourg.
Malvern.
Postmark: 5 May 1912

My dear P.,

We arrived safely here on the Friday, as you know by our telegram, and found that Cherbourg, contrary to all expectations, had come back on Wednesday, and I was late. I did not weep.

On the boat after you had gone, a solid phalanx of 'young persons' lined up on the quay and sang 'let's have a game of ring of roses'. You *would* have enjoyed it. The Malvern weather is exactly like the home – rotten. We have two new masters this term: the 1st a monstrosity of 6 ft., 6 ins height whom I don't like at all, so far as I have any opinion yet. He is called Eden. The other is of reasonable height, and, so far as we can see, fairly decent. But that remains to be seen. There is a new matron, Miss Gosling, who seems to be passably inoffensive – but of course is not nearly as decent as Miss Cowie.⁶ The small master's name is Harris.⁷ I hate starting a new term with an absolutely new staff, and *such* a new staff too.

---

6 The school matron, Miss G.E. Cowie, had been forced to leave, and she was now replaced by Miss Gosling. Writing about Miss Cowie in *SBJ* IV, Lewis said: 'No school ever had a better Matron, more skilled and comforting to boys in sickness, or more cheery and companionable to boys in health...We all loved her; I, the orphan, especially. Now it so happened that Miss C., who seemed old to me, was still in her spiritual immaturity, still hunting...She was...floundering in the mazes of Theosophy, Rosicrucianism, Spiritualism; the whole Anglo-American Occultist tradition...Little by little, unconsciously, unintentionally, she loosened the whole framework, blunted all the sharp edges of my belief. The vagueness, the merely speculative character, of all this Occultism began to spread – yes, and to spread *deliciously* – to the stern truths of the creed. The whole thing became a matter of speculation.'

7 We meet Percy Gerald Kelsal Harris again in the letter of 16 February 1918, but it should be noted that Harris is the master referred to in *SBJ* IV as 'Pogo' and about whom Lewis said: 'Pogo was a wit, Pogo was a dressy man, Pogo was a man about town. Pogo was even a lad. After a week or so of hesitation (for his temper was uncertain) we fell at his feet and adored. Here was sophistication, glossy all over, and (dared one believe it?) ready to impart sophistication to us...After a term of Pogo's society one had the feeling of being not twelve weeks but twelve years older.' P.G.K. Harris was born in Kinver, Staffordshire, on 31 August 1888. From King's School in Taunton he went up to Exeter College, Oxford, in 1907. That he left without a degree may be explained by those very qualities which delighted his pupils at Cherbourg. But he was to show an entirely different sort of mettle in the approaching war. For a photograph of Harris see Walter Hooper, *Through Joy and Beyond: A Pictorial Biography of C.S. Lewis* (1982), p. 30. Harris is the man standing on the left in the back row.

We left Liverpool this time by the 2.40 instead of the 12, and I think we will do so next time; it is a better train.

your loving

son Jack

The Lewis Papers contain no letters from Jack written between that of 5 May 1912 and the one below. The lacuna is possibly explained by the fact that whatever letters he wrote have not survived. However, a more likely explanation is that his energies were being poured into writing of a different sort. His personal 'Renaissance' began when he came across the Christmas issue of The Bookman *for December 1911 and saw the words* Siegfried and the Twilight of the Gods, *with a picture by Rackham illustrating the first part of Richard Wagner's* Ring of the Nibelung *saga. 'Pure "Northernness" engulfed me,' he said, 'a vision of huge, clear spaces hanging above the Atlantic in the endless twilight of Northern summer' (SBJ V). This love of myth led him between the summers of 1912 and 1913 to write 819 lines of an epic called* 'Loki Bound' *which was Norse in subject and Greek in form. He was as well a frequent contributor to* The Cherbourg School Magazine, *in which his articles are remarkable achievements for one so young. But for the moment, however, he had his mind set on winning a Scholarship to Malvern College.*

It was also at this point that Jack became an unbeliever. A major cause was the 'Occultist fancies' he had picked up from the matron of Cherbourg, Miss G.E. Cowie. He got into his head that 'No clause of my prayer was to be allowed to pass muster unless it was accompanied by what I called a "realisation", by which I meant a certain vividness of the imagination and the affections. My nightly task was to produce by sheer will-power a phenomenon which will-power could never produce' (SBJ IV). There were also unconscious causes of doubt.

> *One came from reading the classics. Here, especially in Virgil, one was presented with a mass of religious ideas; and all teachers and editors took it for granted from the outset that these religious ideas were sheer illusion. No one ever attempted to show in what sense Christianity fulfilled Paganism or Paganism prefigured Christianity...Little by little, with fluctuations which I cannot now trace, I became an apostate, dropping my faith with no sense of loss but with the greatest relief. (SBJ IV)*

1913

—— ≈ ——

TO HIS FATHER (LP IV: 1):

Cherbourg.
Sunday.
Postmark: 6 January 1913

My dear Papy,

This scholarship question is going to be settled then once for all, in the coming week; the best or the worst will soon be known. It always seems to me a comforting fact before any important event concerning whose result one is anxious, that one's own varying expectations about it can make no difference to the event. At any rate, I have tried, and the rest must remain to be seen. Tubbs was talking to our friend S.R. James[1] the other day about the affair, and we learn thence that Greek, which has been somewhat of a bugbear, is not a very important subject – that the most necessary things are French and English; my French of course is rather poor, but I think I can do alright in English. But perhaps we had better not think too much about the event until it is over. What shall happen shall happen, and in the mean time we hope.

I expect I shall see W. down at the Coll. when I am there, which will be a good thing, as I have not heard from him for a long time.

On Wednesday we went to see Benson's company in 'Julius Caesar'[2] which was very enjoyable. Benson himself as Mark Anthony acted as badly as anyone possibly could, overdoing his part exceedingly, and in places singing rather than speaking the words. Thus in the famous speech to the people we hear 'all' pronounced with four syllables in the passage – 'So are they all, all honourable men'. The rest of the company were however good, especially a man called Carrington as Brutus, and

---

1 The Rev. Canon Sydney Rhodes James (1855–1934) was the headmaster of Malvern College 1897–1914. His story is told in *Seventy Years: Random Reminiscences and Reflections* (1926).

2 William Shakespeare, *Julius Caesar* (1623).

Johnston as Caesar. Although I do not join with Warnie in condemning Shakespeare, I must say that in a good many plays he has missed alike the realism of modern plays and the statliness of Greek tragedies. Julius Caesar is one of his best in some ways.

The cricket trousers arrived thank you, and fit excellently. Will you please send me some envelopes.

your loving
son Jack.

TO HIS FATHER (LP IV: 26-7):

[Cherbourg School]
June 7, 1913
Saturday.

My dear Papy,

As you say, it was most unfortunate, more than unfortunate, that I should fall ill just now.[3] I had, as I thought, discussed the coming exam with myself in every possible light, but just the one thing I had not taken into account happened. For a while I thought I should not be able to do the papers at all, so that even the chance of doing them in bed was a relief. I did not start till late on Tuesday evening when I did Latin and Greek grammar and Latin Prose: I am afraid I did horribly badly in the Greek, though tolerably well in that days Latin and in the Latin translation and verses which came on Wednesday.

That afternoon came the essay paper which was one after my own heart, the three alternative subjects being 'The qualities of a successful soldier' 'The possibility of an universal language', and 'West is west and East is east, and never the twain shall meet'. I chose the last and applied it chiefly to the Indian question. It was much admired by Tubbs and by some masters at the College.

On Thursday I had a 'General paper' including History and Geography, Scripture and English, in which I got on alright but had not time to finish, a rather difficult French paper, and as a finale, Arithmetic and Algebra, which I think I did rather better than I anticipated.

Thus you have a brief schedule of my three days in bed. Not what one would choose for pleasure, but still what might have been worse. And I

---

3 Jack fell ill on about 1 June and had to retire to bed. He nevertheless managed to take the exams in the infirmary between 3 and 5 June.

hear you have written something to our common respected friend on the subject of a scholarship elsewhere, to the effect that I have some objection to going to any other school than Malvern but that you keep an open mind.[4] Very true. As a natural result I am honoured by the very well meant but rather importunate advice of the said respected friend that I should try for a scholarship elsewhere if I fail here. He is a great man for sticking to his guns; a man of purpose. I foresee that I shall find it very difficult to help taking his advice, which I by no means want to take. The good pedagogue has Uppingham at present in his eye for me. Now of this school I know absolutely nothing, good or bad. For this reason I do not like the idea of it – it is a leap in the dark. Of course for that matter Cherbourg, which has proved a success, was also a leap in the dark to a certain extent. But don't write anything of this to the good pedagogue. I have so far looked with ostensible favour on Uppingham when talking with him of the matter, as, having been ill and working hard on scant food for some days, I do not really feel disposed yet to enter into a controversy which I know will prove sharp. I suppose by going in for an Uppingham scholarship I do not bind myself to go to that school.

I cannot help wanting to go to the Coll. For one thing for two years now – and two years recollect are quite a long time at the age of fourteen – I have been expecting to go to Malvern, not indeed with any great fervour, for I am happy here, but with as much pleasure as I look on any public school, and it has become rather a rooted idea. Then again, I know a good deal more of Malvern than I do of any where else, and it is in a sense familiar already. As well, I shall still be at the town of Malvern, and since I must needs spend the greater part of the year in England I had sooner do it here than anywhere else.

I am very glad indeed that Warnie has at last decided definitely on some career, as I know this will lift a great weight from your mind. I confess that I don't know why you speak – as you have always spoken – so disparagingly of the Army Service Corps. It cannot be, can it, that you really liked the idea of putting W.[5] into the L.N.W.R.? I admit that there are great and lucrative posts to be gained in this company; greater than in the Army Service Corps. But the depths of drudgery for the less

4 He was referring to Mr Allen who on 2 June wrote to Albert saying, 'I believe you want him to go to the college here; if not, he might have a try for some other school which holds its Exams later' (LP IV: 25).

5 Warnie was very often referred to in correspondence with family and friends as 'W.'

successful are also greater. In the A.S.C., W., it is true, may not follow a great career, but, what is far more important, he will be always doing congenial work and mixing with other gentlemen; not with every railway clerk who may wear loud spats and button the last button of his waistcoat.[6]

I have got up today for a short time (Saturday), and am feeling almost all right. Hoping that your boils are better, and you are otherwise in good health, I am

your loving son,

Jack

TO HIS BROTHER (LP IV: 49–50):

Cherbourg.

Gt. Malvern.

[1? July 1913]

Dear old W.,

I have just heard from home the following statement, 'I suppose you know that I am in further and worse trouble about Warnie'.[7] What has happened? You haven't been sacked have you? Whatever it is, I should be the last person to tell you that the plate is hot after you had burned your fingers, so we will look on the bright side as much as possible. After all we have always been justly famed for extracting the maximum of pleasure from the most depressing circumstances: let us live up to it.

I am afraid P. will be in a very cheerless mood for the hols. If we cannot have mental enjoyment from the atmosphere of Leeborough[8] we can always fall back on our own resources and make the most of the physical comfort which, at their worst, the holidays always afford. Rows after tea

---

6 Warnie had just begun thinking of entering the Army Service Corps, the one career he was always sure he wanted, while his father favoured a job with the London and North Western Railway.

The Army Service Corps, which supplied food, weapons and other necessities to the troops, began in 1794 as the Corps of Waggoners. Over time it evolved until in 1888 it was recreated the Army Service Corps. In 1918, in recognition of its good work, it became the Royal Army Service Corps. It was renamed the Royal Corps of Transport in 1965. See John Fortescue, *The Royal Army Service Corps: A History of Transport and Supplies in the British Army*, vol. I (1930). Volume II by R. H. Beadon was published in 1931.

7 Albert's letter to Jack of 30 June 1913 (LP IV: 41). Warnie had been caught smoking.

8 'Leeborough' was Jack's and Warnie's private name for Little Lea. It had the advantage of yielding the adjectives 'Leeburian' and 'Leborough', as in a volume of their Boxen drawings called 'Leborough Studies Ranging from 1905–1916'.

and penitentiary strolls in the garden are not pleasant: but a soft bed, a nice Abdullah, a lazy walk with Tim, an occasional Hippodrome or Opera House, have their consolation and a sound gramophone can always refresh the jaded ear. But even now, in a rather dark hour, I do not dispair of P's cheering up a bit for the hols; for, as good luck would have it, my scholarship has brightened things.

Please write soon (how often have I made that request and received no answer to it), and tell me exactly what has happened, and also tell me your arrangements for the journey home. We break up on Tuesday 29th July, and you as I understand, the following Wednesday. So I suppose we shall go on the Tuesday. *Do* write immediately and tell me about this matter. Don't spend all your journey money. Cheer up.

your affect.
brother Jack.

P.S. Send a cab up for me first, and then down to S.H., and let it be in *plenty* of time. J.

In a letter to his father of 12 December 1912, Warnie told his father that, while he knew smoking was against the rules at Malvern College, he would like his permission to smoke 'in moderation' elsewhere (LP III: 317). Mr Lewis replied on 14 December, 'School smoking I condemn unreservedly...But outside that – at dinners etc., where it would make you odd or uncomfortable not to smoke a cigarette – smoke it and smoke it with a clear conscience, knowing that you would not be ashamed to tell your father what you had done. But in school it is different' (LP III: 318). No trouble seems to have come of this and Warnie was made a prefect on 9 March 1913. About this time he decided on a career in the army and, careless of College rules, he was involved in several escapades. In June 1913 he was degraded from the prefect-ship after being caught smoking at school. Warnie had hoped to remain at Malvern until Christmas 1913 so that he could be there for Jack's first term, but while the headmaster, Canon S.R. James, was willing to reinstate him in his position as a prefect in July 1913 he would not allow him to remain another term. It was Warnie's wish at this time to enter the Royal Military College at Sandhurst and pass from there into the Army Service Corps (ASC). For this Warnie would need to pass the entrance examination to Sandhurst and his father began considering how he might prepare for this.

TO HIS FATHER (LP IV: 44–5):

Cherbourg.
6/6/13 [6 July 1913]

My dear Papy,

I have been extremely worried since I got your last letter. No: I do not know what has happened to W. I have had no news either of him or from him since the day when I heard that he had been degraded. What has happened? Surely he has not been expelled? I often had fears as to what he might do at Malvern, but I never thought it would come to this. It is of no use my writing to him for information, as he seems to consider the answering of letters a superfluous occupation. Of course I know that all this is worse for you than for me, but it is very unpleasant for both of us: what has he himself got to say upon the matter? However, please let me know as soon as you can what the exact position of affairs is: in the meantime I can only hope that my fears have no foundation; for after all, the great majority of the troubles which I have at one time or another anticipated, have never come to pass. But after all, the process of self consolation, if it were not such a terrible business, would be almost funny. We are ready to turn and twist the facts until they bear no resemblance to the original thing. Perhaps one could not go on at all without doing so. Perhaps however if W's school career has been a failure, he may do better in the future.

Thank you very, very much for your kind suggestion about the present. You are really making too much of this scholarship.[9] Nevertheless, there is nothing that I should prize more than a nice edition of Kipling, whose poems I am just beginning to read and to wonder why I never read them before – a usual state of mind, in the literary way, for me at Leeborough.

Today we leave our letters open and the authorities insert a printed notice of the date of breaking up. Its rather singular to notice the familiar landmarks – in a metaphorical sense – that cluster round as we reach the last weeks of the term – and there are only three more now. Nevertheless I hardly watch the flight of time with my usual eagerness. In spite of several rows both fierce and long drawn out, both with masters and boys, I have really been very happy at Cherbourg; and Malvern is unknown ground. More important than this is the fact that we shall see each other again in a short time.

---

9 On 9 June Jack won a classical entrance scholarship to Malvern College.

Looking forward to which, I am,
your loving
son Jack.

TO HIS FATHER (LP IV: 45–6):

Cherbourg.
Gt. Malvern.
8/7/13.

My dear Papy,

I was more pleased than I can say to get your letter. Bad as the news is, it is not the worst, and it is always a relief to have certainty after a prolonged spell of suspense. I am afraid I cannot carry out your suggestion of letting W. speak first: shortly after I wrote my letter to you, I decided to write to him, partly because I hoped for an answer from the College which would naturally reach me before one from Belfast, and I could bear it no longer, partly to cheer W. up since no recriminations can improve the accomplished facts, and partly to settle arrangements about the journey home. In this letter I asked him of course, what exactly had happened, but I have received your answer. You are right in your supposition that I should resent being left in the dark, and I am very thankful that you wrote and told me everything.

Do not say in a letter that 'you must stop, or else begin to pour out all your troubles, which would be unfair'. It would not be unfair; it would be wise. For, in the first place you would derive some comfort from the mere action of putting them into words, and, in the second place, I trust that they would be lighter after we had talked them over together in our letters. This small thing, this act of discussing and sympathizing over matters, is all the help I can give you at present, but, such as it is, I give it, as you know, very gladly.

Perhaps you will be somewhat cheered up by the visit of our Scotch relatives: but to be honest, I have spoken too fiercely and too often against society to endeavour now to preach in its favour.

I was very interested by what you told me about Jordan.[10] Who knows

---

10 In a little piece called 'My Life During the Exmas Holadys of 1907', Jack paid tribute to the postman: 'Our postman is called Gordon [Jordan] and is a very nice and sensible man, and often sets me an essay to wright, the subject of which he provides' (LP III: 90). In his letter to Jack of 30 June 1913, Mr Lewis congratulated Jack on his scholarship, saying: 'I met Jordan the postman the other night, and as he used to set you essays, I thought I would tell him. He was as pleased as Punch. He said "Sir, the next time you're writing will you say – Jordan is delighted." ' (LP IV: 41).

but that I owe more to those early little essays in the old days than you or I imagine? For it is to this uneducated postman that I owe the fact that I was acquainted with the theory of essay writing, in however crude a form, at an age when most boys hardly know the meaning of the word. To him, of course, next to you and to the fact of my being born in a race rich in literary feeling and mastery of their own tongue, and in that atmosphere of culture which has always shrouded the study both at Dundela and Leeborough. Nowhere else have I met that peculiar feeling – that literary ether. Perhaps Archburn would have it were it not for the cats. No school ever had it, and libraries are too public. Thank goodness I shall soon be in it and with you.

Yet I do not enjoy saying goodbye to Cherbourg: a good many things happy and unhappy have happened there, and I like the place.

What a curious business about that post card. Thanks for sending it. Its rather alarming to think that our letters can go astray like that.

your loving
son Jack.

At the beginning of September Albert Lewis thought of asking his old head-master at Lurgan College in County Armagh, William T. Kirkpatrick[11] (1848–1921) if he would prepare Warnie for the Sandhurst examination. Following his retirement from Lurgan in 1899 Mr Kirkpatrick had moved with his wife to 'Gastons', Great Bookham in Surrey, where he usually had one residential pupil each year whom he prepared for university or college examinations. He agreed to tutor Warnie and the latter arrived at Great Bookham on 10 September 1913.

Jack arrived in Malvern on 18 September to begin his first term as a scholar of Malvern College – or 'Wyvern' as he called it in his autobiography. Like Warnie before him, Jack was a member of School House.

---

11 See **William Thompson Kirkpatrick** in the Biographical Appendix. Mr Kirkpatrick had a number of nicknames, including 'The Great Knock', 'Knock' and 'Kirk'.

TO HIS FATHER (LP IV: 71–2):

[Malvern College,
Malvern.
21? September 1913]

My dear P.,

I arrived safely as you know by the telegram – reaching Malvern at about half past five. Most of the other new boys had arrived, but one or two didn't come until the following day. So far everything has been very pleasant indeed.

Luckily I am going to get a study out of which the old occupants are moving today. There will be three other people in it – Hardman,[12] Anderson,[13] and Lodge.[14] The last of these is an intolerable nuisance, but the Old Boy manages these things and it can't be helped.

I have seen quite a lot of W's friend Hichens,[15] who seems frightfully pleased at being head of the house; going about with a huge note book and a blue pencil, taking down quite unneccesary things.

Yesterday we made our first acquaintance of Smugie[16] – a queer, but very nice old man who goes on as if taking a form were a social function – 'a quaint old world courtesy' as you read in some book. There is one

---

12 (Sir) Donald Innes Hardman (1899–1982) was Jack's study-mate in School House. On leaving Malvern he went to Hertford College, Oxford. While serving in the First World War during 1916–19 he joined the Royal Air Force and became a professional serviceman. He was promoted to wing commander in 1939, air commander in 1941, air commander of South East Asia 1946–47, and was chief of air staff and organization 1954–57, retiring in 1958.

13 Edward Anderson (1898–1928) was a member of School House 1913–17. After leaving Malvern he served in the war as a 2nd lieutenant. He later moved to Northern Rhodesia, dying there in November 1928.

14 Kenneth Ernest Lodge (1899–?) was a member of School House 1913–17. During the war he served overseas as a 2nd lieutenant with the Duke of Lancaster's Own Yeomanry. He was promoted to captain and remained in the army.

15 Fitzgerald Charles Cecil Baron Hichens (1895–1977) was at Malvern 1909–14 and was the head of School House when Jack arrived in 1913. From Malvern he went to Exeter College, Oxford, but soon left there for Sandhurst from where he passed into the Duke of Cornwall's Light Infantry in 1915, becoming a captain in 1918. Following the war he resigned from the army and obtained a regular commission in the Royal Air Force, in which he became a wing commander. He retired in 1943.

16 'Smugie' or 'Smewgy' was Harry Wakelyn Smith (1861–1918) who taught Classics and English to the Upper Fifth and for whom Jack was to have great affection. He had been educated at St John's College, Oxford, and he joined the staff of Malvern in 1885. In *SBJ* VII, Lewis said: 'Except at Oldie's I had been fortunate in my teachers ever since I was born; but Smewgy was "beyond expectation, beyond hope". He was a grey-head with large spectacles and a wide mouth which combined to give him a froglike

other new boy from the School House in the Upper V – Cooper, who is quite all right.[17] We begin ordinary work on Monday.

Could you please send me some plain socks, black, which are 'de rigeur' here. My size is rather uncertain, but get them almost as big as your own, for I have a large foot. I have not heard from W. yet. Hoping you are not 'thinking long', I am,

your loving
son Jack

TO HIS FATHER (LP IV: 77):

Malvern.
28/9/13.

My dear Papy,

I hope you don't object to the use of red ink, which is unavoidable, as our study has no black. Thanks very much for the money, note paper and socks. As you advise, I am being careful not to be rooked, and have already refused countless offers of utterly worthless merchandise. I have made the acquaintance of W's friend Captain Tassell, who is quite an interesting study.[18]

---

expression, but nothing could be less froglike than his voice. He was honey-tongued. Every verse he read turned into music on his lips...He first taught me the right sensuality of poetry, how it should be savoured and mouthed in solitude...Had he taught us nothing else, to be in Smewgy's form was to be in a measure ennobled. Amidst all the banal ambition and flashy splendours of school life he stood as a permanent reminder of things more gracious, more humane, larger and cooler. But his teaching, in the narrower sense, was equally good. He could enchant but he could also analyse. An idiom or a textual crux, once expounded by Smewgy, became clear as day.' This deeply loved man died in his little house in the school grounds, where he lived alone, on 13 November 1918, a victim of the influenza sweeping Europe that year.

17 Harry Richard Lucas Cooper (1899–1936), of Oxford, entered Malvern as a minor scholar in 1913. When he left in 1918 he ranked as the second boy in the school, head of School House, a cadet officer in the OTC and a football star. From Malvern he went to Christ Church, Oxford, where he took his BA in 1922. He worked for the Imperial Bank of India, and in 1924 was employed in the Calcutta office.

18 Douglas Spencer Montague Tassell (1872–1956) took a BA in 'Greats' at Christ Church, Oxford, in 1894 and began teaching classics at Malvern in 1905. On the retirement of the geography master in 1928 he took over the teaching of geography. Perhaps his greatest work, and that which gave him most satisfaction, was with the Officers' Training Corps. In 1909 he was put in charge of the Malvern contingent of the OTC, which he commanded until 1919 when he was awarded the Territorial Decoration. Warnie wrote of him: 'In appearance he was a jaunty, dark haired, short mustached, dark eyed little man, very much the soldier with a permanent expression of busy irritation' (LP IV: 73). It was he who first reported Warnie for smoking.

Talking about W., I have heard from him since I came back. He seems to be settling down to the routine a la maison Gastons.

The work here is very heavy going, and it is rather hard to find time for it in the breathless life we lead here. So far that 'breathlessness' is the worst feature of the place. You never get a 'wink of peace'. It is a perpetual rush, at high pressure, with short intervals spent in waiting for another bell. Roll is called several times each day, which of course helps to crowd up the time. However, I suppose this sense of being eternally hustled will wear off as things settle down. On the whole, it is very pleasant so far, and, which is a help, I like Smugie.

There is another thing that is worrying me rather. That is the fact that I miss Lea Shakespeare hours for drawing. Both of these subjects I should like to continue, but one must be dropped. What do you advise me to do? If we decide to give up the drawing, I suppose you can arrange that with the authorities.

I get on very well with the people in my own study, which is a great comfort. How is every thing at Leeborough?

your loving
son Jack

TO HIS BROTHER (LP IV: 78–9):

[Malvern
15? October 1913]

My dear W.,

I was very glad to hear from you and acknowledge my remisness in writing, but honestly I am being worked to death by Smugy – with whom however I get on very well – not a moment of peace.

True, no 24 is rather near the pres. room, but both Hardman and I have extraordinary luck about fagging. One thing is that we are in the same study as that fat beast Lodge, whom everyone hates, so that if a pre. comes in he is sure to fag Lodge before us. I have only had to clean boots twice so far.

I have, among other things, written an article to appear in the 'Malvernian' under the name Hichens – whom I like best of the pres.[19]

---

19 For whatever reason his article did not appear in *The Malvernian*.

I don't see all the horrors which you heaped on Browning.[20] He's always very decent to me. Bourne gets very much mobbed as a pre.[21] I am in Walter Lowe's math set.[22] Were you ever there?

Two very exciting things have happened. A drawing of mine, which we had to do for Smugy as one of the questions in W.E., was pinned up on the Upper V door for a week, and the James came down and said it was spirited. Also an English poem of mine in imitation of Horace was 'sent up for good' to Jimmy.[23] Consequently I have to go down to South Lodge and copy the poem into his great book tomorrow.

Isn't the Fish a glorious man?[24] Smugy keeps on asking about you. As he is so interested in O.M's., you ought to write to him if you have time. He *is* a decent old Kod,[25] isn't he? Recruit drill is at present the chief joy of my life. I got a Coll. pres. for skipping clubs the other day. Jervis I

20 Stanley Forrester Browning (1896–1917) became a member of School House in 1910 and by the time he left at the end of summer term of 1914, he had been a house prefect and in the second eleven at football. In 1914 he joined the Royal Flying Corps, and was a captain in that branch of the service when he was killed in action 3 May 1917.

21 John Arthur Watson Bourne (1896–1943) was at School House 1910–14, during which time he was a house prefect. During World War I he was a captain in the RAF. He then worked as an engineer in the technical and research department of a petroleum company. During World War II he served as a captain in the Royal Signal Corps. He died in March 1943.

22 William Walter Lowe (1873–1945) entered Malvern in the winter of 1888. When he left in 1893 he was junior chapel prefect, captain of the football eleven, and had been four years in the cricket eleven. From Malvern he went to Pembroke College, Cambridge, where he received a BA in 1896. He returned to Malvern as an assistant master in 1896, and was house master 1913–32. He retired in 1932 and died in May 1945.

23 i.e. Canon James, the headmaster.

24 'The Fish' was Henry Geoffrey Curwen Salmon (1870–1933) who went up to Jesus College, Oxford, in 1888 on a Classics scholarship. He joined the staff of Malvern College in 1901 and taught French and German to the sixth form. In 1914 he helped prepare the third edition of the *Malvern Register*, and he was entirely responsible for the fourth edition of 1924. When he retired from teaching in 1929 he was appointed secretary of the Malvernian Society, which work he undertook with enthusiasm for the rest of his life.

25 In his *Glossary of Words in Use in the Counties of Antrim and Down* (1880), William Hugh Patterson (1835–1918) defined 'cod' as '(1) *sb.* a silly, troublesome fellow. (2) *v.* to humbug or quiz a person; to hoax; to idle about. "Quit your *coddin'*."' (p. 22). Warnie said, 'It has however a third meaning, namely an expression of humourous and insincere self depreciation; an Ulsterman will say of himself, "Amn't I the square oul' cod to be doin' so and so?"' (LP IV: 306). Jack Lewis used the expression often, and he seems to have invented the diminutive 'codotta' or 'Kodotta' which appears occasionally in his letters. A notebook of his poems written about this time was entitled 'Metrical Meditations of a Cod'.

rather like,[26] but Bull II hasn't come back yet.[27] It is a good business that I have got into a study with a decent lad. I like Hardman II very much.[28]

By the way, you *don't* enclose the Col. Rena May [list] whatever you may think you do. How goes the History? You must manage to come down to the House Supper. Everyone would be awfully bucked to see you. I shall write and tell P. that I am nervous about going home alone if you like. This is being written in the breathless interval between Supper and Prayers, so I must chuck it now.

your loving
brother Jack

TO HIS FATHER (LP IV: 87–8):

[Malvern]
Postmark: 19 October 1913

My dear P.,

I hope you did not think that I was incurring reckless expense when I wrote to you for the money. The way you are rooked at Malvern by subscriptions, loans, and the fines which are shabbily arranged, is perfectly appalling. Thanks very much indeed for the five shillings.

The poem after Horace was, I am glad to tell you, somewhat in the nature of a success. It was top of the form and was sent up to the James. 'Being sent up for good' is a privilege enjoyed only by our form and the Upper Sixth and is rather a ceremony. I had to go down to Smugy's house and copy the poem into a vast old volume of his, containing the works and signatures of all those who have been 'sent up for good' since 1895. I was of course greatly interested to read the other poems and things in the book: some of them are really very good. I enclose the

---

26 Edwin Cyril Jervis (1896–?) was at School House 1911–15. On leaving Malvern he went to Sandhurst. He joined the Duke of Wellington's Regiment in 1916, was made a lieutenant in 1917 and during the war was seriously wounded. He received the Military Cross.

27 Charles Edward Bristow Bull (1900–77) was at School House 1912–15. During the war he served in the OTC. After the war he was private secretary to Aylesbury Brewery Co. Ltd, and also an actor.

28 This was the younger brother of Jack's study companion. Wallace George Hardman (1897–1917) was at School House 1911–14. After leaving Malvern he was a 2nd lieutenant in the Manchester Regiment, and was killed in action near Kut on 9 January 1917.

poem which it may interest you to see. Smugy's house is a queer little nook of the world, exactly typical of its owner.

I am inclined to agree with you that it will be a pity to lose Mr. Peacocke. He was neither a great preacher nor reader, but he was an educated gentleman, which is something to say in these times.[29]

I hope this business of Aunt Minnie[30] will turn out all right. Coming on top of the trouble about Norman it is very hard lines, and I should imagine that the Moorgate household is one of the worst fitted to receive trouble, as there is always, even when things are at their brightest, a certain gloom there.

It certainly is a grievous pity that Shakespeare filled Romeo and Juliet[31] with those appalling rhymes. But the worst thing in the play is old Capulet's preposterous speech to the guests. Still, it is a very fine tragedy. So is the Greek play that we are doing. It is quite unlike all that stiff bombast which we are accustomed to associate with Greek tragedy. There is life and character in it.

your loving
son Jacks

'"Carpe Diem" after Horace'
'In the metre of "Locksley Hall"' (Tennyson)

When, in haughty exultation, thou durst laugh in
Fortune's face,
Or when thou hast sunk down weary, trampled in
The ceaseless race,
Dellius, think on this I pray thee – but the
Twinkling of an eye,

---

29 The Rev. Gerald Peacocke, who succeeded Thomas Hamilton as rector of St Mark's, was leaving. He was the son of the Most Rev. Joseph Ferguson Peacocke, Archbishop of Dublin, and was educated at Trinity College, Dublin where he took the Hebrew Prize in 1892. He was ordained priest in 1894, and was curate of Carnmoney, Co. Antrim, 1893–6. After four years in Holywood, Co. Down, he was rector of St Mark's, Dundela, 1900–14. He was prebendery of Geashill, Co. Offaly, 1914–23, and Archdeacon of Kildare 1923–44.

30 Aunt Minnie was the wife of Albert's brother, William Lewis (1859–1946). See **The Lewis Family** in the Biographical Appendix.

31 William Shakespeare, *Romeo and Juliet* (1597).

May endure thy pain or pleasure; for thou knowest
Thou shalt die,
Whether on some breeze-kissed upland, with a
Flask of mellow wine,
Thou hast all the world forgotten, stretched be-
Neath the friendly pine,
Or, in foolish toil consuming all the springtime
Of thy life,
Thou hast worked for useless silver and endured
The bitter strife:
Still unchanged thy doom remaineth. Thou art
Set towards thy goal,
Out into the empty breezes soon shall flicker
Forth thy soul,
Here then by the plashing streamlet fill the
Tinkling glass I pray
Bring the short lived rosy garlands, and be
Happy – FOR TODAY.

TO HIS FATHER (LP IV: 90–1):

[Malvern]
Postmark: 26 October 1913

My dear P.,

I hope it did not seem that my act of sending you the poem was meant for a 'draw', which it was not. All the same, thanks very much for the P.O. which has restored 'the firm' to its pristine health and prosperity.

Anderson, one of the people in our study, has just received a huge crate of pictures from home which will enable us to sell some of our older pictures and raise capital. I had not been able to see about the extra copies of the Cherbourg magazine, as I have not yet been up to see Tubbs. I think however that I am going up today, when I shall be able to transact all my business.

On Thursday we had our field day and it was really a great affair. We started for the place, which is quite near Malvern about an hours march, at ten o'clock. W's friend Captain Tassell was in great form, mounted on a steed of which he was obviously terrified. Of course no one knew in the least what was meant to be happening, but we all dashed about, lying down and firing at intervals: on the whole it was very enjoyable.

You ask me what type of person one meets at Malvern: I will tell you. The average Malvernian may be, in fact usually is, a very good fellow in reality, but he always does his best to make himself out as bad as possible. Never believe his own account of his thoughts, deeds, or ideals. It is always far worse than the truth. Beyond this very childish and thoroughly British foible, there are very few faults in him. When you break through the shell of foolish affectation, you find him an honest kind hearted manly enough sort of fellow. At least that is how six weeks acquaintance of him strikes me. To use for once the phrase you have condemned, 'I may be wrong'. But I think not.

Yesterday there was a lecture in the Gym by that man Kearton who came to the Hippodrome last holidays. I must confess that I thought him very poor indeed. So we did not miss much by leaving that 'popular house of entertainment' alone.

The mother of Stone,[32] one of our House Pres., has died this week and he has consequently gone home. It is a very nasty business.

your loving

son Jack.

TO HIS BROTHER (LP IV: 96):

[Malvern
2? November 1913]

My dear W.,

Although always quite ready to fall in with your wishes whenever they are within the bounds of possibility, I always like to point out some of the more glaring absurdities in the same. It has not occurred to you that this simultaneous attack on the paternal purse will savour somewhat too much of preparation. But to proceed. The following is what I intend to write home, coming at the end of a long and cheerful letter, when he will be bucked.

'I have heard from W. again in the course of this week, and he seems to be comfortable with Kirk, although still working at high pressure. He mentions in this last letter, as he has done frequently before, that he entertains an idea of coming down here at the end of the term and

---

32 Noel Herbert Stone (1895–1918) was at Malvern 1910–14. After training at Sandhurst he joined the Worcestershire Regiment and was promoted to captain in 1917. He fought in France and was killed in action near Amiens on 27 April 1918.

travelling home with me as we did in the old times. This of course would be exceedingly pleasant for me, especially as most of the other new boys here have got friends coming down at the end of term; and it is undoubtedly pleasanter as well as more economical to travel in pairs than singly. The Old Boy, who by the way is one of the real good points about Malvern, has asked once or twice after W., and expressed a hope that W. will come down some time soon. Of course I am aware all this has nothing to do with me, but still he seems to have set his heart on it, and as I gather from the tone of his letter he has not mentioned it to you...'

As I said, it looks rather artificial, and can't be made much better. How are you getting on, old man? I hope this thing will work, as I am looking forward to another journey in the good old style. As you will notice in my epistle, I have made it the Oldish and not the James who wants you to come down.[33] I think that his name will carry more weight.

So far I am having a very good time here. You ask me what I think about Jacks.[34] I'll tell you. He's always most awfully nice to me, spends half hall talking to me about you and Smugy and things, and never fags me or drops me; but all the same I can't blind myself to the fact that he is an absolute _____ to most other people. But of course that doesn't worry me.

We had field day on Thursday at Malvern. I have managed to get into my house section, 'mirable dictu',[35] although I mob all the recruit drill. I can't go on now.

your affect.

brother Jack

---

33 'The Old Boy' or 'The Oldish' was George Gordon Fraser (1870–1958), the headmaster's assistant in the management of School House. He entered the College as a day boy in 1879 and remained until 1885. On leaving there he went to London University where he obtained a degree in 1889. In 1895 he became an assistant master at Lord William's School, Thame, and in 1895 he went in the same capacity to Forest School. In 1901 he was appointed an assistant master at Malvern, and in 1917 he became house master of No. 9 House, which position he held until 1927.

34 Stopford Brooke Ludlow Jacks, JP, FRSA (1894–1988), son of Professor L.P. Jacks, entered School House in 1910 and left in 1915. During the war he served with the artillery, became a major, and won the Military Cross. He took a Diploma in Economics in 1920 from Balliol College, Oxford, and became a director of Messrs. Greg and Co., cotton spinners, Manchester. He served as a governor of the Royal College of Arts, chairman of HM Prisons for Women, president of the Prestbury Petty Sessions, and a governor of Malvern College.

35 *Mirabile dictu*, 'Wonderful to relate'.

TO HIS BROTHER (LP IV: 101–2):

[Malvern
9? November 1913]

My dear W.,

You don't seem to be having a bad time at Gt. Bookham with your visits to 'The Laughing Husband' and the Hippodrome etc. I wouldn't boom these diversions over loudly in the paternal ear, as, innocent though they may be in themselves, yet they would not convey an impression of 'good hard work'. You may bet your boots I've heard enough about 'warm singlets and drawers etc.' to last me for a life time. P. tells me that 'when I come home he's going to take me in hand and see that that chest of mine gets as sound as a bell'. I wonder what that means?

I don't really know that a house tie would be worn with a black suit, but we'll see. Anyhow you must provide the tie as I am too 'stoney' for anything. I am amused to see that you have fallen into the excellent Marathon trap of spending 20/- where 5/- would do. As well, I wonder if 'Miss Thompson' would have heard about it. No one in T. Eden's shop ever seems to have heard of anything, do they?

It'll be a great weight off your chest when this filthy exam is over, so I am glad that it is comparatively soon.[36] I should think you ought to pass fairly easily if you've been oiling with Kirk. I am longing to find out from you in the hols what Kirk is really like. A *kod* of the first water I should imagine by all reports.

At the end of this term we really must get Jarnfeldt's Preludium.[37] I heard it again at the Classical Orchestral Concert, and was more than ever charmed with it. Perhaps too you are right about this Marathon scheme. We can talk that over anon.

P. of course refuses to accept your scheme of taking the trip to Malvern as a birthday and Xmas gift. At least he writes to me, 'W of course with his usual ingenuity says that this trip is going to be his Christmas and birthday present. But that is not quite the way I do things'. By the way, are we travelling home a day early or do you want to stay for the House Supper? I don't mind staying a bit if you like, only it is so close to Xmas with that fearful problem of P's present.

yours Jack.

---

36 Warnie was preparing to take the entrance examinations (25 November–2 December) for Woolwich and the Royal Military College at Sandhurst.
37 Armas Järnefelt, *Praeludium* (1904).

TO HIS FATHER (LP IV: 104–5):

[The Sanatorium,
Malvern]
Postmark: 24 November 1913

My dear Papy,

I am sorry to hear that you are 'thinking long', but, as you know, there is a good reason for the absence of letters as this is the first day I have been able to write. As you say, I have a lot of things to talk about and the first is Smugy's half term report.

I must confess that I was very disappointed in it. But I should have expected it all. For, the fact of the matter is about this Greek Grammar, that I know very little indeed: and the consequence of this is that what the rest of the form are running over in a sort of casual way for the third or fourth time, I am often learning for the first time in my life. This of course makes it rather difficult to keep up with the running. Then again, there are a lot of points of Greek grammar which I learnt up in furious haste at Cherbourg in the last few moments before the exam – and of course forgot again. These have to be faced with a half knowledge which is worse than ignorance, because it only muddles one's brain. But all these things should come right in time; as I flatter myself I am not cursed with 'an inability to grasp the elements' of any reasonable subject. As for the place in form, I was prepared for it to be poor, as the general standard of the form is rather beyond me – seeing that with the exception of the other scholars it consists of people who have filtered through to Smugy's care just at the end of their Malvern career. However, I get on well with Smugy and really that is half the battle.

You need not have been so worried about my temporary indisposition. It is only one of those trifling, although irritating chills to which I am subject in the winter months. Anyway, the worst of it is over now, as I am up in my room at the San. today. The San. is about the most curious place I have ever been in. I arrived here a week ago on Friday and was placed in a bed in a large and many windowed apartment, in one corner of which a fire was cheerfully engaged in belching forth dense clouds of smoke, which rendered it well nigh impossible to see or breathe. Conquering a natural terror of at once becoming unconscious in such an atmosphere, I resigned my self to sleep that night – but not for long. I soon discovered to my cost that the room in which I had been deposited was directly over the kitchen. I was apprised of this fact by the musical efforts of the domestic staff, whose vigorous and unwholesome concert was prolonged far into the night. But the funniest thing about this place is the noises that one hears in the morning. I really cannot imagine what the staff do. Judging from the loud peals of laughter and the metallic clangs which strike my ears before breakfast daily, they engage in hand to hand combat with the fire irons.

After a short period of the smoky room I was removed to a smaller but much more comfortable chamber where I still remain. Here my only trouble is the determined 'quacking' of a body of geese imprisoned somewhere in the neighbourhood.

As for your kind enquiries about the approaching natal gift, I have made up my mind that I should like 'The Rhinegold and the Valkyries' to match the 'Siegfried and Twilight of the Gods' which I have got.[38] I think however that the purchase of the book had better be deferred until Xmas when I can talk to my friend Carson in person.

I am glad to hear that W. is coming down at the end of the term as it is nicer travelling 'in comp.' than alone. I must stop now. How are you yourself keeping these days?

> your loving
> son,
> Jack.

TO HIS FATHER (LP IV: 108–9):

> The Sanatorium,
> Thursday or Friday.
> (I am not quite sure what
> day it is today)
> Postmark: 28 November 1913

My dear Papy,

I have advanced yet another stage and am now enjoying the priv-eledge of being downstairs in the San. That is, instead of sitting up in my bedroom, I have been moved to a sitting room where I can look out upon the hideously ugly garden of the San. And yet there is a homely

---

38 Jack already had the last two parts of Wagner's *Ring* cycle, *Siegfried and the Twilight of the Gods*, translated by Margaret Armour, with illustrations by Arthur Rackham (1911). For Christmas his father gave him the volume containing the first two parts, *The Rhinegold & The Valkyrie* (1910).

touch about this garden. It is full of laurels that will never grow because of the wind: we've seen these before haven't we?

I have been condemned by the school doctor, as soon as I go back, to join the ranks of people who do 'special exercises for delicate chests' in the gym. This is a piece of 'sconce' after your own heart, and I have no doubt that you will be more pleased to hear about it than I was. Your remarks about the sealskin etc. strike me as being both in questionable taste and the products of a fevered imagination rather than of a sane mind. But still, the human mind is so constituted that the bizarre must ever appeal more potently than the normal. Which is a consolation.

Congratulations on your victory at the Pattersonian musical festival. You'll be becoming quite a noted Strandtown diner out if you are not careful.

Talking about social functions reminds me of some wild fantastic talk of another dance this year.[39] Don't let us spoil the Xmas holidays by a chore as colossal as it is disagreeable, and as disagreeable as it is unnecessary. No one else gives a dance on two consecutive years. Nip this matter in the bud 'which has a bitter taste' and of which 'sweet will *not* be the flower'. (Do you remember the quotation?) But seriously, I hope no such folly is really toward. It is quite bad enough having to attend the functions of others without adding to the nuisance ourselves. Please convey to Aunt Annie and the other conspirators that you are determined not to hear of it, as I am sure you are. For one thing it is a considerable and uncalled for expense, and an expense of the most annoying kind – namely where you get absolutely no return for your money: unless *you* derive any great pleasure from hovering about among the noisy and objectionable throng who have invaded the pristine seclusion of Leeborough. But I don't fancy that you do. I am certain that I don't.

---

39 'Christmas will be here almost immediately,' Albert wrote to Warnie on 9 November 1913, 'and amongst other questions that must be decided is the all important one – are we to have a dance or not? No doubt our friends expect it. To me of course the thing is an expensive nuisance. But I don't want you and Jacks to drop out of things here' (LP IV: 99). 'No dance!!' replied Warnie on 10 October (LP IV: 101). Jack hated dancing, and years later he wrote in *SBJ* III: 'It was the custom of the neighbourhood to give parties which were really dances for adults but to which, none the less, mere schoolboys and schoolgirls were asked...To me these dances were a torment...How a small boy who can neither flirt nor drink should be expected to enjoy prancing about on a polished floor till the small hours of the morning, is beyond my conception.'

One good thing is that there are only three more weeks or so this term. I suppose W. will have both tickets when it comes to travelling. Is it next Tuesday or the Tuesday after that his exam comes off?

As to your remarks about the school san., in spite of smoky chimneys and a villainous domestic staff, there are a good many worse places to spend a few weeks of a long winter term. There are plenty of books and fires, and I always derive a certain savage pleasure in sitting with my feet on the fender, watching through the window a body of my unfortunate fellow beings setting off for a run across that cold, dismal golf links that always reminds me of the moorland in 'Locksley Hall'.

Talking about 'Locksley Hall', I have discovered a tattered copy of Tennyson's works here, buried among the sixpenny novels and illustrated weeklies, with which I have spent a few enjoyable afternoons reading 'In memoriam'[40] and some other things that one ought to know.

your loving

son Jack.

TO HIS FATHER (LP IV: 111):

> The Sanatorium,
> St. Andrew's Rd.,
> Sunday.
> Postmark: 30 November 1913

My dear P.,

I am now I think really quite better and shall be leaving the San. in a few days. It is funny, isn't it, how soon you get accustomed to a new kind of life? I've been down here for a fortnight or so, and I have grown so used to it that I could almost believe that Malvern never existed. But I shall be amply reminded of its life shortly. I am beginning to go out now on those intensely dull convalescent walks – progressing at two miles an hour, muffled up like an arctic explorer, and getting in the bits of sunshine. Thanks very much for the postal order which arrived yesterday. One good thing about being down at the san. is that it prevents your spending money, which is always an advantage.

For three days during this week I have had a companion – one Waley[41]

---

40 Alfred, Lord Tennyson, *Locksley Hall* (1842), *In Memoriam A.H.H.* (1850).
41 Reginald Philip Simon Waley (1897–1951) was a member of School House 1911–15. On leaving Malvern he served as a 2nd lieutenant in the Royal West Kent Regiment. In 1923 he went to work on the Stock Exchange.

of the School House, who had a boil on his arm and talked an amazing amount of agreeable nonsense. I pretended to be interested in and to understand his explanation of how an aeroplane engine works, and said 'yes' and 'I see' and 'really' at suitable intervals. I think I did all that was required very well.

However I am very pleased that he's gone, as I find my own society infinitely more agreeable than his, and prefer Tennyson to lectures, however learned, on aeronautics. That's just the perversity of fate. Anyone else who'd been down here alone for a fortnight would have been longing for a companion and of course wouldn't get one, while I, who have been thoroughly enjoying the solitude, (so rare a blessing at school), must have not only a companion, but a talkative one, dumped down. However it was only for three days.

You were saying the other day that when you sat doing nothing of an evening you passed the time in day dreams. I used to day dream a tremendous lot, but these last few days I find when I sit down in a nice chair in front of the fire that I get up an hour later and realise that I've been thinking about absolutely nothing. Is this a sort of mental stagnation I wonder.

Have you seen to the quashing of that dance conspiracy yet? Don't dare to answer in the negative. At any rate there *must* be no dance *for me*; nor for any other rational being I hope. So let that matter receive your immediate attention. You have your orders. Now we may go on.

I suppose the winter has set in at home by now, as it has here. But a very different kind of winter is the good old Belfast 'rainy season' from the English equivalent. Have you been winning any more musical laurels? That is a deed of daring do which should be set up in 'letters all of gold' (vide 'brave Horatius')[42] under a statue in the hall representing you with a symbolical lyre and 'plectrum'. (Look 'plectrum' out in a dictionary of classical terms).

　　your loving
　　son Jack.

---

42 Thomas Babington Macaulay, *Lays of Ancient Rome*, 'Horatius', LXVI, 6.

TO HIS FATHER (LP IV: 115):

School House,
Malvern College.
Postmark: 8 December 1913

My dear Papy,

I am now once more safely ensconced in the house, and so my illness is officially dead and buried. Unfortunately I have missed the Lea Shakespeare exam., in which I think I might have done something. However, these things will happen. There are only two more weeks 'and odd days' as they say in Romeo and Juliet,[43] now. I suppose we shall revise this week and have exams. next, so that the routine is practically over. Write and tell me about W's exam as soon as possible.

We have settled down into real winter weather here, which is always rather pleasing.

I notice in your recent correspondance an absence of any answer to my remarks re the quashing of the dance conspiracy. What is the meaning of this? Am I to understand that it has not been duly slain and buried? If not, why not? As I said before – 'you have your orders'. They were put before you in a plain and forcible manner so that you have no excuse for misunderstanding them. I hope to hear by return of post that the matter is now a thing of the past.

I can quite believe that the Peacockean platitudes were a come down after grandfather's production.[44] Yes: that is a very appropriate text.

During the course of my walks abroad while I was at the San., I met Mr. Taylor, the old Cherbourg drawing master whom you met. He was very distressed because he had heard that I had given up my drawing at the Coll., but was consoled by my assurance that it was only a temporary fixture so long as it clashed with English. We had a very pleasant little chat indeed.

Today was the Repton match, and I suppose Cherbourg was there, but I didn't notice them. It ended in a draw of one all after a very exciting game.

---

43 Shakespeare, *Romeo and Juliet*, I, iii, 15.
44 Mr Peacocke, the rector, gave his last sermon at St Mark's on 30 November. Remembering Thomas Hamilton's farewell sermon from the same pulpit, Albert wrote to Warnie on 30 November saying that Mr Peacocke's sermon was 'an extraordinarily poor performance even for him. I remember an old man some thirteen years ago preaching a farewell sermon from the same place, and I have never been more deeply touched by spoken words in my life' (LP IV: 110).

Allow me to observe that your noisy salutations to this insolent physician are not at all apropos and also were in somewhat questionable taste. I cannot write any more now.

your loving
son Jack.

1914

The year began with anxiety about the entrance examination to Sand-hurst that Warnie had taken in November. But more than that was at stake. Albert was worried about what his son could do with his life, and this had been a question he put to Mr Kirkpatrick more than once. After tutoring him for four months, in preparation for Sandhurst, Mr Kirkpatrick wrote to Albert on 18 December 1913, saying:

> _You ask me as to his abilities. They seem to be good enough. But observe, a question of that nature cannot be answered in the abstract, for the will power, the moral element is involved. You never know what you can do until you try, and very few try unless they have to. Warren had a nice easy time, but no more so than the other fellows he associated with, many of whom were so well off that it did not matter from the economic point of view if they ever did anything or not. Years of association with such boys must have an effect in modifying the outlook. I do not see anything wrong with Warren apart from this slack, easy going quality. He has been blessed by Nature with two of her best gifts – good health and good nature. But it is too late now to make him interested in knowledge. The day for that has gone by. What he needs now is to be at work of some kind, and as soon as possible. I trust there can be little doubt of his passing, and if so, he should go to Sandhurst at once. The life may not be too strenuous, but it will be strenuous enough for him. The mere fact that he has set his mind on it is most important, and I think the army is now no bed of ease. Is he adapted for the life and will he succeed? These are questions very hard to answer. He does not want to go into any business, and dislikes exertion, drudgery, push and all the rest of it. He will probably discover that he cannot escape these things, even in the army. I should like to see a little more ambition in his composition – that_

is the main defect; but something of the kind may come in time. I have warned him that his present ideas may not be his ideas when he is a little older – a hard saying for a boy of course. (LP IV: 118–19)

On 9 January the Civil Service Commissioners published the results of the November examinations, and the Lewises were elated to learn that Warnie passed 21st out of 201 successful candidates for Sandhurst. The first 25 candidates were awarded 'Prize Cadetships' which secured them admission to the College at half fees, and a grant of £50 on obtaining a commission. On 3 February Warnie and Jack crossed, Warnie to the Royal Military College, Camberley, Surrey, for the first time, and Jack back to Malvern.

TO HIS FATHER (LP IV: 130–1):

Gt. Malvern,
Sunday.
7th Feb. [1914]

My dear P.,

Thanks for the cutting which has been read with great interest. In addition to the natural unpleasantness of crossing on a bad night, I am annoyed at having broken my record, as I was sea sick on Tuesday for the first time in my life. It is not a pleasant experience. W. was very ill too, which is strange, as we both thought to have got over that danger.

The rest of the journey to Malvern was pleasant enough, and on my arrival I was pleased to find that Hardman and Quennel[1] had moved into the new study, which is a great success. Like somebody's cocoa, it is 'grateful and comforting'. So far, to my surprise, the weather has been quite mild and springlike, so I hope to get rid of the cold I had when I left home.

Smugy, I am sorry to say, waxed humorous over my illness, observing in that hoarse whisper of his that I must be 'a very delicate flower'. He must be excused of course, as the opportunity was too good for him to

---

1 William Eyre Hamilton Quennel (1898–?) entered School House the same term as Jack, and left Malvern in 1916. From there he went to Sandhurst, and in 1917 was gazetted into the 7th Dragoon Guards. He was promoted to lieutenant the same year. After the war he trained to be a doctor at St Bartholomew's Hospital, London. During World War II he served as medical officer in the Essex Yeomanry.

miss. I suppose it is a priviledge of old age. Otherwise he has been very pleasant, almost effusive, which is an unusual state of affairs with him.

I find there are even less than eight weeks more this term, which of course is good news for both of us. Quennel has already disappeared from the arena with a cold and an ear ache. We hear to our inexpressible joy that the good matron is leaving this term. More than we dared to hope. And, in considering about future possibles, it is a comfort to know that whatever happens, we can't get anything worse.[2]

There must be a lot of talk at home about the Greeves affair. What was the dinner like? When you write be sure and tell me all the latest developments. 'The case', as Sherlock Holmes would say, 'is not devoid of interest.'

What is W's address? I know it is Camberley, but there are a lot of codotta about companies and so forth, are there not?

I am afraid I must again 'bite your ear' for ten shillings. An unexpected outrage has occurred. A tax of five shillings a head is being levied for the Old Boy's leaving present, and another five for that of the James. I consider this rather stiff, but I am afraid it must be done. Please send it as soon as possible. I suppose the hat will be going round for various leaving presents all through this term. Another of the fees one has to pay for the benefit of a Public School education. But I think these places are doomed. Books like 'The Horrovians' form the thin end of the wedge.[3] It will end in a terrible debacle. I must stop now.

your loving
son Jack.

TO HIS FATHER (LP IV: 137–8):

[Malvern College]
Postmark: 16 February 1914

My dear Papy,

Thanks very much indeed for the unexpected donation and also for the exacted fund. 'An excellent thing – money' as an old friend of ours is wont to observe.

---

2 'The good matron' was Miss Backhurst, of whom Warnie wrote: 'She was better known and abominated by many generations of School House boys under her usual appellation of "The Old Bitch". She was a weak, spiteful, fussy, prying old woman, absurdly sensitive on the point of dignity, and like so many stupid women, always seeing ridicule where none was intended' (LP IV: 131).
3 Sir Arnold Lunn, *The Harrovians* (1913).

Although others at Malvern have proved wanting in perspicacity with regard to Warnie's brilliant successes, I was glad to see that Smugy was free from the general reproach. He lost no time in congratulating me warmly, and asking me to convey all the appropriate remarks to W. in my next letter. Such things are perhaps not great acts of kindness. But they serve to mark the difference between those who care for their old pupils and those who do not. Indeed the more I see of that remarkable old man, the more I like and admire him. I wish you knew him. If ever you come to visit Malvern again, you must not leave without making his acquaintance.

This week he has set us a job at which I hope to be able to do something. The alternatives were,

a   poem in imitation of Horace asking a friend to stay with you at the most beautiful spot you know.

b   A picture of a specified scene from Sophocles.

c   An original ghost story.

As you have probably guessed, I chose the first. I invited an imaginary friend to stay at Castlerock. As that would be impossible in verse I changed it to Moville, which is a little village near the former, as you remember. I treated the cliffs, seas, etc. at some length, and have taken pains over it. It is to be shown up tomorrow, and I hope it will be a success. I have written again in the metre of Locksley Hall; it is to be hoped that Smugy will not think that this shows a lack of invention or variety. If he does, I shall point out that some people like Pope and Addison wrote all their poems in the same metre. But of course Horace was a greater man than either of those. However, after a lot of thinking I came to the conclusion that no other metre would do as well. Horace is really impossible to translate: but I think we can imitate him in tolerable style. Everything so far is very pleasant in the Upper V.

How can people advocate a 'modern' education? What could be better or more enjoyable than reading the greatest masterpieces of all time, under a man who has made them part of himself? And against this some are foolish enough to oppose algebra and French verbs! The Greek Grammar has not yet put in an appearance. We are turning our attention to Latin where, of course I get on better.

I have seen Dr. Mackay who orders me to continue those annoying breathing exercises and not to play footer. The latter is a great comfort. The other a useful annoyance.

By the way I find I need another coat here. The present one is getting, not shabby, but tired looking, and the other is too small. Could you get Cummings to make me a new black coat to *exactly* the same measurements as the last. Only three buttons. Or, if it be more convenient, is there an old one of W's that would do?

Hichens has been down at the Sanatorium and has just come back. On a walk today I met Tubbs who asked me to go up to Cherbourg tomorrow. I think I shall.

your loving
son Jack.

TO HIS FATHER (LP IV: 152):

[Malvern College]
Postmark: 18 March 1914

My dear Papy,

Please excuse my delay in answering your letter. But I have had no time for any of my private affairs for all this week. I think that your criticism on the report are perfectly just; but I would like to remind you that not only does this persecution get harder to bear as time goes on, but that it is actually getting more severe. As for the work indeed, things are now much brighter, and I have been getting on all right since half term.

But, out of school, life gets more and more dreary; all the prefects detest me and lose no opportunity of venting their spite. Today, for not being able to find a cap which one gentleman wanted, I have been sentenced to clean his boots every day after breakfast for a week. It is after breakfast that the form goes through their translation together. From this I am cut off. When I asked if I might clean them in the evening (an arrangement which you observe would have made no difference to him), I received a refusal, strengthened by being kicked downstairs.

So we go on. These brutes of illiterate, ill-managed English prefects are always watching for an opportunity to drop upon you. There is no escape from them, night or day. There is some consolation in knowing that every one else is in the same box: all my friends too, are utterly miserable and tired of life. Perhaps you ask why we don't complain to the Old Boy. Sometimes a poor creature, driven wild by injustice and oppression, does try it. The Old Boy of course does his best: but what is the result? The prefects return to the persecution of the boy with renewed vigour. The place is systematically made uninhabitable for him, and he usually leaves. So that way is barred.

Please take me out of this as soon as possible but don't, whatever you do, write to the James or the Old Boy, as that would only make matters worse. Thank goodness there are only 2 weeks more; that must be our wee bit of 'silver lining'. You can't think how I'm longing to get back to you and Leeborough again. See and keep quite well yourself.

your loving
son Jack.

TO HIS FATHER (LP IV: 155):

[Malvern College]
Postmark: 22 March 1914

My dear Papy,

What a good thing the police did *not* turn up to arrest Craig.[4] If they had, I suppose you would be in the thick of it now.

No: I think I had better wait till the Tuesday and attend the House Supper. Not that I want to of course, but Maxwell and all the other Irish boys are waiting as it is Jimmy's last term, and you can't very well go early this time. So please book the berth for that night.

In common justice I feel that I ought to correct the notion which, very naturally, I have given you of Hichens. It is only fair to say that he is always ready to do anything he can for me or for anyone else. But the truth of the matter is that, though nominally head of the house, he has to mind his P's and Q's very carefully. The *real* head of the house is a splendid physical animal called Browning, who is one of the worst cads I have ever met. But he certainly *has* got 'guts' and bends the other prefects to his will with a rod of iron. They are all afraid of him. But Hichens, although neither clever or strong minded, is a kindly and gentlemanly sort of person. I have no complaints against him. But we are now so near

---

4 James Craig, first Viscount Craigavon (1871–1940), statesman. He was born in Belfast and was the MP for East Down 1906–18; MP for Mid-Down 1918–21; parliamentary secretary to the Ministry of Pensions 1919–20 and to the Admiralty 1920–1. He was chief secretary to Sir Edward Carson in opposing home rule, and was active in organizing means of resistance in Ulster. He was the first prime minister of Northern Ireland 1921–40. Captain Craig, as he was in 1914, was a very popular figure in the North of Ireland, and his house was about a hundred yards from Little Lea.

the end of the term that I am beginning to take a philosophical view of things: all will soon be over.

Although the papers are full of it, the people here don't seem to grasp the Ulster situation very much: one person asked me this morning if it was *for* Home Rule or against it that the volunteers were being formed.

Last night we had a lecture about Russia which was quite interesting.
your loving
son Jack.

Jack arrived at Little Lea on 25 March. His father, knowing how desperately unhappy he was at Malvern, was already in correspondence with Warnie about the matter. 'Your news about Jack is unpleasant,' Warnie said on 23 March,

> but to me at least, not unexpected: from the moment he first came home and told me his opinion of the Coll., I was afraid it could only be a matter of time until he made the place too hot to hold him. I remember asking if it was not a splendid feeling at the end of a house match when you realised that your own house had won: "I saw a lot of boys throwing their caps in the air and making unpleasant noises: yes, I suppose it is an interesting study"...I had an idea that Malvern would weave its influence round Jacks as it did around me, and give him four very happy years and memories and friendships which he would carry with him to the grave...I am all in favour of sending him to Kirk. There would be no one there except Mr and Mrs K for him to talk to, and he could amuse himself by detonating his little stock of cheap intellectual fireworks under old K's nose. (LP IV: 156–7)

Albert replied on 29 March:

> I honestly confess that knowing Jack's mind and character, I am not greatly surprised to find him and a Public School unsuited to one another. In saying that I blame neither the one nor the other. He is simply out of his proper environment, and would possibly wither and decay rather than grow if kept in such surroundings...What is to be done? For a boy like Jacks to spend the next

three or four years alone with an old man like Kirk is almost certain to strengthen the very faults that are strongest in his disposition. He will make no acquaintances. He will see few people and he will grow more into a hermit than ever. The position is a difficult one and gives me many anxious hours. (LP IV: 160)

Albert asked Mr Kirkpatrick what he advised, and in his letter of 17 April he suggested that he send Jack back to Campbell College in Belfast. 'The Campbell College is at your door,' he said. 'If he went there, he would be in contact with you, which ought surely to count for much at this period of growth...It is very kind of you to think of sending him to me, but do you not think it a little premature?' (LP IV: 165). Mr Lewis persisted, almost begging Mr Kirkpatrick to accept him. 'If he can hold on through this summer,' Mr Kirkpatrick replied on 30 April, 'I hope I shall be ready (if I am spared) to receive him in the autumn, if you are still in the same mind then. And here let me say that I feel almost overwhelmed by the compliment to myself personally which your letter expresses. To have been the teacher of the father and his two sons is surely a unique experience' (LP IV: 167). Although Jack didn't want to go back to Malvern for even one more term, Mr Lewis got him to agree to it as an 'experiment'. If it became too bad, he would leave.

Sometime in mid-April, while this debate was going on, Jack came to know his 'First Friend'. 'His name was Arthur [Greeves]' he wrote in SBJ VIII,

> and he was my brother's exact contemporary; he and I had been at Campbell together though we never met...I received a message saying that Arthur was in bed, convalescent, and would welcome a visit. I can't remember what led me to accept this invitation, but for some reason I did.
>
> I found Arthur sitting up in bed. On the table beside him lay a copy of Myths of the Norsemen.[5]
>
> 'Do you like that?' said I.
>
> 'Do you like that?' said he.
>
> Next moment the book was in our hands, our heads were bent close together, we were pointing, quoting, talking – soon almost

---

5 H.M.A. Guerber, *Myths of the Norsemen from the Eddas and Sagas* (1908).

shouting – discovering in a torrent of questions that we liked not only the same thing, but the same parts of it and in the same way...Many thousands of people have had the experience of finding the first friend, and it is none the less a wonder; as great a wonder...as first love, or even a greater. I had been so far from thinking such a friend possible that I had never even longed for one; no more than I longed to be King of England.

TO HIS FATHER (LP IV: 169–70):

[Malvern College]
Postmark: 3 May 1914

My dear Papy,

I suppose, when I come to think of the matter, it was rather foolish of me to write and ask for 'a coat', without specifying what kind. One is apt to imagine at times that the person to whom you speak can keep up with your thoughts, whether they are expressed or not. What I want is a common or garden jacket coat, same measurements as the last, and with not more than three buttons on the front.

There are now only some five weeks more. Thank goodness!! For to tell the truth, Malvern is hardly the place for a long stay. I think it would be as well to stick to our original plan of leaving at the end of the term. It is rather heavy going; the ceaseless round of fagging, hunting for clothes and books that have been 'borrowed', and other jobs that have to be done in what is euphemistically known as your 'spare time', gets very trying. It is literally true that from the time you get up in the morning till the time you go to bed at night, you have not a moment to spare.

And the worst of it all seems to be that I am not getting on too well in form. It's discouraging. Whether it is that I haven't time to do it, or that I'm losing my mental faculties, or the fact that it is getting harder, I don't know: but the fact remains that things aren't as they should be. Goodness knows, I work as hard as I can. But it's all uphill. For instance, if you are hoping to do some of your surplus work in the interval between breakfast and morning school, it is very hard to have to give up that time to cleaning boots for some great big brute of a prefect at the bottom of the school. Then of course, as all your arrangements have been thrown out of joint, you don't know the lesson. And you can't give Smugy the real explanation. My chief dread is that he may get a bad impression, and I prize his opinion as much as that of any one. Then again, the whole atmosphere of the place is so brutal and unsavoury. In one word, it *won't do.*

Of course this is no new discovery. We both agreed last holidays that it was only an experiment, and I am now giving the result of that experiment. There is no need for you to worry or to do anything other than we have already thought of. But I consider it better to let you know straight away that this place is a failure, than to leave the botch over until it is irreparable. I suppose Kirk's is the best place for me. At any rate one of these 'English Public Schools', so famed in song and story, is not. To get on well at one of these, one needs to have a constitution of iron, a hide so thick that no insult will penetrate it, a brain that will never tire, and an intelligence able and ready to cope with the sharp gentlemen who surround you.

But these places are doomed. Books like the 'Harrovians' are the thin end of the wedge: and I don't mind saying that if you came back in a couple of hundred years, there would be no Public Schools left. That is a sort of consolation: for, among other things, one learns here a power of hating with an almost incredible intensity. However, I suppose this sort of education is found to be suitable for some people. But on others it comes rather hard.

To turn to a brighter topic, I am very pleased to hear that W. is getting on well at Sandhurst. His letters to me are very cheerful, and at the same time more serious than some of his communications have been. All these facts point in the right direction.

In the mean time, how are things in the ancient and honourable city of Belfast? Perhaps all this unpleasantness in a foreign land has its use, in that it teaches one to love home and things connected with home all the more, by contrast. I suppose the aggravation of the social nuisance, which always accompanies Xmas has now died down. And what are the attractions at the popular houses of entertainment? Among other things that I want to know, has the great fire mystery been solved yet? It destroys my mental picture of Leeborough if I am not sure whether there still be a wall between the hall and the study or not. However, I am glad to say that I shall be able to see the whole thing for myself at no very distant date.

It is now half term, and there are only four or five weeks more. They will not be long in the going. I wonder is there any truth in the idea that a wise man can be equally happy in any circumstances. It suddenly struck me the other day that if you could imagine you were at home during the term, it would be just as good as the reality.

your loving

son Jack

TO HIS FATHER (LP IV: 173–4):

[Malvern College]
Postmark: 17 May 1914

My dear P.,

I must really apologise elaborately and profusely for having left you letterless this week: but the fact is that this has been my first opportunity.

First of all, you will be interested to learn that our friend Browning has not, as he anticipated, been raised from the position of House Pre. to that of School Pre. Instead, a humble and inoffensive person named Parker[6] has been placed above him; at which you may well imagine his chagrin and my delight.

The new headmaster[7] has created a good impression here already by making the servants clean our boots – thereby abolishing the most obnoxious source of fagging. So far he has spoken very little indeed, but when he speaks it is in a pleasant voice and in good English. He wastes no time. All this shapes very well, although (thank goodness) I shall not see much of his career.

Smugy's wit on my late return did not exercise itself in my presence. But on the first day, as I am told, he expressed a fear lest I had been 'killed in the war'. Ah, well! These people will soon learn that war is not a subject for joking; so for that shall we too.

The worst part of the summer term is the fact that we have to keep out of doors nearly all our time; but here one notices the great advantage of being in the Upper School, and therefore allowed to go into the

---

6 Gerard Parker (1896–?) was in School House 1910–14, and was school prefect. After leaving Malvern he went to Sandhurst, passing from there in 1915 into the Devon Regiment. He was promoted to lieutenant in 1917 and during the war he was mentioned in despatches. He made captain in 1926, and retired in 1931.

7 Canon James had been succeeded as headmaster by Frank Sansome Preston (1875–1970) who had been educated at Marlborough College and Pembroke College, Cambridge. He was an assistant master at Marlborough 1899–1914, and headmaster of Malvern 1914–37.

Grundy Library at all hours of the day – it proves a great refuge when the 'house' is out of bounds.[8]

I have received a letter from Arthur Greeves. Intimate to him the fact that a suitable reply is being composed at our leisure. Note the royal plural. Well, it's a good thing that two weeks at any rate have gone. How are the 'rheumatics' keeping? I suppose by this time you are in the depths of the house cleaning ceremony: have the study and hall been knocked into one, or any other funny thing happened?

This term in the Grundy I have discovered a new poet whom I must get, Yeats. I never read any of his works before, and both what he says and the way he says it, please me immensely. Do you know him or care for him at all?

Just one bit of 'Kodotto' before we stop. In the study or in *your* dressing room (not mine), you will find a little black book of Warnie's, a Greek Testament. I should be very glad if you would send it here as soon as possible.

> your loving
> son Jack

TO HIS FATHER (LP IV: 179–80):

[Malvern College]
Postmark: 31 May 1914

My dear Papy,

Many apologies again for these same 'epistolary shortcomings'. But the days this term are so very full, and are spent so much out of doors that it is very hard to polish off the weekly letter with anything like regularity.

What a nuisance that old arm is to be sure. However, I expect that when the fine weather sets in it will improve. I am sorry that in asking you to procure my Attic pentateuch I was compelling you to embark upon a voyage at once perilous and disagreeable and arduous (Johnsonese again). I hope that by the time this letter reaches you, the study wall will have been replaced and the stately hall of Leeborough will smile upon guest and inhabitant with its pristine splendour and hospitality. Of

---

8 In *SBJ* VII Lewis said that while 'Smewgy' was the major blessing of Malvern, the other 'undisguised blessing of the Coll was "the Gurney", the school library; not because it was a library, but because it was a sanctuary. As the negro used to become free on touching English soil, so the meanest boy was "unfaggable" once he was inside the Gurney.'

course in restoring the 'main library' you are careful to alter the appearance of the room as little as possible. It would be a pity if I came home to a strange house. In the meantime I hope that the small library has been allowed to remain untouched?

This week I am glad to say that the Greek grammar has been going a good deal better; I hope this will continue, as it would be a pleasure to secure a good report of these people before I left. Happily Browning has been ill at the Sanatorium since last Monday, which has kept him out of mischief for *one* week at least. Last week I got out of the library the works of our present poet laureate, Bridges, who did not impress me a bit;[9] but I have now struck better ground in Charlotte Bronte's 'Wuthering Heights',[10] which although melodramatic like all her books, shapes very well indeed.

Before I close I must request you to forward a little of the 'ready' as owing to exorbitant subscriptions, fines, and the expenses of the summer term, our whole study has run out of cash. As long as one of us was flush the other two could live upon him, but when all three are in this condition it is impossible.

I hope that your arm will not remain 'hors de combat' very long.

Your loving

son Jack

TO ARTHUR GREEVES (W/LP IV: 180–1):

[Malvern College
5 June 1914]

Dear Arthur,

I really must apologize for having kept such a long and unjustifiable – silence. But the readiest means of mending that fault are those of writing fully and at once – which I now propose to do. To begin at the beginning, you had hardly been outside Little Lea for twenty minutes when a chance of not going back seemed to be held out to me, only, as you may guess, to be snatched away again. When we came to pack up my last few belongings, what should happen but that no key was to be found for my trunk! High and low we searched, but not a sign of it. My father

---

9 Robert Bridges (1844–1930), Poet Laureate from 1913. His poetry appeared in a single volume in 1912, and this was probably what Lewis was reading.

10 Emily Brontë, *Wuthering Heights* (1847).

was in despair: how was I to go back? How long would it take to have a new lock fitted? For a few moments I had a wild hope of staying at home. What was my disgust, when, almost at the last moment, Annie[11] turned up with the required artical, and off I had to go!

Since then, I have lived or existed as one does at School. How dreary it all is! I could make some shift to put up with the work, the discomfort, and the school feeding: such inconveniences are only to be expected. But what irritates me more than anything else is the absolute lack of appreciation of anything like music or books which prevails among the people whom I am forced to call my companions. Can you imagine what it is like to live for twelve weeks among boys whose thoughts never rise above the dull daily round of cricket and work and eating? But I must not complain like this, I suppose. Malvern has its good points. It teaches one to appreciate home, and to despise that sort of lifelessness. If I had never seen the horrible spectacle which these coarse, brainless English schoolboys present, there might be a danger of my sometimes becoming like that myself. But, as it is, I have had warning enough for a lifetime. Another good point about Malvern is the Library, which is one of the best-stocked I have ever been in – not that anyone but myself and two or three others care twopence about it, of course! I have here discovered an author exactly after my own heart, whom I am sure you would delight in, W.B. Yeats. He writes plays and poems of rare spirit and beauty about our old Irish mythology. I must really get my father to buy his books when I come home. His works have all got that strange, eerie feeling about them, of which we are both proffessed admirers. I must get hold of them, certainly.

You can hardly tell how glad I was to hear that you were learning theory. It is a positive shame that you should go about with all those lofty strains running in your head, and yet never set pen to paper to perpetuate them. Of course, take the 'Loki Bound' MS.[12] over to Bernagh,[13] anytime you feel inclined to compose a little operatic music. Thank you very much indeed for undertaking the job of the gramaphone. I suppose by this time it is restored to its former condition. It makes me furious to think of your being able to walk about your house and ours and all the

---

11 Annie Strahan was the cook-housekeeper at Little Lea, 1911–17.
12 The tragedy, Norse in subject and Greek in form, which Lewis was writing.
13 The Greeves's home in Circular Road was directly across from Little Lea.

beautiful places we know in the country, while I am cooped up in this hot, ugly country of England. Where is your favourite walk? I hope that by this time you are quite recovered and are able to go about freely without fear of injury. County Down must be looking glorious just now: I can just picture the view of the Lough and Cave Hill from beside the Shepard's Hut. Sometime next holydays, you and I must make a journey up their before breakfast. Have you ever done that? The sunrise over the Holywood Hills, and the fresh stillness of the early morning are well worth the trouble of early rising, I can assure you.

Since I have touched on the subject of health, I must ask a few questions of a disagreeable nature, on a matter which I have very near my heart. I have now had no direct letter from my father for over three weeks, and I hear that he is very ill. I would be very thankful indeed if you would go over and see him sometimes, and try and cheer him up: then you could tell me exactly how he is, and whether what I have heard has been exagerated or not – although I really don't deserve a reply to this after the shameful way I have treated you with regard to letters. But I feel sure you won't mind writing just a few lines, to tell me about yourself and family, and the state of various other things, besides my father's health. As I am sure you are tired by this time of a long and melancholy letter, I will stop.

Yours affectionately
Jack Lewis

TO HIS FATHER (LP IV: 190–1):

[Malvern College]
Postmark: 22 June 1914

My dear Papy,

Since I last wrote to you, I received, with your knowledge as I gather, a letter from Annie, short and comfortless enough to be sure, but still something to keep me from alarm. The most promising thing about her communication was that she promises me a letter from you at no very distant date. Do not force yourself to write until you feel thoroughly fit – but when you can, let me have a rare budget of news and reflections to compensate for the weeks 'that the locust hath eaten'.[14] Above all, don't forget to tell me all about yourself. I will spare you the trite expressions

---

14 Joel 1:4.

of sorrow and hope for your recovery; between those who know each other so well, such remarks are out of place, and I am sure you have had enough of that sort of thing. I should like to encourage you to cheer up if I thought I should have any success in that line; I must at any rate mention one consoling circumstance – namely that it is now half way through this dreary term, and is only five weeks till we shall be together again. This week you will get the report: and I hope and pray, not without confidence, that it will do nothing to add to your discomfort. I think I have now crossed the Rubicon in Greek Grammar, and am now happily arrived at the safe side of it. Mr. Smith [Smugy] has been very kind to me indeed, and I think we shall part friends.

This week I have been reading a most remarkable book which has created a great impression. It is 'The Upton Letters',[15] a series of letters from a school master at 'Upton College' to a friend whose health confines him in Madeira. They purport to have been actually written on such an occasion and not for publication; and indeed the utter absence of plot, or in some cases even of connection, make this seem to be true, although their wonderful beauty argues against it. But to come to my point: the great revelation of the book is the statement made somewhere that we 'ought not to write about our actions but about our thoughts'. How wonderfully true. We busy ourselves, you and I, telling each other about the weather and the little trivial happenings of each day, while the thoughts of our hearts, the really great experiences of our selves, are seldom spoken of. Of course this is rather rhetorical and letters written entirely on those lines would tend to become monotonous. But the saying struck me so forcibly at the time that I thought I would mention it to you.

This week the natural course of our life has been torn up as it were, by a cyclone in the form of speech day. I suppose you will be able to read Preston's speech in the Times, and give your own verdict upon it.[16] For my part, I did not see much merit in it – a few trite maxims, a few of the usual jokes, and that was all. In fact if the truth must be told, Preston is not a big man. He is, as far as I can see, a learned and courtly gentleman of captivating manners, but not the person who can save the ruin of a tottering school. Malvern would seem to be fated by the gods never to

---

15 Arthur Christopher Benson, *The Upton Letters* (1905).
16 *The Times* (2 June 1914), p. 9.

secure the right man as her headmaster. It is gratifying for me to think that I may live to see the end of this place. Perhaps that is an ungenerous thought: and I should hesitate to bestow my loathing so heartily on anything, even an inanimate object, if I did not think that it would be a real benefit for the country if this place were suppressed.

At this time of the year especially, one sees how awfully the place misses its mark. The whole of our spare time is given up to the great business of our life – cricket. Cricket is played with intense seriousness, and the players are usually in a very bad temper with themselves and everyone else, owing to the strain put on their minds by such a stupendous affair. Now for me, work is the business of the term: I am tired when I come out of school, and should like some recreation. Unfortunately, I am frankly and desperately bored by the recreations that are forced upon me. And yet it is obvious that one must have compulsory games at school: but if you do, as it seems, they are given this ludicrous preponderance and become for some the absorbing interest of their life, and for others a bogie and an incubus.

I enclose a few verses in imitation of Ovid, which were top of the form last week and well spoken of by Smugy. Do you care for that metre? There are a great many rhymes in it, which makes it difficult; but the thing that I want to learn is 'to move easily in shackles' (I wonder who said that? Do you know?)

Before I close I must again make shift to bite the paternal ear; as the 10/- which you were kind enough to send has been absorbed in paying off old debts and buying back for the study things which had been sold in the days of extreme embarrasment. I hope you won't think this extravagant.

See you take care of yourself, and write as soon as you are able.

your loving

son Jack

The following poem was enclosed with the letter above. The words underlined by 'Smewgy' are in capital type, and his remarks are in brackets.

'Ovid's "Pars estis pauci"'

(Metre copied from a chorus in Swinburne's 'Atalanta in Calydon')

I.

Of the host whom I NAMED
As friend, ye alone
Dear few!, were ashamed
In troubles unknown
To leave me deserted; but boldly ye cherished my cause as
your own.
(Yes.)

II.

My thanks shall endure
— The poor tribute I paid
To a faith that was pure —
Till my ashes be laid
In the urn; and the Stygian boatmen I seek, an
impalpable shade.
(Yes, but not Ovid.)

III.

But nay! For the days
Of a mortal are few;
Shall they limit your praise
Nay rather to you
Each new generation shall offer — if aught be
remembered — your due.

IV.

For the lofty frame (hardly scans.)
That my VERSES ENFOLD,
Men still shall acclaim
Thro' ages untold;
And still shall they speak of your virtue; your honour
they still shall uphold.
(Yes.)

TO HIS FATHER (LP IV: 192–3):

[Malvern College]
Postmark: 29 June 1914

My dear Papy,

On Friday I got a letter from you for the first time since this trouble, and glad I was to get it. It has been a bad business, but I am glad to see that you are over the worst of it now. Be careful of yourself, and take care that you don't go back to your ordinary routine until you are thoroughly fit.

My mental picture of home is disturbed to a certain extent by your mention of a fire. Here, we are in the middle of a magnificent summer: day succeeds day with the same cloudless sky and parched earth, and the nights are hot and comfortless. But on the whole, fine weather is agreeable, and has, I think, a certain effect on the spirits. Thank you very much for the money, which will enable 'the firm' to live 'en prince' until the time of our exile be over, and I return to a lovelier country to lead a happier life.

On the Tuesday of this week an unusual thing happened. Smugy asked myself and another boy in the same form and house, by name Cooper, to motor over with him to a little place called Birchwood in the country, where we had tea at an inn, and took a long delightful walk through fields and woods to a place where we were again picked up by the car, and thus home again. It was indeed very kind of the old man, as I am sure he sees quite enough of us in school hours. We went through a very beautiful piece of country, far, far away to the N. West of the hills where we could never go in an ordinary walk. To me, tired as I was of the flat, plain, and ugly hills of Malvern, this region, with its long masses of rolling hills and valleys, variegated by close mysterious woods and cornfields, together with one or two streams, was an enchanted ground. The Malvern hills loomed as a dark mass not far off the horizon: seen at this distance, they had lost their sharpness of outline, and looked weird and unreal, but very beautiful.

Here, in the middle of all this, we came upon the little cottage which used to be the summer resort of Elgar,[17] the composer, formerly an intimate friend of Smugy's. The latter told us that Elgar used to say he was

---

17 Sir Edward Elgar (1857–1934), composer, who rose to international fame about 1900
through his choral and orchestral music. He was living in Worcester at this time.

able to read a musical score in his hand, and hear in his mind not only the main theme of the music, but also the different instruments and all the side currents of sound. What a wonderful state of mind!

This week I have taken a course of A.C. Benson's essays, which have impressed me very favourably indeed. Do you know them? He has a clear, simple, but melodious style, second as I think only to Ruskin, and the matter is always suggestive, weighty, and original. He always makes you think, which a book ought to.

your loving
son Jack

TO HIS FATHER (LP IV: 196–7):

[Malvern College]
6/7/14

My dear Papy,

I was glad to get your letter on Saturday, as I was beginning to grow somewhat anxious about you. I am glad indeed to hear that you are on the mend, and hope that the term 'mending' will soon be out of place. So the report has come at last. Though I could have wished for something more effusive, still it is pleasing to note that it is an improvement on the last one, and I hope that the next in its turn will be a proportionate advance. Yes. I think the old man has some regard for me, but, it must be remembered that even if I were to return next winter, I should no longer be under him, as all our form are getting a shove to make way for the influx of new scholarship people.

This week I have enjoyed the doubtful privilege of having two teeth extracted, both of which had been bothering me a good deal off and on this term. The dentist, who is a thoroughly competent official, pronounced his verdict that as they had been tinkered with over and over again, and were now hopelessly rotten, they had better come out. So out they came, with gas, and I think it was a good job.

I am at present engaged in reading Newman's poems:[18] do you know them at all? They are very, very delicate and pretty, and are like nothing more than one of those valuable painted Chinese vases which a touch would destroy. I must except from this criticism the 'Dream of

---

18 John Henry Newman, *Verses on Various Occasions* (1868).

Gerontius',[19] which is very strongly written. But the rest are almost too delicate for my taste: it is a kind of beauty that I can't very much appreciate.

We have had two thunderstorms this week, and their combined efforts have left the ground pretty much under water, which is a great relief, as it puts an end to that eternal cricket. I wonder which is the more fatiguing, being made to play oneself, or watching others play it? We have plenty of both here, and both are compulsory.

But to turn to a better theme, do you realise that there is barely a month more this term; and I am already beginning to look forward to the end of it. That, I think, is one of the really priceless pleasures of youth – this joy of home coming, the gradual approach to the familiar surroundings etc. – as an old friend of ours once said on another subject, 'it can't be beat'.

Which reminds me, has Arthur got the gramophone mended yet?

your loving

son Jack

TO HIS FATHER (LP IV: 197–8):

[Malvern College]
Postmark: 13 July 1914

My dear Papy,

Although there has been no letter this week, I do hope that you have not had a relapse or anything, and that you are getting on all right.

This week we have had a Repton match here, and other things which must now be told. A nice impression truly these people will take back of Malvern and the Malvernians! One evening, during the game called 'crockets' (which is a kind of impromptu cricket played with soft balls on the stretch of gravel outside S.H.), two real knuts from Repton strolled up, and began watching at a distance: this is what they saw. Browning, whose ball had been hit over into Mr. Preston's garden, turned round to

---

19 Newman's *Dream of Gerontius* depicts the journey of the soul to God at the hour of death. In 1900 it was set to music by Elgar, who regarded the work as his masterpiece. Lewis came to like the *Dream* very much in later life and in a discussion of Purgatory in chapter 20 of *Letters to Malcolm* (1964) he said 'the right view returns magnificently in Newman's *Dream*'.

an inoffensive person called Hamley,[20] who has just been made a prefect, and demanded the latter's ball. This request was very naturally refused: whereupon our friend Browning proceeds to take it by force, and with many blows and oaths, succeeded in ejecting the other down the bank. Then, noticing the not unnatural mirth of the Reptonians at the sight of two public school prefects fighting and rolling in the mud like street boys, he turned round and told them in terms which I cannot reproduce, 'not to grin at *him*', with a great emphasis on the last word.

So this is our public school dignity, politeness and hospitality which we are always hearing about! These are the institutions that all other civilised countries envy us for, and would imitate if they could. Bah! I for one, will be glad to be rid of them all, and would like to see the day when they are abolished. But as for this Browning, perhaps we judged him too harshly. It is very true that we never know the data for any case but our own. I hear he is not happy at home: so that, although it may be that he is such a beast that he cannot be well treated, yet on the other hand it may be that he has been made into a beast. One never knows.

Last week we had an essay on the difference between Genius and Talent, and mine has been 'sent up for good', the ceremony which I told you of.[21] Only three weeks more now.

　　your loving
　　son Jacks

On Saturday, 19 September 1914 Jack arrived at Great Bookham to be met at the station by the man he'd heard about all his life, W.T. Kirkpatrick. 'I came prepared,' he later wrote in SBJ IX,

> *to endure a perpetual luke-warm shower bath of sentimentality. That was the price I was ready to pay for the infinite blessedness of escaping school...One story of my father's, in particular, gave me the most embarrassing forebodings. He had loved to tell how once*

20　Cedric Edwin Hamley (1899–1997) was an exact contemporary of Jack Lewis in School House, having arrived in the third term of 1913. He left in 1915 and served in the war with the London Rifle Brigade. He was afterwards a 2nd lieutenant in the RAF, and a captain in the 3rd London Fusiliers from 1922–28. He worked in the family business, C. Hamley Ltd. in London.

21　It is reproduced in LP IV: 198–200.

at Lurgan when he was in some kind of trouble or difficulty, the Old Knock, or the dear Old Knock, had drawn him aside and there 'quietly and naturally' slid his arm round him and rubbed his dear old whiskers against my father's youthful cheek and whispered a few words of comfort...And here was Bookham at last, and there was the arch-sentimentalist himself waiting to meet me...He was over six feet tall, very shabbily dressed...lean as a rake, and immensely muscular. His wrinkling face seemed to consist entirely of muscles, so far as it was visible; for he wore moustache and side whiskers with a clean-shaven chin like Emperor Franz Joseph. The whiskers, you will understand, concerned me very much at that moment. My cheek tingled in anticipation...

Apparently, however, the old man was holding his fire. We shook hands, and though his grip was like iron pincers it was not lingering. A few minutes later we were walking away from the station. 'You are now,' said Kirk, 'proceeding along the principal artery between Great and Little Bookham.' I stole a glance at him. Was this geographical exordium a heavy joke? Or was he trying to conceal his emotions? His face, however, showed only an inflexible gravity. I began to 'make conversation' in the deplorable manner which I had acquired at those evening parties and indeed found increasingly necessary to use with my father. I said I was surprised at the 'scenery' of Surrey; it was much 'wilder' than I had expected.

'Stop!' shouted Kirk with a suddenness that made me jump. 'What do you mean by wildness and what grounds had you for not expecting it?' I replied I don't know what, still 'making conversation'. As answer after answer was torn to shreds it at last dawned upon me that he really wanted to know. He was not making conversation, nor joking, nor snubbing me; he wanted to know. I was stung into attempting a real answer. A few passes sufficed to show that I had no clear and distinct idea corresponding to the word 'wildness', and that, in so far as I had any idea at all, 'wildness' was a singularly inept word. 'Do you not see, then,' concluded the Great Knock, 'that your remark was meaningless?'...By this time our acquaintance had lasted about three and a half minutes; but the tone set by this first conversation was preserved without a single break during all the years I spent at Bookham...If ever a man *came near to being a purely logical entity, that man was Kirk...Some boys would not have liked it; to me it was red beef and strong beer.*

TO HIS FATHER (LP IV: 212):

[Gastons,
Great Bookham,
Surrey]
Sept. 21st [1914]

My dear Papy,

I arrived, as you heard by the telegram, at Great Bookham in perfect safety and with all my effects. Today is Monday and you must excuse my not writing yesterday as some friends of Mine Host's called in the afternoon when I had intended to do this.

Need I say how thoroughly satisfied I am with Bookham, Gastons, and their inhabitants. You already know all about Kirk – more than I do probably – and W. has spoken of Mrs. K., whom I like exceedingly.

The country is absolutely glorious. I took my first tour of exploration this afternoon, and went through the outskirts of a large forest. One was strongly reminded of 'As you like it'.[22] The village is one such as I have often read of, but never before seen. The little row of red roofed cottages, the old inn, and the church dating from the Conquest might all have stepped out of the Vicar of Wakefield.[23] How Arthur would enjoy this place!

Another point of gratification is that I have at last, triumphantly, found a dirtier railway than the Co. Down. (I wonder have you any shares in the London & S. Western?) Kirk's son,[24] who is in a volunteer camp near here called for an hour or so last night. We get the 'Whig' here, which gives a touch of home. I hope you are keeping in good health

---

22 William Shakespeare, *As You Like It* (1623).
23 Oliver Goldsmith, *The Vicar of Wakefield* (1766).
24 George Louis Kirkpatrick (1882–1943) was the only child of Mr and Mrs Kirkpatrick. He was born 23 May 1882 when his father was still headmaster of Lurgan College, and educated in England at Charterhouse 1896–99. From there he went to work for the electrical engineers, Browett, Lindley & Co., English Makers of Patricroft, Manchester. When Mr Kirkpatrick retired from Lurgan he and Mrs Kirkpatrick moved to Manchester to be near him. Now Louis was in a camp near Great Bookham. He was general manager of Bruce Peebles & Co. (Engineers) in Edinburgh from 1932 until his death in 1943.

and spirits and letting Tim sleep indoors. Of course there are sewing meetings and all the usual war codotta at Bookham. To finish up – it is a brilliant success.

　your loving
　son Jack

P.S. Any signs of the photos? J.

TO ARTHUR GREEVES (W/LP IV: 212–13):

'Gastons'
Grt. Bookham.
Surrey.
Saturday
Sept / 14
[26 September 1914]

　My dear Arthur,

　If it were not that you could answer me with my own argument, I should upbraid you with not having written to me. See to it that you do as soon as you have read this.

　And now – what do I think of it? After a week's trial I have come to the conclusion that I am going to have the time of my life: nevertheless, much as I am enjoying the new arrangement, I feel sure that you would appreciate it even more than I. As for the country, I can hardly describe it. The wide expanse of rolling hill and dale, all thickly wooded with hazel and pine (so different from our bare and balder hills in Down) that is called Surrey, is to me, a great delight. Seen at present, in all the glory of a fine Autumn, it may be better imagined than described. How I wish that I could paint! Then I could carry home a few experiences on paper for my own remembrance and your information. But the village wd. please you even better. I have never seen anything like it outside a book. There is a quaint old inn that might have stepped out of the 'Vicar of Wakefield', and a church that dates from before the conquest. But it is no good enumerating things: I cannot convey the impression of perfect restfulness that this place imparts. We have all often read of places that 'Time has forgotten' – well, Great Bookham is one of these!

　I have only just discovered that you put my name in that book.[25]

---

25 Arthur had given him H.G. Wells' *The Country of the Blind, and Other Stories* [1911].

If I had seen it earlier I shd. have sent it back. You have no right to be so foolishly generous! However – many, many thanks. When one has set aside the rubbish that H. G. Wells always puts in, there remains a great deal of original, thoughtful and suggestive work in it. The 'Door in the Wall', for instance, moved me in a way I can hardly describe! How true it all is: the *SEEING ONE* walks out into joy and happiness unthinkable, where the dull, senseless eyes of the world see only destruction & death. 'The Plattner Story' & 'Under the Knife' are the next best: they have given me a great deal of pleasure. I am now engaged in reading 'Sense & Sensibility'. It is, undoubtedly, one of her best. Do you remember the Palmer family?[26]

In Greek, I have started to read Homer's Iliad,[27] of which, of course, you must often have heard. Although you don't know Greek & don't care for poetry, I cannot resist the temptation of telling you how stirring it is. Those fine, simple, euphonious lines, as they roll on with a roar like that of the ocean, strike a chord in one's mind that no modern literature approaches. Better or worse it may be: but different it is for certain.

I hope everything went off successfully on the eventful Teusday, and also that you are now recovered from your cold. You know my address: you have no excuse for silence, Sir!! No Philip's concerts this year at Belfast, I am told.

Yrs. (Expecting a letter)

C. S. Lewis

---

26 In Jane Austen's *Sense and Sensibility* (1811).

27 Homer, the Greek poet generally believed to have lived in about the eighth century BC, is famous for his two epics, the *Iliad* and the *Odyssey*. Mr Kirkpatrick wasted no time preparing Lewis to undertake these Greek masterpieces. 'We opened our books at *Iliad*, Book I,' Lewis wrote in *SBJ* IX. 'Without a word of introduction Knock read aloud the first twenty lines or so in the "new" pronunciation, which I had never heard before...He then translated, with a few, a very few explanations, about a hundred lines. I had never seen a classical author taken in such large gulps before. When he had finished he handed me over Crusius' *Lexicon* and, having told me to go through again as much as I could of what he had done, left the room. It seems an odd method of teaching, but it worked. At first I could travel only a very short way along the trail he had blazed, but every day I could travel further...I was beginning to think in Greek. That is the great Rubicon to cross in learning any language.' Lewis was using Gottlieb Christian Crusius, *A Complete Greek and English Lexicon for the Poems of Homer and the Homeridae: Illustrating the Domestic, Religious, Political, and Military Condition of the Heroic Age, and Explaining the Most Difficult Passages*. Translated with corrections and additions by Henry Smith. New Edition revised and edited by Thomas Kerchever Arnold (1862).

TO HIS FATHER (LP IV: 214):

[Gastons]
Monday.
Postmark: 30 September 1914

My dear Papy,

Thanks very much for the two letters which I received all in due course. Yes: I think that will be the best plan about the photos. Only, please send me two copies, as I want to give one to some one else at Malvern.

I am now at the end of my first week at Bookham, and can again tell you that it is everything that can possibly be desired. Both in work and leisure it is of course incomparably beyond any of the arrangements we have tried yet.

This week end an old pupil and friend of Kirk's was staying with us – one Oswald Smythe, who hies from Bembridge and is about twenty five years of age. Do you know who that would be? We are going on with friend Homer at what – to my ex-Malvernian mind – is a prodigious rate: that is to say we have polished off a book in the first week. At Malvern we always took a term to read a book of that sort of stuff.

Today I did a thing that would have gladdened your heart: walked to Leatherhead (for Bookham does not boast a barber) to get my hair cut. And am now looking like a convict – Yes thanks I have plenty of under-clothing, and the cold is a good deal better!

There is a good deal of war fever raging here, as is natural. I am glad to hear that those 'five righteous' have been found. But five thousand would be more to the point. What is all the local news? Tell Arthur the next time you see him that I am eagerly expecting a reply to my letter. I suppose the winter has closed in at home by this time: but we are still having quite summer weather here – which I rather resent. Mrs. Kirk plays the piano beautifully, which is one of the great assets of Bookham. There is also a movement on foot to make me learn to play bridge: but I am wriggling as hard as is compatible with manners.

your loving
son Jack

P.S. Who is the 'Mr. Dods'[28] that Kirk mentions?

War had been building up for some time, and it was now imminent. The heir to the Hapsburg empire, Archduke Franz Ferdinand, was assassinated in Sarajevo on 28 June 1914. Linking the assassination to the government of Belgrade, on 23 July Austria despatched to Serbia an ultimatum which could only be answered in two ways: Serbia must become for all practical purposes a conquered province of the Austrian Empire, or it must accept a declaration of war. On 28 July Austria declared war on Serbia, and on 29 July Russia mobilized her south-western army. That same day in London, Winston Churchill proposed to the British Cabinet that the European sovereigns should 'be brought together for the sake of peace'.[29] Germany refused, and on 31 July Russia mobilized against Germany. That same day Britain asked France and Germany to respect Belgian neutrality, to the maintenance of which Britain was committed by a treaty signed in 1839. France agreed to do so, but Germany gave no answer. Then, on 3 August Germany declared war on France. Hitherto Britain had stood aside, but the question of Belgian neutrality raised a problem and on 3 August Britain sent an ultimatum to Berlin demanding there be no attack on Belgium. On 4 August Germany entered Belgium, and that night Britain declared war on Germany. By midnight on 4 August five empires were at war: the Austro-Hungarian Empire against Serbia; the German Empire against France, Britain and Russia; the Russian Empire against Germany and Austria-Hungary; and the British and French Empires against Germany.

Because of war-time needs, Warnie's training had been accelerated from two years to only nine months. On 1 October he was commissioned a 2nd lieutenant in the Army Service Corps and sent to the base at Aldershot in preparation for being sent to France on 4 November.

---

28 Eric Robertson Dodds (1893–1979), classical scholar, was from Banbridge, County Down. He was educated at Campbell College, and University College, Oxford. At this time he was reading *Literae Humaniores* at University College. He took his BA in 1917. Dodds was Lecturer in Classics at University College, Reading 1919–24, Professor of Greek at the University of Birmingham 1924–36 and Regius Professor of Greek in the University of Oxford, 1936–60. See his autobiography, *Missing Persons* (1977).

29 Martin Gilbert, *First World War* (1994), p. 25.

TO HIS FATHER (LP IV: 225–6):

[Gastons]
Monday [5?] Oct./14

My dear Papy,

Thanks very much for the photographs, which I have duly received and studied. They are artistically got up and touched in: in fact everything that could be desired – only, do I really tie my tie like that? Do I really brush my hair like that? Am I really as fat as that? Do I really look so sleepy? However, I suppose that thing in the photo is the one thing I am saddled with for ever and ever, so I had better learn to like it. Isn't it curious that we know any one else better than we do ourselves? Possibly a merciful delusion.

You ask about our church at Bookham.[30] I thought I had mentioned it in my first description of the village. However, at the risk of repetition, you shall be informed. It is of pre-Norman structure, and is, like all these old churches, no particular shape. There are various plates of bronze dedicated by 'So and so, gentleman, to his beloved ladye who etc., etc.' The organ is out of tune: the singing execrable. The Vicar is a hard working, sincere and cheerful fellow, but, as Miss Austen would say, of 'no parts'. It is, in its own way, very, very beautiful. Yes, I go every Sunday.

I wonder did you notice the article on Nietzche in last Sunday's Times Literary Supplement,[31] which demonstrates that although we have been told to regard Nietzche as the indirect author of this war, nothing could be farther removed from the spirit and letter of his teaching? It just shows how we can be duped by an ignorant and loud mouthed cheap press. Kirk, who knows something about N., had anticipated that article with us, and is in high glee at seeing the blunder 'proclaimed on the housetops.'

I am very glad to hear that Warnie has at last safely arrived in that state of bliss, our British Army. What happens to him now, do you know?

The weather here is perfectly ideal: sharp frosts at night, and clear, mild sunshine in the day: this is really the nicest country I have ever seen, outside – of course – Co. Down. The places about here in the

---

30 St Nicolas Church, the earliest parts of which were built in the 11th century, is mentioned in the Domesday Book. The Reverend George Shepheard Bird was rector 1905–26. Jane Austen went to St Nicolas often when her godfather was vicar.

31 'The Nietzschean Way', *The Times Literary Supplement* (1 October 1914), p. 442.

woods are alive with pheasants, as the usual shots are at the front: they are so tame that you can come within a few paces of them.

On Saturday the household went over to the famous Boxhill, which however I thought not nearly so pretty as some of the places nearer Gastons.

I can still say that a larger knowledge of our new stunt gives nothing but deeper satisfaction. We have at last struck the real thing in education, in comfort, in pleasure, and in companions. I could almost believe that Malvern had never existed, or was merely a nightmare which I am glad to forget. Paper and time at an end.

yr. loving son,
Jack

TO ARTHUR GREEVES (W/LP IV: 214–7):

Gt. Bookham
[6 October 1914]

Dear Arthur,

I will begin by answering your questions & then we can get on to more interesting topics. The plot of my would-be tragedy is as follows: (The action is divided into the technical parts of a Grk. tragedy: so:)

I. Prologos.

Loki, *alone before Asgard, explains the reason of his quarrel of the gods: 'he had seen what an injustice the creation of man would be and tried to prevent it!* Odin, *by his magic had got the better of him, and now holds him as a slave.* Odin *himself now enters, with bad news.* Loki *(as is shewn in the dialogue) had persuaded the gods to make the following bargain with the Giant,* Fasold: *that if F., in one single winter, built a wall round Asgard, the goddess Freya should be given him as his concubine. The work is all but finished: the gods, repenting of the plan, are claiming Loki's blood.*

II. Parodos.

Thor, Freya & *the* Chorus *enter. After a short ode by the latter, Thor complains that* Loki, *who is always the gods' enemy has persuaded them to this plan, well knowing that it would come to no good.* Loki *defends his actions in a very scornful speech, and the two are only kept from blows at the request of* Odin & Freya.

Odin, *though feeling qualms on account of their ancient friendship, agrees to* Loki's *being punished if the latter cannot devise some way out of the difficulty by the next day, (when 'the appointed Winter' is up). The others then withdraw leaving* Loki *alone with the* Chorus. *He has been cringing to* Odin *up till now, but on his exit bursts out into angry curses.*

III. *Episode I.*
The Chorus *pray to the 'spirits of invocation' to help* Loki *to find a plan. His only desire is to be able to save his own head and plunge the gods into even deeper morasses. A long dialogue ensues between him & the* Chorus, *the result of which is this plan: that* Loki *will send a spirit of madness into* Fasold's *horse which always accomplishes the greater part of the work. (Vide 'Myths of the Norsemen'). The* Chorus *agree &* Loki *sets off to Jarnvid (Ironwood) to instruct the spirit.*

IV. *Episode II.*
It is now quite dark. The Chorus *are singing a song of hope & fate, when* Fasold *enters with his horse, dragging the last great stone. He stops & converses with the* Chorus. *In the dialogue which follows, the genial, honest, blundering mind of* Fasold *is laid open: and his frank confession of his fears & hopes for* Freya, *and his labours, forms a contrast to the subtle intrigues of the gods. At last he decides to move on. He urges the horse: but at that moment the frenzy siezes it: it breaks from its traces & gallops off, kicking its master and leaving him senseless in the snow. Presently he recovers, and after a very sad & indignant accusation of the gods, goes off to mourn 'his vanished hope'. He cannot now hope to gain the 'dear prize' for which 'he laboured all those months'! The morning is all ready at hand*

V. *Episode III.*
Loki, Thor *&* Freya *return. All are in high spirits, and exult over the success of the plan. To them enters* Odin. *By the appearance of the god, we guess that something is wrong. On being questioned his explanation (greatly condensed) is this. 'The gods' empire rests on treaties. Therefore on honour. When that honour is broken their*

doom is at hand. Loki has conquered the Giant, how? By Fraud. We have broken faith and must prepare for the twilight of the gods.' As soon as the general shock has passed off, Thor *turns upon* Loki *and says that he is the cause of all this.* Loki, *seeing that he has accomplished his design, throws off the mask of humility that he has been wearing, and, confessing that it was all his plan, bursts forth into fearful [cursings?] upon* Thor *and* Odin. *Since* Loki *cannot be killed by any known weapon,* Thor *purposes to pinion him on an adjacent boulder (etc. Vide 'Myths of the N's') as a punishment.* Odin, *though without enthusiasm consents, and he is bound. (*Thor, Freya, Odin *go off).*

VI. Exodos.
Loki, *bound to the rock, is indulging in a satyric dialogue with the* Chorus, *when* Odin *returns. As soon as* Loki *sees him he bursts into violent abuse.* Odin *has come to offer him pardon &* release: *'He (*Odin*) is a lonely god: men, gods, & giants are all only his own creatures, not his equals & he has no friend – merely a crowd of slaves.* Loki, *who had been brought forth with & (not by) him by Fate, had supplied one. Will he be reconciled?'* Loki, *however, casts his offer back in his teeth, with many taunts. Seeing that they can effect nothing* Odin *&* Chorus *withdraw & the tragedy ends.*

Such then, in brief, is the skeleton of my poor effort poor indeed in its intrinsic worth, and yet not so poor if you could set it to soul-stirring music. As an opera the parts would be like this.

LOKI	Tenor (?)
ODIN	Baritone
THOR	Basso (of course)
FREYA	Soprano
FASOLD	Basso
LEADER of the CHORUS	Contralto (she has quite a lot to do, here & there)

Of course you would readily see what musical points could be made. Nevertheless I cannot refrain from giving you a few of my ideas. To begin with, Loki's opening speech would be sombre and eerie, – expressive of the fire-god's intrigueing soul, and endless hatred. Then (*Parados*) the first song of the chorus would be bright and tuneful, as a relief to the dramatic duet that precedes it. The next great opportunity for 'atmospheric' music comes (Episode I) where the theme of the 'spirit of madness' is introduced. *You* can well imagine what it ought to be like. Then (Episode II) we would have a bluff, swinging ballad for the huge, hearty giant; and of course the 'madness motive' again, where the horse breaks lose. Then some 'Dawn' music as a prelude to (Episode III) and Odin's speech about their position! What an opening for majestic & mournful themes. But the real gem would be some inexpressibly sad, yearning little theme, where (Exodos) Odin expresses his eternal loneliness. But enough!, enough! I have let my pen run away with me on so congenial a subject & must try & get back to daily life.

As for my average 'Bookham' day, there is not much to tell. Breakfast at 8.0, where I am glad to see good Irish soda-bread on the table begins the day. I then proceed to take the air (we are having some delightful, crisp autumn mornings) till 9.15, when I come in & have the honour of reading that glorious Iliad, which I will not insult with my poor praise. 11–11.15 is a little break, & then we go on with Latin till luncheon, at 1.0. From 1.–5.0, the time is at my own disposal, to read, write or moon about in the golden tinted woods and vallies of this county. 5–7.0, we work again. 7.30, dinner. After that I have the pleasant task of reading a course of English Literature mapped out by Himself.[32] Of course, that doesn't include novels, which I read at other times. I am at present occupied with (as Eng. Lit.) Buckle's 'Civilization of England',[33] and (of my own accord) Ibsen's plays. Hoping to hear from you soon, with all your views & suggestions for Loki, I am.

Yrs. sincerely

C. S. Lewis

P.S. If you begin composing in earnest you'll find the libretto in my study upstairs. J.

---

32 i.e. Mr Kirkpatrick.
33 H.T. Buckle, *History of Civilization in England* (1857; 1861).

TO HIS FATHER (LP IV: 229–39):

[Gastons]
Postmark: 13 October 1914

My dear Papy,

I am astonished to hear that the Glenmachonians[34] are still so foolish as to stick to the Russian delusion: as Kirk has pointed out several times, this extraordinary rumour, and the credit paid to it, is a striking illustration of the way in which a mythology grew up in barbarous or semi-barbarous ages. If we, with all our modern knowledge fall into an error so ludicrous and so unfounded, it is hardly to be wondered at if primitive man believed a good deal of nonsense.

Our household has an addition this week in the person of Mrs. K's theatrical friend Miss MacMullen, who is staying here for a week or ten days. 'Soul! She's a boy!' Altho' perfectly well she sees fit to travel down to Gastons with a bath chair, a maid, and a bull dog. However, they are the only faults, and they are amusing Kodotta.

This is the most extraordinary place I have ever seen for weather: we have had bright sunshine, frost, and not a spot of rain ever since I arrived. The touch of frost, unaccompanied by any wind to blow the leaves off their branches, has converted the country into a veritable paradise of gold and copper. I have never seen anything like it. Everyone at Bookham is engaged in a conspiracy for 'getting up' a cottage for Belgian refugees:[35] a noble scheme I admit: carried out however in a typical fussy 'Parishional' way. Some of Kirk's comments are very funny.

Any news from the Colonel?[36] When is he off to the front? Did you ever at Lurgan read the 4th Georgic?[37] It is the funniest example of the colossal ignorance of a great poet that I know. It's about bees, and Virgil's natural history is very quaint: bees, he thinks, are all males: they find the young in the pollen of flowers. They must be soothed by flute playing when anything goes wrong etc., etc.

---

34 The Ewart family who lived in nearby Glenmachan House. See **The Ewart Family** in the Biographical Appendix.

35 For some weeks the Germans had been intent on reaching the Belgian and French coastline. In an attempt to prolong the defence of their port city, Antwerp, the Belgian government appealed to Britain for troops. Thousands of British troops rushed to the aid of Antwerp, but by 10 October it was impossible to hold it against the Germans. By this time tens of thousands of Belgian refugees had arrived in England.

36 A nickname given Warnie by his father and brother.

37 Virgil (70–19 BC), the greatest Roman poet, wrote four 'Georgics', which are didactic poems in hexameters on Italy and traditional ways of rural life.

I hope that your dental troubles are now gone and that you are quite well in other ways (Yes – it is a bad cold Joffer!) I am scanning the horizon for a brown suit. I suppose you have settled down to winter weather and customs by now at home.

your loving
son Jack

TO ARTHUR GREEVES: (W/LP IV: 220–2)

Wednesday
[14 October 1914]
Bookham

My dear Arthur,

Although delighted, as always, to find your letters on my plate, I was very sorry to hear that you were once again laid up: I hope, however, that it is nothing more than a cold, and will soon pass away.

I was very glad to hear your favourable criticism of 'Loki' (and I hope it is genuine) and to see that you are taking an interest in it. Of course your supposed difficulty about scoring is a 'phantasm'. For, in the first place, if we do compose this opera, it will in all probability never have the chance of being played by an orchestra: and, in the second place, if by any chance it were ever to be produced, the job of scoring it would be given – as is customary – to a hireling. Now, as to your budget of tasteful and fascinating suggestions. Your idea of introducing a dance after the exit of Odin etc, is a very good one, altho' it will occasion some trifling alterations in the text: and, speaking of dances in general, I think that you are quite right in saying that they add a certain finish to both dramatic & operatic works. Indeed, when I was writing them, there were certain lines in the play which I felt would be greatly 'helped out' by appropriate movements. Thus the lines

'The moon already with her silvery glance, –
The hornèd moon that bids the high gods dance'

would suggest some good moonlight music both in motion and orchestra.

Turning to your remarks about illustrations, I must confess that I have often entertained that idea myself; but, thinking that, since you never spoke of it, there was some radical objection on your part, I never liked to suggest it. Now that I am undeceived in *that* direction, however, need I say that I am delighted with the idea? Your skill with the brush, tho' by no means superior to your musical abilities, has yet a greater mastery of the technical difficulties. I have only to cast my eyes over the libretto to conjure up a dozen good ideas for illustrations. (1) First of all, the vast, dreary waste of tumbled volcanic rock with Asgard gleaming high above in the background thrown out into sharp relief by the lurid sunset: then in the foreground there is the lithe, crouching figure of Loki, glaring with satanic malignity at the city he purposes to destroy. That is my conception of the Prologos. (2) Then Odin, thundering through the twilit sky on his eight footed steed! (what a picture.) (3) Again, Freya, beautiful, pathetic and terrified making her anguished entreaty for protection. (4) A sombre study of the moonlight choral dance that you so wisely suggested. (5) The love-sick Fasold raging in impotent fury when he discovers that he has been cheated. And (6) last of all, Loki, bound to his rock, glaring up to the frosty stars in calm, imperturbable and deadly hatred! And so on & so on. But you, with your artist's brain will doubtless think of lots of other openings. I do sincerely hope that this idea will materialise, and that I shall find on my return a whole drawer full of your best.

I am afraid this is rather a 'Loki' letter, and I know that I must not expect others to doat on the subject as foolishly as do I. I am going to ask for 'Myths and legends of the Celtic Race'[38] as part of my Xmas box from my father: so that, as soon as I put the finishing touches to 'Loki Bound', I can turn my attention to the composition of an Irish drama – or perhaps, this time, a narrative poem.[39] The character of Maeve, the mythical warrior Queen of Ireland, will probably furnish me with a dignified & suggestive theme. But, we shall see all in good time.

Mrs Kirkpatrick, the lady of this house, had not played to me at the time of writing my last epistle. But since then she has given me a most delightful hour or so: introducing some of Chopin's preludes, 'Chanson Triste',[40] Beethoven's moonlight Sonata,[41] Chopin's March

38 T.W. Rolleston, *Myths and Legends of the Celtic Race* (1912).
39 Whether Arthur Greeves ever attempted any part of his share in the musical drama is not known, but Lewis's lyric text of 'Loki Bound' filled 32 pages of a notebook. The only part of this which has survived consists of 819 lines reproduced in LP IV: 218–20.
40 Pyotr Il'yich Tchaikovsky's *Chanson Triste* was first performed in 1878.
41 The nickname of Ludwig van Beethoven's piano sonata No. 14 in C sharp, Opus 27, No. 2 (1802).

Funebre,[42] The Peer Gynt Suite[43] & several other of our old favourites. Of course I do not know enough about music to be an authoritative critic, but she seemed to me to play with accuracy, taste & true feeling. So that there is added another source of attraction to Great Bookham. For the value of Mrs K's music is to me two fold: first it gives me the pleasure that beautiful harmonies well executed must always give: and secondly, the familiar airs carry me back in mind to countless happy afternoons spent together at Bernagh or Little Lea!

Strange indeed is my position, suddenly whirled from a state of abject terrorism, misery and hopelessness at Malvern, to a comfort and prosperity far above the average. If you envy my present situation, you must always remember that after so many years of unhappiness there should be something by way of compensation. All I hope is that there will not come a corresponding depression after this: I never quite trust the 'Norns'.[44]

I have come to the end now of my time & paper and, I daresay, of your patience. While I remember; it would be as well for you to keep that sketch of the plot of Loki, so that we can refer to it in our correspondence, when necessary.

Yrs. very sincerely

Jack Lewis

P.S. Have the Honeymooners come home from Scotland yet? (J.)[45]

TO HIS FATHER (LP IV: 232):

[Gastons]
Postmark: 18 October 1914

My dear Papy,

Although fully alive to the gravity of the situation and grateful for the kindness of your suggestion, it was not without a smile that I read your last letter. I hardly think that the siege of Bookham will begin before Xmas, so that I need not come home just yet. And seriously, why not study the lilies of the field?[46] All your worry and anxiety will not help

---

42 Frédéric Chopin's *Marche Funèbre* was first performed in 1827.

43 Edvard Grieg's piano solo, the *Peer Gynt Suite* No. 2 (1893).

44 The female Fates of Norse mythology.

45 The 'Honeymooners' were probably Arthur's brother, Thomas Greeves, and Winifred Lynas, who were married on 22 September 1914.

the war at all: and the truest service that we who are not fighting can do is to conduct our lives in an ordinary way and not yield to panic.

The good ladies of Bookham are now in the highest state of felicity, having secured a formidable family of seven Belgian refugees, which they have duly installed in a cottage selected for the purpose. Luckily the mother of the family speaks French, so that the educated ladies of Bookham can talk to her: but the rest of the family speak nothing but Flemish. Yesterday I went with Mrs. K. to see them: tried my French on the mother and bombarded the others out of a phrase book with subtile converse like 'Good morning: are you well: we are well: is the child well: it is fine: it is wet: is it wet etc.' Of course they are not gentlemen; but very respectable and intelligent bourgeois.

Young Kirk was employed at his camp the other day in unloading a train of seriously wounded soldiers from the front: from whom he learned that the newspaper stories of German atrocities (mutilation of nurses, killing wounded etc.) were not in the least exaggerated.

I hope the dental troubles are a thing of the past. I suppose the Scotch Greevous honeymooners have returned by now, and that Arthur is back to work. He tells me that there is some talk of his going to Portrush with Mrs. Greeves,[47] which I should think was a chilly operation at this time of year.

The Gastonian arrangement continues to give every possible satisfaction that anybody could ask for: and the country is lovelier than ever. The theatrical lady is still here, so that when young Kirk comes down from his camp to spend the week end, we are quite a pleasant sized party. I am off to bed now, so good night.

> your loving
> son Jack

TO ARTHUR GREEVES (W/LP IV: 222–3):

[Gastons
20 October 1914]

My dear Arthur,

Many thanks for the letter, which I hope is becoming a regular 'institution', and apologies for my comparative slackness in replying.

---

46 Matthew 6:28: 'Consider the lilies of the field, how they grow; they toil not, neither do they spin.'

47 This was Arthur's mother, Mrs Mary Margretta (Gribbon) Greeves. See **Arthur Greeves** in the Biographical Appendix.

When I read your description of the boring evening I thought for a while of writing you a letter full of 'war' – to hear your views afterwards. But, to be serious, what would you? Is the trivial round of family conversation ever worth listening to, whether we are at war or no? I can promise you that it is not at Little Lea and if Bernagh is different it must be an exceptional household. The vast majority of people, too, whom one meets outside the household, have nothing to say that we can be interested in. Their circle of interests is sternly practical, and it is only the few who can talk about the really important things – literature, science, music & art. In fact, this deadly *practicalness* is so impressed on my mind, that, when I have finished Loki, I am resolved to write a play against it.

The following idea has occurred to me: in Irish mythology the ruling deities are the light & beautiful Shee: but, we are told, before these came, the world was ruled by the Formons, hideous and monstrous oppressors. What are the exact details of the struggle between the two parties I do not know. But it ought to make a good allegorical story, in which the Formons could be taken as typical of the stern, ugly, money grubbing spirit, finally conquered by that of art & beauty, as exemplified by the lovely folk of the Shee. However, of course, this is only a castle in the air.

I sympathize with your difficulty in drawing a horse, as I have often made the attempt in the days when I fancied myself in that line. But of course that counts for nothing: as the easiest of your sketches would be impossible for me. But there are heaps of pictures in which you need not introduce the animal. I hope the music has started in real earnest by now. The longer I stay at this place, the better I like it. Mrs. K., like all good players – including yourself – is lazy and needs a lot of inducement before she performs.

yours sincerely
C. S. Lewis

TO HIS FATHER (LP IV: 234):

[Gastons
25? October 1914]

My dear Papy,
You have surpassed yourself. The popular press, of whose reliability the Russian rumour is an example, remarks on the possibility of an invasion: the idea, after being turned over in your mind, appears in your

next letter, clothed as 'it is *absolutely certain* that he is going to invade England'[48] Surely, Joffer, this is rather hyperbole? The one thing that Britain can depend upon is her fleet: and in any case Germany has her hands full enough. You will perhaps say that I am living in a fool's paradise. 'Maybe thon'. But, providing it only be a paradise is that not preferable to a wise and calculating inferno? Let us have wisdom by all means, so long as it makes us happy: but as soon as it runs against our peace of mind, let us throw it away and 'carpe diem'.[49] I often wonder how you came to have such a profound and genuine philosopher for your son, don't you?

I received and duly posted your letter to the Colonel: though why it should reach him any more easily from Bookham than from Belfast I don't know. It seems to me outrageous that you can't get a letter through. I suppose he *is* still at Aldershot and that they are allowed to receive letters? I think the 'my bankers'[50] wheeze is immense. The brother of that Smythe fellow, who was staying here some days ago, has lost his arm and is coming home. It begins to come home to you as a personal element, doesn't it? At present the only solution which Kirk will allow probable, is the absolute exhaustion of one, or more likely both parties: and that is a revolting prospect, is it not?

Last week I went up to town with Mrs. K. and the theatrical lady to the Coliseum to see the Russian ballet, which was very good: but the rest of the show seemed to me to be neither better nor worse than an average bill at our own old Hippodrome.

---

48 The rumour that Germany would invade England persisted for a long time and worried Albert greatly. It may have started with an article in *The Times* (15 October 1914) entitled 'Will Invasion be Tried?' in which the war correspondent said: 'Now that the war is reaching the climax of its violence we must anticipate that all the living forces of Germany will be thrown into the conflict, and that the German navy will no longer remain inert. We must expect to be attacked at home, and must not rest under any comforting illusions that we shall not be assailed. As an attack upon us can have no serious object, unless the intention is to land an expedition in England for the purposes of compelling us to sign a disastrous peace, it is well that we should look the situation calmly in the face, and reckon up not only Germany's power to do us harm, but also our power of resistance and means for improving it' (p. 4).

49 'Seize the day'. Horace, *Odes*, Book I, Ode 11, l.8, in which the poet urges Leuconoe to take thought for the present and not to worry inordinately about the future.

50 In a letter of 12 October, in which Warnie asked his father for a loan, he explained that he was owed money by Sandhurst and that 'I have communicated with my bankers' (LP IV: 229).

I hear from my Malvern correspondent, in the thankfulness of his soul, that it is half term. How different is his lot as he counts up the tardy lapse of hard, dreary, cheerless week after week, to mine: where the weeks slip away unasked and unobserved as at home. I am glad to see that the Captain was mentioned in despatches, and cannot see that there would be anything wrong in congratulating Hope.[51] I am giving up the usual end of the letter tag about Gastons 'giving all satisfaction', as you may safely assume that things continue better than I could describe.

your loving
son Jack

TO ARTHUR GREEVES (W/LP IV: 233–4):

Gt. Bookham
Wednesday
[28 October 1914]

Dear Arthur,

You ask me what a shee is: I reply that there is no such thing as '*A*' Shee. The word (which, tho' pronounced as I have spelled it, is properly in Irish spelled 'Shidhe') is a collective noun, signifying 'the fairies', or the gods, – since, in Irish these powers are identical. The common phraze 'Banshee', is derived from 'Beän Shidhe' which means 'a woman of the Shee': and the gods, as a whole, are often called 'Aes Shidhe', or 'people of the S.' The resemblance between this word '*Aes*' and the Norse '*Aesir*' has often been noted as indicating a common origin for Celtic & Teutonic races. So much for the etymology. But the word has a secondary meaning, developed from the first. It is used to indicate the 'faery forts' or dwelling places of the Shee: these are usually subterranean workings, often paved and roofed with stone & showing an advanced stage of civilization. These can be seen in a good many parts of Ireland. Who *really* built them is uncertain: but scholars, judging by the rude patterns on the door posts, put them down to the Danes. Another set say that they were made by the original inhabitants of Ireland, previous *even* to the Celts, – who of course, like all other Aryan people primarily came from Asia.

---

51 Their cousin, Hope Ewart (1882–1934), married Captain George Harding (1877–1957) in 1911 and they went to live in Dublin. Harding joined the army in 1900 and had been a member of the Army Service Corps since 1901. He was promoted to major in October 1914. He gained the DSO during the war and retired in 1928 with the rank of colonel.

I am sorry that my epistle is rather late in arrival this week: but what with people bothering from Malvern, and letters to be written home, I have not had many free evenings. I feel confidant of your always understanding that, when my letters fail to arrive, there is a good, or at least a reasonable explanation. Now that I have threshed out the question of Shee, and apologized, I don't know that there is much to write beyond hoping that 'Loki' is proceding expeditiously in music & illustration.

Last week I was up with these people to the Coliseum: and, though of course (which by the way I see no prospect of) I had sooner have gone to some musical thing, yet I enjoyed myself. The Russian Ballet – and especially the music to it – was magnificent, and G. P. Huntley in a new sketch provoked some laughter. The rest of the show trivial & boring as music halls usually are.[52] At 'Gastons' however, I have no lack of entertainment, having been recently introduced to Chopin's Mazurkas, & Beethoven's 'Sonate Pathétique'.[53]

No: there is no talk yet of going home. And, to tell you the truth, I am not sorry: firstly, I am very happy at Bookham, and secondly, a week at home, if it is to be spent in pulling long faces in Church & getting confirmed, is no great pleasure – a statement, I need hardly say, for yourself alone.

Yrs.

Jack Lewis

TO HIS FATHER (LP IV: 239–49):

[Gastons]
Postmark: 3 November 1914

My dear Papy,

If suddenly there descends upon innocent Leeborough a monstrosity of brown paper containing school books from Malvern, don't lose your head: or in other words, Porch[54] having asked me what to do with some books I had forgotten, was asked by me to send them home, which he may do at any time. I do *not* want you to send them on.

---

52 The programme at the London Coliseum between 19 and 24 October included the Imperial Russian Ballet's performance of *Fleurs d'Orange* and G.P. Huntley acting in Eric Blore's *A Burlington Arcadian*.

53 Ludwig van Beethoven, Sonata No. 8, 'Pathétique' (1799).

54 Robert Bagehot Porch (1875–1962) was a pupil at Malvern College 1888–94. From there he went to Trinity College, Oxford, receiving his BA in 1898. He joined the staff of Malvern College in 1904 and taught there most of his life.

This fellow Smythe who lost his arm at the front, has been telling all sorts of interesting things to Mrs. K., who was up to town to see him last week. I think they ought to be collected and published under the title of 'The right way to get shot'. One is relieved to hear that it is not painful at the time.

What do you think of this latest outrage perpetuated by the slander, ignorance, and prejudice of the British nation on those who alone can support it? I mean of course the shameful way in which Prince Louis of Battenberg has been forced to resign.[55] He is, I hear, the only man in the Admiralty who knows his job: he has lived all his life in England: his patriotism, loyalty, and efficiency are admitted by all who have a right to judge. And yet, because a number of ignorant and illiterate clods (who have no better employment than that of abusing their betters) so choose, he must resign. This is what comes of letting a nation be governed by 'the people'. 'Vox populi, vox Diaboli',[56] we might say, reversing an old but foolish proverb.

I suppose things in Belfast are much in the same condition as usual. I hope a few people are clearing off to the front. Some of those people one meets on the Low Holywood Road would be improved by shooting. Any news from *our* representative in the Army? I suppose he will hardly be out of England yet? I am so pleased at not forgetting to post the letter you sent to him that I shall be furious if you don't get an answer. Has it ever struck you that one of the most serious consequences of this war is what Kirk calls 'the survival of the *un*fittest'? All those who have the courage to do so and are physically sound, are going off to be shot: those who survive are moral and physical weeds – a fact which does not promise favourably for the next generation.

We are beginning to make a feeble attempt at winter here, but the weather is still beautifully mild. I hope you are keeping fit and in good spirits – (Yes thank you Papy, my cold is a good deal better!)

> your loving son,
> Jack

---

55 Prince Louis of Battenburg (1854–1921) was born in Austria. He moved to England when he was a boy and had risen through the ranks of the Royal Navy to become First Sea Lord. Despite all that Winston Churchill could do, as first lord of the Admiralty, Prince Louis was forced to resign. He relinquished his German titles and the family name was changed to Mountbatten.

56 'The voice of the people is the voice of the Devil'.

TO ARTHUR GREEVES (W/LP IV: 236–7):

[Gastons
4 November 1914]

Dear Arthur,

I suppose that I should, as is usual in my case begin my epistle with an apology for its tardiness: but that form of adress is becoming so habitual as to be monotonous, so that it may be taken for granted.

I was, if I may say so, not a little amused to hear you say in an off-hand manner 'The Celts used to retire to them in time of war', when antiquarians have been disputing for ages: but of course you have grounds for your statement I admit. Your souteraines are, I imagine, but another variety of the same phenomena as my Shidhes: when I said 'doorposts' I did not imply the existence of doors, meaning only the stone pillars, commonly (I believe) found at the entrances to these excavations.

Great Bookham and the present arrangement continue to give every satisfaction which is possible. But there is one comfort which must inevitably be wanting anywhere except at home – namely, the ability to write whenever one wishes. For, though of course there is no formal obstacle, you will readily see that it is impossible to take out one's manuscript and start to work in another's house. And, when ideas come flowing upon me, so great is the desire of framing them into words, words into sentences, and sentences into metre, that the inability to do so, is no light affliction. You, when you are cut off for a few weeks from a piano, must experience much the same sensations. But it would be ridiculous for me to pretend that, in spite of this unavoidable trouble, I was not comfortable. Work and liesure, each perfect and complete of its kind, form an agreeable supplent to the other, strikingly different to the dreary labour and compulsory pasttimes of Malvern life. The glorious pageant of the waning year, lavishing her autumn glories on a lovely countryside, fills me, whenever I take a solitary walk among the neighbouring hills, with a great sense of comfort & peace.

So great is the selfishness of human nature, that I can look out from my snug nest with the same equanimity on the horrid desolation of the war, and the well known sorrows of my old school. I feel that this ought not to be so: but I can no more alter my disposition than I can change the height of my stature or the colour of my hair. It would be mere affectation to pretend that sympathy with those whose lot is not so happy as mine, seriously disturbs the tenour of my complacence. Whether this is the egotism of youth, some blemish in my personal character, or the common inheritance of humanity, I do not know. What is your opinion?

I am reading at present, for the second time, the Celtic plays of Yeats.[57] I must try & get them next time I am at home. Write soon, and tell me all that you are doing, reading & thinking.

Yours,

C. S. Lewis

TO HIS FATHER (LP IV: 240–1):

[Gastons
8? November 1914]

My dear Papy,

If bounty on the part of his weary audience could stop the sermon of the philosopher, I should be compelled to close our controversy of the paradise and inferno: but even the four, crisp, dainty postal orders (for which many thanks) cannot deter me from exposing the logical weakness of your position. The arguments, as you will recollect, upon which I based my theory, were briefly as follows: that when evils cannot be averted by him who suffers them, i.e. you and I, who *cannot* go into the army – he would do well to shut his eyes and pretend that they do not exist. For the evil, being in itself a fixed quantity, can neither be multiplied or diminished when it actually descends: but the agony of anticipation may be attenuated to nothing. Bearing these facts in mind, your imaginary dialogue, lively and picturesque tho' it may be, is irrelevant: since your two friends are presumably in a position to volunteer, and their case therefore offers no parallel to our own. In short, you have shifted the ground of argument by substituting the description of a satanist for the demonstrations of a philosopher.

I carried out to the letter your directions about Warnie: or in other words, as he arranged nowhere I met him nowhere. A pity. But who are we to cavil at the arrangements of this great man. Seriously however, I know what your feelings must be when, to the annoyance arising from his shipshod methods at such a moment, is added the anxiety of his

---

57 W.B. Yeats had published many Celtic plays. Lewis may have been thinking of his *Plays for an Irish Theatre* (1911).

present position at the front.[58] Let me offer however such consolations as the case permits of. If, by the Grace of God, he returns unscathed from this hideous masque of death, it will be a sadder and wiser Warnie than he who went away: the indiscretions of a raw Malvern school boy. If, as we both hope and pray, this turns out to be the case, we may indeed feel, that in one home at least, this outburst of the primitive savagery of man will not have been without a compensation.

In the meantime, your worry about Palmes[59] need not be of much importance. I had the honour of meeting this gentleman on one of W's visits to Malvern: he is a harmless, amiable idiot who will make no fuss, and the sum that he lent is, I believe, trifling. Surely too, it is rather hard to call a man a cad, just because he demands his own money back: even if he does so (I am convinced through sheer empty headedness) on a P.C.

Hoping that this will find you in good health and tolerable spirits, I remain,

your loving son,

Jack

TO ARTHUR GREEVES (W/LP IV: 239):

[Gastons
10 November 1914]

Dear Arthur,

It is the immemorial privilege of letter-writers to commit to paper things they would not say: to write in a more grandiose manner than that in which they speak: and to enlarge upon feelings which would be passed by unnoticed in conversation. For this reason I do not attach much importance to your yearnings for an early grave: not, indeed, because I think, as you suggest, that the wish for death is wrong or even foolish, but because I know that a cold in the head is quite an insufficient cause to provoke such feelings. I am glad Monday found you in a more reasonable frame of mind.

---

58 Warnie crossed to France with the Army Service Corps on 4 November. They were part of the British Expeditionary Force stationed at Le Havre.

59 Guy Nicholas Palmes (1894–1915) entered Malvern in 1908, and left in 1911 for the Royal Military College at Sandhurst. He joined the Yorkshire Light Infantry at the beginning of the war and was promoted to lieutenant in 1915. He was killed in action near Ypres on 9 May 1915.

By the way, I hear nothing about music or illustrations now! Eh? I hope that this can be accounted for by the fact that both are finished. I suppose the former has been performed in the Ulster Hall, by this time, and the latter exhibited – where? Here the sentence comes to a stop: for I have suddenly realized that there is no picture gallery in Belfast. It never occurred to me before what a disgrace that was. I notice, too, that you answer my questions about 'doing' and 'reading' but keep a modest silence about 'thinking'. It is often difficult to tell, is not it? And seldom advisable: which makes me think about the hard question of truth. Is it always advisable to tell the truth? Certainly not, say I: sometimes actually criminal. And yet, useful as it is for everyday life, that doctrine will land one in sad sophistries if carried to its conclusion. What is your view?

The other day I was in Guildford (it is a glorious old English town with those houses that [get] bigger towards the top; a Norman castle; a street built up a preposterous hill; and beautiful environments) where I picked up a volume of Wm. Morris's lyric poems in that same edition in which you have 'The Wood at the Worlds end'.[60] So delighted was I with my purchase, that I have written up to the publisher for the same author's 'Sigurd the Volsung':[61] which, as I need hardly tell you, is a narrative poem, dealing with Siegfried (=Sigurd) & Brünhilde, as described in the legends of Iceland, earlier than those of Germany. What is your opinion of Ainsworth? I see you are reading his 'Old St. Pauls'.[62] I must confess I find him dreary – a faint echo of Scott, with all the latter's faults of lengthiness and verbosity and not of his merits of lively narrative & carefully-welded plots.

When you talk about the difficulty of getting the necessary materials for one's pursuits, I am thankful that, in my case, when the opportunity is at hand, the means – paper & pen – is easily found. Whereas you, unfortunately, need a piano or a box of paints and a block of drawing paper.

I hope there will be some relics of us left when we have settled that question of souteraines.

Yrs sincerely
Jack Lewis

---

60 He meant William Morris's *The Well at the World's End* (1896).
61 William Morris, *Sigurd the Volsung* (1876).
62 William Harrison Ainsworth, *Old St Paul's* (1841).

TO HIS FATHER (LP IV: 244-5):

[Gastons
13? November 1914]

My dear Papy,

I was glad to receive your letter this evening (Friday) as I was beginning to get anxious: and thought that I would write my reply at once while your words were still in my head. I must admit that my defence of Palmes was founded on a misconception of his plans – which is excusable, in as much as, if you saw the gentleman in the flesh, you would never imagine that he had the intelligence for such an idea.

After this magnanimous confession of my defeat, I cannot refrain from observing that there is no reply to my last step in the 'Paradise-Inferno' controversy. But as no further disputation is possible after my crushing and exhaustive demonstration, that is not much to be wondered at.

Although perhaps the occasion demands a graver view, I cannot restrain a smile when I think of the colonel staying at a first class hotel in 'Haver' and strutting about in his uniform like a musical comedy hero.

It seems a great pity this confirmation should occur when it does, thus cutting out at least a week of valuable time. Although fully sensible that it is of course of more importance than the work, yet if it could possibly be managed at some more convenient date in the near future, I should think it an advantage. I believe there is one held at Easter, which I might attend with less derangement of our plans. I would ask you to consider this point before mentioning the matter to Kirk. I am not quite clear from your letter as to what you propose to do. As I read it, three interpretations are admissable.

a   That you bring me home for the necessary time and send me back for the odd weeks.
b   That you add from Dec. 6th – Xmas on to the ordinary holidays.
c   That you have ordinary length holidays, only beginning on the 6th and ending earlier.

Of these alternatives, (a) is practicable enough, but necessitates a tiresome and expensive amount of extra travelling: (b) is agreeable, but wasteful of time and quite unthinkable. (c) is not only extremely alien from all our usual plans, but would also put Kirk to a great deal of trouble and annoyance. So that none of the three is really satisfactory. However, you will discuss the point in your next letter. If this Kodotta about cross channel boats goes on much longer, the matter will not rest in our hands.

Hoping for a continuance of health on your part, as well as an improvement in spirits, I am

your loving son,

Jack

TO ARTHUR GREEVES (W/LP IV: 282):

[Gastons
17 November 1914]

My dear Arthur,

Do you ever wake up in the morning and suddenly wonder why you have not bought such-and-such a book long ago, and then decided that life without it will be quite unbearable? I do frequently: the last attack was this morning à propos of Malory's 'Morte D'Arthur', and I have just this moment written to Dent's for it. I am drawing a bow at a venture and getting the Everyman two-shilling 'Library' edition.[63] What is it like, do you know? As for the book itself, I really can't think why I have not got it before. It is really the English national epic, for Paradise Lost[64] is a purely literary poem, while it is the essence of an epic to be genuine folk-lore. Also, Malory was the Master from whom William Morriss copied the style of his prose Tales.

Which reminds me of your criticism of the 'Well'. I quite see your point, and, of course, agree that the interests of the tale reach their climax in the great scene at the World's End: my reply is that the interest of the journey home is of quite a different nature. It is pleasant to pick up all the familiar places and characters and see the same circumstances applied to the heroe's new role of 'Friend of the Well'. The Battle-piece at the end is very fine, and the ending, tho', as was inevitable, conventional, leaves one in a pleasant, satisfied state of mind. The only part that I found really tedious was Roger's historical survey of the Burg & the

---

63 *Le Morte D'Arthur* is the title generally given to the cycle of Arthurian legends by Sir Thomas Malory, finished in 1470 and printed by Caxton in 1485. The version Lewis began with was *Le Morte d'Arthur by Sir Thomas Malory*, with an introduction by Professor Rhys, 2 vols., Everyman's Edition [1906].

64 John Milton, *Paradise Lost* (1667).

Scaur. In fact, Roger was only a lay-figure brought in to conduct the Ladye's machinations with Ralph, and why he was not allowed to drop into oblivion when they were over, I cannot imagine.

How I run on! And yet, however many pages one may fill in a letter, it is only a tithe of what ten minutes conversation would cover: it is curious, too, how the thoughts that bubble up so freely when one meets a friend, seem to congeal on paper, when writing to him.

I wonder what you, who complain of loneliness when surrounded by a numerous family and wide circle of friends, would do if you could change places with me. Except my grinder and his wife, I think I have not spoken to a soul this week: not of course that I mind, much less complain; on the contrary, I find that the people whose society I prefer to my own are very few and far between. The only one of that class in Bookham, is still in the house, though they tell me she is up and about.[65] Of course, as they say at home, this solitude is a kind of egotism: and yet I don't know that they are right. The usual idea is that if you don't want to talk to people, you do so because you think they're intellectually your inferiors. But its not a question of inferiority: if a man talks to me for an hour about golf, war & politics, I know that his mind is built on different lines from mine: but whether better or worse is not to the point.

My only regret at present is that I cannot see Co. Down in the snow: I am sure some of our favourite haunts look very fine. We have been deeply covered with it all week, and the pine wood near hear, with the white masses on ground and trees, forms a beautiful sight. One almost expects a 'march of dwarfs' to come dashing past! How I long to break away into a world where such things were true: this real, hard, dirty, Monday morning modern world stifles one. Progress in health and spirits and music! Write soon and give all your thoughts, actions, readings and any local gossip, for the benefit of

yours sincerely
Jack Lewis

---

65 This was probably Mrs Kirkpatrick's 'theatrical' friend, Miss MacMullen, whom Lewis mentioned to his father on 13 October.

TO HIS FATHER (LP IV: 246):

[Gastons]

Postmark: 20 November 1914

My dear Papy,

I received your answer this evening and decided to be guided by your views, or in other words my objections to the 'Monstre' holiday are not insuperable. Break the news gently to Kirk, as I am not sure he will relish the interruption.

I hope you will enjoy prosecuting dear Mr. Russell:[66] he will probably give you 'something to be going on with' in the way of back chat. Tell me any news of Warnie as soon as you hear it. I will stop now, as this is only a 'letter extraordinary'.

your loving

son Jack

Lewis returned to Belfast on 28 November and was confirmed in St Mark's on 6 December. Writing of this in SBJ X, he said: 'My relations to my father help to explain (I am not suggesting they excuse) one of the worst acts of my life. I allowed myself to be prepared for confirmation, and confirmed, and to make my first Communion, in total disbelief, acting a part, eating and drinking my own condemnation.'

TO HIS BROTHER (LP IV: 276–7):

[Little Lea,

Strandtown.

[22 December 1914]

Ω ἀδελφὲ φίλτατε

Αἰτέω συγγνώμην μόι μη γραφαῖ[67] – but perhaps I'd better write in English. This has become such a habit you know, but I beg your pardon.

It is a pity that you happen to be at the front just now, as – at last – an Opera Company came to Belfast while you were away. It was the 'Moody Manners', but that you have heard P. talking about. They were quite good, though somewhat early Victorian in the way of scenery and

---

66 Mr Russell was a harmless, but terrifying, lunatic who was for many years a well-known figure in and around St Mark's.

67 'O dearest brother, I am sorry not to have written.'

gestures. We went to 'Faust'[68] and 'Trovatore'.[69] The former was perfectly glorious, well sung and everything. It is a very good opera and of course knowing a good deal of the music and having read Goethe, I enjoyed it very well. Of course I have discovered that it is no use expecting to hear the overture or preludes to the acts at Belfast, as everyone talks all the time as if nothing were going on. Il Trovatore, as we have always agreed, is a very mediocre thing anyway, and, with the exception of the soprano and baritone, was villainously sung. I don't want to hear it again.

On the following Friday we got badly let down: the Glenmachonians Greeves's and I had made up a party to go to 'Samson and Delilah',[70] which we were all looking forward to immensely. Imagine our feelings when the cod at the door told us it has been changed to 'Fra Diavolo' – a very inferior comic opera of Auber's![71] I seem to be fated never to get fair treatment from that theatre management. Fra Diavolo impresses on one how very badly the comic opera needed reform when Gilbert and Sullivan came to the rescue:[72] it is the old style – bandits, a foolish English earl, innkeepers 'and sich'. It was without exception the greatest drivel I ever listened to. There has been nothing worth noticing at the Hippodrome lately. Those two people – I've forgotten their names – who do the sketch about the broken mirror, were at the Opera House last week. The Opera House is now in the grip of that annual monstrosity the Grand Xmas Panto. I suppose I ought to be reconciled to it as fate by now. One good thing is that Tom Foy is coming, but of course the whole thing will be awfully patriotic.

I like your asking why I didn't go to meet you in town. You omitted the trifling precaution of telling me your address – or did you intend that I should go up to a policeman in Piccadilly and ask, 'Have you seen my brother anywhere?'

---

68 An opera by Charles Gounod, based on the *Faust* of Johann Wolfgang von Goethe, and first produced in 1859.

69 *Il Trovatore*, an opera by Giuseppe Verdi, was first performed in 1853.

70 *Samson et Dalila,* an opera by Camille Saint-Saëns, was first performed in 1877.

71 Daniel Auber's opera *Fra Diavolo* was first performed in 1830.

72 W.S. Gilbert (1836–1911), playwright and librettist, and Arthur Sullivan (1842–1900), composer, together wrote many very popular operettas. They include *The Pirates of Penzance* performed in 1879, *The Mikado* performed in 1885, and *The Yeoman of the Guard* performed in 1888.

The new records are a most interesting and varied selection, comprising 'The calf of gold' from Faust, with a vocal 'Star of Eve'[73] on the other
side: the Drinking and Duel scenes from Faust: Saint Saen's 'Danse
Macabre':[74] Grieg's 'March of the Dwarfs':[75] and 'Salve Minerva' from
Faust. There are also several new books, but most of them are not in
your line: the only two you might care for are the works of Shelley and
Keats.

We were up at Glenmachan yesterday (Monday) evening to a supper
party of Kelsie's where you went representing a novel.[76] All the usual
push were there of course, and I quite enjoyed it. A number of people
besides, whom I had never seen before, also turned up. There was one
rather pretty thing whom Lily[77] is arranging as 'suitable' for Willie
Greeves[78] – in opposition I suppose to the Taylor affair. Of course it is all
very nice, but don't you thank the gods you haven't got a sister?

---

73 'Bright Star of Eve' is from Charles Gounod's *New Part Songs* (1872 or 1873).

74 Camille Saint-Saëns's orchestral work *Danse Macabre* was first performed in 1872.

75 'March of the Dwarfs' is a piano piece in Edvard Grieg's *Lyriske Stykker* (1891).

76 Their mother's sister, Mrs Lilian 'Lily' Suffern (1860–1934), wrote to Warnie on
3 February 1915 about the book party. 'On 21st Dec.,' she said, 'Kelsie gave a book
party which was very amusing....Some of the books were very good – too good for me,
for I couldn't guess them. Your father's was *Edged Tools*, a fan and a knife. Clive's was
The Three Musketeers – a bit of paper with "Soldier's Three" on it, it made us all mad
because it was so plain, and we did not (many) guess it. Miss Murray's was a cutting
from that day's Newsletter of the birthdays – *The Newcomes*. Another cutting from the
Newsletter won the prize – Advt. of rise in the price of coals – *The Sorrows of Satan*.
No one hardly guessed Hugh McCreddy's – yet it was very good – a picture of a man
with his mouth wide open in a laugh – *L'Homme Qui Rit*. I had a picture of the Kaiser,
nicely framed in ribbon – *The Egoist* (Meredith). Everyone guessed it *The Lunatic at
Large*. Three old ladys sitting talking (picture of), tied with green ribbon was *Gossips
Green*. Willie Jaffe's was bad – a black African with a white line down it – *Across the
Dark Continent*' (LP IV: 289–90).

(Henry Seton Merriman wrote *With Edged Tools* (1894); Alexandre Dumas wrote
The Three Musketeers (1844–5); William Makepeace Thackeray wrote *The Newcomes*
(1853–4); Marie Corelli wrote *The Sorrows of Satan* (1895); Victor Hugo wrote
L'Homme Qui Rit (1869); George Meredith wrote *The Egoist* (1879); Joseph Storer
Clouston wrote *The Lunatic at Large* (1899); Alice Dudeney wrote *Gossips Green*
(1906); and Sir Henry Morton Stanley wrote *Through the Dark Continent* (1878).)

Kelso Ewart (1886–1966) was the fourth child of Lady Ewart, the cousin of Flora
Lewis, and her husband Sir William. See **The Ewart Family** in the Biographical
Appendix.

77 Mary Elizabeth 'Lily' Greeves (1888–1976) was Arthur Greeves's sister. She married
Lewis's cousin Charles Gordon Ewart (1885–1936) on 15 December 1915. See **The
Ewart Family** in the Biographical Appendix.

78 This was Arthur's brother, William Edward Greeves (1890–1960).

One other piece of local gossip is so funny that you really must hear it. Do you know a vulgar, hideous old harridan on the wrong side of 40, a Miss Henderson, who lives at Norwood Towers? She's just the sort of creature who would live there. Well the latest wheeze is that you meet her every time you go to Glenmachan, running after Bob.[79] And the beauty of the thing is that she makes Bob bustle about and talk to her and flirt with her. I know you can't imagine Bob 'courtin'. I promise you it is a thing of beauty. While admiring the creature's energy in getting a move on anyone like him, I don't want her to get into the connection even as remotely as the sister in law of my second cousins.

You're becoming quite a hero in your absence, and I can always command a large and attentive audience by spinning yarns about 'The other day my brother, who is at the front etc.' Hope is here now, and the Captain was home for a few days – I suppose you saw that he is now a Major? Why couldn't you manage to get a few days off? You would at any rate have a change of clothes and diet if you did. Last week we went to the Messiah with Carrie Tubb[80] as soprano – she can sing, but she's as ugly as the day is long. The contralto, altho she hadn't much of a voice, was an improvement in that way – really quite a magnificent creature. Rather like the woman whom we met in France going about with the Katinarsky's. I wondered if it was the same, but I suppose not, as the other would be younger. Of course Handel is not your ideal or mine as a composer: but it is always fair to remember that he wrote in the days of spinets and harpsichords, before anyone had discovered that there could be any point in music beyond a sort of abstract prettiness. Of course the inappropriateness of his tunes is appalling – as for instance where he makes the chorus repeat some twenty times that they have all gone astray like sheep in the same tone of cheerful placidity that they'd use for saying it was a fine evening.

Yes: the Kirk arrangement is absolutely *it*. The war is mainly interesting to him as illustrating some remark he made to 'Mr. Dods' fifty years ago. The only trouble about Bookham is our dear Mrs. Crutwell. I don't know if it was the same in your time, but she has lately developed a

---

79 Robert Heard Ewart (1879–1939). See **The Ewart Family** in the Biographical Appendix.

80 Carrie Tubb (1876–1976) was an English soprano much in demand as an oratorio singer. She was a favourite singer of operatic excepts, notably the final scene of Richard Wagner's *Götterdämmerung*.

mania for 'seeing young people enjoying themselves' – and you know what that means. Write some time.

Yours, Jack

P.S. Did you ever get the letter I wrote from Larne?

1915

—— ❦ ——

TO HIS FATHER (LP IV: 285‒6):

[Gastons
24? January 1915][1]

My dear Papy,

I have arrived and settled down here in due course, and everything progresses favourably, including the German. We had it snowing hard all day on Thursday, beautiful snow and bright frosty sun until Saturday, and are now enduring the thaw. (Yes; I did change my socks. No; there are no holes in my shoes. Yes, thanks, I have plenty of warm underclothing.) I hope you have by this time got rid of your cough, and, did I not know the utter futility of so doing, I should advise you to be careful. However, as you will doubtless reply, my playing the anxious adviser of a patient who will not obey orders, is rather like Satan rebuking sin.[2] But all joking apart, do take any care of yourself that you reasonably can, and don't refuse harmless precautions for no reason.

That Smythe boy, the brother of the one who lost his arm, was home for a few days and lunched at Gastons on Wednesday: he tells us that his brother is going out again as soon as he is better – so hard are we pressed that even cripples whose worth is known will be taken in some departments! What this argues as to the paucity of our troops in general, and the old officer's contempt for the new volunteers who are to come, you will readily imagine. Smythe also directly contradicts the reports of the newspapers about the Indian troops whom he declares to be worthless, and absolutely unfitted for trench fighting: they have too, an unpleasant habit of not burying their dead, which contributes a good deal to the

---

1 Albert Lewis, like so many others, had for some months previously feared that England would be invaded by the Germans, and this explains why his son was not allowed to return to Great Bookham until 16 January 1915.

2 Mark 3:26: 'If Satan rise up against himself, and be divided, he cannot stand, but hath an end.'

discomfort of European men anywhere near. But of course this is only one man's story, and the longer this war goes on the less credulous we become. Kirk has many amusing reflections, as usual, on the present crisis, especially when the curate came in yesterday at afternoon tea and told a number of patriotic lies about Germany and the Germans. Kirk then proceeded with great deliberation to prove step by step that his statements were fallacious, impossible, and ridiculous. The rest of the party including Mrs. K., Louis, and myself enjoyed it hugeously.

Thanks for my Classical Library which I have received. In the course of the week I shall return Munro's Iliad I–XII[3] which was *not* asked for: after which fact has been explained gently to Carson you will tell his remains to give you in exchange Merry's Odyssey I–XII,[4] which *was* asked for. Kirk also tells me to ask for 'Tacitus's Agricola',[5] any edition *except* Macmillan's.

your loving son,
Jack

TO ARTHUR GREEVES (W/LP IV: 286–7):

[Gastons
26 January 1915]

My dear Arthur,

I wonder would hunting be good sport? The matter ocurred to me, not because I am really interested in it, but because I have just returned from a compulsory chase – trying to find out where the bit at the top of page 2 of your letter was meant to come in. Now, faint & perspiring, I am enjoying the fruits of my labours.

By this time you will probably have finished 'Villette'.[6] What do you think of the ending? I can just hear you saying, 'Cracked – absolutely!'. It certainly is most unsatisfactory, but yet a touch of genius. I fancy it is the only novel in existence that leaves you in a like uncertainty. Merriman is a far cry from the Brontes. Both of course are good, but while they should be sipped with luxurious slowness in the winter evening, he may

---

3 Homer, *Iliad, Books I–XII*, with an introduction, a brief Homeric grammar, and notes by D.B. Monro (1884).

4 Homer, *Odyssey, Books I–XII*, with an introduction, notes, etc. by W.W. Merry (1870).

5 Cornelius Tacitus (c. AD 55–117), the greatest historian of ancient Rome, in AD 98 published *Agricola*, a biography of his father-in-law, Julius Agricola.

6 Charlotte Brontë, *Villette* (1853).

be read in a cheap copy on top of a tram. And yet I don't know: of course his novels are melodrama, but then they are the best melodrama ever written, while passages like the 'Storm' or the 'Wreck' in the Grey Lady, or the Reconciliation between the hero and his father in 'Edged Tools', are as good things as English prose contains.[7]

The remark about the Maiden Islands was really quite smart for you. You might have it framed? Also such gems of orthography as 'simpathise' and 'phisically' which appeared in your last correspondance, tho' of course I, being almost as bad, have no right to complain.

The weather here is perfectly damnable, there having been scarcely a couple of hours' sunshine since I left home. Now that my friends have gone, there is nothing to do but sit & read or write when it rains, and consequently I have nearly finished The Morte D'arthur. I am more pleased at having bought it every day, as it has opened up a new world to me. I had no idea that the Arthurian legends were so fine (The name is against them, isn't it??) Malory is really not a great author, but he has two excellent gifts, (1) that of lively narrative and (2) the power of getting you to know characters by gradual association. What I mean is, that, although he never sits down – as the moderns do – to describe a man's character, yet, by the end of the first volume Launcelot & Tristan, Balin & Pellinore, Morgan Le Fay & Isoud are all just as much real, live people as Paul Emanuel or Mme Beck.[8] The very names of the chapters, as they spring to meet the eye, bear with them a fresh, sweet breath from the old-time, faery world, wherein the author moves. Who can read 'How Launcelot in the Chapel Perilous gat a cloth from a Dead corpse' or 'How Pellinore found a damosel by a Fountain, and of the Jousts in the Castle of Four Stones', and not hasten to find out what it's all about?

To obey my own theory that a letter should tell of doings, readings, thinkings, I will conclude by saying that I am trying to find some suitable theme for my Celtic narrative Poem: there are heaps of stories but mostly too long. Fare-thee-well.

Yours sincerely

C. S. Lewis

N.B. This was written on the same day as I got your letter, but I forgot to post it. Mille pardons. J.

---

7 Henry Seton Merriman, *The Grey Lady* (1895); *With Edged Tools* (1894).
8 Paul Emanuel and Mme Beck are characters in *Villette*.

TO ARTHUR GREEVES (W):

[Gastons
2 February 1915]

Dear Arthur,

The first essential point for a letter writer to master is that of making himself intelligable to his reader. Or, to come down from my high horse, what was the (it?) in brackets meant for? A thousand pardons for my dulness, only I utterly failed to follow your wheeze: please explain in your next epistle.

I am deep in Morte D'Arthur by this time, and it is really the greatest thing I've ever read. It is strangely different from William Morris, although by subject & language they challenge comparison. One is genuine, and the other, tho' delightful, must, of course, be only an artificial reproduction. You really ought to read your copy of it, or at any rate parts of it, as the connecting chain between book and book is not very tightly drawn. I don't think it can be the Library Edition, that those people have sent me, as it does not agree with your description at all, being bound in plum-coloured leather, with pale-blue marker attached. However, partly through my keenness to read the book & partly because it was a very handsome binding, I did not send it back.

By the way, is there anything the matter with my father, as I have not heard from him for some time now? Or perhaps it is only this submarine nonsense that makes the conveyance of letters uncertain: which reminds me, that, though I do not usually take much interest in the war, yet it would be unpleasantly brought home to me if I had to spend my holydays in England.[9]

Your remarks á propos of loneliness are quite true, and I admit that what I said before was rather not, as uncongenial companions produce in reality a worse desolation than actual solitude.

I am glad to hear you have read Esmond:[10] it is one of my favourite novels, and I hardly know which to praise most, the wonderful, musical, Queen Anne English, or the delicate beauty of the story. True, I did rather resent the history, and still maintain, that when a man sets out to

---

9 There were, in fact, a good many German submarines operating in the Irish Sea at this time. Lewis's father was particularly upset over the raid near Fleetwood on 30 January 1915 when the Germans sank the *Kilcoan*, a collier designed by his brother Joseph.

10 William Makepeace Thackeray, *Henry Esmond* (1852).

write a novel he has no right to ram an European War down your throat – it is like going back to Henty![11] Did you ever try that arch-fiend?

I am surprised that there is no snow in Ulster as we had a week of good, thick, firm, 'picture' snow – and very much I enjoyed it. And other things too! She is better now, up & about, and we have progressed very rapidly. In fact the great event is actually fixed – fixed! – do you realize that? I don't think I've ever been so bucked about anything in my life, she's an awfully decent sort.[12] But I suppose this is boring you, so I must cut short my raptures – & my letter.

Yours

Jack

TO HIS FATHER (LP IV: 292–3):

[Gastons]
Postmark: 3 February 1915

My dear Papy,

As you will be by this time accustomed to my using 'this week' as synonymous with 'next week', I will make no further mention of that matter than to say that the Iliad which you are to exchange is being sent by the same post as this. I must confess to extraordinary dullness in failing to catch any point – if point there be – in your remark, 'now for a nasty one': 'I found a Homer'. Why a nasty one? The fact that you have begun to suffer from a mania for sending poor, unnecessary unoffending books about the channel is nothing which should disturb the peace of mind of the philosophers of Gastons.

Talking about the channel reminds me of this morning's news. Of course the really important feature of this submarine work is not so much the actual danger to goods and individuals as the inevitable 'scare' which it will cause, and the injury to business arising from that. I suppose this was their intention. As for the Zepplin talk, it seems to me to be

---

11 George Henty (1832–1902), while serving with the army in the Crimea, became a war correspondent. Following this career in many countries, he became successful as the author of stories for boys mainly based on military history. *Out in the Pampas* (1868) was followed by some 35 other titles.

12 A family of Belgian refugees were evacuated to Great Bookham in the autumn of 1914. Lewis began visiting them with Mrs Kirkpatrick, and became infatuated with one of the young girls in the family. He doubtless discussed his feelings for her with Arthur Greeves during the Christmas holidays. As to how much truth there was in what he wrote and said about the Belgian girl, see Lewis's letter of 1 October 1931.

rather childish folly on the part of the Germans: a few babies and an odd chimney stack cannot afford a recompense proportionate to the labour, expense and danger of managing an aerial raid. The only point is the moral influence, which again depends entirely on the amount of 'guts' of the victims.

I am glad to hear that the new Kiplings are poems, as we have had none of them yet. The question as to whether he was a greater poet or proseur is one of those everlasting things. Perhaps however, we may admit that someone else might possibly have written his best poems, but there is only one man alive who could have written 'Kim' or the 'Jungle books' or 'Puck'.[13] I am not sure whether I have read the Seven Seas or not. Is it there that the ballads about the prehistoric Song-Man and Picture Man (the story of Ung) occurs?[14] I remember they make a very interesting criticism on artists and their public, ancient and modern, and impressed me greatly.

We have had one day of spring and are now paying for it by a wind and a rain that would take you off your feet. My German is progressing with such alarming success that I am rather afraid they will put me under suspicious as a spy! Keep well.

your loving son,
Jack

TO HIS FATHER (LP IV: 296–7):

[Gastons]
Postmark: 13 February 1915

My dear Papy,

As Spenser naively remarks at the beginning of about the thousandth canto of his poem,

'Oh, what an endlesse work I have in hand',[15]

so might a parent doomed to supply an ignorant philosopher with the forgotten necessities of life echo the sentiment. Or in other words there

---

13 Rudyard Kipling, *Kim* (1901), *The Jungle Book* (1894); *The Second Jungle Book* (1895); *Puck of Pook's Hill* (1906).

14 Albert Lewis had just acquired Kipling's *The Seven Seas* (1896), which contains 'The Story of Ung'.

15 Edmund Spenser, *The Faerie Queene* (1590, 1596), Book IV, Canto xii, 1.

is 'still one river to cross', and I really do think this will be the end. What I want is a copy of the *Helena* of Euripides,[16] which you will find kicking its heels somewhere in the little end room. The shoes have just arrived, for which many thanks: and by the way, when I want to pay for anything, we'll let you know boss, don't worry.

I am very annoyed that an opera company should come while I am away from home, although indeed it is a common enough state of affairs. Perhaps we are accustomed to regard John Harrison as an oratorio singer and it would be rather a shock to hear him in opera, although I have often seen records of him in operatic songs. I think you would be wise if you raised the energy to go. Perhaps Uncle Hamilton and Aunt Annie would care to take you – do you think so?

They must be having a rotten time at Glenmachan: 'les jeunes maries' particularly are making a bright start, aren't they? What one always feels about these troubles is that they are so hard on poor Bob.[17] Is it not cruel when a poor fellow is doing his best, working away at his music all night and slaving like a nigger to make things bright and cheerful for everyone else, never letting his conversation flag, saving many a dull hour from ennui and always unselfishly making his wishes subservient to the comfort of the household – is it not hard that he should meet trouble like this? And yet – you will hardly believe it – I have heard people so brutal as to suggest that this 'angel in the house' ought to be at the front!

Everything here is pretty much as usual. The weather is delightful and Kirk's thoughts turn even lightlier than of old to agriculture. His chief 'stunt' at present is to point out the fact that he is the same age as Balfour,[18] and ask whether he (K) would stand any chance of getting a job as Headmaster now: and if not, is he to understand that the care of a few schoolboys calls for more qualities of youthful energy and intellect than that of the British Empire? Well, perhaps he's right; we have often heard him say so at any rate.

I have been reading this week a book by Swinburne from the Library, a 'Study on Shakespeare'.[19] This is my first experience of his prose, and I think I shall make it the last. 'Apt alliteration's artful aid' may be all right in verse, but it is undoubtedly vicious in prose, as also are words like

---

16 *Helena*, a play by the Greek poet Euripides, was produced in 412 BC.
17 Lewis is mocking his cousin Robert Heard Ewart.
18 Mr Kirkpatrick and Lord Balfour (1848–1930), were born in 1848, making them 67.
19 Algernon Charles Swinburne, *A Study of Shakespeare* (1880).

'plenilune', 'Mellisonant', 'tautologous', 'intromission'. And yet at the same time there is great force in the book, and his appreciation of the subject is very infectious.

your loving son,
Jack

P.S. You might give me the Colonel's address in your next letter. J.

TO ARTHUR GREEVES (W):

[Gastons
16 February 1915]

Dear Arthur,

When I received your epistle, which certainly did not weary one by its length, I was in one of my black moods: like Saul, my evil spirit was upon me.[20] Having just had a sufficient glimpse of home and of my brother to tantalize but not to satisfy:[21] having lost, if not for good, at least for this term, an unparalleled opportunity: and finding a very objectionable visitor in possession of my grinder's house, you may well imagine that I was in no mood for an extra irritation. I had just, too, been out for a walk, mon dieu, a nightmare! Splashing thro great puddles beneath a leaden sky that rained and rained! However, enough of this.

You ask me what was the matter with me when I was at home. Thank you: I believe I enjoyed excellent health. Of course it is true, that we saw a good deal more of our relations than we wanted, and had none too much time to ourselves: but of course, you, or any member of your household, are always welcome.

As to the other grievance, it really is phenominal ill luck. Of course, like all the rest of her sex she is incapable of seeing anything fair, and when she had been persuaded after a good deal of difficulty to do this, and then I failed to turn up, it is only to be expected that I am 'left'. In any case, it would be impossible now; as she has gone with her mother for a week to visit some other Belgians in Birmingham.[22] But perhaps you are tired of my 'affaires'.

---

20 1 Samuel 16:23: 'The evil spirit from God was upon Saul.'
21 Warren had only just returned from France, and having a week's leave, he and Jack spent part of it together at home. Jack returned to Great Bookham on 9 February.
22 Presumably the Belgian girl he had written about in his previous letter.

To go back to the question of holydays (I started to try and write an 'essay-letter', but can't keep it up; excuse me if I meaunder a bit), the last straw came on Sunday afternoon when we were snatching a few moments rest before going off to visit our various relations: who should walk in – but – but – but – Henry Stokes!!!! Dear boy! How thoughtful of him! How kind! What a pleasure for us all! After that, my brother suggested that if ever he got another week's leave, we should spend it on the Maidens.

You must imagine me writing this in my bedroom at about 11 o'clock, as that damned guest makes it impossible to be comfortable downstairs. Although it was quite spring weather before I went home, a thin snow mixed with rain is falling outside. In spite of all my troubles, I am quite bucked with life to night, and if only the water were hot enough for a bath I should be in heaven. I wonder what you are doing just now?

Which reminds me, you are drifting into a habit of morbid self-pity lately: all your letters are laments. Beware of the awful fate of growing up like that. I never, for my part, saw what was meant by such terms as 'the releif of confiding ones troubles' and the 'consolations of sympathy': my view is, that to mention trouble at all, *in a complaining way*, is to introduce into the conversation an element equally painful for everyone, including the speaker. Of course, it all depends on the way it is done: I mean, simply to mention them, is not wrong, but, by words or expression to call for sympathy which your hearer will feel bound to pump up, is a nuiscance.

What a good friend I am, to sit up writing all this stuff to a creature who, just because he 'doesn't feel like it' gives me no more than a couple of lines. Write soon, like a good friend, and tell me all about yourself, and all the local gossip. I am damnably tired, and there's something the matter with the gas, and I've come to the end of my paper. So I must dry up.

Yours
Jack

TO HIS FATHER (LP IV: 302–3):

[Gastons]
Postmark: 3 March 1915

My dear Papy,

I hope this pause in your correspondence does not mean a pause in your health; it is now, in the words of the poet, 'a long time, in fact a ver-ray considerable time' since your hand writing appeared on the hall table. One might write a paper on characters according to different days of the week: how a Monday table is associated with a letter from Arthur and a Tuesday table with one from you: although, as it would appear sir, in this case it has lately joined

'The inheritors of unfullfilled renown'[23]

and become as blank and barren as its surly brothers of Saturday and Sunday. Of course we would not forget Wednesday with its 'Punch' or Thursday with its Literary Supplement, which is getting by the way poorer and poorer every week (like chalk, you know.)

I don't know that anything of world shaking importance has happened here: we have had snow and thaw, snow and thaw alternately, with plenty of rain, wind and frost thrown in to make things pleasant. Since Saturday however, there has been some sunshine, and we are hoping for better things.

The good ladies of Bookham still come regularly to tea, and I have the priviledge of hearing what Mrs. Grant-Murray would do if she were in Kitchener's place,[24] and all about Miss Milne's new maid. The discovery of German spies too, is an art in which they excell: how I wish I knew enough German to let drop a few words occasionally, just as if I had slipped into it by accident! It is a great pity that Kirk won't come in to afternoon tea, as his commentaries on the whole kodotta would be great.

I essayed a new author the other day whom we have often heard praised and of whom I hoped great things – Landor: but the book I got, a series of imaginary letters called 'Pericles and Aspasia'[25] proved rather disappointing. Indeed I am afraid my appreciation of English prose is

---

23 Percy Bysshe Shelley, *Adonais* (1821), XLV, 397.

24 Lord Kitchener (1850–1916) was Secretary of State for War.

25 Walter Savage Landor, *Pericles and Aspasia* (1836–7).

very limited, and I certainly cannot fatten on mere prose when the matter is not interesting. However, as the Colonel said in his essay on 'Kenilworth',[26] the 'book is not wholly without merit'. I forget whether you said you had ever read him or not?

I suppose we must soon begin to make arrangements about the Easter Holydays – I will not give up that spelling: however there is no hurry as the actual feast comes very late, and it is better to take off the summer term and add on to this. One might observe in passing – purely as a matter of general interest of course – that we must by now have got past half term.

Write soon if you are alright, and tell me all the gossip.

your loving

son Jack

P.S. Has that English word 'got' ever struck you? In reading this letter I couldn't help thinking of it. It is made to mean almost anything – J.

TO HIS FATHER (LP IV: 303):

[Gastons
7? March 1915]

My dear Papy,

In the bad old days when I was still in the gall of bitterness at Malvern, we used sometimes to hear of schools that had a mid term holiday, and congratulate ourselves on being superior to such kodotta. But it proves to be no bad institution after all. Of course it is short: but then how pleasant to feel at the end that one has only half a term to get through. And one appreciates a week at half term more than the same time in the middle of the holiday. I have not heard from the Colonel since we parted at Euston, but I suppose he arrived at Saille all right – (if that is how you spell it.)

That Gerald Smythe of whom I told you, who lost an arm in the war, was staying with us last week. He is really wonderful: he has only been out of bed about a month and is going back to the front again next week. It does one good to see a person thoroughly cheerful under circumstances like his, and actually eager to be there again. Even in so short a time he has learnt to be quite independant, and can cut his food, light

---

26 Sir Walter Scott, *Kenilworth* (1821).

his pipe, and dress – tho' how a man can tie a tie with one arm, I don't know.

Did you read Lloyd George's speech the other day introducing the remark about the German potato bread – 'I fear that potato bread more than all Von Kluck's strategy'.[27] Although, as you have seen, I don't often read the newspapers, I was glad when Kirk pointed that out to me. Most of the people one hears rather laugh at that bread 'wheeze', but I rather think Lloyd George's is the wiser view. In the way of reading, I have been taking a course of 'Poems and Ballads', which, with the exception of the 'Coign of a cliff'[28] I had almost forgotten. It is rather pleasant to discover a book which is already at home for future use.

The weather here is very miserable, and I don't think there has been an hour's sunshine since I came back. Kirk asked me to write for Aeneid VII and VIII, published at 1/6 each by Cambridge University Press, editor Sedgwick.[29] I am afraid these requests for books are rather numerous, but of course it is Kirk's to command, mine not to question why, etc.

I have heard nothing from you now since the holydays, except the scant note of which you so rightly said 'This is not a letter'. I sincerely hope you are not hors de combat. Do drop me a line soon and let me know.

your loving son,
Jack

---

27 David Lloyd George (1863–1945), Minister of Munitions, gave a speech on 28 February in which he appealed for an end to labour disputes. 'We laugh at things in Germany,' he said, 'that ought to terrify us. We say, "Look at the way they are making their bread – out of potatoes, ha, ha." Aye, that potato bread spirit is something which is more to dread than to mock at. I fear that more than I do even von Hindenburg's strategy, efficient as it may be. That is the spirit in which a country should meet a great emergency, and instead of mocking at it we ought to emulate it.' *The Times* (1 March 1915), p. 10.

28 Algernon Charles Swinburne, *Poems and Ballads*, Second Series (1878). The poem entitled 'A Forsaken Garden' begins 'In a coign of the cliff between lowland and highland'.

29 *Publius Vergili Maronis Aeneidos: Liber VII*, edited by Arthur Sidgwick (1879); *The Aeneid of Vergil: Book VIII*, edited with notes and vocabulary by Arthur Sidgwick (1879).

TO HIS FATHER (LP IV: 304):

My dear Papy,

In connection with the 'question before the house', I have, as you may have anticipated, only one answer. Apart from the natural inclination to go home if possible, it occurs to me that there is no knowing where such a period of non-homecoming might end. If we could be sure that this policy of frightfulness would be over by midsummer, I should not hesitate to spend Easter in England. But it would be illogical to stay here *now* on account of the submarines and cross *then* in spite of them. So that there is the frightful prospect of living on opposite sides of the channel for two, five, or six years.

That of course is unthinkable; and it is on that ground chiefly that I should recommend going home.

A minor point to be considered is that it would be as well to make use of my return ticket while it is still available. The same idea would make me inclined to travel by Fleetwood – for which my ticket is available – in preference to Larne and Stranraer. The difference in the length of the crossing is, I should say, by no means commensurate with the extra expense, and in comfort Fleetwood is probably superior. If these ideas fall in at all with your own, I should suggest that I leave Bookham on Thursday week (the 1st April), which would mean arriving home on the morning of Good Friday. That just leaves a comfortable space of time in which you can write to K. about it.

Last week end was busily employed in reading through De Quincey's 'Confessions'[30] as a whole, for the first time, from which I derived great satisfaction. How much of it is true? The whole thing reads so like a novel that I am rather incredulous. Anyway it is certainly a splendid piece of English prose, especially in the rhetorical passages where he shows such a happy knack of getting pleasantly off the point. Thanks for the Aeneids: though, with the holydays near, if I had thought, I might have let it stand over.

As you say, our inability to cope with the submarine menace is a very serious thing; but not half so far reaching, so degrading, so essentially rotten as the behaviour of our working classes, who, tho' so highly paid

---

30 Thomas De Quincey, *Confessions of an English Opium Eater* (1822).

that they can afford to have three days off per week when nominally at work, yet because of some petty jealousies of their own are refusing to turn out the goods necessary to the military operations which the country is engaged upon. As K. points out, we are the only country which when the war broke out was 'free' from militarism, and yet about to engage in civil war: and we are now the only one that cannot secure peace among its working classes. But enough of all this. The weather, as usual of late, is disgusting except for one 'pet' day on Sunday. Hope to see you next week.

your loving son,
Jack

TO ARTHUR GREEVES (W):

[Gastons
30 March 1915]

Dear Arthur,

How I pity you people who never have known the pleasures and the pains – which are an integral part of the pleasures – of a regular interchange of home-coming and school going. Even the terrors of Malvern were almost justified by the raptures with which one hailed the periodic deliverance. Here, where the minor disadvantages of my sojourns at Bookham are just enough to act as a foil to the pleasures of home, but not so great as to make the earlier part of the term unhappy, the arrangement is ideal. The satisfaction with which a day boy looks forward to a period of rest from his work, can be but the faintest shadow of a boarder's feeling towards his return from temporary exile.

These last few days! Every little nuisance, every stale or tiresome bit of work, every feeling of that estrangement which I never quite get over in another country, serves as a delightful reminder of how different it will all be soon. Already one's mind dwells upon the sights and sounds and smells of home, the distant murmuring of the 'yards', the broad sweep of the lough, the noble front of the cave hill, and the fragrant little glens and breezy meadows of our *own* hills! And the sea! I cannot bear to live too far away from it. At Belfast, whether hidden or in sight, still it dominates the general impression of nature's face, lending its own crisp flavour to the winds and its own subtle magic to horizons, even when they conceal it. A sort of feeling of space, and clean fresh vigour hangs over all in a country by the sea: how different from the stuffiness of

Bookham: here the wind – that is to say, the true, brisk, boisterous irre-
sistable wind – never comes.

And yet, I would not for a moment disparage the beauty of Surrey:
these slumbering little vallies, and quaint farmsteads have a mellow
charm of their own, that Ulster has not. But just now my End-of-Term
feelings will not allow me to think of that. 'But why', you will ask 'am I
treated to these lyrical raptures?' Indeed, Sir, I hardly know. My father
wrote a few days ago, and asked if we should risk the submarines and
come home, or not. I of course said that we should, – advancing many
sage arguments thereto, and suggested leaving here next Friday. I have
not been answered yet, but hope to goodness it is coming off. Anyway, a
wave of End-of-Terminess came over me to night, and, as I had to communicate with someone, so you, poor fellow, got let in for this!

I had a letter from 'Her'[31] the other day, which is all satisfactory, Must
shut up now.

Yours
Jack

*Jack arrived in Belfast for his Easter holidays on 1 April and was there till
30 April. During this time he wrote the first poems he considered worthy of
preservation. One of those written during this holiday was 'The Hills of
Down', and it is found in his* Collected Poems *(1994). From this time until
he went up to Oxford in 1917 Lewis wrote 52 poems which he copied into a
notebook bearing the name 'Metrical Meditations of a Cod'. Fourteen of the
'metrical meditations' are found in* Spirits in Bondage.

TO ARTHUR GREEVES (W):

[Gastons
4 May 1915]

Dear Galahad,[32]

I am surprised! Have you actually come down to enjoying such
stuff as 'The Breed of the Treshams'?[33] I never (for which the gods be

---

31 i.e. the Belgian girl.
32 Lewis has borrowed the name from Malory. In *Le Morte d'Arthur* Galahad is the son of
Launcelot and Elaine, and destined because of his immaculate purity to achieve the
Holy Grail.
33 John Rutherford, *The Bread of the Treshams* (1903).

thanked) saw or read it, but the name is enough. I admit, I should like to have seen The Shrew,[34] and novelties in the way of staging are always rather interesting. I much prefer on the stage – and everywhere for that matter – quiet, tasteful, plain decorations, to tawdry, splendid things.

I feel my fame as a 'Man-about-the-Gramaphone' greatly put out by your remarks à propos of Lohengrin Prelude Act III,[35] as, I must confess, I never heard of it on Columbia. I do hope it is a good *record*, as I should like to have it very much: what is the Venusbury music like?[36] Is it that wild part that comes at the end of the Tannhaüser overture? Of course you know the Columbia edition of Schubert's Rosamunde[37] has long been at Little Lea, but when last I played it to you, I seem to remember a *non* favourable verdict from you. I am so glad that you have gotten (That's correct, you know. 'Got' isn't) the Fire Music,[38] as I have been hesitating over it for ages, and your success or failure will decide me. Oh! I had better stop writing about this, as it makes me 'think long': not, if you please, in a sentimental way, but with a sensible desire for my books and you and our Gramaphones etc.[39]

However, I have gott*en* (notice – again) one great addition to my comfort here, in the discovery of a 'Soaking-machine', which conveniences are very scarce in England, owing to the strict customs which prevent the mildest trespassing. My new palace, is at the foot of a great oak, a few yards off a lane, and hidden therefrom by a little row of shrubs and small trees. Completely private, safe from sun, wind or rain, and on the ridge of the only rising ground (you wouldn't call it a hill) about here. There, with a note book and pencil, I can be as free to write, etc, as at home. So if your next letter comes in pencil, on a sheet torn from a pocket book, you needn't be surprised. I must find some more of these places as summer goes on, for it is already too hot to walk far.

---

34 William Shakespeare, *The Taming of the Shrew* (1623).

35 Richard Wagner's opera *Lohengrin* was first performed in 1850.

36 The title Richard Warner had chosen for his opera was *The Venusberg*, but he changed it to *Tannhäuser* when he learned that certain wits were making a joke of it. The opera was first performed in 1845.

37 Franz Schubert's *Rosamund* was first performed in 1823.

38 The 'Fire Music' is the Interlude to Act III, scene 3 of Richard Wagner's opera *Die Walküre*, or *The Valkyrie*, first performed in 1870 and part of his *Ring of the Nibelung* cycle.

39 For information on music recorded on gramophone records see Francis F. Clough and G.J. Cuming, *The World's Encyclopaedia of Recorded Music* (1952).

I bought yesterday a little shilling book about Wm. Morris, his life and his work,[40] which is rather interesting. To me, at least, for I am afraid *you* have given up that old friend of ours.

To say that you have something 'sentimental' to say, and not to say it, is to be like Janie McN.[41] with the latest scandal, that everyone is told *about* and no one is told. I don't quite follow your letter in places. What is the connection between all the rubbish about 'that nuisance Arthur' (you know how all your friends ridicule and dislike that sort of talk) and the wish that I should become sentimental perforce? By the way, I am perhaps more sentimental than you, but I don't blow a trumpet about it. Indeed, I am rather ashamed of it. Feelings ought to be kept for litera-ture and art, where they are delightful and not intruded into life where they are merely a nuisance.

I have just finished 'Shirley'; which I think better than either 'Jane Eyre'[42] or 'Villette'. You must read it. What a letter; every sentence seems to begin 'I'. However, a good healthy dose of egotism is what you need, while you might pass on a little of your superfluous modesty to Bookham. Sorry you've returned the old Meistersingers,[43] but think the Beka better value.

Yours

Jack

P.S. What is the name of the 'Galloping Horse' piece by Chopin,[44] I want to make Mrs K. play it.

---

40 Arthur Clutton-Brock, *William Morris: His Work and Influence* (1914).

41 Jane ('Janie') Agnes McNeill (1889–1959) was the daughter of James Adams McNeill (1853–1907), headmaster of Campbell College 1890–1907, and Margaret Cunningham McNeill. Mr McNeill had at one time been Flora Lewis's teacher, and he and his wife and daughter lived near the Lewises in 'Lisnadene', 191 Belmont Road, Strandtown. When he was young Jack Lewis both liked and disliked Janie. As time went on he realized that Jane, who would have liked to have gone to university, had remained home to look after her mother. He came to admire her much, and in time they became devoted friends. He was also close to Mrs McNeill, whose company he greatly enjoyed. *That Hideous Strength* is dedicated to Janie. See her biography in *CG*.

42 Charlotte Brontë, *Shirley* (1849); *Jane Eyre* (1847).

43 *Die Meistersinger von Nürnberg*, an opera by Richard Wagner, was first performed in 1868.

44 Arthur did not seem entirely sure what this 'Galloping Horse' piece was. In Lewis's next letter of 11 May, he said to Arthur, 'Why didn't you give me the number of the Polonaise: and what cheek to say "I think it is in A Flat" – when a journey downstairs would make sure.' If he had looked carefully Arthur might have discovered that it was not one of Chopin's Polonaises, but one of his Mazurkas.

TO ARTHUR GREEVES (W/LP IV: 316-17):

[Gastons
11 May 1915]

Dear Galahad,

Tut! Tut! Must I change your soubriquet? From being the spotless knight of the Grail, are you going to turn philosopher and meet me on my own ground to dispute my shadowy quibbles about the proper sphere of sentiment? Galahad becomes Merlin: who knows but that you may 'grow besotted of a damosel', like him, and like him, I may find you when I come home bound fast under a great stone, making a piteous wail to all who pass. And what a relief for the neighbourhood! I think I shall nominate a suitable damosel – say Miss Bradley or Sal Stokes – to besott and bind you. By the way, à propos of Miss Bradley, has she yet recovered (or better still died) from that peculiarly interminable complaint of hers, which prevents the gramaphone being played up at Glenmachen?

But to go back to the sentiment controversy, your objection is nonsense. You argue that sentiment is delightful in art, because it is a part of human nature. Quite right. From that, you deduce that it ought not to be confined to that sphere of human nature where it *is* delightful – viz. art. That is almost as sensible as to say that trousers are delightful only because they are a part of human clothes: therefore they ought to be worn, not only on the legs, but every where else. Do you maintain that it is a highly commendable and philosophical act to wear trousers, say, on your head? My point is that art is a recepticacle of human thought: sentiment, emotion etc make up that section of human thought which are best suited to fill that definite receptical – and no other. For why, when we have found the best place to keep a thing, should we keep it in other places as well, or instead? By the analogy of the trousers I have shown how ridiculous that would be. As for your idea that to be young, one must be sentimental, let us go into it. Young children are practically devoid of sentiment: they are moved only by bodily pain: young men are a little more sentimental, middle aged ones considerably more so, and old ones the most mawkishly so of all. Sentiment, you see, is a distinct mark of age.

Ah! Having gott*en* (N.B.) that off our chest, we can proceed to other matters. That little book about Wm. Morris has interested me so much – or re-awakened the old interest – in him, that I have just written up for

'The Roots of the Mountains' in Longman's pocket edition:[45] it is about the Goths, and is praised in that book as one of the best of the prose Romances. What is the good of getting Anderson in Everyman?[46] It is true, the tales have considerable merit in ipso (that's Latin and means 'in themselves', Ignorant!): but yet, if any book ever needed or was greatly improved by fancy binding, that is it.

The word Soaking-Machine can hardly be styled 'slang', being, as it is, coined by myself for private circulation: I thought you knew what it meant. The word 'soak' means to sit idly or sleepily doing nothing, and a S'ing machine is [a] place for this operation, i.e. a comfortable seat. Surely I must often have said to you in the course of our walks 'Let's find a soaking-machine' or 'Here's a good soaking-machine'?

I despair of making head or tail of any of your gramaphonic talk, where your extraordinary loose and obscure use of words like 'latter' etc makes havoc of the sense. Do you mean that you had another record of the Venusburg music, before you heard it with Lohengrin, à l'autre côté? Or do you know what you mean? Or, lastly, do you mean anything at all. I write such enormous letters (which you probably never read to the end) that, from the way Mrs K. keeps looking at me, I believe she fancies it a billet doux. Why didn't you give me the number of the Polonaise: and what cheek to say 'I think it is in A Flat', when a journey downstairs would make sure.

It has been raining for almost 36 hours here, which is not very cheerful. The idea of spelling melodrama 'mello-drama' is really quite 'chic': I should take out a patent on it, if I were you. I hope you are in good spirits these days, and that the lady of the office window is kind & in good health. Write soon: you've know idea how welcome your letters are. By the by, you might tell the girl in Osborne's to send on the monthly catalogues to my address here, which you can tell her – Columbia, H.M.V., Zono, Beka, are the chief. Valde.

Yours

Jack

---

45 William Morris, *The Roots of the Mountains* (1890). The Longman's Pocket Library edition was published in two volumes in 1913.

46 Hans Christian Andersen, *The Mermaid and Other Fairy Tales*, translated by Mrs Edgar Lucas, with coloured illustrations by Maxwell Armfield, Everyman's Library [1914].

TO HIS FATHER (LP IV: 312–13):

[Gastons]
Postmark: 13 May 1915

My dear Papy,

I suppose I must apologise for being a little behindhand with my bulletin; but I confess I don't understand the remark about 'punishing accidents'. I am really sorry if you have been nervous, but I thought the telegram would suffice to set you at ease. However, let me assure you here and now that I and my luggage arrived quite safely at Bookham: there has been no question of accidents at all.

Hard times these must be at Leeboro: I have managed to escape the spring gales both at home and here. Thanks for your exertions about my room, which I hope will prove successful in keeping it from shifting. Perhaps 'key-lashing' as an extreme measure would be advisable.

I think the idea of permanent Sunday luncheon at the Rectory is excellent:[47] perhaps a series of weekly lectures under the title of 'Anticipation and Realization; their genesis, distinctions and development: together with an excursus on their relations to the Greenshaketything', would contribute greatly to the gaiety of the occasion. With that disinterested devotion to science, that noble generosity which has always characterised my actions, I not only place the material at your disposal but actually relinquish all claim to authorship. It would be but folly to deny that I experience some natural pangs – but no! Far be it from me to

---

47 Albert and his sons were delighted with the new rector of St Mark's. This was the Reverend Arthur William Barton (1881–1962) who was born in Dublin and had gone, like Warnie and Jack, to Wynyard School. He took his BA from Trinity College, Dublin in 1903, and his BD in 1906. He was ordained in 1905 and was curate at St George's, Dublin, from 1904 until 1905, and curate of Howth from 1905 to 1913. From 1912 to 1914 he was head of the university settlement at Trinity College Mission in Belfast. He was instituted as rector of St Mark's, Dundela, on 6 April 1914, and remained there until 1925 when he became rector of Bangor. In 1927 he was made Archdeacon of Down, and in 1930 he became Bishop of Kilmore, Elphin and Ardagh. In 1939 Barton became Archbishop of Dublin and Primate of Ireland, which post he held until his retirement in 1956. In his description of Barton Warnie said, 'There must have been few who met him and did not like him, and he was soon to become a constant and welcome visitor at Little Lea. He was a man of sunny temperament, with a great sense of fun, and a caressing voice; he brought into the rather narrow air of a Belfast suburb the breath of a wider culture and a more humane outlook; his society was refreshing. What was of more importance, he was an excellent and conscientious Priest, who found the religion of his parish sunk into mere formalism under the regime of his slothful predecessor, and who set on foot a renaissance' (LP IV: 178).

divert the publication of philosophical enlightenment into a channel for the aggrandisment of personal glory. No! Not even when, from the stately halls of Purdysburn[48] conferred upon you by a grateful and adoring country, you watch the fame of my achievements heaping its most succulent favours upon your own head – not even then, I say, will a sigh of regret escape from the gullet of self sacrifice.

We had some real summer weather for a few days after I came back, but it has seen fit to pour in torrents today. There is nothing of much interest here except that I have heard a nightingale for the first time. I think I mentioned before that they are as common as sparrows about here – in fact they are rather too numerous. In my conceit (Elizabethan), the song of these birds is one of those few things that does really come up to its reputation: at any rate I never heard anything else at all like it.

'But enough of these tropes' (as Bacon says at the end of an essay about Masques and stage plays.):[49] let me soon have another letter as long as a Lurgan spade. The coat has arrived.

your loving son,
Jack

P.S. That cat about *accidence*, I guess has cold feet about jumping, eh?

TO ARTHUR GREEVES (W/LP IV: 323–4):

[Gastons
25 May 1915]

Dear Galahad,

B-r-r-r! Behold me coming with locusts & wild honey about my loins (or is it sackcloth & ashes) to kneel and tremble and apologise for my letterless week. However, qui s'excuse, s'accuse, as the French say, and if you want to seek the real author of the mischief you must go up to heaven, and find the four and twenty elders sitting in a row, as St John says, falling on their faces on the sea of glass[50] (which must hurt rather but apparently is the 'thing' up yonder), and William Morris in white raiment with a halo.

---

48 Purdysburn was a lunatic asylum.
49 'But enough of these toys', Francis Bacon said in 'Of Masques and Triumphs', *Essays or Counsels, Civil and Moral* (1625).
50 Revelation 4:4–10.

Or, in other words, 'The Roots of the Mountains' is the chief cause of my silence. It is not, however, in spite of all this, nearly so good as the first volume of 'The Well at the World's End', although the interest is better sustained throughout. To begin with, I was desparately dissapointed to find that there is nothing, supernatural, faery or unearthly in it at all: in fact, it is more like an ordinary novel. And yet there are many compensations: for, tho' more ordinary than the 'Well', it is still utterly different from any novel you ever read. Apart from the quaint and beautiful old English, which means so much to me, the supernatural element, tho' it does not enter into the plot, yet hovers on the margin all the time: we have 'the wildwood wherein dwell wights that love not men, to whom the groan of the children of men is as the scrape of a fiddle-bow: there too abide the kelpies, and the ghosts of them that rest not',[51] and such delightful names as The Dusky Men, The Shadowy Vale, The Shivering Flood, The Weltering Water etc. Another thing I like about it is that the characters are not mediaeval knights but Norse mountain tribes with axe & long-sword instead of horses & lances and so forth. However, though it is worth having and well worth reading, I don't know if its really worth buying. The next time I get a Morris Romance it will be one of the later ones, as the 'Roots' is one of the first, when, apparently, he hadn't yet found his feet in prose work.

On Saturday last we were over at a little village near here, where Watts the painter lived:[52] there is a little gallery, a lovely building, designed by himself, containing some of his quite famous pictures like 'Orpheus & Euridyce', 'Endymion', 'Sir Galahad' etc, which I always thought were in the Louvre or the Tate or some such place. Of course I don't really quite understand good painting, but I did my best, and succeeded in really enjoying some myself, & persuading the other people that I knew a tremendous lot about them all.

What a grand dialectician, our Little Arthur is!![53] You reply to my elegant tirade against sentiment by stating your old thesis that it ought

---

51 *Roots of the Mountains*, op. cit., vol. I, ch. 3, pp. 24–5: 'Therein are Kobbolds, and Wights that love not men, things unto whom the grief of men is as the sound of the fiddle-bow unto us. And there abide the ghosts of those that may not rest; and there wander the dwarfs and the mountain-dwellers, the dealers in marvels, the givers of gifts that destroy Houses.'

52 The painter and sculptor George Frederic Watts (1817–1904) who lived for some years at 'Limneslease' near Compton in Surrey.

53 Presumably a reference to the notorious Victorian children's lesson book *Little Arthur's England* (1835) by Lady Calcott.

not to be suppressed, without a single reason. You don't admit my arguments, and yet make no endeavour to answer them. And because I choose trousers for an example you say that it is 'very funny'. Moi, I didn't know trousers were funny. If you do, I picture your progress from the tram to the office something thus: 'Hullo! Good lord, there's a fellow with trousers over there! And there's another. Ha-Ha – Oh this is too screaming. Look – one-two-three more – ' and you collapse in a fit of uncontrollable merriment. Doesn't this sort of truck fill up the paper? But in point of fact, I've lost your last letter, and so don't quite know what to talk about.

Thanks for carrying out my message to Miss Whatdoyoucallher? about the monthly catalogues, which are now arriving in due order. That's rather a pretty girl, the H.M.V. infant prodigy 18 year old soprano, but she doesn't seem to sing anything worth hearing. Hear your brethren are going to join a friend's ambulance corps, whatever that may be. Give them my congratulations and all the usual nonsense one ought to say on such an occasion. I hope they will get on famously and come back with Victoria crosses and eye-glasses, which seem to be the two goals of military ambition.

It is hot as our future home down below, here, but the country is looking delightful, & I have found one or two more SOAKING MACHINES (I will use that word if I want to) and so am quite comfortable. I hear you have taken to getting heart fits in the middle of the sermon at Saint Marks and coming out – I only wish you'd teach me the trick.

And now, the kind reader, if there still is one, is going to be left in peace. Do write soon, and forgive your suppliant

Jack

TO HIS FATHER (LP IV: 313–14):

[Gastons]
Postmark: 25 May 1915

Dear Papy,

I don't seem to have heard from you for some time now, but I suppose I am a little behindhand myself. There has been great excitement here this week end: when I came home from Church on Sunday morning I found a note waiting for me to say that Kirk and Mrs. Kirk had gone to Bristol where they had heard by a telegraph that Louis was in hospital. It appears he got a mild species of sun stroke while working with big guns down there at a place called Lydd. It was not very serious – in fact I gather somewhat of a mares nest – and K. is back this evening while Mrs. K. is staying at Bristol for a few days.

We have started our real summer here, and it is pretty warm. How does the weather suit the home farm, where I hope the tragic gardeners are in good form? What between pigeons and gardeners and white Homburg hats, Leeborough must present quite a seasonable spring idyll (with a double 'l'.)

Mrs. K. and I were over at a place called Compton beyond Guildford on Saturday, where the attraction is a little pottery for fancy tiles and sich, founded by my friend William [Morris], who, as you know, besides being a poet was a wall paper designer, a potter, a hand loom weaver and everything else you can think of. Nearby is a gallery of Watts's pictures. He, it appears, was one of that same set, and there are a lot of quite swell things there, such as his 'Paolo and Francesco', 'Orpheus and Euridyce', and 'Found Drowned' etc., which I always imagined to be in some big place like the Louvre or Tate. It was quite interesting.

Any news from the Colonel lately? I have not heard from any one except Arthur for a long time now, so do try and raise a letter soon. Or is this silence a result of a literal obedience to my last advice a propos of lectures to the members of the Select Vestry? I hope the doctors don't think it serious.

There are plenty of nightingales about now, and in fact they are rather a nuisance. I am afraid this is rather a scrappy letter, but I am writing rather late at night, just before going to bed, and am a bit sleepy. I should like to know what is going on at Leeborough just now. I suppose these are the days of no fires, and sunset on the seat behind the laurels, with the crows coming home overhead, and Tim on the look out for wasps.

I hope you are keeping well and cheerful. Write again soon.

your loving,

son,

Jack

TO HIS FATHER (LP IV: 322–3):

[Gastons
28? May 1915]

My dear Papy,

I am sorry to hear that the mental digestion of my parent is so weak, and blame myself for giving it such strong meat. Perhaps a course of 'Decalettes, pure and simple things', or nursery rhymes would meet the case. (Now we can proceed to the letter.)

Of course it is a very good thing that Bernagh is contributing to the forces, but one cannot help thinking that a better choice than the 'Friend's Ambulance Corps' – which really does sound rather sleepy – might have been made.[54] However, I suppose 'those also serve'[55] though the trenches impress the outside spectator more than an ambulance corps. A propos of conscription, I sincerely hope that one of two things may happen. Either that the war may be over before I am eighteen, or that conscription may not come into force before I have volunteered. I shouldn't fancy going out to meet the others – as a conscript. I see the *Daily Mail* is being burnt everywhere for advocating the plan.[56] How excellent a proof of the necessity of a petty little plan like sending an envelope full of ashes – or most likely it was a woman. There is absolutely no news here, and the weather is very hot. Mrs. K. has now returned again from Bristol where she left Louis getting on all right.

I like your garden picture. I can imagine the whole scene, and especially the conversation with the Greeve's on the road, we have heard so many like it before. The country at home must be looking delightful now, and I wish I could see it, but most of all the sea. If Bookham were not so far inland it would be delightful too – and indeed to do it justice it is very pretty. The remark about the fates is excellent from a literary point of view, only I don't like to think of you thinking those sort of things in such a place – and with a white Homburg hat too. And yet I

---

54 Several generations of the Greeves family had been members of the Society of Friends (Quakers). However, Arthur Greeves's grandparents had been converts to the Plymouth Brethren and it was in this denomination that Arthur had been brought up. The family retained its connection to the Friends.

55 John Milton, Sonnet 16, 'When I consider how my light is spent' (1673): 'They also serve who only stand and wait.'

remember that Swinburne has some remark about the impossibility of changing 'wings for feet, or feet for wings'. I suppose if we Lewis's are made in that mould of reflective gravity which troubles deepen into melancholy, it is the price which we pay for a thoughtful and feeling mind. About the question of retrospect and anticipation (dangerous word for you, sir), there is a sentence in one of W. Morris's prose tales that I am reading at present, which tho' perhaps not strictly in point, is yet well worth remembering in its archaic charm and quaint nobility: – 'Thus then lived this folk in much plenty and ease of life, though not delicately nor desiring things out of measure. They wrought with their hands and wearied themselves: they rested from their toil and feasted and were merry: tomorrow was not a burden unto them, nor yesterday a thing that they would fain forget: life shamed them not, nor did death make them afraid.'[57] There is another way of looking at life: impossible it may be in a sophisticated age, and yet I think he would be a happy man who could do so.

What time do my letters reach you in the day? In letter writing one ought to know when and where the other person reads, as it makes more of a semblance to real conversation. I must dry up now.

your loving son,

Jack

TO ARTHUR GREEVES (W):

[Gastons
1 June 1915]

Dear Galahad,

Your interesting epistle which I have read with wonder and delight, contains the following gems of Arthurian style

A. 'I don't suppose you will object to *my* coming with *me*.'

B. 'Read this with *discust*.'

C. 'I am talking now of *sensulity*.'

Dear old Galahad! That's an unusually good budget even for you: I am afraid this 'sensulity' of yours – I never saw the word before but I suppose you know what it means – must be beginning to tell on you.

As to your first question, the only holyday I propose to take is a week or so with my relations at Larne, and my father's offer, which I take to be

---

57 *Roots of the Mountains*, op cit., vol. I, ch. 1, p. 13.

purely formal, I would not much care to accept. I hope you will be sensible enough to spend your holydays at home with me, seeing each other and talking & going for long walks over the hills, instead of going off to some godless place by the sea. My point is that I should be going to my Aunt's in any case, and 1 week or so from home is quite enough for me: as well, I don't think it very decent to leave my father any longer. But don't let this prevent your going somewhere. All I want to point out is, that my refusal of a joint holyday, is not from a design to avoid you, but because I don't want to be away from home too long. Of course, if you would condescend to honour Larne with your presence while I am at my Aunt's, I should be very bucked to see you: but you might be bored. However, we can talk all this over when we meet at the end of July.

Odeon records are the most fascinating and delusive bait on the Gramaphone market. Cheap, classical, performed by good artistes, they present a jolly attractive list: but they wear out in a month. Of course there are exceptions, and I can play you some selections from Lohengrin which I have on that make, and which have worn well. On the whole however, I wouldn't advise anyone to get Odeon records, as a short-lived record is one of the most dissapointing of things. I foresee, by the way, that your way of getting records is like Jane McNeil's way of getting books – that is you use a shop like a free library: whenever a record is worn out, back it goes to the shop, and you have a new one in its place. Which reminds me, my monthly catalogues for this month haven't turned up yet, so you must shout at Miss Thompson.

With reference to your remarks about sensuality – je vous demande pardon – 'sensulity', I don't know I am sure, why you have been suffering especially in this way just now. Of course when I was particularly so last term, there was a reason, about whom you heard perhaps more than you wanted. You ought to be past the age of violent attacks of 'ΕΡΩΤΊΚΑ (Greek); as well you are Galahad the spotless whose 'strength is as the strength of ten, because your heart is pure'. Perhaps you would understand now, what you didn't understand when I started the subject last hols, <what I mean by the 'sensuality of cruelty': again perhaps you would not.>

Last week I got a copy of that little book of yours on Icelandic Sagas, which I found very interesting, and as a result I have now bought a translation of the 'Laxdaela Saga'[58] in the Temple Classics edition. I never saw a Temple Classic before; did you? In binding, paper, & 'forma' (by which I include the aspect of a typical page, its shape, spacing, lettering etc) they are tip top, and justify the boast of 'elegance' made in their advertisements. They are, I think, far better value than Everyman's at the same price.

As to the Saga itself I am very pleased with it indeed: if the brief, simple, nervous style of the translation is a good copy of the original it must be very fine. The story, tho', like most sagas, it loses unity, by being spread over two or three generations, is thoroughly interesting. Just as it was interesting after the 'Well at the World's End' to read the 'Morte', so after the 'Roots', a real saga is interesting. I must admit that here again the primitive type is far better than Morris's reproduction. But that of course is inevitable, just as Homer is better than Vergil.

Sorry to hear my father is so low, but I write to him regularly, and the last was really rather a long and good effort. Hope you're all well at Bernagh.

Yours
Jack

TO ARTHUR GREEVES (W):

[Gastons
8 June 1915]

Dear Galahad,

I seem to have trod on somebody's corns over this question of a holyday: I expressly said that I did not wish to keep you at home on my account if you wished to go elsewhither. To be brief, my whole answer was that I refused your kind proposal because I was already booked, adding that I should not care to take another holyday in addition to that at Larne. Now what is your grievance – for grievance you must have or you would not write such good grammar. Is it because I won't throw up my previous invitation in favour of yours? That would be rude. Is it because I will not accompany you on another holyday? That is selfish of you, to expect me to give [up] my fleeting sojourn at Leeborough for

---

58 *Laxdaela Saga*, translated by M.A.C. Press, Temple Classics (1899). This 13th century Icelandic saga is the tragic story of several generations of an Iceland family, and in particular of Gudrun who causes the death of a man she loves but fails to marry.

your amusement. Is it because I mildly suggested that you need not go for a holyday? There was never any obligation on you to accept such a scheme. And as for your hot weather – je me moque de cette là, it is bitterly cold to-night! How funny that I always prove everything I want in argument with you but never convince you!

Now, having despatched our inevitable weekly dialectical passage-at-arms (by the way, you have never replied to my theory of trousers), we may proceed to the letter. I admit that the 'I hope you are all well' is a blot on my character that can hardly be wiped out: I didn't think I had sunken so low as that, and will try to reform.

I thought you would agree with me about Mansfield park:[59] I should almost say it was her best. I don't remember the names very well, but I think I rather liked Edmund. Do get a Temple Classic. You will bless me ever after, as they are really the best shillings worth on the market. I hope I may prove a false prophet about the Odeon records, and that you will have better luck in them than I. Now that it is drawing a little nearer my return, I begin to hanker again for my gramaphone: but I am not consoled even with the catalogues, so you must stir up the damosel again. I am still at the 'Laxdaela Saga' which is as good as ever, and I insist upon your reading it too.

On Saturday I met the prettiest girl I have ever seen in my life (don't be afraid, you're not going to have to listen to another love-affair). But it is not her prettiness I wanted to tell you about, but the fact that she is just like that grave movement in the Hungarian Rhapsody (or is it the 'dance'?) that I love so much.[60] Of course to you I needn't explain how a person can be like a piece of music, – you will know: and if you play that record over, trying to turn the music into a person, you will know just how she looked and talked. Just 18, and off to do some ridiculous war-work, nursing or something like that at Dover of all places – what a shame!

By the way, that would be a rather interesting amusement, trying to find musical interpretations for all our friends. Thus Gordon[61] is like the Pilgrims chorus from Tannhaüser, Kelsie a bit like the Valkyries[62] only

---

59 Jane Austen, *Mansfield Park* (1814).
60 He had in mind Franz Liszt's Hungarian Rhapsody No. 1, first performed in 1851.
61 Charles Gordon Ewart (1885–1936) was the second son of Sir William Quartus Ewart. See **The Ewart Family** in the Biographical Appendix.
62 He means her character was like Wagner's *Die Walküre*.

not so loud, Gundred[63] like the dance-movement in Danse Macabre, and Bob like a Salvation army hymn. We might add yourself as a mazurka by Chopin, wild, rather plaintful, and disjointed, and Lily like, well – a thing of Grieg's called 'The Watchman's Song'[64] that you haven't heard. I think I must write a book on it.

By the way (all my sentences seem to begin like that) I am very sorry this is a bit late, but I was writing to my father and brother last night. Now, good night, Galahad, and be good and talk sense the next time you do me the honour of arguing with me.

Yours
Jack

P.S. What about the question of 'sensulity'?

TO HIS FATHER (LP IV: 319–20):

[Gastons]
Friday [18 June 1915]

My dear Papy,

I am writing this immediately after reading your letter, but I mean it to belong to next week. Perhaps I shall not post it till Monday to equalize the dates, but at any rate it is much easier to write to you just after reading yours. I somehow seem to be unable to write to you properly now-a-days: perhaps because we make jokes nearly all the time when we are together, and household humour, though the funniest of all things to those who understand (a propos of which, read the first Roman story in 'Puck of Pook's Hill'),[65] can't really be written down. Whereas if I try to be serious, I merely succeed in being 'stuffy'. The last word describes exactly what I mean. However, as Plato says, the written word is only a poor faint shadow of real conversation, in which, among people who know each other well, the merest suggestion explains a train of thought which the most elaborate written explanation leaves obscure, lifeless and formal.[66] Still, as it would be expensive to telephone to you every week

---

63 Gundreda Ewart (1888–1975) was one of the daughters of Sir William Quartus Ewart. See **The Ewart Family** in the Biographical Appendix.

64 From Edvard Grieg's *Lyriske Smaastykker* (1867).

65 i.e. 'A British Roman Song'.

66 He is referring to Plato's *Phaedrus*, 278a.

with trunk calls – do you remember the lady in 'The Whip'?[67] – we must do the best we can.

I think we may reasonably hope that the war will be over before it begins to concern me personally. At the same time, the knowledge that I had gone as soon as possible to the front would not, I fancy, be a very substantial comfort to me if I arrived there as a conscript. All the people on whom that name has fallen would be lumped together without distinction in the minds of our Tommies – who indeed might be excused for feeling some warmth in the circumstances. Then there is the other possibility that Europe will be at peace before I am eighteen. In that case I believe my career at Oxford would be, if anything, a little easier than usual, owing to lack of competition. It would be ghastly however to reckon up that condition as an advantage – when we remember what it means. I am sorry for your sake that 'Mr. Carr'[68] has gone, but after all, from his point of view, it was inevitable. There is not much objection made to the teeth now, it seems!

I will certainly write to the Colonel as soon as you send me his address, which I am not quite sure of. I don't think I will make it a birthday letter, which – from me at any rate – would not appeal to him: I may find some 'crack' however to interest him. Isn't it interesting to note the different things we expect from different people? If I imitated your style exactly, and could write a letter to the Colonel almost the same as a typical one of yours, the result would be merely irritating: if you tried the same experiment with my style, or absence of style, the result would be the same. Yet both, I believe, would be acceptable from the right authors.

This is a digression: to go back to Warnie, it certainly must be very depressing to see so many of the Malvern lot – for whom he had a regard as genuine as it was inexplicable – dropping off like this. 'It is an ill wind' – the proverb is rather old. But one result of the war to us seems to be that you and W., if I may say so, understand each other better than you have done for some time.

I am learning lots of things here besides the Classics – one of them being to take cold baths: and such an artist I am becoming that you will hardly know me when I get home for the brevity of my sojourn in the

---

67 *The Whip*, a play by Cecil Raleigh and Henry Hamilton, had been performed for the first time in 1909 and was having a revival.

68 Willie Carr, Albert's managing clerk, apparently after being rejected for the army on account of his teeth in the earlier days of the war, had now been accepted.

bath room and the prodigious amount of noise I make over it. The weather is still hot and a trifle oppressive here, but agreeable in the morning and evening.

I have been devoting this week to the reading of Othello,[69] which I like as well as any Shakesperian play I have read. The part of Iago, to my mind, is something of a blemish, and the fact that his pitiless malignity has absolutely no motive leaves him rather a monster (in the Classical, not the newspaper sense of the word), than a human character. But then of course Shakespeare at his best always works on titanic lines, and the vices and virtues of Lear, Macbeth, Hamlet, Othello, Desdemona, etc., are magnified to a pitch more splendid and terrible than anything in real life.[70]

If I leave here on the 30th July, so as to arrive home on the last Saturday of that month, the exact half of the term ought to have fallen about four hours ago. That will make the usual twelve weeks. Only six more now! That sounds perhaps too like the old days at Malvern, but don't suppose that because I will be glad to see you again, I am not happy and more than happy at the K's.

your loving,

son,

Jack

TO ARTHUR GREEVES (W):

[Gastons
29 June 1915]

Dear Galahad,

Did the Norns or Dana holy mother of them that die not, weave for us in that hour wherein our mothers bare us, that never should we write to each other without the first page being occupied by argument? Because, whether by the decree of fate or no, this has always been the case. First it was Shee v. Souteraines, then Tears v. Trousers, and now Larne v. Leeborough – which by the way means Little Lea. How you can have known me so long without picking up the words & tags which I use every day passes my understanding – unless I am to conclude that you are asleep half the time I am talking to you, which is very probably so.

---

69 William Shakespeare, *Othello, The Moor of Venice* (1622).

70 These are the central characters in William Shakespeare's plays *King Lear* (1608), *Macbeth* (1623), *Hamlet* (1603) and *Othello*.

Well about this infernal holyday: as your infantile brain – for which I have catered on this envelope – is incapable of swallowing my previous very elementary argument, I will explain my position once more in very simple terms, as follows: –

I have eight weeks vacations.

I have been invited to stay 10 days with Mrs Hamilton.[71]

I have accepted her invitation.

I intend to keep that promise

I don't want to be any longer away than 10 days.

I don't want to keep you at home on that account.

I therefore decline your kind proposal.

I am very sorry

I hope you understand. How's that?

It may be true that it is easier to assign music to people we know, than to conjure up people to fit the music, but I deny that anyone's character is really unlike their appearance. The physical appearance, to my mind, is the expression and result of the other thing – soul, ego, ψυχη, intellect – call it what you will. And this outward expression cannot really differ from the soul. If the correspondence between a soul & body is not obvious at first, then your conception either of that soul or that body must be wrong. Thus, I am 'chubby' – to use your impertinent epithet, because I have a material side to me: because I like sleeping late, good food & clothes etc as well as sonnets & thunderstorms. The idealistic side of me must find an outlet somewhere, perhaps in my eye, my voice or anything else – you can judge better than I. And the other side of me exists in my countenance because it exists also in my character.

'But', I hear you saying, 'this is all very well. Only what about the practised flirt with the innocent schoolgirl face & the murderer with a smile like an old woman?' These are only seeming exceptions. The girl has or imagines she has that sort of disposition somewhere in her, or it wouldn't be on her face: as a matter of fact, it is always 'innocent' (which means ignorant) people who do the most outrageous things. The murderer too, may be really a peaceful, kindly 'crittur', and if circumstances drive him to violence, the initial mould of the character and therefore of the face remain just the same.

---

71 This was Jack's maternal grandmother, Mrs Mary Hamilton, then living at Archburn, Knock. See **The Hamilton Family** in the Biographical Appendix.

I remember reading in a book called 'The open Road'[72] an extract from Hewlet's 'Pan and the Young Shepherd'[73] which I thought splendid. Thanks to our Galahad's detestable handwriting I can't tell whether your book is the 'Lore' or the 'Love' of P. In any case I have never heard of it before, but, from your description, am very eager to read it. I also saw a copy of this author's 'Forest Lovers'[74] in Carson's last hols, but it did not attract me much. Is this new one in a decent edition?

I am glad to hear that you are keeping up the 'illustrative' side of your art, and shall want you to do some for my lyric poems. You can begin a picture of my 'dream garden' where the 'West winds blow'. As directions I inform you it is 'girt about with mists', and is in 'the shadowy country neither life nor sleep', and is the home of 'faint dreams'. With this Bädekers guide to it, you can start a picture. You remember, I scribble at pen and ink sketches a bit, and have begun to practise female faces which have always been my difficulty. I am improving a very little I think, and the margins of my old Greek lexicon as well as my pocket book now swarm with 'studies'.

Only four weeks now till I shall be home again! Isn't that a buck, at least for me – and no one else in the world really counts of course. What nonsense you talk about that 'poor man', my father. I am afraid it is true that he must bore Lily, but there is no fear of her boring him. I sympathize however, with the havoc which he must have wrought with a serious musical evening.

How is your gramaphone progressing, by the way, and how many records have you listed up to date? I am so sorry if this Liliputian writing has blinded you for life, but we have run out of the other sort of note paper.

Well καῖρε μοὶ (Farewel)

Jack

P.S. Have begun the 'Proffessor'[75] and as read far as the heroe's arrival at Brussels. It is shaping very well. I believe you have read it have you not – J.

---

72 *The Open Road*, compiled by E.V. Lucas (1905).

73 Maurice Hewlett, *Pan and the Young Shepherd* (1898).

74 Maurice Hewlett, *Lore of Proserpine* (1913); *Forest Lovers* (1898).

75 Charlotte Brontë, *The Professor* (1857).

Warnie arrived in Bookham from France on 4 July 1915 and Jack, after some resistance from Mr Kirkpatrick, was permitted to accompany him home. He returned to Bookham on 9 July.

TO HIS FATHER (LP V: 1–2):

[Gastons
10? July 1915]

My dear Papy,

In reply to your note which has just this minute been handed to me, I suggest to your notice the following considerations. In the first place you ask 'why were you told £1-10s?' I am not aware that I ever told you anything at all about the subject: the sum of money – whatever it was – was handed by Kirk to Warnie at the request of the latter, who took charge of it throughout, together with both tickets and every other arrangement. It never passed through my hands, and I am not prepared to say with any certainty what it amounted to. I do not remember mentioning the matter while at home. You have therefore applied to the wrong quarter.

Secondly, supposing for purposes of argument that I did tell you that it was £1-10s, what then? As I have already pointed out, I had nothing to do with the money, and Warnie not I, was responsible for its being borrowed. It follows that I could have had no conceivable motive for misrepresenting the amount. If there was to be any blame attached, it was not I who incurred it: I need never even have mentioned it. Accordingly, if I said anything untrue, it must have been through a mere error – and even at that an error by which I could gain nothing.

Thirdly, do not be annoyed if I descend to a rather crude, a fortiori line of argument. The tone of your letter, no less than the haste with which it was dispatched, suggests an ugly suspicion. This can of course be very easily answered. Setting aside all question of honour, I ask you to credit Warnie and myself with commonsense. Granted then, that for some inscrutable reason we wanted to conceal the amount he borrowed from Kirk, would we have been such fools as to have told a lie which must inevitably be detected as soon as the latter wrote to you? And of course, we would have known that K. must write to you to get his money back.

And so, it follows that either Kirk is wrong, or else if Warnie gave you the wrong figures it must have been by accident. That I knew nothing of it, and was not concerned in the transaction, has already been shown.

Last of all, if anything in this letter should seem to indicate that I am hurt or offended, I assure you it is not the case. I am perfectly convinced that your note was not meant to be insulting, though, from its nature, it could hardly help it. In any case it is as well to make things clear, even at the risk of some little superfluous violence. I am,

your loving son,
Jack

TO HIS FATHER (LP IV: 321–2):

[Gastons
19? July 1915]

My dear Papy,

I sincerely hope this silence of yours doesn't mean anything wrong with your health. Arthur says you didn't seem very well the last time he was over at Leeborough, so I am not quite easy in my mind. If however anything is wrong, you might tell Aunt Annie to write to me with particulars, and also to forward W's address, which since I wrote for it in my last letter has become even more necessary as he has now written to me. I should not like him to think that he is forgotten or that his letter has not reached me, but I cannot reply to him until I hear from you.

Not even in Bookham can one be safe from the hoi polloi; a stubborn refusal to learn tennis is no longer a protection among people who will inflict croquet instead. I was out on Wednesday for tea and croquet and again today (Saturday) for the same entertainment, plus a great deal of conversation. However, this I suppose is part of the curse inherited from our first parents: my private opinion is that after the words 'In the sweat of thy brow shalt thou earn thy bread'[76] another clause has dropped out from the original text, running 'In the exasperation of thy souls shalt thou attend social functions'. On the whole, though I do not of course know anyone as well as at home, I like a good many of those I meet: the world indeed (as you have reminded me on innumerable occasions), is full of nice people. And if it must be full at all, I suppose it is as well that they should be nice.

Talk, of course, runs mostly on the war. I have always thought it ridiculous for people to talk so much on a subject of which, in the

---

76 Genesis 3:19.

majority of cases, they are really very ignorant. Books, art, etc., passing trivialities and even gossip are topics on which everyone can speak with more or less authority. We prefer however to pass our time in criticism of politics, or at present the war – subjects on which only specialists should speak. This endless criticism by ignorant men and women of public men, whose positions they do not understand, I always hear with annoyance.

The Colonel writes to me cheerfully though briefly, and wants an answer. I suppose he tells me nothing that you don't know already. Bathing and a sack of books seem to be his chief consolations in 'this detestable country.'

I have been reading nothing since Othello but a translation from the Icelandic, and stray articles etc. In Greek we have begun Demosthenes. Of course oratory is not a sort of literature that I appreciate or understand in any language, so that I am hardly qualified to express an opinion on our friend with the mouthful of pebbles. However, compared with Cicero, he strikes me as a man with something to say, intent only upon saying it clearly and shortly. One misses the beautiful roll of the Ciceronian period, but on the other hand, he is not such a — blether.[77]

Do try and write soon, or, if the worst comes to the worst, get Aunt Annie to do so.

your loving,

son,

Jack

TO ARTHUR GREEVES (W/LP IV: 299–300):

[Gastons
24 July 1915]

Dear Galahad,

I have debated more than once as to whether you would prefer a tired and perfunctory letter written in good time during the week, or a fresh and willing [one] a few days late on Saturday evening. Thinking that you would choose the latter, and knowing I would – here we are.

---

77 Demosthenes (383–322 BC) was a great Athenian orator and statesman, and Cicero (106–43 BC) a great Roman orator and statesman. Neither, however, attracted Lewis, who writing years later in *SBJ* IX said: 'Kirk did not, of course, make me read nothing but Homer. The Two Great Bores (Demosthenes and Cicero) could not be avoided.'

What on earth are you doing reading the Sowers?[78] A Russian mystery-story full of wise diplomatists and impossible women – it ought to be clad in a bright red cover, with a crude picture of Steinmitz saying 'The Moscow Doctor – and your prince!!!' from the head of the stairs, and set on a railway bookstall. But, perhaps I am wrong. Of course it has points, but you are worthy of better things. Never read any George Eliot[79] myself, being no great hand at novels but admire your energy in that line.

Talking about books, I am determined to teach you to like poetry, and will begin next hols. on Coleridges 'Christabel'. Don't be put off by the name. It is exactly the sort of romantic strangeness and dreaminess you & I like, a sort of partner to the Ancient Mariner,[80] as Danse Macabre is to the March of the Dwarfs.

Also – I hope all these schemes aren't boring you – you are going to help me to improve my drawing next hols. Figures I can do tolerably, but from you I must learn the technique of the game – shading, curves, how to do a background without swamping the figures etc. Of course this will all be in pen and ink which is the best medium for my kind of work – I can imagine your smile at my calling such scribbles 'work', but no matter. I am longing to get home again now, and expect I shall arrive next Saturday.

Yes Mrs K. has played the Polonaise; we found the right one without difficulty, and tho' she made some remarks about the hardness of it I at length persuaded her. Now, you know, I never flatter: so you may take it as solemn truth when I tell you that, if I admired your playing before, I understood its true value far better when I compared [it] with Mrs K. – by no means a contemptible craftsman. To hear the lovely galloping passages rendered correctly, even well, but without your own frank enjoyment of the work, your sympathy with the composer and your inimitable fire and abandonment (this sounds like an essay but I mean every word of it), was a revelation. You threw yourself into it, and forgot yourself in the composer: Mrs K sat there, amiable, complacent and correct, as if she were pouring out tea. Now, while they're not all as bad as she, still you alone of the people I have heard play set to the matter

---

78 Henry Seton Merriman, *The Sowers* (1896).
79 George Eliot (1819–80), the English novelist whose real name was Mary Ann Evans.
80 Samuel Taylor Coleridge, *Christabel and Other Poems* (1816); *The Rime of the Ancient Mariner* (1798).

properly. And for that reason, a piece, by you, if it were full of mistakes (tho' of course it wouldn't be) would be better than the same piece fault-lessly played by – say, Hope Harding.[81] This is a rare gift of yours: you should yet do great things with it: you are a fool if you don't cultivate it. Perhaps, because you paint and read as well as play, you realize the imag-ination of a composer's mind perfectly, and can always bring out to a sensible (in the old sense of the word) listener anything at all that there is in the notes. Of course, all this is the praise of an amateur: but the praise of an honest amateur who has a genuine, tho' non-technical taste for music, is worth something at least.

I agree with you that the music of Lohengrin, so far as I know it is delightful: nor do I see what is wrong with the story, tho' of course the splendid wildness of the 'Ring'[82] must be lacking. On the whole, however, I am not sure that any music from it I know, is not perhaps cast in a lower mould than 'Parsifal'[83] & the 'Ring'. Although, indeed the prelude – which you wouldn't listen to when I played it – is quite as fine I think as that from 'Parsifal'.

What is your opinion of W. Jaffe – little Vee-Lee?[84] He did one thing for which he can never be forgiven – dropping in and staying till eleven on the first night of my brother's leave. The Hamiltons came over on another, so we had only one evening alone together in peace and com-fort. On the whole, tho', he is a decent crittur, I suppose. Have you ever heard their gramaphone? I wonder what its like.

Which reminds me, did you hear the new Glenmachen record – a solo by the Russian base – Chaliapin[85] from 'Robert Le Diable'.[86] The orchestration is absolutely magnificent and the singing as good. I only wish I could afford 'the like of them', don't you?

81 i.e. Lewis's cousin, Mrs George Harding (née Charlotte Hope Ewart, 1882–1934).
82 Lewis loved all Richard Wagner's music, especially the *Ring of the Nibelung* cycle comprising *Das Rheingold* (*The Rhinegold*) first performed in 1869; *Die Walküre* (*The Valkyrie*), first performed in 1870; *Siegfried* and *Götterdämmerung* (*The Dusk of the Gods*), both performed for the first time in 1876.
83 *Parsifal*, an opera by Wagner, first performed in 1882.
84 William Jaffé, a friend of Albert Lewis, was the son of Sir Otto Jaffé who was twice Lord Mayor of Belfast.
85 Chaliapin was Fyodor Ivanovich Shalyalpin (1873–1938) who was generally considered the greatest singer of his day.
86 *Robert le Diable*, an opera by Giacomo Meyerbeer, was first performed in 1831.

I shan't write again this term now – jolly glad it's so near the end.
Yours
Jack

TO HIS FATHER (LP V: 9):

[Gastons]
Moon Day.
(A good codotta that.)
[28 July 1915]

My dear Papy,

I was very glad to get both your letters, and sorry if I worried you at a busy moment. Willie's absence must be a great discomfort, and of course I shall understand if letters are short or overdue just at present. No. A registered letter is no equivalent to 'speaking sharply' to one, and I am therefore in no need to the German gentleman's remorse – or 'again-bite' to be Teutonic. But at sixteen we will do much for excitement, a new experience. 'What' said I to myself 'tho' the shades of Plato and Sophocles wait upon my pleasure, the treasures of Rome, the brilliance of France, the knowledge of Germany attend my nod? I am out of the world here. While the great war of all histories, nations and languages is waged hard by, shall I remain like a dormouse, inactive, apathetic. A thousand times no', (as a friend of yours in Punch said on a memorable occasion), 'I will have excitement I will taste of new experiences, soul-stir-ring adventures' – and gripping my hat with a cry of 'D'audace et tou-jours d'audace'[87] I rushed out into the night and – sent a registered letter!

I don't know that there is any news here: that Macmullen girl, the the-atrical lady, is staying here just at present. The summer here is one of the worst Kirk remembers, being very wet and making a special point of rain-ing whenever the poor people are trying to mow or make hay. Fortu-nately the amount of corn we grow at home is insignificant as regards the country's needs. All the same, at a time like the present every little counts, and if this sort of thing is going on all over England it is rather a pity.

(Later on.) I have spent a ghastly evening being used as a lay figure by Miss Macmullen for bandages – as she is going to volunteer to some-thing or other. I have been treated successively for a broken arm, a

---

87 ' "Boldness and ever more boldness" from G. J. Danton in *Le Moniteur* (4 September 1792).'

sprained ankle, and a wound in the head. This, with the adjoining complement of pins, small talk etc., is a good night's work. I can now sympathise with your attitude towards the excellent game of 'hair cut or shaved'. Ah well, I suppose half an hour's codotta with some bits of lint is not a great sacrifice to the war. Still, I am really too exhausted to write any longer, and everyone is going to bed.

> your loving
> son Jack

Jack arrived in Belfast on 31 July and was there for the next eight weeks. Mr Kirkpatrick expected him to continue with some work, and he wrote to him on 17 August saying:

> *I suggest you should order...the following: Plato:* The Phaedo, *if you have not got it. Demosthenes:* De Corona. *Tacitus:* The Annals. *Aeschylus:* The Agamemnon...*I expect you are browsing at present on the pastures of general literature, and this of course is as it should be. If however you find English too easy and sigh for more worlds to conquer, I recommend the perusal of any German book you may happen to come across.* (LP V: 12)

During this time Lewis added six more poems to his 'Metrical Meditations of a Cod', at least two of which are included in his Collected Poems.

TO HIS FATHER (LP V: 128–9):

> [Gastons
> 17? September 1915]

My dear Papy,

After a week of mutual waiting for a letter, I suppose it is my duty to take up the pen. Things have been so developing here in various ways that I have not really had time to settle down. A wonderful thing has happened – yesterday I got a fellow pupil![88] It is a nephew of Mrs. Howard Ferguson's who is to come and read with Kirk for the paymaster's

---

88 The fellow pupil was Terence Forde (1899–?), the ward of Mrs Howard Ferguson. He had been brought up in Manchester, and after moving to Ireland he attended Campbell College, from which school he was sent to Mr Kirkpatrick.

department of the navy, and is about my own age. Of course it is just a bit of crumpled rose leaf to have this inroad, but as he will spend nearly all his time at Leatherhead taking special classes for chemistry and solid mathematics – whatever that name of terror may mean – one cannot complain. He seems a decent poor creature, though of course not wildly interesting. Mrs. Ferguson came down with him on Saturday and went away the same evening. I suppose you have met her? I thought she was exceedingly nice, and was interested to hear all the Lurgan and Banbridge gossip which Mrs. K's questions called forth, until Kirk could stand it no longer and broke in with a fifteen minute lecture on the Budget.

The boy himself was at Campbell before he came here, and I can still remember enough to pick up acquaintance in common and to criticise 'the old place'. I hear to my surprise that Joey[89] is a 'knut' cricketer in his House Eleven: one never hears these tit-bits at home.

It is a good deal warmer here than in Ireland and my cold is consequently getting better – you will be relieved to hear. Kirk is still going strong and Bookham is looking its prettiest. Any sign of the new overcoat yet? But of course it will not really be needed till much later in the year. Tell me too if you hear anything from W. I must now stop and go to bed, which I feel justified in doing because I am one up on you in the way of letters.

your loving
son Jack

P.S. Don't forget to tell me when you write, how that cold of yours is. Jack.

TO ARTHUR GREEVES (W/LP V: 21–2):

[Gastons
5 October 1915]

My dear Galahad,

I can't really see why you have any more right to grouse at my not writing than I at you, but we will let it pass. And in the meantime, what

---

89 This is Jack's cousin, Joseph 'Joey' Tegart Lewis. See note 21 to letter of 27 November 1908. Joey entered Campbell College, Belfast, in 1906, and was still a pupil there. See **The Lewis Family** in the Biographical Appendix.

do you think? It is a bit thick when one has fled from Malvern to shun one's compeers in the seclusion of Surrey wilds, to be met by a damned fellow pupil of my own age – and sex![90] Isn't it the limit? Moreover he is a hopeless fellow with whom I despair of striking up any friendship that can be at all amusing – you know, the usual sort with absolutely no interest in any of the things that matter. Luckily, however he spends the greater part of his time taking special classes at Leatherhead, so that I still have my afternoon walk alone. Indeed, I suppose it is easier to put up with one philistine at Bookham than with five-hundred at Malvern, but still, the thing is a nuisance on which I had not counted.

I wish indeed that I had been with you at Portrush, of which your description sounds most attractive. I once visited Dunluce Castle years ago when I was staying at 'Castle Rock', but being a kid did not of course appreciate it as much as I would now.

It is very annoying that after waiting all the holydays for those Columbia records, I should just manage to miss them: mind you tell the girl to send me on the monthly lists of Zono, Columbia & H.M.V. I noticed by the way that the Zono list contains an attractive record with the 'Seranade' and 'Church Scene' from Faust.[91] Do you remember the latter – that magnificent duet outside the Church, with organ accompaniment where Gretchen is hunted about the stage with Mephisto behind her? You must hear it and tell me your impressions.

I thought you would enjoy 'Shirley'. Don't you see now what I meant when I said that love, apart from physical feelings, was quite different to friendship? If not you must have a brain like a cheese. There is not really much resemblance either between Louis & Gordon or Shirley & Lily. Can you imagine G. behaving to Lily the way Louis does at times to Shirley? I am afraid that, much as I like him, G. hasn't got it in him. Lily of course is not unlike S., but not so much of a 'grande dame', if you know what I mean.[92] When I said that K.[elsie Ewart] was like a valkyrie I meant of course in her appearance – or rather in her open-air appearance. When however you see her in artificial light, both in clothing & natural colouring she is like some thoughtful, exquisite piano piece of Chopin's – you'd know which better than I.

---

90 i.e. Terence Forde.

91 i.e. the opera by Charles Gounod.

92 The comparison is between Louis and Shirley, characters in Charlotte Brontë's *Shirley*, and Gordon Ewart and Lily Greeves who were to be married on 14 December 1915.

By the way, tell your sister that I have already written to thank her for the boot-bags, and that when the love she says she's sending arrives I will write and thank her for it too.

I have been reading the 'Faerie Queen' in Everymans both here and at home ever since I left you and am now half way thro' Book II.[93] Of course it has dull and even childish passages, but on the whole I am charmed, and when I have made you read certain parts I think you will appreciate it too.

Talking about poetry, if you have not done so already, go over to Little Lea and borrow Swinburne's 'Poems and Ballads' 2nd Series at once. Read 'The Forsaken Garden', 'At Parting' (I think that is the name, it begins 'For a day and a night love stayed with us, played with us')[94] 'Triads' 'The Wasted Vigil' and 'At a month's End'. The latter especially you must read from end to end as a commentary on the love parts of 'Shirley', only that in this case the man who tried to tame some such fierce & wonderful character failed instead of succeeding. Then you will relish all the lovely verses at the end, especially that beginning 'Who strives to snare in fear and danger / Some supple beast of fiery kin'.[95] Then tell me your impressions. Hope this hasn't bored you.

I am jolly glad to hear that you are at last starting with Dr Walker[96] and shall expect to find great 'doings' in your musical line when I come back. Write soon and don't forget the catalogues

Yours
Jack

TO ARTHUR GREEVES (W):

[Gastons
12 October 1915]

My dear Galahad,

I am frightfully annoyed. I have just been to Guildford to hear Ysaye[97] and enjoyed it no more than I do the barking of a dog. The

---

93 Edmund Spenser, *The Faerie Queene*, 2 vols., Everyman's Library [1910].

94 Swinburne, *Poems and Ballads*, op. cit. 'At Parting' begins: 'For a day and a night Love sang to us, played with us.'

95 The lines from 'At a Month's End' are: 'Who snares and tames with fear and danger/ A bright beast of a fiery kin.'

96 Dr Lawrence Walker of Belfast was a teacher of music.

97 Eugène Ysaÿe (1858–1931), the Belgian violinist and conductor whose style of playing was considered unconventional and highly original.

apalling thought comes over me that I am losing by degrees my musical faculty: already, as you know, I cannot enjoy things that used to drive me wild with delight, and I suppose in the course of time I shall become absolutely insensible – just like Henry Stokes or my brother or anyone else. There was also a woman called Stralia, a soprano, who sang one lovely thing from 'Madame Butterfly'[98] and lots of stuff I didn't understand. I havenot the faintest idea what Ysaye played, and I never want to hear it again. I listened as hard as I could, shutting my eyes and trying in vain to concentrate my attention, but it was all just meaningless sound. Of course violin solos were never much in my line but even so, it should not be so bad as this. Now I suppose I have lost your sympathy forever and am set down – who knows but it may be rightly – as a Goth and philistine. But it really is torture to feel things going out of you like that. Perhaps after all, the taste in music developed by a gramaphone is a bad, artificial, exotic one that dissapears after a certain point ... The Lord knows!

You ask me how I spend my time, and though I am more interested in thoughts and feelings, we'll come down to facts. I am awakened up in the morning by Kirk splashing in his bath, about 20 minutes after which I get up myself and come down. After breakfast & a short walk we start work on Thucydides – a desperately dull and tedious Greek historian[99] (I daresay tho', you'd find him interesting) and on Homer whom I worship. After quarter of an hour's rest we go on with Tacitus till lunch at 1. I am then free till tea at 4.30: of course I am always anxious at this meal to see if Mrs K. is out, for Kirk never takes it. If she is I lounge in an arm chair with my book by the fire, reading over a leisurely and bountiful meal. If she's in, or worse still has 'some people' to tea, it means sitting on a right angled chair and sipping a meagrue allowance of tea and making intelligent remarks about the war, the parish and the shortcomings of everyones servants. At 5, we do Plato and Horace, who are both charming, till supper at 7.30, after which comes German and French till about 9. Then I am free to go to bed whenever I like which is usually about 10.20.

As soon as my bed room door is shut I get into my dressing gown, draw up a chair to my table and produce – like Louis Moore, note book

---

98 *Madame Butterfly*, an opera by Giacomo Puccini, was first performed in 1904.
99 Thucydides (c. 460–c. 400 BC) wrote a history of the Peloponnesian War which is one of the greatest historical works of all time. One of its most noteworthy passages is Pericles's Funeral Oration over the Athenians who had died in the war.

and pencil. Here I write up my diary for the day, and then turning to the other end of the book devote myself to poetry, either new stuff or polishing the old. If I am not in the mood for that I draw faces and hands and feet etc for practice. This is the best part of the day of course, and I am usually in a very happy frame of mind by the time I slip into bed. And talking about bed, I wish you and your family would have the goodness to keep out of my dreams. You remember my telling you that I dreamed that you and Lily & I were walking along North Street when I saw a ghost but you & she didn't? That was at Port Salon. Well, last night found the same 3 walking somewhere in town, only this time the place had been captured by the Germans. Everyone had escaped and we were hurrying along in terror through the deserted streets with the German soldiers always just round the corner, going to catch us up and do something terrible. Dreams are queer things.

You ask me whether I have ever been in love: fool as I am, I am not quite such a fool as all that. But if one is only to talk from firsthand experience on any subject, conversation would be a very poor business. But though I have no personal experience of the thing they call love, I have what is better – the experience of Sapho,[100] of Euripides of Catullus[101] of Shakespeare of Spenser of Austen of Bronte of, of – anyone else I have read. We see through their eyes. And as the greater includes the less, the passion of a great mind includes all the qualities of the passion of a small one. Accordingly, we have every right to talk about it. And if you read any of the great love-literature of any time or country, you will find they all agree with me, and have nothing to say about your theory that 'love=friendship+sensual feelings'. Take the case I mentioned before. Were Louis & Shirley ever friends, or could they ever be? Bah! Don't talk twaddle. On the contrary, the mental love may exist without the sensual or vice versa, but I doubt if either could exist together with friendship. What nonsense we both talk, don't we? If any third person saw our letters they would have great 'diversion' wouldn't they?

In the meantime, why have no catalogues reached me yet? By the time this reaches you, you will I hope have read your course of Swinburne I mapped out, and can send me your views. So glad you too like the

---

100 Sappho (b. c. mid-7th cent. BC), a poetess born in Lesbos. Only 12 of her poems have survived.
101 Gaius Valerius Catullus (c. 84–c. 54 BC), one of the most versatile of Roman poets, who wrote love poems, elegies and satirical epigrams with equal success.

'Faerie Queen', isn't it great? I have been reading a horrible book of Jack London's called 'The Jacket'.[102] If you come across [it] anywhere, don't read it. It is about the ill-treatment in an American prison, and has me quite miserabl. Write soon.

Yours

Jack

TO HIS FATHER (LP V: 24-5):

[Gastons]
Postmark: 22 October 1915

My dear Papy,

The state of our library at Leeborough must be perfectly apalling: how such a collection of ignorances and carelessnesses could have got together on the shelves of our room passes my comprehension. As well, where is the beautiful quarto edition? What is a quarto? I don't believe you have the vaguest idea, and should not be surprised if the edition in question is merely an 8vo., (– no, that doesn't mean 'in eight volumes', though I too thought so once.) In fact there are a whole lot of things in your letter that I don't understand. What are 'vagrom' men might I ask? I have consulted all the dictionaries at Gastons and failed to find the word. 'But enough of these toys' as Verulam remarks.[103]

Kirk has just called my attention to an amusing article in the papers which I daresay you have read.[104] It appears that a Radley boy who had been allowed home for a day to see his brother who was going to the front, overstayed his leave by permission of his father, and on his return was flogged by the Head. If you remember, there was good reason because it turned out that the journey was out of joint or something, so that the fellow couldn't get home and back in time. Moreover, the father sent a telegram. Well the boy and the father have brought an action, and now we come to the point. One of the witnesses called by the schoolmaster to defend his conduct was a certain Canon Sydney Rhodes James, sometime headmaster of Malvern. As Kirk points out, it is amusing to see that he alone was picked out of all England to defend a pedagogue from the boy he had flogged: so far he 'outshone millions tho' bright'.

---

102 Jack London, *The Jacket* (1915).

103 This is from the essay by Francis Bacon referred to in the letter of 13 May 1915. Bacon was the Baron of Verulam.

104 See *The Times* (21 October 1915), p. 4 and (22 October 1915), p. 5.

Unfortunately the judge, who I fancy must have known his man, decided that Jimmy's theories of school management would be off the point, and did not call him. The evidence I suppose would have consisted in an illuminated discourse on 'the young squirm's' conduct.

The chief amusement here is the Zeppelins. We saw the bombardment of Waterloo station going on that last time they were here: at least that is what we were told it was. All you could see were some electrical flashes in the sky caused by the bombs, and of course it was too far away to hear anything. Now that people know that they are about, we are always hearing them going over at nights, but it usually turns out to be a motor byke in the distance. Once we heard the noise of the thump of a hammer at Guildford, and people said that was the dropping of bombs, but I have my doubts.

Isn't Jimmy good this week in Punch? I am glad to hear that Lily and Gordon are not going out of the neighbourhood, as they would make a bad gap. The sponge etc. must be having a long journey, but I hope they are like the mills of the Gods.[105]

your loving
son Jack

TO HIS FATHER (LP V: 31):

[Gastons]
Postmark: 11 November 1915

My dear Papy,

As sole companion on a desert island, as a friend to talk to on the night before one was hanged, or, as in the present case, for a helper when one lies stunned in a muddy road, whom would we choose rather than Bill Patterson?[106] Ah! Bill. He is a joy for ever, is he not? – to himself. When you talk about the collision as you do, I take it to be mostly codotta: if I thought otherwise, I would be seriously alarmed. In any case, you must not allow this tendency to dissipation to run away with

---

105 'Though the mills of God grind slowly, yet they grind exceedingly small.' Friedrich von Logau, *Sinnegedichte* (1654), 'Desz Dritten Tausend, Andres Hundert' no. 24 (translated by Henry Wadsworth Longfellow).

106 William H.F. 'Bill' Patterson, the son of William Hugh Patterson (1835–1918) who wrote *A Glossary of Words in Use in the Counties of Antrim and Down* (1880), was addicted to puns and was a recognized Strandtown wit. He published a volume of verse under the initials W.H.F., *Songs of a Port* (Belfast, 1920).

you at a time like the present when one sees the angel of death flapping his wings from the shores of Totting to hordes that dwell in the skirts of the rising sun, and things of that sort – instead of which, you go about indulging in debauches at the dentist's. Is this not worthy of the severest censure?

I see no reason to congratulate the Times on its recruiting supplement in any way, nor the country on the necessity (which it allows to remain) for such publications being made. I am afraid that we must admit that Kipling's career as a poet is over. The line to which you refer is the merest prose, as well as very bad metre. And why is the word 'stone' introduced, except to rhyme with o'erthrown?[107] On the other hand, if his career be over, we may say that it is creditably over, and if I, for one, had such a record of poetry behind me I should be well satisfied. I conceive that Kipling is one of those writers who has the misfortune in common with Longfellow, of always being known and liked for his worst works. I mean his poetry to the agaraioi means merely the Barrack Room Ballads,[108] which, however original and clever, are not poetry at all. 'The brightest jewels in his crown' as the hymnal would say, are, I suppose, 'The Brushwood boy',[109] 'Puck of Pook's Hill', 'The jungle book' and various of the scattered poems, among which I should place first the dedication piece about 'my brother's spirit' and 'gentlemen unafraid'. 'The last rhyme of true Thomas', 'The first and last Chantry' and several others which I forget.[110] He is less of a scholar than

---

107 Included in *The Times* of 3 November 1915 was *The Times Recruiting Supplement*, on page 16 of which was a poem Rudyard Kipling composed for the occasion. The first verse of the poem, 'For All We Have and Are', is as follows:

For all we have and are,
For all our children's fate,
Stand up and meet the war,
The Hun is at the gate!
Our world has passed away
In wantonness o'erthrown.
There is nothing left to-day
But steel and fire and stone.

108 Rudyard Kipling, *Barrack-Room Ballads and Other Verses* (1892).
109 'The Brushwood Boy' is one of the stories in Kipling's *The Day's Work* (1908).
110 The 'dedication piece' which refers to 'my brother's spirit' and 'gentlemen unafraid' is the dedication poem to Wolcott Balestier in *Barrack-Room Ballads*; 'The Last Rhyme of True Thomas', 'The First Chantey' and 'The Last Chantey' are found in *The Seven Seas*.

Newbolt,[111] but he is also freer from conventional and obvious senti-ment: his metres are often too clever. With it all however, I think he will survive, if any of the present crew do. Except Yeats, I don't know of any other who is in the least likely to.

I myself have been reading this week a book by a man named Love Peacock, of whom I had not heard, but who seems to be famous. He was a contemporary of Lamb, Hazlitt, Byron etc., and an intimate friend of Shelly. The book is a farcical novel called 'Headlong Hall',[112] and very amusing.

As to the overcoat, I agree with you that it will be better to leave the business till the holydays, as the effort to make Bamford understand any-thing at all under any circumstances whatever is by no means child's play. I hope you have not any urgent desire for the other one. According to my computations the half term was about three days ago. As I must now go and add to the glories of Greek literature by a very choice frag-ment of Attic prose, good night.

your loving son,
Jack

TO HIS FATHER (LP V: 22):

[Gastons
15? November 1915]

My dear Papy,

The youth's name is Terence Ford, and I know nothing more about him except that he lived in the suburbs of Manchester during his father's lifetime. As I never see anything of him except on Sundays – for he spends all day at Leatherhead – I am quite reconciled to his presence and even enjoy hearing his talk about Campbell, which makes me by contrast more sensible of my present good luck. By the way, who is your friend Lord Bacon? I don't remember any such name in English literature: in fact the name Bacon itself never occurs, to my knowledge, except as the family name of Lord Verulam. (Ahh! A body blow, eh?).

I am sorry to hear about your gums. Are you sure your dental artist is a competent man? A change of advisers often works wonders in medical

---

111 Sir Henry John Newbolt (1862–1938) was educated at Clifton College and Corpus Christi College, Oxford. He is remembered particularly for his nautical ballads published in *Admirals All and Other Verses* (1897).

112 Thomas Love Peacock, *Headlong Hall* (1816).

matters. I always envy the Chinese for their excellent arrangement of paying the doctor while in health and, on falling ill, ceasing it until a cure has been effected. Perhaps you might suggest such an arrangement to the dentist.

I am still busy with my 'heavy winged Pegasus' as you call Spenser, and still find him delightful. He is a very lotus land, a garden of Proserpine to people who like pure romance and the 'stretched metre of an antique song'.[113] You should give him another trial some time, though not in our abridged edition which leaves out a lot of valuable stuff. I have also been reading in library copies, Schopenhauer's 'Will and idea',[114] and Swinburne's 'Erectheus' which is another tragedy on Greek lines like 'Atalanta',[115] though not so good in my opinion. Schopenhauer is abstruse and depressing, but has some very interesting remarks on the theory of music and poetry.

Kirk, I need hardly say, is strong on him, and will talk on the subject for hours – by the way, the real subject to get him on just now is the Mons angels.[116] You should drop him a cue in your next letter: you know – 'a man was telling me the other day that he had seen with his own eyes' or something of the kind. And while we are on the subject of the war, I am sure you have noticed the excellent blank verse poem in this week's 'Punch' entitled 'Killed in action'.[117] I read it with great pleasure, and thought at the time that it would appeal to you.

The weather here is a perfect joke, warmer than July, bright sunshine and gentle breezes. Personally I have had quite enough summer, and should not be sorry to bid it goodbye, though Kirk persistently denounces this as a most unnatural state of mind. I am rather curious to know what the new case of books at home contains. Tell Arthur if you see him, that there is a letter owing to me.

---

113 William Shakespeare, Sonnet 17 (1609).

114 Arthur Schopenhauer, *The World as Will and Idea* (1883–6).

115 Algernon Charles Swinburne, *Erechtheus* (1876); *Atalanta in Calydon* (1865).

116 The Battle of Mons, on the Western Front, began on 23 August 1914. For the whole of that day the British held the line against the Germans with greatly inferior numbers. A legend began within two weeks of the battle that an angel had appeared 'on the traditional white horse and clad all in white with flaming sword'. Facing the advancing Germans the angel 'forbade their further progress'. Martin Gilbert, *First World War* (1994), p. 58.

117 'Killed in Action' by R.C.L. is found in *Punch*, Vol. CXLIX (13 November 1915), p. 310.

your loving
son Jack

P.S. Was there any talk about Lord Bacon?

TO ARTHUR GREEVES (W/LP V: 23–4):

[Gastons
16 November 1915]

My Furious Galahad,

Horace has pointed out that if you buy an article after knowing all its defects, you have no right to quarrel with the seller if you are dissatisfied.[118] In the present case, since I told you how slack I was, and openly admitted that I could not promise to keep up a regular correspondance, you have no ground for grumbling if you find that I was speaking the truth. Should you, however, show any disposition to a brief exercise in that fascinating art, I have another excellent excuse: your letters are always shorter than mine: so much so that if I remain silent for a week or so, my amount of letter-writing for the term will still be a good bit bigger than yours.

As a matter of fact I have really had nothing to say, and thought it better to write nothing than to try and pump up 'conversation' – in the philistine sense of the word. I have read nothing new and done nothing new for ages. I am still at the Faerie Queene, and in fact have finished the first volume, which contains the first three books. As I now think it far too good a book to get in ordinary Everyman's I am very much wondering what edition would be the best. Of course I might get my father to give me that big edition we saw in Mullans' for a birthday or Xmas present: but then I don't really care for it much. The pictures are tolerable but the print, if I remember, rather coarse (you know what I mean) and the cover detestable. Your little edition is very nice, but rather too small, and not enough of a library-looking book. How much is it, and what publisher is it by? I believe I have heard you say that it can be got in the same edition as your 'Odyssey', but then that is rather risky, because the illustrations might be hopeless. Write, anyway, and tell me your advice.

By the way those catalogues have never come yet; you might wake the girlinosborne's up. I hope you are right about my music not being a

118 Horace, *Epistles*, 2. 2. 17–19.

whim: could you imagine anything more awful than to have all your tastes gradually fade away? Not a bad subject for a certain sort of novel! And talking about music, how did you enjoy Ysaye:[119] you don't say in your letter. Yes: his brother did play when they were at Guildford: one of his things was a Liebestraum by Liszt, which I did appreciate to a certain extent. Mrs K. has got a new book of Grieg's with a lot of things in it that I am just longing to hear you play: the best is 'Auf den Bergen',[120] do you know it? A lovely scene on mountains by the sea (I imagine) and belled cattle in the distance, and the snow and pines and blue sky, and blue, still, sad water. There's a sort of little refrain in it that you would love. You must try and get hold of it.

Since finishing the first volume of Spenser I have been reading again 'The Well at the World's End', and it has completely ravished me. There is something awfully nice about reading a book again, with all the half-unconscious memories it brings back. 'The Well' always brings to mind our lovely hill-walk in the frost and fog – you remember – because I was reading it then. The very names of chapters and places make me happy: 'Another adventure in the Wood Perilous', 'Ralph rides the Downs to Higham-on-the-Way', 'The Dry Tree', 'Ralp reads in a book concerning the Well at the World's End'.

Why is it that one can never think of the past without wanting to go back? We were neither of us better off last year than we are now, and yet I would love it to be last Xmas, wouldn't you? Still I am longing for next holydays too: do you know they are only five weeks off.

By the way, I hope you have read 'your Swinburne' by now: anyway, when you go up to night to the room I know so well you must go and have a look at the 'Well at the W's End'. Good-night.

Yours

Jacks

---

119 This is Théo Ysaÿe (1865–1918), a pianist and composer, brother of Eugène.
120 'Auf' den Bergen' is a piano solo from Edvard Grieg's *Folkelivsbilleder* (1872).

TO HIS FATHER (LP V: 33):

[Gastons]
Postmark: 19 November 1915

My dear Papy,

By all accounts I have missed a treat by being lost in a Surrey village during these recent 'elemental disturbances' as the man in Bret Harte says – or was it Mark Twain? I love this sort of melodrama in weather, and a night when the cross-channel boats can't put out is just in my line. Of course we never have any real wind here. The winter however has now set in for good, and ever since Monday there has been a hard frost with a little snow. They have been glorious days all the same, mostly without a cloud in the sky, and a blazing sun that is bright and dazzling but quite cold – grand weather for walking. I love the afternoons now, don't you? There is something weird and desolate about the perfectly round orange coloured sun dropping down clear against a slatey grey sky seen through bare trees that pleases me better than all those cloud-cities and mountains that we used to see in summer over the Lough in the old days when the crows were going home. There never seem to be such sunsets latterly, do there?

Your friend Byron is not (I devoutly hope) immortal, though his poem about the Assyrians unfortunately is.[121] It shares that rather deluding longevity with about half a dozen other nightmares such as 'The village clock has just struck four', 'It was the schooner Hesperus', 'Under the spreading chestnut tree'[122] etc.: to which list one might add the poems of Ovid, the novels of Dickens, and the complete works of Wordsworth.

Many thanks for the welcome postal order. Talking about money, when you next write to Warnie you might remind him of a business matter which seems to be rather hanging fire, and tell him that I am not only like Barkis, willing but also waiting.[123] I have acted upon your excellent advice and at last written to Arthur. There is, as yet, no answer, but

121 George Gordon, Lord Byron, *The Destruction of Sennacherib* (1815), l. 1: 'The Assyrian came down like the wolf on the fold'.

122 'It was the schooner Hesperus' is l. 1 of Henry Wadsworth Longfellow's *The Wreck of the Hesperus* (1839); 'Under the spreading chestnut tree' is l. 1 of Longfellow's *The Village Blacksmith* (1839).

123 Barkis is the character in Charles Dickens' *David Copperfield* (1849–50) who sent a message by David to Clara Peggotty that 'Barkis is willin'.'

in the meantime I am investing in a very good suit of sackcloth reach-me-downs and a dozen bottles of best quality ashes.

I am glad that you have been installed as a member of the permanent staff of St. Mark's, and hope that 'the management will continue to secure the services of this enterprising artist during the forthcoming season' as the critics say in another department of life.[124] Yes: I am sure you will read the lesson as it has not been read in St. Mark's for some time, although perhaps as you say, you appreciate it too well to do it justice.

I am rather sorry to hear that I have missed an opera company at all, even if a bad one. I suppose it is useless to ask if you have patronized it – unless perhaps you have been compelled to by Uncle Hamilton on the look out for a free stall.

Hoping the results of the accident are disappearing, I am

your loving,

son,

Jack

TO HIS FATHER (LP V: 33–4):

[Gastons]
Postmark: 24 November 1915

My dear Papy,

I am sorry if my intentional silence on this subject in my last letter has proved, as it well might, rather provoking. You will readily understand however my motives for not wishing to take any unnecessary responsibility in so delicate a point. My position, like that of Gilbert's policeman, 'is not a happy one'.[125] While really anxious not to add in the least to your worries, at the same time I have no wish to do anything that Warnie would afterwards consider mean or unpleasant. Since however you ask my opinion, I reply that the new point of this being the last leave he is likely to get certainly makes a considerable difference from our point of view as well as from that of K. It is no business of mine to sit in judgement on Warnie's actions, and from that it seems to me to be hard luck that he should not get a few days at home with us both before settling down to – an indefinite period. Of course, as you say, he may be exaggerating, but I can only go upon the information that we get.

---

124 Albert had been appointed a church warden at St Mark's for the third time.
125 W.S. Gilbert and Arthur Sullivan, *The Pirates of Penzance* (1879), Act II.

You will understand I am sure that it is almost entirely for his sake that I should suggest such an arrangement. A few rather breathless days at home are not such a prize that I should make much exertion to secure them on my own account. In the absence of any authority from you I have judged it better not to make any mention of the matter to K. I hope this was right as I was not at all sure what I ought to do.

Believe me Papy I am very sorry indeed that we are all worrying you in this way. I have told you what I feel about it, but it remains really a question between you and him. I wish only to act, if possible, in a manner agreeable to you both, or failing that, to help *you* as far as I can and fall in with your wishes. I am not at all sure that I have said exactly what I wanted in this letter, or made my position perfectly clear. The post with your letter came in very late, just as I was going to bed, and I am writing this rather hastily. It cannot be posted till tomorrow morning (Wednesday). I hope your side is getting better, as also the teeth.

your loving
son Jack.

P.S. I need not of course point out to you that I should hardly like to have any of this letter quoted to Warnie – but of course you understand that. J.[126]

TO HIS FATHER (LP V: 36–7):

[Gastons]
Postmark: 4 December 1915

My dear Papy,
This has been a week of surprises. As Chaucer says,

'One might a book make of it in a story'[127]

---

126 Albert replied on 26 November 1915: 'I was glad to get your kind and sympathetic letter. I have done as you would wish. I have just written to Warnie to say that inasmuch as he says he will not get leave again until the end of the war, I have altered my decision and have written to you to hold yourself in readiness to leave when he calls. I shall write to K. and send your travelling money later. You may tell K. what is impending if you like' (LP V: 34).

127 Chaucer, *Troilus and Criseyde*, bk. V, l. 585: 'Men mighte a book make of it, lik a storie!'

On Thursday, having a faint suspicion that things wouldn't pan out as we expected, like Dido 'Omnia tuta timens'[128] I made no preparation beyond walking down to the station to meet what I judged a likely train (excuse the 'ation' jingle in that sentence). Today however, being convinced that Warnie would really turn up, I clothed myself in glad rags, packed my handbag and was just putting on my shoes preparatory to a second walk to the station when your telegram arrived. So we must expect him on Sunday week!

Kirk advised me to make an arrangement about meeting him in town, since it will be a Sunday and the trains therefore different, he might not find time to come down here between his arrival in London and the departure of the boat train. Entre nous I don't think such a plan desirable – I hate meeting people in strange places, and especially W., as we always manage to bungle things in between us. Nor indeed should it be necessary: on the last occasion, as you will remember, he crossed on a Sunday and found no difficulty. Moreover, even if you wrote to arrange it with him as soon as you get this, your letter would scarcely reach him in time, and he would certainly have no time in which to reply. If you think otherwise, of course you will arrange accordingly and let me know.

It has rained steadily for several days now, and in spite of the unsettled conditions I have been reading a lot. I have now finished the first volume of the Faerie Queene and am going through an English Literature of Kirk's by Andrew Lang.[129] Lang is always charming whatever he does – or 'did' as we must unfortunately say, and this book is very good. More a rambling record of personal tastes than a set handbook, but all the better for that reason. There has also been from the London Library a book called 'Springs of Helicon' by Mackail[130] – you know, Professor of Poetry at Oxford and *the* man on Wm. Morris. This is a study on Chaucer, Spenser and Milton and I enjoyed it immensely. He has quite infected me with his enthusiasm for the former, whom I must begin to read. He talks of other works, 'the legend of good women', 'Troilus and Cresseide' as being better than the tales.[131] It is from Troilus and

---

128 Virgil, *Aeneid*, IV, 298: 'Incline to fear where all was safe...'

129 Andrew Lang, *History of English Literature* (1912).

130 John William Mackail, *Springs of Helicon: A Study in the Progress of English Poetry from Chaucer to Milton* (1909); *The Life of William Morris*, 2 vols. (1899).

131 i.e. Chaucer's *Legend of Good Women* and *Troilus and Criseyde* are better than his most popular work, *The Canterbury Tales* (composed 1387–1400).

Cresseide that he quotes that priceless line to which I treated you on the first page: I think it is rather great, don't you?

There is also a 'Greek Literature' by Gilbert Murray,[132] the bad verse-translator, which I have read with dire anger, as he degrades Homer from a poet into a 'question' and prefers that snivelling metaphysician Euripides to Aeschylus.

I suppose the great wedding is over by now? Or shall W. and I be let in for it? I hope you have not let the news of the coming visit trickle through to the ears of the sociable ἀγοραῖοι?[133] Thanks for the 'crowns for convoy', which I am sure will be quite sufficient.

your loving son,
Jack

Jack was home from 21 December 1915 until he returned to Great Bookham on 21 January 1916. Warnie was on leave from France, and Mr Lewis had both his sons home together.

---

132 Gilbert Murray, *A History of Ancient Greek Literature* (1897). Murray (1866–1957) was Regius Professor of Greek at Oxford 1908–36, and a distinguished translator of Greek plays.

133 People who frequent the agora (market place), i.e. the common people.

1916

— ≈ —

Jack was at Little Lea when, on 8 January, The Times published the Military Service Act, which was expected to come into effect soon. In a section concerning the 'Obligation of unmarried men to serve' it stated that included among those who would have to serve were: 'Every male British subject who, on the fifteenth day of August nineteen hundred and fifteen – (a) was ordinarily resident in Great Britain; and (b) had attained the age of eighteen years and had not attained the age of forty-one years; and (c) was unmarried or was a widower without children dependent on him' (p. 8).

In a 'Service Act Proclamation' published in The Times *on 4 February 1916 King George V ordered that the Military Service Act come into operation on 10 February 1916. Even then, Jack had reason at this time to think he might not be required to serve.* The Times *of 8 January had published, along with the Military Service Act, notification of 'A Bill to make provisions with respect to Military Service in connection with the present war' (p. 8). 'Exemptions,' it declared, would include 'Men who are resident in Great Britain for the purpose only of their education or for some other purpose.'*

While the Military Service Act went into effect on 10 February, the question of exemptions for Irishmen was debated by the Government for many months, during which time Jack did not know whether he would qualify for exemption or not. By the time it was clear that exemption would apply to him, and that he was not required to serve, he had decided that he should serve nevertheless.

TO HIS FATHER (LP V: 48–9):

[Gastons]
Postmark: 31 January 1916

My dear Papy,

One of the small consolations that a long experience of the continual change from term to holidays and vice versa brings, is the ability to settle down at once. I feel now as if I had been here for several months and have quite got into the old routine again. Everything at Bookham is of course in statu quo – I believe it would still be a hundred years hence. It is beautiful spring weather, as it was at home when I left you, and if only one could have that matutinal cup of tea, life would have nothing more to offer.

I spent the afternoon last Saturday in town, at the Shaftesbury, where there was a matinée of Carmen:[1] the singing was very poor, especially our friend the bass, whose rendition – I fancy that is the correct term – of the Toreador song was a thing to make the angels weep. Carmen herself however was quite good, and the tenor tolerable, so that on the whole I might have fared worse. With the opera itself, apart from the performance, I was very pleased. Just about the right percentage of the tunes was (it ought to be 'was' not 'were' oughtn't it?) familiar to me, and the ones which I had not heard before 'discoveries'.

This afternoon I have been a long walk to a perfectly delightful village[2] that I had never found out before, and I wish you could see it. It is rather like some of the places described in the 'Upton Letters' only more so. One old house – a thing as thick as a cottage and a good deal longer than Leeborough, all built on different levels, bears the legend '1666'. The best things however are the dragons and other monsters on the roof. Another most excellent codotta is the White Horse where you can drink tea, and a parlour that was used in the coaching days, and has not, by the look of it, been furnished since. If only they would dust the butter it would be quite ideal.

The 'Faerie Queen' which I told Mullens to send here as soon as it came has now arrived, and I am very pleased with it. If a bill comes from Osbornes for those records, please send it on at once as I have a cheque of W's. made out (or whatever the phrase is) to T.E.Osborne to pay it withal. However, no bill ought to arrive as I am asking Arthur to tell the 'young person' to send it here. And by the by, talking about cheques, I am not sure whether I asked you to take the cheque out of my cash box in the little end room and turn it into money some time before next holidays. Would you please do this? Hoping you are carrying on all right.

your loving
son Jack

---

1 *Carmen*, an opera by Georges Bizet, first performed in 1875.
2 The village in question was Dorking.

TO ARTHUR GREEVES (LP V: 50–1):

[Gastons
1 February 1916]

Dear little Archie,

Oh Gods of friendship, has such devotion ever been witnessed as mine! I am just at the beginning of a heavenly new book, I am just at the end of a long day's work, and yet I spend my spare time in writing letters. I hope you duly appreciate the sacrifice of a fresh young heart offered up on the savage altar of[3] – well to get on.

On the Saturday[4] in London I wasted 7/6 on going to a matinee of Carmen. There was no one in the cast of whom I had heard before and no one whom I want to hear again. Carmen herself was tolerable, but the rest, especially the Toreador, were fiendish. With the opera too I was awfully disappointed, although there is certainly a lot of beautiful music in it – particularly in the preludes to the acts (oh, one thing was good – the orchestra: they played that intermezzo that I have exquisitely) and in the scene among the mountains. But one does get so sick of all the tedious melodrama, all the blustering orchestration, and sticky tunes of good old fashioned operas. Then too there are a pair of villains in it who have a ghastly resemblance in their clownings to that other pair in Fra Diavolo – do you remember those awful creatures? So on the whole I was very fed up with this world by the time I reached dear Bookham. I find – of course – my beloved fellow pupil.

Since then I have been cheered up by the arrival of my new 'Faerie Queen' in the red leather Everyman. I can't see why you so dislike this edition: and if you have noticed the effect that their backs have when two or three are together in a shelf I am sure you do really appreciate them. I have read a good chunk of this and have also re-read Jane Eyre from beginning to end – it is a magnificent novel. Some of those long, long dialogues between her and Rochester are really like duets from a splendid opera, aren't they? And do you remember the description of the night she slept on the moor and of the dawn? You really lose a lot by never reading books again.

The other book – which I am denying myself to write to YOU, yes YOU of all people – is from the library by Blackwood called 'Uncle Paul'.[5]

---

3 Algernon Charles Swinburne, *A Forsaken Garden* (1878): 'As a god self-slain on his own strange altar'.

4 29 January 1916.

5 Algernon Blackwood, *The Education of Uncle Paul* (1909).

Oh, I have never read anything like it, except perhaps the 'Lore of Proserpine'. When you have got it out of your library and read how Nixie and Uncle Paul get into a dream together and went to a primaeval forest at dawn to 'see the winds awake' and how they went to the 'Crack between yesterday and tomorrow'[6] you will agree with me.

It was most annoying not getting my new records before I came back, wasn't it? Tell the girlinosbornes – the next time you go to see Olive – to send the bill for them to my address here at once. I do hope my Caruso[7] 'E lucevan e stella'[8] is going to be a success. Talking about that thing, does it convey anything to you? To me it seems to be just abstract melody. The actual scene I believe is a man on the battlement of a castle writing a letter – but you have probably read Tosca in that beastly potted opera book.

I was interested in what you said about the 'Brut'.[9] You ought to get it in Everyman.

Yours
Jack

TO HIS FATHER (LP V: 51–2):

[Gastons
6? February 1916]

My dear Papy,

Thanks very much for the cheque, which I enclose, signed as you told me. I am afraid however that I must trouble you again: one of my pairs of shoes has finally given out 'beyond the hope of uttermost recall' and I want you please to get me a new pair, or else tell Annie to do so. The mysterious piece of paper which I am sending is a map of my foot so that the knave in the shop will know what size to give you. I am very sorry if this is a nuisance, and will take care next term to set out well equipped with hats, coats, shoes and other garments, like the men in the furnace.

---

6 ibid., ch. X, p. 130; ch. XIV, p. 182.
7 Enrico Caruso (1873–1921), Italian tenor who made his first public appearance in Naples in 1894, and whose powerful, wonderfully pure voice made him one of the greatest singers of the century.
8 'E lucevan le stelle'—'and the stars shone'— is a song from Giacomo Puccini's opera *La Tosca*, which was first performed in 1900.
9 Layamon (*fl.*1200), *Brut*. Lewis was referring to *Arthurian Chronicles, Represented by Wace and Layamon*, translated by Eugene Mason, with an introduction by Lucy Allen Paton, Everyman's Library [1912].

That business about Warnie's commission, though of course important in itself, is as you say a nice example of war office methods. If big
things are managed in the same way as these small ones, it promises well
for the success of the war doesn't it? Another thing also struck me: we
have often wondered and laughed at some of the people who have commissions. It becomes even funnier when one reads the formula, 'reposing
special trust and confidence in your loyalty, courage, and good conduct':
we remember that the Jarvey[10] who drove the Colonel up to the office
last time was one of those who hoped soon to enjoy this 'special trust
and confidence.'

By the way, you should get that 'Spirit of Man', Bridge's anthology,[11]
that everyone is talking about. Mrs. K. has it from the library at present:
it is one of the prettiest little books I have seen for a long time, and there
is a lot of good stuff in it. One 'nice point' is that the names of the
authors are printed at the end of the volume and not under each piece: it
is very amusing – and somewhat humiliating – to see how many you
know.

This business about matriculation and enlisting is 'very tiresome', as
the Mikado said.[12] Are you [sure] that it applies to those who are under
age, and who are also Irish? If so, as you say, we must think it over
together. Of course in dealing with such a point we must always remember that a period of something more than a year elapses between the
time of joining up and one's getting any where near the front.[13] However,
it can wait until we are together at Easter.

And now my dear parent, as the time alloted to correspondence is
drawing to its close, I fear I must relinquish – or in other words it is time
for Church. You will observe that this is one of those houses where we
rise so early on Sundays that there is a long interval between breakfast
and our Calvinistic exercises.

your loving son,
Jack

---

10 i.e. a hackney-coachman.
11 Robert Bridges, *The Spirit of Man: An Anthology in English and French From the
Philosophers & Poets made by the Poet Laureate in 1915 & Dedicated by gracious
permission to His Majesty the King* (1916).
12 W.S. Gilbert and Arthur Sullivan, *The Mikado* (1885), Act II.
13 The preliminary selections of persons to be conscripted were apparently going on at
this time.

TO ARTHUR GREEVES (LP V: 53–4):

[Gastons
8 February 1916]

My dear Arthur,

You lucky devil! It makes me very envious to hear of all these good things going on at home while I am languishing in the wilds of Surrey.

I am surprised to hear that you never heard of Barkworth,[14] as I have seen his name in the musical part of the Times and other papers: I believe he is one of the promising musicians of the day – that is if there are ever going to be English musicians and an English school of opera. Personally I should have been very much interested to hear his 'Romeo and Juliet'. If the only fault is that it is blustering, you might say the same of the 'Flying Dutchman'[15] or the 'Valkyrie', mightn't you? What did poor Willie Jaffe think of it? (I suppose you mean him by W.J. –) Hardly in his line I should fancy. I am sure 'Pagliaci' and 'Cavalleria' were lovely, and I would especially like to have seen 'Rigoletto', because I know the plot.[16]

I quite agree with you that a gramophone spoils one for hearing opera: the real difficulty is to find for what a gramophone does not spoil one. True, it improves your musical taste and gives you opportunities of hearing things that you might otherwise never know: but what is the use of that when immediately afterwards it teaches you to expect a standard of performance which you can't get, or else satiates you with all the best things so that they are stale before you have heard them once on the stage? Or in other words, like everything else it is a disappointment, like every other pleasure it just slips out of your hand when you think you've got it. The most striking example of this is the holiday which one looks forward to all the term and which is over and gone while one is still thinking how best to enjoy it.

By all this you will gather that I am in a bad temper: well, so I am – that bloody little beast my fellow pupil has sneaked upstairs for a bath

---

14 John Edmund Barkworth (1858–1929) was an English composer educated at Rugby, Oxford and the Royal College of Music. His chief work, an opera based on Shakespeare's *Romeo and Juliet*, was first performed on 7 January 1916.

15 *Der Fliegende Hollander* ('The Flying Dutchman'), an opera by Richard Wagner (1843).

16 *I Pagliacci* (1892) is a short opera by Ruggiero Leoncavallo; *Cavalleria Rusticana* (1890) a short opera by Pietro Mascagni; and *Rigoletto* (1851) is an opera by Giuseppe Verdi.

and I can now hear him enjoying it and I know there will be no hot water left for me. They only raise hot water here about once a month.

However. Let us proceed: do you read Ruskin at all? I am sure you don't. Well I am reading a book of his at present called 'A joy for ever',[17] which is charming, though I am not sure you would care for it. I also still employ the week ends with the Faerie Queene. I am now in the last three books, which, though not much read as a rule, are full of good things. When I have finished it, I am going to get another of Morris' romances, or his translation of one of the sagas – perhaps that of Grettir the Strong.[18] This can be got either for 5/- in the Library edition (my 'Sigurd the Volsung'[19] one) or for 3/6 in the 'Silver Library' (like my 'Pearl Maiden').[20] Which would you advise?

By the way, why is your letter dated Wednesday? It has arrived here this evening – Tuesday – am I to understand that you posted it tomorrow, or that you have been carrying it about in your pocket for a week?

Isn't it awful about Harding? I hear from my father that Hope is going out.[21] I suppose that by this time the jeunes mariés have got into Schomberg.[22] Why are your letters always so much shorter than mine? Therefore I stop.

Yours,
Jack

---

17 John Ruskin, *The Political Economy of Art* (1857), the title of which was later changed to *A Joy for Ever*.

18 William Morris, *Grettir Saga: The Story of Grettir the Strong*, translated from the Icelandic by Eiríkr Magnússon and William Morris (1869).

19 William Morris, *Völsunga Saga: The Story of the Volsungs and Niblungs, with Certain Songs from the Elder Edda*, translated from the Icelandic by Eiríkr Magnússon and William Morris (1888).

20 Henry Rider Haggard, *Pearl Maiden* (1903).

21 Major George Harding, who was married to the former Charlotte Hope Ewart, had contracted double pneumonia in Sicily, where he had been sent to make the preliminary administrative arrangements for the transfer of a British Expeditionary Force to the Italian front. His wife was allowed to join him in Sicily, and she travelled overland alone via France and Italy.

22 The home of the newlyweds, Gordon and Lily Ewart.

TO HIS FATHER (LP V: 56–7):

[Gastons]
Postmark: 26 February 1916

My dear Papy,

'Well I calls it 'ard' as your friend used to say of the 'alf hour: I am accustomed, nay I am hardened to missing opera companies: but that I should be exiled in the wilds of England while Robin W. Gribbon and Lucius O'Brien[23] are visiting Belfast – this is too utterly all but. But why might I ask are these nonconformist canals reciting in the school house of Saint Mark?[24] What have they to do with us? Let them get behind us. Joking apart, one might get a 'running river of innocent merriment' out of their efforts, 'extremely stretched and conned with cruel pains'. Perhaps however you have your own reasons for reverencing the school house. Is it not the theatre of an immortal rendition of that 'powerful' role of Gesler,[25] and also of an immortal brick-dropping re an immortal preacher? There too the honey tongued tenor of Garranard – but we will draw a veil over the painful scene.

There is a certain symmetry of design in your list of books, a curiosa felicitas, a chaste eloquence and sombre pathos in the comments, 'See no. 40' and 'see no. 2' which I cannot but admire. I don't know how they have bungled it, but so long as I actually have two copies of the 'Helena' it will be all right, as Mullen's will make no difficulty about exchanging the unused one. If however the second copy exist (not exists) only on paper – why there we have the sombre pathos.

I am rather surprised at your criticism on 'The Spirit of man', and consider the reference to 'rescuing' both otiose and in doubtful taste. Of course it must be read, not merely as an anthology, but in the light of its title and avowed purpose, and we must not be disappointed when we

---

23 Robin W. Gribbon of 'Ardvarna', Strandtown, was Arthur Greeves's cousin on his father's side. His son, Charles Edward Gribbon (1898–1938), achieved distinction as an artist. (Sir) Frederick Lucius O'Brien (1869–1974) was Arthur's cousin on his mother's side. He had been educated at the Friends' School, Lisburn, and Bootham School in York. He was the first chairman of the Northern Ireland Housing Trust, 1945–60, and during his life he held many civil and governmental positions in Belfast. He and Arthur often travelled together.

24 They were both Quakers.

25 He is referring to Gioacchino Rossini's opera, *Guillaume Tell*, first performed in 1829. The opera is based on Friedrich von Schiller's play, *William Tell* (1804). William Tell is arrested for failing to salute the Austrian hat which is set upon a pole, and compelled by Gesler to shoot at the apple which is placed upon his son's head.

find certain favourites left out because they could not rightly claim a place in such a scheme. In this sense indeed the book is rather an original work than a collection of poems: for just as the musician may weave together a symphony by using the melodies of others arranged to express himself, so I take it Bridges is here working out an idea of his own: and the medium he chooses – as one might choose marble and another chalk (which you know is deteriorating terribly) – is the collective poetry of his predecessors. Or indeed, if I am reading too much into him, this would be a plan for a better anthology than has yet been written. One thing in the book I admit is indefensible – the detestable translation from Homer, which, though you may hardly recognise it, is meant to be in the metre of 'Oh! let us try'. For this Bridges ought to get 'something with boiling oil'.[26]

After a January so warm and mild that one could almost have sat in the garden, we have suddenly been whisked back to winter. It has snowed all day today, and is freezing hard tonight on top of it. I am very sorry to hear what you tell me about Hope: as you say, it must be terribly lonely and trying for her out there, and I am afraid the patient brings a very second rate constitution to the struggle.

your loving son,
Jack

P.S. I forgot to say the list of books, with one exception, is correct. J.

TO ARTHUR GREEVES (W):

[Gastons
28 February 1916]
Monday

My dear Galahad,

I suppose that by this time there is wrath and fury against me: however, there is no excuse, and you must just thole, as they say.

I don't know what it is like with you, but for this last week we have had the most lovely snow here. There is no wind, so where the snow 'falleth, there shall it lie':[27] which means that when you walk through the

---

26 He means Robert Bridges is to blame because he translated the two pieces from Homer in *The Spirit of Man*.
27 Ecclesiastes 11:3: 'In the place where the tree falleth, there shall it be.'

woods every branch is laden like a Christmas tree, and the mass of white arranged in every fantastic shape and grouping on the trees is really wonderful. Don't you love to walk while it is actually snowing? I love to feel the soft, little touches on your face and see the country through a sort of haze: it is so exquisitly desolate. It reminds one of that scene in 'The Lore of Proserpine'.

Poor thing! I do like the way, because a fellow asks you to join a corps, that you complain about 'your troubles'. May you never do worse! It reminds me of the story of Wellesly and his rich friend: W. had been going on one of his preaching tours round the country, riding alone in all weather, being put in the stocks, insulted, & stoned by the mob, in the course of all which he stayed for a night at the luxurious mansion of the friend. During the evening, a puff of smoke blew out of the grate, where-upon the host exclaimed 'You see, Sir, these are some of the crosses which I have to bear!'[28] Indeed, however, I 'can't talk' as you would say, for of course I am an inveterate grumbler myself – as you, of all people have best reason to know.

By the way, do you know a series of rather commonplace little vol-umes at 1/6 each called the Walter Scott Library? I have just run across them: they are not particularly nice – though tolerable – but the point is that they sell some things I have often wanted to get: among others Mor-ris' translation of the 'Volsunga Saga' (not the poem, you know, that I have, but a translation of the old Icelandic prose saga) which cannot be got in any other edition except the twelve guinea 'Works', of which you can't get the volumes separately.[29] If only the edition were a little decen-ter I'd certainly get it.

---

28 *The Works of John Wesley*, ed. Albert C. Outler, vol. 3 (1986), Sermon 108 'On Riches', para. 8: 'Nearly related to anger, if not a species of it, are *fretfulness* and *peevishness*. But are the rich more assaulted by these than the poor? All experience shows that they are. One remarkable instance I was a witness of many years ago. A gentleman of large fortune, while we were seriously conversing, ordered a servant to throw some coals on the fire. A puff of smoke came out. He threw himself back in his chair and cried out, "O Mr Wesley, these are the crosses which I meet with every day!" I could not help asking, "Pray, Sir John, are these the heaviest crosses you meet with?" Surely these crosses would not have fretted him so much if he had had fifty instead of five thousand pounds a year!' (pp. 526–7). The 'gentleman of large fortune' was Sir John Phillipps (c. 1701–64).

29 *The Collected Works of William Morris*, with introduction by his daughter May Morris, 23 vols. (1910–15). The *Works* were limited to 1,050 copies.

Perhaps you laugh at my everlasting talk about buying books which I never really get: the real reason is that I have so little time here – indeed only the week-ends as I spend all the spare time on week-days in reading French books, which I want to get more fluent in. However, I am now nearing the end of the 'Faerie Queene', and when that is done the Saturdays & Sundays will be free for something else. Really, whatever you say, you have much more time than I.

I wonder why Osborne's have sent no bill to me yet? I am not sure whether I asked you to give them my adress and tell them to send in the account or not: anyway, be a sport, and do so – AT ONCE. I have had a grisly dissapointment this week: Mrs K. said she was going away for a fortnight & I was gloating in the prospect of privacy & peace. But it has turned out a mare's nest. Ochone!

be good,
Jack

TO ARTHUR GREEVES (LP V: 58–9):

[Gastons
7 March 1916]
Tuesday

My dear Galahad,

I was very glad to get your interesting letter – which was fortunately longer than some of them – as I was beginning to wonder what had become of you; I think your 'lapse' this term puts you on a level with mine last, so that we can cry quits and admit that we are both sinners.

I have had a great literary experience this week. I have discovered yet another author to add to our circle – our very own set: never since I first read 'The well at the world's end' have I enjoyed a book so much – and indeed I think my new 'find' is quite as good as Malory or Morris himself. The book, to get to the point, is George Macdonald's 'Faerie Romance', *Phantastes*,[30] which I picked up by hazard in a rather tired Everyman copy – by the way isn't it funny, they cost 1/1d. now – on our station bookstall last Saturday. Have you read it? I suppose not, as if you had, you could not have helped telling me about it. At any rate, whatever

---

30 George MacDonald, *Phantastes: a Faerie Romance* (1858). Lewis was reading the Everyman's Library edition of 1915.

the book you are reading now, you simply MUST get this at once: and it is quite worth getting in a superior Everyman binding too.

Of course it is hopeless for me to try and describe it, but when you have followed the hero Anodos along that little stream to the faery wood, have heard about the terrible ash tree and how the shadow of his gnarled, knotted hand falls upon the book the hero is reading, when you have read about the faery palace – just like that picture in the Dulac book – and heard the episode of Cosmo, I know that you will quite agree with me. You must not be disappointed at the first chapter which is rather conventional faery tale style, and after it you won't be able to stop until you have finished. There are one or two poems in the tale – as in the Morris tales you know – which, with one or two exceptions are shockingly bad, so don't TRY to appreciate them: it is just a sign, isn't it, of how some geniuses can't work in metrical forms – another example being the Brontes.

I quite agree with what you say about buying books, and love all the planning and scheming beforehand, and if they come by post, finding the neat little parcel waiting for you on the hall table and rushing upstairs to open it in the privacy of your own room. Some people – my father for instance – laugh at us for being so serious over our pleasures, but I think a thing can't be properly enjoyed unless you take it in earnest, don't you? What I can't understand about you though is how you can get a nice new book and still go on stolidly with the one you are at: I always like to be able to start the new one on the day I get it, and for that reason wait to buy it until the old one is done But then of course you have so much more money to throw about than I.

Talking about finishing books, I have at last come to the end of the Faerie Queene: and though I say 'at last', I almost wish he had lived to write six books more as he hoped to do – so much have I enjoyed it. The two cantos of 'Mutabilitie' with which it ends are perhaps the finest thing in it, and if you have not done so already, you should read them whenever you have the time to spare.

I am now – by the same post – writing for a book called 'British Ballads' (Everyman)[31] in the chocolate binding of which I used to disapprove: so you see I am gradually becoming converted to all your views.

---

31 *British Ballads: English Literature for Schools*, ed. Arthur Burrell, Everyman's Library [1914].

Perhaps one of these days you may even make a Christian of me. Yes: I have at last heard from the girlinosbornes: but like the minstrel in Scott,

> '*Perhaps he wished the boon denied*'[32]

as the bill is rather a staggerer and my finances are not very blooming at present – I am thinking of sending it out to my brother to pay.

I well remember the glorious walk of which you speak, how we lay drenched with sunshine on the 'moss' and were for a short time perfectly happy – which is a rare enough condition, God knows. As Keats says 'Rarely, rarely comest thou, spirit of Delight'.[33] I do hope we shall have many more pleasant hours such as that the days are running in so fast now, and it makes me so sad to think that I shall have only two more sets of holidays of the good old type, for in November comes my 18th birthday, military age, and the 'vasty fields'[34] of France, which I have no ambition to face. If there is good weather and you get some days off next hols., we should go for some walks before breakfast – the feel of the air is so exquisite. I don't know when I can expect to come home.

Jack

TO HIS FATHER (LP V: 60–1):

[Gastons]
Postmark: 10 March 1916

My dear Papy,

'I wonder' said Demetrius, and so do I. You know it is a terrible thing for a young boy to get into the hands of a rascally old firm of solicitors to be cajoled into signing all sorts of mysterious documents. How do I know to what I have committed myself? Perhaps my three moors are being made over, or you are putting an entail on my little place in Rome. (What is an entail) Ha! Ha! The missing heir. Indeed the whole proceeding savours of the novelette: you must cut your moustache shorter and call yourself Richard or Rupert. However, I herewith enclose the enigmatic slip of paper, with the forged signature inked over 'avec d'empresment' (French language). By the way, I see that I have acknowledged £16-13-10. Well what became of this...this...business...this tea business?

---

32 Sir Walter Scott, *The Lay of the Last Minstrel* (1805), Introduction.
33 The lines are in fact from Shelley's 'Song' (1824).
34 William Shakespeare, *Henry V* (1600), Prologue, 12.

I hope you have read your Times Literary Supplement this week: do you see that the commonwealth of letters is the richer by a great new poet? Now let the stars retire for the sun has risen: let Hemans and M'Kitrick Ros[35] be silent, for Mr. Little has come! It is really too good to be missed. I love the fine impassioned address to the sea, as much greater than Tennyson's 'Break, break, break'[36] as that is than the one in the Prometheus, the one you will have noticed beginning

> 'Oh, wave! Thy clemency is open
> To shrewd suspicion'.[37]

What melody! What masterly phrasing and gorgeous imagery! We may pass over such minor beauties as the lioness which becomes the 'formidable sultaness' and go on to the last piece which contains the gems about the 'golden brawn' of the sunrise, the 'various viands of the rainbow' and nature 'gorgeous, great, gratuitous'. Why this is a more exquisite song than the other about 'Presumption, pride, pomposity', though there is a certain likeness. This I suppose is the modern school that has got beyond Tennyson. Well perhaps they have: but I for one had sooner walk on the earth than soar on any Pegasus which bears such a disquieting resemblance to a rocking horse.

St. John's, the school at Leatherhead whither my fellow pupil is wont daily to repair for gentlemanly and vertuous discipline and schooling in the humane letters, has got an epidemic of influenza and is breaking up for the term. So I suppose we shall have our well beloved Ford more in evidence now. Tell Arthur to write. I am sorry to hear what you say about Grandmother: I feel that we ought to have seen more of her, but it was not easy.[38] Your loving,

son,

Jack

---

35 Two terrible poets. Mrs Felicia Dorothea Hemans (1793–1835) published her first volume of *Poems* when she was 15. Amanda McKittrick Ros (1860–1939), known as 'the World's Worst Writer', was the author of *Irene Iddesleigh* (1897) and *Poems of Puncture* (1915). It became a customary feature of Lewis's Inklings meetings at Magdalen College to bet that no one could read a passage from *Irene Iddlesleigh* without a smile.

36 Alfred, Lord Tennyson, *Break, Break, Break* (1842), ll. 1–2: 'Break, break, break, / On thy cold grey stones, O Sea'.

37 Philip Francis Little, *Thermopylae and Other Poems* (1916), reviewed as 'An Uncertain Voice' in *The Times Literary Supplement* (9 March 1916), p. 116.

38 Lewis's mother's mother, Mary Warren Hamilton (b. 16 December 1826) died on 22 March 1916. See **The Hamilton Family** in the Biographical Appendix.

TO ARTHUR GREEVES (LP V: 63–4):

[Gastons
14 March 1916]
(You ought to know the date.)

My dear Galahad,

It must have been a very old Everyman list on which you found 'Phantastes' as one of the new ones, since, to my knowledge, the copy I got had been on the bookstall for weeks. Everymans with us have gone up 1d. in the shilling: I suppose it is just the same at home? By the time you get this you will probably have finished Phantastes, so you must give me your verdict on it as a whole: when one has read a book, I think there is nothing so nice as discussing it with some one else – even though it sometimes produces rather fierce arguments.

I too am rather disappointed. The 'British Ballads' has come, and though I am awfully bucked with the edition – I can't think why I didn't appreciate it before. This must be a triumph for you – the reading matter is not nearly so good as I expected. For one thing, instead of being all made up of real old ballads as I hoped, it is half full of silly modern imitations and even funny ones. Don't you loathe 'funny' poetry? However, as it is not your style of book, I suppose I am boring you.

All the same, when you begin to write a letter you just go on babbling – at least I do – without thinking whether the person at the other end is interested or not, till you come to the last page and find that you haven't really said what you wanted to. But perhaps that sort of rambling is the right kind of letter. I don't know whether you personally write that way or not, but the result is charming, and you can't think how eager I am to see the atrocious but familiar scroll waiting for me on the hall table. And yet, every letter is a disappointment: for a minute or two I was carried back to your room at Bernagh – don't you remember rooms by their smells? Each one has its own – and seem to be talking to you, and then suddenly I come to the end and it's all only a little bit of paper in my hand and Gastons again. But come. We are being mawkish. I think you and I ought to publish our letters (they'd be a jolly interesting book by the way) under the title of lamentations, as we are always jawing about our sorrows. I gather it was that beastly girl in Mayne's who 'flared up' as you say. Aren't they rude in that place? I think we ought to start a movement in the neighbourhood to boycott them. Only we'd have to join in it ourselves, which would be a pity.

No: I have never yet seen Kelsie's book. I daresay she doesn't know that I take an interest in such things, and you are lucky in having a reputation as a connoisseur which makes you free of every library in Belmont – tho' there aren't very many to be sure. I am afraid our Galahad will be growing a very stodgy mind if he reads nothing but Trollope and Goldsmith and Austen. Of course they are all very good, but I don't think myself I could stand such a dose of stolidity. I suppose you will reply that I am too much the other way, and will grow a very unbalanced mind if I read nothing but lyrics and fairy tales. I believe you are right, but I find it so hard to start a fresh novel: I have a lazy desire to dally with the old favourites again. I think you'll have to take me in hand and set me a 'course' when I come home.

By the way what about the piano and the gramophone these days? We don't seem to talk of music so much now as we did: of course your knowledge on that subject is so much greater than mine that I can really only express a philistine's taste. Are you still going to Walker? For my part, I have found my musical soul again – you will be relieved to hear – this time in the preludes of Chopin. I suppose you must have played them to me, but I never noticed them before. Aren't they wonderful? Although Mrs K. doesn't play them well, they are so passionate, so hopeless, I could almost cry over them: they are unbearable. I will find out the numbers of the ones I mean and we will have a feast next holidays.

By the way, you speak in your last letter of the difference between music and books: I think (to get back to an old argument) it is just the same difference as between friendship and love. The one is a calm and easy going satisfaction, the other a sort of madness: we take possession of one, the other takes possession of us: the one is always pleasant the other in its greatest moments of joy is painful. But perhaps I am rating books and friendship too low, because poetry and great novels do sometimes rouse you almost as much as music: the great love scenes in Shirley for instance, or the best parts of Swinburne etc.

I am sorry I always make the mistake about your address. Hullo – I've done it again.

Yours,
Jack

TO ARTHUR GREEVES (LP V: 64–5):

[Gastons
21 March 1916]

My dear Galahad,

So here we are at the weekly letter, and very glad I am too; but Heavens! – how the weeks run on don't they? While I was at Malvern I used to count the days and long for the end of term, so of course time crawled; now-a-days when I am quite comfortable the whole thing goes on far too quickly. And it's all so many days, months etc., not of the term or the year, but of one's life – which is tiresome. 'Help!' I hear you muttering, 'Is he going to moralize for four pages?' (Cheer up, I'll try to hold it in.)

I'm awfully bucked to hear that you think the same about Phantastes as I, though if you only began to enjoy it in the eleventh chapter, you must have missed what I thought were the best parts – that is to say the forest scene and the faery palace – or does that come after chapter XI? You will gather that the book is upstairs and that I am too lazy to go and get it. I hope that by this time you have bought 'Sir Gibbie'[39] and will be able to advise me on it. Some of the titles of his other books are, to me at least, even more alluring than the one you quote: for instance 'At the back of the north wind'.[40]

Isn't it funny the way some combinations of words can give you – almost apart from their meaning – a thrill like music? It is because I know that you can feel this magic of words AS words that I do not despair of teaching you to appreciate poetry: or rather to appreciate all good poetry, as you now appreciate some. This is however off the point: what I meant to say was that lots of his titles give me that feeling. I wish there were more in Everymans, don't you?

Talking about Everymans, do you know what their 1/6 binding is like? I can't remember whether you have anything in it or not, but I have been thinking of trying it, so tell me what you know on the subject. What? you ask, still new books? Well really the length of the Faerie Queene was a godsend, because so long as I turned to it every week-end with the regularity of clockwork I could keep my money in my pockets: now however the temptation to get a nice new book for the longed for Sunday rest is overwhelming.

---

39 George MacDonald, *Sir Gibbie* (1879).
40 George MacDonald, *At the Back of the North Wind* (1871).

I am glad to hear that you have moved into Lily's room as I think you – or 'we' shall I say in selfishness – will be more comfortable there: at the same time I have a sort of affection for the old one where we have had such good times: we should call it 'joyous garde'.[41] Still, I am longing to find myself in your new quarters with all the old talk, the old music, and the old fingering of rich, friendly books.

You know, Galahad, that though I try to hide it with silly jokes that annoy you, I am very conscious of how unfair our friendship is, and how you ask me over continually and give me an awfully good time, while I hardly ever bring you to us: indeed though he is a good father to me, I must confess that he – my father – is an obstacle. I do hope you understand? You know how I would love if I could have you any time I liked up in my little room with the gramophone and a fire of our own, to be merry and foolish to our hearts content: or even if I could always readily accept your invitations without feeling a rotter for leaving him alone. I don't know why I've gone off into this discussion, but perhaps it is just as well. Indeed the only thing to be done is to get my father married as quickly as may be – say to Mary Bradley. Or lets poison old Stokes and give him the widow. In which case of course our imagined snuggery in the little end room would be brightened up by a charming circle of brothers and sisters in law.

I know quite well that feeling of something strange and wonderful that ought to happen, and wish I could think like you that this hope will some day be fulfilled. And yet I don't know: suppose that when you had opened the door the Ash had REALLY confronted you and turning to fly, you had found the house melting into a haunted wood – mightn't you have wished for the old 'dull' world again? Perhaps indeed the chance of a change into some world of Terreauty (a word I've coined to mean terror and beauty) is in reality in some allegorical way daily offered to us if we had the courage to take it. I mean one has occasionally felt that this cowardice, this human loathing of spirits just because they are such may be keeping doors shut? Who knows? Of course this is all nonsense and the explanation is that through reading Maeterlink,[42] to improve my French, too late at night, I have developed a penchant for mystical

---

41 Sir Launcelot's castle in the Arthurian legend.
42 Maurice Maeterlinck (1862–1949), Belgian poetic dramatist and essayist, achieved great popularity with *L'Oiseau bleu* (1908) and its translation *The Blue Bird* (1909).

philosophy – greatly doubtless to the discomfort of my long suffering reader.

By the way, is the girlinosbornes beginning to ask about my bill yet – which is not paid? Write soon AND LONG mon vieux, to,

yours,

Jack

TO HIS FATHER (LP V: 70):

[Gastons]
Postmark: 1 April 1916

My dear Papy,

The little plans of mice and men, it would seem, must a' gang aft aglee.[43] You ask me when I am thinking of going home. Well I *was* thinking of the 15th, as instructed by the Colonel, so that his next leave would fall nicely at the end of my holydays. Mrs. K. suddenly turns up with the pleasing news that Terry is going on Tuesday the 4th., and Osbert Smythe with mother is coming down on the same date to convalesce from a wound, and – ah – when was I thinking of going home? Or in other words, after a little pow-pow, I have been 'kicked out' (Perhaps they were right to dissemble their love, but why –).[44] So I fear me Tuesday it must be. I hardly think a letter from you can reach me before that, so I shall borrow from K. By the way, Terry tells me that all the Belfast boats are off; if this is so, will you please wire and tell me, as in that case I shall have to go by Larne: I suppose the same ticket and payment of difference will do – or is the fare by Larne just the same? Of course if Liverpool and Fleetwood are still running, I will go by either – whichever is running on Tuesday night. In any case please wire and tell me. I am sorry to be such a nuisance, but it is quite as annoying for me, and more so for W. Sunt lacrimae rerum.[45]

your loving son,

Jack

---

43 Robert Burns, 'To a Mouse' (1786): 'The best laid schemes o' mice an' men / Gang aft a-gley.'

44 Isaac Bickerstaffe, *An Expostulation* (1789): 'Perhaps it was right to dissemble your love, / But – why did you kick me downstairs?'

45 Virgil, *Aeneid*, I, 462: 'Sunt lachrimae rerum et mentem mortalia tangunt' ('There are tears for those things and they touch the minds of men.')

P.S. On second thoughts, Monday would be better if you get this in time; if I go on Tuesday I shall have to travel with Terry and a lot of his friends, which would be terrible – for one thing I know they don't want me. So Monday be it: please wire. J.

Lewis was at home from 5 April to 11 May 1916. Writing to Albert about him on 7 April 1916, Mr Kirkpatrick said:

> *The very idea of urging or stimulating him to increased exertion makes me remind him that it is inadvisable for him to read after 11 p.m. If he were not blessed with such a store of physical health and strength, he wd. surely grow weary now and then. But he never does. He hardly realizes – how could he at his age – with what a liberal hand nature has bestowed her bounties on him...I notice that you feel adverse at present to let him enter the university at the close of next Autumn...But as far as preparation is concerned, it is difficult to conceive of any candidate who ought to be in better position to face the ordeal. He has read more classics than any boy I ever had – or indeed I might add than any I ever heard of, unless it be an Addison or Landor or Macaulay. These are people we read of, but I have never met any.* (LP V: 74)

Mr Kirkpatrick wrote again on 5 May 1916:

> *The case of Clive is very perplexing, but let us make a few points clear. I think he ought to be able to gain a classical scholarship or exhibition at entrance in any of the Oxford Colleges next Novr. or Dec., when the exams are held. But suppose I gave my opinion that he could with advantage do another years work with me. Do you not see what you are in for? Clive will be 18 in Dec., and if he remains in this country after that date, strictly speaking one month after that date, he will be liable for military service. There is no escape from that now...Ireland is exempt from the Act. Will it be brought in, as Carson[46] before, and now Captain Craig have asked?*

---

46 Edward Henry Carson, Baron Carson (1854–1935), Ulster leader, was attorney general of Ireland.

I find it hard to believe it. But we shall see. At any rate we may give up the idea that the war may be over before Jany. 1917...What is to become of the Eng. Universities under this new Conscription Act? I cannot say, but I do not see how they are to go on. Suppose Clive gained an entrance exhibn. next Decr. He would not be able to attend lectures. At the end of one month he would be liable to conscription. (LP V: 78–9)

Albert replied on 8 May 1916: 'Clive has decided to serve, but he also wishes to try his fortune at Oxford' (LP V: 79).

TO ARTHUR GREEVES (LP V: 80–1):

[Gastons
16 May 1916]

My dear Galahad,

I wonder what you are doing tonight? It is nearly ten o'clock and I suppose you are thinking of bed: perhaps you are at this moment staring into the good old bookcase and gloating over your treasures. How well I can see it all, exactly as we arranged it a few days ago: it is rather consoling for me to be able to follow you in imagination like this and feel as if I were back in the well-known places.

Now let us get on with what you really want to hear; no, I did not go to the 'Starlight Express'[47] nor could I see it in the 'Times' list of entertainments. Perhaps after all it is not an opera but a cantata or something. What I did go to see was a play called 'Disraeli'[48] which I liked immensely, though I am not sure the Meccecaplex would have cared for it. It's about the real Disraeli[49] you know, the part being taken by Dennis Eadie – whom you saw in 'Milestones'[50] didn't you; he looks exactly like the pictures of the said politician in the old Punches. However, it is a thoroughly interesting play and I shall never repent of having seen it:

---

47 *The Starlight Express*, a play based on Algernon Blackwood's *A Prisoner in Fairyland* (1913), with incidental music by Edward Elgar, was first performed on 29 December 1915.

48 Louis Napoleon Parker's *Disraeli* was first performed on 23 January 1911.

49 Benjamin Disraeli (1804–81), first Earl of Beaconsfield, was Prime Minister 1868 and 1874–80. He published a number of novels, including *Vivian Grey* (1826), *Coningsby* (1844), *Sybil* (1845) and *Tancred* (1847).

50 Arnold Bennett and Edward Knoblauch's play *Milestones* (1912).

I think you agree with me that a good sensible play is far better than a second rate opera, don't you?

By the way, you have really no right to this letter, old man: that one of yours which you have been talking about all the holidays is not here, and Mrs K. says that nothing came for me while I was away. So now I shall be no longer content with your continual 'as I said in my letter', but will expect it all over again – especially the remarks about 'The Back of the Northwind' (by the way doesn't it sound much better if you pronounce that last word 'Northwind' as one word, with the accent slightly on the first syllable?).

Talking of books – you might ask, when do I talk of anything else – I have read and finished 'The Green Knight',[51] which is absolutely top-hole: in fact the only fault I have to find with it is that it is too short – in itself a compliment. It never wearies you from first to last, and considering the time when it was written, some things about it, the writer's power of getting up atmosphere for instance, quite in the Bronte manner, are little short of marvellous: the descriptions of the winter landscapes around the old castle, and the contrast between them and the blazing hearth inside, are splendid. The last scene too, in the valley where the terrible knight comes to claim his wager, is very impressive.

Since finishing it I have started – don't be surprised – 'Rob Roy',[52] which I suppose you have read long ago. I really don't know how I came to open it: I was just looking for a book in the horribly scanty library of Gastons, and this caught my eye. I must admit that it was a very lucky choice, as I am now revelling in it. Isn't Die Vernon a good heroine – almost as good as Shirley? And the hero's approach through the wild country round his Uncle's hall in Northumberland is awfully good too.

In fact, taking all things round, the world is smiling for me quite pleasantly just at present. The country round here is looking absolutely lovely: not with the stern beauty we like of course: but still, the sunny fields full of buttercups and nice clean cows, the great century old shady trees, and the quaint steeples and tiled roofs of the villages peeping up in their little valleys – all these are nice too, in their humble way. I imagine

---

51 The 14th century poem *Sir Gawain and the Green Knight*. Lewis was reading the prose translation by E.J.B. Kirtlan (1912).
52 Sir Walter Scott, *Rob Roy* (1818).

(am I right?) that 'Our Village'[53] gives one that kind of feeling. Tell me all about your own 'estate' as Spenser would say, when you write.

Have you finished 'Persuasion'[54] and has the De Quincy come yet, and what do you think of both? Have there been any particular beauties of sun and sky since I left? I know all that sounds as though I were trying to talk like a book, but you will understand that I can't put it any other way and that I really do want to hear about those kind of things.

This letter brings you the first instalment of my romance: I expect you'll find it deadly dull: of course the first chapter or so must be in any case, and it'll probably never get beyond them. By the way it is headed as you see 'The Quest of Bleheris'. That's a rotten title of course, and I don't mean it to be permanent: when it's got on a bit, I must try to think of another, really poetic and suggestive: perhaps you can help me in this when you know a bit more what the story is about.

Now I really must shut up. (That's the paper equivalent of 'Arthur, I'm afraid I shall have to go in a minute'.) Oh, I was forgetting all about Frankenstein.[55] What's it like? 'Really Horrid'?, as they say in 'Northanger Abbey'.[56] Write soon before I have time to feel lonely.

Yours,

Jack

TO ARTHUR GREEVES (LP V: 82–4):

[Gastons
22 May 1916]
Monday. 10 o'clock.

My dear Arthur,

Many, many thanks for the nice long letter, which I hope you will keep up for the rest of the term, in length. I see that it has taken four days to reach me, as it came only this morning, so I don't know when you will be reading this.

I am rather surprised at your remark about 'Persuasion', as it seemed to me very good – though not quite in her usual manner. I mean it is more romantic and less humorous than the others, while the inevitable

---

53 Mary Russell Mitford, *Our Village: Sketches of Rural Life, Character, and Scenery*, 5 vols. (1824–32).

54 Jane Austen, *Persuasion* (1818).

55 Mary Wollstonecraft Shelley, *Frankenstein* (1818; 1831).

56 Jane Austen, *Northanger Abbey* (1818).

love interest, instead of being perfunctory as in 'Emma'[57] and 'Mansfield Park' is the real point of the story. Of course I admit that's not quite the style we have learned to expect from Jane Austen, but still don't you think it is rather interesting to see an author trying his – or her – hand at something outside their own 'line of business'? Just as it is interesting to see Verdi in 'Aida'[58] rising above himself – though I suppose I have no right to talk musical criticism to you – or indeed to anybody.

I am glad that you are bucked with your De Quincy, and am eager to see the paper. By the way I suppose you notice that the same series can be got in leather for 5/-. I wonder what that would be like. I am thinking of getting the two volumes of Milton in it, as soon as I am flush or have a present of any sort due to me: one wants to get a person like Milton in a really worthy edition you know. Tell me what you think about this.

On Wednesday I had a great joy: I went up to town with the old woman[59] (by the way I have just seen the point of your joke about 'byre' and liar. Ha! Ha!) to see the Academy.[60] I have never been to one before, and therefore cannot say whether this year's was good as they go: but anyway I enjoyed it immensely and only one thing – your company – was lacking to make it perfect. How I wish we could have been there to enjoy some things together – for there were ones that would have sent you into raptures. Particularly there was a picture called 'Nature groaning' that exactly reminded me of that wet walk of ours, although the scene was different: it represented a dull, gloomy pool in a wood in autumn, with a fierce scudding rain blown slantways across it, dashing withered leaves from the branches and beating the sedge at the sides. I don't suppose that makes you realize it at all, but there was a beautiful dreariness about it that would have appealed to you. But of course it is really no good trying to describe them: I wish you would get that Academy book which one always finds in a dentist's waiting room so that we could compare notes. If you do, you must particularly notice 'The Egyptian Dancers' ['A Dancer of Ancient Egypt'], 'The Valley of the Weugh or Sleugh' or something like that ['The Valley of the Feugh'] (a glorious snow Scene), 'The deep places of the earth', 'The watcher' and a lovely faery scene from Christina Rosetti's 'Goblin Market'. It costs only a

---

57 Jane Austen, *Emma* (1816).
58 *Aida*, an opera by Giuseppe Verdi, first performed in 1871.
59 Mrs Kirkpatrick.
60 The Royal Academy of Art, London.

shilling I think and tho' of course the black and white reproductions lose a lot, still they are quite enjoyable.[61]

Talking about pictures etc., I was very pleased with your description of the mist and the night sky: you are by no means such a contemptable artist in words as you would like people to believe – in fact to be honest, if you weren't lazy you could do big things – and you have brought a very clear picture to my mind: one does get topping effects over the Lough sometimes, doesn't one? Really, after all, for sheer beauty of nearly every kind, there is no place I know like our own good county Down.

I am still at 'Rob Roy' which I like immensely, and am writing by this post for the first volume of Chaucer's 'Canterbury Tales' in the Everyman 2/2 edition:[62] am I wise? I have dipped into them very often latterly in the Kirk's horrible old copy, and think I shall like them, while, as I told you before, the paper of that Everyman is especially nice. I have also got a French prose romance of 'Tristan and Iseut'[63] which promises very well as far as I can see: in the meantime however since like all French firms' books it is paper back, I have sent it away to be bound in a very tasty binding of my own choice. Tell me more about 'Frankenstein' in your next letter so that I may decide whether to buy it or no. Any new records? I imagine that the success of your late venture may buck up your taste for your gramophone may it not?

This brings you the next chapter of my infliction. By the way I don't know how I actually wrote it, but I certainly meant to say 'The quest of Bleheris' and [not] 'of THE Bleheris', since Bleheris is a man's name. However, as I wrote to you before, that title is only waiting until I can get another better one. Your advice as to fighting and brasting exactly falls in with my own ideas since like Milton I am,

> 'Not sedulous by nature to indite
> Wars............'[64]

---

61 A complete list of the art works at the Royal Academy Exhibition can be found in *The Exhibition of the Royal Academy of Arts*, no. 148 (1916). But Lewis is referring to *The Royal Academy Illustrated* (1916) which contains photographs of most of the paintings mentioned here.

62 *Chaucer's Canterbury Tales for the Modern Reader*, prepared and edited by A. Burrell, Everyman's Library (1908).

63 *Le Roman de Tristan et Iseut*, Traduit et Restauré par Joseph Bédier, Préface de Gaston Paris (Paris [1900]).

64 Milton, *Paradise Lost*, IX, 27–8.

I am afraid indeed that like 'Westward Ho'[65] my tale will have to dawdle about a bit in the 'City of Nesses' before I can get poor Bleheris off on his adventures: still you must do your best.

Oh vanity! vanity! to think that I can waste all this time jawing about my own work. Oh, one thing: I can't agree with you that Kelsie is at all like Diana Vernon: for if – to talk like Rashleigh,[66] 'My fair cousin' has a fault, it is a certain deadly propriety and matter-of-factness that will creep in even when she's at her best, don't you think so.

And now I've scrawled for a whole hour (it's just striking) so good night.

Jack

TO HIS FATHER (LP V: 81–2):

Gastons,
Great Bookham.
28/5/16.

My dear Papy,

I hear from the colonel that you are expecting a letter:[67] so, as they say of a sheep in a picture book, 'here it is', although, to be exact, I don't see why I should owe you one – the score so far this term being exactly equal on both sides.

Well, how have things been since I left home? I hope the laurels are coming on nicely. Everything here is of course very much the same, and the weather is glorious. On my way back I went to a play that would have appealed to you – 'Disraeli', which you will remember to have seen reviewed in Punch's 'At the play'.[68] If the real man was at all like the character in the piece he certainly must have been a prince of cards. I suppose that most of the bon mots that I heard at the Royalty are actual historic ones, preserved in his letters and so forth. I wonder too whether it be true to life when, having said good thing, he is represented as making his secretary take a note of it 'For Manchester next week: that'll just about suit Manchester'. Which reminds me how are you getting on with the fourteenth – or is the twentieth volume of his life?[69]

---

65 Charles Kingsley, *Westward Ho!* (1855).
66 Diana Vernon and Rashleigh are characters in *Rob Roy*.
67 Warnie was on leave, and at Little Lea, 19–25 May.
68 *Punch*, vol. CL (12 April 1916), p. 252.
69 Mr Lewis had probably been reading William Flavelle Monypenny's *The Life of Benjamin Disraeli*, 6 vols. (1910–20).

The only other excitement I can think of was a jaunt up to town with Mrs. K. to see the Academy, last Saturday. I had never been to one before, and therefore cannot say whether this was good, as they go, or not. At any rate it seemed to me that there were a lot of very nice things there, while even watching the other watchers was a great amusement.

My reading at present is very sober and old fashioned – 'Rob Roy' and the 'Canterbury Tales', both of which are most satisfactory. The former I suppose you have read years ago: at least I have tracked to its lair one of your favourite quotations, 'Do not mister or Campbell me: my foot is on my native heath and my name is MacGregor'.[70] But what a pity it is to see such good 'yarning' as Scott's spoilt and tripped up at every turn by his intolerably stilted and pedantic English. I suppose we must thank Dr. Johnson and 'Glorious John'[71] for first making such prose possible.

I met Warnie on Friday, according to instructions, and saw him go off by his 4.0 troop train. I am sorry to hear from him that you are bothered with some sort of rheumatism, and hope that it is now on the mend.

your loving
son Jack

P.S. I am one up in letter now: so don't forget to write soon. J.

TO ARTHUR GREEVES (LP XI: 259–60):

[Gastons
30 May 1916]

My dear Galahad,

I don't know whether you quite realized how mysterious your last letter was: on page III I read 'have just begun a tale called "Alice for short"'. Very good, say I, remembering William de Morgan's novel of that name:[72] but you are 'doubtful whether you'll finish it': remembering the size of the volume on our landing book case I am not surprised: then I read on a bit and see that you 'daren't let it out of your hands, even to me'. Ah! Ce devient interèssant (is there an accent on that word?), I think something tremendously improper. But imagine my even greater confusion on learning that de Morgan's long and heavy looking novel is a

---

70 *Rob Roy*, ch. XXXIV.
71 John Dryden (1631–1700), so called both for his writings and for the fact that he was the first Poet Laureate to be officially so designated.
72 William De Morgan, *Alice-for-Short* (1907).

continuation of Alice in Wonderland![73] Of course as soon as I turned the page I saw that you meant 'began to write' and not 'began to read' as I had naturally thought, being as you know cracked absolutely.

Well as to the information itself: I cannot urge you too strongly to go on and write something, anything, but at any rate WRITE. Of course everyone knows his own strength best, but if I may give any advice, I would say as I did before, that humour is a dangerous thing to try: as well, there are so many funny books in the world that it seems a shame to make any more, while the army of weird and beautiful or homely and passionate works could well do with recruits. But perhaps your 'Alice' is not so much humorous as lyric and fantastic? Anyway, you might as well send me along what you have done and let me have a look at it: at the worst it can't be more boring than 'Bleheris' and of course it's much easier to criticise each other's things on paper than viva voce: at least I think so.

And by the way, while I'm on this subject, there's one thing I want to say: I do hope that in things like this you'll always tell me the absolute truth about my work, just as if it were by someone else whom we did not know: I will promise to do the same for you. Because otherwise there is no point in sending them, and I have sometimes thought that you are inclined not to. (Not to be candid I mean). So I shall expect your MS – 'Alice' or anything else you have done – next week.

'Rob Roy' is done now, and (to pay you out for your remarks about 'Persuasion') I must admit that I only skimmed the last three or four chapters: the worst of a book with a plot is that when the plot is over, the obvious 'fixing up' is desperately tedious. On the whole however it was jolly good, and some of the scenery passages, as you say, are gorgeous: particularly where Frank is riding 'near the line' with the Bailey and the latter points out the Highland Hills – do you remember? That bit is almost as good as the scene where Clement Chapman shows Ralph the Wall of the World. But I suppose you would think it sacriledge to compare Morris to Scott. So would I for that matter, only the other way round.

You ask about the binding of my 'Tristram': well of course, apart from the binding itself, all French books are far poorer than ours: this one for instance cost 2/- (2fr.50) although it was only a paper back, of about the

---

73 Lewis Carroll, *Alice's Adventures in Wonderland* (1865).

same size as my Gawain: the binding will come to another 2/- or perhaps 2/6. That sounds a lot: but after all if you saw a nice leather bound book in a shop of that size and were told it cost 4/-, I don't think it would seem very dear. Of course it is true I may very likely be disappointed in it, but then, not being a prudent youth like you, I have to take risks occasionally.

With the Chaucer I am most awfully bucked: it is in the very best Everyman style – lovely paper, strong boards, and – aren't you envious – not one but two bits of tissue paper. When I've collected enough in that way, I shall be able to put tissue in all my better class Everymans. As to the contents, although I looked forward to them immensely, they have proved even better than I hoped: I have only had time so far to read the 'Prologue' and 'The Knight's Tale' (that's Palamon and Arcite you know), but I adore them. The tale is a perfect poem of chivalry, isn't it? And the pathos of Arcite's death is really wonderful, with the last broken appeal,

'Forget nat Palamon that gentil man'[74]

and the cry of 'Mercy Emelye'.[75]

But God! there I go on talking like a book again, and you a poor invalid who ought to be consoled. Seriously though, I hope you'll be quite alright by the time you read this: I don't like to hear of your being in bed so often, especially as it affects your spirits so. However, cheer up, and whenever you are fed up with life, start writing: ink is the great cure for all human ills, as I have found out long ago.

I quite appreciate what you say about my father, to whom I wrote on Sunday: but after all he hasn't written to me, and as he had Warnie with him I thought he could 'thole'. Still you are quite right in what you say and I must be more regular in future.

I thought you would like De Quincy, and hope you will go on reading him: it is always nice to feel that one has got a new friend among the book world, isn't it? What an old miser you are though. I suppose I shall have to buy the Academy book myself now: and rest assured that you will never see one page of it. It is strange that 'Frankenstein' should be badly written: one would expect the wife of Shelley to be a woman of taste, wouldn't one?

---

74 *The Canterbury Tales*, 2797.
75 ibid., 2808.

As to my brother's talk about another 'E Lucevan le Stelle' I'm afraid the front must have turned the poor boy's brain: considering how I pined after your copy for over a year it wasn't very likely that I should have forgotten one if I had it. What put the idea into his head I can't think.

Have been to Leatherhead baths for a swim today and am terribly stiff, as I always am after the first bathe of the year. Sorry this is not much of a letter this week, old man, but it's after 11, and everyone is going to bed. This brings you the next instalment of Bleheris – criticise freely.

Yours,
Jack

TO ARTHUR GREEVES (LP V: 84–6):

[Gastons
6 June 1916]

My dear Arthur,

I was rather surprised to see the note paper of your last letter, and certainly wish that I could have been with you: I have some vague memories of the cliffs round there and of Dunluce Castle, and some memories which are not vague at all of the same coast a little further on at Castlerock, where we used to go in the old days. Don't you love a windy day at a place like that? Waves make one kind of music on rocks and another on sand, and I don't know which of the two I would rather have.

As to your remarks about my 'promise' to join you on some future holiday, I must call your attention to the fact that all I promised was not to contract any engagement with my Aunt that could stand in the way of it, always warning you that I might not go anywhere. However I hope to do so, and will certainly try my best.

By the way, in future, if possible, don't write your letter on so many different 'levels', so to speak: I keep them all on a pin now, and so far, all being written the same way up, I have been able to turn to any one I wanted, like a book: the latest one is a hard nut to crack. Always grumbling you see.

You may well ask 'when' my 'Tristan' is coming: I have asked the same question myself more than once, and it's beginning to be like those famous Columbia records the holydays before last. As to the binding, if it is what the girl in the shop told me, it will be boards with leather back, and those little triangular pieces of leather on the corners. I don't know if you understand this description, so I have drawn it for you: though perhaps indeed you find the picture quite as hard. In other words it is a glorified edition of the 2/- Everyman. The reason I'm not quite certain is that the girl showed me a much larger book done in the same style, only red. As I didn't care for the colour, she said she thought it could be done like that in brown; so I'm still waiting the result.

With my last parcel – the Canterbury Tales – I got Macmillan's and Dent's catalogues, where I find much of interest: I suppose you know it all already however. For instance I never knew before that Macmillans would send you – through a bookseller – books on approval. Of course when things are so out of joint as you're only allowed to keep them for a week, perhaps you could hardly manage it over in Ireland. Being so near town myself, I think I shall try it, wouldn't you? I also notice that Dents have a series of 'Classiques Francaises' corresponding to the English Everymans Library. Does that mean that they'd be bound the same way? Among them I'm very pleased to find a rendering of the 'Chanson de Roland' into modern French:[76] this, as you probably know, is the old French epic, equivalent to our Beowulf,[77] and for years I have been wondering how to get it. Now, as things sometimes do, it just turns up. Of course talking about Beowulf reminds me again what hundreds of things there still are to buy: if you remember it has been 'the next book I'll get' ever since you have known me.

I know very well what you mean by books getting tiresome half way through, but don't think it always happens: for instance 'Phantastes', 'Jane Eyre', 'Shirley' (which in fact only begins to get interesting about then) might be cited – good word that – as examples. Tell me more about 'John Silence'[78] when you write, and also let me know the publisher and price, as I have forgotten again and may want it one of these days.

I don't like the way you say 'don't tell anyone' that you thought 'Frankenstein' badly written, and at once draw in your critical horns with the 'of course I'm no judge' theory. Rot! You are a very good judge

---

76 *La Chanson de Roland*, Traduction Nouvelle D'Après les Textes Originaux [1911].
77 *Beowulf*, a poem in Old English generally dated to the eighth century and surviving in a 10th century manuscript. It tells the story of the Geatish hero, Beowulf, and is the most important poem in Old English.
78 Algernon Blackwood, *John Silence: Physician Extraordinary* (1908).

for me because our tastes run in the same direction. And you ought to rely more on yourself than on anyone else in matters of books – that is if you're out for enjoyment and not for improvement or any nonsense of that sort. Which reminds me, I came on a phrase in Maeterlinck the other day which just suits my views about youth and silly scientific learning. 'L'ignorance lumineuse de la jeunesse',[79] the luminous ignorance of youth is exactly our strong point, isn't it?

Great God, how I must be boring you! But you ought to know by now that your friend Chubs with a pen in his hand is a very dangerous object: that extemporising goes a bit far at times: though seriously, to harp back to the eternal subject of self – I think Bleheris has killed my muse – always rather a sickly child. At any rate my verse, both in quality and in quantity for the last three weeks is deplorable!! Before you get any further in the aforesaid romance, let me hasten to warn you that when I said [of] the first chapter, that Bleheris was like you, I hadn't really thought of what I should make him. However I take that back, so that in future when my poor hero does anything mean you won't think I am covertly preaching at you.

In odd moments last week I read an excellent novel by – you'd never guess – Bernard Shaw. It is called 'Love among the Artists', and is published in Constable's shilling series.[80] I want you to get it: there are one or two extraordinary characters in it, and I think the whole gist of the thing, all about music, art etc. would appeal to you very strongly. Tell me if you do. I wonder what the good author who takes his own works so seriously would think if he knew that he was read for pleasure to fill up the odd moments of a schoolboy. If you do get the book, don't forget to read the preface which is very amusing.

I can't understand why you are willing to let me see your tale in the holydays, but are unwilling to send it by post. I refuse point blank to read it in your presence: that means that you spend your time thinking of what the other person is thinking and have no attention left to give to the work itself. So you may as well send it along.

Since I last wrote to you I have found the thought of a book done and yet not done intolerable, and therefore gone back and finished 'Rob Roy'.

---

79 The phrase is from Maurice Maeterlinck's 'L'Intelligence des Fleurs', which Lewis found in his *Morceaux Choisis*, with an Introduction by Georgette Leblanc (Paris, 1911), p. 181.

80 George Bernard Shaw, *Love Among the Artists*, Constable's 1/- Series (1914).

I am very glad I did so, as otherwise I should have missed the very vigorous scene in the library, and the equally satisfactory death of Rashleigh.

I have written from 10 to quarter past 11 and the others are going up; so good night my Galahad,

from yours,

Jack

TO ARTHUR GREEVES (LP V: 89–90):

[Gastons
14 June 1916]

My dear Arthur,

I must begin by apologizing for being a day late this week: I suppose by this time you have worked up quite a flourishing grievance. However, you will be glad to know that there is a genuine excuse this time – not just laziness. The reason is that there were visitors here last night, and tho I don't usually turn up on these occasions, I was so warmly urged 'just to come into the drawing room for a minute or two when I had finished my work' that I really couldn't refuse. So the hour between 10 and 11 which on Tuesday nights is usually taken up with your letter was lost.

The reason why Mrs K. pressed me was that the visitors were some neighbours of ours and with them a girl who is staying with them – that's an elegantly arranged sentence for a literary man – who has a voice and is being trained for opera. Well I am certainly glad I didn't miss it, as she has a very fine contralto and sang two good songs – your record from 'Orfeo'[81] and a very queer thing of Debussy's which I would like to hear again. Of course with that exception she sang rubbish, as the fools asked for it: horrible old ballads like 'Annie Laurie' etc. Still it was worth sitting talking about the war and wasting my time even for two good things. Why are singers always so plain I wonder?

I can't help smiling at the thought of your sitting in the garden on Sunday morning, as we have had nothing but thunderstorms for the last week and it has just now turned so cold that we've gone back to fires. There, I'm talking about the weather! By the way I don't know if you ever noticed how topping it is to see a fire again suddenly in the middle of June: it is so homely and cozy and is like having a bit of the good old Winter back again.

---

81 *L'Orfeo*, an opera by Luigi Rossi, was first performed in 1647.

The remark about the cows with which you credit me really comes from your newly made friend De Quincy. I think it is just before the description of the flood – the 'Bore' as he calls it. Look it up and see if I'm right.[82] Anyway I quite agree with it: but perhaps even nicer is a humorous looking old horse, living contentedly in a field by himself, it's those little things that keep one from being lonely on a walk – there is one horse here that I have got to know quite well by giving him sugar. Perhaps he may save me from a witch some day or lead me home in a fog?

You will be amused to hear that my 'Tristen' has not YET come: that is nearly three weeks now, and I am beginning to get angry. You ask at what shop it's being done: well you see it's being worked indirectly through the village stationer here who will send books to be bound for you in London, I don't know where. The reason for its taking so long, I imagine is that the wretch really waits until he has several to do and then makes one parcel of them so as to save himself the postage. In any case I shall not give him another opportunity, as there are people in the neighbouring town of Leatherhead who bind books themselves.

I am glad you like 'John Silence' and must get it too. I have now read all the tales of Chaucer which I ever expected to read, and feel that I may consider the book as finished: some of them are quite impossible. On the whole, with one or two splendid exceptions such as the Knight's and the Franklin's tales, he is disappointing when you get to know him. He has most of the faults of the Middle Ages – garrulity and coarseness – without their romantic charm which we find in the 'Green Knight' or in Malory. Still, I only really expected to enjoy some of the Tales, and feel that the book was worth getting for their sake. I am not sure whether you would like him or not, but you should certainly not start poetry with him.

Which reminds me, have you ever carried out your plans of reading 'Jason'?[83] I am wondering what I ought to get next, or whether I ought to save money and read some of the Gastons books – perhaps finish the Brontes or take up another Scott. I have found that Sidney's romance the 'Arcadia'[84] is published at 4/6 by the Cambridge University Press (what

---

82 The passage occurs in the 'Introductory Narration' of Thomas De Quincey's *Confessions of an English Opium Eater* (enlarged edition, 1856).

83 William Morris, *The Life and Death of Jason* (1867).

84 Sir Philip Sidney, *The Countesse of Pembrokes Arcadia* (1590).

are they like?) and am strongly tempted to get it. One thing that interests me is that Sidney wrote it for his sister, the Countess of Pembroke, sending it to her chapter by chapter as he wrote it as I send you 'Bleheris'. Perhaps we were those two in a former state of existence – and that is why your handwriting is so like a girl's. Though even my self conceit will hardly go as far as to compare myself with Sidney.

What a queer compound you are. You talk about your shyness and won't send me the MS of 'Alice', yet say that you are willing to read it to me – as if reading your own work aloud wasn't far more of an ordeal. By the way I hope that you are either going on with 'Alice' or starting something else: you have plenty of imagination, and what you want is practice, practice, practice. It doesn't matter what we write (at least this is my view) at our age, so long as we write continually as well as we can. I feel that every time I write a page either of prose or of verse, with real effort, even if it's thrown into the fire next minute, I am so much further on. And you too who have been so disappointed at the technical difficulties of composing, won't you find it a relief to turn to writing where you can splash about, so to speak, as you like, and gradually get better and better by experience? Or in other words, I shall expect an MS of some sort with your next week's letter: if I don't get it, I may have recourse to serious measures.

I like the way you say 'why don't' I 'take' a day in town! As if I could just stroll down one morning and say that I wasn't going to do any work today: no Galahad, that sort of thing may do in Franklin Street, but where people WORK – note that word, you may not have met it before – it can't be did.

I am being fearfully lacerated at present: thinking that Pindar is a difficult author whom we haven't time to read properly, Kirk has made me get it in the Loeb library – nice little books that have the translation as well as the text.[85] I have now the pleasure of seeing a pretty, 5/- volume ruined by a reader who bends the boards back and won't wash his filthy hands: while, without being rude, I can't do anything to save it. Of course it is a very little thing I suppose, but I must say it makes me quite sick whenever I think of it.

In case you despair of ever getting rid of the 'City of the Nesses', I promise you that in the next chapter after this one Bleheris actually does

---

85 *The Odes of Pindar, including the Principal Fragments*, with an introduction and an English translation by Sir John Edwin Sandys, Loeb Classical Library (1915).

get away. Don't forget the MS when you write, and tell me everything about yourself. Isn't this writing damnable?

Yours,

Jack

The time had come for Lewis to apply to an Oxford college, and it was to this end that Mr Kirkpatrick had been preparing him. Seventeen colleges then made up the University of Oxford, and the question before Lewis was which to apply for. The practice at the time was to list at least three on the entry form, stating one's order of preference. The 'big group' of colleges mentioned in the following letter to his father included New College, Corpus Christi, Christ Church, Oriel, Trinity and Wadham, and of these New College became Lewis's first choice. Before being accepted by a college, Jack had to sit a scholarship examination in the subject he wished to read, Literae Humaniores, or Classics, to be given in December 1917. If accepted by an Oxford college, this would not make him a member of Oxford University. For that he would need to pass Responsions, the entrance examination administered by the University. Meanwhile, in preparation for the scholarship examination, Mr Kirkpatrick obtained some of the examination questions used in previous years so that he and Jack would have a better idea of how to prepare.

TO ARTHUR GREEVES (LP V: 93–5):

[Gastons
20 June 1916]

My dear Arthur,

I do wish you would be serious about 'Alice': whatever else is a matter for joking, work – in this particular sense of the word – certainly is not. I do really want to see something of yours, and you must know that it is impossible to write one's best if nobody else ever has a look at the result.

However, I told you I would proceed to serious measures, so here is my manifesto. I, Clive Staples Lewis, student, do hereby give notice that unless some literary composition of Arthur Greeves be in my possession on or before midnight on the last night of June in the year nineteen hundred and sixteen, I shall discontinue from that date forward, all communication to the said Arthur Greeves of every kind, manner, and description whatsoever, until such composition or compositions be forwarded. 'So there' as the children say. Now let us go on.

'Oh rage, Oh desespoir'! Alas I am undone. All men are liars. Never, never get a book bound. You will gather from this that 'Tristan' has arrived and is a complete and absolute failure. When I told them to bind it in brown leather, with corner pieces etc., I imagined that it would look something like Kelsie's Dickens or like a 2/- Everyman. Wouldn't you have thought so? Well as a matter of fact, though in a sense they have done what I told them, yet the total effect, instead of being booky and library like, is somehow exactly like a bank book or a ledger. For one thing the leather – though I must say excellent in quality – is very dark and commercial looking, and the cloth between the back and triangular bits is the absolute abomination of desolation. As if this wasn't enough – the edges of the paper were before nice, and artistically rough. Well what do you think the brutes have done? They have smoothed them down and coloured them a horrible speckled red colour, such as you see in account books. You can imagine my absolute fury.

True, it is some consolation to find the book itself good beyond what I had expected: it gets the romantic note (which the French don't usually understand) very well indeed. One or two little descriptions are full of atmosphere. In particular, what could be better for Lyonesse – glorious name – as we imagine it, than this simple sentence: 'Climbing to the top of the cliff he saw a land full of vallies where forest stretched itself without end.' I don't know whether you will agree with me, but that gives me a perfect impression of loneliness and mystery. Besides its other good points, it is very, very simple French, so that if you think of starting to read that language this would make a very good beginning.

I am sorry to hear about the 'Beowulf', and if it is at all like what I imagine, surprised as well. Of course you were always less patient of the old fashioned things than I, and perhaps it is not a good translation. However (seriously) I may buy it from you at a reasonable price, if I like the look of it, just to match my 'Gawaine' – that is unless I get Morris's 'Beowulf'[86] instead, which is rather too dear at 5/-.

Your remarks about music would seem to lead back to my old idea about a face being always a true index of character: for in that case, if you imagined from the music of the soul either of Gordon or of this

---

86 *Beowulf,* translated by William Morris and A.J. Wyatt (1892).

mysterious 'fille aux cheveux de lin'[87] one would be bound to imagine the face too – not of course exactly, but its general tone. What type of person is this girl of whom Debussy has been talking to you? As to your other suggestions about old composers like Schubert or Beethoven, I imagine that, while modern music expresses both feeling, thought and imagination, they expressed pure feeling. And you know all day sitting at work, eating, walking etc., you have hundreds of feelings that can't (as you say) be put into words or even into thought, but which would naturally come out in music. And that is why I think that in a sense music is the highest of the arts, because it really begins where the others leave off. Painting can only express visible beauty, poetry can only express feeling that can be analysed – conscious feeling in fact: but music – however if I let myself go on such a fruitful subject I should take up the rest of this letter, whereas I have other things to tell you.

What is nicer than to get a book – doubtful both about reading matter and edition, and then to find both are topping? By way of balancing my disappointment in 'Tristan' I have just had this pleasure in Sidney's 'Arcadia'. Oh Arthur, you simply must get it – though indeed I have so often disappointed you that I oughtn't to advise. Still, when you see the book yourself, you will be green with envy. To begin with, it is exactly the sort of edition you describe in your last letter – strong, plain, scholarly looking and delightfully – what shall I say – solid: that word doesn't really do, but I mean it is the exact opposite of the 'little book' type we're beginning to get tired of. The paper is beautiful, and the type also.

The book itself is a glorious feast: I don't know how to explain its particular charm, because it is not at all like anything I ever read before: and yet in places like all of them. Sometimes it is like Malory, often like Spenser, and yet different from either. For one thing, there is a fine description of scenery in it (only one so far, but I hope for more) which neither of them could have done. Then again the figure of the shepherd boy, 'piping as though he would never be old'[88] rather reminds me of the 'Crock of Gold'.[89] But all this comes to is that Sidney is not like anyone else, but is just himself. The story is much more connected than Malory: there is a great deal of love making, and just enough 'brasting and

---

87 'Flaxen-haired girl'. Lewis was thinking of the prelude by Claude Debussy, 'La Fille aux cheveux de lin'.

88 Sidney, *Arcadia*, Bk. I, ch. 2.

89 James Stephens, *The Crock of Gold* (1912).

fighting' to give a sort of impression of all the old doings of chivalry in the background without becoming tedious: there is a definite set of characters all the time instead of a huge drifting mass, and some of them really alive. Comic relief is supplied by the fussy old king of Arcadia – rather like Mr Woodhouse in Emma – and his boor, Dametas. The only real fault is that all the people talk too much and with a tendency to rhetoric, and the author insists on making bad puns from time to time, such as 'Alas, that that word last should so long last'.[90] But these are only small things: true, there is a good deal of poetry scattered through it which is all detestable, but then that has nothing to do with the story and can be skipped. I'm afraid this description won't help much, but I am just longing for Saturday when I can plunge into it again. (I mean the book, not the description.)

So much have I chattered that I have hardly any more room left. No, I have never yet read any of Christina Rosetti's poems, though, as you have heard me say, I love her brother Gabriel Rosetti. I believe she is very good, and a faery picture illustrating the 'Goblin market'[91] which I saw in the Academy attracted me very much. That is certainly a lovely edition of Lily's, though of course not worth [getting], unless somebody presented it to you. A nice sentiment truly! But you understand.

I see that I have scribbled a note about illustrations on this week's instalment (of course each is written a fortnight before you get it). Well do have a try: or rather that is a patronizing thing to say: I mean, do exert yourself. I am afraid my poor description won't inspire you much. I wonder do you really know what Cloudy Pass[92] looks like?

Well, they're going to bed now. It is eleven o'clock so I suppose you yourself are already in that happy place. Don't forget my manifesto.

Yours,

Jack

---

90 Sidney, *Arcadia*, Bk. I, ch. 1.
91 The picture was by Hilda Hechle.
92 In his story *The Quest of Bleheris*.

TO HIS FATHER (LP V: 86-7):

[Gastons
23 June 1916]

My dear Papy,

There is certainly something mysterious about the 'machinations of the Knock', as one might put it in the title of a novel; because, though I had not thought of it before, his success with Warnie is an unanswerable point against him. As to the Smythe business, however, I understand that mathematics were taught by him at some school in Manchester to which he went every day. But still, we are not flying so high as Woolwich. Tell me what Kirk says in answer to your letter. I do not think that there is anyone at Malvern whose advice I should prefer to Kirk's on the question of Oxford: unless indeed I were to amuse myself by writing to Smugy and asking in an off-hand way whether it was Oxford or Cambridge he was at!

No; to be serious, I think we must rely chiefly on K. and on our own judgement. There is of course a considerable temptation to risk it and try for a Balliol: it was Balliol we always thought of, before we knew as much as we do now, and I must admit there is still a glamour about the name. On the other hand, Dodds says in his letter that the prestige of Balliol is on the decline, and quotes as Colleges in the big group, New, Corpus, Christ Church, Oriel, Trinity, and Wadham. Of course these are all merely names to us both, but the first three and Trinity are generally admitted to be in the first rank, while Dodds speaks with particular admiration of New, and Kirk assures me that now-a-days Christ Church is little if at all inferior to Balliol in scholarship. Bearing all this in mind I am afraid we should hardly be well advised in following,

'The desire of the moth for the star'[93]

when the star in this case is so perilous, and perhaps after all does not differ from another in glory so much as we have been led to expect. A further point to remember is that New College – of which Kirk has got a prospectus – substitutes for verse a paper of French and German translation instead of prose; which of course is far better from our point of view.

---

93 Percy Bysshe Shelley, 'To—: One word is too often profaned' (1824).

If then we decide to enter the big group, as I think we must, it remains to consider in what order we shall put down our Colleges. I should suggest Christ Church first, as undoubtedly the biggest name of the six, and after it perhaps New: and then the others in any order, keeping Wadham to the last.

It is a great relief to hear your news about the exact terms of the Military Service Act, as in this case I ought to be able to get a commission of some sort at home, or even a nomination from Oxford. At any rate, since there is no hurry – detestable expression, but let it pass – we can leave the matter to be discussed at ease in the seclusion of Leeborough.

If you have had even two hot days at home, you need not complain of the weather. We have had,

> 'Clouds instead an ever during dark'[94]

continual rain, and such bitter cold that on one or two evenings we have been obliged to light the fire: I believe it is just as bad all over England.

I am at present enjoying a new literary find in the shape of Sir Philip Sidney's 'Arcadia', which I got at a venture and found better than I expected: though like De Quincy's and Southey's epics, 'I expect that I enjoy the priveledge of being the sole reader of this work'. Talking about books, I hope you noticed the leader in this week's Literary Supplement – on Edgar Allen Poe?[95] I never heard such affectation and preciosity; the man who thinks the 'Raven' tawdry just because it is easily appreciated, and says that in 'The choice of words Poe has touched greater heights than De Quincy' ought – well, what can we say of him?

I am sorry to hear what you say about Cousin Quartus:[96] he seemed to be as brave and cheerful as usual last holydays.

By the way I have had to expend 6/6 on a Pindar and a Lucan which K. wanted me to get from London, thinking that Mullan's would be too slow. If a kind parent would like to refund – !

your loving son,

Jack

---

94 Milton, *Paradise Lost*, III, 45: 'But cloud instead and ever-during dark'.

95 *The Times Literary Supplement* (22 June 1916), pp. 1–2.

96 This was Sir William Quartus Ewart (1844–1919) of Glenmachan House. See **The Ewart Family** in the Biographical Appendix.

TO ARTHUR GREEVES (LP V: 97–8):

[Gastons
28 June 1916]

My dear Arthur,

For some reason your letter didn't reach me until this morning (Wednesday) so I am afraid that this will be a day late. I have been longing to get to my answer all day: and now that the time is come I hardly know how to collect my thoughts – they have been buzzing so in my head ever since breakfast.

First, ten thousand thanks for the enclosure. You know that I never flatter my friends – in fact my faults are in the other direction: so you may accept as a truth how this first sample of your work has knocked me all of a heap. Really, Galahad, I had no idea you could do anything like this: it is splendid. The only fault I have to find is that there is not enough of it. The idea of all the things round the river being in love with your hero – and I suppose the river too – showing their affection – is beautifully suggestive: I am longing to see it worked out – for by the way, on no account must you think of giving up after so happy a beginning. What I like particularly is the way which – according to the advice of friend Horace – you get straight into the middle of your theme right away, without any such dull descriptions as open Bleheris. The whole description of the river, etc., is done (in my poor opinion) with great skill: it sort of carries you away from the world into a dim, summery dream in some landscape more lovely than reality. Isn't the very word 'punt' very descriptive of summer and cool green reaches?

And now I am going to be so bold as to make a few suggestions: not that I think I am better 'up' in such things than you, but because it is good for both parties to be criticised, and I wish you would do the same to me. Well then, I don't know if it be true with other people, but in my own case, I have always found that if you are in at all good form when you write, corrections made afterwards are usually for the worse. Certainly most of yours are not improvements: for instance in several cases you have changed the word 'that' to which, as

> *that) happened long ago.*
> *which)*

Of course it is a small point, but don't you think 'that' is more simple, natural, and dignified than 'which'? The latter is indeed rather business like. Nor do I see why 'extremely old' should be written over the plain 'very old'. The second point is this: does your own judgement approve the sentence, 'shook her silvery sheen'? The alliteration, I think, would be a bit daring even in verse, and I am sure cannot be allowed in prose.

Now, I suppose you think me meddlesome and impudent. Well, though perhaps I am given to finding spots in the sun, I still appreciate its brightness: I repeat, though my opinion of you as a friend could not be higher than it was, my opinion of you as an author has risen by leaps and bounds since this morning. You MUST go on with this exquisite tale: you have it in you, and only laziness – yes, Sir, laziness – can keep you from doing something good, really good. By the way, before we go any further, I must say in fairness, that when you find those roses playing a more prominent part in the life of my Bleheris, it is not cribbed from your willow tree! I had thought out my plot – what there is of it – before I left home.

I am very glad to hear that you have bought C. Rossetti's poems: partly because I want to be able to look at it myself in the comfort of your sofa – mind the springs – and also I am glad you are beginning to read poetry. Which reminds me, a propos of your tale, you should read the bit in Morris's 'Jason' about Hylas and the water nymphs. I think it is in Book II – at any rate you can see from the headings – and it would not take you more than half an hour. As to the illustrated edition of his early poems, I believe we once saw it together in Mullen's, but so far as I remember, weren't greatly impressed; or am I thinking of something else? You don't tell me what you are actually reading at present, for you can't be living entirely on lyrics: have you finished 'John Silence' yet, and what is your final verdict on it?

In the mean time the 'Arcadia' continues beautiful: in fact it gets better and better. There has been one part that Charlotte Bronte could not have bettered: where Philoclea the heroine, or rather one of the heroines, is beginning to fall in love unconsciously with a man disguised as a girl: and she does not know the secret: the delicacy and pathos of her wrestlings with a feeling which of course she can't understand, as told by Sidney are – well I can't explain what they are like: there is one scene where she goes out by moonlight to an old grove, an haunted place, where there is an altar to 'the wood gods of old',[97] and lies looking up at the stars and puzzling about things, that is equal to if not better than the scene where Jane Eyre wakes up on the moor – do you remember? On the other hand, of course there are parts YOU might not have patience with: in the old style, where people relate their own adventures with no direct bearing on the main story: yet even this, to me, is interesting – so quaint and so suggestive of the old romantic world.

Besides this, I have read nothing lately, except a foolish modern novel which I read at one sitting – or rather one lying on the sofa, this afternoon in the middle of a terrible thunderstorm. I think, that if modern novels are to be read at all, they should be taken like this, at one gulp, and then thrown away – preferably into the fire (that is if they are not in one's own edition). Not that I despise them because they are modern, but really most of them are pretty sickly with their everlasting problems.

I am glad to hear that you have started illustrating my tale: your criticism about not making long conversations is a very sound one, though I fear I can't keep up to it. For instance, after this chapter the next two are, I am afraid, taken up with a conversation between Bleheris and the people he meets at an inn. Still, as it is necessary to what follows, you must try and get through it. This chapter is a failure: I particularly wanted to show what sort of a person he is and how he develops, but have only made him ridiculous.

I am interested in what you tell me of the Bronte country. Fancy a real living original of Heathcliffe?[98] What must he have been like.

Now it is time for bed, so good night mon vieux, and don't forget another instalment in your next letter.

Yours,
Jack

TO HIS FATHER (LP V: 91–2):

[Gastons
30? June 1916]

My dear Papy,

I can't understand why Kirk has not answered your letter. He never mentioned it to me, and until I heard from you I did not know that you

---

97 Sidney, *Arcadia*, Bk. II, ch. 4.
98 Heathcliff is the central figure in Emily Brontë's *Wuthering Heights*.

had written: perhaps it has gone astray – like your subscription to the chocolate fund!

At any rate, after reading what you said, I asked him whether a modern language could be substituted as you suggest: he replied that he thought this was so, but pointed out that of course this did not include mathematics, and that the latter would consist of a good deal of graphical work and other things which he – though goodness only knows why – does not feel fit to teach. If the worst comes to the worst, I suppose I could grind mathematics in the holidays: but all things considered I think we should look on the Sandhurst scheme as a "pis aller"[99] if it be found impossible to get a commission by influence or any other way.

You see the difficulties of entrance, though not insurmountable, are still serious, and it is well to remember that, as Harding told us, if I get a permanent commission, it may not be easy to leave the army immediately after the war. Do you think we could manage to work the business through our political friends? Kirk assures me that even now this is not difficult, and if it could be done, it would certainly be far the best plan. Failing this, I should suggest some volunteer institution from Ulster if any of these are still in existence.

Since we last wrote, I have been in communication with Oxford: missives have been elicited from Balliol, and I was glad to hear that if you go in for a scholarship, you are not expected to matriculate as well. It is rather a question however whether Balliol should be our mark: in order to prevent it getting the pick of the candidates, there is an arrangement by which Balliol and one or two insignificant colleges stand in a group by themselves outside the 'big group' which, like 'Pooh-Bah'[100] comprises 'everything else' worth talking about. Now in each of these two groups you put down the Colleges in the order you wish, and are put into one of them according to your place in the exam. You are of course 'stuck' in the group for which you enter. Under these circumstances, unless you are absolutely sure of success, it might be better to leave Balliol alone, seeing that if I miss it I have only a very few fall-backs, and those not of the first water. Tell me what you think? At any rate it is one comfort that Kirk's talk about matriculation was all moonshine: the scholarship exams take place in December. What between Oxford and the Army I am beginning to think that we would be better advised to sell all we have, take a cottage

---

99 'The thing to do if the worst happens.'
100 A character ('Lord High Everything Else') in Gilbert and Sullivan's *The Mikado*.

in Donegal, and cultivate potatoes for the good of the nation. Still, I suppose we really have very little to grumble at.

If it is not strange to say so, I am glad to hear that Dick is safely wounded:[101] it is by far the best thing that can happen to a man in the trenches, and the really unlucky ones are those who 'bear the labour and heat of the day'[102] unhurt for over a year – always it would seem in the long run to be killed after returning from a leave.

Things look pretty black at present, don't they? The North Sea battle, though perhaps not so bad as we thought at first, is certainly a very serious business, and our attitude towards the 'rats' was rather that of friend Tim than of the sportsman 'digging them out'. What exactly will the loss of Kitchener mean?[103] 'De mortuis...'[104] now of course, and for my own part I never approved of arm chair criticism.

How noble of poor Bob to give up his sister to the war!

Your loving

son Jack

As we have seen, for some time now letters had been passing between father and son, and father and Mr Kirkpatrick, regarding Jack's future. All were agreed that he should try for a place at Oxford, and Jack was due to sit for a scholarship examination there on 5 December. However, with one son already in the army, and the war growing worse every day, Albert Lewis was very anxious to keep Jack out of the service. According to the Military Service Act 'every male British subject who had attained the age of eighteen and ordinarily resident in Great Britain' was liable for enlistment in the army. On the other hand, the exemption mentioned at the beginning of this chapter – that of a man resident in Great Britain 'for the purposes of his

---

101 'Dick' who had been 'safely wounded' in France is Richard Lewis (1890–), eldest son of Joseph Lewis (1856–1908), and thus Albert's nephew. He joined the Sports Battalion in 1914 and finished the war as a company sergeant major, with a Distinguished Conduct Medal.

102 Matthew 20:12: 'These last have wrought but one hour, and thou has made them equal unto us, which have borne the burden and heat of the day.'

103 Lord Kitchener, Secretary of State for War, was in the British cruiser, the *Hampshire*, on the way to Russia when on 5 June it was sunk by a German submarine. Kitchener was killed.

104 The phrase 'De mortuis nil nisi bonum' ('Speak not evil of the dead') is originally a Greek expression ascribed to Chilon, a Spartan ephor of the sixth century BC. It is not known who first translated the original Greek into the proverbial Latin that we have.

education only' was now in effect. Jack was Irish, and the exemption applied to him. But contrary to his father's wishes, Jack insisted that he would not apply for the exemption, and he was determined not to be talked out of it by either father or tutor.

TO ARTHUR GREEVES (LP V: 103–5):

[Gastons
4 July 1916]

My dear Arthur,

So you feel hurt that I should think you worth talking to only about books, music, etc.: in other words that I keep my friendship with you only for the highest plane of life: that I leave to others all the sordid and uninteresting worries about so-called practical life, and share with you those joys and experiences which make that life desirable: that – but now I am getting rhetorical. It must be the influence of dear Sidney and his euphuism I suppose. But seriously, what can you have been thinking about when you said 'only' books, music, etc., just as if these weren't the real things!

However, if I had thought for a moment that it would interest you, of course you are perfectly welcome to a full knowledge of my plans – such as they are. Indeed I imagined that you had a pretty clear idea about them: well, 'let us go forward', to quote from a certain romance: being Irish, I hear from my father that the fact of my being educated in England will not bring me under the new act. I am therefore going to remain as I am until December when my Oxford exam comes off. After that, I shall of course join the army: but in what exact way, I don't at present know any more than you do. So there you have the whole yarn.

I may just remark in passing that you should by this time know better than to waste pity on your friend Chubs for 'worrying' about it: did you ever see him worrying about anything? I have learnt by now that whatever plans you make in this world, everything always turns out quite differently, so what is the use of bothering? To be honest, the question has hardly crossed my mind once this term. Now I don't mind in the least telling you all this, and if you wanted to know I don't see why you never asked before. But then I am a coarse-grained creature who never could follow the feelings of refined – might I say super-refined? – natures like my Galahad's.

The annoying part is that you have taken up your letter (and here am I taking up mine!!) with this, to the exclusion of all sorts of interesting things that I wanted to hear: for instance, you must tell me more about Hardy. We have all heard of him till we are sick of it, and so I should like to hear the opinion of someone I know. What sort of a novel is it? Would I like it?

But of course the first thing I looked for in this evening's letter was to see if there was an instalment there. I have now read it over again with last week's to get the continuous narrative, and with the same pleasure. Did you quite realise what a splendid touch it was for Dennis to hope 'nobody would steal his clothes'? Somehow the practical, commonsense realism of that, increases the fairy-like effect of what follows enormously. I don't know if I can explain it, but it sort of brings the thing just enough in touch with reality to make it convincing, without spoiling its dreaminess. Also the idea of his seeing her face not directly, but in the water, is somehow very romantic. By the way, I hope you don't really think that I hinted for a moment that your willow was borrowed from my roses: how could you know what my roses were going to do about five chapters ahead? Above all, don't change anything in the plan of your tale on that account. Perhaps, as you say, we both took it unconsciously from 'Phantastes', who in his turn borrowed it from the dryads, etc. of classical mythology, who are a development of the primitive savage idea that everything has a spirit (just as your precious Jehovah is an old Hebrew thunder spirit): so we needn't be ashamed of borrowing our trees, since they are really common property.

Your reply to my criticism is typically Galahadian: but though in your case I am sure it is more sincere than it looks, still this excessive modesty is rather absurd. You may be dissatisfied with it (though I don't see why), you may be uncertain of yourself, but still in your heart of hearts you don't think of 'The Water Sprite' as 'that rubbish of mine', now do you?

Do you know what your tale has done? It has made me sorry that I began Bleheris in the old style: I see now that though it is harder to work some effects in modern English, yet on the whole my way of writing is a sort of jargon: however, we must do the best we can. I was very glad to hear that you liked the Sunken Wood, especially as the next two chapters are stodgy conversation. I am afraid Bleheris never gets into the wood: but you ought to know that the 'little, hobbling shadow' doesn't live more in that wood than anywhere else. It follows nervous children upstairs to bed, when they daren't look over their shoulders, and comes and sits on your grandfather's summer seat beside two friends when they have talked too much nonsense in the dark. I hope you have an illustration ready for this chapter?

I am still at the 'Arcadia', which you will gather from this is a long book, though not a bit too long. I won't make you sick of it before you see it by starting to sing its praises again: I only promise you that I am still as keen on it as when I began. By the way, now that we are both writing, and know how much work there is in a short instalment that can be read in a few minutes, you begin to realize the labour of writing a thing say like the 'Morte D'Arthur'.

I gather from your silence that you are doing nothing in the gramophone way? Ask the Girlinosbornes whether my new record of 'Is not His word like a fire'[105] (ordered last holidays) has come yet or not. I hope it will be waiting for me when I get home: which event – do you realize – will happen in about a month. This term has gone terribly quickly and been very pleasant, but all the same I shall not be sorry to take up my other life again.

What new books are there of yours to see? I am longing to have a look at your De Quincey and 'Rossetti'. By the way, I suppose you never looked up the passage about the 'bore' nor the one in William Morris about Hylas and the nymphs? I have now finished my Tristan, which is really delightful: it is the saddest story on earth I think, don't you? I have written for the French Everyman translation of 'Roland' which ought to have come by now, but hasn't. I am interested to see what the binding is like, aren't you?

You will see by the scrawl that I am trying to write about a million miles an hour as everyone has gone to bed. So goodnight old man: send another instalment next week, I am so interested in your adorable fairy.

Yrs.,
Jack

P.S. By the way, one criticism just to keep you from getting your head turned. Don't talk about Dennis as 'our young friend' or 'our hero' – the last is like a newspaper: at least you may take it as a suggestion just for what it is worth. – J.

---

105 From Felix Mendelssohn's oratorio *Elijah*, first performed in 1846.

TO HIS FATHER (LP V: 102–3):

[Gastons
7 July 1916]

My dear Papy,

Your 'essay' and letter arrived, and Kirk read me a great part of the former. I think what you say about Christ Church is probably right, although Kirk tells me that there is most certainly a reading set, which one could live in. However, Dod[d]s specially recommends New, and as you say yourself, both it and Oriel are in the first rank. On the other hand, I am afraid that there will be no more 'Guards Regiments' anywhere by the time I reach Oxford: the old 'bloods' have mostly been shot, and the atmosphere of an after-war England will not be conductive to the birth of a new generation. Fortunately, there is no hurry about the question, and we can talk it over together in comfort next holidays.

Yes! It would be true irony if we ran upon something of the James or Capron type again; our little portrait gallery for that never-written novel is already getting crowded. By the way, what do you think of the new arrangement about Ulster? Kirk has talked about it for nearly a week: not that he has any views on either side, but he seems to find a pleasure in balancing off all the arguments for and against the proposal: so well has he succeeded that I am beginning to think 'That way lies madness.'[106] No sooner have we made up our minds on one side, than we are immediately floored by a new point that he brings up on the other. What do you think about it?

I must deprecate those very questionable references to my unfortunate last term's exodus from Gastons: if I saw that the goodwife of the house was, like Martha 'careful over many things,'[107] and then tactfully suggested that I might go home, what do you find extraordinary in such an action? At any rate, though we have our faults, we don't make ourselves ridiculous in an open carriage, nor lose our way in a country we have known from childhood. To be sensible, I suppose the term will end, as you say, at the end of July.

Many thanks for both your enclosures. The letter was from my old Malvern study companion Hardman: he is going to be conscripted at Christmas, and wants to know what I am going to do. I am writing to say

---

106 Shakespeare, *King Lear*, III, iii, 21: 'O! That way madness lies; let me shun that.'
107 Luke 10:41.

that I don't know yet, but will tell him as soon as our plans are settled. Of course if it turned out to be convenient, I should like to have a friend with me in the army, but it is hardly worth while making any special provisions for so small a matter. We shall see how it all works out.

Your reference to the two books is tantalizing. I quite agree with you that they should be put in a safe place: and the safest place in Leeborough is a certain 'little end room' where all the footsteps point one way. I for my part am still at my 'Arcadia' which I find excellent.

The weather here is ridiculous: wintry colds alternating with hot, close fogs, and an occasional thunder shower. I don't know what the farmers will do.

your loving
son Jack

TO ARTHUR GREEVES (LP V: 106–8):

[Gastons
11 July 1916]

My dear Arthur,

I am very glad to hear that you are getting to like Jason: I agree with you that the whole description of Medea – glorious character – going out by night, and of her sorceries in the wood is absolutely wonderful, and there are other bits later on, such as the description of the 'Winter by the Northern River' and the garden of the Hesperides, which I think quite as good. Curiously enough I have just started the 'Argonautica'[108] the Greek poem on the same subject, and though I haven't got very far – only in fact to the launching of Argo – it is shaping very well. It will be interesting to compare this version with Morris's, although indeed the story of the Golden Fleece is so perfect in itself that it really can't be spoiled in the telling. Don't you find the very names 'Argo' and 'Argonauts' somehow stirring?

I thought a person like you would sooner or later come to like poetry: by the way, of course you are quite right when you talk about thinking more of the matter than of the form. All I meant when I talked about the importance of form was to carry a little further what you already feel in prose – that is how some phrases such as the Wall of the World, or at the Back of the North Wind affect you, partly by sound partly by association,

---

108 Apollonius Rhodius (c. 295–215 BC), *Argonautica*.

more than the same meaning would if otherwise expressed. The only difference is that poetry makes use of that sort of feeling much more than prose and produces those effects by metre as well as by phrase. In fact, the metre and the magic of the words should be like the orchestration of a Wagnerian opera – should sort of fill the matter by expressing things that can't be directly told – that is, it expresses feeling while the matter expresses thought. But I daresay I have given you my views on the subject before. I am very flattered that you remember that old line about the 'garden where the west wind' all these months, and will certainly copy out anything that is worth it if you can find me a shop in dear Belfast where I can buy a decent MS book: I have failed in that endeavour so far.

So we are to be treated to more and more modesty? Indeed Arthur if I could get a little of your diffidence, and you a little of my conceit we should both be very fine fellows. This week's instalment is quite worthy of the other two, and I was quite disappointed when it broke off. The reeds 'frightened out of their senses' and shouting in 'their loudest whisper' are delightful. 'Our Lady of the Leaf' might be kept in mind as a possible title if you don't care for the present one.

You are rather naive in telling me that you 'have to sit for a minute thinking' and 'find the same word coming in again' as if these weren't the common experiences of everyone who has ever written. I haven't noticed any smallness in the vocabulary you employ for your tale, and anyway that's just a matter of practice. By the way, even if you didn't mean it, I hope you see now what I am driving at about the remark of Dennis as to his clothes. As to the 'sitting for ten minutes', I don't believe that good work is ever done in a hurry: even if one does write quickly in a burst of good form, it always has to be tamed down afterwards. I usually make up my instalment in my head on a walk because I find that my imagination only works when I am exercising.

Can you guess what I have been reading this week? Of all things in the world 'Pendennis'![109] Isn't this the one you find too much for you? I am nearly through the first volume and like it well so far: of course one gets rather sick of Pen's everlasting misbehaviour and the inevitable repentance going round and round like a mill wheel and there doesn't seem much connection between one episode and another. All the same, it has a sort of way with it.

---

109 William Makepeace Thackeray, *The History of Pendennis* (1849–50).

That feast the 'Arcadia' is nearly ended: in some ways the last book is the best (though a little spoiled I admit by brasting) and here the story is so like the part of Ivanhoe where they are all in Front-de-Boeuf's castle, that I think Scott must have borrowed it.[110] Your remarks about C. Rosetti's poems are very tantalizing and I am longing to see them. How I do love expensive books if only I could afford them. Apropos of which, do you know anything of the artist Beardesley?[111] I fancy he was the man who started the modern school of 'queer' illustrations and the like: well I see you can get for £1.5s. a 1 vol. edition of Malory with his illustrations, published by Dent. What do you think it would be like? I only wish it was Macmillan and so we could have it on approval.

You are quite wrong old man in saying I can draw 'when I like'. On the contrary, if I ever can draw, it is exactly when I don't like. If I sit down solemnly with the purpose of drawing, it is a sight to make me 'ridiculous to the pedestrian population of the etc.'. The only decent things I do are scribbled in the margins of my dictionary – like Shirley – or the backs of old envelopes, when I ought to be attending to something else.

I am quite as sorry as you that I can't see my way to working Bleheris back into the Sunken Wood, for I think the idea might be worked a bit more: but don't see how it is to be done without changing the whole plan of the story.

The immediate prospects of my getting married 'agreeably or otherwise' as you kindly suggest, are not very numerous: but if you are getting uneasy about an invitation, rest assured, when the event comes off, if you behave you shall have one.

It was strange that Mrs K. should get Hardy's 'Under the Greenwood Tree'[112] out of the library last week, though I never got a chance of looking into it: somehow I don't fancy Hardy is in my line, but then I always have a prejudice against people whom you're always hearing about.

You say nothing about music now-a-days, and I am afraid I scarcely think of it: it annoys me hugely to think of the whole world of pleasures that I used to have and can't enjoy now. Did you see a long article in the Times Literary Supplement[113] about the 'Magic Flute'[114] which is on at the

---

110 Sir Walter Scott, *Ivanhoe* (1819), ch. XXI.
111 Aubrey Vincent Beardsley (1872–98).
112 Thomas Hardy, *Under the Greenwood Tree* (1872).
113 'The Magic Flute' (unsigned), *The Times Literary Supplement* (29 June 1916), pp. 1–2.
114 Wolfgang Amadeus Mozart's opera *The Magic Flute* was first performed in 1791.

Shaftesbury? How I wish I could go up and hear it and also 'Tristan and Isolde'[115] – though if I did it would be a disappointment in all probability.

I am furious because in answer to my order for the 'Chanson de Roland' I am told it is out of print, which is very tiresome. Here I enclose another chapter, really all conversation this time, but can promise you a move next week. Don't forget your own instalment which I look forward to very eagerly. Good night.

Yours,

Jack

TO HIS FATHER (LP V: 105–6):

[Gastons
14? July 1916]

My dear Papy,

This must be nipped in the bud: there can be no question of that. Get your lady friend's visit over before the end of this month, at all costs, or else bid them avaunt till the winter.[116] What should I do, left alone all day to face a situation of that sort? As well, the whole thing is tyranny, extortion, infliction, profligacy and arrogance of the worst sort, and therefore not to be borne. Have they not already taken more than their fair share of reprisals for our own visit so long ago? This 'breakfast is a charming meal' business can be overdone: however, a man can but die once, so I suppose destiny must take its course.

This is big news from the front, though whether it will have any permanent effect or not, of course we can't say. The Ulster Division – what there are of them now – must have silenced the yapping politicians for ever.[117] I suppose the losses are felt very heavily in Belfast: here, nobody seems to have noticed anything.

Yes, that wheeze about 'pulled through' ought to 'supply a long felt want': it can be used on every occasion and ought to live for a very long time. I am sorry if any obscurity on my part gave rise to the 'savage emphasis,' but then his ordinary style of conversation is so – I think the

---

115 *Tristan and Isolde*, an opera by Richard Wagner, was first performed in 1865.

116 Albert's brother William, with his wife and daughter, were proposing a visit. See **The Lewis Family** in the Biographical Appendix.

117 Since the beginning of the war, the Ulster Volunteer Force had been gathering momentum, and they had now forced the War Department to accept them as an integral part of the British army.

word is 'nervous' in its 18th Century sense, that best describes it – that we must not pay too much attention to such things. I think, as you say, that things point to New, but of course we will keep an open mind in the meantime.

The literary event of the week is our respected laureate's ode in the Times Literary Supplement:[118] truly a most remarkable production, though I am afraid like the honest Major in 'Patience,' I must confess that 'it seems to me nonsense'.[119] To do the man justice, the lines about Homer, the ones about the birds, the beginning of the vision, and a few other passages, are rather fine. But the habit of throwing in an odd rhyme here and there is rather uncomfortable: still, if you can lay your hand upon it (the Pattersonian pun is quite a mistake, owing to haste, as it is getting late and the others are going up) you might keep this number.

I am at present in the middle of a book called 'Pendennis' which I should advise you to read unless I knew your prejudice against the author: however, one of these days you will come round and 'see my point.'

your loving,

son,

Jack

TO ARTHUR GREEVES (LP V: 111–13):

[Gastons]
Tuesday evening, the I
don't know whath,
[18] July /16.

My dear Arthur,

I can't understand why you should want to know the dates on which these gems of wit were written: if you should ever happen to look at them in the future, a date is a meaningless thing and it won't really help you to see a few numbers written on the top. For my part, when I read your old letters, I don't think about such nonsense. I classify them not by time but by the stage in our thoughts at which they were written:

---

118 He was referring to Robert Bridges' 'Ode on the Tercentenary Commemoration of Shakespeare', *The Times Literary Supplement* (6 July 1916), p. 319.
119 Gilbert and Sullivan, *Patience*, Act I. It is Patience who says: 'Well, it seems to me to be nonsense.'

I say 'Ah, that was when we were talking about Loki, this was when we talked much about music and little about books, we didn't know each other so well when this was written' and so on. Which is far more sensible than saying, 'This was September 1914, that was August 1915.' As well, the fact that everyone else puts a date on their letters is to me an excellent reason for not doing so. Still, if you are really concerned about it, I suppose I must 'bow myself in the house of Rimmon'.[120] Since I have gone so far as to put a date however, you can't be so unreasonable as to suggest that it should be the right one.

I am awfully bucked about 'Twelfth Night':[121] I thought at the time you remember, that Heath Robinson's illustrations were absolutely perfect – quite as good as Rackham's, though of course in a different style. If I remember aright there is a splendid one on the line 'How full of shapes is fancy'[122] and also some fine evening cloud effects – not to mention the jester in the rain and the delightfully 'old English' garden scenes.

I am longing, as you say, to be at home and to go over all our treasures both old and new: – so of course we shall be disappointed in some way. As you say, you are extravagant, but I too at present buy one book as soon as I have finished another.

The 'Arcadia' is finished: or rather I have read all there is of it, for unfortunately it breaks off at a most exciting passage in the middle of a sentence. I will not praise it again, beyond saying that this last 3rd. book, though it has no such fine love passages as the 2nd., yet (despite the brasting), for really tip-top narrative working the interest up and up as it goes along, is quite worthy of Scott.

This week's new purchase consisted of Milton's 'Paradise Lost' – in the same edition as my Mandeville[123] – and 'John Silence' in the 7d. edition. Just as one sometimes has a spell of being disappointed in new books, so at other times you keep on getting one treat after another. For the first few pages of John Silence I was hardly in the right mood: but after that it fairly swept me off my feet, so that on Saturday night I hardly dared to go upstairs. I left off – until next week end – in the middle of the 'Nemesis of Fire' – Oh, Arthur, aren't they priceless? Particularly the 'Ancient Sorceries' one, which I think I shall remember all my life. Oh, that evil

---

120 2 Kings 5:18.

121 *Shakespeare's Comedy of Twelfth Night*, with illustrations by W.H. Robinson [1908].

122 William Shakespeare, *Twelfth Night* (1601), I, i, 14.

123 *The Travels of Sir John Mandeville*, modernized and edited by A.W. Pollard (1900).

dance, and the 'muttering the old, old incantation'! The feeling of it all chimed with a lovely bit of 'Paradise Lost' which I read the same evening where it talked of the hounds that,

> '. . . *Follow the night hag, when, called*
> *In secret riding through the air she comes*
> *Lured with the smell of infant blood, to dance*
> *With Leopard witches, while the labouring moon*
> *Eclipses at their charms.*'[124]

Don't you like the Leopard witches? How you will love Milton some day! By the way we may remark in passing that John Silence is one of the nicest 7d's in paper and so forth that I have ever seen. I wonder how people would laugh if they could hear us smacking our lips over our 7d's and Everymans just as others gloat over rare folios and an Editio Princeps? But after all, we are surely right to get all the pleasure we can, and even in the cheapest books there is a difference between coarse and nice get up. I wonder what a book called 'Letters from Hell' published at 1/- by Macmillan would be like?'[125]

This week's instalment I enjoyed especially: the idea of the hair so beautiful to the eye so coarse to the touch is very suggestive, and you keep us in fine doubt as to whether your faery is going to turn out good and benevolent or terrible. You complain that your tale is commonplace, but I don't know anything that you think is like it, and I hope that you will really never think of giving it up unfinished – all the same, if you do – for which I can see no earthly reason – don't be discouraged, because we very rarely succeed in finishing a first work. If you saw the number of 'beginnings' I have made! By the by, there is one little point I must grouse at this week. You say that the faery resumed her 'normal' size. What was her normal size? We saw her first as a little figure on a leaf, and she hasn't changed since. Do you mean that she took on human size? Of

---

124 Milton, *Paradise Lost*, II, 662.

125 [Valdemar Adolph Thisted], *Letters from Hell*, Given in English by Julie Sutter, with a Preface by George MacDonald (Richard Bentley & Son 1885; reprinted by Macmillan, 1911). This curious book was first published in Denmark in 1866, and later translated into German. Julie Sutter's English translation of 1885 was made from the German version. Who knows? the book may have played some part, years later, in the genesis of Lewis's *Screwtape Letters* (1942).

course a few trifling changes when you revise will make this quite clear. The point of names is rather difficult: 'Dennis' I like, but the old Irish attractions of 'Desmond' are very strong. I really don't know what I should advise.

I am sorry you disapprove of my remarks in the romance. But you must remember that it is not Christianity itself I am sneering at, but Christianity as taught by a formal old priest like Ulfin, and accepted by a rather priggish young man like Bleheris.[126] Still, I fear you will like the main gist of the story even less when you grasp it – if you ever do, for as is proper in romance, the inner meaning is carefully hidden.

I am really very sorry to hear about your new record, but so many of your Odeons have been successful that I cannot reasonably have the pleasure of saying 'I told you so'. Talking about music, I have at last found out the exact number of the Chopin piece I like so well – it is the 21st Prelude. Look it out, and tell me if it is not the best music in the world?

I am afraid it is mere foolishness to praise that rhyme of mine as you do. Remember, you know exactly the occasion that gave rise to it, and can read between the lines, while to others it would perhaps be scarcely intelligible: still it is nice to be able to please even one reader – as you do too, for all your talk. In a way that sort of double-meaning in the title 'Lady of the Leaf' would be rather fascinating I think.

I am glad to hear your remarks about the different pleasures of painting, writing etc. I quite agree with you, 'work' of this kind, though it worries and tortures us, tho' we get sick of it and dissatisfied with it and angry, after all it is the greatest pleasure in life – there is nothing like it. Good night old man.

Jack

P.S. Is Dennis in bathing things all this time, or 'au naturel'? The point is not without interest.

---

126 The passage Arthur probably objected to occurs in Chapter V, where we are told that before Bleheris set out on his quest: 'He made his confession devoutly to father Ulfin, and was shriven of his sins, and took holy water in a little flask to bear with him for a defence, if he met any evil thing by the way. Poor boy!, that deemed in his folly that a priest's bauble, a dream-thing woven out of the hopes of man's self and then called "holy", might avail him aught against the great and terrible powers of the earth!'

P.P.S. Up in my room I have just read over the whole 'Watersprite' again. I have not done it justice in this letter, the whole story is topping and the air of mystery that hangs about Her makes one very keen to go on. I am not putting this in because I want to pleasure you, but because it just strikes me at the moment and must come out. Go on and prosper – there goes half past. So gute nacht du lieber kamarad, bon soir mon vieux.

J.

TO HIS FATHER (LP V: 114–15):

[Gastons]
21st July 1916.

My dear Papy,

I was just beginning to get up what I considered a very legitimate 'grouse', but must admit that you offer the best of reasons for the offence. I am glad that you enjoyed their visit,[127] and wish that I could have been one of the party: – at least so I may now say with safety when 'the tyranny is over past'.[128] Many thanks for your indulgent permission to take a Scotch trip – never fear, we'll keep your place in order.

Kirk tells me he has sent you a list of the Scholarships and Exhibitions at colleges in the big group, which we will be able to go over together in the holidays. It is cheering to see that we have some fifteen to come and go over, most of them in the first rank.

My fellow sojourner at Gastons is going home this day (Friday) week, so I think it would be best for me to choose the following Monday. I forget what state the cross-channel routes are in at present, but if Fleetwood is going I had sooner travel by it: failing that by Liverpool with Larne as a pis aller. So if you could book a stateroom for the 31st, and forward a few 'crowns for convoy' I shall do myself the honour of waiting on you at Leeborough on Tuesday morning the first. (You may notice the phrasing of the last sentence, the insidious influence of that excellent man, Major Pendennis.)[129]

I had not heard before about Dick[130] and was very glad and proud of

---

127 Albert's brother William, his wife Minnie, and their daughter Clare, were at Little Lea from 7 to 13 July.
128 Psalm 57:1.
129 A character in Thackeray's *Pendennis*.
130 i.e. Richard Lewis, the son of Joseph Lewis. See note 101 to letter of 30? June 1916.

the news. As you say, he has plenty of 'guts' if only he has the luck to stick out. Things look a little brighter at the front now, though I am afraid it will need many such successes to bring the business to an end. Kirk went up to London on Wednesday to see the elder Smythe boy, who is at home wounded, for the third time.

'Summer is a-cummen in'[131] here at last, and we have actually had no rain since Saturday.

your loving

son Jack

TO ARTHUR GREEVES (LP V: 115–17):

[Gastons]

July 25 1916 and be d-d to you.

My dear Arthur,

That thrice accursed fellow pupil of mine is at present sitting up in the work room so I cannot go and steal a page from his exercise book to write on, as I have been doing all the term – you must be content therefore with these odd scraps: indeed I don't see why I should write at all, as by writing both the first and the last letter of this term I have treated you to two more than you deserve; however, I will make a note that it is your turn to begin after the holidays.

You are quite mistaken if you suppose that in asking about Dennis' bathing things I suggested that he OUGHT to have them on – I only wanted to get a perfectly clear picture: still I don't see any parallel between him and Bleheris in knickerbockers (a very funny word – that or Bickerknocker would be a good name for a dwarf if either of us should want one), because I take it your story is modern. But of course I quite agree that your hero is far better without them. It seems rather unnatural though to pass over any question of embarrassment in absolute silence: the fey of course, as a non-human being, may be excused, but poor Dennis might at least be allowed to blush when he comes round. Handled delicately and without any foolish humour – I am quite serious – the point might be worked a little more: what think you? Morris – who I always think manages to be as good as gold and at the same time beautifully sensuous, would have revelled in it. This week's instalment is excellent, and your references to the Sea and the sea

---

131 Anonymous, *Cuckoo Song* (c. 1250), l. 1: 'Sumer is icumen in'.

gods give me great anticipation of what may happen next: that next number which I am longing to get – from your own hand.

You must be easily satisfied if you think that I flatter you – when I scarcely let a sentence go past without pricking holes in it: you must also have funny ideas about my rate of composition if you think I have already finished Bleheris. As a matter of fact I write one chapter every Sunday afternoon, and having started before I came back, am always two instalments ahead of the one you get: the general course of the story was mapped out from the start, but of course is changed pretty freely whenever I like. When I said that you wouldn't like the 'gist' of the thing, I meant nothing to do with what you call 'shocked' or 'immodest' (though I admit that when the heroine turns up she is in fairly sharp contrast to Alice the Saint), but that the meaning of it all is somewhat anti-Christian: however, the story and not the allegory is the important part.

I have now finished that adorable (to quote our friend Ch-anie)[132] 'John Silence': I still think 'Ancient Sorceries' the best, though indeed all, particularly the 'Fire' one, are glorious. In the last one the opening part, all about those lovely Northern Islands and the camp life – wouldn't you love to go there? – is so very beautiful that you feel almost sorry to have the supernatural dragged in. Though the idea of the were-wolf is splendid. At what point of the story did you begin to guess the truth?

My last budget of books includes a French Everyman copy of a poet called Chenier[133] (a poet you might perhaps like some day, when you come to read French verse) and a 13d. Macmillan copy of Walter Pater's 'Renaissance',[134] in the same edition as the 'Letters from Hell' I suppose. That book (Hell) by the way is not by Dostoevsky I think, because I fancy I read somewhere that it is translated not from the Russian but from the Swedish: I have noticed too (did I tell you before) that this edition has a preface by our friend Macdonald, the author of Phantastes. We must certainly get it, as the Macmillan 1/- series are, to my mind, very nicely got up. The French Everyman is quite different from the English

---

132 The pronunciation of the name of their friend Jane or 'Janie' (thus 'Ch-anie' and even 'Tchanie') McNeill by 'Ch-anie's' mother – which pronunciation Lewis delighted in imitating.

133 André Chénier (1762–94), *Poésies*, Classiques Françaises [1916].

134 Walter Pater, *The Renaissance: Studies in Art and Poetry*, Second Edition, Revised (1912).

one – I am not sure yet whether I like it more, or less – you must judge for yourself.

It is a terrible responsibility to have to guide my Galahad in poetry: a false step might turn you away altogether! I don't think I should advise Milton: while there are lots of things in him you would love – the descriptions of Hell and Chaos and Paradise and Adam and Eve and Satan's flight down through the stars, on the other hand his classical allusions, his rather crooked style of English, and his long speeches, might be tedious. Besides it is written in blank verse (without rhymes) and people who are beginning to read poetry don't usually care for that. But of course you are different, and for all I know you might. You must have a good look at it in my copy and see what you think.

Endymion[135] is top-hole in places, in fact nearly all the time, though somewhat 'sticky': it would be a very good thing to try, I think, if you would not scruple to skip whenever you found it dull: the third book especially, where he wanders at the bottom of the sea, would appeal to you strongly. The only other poems I can suggest are Arnold's 'Tristan and Isolde' or 'Balder Dead'[136] (though this is in blank verse) or some of the stories in Morris' 'Earthly Paradise'[137] or perhaps some of the other Rossetti's pieces; these of course you could finish in a few hours, and some of them are not really very good. If you get an edition of Keats perhaps you would like 'St Agnes Eve'[138] – it is shorter than Endymion, written in Spenser's metre, and very romantic – though perhaps rather 'sticky' also. In sympathy with your new investment, having finished 'Pendennis' of which I am heartily sick by now, I have begun to read 'Twelfth Night' which is a charming little romance, don't you think? The opening speech about the music is the best.

Can't understand it being 'too hot to practise' as it is absolute winter here. Bah, there you see I am talking about the weather, like any fool! If I can get away – I haven't promised, mind – I should be pleased with all my heart to go to Portsalon: indeed whenever (correctly used in this sentence) I have thought of a holiday with you, that place has come into my mind: however, we can discuss all this when we meet – next week. Can you realize? I am so looking forward to seeing you again old man, and I

---

135 John Keats, *Endymion* (1818).
136 Matthew Arnold, *Tristram and Iseult* (1852); *Balder Dead* (1853).
137 William Morris, *The Earthly Paradise* (1868–70).
138 John Keats, *The Eve of St Agnes* (1820).

do hope and pray that nothing will turn up to disappoint us. I expect to arrive home on Tuesday: there is some faint danger of my father's staying at home, but if not, perhaps you could get a day off? Oh, how we will look over all these new books together: I have something ravishing to show you in the way of paper, but that can wait.

I am writing at present a rather lengthy (for me that is) poem about Hylas, which you shall see if it is a success: but perhaps it will never be finished. By the way, I have come to the Hylas part in the Greek Argonautica. He doesn't go into it nearly as fully as Morris, but in some ways it is better. In this version the various nymphs – mountains, Oreads, wood nymphs etc., are dancing by moonlight when they hear a mortal blundering through the wood. So they all scatter to their various trees, streams etc., and this particular one, as Hylas bent down to fill his pitcher, caught him round the neck and pulled him down; and so to bed, bon soir tu excessivement pudibonde.

Jack

TO ARTHUR GREEVES (LP V: 121–2):

> [Little Lea,
> Strandtown,
> Belfast]
> 18/9/16.[139]

My Dear Galahad,

It seems a mockery to think that we were talking so lately about how much better we were in our letters than in conversation – I don't feel like that when I actually sit down to write for the first time. Somehow my being at home instead of at Bookham makes it seem strange to be away from you: it is only so few days ago that we were ragging about together in your bedroom. And now you must brush your teeth alone!

But first of all I will answer your questions. The journey home was absolutely damnable: I had to wait an hour at Letterkenny, and an hour and a quarter at Strabane. You may judge of my boredom when I tell you that I was reduced to buying a 'Novel' magazine[140] – because everything

---

139 Some time after Lewis arrived home on 1 August, he and Arthur went on holiday to Portsalon in Co. Donegal. While Arthur stayed on at Portsalon – this letter being addressed to him there – Lewis returned to Belfast. He crossed over to England on 22 September.

140 *The Novel Magazine* was published between 1905 and 1936.

else on the bookstall was even more impossible. My father seemed in very poor form when I got home, and fussed a lot about my cold: so everything is beastly, and I have decided – of course – to commit suicide again.

This morning I visited Mullans on your little job, but their copy of the Kaleva[141] was much too old and shop-soiled to satisfy you, while I couldn't find one in Maynes at all: this being so I didn't know quite whether you meant me to order one or not – at any rate I did NOT. I am sending you – as a peace offering – a little present, which may arrive by the end of this week: change it if you don't care for it – or when you have read it.

I was very much interested in your description of those lakes, tho' I must say that considering my eager desire to see them, both this year and last, it was particularly kind of you to go just after I had left – but not a word of that to the others. I can quite imagine how fine it must have been – rather like the 'Star Bath'[142] as I picture them. The mist's gradual creeping up would have been great. After all, mountain scenery is in some ways the best, isn't it – excepting our own hills with their exquisite little corners of such homely and 'intime' beauty, which are in a different class. How I do wish I could still be with you during the next fortnight! You must let me know whatever you do, and tell me all the funny or exciting 'adventures' that turn up, and I won't feel quite out of it.

To go back to books: I found my Milton Vol. II waiting at Mullans and am very pleased with it, except that the yellow wrapper is in bad condition and can't be worn when it is on its shelf. I have also bought a 7d. Macmillan book by Algernon Blackwood called 'Jimbo, a fantasy'.[143] Although you have never mentioned it, I dare say you know that there is such a book – I never heard of it myself. I am keeping it to read in the train when I go back (Friday night), but I have to restrain myself every moment – it looks so awfully appetizing. If it turns out to be good, of course I will let you know. What are you reading? Try Phrynette[144] if you

---

141 *Kalevala* ('Land of Heroes') is the national epic poem of Finland.
142 During his Easter holiday Lewis added seven more poems to his 'Metrical Meditations of a Cod'. One of these was 'Star Bath' which was possibly suggested by an account of some lakes near Portsalon and was later included in *Spirits in Bondage: A Cycle of Lyrics* (1919).
143 Algernon Blackwood, *Jimbo: A Fantasy* (1909).
144 Marthe Troly-Curtin, *Phrynette and London* (1911); *Phrynette Married* (1912).

can't get anything else. I am still at The Newcomes and the Faerie Queene, reserving the Milton for next term, while in the mornings in bed I am going over 'Sense and Sensibility' again – which I had nearly forgotten. Do you remember Mrs Jennings and Marianne Dashwood and the rest?

On Sunday night my father and I had supper at Glenmachan, whither came the Hamiltons from Knock. K.[elsie] has a scheme for going down with them and me to Larne for a day, which I hope will come off, as I am very dull, and lonely and fed up – indeed I shall not be sorry to leave home.

I needn't apologize for giving you no instalment this week, as you are in the same state, but I will try and do better next time. This letter is perhaps a bit short, but so is yours – we have neither of us yet got our sea legs. Let me hear from you by Tuesday at the very latest, a good long one, as I need a lot of cheering up. Good bye old man,

yours,

Jack

TO HIS FATHER (LP V: 125):

[Gastons]
27/9/16.

My dear Papy,

I hope you got the telegram all right this time: at least it was sent on Saturday afternoon. I had a very tolerable journey, and I think my cold is gone. How is yours? Kirk is very pleased with the Trinity papers and we find them very useful: most of them of course are rather harder than those I shall have, as a Trinity Scholarship is not an entrance scholarship at all, but is taken when you have been 'up' for a year – at least so I am assured. But of course the greater includes the less, and if we master these the other will be all the safer. I am sending back some of the German books which he thinks unsuitable, but we have enough for the present.

Thanks for the letter from Arthur which you forwarded. When he wrote, 'the gaiety of nations'[145] had been increased by Gordon's developing a bad knee which prevented him from walking! On the whole it must

---

145 Samuel Johnson, *Lives of the English Poets* (1779–81). In the life of 'Edmund Smith' Dr Johnson said the death of David Garrick 'eclipsed the gaiety of nations'.

have been a cheery little party after my leaving them – tho' *that* in itself was perhaps enough to depress any holiday-makers. But of course you will never hint for a moment to anyone that I had anything but pane-gyrics to say about Portsalon. These people are all so throughother [*sic*] that you never know who will hear what, as Mrs. K. would say.

Everyone here says that they heard the last London raid, though I ingloriously slept all night. With that exception, everything in the war way seems to be going well, doesn't it? It is hot summer weather here without the least suggestion of autumn, which I dislike very much. Kirk is in very good form, although he does not remember M. Henry. About the Westminster confession I have not yet asked.

The collars which Annie was to send me have arrived. I don't know exactly how postage rates are running, but I hope you didn't sell the gramophone or your new picture to raise it. Some day when you have a lot of money and time to spare, I might ask you to send me three cata-logues – Macmillan's, Dent's and a French one, which you will find on the table farthest from the window, on the microscope box, in the little end room. Of course at present, ruined as you are by these freights of cellar linen, I shouldn't dare!

your loving
son Jack

TO ARTHUR GREEVES (LP V: 123−4):

[Gastons]
27th./9/16.

My dear Galahad,

I think you must be going dotty with all your talk about when I'm going back, seeing that I said in my first letter that Friday (last) was already fixed. At any rate you must have found out by now, and will understand why I am late in answering your letter, which only reached me today. As you say, it seems years and years since I left: I have quite dropped back into the not unpleasant, though monotonous routine of Bookham, and could almost believe that I had never left it. Portsalon is like a dream. I heartily agree with you that it must have been nice to have the Lounge all to yourselves.

Now to books: I told you didn't I that I had bought Blackwood's Jimbo did I not? I finished it on Sunday and am awfully bucked with it – a very good 7d. worth. It is quite in Blackwood's best manner, and you will specially love the last thirty pages or so – they are terrific. Get it at once. I hope you are not praising 'Letters from Hell' out of politeness, for I really want to know what it is like. I saw it once in a second hand book-shop at Guildford nearly a year ago: looking over the first few pages I thought it excellent, but of course it may not be so good later on. How many books seem to promise such a lot at the start and then turn out disappointing. Whereas good, stodgy books like Scott have all their interesting parts in the middle and begin with reams of dry-as-dust. Talking about stodge, I finished 'The Newcomes' before leaving home, and certainly enjoyed the end better than any parts except the scenes at Baden. Of course it is a great novel, but I am very thankful to have got it off my chest. I should advise you to get the 2/6 volume containing Milton's minor poems,[146] which I am now reading: I am sure they are better to begin on than P.L. I am now at 'Comus', which is an absolute dream of delight. I am sure you would love it: it is like a play written on an episode from the Faerie Queene, all magic and distressed ladies and haunted woods. It is lovely in books the way you can just turn from one sort of beauty to another and never get tired.

I was sorry to find no instalment in your last letter, tho' of course if you have completely lost interest in poor Papillon it is no good forcing yourself. I will consent to your trying a novel only on the condition that it be sent to me, chapter by chapter. I too am wondering whether I should not chuck Bleheris and start something else: partly I have so many ideas and also I think the old fashioned English is a fatal mistake. Any good things that are in it or would be later on, can be worked in elsewhere. In a way it is disheartening to remember how keenly we were both starting out on our tales this time last term and see the result. But still we have both much experience and practice gained, and we got a lot of pleasure out of them while they lasted: the danger is that we get to turn too easily from one thing to another and never get anything done.

I didn't go to see anything in London, I really don't know why – I was a bit tired, nothing seemed to attract me much, and also, having started 'Jimbo' in the train, was eager to get to it again. One part of my journey I enjoyed very much was the first few miles out of Liverpool: because it was one of the most wonderful mornings I have ever seen – one of those lovely white misty ones when you can't see 10 yards. You could just see

---

146 John Milton, *Paradise Regained and Minor Poems*, ed. F.E. Bumby [1910].

the nearest trees and houses, a little ghostly in appearance, and beyond that everything was a clean white blank. It felt as if the train was alone in space, if you know what I mean.

I think you are very wise not to take that puppy from K[elso Ewart]. Unless you are a person with plenty of spare time and real knowledge, it is a mistake to keep dogs – and cruel to them. Have you got the Kaleva yet, tell me when you do and what you think of it. I wonder where you are at this moment? Have you reached home yet? Tell me all the news when you write, what you're reading etc. and whether you are going back to your taskmaster Tom at once.[147] I am not nearly so fed up now as I was, and hope you are the same. The country at home was beginning to look nice and autumn-y, with dead leaves in the lanes and a nice nutty smell (you know what I mean) so I suppose it is getting better still. Here it is horrible bright summer which I hate. Love to all our friends such as the hedgepig etc.

Yours,
Jack.

TO ARTHUR GREEVES (W):

[Gastons]
Oct. Ugh! 10/4/16!! [4 October 1916]

My dear Arthur,

I believe it is Lamb who says somewhere that he does not know whether it is more delightful to set out for a holiday or return from one: perhaps you hardly agree with him! Though I am sure he hated his office (read 'The Superannuated Man')[148] quite as much as you do. But of course he means, I suppose, the getting back to home, to ones books etc and not to work. However I suppose you are gradually getting 'broken in'.

The beastly summer is at last over here, and good old Autumn colours & smells and temperatures have come back. Thanks to this we had a most glorious walk on Saturday: it was a fine cool, windy day & we set out after lunch to go to a place called 'Friday Street' which is a very long walk from here through beautiful woods and vallies that I don't know well.[149] After several hours wandering over fields & woods etc. with

---

147 Arthur was assisting Tom Greeves in his brother's business.
148 Collected in Charles Lamb's *Essays of Elia* (1823).
149 Friday Street, Surrey, about 10 miles south of Great Bookham.

the aid of a map we began to get lost and suddenly at about 4 o'clock – we had expected to reach the place by that time – we found ourselves in a place where we had been an hour before! *You* will understand that while the others were only annoyed at this, I felt je ne sais quoi de dreamlike and terrifying sensation at the idea of wandering round in circles through these big, solemn woods; also there was a certain tinge of 'Alice-in-W-ism' about it. We had a lot of difficulty in at last reaching the place, but it was glorious when we got there. You are walking in the middle of a wood when all of a sudden you go downwards and come to a little open hollow just big enough for a little lake and some old, old red-tiled houses: all round it the trees tower up on rising ground and every road from it is at once swallowed up in them. You might walk within a few feet of it & suspect nothing unless you saw the smoke rising up from some cottage chimney. Can you imagine what it was like? Best of all, we came down to the little inn of the village and had tea there with – glory of glories – an old tame jackdaw hopping about our feet and asking for crumbs. He is called Jack and will answer to his name.

The inn has three tiny but spotlessly clean bedrooms, so some day, – if the gods will, you & I are going to stay there. The inn is called the 'Stephen Langton' and dates from the time of that gentleman's wars against the king or the barons or somebody (you'll know I expect),[150] tho' of course it has been rebuilt since. I don't like playing the guide-book, but it was so ravishing that I had to tell you. We were so late getting there that it was dark soon after we left, and often going astray we didn't get home till ten o'clock – dead beat but happy.

Partly because the country we saw that day was so like it I have been reading again the second volume of Malory, especially the part of the 'Sangreal' which I had forgotten. With all its faults, in small doses this book is tip-top: those mystic parts are very good to read late at night when you are drowsy and tired and get into a sort of 'exalted' mood. Do you know what I mean? You so often share feelings of mine which I can't explain that I hope you do: mention this subject when you next write. Besides this I have finished 'Comus' with great enjoyment: I have also re-read for the thousandth time 'Rapunzel' and some other favourite bits of Morris, while through the week I have read an excellent novel of

---

150 Stephen Langton (d. 1228), Archbishop of Canterbury, in his later life supported the regency in its struggles against baronial insubordination.

Vachell's 'The Paladin'[151] which you have probably read too and also dipped often into Boswell's 'Life of Johnson'.[152] Being entirely made up of conversation I don't think it is a book to be read continuously, tho' it is very good fun in bits: you are thinking of getting it I believe. I agree with you that I must read some more books in the particular 'genre' of 'Our Village' etc, but there are so many things to read that I don't know where to begin. I forget what edition you are getting of the 'Scenes of Clerical life'[153]

As to the fate of sad Papillon, I will look at the exact place of leaving-off when I go upstairs & write it down somewhere in pencil: unless you decide to go on with it don't waste time & energy copying the rest but send me instead the first drafts of your new work. I should be glad, though, to see you going on with it and have the complete tale, for there is good stuff in it: however, I can't preach in this respect now! Loki & Dennis & Bleheris, all our operas, plays etc go one way; perhaps they are caught like Wan Jadis in the Grey Marish on the way to the country of the past![154] For my part I am at present engaged in making huge plans both for prose and verse none of which I shall try. I begin to see that short, slight stories & poems are all I am fit for at present & that it would be better to write & finish one of such than to begin & leave twenty ambitious epic-poems or romances. I wait eagerly either for another instalment of the Watersprite or else some new venture from you: you shall have the first thing I do, if I ever do anything.

How I wish I had been with you at Mr Thompson's.[155] Everything seems to have happened well after my departure – I suppose you say no wonder! what a female-minded person I am getting! I would cross out that remark as peevish & 'cattish', but it would make a mess and you would only wonder what was underneath. Take it as unsaid.

Have you got or begun the 'Kalevala' yet? Give me your first impressions when you do. Papillon has got to where they are both under the

---

151 Horace Annesley Vachell, *The Paladin, As Beheld by a Woman of Temperament* (1909).
152 James Boswell, *The Life of Samuel Johnson* (1791).
153 George Eliot, *Scenes of Clerical Life* (1858).
154 Wan Jadis is a young man in Lewis's 'Bleheris'. In chapter XI this 'sweet and comely youth' is caught in a swamp named the 'Grey Marish'. Lewis was later to use the name 'Jadis' in the Chronicles of Narnia for the Queen of Charn who becomes the White Witch.
155 James A. Thompson was a resident of Strandtown and of some consequence in the congregation of St Mark's, Dundela.

water and ends with the words 'it shot him much farther than he had intended so that he nearly lost sight of the fairy'. Looking at it revives my enthusiasm. Do go on with it if you can: certainly send me the rest provided this doesn't interfere with any new work. Now good night Galahad the 'haut prince' as Malory [would] say,

yours
Jack

P.S. Poor puppy!! What a life it'll have! I shall poison it in kindness when I come home!

P.P.S. Why do your letters never come till Wednesday now?

TO HIS FATHER (LP V: 129–30):

[Gastons]
10/6/16 [6 October 1916]

My dear Papy,

Many thanks for the catalogues, which were necessary to my peace of mind. I shouldn't try the 'conceit' if I were you, as two can play at that game, and you might get a number of strange parcels.

Since I last wrote, that awe-inspiring person the Tutor for Entrances of Balliol has deigned to forward us last year's scholarship papers for that college – although we are I think quite determined now on the big group. He distinguished himself by doing the very thing that we have so often discussed – addressing his envelope to the 'Rev. T.W. Kirkpatrick', thinking I suppose that no one except a clergyman could possibly be entrusted with the youth of a nation. The papers themselves were pretty much what we expected, and not discouraging. The subject for an English essay – with no alternative – was 'Diplomacy' which is rather a mouthful. It would involve a good deal of history. Kirk has been growing very enthusiastic on the superior composition of these papers to the Trinity ones, which indeed were rather unintelligently drawn up. Some of the pieces in the scholarship exams are desperately hard, while others in the Fellowship ones are ridiculously easy: of course it is the competition and the standard required which really makes the difference. I agree with you that a 'course' would be much worse than this scheme: for while it is true that a man can always learn a course, another can always learn it better.

I am reading at present a book whose scene is laid in Oxford and which tells one a good deal about the University (not Tom Brown),[156] 'Lady Connie' by Mrs. Humphrey Ward.[157] She is a favourite of yours, is she not? I have never read her until now, and she seems to have many points. She is rather a pedant tho', insists too much on her 'culture', and tells us a great deal about tanagra Statues, Titainesque effects, discoveries in Crete, Euripides, Goethe, etc., etc. You know what I mean.

We have yet another pupil here now – a boy who comes every morning to do Spanish. He is reading for the Foreign Office. It seems a lovely language, and so easy that I can imagine 'even Warnie' taking to it. I wish I could prevent Arthur's invasions, but don't know quite how to do it.

your loving
son Jack.

TO ARTHUR GREEVES (W):

[Gastons]
(The 12th. Oct., I think) [1916]

My dear Arthur,

It was unfortunate that I should choose a word like 'exaltation' which is so often used in connection with religion and so give you a wrong impression of my meaning. I will try to explain again: have you ever sat over the fire late, late at night when you are very drowzy & muddle headed, and it is no use trying to go on with your book? Everything seems like a dream, you are absolutely contented, and 'out of the world'. Anything seems possible, and all sorts of queer ideas float through your mind & sort of vaguely thrill you but only mildly & calmly. It is in this sort of mood that the quaint, old mystical parts of Malory are exactly suitable: you can read a chapter or two in a sort of dream & find the forests of 'Logres & of Lyonesse' very agreeable at such a time – at least I do.

As to the other question about religion, I was sad to read your letter. You ask me my religious views: you know, I think, that I beleive in no religion. There is absolutely no proof for any of them, and from a philosophical standpoint Christianity is not even the best. All religions, that is, all mythologies to give them their proper name are merely man's own

---

156 Thomas Hughes, *Tom Brown's Schooldays* (1857); *Tom Brown at Oxford* (1861).
157 Mrs Humphrey Ward (Mary Augusta Ward), *Lady Connie* (1916).

invention – Christ as much as Loki. Primitive man found himself surrounded by all sorts of terrible things he didn't understand – thunder, pestilence, snakes etc: what more natural than to suppose that these were animated by evil spirits trying to torture him. These he kept off by cringing to them, singing songs and making sacrifices etc. Gradually from being mere nature-spirits these supposed being[s] were elevated into more elaborate ideas, such as the old gods: and when man became more refined he pretended that these spirits were good as well as powerful.

Thus religion, that is to say mythology grew up. Often, too, great men were regarded as gods after their death – such as Heracles or Odin: thus after the death of a Hebrew philosopher Yeshua (whose name we have corrupted into Jesus) he became regarded as a god, a cult sprang up, which was afterwards connected with the ancient Hebrew Jahweh-worship, and so Christianity came into being – one mythology among many, but the one that we happen to have been brought up in.

Now all this you must have heard before: it is the recognised scientific account of the growth of religions. Superstition of course in every age has held the common people, but in every age the educated and thinking ones have stood outside it, though usually outwardly conceding to it for convenience. I had thought that you were gradually being emancipated from the old beliefs, but if this is not so, I hope we are too sensible to quarrel about abstract ideas. I must only add that ones views on religious subjects don't make any difference in morals, of course. A good member of society must of course try to be honest, chaste, truthful, kindly etc: these are things we owe to our own manhood & dignity and not to any imagined god or gods.

Of course, mind you, I am not laying down as a certainty that there is nothing outside the material world: considering the discoveries that are always being made, this would be foolish. Anything MAY exist: but until we know that it does, we can't make any assumptions. The universe is an absolute mystery: man has made many guesses at it, but the answer is yet to seek. Whenever any new light can be got as to such matters, I will be glad to welcome it. In the meantime I am not going to go back to the bondage of believing in any old (& already decaying) superstition.

See! I have wasted ¾ of my letter on all these dry bones. However, old man, you started the subject and I had to have my turn. Yes, I wish you had really been with me on the walk to Friday-Street: how you and I, alone, would have gloried in those woods and vallies! But some day we will go and spend a week there at the inn, get up at 5 every morning & go to bed at 8, spending the interval sitting by the lake and talking to the Jackdaw. He can only say 'Caw' so that will be a nice change after my torrents of conversation!

I have written up for 'Letters from Hell' and it ought to be here by the end of the week. I am looking forward to it immensely and will enjoy being able to talk it over with you. You ask me what 'special' book I am reading at present: you must remember that I read seriously only on week-ends. When I last wrote my week-end books were 'Comus' and the Morte Darthur; last week-end, 'Comus' being finished, its place was taken by Shelley's 'Prometheus Unbound'[158] which I got half through. It is an amazing work. I don't know how to describe it to you; it is more wild & out of the world than any poem I ever read, and contains some wonderful descriptions. Shelley had a great genius, but his carelessness about rhymes, metre, choice of words etc, just prevents him being as good as he might be. To me, when you're in the middle of a fine passage and come to a 'cockney' rhyme like 'ru*in*' & 'pursu*ing*', it spoils the whole thing – makes it vulgar and grotesque. However some parts are so splendid that I could forgive him anything. I am now, through the week, reading Scott's 'Antiquary'.[159] I suppose you have read it long ago: I am very pleased with it, especially the character of the Antiquary himself, the description of his room, and the old beggar. Tell me your views when you write – it is nice gradually to get more & more into each other's style of reading, is it not – you with poetry and I with classical novels?

As to Bleheris, he is dead and I shan't trouble his grave.[160] I will try and write something new soon – a short tale, I expect – but am rather taken up with verse at present, in my spare-time; which gets less and less as the exam. draws nearer. However I look eagerly for the first chapter of your novel, or failing that, the next leaf of Dennis.

It is an amazing thing to call the 'Kalevala' tame: whatever else it is, it is not tame. If a poem all about floods & primeval spirits and magic and talking beasts & monsters is not wild enough, I really don't know what to say! However, chacun à son gout! As to the Milton I daren't advise you –

---

158 Percy Bysshe Shelley, *Prometheus Unbound* (1820).
159 Sir Walter Scott, *The Antiquary* (1816).
160 'The Quest of Bleheris' lies in a very distinguished 'grave'. The manuscript is now in the Bodleian Library (MS. Eng. lett. c. 220/5, fols. 5–43).

both volumes are so good, if you care for him. You don't give any criticism on 'Evelina';[161] do so, when you write.

It is a lovely moonlight night (a brau' brich' minlich' nicht, do you remember). I wish you were here. Goodnight

J.

TO HIS FATHER (LP V: 132):

[Gastons]
12th October 1916

My dear Papy,

We have all been plunged in misery here for the last week because no one can remember the context or the author of a quotation that we all know as well as our own names. It started by Mrs. K. seeing it in the 'In Memoriam' part of the paper and asking casually what it was from: since then we have ransacked our memories and books of reference in vain. You will laugh us to scorn when I tell you that it is the familiar,

> 'E'en as he trod that day to God
> So walked he from his birth,
> In simpleness and gentleness
> And honour and clean mirth.'[162]

but I am dashed if I can remember where it comes from. Some time I am sure it is Kipling, and again in other moods it seems impossible. Try and enlighten us.

You are rather too severe on the 'Diplomacy' essay: it is not – in my poor conceit – that the subject is not bounded enough, but that it is too bounded. It hems the candidate down to a field of historical and even technical knowledge that they have no right to expect of him. Now an essay on 'air' in a scientific exam would be very proper, and even an essay on virtue would have no vice about it. You may produce that 'mot' as one of your own when you next meet Bill Patterson 'that sprightly caliph' on the top of his tramcar. Before leaving the subject of exams, I must remark that the Oxford papers do not include one on 'accidents' which is

---

161 Frances Burney, *Evelina* (1778).
162 See note 167 to letter of 19 October 1916 for the actual source of this quotation.

a relief: tho' of course if I am going to break down in that way, I shall have plenty of opportunities in the composition.

I am sorry to hear of your being laid up, and even Arthur's assurance that he is 'going to call on my father some time soon' does not quite make up for it. If the weather at home is the same medley that we have here, I am not surprised. It is alternately hot, damp and warm, or cold and windy. I wish we could settle down to good winter weather and habits.

I have finished 'Lady Connie' and though it does not end as well as it begins, it was good enough to make me determine to read some more of hers next holidays. Since then I have been dipping into Boswell, whom I grow to like better and better.

Thanks for the enclosure which was a letter from my old Malvern study companion, who is in some mysterious affair called the 'Artist's Rifle.' Did you ever hear of it? I confess I don't know what claim Hardman has to be an artist.

Hoping you are quite set up again by now,

I am,

your loving

son Jack.

TO ARTHUR GREEVES (W):

[Gastons]
(Forgotten the date) [18 October 1916]

My dear Arthur,

Frequently in arguing with you by letter I have had to ask you to read what I say carefully before you rush on to answer it. I distinctly said that there was once a Hebrew called Yeshua, I think on p. 2 (II!!) of my letter: when I say 'Christ' of course I mean the mythological being into whom he was afterwards converted by popular imagination, and I am thinking of the legends about his magic performances and resurrection etc. That the man Yeshua or Jesus did actually exist, is as certain as that the Buddha did actually exist: Tacitus mentions his execution in the Annals.[163] But all the other tomfoolery about virgin birth, magic healings, apparitions and so forth is on exactly the same footing as any other mythology. After all even your namesake king Arthur really lived once (if

---

163 Cornelius Tacitus, *Annals* (c. 116), Bk. XV, sect. 44.

we are to believe the latest theories) but it doesn't follow that Malory's old book is history. In the same way there was such a person as Alexander the Great, but the adventures which the Middle Ages related of him are nonsense. It is generally thought, too, that there was such a man as Odin, who was deified after his death: so you see most legends have a kernel of fact in them somewhere. Indeed, these distinctions are so very obvious, that if you were not my best friend I should almost suspect you of wilfully misunderstanding me through temper.

Later on you ask me why I am sad, and suggest that it is because I have no hope of a 'happy life hereafter'. No; strange as it may appear I am quite content to live without beleiving in a bogey who is prepared to torture me forever and ever if I should fail in coming up to an almost impossible ideal (which is a part of the Christian mythology, however much you try to explain it away). In fact I should think it horrible to feel that if life got too bad, I daren't escape for fear of a spirit more cruel and barbarous than any man. Then you are good enough to ask me why I don't kill myself. Because – as I have said to you before – in spite of occasional fits of depression I am very well pleased with life and have a very happy time on the whole. The only reason I was sad was because I was dissapointed in my hope that you were gradually escaping from beleifs which, in my case, always considerably lessened my happiness: if, however, it has the opposite effect on you, tant mieux pour vous! As to the immortality of the soul, though it is a fascinating theme for day-dreaming, I neither beleive nor disbeleive: I simply don't know anything at all, there is no evidence either way. Now let us take off our armour, hang up our swords and talk about things where there is no danger of coming to blows!

Yes, I quite agree that the metre of the Kalevala is tedious & the word 'tame' exactly describes it. It doesn't sort of rise to the subject at all, but is always the same whatever is happening. If you give this up – and there is no point in going on unless it takes your fancy – don't let it quench your rising taste for poetry. I must really fulfill my long standing purpose and settle down to some more books of the 'Cranford'[164] type: your description has made me quite enthusiastic, so without fail tell me the edition you have got it & all your Austens etc in? I finished 'The Antiquary' this afternoon, and it thoroughly denies our old wheeze about

---

164 Elizabeth Cleghorn Gaskell, *Cranford* (1853).

most books getting tiresome halfway through. It gets better and better as it goes on, and I have not enjoyed anything so much for a long time. I believe I shall soon become almost as devoted to Scott as you are: I begin to feel that sort of 'repose', which you like, in turning to him. Which of his should I try next? I shall be glad to hear your views on 'Lavengro'[165] when you have read it, also by whom this mysterious 1/- edition is published.

And now I must turn to 'Letters of Hell'. I suppose I must have looked forward to it too much: at any rate – I will tell the truth – I have failed to read it, have not enjoyed it a bit and have put it away in my drawer unfinished. There! Am I fallen in your eyes forever? I don't really know why I disliked it so much, because I could see all the time that there was good in it if only I could appreciate it – which makes it all the more annoying. For one thing I expected beauties of the phantastic type, and in reality it turns out only a novel. For the parts about Hell are after all only a setting for the story of his previous life – a story which seemed to me so far as I read it supremely commonplace. The characters are all absolutely crude – wicked rich men of the melodramatic type and miraculously innocent angels of heroines. The only part I liked was the vision of paradise, which struck me as good. Still, when both you and Macdonald praise the book, I am ready to beleive that the fault must be in me and not in it.

Thanks for the instalment: as the post only came in at 9 o'clock I can't read it yet or I won't get my letter to you done till bedtime – but you shall have my verdict ('impudence' say you) next week. Do either go on with this tale or start something new: I am trying to make out the plan of a short tale but nothing 'comes'. That is an awful waste, that book W[arnie] gave my father: wouldn't you love an edition with that binding and paper, only the size of my Kipling, say of the Brontës or James Stephens or Macdonald? Talking about Kipling it is time you began him: try 'Rewards & Fairies'[166] and if the first story in it 'Cold Iron' doesn't knock you head over heels, I don't know what will. Good night, they're all gone up, and I have tired you by now 'I *do* talk *so.*'

Jack

---

165 George Borrow, *Lavengro* (1851).

166 Rudyard Kipling, *Rewards and Fairies* (1910).

P.S. (In the bedroom) It is much more wintry to night, and when I came up the curtains were not drawn and the room was full of moonlight, bright bright as anything. It is too cold to sit looking at the glorious night but it *is* beautiful! I shake your hand. Goodnight. I wish you could come & 'grind' at Gastons. Ugh. Horrible cold sheets now

J.

TO HIS FATHER (LP V: 133–4):

[Gastons]
19/Oct./16.

My dear Papy,

Yes! That was a bad lapse of memory, and now that the mystery is solved, I wonder how I could possibly have forgotten it. Perhaps the fact of its being printed as 3 lines (the 'God' and 'trod' rhymes having lines to themselves) had something to do with it. Still, it was a nasty blunder, and I thought I knew my Kipling better than that. Like all quotations from good authors, it is much finer in its setting than when we read it alone: that whole poem ought to settle for good and all K's question as to whether Kipling be a poet.[167] He could be 'spoken to' as poor Uncle Bill was on a similar occasion.

Many thanks for the 'Spectator' which I shall certainly keep for the sake of the poem. It is, I quite agree with you, a really notable piece of work, quite above the average. The verse beginning 'Life? – 'Twas a little thing to give' is glorious, and also the last two lines

> 'Who bartered for Youth's diadem
> The dross of after years.'[168]

I wonder is there any country outside these islands where about every 10th man is a poet, as seems to be the case with us? I wish somebody of real taste would collect all the verse that is appearing in the papers at present and make a selection – it would be the best anthology ever published. As to F.S. Boas I know him well from a book of his on

---

167 The Kipling quotation comes from the prefatory/dedicatory poem to the *Barrack-Room Ballads* (1892). It has no title in the original but simply follows a separate dedicatory page to Wolcott Balestier.

168 'Ulster on the Somme' by F.S. Boas, *The Spectator* (14 October 1916), p. 443.

Shakespeare[169] that Kirk has, but it never struck me that there was any relationship. Perhaps it was he who 'lectured on Herrick'? The nephew I don't remember, though he must have been at Campbell in my time.

The other article has a lot of sense in it: the writer must be like K's friend, of whom I told you, who could give anyone points in classical literature without knowing Latin or Greek. That Butcher and Lang translation of Homer[170] is very good, and so is Bacon's bit of Lucretius, tho' not as beautiful as his own suggestion that 'it be with pity'. Of course I suppose only the very greatest poetry will stand translation: fancy a French prose version of Swinburne.

I am at present reading a book which you would enjoy, 'The letters of Dorothy Osborne to Sir William Temple'.[171] In case you have forgotten who they were, you can turn to Macaulay's essay on the latter.[172] They lived in Cromwell's time, and the letters are very quaint. In the notes the editor also quotes an account of the 'remove these baubles' scene by an eye-witness, who was apparently a member of the old aristocracy and tells us indignantly how the Lord Protector came into the House in 'grey worsted stockings'.[173] They had their own way of writing love letters in those days: Mistress Osborne begins hers 'Sir' like a letter to a newspaper, and ends up 'your humble servant' or 'your faithful friend'. Almost a la Gordon.

your loving
son Jack.

TO ARTHUR GREEVES (W):

[Gastons]
25th Oct 1916

My dear Galahad,

As usually happens in these sort of things the violent controversy that we have been having for the last three weeks (& which I quite agree with you in giving up) has obscured the original subject of the discussion 'exaltation'. I want to know if you understand that sort of 'fey'

---

169 Frederick Samuel Boas, *Shakespeare and his Predecessors* (1896).
170 *The Odyssey of Homer*, done into English by Samuel Henry Butcher and Andrew Lang (1879).
171 *Letters from Dorothy Osborne to Sir William Temple: 1652–4*, ed. E.A. Parry (1888).
172 'Sir William Temple', *The Works of Lord Macaulay*, 12 vols. (1898), vol. IX, pp. 1–110.
173 *Letters from Dorothy Osborne*, introduction to letter 17 (24 April 1653), pp. 75–6.

state of mind which I described, or tried to describe, as coming on when one is very drowzy. Say what you think of this in your next letter. The question arose out of the 'Morte' which I have now read from the beginning of the Quest of the Grael to the end, thus finishing the whole thing. I certainly enjoyed it much better than before, and wished that I had the first volume here as well. The quietness of the end, and the description of Arthur's death are particularly good – you must give it another try sometime.

It was silly of me to ask you about 'Cranford' etc, as I have a MacMillan's list here and could have looked them up myself if I had had the sense: but I suppose you regard that as a big 'if'! I can understand that it is not pleasing to have these in the same edition as the Jane Austens, tho' for me of course it would make a nice change. I don't know when I shall buy some new books, as I am at present suffering from a flash of poverty – poverty comes in flashes like dulness or pleasure. When I do it will be either 'Our Village', 'Cranford' or Chaucer's 'Troilus & Cressida', if I can get a decent edition of it. By all accounts it is much more in my line than the 'Canterbury Tales', and anyway I can take no more interest in them since I have discovered that my Everyman edition is abridged & otherwise mutilated. I wish they wouldn't do that ('Lockhart',[174] you say, is another case) without telling you. I can't bear to have anything but what a man really wrote.

I have been reading the quaintest book this week, 'The Letters of Dorothy Osborne to Sir William Temple' in Everyman. I suppose, as a historian you will know all about those two, but in case you don't they lived in Cromwell's time. It is very interesting to read the ordinary everyday life of a girl in those days, and, tho' of course they are often dull there is a lot in them you would like: especially a description of how she spends the day and another of a summer evening in the garden. It is funny too, to notice that, just like us, she says that she never wished very hard for anything in her life without being dissapointed. But then I suppose everyone in the world has said that sometime or other. It is perhaps not a book to read straight through but well worth having.

My other reading – in French – has been Maeterlinck's 'Oiseau Bleu': of course I have read it before in English and seen it on the stage, as you know, but I am absolutely delighted to read it again. Now that I have the

---

174 John Gibson Lockhart, *Memoirs of the Life of Sir Walter Scott*, 7 vols. (1937–8).

original I wish you would adopt my English version, which is yours for-ever for the taking whenever you care to walk up to my room at home and find it on the little open bookcase. You could do it to day when you are home for lunch: I don't know why you have never read this glorious book before, but please do as I suggest & (though it is always dangerous, as we know, to recommend) I think you will have some real joy out of it. The scenes in the Temple of Night and in the Kingdom of the Future are exactly in our line.

Unfortunately we have not got a complete set of Scott here – only odd Everyman copies of which 'The Fair Maid of Perth' is not one. The ear-lier period is of course all the better for me, in fact to be honest I am childish enough to like 'Ivanhoe' better than any of his, and next to it 'Quentin Durward'. What is 'Guy Mannering' like? The alternative title of 'The Astrologer' sounds attractive but of course it may not have much to do with it.[175]

How's the poor, miserable, ill-fated, star-crossed, hapless, lonely, neglected, misunderstood puppy getting along? What are you going to call him, or rather, to speak properly, how hight he? Don't give him any commonplace name, and above all let it suit his character & appearance. Something like Sigurd, Pelleas or Mars if he is brisk and warlike, or Mime, Bickernocker or Knutt if he is ugly and quaint. Or perhaps he is dead by now, poor little devil!

The book you refer to is 'How to Form a Literary Taste' by Arnold Benett:[176] the edition is pretty but the book is not of any value. The very title – as if you set out to 'learn' literature the way you learn golf – shews that the author is not a real book-lover but only a priggish hack. I never read any of his novels & don't want to. Have you? By the way, he is a rather violent atheist, so I suppose I shall meet him by

'The fiery, flaming flood of Phlegethon',[177]

as good old Spencer has it. I am sure Lockhart's Life of Scott would be good, but 5 vols. at 3/6 each is too much: at any rate I had sooner get

---

175 Sir Walter Scott, *The Fair Maid of Perth* (1828); *Ivanhoe* (1820); *Quentin Durward* (1823); *Guy Mannering* (1815).

176 Arnold Bennett, *Literary Taste: How to Form It, with Detailed Instructions for Collecting a Complete Library of English Literature* (1909).

177 Spenser, *Faerie Queene*, I, v, 33, 3: 'And come to fiery flood of *Phlegeton*'.

Boswell if I were going to make a start on biography. I have read to day – there's absolutely no head or tale in this letter but you ought to be used to that by now – some 10 pages of 'Tristam Shandy'[178] and am wondering whether I like it. It is certainly the maddest book ever written or 'ever wrote' as dear Dorothy Osborne would say. It gives you the impression of an escaped lunatic's conversation while chasing his hat on a windy May morning. Yet there are beautiful serious parts in it though of a sentimental kind, as I know from my father. Have you ever come across it?

Tang-Tang there goes eleven o'clock 'Tis almost faery time'.[179] Don't you simply love going to bed. To curl up warmly in a nice warm bed, in the lovely darkness, that is so restful & then gradually drift away into sleep...Perhaps to enjoy this properly you must stay up till 11 working fairly hard at something – even a letter like this – so as to be really hungry for sleep. At home, like you, I often get started off on a train of thought which keeps me awake: here I am always too tired tho' goodness knows, eleven is early enough compared with some peoples times. It is strange, somehow, to read about concerts & Bill Patterson's visits etc; when I am at Bookham everything at home seems a little unreal. Each of you (i.e. my friends) is quite real by him or herself but 'en bloc' you seem like something out of a book. I wish I had been with you at D. Garrick.[180] I have always heard it was good. I shall not soon forget that morning at the far end of the strand, with the pleasant 'Frightfulness' of the Waves. I can still remember exactly what it felt like in the water and also running up to the cave. Take it all in all, we've had many pleasant times in our lives, & of these many (in my case) the most part together. You'd think I was bidding you an eternal farewell the way I'm going on. There's quarter past, so I'll say 'Good morning' not 'Night' for you read this at breakfast, don't you? I'm turning out the gas. Bon soir!

Jack

By the way, what sort of voice has a 'cracked turnip'. See your last letter.

---

178 Laurence Sterne, *The Life and Opinions of Tristram Shandy*, 9 vols (1760–7).
179 William Shakespeare, *A Midsummer Night's Dream* (1600), V, i, 372.
180 Thomas William Robertson, *David Garrick* (1864), a comedy in three acts.

TO HIS FATHER (LP V: 134–5):

[Gastons]
27/Oct./16.

My dear Papy,

Far be it from me to plead in extenuation of the disgusting freak of Algy that it was only fun. The debauches of a ruffian are not the less disgraceful because they are the product of levity, and Nero is said to have fiddled – about which I have my own views – on a famous occasion. As a matter of fact, to be serious, if Elia's theory that 'the best puns are the worst'[181] is true also of Limericks, Swinburne's Majorca one is a masterpiece, and so is the next one about Birmingham – though on the whole I would agree with you in preferring the 'deserted garden'.

I was very sorry to hear of the death of 'A Student in arms', whose book I read last holidays as you may remember.[182] I never met anything exactly like it before, it is wonderfully original and beautiful. Nothing in it however, if I remember aright, quite reaches the level of this last article, a wise and charming piece of work – and doubly so from the exquisite appropriateness with which it comes from the pen of a man who died a few days after writing it. As you say, there is almost something divine about the way in which he sums up his beliefs and his views on death, just as though he knew the end was coming and meant to finish off his work. The substance of this paper resembles Bernard Shaw's cry, 'Why not give Christianity a trial?' – so far at least as the writing of a scholar and a gentleman can resemble that of a Philistine. Indeed nowadays there seems to be a tendency in that direction: there is some possibility of getting back it appears, to what Christ actually did teach, and clearing away all the additions His followers have been tacking on for the last twenty centuries.

Before leaving the subject of 'Student in Arms', I must draw your attention to what seems a mis-print in the sentence marked. Surely the full stop should come after 'discouraged', and not after 'offend'. The author first states a general principle 'Anxious responsibility is discouraged', and then

---

181 Charles Lamb, 'That the Worst Puns are the Best', *The Last Essays of Elia* (1833).
182 *A Student in Arms*, with an Introduction by John St Loe Stracher (1916) was published anonymously. Lewis and his father had seen a piece in *The Spectator*, vol. 117 (21 October 1916), pp. 466–7, entitled 'In Memory of "A Student in Arms" (Second Lieutenant Donald Hankey, Killed in Action on the Somme, October 12th, 1916).'

goes on to quote as an example of this, the fact that 'if our limbs offend etc.'. As it stands, the sense is not so clear.[183]

I am glad that all these 'manifestations' of Boas prove to emanate from the same 'quella' as editors of MSS. say: perhaps some day, he might be of use to us. Congratulate Dick from me on his decoration and Joey on his scholarship – as to which we can only pray 'adsit omen.'

That is rather a fine article on Hackluyt in this weeks Literary Supplement[184] and a good deal of it might stand as an apology – in the Newman sense of course – for my hours spent on poor Mandeville. The quotation about the deer coming down to the water 'as we rowed'[185] is particularly attractive.

How goes the picture? Even if Mr. Baker[186] is not the society you would choose, still even a compulsory companion (that's a pretty sounding mouthful) to swallow up some part of your solitary week ends is a

---

183 Following the tribute to 'A Student in Arms' in *The Spectator* of 21 October 1916 was a piece written weeks before by Lieutenant Hankey entitled 'Don't Worry, by a Student in Arms'. The sentence which Lewis believed to contain a misprint occurred in a passage in which Lieutenant Hankey said: 'We are not told to set a high value on our lives, and to spend them with care for the good of the Kingdom. On the contrary, we are told to risk our lives recklessly if we would preserve them. A sense of anxious responsibility is discouraged if our limbs cause us to offend. We are advised to cut them off' (p. 468). For more information on this remarkable young man see Kenneth G. Budd, *The Story of Donald Hankey* (1931).

184 'The Great Adventurer (Richard Hakluyt, 1552–1616)', *The Times Literary Supplement* (26 October 1916), pp. 505–6.

185 ibid., p. 506.

186 Warnie adds this note in LP V: 135: 'Mr. Baker was a local artist of some repute; he had painted Richard II in 1897 – a really admirable water colour – The Revd. Thomas Hamilton in 1903 in oils, and the portrait here referred to of Albert in water colour; the latter is signed and dated "A.R. Baker. 1917." All three portraits were the property of Albert, and now (1934) hang in Clive's rooms in Magdalen College. Mr. Baker's wife was a violent Suffragette and a friend of Lily Suffren's. The Albert portrait, though not without merit, is the least satisfactory of the three.'

When C.S. Lewis moved to Cambridge in 1955 he took the portraits of Grandfather Lewis (Richard II) and Grandfather Hamilton (Rev. Thomas Hamilton) with him. Then, when he died, the portrait of Grandfather Hamilton went to the Church of St Mark's, Dundela, where it hangs in the Rectory, and the portrait of Grandfather Lewis went to a Lewis cousin. For years Baker's portrait of Albert Lewis was lost sight of. Then in 1994 it was found in Magdalen College, Oxford, where it had been since it was brought over from Belfast in 1930. There is a photograph of the painting in Walter Hooper, 'The Lewis That Stayed Behind', *Magdalen College Record* (1995).

good thing. Indeed logically, the more disagreeable the companion the more he ought to reconcile you to subsequent loneliness.

your loving

son Jack.

TO ARTHUR GREEVES (W):

[Gastons
1 November 1916]

My dear Galahad,

I can't let it pass unchallegend that you should put 'Boewulf' and 'Malory' together as if they belonged to the same class. One is a mediaeval, English prose romance and the other an Anglo Saxon epic poem: one is Christian, the other heathen: one we read just as it was actually written, the other in a translation. So you can like one without the other, and any way you must like or dislike them both for different reasons. It is always very difficult of course to explain to another person the good points of a book he doesn't like. I know what you mean by that 'crampy' feeling: you mean there are no descriptions in Beowulf as in a modern book, so little is told you & you have to imagine so much for yourself.

Well, for one thing, remember that nearly all your reading is confined to about 150 years of one particular country: this is no disgrace to you, most people's circle is far smaller. But still, compared with the world this one little period of English literature is very small, and tho' you (and I of course) are so accustomed to the particular kinds of art we find inside it, yet we must remember that there are an infinite variety outside it, quite as good in different ways. And so, if you suddenly go back to an Anglo-Saxon gleeman's lay, you come up against something absolutely different – a different world. If you are to enjoy it, you must forget your previous ideas of what a book should be and try and put yourself back in the position of the people for whom it was first made. When I was reading it I tried to imagine myself as an old Saxon thane sitting in my hall of a winter's night, with the wolves & storm outside and the old fellow singing his story. In this way you get the atmosphere of terror that runs through it – the horror of the old barbarous days when the land was all forests and when you thought that a demon might come to your house any night & carry you off. The description of Grendel stalking up from his 'fen and fastness' thrilled me. Besides, I loved the simplicity of the old life it represents: it comes as a relief to get away from all complications about characters & 'problems' to a time when hunting, fighting, eating, drinking & loving were all a man had to think of it. And lastly, always remember it's a translation which spoils most things.

As to 'Malory' I liked it so awfully this time – far better than before – that I don't know what to say. How can I explain? For one thing, to me it is a world of its own, like Jane Austen. Though impossible, it is very fully realized, and all the characters are old friends, we know them so well: you get right away in those forests and somehow to me all the adventures & meetings & dragons seem very real. (I don't beleive that last sentence conveys my meaning a bit) Then too I find in it a rest as you do in Scott: he (M. I mean) is so quiet after our modern writers & thinks of his 'art' so little: he is not self-conscious. Of course he doesn't describe as Morris does, but then he doesn't need to: in the 'Well' you feel it is only a tale suddenly invented and therefore everything has to be described. But the Round Table is different: it *was* a hundred years ago & shall be a hundred years hence. It wasn't just made up like an ordinary tale, it grew. Malory seems to me almost a historian: his world is real to me, his characters are old friends whom you get to know better & better as you go on – he is a companiabl author & good when you're lonely.

I suppose this sounds all rot? But after all when you say it 'doesn't suit you' you strike at the root of the matter. Perhaps you can't enjoy it just as I couldn't enjoy Green's Short History:[187] it is not my fault that I don't like oysters but no reasoning will make me like them. This controversy has proved even more expansive than the other: if you had given me any excuse for going on with the 'exaltation' one I'm afraid I should never get to bed to-night. By the way I suppose at 10 o'clock when I am beginning your letter you are just getting into bed? Remember at 10 next Wednesday night to imagine me just spreading out your one in front of me and starting to jaw. But seriously, do I bore you. I have taken up such reams about 'Boewulf' etc. It is easy to explain a thought, but to explain a feeling is very hard.

Last week-end I spent in reading 'The Professor'. It forms a nice sort of suppliment to Villette – something [like] the same story told from the man's side. I liked the description of Hunsden extremely & also the detestable brother. I do wish she had left out the awful poetry in the proposal scene: they are the worst verses in the language I should think. Its

---

187 John Richard Green, *Short History of the English People* (1874).

difficult to understand how a woman of Ch. Brontës genius could help seeing how bad they were. But on the whole it is a very enjoyable book, tho' not of course to be compared with her other three. What did you think of it?

Yes, I shall be home for Xmas, rather earlier in fact. This exam.[188] will take place in the first week of December and when it is over I shall come straight home. I am beginning to funk it rather: I wish you were in for it with me (so as to be sure of one, at least, worse than myself). I wish I could see 'The Winter's Tale': it, 'The Midsummer's Nights Dream' & the Tempest are the only things of Shakespeare I really appreciate, except the Sonnets.[189] It is a very sweet, sort of old fairy-tale style of thing. You must certainly see it. As to Bennet's book, if a person was really a book-lover, however ignorant, he wouldn't go and look up a text book to see what to buy, as if literature was a subject to be learned like algebra: one thing would lead him to another & he would go through the usual mistakes & gain experience. I hate this idea of 'forming a taste'. If anyone like the feuilletons in the 'Sketch' better than Spenser, for Heaven's sake let him read them: anything is better than to read things he doesn't really like because they are thought classical. I say, old man, it's beastly kind of you to keep the 'Country of the Blind' till I come. Of course if you hadn't told me I should have thought you would throw it off the top of the tram. Ha-Ha-Ha-Ha, likewise He-He-He! (You do love that sort of writing!) By the way why do you call it your dog if it lives at Glenmachen? I suppose in the same way as you like Shakespeare but I don't like reading him? Can't write more to night, your last letter was very short –

J.

TO HIS FATHER (LP V: 142):

[Gastons]
3/11/16.

My dear Papy,

This is a surprise. I can hardly account for it, if it be true – a jump from the rank of second Lieutenant to that of Captain is very unusual, is it not?[190] Even among the temporary people. However, I suppose you will

---

188 The scholarship examination for Oxford.

189 William Shakespeare, *The Winter's Tale* (1623); *The Tempest* (1623); *Sonnets* (1609).

190 Warnie, who was with the 3rd Company 7th Division in France, had been promoted to temporary captain on 1 October.

know all about it in your next letter from Big Brother, who will doubtless communicate the facts with much codotto. I only hope we shall not be disappointed in any way.

I thought that I had told you about the colleges, but apparently not. We have finally burned our boats and sent in my name for the big group. This has not been without a good deal of hesitation, but I think on the whole it was the wisest plan. There are very strong arguments on both sides, and we can only hope for the best. The man at New tells us that the candidates for scholarships will be either lodged in the colleges or directed to 'digs' selected by the University – apparently Alma Mater takes more care than we supposed, for even her sons elect (Bow! Bow!). He is going to write again of course, and indeed I am surprised that we have not heard from him yet. As to the 'Accidents' I really can't see on what principle my Latin and Greek proses may be quite good for five days and come out with some awful blunder on the sixth – which is what happens. I am sure I take as much trouble on one day as on another. It is at times a bit disheartening, but we pray that the exam may not come on an 'off' day. In the German Kirk thinks I am doing better.

I am reading at present, what do you think? Our own friend 'Pilgrim's Progress'.[191] It is one of those books that are usually read too early to appreciate, and perhaps don't come back to. I am very glad however to have discovered it. The allegory of course is obvious and even childish, but just as a romance it is unsurpassed, and also as a specimen of real English. Try a bit of your Ruskin or Macaulay after it, and see the difference between diamonds and tinsel.

It is one of those afternoons here when the sky is the colour of putty and the rain comes down in sheets for hour after hour: perhaps we are beginning the winter at last. Tell me all the further news about the 'captaincy' as soon as you know anything.

your loving
son Jack.

---

191 John Bunyan, *The Pilgrim's Progress* (1678; 1684).

TO ARTHUR GREEVES (W):

[Gastons
8 November 1916]

My dear Arthur,

You certainly have all the luck! I should give anything to be at home for these operas. (Cant get a decent pen so you'll have to do with pencil this week) As I can't see them myself I can only hope & pray devoutly that they will be badly sung & staged, your seat be uncomfortable, yr. neighbours talkative & your escapade detected by your terrible parent – Amen.

To be serious: if I were going to three of them I should choose Aida & the Zauberflut[192] straight off without hesitation: the latter is of course old fashioned but, to me – tho' of course my views on music are those of an ignoramus – the formal old beauty of old music has something very attractive about it. At all events a thing with an overture like that must be good. As to the libretto, my ideas are rather hazy, but an article on it which I read last year in the 'Times' gave me the impression of something rather nice & fantastic. These two then I'd certainly go to: in the third it is more difficult to decide. 'Tales of Hoffman'[193] I thought was a comic opera – at any rate I am sure it's not in the first rank. 'Carmen' & 'the Lily'[194] are out of the question – the latter being an awful hurdy-gurdy, tawdry business by all accounts. Perhaps on the whole you would get more pleasure out of 'Faust' than any: here too you'd have the dramatic interest as well. 'Pagliacci' & 'Cavaleria' you have seen haven't you? – Though of course that's no reason why you shouldn't see them again.

'En passant' I don't exactly 'despise' your opera-book. I think it very useful like a Greek grammar or a time-table, but no more a 'book' in the proper sense than they are. For instance I should never think of getting 'Bradshaw's Railway Guide' printed on hand made paper with illustrations by Rackham, wd you? And talking about Rackham I saw in my French list the other day an edition of Perrault's 'Contes'[195] 'avec gravures en couleurs de Rackham' for 1 fr. 95 (at the present rate of exchange

---

192 i.e. Mozart's opera *Die Zauberflöte* (*The Magic Flute*).

193 *Tales of Hoffman*, an opera by Jacques Offenbach, first performed in 1881.

194 *The Lily of Killarney*, an opera by Julius Benedick (with libretto by John Oxenford and Dion Boucicault, based on the latter's play, *The Colleen Bawn*), was first performed in 1862.

195 Charles Perrault, *Histoires et Contes du Temps Passé* (1697).

about 1/6, I suppose). If its the same Rackham that wd. be wonderful value, wouldn't it? Though I daresay Perrault himself (the French 'Hans Anderson') would not be up to much, – coming as he did of the most prosaic nation on earth.

It is hardly fair to be sarcastick about my 'controversies' as you deliberately asked for both of them. I am afraid I have not made my views on old literature very clear but it can't be helped. The word 'feuilleton' is French, I suppose, originally but quite naturalized. (By the way can the whole of Bernagh not raise a French dictionary? I might give you one in calf for an Xmas box!) It means the horrible serial stories that run in the daily papers: if you've never happened to glance at one it's worth your while. They are unique! Yes, Sir!, it IS correct to say 'if he like' & not 'if he likes' – tho' a little pedantic.

I thought you would enjoy 'The Antiquary'. The scene on the beach is fine & tho' it hadn't struck me before the whole scenery of 'Fairport' is rather like Portsalon. What I liked best was the description of the antiquary's room at Monkbarns – I wish I could fill up my room with old things like that – also the scene where the doting old woman sings them the ballad at her cottage, but perhaps you haven't come to that yet. Of course the hero – as usual in Scott – is a mere puppet, but there are so many other good characters that it doesn't much matter.

What fiddlesticks about Malory being only a translation: I wish you were here that I could have the pleasure of stripping every shred of skin from your bones and giving your intestines to the birds of the air. What do you mean by saying 'It' is 'an old French legend': the 'Morte' includes a hundred different Arthurian legends & as you know the Arthur myth is Welsh. Of course he didn't invent the legends any more than Morris invented the Jason legends: but his book is an original work all the same. Just as the famous 'Loki Bound' of Lewis is based upon a story in the Edda, but still the poem is original – the materials being re-created by the genius of that incomparable poet. As a matter of fact I am at present reading a real 'old french' romance 'The High History of the Holy Graal' translated in the lovely 'Temple Classics'.[196] If I dared to advise you any longer – . It is absolute heaven: it is more mystic & eerie than the 'Morte'

---

196 *The High History of the Holy Graal* was translated (from the first volume of *Perceval le Gallois*, ed. C. Potvin) by Sebastian Evans, with illustrations by Edward Burne-Jones (1898).

& has [a] more connected plot. I think there are parts of it even you'd like.

I am also reading Chaucer's minor poems ('World's Classics',[197] a scrubby edition but the only one I can find) and am half way thr[ough] 'The House of Fame', a dream poem half funny & half fantastic that I like very much. But the print, tho' clear, is very small. As to 'The Letters of D.O. to W.T.' I suggest you had better have a look at them in my copy before you do anything. There is a lot in them I think you would like but also a good deal that is dull.

I got this morning a letter from His Majesty the King of the Fiji isles expressing his pleasure at your gift. How much he appreciates it may be seen in his own terse and elegant words 'Oor mi dalara bo chorabu plat-lark pho'.

We have had glorious storms here & a big old elm at the bottom of the garden is down by the roots. There is something majestic about a giant tree lying dead like this.

By the way take care of that weak heart of yours: it seems pretty sure that CONSCRIPTION is coming to Ireland now. I for one shall be jolly glad to see some relations of mine (and some of yours) made to behave like men at last. Goodnight, old man –

Jack

TO HIS FATHER (LP V: 143):

[Gastons]
9th Nov. 1916.

My dear Papy,

As it happened I had heard from Warnie himself shortly after my letter to you and thus got the truth about the promotion.[198] I think we really have a right to plume ourselves on this – the double step is so very rare. You say 'if inside the next year it is made permanent': is there any prospect of that's happening? If so we had better go and live with him or else get him to make us a separation allowance each. In the mean time avoid your bricklaying friend who may have something to say to you on

---

197 Chaucer, *The Minor Poems*, ed. Walter W. Skeat (1888).

198 Warnie wrote to his father on 30 October saying: 'I have at last got my step. I have got the temp. rank of Captain, dated back to 1/10/16 – exactly two years from the date I got my Commission' (LP V: 139).

the subject of 'temporary' commands. (Ah, these conversations between a brick layer and a brick dropper!)

Your encouragements – even the salts – are very pleasant to read, and it is always a great comfort to be assured that if I lose, I lose nothing more than a scholarship. As to the real prospects of that, they are on the knees of the gods, and possibly the 'putty sky' when I last wrote to you had something to do with my impressions. The consolation of having deserved a thing is perhaps one we should all rather apply to our rivals than to ourselves.

I don't think I shall need any new clothes as I have three good suits (1) besides my everyday one, and two should be enough to take with me. Should I take the dress suit now that we know I shall not go to an hotel? And by the way, when the man says lodgings are to be 'found', does he mean that we get them free?

The hero of 'Lady Connie' was certainly a detestable fellow, though I must admit that in places I found something rather attractive about him. At the auction of the pictures he is particularly great. But on the whole, as you say, the book is unsatisfactory, and she ought to have married the Pole What's his name. We are all reading Clodd's memoirs[199] here, which you will have seen reviewed everywhere. It is rather disappointing though, and the best story in it is the one about the Shah of Persia quoted in the Spectator 'Library Supplement'. There is a certain vulgarity about Clodd: he seems rather too pleased with his famous friends. I like last week's 'Romance' by the Student in Arms very much – in some ways as much as the other, tho' perhaps you will not agree with me.[200]

We have got over the rain at last after one or two fearful storms in which a fine old elm at the bottom of the garden, the pride of Kirk's

---

199 Edward Clodd (1840–1930), banker and author, had just published his *Memoirs* (1916).

200 An essay entitled 'Romance' by 'A Student at Arms' (Donald Hankey) was published posthumously in *The Spectator*, vol. 117 (4 November 1916), pp. 544–5. The sentiments expressed by the young soldier are so like those Lewis was later to hold that they are worth illustrating by these last sentences of the essay: 'For those boys who hate the war, and suffer and endure with the smile that is sometimes so difficult, and long with a great longing for home and peace – some day some of them will look back on these days and will tell themselves that after all it was "Romance," the adventure which made their lives worth while. And they will long to feel once again the stirring of the old comradeship and love and loyalty, to dip their clasp-knives into the same pot of jam, and lie in the same dug-out, and work on the same bit of wire with the same machine gun striking terror into their hearts, and look into each other's

heart, and of fabulous age, has come down. Today it is sunny and cold. That was a bad business in the Irish Sea, wasn't it?

 your loving
 son Jack.

(1). That's a funny mistake. I suppose I'm trying to make adjectives agree in English. – J.

TO ARTHUR GREEVES (W):

[Gastons
15 November 1916]

 Dear Arthur,

 I must begin my letter this week by heartily apologizing for some foolish remarks which I thoughtlessly directed against a book for whose merits your approval should have been to me and to all who enjoy the honour of your friendship a sufficient guarantee. As you very properly remind me, I am profoundly ignorant of the scientific side of music in which you specially excel, while my aesthetic judgements on the subject are modelled upon the sane and temperate example of your own criticism. What amends I can make by studying with diligence the admirable work which you commend, shall immediately be made: for, believe me, I am not insensible of the kindness and indulgence which a man of your education has displayed in such musical discussions to a boy so ill informed as I.

 Your verdict upon Macdonald's tale was worthy of so shrewd and serious a gentleman as yourself: I can well understand that the puerilities which attract a schoolboy may indeed seem [a] waste of time to an experienced business man. I am not a little ashamed of my own light-headedness, and am resolved to turn my attention to that excellent study of history with which you beguile your leisure. Here may I take the liberty of expressing my ardent and continued admiration of those

---

eyes for the same courageous smile. For Romance, after all, is woven of the emotions, especially the elemental ones of love and loyalty and fear and pain. We men are never content! In the dull routine of normal life we sigh for Romance, and sometimes seek to create it artificially, stimulating spurious passions, plunging into muddy depths in search of it. Now we have got it we sigh for a quiet life. But some day those who have not died will say: "Thank God I have lived! I have loved, and endured, and trembled, and trembling, dared. I have had my romance'" (p. 545).

qualities which make you the ornament of the society to which you belong: first and foremost the practical nature of your character which enables you to relinquish in a moment those trivial fairy tales and such like useless inventions: then your habits of economy and regularity, your sound knowledge of the Lord's Word, your unaffected piety, your knowledge of modern thought, the perfect control of your temper, the justness of your sentiments and – above all – the elegance of your language.

Well! we'll drop it now, as I want some room left for a chat: but honestly thats the sort of answer your last letter seemed to expect. Goodness!, you gave me an awful dressing down! And all because I dared to make a joke on a book of yours that has been a recognised subject for fooling this year or so. Perhaps, however, you just happened to be in bad form when you wrote, so I needn't take it too seriously. Or, what is more likely, J. M.[201] has been annoying you and I come in for the aftermath. Anyway, language such as I have just read is not pleasant, and I was on the point of writing a very rude letter. But I remembered, what I do hope you will remember old man, that real friendships are very, very rare and one doesn't want to endanger them by quarrelling over trifles. We seem to be always sparing now a days: I dare say its largely my fault (tho' in this case I really don't know why you're so angry) but anyway do let us stop it. Perhaps my nerves are a bit on edge as I get nearer to this abominable exam., and that makes me irritable. But I'll try to do my best if you will.

So I may imagine you this evening just about now coming from dinner at Lily's with Mr. Thompson, with the memory of 'Aida' from last night and the prospect of the 'Magic Flute' to-morrow! I would give much to be in your place, and more to be in the same place with both of us there. I am very interested to hear what you think of the 'Flute', so mind you give me a special account of it – and accounts of the others also. Aida, of course, if well sung and staged must be enjoyable. I do hope you found them all three so, for that matter.

It must be lovely to really appreciate music (I am not fooling now). My taste for it was always that of a philistine and I am afraid even that is leaving me now. Perhaps it is as well I was not with you, or I might just have sat eating my heart out because I couldn't enjoy what I would have enjoyed in those delightful days when we first 'discovered' one another. But even if music fails I still have books!

---

201 Janie McNeill.

And talking about books I am surprised that you don't say more of the 'Golden Key':[202] to me it was absolute heaven from the moment when Tangle ran into the wood to the glorious end in those mysterious caves. What a lovely idea 'The country from which the shadows fall'! It is funny that we should both have the same idea about the Temple Classics. I was almost sure they were out of print and only wrote on the off chance for the Pilgrims' Progress (did I mention it? I have read it again and am awfully bucked) and then for the 'Grael'. I wonder would Mullan's tell you a thing was out of print just because they didn't think it worth while to get you the few we'd want At any rate, for paper etc they are far the prettiest cheap books I know, and if you still think of getting 'The Compleat Angler'[203] I should advise you to try this edition. The 'set' of the print and the notes in the nice broad margin are what I particularly like – Also the frontispieces – in some. My 'Grael' has a lovely one (in the extreme mediaeval style of course) in each volume by Burne-Jones & a title page design that reminds me of the Goodfridaymusic. I envy you, having your Letters of D.O. to W.T. in the Wayfarers – a very nice series except for the end leaf if I remember right – mine is only the 1/- Everyman and rather shop-soiled at that!

Was Mr. Thompson as nice as ever last night? He is a man I should love to meet again – but here too you have all the luck. Are you still reading 'The Antiquary' and does it still please you as much as ever? Here I am at the end of my letter and I had meant to give you a long jaw about some beautiful frost & mist effects I saw on Saturday evening (like Oldbuck's article on Castrametation) but you will have to pine without it. I must say I heartily agree with your remarks about autumn. There are some lovely colours here, & though I fancy there are finer 'cold' looking afternoons at home, the woods here are perhaps even richer.

Time to dry up now. My head is splitting, & my feet are like ice so I suppose if you were here you'd explain to me how & why I was in for a cold. Well I'd be glad to have you even on those terms. Good-night & do be indulgent to my many failings. There's a frost –

J.

202 George MacDonald, *Short Stories* ('The Light Princess', 'The Giant's Heart', 'The Golden Key') (1928).
203 Izaak Walton, *The Compleat Angler* (1653).

TO HIS FATHER (LP V: 145–6):

[Gastons]
19th Nov. 1916.

My dear Papy,

It is Sunday – though not very early in the morning – and so I am afraid this letter will be late: but yours did not arrive until yesterday and this is really the first time I have had. I have heard of the failing of my spelling in many places, at many seasons, and from many sources (even the 'for a boy of your age it is scandalous' or sometimes 'ludicrous' has a familiar ring) and I am only too well aware of the truth. However, we must hope for the best. As to the other little episode, we must record 'marker, one up!' But you have forgotten to say what the word was: I should like to know.

In spite of the tutor's obliging promise to find, or to use the safer form 'discover' lodgings, a letter arrived from him two or three days ago with a form for entrance in which, among other things, he wants 'your adress during examination' – but no word of advice. I accordingly wrote at once to my Malvern friend, who replied saying that he could not tell of any place, but that candidates as a rule write and ask the college. I did this and got an answer saying he would let me know of some place 'presently' and in the meantime I am to fill up the rest of the form and send it. This I am doing today, putting down the colleges in the order we arranged. He also asks for my birth certificate, which is rather a nuisance. Perhaps you had better see about that exemption business.

I was very sorry when I read the letter from my friend Cooper. His people have gone bankrupt and he has come through a very rough time, although he does not say anything about leaving the Coll. It must be very hard lines on him and he was a thoroughly good fellow. I had asked to be remembered to Smugy and the old man has wished me every success and advised me to read my 'Little Thompson' via Cooper.

It is snowing fast as I write, and has been since yesterday evening. Kirk is actually in bed this morning 'with a cold'. This is so very rare with him that I confess it makes me a little uneasy. Thanks very much but I think your suit case or Warnie's will do very well for the present trip, and we can talk about the other later on.

your loving
son Jack.

TO ARTHUR GREEVES (W):

[Gastons
22 November 1916]

My dear Arthur,

I quite agree with you and hope we shall have no more controversies at any rate for the present: for, as you say, it is too much to hope that we should live in peace and good will for more than a few weeks continuously. In passing I must explain that when I said your 'language was not pleasant' I only meant the general tone of what you said – 'diction' or 'sentiments' as Jane Austin would have delighted to put it. I wasn't using 'language' in the slang sense of the word meaning swearing – for of course I don't mind 'language' of that sort in itself. However, this is only a lesson in English & has nothing to do with the argument, which we will consign to the swarthy mere of Acheron!

Which reminds me I am no longer in a position to take your advice about 'Letters from Hell' as we had a jumble sale for the red cross or something in 'our village' last week and I contributed this. A mean enough offering indeed but they tell me it sold for 1/6! I am at present enjoying the malicious pleasure of expecting that the buyer will be as dissapointed as I was.

What a pity about the 'Magic Flute': I particularly wanted to hear your impressions of it. I am surprised to learn that it is 'comic' (a horrid word to describe a horrid thing) tho' of course it may only be nice humour of the fantastic kind. Your description of Aida is most tantalizing, and I would love to have been there. Even if I had found that I could no longer enjoy the music – tho' I think I am still up to Verdi – I could always have amused myself by talking to you or coughing loudly in the middle of the best passages! Seriously, did they play that lovely prelude well and did the Belfast boors give you a chance to hear it in peace? I daresay I am wrong about the 'Wayfarer's Library': but whatever the end-leaves be like I remember that the whole effect is good. Have you looked at 'Dorothy Osborne' yet and do you think you will like her? I am desperately in love with her and have accordingly made arrangements to commit suicide from 10 till 4 to-morrow precisely. I wonder does the 'Wayfarer' series publish my latest discovery – the most glorious novel (almost) that I have ever read. I daresay you have read it already or at any rate you must have hearded it praised too often to need my advice. It is Nathaniel Hawthorne's 'House with the Seven

Gables'.[204] I love the idea of a house with a curse! And although there is nothing supernatural in the story itself there is a brooding sense of mystery and fate over the whole thing: Have you read it? See if it is in the 'Wayfarers' as I want to get an edition of my own as soon as possible.

I am afraid I have really no memories! I had clean forgotten your ever speaking to me about the 'Golden Key': tho' I well remember setting off in the cab that grey, early morning and waiting for L. & G.[205] at the station! How funny Gordon was with his stiff back! That sounds a strange thing to say but you know what I mean. But after all has not Hewlett (or is it some one else) told us that the fairies have the shortest memories of all! So short that they cannot even remember their lovers from one new moon till the next.

I must say I admire your pluck in taking back 'The Antiquary' after so many years! But as you say the books we buy or return doesnt make much matter to Macmullans. I was sure you'd like the Antiquary very much. I tried to start 'Guy Mannering' on Saturday but some how it didn't grip me. As to the 'mist scene' I am afraid tho' it was very beautiful at the time it will hardly come to life again,

> 'inimitable on earth
> By modle or by shading pencil drawn.'

I will leave you to imagine it.

Your imagination by the way has had a long enough rest by now. I have so far purposely refrained from saying anything about further instalments of 'Papillon', for fear, since you seemed to have no inclination to go on with it, that it might only hinder you from starting something new. But apparently this is not coming off. Do let us have something – tale, novel, what you will. I am revolving plans for a sort of fantasy much shorter than Bleheris and – which I hope will be an improvement – in modern English. I don't know exactly when I shall inflict the first instalment upon you, but like the people in Northanger Abbey you may be prepared for something 'really horrible'.

Talking about 'Northanger' I have been condemned during this last week to watch Mrs K. reading it in her own edition – your one. I wish

---

204 Nathaniel Hawthorne, *The House of the Seven Gables* (1851).
205 Lily and Gordon Ewart.

you could have seen it. It is not that she actually dirtied it, but what is almost worse she held it so rudely and so close over the fire that the boards have developed a permanent curve and the whole book has a horrible twist! It went to my heart all the more because it was your copy: at least I couldn't get that idea out of my head[.] Must stop now sorry I was late starting to night.

Jack

TO HIS FATHER (LP V: 146-7):

[Gastons]
Tues. 28th Nov. 1916.

My dear Papy,

This is not a proper letter – I will write you that later on when I have got yours. Meanwhile I am writing only to ask you to send me either your suit case or Warnie's as soon as you get this, for the fateful day is next Tuesday. Although the tutor said he would write and tell me of lodgings and also the place of the exam he has as yet done neither of these things: but I suppose its alright. Write soon to your

loving son,
Jack.

TO ARTHUR GREEVES (W):

[Gastons
29 November 1916]

Although by experience I am somewhat shy of recommending books to other people I think I am quite safe in earnestly advising you to make 'the Gables' your next purchase. By the way I shouldn't have said 'mystery', there is really no mystery in the proper sense of the word, but a sort of feeling of fate & inevitable horror as in 'Wuthering Heights'. I really think I have never enjoyed a novel more. There is one lovely scene where the villain – Judge Phycheon – has suddenly died in his chair, all alone in the old house, and it describes the corpse sitting there as the day wears on and the room grows darker – darker – and the ticking of his watch. But that sort of bald description is no use! I must leave you to read that wonderful chapter to yourself. There is also a very good 'story in a story' – curiously resembling the Cosmo one[206] tho' of course not so

---

206 Cosmo von Wehrstahl in MacDonald's *Phantastes*.

openly impossible. I intend to read all Hawthorne after this. What a pity such a genius should be a beastly American!

I am sorry to hear of your infatuation (very much inFATuation)* for a certain lady, but you need not despair, nor do I propose to call you out; we will divide mother & daughter between us, and you can have first choice! I really don't know which would be the worse do you?

That is certainly a glorious prelude to Aida. Do you remember that first afternoon last hols! How dissappointed we were at first and yet how we enjoyed ourselves afterwards sitting under those trees in the evening (or rather late afternoon) sunlight & throwing pencils & poems from one to the other? Well, we shall soon be there again if all goes well. I am going up for this damnable exam next Monday, shall be back here not later than Saturday & home on the following Monday if not sooner. So that is all well, but I wish to hell next week was over. Don't you sympathise with me? Pray for me to all your gods and goddesses like a good man!

No the Meagre One was not born with a squint: but long, long, long ago, so long ago that Stonehenge had a roof and walls & was a new built temple, he killed a spider. The good people of his day, outraged at this barbarity, stuck a dagger thro his nerve centre which paralyzed him without making him unconscious, seated him on the altar at St. Henge's temple & locked him up with the spiders son. The latter began to spin a solid mass of cobwebs from the Opposite corner. Very very slowly through countless years the web grew while the poor Meagre One – who couldn't die – developed a squint from watching it getting nearer. At last after countless ages Stonehenge dissapeared under an enormous mass of web & remained thus till one day Merlin hapenned to set a match to it and so discover what was inside: hence the myth of Merlin's having 'built' St. Henge's. To this day if you go there at sunrise & run round it 7 times, looking over your shoulder you can see again the wretched prisoner trying to struggle as the horrid sticky strands close round him. Cheap excursion trains are run for those who wish to try it.

The Tales of a Grandfather[207] in a rather scrubby but old edition has lived in the study these ten years, so you may try a taste of it before risking your money. I imagine it is in rather a childish style, tho' of course you know more about Scott than I do.

207 Sir Walter Scott, *Tales of a Grandfather* (1745–6).

I am sorry to hear that you have not yet begun your novel, and as I am sending you four pages of punishment I trust you will let me have something in your next letter. Which reminds [me] I don't know what my address will be at Oxford so you must just write to Bookham as usual. Do go on with the good work. What about taking that magic story Mr Thompson told us, for instance, toning down the supernatural parts a bit & making a Donegal novel of the Bronte type? Or else working that local idea of the Easelys[208] and all. Remember the second attempt will be easier & pleasanter than the first, and the third than the second.

Talking about the Easeleys, whether I read 'Guy Mannering' or no I shall not take to skimming as Kelsie does – for much as we esteem our beautiful and accomplished cousin – as Mr Collins[209] would have said – I don't think I shall follow her in literary matters. I am quite sure that every thing bad is true of your cousin Florence: she and her sister are young women who need transportation – as also my cousins at Bloomfield.[210] But indeed if only those who deserved to have books had them! – who besides you & me would there be to support the booksellers?

We have had some glorious frosty mornings here, with the fields all white & the sun coming up late like a red hot ball behind the bare woods. How I do love winter. We have had a book of Yeats' prose out of the library, and this has revived my taste for things Gaelic & mystic. Ask Mullan's if he knows a book called 'The Rosacrutian Cosmo Conception' or any on that subject. Gute Nacht. I wish I were dead –

Jack

*Ha! Ha! Poor little Bill, he only tries to be agreeee-able.

---

208 Lewis was to remember this idea of a novel cast in modern-day Ulster. In about 1928 he wrote two chapters of a novel about a family called Easley, which fragment is which is found in LP IX: 291–300.

209 The pompous and silly clergyman in *Pride and Prejudice* who was so obsequious to persons of high social station.

210 The wife and children of Joseph Lewis (1856–1908). See **The Lewis Family** in the Biographical Appendix.

TO HIS FATHER (LP V: 152–3):

[Gastons]
Friday Dec. 1st 1916

My dear Papy,

I am sorry I did not tell you earlier that the exam was so soon, but the idea was so familiar in my own mind that I only just realized, the day when I wrote to you, that I had never given you the date. I suppose by the time this reaches you, you will have sent off the suit case etc., but even if you have not had time, I dare say Mrs. K. would have something that would serve. So far, that pestilent knave at New College has failed to keep his promise of letting me know about lodgings: however, if the worst comes to the worst I can always go to an hotel, though of course this will be more expensive for you and less convenient for me.

We have also seen about this exemption business. K. and I both thought the matter beyond us, so we decided to consult my solicitors (Don't forget the 'my' – or is 'my man of business' the better expression) at Leatherhead. Having only a limited knowledge of solicitor's offices – purely provincial in fact – I was duly impressed. He was a state solicitor – a little, bald, figetty man, in a dingy black suit, and he advised me to put my case before the Chief Recruiting officer at Guildford. I wrote to the latter and today, after a long interval, have a reply saying that I am exempt from the Military Service Act, but that I must get registered at once: which I shall do either this afternoon or tomorrow.

The cold here is quite as bad as with you, and it freezes every night. This week I have been reading 'The House of the Seven Gables' which I have often heard praised but never met before. Have you? It is well worth the reading. As to coming home, the Oxford authorities, whose principle apparently is to worry the candidate by every concievable sort of mystery, have given me no idea how long the exam lasts. But I shall write to you about that from Oxford next week. I suppose I want only a day or two to get back from here and bring my trunk from Bookham. Many thanks for the enclosure – I wish it were for my sixteenth birthday, with two years more of Gastons life ahead.

your loving
son Jack.

Lewis went up to Oxford for the first time on Monday, 4 December 1916, to sit for a scholarship examination. He described this visit in SBJ XII where he says he found lodgings in the first house 'on the right as you turn into Mansfield Road out of Holywell'. The examination, given in Oriel College, took place between 5 and 9 December, after which he returned to Great Bookham.

TO HIS FATHER (LP V: 156):

[1 Mansfield Road,
Oxford
7 December 1916]

My dear P.,

This is Thursday and our last papers are on Saturday morning so I will cross on Monday night if you will kindly make the arrangements. We have so far had General Paper, Latin Prose, Greek and Latin unseen, and English essay. The subject for the latter was Johnson's 'People confound liberty of thinking with liberty of talking'[211] – rather suggestive, tho' to judge by faces, some did not find it so.

I don't know exactly how I am doing, because my most dangerous things – the two proses – are things you can't judge for yourself. The General paper was ideal and each of the unseens contained a piece I had done before. I am surprised at the number of candidates, tho' I can find only one going to New, a Harrow boy who sits opposite me.

The place has surpassed my wildest dreams: I never saw anything so beautiful, especially on these frosty moonlight nights: tho' in the Hall of Oriel where we do our papers it is fearfully cold at about four o'clock on these afternoons. We have most of us tried with varying success to write in our gloves. I will see you then on Tuesday morning.

your loving son,
Jack.

---

211 *Boswell's Life of Johnson*, ed. George Birkbeck Hill, 6 vols. (Oxford: Clarendon Press, 1934), 7 May 1773, vol. II, p. 249.

He crossed over to Belfast on 11 December and his rather fearful worries about the examination were laid to rest when he received a letter of 13 December from the Master of University College, Reginald W. Macan,[212] *who said: 'This College elects you to a Scholarship (New College having passed you over). Owing to your having furnished us with no Oxford address, I am obliged to send this to your home. I should have been glad to see you and ascertain your plans. Will you be so good now as to write to me and let me know what you propose to be doing between this time and next October' (LP V: 159–60). An announcement of this award appeared in* The Times *of 14 December, along with the news that University College had awarded Jack not only a Scholarship but an Exhibition – an additional financial endowment.*

The question for Jack, his father, and Mr Kirkpatrick was what Jack should do until the following October. Jack was keen to begin his studies, and in replying to the Master of University College, he said he had 'formed no plans for the intervening time' and that he would be glad of the Master's 'guidance in the matter' (LP V: 160).

While they waited to hear from the Master, Albert Lewis wrote at once to thank Mr Kirkpatrick for all he had done to secure Jack the Scholarship. Those who have read C. S. Lewis's tribute to Mr Kirkpatrick in Surprised by Joy *will be interested in what the 'Great Knock' thought of his pupil. In his letter to Albert Lewis of 20 December, Mr Kirkpatrick said:*

> The generosity of your heart has led you to express yourself in terms altogether too complimentary to me. I ask you, what could I have done with Clive if he had not been gifted with literary taste and the moral virtue of perseverance? Now to whom is Clive indebted for his brains? Beyond all question to his father and mother. And I hold that he is equally indebted to them for those moral qualities which though less obvious and striking than the intellectual, are equally necessary for the accomplishment of any great object in life – I mean fixity of purpose, determination of

---

212 Reginald Walter Macan (1848–1941), Master of University College 1906–23, was born in Dublin. He was educated at Christ Church, Oxford, where he took Firsts in the subjects Lewis would be reading, Classical Honour Moderations (Greek and Latin classical writers) and *Literae Humaniores* or 'Greats' (philosophy and ancient history). His publications include *Goethe in Rome* (1914) and *Herodotus and Thucydides* (1927).

character, persevering energy. These are the qualities that carried him through. I did not create them, and if they had not been there, I could not have accomplished anything. All this is so perfectly obvious that it is hardly worth emphasizing...As a dialectician, an intellectual disputant, I shall miss him, and he will have no successor. Clive can hold his own in any discussion, and the higher the range of the conversation, the more he feels himself at home. (LP V: 165)

Over Christmas Jack received a letter from the Master of University College. It has not survived, but Albert Lewis provided the gist of it in a letter to Warnie of 31 December. Dr Macan, he said, wrote to Jack

asking him what his intentions were in regard to Military Service, and informing him at the same time that all their Scholars are with the Colours, save one who is hopelessly unfit physically. Pretty plain speaking that! So now I have to start to look for a commission for Jacks. Failing that, I am afraid that he must either chuck Oxford or go into the ranks. Apparently it is a moral impossibility for a healthy man over 18 years of age to go into residence at Oxford. (LP V: 172–3)

Mr Kirkpatrick, again, solved the deadlock. He thought Jack should take Responsions, the University entrance examinations, and have this out of the way. In his letter to Albert of 2 January 1917 he pointed out that Mathematics 'form an important element in this exam.' and that Jack 'could very usefully employ a good part of the day in working up a subject for which he has not only no taste, but on the contrary a distinct aversion' (LP V: 174). It was further decided, as Jack mentioned in the letter to his father of 8 February, that if all his ideas about Oxford 'fell through', he would try for the Foreign Office. For this reason Mr Kirkpatrick planned for him to learn Italian, German and Spanish.

1917

___ ~ ___

TO HIS BROTHER (LP V: 176–7):

[Little Lea]
Postmark: 8 January 1917

My dear APB,[1]

Many thanks indeed for the letter and the most acceptable enclosure, which arrived, thank goodness, while P.[apy] was out, and so was saved from going the same road as my poor legacy. For you know I got £21 (is that the amount?) the same as you, but of course I have never seen a penny of it: my humble suggestion that I might have a pound or two was greeted with the traditional 'Ah, such nonsense.'

Congers on being made a real Lieut., which of course I suppose is far more important than the temporary Captaincy. Is there any chance of your being made a real Captain when this war is over – which I hope to God will be before my valuable person gets anywhere near it.

I quite agree with what you say about 'C. S. Lewis (Malvern.)'. Though of course I pulled a long face about it, I took very good care that Malvern should appear in the form I filled up: moreover, when people asked me what Coll. I was at I replied in the best manner 'Mawan': I saw no necessary to add 'two years ago'. It has been very comfortable at K's but there's no need to publish the fact: indeed I have now got to that stage when I am beginning to sentimentalize about the Coll. I had a very decent letter from old Smugy in which he also congratulated you.

---

1 Jack sometimes addressed Warnie as 'APB' and, in turn, Warnie addressed his brother as 'SPB'. When Warnie and Jack were very young their nurse, Lizzie Endicott, when drying them after a bath, threatened to smack their 'pigieboties' or 'piggiebottoms'. In time the brothers decided that Warnie was the 'Archpiggiebotham' and Jack the 'Smallpiggie-botham' or 'APB' and 'SPB'. Thereafter they used these terms of one another, particularly in their correspondence. For a discussion of 'pigiebotism' see the letter to Warnie of 2 August 1928.

Oxford is absolutely topping, I am awfully bucked with it and longing to go up, tho' apparently I am not to do this until next October. I hope you'll be somewhere near in England when I am at O. after the war, and will be able to come over and look me up in 'my new home' as the private school prospectuses say.

A large parcel of records to you arrived the day before yesterday and we took the liberty of opening them. As you know, they contain the 'Persian Garden' set and the 'Bing Boy' ones. The former are very satisfactory; have you heard them yourself, or did you get them on chance? The others of course aren't my line, but are very good in their own genre, tho' the patter in some of the Geo. Robey[2] ones is not very easy to hear until you 'get used to them like'.

I am going back to the Knock to read for my next exam. Responsions[3] (whatever that may be) on the 18th or 20th of January. After I've passed them, unless I hear against from my Coll. I shall probably join up here at home and not go up till after the war. Is there any possibility of leave?

yours,
SPB

P.S. Quite agree with your remarks about Wilson[4] and his friends. But what else do you expect from a set of squatters and damned money grubbing puritans like the Yanks? You remember Wilde's wheeze, 'When good Americans die they go to Paris' – 'But where do bad Americans go when they die?' – 'Oh, they go to America'. – J.

Lewis left Belfast on 25 January 1917, arrived in Oxford on the 26th, and called on the Master of University College on the 27th. The Master promised that if he passed the Responsions to be given between 20 and 26 March he could come up to Oxford at the beginning of Trinity Term in April. From Oxford, Lewis returned to Great Bookham on 27 January to prepare for the forthcoming examinations.

---

2 (Sir) George Robey (1869–1954), a music-hall comedian who appeared in a number of silent comedy films.
3 Oxford's entrance examination.
4 Woodrow Wilson (1856–1924), President of the United States from 1913 to 1921.

TO HIS FATHER (LP V: 179):

Great Bookham
[28 January 1917]

My dear Papy,

You will know from my two telegraphs that I got through my journey all right, tho' with some annoyance from very crowded trains and long stops at unheard of stations.

At about half past 11 on the Saturday morning I went to Univ. and was led across two quads, one behind the other, to a house in a beautiful old walled garden. This was the ogre's castle. He was a clean shaven, white haired, jolly old man, and was very nice indeed.[5] He treated me to about half an hour's 'Oxford Manner', and then came gradually round to my own business. Since writing last, he had made enquiries, and it seems that if I pass Responsions in March I could 'come up' in the following term and join the O.T.C.[6] This plan he thinks the best, because I should have far more chance of a commission from the Oxford O.T.C. than from anything else of the sort. The only disadvantage is that, as my scholarship doesn't begin until next October, I should not get any 'emolument'. However as he says, in the meantime I am to go on reading for Responsions, and the rest can be settled as we go along. After that he made me stay to lunch with his wife and niece and 'so to the station'. I am very pleased with my ogre after all.

It is colder in England, both here and at Oxford, than I have ever felt it anywhere in my life – perfectly awful. I hope you stayed in the house last week and will be able to do so for some part of the next until you have shaken off your cough. As usual, that 'shockin' cold of mine is disappearing on this side, to be replaced by the usual term time chilblains. The Knock is in very good form, although I have heard no talk about the 'carte blanche' so far.

Let me hear from you soon, and have good news of the cough.

your loving
son Jack.

---

5 The Master of University College.
6 Officers' Training Corps.

TO ARTHUR GREEVES (W):

[Gastons
28 January 1917]

My dear Galahad,

(If you are still to be Galahad after all) here I am at last, on Sunday evening, once more starting the first letter of a term. Well, I left you on the telephone at four of the clock, and I will go over my adventures, to get you thoroughly bored before we start talking.

The crossing was rough and cold, and we were late getting into Fleetwood; after which the train thought it wd. be best to wait for an hour before starting. We dawdled on to Crewe and there waited for another hour, tho' I didn't mind this as it gave me an opportunity of breaking my fast. So by very slow stages I got to Oxford at 6 o'clock. I took the same rooms as before, had a comfortable night, rose at 9.30, bathed, shaved, breakfasted in great ease and so sallied forth.

After wandering about the place and buying a second-hand copy of the 'Gesta Romanorum'[7] (of which more anon) I took my courage in both hands and knocked up the Master of University. He turned out to be a very, very nice old boy and after settling our business he made me stay to lunch. His wife and niece were there, both very decent, <indeed the latter wouldn't be a bad subject for the lash.> But what pleased me most was the masses upon masses of books in his house: among which I saw, tho' of course I couldn't look at it properly, a volume of that glorious new Malory – the one like my 'Psyche'[8] you know. So you may imagine I left Univ. very much relieved and delighted.

(Here my borrowed fountain pen loses its temper) The 'Gesta Romanorum' (you read about it in Mackail's 'Life of W.M.')[9] is a collection of mediaeval tales with morals attached to them: they are very like the Arabian Nights, tho' of course the characters and setting are chivalric instead of Eastern. It is not a first class book but it only cost me 1/- and

---

7 The *Gesta Romanorum* is a collection of fictitious stories in Latin, compiled in the 14th century and first published about 1472.

8 The story of 'Cupid and Psyche', which Lewis read over Christmas, is one episode in *The Golden Ass* of Apuleius (b. c. AD 114). He read it in *The Story of Cupid and Psyche*, translated by William Aldington, Temple Classics (1903). The long gestation of Lewis's *Till We Have Faces* (1956) probably began with this reading of the 'Cupid and Psyche' story.

9 J.W. Mackail's *The Life of William Morris*.

helps to while away an hour or so between serious things. I also bought at Oxford a copy of the poet Collins in the same edition as my Gray[10] (you know?) I don't know if you would care for him, but I like him quite well: you can look him up in your History of Literature and see what it says. I also bought a French Book on the Poetry of the middle ages[11] – so you see dear Oxford is a dangerous place for a book lover. Every second shop has something you want. Meanwhile I am going on with the 'Life' and besides Collins have read over the 1st Book of Paradise Lost again. I think I shall go through the whole poem this term, and if you begin it some day soon it would be interestin to keep side by side. About books, don't forget to tell Walter to send hither the Lambs & the Macaulay so soon as they come. The cold here is beyond words.

I can see my way clear to the end of 'Dymer'[12] now and will let you have an instalment next Sunday: three more will finish him, and after that I shall expect something from you. For my own part, I should like to write some short narrative poem if I could – about the length of a Book of 'Jason'.[13] I am tryin to think of some subject, at once romantic, voluptuous and homely. You must excuse (tho' Im sure I don't care a damn if you don't, mon vieux!) this writing, as it is being done across my knee.

<'Across my knee' of course makes one think of positions for Whipping: or rather not for whipping (you couldn't get any swing) but for that torture with brushes. This position, with its childish, nursery associations wd. have something beautifully intimate and also very humiliating for the victim.>

Quite enough for a first letter. Good bye, my old Archibald (you are fut a-a-ille) –

Jack

---

10 *The Poetical Works of Gray and Collins*, ed. Austin Lane Poole, Oxford Editions (1917). The poets are William Collins (1721–59) and Thomas Gray (1716–71).

11 Gaston Paris, *Littérature Française du Moyen Age* (1912).

12 Over the Christmas holiday, Lewis began a prose tale called 'Dymer'. Though the prose 'Dymer' is no longer extant, he was to begin a narrative poem about the same hero in 1918, which poem was to go through many revisions until it was eventually published in 1926 under his pseudonym 'Clive Hamilton'.

13 Morris, *The Life and Death of Jason*.

TO ARTHUR GREEVES (W):

[Gastons
31 January 1917]

My dear Arthur,

I was specially glad to get this letter of yours, both because it is longer than your usual ones (I hope you will keep this up) and because there are several good items in it.

First, I am glad you are starting French: I knew you would find no difficulty if once you began. Dont slack off after the first week or so, but don't read French on ordinary work day evenings when you are tired. Keep it for week ends. I should think 'Les Miserables'[14] pretty tough reading in any language, but then you like that sort of thing. As well, you always have your translation to save you dictionary turning. By the way, whether in French or English, you simply must read this book of Maeterlink's on death.[15] It is full of most interesting stuff, and even where you don't believe his theories they always have a sort of romantic interest. One case he tells of reminds me of 'John Silence'!, it is so wierd: but I mustn't spoil it by an outline.

I was also glad of your adventure in the billiard room. See how the Gods lead you on of their own accord! <I am given to understand that the idea of suffering yourself appeals to you more than that of inflicting. It used to be so with me, and perhaps the experienced victim does get a more vivid voluptuous sensation than the operator – at first. But of course once you are really in pain you can't think of anything else while the operator grows keener all the time.>

(In passing, can you imagine a horribler book, in paper, illustrations & binding than the 'History'?) Just before supper I finished the 2nd volume of Mackail's 'Life of W.M.' There is nothing nicer than to lay aside a book with a certain satisfaction at getting it settled with and yet having enjoyed it thoroughly, is there? I certainly know Morris better than I did before, tho' in a way his character is a dissapointment. You can't really think there's any resemblance between him and me? Of course I would give mine eyes to be like him in some ways, but I don't honestly think my temper is quite so bad.

As to the other point I often think he must have been <a special devotee of the rod.> Do you remember in the 'Well at the World's End' where

14 Victor Hugo, *Les Misérables* (1862).
15 Maurice Maeterlinck, *La Mort* (1913).

a man at the Birg of the Four Friths says that the advantage of slave girls as opposed to wives is that we need care nothing for their ill humours <'so long as the twigs smart and the whips sting'? That sentence is dragged in quite unnecessarily and is exquisitely worded.>

Item (as Morris says in his letters) the 2nd Vol. of Macaulay[16] is come, in excellent condition. The leaves are all stuck together and lump in ridges and make the right crackly noise. Thanks for sending it, old man: I wish indeed you were coming the same journey. How perfectly happy we could be here, walking and talking together and both doing work we liked.

Your suggestion that I did not want your company in the cab, is purely rhetorical, I hope. You must know that I wanted it very much, although I cant talk about those sort of things the way you do. It seems to me indecent somehow, if you know what I mean.

I am sorry to hear that you're fed up, and, although nobody who gets enough food and clothing in a world where most are hungry and cold has any business to talk about 'misery' I do sympathise with you exceedingly. I wish to goodness (or to Jeshua shall we say?) that you could get out of the office. If only you had work that you liked you'd feel a different being in spite of loneliness and so on. I know I can always turn to pleasant work for comfort as a last resource. But what's the good of telling you this! I think your father and mother should be shot for keepin' you in that hole, <while the only other member of your family whom I am interested in could be punished in an other way – to the general enjoyment of the operator, and to the great good of her soul.>

Dear! Dear! How the theme comes back. To change it, I had a lovely walk this afternoon in the snow. As I walked up the village street the ground and house tops were thick, and it was coming fluttering down à la Debussy. But best of all, the blacksmith's place was open, and you could see the red forge glowing inside. Can't you imagine it?

I long to see the picture you have made of that lane in THE wood. Any more designs for the 'Poems'? That first little one is such a success that you must do lots of tail-peaces and such.

No: I didn't see 'La Bohème',[17] and it took from 2–6 to get from Oxford to here. Good night, old sinner, <and imagine yourself the slave

---

16 Thomas Babington Macaulay, *History of England*, 5 vols. (1849–61).
17 *La Bohème*, an opera by Giacomo Puccini, was first performed in 1897.

of some Eastern queen who whips you – I mean when you next go North.>

I am just going to have the first bath since seeing you, as there has been no hot water. –

<Philomastix>

TO ARTHUR GREEVES (W):

[Gastons
1 February 1917]

Just a scrape to thank you a thousand times for the books[18] which have just come. Can you really spare them? It is most awfully good of you and I am very pleased with them, especially when I think of the other edition which is certainly not so nice, tho' I hope you will come to think otherwise.

I wrote to you on Wednesday as usual, which letter will now have reached [you] & will write again next Wednesday after getting your next. You say 'Arethusa'[19] is lovely: have you bought it or got a copy from the library? In any case I am very glad you have started it. Isn't Omobono a lovely character, and also the slave dealer's wife? I think it a very good romance all round. Having finished Morris I am reading a silly book of Anstey's 'The Talking Horse',[20] before settling down to Macaulay. I never heard you speak of Anstey, but you should read him certainly: this book is fantastic & almost as ridiculous as 'Alice' tho' of course in a more ordinary way.

The snow is nearly gone now, but the country still keeps a wintry look which is lovely & the mornings a wintry nip which is not. You'll be glad to hear that I've started a 'friendly' tobacco-pipe instead of the cigarettes you so object to. Glad your interest in R. is increasing, but more of this elsewhere – Addio,

Jack

---

18 Charles Lamb's *Essays of Elia*.
19 Francis Marion Crawford, *Arethusa* (1907).
20 F. Anstey, *The Talking Horse and Other Tales* (1892).

TO ARTHUR GREEVES (W):

[Gastons
7 February 1917]

My dear Arthur

I must begin by explaining why there is no instalment with this letter. On Sunday, when I should have written one I spent the whole day most delightfully skating on a lake at a place called Wisley near here, which you reach by a road through the woods. As it is now thick snow again you can imagine what a topping walk it is. The winding road covered with snow, the bare trees with their snow covered branches & the sunlight falling thro' them in bars on the ground also covered with snow. Absolutely lovely, especially as the air is very dry and the sky clear.

To day I have been to the same place to skate again & the ice is now rather cut up. I was in pleasant company (NO – not that sort) and enjoyed it greatly, especially the walk back. The moon was out, & starting under a clear starry sky we gradually walked into a cold white fog. The white of the ground and the white of the fog became indistinguishable and you seemed to be floating in a sort of silver cloud, broken by the red light of a railway signal at the station. This is a vague description, but I think you'll understand.

How I do love *real* winter like this! The thermometer in the hall stands at 7° to night, the water in my jug is solid to the bottom and all the pipes are frozen up. If you look out for a moment through the willow-pattern of frost on the windows you see this lovely haze of snow & mist & moonlight. What with the general beauty of the world and my lovely hours of skating I have not been so bucked for a long time.

My French is under rather different conditions from yours, as I read from 10–11 every night except on Wednesdays when I write to you. I have really never counted exactly how much I cover and it wd. not be accurate to count by pages, as they vary so in size and in type. I shouldn't read for more than an hour at a time in your case, certainly not for a whole afternoon. I never read Perrault myself but I am sure he is good (A. Lang praises him) and you may remember that there is an edition of him with illustraggers by Arthur Rackham – I forget the details however. What would you say to the 'Contes Fantastiques' of Charles Nodier, in that nice blue Collection Gallia at 1/-?[21] Some of these tales you would

---

21 Jean Charles Nodier, *Contes Fantastiques* (1914).

like tho' some seemed to me dull. Then again why not get something in that 1/6 Dents edition with the lovely paper, say Voltaire's 'Contes' (very amusing) or the shorter tales of Georges Sand, – you can see the list. I have now made a good start on my second volume of Macaulay, which is admirable. What a nice man James must have been! But before starting this I read in a library copy two of F. W. Bains Indian Tales 'The Descent of the Sun' & 'The Heifer of the Dawn'.[22] They are translations from the Sanskrit and are 'really rather adorable'. A little too weird, perhaps, for your solid tastes; but you should certainly have a look at them in Lily's copies.

It is most exasperating of you to say you have come to a conclusion which will dissapoint me, but you don't want to put it in paper. What tawdry nonsense! If any person did read our letters, he would be an ill-bred cad & therefore we shouldn't mind what he saw. But anyway I will be really annoyed if you don't clear up the mystery in your next letter. My own <Philomastix> is only a harmless piece of Greek affectation: 'philo' is the same word you see in 'philosopher' 'philologist' etc, and means 'fond of' while <'mastix' is the ordinary word for a whip.>

I think I can understand your getting tired of Iceland before Morris left it: but didn't you like the Faroe Islands? That part reminded me of our mountain walks at Portsalon, didnot it you? I rather expected some fuller criticism on Arethusa, and would like to know your final verdict when you write. Tho' of course it's not in the rank of 'real books', I have a sentimental affection for it from reading it over ever since I was about ten. I am now through the first two Books of Paradise L. and really love Milton better every time I come back to him, &, what is more to the point, I think his merits are of a [kind] you'd appreciate. However, if Harrap won't let you have a copy till 1919, our plan [of] reading in harness goes 'off'. I can quite understand the interest of the Welsh marches at the time of the Wars of the Roses – especially as it was in that place & that time that our good friend Thomas Malory lived (see introduction to the Morte). I am now reading in French this book on French literature of the Middle Ages which to me at least is very interestin. By the way Maeterlink's book on Death is in the usual horrid, expensive continental paper back – still this gives you the exciting task of getting it bound.

Good night for the present – <Philomastix ΦΙΛΟΜΑΣΤΙΞ,> you can learn that amount of Gk. letters to mystify the unlettered!)

---

22 Francis William Bain, *The Descent of the Sun* (1903); *A Heifer of the Dawn* (1904).

Next morning – colder still! Remember to clear up the mystery when you write & if you like I'll destroy the letter –

J.

TO HIS FATHER (LP V: 185):

[Gastons]
Postmark: 8 February 1917

My dear Papy,

The 'momentous decision' about German was simply – that we had dropped it and taken up Italian instead! I thought K. would have explained this in his letter, but it makes no difference as, by a little management we have found it possible to fit in both. This means that if all my dreams of Oxford fall through and I were reduced to something really desperate like trying for the Foreign Office, I should have three modern languages in my pocket. Italian quite comes up to K's promises about its easiness and on Sunday I read the first 200 lines of Dante with much success. By the end of term I should be able to read it as easily as French.

And talking about the end of the term, would you please send me £2/2 some time soon, which is the fee to the University for entrance at Responsions?

You are certainly most unfortunate in getting this kind of weather for your convalescence. Is it as bad at home as it is here? We are having real winter, and so far I have had three days excellent skating. Besides the ice, there is fine dry snow everywhere, usually with bright sunshine, which is very pleasant. The water in my 'giraffe' is solid, right through to the bottom, every night, and yesterday evening the thermometer in the hall was at 7 degrees. However, on the whole, I like this sort of weather, tho' the pipes are now all frozen up, which makes rather a nuisance. I suppose however you have already seen all this in the papers.

What do you think about America? Kirk says it will be a great disadvantage if she comes in, tho' I don't quite understand how: he also assures us that we shall be starving before next summer, which indeed (unless you are right in hoping to see it over by then) seems like to be.

your loving
son Jack.

P.S. If you are sending me some of that thermogenic wool, wouldn't it be kind to let the Knock have a little too?

TO ARTHUR GREEVES (W):

[Gastons
15 February 1917]

You begin on this page

Cher Ami,

One of the vertues of snow is that it chiefly teacheth and instructeth us for to loven and cherish the greene grasse – certainly I never appreciated grass until about Teusday when the snow began to melt and after so many days whiteness it was nice to see the old homely fields again, all pale and washed looking, with drifts still lying in the hollows.

Your letter, although dated a long while ago (9th) only arrived this morning, Thursday: so that I am afraid this will not come to your hands at its wonted time. Which is your fault, not mine.

<If the whole mystery was that you didn't love the Rod as I do – well there's no mystery about that. Very, very few are affected in this strange way and I am only surprised that you can enter into my feelings even so much as you do. As a matter of fact, just as the other – the normal desire has a poignant sensual side and a vague sentimental side, so that has too. I can understand your being able to like the *idea*, and yet not having your physical feelings raised by the thought of the 'mastix' – . . . .[23] Is this at all your state of mind? Yes, that business about stepping on Zoe appeals> strongly to the sentimental or theoretical side of this feeling. But we are getting too sticky. Passez outre!

Item, I am reading such a splendid book in German, by a man called Chamisso 'Peter Schlemichl's Wundersame Geschichte' (The Amazing Adventures of Peter Schlemichl).[24] It is about a man (modern) who sells his shadow to a wizard: his subsequent adventures are treated chiefly in the absurd 'Alice' style but there is a sort of core of horror lurking in it all the time, that is to me very attractive. I see from the introduction to my copy that there are several translations: I should certainly advise you to get it out of the library – except in a specially nice edition it is perhaps hardly worth buying. I am writing to night to see about an edition of 'Undine' in the original. I also have seen in a book on German literature

---

23 The dots represent the approximately 15 letters that Arthur had written over, and which are indecipherable.
24 Adelbert von Chamisso, *Peter Schlemihls Wunderbare Geschichte* (1853).

the name of some of Fouqués other books – Thiodolf the Icelander, The Magic Ring etc.[25] Sweet lord! how one does want to read everything. I am nearly through Macaulay Vol. II, which I have enjoyed immensely, especially the part about Oxford: I am sorry Obadiah Walker should have been at Univ![26] However, Shelley & I goin there should make up for it.[27]

Cher ami, j'ai a confession to make. I have thee told a lie. A certain operation is NOT called going North at Malvern. I invented this phraze so that you & I might have some convenient & safe way of referring to that thing. It wd. be unpleasant to have to use the ugly expressions which slang has evolved & this one has the advantage of being quite meaningless to an outsider. But I couldn't have stopped and explained all this to you in the middle of that breathless night walk.

I do so hope you will enjoy the opera: and if I could only be at home worrying you & making little plans for going to them (I couldn't leave my father of course) I'd risk being dissapointed. One sort of music still holds me as much, or indeed more than ever – piano music. I suppose the gods are doing this to console me. By the way, here's a bright idea, perhaps the gods have a touch of my disease & that is why the world is tortured so every day. I wonder could that be work[ed] into a mystical story. Which reminds me, when is your novel comin? The Bible (which you don't read) has very hard things to say of people who put their hand to the plough and turn back.[28] There was great promise in poor 'Papillon' – imagination, charm – the technical part you will learn by practice. Buck up!

At any rate I am sending you Dymer's next excursion, and have begun the poem. The subject is 'The childhood of Medea', & it will leave off where the most poems about her begin – shortly after her meeting with Jason. It will describe her lonely, frightened childhood away in a castle with the terrible old king her father & how she is gradually made to

---

25 Friedrich Fouqué, Baron de la Motte, *Undine* (1811); *Thiodolf the Icelander* (1815); *The Magic Ring* (1812).

26 Possibly because Obadiah Walker (1612–99), the Master of University College 1676–88, was a Roman Catholic who was imprisoned in the Tower because of his religious beliefs. See the two-part essay 'Obadiah Walker' by A.E. Firth in *University College Record*, Vol. IV (September 1962), pp. 95–106 and Vol. IV (October 1964), pp. 261–73.

27 Shelley was expelled from University College in 1811 for circulating a pamphlet, *The Necessity of Atheism* (1811), which he had written with Thomas Jefferson Hogg.

28 Luke 9:62: 'And Jesus said unto him, No man, having put his hand to the plough, and looking back, is fit for the kingdom of God.'

learn magic against her will.[29] Of course I'll make a mess of it 'cracked absolutely', but there's a fine subject in all that for someone who knew how to manage it. I wish Morris or Apollonius had made a poem about that. Descriptions of childhoods & gradual growing up are very fascinating I think.

Glad you are coming to like your Lamb, tho I don't think you can love it so well as I do mine. His novel is called 'Rosamund Gray' isn't it?[30] It was published anonymously and some one (someone like poor little Bill,[31] I suppose) said that

> Friends coming up to examine it
> Observe a good deal of Charles Lamb in it.

What is it like. Yes!, isn't the collection Gallia awfully dainty. As soon as I've finished my book on French Literature of the Middle Ages I think I'm going to tackle 'Notre Dame';[32] It is rather in your line & mine too, isn't it? Do you know I believe I shall come to like history kwite as much as u do? What nonsense about the Heiffer of the Dawn; you never told me a syllable. The Silver library is very nice but is the Library Edition (like My Sigurd[33] you know) not worth the difference? I heartily recomend the E[arthly] Paradise (never having read it) and intend to buy a copy myself as soon as I have finished the Paradise Lost. Have been reading Malory, the 'Beaumains' part again & cant understand how anyone can help loving him. But you always were a cross sent to try me, cher ami, so cher ami good night. Is this letter long enough, because it's all your going to get anyway.

<ΦΙΛΟΜΑΣΤΙΞ>

29 Lewis's primary sources for the story of Medea were Apollonius Rhodius's *Argonautica* and William Morris's *Life and Death of Jason*, both of which are mentioned in his letter of 11 July 1916.

30 Charles Lamb, *A Tale of Rosamund Gray and Old Blind Margaret* (1798). It was not published anonymously as Lewis thought.

31 William Hazlitt (1778–1830), who was a friend of Charles Lamb.

32 Victor Hugo, *Notre Dame de Paris* (1831).

33 Morris, *Sigurd the Volsung*. See note 61 to letter of 10 November 1914.

TO HIS FATHER (LP V: 187):

[Gastons]
Friday.
Postmark: 16 February 1917

My dear Papy,

First of all, many thanks for the enclosure which I have sent off to the pundits, and thus got the whole of that business off my chest. After mature deliberation I decided that it would be just as well not to send £1-19-6 with a note, '6d. deducted for telegraphic peculation' – the plan which first occurred to me.

I am sorry that my last letter did not arrive in time to prevent you from discharging your volley of pebbles. K. told me that he heard from you and that he was writing to 'put you in possession of the facts', which I suppose means that you are being put in your place.[34] At any rate I hope you will approve of the present arrangement. Certainly Italian gets better and better, and will be an excellent counterblast to Big Brother's 'fine wandering knowledge of the Spanish language'. I think that after some twenty years work, I may be able to make something out of German too.

Talking about Big Brother, I heard from him yesterday. He seems to have had a touch of fever again, and wants to know why there are no letters from Little Lea. This weather out there must be rather offensive. The snow is gone here, but the frost has kindly come back again, just to keep us from thinking long. I am very glad to hear the news of your recovery, and hope it will be permanent.

---

34 In his letter to Albert of 14 February Mr Kirkpatrick said: '[Clive] has actually dropped nothing, only that the amount of Classical reading has been somewhat curtailed. He goes on with German, which, tho' not directly required at Oxford, will we hope be of service to him in the future. But he has taken on a new language – Italian. This may seem a bold venture to be accomplished in seven weeks. And, no doubt, there are many teachers who would pronounce the proposal little better than folly. But you may be quite sure I wd. not have undertaken such a task if I had not seen my way to make it a success. Italian is just the kind of language that Clive can get into easily, and already inside a fortnight he is reading *I Promessi Sposi* (a Senior Grade book) with more success and a great deal more interest than anything he has done in German. Of course his knowledge of Latin is a great service to him in the new venture, and with an ordinary pupil I should not have thought of making such an experiment. If he gets a good grammatical knowledge here before he goes, it is half the victory. All he wants afterwards is Spanish, and then he will have the full complement of modern languages required for the Foreign Office' (LP V: 186–7). *I Promessi Sposi* (1827) – 'The Betrothed' – by Alessandro Manzoni is held by many to be the greatest Italian literary work after Dante's *Divine Comedy*.

Yes! This is not the first time that I have had buttons sewn on me by an opera company. However, I am sure I shall have a full account of their performances by an 'eye-witness'.

> your loving
> son,
> Jack.

TO ARTHUR GREEVES (W):

[Gastons
20 February 1917]

Cher Ami,

Il y a je ne sais quoi de charme in your style of writing a letter on a number of loose sheets in devil knows what order. It is so nice when you think that the pleasure of reading it is over to suddenly come on half a page more hiding somewhere. I wish I wasn't such friends with you – it takes away from ones independance: I hang on Teusday evenings and Wednesday mornings for your letter just like a schoolgirl and am quite put out if it doesn't turn up.

Item, it is very annoying for a habitual liar like me, when he does tell the truth for once to be accused of invention: however, tho' my little confession was quite true, many of my statements are so 'Of imagination all compact'[35] that I can't blame you for disbelieving this one. It is a pity tho' that you always fix on the true ones to suspect and swallow down the lies with avidity!

I am sorry that you don't like Mackail's second volume. I suppose I am a bundle of contradictions, but I must say socialism does interest me. When you think of the way labourers in the factory live at home, – men & women slaving from half past five in the morning to six at night at hard, monotonous work in hideous rooms full of shrieking machinery year after year, with never a moments pleasure except when they are drunk (and you can't blame them) it really does make you feel that the whole thing is wrong. Aren't you ashamed to think of us, blessèd prigs, with our books and music and little grumbles about nothing, dawdling along (your office is absolute Paradise & idleness compared with their lives) while half or more than half the people are slaves. As much slaves as ever there were in Rome, their only liberty being liberty to starve

---

35 Shakespeare, *A Midsummer Night's Dream*, V, i, 8.

when the torture becomes unbearable! However I am not going to afflict my cher ami with a political letter, but I just wanted to explain why I can't help thinking about those things.

By the way, what do you mean by <the whip in music? At any rate the mere sound of a whip doesn't affect me in the least. There's no special virtue in a whip – hundreds of other methods of mild torture are just as good.>

I am glad I wasn't there to have the last remnants of my Wagnerian taste murdered by a garbled Tannhäuser. Aye me! how our tastes and feelings have changed since the days when Wagner was the great common ground of talk, when Morris was only a name (perhaps you wish he were still) and I had never read Charlotte Brontë. A propos of which, having finished Macaulay (an admirable book, tho' of course the writer is too much of a whig and puritan for my taste: the old cavaliers were at any rate gentlemen) I am beginning 'Mansfield Park' again, after a futile effort to read 'Vanity Fair'.[36] I waded knee deep into the marish of endless characters, sentimentalism & platitude and then really could not go on. Why is it I can't appreciate Thackeray?

It is difficult to choose between two such perfect flowers as the 'Crock of Gold' & 'Phantastes'. The former has a beautiful sense of nature and open air, and a certain voluptuousness that the other ha'nt, but then there is nothing in it quite so fine as the faery palace[37] or the place where Anodos comes out on the sad sea shore and throws himself into the waves[38] – or

---

36 William Makepeace Thackeray, *Vanity Fair* (1848).

37 *Phantastes*, ch. X: 'The stream bore my little boat with a gentle sweep round a bend of the river; and lo! on a broad lawn, which rose from the water's edge with a long green slope to a clear elevation from which the trees receded on all sides, stood a stately palace glimmering ghostly in the moonshine: it seemed to be built throughout of the whitest marble. There was no reflection of moonlight from windows – there seemed to be none; so there was no cold glitter; only, as I said, a ghostly shimmer. Numberless shadows tempered the shine, from column and balcony and tower. For everywhere galleries ran along the face of the buildings; wings were extended in many directions; and numberless openings, through which the moonbeams vanished into the interior, and which served both for doors and windows, had their separate balconies in front, communicating with a common gallery that rose on its own pillars...Though I was there for many days, I did not succeed in mastering the inner topography of the building, so extensive and complicated it was.'

38 ibid., ch. XVIII: 'I stood one moment and gazed into the heaving abyss beneath me; then plunged headlong into the mounting wave below. A blessing, like the kiss of a mother, seemed to alight on my soul; a calm, deeper than that which accompanies a hope deferred, bathed my spirit. I sank far into the waves, and sought not to return...'

the story of Cosmo.[39] You see!, what memories crowd up. Still the homely, Irish beauty of the other is topping: so is the humour both of the philosopher and the policemen. The philosophical parts (I mean the serious philosophical parts at the beginning of some chapters) I don't understand, but they stir me in some strange way that they probably wouldn't if I really could follow them.

<By the way, cher ami, you must have a very depraved taste if you like THAT passage best in Dymer tho'> I admit twas pleasant to write. Perhaps it is true what the Greek poet in the Anthology says: 'Sweet is water to the thirsty man, and to the weary mariners sight of land is sweet. But sweeter than all it is when one bed holds twain that love, and the queen of Cypris is praised of both.'[40] Queen of Cypris, you know, is Aphrodite. I have no intention of giving up Dymer, tho' I fear he will dissapoint you.

The childhood of Medea has progressed to some two hundred and twenty lines, in the metre of 'Jason' – tho' I am trying not to imitate Morris too much. The subject of course is far too good for a schoolboy of eighteen to blunder at, but I think I shall try & go on. I write it whenever the fit takes me, in a pocket book, so you will not see it till tis done.

My Responsions exam begins on Teusday 20th of March and I cast me to be home before the following Monday. You say you hope to have some more 'breathless' walks. I can undertake to manage the 'breathless' part either by strapping a sponge bag onto your head, or by compelling you to advance up the steepest hills at the double. I have finished my book on French Literature (admirable, excellent, exquisite) and started a very interesting work 'Les Confessions' de Rousseau[41] – <qui avait, lui aussi, un penchant pour la verge qui consacre a ce sujet adorable quatre pages.>[42] Altogether a 'really rather lovely' book. <His taste is altogether for suffering rather than inflicting: which I can feel too, but it is a feeling more proper to the other sex.>

I opened my eyes; and, looking first up, saw above me the deep violent sky of a warm southern night; and then, lifting my head, saw that I was sailing fast upon a summer sea, in the last border of a southern twilight.'

39 Cosmo von Wehrstahl whose story is told in chapter XIII.

40 The *Greek Anthology* contains over six thousand epigrams found in various Greek authors and ranging over 17 centuries. The words Lewis quoted are from a poem by Asclepiades, found in the *Greek Anthology*, bk. 5, poem 169.

41 Jean-Jacques Rousseau, *Les Confessions* (1781–8).

42 'who had, he too, a penchant for the rod, [and] who dedicates to this delightful subject four pages'.

The pleasures of spring have been jawed about so often that I am rather shy of saying anything about the lovely weather that has succeeded to the snow here. Do you know what it feels like when you go out for the first time without an overcoat and feel all the nerves funny up the back of your legs and see the clouds blowing about a really blue sky? All the same I know spring too well to really like her. She invariably makes you feel lonely & dissatisfied & long for

> 'The land where I shall never be
> The love that I shall never see.'[43]

You know what I mean?
  Yrs.,
  J.
  <Philom.>

  <VERGERS POUR LES VIERGES>

TO ARTHUR GREEVES (W):

[Gastons
28 February 1917]

  Cher Ami,
  Thou art fool: you take tremendous care about putting in anything too <*philomastigian*> for fear it should be seen and then go and stick in a reference to a certain lady of my passion, making it quite clear whom you mean so that it *really would* matter if somebody got hold of it. However, they shan't.
  But as to that lady, I remember that you did not agree when I suggested <her as a suitable subject for the lash>, on that eventful night. But surely now that you have seen her again you must agree with me. Is she not absolutely perfect from head to heel – and moreover <the necessary part of the body – one of the most beautiful parts anyway – shaped with an almost intolerable grace? The gods> – whom I'm always abusing – certainly produced a masterpiece in her: even to see her walk across the room is a liberal education. Ah me, <if she had suffered indeed half the stripes that have fallen upon her in imagination she would be well

---

43 For the source of these lines see note 44 to the letter of 28 February 1917.

disciplined.> Of course I don't say that it is quite my own ideal type of beauty. But then who ever is? After all 'The love that I shall never see' is better both in body and soul than all the real women on earth.

Which reminds me, that couplet (a beauty isn't it) is NOT by me – I wish it were. Andrew Lang quotes it somewhere, but I have never been able to discover the author. Whoever it be, he deserves immortality for those two lines alone.[44]

Item, I have read nearly all Tacitus, his short works the Agricola & Germania, the Histories & am now at the Annals.[45] At first I absolutely hated him, partly because I had not then learned to appreciate history, partly because his twisted and obscure style (he is called 'the Latin Carlyle' & 'the Latin Meredith', so you can imagine) at first repelled me. Now, however, I am grown to be very fond of him indeed. I have just finished the 14th and am beginning the 15th book of the Annals – all about Nero. Some of N's depravities are so fearful as to be almost funny, aren't they? I expect that like me, it will especially interest you as being the source of 'Quo Vadis'.[46] The only other author of ancient history I can recommend is the Greek historian Herodotus.[47] He combines the pleasure of real history & the charm of romance: he tells all about Egypt & Persia and the wonder of Babylon & the Hyperboreans who live beyond the North Wind, & the gryphons who guard their gold in the Scythian deserts etc. I am sure a good translation of him would provide you with agreeable reading.

Since writing last I have read for the first time 'The Tenant of Wildfell Hall'.[48] In spite of some excellent passages it is a bad book. People who have been brought up as gentleman don't even when drunk, fight and beat their wives in their hostesse's drawing room. It is all very melodramatic & gives you the impression of being written by a lady's maid. However the beginning and the end, the part outside Helen's own

---

44 The lines 'The land where I shall never be / The love that I shall never see' are by Andrew Lang and are found in his *History of English Literature* (1912), p. 579, which book Lewis was reading in 1915. Lewis was, however, quoting from memory. Lang's actual lines are 'The love whom I shall never meet, / The Land where I shall never be'.

45 Cornelius Tacitus, *The Life of Agricola* (c. 98); *Germania* (98); *Histories* (c. 116).

46 Henryk Sienkiewicz, *Quo Vadis?* (1896).

47 Herodotus (c. 480–c. 425 BC) is known as the 'father of history'. His *Histories*, the first great prose work in European literature, deal with the struggle between Asia and Europe and culminate with the Persian invasions of Greece.

48 Anne Brontë, *The Tenant of Wildfell Hall* (1848).

narrative, are topping & I had rather have read it than not. I am now beginning Mrs. Gaskell's 'Life'[49] in the household edition & love it already. The description of Haworth with the moors going up behind it is heavenly – wouldn't you like that sort of country – tho' of course not better than our own. You will be glad to hear that in the introduction to this copy, that ill-bred journalist Clement Shorter gets well slated & is shown to have most maliciously [mis]represented lots of things.

Your description of 'John Inglesant'[50] is not very appetising: as to the subject about Catholics and Protestants, I fear me that my views would only annoy you (comment 'Has that ever prevented you from stating them if you wanted to?' Ah well! ...) Doesn't it seem ages ago, cher ami, since we sat that day in the library looking down on the street and trying to talk? I *am* looking forward to a return homeward. Responsions is the entrance exam to the University: for you see, tho' I have got a scholarship at one college, I don't belong to the whole show.

'The Confessions' of Rousseau (to jump from one subject to another) quite apart from THAT splendid passage, continue very interesting indeed. The description of his wanderings and adventures is rather like that of De Quincey – perhaps even better. It would be rather long for you at present but you should keep it in your mental list of French books to be got.

I do hope you are really speaking the truth about Dymer in all your flattery. As he draws near his end I am getting quite anxious lest I should not finish him. You will understand with what pleasure I look forward to being able to say 'Well, there is a book written: long or short, good or bad, there it is by itself and done.' How I wish I could make you start writing again so that we could have all these little wheezes in common as we do everything else.

Item, the

'*springs voluptuous pantings*'[51]

still go on, damn them! It has now got to the stage when real comfort in bed must be given up till next winter. If you keep on the clothes you had

---

49 Elizabeth Cleghorn Gaskell, *The Life of Charlotte Brontë* (1857).
50 Joseph Henry Shorthouse, *John Inglesant* (1881).
51 Percy Bysshe Shelley, *Alastor* (1815), l. 11.

last week you will be asphyxiated, if you lay them off you will have, not cold, but a lonely, comfortless sense of thinness. All the same I must admit it is lovely to hear the birds of a morning and feel the sun on your back as you're getting into your bath. Voilà de l'éloquence à propos d'a worn out theme: but honest all the same, and therefore pardonable. Do you know, cher ami, that it is at great cost I write hard like this up to the very moment of going to bed? I never sleep well on the nights of writing – all the ideas buzzing in my head keep me awake.

Which reminds me, you will be relieved to hear that 'Medea's Childhood' after struggling on for 300 turgid lines has been quietly made into spills for my 'tobacco pipe' – all those fine landscapes and vigorous speeches, devoted to real use at last![52] En effet, it is a failure. I can quite share your annoyance about the Essays. There are a hundred things I meant to say in this letter and haven't. My feet are cold & there is a moon. Look at the lady we mentioned & think. Good night old fool: have finished P. Schlemihl.

TO HIS FATHER (LP V: 189–90):

[Gastons]
Thursday.
1st March 1917.

My dear Papy,

I have waited thus long in the hope of dragging some communication out of you: for to treat the parcel of Greek grammar – for which however many thanks – as a substitute for your weekly letter would be a very bad precedent. However, although you are not entitled to one now, I suppose I must make allowances. 'Colonial manners' don't you know. By the way, I hope the letterlessness, to coin a pretty word, of last week doesn't mean that you are laid up again? Arthur says that he met you 'the other day', but of course I don't know when that was. So try and let me have a letter some time soon, just to see how things are going.

This Responsions exam. begins Tuesday the 20th of this month, and I hope to be with you on the following Monday at the latest, but much

---

52 While Lewis may have destroyed the version of 'Medea's Childhood' he first mentioned in his letter of 15 February 1917, he returned to the theme a year and half later. In his letter to Arthur of 14 July 1919 he said of the second version, 'The "Medea" is very nearly finished, and will be about twelve hundred lines.' For the only surviving lines of the poem see the letter of 18 September 1919.

more likely on the Friday. If the exam does not end until the Saturday I may have to stay in Oxford over the Sunday, which will be rather a nuisance – tho' of course there would be points about it too. The spring is coming on by leaps and bounds here, but I'm afraid I can't share the usual raptures. Mrs. K. is already beginning to say 'Really it's almost too hot with the fire today' which is a very disconcerting sign. I must admit there is something nice about those birds in the mornings – the creatures that you and I would call swallows, but which Kirk (after a short preamble on the amazing ignorance of elementary natural history shown by some people), puts down as 'house martins'. I think Blodo's 'Oh no sir', delivered in the Blodo voice would be a suitable reply.

My condiscipulus Terry, whom I am beginning rather to like, was 'called up' last week, but managed to get exempted after some bother. How glad I am that my fate is once for all settled for good or bad.

I have got out of the library an old name of ours, 'The Chronicles of Froissart'[53] in two enormous folios from the Kelmscott Press – Morris's thing you know. But it is rather dull after all. I foresee great difficulty in getting German and Italian books later on, but I suppose the covers of Oxford may yield to beating.

Let me hear from you soon.

your loving
son Jack.

TO ARTHUR GREEVES (W):

[Gastons
6 March 1917]

Cher Ami,

I think sometimes that we have spoiled everything by starting this subject. For one thing, we always are like the ladies in Jane Austin, who each want to talk about her own concerns and neither to hear the other's. <I mean, you are interested in a brand of *That* which doesn't appeal to me, and I in one that doesn't appeal to you.>

But it is not only that: I happened this morning on an old letter of yours from the days of Papillon, full of enthusiasm about books and music and scenery, which somehow made me feel that we were on a

---

53 *Froissart's Chronicles*, Kelmscott Press, 2 vols. limited to 160 copies on vellum (1897). The *Chronicles* of Jean Froissart (c. 1337–c. 1410) were first translated into English by John Bourchier in 1523–5.

much higher level then, much more removed from the common mob. And yet I do not see that it is sensible to pretend that these things don't exist, when we are both really very sensual at heart. Rather, when we first started the subject, I didn't think it would be quite the same: I fancied there was a way of treating such themes with gravity, delicacy and real, honest appreciation of the good things of the world, that could sort of fall into line with our other interest in literature and so on: that we could raise the subject to our level instead of falling to its. Nor can I see exactly how we have failed in that ideal: yet – without blaming you in the very, very, least – when I had read your letter this evening I felt that something was wrong.

Perhaps I was just in a particular kind of mood, but more likely it was the unhappy reference to Catullus that finished me. For Catullus (you saw him in my big Medici volume) though I have only read ⅓ or so of him, is to me one of the really sacred poets, some of his tiny little things leave me really breathless – in particular one bit about that wander-lust feeling in the Spring, which he describes beautifully; in fact he is one of my gods, I put him on a level with Morris or Keats. You can understand what a sudden shock it gave me <to think of anyone approaching him from your point of view. It was blasphemy>: mind, I don't blame you in the very least, still less do I suggest that I wouldn't have felt just the same in your position <(I may remark in passing that in the parts of Catullus I have read there is no allusion to your particular taste).> All the same it set me thinking – and I have just tried to jot down the substance of it. In a way we have spoiled our paradise.

All the same, having gone thus far, there is no good trying to go back – it would be horrible to keep an artificial silence and feel that there was something there all the time. Let us talk of these things when we want, but always keep them on the side that tends to beauty, and avoid everything that tends to sordid-ness <and beastly police court sort of scandal out of grim real life (like the O. Wilde story).> Cher ami, please, please don't think this is preaching. I don't pretend that I have done so any better than you, but I am only suggesting plans for the future: for I am sure you have felt at times as I do now.

You will have gathered that I am in bad form to-night:

> 'Oh Galahad, my Galahad,
> The world is very lone and sad,

The world is old and gray with pain
And all the ways thereof are bad.'

For one thing it is most annoying to think that I shall only have 3 weeks holiday this Easter: for another, as it draws to its close, I begin to regret the very happy time I have spent at Bookham. As well Mrs Gaskell's Life, though a book quite beyond all praise, especially in the description of scenery, has regularly given me the blues, so sad is the story it tells. When God can get hold of a really first rate character like Charlotte Brontë to torture, he's just in his element: cruelty after cruelty without any escape. How little right we have to grumble at any little discomforts of ours.

Cher ami, of course that lady is not my ideal, and I agree with you that she is much too big. I wonder would you think my ideal even pretty if I could produce her in bodily form! I have her very clearly in my mind however & could recognize her at once if such a person came into existance. The girl in the last instalment of Dymer is the one from the witch's house of course: it was dark when they met there, and in the morning Dymer left her still sleeping – so of course he knew her but she had never seen him. But I admit, that was so long ago that you may be pardoned for having forgotten. I am afraid this instalment is a failure. I have made three attempts at it and am not at all satisfied. Both in prose & verse & my everyday work the thing I take most pains with are always the poorest. Regardez comme je suis égoiste! Half the time I talk about the state of my soul & the other half of my own book.

Item, 'Peter Schlemihl' is the name of that German 'admirable' book about the man who sold his shadow. I am very pleased to have read it. I am now (in German) at 'Sintram'[54] a tale by Fouqué. It has some good eerie touches in it, but none of the homely beauty of 'Undine' – indeed 'tis rather tawdry as a whole. The edition is so horrible that it ought to emanate from 'Satan & Co.' & sometimes I have a ghastly suspicion that it is 'scripted': for these school editors are absolutely without conscience & wouldn't hesitate to mutilate a book and then publish it without a word of explanation.

By the way, did you know that the 1/- Nelson French series had several other bindings? I have got a 4/- 'half-polished morocco' one at

---

54 Friedrich Fouqué, Baron de la Motte, *Sintram* (1862).

which you will 'fly with delight'. It is Victor Hugo's 'Hans d'Islande'[55] (Islande=Iceland, not island, you know) of which a book on F. literature says 'it is founded on a modern Icelandic tradition of a man-beast who lives among the mountains.' So I hope it will be good. The whole set of Hugo built up in that binding would be splendid.

I have finished 'Paradise Lost' again, enjoying it even more than before. Really you must read it sometime soon. In Milton is everything you get everywhere else, only better. He is as voluptuous as Keats, as romantic as Morris, as grand as Wagner, as wierd as Poe, and a better lover of nature than even the Brontes. A propos of which, there are certainly some true Bronte touches in 'The Tenant of Wildfell (lovely name) Hall', especially in the homely gathering of the first chapter and some fine descriptions of the moors. Those moors must be lovely. Mrs. Gaskell's excellent description has quite fired me – not that any scenery could quite fill the place of our own dear glens and fields. I do hope we shall have some really good rambles among them soon: we must be careful never to talk of 'That' in the precincts of the Sacred Wood – as well, our vegetable loves, the hazels & brambles, might be jealous. Have your 'Essays' come yet? I wrote to Mullans a long time ago for the 3rd volume of the History which of course has not come. If this goes on I shall get all my books from London both in term and holydays. Yet that would be against all my principles.

'Our azure sister of the Spring'[56] is so annoyed at my praises of winter that she has retired and left the field to snow and slush. And the bare trees are all waving to and fro and sighing, and the drenching rain is blowing sideways out of a gray sky today altogether a very fine spectacle. I got onto one of the big Roman roads (theres something fine about feeling that a road runs away to Carlisle behind you) and trudged for miles watching the dead leaves floating along the swollen gutters. A most fascinating amusement, have you ever tried it?

I have written for the 'Faithful Shepheardess'[57] in the Temple Dramatists. What are they like? I have also got a Chatto & Windus list with some interesting news in it. My usual smoking nowadays is one of those

---

55 Victor Hugo, *Han d'Islande* (1823).

56 Percy Bysshe Shelley, 'Ode to the West Wind' (1819), l. 9: 'Thine azure sister of the spring'.

57 John Fletcher, *The Faithful Shepherdess* (1610).

very long old fashioned clay pipes. The sort that Milton may have smoked. You should try one. It is the cheapest and one of the best ways of smoking & you can understand the 'old world charm' of it. I wish there wasn't a week to wait for your next letter, make it as long as long as long. Good night, mon vieux.

TO HIS FATHER (LP V: 192):

[Gastons]
8/3/17.

My dear Papy,

I am very sorry that you should feel hurt about the boots. I must admit that I was hitherto under the impression that Warnie proposed to write and pay for them himself, in which case there would have been no reason to bring to your notice what I was sure you would regard as an extravagance. I argued that at any rate it was his affair and not mine, that it was not my business. Whenever I am in doubt what to do, it is always my rule to do nothing. I suppose I was wrong to follow it in this case, and am very sorry you should have been troubled.

The Oxford arrangement is rather more than an assurance that 'nothing will be decided until I go into residence'. I take it that we have settled that my military career will begin through the Oxford O.T.C. next term, and after that everything will be in the hands of the authorities – so that we have nothing more to worry about. At any rate that is what I meant in my last letter. The exam, as you know, begins next Tuesday week. With many abject apologies for my old, old offence, may I ask you to send me before that time, the waistcoat of my new brown suit? There are several brown waistcoats in my room, but you will know this one by the bright blue lining.

The food allowances are beginning to be short enough here. Like you, we find the meat plenty, but the bread rather short. Potatoes have almost disappeared among the poorer people and are no longer an every day dish anywhere. Of course it would be absurd to complain at present but it looks very black for the future, if this submarine business goes on. Kirk complains of the surplus potatoes held up in Ireland. By the way how is our ill fated front lawn coming on?

Some time before I arrive home I am posting a parcel addressed to you, with as many books as possible, to gain weight, and room in the suit case. At present I am reading Mrs. Gaskell's 'Life of Charlotte Bronte' which is admirable. After a glimpse of spring, we are back to a blowing frost.

your loving
son Jack.

TO HIS FATHER (LP V: 193–4):

[Gastons]
14th March /17.

My dear Papy,

It is rather difficult to give you any idea of what monies numbered I shall need for this trip. Last time, the journey to Oxford and back and the stay there came to a little over £5, did it not. This time of course there will be the journey from Oxford to Liverpool (or Fleetwood) as well.

Which reminds me, I will write and tell you as soon as I know which will be the better way and on what night I am crossing. If my examination takes me till midday on its last day, I might have difficulty in catching that evening's boat and so have to waste another day. I don't know when Malvern breaks up, but I have hopes of seeing my friend Cooper this time.

I suppose the wierd looking parcels of my books have arrived by now, and shall be glad to hear of their safety. I spent a long morning on Saturday rummaging the second hand dealers of Charing Cross Road (vide Lamb) for them: these foreign books (except French of course) are a great difficulty now.

Of course there is no formal promise about military service, but even if we wanted to (which we don't) we couldn't very well help joining the O.T.C. next term, when I am being allowed to go up for that very purpose. You don't mention your health, so I hope the cough has disappeared. We have had some more snow and several days and half days of the densest clamniest fog you ever heard of outside London.

Another of Mrs. K's nieces is staying here at present: they seem to be inexhaustable. I am looking forward to a glorious vista of potatoes in plentiful Ireland.

your loving
son Jack.

TO ARTHUR GREEVES (W):

[Gastons
14 March 1917]

Cher Ami,

I have just been debating whether the pleasure of getting a letter will outweigh the dissapointment of finding a very short one: for without anything from you to provoke argument I don't know how long I can go on gassing. See how concieted I am grown, as if in my letters shortness would not be the best recommendation.

Well to proceed (and recite the following verses of the poet) I was delighted to hear of your illness, which I did yesterday from M. mon père and to day from Mme. vôtre mère & your own scrawl. I hope you will be just nicely convalescing when I turn up – well enough to go out, but of course not nearly well enough for Niffleheim (or Frankleheim). Seriously, unless it is [a] very painful or opressive illness I always get some pleasure out of 'keeping my bed'. Especially if you are sick enough to have a fire! There is something beautifully cosy about meals brought up on a tray, and after a frugal but thoroughly enjoyable breakfast I love to pile up my pillows, call for a choice pile of bright volumes and settle down to an endless read: if there be snow falling so much the better.

I say 'bright volumes' advisedly, because all books are not suitable for bed reading. Books of the 'Phantastes' & 'Crock of Gold' type are best; some new ones if possible, several old favourites, a trashy novel from the library (trashy, but not bad, if you know what I mean) AND some picture books of the Rackham & Robinson type. I should find 'Jason' very good company too. By the way don't imagine I'm trotting all this out as sort of 'advice to invalids': its only that the subject naturally came up & I couldn't lose an opportunity of airing my own tastes. Expect you wont agree with any of them. I suppose the Titian print is great company: or can you see nothing but reflexions in it's glass from where you sit?

Cher ami, 'Han d'Islande' in its lovely binding is the best book I've read for many a day. It is about Norway in the 16th century, a good historical romance, gets along quicker than Scott tho' without any of the hiccupping style that annoys us in Dumas. Although there is no supernatural element there is a great deal of the terrifying and the 'macabre'. Hans himself, a sort of ugly & ferocious Rob Roy, with a dash of Alberich in his character and appearance is a real treat. There are also excellent descriptions of scenery among the mountains and ruins. Altogether a book I should very heartily recommend you. Amn't I good to write to you instead of readin it at this moment? The III vol. of my Macaulay has come at last in a shocking shop soiled copy, but I suppose I shall have to keep it.

You will see from the tag in this week's Dymer that I have begun Italian, which is the easiest language of the world.[58] I shall be able to shew you one charming edition in that language next hols. My adress after Teusday is,

> C/o Mrs Etheridge,
> 1 Mansfield Road,
> Oxford.

'No more now' as the housemaids say. Goodnight.

P.S. I wonder what you really thought of my last letter

Lewis returned to Oxford on 20 March and lodged in the same digs as before. Responsions began on the 21st and he returned home on 27 March, soon afterwards learning that he had been ploughed in algebra. He was, however, allowed to come into residence in Trinity Term so as to be able to pass into the army by way of the University Officers' Training Corps. He arrived in Oxford on 26 April and matriculated on the 28th. From an academic point of view he was supposed to be reading for Responsions, and shortly after his arrival he began algebra lessons with John Edward Campbell (1862–1924) of Hertford College.

On 30 April Lewis joined the Officers' Training Corps and had a physical examination. He weighed 13 stone, or 182 pounds, and measured 5 feet 10³/₄ inches. In the official records, the officer commanding wrote under 'Special Remarks': 'Likely to make a useful officer but will not have had sufficient training for admission to an O.C.U.[59] before end of June.'

---

58 Writing to Jack's father on 18 April 1917, Mr Kirkpatrick said: 'I conceived, with the enthusiastic assent of the pupil, of course, the bold conception of mastering the Italian language in half a term. And we did it. None but a quite exceptional student could have attempted it, much less succeeded in it.' (LP V: 203).

59 Officer Cadet Unit.

TO HIS FATHER (LP V: 194):

[University College,
Oxford]
Postmark: 20 March 1917

My dear P.,

Many thanks for the money: I am sorry to have given you the trouble of wiring it. I find I can cross by Fleetwood on Friday night. Have arrived here this morning and exams begin to morrow. Your letter came just before I left Bookham. As usual it is colder here than any where else. This is our shop: second tower belongs to some other coll.

yours J.

TO HIS FATHER (LP V: 206–7):

[University College]
Postmark: 28 April 1917

My dear Papy,

I hope that you have got both my wires. The second I could not send off till the morning, as the post offices were all shut by the time I knew anything to tell you last night.

The effect of the war here is much more startling than I could have expected, and everything is very homely and out of order. The College at present numbers 6 men, of whom 4 are freshmen! Others are coming all the time, but I do not think we shall be more than eleven all told. Last night we had dinner not in Hall but in a small lecture room, and none of the dons appeared. Hall is in possession of the blue-coated wounded, who occupy the whole of one quad: incidentally, the second tower (in the p. card) does belong to us after all.

The first thing that strikes you is the enormous size of the rooms. I imagined a 'sitter' something smaller than the little end room. The first one they showed me was rather larger than our drawing room and full of most beautiful oak. I wasn't left there however, and am now in a much humbler, and very nice set, on the other side of the quad.[60] It is a pity in a way that all the furniture and pictures really belong to a man who may be coming back after the war – it saves me expenses, but it prevents me from having what I want.

---

60 Lewis was in set no. 5 on Staircase XII of the Radcliffe Quad. Most of the rooms in this quad were occupied by the wounded.

I have been to see the Dean,[61] who turns out to be a beardless boy of about 25, and also my tutor, who is also the bursar.[62] They don't appear to suggest any real reading while I am in the Corps, but the Bursar has promised to find me a coach for elementary mathematics, if possible. Corps does not begin till Monday evening for which short respite I am very thankful. I think it will be quite cheap living in this 'vast solitude': the only serious expenses so far have been £2-10 for uniform (which seems very reasonable), and £1-9 for cap and gown (which does not). It seems that the adress of 'University Coll.' will find me quite safely. Hoping that you are keeping well and cheerful and that you will soon write,

I am,

your loving son,

Jack.

TO ARTHUR GREEVES (W):

[University College
28 April 1917]

Cher Ami,

I wonder how much description will be tolerable for you to hear and me to write. I am so full of new things that I don't know where to begin, and yet nothing has really happened so far. I will try to tell you at least my first adventures in some detail.

Heavily laden with suitcase, parcels and coats I arrived at the great gate of Univ. at about 5 o'clock. From the porter's lodge a sandy-haired man emerged and shouted 'Jo'. Somewhat timidly I came further in and asked 'Can you tell me where my rooms are, – my name is Lewis.' Yes, Sir,' said the man. 'Can't say where you'll be, Sir, the Dean hasn't come up yet – Jo!' Jo now appeared.[63] 'Show Mr Lewis into Mr

---

61 John Clifford Valentine Behan (1881–1957) was Dean 1914–17. He was the first Rhodes Scholar to come from the state of Victoria, Australia, and he was made a Fellow of Law at University College in 1909.

62 Arthur Blackburne Poynton (1876–1944), Lewis's tutor. He came up to Balliol College in 1885 and was one of the most distinguished undergraduates of his generation. After taking a First in Classical Honour Moderations in 1889 and a First in *Literae Humaniores* in 1890 he was elected a Fellow of Hertford College. In 1894 he moved to University College as Fellow and Praelector in Greek. He was the Master of University College from 1935 to 1937.

63 Cyril 'Joe' Haggis (1890–1967), a college scout, came to the College in 1908, and retired, at the age of 65, after 43 years of service. See *University College Record*, Vol. V (September 1967), pp. 111–12.

Crawford's[64] old rooms' said the sandy haired man. Jo took my various baggage and led the way along one side of the quad (I was very relieved to see no one about). Then he led me up three very bare noisy flights of stairs, between stone walls, dark with tiny windows, halted before a room, and throwing open the 'oak' and the inner door said 'Here you are, Sir. Your servant'll be here in arf an hour, and if these aren't the right rooms, he'll tell you Sir.'

You can imagine, ami, with what intense excitement I stepped into the first varsity rooms I'd ever seen. The first thing that struck me with amazement was the size. I had expected something rather less than the little end room at home. What I saw was a very low-roofed, rather uneven-floored room somewhat larger than the study at home. The furniture was of dark oak very richly carved, and valuable I should think. On the floor was a red carpet with great profusion of rugs. Besides the old furniture was a big modern sofa & several very easy chairs. There was also a little bed-room and a cupboard. I was awfully bucked with it and went on sitting down in one chair after another, and opening and shutting the 'oak' after Jo had left me.

I looked down on the quad. and saw a tall youth in spectacles talking to the porter. I began to wonder what I should do. Did one wear a gown for hall? How did one sit in hall? The question of wearing a gown was solved soon, because I heard someone in the opposite room saying to someone else 'Oh no, no gowns.' Presently I went down into the quad to prospect – but be of good cheer, cher ami, I am not going to keep up this detailed description much longer. I must try and give you a general account of the college in shorter terms.

The rooms I am in now are very nice tho' not so magnificent as the first ones (which turned out to be wrong). They really belong to a tremendous blood who is at the front – at least the furniture is all his. Of course this takes away from me the pleasure of choosing the things for myself; but then it is much better done than I could have afforded. There is a grand piano – couldn't we have great times, ami? It is getting to be

---

64 Edward Hugh Martin Crawford (1894–1973) was a graduate of Dalhousie University, Nova Scotia. He matriculated in 1914 as a Rhodes Scholar. He took a Second in Jurisprudence in 1916, and a BCL in 1920. He was called to the Canadian Bar in 1920, having spent the latter years of the war in a munitions factory. During World War II he served with the Royal Canadian Air Force.

quite homely to me this room, especially when I come back to it by fire-light and find the kettle boiling. How I love kettles!

Dinner is not in Hall now, as there are only 12 men in college, but in a small lecture room, and the dons don't turn up. For all other meals the scout brings you a cover in your rooms; tea etc you make for yourself. So far, I have done absolutely nothing. The Dean refuses to map out any plans for me, on the ground that the Corps will take me all my time. Corps doesn't begin till Monday afternoon.

Now as to the human part of the place. None of the older men (from last or previous terms, I mean) take any notice of us freshmen, except to ask us for the salt and that sort of thing. There are 3 freshmen counting myself. One of them is quite impossible, and I and the other one, a certain Edgell,[65] have lived mostly together so far. He is writing letters in my rooms at the moment. Well what like is he? I can hardly say. First of all, in tastes he is no friend of ours. He doesn't read, and is interested in mechanics – ugh! However, he can talk not without interest on a good many subjects, among which we reached religion, when I was foolish enough to tell him my own views. 'Natheless he so endured.'[66] He is very useful to me, because his father was at Univ. and has told him all the tricks of the trade. He also makes excellent cofee, and so I am sticking to him at present. Later on, as I get to know more people, perhaps I shall find some real friends here also.

The only other thing I can think of that may interest you – in that way – is the Shelley memorial which you would love. I pass it every morning on the way to my bath. On a slab of black marble, carved underneath with weeping muses, lies in white stone the nude figure of Shelley, as he was cast up by the sea – all tossed into curious attitudes with lovely ripples of muscle and strained limbs. He is lovely.[67] <(No – not since I came back. Somehow I haven't even thought of it.)>

---

65 Lawrence Fayrer Arnold Edgell (1898–1950) after receiving his BA in 1923, read Theology at Wycliffe Hall, Oxford, and was ordained in the Church of England in 1927. After some years with the Church Missionary Society in Persia, he returned home and was the vicar of several churches, his last being in Shalford, Essex, from 1946 until his death.

66 Milton, *Paradise Lost*, I, 299.

67 The drowned figure of Shelley lying on a slab of Connemara marble was carved by Edward Onslow Ford. It lies under a dome designed by Basil Champneys. The monument was originally intended for the Protestant cemetery in Rome, where Shelley is buried, but it was presented to the college by Lady Shelley.

Well, there you have all my news. Now let us talk about yourself. So write at once and tell me everything, and be of good cheer. We get potatoes every day here. – Addio,

Jack

TO HIS FATHER (LP V: 208–9):

[University College]
Wednesday.
Postmark: 3 May 1917

My dear Papy,

I was delighted to see your letter at the bottom of my staircase this morning, and was only sorry to hear that you are 'hipped'. Of course I know that that can hardly be otherwise,

> *'and on my knees*
> *I too have prayed that it should be amended'*

though I do not know how. It is terrible to think of the lonely life you now have to lead, and I do most earnestly hope and pray that you may find some way out of it. So far as the knowledge of my comfortable and healthy circumstances here can add to your happiness – well 'Make it so'; I have nothing but good to report so far. The Corps proves very much more agreeable than the Malvern one – every one is so friendly and reasonable, you feel that you are there to learn, and not merely to be bullied by sergeants. I have found a mathematical coach, a very pleasant Scotsman, a Mr. Campbell of Hertford, who has almost promised to get me through 'Smalls' [Responsions] next term.

As to the other matters, whatever vices one is likely to develop here must be those native to the University: the huge mass of military people who are settled in Oxford count for nothing. You see the actual varsity O.T.C. is only a small body: outside it is a mob of cadets freshly come from other O.T.C.'s, and here training for commissions. They are rather a bad lot, and certainly an ill bred lot, especially the Flying Corps, who, like most people in dangerous things, are busily engaged in eating and drinking on their splendid pay, for tomorrow they die. Against all these the old feud of TOWN and GOWN is rather in force. Thank goodness none are quartered in Univ. But even then we shouldn't know them. Beyond the 'commons' mug of ale supplied with our lunch, bread and cheese, I see no drinking here.

I have met several Malvernians, including my sometime study companion Hardman, whom I was sorry to find in the ill-famed Flying Corps, quartered opposite us in Queen's. However, I was glad to have a crack with him over old times: some people, like some books, do not read so well when we open them after a long interval. Yet the charm of 'Do you remember' will carry on a conversation with anyone.

I paid cash for the gown but not for the uniform. The bills will come in at the end of term, and I think will include nothing but tailor, grocer (for necessaries not supplied by College, tea, sugar, butter etc.) and Battels. These are sent me weekly to check, but aren't paid till the vac. Of course I shall try to keep everything down, tho' my fresher's ignorance of shops sometimes makes me pay more for something than I need have done. Am learning to row.

your loving son,
Jack.

P.S. Please let me have Warnie's adress, of which I am not quite sure. J.

TO ARTHUR GREEVES (W):

[University College
6 May 1917]

My dear Galahad,

I am afraid this letter is not punctual and I am further afraid that many of my letters this term will not be punctual. We do not do really much here, but somehow the whole day is frittered away in little things. As for going on to my diabolical romance – tis out of the question. Your last letter is lost, so what shall I jaw about?

Well first, let me most earnestly advise you to get Gautier's 'Un Trio de Romans'[68] when you next want a French book. It is really excellent; one story rather reminds me of the Cosmo episode in 'Phantastes'. I am afraid I shall get too many in that edition, it is so very convenient. The 2nd vol. of the Earthly Paradise stands in my bookcase here, but I have progressed only a few pages since coming up. However I am going to make out a regular time-table for each day & try if I cannot get more

---

68 Théophile Gautier, *Un Trio de Romans* (1852).

time like that. When you are not made to work and when there is such a lot to do, it is very hard to get on with things.

It is most glorious weather here now and we spend most of our spare afternoons on the river. Edgell knows something about rowing, so I am gradually learning through many blunders. We ran someone down today (Sunday) greatly to the amusement of the assembled river: but as the other wasn't a varsity man of course it didn't matter!

My chief 'cross' at present is my friend, or rather my companion, Edgell, whose limitless piety I don't think I can endure any longer. He has all your particular faults, cher ami, with none of your merits. He is economical, methodical to the verge of insanity. He is fully convinced of his own moral superiority, and lectures me on my 'weakness of character'. Still, I suppose I must stick to him until I get to know some of the senior men a bit better!

Don't imagine however that I'm grumbling. The place is on the whole absolutely ripping. If only you saw the quad. on these moonlit nights with the long shadows lying half across the level, perfect grass and the tangle of spires & towers rising beyond in the dark! Oh ami, ami, what times we could have here together: you really must come. What talks we could have in the privacy of these rooms by firelight while the kettle was boiling. Item, you must get a ground room if you come, as even I begin to find the dashing up & down stairs rather tiring. I am finding a whole lot of Malvernians here – a new one every day. How lovely the country must be at home now – I hope you are still on half time and are having some nice afternoons <(– in that way?)> in the garden. Which reminds me, I have 'Digestive' biscuits every day for tea, & always wish I was sharing them with you instead of with that six feet of spectacled priggery!

The book shops here are rather adorable, and also our college library. Still better is the Library of the Union Society (a club everyone belongs to) where I spent this morning turning over one book after another and enjoying myself hugely. My books have not finished binding yet, but of course I shall give you a full account so soon as they arrive. The Maeterlink's are to be plain dark blue cloth, and the 'Literature Française au Moyen Age' in green linnen. I'm afraid this [is] all the length of letter I can raise. Do reply soon and at full length.

TO HIS FATHER (LP V: 210–11):

[University College]
Postmark: 12 May 1917

My dear Papy,

I hope you will forgive a little delay in my answering your last letter, as I wanted to wait until I had seen my coach Mr. Campbell again, and could give an answer to your question. A rather awkward and at the same time rather pleasing thing has happened. (Incidentally Mr. Campbell turns out to be the uncle of my Malvern friend Hardman, who, as I told you, is here in the Flying Corps). Well, when I asked him about fees, he said he didn't want any. I replied, with very many thanks, that the matter of course concerned my father and not me, and that I was sure you wouldn't allow him to do any such thing. He said that he regarded the thing as a service done to Univ., to which society he was under many obligations: that if my father wanted to get rid of some money, he could give it to some deserving charity: and that if you sent it to him, that is what he would do with it. I repeated that of course it had nothing to do with me – that I would write to you about it. I then bear my retreat, with renewed thanks. Whatever you decide to do, I suppose you will write to him. The address is:

> J.A.Campbell Esq.
> Hertford College,
> Oxford.

When you imagine how boring it must be for a real mathematician and an F.R.S. to teach such elementary stuff, you will understand the extent of his goodness. I have liked him exceedingly from the first. As you say, it is a thousand pities that this is not the real Oxford. The more I stay here the more I hope that I shall see it again as it ought to be.

Of course I am keeping my classics up as much as I can, tho' it is not always easy to find time for everything, especially as 'sporting your oak' is not allowed when there are so few men in College. Yes, there are plenty of shellfish of the crab kind to be found in the waters both of the 'Isis' and the Cherwell: also knocks on the chin, and eloquence from people you collide with. Some other freshers and I had 'brekker' with the Master this morning – a thoroughly enjoyable function. How very nice everyone I've met so far seems to be! The only possible exception is the Dean, who is – in manner – like Uncle Pumblechook,[69] only more so: his favourite conversational fallback is that chilling word 'Oh.' Your friend David Garrick was here last week, but I didn't go.

your loving

son Jack.

TO ARTHUR GREEVES (W):

[University College
13 May 1917]

Cher Ami,

As you seem able to bear my boring accounts of life here, I may give you a little more. To-day, for instance, (Sunday) has so far been a very prosperous and a not untypical day. I woke at about 7 o'clock with the pleasing reflection that there was no early parade and read Wm. Morris and Gautier till 8.30. I then went down to the bathroom and had first a hot & then a cold bath – which is 'done' here.

We are gradually getting to know people and a very senior man, Butler,[70] has asked us to 'brekker' (breakfast) this morning. I arrived in his rooms a little too early, and thus had an opportunity of studying his books, which I always consider the best introduction to a new acquaintance. I was pleased to find Keats, Shelley, Oscar Wilde, Dante & Villon, as well as Plutarch & one of the lately executed Sinn Fein poets:[71] for Butler is an Irishman & a nationalist. I was just trying to find out the publisher of the nice Plutarch when Butler arrived with the other guests, Edgell & a certain Edwards[72] & we sat down to brekker. I like Butler exceedingly. Of

---

69 'Uncle Pumblechook' was the Lewises' nickname for G. Herbert Ewart (1857–1924), the brother of Sir William Quartus Ewart, and the managing director of the family business of William Ewart and Son, Belfast.

70 Theobald Richard Fitzwalter Butler (1894–1976) who was to achieve great distinction as a lawyer, was called to the Bar, Inner Temple, in 1921, became Master of the Bench in 1960, and Chancellor of the Diocese of Peterborough in 1962.

71 He is referring to Joseph Mary Plunkett (1887–1916), known as one of 'The 1916 Poets'.

72 John Robert Edwards (1897–1992) grew up in Manchester and attended Manchester Grammar School. He graduated from Univ. in 1920 with a Second in Greats. He began work in business, but he could not be parted from the Greek and Latin classics, and he had a remarkable career as a teacher. He taught classics at Chigwell School and Merchant Taylor's School, Crosby, until 1931. He was then appointed headmaster of Grove Park Grammar School, Wrexham, where he remained until 1935. He went from there to the Liverpool Institute High School as headmaster where he remained until his

course he talked a good deal to me about Ireland: it seems that he knows Yeats quite well, & also Gilbert Murray. Otherwise the talk turned on books. Can I confess that I had certain spiteful pleasure in seeing Edgell, who has been lecturing me on morals & motor bykes for the last fortnight, very much out of his element in such a conversation?

After brekker we all decided that a bathe would be a very sound plan. Some kind friend lent me a bycyle and thus we set out. It was a perfectly lovely morning with a deep blue sky, all the towers & pinnacles gleaming in the sun & bells ringing everywhere. We past down through quieter streets among colleges and gardens to the river, & after about quarter of an hour's ride along the bank came to the bathing places. Here, without the tiresome convention of bathing things we enjoyed a swim. The bathing place is a lovely backwater surrounded by those *level* (you know the sort) daisied & buttercuped fields & overhung by those short fluffy trees – named – I don't know.[73]

So about 11.30 we arrived back at college and I am come straight thence to the Union. 'The Union' is a club to which nearly everyone in the varsity belongs. It has a writing room of strictest silence, where I am scribbling this, and an admirable library where I have already passed many happy hours and hope to pass many more. Oh, Galahad, you simply must come up after the war. This at present is only a shadow of the real Oxford, yet even so I never was happier in my life. Do make an effort!

By the way my books have finished binding and are absolutely ripping. In a fit of extravagance I am getting two more done. One is an Apuleius: he as you know wrote the book in which the 'Cupid & Psyche' story occurs. I have found his complete works in the college library and their brooding magic no less than their occasional voluptuousness &

---

retirement in 1961. Writing to me on 6 January 1978, he recalls that Lewis in 1917 'could join in any discussion on any subject and talk fluently and knowledgeably; he was particularly interested in those early days in religion and was particularly challenging in his scepticism'. See *University College Record*, Vol. X, No. 4 (1992), pp. 93–4.

73 'Parson's Pleasure' lay north of Magdalen College, where two branches of the Cherwell come together to form the area known as 'Mesopotamia', after the ancient country between the Tigris and the Euphrates. It was known as 'Parson's Pleasure' in the 17th century and it seems always to have been used by men for bathing and sunbathing in the nude. It was customary for ladies to disembark from their punts before reaching 'Parson's Pleasure' and walk around to a series of metal rollers where they could pick them up again. In recent years it has been turned into a park.

ridiculous passages have made me feel that I must get a copy of my own. What lots I shall have to show you when I come down!

But voila que je suis égoiste![74] I have done nothing but jaw about myself. However reply by jawing about yourself & tell me all you are reading & thinking & how things go forward at home.

Jack

TO HIS FATHER (LP V: 212-13):

[University College]
Postmark: 17 May 1917

My dear Papy,

I think your note to Campbell will fit the occasion very well. His job at Hertford is that of Bursar – but I fancy he is undertaking this only for the time of the war. He is a fellow (all people like Bursars and Deans are Fellows as well it would appear), and a mathematical tutor. I am often alone in his room at Hertford, but I have not seen anything but technical books so far, except one vol. of our own edition of De Quincy. However, I must take further reconnaissances. He is really an awfully nice chap, though very Scotch.

Our 'military duties' are as light as they well could be. We have a morning parade from 7 till 7.45, and another from 2 till 4, with occasional evening lectures on map reading and such like subjects. I am afraid I must tell you that the chances of getting into the gunners are pretty pale, as 'Only those cadets who can be shown to have some special knowledge of mathematics' will be recommended for them.

The early morning parade of course makes it impossible for us to go to chapel, except to the Celebration on Sundays. I am afraid that I usually find the place in possession only of us freshers and the dons. As to St Mary's,[75] I have not been yet. The last two Sundays were so fine that having been to the early service, I felt justified in going off to bathe after 'brekker'. I have however found out enough about it to realize that it is rather different from what we imagine. There are only a few prayers, and a very long sermon, usually more of a philosophical and political than of

---

74 'But there it is: what an egoist I am!'

75 The Church of St Mary the Virgin. This medieval church, which was largely rebuilt in the 15th and early 16th centuries, dominates the High Street and is directly across the street from Univ. It has for centuries been closely associated with the University, and is referred to as the 'University Church'.

a religious nature: in fact it is more a Sunday lecture room than a church in the true sense. The best place to go for a fine service is the Cathedral at 'The House' as Christ Church is called: it is typical of the House that it should have the Cathedral of the diocese for its chapel!

Getting the right to use the Bodleian is a long job; I have been recommended for a 'reader' by my tutor, but must wait a week or so until I am elected. In the mean time the College Library and the 'Union' library supply me with more books than I am ever likely to read. The Union is particularly interesting to me because it bears on its walls the remains of the frescoes which Morris, Burne-Jones, Watts and Rosetti painted – only to fade immediately through some impurity in the plaster.

How I hope that you'll be able to come up and see me here some day when this troublesome war is over! I see Wells has written a new book – apparently working out some of the theories hinted at in 'Mr. Britling'.[76] We have had a round of dissipation this week, going to 'brekker' with nearly all the senior men. It appears that they ask you, but that freshers aren't supposed to ask anyone to anything their first term. There is an Irishman here called Butler who was in Serbia with Dod[d]s and worked his passage home with him: he is a violent Home Ruler.

your loving
son Jack.

TO ARTHUR GREEVES (W):

[University College
20 May 1917]

Cher Ami,

I wonder if we could not arrange our letters so that they don't always cross. I mean, as things at present are, you will not have got this until you have written your own replying to my last. This spoils the 'conversational' effect of letter writing. However, I am afraid Sunday is now my only possible time, and if it is yours too I am afraid there is no help for us.

I am glad to hear that you like Milton: I was sure he would appeal to you. The language is, I admit, not always easily understood: tho' using English words, he often builds his sentences on a Latin framework which

---

76 H.G. Wells, *The Soul of a Bishop: A Novel – with just a little love in it – and Conscience and Religion and the real Troubles of Life* (1917); *Mr Britling Sees it Through* (1916).

makes it almost meaningless to a purely English reader. Some words, too, he uses in very strange ways. For instance, when, at the opening of the 3rd Book you come to the line

'Or hear'st thou rather pure ethereal stream'[77]

remember that 'hear' means in this place 'hight', i.e. 'to be called'. What he wants to say is 'Shall I call thee rather "Pure, ethereal stream." ' Don't you love all the descriptions of Hell? (Item. When reading about the Shetlands in 'The Pirate'[78] I was disconsolate because I thought I should never see them. In reading about the scenery of Hell, I need have no such uneasiness!) You will also love the parts about Eden when you come to them.

The chief event in things of art this week has been my discovery of Albert Dürer. I don't know if you have heard of him before: he was a German engraver of the 16th century, and I have often heard him referred to as the 'most Romantic of engravers', the 'Founder of the Fantastic school in Art' etc. Yesterday I came across some postcard reproductions of his pictures, and bought some. I daresay they will dissapoint you, but I like them greatly: especially one 'Study of an old Man's Head'. Although not a modern, you can easily see that he is the father of Rackham and all this modern school of fantastic illustrators. But all this must wait for full discussion when I come down, & we can go over them side by side.

Life goes on very pleasantly here. Besides Butler (whom I mentioned in my last letter) the other most interesting person here is a man named Edwards. He is not a very attractive person, and has a rather unpleasant accent (tho' not so bad as some of my friends have!): what interests me about him is that he was an atheist till lately, and is now engaged in becoming a Catholic, or is very near it. He came into my rooms last night, and sat till about 12. We had a long talk about religion, Buddhism, poetry and everything else. How I like talking!

As to the other man, Butler, I like him better the more I know him (Item. He often comes to Portsalon so we may see him sometime). He is, however, not an immaculate character. I had often heard that he was

---

77 Milton, *Paradise Lost*, III, 7.
78 Sir Walter Scott, *The Pirate* (1821).

very amusing when drunk, but I had no experience until last night. At about 10, he burst into my room exclaiming 'God bless you, God bless you.' He sank down on my sofa but soon rolled onto the floor, repeating in tragic accents 'I would that I were dead, and lying in the woods with the corpses of the great ones of Erin about me. (This is all out of some nationalist poet) None is unhappier than I, save only the great yellow bittern.' He continued lying on the floor reciting, expressing an ardent desire to go and kiss the Dean, and calling on the 'Holy Mother of God', until Edwards and a rather pointless man called MacNicholl[79] came in to see the fun. We began to try to get him to bed, but he begged in pathetic tones to be left there on the floor for just ten minutes and swore 'by the Holy Ghost and by Venus Aphrodite' that he would go then. By about 11 we did actually succeed in getting him out. His mood had changed now and instead of wanting to lie 'dead in the wood' he wanted 'To be in the pine forest in the white arms of Aphrodite'. You see how a man of taste & reading preserves his natural character even when dead drunk. He used the most beautiful language. I went for a bathe with him this morning and he seemed almost quite recovered. He is going to lend me a copy of the nationalist poet from whom he was quoting from.

I have finished the 2nd vol. of Wm. Morris, all except the last story of 'Ogier the Dane'.[80] I don't think I shall order the next until I come down, as I have so little time for reading here. By the way – don't ever imagine, as I used to, that access to good libraries is an inducement to reading. Among thousands of interesting books it is impossible to settle down to one. Yes, I did and do think of Papillon on the river – especially when we pass pretty people.

Yours
Jack

---

79 John Milne MacNicholl (1898–), son of Douglas McNicholl of Abergele, Denbighshire, matriculated in 1917, but in 1918 enlisted as a 2nd lieutenant in the Royal Horse Artillery and served in Palestine. He did not return to Oxford to finish his degree.
80 'Ogier the Dane' is one of the stories in *The Earthly Paradise*.

TO ARTHUR GREEVES (W):

[University College
27 May 1917]

Cher Ami,

First, lest we forget, I must answer your question. I do not know yet when I shall get down nor for how long: it is certain that we shall not be down for the whole vac., but even so, I think we shall be at home longer than a school holiday. I hope to be able to tell you exactly in my next letter.

You say that your books have come at last from Denny, and then add that you may give up buying books altogether. Am I to gather that this last parcel (consisting of what?) is very dissapointing? Personally I am being rather extravagant. This week's purchases include the poems of Thomson and Renan's 'Vie de Jésus'.[81] The Thomson here mentioned is not the modern but an 18th century man, whose best thing is a poem in Spencerian stanzas called 'The Castle of Indolence'.[82] Tis as good as the title suggests. The other (Nelson's 1/- edition), Renan's 'Vie de Jesus' you will probably have heard of: it is a life of 'Jeshua' written from a free thinker's point of view, and is very beautiful in style. I think you would not care for it, but I like it immensely. I have also ordered a copy of the first volume of Tennyson in a new edition by Macmillan. It is excellent in paper and title page & so on, but the binding is a kind of semi-limp leather that I don't much care for. However, as it is the only tolerable edition of Tennyson that I can hear tell of, I thought it fit to be bought. Dunsany's book was reviewed in the Times Literary Supplement some time ago, where they spoke of him as an experimenter in prose style.[83] I should like to see his 'Tales of Wonder', but I do not think it would be worth 5/-. Another good book I am reading at present (from the Union Library) is Andrew Lang's and R. Haggard's 'The World's Desire'[84] of which you have heard Chainie[85] speak very, very, very often. Item, tell Chainie that I am coaching with a friend of hers, Mr Campbell of Hertford.

---

81 Joseph Ernest Renan, *La Vie de Jésus* (1863).
82 James Thomson, *The Castle of Indolence* (1748).
83 The review of Edward Dunsany's *Tales of Wonder* (1917) is found in *The Times Literary Supplement* (12 April 1917), p. 172.
84 H. Rider Haggard and Andrew Lang, *The World's Desire* (1891).
85 i.e. Janie McNeill.

The other morning I was surprised by Gundrede,[86] (up for the day) Mrs and Cherry Robbins.[87] G. of course has gone but of the other two I have seen a good deal. Cherry is not pretty unfortunately but she is what I call a really ripping kind of person – an awfully good sort, and (greatest recommendation to us) a lover of books.

No – all days are not so pleasant as the Sundays. On week days I am called by my scout at 7.0. I tramp down to the parks for early parade, from which I return to bath and brekker at about 8.45. I then work till 1, have lunch, and set off for another parade from 2 till 4. At 4 I come back, have tea (either in college or at the Union) and go down to the river for a bathe. I get back to college at about 5.30, and then read English until dinner at 7. In the evenings I work mildly or talk or sometimes play cards or even go for a byke ride, getting to bed at about 11. It is on the whole a very pleasant life.

To-day (Sunday) Butler had brekker with me and afterwards we bathed. We had a long talk on the rival merits of Swinburne & Keats, the improbability of God, and Home Rule. Like all Irish people who meet in England we ended by criticisms on the invincible flippancy and dulness of the Anglo-Saxon race. After all, there is no doubt, ami, that the Irish are the only people: with all their faults I would not gladly live or die among another folk.

Edgell – the other fresher of whom I have spoken – gets more and more wearisome every day: he is the most priggish, illiterate and narrow-minded ass I ever met. His chief subject of conversation is his relatives, especially his brother and cousin who have been killed at the front. Well of course I respect them for it, and I sympathise with him for loosing them. At the same time, I don't think they need be dragged into every single conversation, on every opportunity!

The country about here with its two rivers and its tall poplars, though not exciting is now beautifully fresh and green and sleepy. How I look forward to the hills of Down, the little copses and the view over the

---

86 Lewis's cousin, Gundreda Ewart, who was with the Voluntary Aid Detachment, was home on leave from France where she had been nursing at various camps.

87 Mrs Kittie Robbins (wife of Colonel Herbert E. Robbins) was the sister of Mary, Lady Ewart – and so first cousin to Lewis's mother. Her daughter 'Cherry' was with the Voluntary Aid Detachment at a military hospital in Oxford during the war.

lough! I am sorry my letters from here cannot be so long as they were from Bookham, but I really have not time. Addio,

yours,

Jack

TO HIS FATHER (LP V: 215-6):

[University College]
Postmark: 28 May 1917

My dear Papy,

Coals, did you say? At present all my windows are open, my blinds are pulled down on the sunny side; the quad., with its roasting stonework is simply baking under a 'heaven as brass above me'.[88] These sort of days are topping on the river, but not so nice for bayonet practice, and route marches and such like entertainments. I will find out from the Adjutant exactly when we O.T.C. people come down and for how long: rumours vary a good deal, but I think our vac. will be shorter by several weeks than the ordinary one, but as long or longer than a school summer holidays. However, I expect that I shall be able to give you more definite information in my next letter.

This week I have had adventures. On Tuesday in the middle of the morning I had happened to come down and walk across the quad. to see if there were any letters in the porch, when I was hailed as 'Jack' by a group of ladies on the far side. At first I couldn't see who they were, but they turned out to be Gundreda (up for the day), Aunt Kittie and Cherry Robbins. They had come in to look at College quite by accident, not knowing that I was there. Since then I have seen a good deal of them. What a dear old lady Aunt Kittie is! And how typical of her set: we happened to talk about Cromwell the other day, and when Cherry and I ventured on some criticisms, the true greatness of old Noll was explained to us by a reminder that 'Cromwell's mother was some connection of ours'! Here we have the spirit of history; wouldn't it appeal to the Knock?

Dod's friend Butler is a poetical and sentimental complete separationist, interested in the pronunciation of Gaelic: by the way, Dods is

---

88 Lewis possibly had in mind John Webster's *The Duchess of Malfi* (1623), IV, ii, 25:
'Th'heaven ore my head, seems made of molton brasse.' This, in turn, may be related to the curse in Deuteronomy 28:23: 'And thy heaven that is over thy head shall be brass, and the earth that is under thee shall be iron.'

coming up to take his degree at the end of this term, so I shall have an opportunity of meeting him.

I should be glad if you would send the little book on philosophy so soon as you can, as I want to make a start on this subject and the College Library has nothing quite elementary enough for a beginner. At present I am reading Renan's 'Vie de Jésus', which I think an admirable book, and a great lesson in good manners to other free thinkers.

I have had to pay cash (£2.10) to the Quartermaster for my uniform, and 15/6 for a pair of service boots. I don't want to bother you unneccessarily, but this has been rather a drain on resources, and I should be glad if you could refund it.

your loving
son Jack.

TO ARTHUR GREEVES (W):

[University College
3 June 1917]

Cher Ami,

I am delighted to hear that you have at last arriven at 'The Victorians'.[89] The criticism that most of these novels begin with a very interesting part about the childhood and then get more conventional as they go on is only too true – at least for us who are attracted by 'childish things'.[90] In this case I think it is certainly true that the school scenes are the best (very good in every way). But there is no very violent slump in the interest and I for one followed the rest of it very eagerly. She is a most excellent character.

Last Sunday I began reading Blackwood's 'Prisoner in Fairyland'[91] in the Union Library, & liked it immensely. But I think I shall wait until they publish it in the 7d edition & then get it for myself. My other book 'The Castle of Indolence' goes on excellently: it is quite a good imitation of Spencer, and has a certain shy humour mixed with it, which Spencer himself has not. I am also, in Italian, reading Ariosto's 'Orlando Furioso',[92] from which there are many stories in your Andrew Lang romance book. It is in the same edition as my Tasso which you have

---

89 Netta Syrett, *The Victorians* (1915).
90 1 Corinthians 13:11.
91 Algernon Henry Blackwood, *Prisoner in Fairyland* (1913).
92 Ludovico Ariosto, *Orlando Furioso* (1532).

probably forgotten: I am just reading a canto here & a canto there, and it is very good, really suggesting 'Phantastes' more than the Faery Queen.

How beautiful Donegal must be now! I often think how lovely twould be if you could take up this city of Oxford bodily and put it down somewhere

'By a northern sea' [93]

between the mountains of Donegal. I am afraid the river would have to go, though!

I hope you are right as to the possibilities of my finding my particular kind of love. <Butler tells me that the person to read on my subject is a Frenchman of the 17th century called the Visconte de sade>:[94] his books, however, are very hard to come by.

I cannot understand Denny's behaviour to you, as they never gave me any trouble at all. How you would love the shops here! At home you have to hammer what you want into their thick heads: here they know all about publishing and literature (Sanskrit or Russian if you want!) & your only effort is to conceal your ignorance.

I do wish you were here: what long and private talks we could have. Somehow the place seems to lend itself to endless conversation. Butler came in and sate till twenty to two last night. The piano too would be a perpetual joy, for Cherry was playing it when she was in here to tea the other day, and says it is quite good. I suppose Cherry has only met you for a few moments, as I have never heard you speak of her. She is a real sportsman, the sort of person I really like. Quel domage que sa figure n'égale pas son ésprit![95] Yet after all she is plain in rather a pleasing kind of way when you get to know her. Mrs Robbins I also like immensely.

In prose at present I am reading one of those 'Home University Library' books on 'Psychic Research'.[96] It is a subject in which my old interest is awakening: so far the phenomena are certainly extraordinary,

---

93 Lewis probably had in mind Andrew Lang's lines: 'St Andrews by the Northern Sea, / A haunted town it is to me', *Almae Matres* (1884).

94 Comte Donatien Alphonse François de Sade (1740–1814), known as the Marquis de Sade, was a French novelist. His obsession with a particular sexual perversion caused his name to be given to the word 'sadism', meaning a love of cruelty.

95 'It's too bad that her figure isn't in the same class as her wit.'

96 William Fletcher Barrett, *Psychical Research* [1911].

tho' I fear they do not actually prove the agency of real spirits – yet. They tell me that Dodds, who is coming up next week is very interested in the subject also, so I shall be able to have a talk about it.

I quite agree with you that cards are the most utter and senseless and losing waste of time ever invented, and I never play them from inclination but only because you can't go on refusing the same people if you have nothing to do. We have had a college group [photo] of our 9 surviving undergrads. so I will be able to point out to you all these characters.

Item, somebody pointed me out Bridges[97] in the street the other day. How I should like to meet him! Really cannot spare a second longer, now old man. Write soon & LONG, returning good for evil –

Yours
Jack

TO HIS FATHER (LP XI: 261):

[University College
3? June 1917]

My dear Papy,

Thank you for the enclosures and also for the enquiries (a nice, rythmical sentence by the way). I am glad to find that my money 'pans out' quite sufficiently, and is indeed just about the average. I mean the amount of pocket money is about the same as that of other people, though of course many have an allowance out of which they pay all their own bills – in which case the actual pocket money will vary with the ups and downs of their Battels. To give you some idea of the latter, I enclose mine as supplied so far. (These do not include groceries as explained before). I am pleased to see that they decrease from the beginning of term onwards. The first week was necessarily expensive, chiefly through ignorance, 'in which accomplishment' as De Quincey says, 'I excel'.

My scout is a very fatherly old man who has been here for forty-six years, and is really exceedingly good about keeping my expenses down: he once even told me to change my socks when they were wet!!! His only failing is an impentrible (or -able) deafness which causes many conversations of the 'It's a fine day' – 'No, not much to pay' type.

I am afraid you must not build anything on the idea of my rowing, as I have almost given it up in favour of canoeing. You see a row boat can

---

97 i.e. Robert Bridges, the Poet Laureate.

be used only on the big river, where you run into all the real rowing men, as the Cherwell (much prettier and more interesting) soon gets too narrow for rowers to pass each other. Besides, there is to me something very attractive about one of these little canoes – so very light and so all-to-yourself. Perhaps when we all come back again from the war, and there is no O.T.C., I will take up rowing again.

The O.T.C. gets more interesting as we go on. We spend a good deal of our time in 'the trenches' – a complete model system with dug outs, shell holes and – graves. This last touch of realistic scenery seems rather superfluous. But then our C.O., a certain Colonel Stanning, is quite cracked.

I have nearly finished Renan, whom I find delightful. He seems to have written a good many other books on different subjects. I am going to borrow Wells' new book from a man in College called Edwards, who is thinking of becoming a Catholic. He is an ardent Newmanite, and we have some talk on literary subjects. Someone pointed me out our present poet-laureate, Bridges (1), on the river last Wednesday.

your loving son,

Jacks

(1) Its just occurred to me that you might have known the name anyway. Apologies! – J.

On Thursday 7 June, Lewis joined a cadet battalion and was sent across Oxford to be billeted in Keble College for a four-month course in soldiery. It has already been pointed out that as an Irishman Lewis was exempt from the Conscription Act. Normally a member of the OTC is not part of the regular army, and membership in it may be resigned at will. However, during the war members of the OTC were 'embodied', that is, became part of the army. As a result they were liable to be treated as the needs of the army required. Keble College had been used since January 1915 for the training of officers, and Lewis was one of many from Oxford and other places who arrived there on 7 June. He found himself sharing a room with Edward Francis Courtenay ('Paddy') Moore,[98] *who came into the Oxford OTC from Bristol where he had been a pupil at Clifton College.*

---

98 See **Edward Francis Courtenay 'Paddy' Moore** in the Biographical Appendix.

Paddy, who was the same age as Lewis, was born near Dublin of Anglo-Irish parents, Courtenay Edward Moore and Janie King Moore.[99] When they separated in 1907, Mrs Moore took Paddy and his sister Maureen[100] to live in Bristol where she had a brother. When it was known that he would go into the army through the Oxford OTC, Mrs Moore and Maureen came with him and took rooms in Wellington Square.

TO HIS FATHER (LP V: 218):

[Keble College,
Oxford]
Postmark: 8 June 1917

My dear Papy,

Just a line in a hurry, to let you know how things go. I have not been able to write to you before. Well of course this is not an agreeable change, but it was the natural next step in any pilgrimage towards a commission. The cadet batallion, which I joined yesterday (of course it has nothing to do with the varsity) is quartered in Keble. There are several gentlemen among it, and I am fortunate in sharing a room with one. It is a great comfort to be in Oxford, as I shall still be able to see something of my Univ. friends and Cherry.

As to Responsions, I may or may not be able to persuade them to give me three days' leave to do it in: if they do, I should not think that under the circumstances my chances of passing would be very bright. At any rate, six months service with the colours will exempt me from it.

As to the artillery, I am afraid that only those who have 'some special knowledge of mathematics' will be recommended. About leave we don't know anything yet. I am sorry I can't write any more to cheer you up, but we must both of us thole for a while. My tips etc. on leaving College have cleared me out, so could you let me have something to go on with? Write to the old address at Univ. as I can call for letters there at any time.

your loving
son Jack

---

99 See **Janie King Moore** in the Biographical Appendix.
100 See **Dame Maureen Dunbar of Hempriggs** in the Biographical Appendix.

TO HIS FATHER (LP V: 218–9):

My dear Papy,

I am sorry that your last letter had to wait some time for an answer: I am afraid that, whenever I hear from you, I can only reply on a Saturday or a Sunday.

And now for some account of the new life. Well at first when I left my own snug quarters and my own friends at Univ. for a carpetless little cell with two beds (minus sheets or pillows) at Keble, and got into a Tommy's uniform, I will not deny that I thought myself very ill used. However, as What's-his-name said, 'I have had many misfortunes in life, but most of them never happened to me'.

I have quite recovered, and am now leading a very happy life, tho' not of course the life I would have chosen. In many ways it is a better life: I have never worked until now, and it is high time that I began. As to my companions, they are really divided into three lots. The first and largest lot consists of rankers who have been out for some time and have come here to get commissions. These are mostly jolly good chaps: clean, honest, infinitely good natured. As they have come here to be made into 'officers and gentlemen' their own naive conceptions of how gentlemen behave among themselves lead them into an impossible politeness that is really very pathetic. Most of our set get on very well with them. The next lot (about one third of the whole) consists of cads and fools pure and simple. They don't need much description: some of them are vicious, some merely doltish, all vulgar and uninteresting. They drop their h's, spit on the stairs, and talk about what they're going to do when they get to the front – where of course none of them has been. Then comes the third lot, our own set, the public school men and varsity men with all their faults and merits 'already ascertained'.

My chief friend is Somerville, scholar of Eton and scholar of King's, Cambridge, a very quiet sort of person, but very booky and interesting. Moore of Clifton, my room companion, and Sutton of Repton (the company humourist) are also good fellows. The former is a little too childish for real companionship, but I will forgive him much for his appreciation of Newbolt. I must not pass over the knut, De Pass, also of Repton, our regnant authority on all matter of dress, who is reported to wear stays: nor Davy, the Carthusian, who remembers my Sinn Fein friend as a prefect at Charterhouse.[101]

The daily round is of course pretty strenuous, and leaves little time for dreaming or reading. However, I eat and sleep as I have never done before, and am getting rid of some adipose tissue. I will give you full information about leave as soon as I have any. Captain Moberly himself an old Oxonian, is a delightful man, and I am sure he will do anything he can for me about an extension of time for travelling. It would be 'a bit too previous' to ask him at present.

I think I mentioned that Dodds had come up for his schools. Both he and Butler got Firsts, Dodds in Literae Humaniores, Butler in Law. Although of course they should both be serving, still a college with only nine undergraduates cannot help being proud of two Firsts. The conquering heroes gave a dinner on Saturday last, to which I attended and helped to celebrate the event. Both are now gone down, but Butler has promised to write to me.

There is no need to do anything at present about my clothes etc. They are carefully put away in my rooms at Univ., and can stay there till my course is ended, when I can bring the whole lot home together. By the way, my new adress is No. 738 Cadet C. S. Lewis, 'E' Company, Keble College, Oxford. Be of good cheer, your loving son,

Jack

TO ARTHUR GREEVES (W):

[Keble College
10 June 1917]

My dear Arthur,

I must admit that you have a very reasonable ground of complaint against me. But you must remember that my whole way of life has now completely changed, and that I have practically no time for reading or writing except at week-ends. However I will try to do better in future, tho' I hope that you, who have more time to yourself, will give me longer

---

101 Martin Ashworth Somerville (1898–1918) became a member of King's College, Cambridge, in April 1917. During the war he served as a member of the Rifle Brigade in Egypt and Palestine, and died 21 September 1918 of wounds received in action. The others, all born in 1898, were: 'Paddy' Moore of Clifton College, Alexander Gordon Sutton and Denis Howard de Pass of Repton School, and Thomas Kerrison Davey of Charterhouse School. The 'Sinn Fein' friend was Theobald Butler.

letters than you get: just as, when I get to the trenches, tho' I may not be able to write to you at all, I shall hope to hear from you at regular intervals. This may seem a one-sided bargain: yet surely it is fair, that when one of us has escaped and the other has got into this military nonsense, the freeman should make some allowances for the slave.

I will only tell you very shortly of the new life as there is not much of interest. It is a great change to leave my own snug room at Univ. for a carpetless room, with beds without sheets or pillows, kept miserably tidy & shared with another cadet, at Keble. However, tho' the work is very hard & not very interesting, I am by now quite reconciled to my lot. It is doing me a lot of good (days of trench digging and route marching under a blazing sun are a fine cure for tendencies in THAT direction) and I have made a number of excellent friends – especially Somerville, a scholar of Eton & King's (Cambridge) who is very well up in books. My room-mate Moore (of Clifton) is quite a good fellow too, tho' a little too childish and virtuous for 'common nature's daily food'. The advantages of being in Oxford are very great, as I can get week end leave (from 1 o'clock Saturday till 11 o'clock p.m. Sunday) and go to Univ. where I enjoy the rare luxury of sheets & a long sleep.

Last week end was a great success. Butler and Dodds (Dodds a Campbellian and Univ. man whom you must have heard of) both got 'Firsts' in their Schools and gave a dinner to celebrate the event, at which, for the first time in my life, I was royally drunk. <I am afraid I must have given myself away rather as I went round imploring everyone to let me whip them for the sum of 1s. a lash!> All this happened at Exeter in the rooms of an Indian called Gokeldas: but as I was not the only person in that condition, the Dean of Exeter got fed up with the row and sent round a notice that Mr Gokeldas' guests must leave the College at once. I have absolutely no recollection of the walk home, and in fact, tho' I remember leaving Exeter, knew nothing more till I woke up on the floor of my own room at about 9 next morning.[102]

The story that you have a headache after being drunk is apparently quite a lie <(like the other one about going mad from THAT).> But the

---

102 He seems not to have exaggerated the degree of his intoxication: the Indian he calls 'Gokeldas' was Madhavji Dharamsi Moraji Gokuldas (1896–1931), a member of Brasenose College, and it was probably in Brasenose, rather than in Exeter, that the party occurred. The Dean of Brasenose was W.T.S. Stallybrass (1883–1948), who became Principal of the college in 1936.

interesting part is that Butler, having muddled recollections of my last night's <desire to whip,> challenged me on the subject, and we had a long conversation. <He's not himself that way inclined. He has come across the thing in the course of his varied reading. The right name for it is sadism, so called from its great originator of the 16th century, M. Le Vicomte de Sade whose history we looked up in a French 'Dictionaire de la Bibliographie Nationale'.>

Butler (and nearly every one else) has now gone down, so that this week end I have lived very quietly, but no less happily in an empty College, sleeping late, and reading my new volume of Maeterlinck's plays.[103] Two of them I have read before in English ('Pelleas & Melisande', 'L'Interieur') but all could be read with pleasure a score of times. They all have a peculiar mystic dreamlike atmosphere about them, and tho' much more possible are somehow much more wierd than 'L'Oiseau Bleu', especially the 'most musical, most melancholy' 'Alladine et Palomides', where Palomides may be the Malory Palomides or may not.

I have also been spending more time than usual in the College Library, dipping here and there. Did I tell you that there was a queer little volume in Latin by Cornelius Agrippa the great magician (mentioned in Cosmo's episode)? Unfortunately the print is so execrable and the worms have done their work so well that I cannot make much of it: but I love to have it in my hands, and think of all the wizards who have centred their hopes on it – perhaps on this very copy, for it is some 300 years old.[104]

I have also read a good deal of Spencer in a big folio and of my favourite Johnson. On taking up my Homer this morning it was shocking to find how strangely the Greek came to me after three weeks soldiering. I do hope I shall not forget all I know, and come back from the war a great empty-headed military prig!

Yesterday afternoon I spent on the river with Cherry Robbins, in whom I am pleased to find an ardent admirer both of Arthur Rackham & of Wagner. She has heard 'Die Walküre' at Covent Garden & has read the Ring in my edition. She says that the stage is a terrible come down to those who have seen Rackham's pictures first and that she listened with

---

103 Maurice Maeterlinck, *Alladine et Palomides, Intérieur, et La Mort de Tintagiles, Drames Pour Marionnettes* (1894).

104 He is writing about either Vol. I or Vol. II of the *Opera* (Lugduni: Per Beringos Fratres [1531]) of Henricus Cornelius Agrippa (1486–1535) of Nettesheim. The book which he handled is now in the Museum of the History of Science.

her eyes shut most of the time. The 'Wotan' however was splendid, and really terrifying. She is also very keen on Norse mythology, and for this reason praised the Ring above 'Parsifal' or 'Lohengrin'. Although the subject did not arise, I rather think from some phrazes she let fall about Norse & Christian mythology, that I shall find another agnostic here. How sad that so interesting a girl is not beautiful (tho' she is certainly not nearly so plain as I at first imagined) Even sadder that she should like Browning and have a morbid appetite for photography!!

I am in a strangely productive mood at present and spend my few moments of spare time in scribbling verse. When my 4 months course in the cadet battalion is at an end, I shall, supposing I get a commission allright, have a 4 weeks leave before joining my regiment. During it I propose to get together all the stuff I have perpetrated and see if any kind publisher would like to take it. After that, if the fates decide to kill me at the front, I shall enjoy a 9 days immortality while friends who know nothing about poetry imagine that I must have been a genius – what usually happens in such cases. In the meantime my address is

> No 738 Cadet C. S. Lewis
> 'E' Company,
> Keble College
> Oxford.

Write me a nice long letter and help to keep up other interests amid all this damned military show.

Yours as ever
Jack

TO HIS FATHER (LP V: 224–5):

[Keble College]
Postmark: 18 June 1917

My dear Papy,

First of all, many thanks for the liberal enclosure, which has made life much more 'sunny' again: though indeed I have no right to grumble about my present position. The change was bound to come, and could not be expected to be an agreeable one. But this being so, it could not have been better than it is. Being in Oxford is a great comfort, and there is an unusually high percentage of Public School men in this Battalion.

Moore, my room mate, comes from Clifton and is a very decent sort of man; his mother, an Irish lady, is staying up here and I have met her once or twice. As to my friends in Univ., they are accounted for in various ways. The only other two who were in the O.T.C. with me are both under eighteen and a half. Edwards, the embryo Roman Catholic, is physically unfit. Butler, the Home Ruler, is not serving for political reasons.

The weather here is terribly hot, and we are all getting into wonderful training under it: however, I can well afford that sort of thing, as you know. It seems that we get a four days leave after the first month of our course. Unless they will allow me extra time for travelling, I don't exactly know what to do with my four days. If you could come up for a week we could both stay at Univ. (one is allowed to have a guest staying in College), and have a very nice little time. Think about it and see if you couldn't manage – seriously.

I don't know of any special Cadet Batallion (or is it Battalion?) for the artillery. Don't you think it would be better to give up that idea? A person who gets ploughed in Smalls in not likely to master Trigonometry etc: as well, every one else puts up with the Infantry, and I think we ought to do so too.[105]

I hope this kind of weather suits a man who lives in 'a rotten house'. And that the same man is carrying on well and cheerfully. Please explain to Warnie that I have hardly time to write, and ask him to let me have a line or two when he can.

your loving
son Jack

---

105 Albert Lewis was becoming frantic with worry about Jack, and was seeking a way to have his son transferred from the infantry into the artillery, particularly to the gunners, where he believed he would be safer. The infantry was composed of foot-soldiers, who were closest to the enemy and the first to lose their lives. Artillery was the great killer of the First World War; it is thought that artillery fire caused up to 70 per cent of battlefield deaths. But whereas the infantry were in close contact with the enemy, the artillery were firing from some distance behind them, and their position was perhaps somewhat safer.

TO ARTHUR GREEVES (W):

[University College
8 July 1917]

Cher Ami,

The best, in fact the only really important tale in Gautier's little book was the last one 'Avatar',[106] which I would have had you read first & read the other two or not, as might seem worthwhile afterwards. It was this third one that I compared, not to Phantastes as a whole, but to the Cosmo story – which, you know, has rather a different flavour from the main book. I must admit that the resemblance is rather a vague one: still, I am sure that you will like 'Avatar' if you give it a trial. In French I am going on with this new volume of Maeterlinck's plays. The last one 'La Morte de Tintagiles' is even better than Palomides, and quite one of the eeriest and most overwhelming things I have struck yet – though I am not quite sure if I understand what the author is driving at. You must certainly get this volume, or borrow mine someday.

'From a College Window'[107] is one of the 5 or 6 Benson books that I have read: but as the titles are so vague, I never can remember which is which. I enjoyed them all very much, they are nice companionable reading for lonely men. Perhaps the 'Upton Letters' was the one that pleased me best.

I was sure that you wd. like 'Balder Dead': I used to prefer it to 'Sohrab'[108] tho' I don't now. All the same it is a topping piece of work, especially the journey, as you say, and the description of the ghosts, and the ending with its impressive pause before the glorious line

'At last he sighed & set forth back to Heaven.'[109]

Doesn't it all make you think of the dear old days when we were writing our great opera on Loki & Odin & the rest? Indeed I am recalled to our earlier stage by other things as well: for all morning I have been reading the German text of 'Siegfried'. The splendid first Act has quite stirred up my old Wagnerian enthusiasms, & for the first time this twelve months or so I have really felt the want for a gramophone. Of course a great deal

---

106 Théophile Gautier, *Avatar, or, The Double Transformation* (1888).

107 Arthur Christopher Benson, *From a College Window* (1906).

108 Matthew Arnold, *Sohrab and Rustum* (1853).

109 Arnold, *Balder Dead*, III, 566.

of my pleasure in it is owing to Rackham's pictures: still it is lovely wild poetry &, like everything else, much better in its own language. The edition is the same as my one of the Dutchman & I can get the other three parts of the Ring in the same: when I have them all I think I shall bind the 4 thin volumes into one nice book & have a really good edition to my library.

This week end, as you gather, I am again spending in Univ. But the Dean says I can't come any more, as the Scouts are going for the holidays!! Damn him! Do you know, Ami, I am more homesick for this College than ever I was for Little Lea. I love every stone in it: I do wish we could be here together after the war!

Last night, at about nine o'clock I wandered out into the deserted quad. & after 'strolling' for some time went up a staircase where nobody ever goes in these days into the oldest part of the College. The windows here are all tiny & ivy covered & stained so that it was very dark already. I walked up & down long passages with locked rooms on each side, revelling in 'desolation'. The 'oaks' of these rooms were mostly (as I say) locked, but by good luck I found one open & went in. On the inner door the faded name 'Mr Carter' greeted me: inside was a tiny room, smaller than my own at home, very dark & thick with dust. It seemed almost sacrilege to turn on the lights in such a forsaken place, but I simply had to inspect it. The furniture was all just as the owner must have left it & his photos were there on the wall. I also inspected his books (mostly ordinary Everymen) including 'Lavengro', 'Tristram Shandy', [Edmund] Burke's Speeches & 'Tom Jones'.[110] I suppose this sounds trivial to you; but perhaps you can picture the strange poetry of the thing in such a time & place. I wonder who Carter is, and if he has been killed yet, & why he left his pile of music so untidily on the dressing table?[111]

I had another thrill too, when I got up (quite dark by now) into a sort

---

110 Henry Fielding, *Tom Jones* (1749).

111 Arthur Norwood Carter (1891–1983), whose rooms Lewis was in, matriculated as a Rhodes Scholar from New Brunswick, Canada, in 1913. On 4 August 1914 he was commissioned a lieutenant in the 8th York and Lancaster Regiment, and he served in France during 1915. He was awarded the Military Cross on 6 March 1918. On returning to Oxford he took a shortened war course in jurisprudence in 1919, and he received his BCL in 1920. He sent two sons – also Rhodes Scholars – to University College.

of attic place full of old trunks etc. & heard a strange thumping noise just beside me. I was mystified for a while, till I realized that I was just behind the big college clock & this was the ticking of it. You know how sad & grand a big clock sounds in a lonely place! These are all rather conventional remarks, but I really did get into a great mood among all the cobwebs. When I came back into the quad & saw all the empty windows staring at me all round, I turned a bit creepy & was glad to get back to my rooms & settle down on the 'Faerie Queene', & another book, which I must tell you about.

This is a book on William Morris in the 'English Men of Letters Series' by Alfred Noyes[112] which I took out of the Library. It is chiefly interesting for its venomous hostility towards Mackail's great 'Life of W.M.' which it loses no opportunity of attacking. This of course is rather petty: but I must admit that the book has some very good points about it, & certainly appreciates 'Jason' far better than Mackail does.

Yes, I must say that the society of some interesting person of the other sex is a great anodyne in a life like this – especially if it is one of the very few people who share our own pet tastes – Wagner, Rackham and the rest. Cherry has been away on leave this last week, and I find this causes quite a gap in my routine. A propos, when is there any prospect of your long expected visit being paid to Oxford. If you were here for a week-end I could come & stay with you somewhere in the town, & I think that the time would pass pleasantly.

It is pouring with rain outside as I write. If I do ever send my stuff to a publisher, I think I shall try Maunsel, those Dublin people, and so tack myself definitely onto the Irish school. What castles in the air – but still better have a cloud castle than no castle at all –

Yours,
Jack

TO HIS FATHER (LP V: 227-8):

[Keble College]
Postmark: 18 July 1917

My dear Papy,

Many thanks for your nice long letters: as before, it has to wait till Sunday for an answer, but I hope you were not expecting one sooner.

---

112 Alfred Noyes, *William Morris* (1908).

Life here goes on pretty much in the usual way, except that the work gets rather more interesting and involves less actual 'sweat of the brow' than at first. We do a good deal of night work, which I rather like, and which leads to getting up later in the morning. The weather too has grown cooler, and today it is raining.

Dodds' particular foible is also nationalism. I don't know that it is pure cant either in his case or in Butler's: certainly the argument from 'being at an English university' hardly seems very cogent unless you are going to come down on the Englishmen who were at German universities before the war. Does the fact of going to be educated in a country give that country any claim on your services? After all, you *pay* them for the education. Which reminds me that the Bursar has written to say that I am to have my scholarship money for this term and knock off some other term for it after the war. He says that this arrangement has been made with people in my position. I don't know whether we are being 'done' in any subtle way or not, but I suppose there is no objection to the plan so far as you are concerned.

You are allowed week end leave here every week, provided that you do not go out of Oxford. The last four weeks I have spent it over at Univ., enjoying all my old luxuries over again. Now however the Dean – Who as I remarked is a superior person – has vetoed the plan; on the ground that College is kept open in vacation for men who want to read 'and not for use as an hotel'. I suppose he is quite right in a way, but it is rather a pity.

You can't imagine how I have grown to love Univ., especially since I left. Last Saturday evening when I was sleeping there alone, I spent a long time wandering over it, into all sorts of parts where I had never been before, where the mullioned windows are dark with ivy that no one has bothered to cut since the war emptied the rooms they belong to. Some of these rooms were all dust sheeted, others were much as the owners had left them – the pictures still on the wall and the books dust covered in their shelves. It was melancholy in a way, and yet very interesting. I have found one room that I have mapped out to be my own when I come back.

At present I am reading a countryman of ours, Bishop Berkely, 'that silly old man' as Andrew Lang calls him: in fact, one of our few philosophers and a very interesting fellow, whom I always admired for the courage with which you find him standing up to the ogre in Boswell.[113]

Are the other poems in 'The Old Way'[114] man's book as good as the one we know? Talking of modern poetry, some of the rebels who were shot in Easter week seem to have had the root of the matter in them.

Could you let me have some money to get boots for my officer-pattern uniform. I find the cadet school so far much more expensive than the Varsity. When does W. get his leave?

your loving

son Jack

TO HIS FATHER (LP V: 230–1):

University College,
Oxford.
Postmark: 22 July 1917

My dear Papy,

I have to thank you for two letters and for moneys numbered. Pay there was none at first, except for the old soldiers: but the War Office has at last discovered our existence, and on Friday I drew 7/-, the first money I have earned. It ought to be hung on a watch chain.

---

113 Mr Kirkpatrick had encouraged Lewis to read various works of philosophy in preparation for the day when he would begin his studies in *Literae Humaniores*. In the last few months he had become very interested in 'Subjective Idealism' or 'Idealism', the predominant philosophy at Oxford. At this time Lewis was immersing himself in the subjective idealism of Bishop George Berkeley (1685–1753) as propounded in his *Principles of Human Knowledge* (1710). The Bishop held that when we affirm material things to be real, we mean no more than that they are perceived. What annoyed Lewis about 'the ogre in Boswell' – that is, Dr Johnson – was the famous remark recorded in Boswell's *Life of Samuel Johnson*, vol. I, p. 471. On 6 August 1763 Boswell wrote: 'After we came out of the church, we stood talking for some time together of Bishop Berkeley's ingenious sophistry to prove the non-existence of matter, and that every thing in the universe is merely ideal. I observed, that though we are satisfied his doctrine is not true, it is impossible to refute it. I shall never forget the alacrity with which Johnson answered, striking his foot with mighty force against a large stone, till he rebounded from it, "I refute it *thus*."' As Bishop Berkeley never met Dr Johnson, he had no chance of 'standing up' to him. Lewis had confused the Bishop with his son, who was also named George. This George Berkeley (1733–95) met Dr Johnson shortly after he came up to Oxford in 1752, and when Dr Johnson made fun of the Bishop's abortive scheme for a missionary college in Bermuda the young George walked out of the room. He subsequently refused Dr Johnson's repeated requests for permission to write a Life of Bishop Berkeley.

114 Ronald Arthur Hopwood, *The Old Way and Other Poems* (1917).

You say that you should talk to me 'not of the Muse'. Indeed the reverse is quite the truth, for I make every effort to cling to the old life of books, hoping that I may save my soul alive and not become a great, empty headed, conceited military prig. I am finding out that the military ideal in our army differs from the German one only in degree and not in kind. The Sergeant Major told us the other day that 'soldiering is more than 'arf swank. You've got to learn to walk out as if the bloody street belonged to you. See?' We are also encouraged in every way to be pharisees and pat ourselves on the back for being in khaki, and stare rudely at apparently eligible young men whom we meet in mufti. Well I hope that neither I nor any of my friends – and I have done well here in the way of friends – will ever attain to that degree of soldierhood. The promised four days' leave will come in about a fortnight's time: I am sorry that I cannot let you know more definitely. I shall of course come home the quickest way, there being no question of 'lucre' when a paternal government provides you with a pass.

As to your suggestions about the Artillery, I fear I cannot follow you in this matter. Let us have it out. I have put down my name for the artillery first, and after that for the infantry. To which on the advice of my friends, I have added 'King's Own Scottish Borderers' in brackets. Of course this second alternative which I have put in would not make any difference to the first if they were disposed to have me in the gunners. But, as I have mentioned before, they specially insist on a knowledge of advanced mathematics. It is true that you might get me in by influence. But would it not be very wrong for mere reasons of safety, to push me into a responsible position for which I know I am absolutely unfit? If you are fortunate (and how few fathers are today) in having one son in a perfectly safe job, do you think we should try to alter the natural cause of events for the sake of the other? As minor considerations, I may add that I am come to like the idea of the K.O.S.B.'s very much, because two friends of mine will be going at the same time. When you have thought it over, I am sure you will not even want me to change my mind.

On Saturday I drank tea with a dear old gentleman named Goddard, formerly an undergrad. of Balliol and now a don at Trinity.[115] What

---

115 He must have misunderstood the name. There was no don named 'Goddard' at Trinity College in 1917.

interested me most was his opinion of Jowett[116] (here usually pronounced to rhyme with 'poet') who, he said, had spoiled the scholarly tone of Balliol by a vulgar running after lions. Surely Jowett must have trodden on Mr. Goddard's corns some how, or is there any truth in this verdict?

Of Swinburne's prose, I have read the book on Charlotte Bronte, and the smaller one on William Blake.[117] It is undoubtedly very bad prose (I did not find the coarseness) but it is so vigorous that you can forgive it. Don't forget to keep Wells' 'God the invisible King'[118] in the house, as I am longing to read it.

your loving
son Jack

TO HIS FATHER (LP V: 231):

[Keble College]
Postmark: 24 July 1917

My dear Papy,

I am very sorry to have left you so long without a letter: we have been hopelessly rushed for the last week, the idea being I suppose to get the last ounce out of us before we go on our mouthful of leave. Which reminds me, I think that I forgot to tell you the exact date when I should get home – which was just as well, for the date has now been changed. According to the new arrangement, our leave is from 12 noon on Wednesday the 8th of August till 12 midnight on the following Sunday. As they have refused to allow me any extension for travelling, this will mean arriving home on Thursday morning and leaving on Saturday night. However, 'smallest contributions thankfully recieved' must be our spirit I suppose.

As soon as possible I want you to find out whether Fleetwood or Liverpool is running on Wednesday night, book me a berth, and let me know which it is – by wire. (Be careful to put 'E' Company on it, as there

---

116 Benjamin Jowett (1817–93) was the Master of Balliol College from 1870 to 1893. He was ordained in 1845 but his theological liberalism, particularly evident in his essay 'The Interpretation of Scripture', was hotly debated. Jowett's classical learning was, however, almost unrivalled during his years in Oxford. He was an Oxford figure and the subject of innumerable stories.

117 Algernon Charles Swinburne, *Note on Charlotte Brontë* (1877); *William Blake* (1868).

118 H.G. Wells, *God the Invisible King* (1917).

is another C. S. Lewis in another company, also at Keble. I keep on getting letters of his, and vice versa.)

Please forgive me for a short letter, as I want to go to bed. We shall have the more to talk about when I come back.

your loving

son Jack

TO ARTHUR GREEVES (W):

University College,
Oxford.
24/7/17

Cher Ami,

How horribly conventional to be writing on ordinary note paper just like other people – why I'll be putting the date at the top soon if I'm not careful. A propos de Maunsel, you say that the patriotic motive could have no influence on me. Well perhaps that may be deserved: tis true that I have no patriotic feeling for anything in England, except Oxford for which I would live and die. But as to Ireland you know that none loves the hills of Down (or of Donegal) better than I: and indeed, partly from interest in Yeats and Celtic mythology, partly from a natural repulsion to noisy drum-beating, bullying Orange-men and partly from association with Butler, I begin to have a very warm feeling for Ireland in general. I mean the real Ireland of Patsy Macan[119] etc, not so much our protestant north. Indeed, if I ever get interested in politics, I shall probably be a nationalist (another subject for us to quarrel on, you see). Of course one sound reason for choosing Maunsel is that they are only a second-rate house and therefore more likely to give me some attention.

I suppose that by now you are nearly at the end of 'Avatar', and see what I meant by comparing it to the Cosmo story. It is an excellent little novel, I think, as voluptuous and magical as only you and I can appreciate. The titles of Benson's essays which you quote bring back memories of pleasant mornings over my tea in bed at home.

Good God, if only I could get back to it all! And yet I am not nearly so unhappy as I ought to be. This week I have been reading the works of Bishop Berkely, an eighteenth century country man of ours, &

---

119 Patsy Macann is a character in Stephen's *The Demi-Gods* (1914).

philosopher. Published under the title of 'Principles of Human Knowledge etc'[120] in the Everyman. The part I have been reading is 3 dialogues written to prove the existence of God – which he does by disproving the existence of matter. The reasoning is very subtle but not difficult. Look here, oh my Galahad, philosophy is a subject I am just arriving at, so why shouldn't we start abreast & read it side by side. After Berkely I shall try Hume or Descartes also in Everyman. What do you say? Expend 1/- on Berkely and have a go on those 3 Dialogues!

Your idea of the old wizard, up in the clock-tower, the in dwelling spirit of this dear college since Alfred's time,[121] is excellent; and when I am in the mood again I must write on it either in prose or in verse (outher in verse, as Malory would say).

You must remember a copy of Pater's 'Renaissance' badly stained with hair oil in my cupboard. I tried to read it some time syne when I knew even less of liter[ature] and art than I do know now, & I found it rather stiff. Pater is called a great prose stylist – but except Malory, Bunyan, Ruskin and the Authorised Version of the Bible, I am afraid I have not much ear for prose style.

I find that we get 4 days leave in about 3 weeks. Unless they allow me some time for travelling it will mean very little time at home for me, and of that little even less can be devoted to you: though you know my wishes. However I trust we shall have some few hours of happiness together. How I long to see your new books & to shew you mine – especially the ones I got bound, which I hope you will approve. Then too I will choose that present which you have so kindly offered to give me. (And so there will be no sinful waste on postal orders to worry the just.)

I must dry up now. Sorry this letter is late, but I lost it when half finished & have found it again in a pocket only to-day (Teusday).

Yours
Jack

---

120 George Berkeley, *A New Theory of Vision and Other Writings* (*A Treatise Concerning the Principles of Human Knowledge. Three Dialogues between Hylas and Philonous*) (1710), with an introduction by A.D. Lindsay, Everyman's Library [1910].
121 University College, according to some histories, was founded by Alfred the Great.

TO ARTHUR GREEVES (W):

University College,
Oxford.
[4 August 1917]

Cher Ami,

Before I go on to anything interesting I must just have one little growl at you about something in your last epistle. You express a fear that my father 'may take into his head' to stay at home during my day or two of leave. Well I resent this 'take into his head' tone. A man is living absolutely alone: both his sons are in the army and one of them – who will soon be 'out' and in the infantry, not the A.S.C. or the Friends' Ambulance Corps – gets the first day's leave he has had since joining. And then you talk about the man 'taking it into his head' to see something of him! I am afraid that my father will most certainly 'take it into his head' to stay at home. But I hope to be able to see something of my Galahad, though I fear not much.

I was interested to hear that you liked Tristram Shandy – I think I told you about seeing a copy of it in one of the deserted rooms of Univ. Personally I have tried in vain to see the good points of it. The absolute disconnection or scrappiness, the abundant coarseness of an utterly vulgar, non-voluptuous sort and the general smoking-room atmosphere of the book were too much for me. In all these points it is the direct opposite of our quiet, balanced & delicately humourous Jane Austen. Tell me more about it in your next letter and try to shew me its merits: one often learns to appreciate a book through one's friends in this way. What edition are you reading it in?

I am delighted to hear that you enjoyed Comus – it is agreed to be one of the most perfect things in English poetry, and if you prefer it to Paradise Lost you have Saintsbury[122] (but not little me) to back you up. Don't you love the opening speech

'Above the smoke & stir of this dim spot . . .'[123]

– which always reminds me of our walks over the clean hills when we look down into the Nibbelheim below. Also the descriptions of the forest

---

122 George Edward Bateman Saintsbury, *Short History of English Literature* (1898).
123 John Milton, *Comus* (1637), 5.

and the weird sounds that lonely shepheards have heard on its outskirts are very weird. I think the best thing of all is the last song with its allusions to

> 'Hesperus and his daughters three
> That sing about the golden tree',[124]

– so beautifully lonely and romantic. I hope you won't give up your idea of reading Berkely; he is, I should think, a very good philosopher to begin on: perhaps that little book in the Home University series 'Problems of Philosophy'[125] would help too.

By the way I have forgotten to tell you any news about leave. It was going to be from next Friday till next Teusday, but that has been changed. It is now going to start on Wednesday[126] 9th & go on till that Sunday midnight. A lot depends on whether I can get any extension for travelling, which is still

> 'in even poise.'[127]

If I can't it will be pretty poor.

You have started the question of prose style in your letter and ask whether it is anything more than the 'literal meaning of the words'. On the contrary it means less – it means the words themselves. For every thought can be expressed in a number of different ways: and style is the art of expressing a given thought in the most beautiful words and rythms of words. For instance a man might say 'When the constellations which appear at early morning joined in musical exercises and the angelic spirits loudly testified to their satisfaction'. Expressing exactly the same thought, the Authorised Version says 'When the morning stars sang together and all the sons of God shouted for joy.'[128] Thus by the power of style what was nonsense becomes ineffably beautiful. See?

Talking about 'Comus', I forgot to mention my new edition of it. The binding is not interesting. The paper is a kind of parchment (like your

---

124 ibid., 982–3.
125 James Hervey Hyslop, *Problems of Philosophy, or, Principles of Epistemology* (1905).
126 A mistake for Thursday.
127 Milton, *Comus*, 410: 'an equal poise'.
128 Job 38:7.

Omar Khayyam) and it is illustrated by the person who did 'Tchainie's' copy of the 'High History of the Holy Grael'. A thoroughly desirable book of which I hope you will approve.

Have lots to talk about but no time, and too dead tired as we were up till 2 o'clock last night doing 'attack' and then got up at the usual hour of 6.30 again this morning.

Yours
Jack

Albert Lewis recorded in his diary that Jack arrived home in his uniform on Thursday 9 August, and was there until he left Belfast on Saturday 11 August. Warnie was able to get over to see his father from 14 to 21 August, after which he paid Jack a visit in Oxford on 22 August before returning to France.

TO HIS FATHER (LP V: 231–2)

[Keble College]
Postmark: 27 August 1917

My dear Papy,

You must have been wondering what had come over me, but the crowded time I have been having since I left home will serve as some excuse. First of all came the week at Warwick, which was a nightmare. I was billeted with five others in the house of an undertaker and memorial sculptor. We had three beds between six of us, there was of course no bath, and the feeding was execrable. The little back yard full of tomb stones, which we christened 'the quadrangle', was infinitely preferable to the tiny dining room with its horse hair sofa and family photos. When all six of us sat down to meals there together, there was scarcely room to eat, let alone swing the traditional cat round. Altogether it was a memorable experience.

We came back on Saturday, and the following week I spent with Moore at the digs of his mother who, as I mentioned, is staying at Oxford. I like her immensely and thoroughly enjoyed myself.

On Wednesday as you know, Warnie was up here and we had a most enjoyable afternoon and evening together, chiefly at my rooms in Univ. How I wish you could have been there too. But please God I shall be able to see you at Oxford and show you my 'sacred city' in happier times.

Since coming back I have finished 'The angel of pain'[129] (which I give full marks) and started an interesting book of Wells', 'A modern Utopia'.[130] Being interested in an author is a very different thing from liking him, isn't it? I will send you the college group some day next week if I can get cardboard. I have asked the grocers for their bill. Hoping to hear from you soon,

your loving son,

Jack

TO HIS FATHER (LP V: 232–3) :

[Keble College]
Postmark: 10 September 1917

My dear Papy,

I was very glad to get your letter, for, though my own sins in that line are as scarlet, I must admit that I was beginning to get a little bit anxious. It was such a pity that Warnie and I could not be home together – and yet too, in a way, it spread out the 'invasion' of your young hopefuls longer for you. Warnie seems to have thoroughly enjoyed his leave, and I am sure the 'drag' exists only in your imagination.

I can quite understand your refusal of Aunt Hamilton's warm and timely invitation. In three days time I bid fair to understand it still better: for – have I told you – the next amusement on our programme is a three days bivouac up in the Wytham hills. As it has rained all the time for two or three days, our model trenches up there will provide a very unnesseccarily good imitation of Flanders mud. You know how I always disapproved of realism in art!

I will send you 'The angel of Pain' in a few days: just at present my friend Mrs. Moore has borrowed it.

As time gets on towards the end of our course, we are more and more crowded and live only in hope for the fabulous amounts of leave we are going to get before we're gazetted. Tell Arthur I simply *can't* write.

your loving
son Jack

---

129 Edward Frederic Benson, *The Angel of Pain* (1906).
130 H.G. Wells, *A Modern Utopia* (1905).

TO HIS FATHER (LP V: 233):

[Keble College]
Postmark: 24 September 1917

My dear Papy,

I hope I was not grousing in my last letter, for though this may not be the life I had chosen, yet a little hard work never did any one any harm, and I might be much worse off. The sleeping out on Cumnor hills (there were only two nights of it) illustrated some old theories of anticipation etc. – but I needn't go through it. In point of fact, sleeping out of doors proved delightful. You have a waterproof groundsheet, two blankets, and your haversack for a pillow. There was plenty of bracken to make a soft bed, and I slept excellently. You wake up in a flash without any drowsiness, feeling wonderfully fresh. Both nights were fine, but of course it would be horrible in the wet.

Our final exam comes off next Tuesday: and remembering my wonderful faculty for failing in easy exams (vide Smalls) I don't feel too confident. There seems some doubt as to when we get away after it, but probably before the end of this week. In any case I shall stay on here with the Moores over the Sunday, and wire exact date of my crossing to you later. We get a free warrant home, but I should be glad if you would send me the Samaritan's 'two pence' for oil and wine en route. Is the Wilkes you mention the same man who showed his ear in cotton wool to the Commons?

ever your loving
son Jack

P.S. Please send your next letter to University with 'To be called for' on it, as I may be in Keble or at the Moores or anywhere. Yours J.

Jack took his Responsions ('Smalls') examination on Tuesday 25 September. The next day he received a temporary commission in the regular army, and was given a month's leave. His father, waiting in tense anticipation for a visit, was to be deeply hurt by what happened. On Saturday 29 September Jack went with Paddy and his family to their home at 56 Ravenswood Road, Bristol, and remained there until he crossed over to Ireland on Saturday 12 October, giving his father a pittance of a visit. It was while he was there that Paddy learned that he had been placed in the Rifle Brigade, and he crossed to France in October.

This stay with the Moores was to have far-reaching consequences. It was the last time Jack and Paddy were to be together. The slaughter of junior officers at this period in the war was very great, the youngest paying the highest price. Twenty-three per cent of the men in University College lost their lives in the war. Jack and Paddy knew how slim their chances were, and Paddy's sister, Maureen, recalls hearing Paddy and Jack promise one another that if only one survived the war the survivor would look after Paddy's mother and Jack's father. Mrs Moore knew of the promise too, and was later to mention it to Mr Lewis.

TO HIS FATHER (LP V: 234):

56 Ravenswood Road,
Redland,
Bristol
Oct. 3rd [1917]

My dear Papy,

I suppose you must have been wondering what had become of your prodigal son all this time. Rather a chapter of adventures has occurred, and I will hasten to recount them – in the best journalese style.

We got away from Keble on the Saturday, and instead of staying in Oxford with the Moores I came down here to their home at Bristol – within a mile or so of Clifton school. On the Sunday we went and saw the latter, including the Chapel where I failed to find 'Qui procul hinc ante diem etc,' which in fact does not exist. The place is fine, but inferior to Malvern.

On Monday a cold (complete with sore throat) which I had developed at Oxford, went on so merrily that Mrs Moore took my temperature and put me to bed, where I am writing this letter (Wednesday). I am quite better now however, and shall cross on Monday night.

Looking forward to seeing you soon again, I am
your loving
son, Jack

P.S. The exam was alright, as you promised me. They don't publish either places or marks, but only tell you whether you failed or not.

Jack arrived in Belfast on Friday 12 October, and on the 16th he was gazetted into the Somerset Light Infantry. He left home on Thursday 18 October to join his regiment at Crownhill, South Devon.

TO HIS FATHER (LP V: 237–8):

3rd Somerset Light Infantry,
Crownhill,
South Devon
Monday. 5.5 p.m. [22 October 1917]

My dear Papy,

I have waited till now so that I could tell you what an ordinary working day here is like. Incidentally the phrase 'working day' is merely façon de parler: but more of that anon, as you will first be anxious to hear what sort of thieves I have fallen among. I should say the gentlemen are about 65 per cent of the whole crowd of officers, which is quite as large a majority as one has a right to expect now-a-days. One or two of them I think I shall like, though of course it is hard to say at present. It must be admitted that most of them are hardly after my style: the subjects of conversation are shop (Oh! for the ancient taboo that ruled in officers messes in the piping times of peace) sport and theatrical news recurring with a rather dull regularity – that is in the few moments of conversation which interrupt the serious business of bridge and snooker. However, they are for the most part well bred and quite nice to me. So that if this new life rouses no violent enthusiasm in me, it is on the other hand quite bearable or even pleasant.

The 'work' is a very simple matter. All the men nearly are recruits, and the training is carried on by N.C.O.s. All you do is to lead your party onto parade, hand them over to their instructor, and then walk about doing nothing at all. This you do for several hours a day. It is a little tiring to the legs and I think will finally result in atrophy of the brain. However, it is very much better than hard work, and I am quite satisfied.

I was a bit too previous in wiring from Plymouth station that Crownhill was a barracks. It turns out to be a village of wooden huts, set up in the hills amid really very beautiful scenery. Besides the officer's mess – which is a sort of glorified golf club-house – we each have our own room, with a stove in it. When this is lit, it is really very snug, tho' of course huts are always a little more draughty than even 'r-r-r-rotten' houses!

So my verdict you see is quite favourable. The life, so long as I am in England, will be rather dull, but easy and not unpleasant. There is no need to transfer into any other infantry regiment. So at least I think now: of course I may change. I had a rather tiresome journey and got to Bristol at 12.

Hoping that the new domestic is a success[131] and that you are tolerably comfortable.

your loving
son Jack

TO ARTHUR GREEVES (W):

3d Somerset Light Infantry,
Crown Hill,
Plymouth
Sunday [28? October 1917]

Cher Ami,

'At last' you will say, and I admit I should have written long ago. I am the more sorry to have to begin my letter by saying something rather ungracious. Since coming back & meeting a certain person[132] I have begun to realize that it was not at all the right thing for me to tell you so much as I did. I must therefore try to undo my actions as far as possible by asking you to try & forget my various statements & not to refer to the subject. Of course I have perfect trust in you, mon vieux, but still I have no business to go discussing those sort of things with you. So in future that topic must be taboo between us.

And now to tell you all the news. I am quite fairly comfortable here, we are in huts: but I have a room to myself with a fire in it & so am quite snug. The country is glorious – very wild & hilly & we are up a good height ourselves. From the camp I can enjoy a fine landscape – nice cosy little bits of green country with cottages & water & trees, then woodier

---

131 Annie Strahan (1884–1972), the cook-housekeeper at Little Lea since 1910, had decided to retire and set up a cake shop in Belfast. She was to remain a valued friend of the Lewises, and Albert lent his house and resources to her for a wedding party in November 1917 when she married John McCrea. Albert gave his services as a solicitor to the McCreas, and he always took a great interest in their five children. Mrs McCrea was succeeded at Little Lea by Mary Cullen who was to remain with the family until the break-up of Little Lea in 1930.

132 Mrs Moore.

hills rising at last into big, open moors that make up the horizon. It is especially lovely in the mists of early morning or of night.

There is very little work to do here, so you will see that I might be worse off. I even manage to get a little reading done. At present I am engaged on Hawthorne's 'Transformation' in the Bohn's 1/- edition. In spite of repeated advice from me I don't think you have ever read this man. This one is very good indeed & has a lot about painting in it & some fine descriptions of Italian scenery. It is better than 'The Scarlet Letter',[133] but, of course, not so good as 'The House with the Seven Gables'. I have also got the 1st 2 volumes of Malory in the Temple Classics. The frontispieces are from designs by Beardsley.[134] They are v. good in the extremest style of mediaevalism – perhaps rather affected. One is of the finding of Excalibur & the other of someone giving Tristam a shield. In the Excalibur one, Merlin is shewn as a not very old clean-shaven but beautifully wizened man. Not what I'd have imagined him but good all the same. I have also bought in the ordinary Everyman 'Adam Bede' (by George Eliot)[135] because it was the only thing I could find – the bookshops in Plymouth are rotten. I rather like the look of it and it is one of the best kind of Everyman as regards paper & type.

There is a rumour that we are all going to Ireland to quell the Sinn Feiner in a day or two – but the above address is safe to find me. Better not send the MS. book[136] till we're sure where I'll be.

Adieu mon ami, write soon

Jack

TO ARTHUR GREEVES (W):

[Crown Hill,
Plymouth
4? November 1917]

My dear Arthur,

To your last three letters, which, with all respect, indicate a sad falling under influences which I thought we had killed, I might make a

---

133 Nathaniel Hawthorne, *Transformation* or *The Marble Faun* (1860); *The Scarlet Letter* (1850).

134 Malory, *Le Morte d'Arthur*, Temple Classics (1897).

135 George Eliot, *Adam Bede*, Everyman's Library (1859).

136 The manuscript volume of his poems, 'Metrical Meditations of a Cod', some of which he hoped to publish.

very long reply indeed: but as free criticism is notoriously dangerous, even among friends of our standing, I will content myself with saying 'Don't be a damned fool' and je passerai outre.

I am so sorry that you have never heard before that 'Green'[137] arrived safely, for which many thanks. I rather thought I had told Mrs Moore, but perhaps she forgot to pass the information on, or, which is more likely, I forgot to give it in the first place. I approve most thoroughly of this shelter of yours in the garden, it will make a resort where we can always have privacy, even when everyone else is at home.

I shall certainly be in Ireland, by the way, though when & for how long I don't know. By the way (to descend into practical matters) after your leave, you go to a battalion at home until you are posted 'overseas' again. In my case the 3d Somersets to which I shall go is at Holywood Barracks, so that if I have a short respite before going out again, during *that* time also I shall be able to come up and see you of an afternoon. You will be glad to hear that I have revised my former 'patriotic' views about having a hospital in Craigavon: and I now regard a Tommy whether wounded or not as an abominable sight, especially among the scenes of home.

I am much obliged to you for the suggestion that I am now become 'a cheer-oh young man' (by the way, in my experience, only lodging house landladies etc. refer to people as 'young men') and if I had the energy would take my revenge by playing the part of one: but it would be too fatiguing.

I think the only real change that you will find in me is an increasing tendency towards philosophy; which has grown in the course of many interesting talks with my good friend Johnson,[138] whom I hope to meet after the war as a scholar of Queens at Oxford. I think you would like him for his literary tastes and for a morality as strict as your own, but based on reasonable, not religious grounds: in music you would have many a quarrel with him and perhaps consider him a prig when he

---

137 i.e. Green's *Short History of the English People*. See letter of 1 November 1916.

138 Laurence Bertrand Johnson (1898–1918) was elected a scholar of Queen's College, Oxford, in the spring of 1917 but, being commissioned a 2nd lieutenant in the Somerset Light Infantry on 15 April 1917, he was never able to matriculate at the University. Lewis was to see a good deal of him over the next months, and not only did he like him better upon closer acquaintance, but he was to write a deeply affectionate reminiscence of him many years later in *SBJ* XII.

pronounces Chopin to be 'sugary' – his severe tastes apparently do not fall below Bach & Wagner. Debussy, strange to relate, he does not know.

Both he and all the other literary people whom I have met since I left home for Oxford, have made me feel how deep is my ignorance of modern, that is to say, *contemporary*, literature, especially poetry. I have often sat in amazed silence amid glib talk of Rupert Brooke,[139] Masefield,[140] Chesterton,[141] Bottomley[142] etc. But after all I suppose our steady nibbling at older works is a safe-guard against 'crazes' – deadly things that arise so easily about a new writer. At the same time I am often surprised to find how utterly ignored Yeats is among the men I have met: perhaps his appeal is purely Irish – if so, then thank the gods that I am Irish.

But philosophy or metaphysics is my great find at present: all other questions really seem irrelevant till its ones are solved. I think you should take it up – its probings would at least save you from the intellectual stagnation that usually awaits a man who has found complete satisfaction in some traditional religious system.

By the way, you never told me what Carpenter's <'The Intermediate Sex'[143]> was like (– or did you? Yes, I think you did). I don't much fancy a book – 'something like the psalms' – it sounds as if it were that detestable thing known as 'prose-poetry' which is usually the cave of Adullam for those who can write NEITHER prose NOR poetry. But perhaps I have not quite understood you.

Since I have been here I have had one parcel from Denny's containing 'The Ultimate Belief' by Clutton-Brock[144] and 'Eighteenth Century Studies' (in the Wayfarers' Library) by Austin Dobson.[145] Clutton Brock wrote a monograph on Wm. Morris in the 'Home University Series'[146] – that is

---

139 Rupert Brooke (1887–1915), a young poet of beauty and charm whose reputation was enhanced by the posthumous publication of his *1914 and Other Poems* (1915) and *Collected Poems* (1918).

140 John Masefield (1878–1967), perhaps Lewis's favourite modern poet, published over 50 volumes of verse, and became Poet Laureate in 1930.

141 G.K. Chesterton (1874–1936), Catholic poet, novelist, journalist, and Christian apologist. His works were to have a deep and lasting impression on Lewis. His *Orthodoxy* (1909) and *The Everlasting Man* (1925) contributed towards Lewis's conversion.

142 Gordon Bottomley (1874–1948), a poet whose works Lewis wrote to Greeves about on 12 September 1918.

143 Edward Carpenter, *The Intermediate Sex* (1908).

144 Arthur Clutton-Brock, *The Ultimate Belief* (1916).

145 Henry Austin Dobson, *Eighteenth-Century Essays* (1914).

146 i.e. *William Morris: His Work and Influence*, op. cit.

all I knew about him until this new book of his was on everyone's lips. I expected it to be a fat tome at 12/6 but it turned out to be a mere pamphlet in size (though not in format) published by Constable at 2/6. I should like you to read it: it is partly about education, but is of great general interest and has given me new points of view, especially on the subject of morals. Hitherto I had always thought there were only two possible views of morals: either, if you believed in a religion, that they were a god-imposed law: or, if you did not, that they were merely rules for convenience – 'The rules of our prison-house' as Blake called them. This man gives a third possibility which is very interesting – regarding them as a kind of art, an object to be pursued for its own beauty. He says several other good things – also on aesthetics. The other book is just what I expected – pleasant & chatty & good to read in bed tho' not wildly exciting or original.

In your last letter – the 'neglected' one, written apparently on the model of Mrs Gumadge in one of Dicken's books[147] – as far as I remember you don't tell me much about your reading. I was glad to hear in a former letter that you liked Benvenuto Cellini – of course your knowledge of history would make it even more interesting to you than to me. The references to <'That'> were slightly involved and may easily have escaped you: I could scarcely find them again. I think you *would* like Andrew Lang's translation of the Odyssey: the Iliad is much less pleasing,[148] mind you don't try it.

I wonder have those walks in sun & rain vanished forever? I wonder shall I ever live as I lived then? However we must get on as best we can: I shouldn't drop that romance of yours except to begin something else. Burton's advice to the melancholy you know was 'be not idle, be not solitary'[149] – which has been corrected to 'be not idle when you are solitary'.

Good bye, now, cher ami, write to me soon and tell me all your thoughts and doings.

Yours
Jack

---

147 Mrs Gummidge in Charles Dickens' *David Copperfield* (1850) – a 'lone lorn creetur'.
148 Andrew Lang (with S.H. Butcher), *The Odyssey* (1879); (with W. Leaf and E. Myers), *The Iliad* (1883).
149 Robert Burton, *The Anatomy of Melancholy* (1621), part I, sec. ii, mem. 2, subs. 6.

TO HIS FATHER (LP V: 240–1):

[3rd Somerset Light Infantry,
Crownhill,
South Devon]
Postmark: Belfast, 5 November 1917

My dear Papy,

We are all in great excitement here. News has come round that we are under short notice to proceed to Ireland on active service. That means that everything has to be got ready and we may or may not go at the end of it. They sometimes do these things you know just to see how quickly a Battalion can get 'short hove' as grandfather used to say. Of course we are all hoping it is true, as 'active service' in Ireland, whatever exactly it may mean, will be a great deal pleasanter than in France. Have you any idea what it could be about? The wildest rumours are afloat here about new Sinn Fein risings and one man actually says that the Germans have landed on the Shannon!

Apart from all nonsense of that sort, there certainly does seem some hope of a job that might keep us at home, if we are all going to Ireland together. Everything is being taken as if for real work there – ammunition, field dressings, even anti-gas appliances. After all, very probably it will turn out to be only a war office stunt to smarten us up, and nothing may happen.

Thanks muchly for the proofs. I will return them in a day or two after deliberation. The ones of us both together are excellent as photographs, but I think a little theatrical and 'posed'. The ones of me alone are so monstrous in size, aren't they? Warnie's one was much more natural and more what one expects a photograph to be than those enormous heads. The slight blurring of the shoulder in two or three doesn't matter much I think: of the likeness or unlikeness of course I can hardly judge. In the 'joint' photographs, I think the one of you looking at me is excellent: the full face not so good. I will give you my final verdict when I send them.

I have really been very lucky in getting here, as I like most of my companions, and the percentage of gentlemen is distinctly high. Paddy Moore, in the Rifle Brigade, seems to have got in with a most terrible lot of outsiders, so after all our separation was a blessing in disguise. He also seems to be much harder worked than I. Curiously enough there are two

Malvernians here, Perret[150] and Routh,[151] neither of whom I knew at the Coll: the former is quite a good sort. There are also two Oxonians, the Padre, formerly of Christ Church, and a man named John who was up at Exeter.

Thanks. I am well supplied with books just at present. After this Irish business has been settled one way or the other, if I still have time for reading, I may ask you to send me some of my own books from home – in which case of course, I can give you exact geographical descriptions of their disposition.

Hoping that you are well and that the domestic arrangement goes on 'as well as may be expected', I am,

your loving
son Jack

TO HIS FATHER (LP V: 241):

Telegraphed from Bristol
5.55 p.m. 15 November 1917

Have arrived Bristol on 48 hours leave. Report Southampton Saturday. Can you come Bristol. If so meet at station. Reply Mrs. Moore's address 56 Ravenswood Road Redlands Bristol. Jack.[152]

TO HIS FATHER (LP V: 242):

[56 Ravenswood Road,
Redland,
Bristol]
Postmark: 15 November 1917

My dear Papy,

I have just got your wire. I am sending off another to explain things more clearly: I'm awfully sorry, but I can't think how I failed to make it plain in the first. It is perfectly wretched giving me such short leave – 48 hours is no earthly use to a person who lives in Ireland and

---

150 Frank Winter Perrett (1898–), of London entered Malvern in the third term of 1912. After leaving in 1915 he served as a lieutenant in the 3rd Somerset Light Infantry. After the war he worked for some years as a planter.

151 Douglas James Lionel Routh (1895–) entered Malvern in 1913, and served in World War I from 1914–19 as a captain with the Somerset Light Infantry.

152 Mr Lewis wired back: 'Don't understand telegram. Please write. P.'

would have to spend about two days and nights travelling. Please don't worry, I shall probably be a long time at the base as I have had so little training in England. Can't write more now: must go and do some shopping. I return the proofs. I should like one of each I think. I'll let you know my address in France as soon as I can.

your loving
son Jack

TO HIS FATHER (LP V: 242):

Telegraphed from Bristol
11.20 a.m. 16 November 1917

Orders France. Reporting Southampton 4 p.m. on Saty. [17 November][153] If coming, wire immediately. No need alarm. Shall be at base. Jack.

TO HIS FATHER (LP V: 243):

[France]
1st Somerset Light Infty.
3 I.B.D.
21/11/17.

My dear Papy,

This is really a very sudden and unpleasant surprise. I had no notion of it until I was sent off on my 48 hours final leave, in fact I thought they were ragging me when they told me. I am now at a certain very safe base town[154] where we live comfortably in huts as we did at Crownhill. I am being innoculated this afternoon and have 48 hours off duty afterwards. By the way, has Gundrede come out again? You might let me know, as she was at this town before and meant to come back here.

I suppose we have no reason to grumble: this was bound to come sooner or later. There is no need to worry for a good time yet, and I'll try and let you hear every day when there is. Have got to go on parade in a

---

153 Immediately upon their arrival at Southampton on 17 November, Lewis went with his battalion to France.

154 Lewis was at Monchy-Le-Preux. One of the poems in his *Spirits in Bondage* (1919) is named 'French Nocturne (Monchy-Le-Preux)' and if it was not written there, it is about the effect the place had on him.

few minutes, so must stop. Shall be able to write you a proper letter off duty tomorrow.

your loving
son Jack

Albert Lewis was desperately worried about his son, and upon receipt of this letter he wrote to Colonel James Craig – later Viscount Craigavon (1871–1940) – who was MP for the East Division of County Down, asking for his help in getting his son transferred from the infantry to the artillery. He believed he would be safer with the gunners. Colonel Craig replied on 3 December 1917 that 'Before any steps are taken in this matter, it will be necessary for me to have a letter from [CSL.] personally, expressing his wishes to be transferred, and explaining that his present Commanding Officer will recommend him' (LP V: 247). Mr Lewis sent a copy of this correspondence to Jack.

TO HIS FATHER (LP V: 249):

[France]
13 December 1917

My dear Papy,

Your letter arrived today, and I must answer it at once – with apologies. Of course you will understand that work and a certain inevitable share in the life of the regiment do not leave me much time to myself.

The letter of which you forwarded me a copy is rather a surprise, and I hope you will not be disappointed at my answer to it. Some arguments in favour of staying in the infantry have arisen since we were last together. In the first place, I must confess that I have become very much attached to this regiment. I have several friends whom I should be sorry to leave and I am just beginning to know my men and understand the work.

In the second place, if the main reason for going into the gunners is their supposed safety, I hardly think it is enough. On this part of the front the guns are exposed to almost as heavy shelling (and it is shells that count far more than rifle fire) as the infantry: if their casualties are fewer that must be because their total strength is so much smaller. Then, again, nobody holds out any hopes of my getting recommended by the

C.O. He would be sure to reply (and not without reason) that it would be expensive and wasteful to take a half-trained infantry officer home again and turn him into a gunner. Our C.O. – a Lt. Colonel Majendie – is a splendid fellow for whom I have a great admiration, and I should be sorry to cut so poor a figure in his eyes as I must do in trying to back out as I get nearer the real part of my job.[155] Of course I fully understand that it is rather late for me to talk thus; and beyond the right which you have to guide me in any case, you have ample grounds for claiming that I should stick to our arrangement. Yet I think you will sympathize with what I have said above.

I am at present in billets in a certain rather battered town somewhere behind the line. It is quite comfy, but of course the work is hard and (which is worse) irregular. I have just finished 'Adam Bede' which I liked immensely – but don't send me any more of hers as I know a shop (or rather canteen here) that has them – in the Tauchnitz edition.

By the way I owe you some money for the things you bought and which should have been paid for out of my first allowances. I enclose a blank cheque to 'square' it.

Good night. Try not to worry and write soon.

your loving
son Jack

TO ARTHUR GREEVES (W):

[France]
14/12/17

My dear Galahad,

Just the proverbial few lines to answer your letter & to thank you for writing to Mrs Moore – she appreciated it very much and you may perhaps understand how nice & homely it is for me to know that the two people who matter most to me in the world are in touch.

I do get a certain amount of time for reading here, but of course it takes a long time to eat up a whole book in such small mouthfuls. I have just finished 'Adam Bede'. As you know, it is the first of hers I have read,

---

155 Vivian Henry Bruce Majendie (1886–1960) had been educated at Winchester College and Sandhurst. As commander of the 1st Battalion of the Somerset Light Infantry he was eminently suited for writing *A History of the 1st Battalion The Somerset Light Infantry (Prince Albert's) July 1st 1916 to the end of the War* (1921). He ended his long and useful career in the army as a major-general, and he retired in 1946.

and I earnestly advise you to read it. Of course as in so many of the older novelists there is a feeble happy ending stuck on to a tragedy: but the greater part of it is excellent. I am now reading a book of Balzac's called 'Le Père Goriot'.[156] It is rather a grim, realist production but quite good. I am writing home for Boswell, Milton, and another George Eliott in the Everyman.

I don't know when I can give you a decent letter but I may manage a note like this fairly often. Write as often & long as you can, mon ami, it's a great comfort –

ever yours
Jack

(Never tell mon père when I write to you – J)

On 29 November Warnie Lewis, who was still in France with the 4th Company, 7th Divisional Train, was promoted to captain. On 23 December he arrived in St Omer to begin a course at the Mechanical Transport School of Instruction.

TO ARTHUR GREEVES (W):

[France]
New Year's Eve [1917]

Cher Ami,

So glad to hear from you again yesterday evening. My last correspondent from Strandtown was 'Chanie' who wrote me a very typical would-be facetious letter – <she certainly is an apalling woman and I shall> never forget her on various occasions profaning our sacred haunts & soaking machines with her chatter. Do you remember the day we heard or thought we heard her in the wood and fled through many devious paths. Oh I'd just love to have another of those walks, particularly now in the snow – I suppose there's snow at home too, it is just thawing here. Don't think I've lost the taste for all that life.

I hope I have gained the new without losing the old and if we were all three – you know my meaning – together somewhere I'm sure we could be very happy, without any clash of interests. Apologies for not telling

---

156 Honoré de Balzac, *Le Père Goriot* (1834).

you much 'about myself' in my last letter. You know we always avoided practical details & anyway I assume that you hear all that from another source.

I am delighted to find that you appreciate 'Yeats' – I think the eeriness of that opening conversation in 'The Countess Kathleen' is splendid – rather like 'Christabel' in a way

'What can have made the grey hen flutter so?'[157]

By the way will you send on my MS. book – the Metrical Meditations one – to Ravenswood Rd – I have yielded to oft repeated suggestions that it should go there.

Write as much as you can & as often

Yours

Jack

---

157 William Butler Yeats, *The Countess Cathleen* (1892), i, 1.

1918

— ∼ —

TO HIS FATHER (LP V: 256-7):

[France]
4 January 1918

My dear Papy,

Your letter, with the enclosure for which I thank you very much, arrived the day before yesterday. Before going any further, I should say in answer to your question that I find my pay quite sufficient for all my needs and comforts. I am glad that I shall not have to bother you in that way.

I have thought a good deal about the question that is uppermost in both our minds, and talked it over with some of my friends. The arguments in favour of staying where I am seem overwhelming, and I have finally made up my mind to do so. I am very sorry that you should have taken trouble unnecessarily, and I hope that my decision will not be a disappointment to you. From what you say in your last letter, I think you agree with me that the gunners are not really preferable for safety or society. I have been up in the trenches for a few days (which I will speak about later on) attached to a company for instruction, and the number of shells that went singing over our heads to fall on the batteries far away behind, did not – as you may imagine – weaken my affection for the infantry!

I am now back again on a course of bombing, where I live with the bombing officer, a very nice fellow, of literary tastes, in a quite comfortable billet. The work, involving a good deal of chemical and mechanical questions, is not of the sort my brain takes to readily, but as long as one is safe and has an unbroken nights sleep, there is nothing to grouse about I suppose.

You will be anxious to hear my first impressions of trench life. This is a very quiet part of the line and the dug outs are very much more comfortable than one imagines at home. They are very deep, you go down to them by a shaft of about 20 steps: they have wire bunks where a man can sleep quite snugly, and brasiers for warmth and cooking. Indeed, the

351

chief discomfort is that they tend to get *too* hot, while of course the bad air makes one rather headachy. I had quite a pleasant time, and was only once in a situation of unusual danger, owing to a shell falling near the latrines while I was using them.

I think I told you that I had read 'Adam Bede' and am now at 'The Mill on the Floss',[1] which I like even better. Do you know of any life of George Elliot published in a cheap edition? If you can find one, I should like to read it.

Thank you muchly for the smokeables. The pipes have been soaked in whiskey, according to the dictum of experts, and are going very well. I also thank you from my heart for your last letter that defies definition. I am very proud of my father.

With such wishes for the New Year as still seem possible,

I am,

your loving son,

Jack

TO ARTHUR GREEVES (W):

No 10 British Red Cross Hospital[2]

Le Tréport

France.

2/2/18

My dear Galahad,

Here I am safely ensconced in a bed in hospital, miles away from the line, thank the gods, and therefore at last in a position to write you a more or less respectable letter. The news of my illness will have been given you by Mrs Moore, so there is no need to waste words on that.

I was sorry to hear that you were in trouble over the death of your cousin:[3] I did not think that you had been so attached to him. Your letters are always very sad now. I hope you are not letting yourself 'fall into

---

1 George Eliot, *The Mill on the Floss* (1860).

2 After some months on the front line Lewis fell ill with pyrexia, or 'trench fever' as the troops called it. On 1 February he was admitted to this hospital where he was to remain until 28 February.

3 Thomas Malcolmson 'Malcolm' Greeves (1895–1917) was the son of Alfred Greeves of 'Fernbank', Belfast. He attended Campbell College 1907–13. During the war he served as a flight sub-lieutenant with the Royal Navy, and was killed in action on 23 December 1917.

a melancholy' as Johnson would have said in some severe letter to his Boswell. Now is the time to rally all your interests about you & to paint & write for dear life.

I must admit fate has played strange tricks with me since last winter: I feel that I have definitely got into a new epoch of life and one feels extraordinarily helpless over it. How I should love one of our old afternoons again when we sat in your drawing room and discussed our tea and digestive biscuits: we were usually discontented over something but we had many a good laugh. As for the older days of real walks far away in the hills & journies out of town on the top of the tram – ma foi, that was the golden age infinitely remote 'mais ou sont les neiges d'antan'.[4] Perhaps you don't believe that I want all that again, because other things more important have come in: but after all there is room for other things besides love in a man's life. As well, you should trust in me after I have given you so much confidence.

How rude of me! – to come thus far without thanking you for your parcel. Let me hasten to do so. I am still reading the 'Lavengro' (although I'm sorry to say both books were rather crushed when they arrived) & like it very well though of course I am most violently out of sympathy with the author at times – when he is loudly patriotic (as in the idiotic passage about painters in chapter XXI) or when he indulges in vulgar invective against the parent church. Of course *that* is probably agreeable enough to you – eh?, old puritan. I am also reading Boswell vol. II and enjoy very much renewing my acquaintance with all these great old gentlemen. It is the ideal book to read out here and to keep me in touch with all the quiet literary pleasant things in the world – one feels so cut off at times among all these godless philistines. However I'm having an excellent time here doing nothing – if only it could last.

You are lucky you know; it must be grand to look forward to an endless prospect of regular nights' sleep & comfortable chairs & good meals & books & everything decent & civilized.

Well, good bye for the present mon vieux, keep true to the old interests – and don't let your relations influence you too much. You see I begin to fear for you now I can't watch over you & guard you against evil!

Yours

Jack

---

4 François Villon, *Le Grand Testament* (1461), 'Ballade des dames du temps Jadis': 'But where are the snows of yesteryear?'

TO HIS FATHER (LP V: 282):

British Red Cross and Order of St. John[5]

[France]

9 February 1918

My dear P.,

Just a line. I am much better now and hope to be up in a few days. In spite of its alarming name, Pyrexia is not much more serious than influenza. I shouldn't build on the idea of leave in which to recuperate, I'm afraid that's only for people who have been very ill indeed. This little turn is however not a bad thing, as it has kept me out of the line and in a good bed for a season. I will write again and at greater length when I get up.

your loving,

son,

Jack

TO ARTHUR GREEVES (W):

[No. 10 British Red Cross Hospital,

Le Tréport,

France]

12/2/18

My dear Galahad,

Your letter dated the 24th January 1917 (sic) arrived a few days ago. It has certainly been a famous time, – a year and a month – in coming.

Your account of the various meetings with your friend Mr Thompson reads rather like our Boswell. 'I met him at luncheon at so-and-so: I dined with him at etc.' From which you will gather that I am still reading my '*Bozz*-well' (you remember the proper way of pronouncing it?) and enjoying it very much: it is such a rest to come back to after everything else. I also have a confession – to wit that I have given up Lavengro at any rate for the present. I gave up everything, of course, during a bad spell with high temperature which I have had since I last wrote to you: and now I feel no inclination to return to him. I don't object to the scheme of the book; in fact I think that in other hands, say A. C. Benson's, it might

---

5 On 2 February 1918 the War Office informed Albert Lewis that Jack 'was admitted to 10th Red Cross Hospital, Le Tréport on February 1st, suffering from slight Pyrexia'.

be charming. But my lack of sympathy with, nay by now my violent hostility to the author, prevents me from enjoying it. I expect you will think me rather foolish over this.

How do you like the tour to the Hebrides?[6] That book follows naturally after one has read the Life. I remember taking up the Everyman copy of it in a shop in Oxford (oh! for those bookshops in 'The Broad' – how we could ramble there!) & liking the paper and type.

I am sorry 'Tommy' has gone as he must have brightened up your 'circle' a good deal. <Are you still bound to him by the chains of desire as well as by 'pure' friendship?> I consider your reasons for not going to stay with him seem to me, with all due respect to be rot. A person with a weak heart may need quiet & may have to take care not to tire himself etc but Lord-a-mercy, short of actual hardships, why should he be more uncomfortable than other people? Of course you know best, but I must say if I ever thought you were refusing to come and stay with me for like cause I should think pretty poorly of your excuses – and your friendship. Not that I think you would, old man: I flatter myself that you could endure a few discomforts if we were together again.

'Shall we ever be the same again'[?] Oh, how far we have travelled, you and I. To think of the things we've done: do you remember that day we walked up the glen in the rain, & everything was soaking? Or the evening up in Tiglath's field at dusk – the only real evening walk we ever had? Or the days of scheming over Loki when I first shewed you any work of mine, and you used to play over bits from the unborn opera? And the night when we first broached the 'nameless secrets of Aphrodite' and walked up and down that bit of road in the dark? And now – well, umph. However, we may have good times yet, although I have been at a war and although I love someone.

You talk about the days of our book-discussing as being far off, but indeed I think they're the only thing that has survived, I still want to hear all you are reading & I am still buying books. Apropos I have written home (London, I mean) for 'The Autobiography of Benvenuto Cellini' (Everyman)[7] which I'll talk about some other time. Fancy you beginning to care for old books! I was beginning to love some of the old books in

---

6 James Boswell, *The Journal of a Tour to the Hebrides* (1785).
7 *The Memoirs of Benvenuto Cellini written by Himself*, translated by Anne Macdonell, Everyman's Library (1913).

the college library at Univ. Of course London is the place, I suppose, for rumaging second hand shops.

You don't tell me what you are reading: always remember that it keeps us in touch. I'm afraid you'll be on very stodgy stuff – but then I'm getting stodgy too. After Benvenuto I'm thinking of reading Lockhart's 'Life of Scott' or else a life of 'G. Eliot'. Hers ought to be interesting. She had an affair with De Musset.[8] Is there any other edition of Green's Short History than the one that both our fathers have? Please answer this. Good bye now, old man, try to keep in touch and feel to me as you used to –

Yours
Jack

TO HIS FATHER (LP V: 285–6):

No. 10 British Red Cross Hospital,
Le Tréport
16 February 1918

My dear Papy,

Your letter has remained unanswered for some time, and if I had literally fulfilled my promise of 'writing when I got up', I fear the time would have been longer still. 'Trench fever' sounds a formidable name enough – like 'prison fever' in the days of the Bloody Assize I always think, but it is not usually a troublesome business. In this country it is called P.U.O. which, I am told, stands for 'Pyrexia unknown origin': which in plain English means merely a high temperature arising from the general irregularity of life at the front. In my case however, after they had got me down to normal, I had a relapse, and was pretty ill for a day or two. I am now however on the highroad to recovery, though still in bed. I consider this little turn as an unmixed blessing: even if I get no leave by it – and I'm afraid that is not very likely – I shall have had a comfortable rest from the line. The place where I have been dropped down is a little fishing village so far as I can make out. There are cliffs and a grey sea beyond – which one is very glad to see again – and from my own window pleasant wooded country. They tell me Dieppe is about eighteen miles away: and that makes one remember . . . eheu fugaces![9]

---

8 He is probably thinking of Alfred de Musset's affair with the French novelist, George Sand.

9 During part of August and September 1907 the Lewis brothers spent their last holiday with their mother near Dieppe. See letter of 4 September 1907.

This is indeed distressing news about Gunny: I hope the successful backwoodsman does not propose to return to his native heath with his booty, when the war is over.[10] However, we must rejoice that our qualms about a certain Hebrew neighbour were baseless. How is Cousin Quartus – he was in a poor way when I left home.

By the way (I can't remember whether I told you before or not) the Captain of the Company I am in is the Harris who used to be a master at Cherbourg: I think you met him once. He impressed me in those days, but I find him very disappointing. I wonder is it my own fault that so many of my old acquaintances I have run up against since leaving my shell at Bookham 'Please me not'? I suppose these things are to be expected.[11]

---

10 Gundreda Ewart was being courted by Captain Geoffrey Burbage, an army officer from Canada. Their engagement was announced in January 1919 but was broken off a few months later.

11 This is the same Percy Gerald Kelsal Harris, 'Pogo', mentioned in note 7 of the letter of 5 May 1912. Harris was commissioned a lieutenant in the Somerset Light Infantry on 1 February 1915 and on 6 October 1917 he was promoted to captain. He had made a poor showing at Cherbourg House, but he cuts an heroic and dashing figure in Everard Wyrall's official *History of the Somerset Light Infantry (Prince Albert's) 1914–1919* (1927). Wyrall describes the bravery at Verchain which caused Harris to receive the Military Cross with this citation: 'For conspicuous gallantry near Verchain on 24 October 1918. At the river bank, in the darkness, considerable confusion and difficulty were experienced in throwing the bridges, owing to the heavy machine-gun fire. It was entirely due to his example and efforts that the bridges were thrown and that the men were able to cross. He subsequently led his company to a further objective, and carried out a personal reconnaissance across the open under heavy machine-gun fire, obtaining very valuable information' (p. 354). A bar was added to that Cross as a result of Harris's gallantry at Preseau on 1 November 1918. Wyrall wrote of it: '"Preseau" – it was here that the 1st Somerset Light Infantry ended its glorious record of fighting in the Great War...Assisted by Company Sergeant-Major R. Johnson, Captain P.G.K. Harris rallied his men and ordered them to charge. The whole line sprang forward with a cheer and, with the bayonet, flung the Germans back' (p. 356).

It is, however, in Lt Col. Majendie's *History of the 1st Battalion The Somerset Light Infantry* that the Cherbourg 'Pogo' of uncertain temper is seen as a man, not less glossy perhaps, but far more admirable than the one Jack remembered. 'During the clearing of Preseau,' wrote Colonel Majendie, 'Captain P.G.K. Harris, M.C., was the chief performer in an incident which gave rise to some merriment. He was standing at the top of some cellar steps collecting prisoners, when a German came up from below "kamerading" with such enthusiasm that he collided with Captain Harris and knocked him down. Captain Harris sat down violently on top of a dead German, and in his efforts to rise put his hand on the dead man's face. This was too much for Light Company's Commander; he leapt at the offender and, mindful of his Oxford days, caught him such a left under the jaw that the unhappy German did not recover consciousness for some time' (p. 120).

You kindly ask if there is anything you could send. The next time you are in Mullan's, I should be 'beholden' if you would ask them to look out some cheap edition of Burton's 'Anatomy of Melancholy' and send it to me, or the 1st. volume of it. You remember it used to be a fancy of mine, and somebody has recommended it to me lately. If the only edition is in a fairly large book, let them send it all the same – I can find room for it. What are you reading? You see I make some desperate attempt to keep in touch with a life beyond the one which we lead here. I hope you keep well in body: so long as I am in hospital you may keep easy in mind. How I wish your hopes about leave could be realized. Of course it is possible, but I don't think there is much chance. By the way, offer Warnie all my congratulations upon his recent glories when next you write. That at least is a blessing: he won't be doing badly in the soldiering line if he is to be a Captain after the war at his age. Well good bye for the present: write soon again.

> your loving
> son Jack

TO ARTHUR GREEVES (W):

[No. 10 British Red Cross Hospital]
21/2/18

My dear Galahad,

Your last letter would have been answered earlier but for two reasons. 1, that as my last apparently crossed yours I thought you had something to go on with; 2 when I had actually started writing to you the other day, duty suddenly called to me and made me write to M. mon père instead. So you see your good precepts have stood in your own way!

I will dispose of the immensely uninteresting subject of my own health shortly – I am up again now and was out for the first time yesterday. Indeed I am beginning to tremble as to how long I shall be left here – but of course I may have the good luck of another relapse: but I doubt it, the gods hate me – and naturally enough considering my usual attitude towards them.

The country round, so far as I could see in yesterday's walk, quite comes up to expectation. I in vain tried to get onto a road leading to the cliffs and the sea, but, like the house in 'Alice in Wonderland' they evaded me. I struck a very pretty little village however: the houses are mostly clay walled, which gives them a lovely colour, and are very ramshakle.

The roofs are all of old old tiles and there are lots of old stone crucifixes, with their little offerings of grass & beads & things on them. Catholic Christianity is certainly more picturesque than puritanism. But what pleased me most was an old granary with little kinds of arrow slits under the eaves through which you could see oats or corn or whatever it was projecting: it gave you the impression of the place being filled to bursting and was somehow very homely, snug and comfortable. There are also pigeons all over the place, lodged in dovecots of the real old type that you see in pictures. Another nice thing was the orchards, where you could look along the bright grass among the tree stems – very like our wood at home just above and beyond the vicious dog. Wandering about the sleepy country reminded me of Bookham days – what a paradise of peace and quiet interests that was with our weekly letters so full of life & always following up some new idea.

I hardly realized till your last letter that of course from your present liesure you must look back with a kind of horror to the days when you had to go into town. Yet we had a few minutes of 'good talk' sometimes in that sordid old office – which, by the way, if I had a bunk in one corner, I should now regard as an almost incredibly luxurious billet – actually windows and a fireplace.

I am longing to see those old English romances of yours: I think that *is* the kind of book I had rather hunt out second hand than buy brand new and obvious in a shop. If, as I imagine from your account they suffer from being too thin, could you not have them bound together in some good solemn half leather & strong boards. The girl in Ovenell's, Broad St., Oxford assured me they could make a good job of binding books together like that. I am sure your cautious soul would never risk it, but I think you'd be quite safe in sending them to Ovenell's with instructions. She would understand & a good shop like that would certainly do it with taste. If it suits the style of the book you could have a guilt top as well.

I wait anxiously for your answer as to there being any other edition of Green's Short History – but I'm afraid there is NOT. I feel inclined to read history somehow. By the way I must recommend the 'Autobiography' of Benvenuto Cellini which I am now three quarters way through. I expect you know who he was – a Florentine designer born in 1500. The book professes to be a sober 'life' but seems to me most impossible. He lives like a character in a Dumas novel: he is often attacked in the street by five or six men, all of whom he kills wounds, or puts to flight: he is shut up in a castle (with a 'castellan' who is mad & imagines himself to be a bat), and makes a most wonderful escape – letting himself down by a rope of sheets *of course* – He goes with a magician to practice sorcery in the ruins of the Colisseum and after the magician had 'conjured for more than two hours many thousands of spirits began to appear' so that the whole amphitheatre was full of them threatening to come inside the magic circle. And perhaps what would appeal to you most is the background of great historical figures by whom he is patronized – two popes, cardinals both of France and Italy, Lorenzo & Cosimo de' Medici, the King of France and his powerful & spiteful mistress Madame d'Etampes, the Emperor. It is like a grand historical romance, with the added pleasure that it is, at least for the most part, true: how I look forward to reading it in the Italian when (and if) I get back to real life. It is also a good Everyman speciman: the paper is thin & crisp, the print just a comfortable size & the margins larger than usual – making a very pretty page. But I could talk forever about it. I should very, very strongly recommend you to get it as in the historical way it may appeal to you even more than to me. <It touches in one place tho' very briefly on your penchant, and is from time to time interesting in 'that way'.> I expect you are now heartily sick of the subject!

The 1st volume of Johnson has arrived and I am now started on it: I also discovered among the piles of trash of the hospital Blackwood's 'Incredible Adventures'[12] and a ragged copy containing some of Tennyson. Of the former I have read 2 stories, excellent of his style but I feel it a waste of time in these precious days. Tennyson, too, never raises any great enthusiasm in me. I am starting G. Eliot's 'Middlemarch'[13] to night. So, you see I am in clover. Do write soon again or I shall begin to feel neglected –

Yours
Jack

---

12 Algernon Henry Blackwood, *Incredible Adventures* (1914).
13 George Eliot, *Middlemarch* (1871–2).

TO HIS FATHER (LP V: 291-2):

[No. 10 British Red Cross Hospital,]
Le Tréport
22 February 1918

My dear Papy,

Your letter of the 17th has just arrived, with the enclosure, for which many thanks: a widening experience of other people's parents has taught me to value these things more than I once did, both for themselves and what they mean. That suggests literary possibilities: there is already a book called 'Other people's children',[14] but why not a companion volume 'Other people's parents' – in our schooldays we have most of us suffered from time to time at the hands of these irrelevant beings.

It is one of the punishments – to be sure, richly deserved – of a bad correspondant, that when at last he does write, his letter usually crosses the next one from his victim. I hope that you have before this got the longer letter which apparently had not come when you wrote yours.

I don't think there is need to worry if at any future time you hear of my being in hospital merely with illness. Even supposing it to be fairly serious, it is a more natural and easy kind of danger than that of the front: as well, there is always the rest, the unaccustomed comforts, and at the end the possibility of leave. In this case I am afraid I have not been bad enough.

I am sending you in this two photographs of my room at Univ. They were taken by my friend Moore shortly before I left Oxford, but remained undeveloped for a long time and have lately been sent to me by his mother. The room is not of much personal interest, as everything in it belonged to another man – I think I mentioned that at the time. But I daresay you may care to see them. Do you remember it used to be one of my dreams that I might some day entertain you and the Knock there together. As you said, 'That would be a symposium of the gods'. What crack there would have been! With what an added zest we would have drunk in the man's 'statements of fact' in the hope of chuckling over them between ourselves later on. Who knows? At any rate we can hope that you and I will some time see Oxford together.

The picture of our Warnie attending an A-murican proffessor's lecture from the chair of Poker is good. But I'm afraid the psychology of the

---

14 John Habberton, *Other People's Children* (1877).

card player will always baffle me as it has baffled you. I had as soon spend the evening building card houses – much sooner watch the picture in the red of the fire.

I have discovered that optimism about the war increases in an inverse ratio to the optimist's proximity to the line. Was our Colonel so hopeful a month ago? But indeed I'm afraid I must live up to our family reputation, for certainly I can't see any bright prospects at present. The conditions at home are almost as bad as anything we once fabled of starvation in Germany: spirits will be more pacific every day on short commons: there seems to be 'spiritual wickedness in high places'[15] (I think it was Smugy who told us that this text should be rendered 'wickedness of spirits in the upper regions of the air' – Satan being 'Prince of the air' and the evil hosts finding there the parade ground par excellence).

Poor old Mr. Patterson! As you say, we cannot miss a single detail out of the picture of home without a sense of regret. The longer we are absent from it and the more different the scenes in which we are compelled to live, the more eagerly we prize even its most irrelevant features. The sight of Campbell across the fields – the hideous palm like thing beside the front avenue – the broken glass in the etching in the upstairs passage. Mr. Patterson was en[titled] to some fame too for his famous mot 'Not convenient'. We avoided him often in our walks and are sorry that there will be no necessity to avoid him again.[16] He was, in short, one of the 'old familiar faces'.[17]

Now there is a thing we quote very often, but I never read till the other day the little poem of Lambs from which it comes: I don't know if you were in the same plight: if so, it would give you a few minutes pleasure – if it is in any of our imperfect editions of Lamb.

I am ordering a couple of books of Vergil from my bookseller in London, and if I find that I get on with these I shall order something equally pleasant and simple in Greek. German and Italian I fear must go to the wall: of course I read a French book from time to time and seek opportunities of speaking it – but one sees very little of the natives. I am also still at Boswell, and have also begun 'Middlemarch'. You see I am quite 'caught' by George Eliot's books.

---

15 Ephesians 6:12.

16 William Hugh Patterson (see note 25 to letter of 19 October 1913) died on 6 February 1918.

17 Charles Lamb, 'The Old Familiar Faces', l. 3: 'All, all are gone, the old familiar faces'.

I have now almost written my pen out of ink, and – perhaps my reader out of patience: but 'out of the abundance of the heart'[18] and as well there will be days when I cannot write much. I have been out once or twice, and can't say how much longer I shall be here. Write as often and as long (grammar!) as you can.

your loving,

son Jack

TO HIS FATHER (LP V: 301):

[France
5 March 1918]

My dear Papy,

I have been living at such a rush since I left hospital that it needed this battle and your probable anxiety to make me write. I am out of the fighting area, but of course we are not enjoying the old peaceful trench warfare I knew before Le Treport. We have just come back from a four days tour in the front line during which I had about as many hours sleep: then when we got back to this soi-disant rest, we spent the whole night digging. Under these conditions I know you will excuse me from much letter writing: but I will try and let you know that I am safe from time to time.

your loving son

Jack

TO HIS FATHER (LP V: 304):

[France]
8 April 1918

My dear Papy,

Just another hurried line to tell you that I am still safe and well. We have had a fairly rough time, though we were not really in the thick of it. I have lost one or two of my best friends and in particular a fellow called Perrett who used to be at Malvern, and who got a bit in the eye. It is a long time since I heard from you.

your loving son

Jack

---

18 Matthew 12:34.

The Germans launched their great spring offensive on 21 March with the additional troops drawn from the Eastern Front following the collapse of Russia. This was the worst crisis of the war and it galvanized the War Cabinet into action. The Prime Minister, David Lloyd George, took over the direction of the War Office on 23 March and the nation was soon transporting 30,000 men a day to France. Even so, the Allies were disintegrating, and on 3 April Marshal Foch took over supreme command. He was just able to halt the advance of the Germans when they were within 40 miles of Paris. 'With our backs to the wall and believing in the justice of our case, each must fight to the end,' declared Field Marshal Douglas Haig, chief of the British forces on the Western Front. The Germans' second putsch came on 9 to 25 April. On 3 April Lewis was among those who took part in the Battle of Arras. The particular part of the battle he took part in was centred on Riez du Vinage. In his official History of the 1st Battalion The Somerset Light Infantry (Prince Albert's) July 1st 1916 to the end of the War, *Everard Wyrall gives an account of the battle that took place between 14 and 16 April:*

> As the leading Somerset men approached the eastern exits of Riez, the enemy launched a counter-attack from east of the village and the northern end of the Bois de Pacaut. This counter-attack was at once engaged with Lewis-gun and rifle fire and about 50 per cent of the Germans were shot down. Of the remainder about half ran away and the other half ran towards the Somerset men with their hands in the air crying out 'Kamerad!' and were made prisoners...
>
> When dawn broke on the 15th a considerable number of Germans in full marching order were seen: they were advancing in twos and threes into shell holes from houses north and north-east of Riez and from the northern end of Bois de Pacaut. Heavy rifle fire and Lewis-gun fire was opened on them, serious casualties being inflicted, and if a serious counter-attack was intended it was definitely broken up, for no further action was taken by the evening: his stretcher-bearers were busy for the rest of the day...
>
> About noon on the 16th the enemy opened a trench-mortar and artillery fire on the line held by the Somerset men...A little later he was observed massing immediately north-east of Riez with the obvious intention of wresting the village from the Somersets...About 2 p.m. the Germans were seen retiring in twos and

threes: they had given up the struggle, having found the stout opposition put up by the Somersets impossible to break down. The results of this minor enterprise were splendid: (i) The village of Riez du Vinage had been captured; (ii) a battery of British field guns and a battery of 4.5 howitzers, taken by the enemy, had been recaptured; (iii) sixteen light machine guns and four heavy machine guns were taken: a Vickers gun was also recaptured – making a total of 21; (iv) a heavy mortar on wheels was taken, but it was not possible to get it away before the Somersets were relieved; (v) at least one German battalion, or the equivalent, was put out of action; 135 prisoners were taken: 60 dead Germans were seen in the village and probably 200 other casualties were inflicted on the enemy. A statement in the Battalion Diary, however, to the effect that 'never before have such targets been presented, or such execution done by the bullet', is hardly correct, for during the War there were many instances of the enemy's troops advancing in massed formation and being shot down in hundreds, if not in thousands. That the Somerset men had taken full advantage of the opportunities presented them, is shown by the fact that one Lewis gunner fired 2,000 rounds from his gun during the period, whilst a rifleman fired in one day from his own rifle 400 rounds.

The casualties of the 1st Battalion between 14th and 16th April were: 2/Lieut. L. B. Johnson died of wounds (15/4/18) and 2/Lieuts. C. S. Lewis, A. G. Rawlence, J. R. Hill and C. S. Dowding wounded: in other ranks the estimated losses were 210 killed, wounded and missing. (pp. 293–5)

TO HIS FATHER (LP V: 307):

[Liverpool Merchants Mobile Hospital, Étaples]
16 April 1918

My dear Papy,

I am slightly wounded and am now in Hospital and will let you know my definite address as soon as possible.

yours,

Jack[19]

---

19 This note was written in an unknown hand, presumably that of a hospital nurse.

TO HIS FATHER (LP V: 307):

[Liverpool Merchants Mobile Hospital,
Étaples]
17 April 1918

My dear P.,

I have come down the line and my address is 'Liverpool Merchants Mobile Hospital, Etaples'. Getting on all right but cant write properly yet as my left arm is still tied up and its hard to manage with one. Please write soon.

your loving son,
Jack

Shortly after Jack was taken to the hospital at Étaples, on the Strait of Dover, his father received a telegram from the War Office saying: '2nd. Lt. C. S. Lewis Somerset Light Infantry wounded April fifteenth' (LP V: 308). Albert interpreted this to mean 'severely wounded', and was of course very worried. Warnie, having completed the course at the Mechanical Transport School of Instruction, had been stationed at a camp near the village of Behucourt near Doullens since 8 March. On learning from his father on 24 April that Jack had been 'severely wounded', he borrowed a motor bike and rode the 50 miles from Doullens through Frévent, Hesdin and Montreuil to the hospital at Étaples. 'You can't let your mind dwell on imaginary fears,' he told his father on 13 May, 'when you are trying to get your best out of machinery – roaring along the straight bits of road and nursing your engine over the rough' (LP V: 315). He made the return trip as soon as he had seen his brother, and writing to his father on the evening of 24 April, he said:

> I don't know who was responsible for the phrase 'severely wounded', but it gave me a desperately bad fright. As a matter of fact you will be glad to hear that [Jack] is not much the worse, and is in better spirits than I have seen him for a long time. He was in great fettle and we had a long crack...A shell burst close to where he was standing, killing a Sergeant, and luckily for 'It' [Jack] he only stopped three bits: one in the cheek and two in the hands: he then crawled back and was picked up by a stretcher bearer. (LP V: 309)

TO HIS FATHER (LP V: 312–13):

[Liverpool Merchants Mobile Hospital,
Étaples]
4 May [1918]

My dear Papy,

Many thanks for the smokes and also for the letter which I was particularly glad to get, as I had not heard from you for so long. I am very sorry – and angry – that you [have] been through a lot of unnecessary worry and anxiety owing to the carelessness of some fool at the War Office, who – as Arthur informs me – told you some rubbish about my being hit in both arms and in the face.

As a matter of fact I was really hit in the back of the left hand, on the left leg from behind and just above the knee, and in the left side just under the arm pit. All three were only flesh wounds. The myth about being hit in the face arose, I imagine, from the fact that I got a lot of dirt in the left eye which was closed up for a few days, but is now alright. I still can't lie on my side (neither the bad one nor the other one) but otherwise I lead the life of an ordinary mortal and my temperature is alright. So there is no need for any anxiety at all.

I was surprised the day before yesterday by a visit from two ladies – a Miss McConnell and a friend. Apparently you know her brother. Ought I to? For the life of me I can't remember any one of that name. Whoever she is she was very agreeable and it didn't make any difference.

The correspondants of mine – Mrs. Moore and a man called Johns in the Somersets – seem to think that a number of letters to me were sent to my home address when I first went to Le Treport. If you have any letters of mine, will you please send them on? I suppose they haven't been silly enough to send my valise home have they?

Warnie has been down to see me and seems in good health and spirits. If only leave would start again he might manage to be at home with me as he is due for it now.

I hope you are keeping well and not worrying about me, for as you see, I am getting on excellently.

your loving son
Jack

TO HIS FATHER (LP V: 316–17):

Same adress.
[Étaples]
14/6/18 [14 May 1918]

My dear Papy,

Thank you for the letter, the enclosure, and the other 'far wandered' letters. I must confess that when Warnie turned up here I didn't realise through what possible difficulties or by what exertions he had come: I understand now 'video proboque'.[20]

I expect to be sent across in a few days time, of course as a stretcher case: indeed whatever my condition they would have to send me in that way, because I have no clothes. This is a standing joke out here – the mania which people at the dressing stations have for cutting off a wounded man's clothes whether there is any need for it or not. In my case the tunic was probably beyond hope, but I admit that I mourn the undeserved fate of my breeches. Unfortunately I was unconscious when the sacrilege took place and could not very well argue the point.

I am doing exceedingly well and can lie on my right side (not of course on my left), which is a great treat after you have been on your back for a few weeks. In one respect I was wrong in my last account of my wounds: the one under my arm is worse than a flesh wound, as the bit of metal which went in there is now in my chest, high up under my 'pigeon chest' as shown: this however is nothing to worry about as it is doing no harm. They will leave it there and I am told that I can carry it about for the rest of my life without any evil results.

Aunt Lily[21] keeps up a sharp fire of literature – Browning, Emerson, Mill (on 'the subjection of women")[22] and 'The Scotsman'. How on earth can I be supposed to be interested in 'The Scotsman'? However there are

---

20 Ovid, *Metamorphoses*, Book 7, ll. 19–21: 'sed trahit invitam nova vis, aliudque cupido, / mens aliud suadet: video meliora proboque, / deteriora sequor'. 'But a strange force drags me against my will, and desire persuades me one way, reason another: I see the better and even approve it – still, I follow the worse.'

21 Mrs Lilian 'Lily' Hamilton Suffern, who is mentioned in note 73 to the letter of 22 December 1914, was the sister of Florence Hamilton Lewis, and Jack's aunt. She was an ardent suffragette who had quarrelled with everyone in her family. She had been married to a Scotsman, William Suffern, who died in 1913. Although she was constantly on the move, she was living in Edinburgh at the time. Mrs Suffern was particularly fond of Jack and bombarded him with books and a pseudo-metaphysical correspondence. See **The Hamilton Family** in the Biographical Appendix.

22 John Stuart Mill, *The Subjection of Women* (1869).

one or two Scotch patients here to whom I hand it over: so I can truthfully tell her that they 'are read and enjoyed'.

My friend Mrs Moore is in great trouble – Paddy has been missing for over a month and is almost certainly dead. Of all my own particular set at Keble he has been the first to go, and it is pathetic to remember that he at least was always certain that he would come through.

In spite of Aunt Lily's library I have been battening on other fare. 'Old Mortality'[23] which I found disappointing, and now 'Barchester Towers'[24] with which I am delighted. This brings me to Martha's wedding.[25] (The connection being 'What a pity that she too has not married a Bishop, since she could run a diocese at least as well as Mrs. Proudie').[26] Give her any message from me which you think suitable. Hoping that you keep well and cheerful, I am,

your loving son

Jack

Although his mother did not receive confirmation until September, Paddy Moore died in March 1918 during the battle at Pargny. The story of his part in the war was summarized, from information supplied by Mrs Moore, in his school magazine The Cliftonian, *No. CCXCV (May 1918), p. 225:*

> *2nd-Lieutenant E.F.C. Moore. He joined the Rifle Brigade after the usual training, and was in action in France in the great German attack which began on March 21. He was reported missing on March 24, and it is now feared that he cannot have escaped with his life. The Adjutant of his battalion writes: 'I have to tell you that your very gallant son was reported missing on the 24th of last month. He was last seen on the morning of that day with a few men defending a position on a river bank against infinitely superior numbers of the enemy. All the other officers and most of the*

---

23 Sir Walter Scott, *Old Mortality* (1816).

24 Anthony Trollope, *Barchester Towers* (1857).

25 Martha, the cook at Little Lea, was getting ready to marry a clergyman and move to Glenavy, County Antrim.

26 'Mrs. Proudie', a character in *Barchester Towers* and all Trollope's subsequent Barsetshire novels, is the tyrannical wife of the Bishop of Barchester.

*men of his company have become casualties, and I fear it is impos-
sible to obtain more definite information. He did really fine work
on the previous night in beating off a party of Germans who had
succeeded in rushing a bridgehead in our lines. We all feel his loss
very deeply, and I cannot express too strongly our sympathy with
you.'*

TO ARTHUR GREEVES (W):

[Liverpool Merchants Mobile Hospital,
Étaples
23 May 1918]

My dear Arthur,

I was so glad to get your answer to day as it is the first 'answer' I've
had for a long time – thro' my own neglect I admit.

I think your criticisms on my 'Literary Supplement' letter[27] were quite
just, but I must give two reasons why I was led to write in such a style. In
the first place I was rather stung by your gratuitous supposition that I
had become a 'cheer-oh young man', and this naturally urged me into the
opposite extreme of being what somebody calls 'a university prize prig'.
Of course I don't mean to say that I didn't write throughout of things
that really interested me and which I expected to interest you: but the
general tone was probably influenced by that feeling. The second reason
is this. The personal element naturally found a large field in my letters
from Bookham and Univ. where all my life and surroundings were of
interest to us both: but here, where everything I do & suffer is dull and
repulsive, I don't turn to description and details which would bore me to
write and – probably – you to read. If you think that I look to you only
for abstract interests and no longer yearn for the old intimacy, the teas,
the laughter the walks and the comparing of books – you are very much
mistaken, mon ami.

(Talking about comparing of books, if you are still minded to sell your
Trollope you will now find a purchaser in me. A chance copy of 'Barchester Towers' has quite converted me and I am now all a-gog to read his
others, so that I will certainly take your whole set if I may. By the way, this
is an advantage – the only one – of being in the army: I have always
plenty of money for anything I want. To any one in my irresponsible

---

27 So called because of his lengthy comments on Cellini's *Memoirs*.

position the despised pay of a second lieutenant is a never-empty purse, unless he chooses to waste it on prostitutes, restaurants and tailors, as the gentiles do.)

When I see you face to face I will tell you any war impressions quite freely *at your request* – and not otherwise: for it is very proper that you should make use of me if you ever happen to want to know how certain things feel – but on the other hand there is no reason why I should bore you with a subject that we have always disliked, if you do *not* want.

Congratulations old man. I am delighted that you have had the moral courage to form your own opinions <independently,> in defiance of the old taboos. I am not sure that I agree with you: but, as you hint in your letter, <this penchant is a sort of mystery only to be fully understood by those who are made that way – and my views on it can be at best but emotion.>

You will be surprised and I expect, not a little amused to hear that my views at present are getting almost monastic about all the lusts of the flesh. They seem to me to extend the dominion of matter over us: and, out here, where I see spirit continually dodging matter (shells, bullets, animal fears, animal pains) I have formulated my equation Matter= Nature=Satan. And on the other side Beauty, the only spiritual & not-natural thing that I have yet found. Does all this bore you?

I think my stilted style must be due to the fact that I read 'Old Mortality' a short time ago and am at present in the midst of 'Guy Mannering'. The former I thought very disappointing but am quite pleased with the latter, tho', truth to tell, I enjoyed 'Barchester Towers' much more. I have got here but not yet begun Blackwood's new book 'The Promise of the Air':[28] perhaps you read the verdict of the Times L.S. that this is his first really serious book.[29] I hope it may be true.

Strange! how wrongly one can read the simplest sentence: just reading over part of your letter I have realised for the first time that when you say you were 'driven' to town you mean driven in the car: I thought you meant 'driven' by circumstances of some sort. Now theres one of those little things which are useless on paper but would have made us roar with laughter if we were together.

---

28 Algernon Henry Blackwood, *The Promise of Air* (1918).
29 *The Times Literary Supplement* (9 May 1918), p. 219.

By the way, are you allowed to go up & downstairs freely these days? If so, it occurs to me that it would be a very good idea for you to act as a sort of librarian to the little-end-room when I return to my penance. I mean, the key would be left in the bookcase and I should like you to go there frequently & see that they were alright, and borrow or examine anything you wanted & put in suitable places any new volumes I sent you. This would keep me in touch with my books to some extent and save the room from looking disused when I come back. What do you say?

I have only come across a few references to the Dorian customs: I hope Carpenter does not fall into the error common to enthusiasts, of reading into ancient institutions more than is really there. However, of course I have never studied the subject and can't give an opinion.

I was to have been sent across to England last night, but we were heavily bombed, so of course all traffic stopped. It is interesting to note that an air-raid here frightened me much more than anything I encountered at the front: you feel so helpless in bed, knowing you can't walk or anything even if you get out of it. Unless the same things happen again I shall probably go, or at least the night after. I suppose it would be out of the question for you to come and see me in hospital in England for a few days? It would be a great something to look forward to & it would give you an opportunity to meet Mrs Moore.

I am tired now, old man, after a very disturbed night & a stifling day so I will dry up & just enclose a little song I wrote the other day, which I hope you will approve –

Yours ever

Jack

Song

Faeries must be in the woods
Or the satyr's merry broods,
Tritons in the summer sea,
Else how could the dead things be
Half so lovely as they are?
How could wreathèd star on star
Dusted o'er the wintry night,
Fill thy spirit with delight

And lead thee from this care of thine
Through a land of dreams divine
To the dearest heart's-desire,
Unless each pale & drifting fire
Were indeed a happy isle
Where eternal gardens smile
And golden globes of fruit are seen
Twinkling thro' the orchards green
Where the Other People go
On the soft sward to and fro?
Atoms dead could never thus
Wake the human heart of us,
Unless the beauty that we see
Part of endless beauty be,
Thronged with spirits that have trod
Where the bright foot-prints of God
Lie fresh upon the heavenly sod.[30]

TELEGRAM TO HIS FATHER (LP V: 319):

25 May 1918

Am in Endsleigh Palace Hospital, Endsleigh Gardens, London, Jack.

TO ARTHUR GREEVES (W):

[Endsleigh Palace Hospital,
Endsleigh Gardens,
London
29 May 1918]

Cher Ami,

I am sitting up in bed in the middle of a red sunset to answer this evening's letter straightaway. Your letters set me thinking of so many old interests that I cannot go on with my book.

First a word or two as to my present estate: I am in a vastly comfortable hospital, where we are in separate rooms & have tea in the morning & big broad beds & everything the heart of man could desire and best

---

30 This poem was later to appear under the same name, but with considerable alterations, in Lewis's *Spirits in Bondage* (1919), pp. 73–4. It is reprinted in his *Collected Poems* (1994).

of all, in close communication with all the bookshops of London. Of course you can easily understand what other and greater reasons there are for me to be happy. There are still two pieces of shrapnel in my chest, but they give me no discomfort: <Mrs Moore and> I are always hoping that it *will* start to give some trouble and thus secure me a longer illness (This is quite like the Malvern days again, isn't it?).

The thing in your last letter with which I most want to disagree is the remark about Beauty and nature; apparently I did not make myself very clear. You say that nature is beautiful, and that is the view we all start with. But let us see what we mean. If you take a tree, for instance, you call it beautiful because of its shape, colour and motions, and perhaps a little because of association. Now these colours etc are sensations in my eye, produced by vibrations on the aether between me and the tree: the real tree is something quite different – a combination of colourless, shapeless, invisible atoms. It follows then that neither the tree, nor any other material object can be beautiful in itself: I can never see them as they are, and if I could it would give me no delight. The beauty therefore is not in matter at all, but is something purely spiritual, arising mysteriously out of the relation between me & the tree: or perhaps as I suggest in my Song, out of some indwelling spirit behind the matter of the tree – the Dryad in fact.

You see the conviction is gaining ground on me that after all Spirit does exist; and that we come in contact with the spiritual element by means of these 'thrills'. I fancy that there is Something right outside time & place, which did not create matter, as the Christians say, but is matter's great enemy: and that Beauty is the call of the spirit in that something to the spirit in us. You see how frankly I admit that my views have changed: I hope I don't bore you.

<I admit the associations of the word paederasty are unfortunate but you should rise above that. As well what does 'Uranian' mean – it ought to mean 'Heavenly' as far as my knowledge goes, and I will stick to the word that I understand in preference.>

I don't agree with you about Trollope's being mamby pamby: in fact the sentimental part seems to me very slightly sketched and only to serve as a turning point for all the delightful 'Austinesque' work about the Mrs Proudie's etc. I have now read the 'Warden' and am more than half way through 'Dr Thorne'.[31] I cannot understand why you got tired of him, I

---

31 Anthony Trollope, *The Warden* (1855); *Doctor Thorne* (1858).

should have thought he was so very much in your line: but indeed one can never really say what will please another person.

I told you I was reading Blackwood's new one 'The Promise of Air': it is very disappointing, being merely a long & tedious expansion of a theory that could have been explained in a single essay. Although it is in story form nothing ever happens: I'm afraid if he goes on being 'serious' after this fashion we shall have lost a good romancer for a bad mystic.

Can you imagine how I enjoyed my journey to London? First of all the sight and smell of the sea, that I have missed for so many long and weary months, and then the beautiful green country seen from the train: I suppose its because I've been shut up in a hut so long, but I think I never enjoyed anything so much as that scenery – all the white in the hedges, and the fields so full of buttercups that in the distance they seemed to be of solid gold: and everything such a bright, bright green. I am sure our hills look lovely now and the wood must be full of life and sweet smells.

Yes, after all our old conversations I *can* feel otherwise about the lusts of the flesh: is not desire merely a kind of sugar-plum that nature gives us to make us breed, as she does the beetles and toads so that both we and they may beget more creatures to struggle in the same net: Nature, or the common order of things, has really produced in man a sort of Frankenstein who is learning to shake her off. For man alone of all things can master his instincts.

From my window I see a big flat plain of houses and beyond that actually a green hill with trees on it, which I am told is the aristocratic district of High Hampstead. In the foreground is the Euston station hotel – bringing old, old memories. 'Mais ou sont les neiges.'

Your quotation from Pater expresses my attitude to philosophy exactly: I don't really think it will teach me the truth, but I do think it will supply me with thoughts & feelings that I may be able to turn into poetry. As you turn all kinds of nourishment into blood. I was glad to see Willie (I suppose 'Bill' since his marriage)[32] he seems in good form.

Good bye, old man, write by return.

Yours ever

Jack

---

32 Arthur's brother, William Edward Greeves, who married Marion Janet Cadbury on 14 February 1918.

TO HIS FATHER (LP V: 320–1):

Endsleigh Gardens.
[London]
30 May 1918

My dear Papy,

I hope that you got my telegram and that I will soon hear from you, and not only hear but receive a visit in the aristocratic neighbourhood of Euston. You will be able to come over, will you not, if only for a few days? We must get Kirk up to meet you and have a famous crack. In the meantime, will you please send me my new brown suit, and also, if possible, a pair of black brogue shoes: I ought to have several. It is allowed to wear ordinary clothes here until I can get a uniform made. This is merely a note, as you are already heavily in my debt in the matter of letters. Hoping to hear soon, I am

your loving son
Jack

TO ARTHUR GREEVES (W):

[Endsleigh Palace Hospital,
London
3 June 1918]

My dear Arthur,

Your letter of the 1st arrived this morning. I am very sorry that you are getting bored with our 'tree' argument (the Dry Tree as it might well be called from the nature of the discussions to which it gives rise) for I am afraid I cannot let the subject drop without refuting the heresies which you started in to-day's letter.

First, as to the colour of the atom, I would remind you that atoms are regarded as all identically the same – as the original world-stuff, and if therefore they had colour all things would be coloured the same. And to analyse colour ninety-two million miles away the action of certain vibrations in the sun sets up a wave on the ether which travels to the atom under your consideration: this sets up certain other vibrations in the atom which again sends off another wave along the ether towards your eye. When this reaches the tissue of your eye it sets up more action which travels along a nerve and produces in your brain a sensation which we call greenness. Here for the first time we reach the colour – in your brain, not in all these vibrations of atoms. Magnify your atom to infinity, and still your consciousness has no *direct* communion with it. All you can ever say is that certain sensations arise in your brain: you suppose (which in itself was doubted by Berkeley and other idealists) that there is some exterior cause for these: but what that exterior cause is like in itself you do not know and never can know. Suppose this vibration from the atom never happened to strike an eye, but went on for ever into space – where then is your greenness? No – the whole exterior world can only make itself known to us by certain sensations which it produces on our brain in a complicated manner, and it is simply a habit of mind which makes us call these impressions (colour, shape, sound etc) the thing-in-itself. Hence as I said before, beauty cannot be in the material thing.

Of course there is another simpler argument, without going into abstruse regions. If beauty were really in the tree, then two people who both had normal eyes would be bound to see the same beauty. But nothing is easier than to find two people one of whom would see beauty and the other see no beauty in the same tree. Therefore the beauty cannot be in the tree but in some obscure and non-material point of view or relation between the mind of the perciever and the sensations which the tree – very indirectly – causes in that mind. I have done: are you bored beyond endurance?

Perhaps you feel that we are wandering away from the grounds that supplied our earlier interests in common and first brought us together. I hope not: I like to think of our interests as a circle which may increase in size but whose centre is always the same. For myself I think I am true to the old cannons – romantic beauty, eeriness, terror, homeliness, solidity – & absurdity. These were the gods we worshipped in the golden age, were they not mon vieux?

By the same token, I have been reading since this morning an incomparably homely book, of which I am having a copy sent to you – 'The Private Papers of Henry Ryecroft' by G. Gissing (Constable 1/-).[33] Gissing's name I have often heard, but I have no idea what else he wrote. This is a collection of very loose, spontaneous essays, about books and other quiet interests – including food. He has some splendid things to say about the glory of 'tea', so homely & cheery after a long walk. There is hardly a bad piece in the whole book, and it is a very companionable

33 George Robert Gissing, *The Private Papers of Henry Ryecroft* (1903).

volume to fill up the spaces of serious reading with, or to read over a lonely meal.

Are you lonely these days, or are you over-much oppressed with visitors? I should like to hear from you a fuller account of your cousin Gribbon: I remember him – with a shudder – at Campbell. I hear he is enormously clever and knows all things: I expect he will pulverize me – rusted as I am with a year's barbarity – if I should ever meet him.[34] But I mustn't talk thus or you will perhaps think, like somebody in a French play 'que je vous fasse l'honneur d'etre jaloux'.[35]

Spenser, I am sure, would be greatly surprised to hear that Britomart was a type of [illegible] – considering she is represented as loving Artegall the knight of Justice; I don't remember her being described as having a 'man's heart' in the real Faerie Queene, and the book which you mention probably uses that phraze in the conventional sense as 'having a man's courage'. But how I love to hear you say 'I came across so-and-so in a book this morning': it conjures up such visions of those old happy hours when I sat surrounded by my little library and browsed from book to book. You, who have never lost that life, cannot understand the longing with which I look back to it.

By the way, haven't you got a reddy-brown MS. book of mine containing 'Lullaby' and several other of my later poems? I wish you would send it here, as I have decided to copy out all my work of which I approve and get it typed as a step towards possible publishing. Even if nobody will have them a complete typed copy would be a great convenience.

Wouldn't it be glorious if I were writing you the last letter of a term at Bookham, perhaps with an 'instalment', with all the rich harvest of the pleasant term behind me and the glorious liesure of the long summer holidays (with after dinner walks to the shrine of Tigliath-Pileser) before me. I knew then that those were good days, but I think now that I didn't prize them enough. Ahem!, the sunset appears to be making me sentimental: & yet its not sentiment at all but very certain truth. Doesn't the word 'ahem' breathe of old-fashioned novels?

---

34 Arthur's cousin Charles Edward Gribbon (1898–1938), mentioned in note 23 to the letter of 26 February 1916, had been a pupil at Campbell College 1904–14, and became a professional artist. Some of his pictures were bought by the Friends of the National Collection of Ireland.

35 'that I should do you the honour of being jealous'.

You accuse me of talking, 'as your own father might talk': and perhaps that is one thing you may find in me now – a vein of asceticism, almost of puritan practice without the puritan dogma. I believe in no God, least of all in one that would punish me for the 'lusts of the flesh':[36] but I do believe that I have in me a spirit, a chip, shall we say, of universal spirit; and that, since all good & joyful things are spiritual & non-material, I must be careful not to let matter (= nature = Satan, remember) get too great a hold on me, & dull the one spark I have.

Yours ever

Jack

TO HIS FATHER (LP V: 326–7):

Endsleigh Palace Hospital

[London]

12 June 1918

My dear Papy,

Thank you for both the letters, as the 'essay with enclosures' has followed me here, and indeed arrived shortly after the one I wrote, venturing to suggest that my score of letters was still one up. Peccavi: I most humbly apologise. 'And you wid a bronchitis in you.' (By the way it is not a whole shell in me, only a bit of one.) Seriously, I hope that before this you have got over any suggestion of the old trouble: you cannot be too careful in warding it off.

The brown suit arrived safely, together with some collars and ties which I had forgotten to ask for, but which either you or Mary had thoughtfully put in. I am now up and dressed and have been out a few times: you can well imagine how delightful it is for me to wear decent clothes again – to have pockets without buttons, and to be able to change one's tie from day to day. I have written to the transport officer of the battalion about my valise, but so far there is no answer: poor man, I expect he has other things to think about than my kit. And – who knows – perhaps even now a Teutonic unter offizier is sleeping in my blankets and improving his English on my bits of books.[37] Which reminds me,

---

36 *Book of Common Prayer*, the Catechism: 'I should renounce the devil and all his works, the pomps and vanity of this wicked world, and all the sinful lusts of the flesh.'

37 Warnie wrote to his father on 7 June saying: 'It is splendid to know that our "It" [Jack] is safely home at last. I confess it made me very uneasy when I heard that those damned hounds had been bombing base hospitals. And talking about that, did you see

though the reproach is usually the other way, on the only occasion when we took any prisoners, I was able to talk a little German to their officer, though he could speak no English to me.

My first day out here was enlivened by a taxi accident – some girl with a lorry ran into the cab in which I was, causing considerable damage to both machines but doing no harm otherwise. Since then I have had a solicitor's clerk round here asking me interminable questions: I have often been reminded of your friend's answer, 'I thought some damned fool would be sure to ask me, so I measured'. I consider that when the fates arrange little varieties of this sort for a man in search of peace, it is a very doubtful 'jeu d'esprit'.

I have since added to my new knowledge of Trollope 'The Warden' and 'Dr. Thorne'. Although it may seem strange that Warnie and I both neglect books that are at home and then afterwards read them elsewhere, there is a reason. A book must find you in the right mood, and its mere presence on a shelf will not create that mood, tho' it lie there for years: as well, when you meet 'in a strange land'[38] a book that is associated with home, it has for that very reason an attraction which it would not have at ordinary times. I am now at work, and very much at work on Hume's 'Treatise of Human Nature',[39] a new Maeterlinck and a new volume of Swinburne. I keep up a very brisk fire of correspondence on Literary and pseudo-scientific subjects with my Aunt Suffern: at this distance she is entertaining, but in a tête à tête 'no, a thousand times no'.

By the way, I have never seen anything but the proofs of those photos of us both, and I should be glad if you would send me the best. Which reminds me, what was the final verdict on your portrait? Is it still a sojourner in the drawing room? But we must settle all these things when I come home.

It is a great pity that you are laid up: there would be points about London for us two – I should like to go with you to the Abbey and the Temple and a few other places. (Just as I am making Arthur green with envy by my accounts of Charing Cross Road, 'a mile of bookshops'.) On Sunday I am going down to Bookham to see the sage: if only you could

---

that the fellow who was caught red handed was admitted into the hospital he had bombed, and had his wound treated. I'd have given him treatment forsooth.'

38 Exodus 2:22: 'I have been a stranger in a strange land.'

39 David Hume, *A Treatise of Human Nature* (1739).

make the same pilgrimage! I must go and be massaged now, take care of yourself.

your loving son,
Jack

TO ARTHUR GREEVES (W):

[Endsleigh Palace Hospital,
London]
Monday [17 June 1918]

My dear Galahad,

Now will I make you envious. On Friday night I went to Drury Lane to hear 'The Valkyrie'.[40] The dream of years has been realised, and without disillusionment: I have had thrills and delights of the real old sort, I have felt as I felt five years ago.

We had difficulty in getting seats, and from those which we had we could only see one side of the stage. I was also much worried by the people that sat near us. Not that they were philistines and talked, but their very enthusiasm made them a nuisance. One little man in front of me was so moved that at several interesting points he stood up, until at last I became so exasperated that I caught him by his coat tails and pulled him into his seat. Another, who was following the score, kept on giving vent to quite audible criticisms such as 'Louder, Louder!' or 'No, no, no' whenever the conductor's design differed from his own.

But the performance was beyond all words. The first act as you remember is in Hunding's hut with the tree growing in it: and towards the end you remember how Siegmund draws the sword and how they throw open the great doors at the back. This showed us a most beautiful scene of distant snow covered peaks and a wild valley. The lighting gave a really unusual impression of spring moon light, and that combined with the glorious love-music of the orchestra (you remember the spring song?) simply swept you away – and then all the time creeping in under this the faint horn blown motive of the sword and the far-off tinkling hammers to remind you of the Niblungs – oh, ami, it was simply heaven! But the next act which opens in 'A wild rocky place' – represented not conventionally but with real sympathy – and Brünhilde singing 'Moi-a-

---

40 The performance on 14 June of Wagner's *The Valkyrie* was conducted by Sir Thomas Beecham and there is a notice about it in *The Times* (15 June 1918), p. 3.

a-hei' (you know) was even better. She, it is true, was a trifle full-breasted and operatic, but as the interest of the scene went on, one forgot that. Wotan was magnificent whenever he came on, and all his music is splendid – there are whole hours of music just as wonderful as the little bits we know: the singing was in English, and so clear and un-strained that with my knowledge of the story, I could follow nearly all the dialogue, and so all the poetic and romantic pleasure came to help the musical. As a spectacle the third act was the best, where Brünhilde is hiding from Wotan. The stage is almost dark, lit only from time to time by flashes of lightening, as the angry god draws nearer and nearer and at last enters in a glare of red light, glinting on the huge raven-wings of his helmet and the rings of his mail – one gleaming figure in that sinister gloom – and the music, I cannot describe it. Most unfortunately it was so late that I had to come away before the end, and miss the fire music: but I was so full of delights that I could hardly find it in my heart to grumble.

Looking back, what pleases me most was the training of all the singers together and the entire absence of strain: none of your Italian screaming and contortions. There was no famous name in the caste, and no-one except Brünhilde had a voice of any unusual power: but the beauty was that they never tried to sing louder than they could, and were content to sacrifice power to real beauty – playing into each other's hands and making it all musical dialogue NOT mere duets. You felt that they all loved the Ring and took it seriously not merely as an opportunity for noise. Sieglindë particularly, with a sweet voice and clear enunciation, *acted* very well, quietly & naturally not in the usual operatic style. And oh! the blessèd absence of a chorus! So you have my verdict that if the Ring is all like this it quite comes up to our old dreams, and that all Italian opera is merely a passtime compared with the great music-drama of Wagner. In spite of all our efforts we could not get a programme and so I cannot send you one.

To descend from the windswept eerie's of the swan-maidens to a further argument about the Dry Tree may seem bathos: but as you have agreed to go on with it, let us do so. The subject is of great interest too.

Of course we all start with the idea that our senses put us in direct contact with reality – you think that your eyes are windows by which your brain 'sees' the world. But science teaches you that your eye, or rather the nerve of your eye, is merely a telegraph wire. It's vibration produces a feeling in your brain which we call colour etc.: but what the

Something at the other end which starts the vibration may be, of this no human being can have any conception. No increase of our sensory keenness, no microscope or teloscope can put us in any direct relation with the Thing: we still remain dependant on this long chain of communications, travelling by vibration from atom to atom: and we can never have any proof that the sensation which it produces in our brain conveys any true idea of the external Thing. Nay the thing *must* be quite different from our conception of it: for we necessarily concieve it in terms of the senses – we think of any object as having a certain size, shape, colour and feel. But all these are only the names of our own sensations: take size, which may seem at first to be outside ourselves. On the table lies my pipe: if I wish to have an idea of the size of this I naturally handle it: in other words I send out a *will* from my brain (which I call 'moving my hand') and presently a set of impressions come back to me – smoothness, hardness, width and the rest. It is true that at the same time as these come along my touch-nerves another set of brown-ness, shininess, rotundity etc come along my visual-nerves. And if I repeat the action ten times I find that the same set of sight-impressions always accompanies the same set of touch-ones: in other words what looks a pipe, always feels a pipe too. But this brings me no nearer to the real pipe: I can only think of it as long, brown, smooth, hard and rounded: therefore think of it wrongly, since length, smoothness, brown-ness, hardness and rotundity are feelings in my brain, and cannot belong to the real pipe at all. (Shape, which was bothering you, is of course on the same footing as colour or hardness: it can only be apprehended thro' the same chain of communication, by the senses of touch or sight, and therefore is in me not in the external Thing). Hence you see we are driven to the conclusion that we have no knowledge of the external world: that it is concievable that there IS no external world at all, and that if it does exist it must be quite different from our usual ideas of it. A good many modern scientists think that 'matter' consists of atoms which are not (as we used to think) small solid bodies but merely points of force and that all the phenomena of matter can be attributed to the inter-action of these forces. If you are still interested in these subjects I will talk in another letter about the various conclusions which philosophers have drawn from this ignorance which we are forced to acknowledge, and the ways by which they have tried to escape from it.

I have sent you two books from Hatchards' of Picadilly: whether you have them already or would care to have them, I can't say, but you will have no difficulty in changing them. I finished my last letter in rather a hurry, and can't remember whether I referred to your drawing in them: I am glad you are going on with it. The absence of models, as far as hands, limbs, folds of clothes, etc go could be helped by the looking-glass, which I imagine is an excellent teacher. How fine it will be when you can get me up in your room again and show me all your new work and all your new treasures. I too shall have plenty for you to see: I have sent home a fine edition of Yeats which I have been wanting for ages, and have bought here Dent's Malory with designs by Beardesly. It is a beautiful book, with a handsome binding, good paper and a fair page: there are lovely chapter headings and decorations, and somehow a great big book suits Malory, doesn't it? In that same shop, Bain's, where I got this they showed me some of Morris's Kelmscott Press books, including the Chaucer, very rare and now at £82. I suppose it is bad taste on my part, but I don't care for Morris's type, it is much too ornate and difficult to read. Ordinary old black-letter I should much prefer.

By the way, <if you have alone established 'Uranianism' in your own mind as something virtuous and natural, I must remind you that for men in ordinary sexual arrangements, a promiscuous desire for every beautiful person you meet is usually disapproved of. Your talk about continually meeting people and having to conceal your feelings suggests that you have no intention of confining yourself to one love: but perhaps I have misunderstood you.>

On Sunday we were down at Bookham and I called at Gastons. You can imagine how strange it was to go back now among those old scenes and people.

I think I have talked enough now. Addio, write by return.

Yours
Jack

TO HIS FATHER (LP V: 329–31):

> [Endsleigh Palace Hospital,
> London
> 20? June 1918]

My dear Papy,

On Sunday I made my pilgrimage. Even to go to Waterloo was an adventure full of memories, and every station that I passed on the way down seemed to clear away another layer of the time that passed and bring me back to the old life.

Bookham was as its best: a mass of green, very pleasing to one 'that has been long in city pent'.[41] As I walked up to Gastons the familiar road was crowded with good people coming back from church, and I passed many a stuffy old couple whom I remembered well, though none of them recognised me. It was like being a ghost: I opened the gate of Kirk's garden almost with stealth and went on past the house, to the vegetable garden and the little wild orchard with the pond, where I had sat so often on hot Sunday afternoons, and practised skating with Terry when the long frost began two years ago.

And there among the cabbages, in his shirt and 'Sunday' trousers, there sure enough was the old man, still digging and smoking his villainous pipe. His back was towards me and I had come within a few paces of him before he turned and saw me. And so I was led into the house with much triumph and displayed to Mrs K., whom we found fussing with the maid just as of old. I have seldom spent a more delightful afternoon: what 'crack' we had, what reminiscences, how often my opinions were shown to be based ('bazed' as the sage pronounces it) on an insufficient knowledge of the subject! When I told him that it was by an English shell I was hit, it called forth a magnificent Tirade on the 'simple mathematical problem' of calculating how a gun's range would shorten as it got heated by firing – on the 'every school boy knows' lines.

I have bought an edition of Yeats[42] which I ordered the bookseller to send home and which should have arrived by this time. Of course I need not add that you are welcome to open the parcel, if you would care to. Arthur at any rate would like to see it, and if you replace the books in their boxes they will be safe from dust and damp until I come home. I hope you do not think it extravagant in me to have bought such a thing, for I knew it was a limited edition which would be very much dearer in a few years' time. In the same shop where I made this purchase, I'm afraid I gave myself away badly. What first tempted me to go in was a battered copy of Burton's Anatomy: as you know, I had been looking for this and thought here was an opportunity of picking up a cheap second hand

---

41 John Keats, 'To one who has been long in city pent' (1817), l. 1.
42 This was probably *The Collected Works of William Butler Yeats in Verse and Prose* in eight volumes, published in 1908 by the Shakespeare Head Press.

copy. I went in and requested a courtly old gentleman to let me see it. 'H'm', said I, glancing over the dirty little volume, 'it seems rather worn: haven't you a newer copy?' The gentleman looked at me in rather a pained way and said that he had not. 'Well, how much is it?' I asked, expecting a considerable reduction. 'Twenty-five guineas' said my friend with a bland smile. Ye Gods! Just think of it: there was I for the first time in my life fingering a really valuable old edition and asking for a 'NEWER' copy. I turned hot all over: and even you as you read, will blush for the credit of the clan. However, the old gentleman was very forgiving: he turned his treasury inside out for me. He showed me priceless old copies of Vergil and Rabelais, books from the Kelmscott Press, including the Chaucer at £82 and strange forgotten waifs of French literature with stiff engravings 'from the age of snuff boxes and fans'. And so what could I do but bring away the Yeats? Apropos of Beardsley, he told me that the 'fleshly' artist had often been in that shop and had finally gone the way of all mortal things without paying his account. Well, 'et ego in Arcadia Vixi,'[43] it is something to have been in the shop of James Bain even for an hour.

It seems that now-a-days one is sent from hospital to be kept for some time in a 'convalescent home' before going on leave. Of course I have asked to be sent to an Irish one, but there are only a few of these and they are already crowded: we must not therefore expect too much. But wherever I am I know that you will come and see me. You know I have some difficulty in talking of the greatest things: it is the fault of our generation and of the English schools. But at least you will believe that I was never before so eager to cling to every bit of our old home life and to see you. I know I have often been far from what I should in my relations to you, and have undervalued an affection and a generosity which (as I said somewhere else) an experience of 'other people's parents' has shown me in a new light. But, please God, I shall do better in the future. Come and see me. I am homesick, that is the long and the short of it.

I have been once or twice to the English Opera at Drury Lane and seen among other things my long desired 'Valkyrie' and Faust again – full of reminiscences of course. This week Mrs. Moore has been up on a visit to her sister who works at the War Office, and we have seen a good

---

43 'I too have lived in Arcadia.' Lewis was here altering the anonymous tomb inscription, 'Et in Arcadia ego', which is often depicted on classical paintings.

deal of each other. I think it some comfort to her to be with someone who was a friend of Paddy's and is a link with the Oxford days: she has certainly been a very, very good friend to me.

I was much cheered this afternoon by a visit from Kelsie [Ewart]: who is in excellent spirits but looked to me very poorly – perhaps it is my imagination. I will wire to you as soon as there is any talk of my being moved. Do not count on Ireland: but at all events, come. The wound on my leg is still bothering me a bit, although it was the smallest I had. The bandage – just above the knee – is always slipping, and descended to my ankle the other day in the middle of Piccadilly, necessitating urgent calls for a taxi.

Good night: nurse the old chest and write soon and long,

your loving son

Jack

TO HIS FATHER (LP VI: 17–18):

[Ashton Court,
Long Ashton,
Clifton, Bristol
29 June 1918][44]
Saturday.

My dear Papy,

Surely this is the most unfortunate thing that ever happened to us! I was prepared to be disappointed in my efforts to be sent to an Irish convalescent home, but this is the very acme of ill luck. When they finally told me in London that I could not go to Ireland, they asked me to choose some part of England: at first I said London, thinking that this would be more convenient for you than any provincial town, but this could not be done. I then elected Bristol, where I could have the society of Mrs Moore, and also of Perrett of the Somersets, whose being wounded some days before myself I mentioned to you. Little could I foresee what was going to happen: we are still close prisoners, and have had several tests of blood and excreta taken – the one painful, the other disgusting.

All the 'gilded youth' among the patients, who have no interests in themselves, of course grow more troublesome being confined. The place

---

44 Lewis, as he mentions in this letter, hoped to be transferred to an Irish hospital, but he was sent to Ashton Court instead, arriving there on 25 June.

echoes to the crack of their billiard balls and their loud, tuneless whistling: I was very miserable for the first few days until I discovered a little, almost disused writing room at one end of the house. Here I can sit in comparative safety and read Burton's anatomy[45] which I have had sent from town.

If I should happen to get the disease I suppose all my bits of things will be burned. I could sit down and cry over the whole business: and yet of course we have both much to be thankful for. When a man can sleep between sheets as long as he will, sit in arm chairs, and have no fears, it is peevish to complain. If I had not been wounded when I was, I should have gone through a terrible time. Nearly all my friends in the Battalion are gone. Did I ever mention Johnson who was a scholar of Queens? I had hoped to meet him at Oxford some day, and renew the endless talks that we had out there. 'Dis aliter visum',[46] he is dead. I had had him so often in my thoughts, had so often hit on some new point in one of our arguments, and made a note of things in my reading to tell him when we met again, that I can hardly believe he is dead. Don't you find it particularly hard to realise the death of people whose strong personality makes them particularly alive: with the ordinary sons of Belial who eat and drink and are merry, it is not so hard.

But I must not enlarge on a melancholy subject: I have no doubt that we are all three of us pretty low. However, 'better luck next time': this cannot last for ever and I hope yet to have a visit from you. As for my own health it is pretty good, although the wound in the leg – the smallest of the three – is still giving some trouble. The house here is the survival, tho' altered by continual rebuilding, of a thirteenth-century castle: the greater part is now stucco work of the worst Victorian period (à la Norwood Towers) but we have one or two fine old paintings and a ghost. I haven't met it yet and have not much hope to – indeed if poor Johnson's ghost would come walking into the lonely writing room this minute, I should be glad enough. Greatly to my chagrin the library is locked up. The park is several miles in extent, very pleasant and stocked with deer: once or twice while wandering in the bracken I have suddenly come

---

45 Lewis's copy of Burton's *The Anatomy of Melancholy* was one brought out by Chatto & Windus in 1907. Lewis kept this edition all his life and some of its many annotations were no doubt made at Ashton Court.

46 'It seemed otherwise to the gods'. Laurence Bertrand Johnson (see note 138 to letter of 4 November 1917) was killed by the shell which wounded Lewis.

upon the solemn face and branching antlers of a stag, within a few feet of me. He examines me for a moment, then snorts, kicks up his heels, and is gone: a second later, head after head comes up – his panic has reached the rest of the herd, and they too scamper off after him like the wind.

A most generous and welcome consignment of smokeables came this morning. Communication with the town is scanty now of course, and this is a most welcome addition to our diminishing stocks: what is more, such little attentions are infinitely cheering when one is dull, lonely and disappointed. With many thanks and best love, I am

your loving
son Jack

P.S. Please let Arthur know my change of address and tell him that I will write soon. yours, J.

TO ARTHUR GREEVES (W):

[Ashton Court,
Long Ashton,
Clifton, Bristol
17? July 1918]

My dear Arthur,

I am truly sorry to have left you so long without a letter. My best excuse is that already 'my hand aches and my eyes grow weary' with writing, for I am at present busily engaged in copying out the final version of my poems: in a few days the new MS. will be ready for the typist and when it returns thence it will begin the round of the publishers. I shall start with the famous houses and go on until I have exhausted all that I can hear of: even if it is unsuccessful all round, I may pick up some useful criticisms, and at any rate it will be well to have a typed copy.

Of course the book now is very different from the one you have, by the insertion of several new pieces and the alteration or omission of some of the old. The arrangement I find particularly difficult and besides I am beginning to grow nervy and distrust my own judgement. It is so hard to know whether you are improving or spoiling a thing.

This will partly explain my silence, tho' of course I know I should have written. But, ami, you must never suppose when I don't write that this means any change in my feelings or any loss of touch with the old life – put it down to laziness or forgetfulness or other occupations rather than to that. When I have got the MS. off (it used to be my love but is now becoming more my tyrant!) I will write you a longer and better letter. In the meantime I will just run over my news up to date and then say good-bye.

My last adventures before leaving town were a visit to 'Faust' and to 'Tosca'.[47] With the former I was disgusted: the crowded stage, the conventionality, the noisy comic-opera scenes of drinking, the choruses etc were really too much after the 'Valkyrie'. The church scene was very well done I admit: but on the whole I got very little pleasure out of it. Of course if I were a real musician like you I should appreciate this kind of music too 'in its own way' and get a sort of critical & historical interest out of it to make up for the sheer ecstasy of modern music: but then literature is my province, and in music I can only afford to enjoy the music that really suits me. By the way they had the whole ballet, which is very rarely done now I suppose, as a separate scene. The dancing was very uninspired and I didn't care for the music, but you would have agreed with me in praising the setting – which was a wild open place done in the style of Heath Robinson: in the back ground was a typical absurdly beautiful mountain of his, and steep little vallies, and big masses of pink cloud. The whole was lighted to represent early summer morning and gave a fine impression of loneliness.

'Tosca' I revelled in: from beginning to end I enjoyed it, and it seemed to my untutored ears to be very well sung – tho' not of course with the solemnity of the 'Valkyrie' (you see I cannot help harking back to that, it was immeasurably beyond anything I had seen or hoped to see so gloriously un-operatic – in the silly sense). Puccini certainly has a wonderful richness of orchestration and a sort of continuity – hasn't he? None of those nasty gaps that you have in 'Faust' where one 'number' (loathsome word) has ended and the other begins, like pieces in a concert: 'E lucevan le stelle' was quite up to expectations.

The books which you returned did not arrive until I had left London – but don't bother about that: I have decided to keep 'Peacock Pie'[48] and can easily dispose of the others. As it seems impossible to get what would

---

47 The production of Giacomo Puccini's opera, *Tosca* (1900), which Lewis saw on 21 June is reviewed in *The Times* (22 June 1918), p. 3.
48 Walter de la Mare, *Peacock Pie: A Book of Rhymes* (1913).

suit you 'by the light of nature' I am sending you the wherewithal to choose for yourself at Mullan's. This is an unconventional way of giving a present, but you are too sensible to mind that. I will tell you all my details in my next letter. Bear with me.

Yours ever

Jack

TO HIS FATHER (LP VI: 11):

Ashton Court.
Monday.
[29? July 1918]

My dear Papy,

You can imagine how mystified I was by an envelope from the U.V.F. – the contents too were unexpected.[49] In some ways this scheme has given me to think: you see the Board which sate upon me in London gave me two months convalescence which will be finished on the 4th of August. It appears however in this hospital, if you are quiet and inoffensive and keep yourself well out of the notice of the authorities, you may be often left for several weeks after your time. The great danger about this change would be that of getting the reply 'If you are so anxious to move, we will have you boarded at once and discharged from hospital.' Such a procedure would of course hasten my return to France. The amount of leave I get after hospital (whatever it may be) will not be influenced by the time which I have spent in the former, and it is therefore to our interest to prolong the hospital period to the utmost. The smaller Irish hospitals are notoriously strict and up to time with their Boards.

I must admit too, I should be sorry to give up the idea of your coming to visit me here: it would give me great pleasure for you to meet Mrs. Moore, and I feel that this visit to me is the only excuse on which you will ever get away for a while from Belfast and the office. If you were at the office all day and I had to be back at the hospital at 6 or 7 every night, it would be hardly worth while coming to a hospital at home. Here we could have a delightful little holiday together.

I am the more ready to put off any change because of the fact which I had forgotten to tell you – namely that the 3rd Somersets are in

---

49 Albert Lewis was trying to get Jack into the Ulster Volunteer Force, hoping this way to get him transferred to Ireland.

Holywood Barracks, and during the period of home service which will follow my leave I shall be able to dine with you every evening, and perhaps even to sleep at home: I shall also be able to get a week end off from time to time. For all these reasons I have thought it better to make no move in the matter. Write and tell me what you think: I hope you will come over here and talk the matter over in person. This is of course only a 'business' letter: I will write again to take away any reproach in the matter of correspondence.

your loving
son Jack

TO ARTHUR GREEVES (W):

[Ashton Court,
Bristol]
Wednesday [7 August 1918]

My dear Arthur,

The fact of trying to publish a book at once makes you regard publishers in quite a new light. When you sit down to consider where you will send it first, you immediately realize the enormous prestige of Macmillan – when you come to think of it, everyone who is published by them gains a certain importance from that very fact. I looked upon acceptance by them as a goal almost beyond hope, and sent my MS. to them first. Needless to say it has come back, accompanied by the following note: – 'Dear Sir, We duly received your manuscript entitled "Spirits in Prison: A cycle of lyrical poems", by Clive Staples, and regret to say that we do not see our way to undertake its publication. Some of the shorter nature poems seem to us to have no little charm, but we do not feel that the collection as a whole would be likely to appeal to any considerable public. We beg therefore to return the MS. with thanks. We are, yours faithfully, Macmillan and Co. Ltd.'

This is at any rate courteous and I suppose not very discouraging: perhaps, however, they always sweeten their refusals with some little complement. However that may be, I am determined not to lose heart until I have tried all the houses I can hear of. I am sending it to Heinneman next – they seem to publish a fair amount of new poetry. From the title which I have given my collection, you will gather that it differs in many ways from the one which you possess.

I find I am getting very slack and idle. My serious reading at present is

Burton's Anatomy of Melancholy, as published in one big volume by Chatto & Windus at 7/-.[50] The paper and type are of a good, plain quality, but the binding is not attractive. I get on with it very slowly, and have intermixed with it a new book called 'A Schoolmaster's Diary',[51] which interests me being mainly on education and literature. I also read a good deal of Wordsworth in my Everyman. You remember perhaps how violent my criticisms on him once were, but I am becoming a reformed character. I feel very weak and tired these days and inclined to lose interest in anything that needs continued attention. If only I could get my book accepted it would give me a tremendous fillip and take my mind off the future. In my present mood few things have pleased me more than Macdonald's 'The Goblin and the Princess',[52] which I borrowed from Maureen Moore. This child has a well stocked library of fairy tales which form her continual reading – an excellent taste at her age, I think, which will lead her in later life to romance and poetry and not to the twaddling novels that make up the diet of most educated women apparently. I am getting the Life of Thomas More in the Temple Classics.[53]

Forgive me if I don't write any more, I don't feel like it to day. It is terribly hot, which you know I hate.

Yours

Jack

TO ARTHUR GREEVES (W):

[Ashton Court,
Bristol
31 August 1918]

My dear Arthur,

In spite of the loneliness and melancholy of which you complain I must begin by congratulating you on the excellent time which you had in Dublin and the interesting people whom you met. Indeed I think you are

---

50 Richard Burton, *The Anatomy of Melancholy; What it is with all the Kinds Causes Symptoms Prognostics & Several Cures of It, In Three Partitions with the Several Sections Members & Subsections Philosophically Medicinally Historically Opened & Cut Up by 'Democritus Junior' ['Robert Burton'] with a Satirical Preface Conducing to the Following Discourse* (Chatto & Windus, 1907). See note 45 to letter of 29 June 1918.

51 Stuart Petre Brodie Mais, *A Schoolmaster's Diary* (1918).

52 George MacDonald, *The Princess and the Goblin* (1871).

53 Ann Manning, *The Household of Sir Thomas More*, with *The Life of Sir Thomas More* by William Roper, Introduction by Ernest Rhys, Temple Classics (1906).

as much to be envied as anyone I know: you live in comfort, surrounded by interests, in pleasant society, and are not a slave of the state and do not have the menace of France hanging over your head. When you were toiling in the office how you would have looked forward to this time if you had known it was coming! How many men to-day, living in holes and mud heaps, driven, hunted, terrified, verminous, starved for sleep, hopeless, would give their very souls to change places with you even for twenty four hours. And yet of course we can all be discontented in any circumstances, and I dare say I should be just the same in your place.

So you are inclining to the New Ireland school are you? I remember you used rather to laugh at my Irish enthusiasm in the old days when you were still an orthodox Ulsterman. I am glad you begin to think otherwise: a poetry bookshop for Ireland, in Dublin, would be a most praiseworthy undertaking: it might also bring out some monthly journal on Irish literature, containing reviews of contemporary books, articles on classical Gaelic literature and language, and a few poems and sketches. The idea is fascinating: if you could get some big man to take it up. I should like very much indeed to meet your friend Parker: it is a grand idea to build a house after a dream. What talks you all must have had. Were they purely literary or did they talk anything about religion and philosophy? I suppose that set are mostly mystics, rosacrutians and the like. Here I must indulge my love of preaching by warning you not to get too much bound up in a cult. Between your other penchant .... and the Irish school you might get into a sort of little by-way of the intellectual world, off the main track and loose yourself there. Remember that the great minds, Milton, Scott, Mozart and so on, are always sane before all and keep in the broad highway of thought and feel what can be felt by all men, not only by a few. Attractive as they are these side-tracks are always a little decadent if one lives wholly in them. But I suppose your good solid old faith in history and 'stodge' will keep you from that danger.

It is partly through this feeling that I have not begun by sending my MS. to Maunsels: it would associate me too definitely with a cult and partly because their paper and binding are rather poor. I suppose none of your friends have any influence at Maunsels that might be of use to me?

I have just finished reading a very pleasant book called 'The Four Men', by Hillaire Belloc.[54] I always imagined that his books were of a very

---

54 Hilaire Belloc, *The Four Men: A Farrago* [1912].

different kind but this is rather in the style of Lavengro, only, it seems to me, more homely and humorous: in one or two places where the four wanderers sit in a little forest hut smoking and telling tales it rather reminds me of the 'Crock of Gold'. I began to read the 'Egoist'[55] and after five pages came to the conclusion that it was one of the worst books I had ever seen or heard of. I don't know how you can stand Meredith's affectation. By the bye, 'The Four Men' is in the 1/- Nelson blue edition with quite nice pen and ink sketches. I should not advise you to try Burton. I have got stuck with him and I think he would be less in your line than in mine. Oh don't you sometimes feel that everything is dead? I feel, and apparently you feel, a sort of impossibility in getting on solidly with any serious book in the way we used to do.

Yours
Jack

TO HIS FATHER (LP VI: 26–7):

> Ashton Court,
> Long Ashton,
> Clifton.
> 3 September 1918

My dear Papy,

Ever since my last letter to you I have been almost daily expecting to hear from you, and I am rather surprised that neither my answer to your proposal nor my suggestion that you should come over here has met with any reply. Have you not yet decided on a date for coming over? It is four months now since I returned from France, and my friends laughingly suggest that 'my father in Ireland' of whom they hear is a mythical creation like Mrs Harris.[56]

As to my decision, I think you will agree that it has already justified itself. I am now nearly a month over my time, and even if I were boarded tomorrow this would be so much to the good. Of course in the present need for men, being passed fit by a board would mean a pretty quick return to France. I am afraid there is not much possibility of the 'job at home' which you once thought might be the result of my wounds: although not quite well I am almost 'fit' now in the military sense of the

---

55 George Meredith, *The Egoist* (1879).
56 The mythical friend of Mrs Gamp in Charles Dickens' *Martin Chuzzlewit* (1843–4).

word, and depend only on the forgetfulness of the authorities for my continued stay in hospital. Of course this has nothing to do with my leave.

I hope there is nothing wrong and that I shall soon hear from you again and see you here. I know there are difficulties in the way, but I suppose they are no more serious now than when Warnie was at home. With best love, I am,

your loving son,
Jack

TO HIS FATHER (LP VI: 30–1):

Ashton Court,
Long Ashton.
Clifton.
9 September 1918

My dear Papy,

I write in haste to give you a piece of news which I hope will please you not much less than it did me. You are aware that for some years now I have amused myself by writing verses, and a pocket book collection of these followed me through France. Since my return I have occupied myself in revising these, getting them typed with a few additions, and trying to publish them. After a refusal from Macmillans they have, somewhat to my surprise, been accepted by Heinemann. Wm. Heinemann thinks it would 'be well to reconsider the inclusion of one or two pieces which are not perhaps on a level with my best work'. I have sent him some new ones as substitutes for these and things are going on well, although his absence from town on a fortnight's holiday will cause a delay in coming to a definite arrangement about money.

I don't know when I may hope actually to see the book, but of course I will send you a copy at once. It is called 'Spirits in Prison: a cycle of lyrical poems by Clive Staples'. The paper and printing will probably be detestable, as they always are now-a-days. This little success gives me a pleasure which is perhaps childish and yet akin to greater things.

Hoping that I shall soon have some answer from you, I am,
your loving son,
Jack

TO ARTHUR GREEVES (W):

56 Ravenswood Rd.,

Redland,

Bristol.

[12 September 1918]

My dear Arthur,

The best of news! After keeping my MS. for ages Heinemann has actually accepted it. 'Wm. Heinemann' – apparently there is a real Mr Heinnemann – writes to say that he 'will be pleased to become its publisher'. He adds that it may be well to re-consider the inclusion of some of the pieces 'which are not perhaps on a level with my best work'. I wrote back thanking him and telling him there were a few new pieces that he might care to use as substitutions for ones he omits. An answer came back this time from a man called Evans, the managing director asking me to send the new pieces and saying that Heinemann himself was out of town for a week or so.[57] I sent him 5 new poems by return – and so things are going on very well although I'm afraid Heinemann's holiday will cause some delay. You can imagine how pleased I am, and how eagerly I now look at all Heinemann's books and wonder what mine will be like. I'm afraid the paper will be poor as it always is now in new books.

It is going to be called 'Spirits in Prison'[58] by Clive Staples & is mainly strung round the idea that I mentioned to you before – that nature is wholly diabolical & malevolent and that God, if he exists, is outside of and in opposition to the cosmic arrangements. I'm afraid you will find a good many of your favourite ones left out: I thought very carefully over them but I think we all have to follow our own judgement in the end.

On no account tell my father that you know anything about it, as he might be hurt at not having been taken into my confidence: I will let him know myself when I next write (I have written to him since at your instance) and you must hear it from him as news or else pretend that you have just heard. *Of course* don't say anything to the Strandtown fraternity.

I am glad to see that you are more cheerful in your last letter. I don't think I shall follow your advice to try George Meredith again. There is so

---

57 These letters from William Heinemann (1863–1920) and Charles Sheldon Evans (1883–1944) of 3 and 5 September respectively are found in LP VI: 31–2.

58 1 Peter 3:19: Christ 'went and preached unto the spirits in prison'.

much good stuff to read that it is wasteful to spend time on affectations. You are quite right about Emerson.[59] I often pick him up here for an odd quarter of an hour, and go away full of new ideas. Every sentence is weighty: he puts into paragraphs what others, seeking charm, expand into whole essays or chapters. At the same time his tense concentration makes him painful reading, he gives you no rest. I don't know why you object to his style – it seems to me admirable. Quel dommage that such a man should be an American.

I have read (in a borrowed copy) 'King Lear's Wife' and also 'The End of the World' which is in the same volume.[60] Bottomley's play seems very closely copied from Yeats, but very good. I prefer the other on the whole – tho' I think better of humanity and believe that quite ordinary folk would face 'The fire that was before the world was made' with less hysteria than Huff and his circle.[61]

Must stop now – good bye –
Yours
Jack

P.S. Board[62] is overdue & may it continue so.

TO HIS FATHER (LP VI: 34):

Ashton Court,
Long Ashton,
Clifton.
14 September 1918

My dear Papy,

I am sorry that you should have been so troubled as you were when you last wrote to me, and sorrier still that I should have been to any extent the cause of it. At the same time it is only fair to add that I do not entirely acquiesce in the blame which you lay upon me. Above all, the joking reference to 'Mrs Harris' which you take 'au pied de la lettre'

---

59 Ralph Waldo Emerson (1803–82).

60 *Georgian Poetry 1913–1915*, ed. E[dward] M[arsh] (1915). 'King Lear's Wife' is by Gordon Bottomley (pp. 3–47) and 'The End of the World' by Lascelles Abercrombie (pp. 195–239).

61 A line from Act I of 'The End of the World' (p. 205). Huff is a character in that play.

62 The army medical board who would decide whether or not Lewis should return to active duty.

was quite harmlessly meant. I do not choose my friends among people who jeer, nor has a tendency to promiscuous confidence ever been one of my characteristic faults. However perhaps it was tactless, and there is no need to go into it further.

Many thanks for the 'monies numbered' and the parcel. Those Virginian cigarettes which you have sent me several times are a good brand. Are matches obtainable at home? We are very badly off for them here: hardly any tobacconist will give you a box, and grocers only give a small weekly allowance to their regular customers.

I was very much cheered by your telegram. Such things are the most valuable part of the successes which they accompany. I hope I have not led you to expect too much: the publisher is only the first fence in our steeplechase – the book may still be badly reviewed or not reviewed at all, may fail to sell, or your own taste and judgement may be disappointed in it. The news I need hardly say should be communicated with discretion to the 'hoi polloi'. Heinemann is still out of town, so nothing further can be done just at present.

I expect this letter will again cross yours, but it seems our fate.

your loving son,

Jack

TO HIS FATHER (LP VI: 36–7):

Ashton Court,
Long Ashton,
Clifton.
18 September 1918

My dear Papy,

Many thanks for your cheering and encouraging letter and for the enclosure. I knew that I could count on your sharing my interests on this subject and already the suggestions you make are most valuable.

It had quite escaped my notice that Hichens had written a novel called 'Spirits in prison', but now that you mention it, I think that you are right – or perhaps it is 'A spirit in Prison' – the resemblance at any rate is close enough to hit that title on the head.[63] I don't know whether I shall be able to find another that expresses so aptly the general scheme of the book, but we must do our best. The sub-title 'A cycle of lyrical poems' was not

---

63 Robert Hitchens, *A Spirit in Prison* (1908).

given without a reason: the reason is that the book is not a collection of really independant pieces, but the working out, loosely of course and with digressions, of a general idea. If you can imagine 'In Memoriam'[64] with its various parts in different metres it will give you some idea of the form I have tried to adopt. Such merit as it has depends less on the individual than on the combined effect of the pieces. To call it a cycle is to prepare the reader for this plan and to induce him to follow the order of the poems as I have put them. Probably he will not, but we must do our best.

At the same time I admit that the word 'cycle' is a very objectionable one. The only others which I know to express the same thing are 'series' and 'sequence' and of those the former is hardly definite enough and the latter in my opinion more affected and precieux than 'cycle' itself. Of course one could dispense with a sub-title altogether, but I rather approve of the old practice by which a book gives some account of itself – as 'Paradise Lost – a heroic poem in twelve books' – 'The Pilgrim's Progress – being an account of his journey from this world to the next'. Perhaps you can suggest some simpler and more dignified way of saying that the book is a whole and not a collection.

My only reason for choosing a pseudonym at all was a natural feeling that I should not care to have this bit of my life known in the regiment. One doesn't want either officers or men to talk about 'our b—y lyrical poet again' whenever I make a mistake. But perhaps it is silly to attach importance to that. Simply 'Clive Lewis' would be better in many ways than any faked name. The objections to the name 'Staples' had not occurred to me, but I am afraid they are only too true. At one time I thought of anagraming Lewis into 'Wiles' or 'Welis' but I give it up as a trifle fantastic. On the whole it is more straightforward to put ones own name on the cover to take its fortune, and since I agree with you about Staples, we may as well drop the disguise altogether.

Mrs. Moore had received news at last of her son's death: I suppose it is best to know, and fortunately she never cherished any hopes. Never a day passes but I thankfully realize my great good fortune in getting wounded when I did and thus being spared the very deadly months that followed.

With best love,

your loving son,

Jack

---

64 Tennyson, *In Memoriam A.H.H.*

TO HIS FATHER (LP VI: 45–6):

Ashton Court,
Long Ashton,
Clifton.
Postmark: 3 October 1918

My dear Papy,

Thank you for your letter and for the parcel of cigarettes. I am well enough off for underclothing etc., and have been able to get a local tailor to make a quite satisfactory khaki suit to replace the one which was cut up at the dressing station.

Now as to the question of this word 'cycle'. In its primitive sense it does undoubtedly mean, as you say, simply a wheel or circle. I think however that there is lots of precedent for using it to mean a series. For one thing, to use your own example, Wagner's 'Ring' is called a cycle: for another, the German lyric poets have always used the name 'a song cycle' to describe a series of songs, and following them, Tennyson wrote 'The Swallows – A Cycle', which was set to music by Sullivan.[65] Again, in critical books hasn't one often heard it used in that way? 'The cycle of legends clustering round the Grail Story', or say that 'The Iliad probably represents the combination of a whole cycle of "independant lays"'. Why the word should be used in that sense I don't know, but I think there is sufficiently good authority. I think 'Spirits in Bondage' would be a good substitute for the old title and would sound well: 'Spirits in Bonds' would not do so well, and suggests tiresome jokes about whiskey. I think it is only natural to describe it as a Cycle of poems, just to say 'a cycle' is rather unintelligible. After all I'm not claiming that they are good poems – you know the schoolboy's definitions, 'Prose is when the lines go on to the end of the page: poetry is when they don't.'

The more I think of it the less I like anonymity. If it wasn't for the army I'd let my own name take its chance. Don't you think Clive is too famous a surname to take as a nom de plume (just as we thought Staples too notorious)? Of course we must always remember that the people who are most likely to talk of 'our b****y poet' are also the least likely to hear anything about it; they don't haunt bookshops, nor do they read literary papers.

---

65 Those works of Alfred, Lord Tennyson set to music by Arthur Sullivan are *The Foresters* (1892) and *The Window* (1871).

I read and posted the letter which you enclosed for Mrs Moore. It seemed to me up to the high standard of your usual letters on such occasions.[66] I have heard lately that Somerville, whom I have mentioned to you, is gone too. With him the old set completely vanishes.[67]

I hope that the domestic troubles have by now reached some solution. I'm afraid that question will be very acute, even after the war: over here it is a mark of great good luck and of a large income for people in our position to have maids at all.

Your loving
son Jack.

On the following day Germany appealed to President Wilson for an Armistice; the request was either refused or ignored.

---

66 A draft of Albert Lewis's letter to Mrs Moore reads as follows: '[21 September 1918] Dear Mrs. Moore, Two days ago I heard from Jacks that all hope of Paddy's safety must now be abandoned. I hope I may write of him as "Paddy" for I felt as tho' I had known him intimately for a long time. I shall not offer you the commonplaces of consolation – about duty and patriotism. When all that is said – and truthfully said – the terrible fact remains – the irremediable loss – the bitter grief. I do however offer you with intense sincerity my true and earnest and deep sympathy and sorrow in your great loss. For all your kindness to my son which I here again ask permission to acknowledge, I am deeply grateful. Believe me, with much sympathy, yours most sincerely, Albert Lewis' (LP VI: 42).

67 Those who made up 'the old set' are mentioned by name in Lewis's letter from Oxford of 10 June 1917. Paddy Moore died at Pargny in March 1918. Martin Ashworth Somerville, also of the Rifle Brigade, served in Egypt and Palestine and was killed in Palestine on 21 September 1918. Alexander Gordon Sutton, who was with Paddy in the 2nd Battalion of the Rifle Brigade, was killed in action on 2 January 1918. Thomas Kerrison Davy, of the 1st Battalion of the Rifle Brigade, died of wounds received near Arras on 29 March 1918. Lewis assumed that Denis Howard de Pass – 'our regnant authority on all matters of dress, who is reported to wear stays' – had died as well. He was reported 'wounded and missing' on 1 April 1918. As it turned out, de Pass of the 12th Battalion of the Rifle Brigade had been taken prisoner by the Germans. Following the repatriation in December 1918 he not only continued to serve in the First World War but fought in the Second as well. From 1950 until his death in 1973 this once fashionable dresser was a dairy farmer at Polegate in Sussex.

TO ARTHUR GREEVES (W):

No 3 Officers' Mess,
Perham Downs Camp,
Ludgershall, Hants.[68]
[6? October 1918]

My dear Arthur,

No, you were wrong, I have not gone on my leave; I was only out for a night at Mrs Moore's. I have now however had my board, over a month late I'm glad to say, and been sent for further convalescence to a camp here. This is Salisbury Plain, a place much cursed by most army people who are sent there because it is in the heart of the country and cannot therefore afford them the only pleasures of which they are capable. Personally I quite like it: it consists of long low hills, grassy and rather grey looking except in bright sun and very few trees. Of course it is rather spoilt by the city of wooden huts that is called a camp, but even these look quite well towards dusk when there are rows of light in the windows.

By this time you have probably got a parcel containing Beardesly's Malory and the Works of Corneille, which I have sent to you for safe keeping. Be sure and let me know what you think of both. Even if you don't care for the designs (and they are a little decadent and 'genre') I think you will like the general get up of the Malory. The Corneille is in a sort of good, solid old fashioned style, which I have grown to like: the plates of course *as* illustrations are idiotic but there is something solid and grand about them. Corneille is not half such a dull author as some people might imagine – don't take him at Tchaine's valuation. Down here I am reading Dante's 'Purgatorio' in the Temple Classics edition with a crib on the opposite page.[69] So 'ave the mighty fallen.

I told you that Wm. Heinemann was away for a fortnight, but he should be back now and I am expecting to hear from him any day now. I had a shock a short while ago when I saw a book of poems 'Counter-Attack' by Siegfried Sassoon[70] (a horrid man) published by him at 2/6 in a red paper cover and horrid type. I do hope they will give me something better than that.

---

68 Lewis was moved here on 4 October.
69 *The Purgatorio of Dante Alighieri*, the text with a translation by Thomas Okey, edited by H. Oelsner (1900).
70 Siegfried Sassoon, *Counterattack* (1918).

I have also been reading here the 1916–1917 books of Georgian Verse,[71] in which I liked particularly the bits from Robert Nichol's 'Faun's Holiday'. How a man who wrote them could also write such howling gibberish as 'The Assault' must remain a mystery. I believe you have his 'Ardours and Endurances'[72] haven't you? If so you might give me the details as to publisher, price and edition.

Mrs Moore has managed to get rooms in a tiny cottage here, where they keep rabbits and pigs. It is all very rural but not very sanitary. Write soon.

Yours
Jack

P.S. Don't say anything about my being moved, as I don't want my father to start trying to get me moved again.

On 4 October a German and Austrian 'Peace Note' was sent to President Woodrow Wilson, asking him to agree to an armistice. They made it clear that this was not a surrender, but an attempt to end the war without conditions that would be harmful to Germany and Austria. On 8 October Wilson rejected the Peace Note, insisting that a first condition of an armistice was the evacuation of all occupied territories.

TO HIS FATHER (LP VI: 50):

[No. 3 Officers Mess,
Perham Downs Camp,
Ludgershall,
Hants.]
10th [October 1918]

My dear Papy,

Thanks for the parcel, also the little note with enclosure. The 'Kassandra' cigarettes – one wonders vaguely why the 'K' and what language – are a pre-war luxury and much appreciated by us all.

By this time I expect you have my last letter and I may soon hope for your answer. Isn't the news excellent, or do you still distrust it? Peace and

---

71 *Georgian Poetry 1916–1917*, ed. E[dward] M[arsh] (1917).

72 Robert Nichols, *Assault and other War Poems* (1918); *Ardours and Endurances* (1917).

success have been so often held up to us that I admit one scarcely dares to have definite hopes again. I was very pleased however by the wise and temperate tone of Wilson's reply, which contrasted favourably with the blood and thunder vulgarity of the American press. But hush! We must not speak that way now when Britain has come to be mentioned as 'one of the Allies of the States': I never thought I'd live to see that – Wilson the head of the confederacy and England his humble retainer.

With best love,

your loving son,

Jack

TO ARTHUR GREEVES (W):

No 3 Officers Mess,
Perham Downs Camp,
Ludgershall,
Hants.
Sunday [13 October 1918]

My dear Arthur,

'Savernake Woods', doesn't that breathe of romance? It is the sort of name one would expect to find in Maurice Hewlett or Geoffrey Farnol, but as a matter of fact it is not invention at all – I have been in Savernake Woods this morning.

You get clear of the village, cross a couple of fields and then a sunken chalky road leads you right into the wood. It is full of beech and oak but also of those little bushy things that grow out of the earth in four or five different trunks – vide Rackham's woodland scenes in the 'Siegfried' illustrations. In places, too, there has been a good deal of cutting down: some people think this spoils a wood but I find it delightful to come out of the thickets suddenly to a half bare patch full of stumps and stacks of piled wood with the sun glinting thro' the survivors. Green walks of grass with thick wood on either side led off the road and we followed one of these down and found our way back by long détours, tho' not before a comfortable 'soaking machine' had been discovered and enjoyed.

By the way, talking about Siegfried, is it not an abomination the way the Germans have named their trench systems after the heroes of the Ring? The other day they were defending the 'Alberich line' and now they have been driven back to 'Brünnhilde'. Anything more vulgar than the application of that grand old cycle to the wearisome ugliness of modern war I can't imagine.

It was strange the way not only our letters but our thoughts crossed about 'the good old style' of the Corneille: the binding was of my own choice. How had both books stood their journey? As long as our views agree to this extent you need not be afraid of that 'getting farther and farther away' of which you always complain. We shall of course have a great many new subjects to talk of when we meet again, and a good many old ones to talk of quite differently, but that is an advantage.

I only wish I *was* busy 'correcting my proof-sheets': I have heard nothing more from Heinnemann although he must be back from his holiday by now. I have horrid fears sometimes that he may have changed his mind and be getting ready to return them – but then it would have been so easy for him to have done that in the first place.[73] Of course there is none of the fighting element in my book, but I suppose it has some indirect bearing on the war.

Funnily enough I had been reading a little handbook on Schopen-hauer last week:[74] though I have never read him seriously I have often dipped into him at Kirk's and the old man's talk was saturated with Shopenhauer-esque quotations and ideas. There is certainly much worth reading in him: his views on love, for instance, though they are far from being the whole truth, give nevertheless an excellent account of the actual origin of love – what he forgets is that it is man's peculiar glory to make out of something which nature created for her own biological pur-poses something else which is spiritual and which nature would have no interest in. That is our triumph. Of course he is not really a philosopher at all in the technical sense.

Am still going on slowly with the Purgatorio. Write soon a good long screed

Yours

Jack

---

73 Mr Heinemann's enthusiastic letter of 8 October (LP VI: 49) was sent to Ashton Court and had not yet caught up with him.

74 Arthur Schopenhauer (1788–1860). Lewis was probably reading *The Wisdom of Schopenhauer*, ed. W. Jekyll (1911).

TO ARTHUR GREEVES (W):

Teusday [15 October 1918]
Same place.

My dear Arthur,

Many thanks for the book,[75] it was most unexpected and delightful. It is nicely got up, but has suffered a little from tight strings on the journey. I haven't begun to read it seriously yet but all that I have seen pleases me. I at once looked up the poem 'The Gift of Song' which you mentioned, and I thoroughly agree with you. It has a beautiful dreamy movement and the sound follows the sense exactly; also, what is more it has that depth and mystery which a lyric should have if you are to read it again and again. I liked too the 'Canticle' in Danaë and indeed all the Danaë pieces, and there are fine passages in the verses on somebody's death – the ones where the last lines all rhyme to 'Despair'. Didn't you like that description of the snow outside the firelit window at Oxford. The war poetry is, at least, no worse than the rest of its kind. Nichols is very different from that great mass of modern poets, who copy the faults but not the merits of Rupert Brooke, and who are so intolerably clumsy and ugly in form. He stands quite apart and seems to me the best of the younger lot whom I have come across – much better than Brooke himself for instance. I'm afraid I shall never be an orthodox modern – I like lines that will scan and do not care for descriptions of sea-sickness.

Now for a little growl: if you realised what I'd got to go back to you wouldn't be so damned keen on my having another board. And you should understand that the longer it is before you see me the longer that evil day is put off.

Talking about Schopenhauer have you read anything about his views on music? He regards the arts in general as the only escape from the Will, and music in particular as the supreme escape and perhaps in itself the fundamental Reality. It is rather finely worked out and should appeal to you.

I am so glad you have got into that school at last: I hope they will do you good and lead you on to a proper development of your natural bent. After all interesting and arduous work is about the one thing to save us from melancholy – your besetting disease (I had almost written 'sin').

The Purgatorio, or even the whole Divine Comedy with the Inferno and Paradiso, is much shorter than the Faerie Queene. Without Latin I

---

75 i.e. *Ardours and Endurances* by Robert Nichols.

am not sure that even your knowledge of French & the crib would carry you through: but if you would care for a translation remember that Cary's version in blank verse is supposed to be the best piece of verse-translation ever written.[76] Don't get Longfellow's or any of the modern ones, they are all (I'm told) bad. Gilbert Murray is a very sound man, and his translations should be good – I have never more than glanced at them, not being fond of Euripides myself.[77]

I got Mrs Moore's sister in town to call on Heinemanns, which she did on Wednesday last and they said they'd written the day before, but it must have been lost. That of course accounts for the delay and I hope to hear some day soon.

The hills and all our favourite walks should be lovely just now – Hadn't heard about K.'s arm.

Yours
Jack

TO HIS FATHER (LP VI: 53–4):

Officers Mess,
No. 3 Camp,
Perham Down.
Andover,
Hants.
Oct. 18th 1918

My dear Papy,

I have had a board at last, and been moved to this 'Command Depot' for an unspecified period. This is the usual step after leaving hospital, unless one is well enough to be passed for general service. Of course I am still far from this, but one doesn't usually remain here very long. It is a sort of a glorified hospital here, although we live in a mess and wear uniform: the best feature is that we have rooms to ourselves, which is a pleasant change after hospital wards.

I have just had a letter from Heinemann's which has taken some time to come round through Ashton Court. He accepts some new pieces I had sent him and mentions a few he wants rejected. He also objects to a 'too

---

76 *The Vision or Hell, Purgatory and Paradise of Dante Alighieri*, trans. Henry Francis Cary (1814).

77 *Hippolytus and The Bacchae of Euripides, and the Frogs of Aristophanes*, trans. Gilbert Murray (1902).

frequent use of certain words' and points to one or two places that seem weak and which I might alter. 'After that' he suggests we might come to terms, a point on which I am quite ready to agree with him. I am hoping to get a day off some time next week and run up to town and see him: that will be much better than a long series of letters. With most of his omissions and objections I agree, and shall have no difficulty in making changes, tho' there are one or two cases in which I am determined to stick to my guns. One must trust ones own judgements sometimes.

I was quite amused at your story of the origin of 'Spirits in Bondage' tho' that would not be a sufficient argument against it. Of course I remembered the text about 'the spirits which are in prison' and it is that which seemed to give the old title its significance which 'Spirits in bondage' could never have. I think perhaps we should stick to 'Prison'. I shall ask Heinemann whether that novel by Hichens really exists; he ought to know.

By the way, what about Clive Hamilton for a pseudonym? It will be a complete disguise to outsiders, transparent to 'our ain folk', and will be a name which we have the best of reasons to love and honour.[78]

Many thanks for the enclosure. I am very sorry to hear about the drawing room floor which used to be 'the brightest jewel in our crown'.

your loving
son Jack

---

78 'Clive Hamilton' is the pseudonym Lewis eventually chose to appear under. Unluckily for Lewis, in a 'List of Poetry' from Heinemann found in the back pages of *Spirits in Bondage*, the book is advertised as the work of 'George Lewis': 'Crown 8vo. Cloth 3s.6d. net. Lieut. G.S. Lewis, who is 20 years of age, was at Malvern College when the war broke out. In 1916 he took a classical scholarship at University College, Oxford, and a year later received his commission in the Somerset Light Infantry. He was wounded in front of Lillers in April, 1918.' C.S. Evans wrote to Lewis on 7 April 1919 saying, 'I do not know how the "C" became changed into "G" and hence by a natural deduction into "George", except that we have another poet whose name is George Hamilton' (LP VI: 106).

TO HIS FATHER (LP VI: 58–9):

No. 3 Officer's Mess,
Perham Downs Camp.
Ludgershall,
Hants.
27th[26th?] Oct. 1918

My dear Papy,

I succeeded in getting my day off to see Heinemann yesterday, after being stopped last week through a very ridiculous incident of a kind that is common in the army. In order to get leave for a day you have to write down your name, the time of leaving, and your destination in the book which is then signed by the medical officer. Last week the book was lost: no objection was made to my going on either military or medical grounds, but – how could I go without the book? A suggestion that I might write the particulars on a slip of paper which could then afterwards be put in the book was treated as a sort of sacrilege. After a week however it occurred to the Adjutant (who must be a man of bold originality and signal generosity) that we might spend half a crown on a new book, and so I was able to go after all.

Heinemann was out when I reached the office and I was shown in to the Manager, a man called Evans, quite a young fellow and very agreeable. Afterwards Heinemann himself came in and I was with him for about three-quarters of an hour. He produced a typed agreement of which, with many 'hereinafter's and 'aforesaid's, the gist is that they are to publish the book 'at their own expense, in such style and to be sold at such price as they deem best' and that I am 'to receive the following royalty: 10% of the profits on the published price of 12 out of every thirteen copies sold'. It concludes with a stipulation that they should have the refusal of my next work, if any. Whether I am being well or ill treated I am of course too ignorant to say: but I suppose, poetry being such an unprofitable branch of publishing, I have no reason to be dissatisfied. He also told me that John Galsworthy (who publishes with them) had seen my MS and wanted to publish a certain poem in a new monthly called 'Reviellé' which he is bringing out in aid of disabled soldiers and sailors. I naturally consented, both because it is pleasant 'laudari a laudato viro' and because it is an excellent advertisement. Before I left he said he would go on with the printing at once and might be able to have the proofs ready for me in three weeks. He is a fat little man with a bald head, apparently well read, and a trifle fussy – inclined to get his papers mixed up and repeat himself.

Thank you very much for the cigarettes and tobacco – I was just out of the latter. I am sending you the last batch of photos of the child, taken in Bristol some time ago and only now developed. Let me know what you think of them.

Lunch in London on omlettes, fish, hors d'oeuvres and other non-coupon dishes was alright – but what about one scone and cup of tea at 1/6?

your loving son,
Jack

P.S. By the way I've never had any finished copies of those last photos taken at home – could you please send me some. J.

TO ARTHUR GREEVES (W):

[Perham Downs Camp,
Ludgershall]
Saturday [2 November 1918]

My dear Arthur,

Many thanks for your letter (what a conventional opening!) which shows you much more cheerful and contented than you were in the last. I am delighted about these classes at the technical, and I am sure, tho' it may be tiring at times, that you will feel much the better for them both in your painting and spirits. What sort of people do you meet there? I suppose they are of all ages, sexes and classes, but you ought with luck to find plenty of interesting folk in a place of that sort.

I suppose I *was* the last person to whom the bramble spoke. Your reference to her does carry one back to the old days that were so happy although one hardly realized how happy at the time (another frightfully conventional remark, but you can't help feeling that it's true). It is terrible to think how quickly an old order changes and how impossible it is to build it up again exactly the same.

I wonder will there be many changes when we meet again? Maureen told me the other day that I was greatly changed since she first knew me, but, with the impenetrable reticence of a child, declined to say in what way. Personally I don't feel very different. I suppose I am a bit broader – more tolerant of people different from ourselves and readier to see the good points in a well-meaning philistine – but I think my interests and ambitions are pretty much the same. You, I imagine from your letters, are a good deal broader, and have developed considerably, especially in your taste for poetry: your dip into the slightly decadent but charming 'celtic' circle at Dublin has certainly made you less of a Northerner. You were once a trifle bigoted about catholicism: that has passed. I suppose we are each of us different from being away from the other: we had perhaps learned to think & even read too much with an eye on the other's criticism. However we shall have enough to talk about for years, when once we get going.

By the way these rather stuffy reflections are holding up all my real news. Last Friday, or rather last Friday week, I made a journey to London to see Heinemanns.[79] You will understand well how pleasant it was to walk in under a doorway, adorned with the 'windmill' we have so often seen, feeling that I had some right to be there. I offered a card to a young woman who said that she thought Mr H. was out, would I see the manager? I was led through innumerable corridors, thro' all sorts of offices, past armies of typists and shown into a rather dingy room. C. S. Evans, the manager, was a young man, pale and fair &, I think, a gentleman. He was very nice to me and quite enthusiastic about the book and especially about one piece. John Galsworthy, he said, had read the MS. and wanted to put this piece in a new Quarterly which he is bringing out for disabled soldiers & sailors called Reveille: of course I consented.[80] While we were talking he was interrupted to speak on the telephone. I listened to quite a long technical conversation (if you can call *one* end of a telephone conversation) apparently with a female interlocutor on 'some designs for endleaves' – all of which, as you would heartily agree with me, was very interesting.

Later on H. himself came in. He was a little, fat bald man, very agreeable and fussy, but, as far as one could see, a really literary not a mere business man. We fixed up all the formalities about terms and he hopes to let me have the proofs in about three weeks.

---

79 On 25 October.
80 When it was discovered that Robert Hitchens had published a book under the title *Spirits in Prison* in 1908, Lewis (who altered his pseudonym to 'Clive Hamilton') changed the title of his to *Spirits in Bondage*, a phrase borrowed from Milton's *Paradise Lost*, I, 658.

I returned home treading on air and bought a copy of Reveille – the August number & the first. It included only one poem, by Kipling so I suppose I should be satisfied with the company. So at last dreams come to pass and I have sat in the sanctum of a publisher discussing my own book (Notice the hideous vulgarity of success already growing in me). Yet – though it is very pleasant – you will understand me when I say that it has not the utter romance which the promise of it had a year ago. Once a dream has become a fact I suppose it loses something. This isn't affectation: we long & long for a thing and when it comes it turns out to be just a pleasant incident, very much like others.

The country is gorgeous, it is so still that hardly a leaf has fallen & I have never seen such autumn colours anywhere. There are lovely beech woods down beyond Savernake with winding roads thro' them and some fine old houses hidden away. They are all like a big yellow flame now – and a lovely autumn smell. Am sending you a new photo to-morrow

Yours

Jack

TO HIS FATHER (LP VI: 62–3):

No. 3 Officer's Mess,
Perham Downs Camp,
Ludgershall.
Hants.
3 Sept. [November] 1918

My dear Papy,

The first parcel of smokeables *did* arrive safely despite its perilous transit through Ashton Court and was acknowledged in my last letter: I am therefore the richer by your qualms on that subject and acknowledge my 'dutiful thanks' for both.

You may make your mind easy on the question of the War Office's 'tricks', as my removal to a command depot is quite in order. At the same time I am afraid I shall have to disappoint you on the two months leave as I am not likely to get nearly so long. The idea doubtless arose in your mind from the fact that officers discharged from hospital and still convalescent, were formerly sent home and told to report for a board again in two, three or even six months' time. This however was

'*In the olden*
Time long ago'

It was found that the average uniformed bounder had only two interests – alcohol and women – and that two months' undisturbed indulgence in his natural tastes left him very much less fit than when he began. As well, men were continually being forgotten, and there were even cases of officer's desertion: consequently tho' Majors 'et hoc genus omne'[81] still get their sick leave, we unfortunates convalesce in hospitals and depots and get some leave as a sop after we are cured. As usual, the innocent suffer for the guilty, but this is too common an event to surprise either you or me. Any attempt to 'work' things is dangerous: we had a hopelessly unfit man at Ashton, who, on trying to be sent to a different hospital, was boarded and sent to France. It's a way they have in the army.

Since you have asked about the state of the exchequer – I find my pay quite sufficient for ordinary purposes and even for such mild luxuries as I want. It would be quite unfair for a person in my position to expect pocket money from his father. Distinct from these ordinary expenses however, I would mention the quite *extra*-ordinary one of getting a new uniform (for which I am sending you the receipt) and boots, very cheap at 36/-. If you don't agree with me in calling this an extra-ordinary expense, say so of course quite frankly, I shall not be at all hurt. There was also a revolver which I have not replaced. Perhaps indeed the whole bill should be sent in to 'A firer of gun, name and location uncertain'!

I was wrong in calling 'Reviellé' a monthly, it is a quarterly. I have bought a copy of the first number (which is dated August) to spy out the land. It contains only one poem – by Kipling, not at his best, and is rather more technical and propagandist than I had hoped. However, it will be a useful enough means of drawing attention to ones existance.

Yes – a year and six days is a long stretch enough: indeed my life is rapidly becoming divided into two periods, one including all the time before we got into the battle of Arras, the other ever since. Already last year seems a long, long way off. However, there appears to be some prospect of the whole beastly business coming to an end fairly soon.

your loving son,
Jack

---

81 'and all that sort'.

TO HIS FATHER (LP VI: 65–6):

No. 3 Officer's Mess,
Perham Down Camp,
Ludgershall,
Hants.
10th Nov. 1918

My dear Papy,

I have three things to acknowledge with thanks – cigarettes, photos, and a cheque. As to the photos, the only case in which I am really able to judge of the likeness is the 'crack' one. This I think is very good indeed and greatly superior to any of the single photos of you which have yet appeared. It is unfortunate that they all have such serious technical imperfections of blurring. I will direct the Bristol photographer to send you some copies of the new one which you like – of course without the account: this is my show.

Although one does not wish to live in a fool's paradise or be foolishly confident, yet I do think the present course of events is such as to render the question of trying to get a home job rather less important than it was a month ago. In twenty four hours time it may have ceased to have any meaning at all. Of course even if we do get peace, I suppose I shall take some time in escaping from the army. But in no position should I stand a better chance of a speedy discharge than in my present one of convalescent officer at a Command Depot. Our attitude therefore must simply be to 'stand by'. I do not know what your views on the present situation are, but suppose you have reached the situation prophesied by George Harding in which you and Hope will no longer be able to 'have a real good talk'.

Of course the question whether Heinemann is treating me well or no has often been in my mind, and I have come to the conclusion that such an agreement is all that we have a right to expect. We must remember that even when poetry has a 'succès fou' it is still less profitable to the publisher than even fairly good fiction. As Evans said to me, 'We don't expect to make a commercial success out of poetry: we only publish it – well simply because its good'. This of course may be an exaggeration, but surely there is a good deal of truth in it? I was particularly careful to find out exactly what the 'first refusal' clause committed me to. I began by asking if this would prevent me writing a magazine article if ever I wanted to. Evans said 'Of course not' and added, 'All the clause means is this, Mr. Lewis. You send us your next MS. If we don't like it we shan't take it: if you don't like our terms you won't let us have it'. That seems a straight enough proposition. There was no suggestion at all that I should *have* to sell them at the same terms as the first.

Since you ask, such compliments as I was payed by Heinemann were of a somewhat peculiar nature – their object being to impress upon me the great honour that was being done me, and the majesty of the firm. 'Of course Mr. Lewis we never accept poetry unless it is really good' and more in that strain – with mental reservations on my part as I remembered some specimens. He merely said that Galsworthy 'admired' the one he wanted for Reveillé.

We have been innoculated against the influenza here. If it is at all bad at home I should get it done. It is not worth one's while risking ones life over a thing like that and the innoculation is very mild. It proved an effective check in Paris and why it has not been more widely used here, goodness only knows.

With many thanks for everything and best love,

I am your loving son,

Jack

On 11 November, Albert Lewis wrote in his diary: 'Armistice signed. War ended. Thanks be to God.'

TO HIS FATHER (LP VI: 68–9):

> Officers' Command Depot,
> Eastbourne.
> Suffolk [Sussex]
> [17? November 1918]

My dear Papy,

As you see, I have been moved again. That is to say I have in the literal sense covered several hundreds of miles of country, but in the military sense I have not moved at all. In other words, 'Command Depot' itself has moved: as a step towards demobilisation the officers who were scattered at various depots over the country have been collected into a special depot for officers here. As to the great news which is uppermost in our minds, I can only echo what you have already said. The man who can give way to mafficking at such a time is more than indecent – he is mad. I remember five of us at Keble, and I am the only survivor: I think of Mr Sutton, a widower with five sons, all of whom have gone. One cannot help wondering why. Let us be silent and thankful.

The question of how to get most quickly out of the army has of course occupied me too. I wrote to Macan explaining my position and asking whether Colleges propose to make any representations to the powers on behalf of the Sam-Browned freshmen who wanted to get back – for I had heard that something of that kind was being done. He replied in a kind and even cordial letter that I was not likely, so far as he knew, to be discharged for several months, and that the head of the U.T.C.[82] was writing to me. The latter wrote to me saying that if I could get passed by a board as 'unfit for at least three months' I could go back to Oxford in khaki and on army pay, for what they call 'an intensive course of University training' on the chance of not being disturbed again. This seems to me however rather a cat and mouse business, and for another thing, I don't think any board is likely to pass me as unfit for three months. As regards wire pulling, we must remember that there are thousands of other young men in the same position, each thinking that his own claims for an early release are particularly pressing: I doubt if personal influence is likely to alter the plan of demobilisation much. Of course too there is the danger of being passed fit for that army of occupation.

We're a nice pair! In the same letter you say – quite truly – that I have never told you to what extent I am likely to be disabled by the wound, and also that you are in Squeaky's hands for trouble – unspecified.[83] Well let's make a bargain. Here is my health report, and in return I shall look for a full account of your own bother. The effects of the wound in general movement are practically nil. I can do everything except hold my left arm straight above my head, which I don't want to do anyway. The effects on general health are very small: I have had one or two stoppages of breath which I am told are not unusual after a chest wound and which will soon disappear, and of course I still get tired easily and have a few headaches in the evenings. On the nerves there are two effects which will probably go with quiet and rest...[84] The other is nightmares – or rather the same nightmare over and over again. Nearly everyone has it, and

82 University Training Courses.
83 'Squeaky Dick', as Richard Whytock Leslie, MD (1862–1931) was known to many, was the Lewis family doctor.
84 The Lewis brothers removed a passage from this letter when it was typed for the Lewis Papers.

though very unpleasant, it is passing and will do no harm. So you see I am almost 'in statu quo'. I certainly don't think the removal of the piece would be advisable.

The proofs of the book are expected any day and it will probably be out in the Christmas list. I hope you will not be disappointed in it. Have you any news of when Warnie is likely to be home?

With best love and heartiest congratulations on the good fortune we have both shared, I am,

your loving son,

Jack

TO ARTHUR GREEVES (W):

Officers' Command Depôt,
Eastbourne.[85]
Monday 2nd [December 1918]

My dear Arthur,

Many thanks for your letter. I am sorry to have left you so long without anything; the chief reason was the bustle of being moved here. At first I thought it abominable – it is [a] much worse camp than the Ludgershall one – but now that the others[86] have come down of course I spend most of my time out.

You are wrong in supposing that I am doing no reading, indeed I don't know why I have not kept you up to date. I have just finished the life of Browning (Everyman) by Dowden[87] which was a most interesting book – just what the life of a writer should be in my opinion, i.e mainly about his work, not all futile personal details & dates. Moved by this I read his (B's) 'Paracelsus'[88] which I liked much better than I expected. Of course a good deal of it is not what we used to call poetry in the good old days, but there are some bits of the real stuff and it is all full of interest.

But the great event is that I have learned to enjoy Shakespeare. I bought an Everyman copy of the Comedies[89] and am just finishing 'Measure for Measure'. Isn't it funny the way you come round to things you

---

85 Lewis was moved here about the middle of November.
86 Mrs Moore and Maureen.
87 Edward Dowden, *Robert Browning* (1915).
88 Robert Browning, *Paracelsus* (1835).
89 *Shakespeare's Comedies*, with biographical introduction by Oliphant Smeaton and prefatory notes by D.C. Browning (1906).

used to hate? I think the characterisation is excellent & there are fine passages of poetry. Don't you like Claudio's piece about,

> *'worse than worst*
> *Of those that wayward & uncertain thought*
> *Imagines howling'?*[90]

I am also reading Virgil & Euripides 'Alcestis'.[91]

At the same time I am doing a lot of writing again. I have just finished a short narrative, which is a verse version of our old friend 'Dymer', greatly reduced & altered to my new ideas. The main idea is that of development by self-destruction, both of individuals & species (as nature produces man only to conquer her [*sic*], & man produces a future & higher generation to conquer the ideals of the last, or again as an individual produces a nobler mood to undo all that to-day's has done). The background proceeds on the old assumption of good *outside & opposed to* the cosmic order. It is written in the metre of Venus & Adonis:[92] 'Dymer' is changed to 'Ask' (you remember Ask & Embla in the Norse myths) & it is in the 3rd person under the title of 'The Redemption of Ask'. I am wondering what you will think of it. I am also at work on a short blank verse scene (you can hardly call it a play) between Tristram & King Mark & a poem on Ion, which is a failure so far.

By the way have you thought of getting the Xmas Bookman? I suppose not & I am in despair because it has all been bought up in advance. It is a thing I always want to get & it will be especially desirable this year as it may have a review of my book in it. Item, the proofs have NOT come yet but we live in hopes.

It is almost incredible that the war is over, isn't it – not to have that 'going-back' hanging over my head all the time. This time last year I was in the trenches, & now – but, come!, the tendency to moralize is getting the better of me. The child[93] is writing another fairy tale – rather the plan of 'Puck of Pook's Hill' I fancy.

Yours

Jack

---

90 William Shakespeare, *Measure for Measure* (1623), III, i, 124 (slightly misquoted).
91 Euripides (480–406 BC), *Alcestis*.
92 William Shakespeare, *Venus and Adonis* (1593).
93 The 'child' is probably Maureen Moore.

TO HIS FATHER (LP VI: 74–5):

Officer's Command depot,
Eastbourne.
8th Dec. 1918

My dear Papy,

I have put off answering your birthday letter and thanking you for the enclosure in the hope that your answer to my last, which is now due, would arrive. I am anxiously awaiting your views on the University Training Corps business: until I hear these I am rather uneasy about taking even such negative action as is implied in doing nothing.

The first disappointment of 'this publishing business' reached me last week and has probably by now reached you. Of course Galsworthy had every right to change his mind on the merits of my piece, but I will admit that I was rather annoyed to find that neither he nor Heinemann saw fit to tell me the fact. I first knew of it by seeing a copy of 'Reveillé' on the local book stall.[94] However these things are common enough in the lives of even real writers, and there is no need to grouse. Let us go and solace our hearts with Mr. Nichol's more successful chef d'oeuvre.

As you have probably seen in the papers, we are all going to get 12 days 'Christmas leave'. I use the inverted commas advisedly as mine seems likely to be in January. I suppose it would be unreasonable to expect them to let us all go at the same time, and you and I won't quarrel with dates. It has been a long time coming and a time unpleasantly and wastefully spent, but thank God it is over at last. By the way, although, as I understand, I am entitled to a vote, I have not yet received any of the 'Election Communications' which have fallen to the lot of most men I know. Perhaps you can advise the constituency that it is in danger of losing the support of an influential voter! I suppose we are all voting for the Coalition, though I must confess I distrust them most heartily and look for no liberty as long as they are in power. Most of us here would be ready to vote for Lucifer himself if he rose up in red velvet and sulpher whispering the word 'Discharged'. But I see we are not to be 'discharged' but demobilized and kept on a leash for the rest of our lives. Sometimes when I think of this I feel inclined to go and steal a red flag from the neighbouring golf course.

Could you please send me a Greek Lexicon which you will find – I hope – in the little end room, and also Sophocles 'Oedipus Rex' or

---

94 The publishers had decided not to include Lewis's poem in issue No. 2 of *Reveille*.

'O.Tyrrannus'[95] which you will find among three blue volumes of Sopho-cles in the middle of the second shelf from the top of the bookcase fur-thest from the window. If you also had room for Tasso's 'Gerusalemme Liberata'[96] from the top shelf, I should be 'eternally beholden to you'.

At my suggestion Mrs Moore has come down here and is staying in rooms near the camp, where I hope she will remain until I go on leave. It is a great relief to get away from the army atmosphere, although for that matter I have been lucky in finding several decent fellows, including even another aspirant for poetical laurels – a most amusing card. It is fine country down here and I am glad that chance has given me its hills and cliffs to walk on. Certainly, if nothing else, the army has shown me some bits of England that I would not otherwise have seen.

I hope for your letter soon and that it will bring no bad news of that 'trouble' of yours.

With love and thanks,

your loving,

son,

Jack

TO HIS FATHER (LP VI: 76):

Officers Command Depot,
Eastbourne,
Sussex.
Dec. [16?]th, 1918.

My dear Papy,

Thank you very much for the letter and enclosure and also for the two books which arrived today in excellent condition. I have already wired to you the dates of my leave:[97] a list of the periods alloted to each of us has been posted up here, and, as was to be expected, the coveted dates which would include Christmas fall to the Majors and Captains 'et hoc genus omne'. If however you can let Warnie know in time, I should think he would have no difficulty in getting his leave postponed. Everyone of course will be trying to get home for Christmas day, and it ought to be easy to change with someone who had got a later date against his will.

---

95 Sophocles (496–406 BC), one of the great Greek tragedians, wrote *Oedipus Tyrannus*.

96 Torquato Tasso, *Gerusalemme Liberata* (1581).

97 The telegram to his father of 16 December reads: 'Leave tenth to twenty second January.'

I quite agree with you that it would be most disappointing if even now our little gathering were broken up.

Of course I shall be only too pleased if any influence of yours could succeed in getting me a discharge, though at the same time I am afraid it will be a very difficult business. As you have probably seen in the papers, we are to be drafted on our demobilization in 'Class Z Reserve' where I suppose we shall remain ready for the next scrape that some Labour government in the future may get the country into. I don't want to be pessimistic, but there does not seem much hope of ever being quite free of the army again. To get a discharge might be possible on the score of unfitness, but I do not think that my degree of military unfitness will be sufficient to serve our turn.

What you have to say on the Reviellé question makes me feel rather a fool: no doubt it must be as you say. The only thing that bothers me is this. Surely Heinemann will get my book out before the next quarterly season begins? – and if so, is it usual for a periodical to publish an extract from a book *after* that book itself has appeared? However, it is quite an unimportant sideshow.

About the 'University Training Course', I still think as I thought before that it would be almost useless for me to try and get that 3 months verdict from a board. I only wanted to see if you thought the thing so desirable that you would wish me to try on the off chance. Since we both look eye to eye on the matter and are not inclined to jump at any disguised backwater of the army (you can still see the brass buttons under the gown!), we may let it drop.

So far my readings both in Latin and Greek have been a pleasant surprise: I have forgotten less than I feared, and once I get the sound and savour of the language into my head by a spell of reading, composition should not come too hard either. In English I have started friend Trollope again – 'The Small House at Allington'.

I hope that trouble of yours is really better – as you say, it is an unpleasant complaint and leads to a good many inconveniences.

With best love, your loving son,

Jack

TO HIS FATHER (LP VI: 77):

Officers Command Depot,
Eastbourne,
Sussex.
Dec. 22nd. 1918

My dear Papy,

The selection of possible books here was so small that I was really driven to this as a last resource: if you have it already, or if you do not like it, I expect that Mullen's will be gracious and change it.

The slippers were got for the benefit of corns and sore feet. I should like them to have been better, but as you know, the war has pretty well drained the English shops of leather goods.

With my very best love and heartiest wishes for a happy Christmas, a speedy reunion, and a prosperous and peaceful New Year for us all, I am,

your loving son,
Jack

Jack had told his father that his leave was not until 10 to 22 January. Warnie, who was in France, was unable to alter the dates of his leave and he arrived in Belfast on the morning of 23 December. Jack was discharged from the hospital on 24 December, and he found himself demobilized from the army. There was not enough time to alert his father before he set off for home. In his diary of 27 December Warnie wrote: 'A red letter day today. We were sitting in the study about 11 o'clock this morning when we saw a cab coming up the avenue. It was Jacks! He has been demobilized thank God. Needless to say there were great doings. He is looking pretty fit. We had lunch and then all three went for a walk. It was as if the evil dream of four years had passed away and we were still in the year 1915. In the evening there was bubbly for dinner in honour of the event. The first time I have ever had champagne at home. Had the usual long conversation with Jacks after going to bed' (LP VI: 79). Following this reunion, Jack returned to Oxford on 13 January 1919 to begin the Classical Honour Moderations course in Greek and Latin literature. He was living in University College, still in Room 5 on Staircase XII. Mrs Moore and Maureen found rooms nearby in the home of Miss Featherstone at 28 Warneford Road, Oxford. Meanwhile, Jack's father had been urging him to write to the War Office about a possible pension, and the next letter was written in Oxford but 'as from' his home in Belfast.

1919

___ ~ ___

TO THE SECRETARY, WAR OFFICE (PUBLIC RECORD OFFICE):

Little Lea,
Strandtown,
Belfast
Jan 18th 1919

Sir,

On the 26th of September 1917 I was appointed from the Oxford University O.T.C. to a temporary commission in the Regular Army. I joined the Somerset Light Infantry on the 16th October and crossed to France on the 17th of November. I was severely wounded near Lillers on the 15th April 1918 and remained in Hospitals and Command Depôts until the 24th December 1918 when I was demobilised. I have up till now recieved neither gratuity nor pension. I shall be obliged by your informing me when I may expect a communication on the subject.

I am, Sir,

Your obedient servant,

C. S. Lewis

TO ARTHUR GREEVES (W):

[University College,
Oxford
26 January 1919]

My dear Arthur,

I was agreeably surprised to hear from you so soon: perhaps you will be equally surprised to hear that I have already performed your commissions if not to your satisfaction at any rate vastly to my own. I found two complete editions of the Larger Temple Sh.,[1] one new and the other second

---

1 *The Works of Shakespeare*, ed. Israel Gollancz, 12 vols., 'The Larger Temple Shakespeare' (1899).

hand at 36/-. In neither case would they sell separate volumes and I therefore got the 36/- one myself with malicious glee! It is a little bit battered in some volumes but absolutely clean inside and has the real pre-war guilding, and good edges. Slowly as I can afford [it] I must get them re-bound.

As to the Gibbon they showed me specimen volumes of two editions both by Methuen: the larger one at 10/6 a volume was about the size of your 'British Empire' book & very similar in paper and type: the binding was a somewhat unpleasant ribbed blue cloth with elaborate gilding on the back – not unlike my Benedetto Croce. The smaller was the one which my father has, beautifully fresh & clean: I have therefore asked them to order this,[2] explaining that it would be no use unless they could get you the complete set – which they seem fairly confident of doing. I suppose this is what you would like done? I certainly envy you such a nice book if they *do* get a complete set: where will you put it? I am very pleased indeed with my Shakespeare.

Now for some account of myself and my doings. My day is as follows: called at 7.30, bath, chapel and breakfast – in Hall.* Owing to the lack of coal and servants we are having all our meals in Hall this term. Next term we hope to go back to the traditional and much more pleasant arrangement of having breakfast and lunch in our own rooms. After breakfast I work (in the library or a lecture-room which are both warm) or attend lectures until 1 o'clock when I bycycle out to Mrs Moore's.

They are installed in our 'own hired house'[3] (like St Paul only not daily preaching & teaching). The owner of the house has not yet cleared out & we pay a little less than the whole for her still having a room. She is an elderly maiden lady and – I am not joking – a saint. She gets up early every morning and goes to church – very high Anglican – through the bitter frost. In spite of protests she brings Mrs Moore a cup of tea in the morning: she can hardly be persuaded to use her own kitchen, which by the arrangement should be common to us both. Altogether a most remarkable character – and very given to good works. At another house we tried we met a Miss Tennyson, niece of the poet.

After lunch I work until tea, then work again till dinner. After that a little more work, talk and laziness & sometimes bridge then bycycle back

---

2 Edward Gibbon, *The History of the Decline and Fall of the Roman Empire* (1776–88), ed. J.B. Bury, 7 vols., 'Methuen's Standard Library' (1905–6).

3 Acts 28:30: 'And Paul dwelt two whole years in his own hired house, and received all that came in unto him.'

to College at 11. I then light my fire and work or read till 12 o'clock when I retire to sleep the sleep of the just. At this little end of the day I have read three Acts of King John which I like immensely. At that time of life he wrote much more simply: the verse has a more correct flow and the characters are easily understood. Don't you like Constance, especially her speech about death & the scene between Pandulph & the Dauphin just afterwards?[4] Also, whether working or not I always end the day by looking into Bridges. He is so quiet and has something for every mood.

(From this [point] on you may read the letter to my father if you want.) The place is more beautiful than ever in this weather: every morning when I am called I see a lovely picture out of my window: a battlemented tower and three bare trees against the cold, cold red of the morning: then looking out you see the grass of the quad. powdered in white and all the old stone of the roofs white too and pinched with cold. However one can get quite warm in the library or the Junior Common Room: of course it is in the former I work – if only you could smoke there, it would be ideal: the temptation to spend all your time rambling over the interesting modern books & the great old worm-eaten folios has to be sternly resisted!

Now for a piece of good luck – I go to lectures by Gilbert Murray twice a week, on Euripides 'Bacchae'. Luckily I have read the play before and can therefore give him a freeër attention: it is a very wierd play (you have read his translation, have you not?) and he is a real inspiration, – quite as good as his best books, if only he didn't dress so horribly, worse even than most dons. I go to Christchurch to hear him and to Balliol to hear a man called Bailey on Lucretius, who is very amusing.[5] He began by saying 'I hope none of you gentlemen have got my edition of this book[6] as it was written in my unregenerate days.'

One of the things that worries me is that every lecturer you go to tells you of about 5 books 'you should all have access to', which comes expensive. Some, of course, can be got second hand: my regular book-monger keeps his second-hand stock downstairs in a 12th century crypt, at one period haunted by Guy Faulkes.[7] Some of the best bits of Oxford seem to

---

4 William Shakespeare, *King John* (1623), III, i, 29ff.
5 Cyril Bailey (1871–1957) was Classical Tutor at Balliol College.
6 *Lucreti De Rerum Natura Libri Sex. Recognovit brevique adnotatione critica instruxit C. Bailey* [1899].
7 This was Mr H.G. Gadney's bookshop at 2 and 3 Turl Street. It later became the Turl Cash Bookshop – taking its name from the fact that Mr Gadney never gave credit. The 12th century crypt, haunted by Guy Fawkes, is now 'The Crypt' of the Mitre restaurant.

be underground – hidden away beneath prosaic grocers, hotels and tobacconists. Another thing that bothers me is the terrible independence with which you have to work here: I only see my tutor once a week and at other times it is very trying to reflect after a long day's work that you may have been simply wasting your time ever since you got up. On the whole, however, I get on fairly well & the amount of reading I've done stands me in good stead. Of course there is very little time for ordinary reading, which has to be confined to the week-end as it was at Kirk's. At present I am still at the Philosopher book which is excellent.

I have found one old friend, Edwards, who was here when I was last up and, as an 'unfit' has been here all the time. It is good to be back and doing something one is interested in. I bless my good fortune every night when I hear the hours strike, lying in my bed. One chime takes it from another with varying notes, getting fainter & fainter, as though the whole great city were turning over and settling itself to sleep in the cold, cold night. That Debussy thing keeps on running in my head. I hope the biliousness is gone, & that you are getting on with your varying works: anything in the writing line?

Yours

Jack

* I mean breakfast only in hall – not bath & chapel as well.

TO HIS FATHER (LP VI: 82–3):

University College,
Oxford.
Jan. 27th 1919

My dear Papy,

Before giving any account of myself and my doings, I should let you know what we have missed. The letter from Aunt Lily[8] which you forwarded to me announced that she would soon be arriving in Belfast 'for two days'. She proposed to come and see the Hamiltonians 'we could walk down together and have a good talk on the way; perhaps that nice boy Arthur Greeves would join us'. May one be permitted to hope that the good lady has been even better consoled by a good talk with you. I can just see the picture.

---

8 Jack's aunt, Mrs Lilian Hamilton Suffern. See note 21 to the letter of 14 May 1918.

After a quite comfortable journey (which showed me that 1st. Class travelling is very little different from 3rd) I arrived here somewhat late in the evening. The moon was just rising: the porter knew me at once and ushered me into the same old rooms (which by the way I am going to change).[9] It was a great return and something to be very thankful for. I was also pleased to find an old friend, Edwards, who was up with me in 1916, and being unfit, has been there all the time. There is of course already a great difference between this Oxford and the ghost I knew before: true, we are only twenty eight in College, but we *do* dine in Hall again, the Junior Common Room is no longer swathed in dust sheets, and the old round of lectures, debates, games, and whatnot is getting under weigh. The reawakening is a little pathetic: at our first[10] we read the minutes of the last – 1914. I don't know any little thing that has made me realise the absolute suspension and waste of these years more thoroughly.

The Mugger[11] preached a quite memorable sermon on the first Sunday evening. It was very plain, even homely in style, not what one expected, but it grew on one, and I admire the restraint where 'gush' would have been so fatally easy. By the way, I have not been asked to see the Mugger yet, but I gather he has a waiting list and is working slowly through it. We have quite a number of old members who were up before the war and are a kind of dictionary of traditions.

Now as to work: I am 'deemed to have passed' Responsions and Divinity and it was open to me either to take Honour Mods or go straight on to 'Greats'[12] – as you know, the final fence. In consideration of my wish to get a fellowship, Poynton,[13] who is my tutor, strongly advised me not to avail myself of this opportunity of slurring over Mods. I presume I was acting as I should when I followed his advice. Except for the disadvantage of starting eighteen books of Homer to the bad I find

---

9 Room 5 on Staircase XII.

10 i.e. the first meeting of the Junior Common Room.

11 The Master of University College, R.W. Macan.

12 'Greats' or *Literae Humaniores* is the study of philosophy and ancient history. Midway in the student's second year he takes the first public examination in what is called Classical Honour Moderations, an examination in Greek and Latin. It is possible, however, to go directly to 'Greats' which is the second part of *Literae Humaniores*. Given the choice, Lewis decided not to bypass Classical Honour Moderations.

13 Arthur Blackburne Poynton is mentioned in note 62 to the letter of 28 April 1917.

myself fairly alright: of course the great difference after Kirk's is that you are left to work very much on your own. It is a little bit strange at first, but I suppose hard work in any lines will not be wasted. The best thing I go to is the series of lectures by Gilbert Murray, which are very good indeed: I always feel much the better for them.

The coal difficulty is not very serious. We have all our meals in Hall, which, if it abolishes the cosy breakfast in one's rooms and the interchange of 'decencies and proprieties' is a little cheaper: we shall go back to the old arrangement as soon as we can. The library, one lecture room, and the Junior Common Room are always warm, and the two former are quite quiet: then for the evening we can afford a modest blaze at one's 'ain fireside'. Our little body gets on very well together and most of us work. The place is looking more beautiful than ever in the wintry frost: one gets splendid cold colouring at the expense of tingling fingers and red noses.

I hope the water works in front of the dining room windows is being restored, and that you are keeping well. How is the finger?

your loving son,
Jack

TO HIS FATHER (LP VI: 85–6):

University College,
Oxford.
4th Feb. 1919

My dear Papy,

Although, as you say, your letter was not a 'real' one, the absence of a successor to it leads me to believe that the word is again with me. Before this I hope that you have got mine. Thank you for the enclosure which so far I have failed to change as they ask me for my 'certificate'. If you have it I had better get it or else send you the other thing to change. The private letter which you enclose was rather funny: it thanks me for a subscription to the 'Strandtown Sewing Guild' – which I have never heard of. I suppose it was really given by you – or is W. a keen amateur of sewing guilds?

With regard to things in general here I don't know that I have much to add to my last letter. I find the work pretty stiff, but I think I am keeping my head above water. Poynton is, so far as I can judge, quite an exceptionally good tutor, and my visits to him are enjoyable as well as useful – although he objects to my style of Greek prose – 'I don't care very much for treacle *or* barley sugar myself'. So you have bequeathed to me some remnant of the old Macaulese taint after all. I drank tea with him last Sunday. Another man from Univ. went with me and the party consisted of Mrs and Miss Poynton, two girl undergraduates, and ourselves. As a matter of fact our host did nearly all the talking and kept us very well amused: he is an excellent if somewhat unjust raconteur. He came up to Balliol under Jowett and had a lot to say of the great man. It's funny you know, they all laugh at him, they all imitate his little mannerisms, but nobody who ever met him forgets to tell you so.

Much to my surprise I have had 'greatness thrust upon me'.[14] There is a literary club in College called the Martlets, limited to twelve undergraduate members: it is over three hundred years old, and alone of all College Clubs has its minutes preserved in the Bodleian.[15] I have been elected Secretary – the reason being of course that my proposer, Edwards, was afraid of getting the job himself. And so if I am forgotten of all else, at least a specimen of my handwriting will be preserved to posterity. Someone will read a paper on Yeats at our next meeting: we are also going to have one on Masefield and we hope to get Masefield himself (who lives just outside)[16] to come up and listen to it and give a reply.

I have a very bad piece of news for you: Smugy is dead.[17] Sometime in the middle of last term he fell a victim to flu. I suppose I am very inexperienced but I had come to depend on his always being there – to quote a specimen of his Little Thompson, to welcome me back some day to criticise the book. Poor old man! I heard this from my friend Cooper who is up at Christchurch. As he is in a most expensive College and arrayed in glory, I suppose – and hope – that there has been a change in the family fortunes.

---

14 Shakespeare, *Twelfth Night*, II, v, 161.

15 The Martlets somehow acquired the reputation of dating 'from dim antiquity' but their first meeting was in 1892. The minute books are in the Bodleian Library under the shelfmark MS. Top Oxon. d. 95/1–5. There is an article on 'The Martlets' by P.C. Bayley in the *University College Record* (1949–1950). Walter Hooper's 'To the Martlets' in *C.S. Lewis: Speaker and Teacher*, ed. Carolyn Keefe (1971) contains the minutes of the papers Lewis read to the society between 1919 and 1940.

16 i.e. outside Oxford.

17 Harry Wakelyn Smith, who taught Classics and English at Malvern College. See note 16 to the letter of 21 September 1913.

I am afraid all this must sound rather selfish to you in the Bolshevik darkness of Belfast: but you have my sympathy – if only nothing worse comes of it. The Clyde business seems to have been settled without a concession, and that is the best sign we have.[18]

With best love,

your loving son,

Jack

TO ARTHUR GREEVES (W):

[University College
9 February 1919]

My dear Arthur,

I am really sorry that I did not write you your letter as I should last week. At present I am working at such high pressure that if anything unexpected turns up it must swallow something else. So long as nothing interrupts my routine I get on just comfortably, with a little time to spare at week ends for reading: when something does, I am stranded. However I hope to be more regular in future. Last Sunday I had to go out to tea with a don here called Poynton who is my tutor.

The place has been looking just lovely in the snow. As you come out of our college gate you see All Souls and just beyond it the grey spire of St Mary's Church: you know what real Gothic is like: all little pinacles with every kind of ornament on them and in the snow they look like a wintry forest hung up against the dark sky, and always associated in ones mind with the sound of bells. Just beyond St Marys you come into a solemn silent square with the great dome of the Bodleian in the middle: you can imagine how fine it looks with the white carpet underfoot. But I must send you some penny postcards.

I expected my father read you about the 'Martlets', a literary club I have joined: I only hope it won't absorb valuable time. The great treat is the prospect of whistling John Masefield up from his villa in the suburbs of Oxford to read us a paper. I must really get some of his books when

---

18 Over the years the high price of shipbuilding caused the well-known shipbuilders, Messrs. Yarrow and Co., to move their works from the Thames at Poplar up to Scotstoun on the Clyde (near Glasgow). Nevertheless, because labour problems continued to hound shipbuilding even in Scotland, it was announced in *The Times* of 4 February 1919 (p. 9) that Yarrow and Co. would gradually transfer part of their production to the Pacific coast of North America at Vancouver.

I have any time. I see from this week's Supplement[19] that he has just published another volume of narrative poems. Judging by the quotations it is execrably bad.

Tea at the Poynton's was quite amusing by the way: he is a very humorous old man who says the funniest things in a monotonous, melancholy voice. He showed us some books of Russian fairy tales – he is learning the language. They were badly printed on poor paper but exquisitely illustrated and illuminated: the designs were all 'flat' of course but very effective, and in one or two cases very simple colouring produced the best impressions of evening or cold or so forth.

The only man of much interest whom I have met in College is Blunt.[20] His father is a don at Christ Church,[21] and he was at Winchester where he acted a minor part in a production of Yeat's 'On Baile's Strand'[22] with the young Asquith[23] as 'The Fool' – some wd. say an appropriate part! He has also met Kipling and Bergson,[24] neither of whom impressed him in talk tho' he professes to admire the latter. Of course he is a trifle affected and omniscient like all these people who stayed out the whole numbing time at 'one of our great public schools' but he is really appreciative of some kinds of literature, especially Morris, Yeats and Maeterlinck which of course pleases me. I also find that another man in college called Paisley[25] has written some poems which that man Mais (who wrote 'Diary of

19 John Masefield's *A Poem and Two Plays* (1919) was reviewed in *The Times Literary Supplement* (30 January 1919), p. 54.

20 Henry Pyot Blunt (1898–1955) took his BA in 1922. He was with the Bombay Burma Trading Corporation, Rangoon, 1922–26; an assistant master in the Upper Canada College, Toronto, 1927; with the John Lewis Partnership in 1936; Minister of Food in 1939; with the Commercial Corporation in 1942; and Minister of Food 1947–52.

21 Herbert William Blunt (1864–1940) who was Tutor in Philosophy and Librarian of Christ Church 1888–1928.

22 W.B. Yeats, *On Baile's Strand* (1904).

23 The Hon. Anthony Asquith (1902–68), fifth son of the 1st Earl of Oxford and Asquith.

24 Henri Bergson (1859–1941), a French philosopher who developed a philosophical position in opposition to scientific materialism. During his undergraduate years Lewis read Bergson's *Essai* (1889) and *L'Évolution Créatice* (1907).

25 (Sir) Rodney Marshall Pasley (1899–1982) was educated at Sherborne School, after which he served as a 2nd lieutenant in the Royal Field Artillery during 1914–18. He took his BA from University College in 1921, after which he became an assistant master at Alleyn's School, Dulwich, 1921–5; vice-principal of Rajkumar College at Rajkot, India, 1926–8; assistant master at Alleyn's School, 1931–6; headmaster of Barnstaple Grammar School, 1936–43; and headmaster of Central Grammar School, Birmingham, from 1943 until his retirement in 1959.

a Schoolmaster and an introduction to 'The Loom of Youth'[26]) is 'trying to get published'. The thing rather sniffs of modernism, of general Alec-Waugh-ishness. I don't know Paisley very well but I shall be interested to see the book when and if it comes out. I wish I could hear anything of my own: I am sure I shall be white haired before it sees daylight!

In reading I am still at the philosopher book, have finished King John and am reading Troilus & Cressida – a very good play. I progress so slowly that I shall have little to chronicle in this way for a long time. The Gibbon for you has not turned up yet but I shall order them to send it immediately.

'The family' has been greatly taken with your photo: they didn't expect you to be so good-looking! & Mrs Moore asks me to ask you for one for herself and sends her love.

I wonder are you right about George Elliot not living? Perhaps so, for even already one hears less of her than of the Brontes: but there is a sort of balance and sanity, a good-breeding even about them & especially 'Middlemarch' that you don't get in the Brontes. You said you *had* read Gilbert Murray's translation of the Bacchae didn't you? I think I shall write one myself some day: his doesn't satisfy me at all!

I am glad to hear you are still working. Do get on with the writing: as you said yourself it at least needs no physical energy and I am sure you only need to stick at it. The cold here is simply awful – thats not a conventional remark, because it is. Oh, by the way, somebody else *did* ask me who wrote the librettos of Wagner's operas – I nearly expired. Two such ignorami in one world is *too* much.[27]

Yours
Jack

P.S. Nearly all this is fit for 'publication' except one sentence.[28]

TO ARTHUR GREEVES (W):

[University College
16 February 1919]

My dear Arthur,
Many thanks for your letter. Your account of strike life at home

---

26 Alec Waugh, *The Loom of Youth* (1917).
27 Lewis was thinking of Richard Wagner's *Ring of the Nibelung* cycle, for which Wagner wrote both libretto and music.
28 He did not want his father to see the reference to Mrs Moore.

was very amusing – rather trying to have your model eaten! Only why were you painting those sort of things? 'Faute de mieux' I suppose!

About the Gibbon, Blackwell's have at last heard: you can get only three volumes and there is no talk of a reprint. Would you like me to try and get a complete set of that larger edition by the same publisher? I think I described it to you before, but I can't say I should advise it myself: the type is a little bit larger but it has no other advantage & is certainly not worth the difference in price.

I have bought two copies of drawings by Albrecht Dürer. You will find a good article about him in the Encyclopedia Brittanica. I have always looked upon [him] as the founder of the fantastic & illustrative school now represented by Rackham and Heath Robinson. This view is probably quite wrong historically but I am sure you would recognize the similarity in the very lines and shadows. These two are 'S. Jerome' and the 'Prodigal Son'. The first is very dark, and shows a heavy Gothic chamber: in the light of the single window sits an old wizardy figure pouring over a monstrous book. The room contains the typical insignia of mediaeval sorcery – a crocodile hung on the wall. At the saint's feet sleep together a lion and a dog. I do wish Dürer had illustrated 'The Faerie Queene'. The best thing about the 'Prodigal Son' is the drawing of the swine, which are really like great, wild boars, shaggy and tusked, and recalling somehow in their fantastic strength the dwarfs in Rackham. The background containing the thatched buildings of the sty and the 'tangled spires' of a house is – le Romance même. I haven't had time to study the prodigal himself and so don't describe him. I hope they will be framed by Teusday. There are several others in a shop here – from 2/6 each and a few shillings more for framing. I wonder would you like them? There are a lot I would like to get but some of his best backgrounds are spoilt by nude female figures of the most brutal and deliberate ugliness I've ever seen. I can't think what he is trying to do in these cases – whether they are done in malice or whether that seemed beautiful in his day.

I am still reading the philosopher book: there is something to be said for reading so little, you take it in better. Of course in work I am reading as fast [as] I can & am more than half way through the Iliad. I have to read all Homer, all Virgil, all Demosthenes & all Cicero, besides four Greek plays and a special subject instead of verse. I think in my case it will be Logic, but am not quite sure.

By the way when are you going to get Lang's translation of Homer? I suggest you should get 'The World's Desire' the romance about Helen that he wrote in collaboration with Rider Haggard (a good blend!) and then his Oddyssey after that. 'World's Desire' is so Homeric that you would pass from one to the other insensibly. By the way people from Christ Church tell me they have a don there who tells you to translate Homer in the style of Pope and sternly quells anything like Morris or Chaucer. Can you believe that such barbarism survives in the 20th century, such an absolute lack of historical sense?

Did I describe to you our meeting of the 'Martlets' on Yeats,[29] I think I did. I have got to read a paper on Morris at the next but one. I fought hard against undertaking this extra time devouring job, but had to in the end. Luckily I shall have no difficulty in finding things to say, and I really have read nearly all his important works – which is a very rare qualification in people that read papers at college societies.

Winter has broken up here and it is quite warm. Once or twice in the mornings I have been able to sit in my own rooms without a fire and the window open. One of the annual joys is the first day you go out without an overcoat.

I have been talking to Pasely, the man whose poems Mais is trying to get published. He says he is of an old-fashioned type, not at all a modernist and has promised to show me his things. He was at the same school with Alec Waugh and confirms the story of his getting the order of the boot.

You don't say anything about your own writing: mine of course is compulsorily 'off'. I think it would do you [a] lot of good to start something and perhaps send me instalments in the old way.

Many thanks for the photo.

Yours

Jack

Lewis thought he was probably holding a temporary commission in the regular army, with perhaps a small pension, and on 18 February he sent the War Office exactly the same letter he had written to them on 18 January, complaining that he had 'received neither gratuity nor pension', and asking for clarification on the matter. He was to be disappointed and embarrassed by the reply. In their letter of 20 February the War Office said:

---

29 The minutes of this meeting, held on 12 February, are found in the Bodleian: MS. Top. Oxon. d. 95/3, fos. 64–6.

You have been released from actual military duty from 24th December inclusive. Subsequent to this date you will not be entitled to army pay and allowances, neither shall any period during which you are so released count towards any gratuity, nor for non-effective benefits, nor will you be eligible for promotion during that period...You will be liable to recall for Military duty only in the event of urgent military necessity before the termination of the present war, but such liability of service is not a bar to you taking up civil employment, emigration, or repatriation overseas. (Public Record Office and LP VI: 91)

TO HIS FATHER (LP VI: 91–2):

University College,
Oxford.
23rd Feby. 1919

My dear Papy,

Many thanks for your letters and the enclosures. Certainly our friends 'the master starred with gold and splashed with red' have surpassed themselves over my commission. I remember Peard well at Crownhill: I do not remember his having been to France since, so we may suppose that for the last two years he has been able to devote all his energies to the cultivation of his epistolary style. The result is highly praiseworthy. You write complaining that A is B and he replies that on the contrary you can find by reference that B is A. As you say however, we cannot let the matter rest there. The immediate danger you spoke of has been warded off, at any rate for a time, and I think you can safely continue your correspondence with this very worthy young man.

I return the two oracular letters about the gratuity. I can hardly believe that they are trying to cheat me altogether, as it has been repeated time after time in every newspaper that we are all to have them – wounded or unwounded. I met a man from Keble the other day who had never been out, but who was demobilized with a pension of 10/- a week on the strength of 'ill-health contracted while in the service'. Perhaps we might mention to the masters that I went in Class A and came out B: that I can't take any violent exercise: and that I still have other trouble we wot of. Certainly if we do get Bolshevism in England, the treacherous and dishonest beaurocracy has earned it. Have you read the story of the eight officers sent back on leave from Cologne in the middle of the recent cold in a cattle truck without even straw, and no stops – seven of whom died? Save us from our friends.[30]

By the way I notice that the war bond thing you sent me expires on the first of next month. Will you please send me the certificate with your next letter, as they won't change it otherwise. Thank you for the pyjamas which are quite warm enough. Spring has come in with a rush, and once or twice in the morning I have been able to sit in my room with no fire and the windows open.

I am glad to hear that Malvern intends to do the right thing about Smugy. Let me know what the Colonel intends to do and I will do like wise. I should rather like to know the subject they will choose for the H.W. Smith Prize. I suggest the study of Horace as suitable to the old man's tastes. Cooper has a photo of him taken shortly before his death: he seemed to have got much thinner, and that, with the size of his eyes, had given him a somewhat frog like appearance, but it was the same genial face. On the questions of his possible criticisms of the book we are left to endless conjecture: whether he would have thought them too outspoken or not, he would probably have found them too polemical, too turbid, lacking the classical quiet and detachment for which he looked in his favourite books – Horace, Milton, the Arabian Nights, R.L. Stevenson. 'I hate being written *at*' he once said.

I am glad to hear that Belfast has recovered, and hope you are none the worse for the wearisome weeks you have been through.

With best love,
your loving son,
Jack

TO HIS FATHER (LP VI: 86–7):

University College,
Oxford
[28?] Feb. 1919

My dear Papy,

This week we have surpassed ourselves – besides crossing in fact, our letters have crossed in substance as well. It is rather strange that

---

30 Albert Lewis would not allow the matter to rest. After writing to the War Office on behalf of his son, on 28 March they paid Jack a 'wound gratuity' of £145 16s 8d. After further correspondence, and a medical examination, he was paid a 'further wound gratuity' of £104 3s 4d.

Warnie and I should both be foregathering with Old Malvernians so far apart. I am glad to see that affairs at home have not gone beyond inconvenience, although that is bad enough: our own strikers however seem to have shown a certain decency and sense of order which others did not.

We continue here in much the same way and I am beginning to fall into the routine. On Wednesday I drank tea with the Carlyles – Dr. Carlyle, as I think I said, is one of the Don members of the Martlets.[31] He is also the College Chaplain, and in describing our daily services to a lady, Poynton rather maliciously said, 'Carlyle reads as much of the service as he can remember', which is only half justified. He is a foxy looking old gentleman of Scotch extraction with an ultra-clerical voice: wife and daughters not very remarkable. The most interesting thing about him is his house in 'Holywell', one of the oldest streets. It is inconspicuous from outside, as its fine old gables have been cut down into a 'classic' balustrade during the barbarism of the 18th century, but it is almost perfect inside: grand old stone fireplaces, little leaded panes and beamed ceilings. I suspect however that it is a trifle damp and not unknown to the mice.

We have woken up to a white quad (if not quite a white world) for two or three mornings, and I believe there has been some skating. It is certainly very pretty, but I for one shall be glad when it is gone.

By the way, from what you say about 'Mods' and 'Greats' I am inclined to think that I may have given you a wrong impression. It is not really a question of 'cultivating fallow ground' by Mods., for as a matter of fact, 'Greats', being more philosophical and less strictly Classical, would be really rather easier to me as I am at present. The only thing is that when a question of Fellowships rose later on, people might feel that they could never be quite sure of you unless they knew what you had done in Mods. However, from that point of view it is equally the right course to take.

I have had a letter from Aunt Suffern and I gather than the two 'Arundel Prints' are coming. She hopes that 'the prevailing tint of my rooms is

---

31 The Rev. Alexander James Carlyle (1861–1943) was a political philosopher, ecclesiastical historian and social reformer. He was ordained in the Church of England in 1888, and became a Fellow and Chaplain of University College in 1893. He had to give up the fellowship when he married in 1895, but he continued to serve the College as a lecturer in politics and economics and as chaplain. He was the mainstay of the Christian Social Union. His works include the *History of Mediaeval Political Theory in the West*, 6 vols. (1903–36), which he wrote in collaboration with his brother, Sir R.W. Carlyle.

brown' as otherwise they will not enjoy their full splendour. In the present condition of the post I think it is very doubtful if they will ever arrive at all.

Would you please ask the 'skeery old woman' to fish me out a suit of pyjamas and send them?[32] I find I have left myself rather short. I hope that the floods around Leeborough are by now subsiding – or perhaps you have had a little skating in front of the dining room windows. Heinemanns remain as silent as the grave.

your loving son,

Jack

P.S. I have sent off the various army forms. Any news about getting out of that Special Reserve commision?

TO ARTHUR GREEVES (W):

[University College]
Sunday [2 March 1919]

My dear Arthur,

I was rather under the impression that I *had* kept to the weekly arrangement this last time. At any rate you will observe that I am answering your last at once for it only came yesterday.

You seem to be lucky in your theatrical fates at home. I should very much like to have seen 'The Importance of Being Ernest',[33] tho perhaps some of it would be lost on the stage. So far as I can remember I don't agree with you about the feeble ending. The beauty of it is that it entirely rejects probability or sentiment – would that all our society farces did the same – and gives itself up to a sort of glittering and classic nonsense that reminds me strongly of 'Alice in Wonderland'.

I have Layamon's Brut and Wace's translated in the one Everyman volume[34] – or rather the parts of them about the Arthurian period. Wace you remember was 'a french clerke, well could he write' who copied

---

32 The 'skeery old woman' was Mary Cullen, the successor to Annie Strahan in 1917 as cook-housekeeper at Little Lea. She was called this because of a certain breathless manner. She was devoted to Albert Lewis whom she served for the rest of his life. On the break-up of Little Lea in 1930 she became a cook in a public kitchen, and lived in a house which had belonged to Albert, rent free. (LP VI: 87).

33 Oscar Wilde, *The Importance of Being Earnest* (1895).

34 This is the *Arthurian Chronicles, Represented by Wace and Layamon* [1912] mentioned in note 9 to letter of 1 February 1916.

Layamon's poem in French rhyming couplets, with more style but less vigour. Wace is famous for his 'rationalising' remark about a magic fountain he went to see in Broceliande, and, being the wrong sort of man, of course did not find the marvels 'A fool I went, a fool I returned.'[35] Layamon I quite liked tho' I didn't finish it. Of course his battles are fatiguing, but the whole thing is very 'heroic' – much more like Boewulf than Malory. Arthur cleaves the Dane Skallagrim to the teeth and exults over him just like the warriors in the Iliad. On the other hand the passing of Arthur is really more romantic than in Malory, who, you remember, makes Avalon a really existing valley where the great king is buried. Brut, however, knows better 'They say he abideth in Avalon with Argante the fairest of all elves: but ever the Britons think that he will come again to help them at their need'[36] – a great deal of which I copied in a poem rejected by Heinemann – on whom ten thousand maledictions. Every week nearly in the Times Supplement I see a new book of poems published by him, but never mine. I can't think why he took it at all at this rate. I shall probably write to Evans to day – with the usual result.

As your letter arrived yesterday afternoon (Saturday) I couldn't follow your commands about going for the Gibbon-hunt at once. I am still at the philosopher book, tho' nearly finished. The later & more modern chapters are pretty difficult – Spencer and William James etc, who do not so easily fit into formulae as simple minded gentlemen of the Locke or Paley type. I thought you would like 'The Private Papers of Henry Ryecroft'. I don't know that the 'soothing qualities' were what struck me most, but no! – I'm thinking of 'The Corner of Harley Street'.[37] Now I remember: don't you like his remarks about cooking? Also on spiritualism he expresses a feeling I have sometimes experienced – mechanical reaction I suppose. We do get quite good things at the theatre but when should I have time to go? The only one I regret was Maeterlinck's 'Burgomaster of Stilmonde':[38] but it was only two nights, and the waste of an evening and the rush there would have been to get seats put me off.

To go back 'to the last remark but one' for a minute, as Alice says, that book of mine on Epic and Heroic Poetry gives a very good account of Layamon: reading it I have often wished you could get a complete crib

---

35 ibid., p. x.
36 ibid., p. 264.
37 Peter Harding, *The Corner of Harley Street* (1911).
38 Maurice Maeterlinck, *Le Bourgmestre de Stilmonde* (1919).

instead of only the Arthurian bit. Geoffrey of Monmouth is in the Everyman is he not? I am waiting to try and get a copy of him in the Latin[39] – perhaps there is one in the College Library. If only one had time to read a little more: we either get shallow & broad or narrow and deep.

At our last meeting of the Martlets a man called Wyllie read a paper on Newbolt.[40] I hadn't thought the subject *very* promising but he quoted a great many good things I hadn't known – especially a very queer little song about grasshoppers that you must read if you can get hold of it: so different from the usual patriotic business, tho' that is good too, until you've read sixty odd pieces on exactly the same lines. I have had a most interesting talk with Pasely and seen his poems. I mentioned him before, didn't I? Mais is trying to get him published. He has written one long piece that I envy him very much, and a number of pretty enough things – no stuff in them, the sort of things that are as common and not quite as good as wildflowers. But the one piece was really extraordinarily good. I wonder will he do the same again? At the meeting, by the way, some bright person was found to make a defence of vers libre.[41]

I got a letter the other day from an unknown member of the female sex – an undergraduate apparently – asking me to play my part in National Reconstruction by joining the Oxford University Socialist Society. As it was a printed circular I didnt 'feel called upon' to answer it.

I think the ugly figures in Dürer go beyond your suggestion – there is spite in every line: they were probably fancy portraits of ladies who didn't ask him to dinner. But it would be unfair to judge him by these explosions of ill temper. By 'verse' in exams I mean the composition of Latin & Greek verses, which is the usual subject to take: if you don't do them, you do something else. Of course it is nothing to do with the verse or prose that you read.

We are having some lovely days here now, and it must be just glorious in the country: thank goodness there is plenty of greenery in Oxford.

---

39 Geoffrey of Monmouth (d. 1154), *Historia Regum Britanniae* (Paris, 1508); *Histories of the Kings of Britain*, trans. Sebastian Evans, Everyman's Library [1912].

40 Basil Platel Wyllie's paper, read at the meeting on 26 February, was entitled 'The Poetry of Henry Newbolt'. Bodleian: MS. Top. Oxon. d. 95/3, fos. 67–9.

41 'An interesting discussion on "Vers Libre", arising out of one poem quoted by Mr Wyllie, then followed. Mr Pasley maintained that this school was not entirely free from a certain charlatanism, but the Society was interested to find in Mr [Geoffrey Odell] Vinter an enthusiastic defender of this kind of composition.' MS. Top. Oxon. d. 95/3, fo. 69.

There is no decent edition of Chaucer except the fabulously expensive Medici press one and even that only gives the Canterbury Tales – except of course the Everyman Canterbury Tales which is garbled and modernised: by a ridiculous arrangement whenever they come to an obscene passage they slip back into the real language.[42] Chaucer was very like Dickens – a virtuous, bourgeois story teller fond of highly moral vulgarity & indecency for its own sake, incapable (at the Tales period not in his early life) of appreciating romance.

Yours
Jack

TO HIS FATHER (LP VI: 96–7):

University College,
Oxford
5th March 1919

My dear Papy,

I was glad to get your letter, after a somewhat longer interval than usual and a hint that you were rather under the weather. Arthur also tells me that you have not been well. If this flu' is at all bad in Belfast I most strongly advise you to get inoculated. It will cost you only a few hours discomfort and, whatever people may tell you about its efficacy or otherwise, it undoubtedly did stop the pest in our camp at Ludgershall.

Thank you for your offer about the Smugy memorial: but you remember what David said on a similar occasion about 'that which cost naught'.[43] I am sending them a cheque for £2 and if you still wish to, you had better make yours a separate present in your own person. By the way, talking about subscriptions, I was asked the other day for one to a testimonial for the commandant of Ashton Court – a most peevish and ill tempered old maid whom we all hated, patients and nurses alike. I wish the adoring public could know what a few of these 'kind workers for our wounded' are really like.

I return with many thanks the certificate and the other two official documents. The one which promises that I shall not be called up for further service except in the case of another emergency in the present war was very pleasing to me – not that I set any value on their promise, but it

---

42 Charles Cowden Clarke, *Tales from Chaucer*, Everyman's Library [1911].
43 2 Samuel 24:24.

would be nice to be able to show their dishonesty in print if they tried to trick me again. With regard to the other, I am thinking of changing my bank to one in Oxford, as I have to get my cheques cashed at odd shops and depend on their convenience. Have you any advice to give me on this point?

I don't think that anyone who takes the trouble to read my book through will seriously call it blasphemous, whatever criticism he may make on artistic grounds.[44] If he does not, we need not bother about his views. Of course I know there will be a number of people who will open it by chance at some of the gloomiest parts of Part I and decide 'Swinburnian Ballads' and never look at it again. But what would you do? If one writes at all – perhaps like Talleyrand many 'don't see the necessity' – one must be honest. You know who the God I blaspheme is and that it is not the God you or I worship, or any other Christian. But we have talked over this before. Arthur tells me that you have a copy of Reveillé with my thing in it.[45] They have omitted to send me one – 'who am I?' as Knowles said.

I look like having a busy time next week: I am reading in Chapel, saying grace in Hall, writing a paper on Morris for the Martlets, finishing

---

44 Although *Spirits in Bondage* was not published until 20 March 1919, Albert and Warnie Lewis had read it and Jack's atheism was evident to both. Exchanging views about the poems, Albert said to Warnie on 27 January, 'I don't know what your candid opinion may be as we had not an opportunity of comparing notes. Mine is very distinct. Some of the poems I think excellent – one or two better than excellent. The spirit which pervades the book, at times at all events, I should have liked different. But when every word of criticism or disparagement has been spoken, it remains something more than a creditable performance for a boy of 19' (LP VI: 82). 'While I am in complete agreement with you,' Warnie replied on 28 January, 'as to the excellence of parts of "IT'S" book, I am of opinion that it would have been better if it had never been published. Even at 23 one realises that the opinions and convictions of 20 are transient things. Jack's Atheism is I am sure purely academic, but even so, no useful purpose is served by endeavouring to advertise oneself as an Atheist. Setting aside the higher problems involved, it is obvious that a profession of a Christian belief is as necessary a part of a man's mental make up as a belief in the King, the Regular Army, and the Public Schools.' Mr Lewis knew that his younger son's dislike of Malvern was a cause of irritation and embarrassment to the older brother, but when he learned that Warnie had taken Jack to task over the book, he wrote to him on 9 March saying: 'He is young and he will learn in time that a man has not absolutely solved the riddle of the heavens above and the earth beneath and the waters under the earth at twenty. I am not going to slop over but I do think that if Oxford does not spoil him...he may write something that men would not willingly let die' (LP VI: 98).
45 'Death in Battle' from *Spirits in Bondage* appeared in *Reveille*, No. 3 (February 1919).

the Iliad, and dining with the Mugger. I hope to be able to eat and sleep a little as well! As the time goes on I appreciate my hours with Poynton more and more. After Smugy and Kirk I must be rather spoiled in the way of tutors, but this man comes up to either of them, both as a teacher and as a humorous 'card'. Gilbert Murray is, I'm afraid, not very much good for exams., tho' his literary merits are unsurpassed.

I will write to the Bristol photographer and speak 'severely'. What do you think of the Canadian Bolshevists? I wonder is there anyone found now a days to disparage – as we once did – the great Victorian age? 'They were the glory, we are the decline'.

I hope you are better by now. Take care of yourself and don't run risks.

your loving son,
Jack

TO HIS FATHER (LP VI: 100):

University College,
Oxford
Saturday 15th [March 1919]

My dear Papy,

This is 'out of its due time'[46] as you are still in my debt. I am writing to tell you that the 'Varsity term ends today and the College term on Monday. I shall be staying up for a week more, following Poynton's instructions.

After that I shall go down to help Mrs Moore with her move at Bristol: she has had to come back to clear out the house. There seems to be considerable difficulty about getting anywhere else. London and Bristol are both hopeless: I have suggested here, but that seems equally impossible. I can't understand where the influx of people is coming from.

Of course the expenses of the journey I shall pay myself, and not include in the 'Term' – which, by the way, will also not include this term's Battels, as, by an absurd arrangement, we don't get our bills until we come up next term.

My effort in Reveillé – I was sorry to see the old reading – is in curious company, isn't it? No word from Heinemann's still.

---

46 1 Corinthians 15:8.

I was surprised to hear from Aunt Lily that G. had broken off her engagement.[47] I wonder what your view on the subject is?

your loving son,

Jack

TO HIS BROTHER (LP VI: 104):

University College,
Oxford
[2? April 1919]

My dear W.,

Many thanks for both letters. I got the first one alright, and wrote for the French book at once, waiting to answer you until I could send it. The reason of my silence in general is that I have got to work like Hell here – I seem to have forgotten everything I know.

If you are on the look out for a cheap modern edition of Chesterfield's letters,[48] I will see what I can do, but I feel inclined to reply in Tommy's irreverent style, 'Wot 'opes'. About St Simon you will find it much easier to write to Paris for a French edition: when you had finished with it you could send it on to me to be bound and pressed – after which you would find it as good as new. I don't know of a crib to it.[49] To take up P's style, have you ever noticed a book at home 'very much on the same lines', the Memoirs of Count Gramont, written in French by a Hamilton who was a hanger on of the grand monarque, and translated?[50]

In the name of all the gods why do you want to go into the 'Russian Expeditionary Force'? You will drag on a post-less, drink-less, book-less, tobacco-less existence for some months until the Bolshevists finally crush us and then probably end your days at a stake or on a cross.

The typewriting of private letters is the vile invention of business men, but I will forgive you on the ground that you were practising.

---

47 His cousin Gundreda Ewart had just broken off her engagement to Captain Geoffrey Burbage.

48 Philip Dormer Stanhope, Earl of Chesterfield, *Letters to his Son*, 2 vols. (1774); *Letters to his Friends*, 3 vols. (1777–8).

49 Warnie was to remember all his life the discovery in St Omer on 3 March 1919 of an abridgement of the *Mémoirs* of the Duc de Saint-Simon. He was writing to Jack from France for information about the whole of Saint-Simon's *Mémoirs* which he was keen to acquire. Out of this grew his lifelong interest in the court of Louis XIV and the *Grand Siècle*, and the writing of his seven books on that period.

50 *Memoirs of Count Gramont*, ed. Gordon Goodwin (1903).

There doesn't seem to be any week end leave at Oxford except for the U.P.A., which aren't so easily accepted as in the army.

Did you see the 'very insolent' review of me on the back page of the Times Literary Supplement last week?[51] There will be woe and consternation on the home front. I have been meeting a lot of O.M.'s.[52] this term, mostly people who sat under Smugy with me. I'm sorry to give you such a scrappy letter, but – quite bona fide – I really am burning the midnight oil these days.

yours
Jack

P.S. The only echo of Bolshevism in Oxford was the following jeu d'esprit: five or six bright spirits from Balliol sent up a long wire to the Daily Mail telling of an attempt by the 'Red' people to burn down Oxford, which only succeeded in burning down a cabstand: the lie never appeared and seems to have fallen rather flat.

TO ARTHUR GREEVES (W):

[University College]
Monday [5 May 1919][53]

My dear Arthur,

Many thanks for your letter. I had meant to write to you yesterday whether I heard or not, but when the time came I was not feeling well and so it got put off till to-day.

My first news I'm afraid will plunge you into despair. The copy of Morris's Odyssey which I had seen last term is gone and they could produce only a rather dirty one in its place! I felt I had better not order a copy, as you [are] rather afraid of doing that – tho' I think it is a case of 'nothing venture, nothing win', you'll *have* to order a book sometime again.

---

51 *Spirits in Bondage* received the following review in *The Times Literary Supplement* (27 March 1919): 'These lyrics are always graceful and polished, and their varied themes are chosen from those which naturally attract poets – the Autumn Morning, Oxford, Lullaby, The Witch, Milton Read Again, and so on. The thought, when closed with, is found rather often not to rise above the commonplace. The piece which most arrested us was "The Satyr."'

52 Old Malvernians.

53 Lewis would have seen Arthur when he was in Belfast from 2 to 24 April.

I was in some anxiety to see my new rooms, having left them in a ghastly state from my luckless attempt at distempering, and having heard nothing from the man whom I had told to paper them. Of course he hadn't done it, but by way of compensation the distemper had dried out excellently – all my splotches and thick & thin variations had disappeared. It is a nice quiet greyish blue: of course it is rather untidy and splashed about the woodwork a bit, but you don't notice that very much. It suits the two Dürers very well and also the Venus. There is also *one* good piece of furniture, a small bookcase of dark oak. You would agree with me in liking the beam in the ceiling and the deep windows and the old tree that taps against them, recalling Phantastes and Wuthering Heights. When it gets into leaf I shall look out into a mass of greenery with glimpses of the old walls across and of the grass below – such a scene as the redoubtable Heath Robinson did in your 12th night.[54]

But all this you shall see for yourself. I shall go to the dean as my tutor to-morrow and ask him then about the 'guest-room'. By the way I was annoyed to find that I had left behind all the pictures you gave me. Will you please send them as soon as possible: you can understand my desire to get fixed in and see all my household gods around me. How is the Rackham-esque drawing of the hills going on? I hope it will be a great success: it was certainly a splendid idea to do that particular bit in that style.

I have nearly finished the Venus poem and am full of ideas for another, which Gilbert Murray gave me the hint of in a lecture – a very curious legend about Helen, whom Simon Magus, a gnostic magician mentioned in the Acts,[55] found living as a very earthly person in Antioch and gradually recalled to her who she was and took her up to Zeus again, reborn: on their way they had to fight 'the Dynasties' or planets – the evil powers that hold the heaven, between us and something really friendly beyond – I have written some of it, but of course I get hardly any time either for reading or writing.

I have not quite finished the third volume of Gibbon, and it still pleases me as much as ever it did, in fact all the more as I go on. The only attitude you can adopt towards my father's underhand and contemptible efforts to get information out of you (he apparently judges

---

54 Shakespeare's *Twelfth Night*. See note 120 to letter of [18] July 1916.
55 Acts 8:9–24.

your character by his own) is the one you rightly do already – as you say, ignore it; and if he becomes unbearable, go away. You throw out merely a hint about the Glenmachonians' remarks on my book: tell me all they say when you write, you can easily understand how interested I am. I am glad you liked the Patriotism book, many parts of it sounded attractive: the Masefield one I hope to get one of these days.

We have had one meeting of the Martlets at which a very dull looking youth read a surprisingly good paper on Synge:[56] it has really quite encouraged me to try him again, tho' I feel some grains of prejudice against what I remember of him – perhaps because he has become a cult, which few writers escape now a days. I am afraid I have not got to know any of the Balliol poets yet, and am not sure that I shall be able to manage it – I don't see very many people and I don't think Pasely himself meets them very often.

I hope by this time you're sailing the seas of Gibbon (the new counterpart to the old 'Have you read your Swinburne?') and not feeling too depressed with the world in general – that 'The thing's not becoming intolerable!' in fact.

We are having lovely weather here and I shall soon begin to bathe. Don't forget the pictures.

Yours
Jack

TO HIS FATHER (LP VI: 122):

[University College,
Oxford]
11th May 1919

My dear Papy,

Many thanks for your letter and also for the enclosed cheque for £19.12.8. That amount includes all the charges both for tuition and

---

56 Edward Fairchild Watling (1899–1990) matriculated at University College in 1918. He took a Second in Classical Moderations in 1920, and a Third in Greats in 1922. On leaving Oxford he went to King Edward VII School, Sheffield, where he taught classics for 36 years. He will be remembered for his idiomatic and highly readable translations of the classics. These include Sophocles's *Theban Plays* (1947) and Seneca's *Four Tragedies and Octavia* (1966). See *University College Record*, Vol. X, No. 3 (1991), pp. 115–17. He read his paper on 'The Plays of J.M. Synge' at the 192nd meeting of the Martlets on 30 April. Bodleian: MS. Top. Oxon. d. 96/3, fos. 71–2.

college expenses and may serve as a base for future calculation, tho' of course there may be slight differences from term to term.

I was very glad to hear the good news about May:[57] if she was really as bad as they suppose when I left home, they have certainly every reason to be thankful for a very extraordinary recovery.

I have not yet heard from the war office, but, having regard to their usual leisurely methods, I suppose it is not yet time to take any fresh step. I am right, am I not, in supposing that it is from London and not from Dublin that I must expect further communication? We are having real summer weather here, and in our stone walls, without any wind, it is already rather oppressive. The river of course is refreshing, and as my room does not get the morning sun, I can be fairly cool there with all the windows open.

I am sorry that you have no encouraging news from Campbell. Perhaps, after you have given him a fair trial, it might be advisable to see some English surgeon and get a new point of view.

We have all been much amused here by the historic insolence of the German delegates at Versailles. I am afraid however that the matter has a very serious side, and some are already beginning to hint that we may be back in uniform again before it is all over.

Thank you for the letter from Warnie which you sent on: he suggests, as perhaps he has already done to you, that we should go out and see him in France for a few days this summer.

your loving son,
Jack

TO HIS FATHER (LP VI: 126–7):

[University College,
Oxford]
25th May 1919

My dear Papy,

Close upon the heels of your letter came one from the War Office in which I was instructed to place myself in communication with the G.O.C. Southern Command at Salisbury with a view to this Medical Board. I have acknowledged, and shall get myself examined by a local doctor tomorrow.

---

57 May Lewis (b. 1887) was the daughter of Albert's brother, Joseph Lewis.

As for the investments, I think on the whole that the Commercial Debentures would be the most promising: the security, you say, is perfectly good, and in any case I suppose with small sums one should always prefer a good rate to mere safety.

Many thanks for the cake which ate excellently: I enclose a small note of 'appreciation' to the Witch of Endor[58] – it was really rather good of the old creature to suggest the enterprise.

I have not written to Evans, as I found a circular from a Press Association cutting to which I have replied, enclosing 10/-. The results so far have been a very interesting review on 'The Principles of Symbolic Logic' by C. S. Lewis of the University of California. I am writing back to tell them that they have got rather muddled. Symbolic Logic forsooth! I started reading it without noticing the title and was surprised to find myself – as I thought – being commended for a 'scholarly elucidation of a difficult subject'.

As nearly everyone here is a poet himself, they have naturally no time left for lionizing others. Indeed the current literary set is one I could not afford to live in anyway, and tho' many of them have kindly bought copies of the book, their tastes run rather to modernism, 'vers libre' and that sort of thing. I have a holy terror of coteries: I have already been asked to join a Theosophist, a Socialist, and a Celtic society.

By the way, the distinction which one finds in such books as Tom Brown[59] by which the poor, the industrious, and the intellectual, are all in one class, and the rich, brainless and vicious, all in another, does not obtain. Some 'poor scholars' are bad lots, and some of the 'gilded youth' are fond of literature.

I am exceedingly sorry about May. I had hoped that after she turned the corner, the recovery would be easy. The suffering is perhaps the worst feature of the case – danger is so much easier to bear.

I think the work is progressing 'according to plan' and Poynton is still most satisfactory.

We are having a heat wave at present, but manage to survive with the help of bathes. I find I can't swim half the distance I used to, and am

---

58 Mary Cullen, the cook-housekeeper at Little Lea, was often referred to as the 'Witch of Endor'. See note 31 to the letter of 2 March 1919.

59 Hughes, *Tom Brown's Schooldays*.

rather stiff after that. Hoping that your own trouble is on the mend, I am,

your loving son,
Jack

For some time Mr Lewis had been worried about the prominence of Mrs Moore in Jack's life, and he and Warnie were beginning to discuss it. 'The Mrs Moore business is certainly a mystery,' Warnie wrote to his father on 10 May, 'but I think perhaps you are making too much of it. Have you any idea of the footing on which he is with her? Is she an intellectual? It seems to me preposterous that there can be anything in it. But the whole thing irritates me by its freakishness...Probably the whole dread mystery is a product of our own imaginations' (LP VI: 118). 'I confess I do not know what to do or say about Jack's affair,' replied Mr Lewis on 20 May:

> It worries and depresses me greatly. All I know about the lady is that she is old enough to be his mother – that she is separated from her husband and that she is in poor circumstances. I also know that Jacks has frequently drawn cheques in her favour running up to £10 – for what I don't know. If Jacks were not an impetuous, kind hearted creature who could be cajoled by any woman who has been through the mill, I should not be uneasy. Then there is the husband whom I have always been told is a scoundrel – but who some of these days might try a little amiable blackmailing. But outside all these considerations that may be the outcome of a suspicious, police court mind, there is the distraction from work and the folly of the daily letters. (LP VI: 123)

On 3 June Warren wrote to his father saying,

> I am greatly relieved...to hear that Mrs Moore HAS a husband: I understood she was a widow; but as there is a Mr Moore, the whole complexion of the business is altered. We now get the following very unsatisfactory findings. (1) Mrs Moore can't marry Jacks. (2) Mr Moore can't blackmail him because 'IT' hasn't enough to make it a paying risk. (3) You can't be blackmailed because you

wouldn't listen to the proposition for one moment. But the daily letter business does annoy me: especially as I have heard from Jacks once since January of this year. (LP VI: 129)

Although Mrs Moore received a small amount of money from her husband, the main expense of their joint home seems to have fallen on Jack. As Warren mentioned in his 'Memoir': 'since an allowance calculated to suit a bachelor living in college was by no means enough for a householder, Jack found himself miserably poor'. In 1919 the average cost of living in an Oxford college was about £60 a term. (At this time £1 was worth about US$5.) Jack's scholarship from University College was worth about £80 a year, but after paying his college expenses he was left with only about £11 per term. Albert Lewis was giving his son £67 per term, as well as paying incidental expenses.

TO ARTHUR GREEVES (W):

[University College,
Oxford]
Monday [2 June 1919]

My dear Arthur,

I really was ashamed of myself when I got your letter: I had put off my weekly one to you from day to day, hoping to work it in 'some day soon' and hardly realized how long I'd let it go. My letter-writing time last week was rather upset by a long standing debt to Aunt Lily, which simply *had* to be done and an unexpected letter from W.

Now as to all the important questions (1) Come whenever is convenient and let me know beforehand when I may expect you (2) I am afraid you can only get a guests [room] for one or two nights in College, therefore (3) You had better stay in 'The Mitre' in High Street which is the best and also the nearest to College (4) Would you like me to book you a room there.

Thanks very much for the pictures: the two best, the garden one and the tree in the new Soaking Machine are better than I remembered. I am having them both framed. The little Rackhamesque one I am not sure yet how I will treat. It gives me pleasure and has indeed a *special* appeal that the ordinary kind of drawing has not, but I can't find any place I think it would suit. We shall see.

It is perfectly lovely now both in town and country – there are such masses of fruit trees, all white. One big cherry tree stands in the Master's garden just below my windows and a brisk wind this morning had shaken down masses of leaves that lay like snow flakes on the bright smooth grass. Then beyond the lawn you see the gable end of the chapel.

I usually go and bathe before breakfast now at a very nice little place up the Cherwell called 'Parson's Pleasure'.[60] I always swim (on chest) down to a bend, straight towards the sun, see some hills in the distance across the water, then turn and come again to land going on my back and looking up at the willow trees above me. It is a most romantic bathe and rather like William Morris – as one of his characters would 'wash the night off'. I have been reading at breakfast lately 'The Water of the Wondrous Isles',[61] which is more romantic tho' not so well-constructed as 'The Well at the World's End': all the same I have enjoyed it immensely with quite the old thrill, his witches and wanderers I can usually rely on. He is so inexhaustible!

How very funny about Bob, and how typical of Kelsie! Is it that she hides her opinions – I mean on other subjects as well as this – or that she has none.

I have NOT 'woken up and found myself famous' yet but I have slunk into a modicum of notoriety it would seem. At the last meeting of the Martlets I was asked by a man called Hartman[62] whether I was 'the famous Lewis' jokingly of course. It appears that some of the extreme literary set at Balliol and Exeter, the writers of 'vers libre' etc, who run the yearly Books of Oxford Poetry had got the book and asked Hartman if he knew a Lewis at Univ. and if that was the man. The result is that several people are going to buy it who might not have otherwise done so. On Wednesday I am to meet at Hartman's rooms a man called Childe

---

60 See note 73 to letter of 13 May 1917.

61 William Morris, *The Water of the Wondrous Isles* (1897).

62 Cyril Hughes Hartmann (1896–1967), elder son of George Hartmann of Thames Ditton, Surrey, was educated at Charterhouse and matriculated at Oxford in 1914. He took a Third in Modern History in 1920 and a B.Litt. in 1922. On leaving Oxford he became a successful author, writing mainly on literary and historical subjects. His many books include *La Belle Stuart: Memoirs of Court and Society in the Times of Francis Teresa Stuart, Duchess of Richmond and Lennox* (1924), *The Cavalier Spirit and its Influence on the Life and Work of Richard Lovelace (1618–1658)* (1925), *Charles II and Madame* [1934], and *Cudleigh, Lord High Treasurer of England (1630–1673)* [1937].

who edits these books of Oxford Poetry[63] & tho' I am sure I shall disapprove of him and his views it will possibly be useful. Hartman himself is rather an interesting character: his mother was a member of the set that included Oscar Wilde and Whistler[64] and would have included Swinburne if it could. He said he had once met Wilde but did not remember much about it. Lucky man, he was in Spain all thro' the war!

I am afraid I shall never get on with the Gibbon as I go now; although I still like it as much as ever it is awfully hard to keep the connection in my head with so many other irons in the fire. If I once give it up I shall be lost!

Hardly writing anything at all except a few lines yesterday for the Helen poem, and bits for a short one I thought of doing on 'Nimue'. What are the possibilities of the subject? Awfully sorry to hear you've been laid up again: you mustn't do too much when you're here.[65]

Yours
Jack

P.S. Haven't heard from my esteemed parent for some time; has he committed suicide yet?

TO HIS BROTHER (LP VI: 133-4):

University College,
Oxford
9th [June 1919]

My dear W.,

'Sir,' said Dr Johnson, 'you are an unsocial person.' In answer to the charge I can only plead the general atmosphere of the summer term which is the same here as it was at school: whatever energy I have has to be thrown into work and, for the rest, the seductive influence of the river and hot weather must bear the blame. Term ends some time in July, but I shall be staying up for part of the vac. Would the early part of September

---

63 Wilfred Rowland Childe (1890–1952) was the editor (with T.W. Earp and A.L. Huxley) of *Oxford Poetry 1916* (1917) and (with T.W. Earp and Dorothy L. Sayers) of *Oxford Poetry 1917* (1918).

64 The artist James Abbott McNeill Whistler (1834–1903).

65 Arthur visited Lewis in Oxford from about 20 to 28 June, during which time he met the Moores. From Oxford he went to London to consult a heart specialist.

do for your leave: one doesn't get any chance of fine weather or of endurably warm sea water any earlier in Donegal.

I quite agree with you that we could have quite an excellent time together at Portsalon – if we were 'both' there; if, as you suggest, we were 'all' there, I suppose we could endure as we always have endured.

You ask me what is wrong with P......[66] which he describes as exceedingly painful and horribly depressing. I don't meet the doctors myself and therefore, in the case of a man who would hold precisely the same language about a boil or a wasp's sting, it is impossible to say how bad he is: I am afraid however it is rather a serious bother.

There is also a second thing wrong with him – namely that he is fast becoming unbearable. What the difficulties of life with him always were, you know: but I never found it as bad as when I was last at home. I needn't describe the continual fussing, the sulks, the demand to know all one's affairs – you might think I was exaggerating as you have been out of it for so long. I wish to the Lord we had a small income of our own to fall back on in case of emergencies.

The third piece of information was drawn out of Arthur with some difficulty, and will appeal to your sense of humour. It began by a conversation which he overheard between the Gudeman and his lady mother, after they had just met P. The phrases 'It's a pity', 'It's sad to see him going that way', 'I've been afraid for some time' were repeated with true puritan gravity. The real fun began when Arthur managed to drift into the study unannounced one day. There he found our revered parent sprawling in an arm chair, very red in the face and drowsy. For some time he merely stared and refused to give any answer to any remark. Poor Arthur wondered what to do, till his host finally solved the question by saying in a husky voice, 'I'm in great trouble, you'd better go away'. No evidence as to what this 'great trouble' was has ever been forthcoming, so I think we may with probability, if not quite certainty, breathe the magic word of *al-cohol*, 'the subtle alchemist who in a trice' etc.! Of course no one objects to a man getting blind occasionally – although it is interesting to remember his merciless tirades on drink – but there is something unpleasant about this solitary tippling. He might have gathered some of his friends to share the fun.

Thanks very much for getting three copies of the book: one to Jacks, if Jacks père approves of it, might help me to get something into 'The

---

66 Part of this sentence was removed when the letter was copied into the Lewis Papers.

Hibbert', which as you know he edits.[67] I am pleased that you liked 'The Star Bath'[68] as you have been, so far, its only admirer. I have tried with perhaps not very much energy to find those books for you, but Arthur is coming up next week and I shall send him hunting while I want to work. At the same time I should think from my own experience that ordinary English translations are usually too free to be much use as cribs.

The scenery of Donegal would suit us both better than the continent – good old mountains and heather, rather grey and grim. One usually finds quite pleasing people in the hotel which would serve to break up the eternal trio. Write and let me know your plans, I shall try to answer sooner this time.

yours,
Jack

TO HIS FATHER (LP VI: 151–2):

Oxford
Sat. June 29th [1919]

My dear Papy,

I have put off answering your letter until I got Arthur away, who departed with much reluctance yesterday. I have a short note from him this morning telling his first London adventures, which include a discovery of the fact that the specialist whom he went to see has retired some years ago. One would have thought that his people or his home doctor might have found this out before he was sent.

As regards the matter which you particularly mention, there was less need of 'expedition' because I had already communicated with the colonel and had an answer from him: his letter I presume contains substantially the same information which he gave to you.

My own position is this: the academical term has just ended, but owing to 'Comem,' and various schools, hardly anyone has gone down yet. In practice, the summer term really continues for a fortnight or three weeks after its official decease. Beyond this, Poynton has advised me to stay up for some time and work. I am inclined to agree with him: home, while it has every material, has few moral incitements to steady

---

67 Lawrence Pearsall Jacks (1860–1955), the editor of the *Hibbert Journal*, was a lecturer in philosophy at Manchester College, Oxford, from 1903, and Principal of the College 1915–31.

68 One of the poems in *Spirits in Bondage*.

reading. My own books, my MSS, the supply of new literature, our kind friends, and the telephone are all temptations: here, when the oi polloi go down, there is a melancholy desertion which leaves you simply nothing to do but work.

Under these circumstances I should suggest first that Warnie should change his leave, *if possible*. If this is absolutely out of the question I suppose he will divide his time between Leeborough and Oxford. It naturally occurs to me here that you were hoping to get away for a bit this summer. Where could you pass your holiday better than Oxford? The three of us could certainly spend our afternoons in a punt under the willows at least as comfortably as we did at Dunbar, and the Mitre, honoured with so many famous ghosts, would be an improvement on the Railway Hotel! Let me know in your next letter what you propose to do.

I have not been able to get hold of a complete copy of the June 'Bookman', but the cutting which the agency sent me is pasted into a little book in which I am collecting such shreds of criticism as I can get hold of.[69] My friends tell me that I am at a disadvantage for literary success because I lack the 'gift of self advertisement'. My only reply – not expressed aloud – 'thank heaven'!

Murray certainly seems to hold rather moderate views of the Mugger's accomplishments: I have lately been noticing in his history of Greek Literature the references to Mr Macan's conclusions on this and that

---

69 The review of *Spirits in Bondage* in *The Bookman*, vol. LVI (June 1919), p. 108, is the best Lewis received. 'There is nothing indefinite here,' wrote Francis Bickley. 'Mr Hamilton is as positive as Pope. From his forty short poems one can reconstruct his cosmogony. There is, it seems, somewhere "far too far off for thought or any prayer", a god who created the world but subsequently lost interest in it; nearer and more active is a lesser god, who is also Satan, and is responsible, among other unpleasantness, for the war; then there is the world of men, who suffer from and are degraded by this second god's irresponsible iniquities; lastly, there is the world of fairies whither, if one is as fortunate as Mr Hamilton, one may escape for beauty and peace; like Mr Maurice Hewlett, Mr Hamilton is friend of Desponia, and he has seen Angus. And with all these orders of being he deals competently. One might search his book for an accent out of place or a false rhyme; I do not think one will be rewarded. He writes so well that he does not fear to challenge comparison with his greatest predecessors. (He had even the hardihood to collocate the adjectives "old" and "unhappy".) Confidently he claims a place in the great tradition, and I think he makes his claim good. For there is beauty and dignity, a fine bitter vein and a fine courage, in his work, and good craftsmanship is one of the major virtues of poetry.'

subject. They are very polite, and this perhaps is what makes them so desperate.[70]

The town is expecting the news of the peace and preparing for it with all kinds of modern fireworks which 'make a noise exactly like a heavy shell'. I don't know that I am very fond of that kind of noise. Meanwhile they are starving and torturing in Russia and the Polish women are out digging trenches against Hindenburg's invasion. Should one laugh – or cry?

I hope that you are keeping up to the mark and that the old trouble shows some signs of improvement.

your loving son,
Jack

TO ARTHUR GREEVES (W):

[University College
14 July 1919]

My dear Arthur,

I suppose you have already decided about my remissness as a correspondent that 'The thing is intolerable': and perhaps I have been more ready even than usual because I have to convey to you a piece of information which as Miss Austin[71] says may produce 'the cruelest sense of mortification'. It is about the song: on the more technical side of the question Miss Plowman will write to you but I can give you some outline.[72] It appears, to speak frankly, that you will have to learn a great deal more about composition, and even about more elementary points of technique before you can hope to do yourself justice. It is not merely a question of embellishing or pruning what you have done to suit arbitrary rules. As far as I can gather, the real trouble is that your weakness on these points leads you, so to speak, to run your ideas into moulds already prepared by compositions which you unconsciously remember, and therefore appear to be less original than you are. Do I make it clear?

---

70 Gilbert Murray, *A History of Ancient Greek Literature* (1897).

71 i.e. Jane Austen.

72 Mary Plowman was the elocution mistress as well as a teacher of music at Headington School, where Maureen was a pupil. In time she became friends with Maureen's mother and Lewis and was a frequent visitor at their house. During her lifetime she published four books: *Monologues and Duologues* (1909); *The Letters of Paul Durrant* (1918); *The Vicar* (1919); *Get Out of Your Cage* [1934]. Her opinion was sought about a piece of music Arthur had just written.

It seems to me the inevitable result of a lack of formal knowledge: it is like an essay by a schoolboy who gives you a sentence of his own here and there and then ends up the sentence with a remeniscense of Macaulay. I don't think myself that in any art this argues a real lack of originality: it merely shows that he is 'groping about in worlds not realised' and his thought clutches at any ready-made clothing which seems fairly suitable. But Miss Plowman's letter will make all clear.

Now I do hope you won't let yourself be discouraged by what her friends have said. If without any knowledge you had succeeded in giving yourself a chance it would have been very wonderful: that you have not, was only to be expected, and I certainly think you have no reason to give it up. When I was at Bookham I twice went in for the lyric competition in the Bookman, once with 'Night! black Night' and again with the piece which appears as 'Ad Astra' in the MS. & 'Victory' in the printed book.[73] Both were complete failures – failed of the first prize, failed of the second, failed even of a mention. This was much worse than what has now happened to you! Besides you could not be in a better position than you are for going on: you have absolutely unbounded liesure – you don't have to work at odd moments stolen from your 'work' in the other sense like the rest of us: according to this specialist your heart is not so bad as you have supposed: good feeding and a little more exercise which good feeding will enable you to take will set you up. A course of solid but agreeable work with hopes and dreams ever in view would be the best thing for your nerves & spirits. That is, of course, unless you decide to take up painting or writing *really* seriously instead. Now that you have made a sort of landmark in your routine by coming to England, do try not to slip back into the old ways: do not give in to depression – and give everything up as soon as difficulties arise. Remember all we dreamed and did in the golden age of Bookham. I think I have nearly talked myself out now, & it is a wonder if you have put up with it.

Since you left I have read the 'Talisman',[74] merely because Maureen happens to be 'doing it' at school and it was lying about. Of course it is one of his poorest: the rapid episodes and impossible disguises remind us of what monstrosities the Romantic movement could and did commit in its infancy. I imagine Walpole's 'Castle of Otranto'[75] and the 'really

73 *Spirits in Bondage*, p. 16.
74 Sir Walter Scott, *The Talisman* (1825).
75 Horace Walpole, *The Castle of Otranto* (1765).

horrid' Gothic romances of Mrs Whats-her-Name[76] were something in this style. The subject however is fascinating, and Saladin is a great figure. I wonder where one could read something else about the Crusaders & the Saracens – do you know of anything? I suppose for the next six years or so I shall have no time to get thro' Tasso[77] in the original! I am now reading an Everyman crib to 'Marco Polo'.[78] The descriptions of innumerable Eastern towns would probably bore you, not having my appetite for collecting useless information: but I think you would like it once he reaches China and describes the wonderful court of the great Khan Khublai (Coleridge's Khubla Khan): the royal park with its palaces & pavilions and lakes 'full of all kinds of birds and bridges' reminds one of a willow pattern plate. There is also an excellent introduction by John Masefield and as a book this copy is a very favourable specimen of Everyman. This and the Talisman have begun to revive my interest in the East which was swept aside by Morris and Malory about the time I first knew you.

I hope you are avoiding my father as much as possible. Keep me posted however in all that may occur. I wired to him the other day to ask if W. had come home, and as he calls the latter 'Warren' in his reply I conclude he is in a temper about something or other.

The 'Medea' is very nearly finished, and will be about twelve hundred lines.[79] The main interest hangs on the family relations of the horrible old king and his daughter, whom I imagine as a sort of Emily Brontë, only more of a wolf – some of her father's bad blood coming out. The defect of the poem as a whole will be – heaven help us! – dulness.

I picture to myself your pleasure in arranging all your new books and getting settled down again: I do hope you will keep well and do something – perhaps I might get an instalment some day. Give me a full account of what you saw in town, especially about Cyrano.[80] The Minto[81] sends her love & says she is very pleased with the doctor's report on you:

---

76 Mrs Ann Radcliffe who wrote *The Mysteries of Udolpho* (1794).

77 i.e. Tasso's *Gerusalemme Liberata*.

78 *The Travels of Marco Polo the Venetian*, with an Introduction by John Masefield, Everyman's Library [1908].

79 Lewis mentioned an earlier version of the poem 'Medea' in his letters of 15, 20 and 28 February 1917. For more on this second version see his letter of 18 September 1919.

80 Presumably the play *Cyrano de Bergerac* (1898) by Edmond Rostand which Greeves could have seen in London.

81 The nickname used by Lewis and Greeves for Mrs Moore.

she also tells me to add that she has been expecting a letter from you by every post, and her 'face falls' three times a day. The hot weather comes back. Cheer up & write soon & don't shoot yourself yet.

Yours

Jack

TO HIS BROTHER (LP VI: 141–2):

University College,
Oxford
Teusday 22nd [July 1919]

My dear A.P.B.,[82]

I have just got your letter to which I am replying immediately. Of course I see your point, and am greatly relieved to hear from you as I had – of course – lost your adress and wanted to get into touch with you. Now will you please wire me at Univ. and let me know the day and approximate time of your arrival at Oxford: I will then report at the station at a suitable hour. If by any chance I am absent from parade you must drive to Univ. and wait for me, even if I do not turn up at once. The porter will have means of getting on to me if I am out. The programme you sketch is very attractive and it would be grand to have ignorance exposed by the Knock again. You understand why I behave so queerly – the effort to avoid being left alone at Leeborough. With you to back me up however, I have no doubt that we shall depart up to scheduled time. I doubt if this letter will reach you before you leave – in which case I hope it will *not* be forwarded.

yours ever,

Jack

Warnie arrived in Oxford on 23 July to begin his holiday with Jack. They were in London for the next two days, and on the 25th they visited Mr Kirkpatrick in Great Bookham. On 26 July they crossed to Ireland to stay with their father until 22 August.

The already uneasy relations between Jack and his father were considerably worsened by an event described by Mr Lewis in his diary of 6 August:

---

82 'Archpiggiebotham'. See note 1 to letter of 8 January 1917.

Sitting in the study after dinner I began to talk to Jacks about money matters and the cost of maintaining himself at the University. I asked him if he had any money to his credit, and he said about £15. I happened to go up to the little end room and lying on his table was a piece of paper. I took it up and it proved to be a letter from Cox and Co stating that his a/c was overdrawn £12 odd. I came down and told him what I had seen. He then admitted that he had told me a lie. As a reason, he said that he had tried to give me his confidence, but I had never given him mine etc., etc. He referred to incidents of his childhood where I had treated them badly. In further conversation he said he had no respect for me – nor confidence in me. (LP VI: 161)

On 22 August Warnie and Jack set off for Dublin where they visited a friend of Warnie's, Dr Horace Stratford Collins, house surgeon at Doctor Steeven's Hospital, Dublin. Jack returned to Oxford from Dublin on 24 August to find that Mrs Moore had left 28 Warneford Road and taken a flat in the home of Mr and Mrs Albert Morris at 76 Windmill Road, Headington.

This rupture between Jack and his father was to last a long time. On 5 September Mr Lewis wrote in his diary:

I have during the past four weeks passed through one of the most miserable periods of my life – in many respects the most miserable. It began with the estrangement from Jacks. On 6 August he deceived me and said terrible, insulting, and despising things to me. God help me! That all my love and devotion and self-sacrifice should have come to this – that 'he doesn't respect me. That he doesn't trust me, and cares for me in a way.' He has one cause of complaint against me I admit – that I did not visit him while he was in hospital. I should have sacrificed everything to do so and had he not been comfortable and making good progress I should have done so...The other troubles and anxieties which have come upon me can be faced by courage, endurance, and self-denial. The loss of Jacks' affection, if it be permanent, is irreparable and leaves me very miserable and heart sore. (LP VI: 167)

TO ARTHUR GREEVES (W):

Sunday [24 August 1919]
'Hill View'
Windmill Rd.
Highfield
[Oxford]

My dear Arthur,

Just a line to let you know of my arrival and of this change of address – the Minto having left Uplands and come here. Our landlady is a funny old woman, the wife of an Indian engine driver: I sleep on the sofa which quite satisfies my moderate demands on the world's comfort though it would hardly do for you.

We had quite a pleasant day in Dublin. I liked W's friend, who is house-surgeon in Steeven's hospital where he has a very pleasing little set of rooms. Have you ever been in Steeven's? There is a fine little library – despite some shocking portraits – containing some letters of Swift's. This letter begins to read like a guide book, so I will pass on.

Pass on to what? We are all well here and the Minto sends her love and tells me to thank you for all your labours on our behalf in the matter of letters etc[83] and also for the butter which we are still eating. She expects to go to France in a week or so now, which is rather horrible. What a pity you couldn't come over and bear me company in the solitudes of Highfield. By the way there is a thing I want you to do. No sooner had we got outside the gate on Friday than I remembered I had left the Reviews of my book[84] behind, which I particularly wanted to bring. Would you please go across some morning when his Excellenz is out and get them: they are in the bottom shelf of the miniature roller-top desk thing that stands on the table of the little end room nearest the window. They are in a white envelope – please see about it, will you, and send them on.

Have not been doing much in the way of reading so far but the Hell-story is nearly finished. Write soon and tell me all developments.

Yours
Jack

---

83 Lewis and Mrs Moore exchanged daily letters whenever he was in Ireland, and to avoid Albert Lewis knowing about this (though he did in fact know) Mrs Moore addressed hers to Arthur's home.
84 i.e. the reviews of *Spirits in Bondage*.

TO HIS FATHER (LP VI: 168–9):

University College,
Oxford
13th Sept. 1919

My dear Papy,

I was rather under the impression that you were a letter in my debt and have consequently waited from day to day in the expectation of hearing from you. However that may be, you have outdone me in taciturnity and the move falls to me.

We are having very hot weather here until today when it has, to my great relief, broken in mists and rain. However I can usually manage to get cool in my room and am getting through a good deal of work. Having regard to the coal situation, indeed, it is to be hoped that we shall not have a long winter.

From the newspapers you appear to be having a lively time in Ireland. I know of course that there was an extensive 'Papish' party in Belfast, but I am surprised to see that Larne has also been the scene of a raid. I should have thought that it was almost the type of a 'decent wee Presbyterian town' with not a spark of disaffection in it.

While at home I forgot to ask you for the certificate of my War Bond, without which I cannot turn the Dividend Warrant of June 1st into money. Will you therefore please forward it to me? I should also be glad if you would let me have Warnie's latest address.

We are living here in the anticipation of two interesting arrivals – Yeats for good[85] and Bergson for a second visit. The former I hope to meet, but I suppose I shall not see the latter unless he gives a lecture. Such are the important events that exercise our little community.

your loving son,
Jack

TO ARTHUR GREEVES (W):

[University College]
Thursday [18 September 1919]

My dear Arthur,

Your first letter, to quote Dr Johnson, 'was in such a strain of peevish discontent and unmanly resolution as could afford little comfort to a

---

85 The poet W.B. Yeats had moved to 4 Broad Street, Oxford.

friend or satisfaction to a philosopher.' Hem! Well, perhaps it wasn't so bad as all that: but I hope that the bad spirits which seem to have resulted from mountains, sea and pleasant society have been banished by the charms of Bernagh.

You seem to have had some adventures in rescuing my reviews from the jaws of Excellenz! How fortunate that you had really borrowed some books to carry off the scene with. 'De Profundis'[86] is hardly more than a memory to me. I seem to remember that it had considerable beauties, but of course in his serious work one always wonders how much is real and how much is artistic convention. He must have suffered terribly in prison, more perhaps than many a better man. I believe 'The Ballad of Reading Gaol'[87] was written just after he came out, and before he had had time to smelt down his experiences into artificiality, and that *it* rather than 'De Profundis' represents the real effect on his mind. In other words the grim bitterness is true: the resignation not quite so true. Of course one gets very real bitterness in D.P. too – as in the passage where he waited at the railway junction. Hartman's mother was a member of the Wilde set, and Hartman knows the person (referred to in the book by initials) who waited to take off his hat – but I've forgotten who it was. 'The Ideal Husband'[88] is not, I think, one of the best.

I have written to and had an answer from Excellenz. He observes that he was pleased to get my letter and would have been more pleased to see in it 'some expression of regret for the terrible things I had said to him'. You see, he still insists on occupying the position of joint judge, jury and accuser, while relegating me to that of prisoner at the bar. So long as he refuses to acknowledge any faults on his side or to attribute the whole business to anything but my original sin, I do not see how he can expect a real or permanent reconciliation.

The Minto has returned from France: on which subject you will probably hear from her own pen. Since then we have moved into the flat which is very comfortable. Of course there has been a tremendous amount of work settling in but we begin to see daylight now.

On getting back to England I had the pleasure of looking over my 'Medea' of which I told you and finding that it was all hopeless and only fit for the fire! Nothing daunted however I bade it a long farewell – poor

---

86 Oscar Wilde, *De Profundis* (1905).

87 Oscar Wilde, *The Ballad of Reading Gaol* (1898).

88 Oscar Wilde, *An Ideal Husband* (1899).

still-born – and consoled myself by turning the 'Nimue' from a mono-logue into a narrative, in which form it may do. It appears in 'stanzas' of my own invention and is rather indebted to 'St Agnes' Eve' with touches of Christabel and some references to contemporary politics – by way of showing how much better I could manage the country if they made me Prime Minister. Sounds promising, DON'T it? It relates the events of a single evening – Merlin coming back & catching Nimue at last. This is the first stanza, do you think it any good?

> *'There was none stirring in the hall that night,*
> *The dogs slept in the ashes, and the guard*
> *Drowsily nodded in the warm fire-light,*
> *Lulled by the rain and wearied of his ward,*
> *Till, hearing one that knocked without full hard,*
> *Half-dazed he started up in aged fear*
> *And rubbed his eyes and took his tarnished spear*
> *And hobbled to the doorway and unbarred.'* [89]

You will perhaps be surprised to hear that I am reading 'The Prelude'[90] by way of graduating in Wordsworth-ism. What's even funnier, I rather like it! I'm coming to the conclusion that there are two orders of poetry – real poetry and the sort you read while smoking a pipe. 'The Prelude' nearly always on the second level but very comfortable and interesting all the same – better than Rousseau's Confessions in something the same style. You read it, didn't you? I expect like me you recognised lots of the early parts from recollections of your own childhood. I fancy the first Book is the best.[91]

I sent 'Hippolytus' to the Odds & Ends Magazine[92] but I haven't seen it yet. I shall be interested in trying to pick out Mrs Pomeroy's contribu-tion. Does she write prose or verse?

---

89 These are the only surviving lines of Lewis's poem about Medea which he had mentioned frequently in his letters to Arthur. There are two further references to it in his letters of 11 April 1920 and 4 November 1925.

90 William Wordsworth, *The Prelude: or, Growth of a Poet's Mind* (1850).

91 In response to the question put by *The Christian Century* (6 June 1962): 'What books did most to shape your vocational attitude and your philosophy of life?' Lewis listed 10 books, of which one is Wordsworth's *Prelude*. See *CG*, p. 752.

92 Mrs Pomeroy, a Belfast lady and friend of Arthur Greeves, founded and edited the *Odds & Ends Magazine* to which Lewis contributed. I have been unable to discover any

The country is just beginning to think about Autumn. We have had some lovely walks. There are delightful 'rights of way' about here through fields and wood, all over styles made of single old stones – rather Druidical looking.

Write soon again. The family sends their love.

Yours

Jack

TO ARTHUR GREEVES (W):

University College.
[18 October 1919]

My dear Arthur,

I am sorry to have left your last letter so long without an answer: of course the beginning of the term is accompanied with a lot of business which fills up my time. And I am afraid there is another cause which operates against you – namely that the idea of writing to you is inevitably associated with that of writing to Excellenz, a task for which I have so little relish that, in my cowardly way, I keep it as much out of my mind as possible.

I should have spared my 'sarcasm' if I had known that it would 'cut you to the heart': that susceptible and sorely-tried organ of yours should not offer itself so readily to the knife: and, as you see, Johnson was much *more* severe. Not of course that I consider myself entitled to the great man's privilege of colossal rudeness. But we follow as we may.

I am not very fond of Euripides' Medea: but as regards the under-working of the possibilities which you mention, you must remember that the translation has to be rather stiff – tied by the double chains of fidelity to the original and the demands of its own metres, it cannot have the freedom and therefore cannot have the passion of the real thing. As well, even in reading the Greek we must miss a lot. We call it 'statuesque' and 'restrained' because at the distance of 2500 years we cannot catch the subtler points – the associations of a word, the homeliness of some

---

copies of the *Odds & Ends Magazine*. However, among the literary fragments preserved in the Lewis Papers (VIII: 165–7) is a portion of the 'Hippolytus' poem no doubt referred to here. The poem was to go through various transformations, from 'Hippolytus' to 'Wild Hunt' to 'The King of Drum' until it finally became 'The Queen of Drum' which is found in Lewis's *Narrative Poems* (1969).

phrazes and the unexpected strangeness of others. All this we, as foreigners, don't see – and are therefore inclined to assume that it wasn't there.

I quite see the humour of your idea about Excellenz's double life and clandestine marriage. I don't think it *has* evaporated on paper. But, oh ye gods, what fun there would have been if he had been at home when Mrs Pomeroy arrived! What mysteries and suspicions he would have spun.

Yeats has taken up his residence in Oxford, and some of us are going to beard the lion in his den one of these days. Perhaps we shall get him to read a paper to the Martlets: perhaps we shall be kicked out. But I think his vanity is sufficient to secure us a good reception if we come with the obvious purpose of worshipping devoutly.

I finished the Prelude and liked it. It is about as bad as a poem could be in some ways but one considers the great passages not too dearly bought at the price of the rest. Since then I have read Geoffrey of Monmouth's 'History of the Kings of Britain'. I don't think you would care much for it, there are a good many dull battles and his Arthur is merely contemptible. Where he really is good is in the early part. Who would not hear about the first coming of Brut, and Bladud (our first aeronaut, the British counterpart of Daedalus), and the birth of Merlin and the building of Stonehenge (its delightful alternative name being The Dance of Giants) and Vortigern and Lear and Locrine? One learns a little too. 'Kaer' apparently is British for 'city'.[93] Hence Leil builds Kaer-Leil (Carlyle) and Kaer-leon is the city of legion. 'Kaerleon of the legions' (as I call it in Nimue) what a name! Also I have been looking into Macdonald's poems in bookshops lately: now-a-days I am too poor to buy anything without long consideration. They look much better than I thought before. I have been so long with Wordsworth and philosophers that I want something mystical – pure unadulterated imagination.

One gets lovely autumn bits even in town now. The other day I was sitting under the tower of Magdalen on a bus. The big bells were just chiming five and the tower was turning paler and paler every minute. The trees were getting ghostly and everything had just one word 'frost'. I do love to feel the winter coming on.

---

93 Hence 'Cair Paravel', castle of the kings and queens of Narnia in Lewis's Chronicles of Narnia.

The Minto is frightfully busy and hasn't written to a creature except her sister since she came back, but when she has time you will be among the first claimants. We are both delighted to hear that you are coming to London[94] at last and shall expect to see you here for a week end whenever you can come. I do hope the London idea will set you up & start a new 'era' (hideous word) in your life. I am writing to Excellenz tomorrow (Sunday). Owing to the darned strike I have had no copy of Odds and Ends yet but am living in hopes.

Yours
Jack

TO HIS FATHER (LP VI: 170–1):

University College,
Oxford.
Postmark: 20 October 1919

My dear Papy,

I have had rather a miserable time with a heavy cold and sore throat which has sent me to bed early in the evenings and generally kept me from doing the things which I ought. Otherwise I should have answered your letter before. I seem to have got rid of it now.

Many thanks for your packet of War Office papers. I filled them all up, supplying the facts as you suggested, and got more forms in return which I filled up again. Like most of these papers, it involves signing for the money which you haven't yet got, and this signature – rather funnily it seems to me – constitutes a sort of cheque which you pay into your bankers. It is also loaded with deadly threats against 'people making false declarations'.

I had already seen about the death of Cousin Quartus[95] in the Times before I got your telegram. For this I suppose one should have been prepared, and indeed for himself, poor man, it was no tragedy. Yet I had come to think of his always being there: it will be a sad thing to go to Glenmachan now. As far back as I can remember he has always had a big place in our life – always the same kindly, courteous old gentleman. I am of course writing to Cousin Mary, although I think such letters are of little use. There is a great deal that we could all say, and say honestly, but it usually sounds conventional on paper.

---

94 Arthur was thinking of going there to study art.
95 Sir William Quartus Ewart died on 17 October. See **The Ewart Family** in the Biographical Appendix.

It is very cold here, but fortunately I have a fair amount of coal left over from last term and can therefore afford a reasonable period of fire every day.

As regards the other matter of which you spoke in your letters, I must ask you to believe that it would have been much easier for me to have left those things unsaid. They were as painful to me as they were for you. Yet, though I have many things to blame myself for, I should blame myself still more if I had tried to establish the relations you refer to by any other means than that of saying frankly what I thought. I did not speak in anger; still less for the purpose of giving pain. But I am sure you will agree with me that the confidence and affection which we both desire are more likely to be restored by honest effort on both sides and toleration – such as is always necessary between imperfect human creatures – than by any answer of mine which was not perfectly sincere.

your loving son,
Jack

1920

— ∿ —

TO LEO BAKER[1] (B):

> Little Lea,
> Strandtown,
> Belfast.
> 12th Jan. 1920.

My dear Baker,

The fact of being at home, which to me is a synonym for busy triviality, continual interruption and a complete lack of privacy, must be my best excuse for not having written to you before. I should have thanked you, too, long ago for the card which you sent me with my MSS. The poem, seen for the first time in print, was excellent: the first line carries you away into a strange country, a grave childlike kind of Christmasland, homely yet strangely interesting and even awe-inspiring. I find, however, on reading the poem over, plenty of melody but not enough harmony: it does not leave a continuous music in the ear.

This is intolerable, you know, about your health: I had never reckoned on such a sublunary consideration breaking up our salon. Doubtless you have already decided what to do, so any advice on my part comes – happily – too late. 'Safety first' as the posters say, must of course be your motto and no one would advise you to risk your permanent health for even the delights of Pasley's society and mine: but, unless my wishes deceive me, I should think that interest and occupation at Oxford would be better for you than remaining in town with or without a job. I am afraid everything will be broken up if you are staying next term. You are rather a key-stone, you know.[2] Pasley will tend gradually toward modernism, I to mediaevalism; Hartman will go on being brilliant, but

---

1 See **Leo Baker** in the Biographical Appendix.
2 Baker matriculated at Wadham College in October 1919. Because of ill-health he was unsure of coming back to Oxford for the Hilary Term.

there will be no cohesion. I was hoping to have many more conversations with you on the subjects which we have in common, and perhaps become your amateur disciple in mysticism. However – do try and come up.

About Munro's refusal and the new step, if any, to be taken, we can hardly talk without meeting.[3] I feel, as a matter of conscience that we should try to get the thing published, though I do not feel any great joy at the prospect.[4] Everything hinges on our view of Munro's opinion. If he is right we must make him wrong,

yours very truly
Clive Lewis

TO ARTHUR GREEVES (W):

[University College]
Teusday [3? February 1920]

My dear Arthur,

I shall expect to hear from you soon that your plans are settled: I suppose it is useless to hope that you have still any intention of going to Harrogate, though you may tell your advisers, for their comfort, that it is absolutely warm and springlike in England.

You will be surprised when you hear how I employed the return journey – by reading an H. G. Wells novel called 'Marriage',[5] and perhaps more surprised when I say that I thoroughly enjoyed it; one thing you can say for the man is that he really is interested in all the big, outside questions – and the characters are intensely real, especially a Mr Pope who reminds me of Excellenz. It opens new landscapes to me – how one felt that on finding that a new kind of book was waiting for one, in the old days – and I have decided to read some more of his serious books. It is funny that I – and perhaps you – read the old books for pleasure and always turn to contemporaries with the notion of 'improving my mind'. With most, I fancy, the direct opposite is so.

---

3 H.E. Monro (1879–1932) founded a poetry bookshop in 1913 to encourage its sale and for publishing the series *Georgian Poetry*, edited by Sir Edward Marsh. He had refused to publish the poems Lewis sent him.

4 Lewis and Baker were getting together an anthology of poems entitled 'The Way's the Way' which they hoped would be published by Basil Blackwell.

5 H.G. Wells, *Marriage* (1912).

But I must work like ten devils this term and bid good-bye to general reading except for an odd hour on Sundays. I read the Bacchae[6] over yesterday – for the last time before the exam: to rush through great poetry at top speed is not, of course, the right way to appreciate it, but one gets a peculiar value out of such a flying survey now and then. I realized, for one thing, how very quickly the terrible story happens: in the morning the old men with the magic youth in them are going out to the mountains, and before evening you have the stupid anger of Pentheus, the capture of the God and his quiet, ominous words to his captor, his escape, the swift madness of Pentheus, the catastrophe, and then it is all over and the long years of misery follow the one fatal mistake when mortal wisdom met immortal passion. You did like it didn't you?

I was in Baker's rooms with Pasley last night: Pasley departed early and the conversation between us two fell on shadowy subjects – ghosts and spirits and Gods. You may or may not disbelieve what followed. Baker began to tell me about himself: how he had seen things ever since he was a child, and had played about with hypnotism and automatic writing: how he had finally given it all up, till now 'things' were coming back of their own accord. 'At one time' he said 'I was afraid to look round the room for fear of what I might see.' He also stated confidently that anyone could compel a ghost to appear, that there were definite ways of doing it: though of course the thing you 'fished up' might not be what you wanted – indeed *quite* the contrary. The greater part of his views I will reserve for our next meeting: what I wanted to tell you was the effect on me. I got, as it were, dazed and drunk in all he said: then I noticed his eyes: presently I could hardly see anything else: and everything he said was real – incredibly real. When I came away, I moved my eyes off his, with a jerk, so to speak, and suddenly found that I had a splitting headache and was tired and nervous and pulled to pieces. I fancy I was a bit hypnotised. At any rate I had such a fit of superstitious terror as I have never known since childhood and have consequently conceived, for the present, a violent distaste for mysteries and all that kind of business. Perhaps he is a bit mad.

The Minto was so pleased with your bag and so was Maureen with her box which I think is quite charming. I have decided to come out and

---

6 *Bacchae* is a tragedy by Euripides produced c. 405 BC.

'dig' at Headington altogether next term.[7] Hope you're alright.

Yours

Jack

TO HIS FATHER (LP VI: 179):

University College
Sunday.
Postmark: 4 February 1920

My dear Papy,

Many thanks for your letter and also for the instructions to Aunt Suffern. I don't in the least want to consume large quantities of oranges or anything else, but if it must be, I suppose she will rest content with such an arrangement. I only hope she will not waste too much of our substance in riotous living.

The parcel you were asked to register contained my old trench coat which I thought might be better than a big coat for wet but warm days. I had left it with her of Endor and given instructions that it should be sent on and that 'the captain would register and address it'. However it has now arrived safely, and as there have been no 'wet, warm days' the delay has done no harm.

I am preparing to wait upon my great aunt Warren[8] this afternoon, with transports as moderate as those of the Colonel. I think this particular form of introducing strangers by letter, on the theory that blood is thicker than water ('and a good deal nastier' as someone added) is one of the most irritating of social amenities. It always reminds me of two hostile children being shoved into a room and told to 'have a nice game' together.

I hope you will like Mexico:[9] most interesting characters those old 'conquistadors' with their strange mixture of avarice, religion, and

7 Undergraduates were normally required to spend three terms in College, after which they were allowed to move into University-approved 'digs' or lodgings. Lewis meant that at the end of Hilary Term he planned to live with the Moores. About the time this letter was written the Moores moved from 76 Windmill Road, Headington, into the house of Mrs John Jeffrey, a butcher by occupation, in 58 Windmill Road.

8 Warnie included a note about this lady in LP VI: 179: 'I am unable to trace "great aunt Warren"; she cannot however have been a Warren by blood, for all the five sisters of Mary Hamilton [his maternal grandmother] were married. The three brothers of Mary Hamilton were also married, and I presume that it is the wife of one of them who is referred to.'

9 Albert Lewis was probably reading Charles Reginald Enock's *Mexico* (1909).

brutality. I am inclined to agree with you – and Mrs Ward – about the lack of charm in Wells: but there are other qualities as important, if less delightful. I am now reading 'Lavengro' at breakfast every morning and should like it very much if one could cut out the anti-Catholic propaganda.

We are still having wonderful weather here and I hope to get in a good walk today. The new suits have arrived and are most satisfactory.

your loving son,

Jack

TO ARTHUR GREEVES (W):

[University College]
Saturday [14? February 1920]

My dear Arthur,

I was very glad to see from your letter that you have at last escaped from Ireland. New scenery, pleasant society, books to read and an empty hotel to read them in – what could be nicer? I hope you have got over your usual 'unsettlement' at leaving home: certainly it is good that you have left: it is not the disadvantages of home but its comforts that kill – lazy comfort gets hold on one like spiders-web, doesn't it? I hope you told Mrs P.[10] that it was 'lack of time' decided me to give up 'Odds & Ends', not that I thought it pretty bad? You are so tactful you know!

You will be glad to hear that I have started Lavengro again (at breakfast) and though I still dislike the anti-Catholic propaganda and the rhetorical passages where the inspiration failed him and he filled up with the usual style of the period, I feel the charm as I did not feel it before and find the book hard to put down. I think with authors as with people we meet, when one finds an objectional feature the best thing is to trace it back to some central point of character from which it originates. When a thing is explained it loses half its nastiness, 'tout comprende c'est tout pardonner'.[11] I have therefore found an explanation which might account for

---

10 Mrs Pomeroy.

11 Madame de Staël (1766–1817) said in *Corinne* (1807), bk. 18, ch. 5, 'Tout comprendre rend très indulgen' ('To understand everything makes one very indulgent'). There are two similar phrases, 'Comprendre c'est pardonner' ('To understand is to forgive') and 'Tout comprendre c'est tout pardonner' ('To understand everything is to forgive everything') which are attributed to Madame de Staël but are not found in her works. The phrases are probably misquotations of – or indeed improvements on – the sentence in *Corinne*.

Borrow's rampant protestantism – it lies in the extreme Northernness or Saxon-ism of his nature. He thrilled, as we once did, to everything Norse, even the skull of Dane. I am glad to see that he knew the Kalevala. Hence, of course, a thoroughly Southern, Latin & Mediterranean thing like the Church was antipathetic and he worked up reasonable explanations to support the feeling which was really independent of them. I think the descriptions of the walk thro' the snow and the fairy-smith are admirable.

Did you see the Times Review of a new poem 'Mansoul' by Charles Doughty?[12] Doughty is an old poet and traveller whom I have heard mentioned now & then by the 'people who really know', always with a profound if distant respect. The review persuaded me to buy Mansoul, which is the strangest thing to be written in 1920 – an epic poem in 6 books, of which I have read two and a half so far. Now, mark, for this is important if I'm right – I think it was one of the *really* great things that will stand out like Dante or Milton, and, if so, isn't it wonderful to be alive when it has come out. It is very, very difficult, being written in a curious grammar which leaves out nearly all the pronouns: this is wicked, but even through it you can see the signs of a great work. It is a sort of journey into the underworld, where various ancient sages are interviewed on the meaning of life: we have a glimpse of hell, too, and some fine well-at-the-worlds-end kind of scenery in the first book: later on, I see, there are very learned & very English fairy passages. On the whole its more like Spenser than Milton.

Damn Tchaine's impudence for thinking I am to be a critic: the only thing in the world I could criticize really well is her wonderful self.

It is frosty here again, and there has been beautiful twilight to-day with the cold red light behind the black trees. All of us and chiefly the Minto find this place[13] more and more intolerable as time goes on: but all our hopes of a change seem to become will o' the wisps (do you remember that song – at Portsalon – ye gods!!) when we are hottest on the trail.

I have decided to send you some spelling-notes every time I write until you improve. To day I suggest 'digging' and 'asthma' as preferable to 'diging' and 'asma'.

Yours
Jack

---

12 Charles Montagu Doughty, *Mansoul, or the Riddle of the World* (1920). Reviewed in *The Times Literary Supplement* (22 January 1920), p. 49.
13 Mrs Jeffrey's house at 58 Windmill Road.

TO ARTHUR GREEVES (W):

22 Old Cleeve
Washford,
Somerset.
[2 April 1920]

My dear Arthur,

I don't know what you must think of me by now. Sometimes I try to console myself by saying that you would have written again yourself unless you had been sufficiently occupied in the interval. All the same I know the fault is mine – but hear my tale.

First of all came some weeks of hard work before the exam. Then the exam[14], itself for eight days, on the first day of which this swollen gland in my throat appeared again, much larger this time and more painful. I had a night with practically no sleep and could hardly eat anything – I think sanatogen saved me in the end. After the exam, I had a few cheery days packing up all my books etc (heart-breaking task!) preparatory to living at Headington next term. Then when I got out there, relations with our landlady had become so intolerable – the Minto will describe it to you some day – that we had to leave at once – and as the place we are going next term was not ready we had no other alternative but to decamp and leave our effects with various friends. More days of packing, pulling & hawling cases, arranging and re-arranging in boiling weather. We had seen an advertisement of a cottage here for a month and taken it on chance, so desperate were we. Thus finally, after the most loathsome and degrading scenes with our landlady and landlord, who nearly became violent, we departed – all of us pretty nearly done. The Minto and I still dream of the Jeffreys. I shall never get the taste of that woman out of my mind – 'not uglier follow the night-hag'.[15] But now that we are here, to quote Milton again, 'This turn hath made amends.'[16]

You do not, of course, know where old Cleeve is: nor did I till a week ago. It is not far from the end of the world: from a delightful thatched cottage with big low rooms *and* modern arrangements we look out on a

---

14 These were the examinations for Classical Honour Moderations which began on
 4 March. The results were already known and, curiously, Lewis failed to tell his friend
 that he took a First, an announcement of which appeared in *The Times* (1 April 1920),
 p. 18.
15 Milton, *Paradise Lost*, II, 662: 'Nor uglier...'
16 ibid., VIII, 491.

sea of fruit trees. The village is so small as hardly to deserve the name: and all round there is not a single straight line in the landscape. From the sea which is about a mile to our right to the black mountains on our left the hills are piled together like eggs in a basket, with the most charming villages nestling between them and orchards and streams everywhere and primroses as thick as the lights from the town at home on every bank. Across the water is the hazy outline of Wales – the Arthurian country round Kaerleon and the Usk, I believe. Those same 'Black Hills' on the extreme left of our landscape I have been trying to reach for some time and succeeded this morning (Good Friday). They are rather of the same type as Divis[17] – very black and grim. On one side I looked down into our own homely and rolling valley, on the other to more and more hills with deep gorges between where fir woods sometimes straggled up the sides. Then I went half way down a deep fold in the hill where a stream ran under queer gray trees and there were rocks to sit on, for the bracken and heather were wet. There I rested in an enormous silence and gradually the old feeling came into my mind. You know what I mean – a feeling associated with Wagner and the Well at the Worlds End, which I haven't had for over a year now. I wish I had my copy of The Lore of Proserpine here – it is just the place to read it in.

You can't imagine what a relief it is to be down here, away from work and exams and rows and packing and luggage! I am writing a good deal and also reading. Before we left Oxford I read Romola.[18] Certainly there is great comfort in these old-fashioned historical novels with a slow but not languid movement and plenty of work in them. I have forgotten whether you have read it or not. Since then followed Washington Irving's Life of Mahomet,[19] a silly and scanty book on an interesting subject and Lowes Dickinson's 'The Meaning of Good'.[20] You should read the latter if you get hold of it – it introduces you to a good many points of view in philosophy without being at all technical or pedantic. I am now at 'Waverley'[21] which I like very much so far and 'Prometheus Unbound'.

---

17 Mount Divis in Co. Antrim.
18 George Eliot, Romola (1863).
19 Washington Irving, Lives of Mahomet and his Successors (1850). The Life of Mahomet was published separately in Everyman's Library (1911).
20 Lowes Dickinson, The Meaning of Good (1901).
21 Sir Walter Scott, Waverley (1814).

I am writing to my father on Monday to tell him that I shall not be home this Vac. – I really can't face him on top of everything else – but you had better pose as having heard nothing about me or my movements if you should be compelled to meet him.

The Minto has a nasty cold but I think the place is doing her good – she sends her love and hopes that your stay in England has done you good. And now, don't be fed up with me for my long silence: write and tell me how your world goes on – I only hope you are having as good a time as I at present have without the purgatory through which I passed to reach it.

Yours
Jack

TO HIS FATHER (LP VI: 183):

> 22 Old Cleeve,
> Washford,
> Somerset
> 4 April 1920

My dear Papy,

I am glad to be able to begin with a bit of good news. I did get a first after all. Unfortunately that is almost all I can tell you, as the names in each class are given only in alphabetical order and I can see no possibility of finding out places or marks. Now as to our movements: as this is the shortest vac., and also as I felt in need of some 'refresher' I thought it a good opportunity of paying off an engagement with a man who has been asking me for some time to go and 'walk' with him.[22] We are at present at this tiny little village in a perfectly ideal cottage (which is, so to speak, his people's Teigh-na-mara) from which base we shall set out when the weather clears.

We are quite alone and live an idyllic life on eggs, bully beef and – divine treasure – an excellent ham which Aunt Lily very opportunely sent. The country is delightful, consisting of high moors with charming valleys full of orchards between them, and everything is a mass of white blossom. It is on the borders of Somerset and Devon. Our address will of course be moveable but letters sent here will reach me after some delay. I am sorry to desert you for the present, but it had to be polished off sooner or later.

---

22 This of course is a fabrication as Lewis was here with Mrs Moore and Maureen.

I am just getting over a rather tiresome cough and cold and am beginning to feel much better than I have done for a long time. I have brought Waverley to clean out my mind – there is great comfort in these solid old books.

I have celebrated the occasion by sending a poem to the Hibbert Journal, but I very much doubt if they will accept anything by so unknown a person as myself. At any rate they will probably take about a month to deliberate.

Thank you very much for both the cheques. I hope the teeth are now giving no trouble and also that the official shooting season has not set in yet at Belfast. Does the last murder mean that the Orange people are replying?

your loving

son Jack

TO ARTHUR GREEVES (W):

> 22 Old Cleeve,
> Washford,
> Somerset.
> *Sunday* [11 April 1920]

My dear Arthur,

Your letter gave me great pleasure both because it was the first after a long pause (for which I was responsible) and also because it had a cheerfulness and resolution which have long been strangers to you. If the mind really reflects the body you must be enormously better. Is it possible that the good days are at last dawning again? I can't say how pleased I should be to see you strong and able to do things and doing them: above all don't get a relapse either mental or physical, and incidentally excuse what may sound a patronising tone and put it down to the best motives. As we cannot have that 'long talk' you mention, we must try to discuss things as well as possible on paper.

One thing I should take as data – whatever you do, let it be something that will take you from Belfast. Absence cured you: nothing, I fancy, is more likely to un-cure you than a long period at Bernagh. I can't put into words the effect which surroundings familiar even to staleness and the sort of heavy impetus of all that has passed are likely to have. And Ireland itself – much as I love and 'desire it all my days' as Homer says, if other things were equal – I think there is some truth in my own 'Irish

Nocturne'.[23] Look it up, not as a poem but as a theory and tell me if you agree.

It would please me beyond everything if you could realize your plan of coming to Oxford. Though of course I could not see you so often nor so regularly as at home we should be constantly meeting, and once you get 'settled' – which you would in time – I think the life would be splendid for you. You would find an enormous choice of congenial friends, and you can have no idea how the constant friction with other and different minds improves one. You would have none of the reasons (either of circumstance or temperament) which make my circle small and would, I hope, soon 'know everybody'. The difficulty is to find an ostensible pretext for Oxford. What the exact conditions of entering are since Greek has been withdrawn I do not know: but perhaps merely to be here, *not* as an undergraduate would leave you freer to develop on your own lines – though of course a degree is useful in itself and gives you, as you say, some object in life. You might come up to study some particular period of history – not as an undergraduate – and to use the old documents etc in the Bodleian: always provided you can trust yourself to be busy and happy without a definite task and exams. Your father could easily afford it: would he approve. Of course you can frankly use my presence as a reason for wanting to be here!

Except for my own pleasure the Slade[24] is undoubtedly the best plan, and I suppose it is that you really have in view. I don't see on what principle the doctor could veto it and yet allow any of the other plans.

I suppose you are not really serious about the poultry farming? The Minto has plenty of experience in that line and says that IF you could get the ground and house at Headington you could run a partnership with her and she would undertake to make it pay! You know best whether you could really be happy in what is called an outdoor life.

In fact if the doctor forbids the Slade, I suppose it comes down to pursuing something definite in private – but I hope NOT at home. I do most strongly fear the effects of another dull, empty winter at Bernagh. I know you don't like to apply to your father again very soon but if nothing else turns up you should make an effort at all costs to be away, here

---

23 'Irish Nocturne', *Spirits in Bondage*, pp. 18–19: '...I know that the colourless skies / And the blurred horizons breed / Lonely desire and many words and brooding and never a deed.'
24 The Slade School of Fine Art, University College, London.

or anywhere, for as long as possible. You wouldn't care to turn your attention to philosophy – seriously, I mean, not just as ordinary reading? I am just starting it soon for my next exam. and we could keep each other up by letter.

I didn't at all agree with you about the difficulty of 'getting into' Waverley. I personally would not have a sentence of those early chapters curtailed: they showed me Scott in quite a new light, describing the childhood and development of the hero in his world of imagination. I can't help feeling that when he wrote this Scott had a higher sense of responsibility to his own characters – took them more seriously and worked out their natural growth more thoroughly – than in his later novels. Isn't the scene at the end where Waverley finds the old Baron of Bradwardine by the guidance of the idiot David Gellatley simply typical Scott – and delightful.

I saw a scene the other day that was typical Scott too – the Castle of Dunster. It stands on a little wooded hill just at the mouth of a long valley with very steep sides half-covered by fir-woods and just from its gates downwards straggles the single broad street of a drowsy village[25] with an old fountain: and the upper storeys of the cottages project in Elizabethan style. But it can only be described in language of Scott's period.

I am glad you saw 'Dear Brutus'.[26] 'Don't go into the wood!' – how well that first act works up to the supernatural of the second. I hope the 'Dream-child'[27] was good – everything depends on her. And that reminds me, the best news of all in your letter was that you are writing again. I won't repeat all my old wishes on the subject: but I still think it most unlikely that all the romance and imagination which are in you should evaporate in nothing more than appreciation of other people's work. Of course the thing's always difficult for a man who begins after his own critical faculties are fully grown. A child, if easily discouraged, is also easily satisfied and his powers grow with his ideals. But I hope you will make up your mind to go through with a good deal of trouble.

Look at me – I am still working at my poem on Merlin and Nimue. It has been in succession – rhymed monologue – rhymed dialogue – blank verse dialogue – long narrative in stanzas – short narrative in couplets –

---

25 Dunster, Somerset.

26 Sir James Matthew Barrie, *Dear Brutus* (1917).

27 *The Dream-Child* is the young daughter who exists only in the dream-world of Act II of *Dear Brutus*.

and I am at present at work on a blank verse narrative version. I hope I am not wasting my time: but there must be some good in a subject which drags me back to itself so often. You see, as Chaucer says,

> *We toilen ever and poren in the fire*
> *And for all that we fail in our desire.*[28]

Since finishing Waverley I have started Heroes and Hero-Worship[29] and finished the first lecture, which I read long, long ago when I first knew you, in the days when everything to do with the Norse lore was honey to me. Even now, when I have found so much better, I can't help regretting the extraordinary keenness and singleness of *wish* that one had then.

Write soon and I will really try to keep up a regular interchange in the 'good, old' style. I hope that you will go on as you now are: remember how others have kept themselves full of hope and life in worse predicaments – and excuse my ever preaching.

Yours

Jack

P.S. I never got the last letter you mention. If you can please say *when* it was sent, for we are afraid those damned Jeffreys are keeping our letters. Love from all.

TO HIS FATHER (LP VI: 184–5):

22 Old Cleeve,
Washford,
Somerset.
April 11th 1920

My dear Papy,

I was very sorry to hear that I had allowed you first to learn the news about Mods. from a stranger. I had put off writing until I was clear of Oxford and half thought that you might see it in the Times[30] as soon

---

28 Chaucer, *Canterbury Tales,* 'The Canon's Yeoman's Tale', 670–1: 'We blondren evere and pouren in the fir, / And for al that we faille of oure desire.'
29 Thomas Carlyle, *On Heroes, Hero-Worship, and the Heroic in History* (1841).
30 The results of the Classical Moderations examinations were mentioned in *The Times* of 1 April 1920 (p. 18).

as you could have heard it from me. As a matter of fact the Oxford news is so hid in a corner of the paper that it quite naturally escaped you.

I had quite forgotten about Aunt Warren. She must be pretty old, and dresses (with cap and white collar) in a style which makes her look rather more so. At the same time there is nothing senile in her conversation or manner. We talked chiefly about Glenmachan and Irish politics. The only one of 'the girls' present was Daisy, who is, I suppose, over forty. She struck me as being ecclesiastical in a high degree: for instance from her point of view the chief argument in favour of expelling the Turks from Europe was 'that it would re-establish the Patriarch at Constantinople and thus create a balance to the Papacy'. After the Armenian massacres, not to mention the war, *that* would hardly have appeared to me – nor to you I presume – the most important reason. There was a very attractive child whose parents are in India: but I like the old lady the best of the three.

As you see, we have not yet moved: indeed the weather has not encouraged us to set out, though it has not prevented us from a great deal of walking. It is more beautiful here almost than any place I have ever seen – whether in the valleys full of orchards or up on the big heathery hills from which one looks down on the sea and the Welsh coast away on the horizon.

You need not have any fears about our cuisine here. Remember we are almost in Devon and the clotted cream of the country is a host in itself: also – shades of Oldie – the real 'Deevonshire' cider in every thatched and sanded pub.[31]

A few miles away is a little fishing town called Watchet, which saw at least one interesting scene in its obscure history: it was here that Coleridge and the Wordsworths slept (or 'lay' as they would have said) on the first night of their walking tour. During that afternoon the germ of the Ancient Mariner occurred in conversation and in the inn at Watchet the first lines were jotted down.

I should think Brighton is not yet so intolerable as it will become in summer. I fancy the Colonel – and perhaps all of us – stands a good chance of being back in France soon unless the situation clears. God bless the French! and a murrain on Lloyd George and his impudent note!

---

31 Robert Capron ('Oldie'), his former headmaster at Wynyard School, was from Devonshire.

I am sorry to hear that you have been poorly again. Have you ever tried Sanatogen as a tonic? Someone recommended it to me when I had my gland and was feeling rather poorly. It certainly gave me sleep, though not an opiate, and I think bucked me up all round.

your loving son,

Jack

TO HIS FATHER (LP VI: 187–8):

University College,
Oxford.
May 1st 1920

My dear Papy,

I found your letter waiting for me when I came up, and in the business of seeing new tutors, starting new lines of work, lunching with the said new tutors etc., etc., this is almost the first opportunity I have had of answering you.

As to 'finance' I agree with what you say. I understand that the arrangement was for you to lodge £30 at the beginning of each term: and the reason why no dates were mentioned was that doubtless a person with a mind like mine (or 'mentality' as a really modern writer would say – I know you love the word!) never knows the dates of the terms unless he has a calendar by him. I think however that this is sufficiently definite: and if you would kindly send me that amount before the beginning of each term, and also do so now, we shall be alright. You will not mind my applying to you for some 'extra' expenses which may from time to time occur.

I have two tutors now that I am doing 'Greats', one for history[32] and one for philosophy.[33] Of course I am sorry to have parted brass rags with

---

32 George Hope Stevenson (1880–1952), Lewis's history tutor, was born in Glasgow and educated at Glasgow University. He took a First in Greats from Balliol College and in 1906 he was elected Praelector in Ancient History at University College where he remained until his retirement in 1949. His contributions to Roman history include *Roman History* (1930) and *Roman Provincial Administration* (1939). He was a keen Anglo-Catholic and for many years was church warden at St Margaret's Church in Oxford.

33 Edgar Frederick Carritt (1876–1964), Lewis's tutor in philosophy, was Fellow of Philosophy at University College, 1898–1941. He was an excellent lecturer, combining a very logical procedure with commonsense illustrations. In 1902 he was the first member of the faculty to lecture on aesthetics. Some of his lectures were amplified and published

old Poynton: the other two are much younger men, but seem quite nice. We go to the philosophy one in pairs: then one of us reads an essay and all three discuss it. I wish you could hear the 'crack', it is very amusing. Luckily I find that my previous dabbling in the subject stands me in good stead and for some time I shall have only to go over more carefully ground through which I have already meandered on my own.

I expect that what you feel about travel would be endorsed by a great many other people of your own age, who, as you say, have never really wanted a shilling in their lives. As far as I can see it is only the few who can do it without the least sacrifice who bother to see the world at all: the majority will not give up anything for it and would sooner afford a car to go round Stangford on, than see Greece or Cathay – if there really is a Cathay. One is amazed at the resolution of a real traveller like Herodotus, whom I am reading at present: knowing apparently no language but his own and relying on merchant caravans and dragomans with a smattering of Greek, he had yet penetrated to Babylon and seen the hanging gardens and the temple of Bel-Baal I suppose – and up the Nile as far as Elephantine where there were rumours of the land of dwarfs beyond – the Pygmies of course. Or Marco Polo – whom you should read: books of travel are a great resource.

I can't understand the Irish news at all. One of the most curious things is the rapprochement which seems probable between English Trades Unionism and Sinn Fein. I was always confident that the religious differences, the 'odium theologicum' would prevent a junction between the two. If they really do work together I think it is all up for England and Ireland.

How are the teeth getting on?

your loving son,

Jack

---

as *Theory of Beauty* (1914), *Philosophies of Beauty* (1931) and *Ethical and Political Thinking* (1947). Mr Carritt, a Socialist and supporter of the left wing, was not a Christian. An argument he had with Lewis years later is mentioned in Lewis's 'Christianity and Culture' found in *Christian Reflections* (1967). See 'Edgar Carritt' in the *University College Record*, Vol. IV (October 1964), pp. 235–43.

TO ARTHUR GREEVES (W):

[University College]
Monday [3? May 1920]

My dear Arthur,

Your last letter reached me the day after my return here and this is positively the first opportunity I have had of answering it. I must deal first of all with your definite questions. Ist As far as I can make out (for, indeed, the whole subject is still very uncertain) Greek will still be compulsory for Responsions in June but *not* for those in October and after. IInd I do not consider the choice of a college very important, much less so than that of a house at school. There are one or two you should avoid, as Christchurch and Magdalen for their expense, or Keble and Jesus for their vulgarity. Wadham is a very nice, quiet place and not too big. My great friend Baker is there and finds a great many pleasant people. There is no reason why Univ. should be 'out of the question', tho there is equally no reason why you should prefer it, especially now that I am living out. IIId I do not think that most colleges have entrance exams. in addition to Responsions. But on that and on the question of coming up before you take Responsions you had better write to the Bursar of the college you decide on and get definite information. It is much better to open such a correspondence than to rely on unofficial snippets like mine. I should say that you hoped to come up to So-and-So and ask I. for a syllabus of the Responsions subjects, II. whether you must take them before you come up – and any other questions that may occur to you. I do not think that anyone can fail in 'Smalls' after the removal of Greek, unless, like myself, he is incapable of elementary mathematics![34]

I do not quite gather if your going to Oxford is still only a pis-aller for the Slade or whether you now mean to come in any case. I most sincerely hope you will, for I can imagine nothing that would do you more good. I feel rather nervous, lest, if it disappoint you, the responsibility may rest with me. It is a pity Caesar is such a dull book, but I suppose you'll have to stick it. With care and going slowly at first you should easily pick up your Latin again. Perhaps indeed the historian in you may find interest where most of us cannot: of course it is mainly military history but if you once see it in perspective as an important step in the evolution of Europe you may not be too hopelessly bored.

---

34 Lewis was now exempt from having to pass Responsions in mathematics by virtue of being a serviceman.

How splendid to hear of you on the hills again: I can imagine what you felt in reaching at last that Mecca of ours after being exiled so long. There is much better scenery elsewhere no doubt, but as long as I live those little bits of wood and field will be an enchanted country to me. I think you touch on the great problem of writing when you put off describing your walk because the feeling of it is already past. If only the moment of inspiration cd. be identical with that of composition! As Chénier says 'Le Coeur seul est poète'[35] – only the heart, not the poor intellect trying to recapture it with his words and craft. Have you tried anything more in the writing line since? but I daresay your mind and your time are fully occupied in other ways.

We find our new quarters much more to our liking (so far) than we expected, though very expensive.[36] It is a great relief to be living here and not trailing back in every night. Our landlady is a strange character – with a mystery about her: but that needs a whole letter if not an Algernon Blackwood story to describe.

Our Anthology[37] (you know what I mean) goes to the publishers finally to-morrow and will be out for the Autumn sales. I am not just too satisfied with it, but Blackwell[38] seems to think it will pay its way and even leave a little profit with its five authors.

I am very sorry to find that my friend Baker is leaving at the end of this term: he is in every way the best person I have met in Oxford. I wonder what you will think of his poems. I say nothing of reading as I have been busy working and seeing people ever since I came up. The Minto sends her love and is like me delighted to hear of the revolution in your plans.

Just one more thing – if you really believe that painting is your job rather than a life of letters, don't let this obscure that object. There is plenty of time for both, I suppose, but the real thing must always be the background of ones mind, mustn't it? Hoping that nothing will occur to set you back in anyway – how conventional the words are, but I do most intensely mean them.

---

35 André Chénier (1762–94), *Les Elégies*, viii, 2: 'L'art ne fait que des vers, / le coeur seul est poète' ('Art only makes rhymes, / The heart alone is a poet').

36 Lewis and the Moores now had rooms in the home of Mrs Marshall, at 'Courtfield Cottage', 131 Osler Road, Headington.

37 i.e. 'The Way's the Way'.

38 Mr (later Sir) Basil Blackwell (1889–1984), the distinguished Oxford bookseller and publisher. He joined the family firm of B.H. Blackwell in 1913, and that same year established a publications department separate from the bookshop.

Yours
Jack

P.S. Your other letter has turned up.

TO HIS FATHER (LP VI: 188):

[University College,
Oxford]
Wednesday
Postmark: 25 May 1920

My dear Papy,

Please forgive my not having acknowledged your note sooner – I half expected a letter to follow. Many thanks for putting in the cheque. I have been in bed for some days with a mild form of this flu' but am better now. The heat here is something terrible – we are almost a city of dreadful night.

your loving son,
Jack

TO ARTHUR GREEVES (W):

[University College]
Sunday [6? June 1920]

My dear Arthur,

You certainly seem to be working with a vengeance now, and I daresay you find a great deal of effort necessary. I shouldn't go too hard at the beginning: certainly I should not advise work on walks. I am a great believer in having your periods of rest, complete rest, however short they may be: ten minutes absolute 'slack' is far more useful than an hour of the half in between business.

The Latin Constructions did at one time seem rather a 'slough', I remember. The great thing is to pin them onto the nearest English equivalent constructions. Thus, for instance, if you have 'He said I was a fool', instead of thinking mechanically for the Accus. & Inf. rule, remember simply to say in English 'He declared me to be a fool'

dixit
– then you get it at once *declaravit } me stultum esse'.*

Always make the verb of saying 'declare' in English. Similarly the Ablative Absolute has a parallel in the Irish idiom: as you might have '*He kept on talking while I waited*' which in the language of Meehawl Mac-Murrahu would [be] 'He kept on talking, so he did, and me waiting' – there you have it (leaving out the 'and' of course) 'mê expectante'. I am afraid I don't know the difference between a final and consecutive clause in English *or* Latin! – I always do what sounds right in either, but of course you can't begin that way. 'That I may get a copy' would certainly be Pres. Subj. 'ut librum procurem'. I shouldn't kill myself trying to get ready for 'Smalls' by any particular time, though, of course, the sooner the better.

You will be interested to hear that I met your friend Robert Nicholls the other day. He is much less beautiful than the frontispiece to 'Ardours & Endurances' would lead you to suppose: as the particular grin which makes that big mouth tolerable in the photo cannot be kept up in conversation! He also sees fit to wear enormous goggle spectacles rimmed with thick, dark horn which covers most of his cheeks. He is a pleasant fellow, though rather overpowering and Tchanie-like (could a suitable match be arranged? I have no doubt the 'ardours' could be found on her side, but would the 'endurances' on his be forthcoming?) He went over the 'Wild Hunt' with me, suggesting several emendations, most of which I (and Baker) thought definitely bad – or rather he goes on a peculiar theory which may be good for him, but is not good for me.

Certainly the little trivial things such as shaving, cooking, eating and the like run away with a lot of time. I have had some days in bed with flu and been generally very lazy, reading 'Kim'[39] and Trollope's 'Small House at Alington'.[40] I am also, in the evening, reading Virgil through again: I do hope you will someday be able to read Latin with enjoyment – tho' perhaps that seems to you at present a contradiction in terms.

I saw 'Romance'[41] in Oxford in 1917 before I went into the army (antequam militiam suscepi!)[42] and liked it pretty well, though there is really only one character in it – the woman. If she is good, parts of it are really very fine – and oh!, I forgot the other character, Tomaso, the

---

39 Rudyard Kipling, *Kim* (1901).

40 Anthony Trollope, *The Small House at Allington* (1864).

41 The play *Romance* by Edward Brewster Sheldon was performed first in New York on 10 February 1913, and for the first time in England on 30 September 1915.

42 'before I went into the army'.

monkey. I expect you will see in it the same people whom I saw (censeo te in illâ fabulâ visurum esse eosdem histriones quos ego!!)

I hope this last bout of hot weather has not set you back. You really shouldn't grudge any time spent on walks: now that you feel better able to get about it must be delightful to visit the old haunts. By the bye, I hope you keep the week-ends quite free from work: what can be better than to get out a book on Saturday afternoon and thrust all mundane considerations away till next week. You never get the same pleasure out of books as when you come back to them from these periodical exiles. I doubt if the amount of history you'd require for Smalls would really be much use to you afterwards: and I am quite sure that it would for the moment be more troublesome than the literature.

Wonderful to relate W. has been home and back again without giving us the honour of a visit.[43] Miss Plowman was here the other night. The Minto sends her love and hopes to see you soon 'flusht with victory'.

Yrs
Jack

P.S. 'Realize' not 'reallize'. How is Gundred's portrait getting on. How well you'll look in a commoner's gown!

TO HIS FATHER (LP VI: 189–90):

University College,
Oxford
6th June 1920

My dear Papy,

A better case could have been made out for your not writing: technically I might be the defendant, since your letter, of whatever length, was the last given or received. At any rate it's a very nice point. I'm sorry to hear that you also have been ill: I hope it is not a return of the old trouble. Mine of course was nothing more than troublesome and now I am all right.

What exactly is Big Brother doing now? I presume that he hasn't really started to keep a stud of two cars – I suppose one is being sold to get another: perhaps he too is getting sold over the deal. How we all get let down over the things on which we plume ourselves! Nothing will

---

43 Warnie, who was now stationed at Aldershot in Hampshire, was in Belfast on leave from 23 to 29 May.

convince Warnie that he is not a great financier, while I continue in the face of all experience to imagine myself a 'very parfait'[44] traveller. Thus Johnson considered that he was 'a very polite man'.[45]

I thought I had said something about the Anthology. It is being got up as a kind of counterblast to the ruling literary fashion here, which consists in the tendencies called 'Vorticist'. Vorticist poems are usually in 'vers libre' (which means they are printed like verse, but neither rhyme nor scan, a line ending wherever you like). Some of them are clever, the majority merely affected, and a good few – especially among the French ones – indecent: not a sensuous indecency, but one meant to nauseate, the whole genus arising from the 'sick of everything' mood. So some of us others who are not yet sick of everything have decided to bring out a yearly collection of our own things in the hope of persuading the gilded youth that the possibilities of metrical poetry on sane subjects are not yet quite exhausted because the Vorticists are suffering from satiety. Of course we may end by proving just the opposite, but we must risk that: there will be a polemical preface and the first number is to appear in the autumn. We call it 'The way's the way'[46] which is a quotation from Bunyan (a writer of books you know)!

I have had to do some restocking of foot gear as the Somersetshire hills finished some old veterans. The bill for three 'solings' with rubbers (which add to the weight of the foot but keep you dry and make the leather last much longer) and one new pair is £3.18.0. It seems to me rather excessive, but my friends all tell me that it is low for the times. If you think this may fairly be counted an extra, would you please let me have the amount some time?

I don't think even Arthur can fail to pass Responsions now that they have abolished Greek – unless indeed he stumbles, as I did, over elementary mathematics. He tell me you have been 'very kind' in 'giving him advice', which I gather means telling him how to write a letter. I remember once when he was here he had to write a card about getting a room

---

44 Chaucer, *Canterbury Tales*, 'General Prologue', 72: 'He was a verray, parfit gentil knyght.'

45 *Boswell's Life of Johnson*, op. cit., vol. III, p. 54, n. 1.

46 John Bunyan, *The Pilgrim's Progress*, ed. James Blanton Wharey, 2nd ed. revised by Roger Sharrock, Oxford English Texts (Oxford: 1960), pt. II, p. 237: 'Some have wished that the next way to their Fathers House were here, that they might be troubled no more with either Hills or Mountains to go over; but the way is the way, and there's an end.'

in London: we were in committee about that for the best part of twenty four hours. However, judging by his recent letters, there is a great mental and physical improvement.

We have had a bus strike here. The President of the Liberal Club and the President of the Labour Club, with followers, very foolishly addressed the world at large from chairs the other evening: and a warm scene between mixed workers and undergraduates on each side was only interrupted by the appearance of the Proctors: whereupon the under-graduates fled from the Proctors and the Proctors, with less success, fled from the mob. This, you see, is true democracy.

your loving son,
Jack

P.S. I have had my board and am certified for a 20% disability: we shall hear in time what that means.

TO ARTHUR GREEVES (W):

[University College]
Saturday [19 June 1920]

My dear Arthur,

The new syllabus for 'Smalls' certainly looks attractive. Quite putting aside the question of interest, I should advise you to take the lit-erature. There is a lot of work in making up even a short period of his-tory: but, for a person who has acquired the habit of reading, it should be really very easy to pass on the plays and the Milton and even on the Bacon. Of course you will have to read the books several times and make yourself master of all the biographical details etc: since you do not natu-rally remember things 'to quote' you must simply (as many another) learn by heart the 'pivot' passages which illustrate important qualities. Thus in Milton I you would quote 'That to the height of this great argu-ment / I may assert eternal Providence / And justify the ways of God to Man'[47] to illustrate the moral purpose, as a commentator would say, and the passage about 'Faery-elves'[48] (near the end) for his Romanticism: and find out from the notes where he is imitating the classics or the Italians etc. Never having done this kind of thing I can't say what are the best

---

47 Milton, *Paradise Lost*, I, 24–6 (slightly misquoted).
48 ibid., I, 781.

annotated editions of these books: but doubtless any 'English master' at Campbell could tell you. I scarcely think that you ought to need any tuition for the English: nor would I recommend Helen – <the unspeakable Helen>. Can you get hold of any old papers on the subjects to give you an idea of the sort of questions they ask? That is a very great help. The one and only method in reading Latin is to go slowly and scientifically at first, looking for the verb etc in the old childish way: to rush like a bull in a china shop is fatal. As for the composition, it must be taught. Whether you enjoy it or not, the mere working for this exam. will do you an enormous amount of good: you have no idea how routine work and exactness improve the brain. I, for instance, have gained enormously in clearness and honesty of thought from my last year's work. I am reading Bergson now and find all sorts of things plain sailing which were baffling a year ago.

Without a scholarship I do not think you can manage on less than £300 a year: £250 might be just possible, but most uncomfortable and your attention would be everlastingly settled on money matters. (Some colleges, by the way, have musical scholarships: would you have any chance for one of those?).

I hope you won't mind my calling your attention to one other necessity – that of a drastic revision in your methods of spelling, which are at present a trifle too eccentric for general acceptance. I am afraid if the first page of your English paper contained such peculiarities as 'unprepaired', 'Hellen', 'reallized', 'overate' (over-rate?) it might prejudice an examiner! (It has just struck [me] that of course 'overate' would be the past tense of 'over-eat' but that can't be what you mean – I never over-eat your abilities.) This, of course, is a matter which can easily be put right: and I know that you are not bothering about it in a letter to me, as indeed there is no reason why you should.

Our anthology 'The Way's the Way' is to come out in autumn. The contributors are Carola Oman[49] (the daughter of the historian), Margaret Gidding (a friend of Pasley's), Pasley, Baker and myself. My own pieces are 6 in number, one of which is the longish 'Wild Hunt' which I think you saw: it was sent, in a slightly different form to 'Odds & Ends'.

---

49 Carola Mary Anima Oman (Lady Denanton), (1897–). Her father, Sir Charles William Chadwick Oman (1860–1946), had been a Fellow of All Souls College, Oxford, since 1883.

Most of the others I think you have seen, but you would not remember them by their names. Blackwell has the audacity to talk of 'five or six shillings' as a price for the book and seems to hope for a profit: I suppose he ought to know, but I feel dubious.

You ask about Baker, and I hardly know how to describe him. He was at a mixed school of a very modern type, where everyone seems to have written, painted and composed. He is so clairvoyant that in childhood 'he was afraid to look round the room for fear of what he might see'. He got a decoration in France for doing some work in an aeroplane over the lines under very deadly fire: but he maintains that he did nothing, for he was 'out of his body' and could see his own machine with 'someone' in it, 'roaring with laughter'. He has a bad heart. He was a conscientious objector, but went to the war 'because this degradation and sin might be just the very sacrifice which was demanded of him'. He maintains that everything in Algernon Blackwood is quite possible: and though the particular cases may be fictitious, 'things of that sort' are quite common. He is engaged to be married. In appearance, he is about my height, with very fair hair, glasses, remarkable eyes and according to the Minto, rather like you. I like and admire him very much, though at times I have doubts on his sanity. He is almost exactly my own age. He is quite different from Pasley, who represents rather the best type of the average English 'nice boy' and combines literature and athletics.

It is really quite delightful here. I walk into Oxford every morning down a green lane[50] and across the bridges and islands of the Cherwell: they are all white with may and quite deserted at that time. I have had one bathe. The Minto and I 'drank a dish of tea' with Miss Plowman the other day, and came away a trifle 'bethumped with words'.[51] I should like to see her and Tchanie together.

I am trying to imagine what your life is like these days, and always hoping that nothing will turn up to change your mind. What hours do you work? and do you find time to go for walks? You must begin to write something now, whether good or bad, in order to acquire a faculty of expression: for of course, whatever you take up here, you will do a lot of essay writing. It is simply splendid to think of all the difference between now and a few months back: perhaps you are hardly enjoying

---

50 Cuckoo Lane which runs parallel to Headington Hill.
51 Shakespeare, *King John*, II, i, 466: "Zounds! I was never so bethump'd with words.'

the change yet, but I have no doubt there is a good time coming. If you can pass a year or two here with success, learning what you want to know and making friends, you will still be able to go back to the painting. The loss of time is serious: but more, far more than compensated by the extra power and brain you would take to your work. Write soon or I shall augur a relapse.

Yours
Jack

TO HIS FATHER (LP VI: 192):

[University College]
Sunday.
Postmark: 23 June 1920

My dear Papy,

I am very sorry to hear of Mr Henessy's death.[52] Although you did not often mention him I think I have heard you say that he visited you in the office nearly every Saturday: it is just that sort of regularity in a friendship which, on each separate occasion, may be taken for granted and may count for little, but which in its cumulative effect is very strong. I too in a short space of time have lost some of the best friends I had: but of course the long years of intercourse knit a closer bond than even the warmest of friendships which the war cut short after a few months. You are wrong in supposing I never met him: though I do not know when, I distinctly remember him coming out to lunch, long ago, in Mammy's time, and even have some hazy idea of what he looked like. He was a biggish man was he not, and wore a short beard?

Now for a dramatic bit of news. Picture me yesterday strolling along 'the High' neither fearing nor purposing any evil in the world. Suddenly, as happens when one is wool gathering, I found my eyes fixed on a face that came towards me. Curious...I should know it...ah, yes, some woman who happens to be rather like Mrs McNeill. But no: there is a growing uneasiness: it *is* Mrs McNeill[53] and – horror of horrors – 'Tchainie' is with her. Next minute the streets of this learned city echoed to her stentorian greeting. Tomorrow we are 'going to have tea somewhere' for the wonder and admiration of my fellow citizens.

---

52 E.G. Henesy, who died on 9 June 1920, was one of Albert's closest friends. He was the manager of the East Downshire Steamship Co. Ltd. at Dundrum, Co. Down.
53 See note 41 to letter of 4 May 1915.

I know from experience how slow Arthur is to accept alterations in a letter. But is it not true that we are all least ready to be corrected in the things which we do worst? My friend Baker for instance will let you criticize his poetry (which is good) ad infinitum: but any logical argument about his views on religion, philosophy, or politics (which are what Johnson calls 'undigested') is treated with the polite tolerance of unassailed superiority.

Thank you very much for the cheque. An appreciative College has awarded me £5 worth of books as a prize for getting a 1st. The other man in Univ. who did likewise of course had chosen his several weeks ago: I, after nearly giving up the problem as insoluble, have just sent in my list.

I enclose a sketch of the real Poynton. He not only has two sons, but a daughter. Didn't I ever tell you about Carlyle and the daughter's christening?

your loving son,
Jack

TO ARTHUR GREEVES (W):

[University College]
Sunday [27? June 1920]

My dear Arthur,

Do you think Davis[54] is a good teacher? I should be sorry to weaken your confidence in him, but I don't like his just passing over the Oratio-Obliqua and saying you won't get anything as hard in Smalls. I think with care and patience – but so few schoolmasters have any patience – anyone could be led to master a reported speech in Caesar: and it is just possible you might get an equally difficult Unseen. My Unseen was the passage from Statius (Davis will show it you) beginning 'Crimine quo merui juvenis, placidissime divum':[55] it is a lovely little poem; have a look at it and see if you can make it out.

---

54 Robert Furley Davis (1866–1937), who took his BA from St John's College, Cambridge, in 1888 and his MA in 1896, was the senior Classical master at Campbell College from 1902 until his retirement in 1931.

55 Statius, *Silvae*, V, iv, I. The full Latin text is: 'Criminie quo merui, iuvenis placidissime divum, quove errore miser, donis ut solus egerem, Somne, tuis?' which is translated: 'O youthful Sleep, gentlest of the gods, by what crime or by what mistake of mine have I deserved that I alone should lack your gifts?'

I have had a delightful windfall: £5 worth of books as a prize from College for getting a First. Oh ye gods, if this had come four or five years ago, what raptures and debatings, what making and re-making of lists had been! As it was I had great difficulty in making them out at all, being perpetually haunted by the fear that I should afterwards find out that I had got all the things I really did NOT want. It is a dismal sign of breaking up and old age that I look forward to their arrival with very luke warm pleasure. The nicest among them all will be Hall's 'Ancient History of the Nearer East'[56] – which bears to some extent on my work in Herodotus, but goes beyond it.

This subject of ancient history is now one of my absorbing interests: Herodotus is pure delight, and so are the modern writers who comment on [him]. Isn't the magic of mere names wonderful? Babylon, Nineveh, Darius, the Pharaohs – I revel in every trace of them – and to see things piecing together: a story in Herodotus and a story in the Book of Kings, backed up by an inscription newly unearthed in Mesopotamia or a scrap of Persian legend! However, this may not interest you.

'Abraham Lincoln'[57] came here last term and all the world except me went to see it: I have heard it praised by everyone. It is very cheering to see these 'literary' plays with verse in them like the Dynasts[58] and Drinkwater's one, on the stage at all. Fifty years ago I don't suppose they'd have got a hearing.

My imagination boggles at the idea of you – or myself – on a motor byke. When you come up here I suppose you will become one of the young men who toot-toot-toot up and down the High clad in overalls: and instead of the Muses it will be spanners and magnetos and intermezzos and cut-outs and petrol that will fill our conversation. Ah well!, I must move with the times. I can't quite rise to a motorbyke but perhaps I could get a scooter (Picture – Excellenz and myself going to Church on scooters 'Ah – these scooters are r-r-r-otten tools: the thing's intolerable')

This letter was begun I don't know how long ago. 'Sunday' is all I can find at the top: but whether it was a week or a fortnight ago I can't say. I'm sorry: a mood of laziness has been upon me. It has been one of those

---

56 H.R.H. Hall, *The Ancient History of the Near East* (1913).
57 John Drinkwater, *Abraham Lincoln*, first performed 12 October 1918, was published in 1919.
58 Thomas Hardy's *The Dynasts* (1904–8) was first performed as a play on 15 November 1914.

periods when we do nothing because we always feel tired and feel tired because [we] do nothing. Also – Tchanie is here: I have chust returned from lunching with her and her amiable mother, with the usual exhausting effect. Mrs McNeil has made several exquisitely ridiculous remarks in her solemn style, but they would be spoiled on paper. Tchanie has been strongly urging the advantages which would result from your having Helen as a tutor: and, though you may fancy that I have been talked over, I would advise you to think of it. When I said before that you didn't need a tutor for English, I am afraid I was thinking rather of the mere 'getting up' of the books: for essays etc you really do need someone to put you up to those little tricks of vocabulary and rounding off sentences which may seem trivial but which examiners demand. Whether Helen is the best person you can get, is, of course, quite a different story: if you had any authority outside Tchanie's for believing her to be good, I should not let any personal dislike stand in the way. Who are the alternatives? The divine mother & daughter have mentioned some other McNeil at Wadham who appears to be a friend of yours:[59] did you ever speak to me of him? – you know I can never remember names. The publication of our Anthology has been put off to an indefinite date because of a printing strike: I shall improve the interval by correcting my contributions out of recognition.

The only book I have read with satisfaction lately is Mackail's 'Lectures on Poetry':[60] I think he is one of my favourite moderns – he always has just the right point of view and deals with the right subject: he has sent me back to 'Endymion' which I read for some time in a church porch yesterday afternoon. Otherwise books have been absorbed in the general inertia of this time. I hope you are having exactly opposite experiences.

Yours
Jack

---

59 William Martin McNeill, who matriculated in 1919.
60 John William Mackail, *Lectures on Poetry* (1911).

TO HIS FATHER (LP VI: 195–6):

University College,
Oxford
25th July 1920

My dear Papy,

I should have answered you before but I have been engaged in entertaining the Colonel. He, despite the efforts of a tyrannical and slave driving general staff, is still managing to keep body and soul together and to sustain his labours with that equanimity for which he is justly famed. Contrary to your fears, he, as yet, [has] only one car: which he proposes to sell and buy another. As soon as his leave begins he is going to motor me to Liverpool, via Malvern, and so home. I am still debating whether I can sufficiently brace my nerves to such an ordeal.

But indeed one should not at the present moment talk in joke about ordeals: for by all accounts you are approaching a real one at home. Do the 'Times' accounts of the Belfast rioting exaggerate or the reverse?[61] I am glad to note that so far it has been mainly confined to its traditional grounds at the other end of town, and also that it usually takes place 'after hours'. A wise man these days will do well to survey the situation chiefly from the study. When I come home I shall (like Lundy in the play) buy a favour with green on one side and orange on the other, turning the appropriate colour outwards according to circumstances. What between this business at home and the Bolshevists nearly in Germany, one feels inclined to despair. Are all efforts made for the world as utterly barren in results as the terrible effort of this war has undoubtedly proved?

Your mention of the charms of biography reminds me of a book I saw the other day which would be much in your line – a translation of the diary kept by the late Shah of Persia during his tour of Europe. This is indeed to 'see ourselves as others see us'. Thus for instance 'the people of London are taught to pay great respect to their police, who are comely young men in a peculiar uniform: whatsoever offends them is judged worthy of death'. Or again (on the way from Dover) 'the train proceeded at such a speed that fire came out of the wheels and set one of the coaches ablaze: the mechanics extinguished the fire: then we continued

---

61 *The Times* (24 July 1920), p. 12: 'Night fighting in Belfast, 23 July. Little more than a mile away from the City Hall are lying over 100 casualties and at least 13 dead. For the greater part of the night a triangular contest of soldiers, Protestants and Catholics has gone on intermittently in several widely-separated areas.'

our journey'. Still better, (referring to Edward VII as Prince of Wales in kilts): 'Now the peculiarity of Scottish costume is this – that the legs are left bare to the thighs'. This is a greater treasure than the Young Visiters:[62] but I have room for only one more quotation. 'The waves rose and a violent storm began: the great Wazeer, the (here follow several unpronounceable officials) etc. were much disturbed. Thanks to Allah, We retained Our composure'.[63] (Room for an illustration by George Morrow[64] I think!)

I had nearly forgotten to tell you that Uncle and Aunt Hamilton[65] were here for a night on their tour. If any man has ever been successful in screwing the honey out of life it is he. One cannot help admiring the skill with which he knows exactly how far selfishness can go without rebounding on himself: he has learned to a nicety how much every plank will bear. At the same time this worldly wisdom which has an appetite for everything and yet can be content with little, which knows what can be got out of life and does not expect more, would be almost a virtue, so pleasant is it and so sensible, if it were not centred completely on self. He made one good 'mot' here – that 'England would be an excellent country to tour in were it not for the Cathedrals'. I hear that you were very nearly asked to take John in their absence but were finally rejected in favour of Glenmachan. No doubt you feel the affront bitterly. Hoping that you are otherwise well.

your loving son,
Jack

---

62 *The Young Visiters* (1919) is a comic masterpiece. It was written by Daisy Ashford (1881–1972) when she was a child. It was found in 1919 and sent to Chatto & Windus who published it with an introduction by J.M. Barrie, who insisted on meeting the author in order to discover if it was genuine.

63 Nasir Al-Din, *The Diary of H.M. The Shah of Persia during His Tour Through Europe in A.D. 1873*, translated by J.W. Redhouse (1874), ch. IV.

64 George Morrow (1870–1955) was a book illustrator from Belfast who was a regular contributor to *Punch*.

65 Augustus 'Gussie' Warren Hamilton (1866–1945) was the brother of Flora Lewis. He was known as possessing a remarkable degree of 'matter of factness'. After leaving Strandtown School he was apprenticed to the firm of MacIlwaine, Lewis and Co., and on completing his time, he went to sea as an engineer with the Ulster Steamship Company. On one of his voyages he met and fell in love with a young lady from Canada, Anne Sargent Harley (1866–1930), who later became his wife. After leaving the sea, Augustus settled in Belfast and founded the firm of Hamilton & McMaster, marine boilermakers and engineers. 'He was,' Warnie Lewis wrote of him, 'one of that rather uncommon type of man, thoroughly selfish and mean in money matters, who yet possesses qualities which make his society welcomed in any company' (LP II: 155). See **The Hamilton Family** in the Biographical Appendix.

TO HIS FATHER (LP VI: 198–9):

University College,
Oxford
Aug. 11th 1920

My dear Papy,

Thanks for your letter and the enclosure. Of this latter I scarcely know what to make. Your interpretation of it as meaning that I am still in the army seems inevitable. The fact being that hundreds of us who asked for temporary commissions in the regulars were, on the quiet, given permanent commissions in the special reserve. But unless my memory plays me very false, all the newspapers published a statement some time ago to the effect that those in my position would be 'deemed to have resigned' their commissions unless they wrote expressing a wish to the contrary before a certain date. Is it of any use for me to write and mention this? In the meantime I am making all enquiries I can about the subject. If anything should happen so suddenly as to prevent my 'concerting a plan' with you, I could, as a last resource, go to the solicitor here. At all events its no good blinding ourselves to the fact that if another emergency occurs, everyone will be pushed into it again by public opinion or conscription, commission or no: to be out of the army would mean only a few months lease of freedom. I cannot say that I now face such a prospect with anything more than resignation – once was enough. However, I am convinced that this country cannot now go to war: if we try, it will be a case of fighting our English revolutionaries at home, and then we shall all have our backs to the wall and nothing will matter much.

In all seriousness, I think we have now arrived at the point where a wise man can do no more than wait for the end with what grace he can: and it is hard to summon much grace if you meet as many traitors and cranks in our own class as I do here, hankering for the blessing of Soviet rule at once. Only boys of course, as you will say: but it is usually a few fools who start the shooting which the wise heads cannot stop.

I quite forgot to tell you the result of my board: perhaps it was so sweet a morsel that I feared to part with it – I was awarded £20 down in lieu of further pension! I wrote and protested on the ground that even the last board had given me a 20% disability which I understood entitled me to something more. They said the matter could not be reconsidered. The ultimate result of this will be I suppose that I am counted 'fit' again for anything that may turn up: the immediate result is that I shall have to ask you to make up the extra £50 per annum. I am sorry to have to do so, but the necessity of keeping my allowance, as it was with the pension, depends on the same conditions of life everywhere, which makes me reluctant to ask.

Under the unwritten laws of social humbug the Henry's[66] certainty that you would not come if asked did not justify them in passing you by. You were quite right not to send a present. The weather here is almost frosty, and it usually rains. I think it likely that the Colonel and I may advance by rail after all.

your loving son,
Jack

TO LEO BAKER (B):

27 Old Cleeve,
Washford,
Somerset.
[14? August 1920]

My dear Baker,

You tell me you have nothing specific to write about: but I have a thousand such. I could a tale unfold!..but I will not reduce your several hairs to the condition of quills upon the fretful porpentine. Let it suffice to say that I have lived this many a day in the realms of nightmare,

> *– I have sat down by Babylonian streams*
> *And hanged my harp upon funereal trees –*[67]

in a world of incredible problems that offer one the alternative 'Heads I win, tails you lose' of plans feverishly made and remade, of things once deemed impossible yet undertaken, from dire necessity at the last moment. A faint pallor of daylight, however, now streaks the East: we

---

66 The 'Henrys' were contemporaries of Warnie. Robin Henry was something of a character in Strandtown. He and his wife, the former Molly Robertson, had both been pupils of Miss Annie Harper, and they formed a good-looking pair. During the war Robin Henry served in the artillery.

67 Lewis's lines are based on Psalm 137:1–2 (Coverdale version): 'By the waters of Babylon we sat down and wept: when we remembered thee, O Sion. / As for our harps, we hanged them up: upon the trees that are therein.'

have a house in view! But I am not yet 'full of beans' again, either in mind or body.

I was glad to hear that you are reading my two canonical poets: though how you can take Milton and Spenser together, I do not at all understand. All historians of literature have told me, like you, of their points in common: but, tho' interesting, how artificial do these verbal likenesses appear compared with the real difference of the faery atmosphere and the divine. Spenser says 'The waies thro which my wearie steps I guide in this delightful launde of faerie, are so exceedingly spatious, and wide, and sprinkled with such swete varietie...etc',[68] but the other 'Sad task! – yet argument not less but more heroic than the tale of'[69] – I forget the words but you can find them. Or again, to take a passage where the Miltonic thunder seems somehow wearisome and forced beside the 'falling close' of Spenser, compare 'Hurled headlong flaming from the etherial sky to bottomless perdition – there to dwell, with adamantine chains and penal fire'[70] with 'And Nature's selfe was vanished whither no man wist'[71] – surely the most wonderful alexandrine ever written. To see Milton's real greatness one need but notice the fresh joy and reality of his Eden after the over-ripe stanzas which describe the garden of Acasia, tho' that is partly in the subject. I do, however, like to pick up in the Faerie Queene the germs of Milton's phrazes.

This is one of the privileges of art, that all things are in common: imitation, if it is forgotten, matters not, and, if it lives, is justified and does not diminish the originality of the borrower. The notion of literary property was brought by philistines from the valley of the gorribeenmen into Helicon where it has no weight nor meaning. All poetry is one, and I love to see the great notes repeated. Homer and Virgil wrote lines not for their own works alone but for the use of all their followers. A plague on these moderns scrambling for what they call originality – like men trying to lift themselves off the earth by pulling at their own braces: as if by shutting their eyes to the work of the masters they were likely to create new things themselves.

68 Spenser, *Faerie Queene*, VI, Preface, 1, 1–2.
69 Milton, *Paradise Lost*, IX, 13–16: 'Sad task! Yet argument / Not less but more heroic than the wrath / Of stern Achilles on his foe pursued / Thrice fugitive about Troy wall.'
70 ibid., I, 45.
71 Spenser, *Faerie Queene*, VII, vii, 59, 9.

'Damme' says Wellington in the Dynasts 'Where does he suppose I am to get reinforcements from'.[72] Where do you suppose a hermit like myself is to find new recruits for our Guild? About this same Guild, by the way, I went to see Barfield[73] before I left Oxford but found him about an hour gone. We must not make the mistake of trying too hard to beat up followers: indeed perhaps we must not make the mistake of trying too hard about anything: of this sacred Anthology of ours I am heartily sick. It appears now as clear as daylight that Blackwell does not want it, though he may bring it out, for all that, in his own good time. The chief motive for sticking to such a water-logged craft is the disappointment which I think Pasley would feel if he were marooned. I have had his revised version of the old man sent to me, with many corrections, but not of great importance. The more often I read his work in comparison with the rest of the anthology the more do I feel that we have consistently under-estimated him, tho' more by inference and assumption than by direct statement. When all these things reach the public, the modernist vigour of Vision and Tumult and the other one about 'Against the sky rode he' will make a noise that may surprise us, – agreeable, I hope, for the greatness of our hearts. I have done revised versions of Nimue and The Wild Hunt: the latter, I hope, is improved beyond recognition. At least I have reached a state from which I usually augur well – that wherein one looks back on the first version (once pleasing enough) as impossible, and thanks the gods for having escaped it.

Since I began this letter some two or three days ago I have been recuperating in most divine scenery. There are moors here, not so big nor high as those beyond Minehead, but sufficient for perfect beauty and solitude: indeed I have seldom found anywhere quite so alone. For a whole morning I saw nothing but ants (enormous ones) and a hawk: and from them you look down to the most wonderful hills and gorges and more moors on the one side, and on the other to the channel with Wales beyond it. Up there the emptiness, if it says anything, seems to say 'Admire if you will, but you have nor lot nor part in me'. I am constitutionally incapable of the harmony you feel. The more beautiful and desolate it is, the more I feel myself a trespasser: there is always someone waiting over the crest to warn me off. We also rode through glorious hill

---

72 Hardy, *The Dynasts*, VII, vii (slightly misquoted).
73 See **Owen Barfield** in the Biographical Appendix. He came up to Wadham College, Oxford, on a Classical Scholarship in 1919 and was introduced to Lewis by Leo Baker.

country to Porlock and saw Exmoor, far off, as Alan Quartermain saw the mountains of Suliman Berg.[74] This town has a church of St. Dubricius who, you may remember, crowned and annointed Arthur. (I forget whether this is in Malory, but it certainly is in the guide book.)[75]

I am sorry your job has not materilized. It seems as if the best thing you could do would be to return to Oxford. When I come within reach of typists again, I will try to send you the new Wild Hunt.

yours
C. S. Lewis

Is this good, bad or indifferent? –

> Oh that a black ship now were bearing me
>   Between the stars of the sky
> And the answering stars of the sea!, –
>   And the wind to throb, and I
>   On the decks to be sitting, awake
>   Watching the foamdrops break
>   In fire from her prow:
> Passing a moon-drencht island, pale, a Hesperian clime
>   Where the apple hangs on the bough
>   And the blood-red life, with no repining
>   Is full of shouting, a giant, terrible, shining,
> Till the guttering of the candle and the gathering home
> of time.

P.S. I am very sorry that I shall (I hope) be assisting a move into the house at the time you ask me to come to you. But I will tell you latter for certain.[76]

---

74 In Rider Haggard's novel *King Solomon's Mines* (1886).
75 The church in Porlock Lewis wrote about is dedicated to St Dubricius, whose name is sometimes spelled 'Dubric' or 'Dyfrig'. St Dubricius (d. c. 550), as he is usually called, is one of the most important saints of South Wales. He was a monk and a bishop, who worked mainly in the Hereford-Gwent area. Very little is known about him. He does not appear in Malory, but in Geoffrey of Monmouth's 12th-century *Historia Regum Britanniae* (VIII, 12), is given credit for crowning King Arthur.
76 Leo Baker's reply to this letter, dated 16 August 1920, is found in LP VI: 199–200.

On 20 August Jack joined Warnie at Aldershot Camp in Farnham, Hampshire. They travelled in Warnie's motorcycle and sidecar to Liverpool, and from there they crossed the Channel to Belfast, arriving at Little Lea on 26 August. They stayed with their father until 23 September.

TO LEO BAKER (B):

[University College
25 September 1920]

My dear Baker,

I was delighted to get your letter. You seem to have dropped – or dropt, as Pasley would like us to write – into a job which is pleasant though somewhat arduous. What a lucky thing for Harpenden!

Now, to get this damned anthology of[f] my chest: it has been sent back to Basil, who has now kept it in silence for a fortnight. He talked about being able 'to meet us in some way': I pointed out on behalf of the Big Three that we could meet him to precisely the extent of £0.0s.0d. In spite of this he still wanted to see the MS again, but I am quite sure he will never publish it. Pasley and I both think that if he does not, we ought to give up the plan: let me know whether you agree.

I have been absolutely incapable of writing a line for heaven knows how long: as I have to do two essays – one philosophical & one historical – every week and have also been writing a paper for the Martlets, this is perhaps not to be wondered at.

I am more worried by what goes on inside me: my imagination seems to have died: where there used to be pictures that were bright, at least to me, there is now nothing but a repetition of the trivialities and worries of the outer life – I go round and round on the same subjects which are always those I least want to think about. Perhaps, after all, these experiences are not brilliantly original nor wonderfully tragic – so don't think I am taking myself too seriously. After all, what is the object of writing to friends except that of talking oneself into a state of self importance and the belief that ones own perversities are matter of universal sympathy.

Pasley is in great form mentally, tho busily engaged in killing himself in trying to run. He announced his engagement (in deadly secrecy) the other day: so do not assume knowledge of the same unless you had heard before. He is also writing poems in what he calls 'rhythm'. I am using all my powers of persuasion to guide 'rhythm' away from vers libre and towards the unrhymed lyric. Do you remember a poem in unrhymed quatrains, which he showed us both? He has revised it and I think it is now one of his best –

> 'gold and silver moons
> That wonderfully sing their glories up.'

He is certainly much better than he was last term.

Thanks for the theory of poetry. The most valuable part of it, and the part which shd. be insisted on is that 'a poet who is only a poet is not the greatest poet'. The assumption that a great poem must have nothing in it but poetry has 'worked like madness in the brain'[77] of too many of us. On the other hand Coleridge's definition 'the best words in the best order'[78] has always seemed to me bad: for it would apply to good prose: or it would apply even to any piece of writing that fulfilled its purpose. Thus 'The train will leave at 7.30' gives us the best words (for the purpose) in the best order, i.e. we cannot improve upon them. Wordsworth indeed might have written 'The hissing locomotive with her line / Of labouring coaches from the platform side / Shall take departure ere the moving index / On that high, grim chronometer etc': but this wd. be worse words in a worst order. Coleridge's position does not (to me) therefore involve what you say. It is in your 1 (b) 'Words used for the purpose they alone can serve' that you really get to the heart of the matter. All this talk that every critic gives us about vision etc is darkening counsil: for vision, exaltation, criticism of life etc are not poetry, but the subject of poetry: and not the peculiar subject of poetry but the subject of all art. What we want to find is – that which is proper to poetry alone: what is the method by which poetry *and no other art* performs the duties shared with all art? Doubtless you would answer that in the same way as I wd. & come to a definition something like this 'Poetry is the art of utilizing the informal or irrational values of words to express that which can only be symbolized by their formal or conventional meanings.' These values include chiefly sound & association: also of course their 'group' sound or rhythms which are above and beyond their individual sounds: here is the meaning & justification of metre. Hence the value of the test 'Could this be said as well in prose?': if the answer is in the affirmative the poem is

---

77 Coleridge, *Christabel*, II, 413.
78 Samuel Taylor Coleridge, *Biographia Literaria* (1817), Ch. XIV.

condemned. As to all those other things – inspiration, purpose, nobility, wisdom etc, there are two answers. (1.) These are not peculiar to the art of poetry but common to all art: it is unfair, therefore, to include them in the definition of poetry. (2) If a man was not an artist (i.e. had not these other possessions) he cd. not have things inexpressible by ordinary speech to tell us, cd. not therefore be a poet. So our definition, narrow as it may seem at first sight, implies all that is necessary. You see that my theory has nearly everything in common with yours, but I think you still show some confusion between poetry itself and the objects of poetry.

Your invitations are delightfully couched. I have not forgotten at Cornwall 'there are no route marches, no dreadful excursions & no political debates: we do only those things that are proper to hermits'. I hope you won't think it the usual social lie, when I again have to refuse them. Please thank your Aunt and convey my apologies.

I shall have to spend Christmas in Ireland: it is very difficult for me ever to get away. You can understand that when you have a nominal home in one place & a real home somewhere else, the disposal of ones person even for a few days makes demands that can't be met. I am very sorry, not to be able to come. I wish I could ask you to visit us at Oxford sometime when term is over: but the gods only know where or in what quarters we may be then. If your journeyings ever bring you to Oxford I needn't tell you how glad I should be: why you insisted on going down is still a mystery to me.

I haven't had time yet to go and look Barfield up but hope to do so soon: you don't mention the Guild, so I hope it has not gone the way of all ideals.

You will be interested to hear that in the course of my philosophy – on the existence of matter – I have had to postulate some sort of God as the least objectionable theory: but of course we know nothing. At any rate we don't know what the real Good is, and consequently I have stopped defying heaven: it can't know less than I, so perhaps things really are alright. This, to you, will be old news but perhaps you will see it in me as a sign of grace. Don't mistake the position: its no cry of 'all's well with the world':[79] its only a sense that I have no business to object to the universe as long as I have nothing to offer myself – and in that respect we are all bankrupt.

---

79 Robert Browning, *Pippa Passes* (1841), I, 228: 'All's right with the world!'

Write again: forgive my atrocious habits as a correspondant –
Yours
C. S. Lewis

TO HIS FATHER (LP VI: 169):

University College,
Oxford
9th Oct. [1920]

My dear Papy,

Once again, in the words of the immortals, we have resumed our round of steady work, relieved and sweetened by hearty play. I would have written earlier but I have been rather incapacitated by a bite from a playful cat – merely a scratch at the end of my forefinger, but enough for a while to prevent one laying it to a pen with any comfort. It is now alright.

I was sorry to see the other day news of our friend Heineman's sudden death. The papers have been so covering him with eulogy since he went that I begin to feel glad I met him, if only for once – Vergilium vidi tantum!'[80] In this case however I think the virtues are not wholly of the tombstone nature: a great publisher is really something more than a mere machine for making money: he has opportunities for doing things for the best of motives, and if one looks round most of our English houses, I think he avails himself of them as well as anyone can expect. I always put up a fight for the tribe of publishers here where so many young men with manuscripts have nothing too bad to say of them.

We are having the most delightful weather here – it ought to mean a saving of coal against the lean days, if the strike comes off: tho' I suppose the amount of coal used for domestic purposes is trifling compared with the consumption in factories – 'and the like' as Knock says. The look of the streets here has been very much altered by these quaint caps and gowns which the women have started wearing since they came into their inheritance – but I daresay you have read of it in the papers.[81]

---

80 'I have seen the so great Virgil!' Ovid, *Tristia*, IV, x, 51.
81 On 17 February 1920 a statute was passed making women full members of the University.

I hope you are keeping well: it is strange to be once more in circles where Irish politics show only a certain way above the horizons. English people are terribly indifferent.

your loving son,

Jack

TO HIS FATHER (LP VI: 211–12):

University Coll.

Postmark: 8 December 1920

My dear Papy,

I am afraid your opinion of my powers as a correspondant will not have increased. As a matter of fact I have been interrupted by a journey to Cambridge, followed by some days in bed. It is not, I hope, too late to thank you for the cheque and also for Bill's book.[82] A notable work that! I have not yet summoned up enough courage to write to him, nor found words wherewith to congratulate him on this grotesque firstborn. I suppose one can always fall back on comparisons and say which are better than others, even in depths like this.

My journey to Cambridge was on this wise. You may remember that a society of Martlets at Pembroke, Cambridge sent representatives to our society of that name: on this occasion four of us were sent to pay a return match. The trip was rendered both cheaper and pleasanter by the fact that one of the four lives there, and very kindly put us all up. I read them a paper on narrative poetry.[83] Of course I don't know what they thought of it, but at any rate nothing was thrown at me. We dined with them first. It was a wretched night, which having attempted to freeze, had finally decided instead on a sleety rain. The old library of their college, where we had dinner, was very badly heated, and what between that and going about their quadrangle in the chilliness of evening dress and the rain, I got rather a nasty chill – whereof I am just now recovered.

---

82 Their friend of many years, Bill Patterson, had just published under the initials W.H.F. a small volume of verse entitled *Songs of a Port* (Belfast: McCaw, Stevenson & Orr, 1920).

83 This was Lewis's first visit to Cambridge and it took place on his 22nd birthday, 29 November 1920. Lewis was elected President of the Martlets on 15 October 1919 and he was prevailed upon to retain the position until 13 June 1921. The paper he read in Cambridge on 'Narrative Poetry' was the same he had read to the Oxford Martlets on 3 November 1920. The paper has not survived but the minutes of the Oxford meeting are reproduced in Walter Hooper's 'To the Martlets' in *C.S. Lewis: Speaker and Teacher*, op. cit., pp. 44–5.

It was very interesting next day to see Cambridge. In many ways it is a contrast: there is something, I can hardly say whether of colour or of atmosphere, which at once strikes a more northern, a bleaker and a harder note. Perhaps the flatness of the country, suggesting places seen from the railway beyond Crewe, has something to do with it. The streets are narrow and crowded: the non-university parts depressing enough. Some things – such as King's College Chapel, in which I was prepared to be disappointed – are indeed beautiful beyond hope or belief: several little quadrangles I remember, with tiled gables, sun dials and tall chimnies like Tudor houses, were charming. One felt everywhere the touch of Puritanism, of something Whiggish, a little defiant perhaps. It has not so much Church and State in its veins as we. The stained windows in the Halls show figures like Erasmus[84] and Cranmer.[85] Oxford is more magnificent, Cambridge perhaps more intriguing. Our characteristic colour is the pale grey, almost the yellow of old stone: their's the warm brown of old brick. A great many Cambridge buildings remind one of the Tower of London. Most of the undergraduates whom I met I liked very much. Their dons, as judged by those who were at the 'do', are certainly inferior to ours in charm of manners and geniality. One I thought hardly a gentleman.

I am afraid you took my remark about 'a small book' rather too literally – I meant only an essay for my tutor: I am hardly up to writing historical monographs (for publication) just yet. I have however been recommended to try for the Vice Chancellor's Essay Prize next April. The subject is 'Optimism' under which heading one could include almost anything one wanted to write about. My point of view will be mainly metaphysical and rather dry. It would be a splendid advertisement if I could pull it off, but of course competition is very keen.

---

84 Desiderius Erasmus (1466/9–1536), the Dutch humanist, was the most renowned scholar of his age. Besides reviving many Classical texts, he edited the Greek New Testament with his own translation into Classical Latin. Drawn to Cambridge by St John Fisher (1469–1535), Vice-Chancellor of Cambridge University, Erasmus was the first teacher of Greek there.

85 Thomas Cranmer (1489–1556), Archbishop of Canterbury from 1533 to 1553, was educated at Jesus College, Cambridge, and became a Fellow in 1523. He was Henry VIII's chief instrument in overthrowing Papal supremacy in England. His theology was influenced by the Continental Reformers, and he achieved his ambition of providing the Church of England with the *Book of Common Prayer* (1549).

Thanks for the enclosures. I suppose the War Office business is now settled, although apparently the army cannot exist without my services as a full Lieutenant. I really don't think I can go to Mrs Shillington's dance[86] and hang about uselessly cumbering the ground – which is all a non-dancer can do.

The same storm which you mention seems to have done damage all over England. I hope the trouble at Leeborough is not serious.

your loving son,

Jack

P.S. W. was over here some time ago. He says that in the photo Kirk is wearing 'his ordinary expression', which shows how he has changed since the old days.[87]

TO LEO BAKER (B):

[University College
22 December 1920]

My Dear Baker –

The Way's the way to bankruptcy, paying cash down and heavy loss: and for this reason Edmund Gosse those lovely lines will never see. And oh! to think with what a shock we crush the hopes of Clutton Brock;[88] and luckless G. K. Chesterton is fated not to look thereon. The blow has fallen. Basil refuses to publish the dam' thing unless we raise some money – I forget how much, but more than we thought possible. Please find enclosed, our own babes from the ruined crêche. My own feeling of relief is something wonderful and has inspired me to write several immortal poems in the last few days. I am sending you the revised version of the Wild Hunt and await your criticism. I am crossing to Ireland to-morrow, where my address will be Little Lea, Strandtown, Belfast.

---

86 Lewis had been invited to a party at the home of Mrs Shillington in Belfast. He and Warnie were there visiting their father from 24 to 30 December.

87 On 10 October 1920 Warnie took a photograph of Mr and Mrs W.T. Kirkpatrick at their home in Little Bookham, Surrey. It is the only known photograph of the 'Great Knock', and it is reproduced in Walter Hooper, *Through Joy and Beyond: A Pictorial Biography of C.S. Lewis* (1982), p. 35.

88 Lewis is only having fun. He did not expect any of these men to see their poems. Sir Edmund Gosse (1849–1928) was a poet who had been friends with some of the Pre-Raphaelites; Arthur Clutton-Brock (1868–1924) was an essayist, critic and journalist who contributed frequently to *The Times Literary Supplement.*

Heard Lohengrin with great delight, for the first time, since I wrote to you: (this letter is so childish that I almost continued 'It was very nice'). I have not time today to discuss your theory of poetry: we seem to be prettily [*sic*] agreed on fundamentals, tho' there are still points of difference – real ones, not 'misunderstandings'. Am writing again,

yours

C. S. Lewis

1921

—— ≈ ——

TO HIS FATHER (LP VI: 226):

Oxford Union Society
[Oxford]
Jan. 19th [1921]

My dear Papy,

I was sorry to hear that you were not well. I suppose it was the final stage of the nasty cold which you had when I left, and hope that it has now 'dragged its slow length' to completion. Warnie will have told you of our pleasant journey to Liverpool. I travelled the rest of the way in great comfort and had an excellent lunch on the train. After so many lean years during the war it is quite strange to see a dining car again. The country was flooded everywhere as far as Oxford: I have never seen anything like it, and I suppose it will be very serious.

I have been very busy ever since I came up with my essay on Optimism, which I find has to be earlier than I thought. Indeed I have almost lived with my pen to the paper. It has been one of those rare periods that we all have now and then when everything becomes clear and we see the way before us. So I thought I must utilise it at all costs: I felt like the horse in Masefield's new poem, when he was winning the steeple-chase, 'my day, my day, I shall not have another'.[1] For this reason I did not write to you on Sunday.

I don't know that there is anything new here to record: if there is, I have probably missed it, being for the nonce a troglodyte in the truly paternal manner. I have had one of the usual voluminous letters from Aunt Lily. It has turned cold here and very frosty of nights: but it is dry and bracing and pleasanter than the sort of deluge you are perhaps still having at home. Tell big brother that I have e'en now taken his bundles of literature to one he wots of and they will be done in three

---

1 John Masefield, *Right Royal* (1920), Pt. I, p. 8 (slightly misquoted).

515

weeks.[2] You might also tell him to occupy his spare time looking round the study for a little green book called 'Skeleton Outlines of Greek History':[3] and if he will send it, I shall be his debtor. I am writing this at the Union in great haste before lunch, and cannot stay longer: next week I shall not be so busy. Hoping that you are now better and possibly none the worse for a few days Nirvana in bed and away from the Court.

> your loving son,
> Jack

TO HIS FATHER (LP VI: 229–30):

Oxford Union Society
[Oxford]
Friday Jan. 21st [1921][4]

My dear Papy,

I certainly deserve the wrath of all my family, for I had scarcely sent off my last letter to you when I discovered that the missing book had never been taken home at all. Perhaps I should have let you know this: but having heard that you were in bed, I supposed that the quest would be confined to Big Brother and that his usual self restraint would have prevented his researches from being carried to any tedious length. However – !

My history tutor has handed me over to a gentleman at Magdalen whom he recommended by telling me that he was a grandson of Mendelsohn's: a trifle irrelevant I thought. The exchange was presented to me in the form of a compliment and I am quite satisfied with it. The reason I mention it is because the new man deserves to be known to fame. I had not been many minutes in his room until I had an uneasy sense of strange yet familiar neighbours. When he went out for a moment I discovered what it was – pigs! Do not mistake me: not live pigs: but pigs of china, of bronze, of clay, of wood, of stuff and of stone: pigs jovial and pigs quizzical, kindly pigs and severe pigs, Falstaffian pigs and pigs philosophical. I counted 28 in a few seconds and had still not

---

2 Warnie had returned to Belfast on 14 January, to remain with his father until he embarked on 9 March 1921 for Sierra Leone. He had sent his brother four volumes of *Mémoires de Mlle de Montpensier*, ed. Pierre Adolphe Chéruel (Paris: 1858) to be bound.

3 Evelyn Abbott, *A Skeleton Outline of Greek History* (1900).

4 This letter bears the postmark 2 p.m. 29 January 1921.

got beyond the mantelpiece. This porcine seraglio of a lonely old bachelor is one of the little comedies I would not have missed for a good deal. And yet how wise! Here are companions for every mood, who need practically no upkeep and are never untrue or unkind. I think I must give him a new one: perhaps one of those balloon pigs filled with gas, so that it would hover against the ceiling – and be drawn down by a windlass at night to rest, like a Zeppelin in some little 'hangar'.[5]

I am very sorry to hear that you were laid up so long, and hope that you now have quite shaken it off. I have had a bit of a cold, but it is now gone, and beyond the perennial need of having my hair cut, I think you would pass me as 'all present and correct'. I am still smoothing and varnishing the work on Optimism.

Here is a story that will please the Colonel. The other night at the 'Martlets' old Carlyle read a paper. He is a foxy looking old gentleman with a cleanshaven face as red as a berry and straight hair the colour of snuff – a very comical face and a high croaking voice. He began by saying that he ought to apologise for his paper 'because – H'm – to tell you the truth – I had meant to publish it – but – H'm – H'm – it was so unsatisfactory that – I – I just sent it to an American magazine.' That's the proper spirit!

How very like our great army on which the sun never sets – I mean all the muddle about Warnie's sailing: I don't much envy him his voyage if this weather continues.[6] It is a little unkind to tantalise me with these glimpses of the social joys – Pumblechooks party – a quiet chat with John – symposium chez the apple man: this to me a poor scholar in Grub St! But I am sure it was unintentional, and I grudge no one his innocent pleasures.

your loving son,
Jack

---

5 The history tutor was Paul Victor Mendelssohn Benecke (1868–1944), the great-grandson of the composer Felix Mendelssohn. He became a Fellow of Magdalen College in 1893 and taught Classics until his retirement in 1925. He lived in Magdalen with his vast collection of pigs for the rest of his life. Lewis's reminiscences of Benecke are found in Margaret Deneke's *Paul Victor Mendelssohn Benecke (1868–1944)* (Oxford: [1954]), pp. 31–4.

6 The War Office had informed Warnie that he was under orders to sail to Sierra Leone on 12 January, but the orders were sent to Aldershot and forwarded from there to Sierra Leone. As a result, the ship sailed without him, and he had to wait until 9 March to embark on another one.

TO HIS FATHER (LP VI: 242–3):

Oxford Union Society
[Oxford]
16th Feb. [1921]

My dear Papy,

I am afraid I have been on this occasion remiss. I have been pretty busy and that, coupled with the laziness which follows a 'cold in the nose' and one or two outstanding letters to Aunt Suffern and a few others, have kept me going. Correspondance is unhappily no true parallel to conversation: and it is just when one would be most ready for a talk in the odd hour of the day when one shoves ones work from one and lights the pipe of peace, that one is least ready to sit down and write a letter. I often wonder how the born letter writers whose 'works' fill volumes, overcame this difficulty.

The colonel is certainly in luck, and I do not see how even the logic of the army can hold him responsible for not having been ordered abroad. I have a sort of feeling – a mere presentiment – at the back of my mind, that he will never reach Sierra Leone: a fate which will worry him more than you.

My bookseller has just sent me a bill for the books which I have got since I began to read 'Greats'. I tried originally to neutralise the outlay by selling again most of those which I had for 'Mods.', but this did not carry me far. I hope you will not consider it unreasonable if I ask you for a contribution of £5, since I cannot comfortably meet this out of income. Prices of necessary books are appalling: a Joseph's 'Logic'[7] at 12/6, a 'corpus' of Greek inscriptions at 15/-, an edition of Aristotle's Ethics at 12/6 etc., etc. For some reason – presumably because of the increased number of undergraduates – second-hand books have practically disappeared from the market here. One cannot rely entirely on libraries for some works of reference which are constantly in use, tho' I particularly resent expenditure on books which I shall never open once I am through the examination schools. The £5 of course does not include any thing I got 'because I thought I would like to have it', whether bearing on my subject or not.

The tale of Tchanie and Lily's absurd remark about the Strandtown 'season' is good. I met a friend of the said Tchanies the other night at the

---

7 Horace William Brindley Joseph, *An Introduction to Logic* (1906).

Carlyles, a girl called Helen Waddell[8] whom you may have heard of. When last I saw her she was lying face downwards on the floor of Mrs McNeill's drawing room, saying rather good things in a quaint Belfast drawl which poor Allan Smiles[9] himself could hardly have beaten. Though she behaved differently here, it was a strange sensation to see a little bit of our queer native world in such a different milieu. Que diable [allait-il] faire dans cette galere?[10]

I hope Arthur is not really going to the South of France because he is tired of the Slade: if that is so, I am afraid I shall find it hard to feel any sympathy with him again. It will be a disease of the soul rather than of the heart, and an incurable one, which we shall then have to bewail in him.

If the Colonel is at home again, will you show him the cutting which I enclose: he will remember having seen this strange creature here in the Union, and who could forget the 'voluminous trousers'.[11] There is a Chaucerian or Dickensian 'mine host' in a little inn near Cumnor where I sometimes call on my walks abroad who has told me that the old man

---

8 Helen Waddell (1889–1965), medieval scholar and translator, was educated at Victoria College and Queen's University, Belfast. She went up to Somerville College, Oxford, in 1920, and after taking her degree she spent the years 1923-5 in France learning the language and attaining familiarly with the Latin poetry of the fourth to the twelfth centuries. On her return she gave a course of lectures at Lady Margaret Hall, Oxford, on 'The Wandering Scholars'. She lived mostly in London after this, and published many books, the most famous of which are *The Wandering Scholars* (1927), *Medieval Latin Lyrics* (1929) and a novel, *Peter Abelard* (1933). She was a close friend of Jane McNeill, but except for this one reference above neither she nor Lewis mentioned each other in their correspondence. Lewis was, however, an admirer of her books, and in *The Allegory of Love* (1936) he says of *The Wandering Scholars*: 'Of the literary merits of Bernardus, the reader can judge best by comparing the account I have just given with the equally favourable, but differently directed, account of Miss Waddell, who touches nothing which she does not adorn' (ch. II). See Felicitas Corrigan, *Helen Waddell: A Biography* (1986).

9 Alan Smiles was a neighbour of the Lewises. He joined the Royal Irish Rifles in 1914 and was killed in battle in 1916.

10 Molière, *Les Fourberies de Scapin*, II, vii. A literal translation is, 'Why on earth did he ever get on board that galley?' but, in Lewis's context, 'What on earth was he doing there?'

11 Jack sent his father an article from *The Times* (5 February 1921), p. 11, entitled 'Death of an Oxford Character'. 'The death was announced yesterday,' it said, 'of Mr Herbert Jackson, a well-known Oxford "coach" and one of the oldest non-collegiate students. He was a remarkable personality, and his utter indifference to his dress, shown in the cravat, short coat, and voluminous trousers which he habitually wore, made him a distinctive figure in the streets of Oxford and at University ceremonies.'

used often to be there years ago – 'and 'e didn't 'arf look after his self sir.
I've seen 'im polish off an 'ole duck and 'arf a pound of cheese and a
couple of pints o' bitters – reg'lar as anything 'e would' – which sounds
an exaggeration.

It has been very cold here – frost and wind. I often pity the heroes
whom I see on the river in things like summer underclothes. I suppose
they'd pity me too, in a less kindly manner, if they knew that such a
mortal existed.

your loving son,
Jack

TO LEO BAKER (B):

Union Society,
Oxford.
Feb 25th 1921

My dear Baker,

When I read your letter I was so glad that, if I were not a
respectable middle aged suburbanite, I should have gone and got drunk.
I am staying up until this term next year, so, tho I shall pass a little before
you, we have some time before us.

Next to the news of your return – which I accept too thankfully to ask
for reason or motive – I was pleased, tho not maliciously, to hear that you
had entered *questa salva selvaggia ed aspre et forte*,[12] the Dantesque mood,
and begun to doubt. I can foresee clearly your ultimate return to the house
hold of faith, but anticipate great good from your excursion. 'Blind faith' is
indeed unsuitable for us who are alive now: we know too much and see life
too widely and it is culpable not to make use of our widened landscape.
The comfortable little universe with heaven above and hell beneath, an
absolute up and down and a bare six thousand years of recorded history,
could furnish you well enough with a world-view that a man could write in
his pocket book and have done. But we haven't got that now, and I feel that
we ought to use our own data even if they lead only to destruction.

It is hard to criticize the little poem you sent me: I shall try to do so
later on. At present it seems to me like the landscape it describes, full of
mist opening only here and there into oases of something you can get

---

12 *The Vision or Hell, Purgatory and Paradise of Dante Alighieri*, op. cit., Canto I, l. 5: 'That
forest, how robust and rough its growth'.

hold of. I was a bit thrown off the rails by expecting it to be heroic blank verse, but I think it will come on acquaintance to please my ear. The fine rhythm of 'God the father almighty' tho' borrowed from the prayer book, comes in with such a gracious surprise that it becomes your own. But of this more when I have digested it. I look forward to hearing the music: tho' I hope it is not going to mean a permanent turning away from poetry. I suppose it is the stress of work which has absorbed your energy and prevented you from writing anything lately.

The same thing has happened to Pasley – indeed between schools and being engaged he has lost all interest in the muse. At the same time I think I like him better now than ever I did (have I said this before?). There are other things besides vision – lots of them.

What a splendid picture of you as a Nabob! – tho I hope your leg has released you before this from your enforced royalty.

It has been wonderfully springlike here, and I have been reading Prometheus Unbound and going for long walks – particularly interested lately in cloud scenery. This coming luck of yours is unlike things that really happen: like reversing time and raising the dead. Am busy on my old Venus re-cooked as a narrative with Ossian[13] & Niamh[14] instead of Venus & Tannhauser:[15] a wonderful subject 'if answerable style I can obtain'.[16] I shall try to send you something without a letter in a few days.

yrs

C. S. Lewis

TO LEO BAKER (B):

Oxford Union,
[4? March 1921]

My dear Baker,

As you say, this is indeed terrible. A letter railing upon the gods or fates means no great thing in my mouth but I was disturbed to see that

---

13 i.e. Oisin, a legendary Gaelic warrior and bard, as found in W.B. Yeats' narrative poem, *The Wanderings of Oisin* (1889).

14 In Irish mythology, Niamh is the daughter of Manannán the sea-god. She fell in love with Oisin, carried him off, and kept him with her for 300 years. She allowed him to return to his country on condition that he not set foot on the earth. He disregarded the caution and as a result lost his youth and became a blind, old man.

15 Tannhäuser is a German Minnesinger or lyric poet of the 13th century. He becomes enamoured of a beautiful woman who beckons him into the grotto of Venus.

16 Milton, *Paradise Lost*, IX, 20.

they have brought you also to this pass: partly indeed from a certain jealousy wherewith I am used to reserve pessimism to myself and keep my friends as a body of consolers, but partly because I argue from it something seriously wrong. I hope it will turn out to be merely the psychological result of your body's impertinent interference, and not some 'stroke of fortune': I hope you're not in pain: 'pain the perfect misery, the worst / Of cuts', there's nothing else to say about it. As a matter of fact, I fancy you would bear pain a great deal more wisely than I, who am an arrant coward and ready to run to earth even in annihilation at the first touch of our lady Dolores:[17] the enforced idleness and monotony of illness, on the other hand, you probably resent far more than I. There must be a drop of Oriental blood in me: I am so often content to sit or lie still for hours together thinking nothing and hardly even imagining anything. Beyond Suez they call it the Kaf, I think. I am rather like a cow, you see: you, rather more like a blue bottle. In short you probably need the South for your mind as much as for your body – is there any chance of you going abroad?

Barfield, whom I have looked up after a term's inexcusable neglect on both sides, tells me you were in excellent form when he last met you. He has given me his 'Tower' to read, which you have seen, I believe. In spite of many obvious faults – languor of metre, indirect egotism, too great frequency of similes and a forced novelty of phrasing – in spite of all this I am amazed at its power and feel that we have never yet treated him with sufficient respect. Its solid and real and has its feet on terra firma: it is organically connected with life as a whole, not a mere panel of odd experiences, in a word its central. That's what I envy him and what our best moderns, Brooke and Flecker[18] and de la Mare, seem to lack. Yeats even hasn't got it: Masefield has or had it in some degree. The description of the 'musical endings' and 'little blunt verses' remembered from fairy tales and the dream which follows are, I think, really capital. On the other hand, I cannot tolerate the prologue. Tho' in theory all shd. come within the poet's range, yet in practice there are some things one simply can't say without making the reader, or at least a reader like me, either uncomfortable or disposed to mock. At any rate, Barfield can't do it: it

---

17 From Dolour, 'Our Lady of Pain', as Dolour or Pain is sometimes called.
18 James Elroy Flecker (1884–1915), poet and playwright whose Eastern work *Hassan* Lewis wrote about to Arthur Greeves on 23 February 1931.

hasn't come off, tis a shameless piece of spiritual indecency. It is mere instinct given direct and not sublimated by vision. What do you think about it? The recurring motive of the tower, I'm afraid, will give the psycho-analysts something to talk about in their usual vein.

I was interested to hear about your music – you attempt formidable subjects: will there be any chance of your sending either of the songs here. Barfield has a friend called Mitchell, a baritone, who sang pleasantly enough when I was with them the other night. He is also digging with the poet Harwood;[19] do you know any of his work? But I am a little alarmed, all the same, so jealous I am, to see you flirting ever so innocently with the other muse. Even if I could do it, I should feel it a kind of adultery in me and fear to be finally discovered and cast off by both. Which is inconsistent, for I am even now busied with my Essay on Optimism for the Vice Chancellor's prize. I have written four or five poems since the end of last term, one quite recently. I suppose I can hardly expect you to go to the trouble of copying out any of your new ones: if you ever feel so disposed, send them to me, even without a letter if you haven't time.

We must really try to harden ourselves to the difficulties of correspondence, which are very real. It is just those odd hours of the day when one shoves ones work from one and lights a pipe that one would most readily talk if a friend was present and yet is least disposed to write a letter. However we ought to be able to conquer this.

Thanks for your criticisms of the Wild Hunt (Barfield, by the way, condemns it as 'derivative'). Rê the last line, 'sincerity' is a vague word: it is *not* my own view I give, but my own view from the position of Hippolytus – from that mood which makes the subject of the whole poem, and which comes to us all at times and shd. be taken into account. I hope you will be better before this reaches you: don't work yourself to death whatever job you do, you have other functions more important for which you will in 'the perfect witness of all-judging Jove'[20] be more accountable. – and do try to give me another letter soon

Yrs

C. S. Lewis

---

19 See **Cecil Harwood** in the Biographical Appendix. Harwood matriculated at Christ Church, Oxford, in 1919. After taking his BA in 1921 he and Owen Barfield had 'digs' together at Bee Cottage in Beckley, a few miles from Oxford.

20 Milton, *Lycidas*, 82.

P.S. Paisley has won a College prize (£5) for the historical essay: he is full of life and happiness & looking for a job against his going down at th' end of next term. Faces what seems to me awful difficulties in 'the grand manner,' has written no poetry lately and I'm rather afraid he's not likely to.

TO HIS FATHER (LP VII: 261–2):

Oxford Union Society
[Oxford]
19th March [1921]

My dear Papy,

I have put off writing from day to day, partly in the expectation of a letter from you, which your last note seemed to promise, and partly at first because I thought that the Colonel would call here on his way to the world's end. I suppose he has arrived by now at the incredible place.[21] Here, amid cold March winds, my imagination has a sort of shock when it tries to paint those poster like blue skies and to think of him sitting in flannels and panting. I have so long forsaken the illiberal study of geography that I would not now give up my ignorance for a good deal. To me, and I expect to you, everywhere beyond the equator is a vague romance: I have an idea that if Warnie went for a walk a little way south he would come to the coast of Coromandel and be able to get an autograph from the Yongi Bongi Bo himself. Please let me have his address as I have promised ('the triumph of optimism over experience')[22] to try and send him a monthly newsletter.

I have been taken recently to see the mighty Yeats.[23] It was the weirdest show you ever saw, and I fear he is a Kod. You sit on hard antique chairs by candlelight in an oriental looking room and listen in silence while the great man talks about magic and ghosts and mystics: I should have loved to have had Kirk there. What fluttering of the dovecote! It is a pity that the real romance of meeting a man who has written great poetry and

---

21 Warnie sailed on the ship *Appam* for Sierra Leone on 9 March 1921. He arrived at Freetown, Sierra Leone on 19 March.

22 *Boswell's Life of Johnson*, op. cit., vol. II, 7 December 1770, p. 128: 'A gentleman who had been very unhappy in marriage, married immediately after his wife died: Johnson said, it was the triumph of hope over experience.'

23 The meeting with W.B. Yeats took place on 14 March and is described fully in Jack's serial letter to Warnie of March–April 1921.

who has known William Morris and Tagore[24] and Symons[25] should be so overlaid with the sham romance of flame coloured curtains and mumbo-jumbo.

It is bitterly cold here and I have been a little bothered with what would be called growing pains if I were a bit younger, but would now be dignified by the name of rheumatism. I have written a piteous and I hope convincing reply to the letter you enclosed. 'Optimism' is going to the typist next week.

Hoping to hear from you and that you keep well.

your loving son,

Jack

TO HIS BROTHER: (A SERIAL LETTER, WRITTEN ON VARIOUS DATES IN MARCH–APRIL 1921; LP VI: 284–9)

University College.

[Oxford]

My dear W.,

I am waiting to hear your address from M. L'Oiseau Pomme de Terre,[26] and in the meantime have begun – tho' with what promise of continuance I don't know – my journal letter. As nothing ever happens to me it will be filled, if at all, with trivialities and things that have interested me from day to day. As we talk a good deal of odd fragments out of books when we are together, there's no reason why we should not reproduce the same sort of tittle-tattle. Perhaps one of the reasons why letters are so hard to write and so much harder to read is that people confine themselves to news – or in other words think nothing worth writing except that which would not be worth saying. All that should be said by way of preamble has already been better said by Lamb in his letter to a friend at the Antipodes. I feel the same difficulty: I cannot imagine in what kind of melodramatic setting you will be reading this. I hear that

---

24 Rabindranath Tagore (1861–1941), the eminent Bengali poet. His *Gitanjali: Song Offering* (1912) won the Nobel Prize for Literature in 1913.

25 Arthur William Symons (1865–1945) whose early volumes of poetry included *Days and Nights* (1889) and *London Nights* (1895). He is largely remembered as a leading spirit of the Decadence movement and a defender of 'Art for Art's Sake'.

26 The Lewis brothers were enthusiastic nicknamers. Since boyhood they had been amused by their father's 'low' Irish pronunciation of 'potatoes' as 'p'daytas'. As a result, he became 'The P'dayta' or 'The P'daytabird' – and now, with Warnie in Sierra Leone where French is spoken, 'Monsieur L'Oiseau Pomme de Terre'.

your 'preposterous box' on the 'East India-man' was not to your liking. Well, you would be a soldier: you must keep a stiff upper lip about it and button up your coat. Here we have sleet and that sort of wind that freezes you when you go out drest for summer: if you do otherwise, 'the wild winds whist' and the sun comes out a good 80. But I will be on with my journal: the dates are only approximate.

March 1st

Going into College today I met Hamilton-Jenkin[27] in the porch, who carried me to his rooms in Merton Street. Jenkin is a little, pale person with a smooth green face, not unlike a lizard's. He was too young for the war and I always look on him as rather a child, though some people think I am wrong in this. I mention him for the amusing passages he showed me from two books. One was a Tour of the County of Cornwall written in the 17th Century: an admirable codology. Under the heading of Beastes we find (after those of Venerie and Draught) Rats. These are described as 'not only mischievous by day for their devouring of clothes, writings and meats, but cumbersome by night for their rattling and jaunting as they gallop their galliards in the roof'. This sentence I at once learnt by heart. 'The slow six legged crawler' which in Cornwall infest all but the 'cleanly home bred' are also worth recording.[28]

The other book approaches the tall end of your period from a strange angle. It is the newly discovered autobiography of a Cornish smuggler who was one of the first 'methodies': apparently finding this employment compatible with his religion. The joke was that he managed to get himself imprisoned in France with some 'of the best people' waiting to be guillotined. They seem to have been very nice to him and asked him to sing – for in his own Cornwall he was accustomed to go out into a lonely place and sing 'so that I suppose I could be heard for a mile off': which he did 'for fear of giving offence'. He was however worried how to avoid too much society without offending until 'the Lord provided him a little place under the stairs'. This strange character I thought worth mentioning.[29]

---

27 See **Alfred Kenneth Hamilton Jenkin** in the Biographical Appendix. Jenkin was born in Cornwall and matriculated at University College in 1919 where he read English and was a member of the Martlets.

28 Although the passages are slightly misquoted they come from Richard Carew's *The Survey of Cornwall* (1602), p. 22.

29 *The Autobiography of a Cornish Smuggler (Captain Harry Carter, of Prussia Cove) 1748–1809*, with an Introduction and Notes by John B. Cornish (1894).

Jenkin himself is an enthusiastic Cornishman and some are bored with his persistency in talking of his native scenery, habits, language and superstitions. I rather like it. He put on a little linen cap which he wears when 'he goes down mines'. Cornwall of course is all mines: they are full of beings called Nackers whom one hears knocking at the ends of the lonelier galleries. The workmen leave little bits of their food for them, for they are terrible bringers of good and bad luck – rather like Leprechauns as I understand. Jenkins has only one vice: that of writing very sad poetry which he sometimes shows me. It is usually about Cornwall.

March 12th

Everyone was going down today. Such days have all the atmosphere of a school end of term with its joy taken out of it – body without soul. I hate it: and lest empty rooms and stacks of suit cases should not be sufficiently offensive, we have the intolerable institution of Collections.[30] This is the worst relic of barbarism which yet hangs about the University. From 9 until noon the Master with all his 'auxiliar fiends' sits at the high table in Hall and one by one sheepish or truculent undergraduates, as their names are called, walk up the long emptiness, mount the dais, and stand foolishly gaping while he delivers a little homily. In my case he always used to say the same thing. 'Well Mr Lewis, I – ah – I – have nothing but – ah – satisfaction to express as regards – ah – ah. We expect great things of you.' Apparently he has now given up expecting great things of me.

Now you, lolling in your punkah while the lotuses fly over a pagoda coloured sky etc, may think me very weak: but it is extraordinary that any ceremony which is designed to make you feel like an inky schoolboy will succeed in making you feel like an inky schoolboy. I doubt if even the P'daytabird could have invented anything more subtly undermining of one's self-respect than that early morning procession up a big hall to be complimented by an old gentleman at a table. Try to imagine it and then add the idea of nine o'clock in the morning: and that your collar has broken loose from its stud at the back: and that there's a smell of last night's dinner about: a fly on your nose: a shaving cut beginning to bleed – but no, it is too painful.

---

30 'Collections' means either the informal college examination at the beginning of each term to test a student's progress in his work, or the reports given orally at the end of a term by the tutor.

While waiting my turn I had a smart faux pas with an old monument called

> 'A Mr Wilkinson, a clergyman'

(as the immortal line runs) who is reading for the Church.[31] He used to be President of the Martlets when I was secretary and I have had fiery passages with him in 1919. He had been to see the Queen given a degree the day before and I dropped some vague remarks about 'this uphol-stered poker business'. But, would you believe it, I'd stumbled on a true loyalist who thought her a fine woman and gave me a severe telling-off! It was a day of misfortunes. Wilkinson looks very like Gordon[32] grown fatter. He once read us a paper on Drinkwater,[33] holding a little bundle of paper close to his face and speaking a thin whisper out of the corner of his mouth: but it soon developed into a philosophical argument by Wilkinson, which lasted till one o'clock, much to the annoyance of the unphilosophical owner of the rooms, who wanted to go to bed.

March 13th

It being Lord's Day I waited after breakfast on Pasley in his rooms at Unity House: this is a cottage in a lane by Headington Church where the buildings are so ruinous that it looks like a bit of France as the cant goes – well FAIRLY like it. Pasley is my oldest ally: he used to write poetry but is now too engrossed in history and he has also become engaged – that fatal tomb of all lively and interesting men. Unity House is ruled by a strangely ugly woman whose only accomplishment is an illegitimate born to a captain of artillery who once lodged there. So at least she tells Pasley: but I find these villagers are so eager to present the

---

31 Donald Frederick Wilkinson enlisted in the army in 1914. In 1915 he was commissioned a captain and served with the King's (Liverpool Regiment) in France and Belgium 1915–17. He was awarded the Military Cross in 1917. He matriculated at University College in 1918 and read *Literae Humaniores*. He took his BA in 1921, and his MA in 1925. After reading Theology at St Stephen's House, Oxford and Cuddesdon College, Cuddesdon, he was ordained in the Church of England in 1924 for the diocese of Southwark. After a number of impressive appointments, he was Rector of Beckley, Sussex, from 1931 to 1947.

32 i.e. Gordon Ewart.

33 John Drinkwater (1882–1937), a poet and critic, some of whose poems Lewis had seen in the five volumes of *Georgian Poetry* published between 1912 and 1922.

world with a 'gentleman's' son and so proud to have done it, that it may be mere idle boasting. This is no exaggeration but plain truth – they burst with pride and lose their heads in proportion as they lose their figures. Headington is a sink of all the iniquities and improbabilities: but perhaps I shall devote a whole 'Account' to that – and become known as 'Headington Hamilton' which rolls off the tongue at least as well as Corsica Boswell. By the same token I saw an EDITIO PRINCEPS of Bozzy's Corsica[34] for 5/- the other day.

But where was I? Nothing to say after all but that I had an excellent walk with Pasley: he described to me the humours of the new constitution of Tzecho-Slovakia, which I wish I cd. remember. We sat in a wood full of primroses. Damnit, how generations of P'dayta's have teased the language till the very name of a primrose sounds sentimental: when you come to look at them, they are really rather attractive. I walked Pasley off his legs and we lunched chez moi on rabbit pie – our common fare at present – Pasley and Mrs Moore having a lively conversation on money in view of his intent shortly to try 'this marrying business'.

March 14th

I received this morning a letter from my obliging friend Stead.[35] Stead is rather a punt: I think you saw me stop to speak to him one day in the Corn.[36] He is an undergraduate but also curate of a parish in Oxford. He writes poetry. The annoying thing is that it's exactly like

---

34 James Boswell, *An Account of Corsica* (1768).

35 William Force Stead (1884–1967) was born in Washington, DC, and graduated from the University of Virginia in 1908. That same year he was appointed to the US Consular Service, serving as vice-consul in Liverpool and Nottingham. He was ordained in the Church of England in 1915 and served as a curate at Ross-on-Wye until he matriculated at Queen's College, Oxford, in 1917. He took his BA from Queen's in 1921 and his MA in 1925. Stead was Chaplain of St Mark's Anglican Church, Florence, Italy, from 1922 to 1924. He served as Chaplain of Worcester College, Oxford, from 1925 to 1933 when he converted to the Catholic Church. Stead was a friend of T.S. Eliot, whom he baptized on 9 June 1927. He published many volumes of poems, and besides having this interest in common with Lewis, his wife, the former Frances Goldsborough, was the sister of Mary Goldsborough, who married Dr John Askins. Dr Askins was Mrs Moore's brother, so Frances Stead, being sister to Mrs Askins, was Mrs Moore's sister-in-law's sister. At the beginning of World War II, Stead returned to the Consular Service in order to help his country. He went back to the United States in August 1939. His published poems include *Verd Antique* (1920), *The Sweet Miracle* (1922) and *Festival in Tuscany* (1927).

36 i.e. Cornmarket Street, Oxford.

mine, only like the bad parts of mine: this was my own original opinion and it has been confirmed by others. Perhaps you can imagine the sensation I experienced in reading it. Stead's letter was to say that he had mentioned to Yeats – whom he knows – 'my double claim to distinction as an Irishman and a poet' and would I come along this evening and see him?

I accordingly repaired after dinner to Stead's lodging in Canterbury Street. He is a married man: his wife is an American: she is the sister of a woman who is married to a brother of Mrs Moore's. She was a woman of implacable sullenness who refused even to say good evening to me: beside her at the fire sat an American gentleman who was apparently left to console her for the absence of her husband. This was a very amiable person: he was 'studyin'' when I entered, but politely laid his book down. You know the sort of face in which a long promontory of nose (eagle build) projects from between two rounded hills of cheek (cherub build)? Picture this surmounted by a pair of horn spectacles and made of a texture rather like cod's roe: then add that this face beams but can contribute to the crack only by saying 'That's right' at the end of everyone's remark. In these rather nasty surroundings Stead was finishing a very nasty meal of cold fish and cocoa: but he soon put on his coat and after asking his lady why there were no stamps in the house and receiving no answer, swung out with me into the usual Oxford theatrical night. Trusting soul to leave his wife unguarded in such society!

Yeats lives at the end of Broad St, the first house on your right as you leave the town. I can assure you I felt a veritable Bozzy as I reflected that I was now to meet at last WILLIAM BUTLER YEATS![37] But enough of that. We were shown up a long stairway lined with rather wicked pictures by Blake – all devils and monsters – and finally into the presence chamber, lit by tall candles, with orange coloured curtains and full of things which I can't describe because I don't know their names. The poet was very big, about sixty years of age: 'awful' as Bozzy says: grey haired, clean shaven. When he first began to speak I would have thought him French, but the Irish sounds through after a time. Before the fire was a

---

37 William Butler Yeats (1865–1939) and his wife, the former Georgie Hyde-Lees, had moved to 4 Broad Street, Oxford, in April 1919. Lewis admired Yeats' poetry when the poet was a romantic. However, as Yeats moved further and further into mysticism and theosophy, Lewis began to feel repulsed; he had seen other lives ruined by theosophy. Mrs Yeats was pregnant at this time, and on 22 August 1921 she gave birth to their son, Michael Yeats.

circle of hard antique chairs. Present were the poet's wife, a little man who never spoke all evening, and Father Martindale.[38] Father M. is a Catholic Priest, a little twinkling man like a bird, or like Puck, whom I take to be an atheistical dog. I used to go to his lectures in the old days: he is a mocker. Everyone got up as we came in: after the formalities I was humbly preparing to sink into the outlying chair leaving the more honourable to Stead, but the poet sternly and silently motioned us into other ones. The meaning of this I have not fathomed: 'twas very Pumblechookian.[39]

Then the talk began. It was all of magic and cabbalism and 'the Hermetic knowledge'. The great man talked while the priest and Mrs Yeats fed him with judicious questions. The matter I admit was either mediaeval or modern, but the manner was so XVIII Century that I lost my morale. I understood how it is possible for a man to terrify a room into silence: and I had a ghastly presentment that something would presently impel me to up like that 'unknown curate' and say 'Were not Vale Owen's revelations, Sir, addressed to the passions?'[40] And then as Max Beerbohm says 'Bang' the suddenness of it! However I remembered that Johnson WAS really dead and controlled myself. Indeed some good angel guided me: for presently I really had something to say – a case mentioned by

---

38 Father Cyril Charlie Martindale SJ (1879–1963) was a member of the Jesuit college, Campion Hall, and he lectured in the faculty of *Literae Humaniores*. He began life as a bookish little boy, and he took a First in Classical Honour Moderations in 1903 and a First in Greats in 1905. After his ordination to the priesthood in 1911, he taught at Stonyhurst. He returned to Oxford to lecture in Classics in 1916. During the war he surprised everyone with an unsuspected ability to minister to the spiritual needs of the wounded, and a remarkable ability to communicate with people very unlike himself. In 1927 he joined the staff of the Jesuits' Farm Street Church in London, where his spiritual clientele was drawn from every level of society, from dukes to dustmen. He involved himself with numerous good enterprises, including settlements for working-class boys in the East End of London. Far from being an 'atheistical dog', as Lewis suspected, he preceded Lewis as a broadcaster and writer who could translate theological doctrines into simple, everyday language. He published numerous biographies of such contemporaries as Robert Hugh Benson, and many works of Christian apologetics. See Philip Caraman, *C.C. Martindale* (1967).

39 'Pumblechook' was the nickname of G. Herbert Ewart (1857–1924). See note 68 to the letter of 12 May 1917.

40 George Vale Owen (1869–1931) was a clerical spiritualist admired by Sir Arthur Conan Doyle. His *magnum opus* was *The Life Beyond the Veil*, 4 vols (1920–1). He also wrote *Problems which Perplex (mainly psychic) explained by question and answer* (1890), *The Outlands of Heaven* [1923], *What Happens after Death* [1924], and *How Spirits Communicate* [1926].

Coleridge which was most apposite and indeed crying for quotation on something just said. But thank God I didn't: for a minute later the priest did.

> YEATS (thumping his chair): 'Yes – yes – the old woman in Coleridge. That story was published by Coleridge without the slightest evidence. Andrew Lang exposed it. I've never had a conversation on the subject that SOMEONE didn't bring in Coleridge's old woman. It is anonymous in the first place and every one has taken it over without question. It just shows that there's no limit to the unscrupulousness that a sceptical man will go to – '
> MARTINDALE: 'Oh surely Mr Yeats – '
> YEATS: 'Yes! There is a Professor living in Oxford at this moment who is the greatest sceptic in print. The same man has told me that he entered a laboratory where X (some woman whose name I didn't catch) was doing experiments: saw the table floating near the ceiling with X sitting on it: vomited: gave orders that no further experiments were to be done in the laboratories – and refused to let the story be known.'

But it would be only ridiculous to record it all: I should give you the insanity of the man without his eloquence and presence, which are very great. I could never have believed that he was so exactly like his own poetry.

One more joke must be recorded. Stead presently told us a dream he had had: it was so good that I thought it a lie. YEATS (looking to his wife): 'Have you anything to say about that, Georgie?' Apparently Stead's transcendental self, not important enough for the poet, has been committed to Mrs Yeats as a kind of ersatz or secondary magician. Finally we are given sherry or vermouth in long and curiously shaped glasses, except Martindale who has whiskey out of an even longer and more curiously shaped glass, and the orgy is at an end. Try to mix Pumblechook, the lunatic we met at the Mitre, Dr Johnson, the most eloquent drunk Irishman you know, and Yeat's own poetry, all up into one composite figure, and you will have the best impression I can give you.

March 18th etc.
About this time I recieved a letter from Pdaytaheim in which I was informed that 'as the vacation was only ten days long' he supposed I

should not be coming down, tho' it would have been 'very pleasant' if I had. Three cheers for inaccurate information, said I, and flung my hat in the air! For about a week after this we had the most beautiful spring weather. I took to push-biking and slacked off work a good deal. The country round here is not bad: for summer or winter at their best, one wants mountains and sea, but just at present it is quite good enough to be in an ordinary English county. Whatever else you lack you always have fruit trees with white blossom (looking like cauliflowers) and winding road and nice little stone villages, each with its pleasant church and pub: and what, after all, is wrong with a low raftered bar parlour in the Thames valley, with foxes in glass cases and a pint of good draft cider? On such occasions I usually take a little note book and write down whatever occurs to me. On Easter Monday the publican at Garsington was very polite to me and asked me to go into the front parlour 'if I had some writing to do'. I elected to stay where I was: but how true to the countryman's attitude! We 'write', they 'have some writing to do' on rare occasions – just as they might have 'some digging' or 'some darning' TO DO. I usually get back for a late tea and after consuming much soda bread and drinking Johnsonian cups, sit under the one tree in our tiny strip of garden and read a little of the good Plato.

March 19th

Here is a thing worth remembering – a propos of our old discussion of the ancestral conception of God as 'an old gentleman in a blue dressing gown etc'. It is a remark of Chateaubriand's (you will probably think I am inventing it, but it's quite true) quoted by Emerson – 'Si Dieu a fail l'homme a son image, l'homme l'a bien rendu.'[41] Serve him right!

March 21st

Having met Stead yesterday in the Broad with his wife and of course with our friend of the nose, I was told that the great man had expressed himself sorry not to have been able to see more of me owing to his argument with the priest, and would I come again with Stead [the] next night?

41 'Si Dieu nous a faits à son image, nous le lui avons bien rendu' ('If God created us to his image, we returned him the compliment'). The quotation is actually from Voltaire's *Le Sottisier*.

This night we were shown to a study up in the ceiling and entertained by him alone: and, would you believe it, he was almost quite sane, and talked about books and things, still eloquently and quite intelligently? Of course we got on to magic in the end – that was only to be expected. It was really my fault, for I mentioned Bergson. 'Ah yes,' said he, 'Bergson. It was his sister who taught me magic.' The effect of this statement on Aunt Suffern (already in paroxysms of contempt over what I had already told her about Yeats) ought to be amusing.

We spoke of Andrew Lang. YEATS: 'I met him once – at a dinner somewhere. He never said a word. When we began to talk afterwards, he just got up and took his chair into a corner of the room and sat down facing the wall. He stayed there all the evening.' Perhaps Lang didn't like wizards! Of the 'great Victorians' he said: 'The most interesting thing about the Victorian period was their penchant for selecting one typical great man in each department – Tennyson, THE poet, Roberts, THE soldier: and then these types were made into myths. You never heard of anyone else: if you spoke of medicine it meant – (some 'THE Doctor' whose name I've forgotten): if you spoke of politics it was Gladstone.'

This is especially interesting to us as explaining the mental growth of a certain bird we wot of. ('Well all said and done boys, he was a GREAT man.') So home to bed more pleased with our poet than I had been on the last occasion: and rather thankful that L'Oiseau Pomme de Terre hadn't been there to explain that 'you can see he's a disappointed man' after every adverse criticism on any living writer. Oh, before I leave it, Stead told me he had shown Yeats a poem: Yeats said he thought 'IT WOULD DO VERY WELL' to set to music! Stead thinks this is a compliment. H'mh!

TO HIS FATHER (LP VI: 269–70):

University College,
Oxford.
March 28th [1921]

My dear Papy,

I am glad that you sent me the wire. I am a poor reader of papers and should have been very sorry, through ignorance, to let such a thing pass in silence. Poor old Kirk![42] What shall one say of him? It would be a

---

42 Mr W.T. Kirkpatrick died at his home, Gastons, Great Bookham, Surrey, on 22 March 1921.

poor compliment to that memory to be sentimental: indeed, if it were possible, he would himself return to chide the absurdity. It is however no sentiment, but plainest fact to say that I at least owe to him in the intellectual sphere as much as one human being can owe another. That he enabled me to win a scholarship is the least that he did for me. It was an atmosphere of unrelenting clearness and rigid honesty of thought that one breathed from living with him – and this I shall be the better for as long as I live. And if this is the greatest thing, there are others which none of us will forget: his dry humour, his imperturbable good temper and his amazing energy – these it is good to have seen. He was a unique personality with nothing inconsistent about him – except the one foible about the Sunday suit: the more one sees of weakness, affectation and general vagueness in the majority of men, the more one admires that rigid, lonely old figure – more like some ancient Stoic standing fast in the Roman decadence than a modern scholar living in the home counties. Indeed we may almost call him a great man, tho', as it happened, his greatness was doomed to reach so small a circle. I should have liked to have seen him once again before this happened. I have of course written to Mrs K.

You ask whether I am satisfied with my Optimism, and I am afraid I hardly know. For one thing I almost know it by heart, and consequently can least of all judge it impartially: for another, it is so very ill typed that the usually helpful effect of cold print is neutralised by mere irritation. At a charge of £1.7s. for an essay of about 11,000 words I should not have expected such petty annoyances as MEDONISM for HEDONISM, NOW for WORD, paragraphs run together, question marks in the wrong place etc., etc. But, as Knowles says, 'Who am I'.

At any rate, it has given me, in parts, as much trouble as anything I have ever done and I shall be glad to have it launched into the registrar's box for good and all and to leave the rest on the knees of the gods. Only don't expect any results. You see I am afraid I have rather fallen between two stools: it has to aim at being both literary and philosophical, and, in the effort to accomplish the double object, I have made it too literary for the philosophers and too metaphysical for the dons of English Literature. These are the pitfalls with which the walks of Academe are digged. Such things are written for a tiny public of appointed judges, and you never know what their particular point of view is going to be: they are only human beings and must have tastes and tempers of their own, but one can't find these out. It must be difficult to be quite fair to an essay which expresses some view that you have been denouncing to a submissive Senior Common Room for the last half century, however good it may be.

I should dearly love to get away for a bit, but, as you say, for so short a time, the expense and the interruption of work is hardly worth it. The Colonel must have had an unpleasant journey: I wish he would keep a diary which we could compare with that of Grandfather Hamilton in the same waters.[43] Two generations of sub-tropical Atlantic and Hamilton temperament would be worth studying!

I hope you are keeping tolerably well: my growing pains are better. I don't think I 'ever heard tell of' rheumatics being traced to absence of underclothing: but an old wound always gives you some degree of rheumatism as a souvenir. I was asked to the Yeat's again last Saturday: there was only one other guest and the great man was much saner: he talked less of magic and more of literature, including a good story about Andrew Lang for which I haven't room here – but remind me. The country is full of white apple blossom.

your loving son,
Jack

TO HIS BROTHER: (A CONTINUATION OF THE SERIAL LETTER: LP VI: 289–91)

[University College]
April 20? [1921]

I am afraid I had already let my diary languish for some time, less from being tired of it than from shame to repeat endlessly little descriptions of walks and talks, when yours arrived. The mail day for your land is on the 26th, but as term has now begun again I had better keep its adventures, if any, for my next. Whether during term I shall be able to keep a journal I don't know. In the meantime you have not lost many items of interest.

---

43 Warnie, who was still in Sierra Leone, *was* keeping a diary at this time. Their maternal grandfather, the Rev. Thomas Robert Hamilton (1826–1905), was ordained a clergyman in 1853, and in 1854 he was appointed a chaplain in the Royal Navy. He served with the Baltic squadron of the fleet throughout the Crimean War, and in other parts of the world until he retired from the navy in 1870. The diaries he kept during his naval career form part of the Lewis Papers. See **The Hamilton Family** in the Biographical Appendix.

There was a show at the child's[44] school to which I went, sneaking in alone a whimsical and unobserved male among miles of petticoat. Of course they did the ghost scene from Macbeth: great success if some lout in the audience hadn't giggled at the entrance of the ghost. The ghost, I should add in justice, was really very good: but they all took up the laugh like sheep and 'Macbeth's' chances of tragic effect were ruined. Perhaps also I should not let Miss Ploughman pass unrecorded.[45] She is the music mistress at this school, who called here the day after the coal strike had been declared and said 'Well you know, I don't think that there's going to be any strike after all'; she is not however, as this remark seems to imply, brainless, but suffers from an excess of energy, being jerky in her movements. She looks like a Spaniard and pours forth a stream of continuous conversation in a VERY loud voice with the rich intonation of a teacher of elocution. She has published one book.

About the coal strike itself you have, I suppose, heard AD NAUSEAM from the papers: what it means to me personally is that I have done a good deal of wood sawing. Have you ever sawed wood? If not, you probably have an idea that one sets the saw lightly on the log, gets to work, and continues steadily deepening until the two halves fall apart. Not a bit of it: you set the saw lightly on the log and then try to move it. It darts aside with a sound like a swallow, and you wrap a handkerchief round your hand: when the blood has soaked through this you go into the house and get some court plaster. Next time you go more cautiously and after the saw has chirped a whole song, a bit of bark comes off: by this time you are fairly warm. Then you really get to it: back and forward you go, changing uneasily from your left to your right, feeling the blisters arise on your hand, while the shadows lengthen and the sweat pours down. When you go to bed that night, the 'big push' has got about as far as you see in the cut, and you get visions of getting through that log on your thirtieth birthday. I have now become quite good at it and sometimes even get a degree of enjoyment out of it when the day is fine and it goes well. Pasley has turned up the other day: everyone has drifted in since.

Many thanks for your most interesting letter. What a queer end of the world backwater – just like the places we used to imagine out of God

---

44 The 'child' is Maureen Moore, a pupil at Headington School.
45 i.e. Mary Plowman. See note 72 to letter of 14 July 1919.

knows what sea stories but, still more 'all made out of the carver's brain'.[46] I certainly never thought to hear anything like H.M.S. 'Dwarf' in real life: and how very homely to have a telescope and a Lloyd's register! You will have plenty more to tell me in your next letter: I haven't quite got my picture yet. What type of mountains are they? I assume they don't rise to snow: I know they can't be heathery: and I have a suspicion they are not smooth green like the hills at Malvern. So you see I am at a loss for them. The cockchafers[47] are the last word. It is the terror of such specimens of nature's vulgar horseplay which will keep me confined to Europe all my days. You don't mention the white people you meet. Have you heard of a civilian called Bathgate or Wimberley – these are people who Mrs Moore mentions as 'having government jobs' in Sierra Leone. By the way, does Sierra Leone mean in practice just the town, or do people live anywhere else?

I am very glad you have become a convert to Milton: what put you on to him and what parts have you been reading? I wonder will you ever get to the end of the Bible:[48] the undesirable 'primitives' around you will enable you to appreciate the Hebrews who were Class A primitives after all.

What a queer thing that black man (v. Lamb on 'our brothers')[49] is: he's been there as long as anyone else and has never advanced one quarter of a step. Perhaps the really strange thing is that the others have. Let me know when you write if you get the Times Literary Supplement: if not I will send you cuttings that are in your line. Also tell me whether you want this to continue: is there anything you'd like to hear LESS of?

---

46 Coleridge, *Christabel*, I, 179–80: 'Carved with figures strange and sweet, / All made out of the carver's brain.'

47 Cockchafers are a coleopterous insect which come from the chrysalis late in May and fly with a whirring sound.

48 In March Warnie decided to use his free time in Sierra Leone by reading the Bible through. His idea was to read five pages per day, and when he wrote to Jack he had just finished Leviticus.

49 In Charles Lamb's 'Imperfect Sympathies', in *Essays of Elia*, he said: 'In the Negro countenance you will often meet with strong traits of benignity. I have felt yearnings of tenderness towards some of these faces – or rather masks – that have looked out kindly upon one in casual encounters in the streets and highways. I love what Fuller beautifully calls – these "images of God cut in ebony".'

TO HIS FATHER (LP VI: 294–5):

[University College]
April 23rd [1921]

My dear Papy,

I am sorry to hear that you have been unwell. If you have been having our weather I am not surprised – days of bright spring, alternating with frosts, biting winds, and snows, or often all these mixed in one day. It has indeed the charm of variety, but, unlike that other variety 'custom can' easily 'stale it'.[50]

On top of this, or rather arranged by some malicious power to coincide with the cold, comes the strike, and as Pepys says 'Lord knows what disorders we shall fall into'. Once or twice it has looked like becoming a very ugly business. On this subject you are the optimist to my pessimist, and I hope you are right. No doubt it was very wise of the government to call up the reserve, thus meeting at one stroke the unemployment and the results of the unemployment, but these queues of volunteers, the lorries in the streets and the uniformed figures are too unpleasantly familiar to most of us – and suggestive. What a good thing we drew our foot out of that net!

I can of course appreciate your feelings about poor Kirk's funeral.[51] Stripped of all wherewith belief and tradition have clothed it, death appears a little grimmer – a shade more chilly and loathsome – in the eyes of the most matter of fact. At the same time, while this is sad, it would have been not only sad but shocking to have pronounced over Kirk words that he did not believe and performed ceremonies that he himself would have denounced as meaningless. Yet, as you say, he is so indelibly stamped on one's mind once known, so often present in thought, that he makes his own acceptance of annihilation the more unthinkable. I have seen death fairly often and never yet been able to find it anything but extraordinary and rather incredible. The real person

---

50 William Shakespeare, *Antony and Cleopatra* (1623), II, ii, 243: 'Age cannot wither her, nor custom stale'.

51 The Lewises had long known that Mr Kirkpatrick was an atheist. However, writing to Warnie on 21 April, Mr Lewis told him how painful he found the arrangements for Mr Kirkpatrick's body: 'There was not to be a funeral – no service, no ceremony, no flowers, and he was to be cremated. My whole soul rose in revolt at the thought. The dear old man to be spirited away furtively – like an unclean thing – and burned!' (LP VI: 292).

is so very real, so obviously living and different from what is left that one cannot believe something has turned into nothing. It is not faith, it is not reason – just a 'feeling'. 'Feelings' are in the long run a pretty good match for what we call our beliefs.

I have had a letter from Warnie, probably stating much the same as he has written to you. He certainly seems very pleased with his new billet so far: and it must be a breath of home to find his office provided with a Lloyd's Register and a telescope. He is apparently reading Milton and the Old Testament, both I fancy works which enjoy a very limited circulation on the West Coast!

I find that I am run pretty near the end of my tether by now and would be glad if you will put in the new money at once. We are hobbling along on wood fuel at present but that is soon to be limited: gas also is threatened and with it presently, electricity. If this lasts a month longer, England will be in a pretty state.

No news of Optimist yet and no man knoweth when it may be expected – so we can all enjoy our hopes undisturbed by facts for a while longer.

your loving son,
Jack

TO HIS FATHER (LP VI: 308–9):

University College,
Oxford
May 9th [1921]

My dear Papy,

I must apologise for having delayed till now to answer your letter and acknowledge 'the needfull', for which, tho' belated, many thanks. (That's a bad sentence: I mean the THANKS are belated, of course, a confusion that could hardly occur in any language except English. However, letters do not aim at literary precision.)

It seems almost a pity to have cashed the dividend: such relics of civilisation and commerce will soon have a historical interest if this country goes the way it is treading at present. Of course it is not a question of wages: it is one side of the big underground movement which is working other troubles than those of labour at present. The most dangerous feature of the whole thing has developed since you wrote – I mean the 'sack of Aldershot' by the Reservists with a red flag.[52] The levity of English people is incorrigible – and encouraging. Most of the men I have met take the view, having been at Aldershot during some period of their soldiering, that the sooner it is all destroyed the better. As our friend at the Hippodrome says, 'I won't go back to Aldershot'!

I am beginning my period of Roman history and this has sent me back to Tacitus whom I read with Kirk. It is the strangest and in a way the pleasantest sensation. The old phrases come up inevitably in his own voice and manner, not only by the usual force of association, but also because Tacitus is a grim, sardonic author whose hardest sayings Kirk relished and made his own. One seems to remember those days in the little upper room with the photograph of Gladstone and the gas stove all the more often now that they are absolutely finished and shut up.

The weather continues pretty cold here and there are still a good many soldiers passing to and fro. I don't know that the Colonel's letter to me was very discursive: the Lloyd's Register in his office and his dislike of the natives and cockchafers were the chief points. But for the climate it would not be a bad job for troglodytes and readers like ourselves: fortunately he has a streak of that in him. For the average officers with no mind and no resources it must be a terrible business and a nurse of all the solitary vices: it is a curious necessity that always casts these sort of jobs – Lighthouses, wireless stations etc. – on the men least fitted for them by nature.

There is still no news of Optimism, and by now little optimism among those who await the news. I should have thought that they could have decided on the productions before this: an unsettled possibility like that becomes in the end a nuisance at the back of one's mind.

your loving son,
Jack

---

52 *The Times* (9 May 1921), p. 10: 'A riot which caused material damage, and which, it is believed, was instigated by Bolshevist sympathizers in military uniform, occurred in Aldershot last night…The actual rioters may have numbered between 60 and 80; the party who marched with them under the red flag, it is estimated numbered about 500.'

TO HIS BROTHER (LP VI: 315–19):

[University College]
May 10th [1921]

My dear W.,

The younger Pliny has a good letter in which he says to a friend 'If any one asks you at Rome what you have done today, you reply perhaps, I have been to a betrothal, I have assisted at so and so's coming of age, I've been to vote for somebody etc. That day and each day it seems necessary: it is only when you review the series of days from the seclusion of the country that it seems futile.'[53] I quote this a propos: for tho' I have less time to describe things now that term has begun, I don't know that I can spend even that setting down so many nothings.

From your last letter – in which I was sorry to see that you had not got mine – I gather that you don't get the papers. Still, I suppose I needn't describe the coal strike, the split in labour which now alas appears to be healing: nor the calling up of the reserves: nor the sack of Aldershot by 2000 of those same Reservists, a red flag at their head. All this you will get (with appropriate comments) from another source. You may imagine meantime how glad I am to have got safely out of the Ersatz before all this began.

Here term is still new enough to be interesting. It is still pleasant to see fewer foreign visitors pacing the High with guide books and taking photos of spires – where I know they'll get them crooked – and to see one's friends again instead. Pasley was the first to wait upon us, in a blinding snow shower, a few days before term began.

As you will never meet them (nor indeed will I), it is no breach of confidence to touch on the grim humours of his future 'in-laws'. A mother of the Mrs Greeves type, who has all the money but is nevertheless incapable of resisting her husband, a retired army officer, busily engaged in trying to see if his constitution will 'keep' by being sufficiently soaked in spirits. This indeed has been his life work, and the devil of it is that it seems likely to 'keep' a good bit yet. He wd. not be worth mentioning save for one trait which brings him into our circle. After having been on a binge for several days, after having exhausted all the months money, his favourite remark is 'Well, well, after all, we're a happy family.' Another good P'daytism: to the daughter (Pasley's fiancée)

---

53 Pliny the Younger (AD 61 or 62–c. 113), *Letters*, No. 9 to Minicius Fundanus.

reduced to great straits and learning typing, altho' they ought to be fairly comfortably off: 'Don't forget to let me know any time a little money would come in handy.' As Pasley, in the true language of a historian wd. say if he could live in Leeborough a while, 'A very good parallel.'

A great friend of mine, Baker of Wadham, has come up again after being down for a couple of terms. I often amuse myself by thinking how you and he would worry each other: not so much by direct antagonism as by being absolutely unable to understand one another. Have you ever met a person who talks habitually in metaphors and doesn't know that they are metaphors? He has certainly the perverseness and troublesomeness of speech which betoken greatness: his poems are like rooms full of exotic and insolent ornaments, but with nowhere to sit down. However, I introduced him only to lead up to an idea which may tickle you. Seated together in Wadham gardens (one of the few WILD gardens in Oxford, full of bluebells and old trees) during one of our rare glimpses of fine weather, I was talking to him about magic (of course: it's the burning subject) and the difficulty of getting enough data even to disbelieve: then it transpired that the secrets books are attainable only to the esoteric Masons. Now of course all the little P'daytas and Squeakies are fed on EXoteric faked rituals ('so they tell you').[54] But what a fine discourse on the black art we can have one of these days at Leeborough. 'Well the idea of any sane man – ' 'Pa!' (in a warning voice) 'Do you seriously mean Warren – ' 'Brother, here is this man himself initiated into the abominable rites of the most powerful magical association in existance etc. etc.' But the picture of M. L'Oiseau P. de T. as a wizard will remain. Some of the 'Horrid names' used in incantations (Shadai, Gogiol) seem made for his particular intonation.

The only strictly social function I have attended so far this term was tea with the Carlyles in their most charming house in Holywell. It is a place I greatly envy: long uneven rooms with beams in the ceiling and wide stone grates where a little kind of brazier sits in a deep cave of Dutch tiles. I need hardly say that in Oxford houses all such things were unearthed only fairly recently: the XVIII Cent. had very decently covered them over with plaster, 'substituting' as they wd. doubtless have said 'elegance and civility for Gothic rudeness'.

The principles on which tea fights are conducted at the Carlyles is this: you are given a seat by someone and when you have had a reasonable

---

54 He is referring to the fact that Albert Lewis was a member of the Freemasons.

time to get to the interesting part of the conversation, Mrs C., a rather fatuous woman, gets up and says, 'Mr Lewis, go and talk to Professor Smith' or 'Mr Wyllie, I think you know my daughter' or whatever it may be: then every single pair is shuffled. When you've got fairly settled, the same thing happens again: as some one said, it is like nothing so much as a game of cricket with nothing in it but an umpire calling 'over'. I had my longest 'spell' between Pasley and a lady whom the elder Miss C. describes as 'my little sister'. She is reading our School: she is a damned socialist and is contributing moneys to the miners: she laughs all the time: worst of all she is an optimist. Her face suggests an intensely anxious rabbit.

By the rule of the house of course Pasley and I had scarcely started trying to instil a little pessimism when she said, 'Oh, I must get Father to talk to you'. OVER! When that had subsided I recovered consciousness beside Dr Carlyle. He has every reason to be an optimist: a man who can hold a parish AND a College Chaplaincy (you remember Poynton's remark 'Dr Carlyle repeats as much of the service as he can remember') without being a Christian, and who has lived on the bounty of a Royal Foundation for the last century while being a Socialist, ought to be. All the same he's a dear old man with a thin brick red face and very straight white hair and never takes anything seriously. People talk about the Oxford manner and the Oxford life and the Oxford God-knows what else: as if the undergraduates had anything to do with it. Sitting beside this worthy priest I felt that it is really a thing we are quite outside: the real Oxford is a close corporation of jolly, untidy, lazy, good for nothing humorous old men, who have been electing their own successors ever since the world began and who intend to go on with it: they'll squeeze under the Revolution or leap over it somehow when it comes, don't you worry. When I think how little chance I have of ever fighting my way into that unassuming yet impregnable fortress, that modest unremovability, that provokingly intangible stone wall, I think of Keats's poison

> 'Brewed in monkish cell
> To thin the scarlet conclave of old men.'[55]

Which reminds me, did you ever read Daudet's 'L'Immortel'? It is a novel about the Academie Francaise: if you like sheer cool premeditated

---

55 John Keats, *The Fall of Hyperion*, I, 49–50 (slightly misquoted).

insolence you should order this by the next mail – tho' perhaps I should warn you that it is only a couple of hours reading, and you may like books that last, on the world's end. However, it is a book that might have been written by Kirk – I will quote from the preface, which is a good testimony to its character – 'Les insinuations de quelques journaux voulant faire de *L'Immortel* l'expression d'une vulgaire cacune de candidat evincé, m'oligent a mettre en tête [de cette nouvelle édition] la lettre que j'ecrevais il y a cinq ans: "Je ne me presente pas, je ne me suis jamais presenté, je ne me presenterai jamais a L'Academie".'[56] I suppose this is for P'daytas 'Ah, he's a disappointed man you know. I await Moore's Abelard with interest: I have never read anything by him. I gather it is of incredible length.[57]

I mentioned Kirk just now, almost by accident. The resources of conversation are silenced before his death. Is there anything you could say which he wouldn't rise and denounce as 'the grossest absurdity'? Better to treat it in our own way and picture him addressing to Jehovah, when first presented, the famous Voltarian alexandrine

'Je soupçonne entre nous que vous n'existez pas'[58]

or telling Aristotle that his logic (this is a real Kirkian remark which he once made) 'has the distinction of never having been of the slightest use to any human being'. All this is only after all our interpretation of the Miltonic counsel

'[For] so to interpose a little ease
Let our frail thoughts dally with false surmise.'[59]

Today the 11th, little Jenkin[60] appeared after lunch and bade me go for a bike ride. As I had decided to work, I thought this would be an excellent opportunity of breaking my resolution. Jenkin has his own principles of

---

56 Alphonse Daudet, *l'Immortel, Moeurs parisiennes* (1888): 'The insinuations of some newspapers that wish to make the author of *L'Immortel* sound like a common rejected candidate voicing his feelings, force me to start [this new edition] with a letter I wrote [to *Le Figaro*] five years ago: "I am not a candidate to the Académie, I have never been one and never shall be."'

57 George Augustus Moore, *Heloïse and Abelard* (1921).

58 Voltaire: 'Between us, I suspect that you do not exist.'

59 Milton, *Lycidas*, 152.

60 A.K. Hamilton Jenkin.

push biking, the maxim being that 'where I go my machine can go'. He rides over moors and once carried it down a cliff in Cornwall. After stopping for a drop of the negus at Garsington in the same little pub whither I went (v. last letter) on Easter Monday, we rode along the top of a long hill where you look down into a good, woody English valley with the Chilterns, rather sleek and chalky – like greyhounds – on the horizon. It was a grey day with clouds in muddled perspective all round. Just as the first drops of rain began to fall, we found a young man looking as if he were going to be hanged, crossing a field. He turned out to be one Groves[61] of Univ., who is now gone down and incarcerated at a High Church Theological Seminary in the neighbouring village of Cuddesdon. 'He would have liked to ask us in to tea, but couldn't – indeed oughtn't to be talking to us – because they were having a QUIET DAY.' Ye gods: a lot of young men shut up together, all thinking about their souls! Isn't it awful?

After this it was quite fresh and lively to investigate an old wind mill near Wheatley: it has the sort of atmosphere we felt at Doagh and a little copper plate over the door with a figure of a bird on it. Under it was a word variously read by Jenkin and myself as County and Cointy. I do not know what this all was about. Jenkin keeps on picking up stones and telling you that it is iron here.

We rode over Shotover Hill: through sandy lanes with gorse on each side and passing occasional warm comfortable English barns and haystacks. Most attractive sign posts, 'Bridle path to Horsley' – a bridle path always sounds mysterious. And dozens of rabbits and whole bunches of bluebells: and a view far off between the two slopes of Forest Hill and the little house where the first Mrs Milton used to live. About the time he wrote L'Allegro and Il Penseroso he would often be riding over here from his home to court her – God help her!

While on the subject of Milton I should remark that I haven't had time yet to solve your puzzle out of Comus. Give me a hint as to whether the motto refers to (1) Sierra Leone or (2) yourself or (3) Diary writing. If to (1), perhaps you will prefer after a few months, 4 lines from Paradise Lost – about 'a universe of death, which God by curse/Created evil, for evil only good – where nature runs perverse and breeds all

---

61 Sidney John Selby Groves (1897–1970) was ordained in 1922. He was vicar of Sonning from 1942 to 1965 and a canon of Christ Church.

monstrous, all prodigious things etc.'[62] I say this because in your last letter you already seem to be finding it unattractive. You have omitted so far all reference to the human element – the 'other fellows': and I await with interest some account of your visit to H.M.S. Dwarf. What loathsome place to go for a walk in – that's one thing about the Daudel[63] (have you made any use of the same). I suppose snakes can't JUMP into it? Why didn't you try this Cambridge reptile with a whiff of grapeshot or a little of the cannister?

We had a visit this afternoon from Dr Macran.[64] He nearly fills up our little suburbanite garden and his loud, spasmodic Irish conversation can be heard by all the neighbours. (Our neighbours by the way include members of Univ.) Cranny, as we call this atheistical priest, was full of wonderful things that happened. He lives in the tiny village of Childrey, where, judging by his own appearance, he must keep a strange household. Here he recently had the adventure of entertaining compulsorily an old schoolfellow of his son's, who brought down some funny little touring company and insisted on Cranny taking a lorry to the nearest railway station to conduct the company of 14 members. He then proceeded to cover that small village with posters, explaining that the specimens of fine English comedy to be given shortly in the village hall, were 'under the patronage of Dr Macran': this, of course, being unauthorised. Cranny arrived the next evening to see the show: he found the same man conducting a furious quarrel with his leading comedian at the door, after which he fainted. And so on.

Here's another: a neighbouring clergyman while proceeding to Oxford, met a notable thievish charwoman of Childrey in the train. The parson (who must have been blind to the world) insisted on inviting this

---

62 Milton, *Paradise Lost*, II, 622–6:'Created evil, for evil only good; / Where all life dies, death lives, and Nature breeds, / Perverse, all monstrous, all prodigious things, / Abominable, unutterable, and worse.'

63 What Jack refers to as the 'Daudel' or 'Dawdle' was Warnie's motorcycle and sidecar.

64 The Rev. Dr Frederick Walker Macran, 'Cranny' (1866–1947) was an old friend of Mrs Moore and her brother, Dr John Askins. He was born in Ireland and took a BA from Trinity College, Dublin in 1886. After serving in a number of parishes in Co. Down, he moved to England and was the rector of Childrey from 1905 to 1923. He is the man Lewis refers to in *SBJ* XIII as 'an old, dirty, gabbling, tragic, Irish parson who had long since lost his faith but retained his living...All he wanted was the assurance that something he could call "himself" would, on almost any terms, last longer than his bodily life.' There is a good deal about him in *AMR*.

lady to tea somewhere in Oxford: after the meal he said, 'I'm feeling a little faint: you must give me your arm' and proceeded to walk her up and down the Corn telling her scandalous stories about Cranny. Strange mortals these knights of the cloth are! But you would have been amused if you had seen me seated by Cranny in the smoking room of the Union this morning, before an audience of amazed old men: he has 24 hours growth on his face, one trouser turned up and the other down: one tail of his coat was coming away from the main body and he had apparently failed in the arithmetic of his fly buttons. He expounded Thomas Aquinas, modernism, Stead's religious position, the views of a Univ. don called Emmet on the divinity of Christ, of which the point is that he was only a man but you can still apparently go on being a parson if you say 'We don't worship Jesus Christ, only the Christ THAT WAS in Jesus' – a beautiful distinction. Anyway to have heard scraps of our crack would have thought he was delivering 'a straight talk with boys' – however they must have heard it ALL, anyway, so I needn't worry what the effect of 'scraps' would have been.

23rd [May 1921]

Am just finishing this off. Thanks for your other letter: it is very sad to hear that you have not yet got mine, but I hope you will have by this. I suppose I needn't add anything by way of public news: even without papers the main things will reach you – that Egypt is rioting – that the relations and children of R.I.C.[65] men are being murdered in London by Sinn Fein – that the coal strike is still on – that the Japanese Prince has visited Oxford – that sharks and octopuses have appeared on the English coast for the first time within memory. This last is really the climax: a jelly fish was quite enough. Hoping to hear again soon.

yours,
Jack

---

65 Royal Irish Constabulary.

TO HIS FATHER (LP VI: 325–7):

[University College,
Oxford]
29 [May 1921]

My dear Papy,

Thank you very much for your wire and the letter: I am very glad to have been able to send you good news.[66] I had almost lost heart about the thing, it dragged on so long. Everyone has been very nice about it, particularly the Mugger who is delighted, and this ought to be of use to me later on. Some of my congratulations indeed have made me feel rather ashamed, coming from people whom I have been used to class generically as 'louts'. By louts I denote great beefy people unknown to me by name, men with too much money and athletic honour, who stand blocking up passages. If looks could kill I'm afraid they would often have been in danger as I shouldered my way through them. Now they have weighed in with polite remarks and gratified my vanity with the grand-paternal 'No. Does HE know ME?' I suppose the explanation is that in their view we have done so badly on the river that any success – even in so unimportant a field as letters – should be encouraged.

I have also had a letter from Blackwell offering to see me about publishing it, and have, as a formality, written to Heinemann's. In any case I am not sure what to do about that: I shall certainly not spend any money (nor allow you to, tho' I know you gladly would) on forcing it into print if publishers won't take the risk. I have always thought that a bad thing to do. Perhaps publication in some periodical might provide a compromise: it would remind people that I exist and yet it would not give too permanent a form to any opinion or argument that I may outgrow later on. At worst, if any one would like it, it would mean a five pound note and enable you and everyone else to read it decently printed instead of in type. If all these plans fall through, or if they are likely to take a long time, I will get another copy done and send it to you.

You must not expect too much: the trains of argument are rather dull and I am afraid this effect is not neutralised by anything more than adequacy in the form. No purple patches – hardly a faint blue. But I must drop the annoying habit of anticipating your judgement.

---

66 On 24 May the University announced that the Chancellor's Prize for an English Essay was won by C.S. Lewis, and Jack immediately informed his father of this by telegram. No copy of 'Optimism' survives in either the University or the Lewis family papers.

Before I stop egoising I must tell you one other fact. The 'proxime accessit' or next best was, as you have probably seen in the Times, a man called Brundrit[67] of Wadham. He is a frequent speaker in the Union and the editor of an 'advanced' magazine: that is to say he inclines to the Bolshevik left and doubtless managed to make Optimism a political subject. I am very glad to have been able to do even this much towards removing the common reproach that the revolutionaries here have all the brains – indeed it is generally true: the real Tories have nothing but beautiful voices and long banking accounts.

I am very sorry to hear about W's letters going astray. He has apparently not got mine. I can quite understand that letters mean a good deal at the world's end, and I have broken all precedent in giving him long screeds full of English scenery and atmosphere. Do you suppose that he has given us an insufficient address? Let me know if you hear anything that will throw light on the matter. I suppose this is the Government's return for increased rates of postage!

I have been reading the oddest book lately – Newman's 'Loss and Gain.'[68] I never knew that he had written a novel. As fiction or drama it is of course beneath contempt, but it has some real satirical humour. Do you know it? The picture of the then Oxford, with its ecclesiastical controversies etc., is something more remote from my experience whether real or imagined, than ancient Britain or modern Cathay.[69] I haven't heard anything about the prize – I think it is in money – not very much – and there are some books from College.

I too thought about Kirk. We are all old, disillusioned creatures now, and look back on the days of 'buns and coffee' through a long perspective and only seldom come out of our holes: the young men up from school in their immaculate clothes think we have come to clean the windows when they see us. It happens to everyone here. In your first year you drink your sherry and see people: after that your set narrows, you haunt the country lanes more than the High, and cease to play at being the undergraduate of

---

67 Daniel Fernley Brundrit, of Wadham College, took his BA in 1921.
68 John Henry Newman, *Loss and Gain: The Story of a Convert* (1848).
69 He was thinking of the grip of the Church of England on the University since the Reformation. Until 1854–6 no student could take a degree without subscribing to the Thirty-Nine Articles, the set of doctrinal formulae which define the Anglican Church's dogmatic relation to the controversies of the 16th century. It was not until 1871 that religious tests were no longer required of University officials.

fiction. 1919 seems further off than France at times. So I need not avail myself of your kindly suggestion – there will be no revelry by night.

your loving son,

Jack

TO HIS FATHER (LP VII: 14):

[University College,
Oxford]
Postmark: 17 June 1921

My dear Papy,

This is a bad business about the rabbit hole: and it is cold comfort to reflect that your misfortune is to be traced solely to your insatiable desire for the society of your fellow men. I know of few things, in a small way, more painful than a sprain. I hope it has not been so bad as to keep you awake at nights: one can stand any amount of discomfort during the day time, if only one can get sleep: it is after that the real rub comes.

It is not easy to know what to do about publishing my essay. I must begin by thanking you very heartily for your suggestion: if, after you have heard what I have to say and after you have read the essay – which I will try to send this or next week – you still feel the same, I will do as you wish. At the same time I think we should be wiser to let the matter alone. I can only find three motives for publishing anything – fame, money or reputation, in the narrower sense that may help ones career indirectly. I presume that in the present case the last of these three is the important one: and in this, I do not think that publication will be of any use. My essay itself, however treated, will soon be forgotten except by my own family and friends: THE FACT of my having won the prize will be recorded and may some day turn the balance in my favour. Several of our dons have advised me (with infinite degrees of tact which are funny to watch) not to go into print: many have regretted it in similar circumstances: whatever merits there are in prize compositions are much better kept to make the basis of a real book later on, when wider reading and fresh thought have given the chance to make better use of any really original idea you have blundered on. This seems to be the general view, and there is much to be said for it. I do not of course mean that publication would be an absolutely bad thing: but I already regret one or two things in Spirits in Bondage and (however different its sphere) there may be parts of Optimism, both in style and manner, which I shall have outgrown in a few years. I labour the matter because I want you to accept my point of view, if you do accept it, DE JURE and not DE FACTO. At all events it is only reasonable that you should see it yourself before you make any decision. I am tempted to alter one or two sentences (on which you will easily lay your finger) but shall restrain myself – and except for the translation of some quotations it will be as it went into action.

Cousin Mary and Kelsie[70] have been here for a few days – the former looking very aged since I last saw her. I gather she has been sent to England by medical advice. The worthy Graham[71] was with them: he does not approve of Oxford I think.

A friend of mine who is going down this term is starting schoolmastering on £330 a year: on the strength of 'being expected to get a first' – so that even if I had to mark time at that job for a year or two before getting a fellowship, it would not be so bad as it once was. My tutor knows of one or two places which will be vacant here next year: however, if I do well in schools, I have some hope of getting a berth forthwith. I only hope I shall not collapse just at the end into stupidity as many a better man has done.

I have [had] nothing from W. for a long time: hoping the ankle is well again by now.

your loving son,
Jack

TO HIS FATHER (LP VII: 20–1):

[University College,
Oxford]
Monday 27th [June 1921]

My dear Papy,

I ought perhaps to have written before this about a remarkable thing that has happened: but, as you will see when you have read this letter, I have had my full these last three days. The 'thing' is a cheque made out by you to me for £19-8-9 and dated May 1919, wh., greatly to my surprise, I have unearthed between the pages of an old manuscript

---

70 Cousin Mary, the reader may recall, is Lady Ewart of Glenmachan House, Belfast.
 Kelso, or 'Kelsie' is her daughter. See **The Ewart Family** in the Biographical Appendix.
71 Samuel Graham was the Ewart family's coachman and family friend.

book. What the legal and formal position may be in such a case I have no idea; as however the money was intended for me and as its loss at the time, tho' not noted INTELLECTUALLY by such a muddle head as myself, must have occasioned some discomfort and exhausted the remains of my army money, I have felt justified in sending it in. I should not of course have done so, even with a stranger, without letting him know. I hope you will agree with what I have done: if not, you must let me know.

So much for that: the event of last week was one of the unforeseen consequences of my winning Optimism. I had almost forgotten, if I had ever known, that 'prizemen' have to read portions of their compositions at our ceremony of the Encaenia.[72] Being of the troglodytic nature I have never before exerted myself so far as to assist at this show: but having been now compelled, I am glad.

It is a most curious business. We unhappy performers attend (tho' it is at noon) in caps, gowns, and FULL EVENING DRESS. It was held in the Sheldonian Theatre: I think Macaulay has a purple passage about 'the painted roof of the Sheldonian'[73] under which Charles held his last Parliament. During the long wait, while people trickled in, an organ (much too large for the building) gave a recital. The undergraduates and their guests sit round in the galleries: the 'floor' is occupied by the graduates en masse, standing at barriers in all their war paint. At noon the Vice Chancellor enters with his procession of 'Heads of Colleges, Doctors, Proctors, and Noblemen' – a very strange show they make, half splendid and half grotesque, for few don's faces are fit to bear up against the scarlet and blue and silver of their robes.

Then some 'back chat' in Latin from the Vice Chancellor's throne and the Public Orator led in the persons who were to receive honorary degrees: with the exception of Clemenceau and Keyes (the Zeebruge man), they were not well known to the world at large. Keyes was a very

---

72 The Encaenia is Oxford University's annual commemoration of founders and benefactors, at which honorary degrees are given and prize compositions recited.

73 Macaulay, *History of England*, vol. II, ch. viii, p. 446: 'When her Chancellor, the venerable Duke of Ormond, sate in his embroidered mantle on his throne under the painted ceiling of the Sheldonian theatre, surrounded by hundreds of graduates robed according to their rank, while the noblest youths of England were solemnly presented to him as candidates for academical honours, he made an appearance scarcely less regal than that which his master made in the Banqueting House of Whitehall.'

honest looking fellow and Clemenceau the tough, burly 'people's man' whom one expected: but what was beyond everything was the Canon of Notre Dame, a great theologian apparently, with some name like Raffitol.[74] Such a picture of a great priest with all the pale dignity that one had imagined, I never saw. If the words 'love at first sight' were not tied down to one kind of feeling only, I would almost use them to express the way this man attracted me. He would have appealed to you immensely.

After the honorary degrees, the Professor of Poetry[75] made an 'oration' in Latin, chiefly about colleagues who had died during the last year: this was my first experience of spoken Latin and I was pleased to find that I could follow and enjoy it. The performance of us prizemen was of course very small beer after all this. We had been instructed to read for about two minutes each: I had some difficulty in finding a short passage which would be intelligible by itself. I was, of course, nervous: I am also told that I was the first of our little band whom Clemenceau looked at: but as I do not know WITH WHAT EXPRESSION he looked, nor whether he speaks English, we must remain in doubt whether this was a compliment or not.

I have had a good lesson in modesty from thus seeing my fellow prize men. I was hardly prepared for such a collection of scrubby, beetle-like, bespectacled oddities: only one of them appeared to be a gentleman. Any I spoke to sounded very like fools, perhaps like Goldsmith, they 'writ like an angel and talked like poor Poll'.[76] It brings home to one how very little I know of Oxford: I am apt to regard my own set, which consists mainly of literary gents, with a smattering of political, musical and philosophical – as being central, normal, and representative. But step out of it, into the athletes on one side or the pale pot hunters on the other, and it is a strange planet.

---

74 Georges Clemenceau (1841–1929) was Prime Minister and Minister for War of France from 1917 to 1920. Sir Roger Keyes (1881–1929) was Admiral of the Fleet from 1920 to 1929 and the hero of Zeebrugge. The Canon of Notre-Dame de Paris was the Rt. Rev. Monseigneur Pierre Battifol (1861–1929), a distinguished church historian.
75 William Paton Ker (1855–1923), Fellow of All Souls' College, Oxford, and Quain Professor of English Language and Literature at the University of London, was the author of many books on English, Scottish and Scandinavian literature.
76 David Garrick's imaginary epitaph on Oliver Goldsmith.

I have hardly left room to answer your letter. As to 'a berth', that may all be put on one side for the present. I am sorry you didn't go and get yourself made an O.B.E.[77] or something when George-by-the-grace-of-God came to Belfast.[78] I suppose it is useless to hope for any fruit from his speech: from today's paper Ulster seems to be beating her big drum harder than ever, with a zeal excusable more than praiseworthy. You don't mention how the leg is getting on. I hope my MS will reach you next week.

your loving son,
Jack

P.S. By the bye – if you may answer such questions – is there a real difference between Esoteric and Exoteric Masonry: and have the magicians – I know some – any justification for associating all their stuff with the Masonic inner circle. I should be glad of a little hard facts. – J.

TO HIS BROTHER (LP VII: 24–9):

[28 Warneford Road,
Oxford]
July 1st [1921]

My dear W.,

I was delighted to get your letter this morning; for some reason it had been sent first to a non-existent address in Liverpool. I had deliberately written nothing to you since those two you mention: not that I was tired of the job, but because I did not feel disposed to go on posting into the void until I had some assurance that my effusions would reach you. That seemed a process too like prayer for my taste: as I once said to Baker – my mystical friend with the crowded poetry – the trouble about God is that he is like a person who never acknowledges one's letters and so, in time, one comes to the conclusion either that he does not exist or that you have got the address wrong. I admitted that it was of great moment: but what was the use of going on despatching fervent messages – say to Edinburgh – if they all came back through the dead letter office: nay more, if you couldn't even find Edinburgh on the map. His cryptic reply was that it would be almost worth going to Edinburgh to find out.

---

77 Officer (of the Order) of the British Empire.
78 King George V was in Belfast on 22 June to open the Parliament of Northern Ireland.

I am glad however that you have ceased to occupy such a divine position, and will do my best to continue: tho' I hope it won't be for fifteen months.

Here another term has blossomed and faded: that time moves has I believe been observed before. I have lived my usual life: a few lectures, until – as happens about half way through the term – I got tired of them all: work, meetings with friends, walks and rides, solitary or otherwise, and meetings of the Martlets. These birds by the by were all invited to dinner by the don Martlets a few weeks ago, and I again had the opportunity of peeping into the real Oxford: this time through the medium of a very excellent meal ('with wine' as Milton says with the air of a footnote) in cool, brown oaky rooms. I have been thinking of a formula for it all and decided on 'Glenmachan turned male and intellectualised' as fairly good.

The great event of MY term was of course 'Optimism'. I must thank you for your congratulations before going on: THEY were provoked by the event, but the consequences of it will move your ribaldry. 'Prizemen', the Statutes say, 'will read at the Encaenia portions of their exercises (I like that word) – their exercises chosen by the Professor of Poetry and the Public Orator.' Sounds dam' fine, doesn't it? But the Statutes omit to mention the very cream of the whole situation – namely that the prizemen will appear in full evening dress. Fancy me entering the Sheldonian at 11.30 a.m. on a fine June morning in a cap, gown, boiled shirt, pumps, white tie and tails. Of course it was a 'broiling' day as the P'daytabird would say, and of course, for mere decency I had to wear an overcoat.

However, I managed to make myself audible, I am told, and beyond nearly falling as I entered the rostrum, I escaped with success (They DO actually call it a rostrum, so that I was delighted: for the whole gallery of the Damerfesk[79] seemed to gaze at me, and the jarring ghosts of Big, Polonius and Arabudda to lend me countenance.)[80] This was really the fault of one not unlike our Arabudda – old Ker the professor of poetry, who, having earlier in the proceeding delivered his Latin oration,

---

79 The 'Damerfesk' is described in *SBJ* V as the 'common legislative assembly' of Boxen. Unlike that of England, it was not doomed to one fixed meeting place, but could meet anywhere the joint sovereigns chose.

80 Lord Big (a frog), Polonius Green (a parrot) and Sir Charles Arabudda (a fish) are characters from the world of 'Boxen' which Jack and Warnie created as boys. See note 10 to letter of [c. 1906].

decided to remain sitting in the rostrum instead of going back to his own stall. This (in the language of Marie Stopes)[81] 'made entry difficult if not impossible' for us prizemen: in my anxiety to avoid the burly professor, I stumbled over a raised step and nearly fell backwards. This must have appeared curiously enough to those who were on a level with, or higher than the rostrum: but the best effect of all was from the floor, from which, owing to the height of the front barrier and the big velvet cushion on it, I appeared simply to sink through a trap and rise again like a jack-in-the-box. However, I rallied my sang froid and bawled defiant remarks on the universe for two minutes. It is a good thing that the P'daytabird was not present or he would have been sorely put to it – especially if you had been beside him, giddy with laughter (You can imagine his asking me afterwards 'Did you do it to annoy me?').

I will send you a copy of my essay, since you ask for it, though I do not think it will be much in your line. Some of the insolent passages may amuse you: I hope you will like the way I dealt with the difficulty of 'God or no God'. To admit that person's existence would have upset my whole applecart: to deny it seemed inadvisable, on the off chance of there being a Christian among the examiners. I therefore adopted the more Kirkian alternative of proving – at any rate to my own satisfaction – that it 'really made no difference whatsoever' whether there was such a person or no. The second part of my essay you may use as a mild test whether you are ever likely to come to metaphysics or not. I look forward with some trepidation to discussing it at home: for his 'reading of the thing' will doubtless differ vastly from my writing of it.

Clemenceau took an honorary degree at this same ceremony and, tho' an imposing figure, suffered by contrast to the other two Frenchmen presented with him. There's no doubt that a butty, tho' a genius, remains a butty still. With him were Canon de Notre Dame Raffitol, a perfect picture of a great priest, and the Duc de Broglie.[82] From a great deal of snobbish reference, which sounded less vulgar in Latin, I gather he is of a great house. Do you know anything of it?

---

81 Marie Stopes (1880–1958) was an early sex reformer who devoted herself to birth control.

82 Louis-Victor, 7th Duc de Broglie (1892–1987), French physicist of a distinguished noble family, is best known for his research on quantum theory, and for his discovery of the wave nature of electrons. He was awarded the Nobel Prize for Physics in 1929.

I had not meant, in my other letters, to bring any serious charge against the Oxfordshire country. Tried by European standards it takes a lowish rank: but I am not such a fool as to deprecate any decent country now, and rather wrote in deprecation for fear you'd fancy I was 'writing up' a place [in] which you would remember no particular beauties. Of landscapes, as of people, one becomes more tolerant after one's twentieth year (which reminds me to congratulate you on your birthday and ask what age it makes you.[83] The rate at which we both advance towards a responsible age is indecent). We learn to look at them not IN THE FLAT as pictures to be seen, but IN DEPTH as things to be burrowed into. It is not merely a question of lines and colours but of smells, sounds and tastes as well: I often wonder if professional artists don't lose something of the real love of earth by seeing it in eye sensations exclusively?

From the house where we are now living there are few good walks, but several decent rides. Last Saturday we rode to Standlake. In the heat of the day – we are having drought here too – it was an heroic undertaking. Don't come down on me with any traveller's tale about 'what real heat is': I know with my intellect that it is much hotter in Africa, but put any honest man on a treeless road, uphill, in an English summer, and he can't really imagine anything is hotter. We had to begin by climbing the 'warm green muffled Cumnor hills':[84] a long pull, all on foot. You have a fine, but conventional view of Oxford as you look back: but we really enjoyed nothing until beyond Cumnor we sunk into the long grass by the side of the road under one of the deplorably rare trees and tackled our luncheon basket. A local pub supplied beer for me and lemonade for the children, and we had a basket of cherries. After this it became better and when after a long and pleasant decline through corkscrew lanes full of meadowsweet (that's the white, dusty stuff with a nice smell, you know) we reached Bablocke Hythe, it was quite delightful. Beyond this the country is very flat, but tree-y: full of villages rather too 'warm and muffled': they make you feel like a bumble bee that has got into damp cotton wool.

Our objective was a cottage in Standlake about the letting of which during the summer Mrs Moore was going to see. Here (tho' our purpose failed) we were rewarded by meeting a wonderful old woman, the owner,

---

83 Warnie turned 26 on 16 June.
84 Matthew Arnold, *The Scholar-Gipsy*, VII, 9.

Mrs Penfold, who talked of her husband as 'Penfold' without the Mr, just like a character in Jane Austen. This I am afraid you will hardly credit, but it is true all the same. Although flat and almost too blankety for a man to strike a match in, this country is much favoured of the Muse.

A few miles beyond us was Kelmscott, where Wm Morris lived and built that 'red house' whose brick nudity first defied the stucco traditions: from it, all the pretty villas of our day are directly descended. A little to our right at Stanton Harcourt (where Jenkins is always going to take me) is an old Manor with a tower room where Pope wrote his famous parody – which he called a translation – of the Iliad.[85] And of course, as you know, every mile smells of Arnold. We were not far from 'the Fyfield elm': we had 'crossed the stripling Thames'[86] and saw in the distance near Cumnor what I took for the 'plot of forest ground called Thessaly'.[87] Oh by the way I have found the ideally bad edition of Thyrsis and the Scholar Gipsy.[88] It was lying in Blackwells between grey boards with very black type: illustrated with photographs – one to almost every two stanzas. For 'what sedged brooks are Thames's tributaries'[89] you had a bed of rushes taken close, as you would for a plate in a natural history handbook, with a water rat in the middle: but best of all – there's a line somewhere I can't remember, about a 'battered merchant-man coming into port': for this we had two cutter racing yachts!! How are such things possible: and yet people will buy this and like it and be very proud of it. I am writing in our little strip of garden at five past ten and it is getting too dark to see: I will in and drink some of the eveningmilch.

The next time I am in town I will order the books you ask for. Cary's Dante (not the Inferno alone, but the whole Comedy) is published in the Everyman. You may remember I got it last Christmas in the Oxford edition which suffers from intolerably small print, but gains from having Flaxman's interesting designs.[90] It is supposed, as you know, to be one of the very few

---

85 Alexander Pope, *The Iliad*, 6 vols. (1715–20).
86 Arnold, *Scholar-Gypsy*, VIII, 4: 'Crossing the stripling Thames at Bab-lock-hithe'.
87 ibid., XII, 5: 'Above the forest-ground called Thessaly'.
88 Matthew Arnold, *The Oxford Poems of Matthew Arnold* – 'The Scholar Gipsy' and 'Thyrsis' – illustrated...Portrait, Ordnance Map, and 76 photographs. By Henry W. Taunt (Oxford: Henry W. Taunt & Co. [1909]).
89 Matthew Arnold, *Thyrsis* (1866), XI, 10.
90 *The Vision or Hell, Purgatory and Paradise of Dante Alighieri*, trans. H.F. Cary, with Introduction and Notes by E.G. Gardner (London: Everyman's Library, 1908); the same translation, illustrated by John Flaxman (London: Oxford University Press, 1910).

really good translations in existance. If you get sick of the Inferno, you will, on my advice, skip to the Purgatorio: about the last quarter of it is the heart of the whole book – tho' perhaps, as was unkindly said of the Good Friday music – it owes something to its surroundings: perhaps one has to go through the Inferno to appreciate the relief. Rochefocauld[91] I think can be got in the same series as my little volume of Voltaire's Contes.

I agree with your refusal to support George Moore in his blackmail.[92] The theory is that he publishes privately because he can't put up with modern print and paper: tho' I am sufficient of a kod myself to like beautiful type and to be discontented with the usual commercial sort, I think it a bad plan – because it rejects the real reader – who is always a poor man, and admits the parvenu who would buy 'culture'. Incidentally I have an unreasonable and purely A PRIORI belief that Geo. Moore is a bit of a quack. If I were more of a P'dayta I should invent some reasons – or what he wd. take to be reasons – for this idea, but I am ready to leave it admittedly unreasonable.

Since we last communicated, Cousin Mary and Kelsie have visited Oxford. I was summoned for my first audience after dinner on a breathless evening, threatening thunder. Dripping with sweat, I climbed up the stairs of the Mitre to the private room where they had for the nonce established their holy of holies. They had a fire going! They had just finished dinner: a few minutes later a substantial meal of tea, cakes, bread and butter was brought up. The two ladies did it ample justice. I was the only non-juror. The conversation was all of Ireland. The following thesis was put forward. (1) That there were no atrocities committed by the Crown forces. (2) That it was no wonder the Crown forces did ANYTHING considering what they had to put up with. (3) That in any case it was all the fault of the English government.

---

91 François, Duc de La Rochefoucauld, *Réflexions ou Sentences et Maximes Morales* (1665). Lewis was probably talking about *The Moral Maxims and Reflections of the Duc de La Rochefoucauld*, trans. G. Stanhope, with notes by G.H. Powell (1904).

92 George Augustus Moore (1852–1933), the Anglo-Irish novelist, two of whose best known works were *Esther Waters* (1894) and *Heloïse and Abelard* (1921). Jack and Warnie had been reading an article by Moore entitled 'A Communication to Book Collectors' in *The Times Literary Supplement* (10 March 1921), p. 157, in which Moore announces his plans to revive the art of printing. There was no blackmail in the formal sense. Jack was thinking of the difficulty Moore caused the publisher, William Heinemann, over publishing a special edition of *Esther Waters*.

Kelsie tells me that she met Turner[93] in town on the day of the elections: 'he's had one vote in Larne, and another in Belfast, and he'd have another before he went home'. The corruption appears to have been something that wd. make an Englishman's hair rise. I was told that the Sinn Feiners made a great attempt at intimidation. ME: 'But how could that be? I thought they were in a minority?' C.M.: 'Oh, well they thought they'd try anyway.' A story of a 'decent man' shooting Catholics outside one of the booths was advanced – apparently as a proof of Sinn Fein intimidation, and the whole wound up with the statement that 'English people didn't understand'.

Next day at lunch a woman living in N. Oxford and called Cousin Bessie[94] was present: conversation ran on purely family lines. 'And how are Hugh's boys?' – 'Ah, I'm afraid he's wild' – 'Oh my, what a pity' (from C.M.) – 'Of course SHE thought she was going to live at Warrenscourt – oh no, it wouldn't have done at all – poor Uncle Jack – everyone told him you know – and what about the boy – they say he's wild too.' The number of people who were disposed of in the single word 'wild' was very funny. I wonder what exactly it means? Are we wild do you think? Or tame? However the real final deluge of Glenmachonianism and the concerted movement of the whole symphony – came on Saturday evening when I dined alone with Kelsie. She always had her on days and her off days: and for many years now there have been times when I found têtes a têtes with her longer by mental measurement than the clock would vouch for. But on this occasion, honestly it was so boring that there was an air of insanity about it all: connected perhaps with the terrible heat and with that crowded tiny dining room at the Mitre. She never paused. Stories that I have heard from those same lips so often before followed one another: somebody was engaged and somebody else had broken off an engagement: the inevitable discussion of the Greeves's: had I heard about so and so: did I remember what Willie Jaffé had done on such and such an occasion?

---

93 Warnie provided the following information in LP VII: 27: 'Turner had formerly been the Glenmachan butler, and at this time was the Major Domo of the Olderfleet Hotel at Larne Harbour, which in fact I believe he owned. I was once shopping there when some of the Ewarts arrived at the hotel, driven of course by Graham. The latter greeted his former fellow servant in the following encouraging manner – "Well Turner, are ye not dead yet?"'

94 Warnie says of her in LP VII: 27: 'Presumably Bessie Geraldina Gundred [Warren], daughter of Rear Admiral J.B. Warren and Mary St Ledger, and therefore a first cousin of Lady Ewart's: Lady Ewart's mother, Charlotte Heard being a sister of the Admiral's.'

When we went up to the private room again, I could do no more. Wrapping my gown round her head to stifle her cries, I seized our cousin by the left ankle and precipitated her from the window. She flew out over the High in a great arc: the strolling butties and undergraduates looked up and shouted. But to my horror, just as she descended on one of the pinnacles of St Mary's spires, her dress developed a certain balloon like quality: instead of breaking into a thousand pieces she rose up on the giddy ledge and, just as I lost consciousness, I could hear her proclaim distinctly to the whole town 'I once saw an awfully funny thing happen to a girl at Aldershot – .' I can't quite swear to all this having happened exactly as it is here set down: but something like it must have taken place, since the undoubted fact remains that I did get away.

Good old Glenmachan with its faint, unmistakable smell: can't you hear the soft 'whoosh' of the rubber thing on the cloak room door and the 'tuff tuff' of the gas engine a little further off? And then one thinks of all sorts of things – long afternoons in the very old days when we were more like burglars than guests. Do you remember how one used to feel turning down that avenue homeward at about 5 o'c some summer's afternoon when there was a row on? Or at the last day of the holidays? By Jove it was a refuge for battered p.b[95] during their stormy youth. Certainly it has no more convinced disciple than myself: but it won't bear transplanting: move the Court to the Mitre and it is simply a joke as you would realise if you had seen it.

The steps by which you became a Miltonian are very interesting. Can one quite have done by labelling him a republican and a puritan? Puritanism was after all (in some of its exponents) a very different thing from modern 'dissent'. One cannot imagine Milton going about and asking people if they were saved: that intolerable pride is the direct opposite to sentimentalism. He really had the vices and virtues of the aristocracy – writing for 'fit audience tho' few'.[96] He always seems to look down on the vulgar from an almost archducal height. 'How charming is divine philosophy. Not harsh and crabbed as dull fools suppose.'[97] The DULL FOOLS are the ordinary mass of humanity, and though it has its ridiculous side, that deliberate decision of his, taken at my age 'to leave

---

95 'Pigieboties' or 'Piggiebottoms'.
96 Milton, *Paradise Lost*, VII, 31: 'and fit audience find, though few'.
97 Milton, *Comus*, 476.

something so written that posterity wd not willingly let it die'[98] takes a little doing. Paradise Regained I only read once: it is a bit too much for me. In it the Hebrew element finally gets the better of the classical and romantic ingredients. How can people be attracted to things Hebrew? However, old Kirk really summed up Milton when he said 'I would venture to assert that no human being ever called him Johnnie'.

By the way, on a ride the other day I passed an inn which the landlord had seen fit to call 'The Olde Air Balloon'. What a splendid name for the P'daytabird – who, by the way, is threatening to come here in a few days, thanks to the persistent endeavours of Uncle and Aunt Hamilton, backed, according to his account, by your advice. I wish you'd mind your own business, Master P. B. I have told him I've been moved out of College, so the business resolves itself into my presenting my abode here as ordinary digs – and keeping him out of them as much as may be. Luckily Pasley will be up for his viva and 'a friend sharing with me and working very hard' ought to be a sufficient deterrent. I think too, that if I walk the Old Air Balloon out here in the present insupportable heat, once will be enough for him. The temperature is over 90 in the shade: even the water at Parson's Pleasure has reached 71. Though still the only comfortable place (where I spend many a happy hour) this takes the real bite and shock out of a bathe.

One great beauty at present is that they are mowing the meadows on the far side, and as you splash along with your nose just above the dark brown water, you swim into the smell of hay. But to expiate over the delights of an English river would be really unkind to you. You will probably await my next with interest, in which you will hear of the success or failure of the paternal visit. What an anachronism he will be here: of course he may not come: I have suggested that 'if he really is going away, some little place to ourselves later on would be much more enjoyable than a Hamilton obbligato – perhaps N. Wales' – which as the hereditary cradle of true Pdaytism, ought to be a draw.

Thanks for the passage about H. Walpole and the Bozzy bird: its simply splendid. Try and let me hear again soon: I will write as soon as I am out of my present pother.

yrs,

Jack

Books and MSS following on in due course.

---

98 Milton, *The Reason of Church-Government*, Second Book (slightly misquoted).

TO ARTHUR GREEVES (W):

[University College
June 1921]

My dear Arthur, [99]

I am ashamed that this has been so long delayed. Now that you have been caught, though late, in the snares and cares of this wicked world you will be able to understand how the time rushes past, how you have scarcely time to notice a new week beginning before it is Saturday again, and thence at a single stride into the middle of the next. And always like a mountain piles up the list of things that you must put off, books you want to read, people to see, letters to write.

So many things have happened since we last met that it is no use to attempt chronology: I may as well begin with what is, I must admit, uppermost in my mind – this Chancellor's prize, that you ask about. It is set every year for the whole university and decided by seven judges chosen in rotation. The subject this year was 'Optimism'. Suitable to my family, as you probably guess! The actual prize is £20 in money (that is in strict secrecy – I don't want the fact disclosed at home until it has to be) but of course it is much more valuable as a means of self advertisement and may help me towards a job one of these days: it serves a little to mark you out from the crowd. I liked the subject and took a lot of trouble and am consequently very pleased. The essay may possibly be published – I don't know yet: in any case I don't think anyone at home will care much for it – its rather dull and metaphysical.

The other thing which I suppose you would be most interested to hear about will be my two visits to Yeats. I really cannot do this justice in the space of a letter, but will give you something to go on with. His house is in Broad Street: you go up a long staircase lined with pictures by Blake – chiefly the 'Book of Job' and the 'Paradise Lost' ones, which thus, en masse, have a somewhat diabolical appearance. The first time I came I found a priest called Father Martindale, his wife and a little man with a grey beard who never spoke, sitting with him. It was a very funny room: the light was supplied by candles, two of them in those 6-ft. candle-sticks that you see before the altar in some English churches. There were

---

99 Arthur gave up his idea of going to Oxford when he was permitted to enrol in the Slade School of Fine Art in London. He entered the Slade in January 1921 and took lessons three times a week until he left in December 1923. His address while in London was 66 Torrington Square and, later, 49 Leinster Gardens.

flame-coloured curtains, a great many pictures, and some strange for-eign-looking ornaments that I can't describe. The company sat on very hard, straight, antique chairs: except Mrs Yeats who lay on a kind of very broad divan, with bright cushions, in the window. Yeats himself is a very big man – very tall, very fat and very broad: his face also gives one the impression of vast size. There would have been no mistaking which was THE man we had come to see, however many people had been in the room. Grey haired: about sixty years of age: clean shaven: glasses with a thick tape. His voice sounded rather French, I thought, at first, but the Irish shows through after a bit. I have seldom felt less at my ease before anyone than I did before him: I understand the Dr Johnson atmosphere for the first time – it was just like that, you know, we all sit-ting round, putting in judicious questions while the great man played with some old seals on his watch chain and talked.

The subjects of his talk, of course, were the very reverse of Johnson-ian: it was all of magic and apparitions. That room and that voice would make you believe anything. He talks very well and not unlike his own printed prose: one sentence came almost directly out of 'Per Amica Silentia Lunae'.[100] The priest was guardedly sceptical but allowed himself to be argued down. One gets the impression (as I have sometimes got it from others) of a tremendous amount of this sort of thing going on all round us. Yeats – 'learnt magic from Bergson's sister' – 'for a long time I wondered what this dream meant till I came across some Hermetic students in London, who showed me a picture of the same thing I had seen' – 'ah yes – So-and-so: he went in for magic too, but his brain wasn't strong enough and he went mad' – 'at that time I was going through what are known as Lunar meditations etc, etc'. You'll think I'm inventing all this but it's really dead, sober truth. The last two or three years have taught me that all the things we used to like as mere fantasy are held as facts at this moment by lots of people in Europe: perhaps, however, you have run across it in town.

The second time I went to see Yeats, the talk ran more on literature: it also was very interesting, better in some ways than the other, but I haven't time to describe it – beyond recording the fact that he is an enthusiastic admirer of Morris prose romances: which shd. give us confidence.

---

100 W.B. Yeats, *Per Amica Silentia Lunae* (1918).

That constitutes about all my real news: otherwise it has been all the usual thing. I walk and ride out into the country, sometimes with the family, sometimes alone. I work: I wash up and water the peas and beans in our little garden: I try to write: I meet my friends and go to lectures. In other words I combine the life of an Oxford undergraduate with that of a country householder: a feat which I imagine is seldom performed. Such energies as I have left for general reading go almost entirely on poetry – and little enough of that.

If my letters fail by their rarity, yours tell me very little about yourself. I have had no news yet, save very indirect snippets, as to how you are getting on with the Slade. Have you met any interesting people? What is your day made up of ? I await with interest the results of this 're-arrangement of your face'. Have you become infected with futurism and do you intend to practice it on yourself? Will something of this sort be the result? Seriously, I hope you won't have too bad a time.

Like you, I am too hard up to think of leaving Oxford except for a compulsory tête-a-tête with Excellenz. There is an awful suggestion of his coming over to England on a motor tour with the Hamiltons, calling of course at Oxford. What on earth that might lead to I daren't even begin to imagine: my only consolation is that the difficulty of removing him from Little Lea will probably prove insurmountable.

Kelsie and Cousin Mary have been here for a few days & are going to-morrow: I think they intend to 'look you up' in London. Just between ourselves I have been bored to death with them: I came in a thunderously hot evening to find them sitting in a private room at the Mitre with a big fire blazing – then an ample meal of tea & cakes an hour after their dinner. Well I don't know: they have been very kind to me all my life and are in many ways excellent people: but just seeing them here suddenly, out of their setting, the main impression is of provincialism, narrow Ulster bigotry and a certain sleek unreality – so hardly will a rich woman enter into the Kingdom.

Try to let me have an answer to this & I'll try to answer *that*. Let me know *between what dates* you'll be at Bernagh: I must try to get my compulsory visit coinciding with you. The Minto sends her love and sympathies for the nursing home.

Yours
Jack

TO LEO BAKER (B):

28 Warneford Road,
Oxford.
[July 1921]

My dear Baker,

You must have almost given me up by now. I don't know how it has been. I have had a good deal of bothers of one sort and another, that have induced me, in my lazy way, to let work and with it things more obligatory, go their own way. First of all, thanks for the Gospel of Buddha:[101] in so far as it is a gospel, an exposition of ethics etc, it has not perhaps added much to what I knew of the subject, tho' it has been very pleasant reading. On the metaphysical presuppositions of Buddhism, it has given me new light: I did not realize, before, his denial of the Atman: that is very interesting. I cannot at present believe it – to me the Self, as really existing, seems involved in everything we think. No use to talk of 'a bundle of thoughts' etc for, as you know, I always have to ask 'who thinks?' Indeed Buddhism itself does not seem to make much use of the non-Atman doctrine, once it has been stated: and it is only by torture that the theory of re-birth is made compatible with it. Perhaps he has confused a moral truth with a metaphysical fallacy? One sees, of course, its inferiority to Christianity – at any rate as a creed for ordinary men: and though I sometimes feel that complete abnegation is the only real refuge, in my healthier moments I hope that there is something better. This minute I can pine for Nirvana, but when the sky clears I shall prefer something with more positive joy.

I wonder what is to be done about your question of Beauty? The popular theory among contemporaries is that Beauty is simply expression: as soon as a shape or a sound becomes a means by which I find the expression or 'objectification' of myself, it is beautiful. That is why (they say) that even things 'uncomely & broken' find their aesthetic value in the right place. Not satisfied with this view myself: for it makes it indifferent *what* is expressed. E.g. a face that expressed cruelty, stupidity or greed would be beautiful if only it expressed them thoroughly. They wd. probably say that greed etc are themselves 'inexpressive' of the *idea* of the individual – the thing he is tending to be, his potential completeness. To me it seems that a great many different emotions are united in the

---

101 Paul Carus, *The Gospel of Buddha According to Old Records* (1895).

perception of beauty: it may turn out to be not a simple thing but a result of unions. For one thing nearly all beautiful sights are to me chiefly important as *reminders* of other beautiful sights: without memory twould be a poor affair. The process presumably has a beginning but once going it grows like a snowball. Could it be that joy remembered ('Which now is sad because it has been sweet')[102] is a necessary element in Beauty? There is too, I think, a purely sensuous element: that such and such notes or tints (*in themselves* – not in their combinations) just happen to satisfy our nerves of hearing & sight – as certain foods satisfy those of tastes. This wd. be rather a condition of beauty, perhaps, than an element in it. One thing is plain, that the statements continually made about Beauty's being pure contemplation, stirring no impulse, being the antithesis of the practical or energizing side of us, are wrong. On the contrary beauty seems to me to be always an invitation of some sort & usually an invitation to we don't know what. A wood seen as 'picturesque' by a fool (who'd like a frame round it) may be purely contemplated: seen as 'beautiful' it seems rather to say 'come into me'. But this is getting away from your point – much more important – whether its objective & has a real right & wrong apart from our opinions. One always feels that it has. But I don't understand: it must be objective & yet how can it? Don't quite know what you mean about the organs of generation appearing beautiful: I never thought that.

Pasley is with us at present for his viva: he is very worn out and somewhat depressed – changing in the most curious way. He has got into spiritualism and is very keen. It was only the end of last term he said to me that he had no interest in immortality – 'with ordinary luck a man ought to have lived all there was in him to live by the time he reaches old age'. That's quite changed now & he finds life 'weary stale unprofitable'[103] if theres no immortality. See how they run!

I have been very busy – as I had been some time ago – writing a new & v. different version of the 'Foster' poem: it is being very troublesome & at present will not get itself finished but now & then I have great hopes of it. I am afraid this [is] rather a spidery letter. By the way I hope you are vastly improved before this in body & mind and have met good

---

102 Shelley, *Prometheus Unbound*, II, i, 9.

103 Shakespeare, *Hamlet*, I, ii, 133–4: 'How weary, stale, flat, and unprofitable / Seem to me all the uses of this world.'

adventure. I shall try to write again, and shall be greatly delighted to hear from you.

Yrs

C. S. Lewis

TO HIS FATHER (LP VII: 33):

University College,
Oxford
9th July [1921]

My dear Papy,

Many thanks for your letter and for 'this of' the cheque. It was no one's fault but my own that it was not sent in at the proper time: my brain seems to be a very poor engine for carrying the day to day facts of existance in my head.

The colonel seems to write to us both about the same time: and what you tell me of his letters would sometimes suggest that he kills two birds with one stone by means of carbon paper – if his ink did not disprove it. I am very glad, at last, to find that my letters are now reaching him. I think the introduction of monkeys at Leeborough would be a dangerous precedent. Tim, for one, would go off his head.

I am truly delighted to hear that you think it at last possible to weigh anchor from home: and there are certainly great attractions about your coming here. Is it safe – I am so afraid that any change may mean a change to the negative course of status quo – to suggest that if you can get away, we might utilise the opportunity better? Here of course there is the charm of much which I do not underrate because it is now family, and which would naturally have a peculiar interest for you. On the other hand there will be very little privacy. I have been moved out of College and you will probably find me sharing with a man who is up to his eyes in work. That means we can't spend much time on my own hearth: and, for the rest, I think we should prefer each other neat rather than with a permanent Hamilton soda (Hamilton paying the soda of course?). What do you say to a few weeks later on somewhere in Westmorland or N. Wales? We might 'do' a little bit of country by walks, rather than a big bit by motor. But let me know. It is in these directions that my own fancy inclines: the great thing is to GET AWAY – hither if you like, elsewhere if you like – but AWAY.

Have you seen a recent amusing illustration of Wilde's theory that nature copies art? that a real Captain Kettle has appeared in the bay of

Syracuse: complete even to the beard: and told the public prosecutor, the British Consul, and the Italian officers 'The minute any of you gentlemen sets foot on my deck, I'll brown her up'. By James!

I have been looking at Shaw's new books in the library once or twice. It seems 'curiouser and curiouser'[104] as Alice said. The drought and the heat wave here are something beyond description.

　　your loving son,
　　Jack

In the end, Mr Lewis decided to visit his son in Oxford, and he set off on one of his rare holidays, the last and the most enterprising he was ever to take. On 20 July he joined his brother-in-law and sister-in-law, Augustus and Anne Hamilton, and they travelled in their car across Wales. At Albert's request, the party spent their first night in Betws-y-Coed, Caernarvonshire, for it was here in 1894 that Albert and Flora spent the first part of their honeymoon. They then proceeded to Oxford where they were joined by Jack on 24 July. Together they toured much of southern England.

TO HIS BROTHER (LP VII: 49–58):

28 Warneford Road
Oxford
7 August [1921]

　　My dear W.,

　　You heard in my last letter of the consternation into which our little household was thrown by the threatened and hardly precedented migration of the P'daytabird. I have so much history to record that I must bustle on from that point. By rights I should tell you of all the preparations that were made: how Pasley came up at a whistle, like the faithful comrade in arms he is, to be the man who was digging with me and to 'lend artistic verisimilitude':[105] how the little back room was dressed up in the semblance of an undergraduate's digs, where women never set foot. But the story would be too long. The gods spared me the

---

104　Carroll, *Alice's Adventures in Wonderland*, ch. 2.
105　Gilbert and Sullivan, *The Mikado*, Act II. Pooh says: 'Merely corroborative detail, intended to give artistic verisimilitude to an otherwise bald and unconvincing narrative.' It is repeated in the letter of 28 May 1923.

need of this Palais Royal farce with its uneasy tendency to degenerate into something more like Grand Guignol.[106]

It so worked out that the Irish party only stopt at Oxford for their midday eating and then took me with them for a week. My compulsory holiday took me through so much good country and supplied me with such a rare crop of P'daytisms that it gives me really too much epic matter to write about. I shall try to give you any information that may interest you as prospective pilot of the Dawdle through the same parts: but of course you must not take it for as accurate as Michelin.

The first and by far the funniest piece of scenery I saw was my first glimpse of the Old Air Balloon himself, outside the Clarendon in Cornmarket. You've no idea how odd he looked, almost a bit shrunk: pacing along with that expression peculiar to him on a holiday – the eyebrows half way up his forehead. I was very warmly greeted by all; and with the exception of Aunt Annie, we took a short stroll before lunch. I was in a great flutter for fear of meeting some fool who might out with any irrelevance, but everything passed off well.

I learned that he found the heat intolerable, that he had not slept a wink since he left home, that he had a feather bed last night at Worcester – which Uncle Hamilton thought a great joke. He seemed dazed by his surroundings and showed no disposition to go and see my rooms, tho' he observed that College had 'treated me very shabbily as they distinctly mentioned free rooms as one of the privileges of scholars' – a statute by the by completely unknown at Oxford, however familiar at Leeborough. We lunched heavily at the Clarendon: I succeeded in getting some cold meats (suitable to a shade temperature of near 90) in spite of the frequently advanced proposition that it would be 'better' (how or why?) for us 'all to have the table d'hote'.

We addressed ourselves to the road as soon as the meal was over.[107]

---

106 The Grand Guignol was a type of English theatre which made its appearance in Britain in 1908 and which has appeared from time to time ever since. It specialized in short, one-act horror plays. There was for a time an English company which called itself 'Grand Grignol'. Both took their name from the Théâtre du Grand Grignol which operated in Montmartre during the 19th century and which specialized in short plays of violence, murder, rape, ghostly apparitions and suicide.

107 In his letter to Warnie of 22 August Mr Lewis wrote: 'Shortly after our arrival, the "Lad" drifted in with a few belongings in a borrowed handbag. He looked a bit washed out, but was in great spirits. After a capital lunch we started out again. I had not much time in Oxford...I did not see the river or Univ. "It" seemed a bit shy of the role of showman and of course I did not press for more than he offered' (LP VII: 73).

Uncle Hamilton's car is a 4-seater Wolsley: I have forgotten the horse power. It is pale grey and wears a light hood. Our direction was South and West, so we ran out over Folly Bridge and towards Berkshire, thro' pleasant but tame wooded country. The weather was oppressively hot, even in an open car which our uncle keeps almost permanently over thirty-five miles an hour: when you dropped to twenty at a turn or a village a stifling heat leaps up round you at once. This first run was almost the only one where Excellency sat behind me, and it was about half an hour south of Oxford that he made his first mot, and one of the best of his life, by asking 'Are we IN CORNWALL YET?' Honest Injun, he did!

I don't know if you have a map with you: we drove by Nailsworth, Cirencester, Tetbury (I think) to Malmesbury ('MAWMSbury, Gussie' from the O.A.B.) where we hoped to lie. The people here have a very barbarous, uncivil custom of closing hotels, even to resident visitors, on a Sunday – this being Sunday. In this quandary various proposals were raised: the P'daytabird was in favour of going on to Bath and going to the largest hotel there – being reduced to a painful uneasiness when we told him that he could get supper, not dinner, of a Sunday evening in these small towns. Here and elsewhere through the tour Uncle H. displayed great skill in his family tactics of amusing all parties with a frivolous appearance of a discussion while he was preparing his own plans.

It ended by our pushing on to a place called Chippenham, which we made about five o'clock, and, liking the house where we had tea, we took rooms for the night. Aunt A. and I were sent to look at them, and the O.A.B., despite of all his pother of the feather bed overnight refused (of course) to look at them. 'If they satisfy you, Annie, they'll satisfy me.' Chippenham is one of (I suppose) a thousand English towns that one has never heard of, but once having seen, remembers kindly. It is perhaps about the size of Wrexham, but as different as the south from the north. Here are quiet streets with nice old ivied houses, at a strange variety of levels, so that you can look into their gardens, with a little river running through them, and very fine trees. These streets widen occasionally into what are called squares, being, after the manner of English country towns, any other shape in Euclid rather than a square.

Our hotel was very comfortable and nearly empty. After dinner of course we 'strolled'. I had some Leeburian talk with the O.A.B. and afterwards some, of another sort, with our uncle – about God: a monstrous unlikely subject under such conditions. He finds the proof of intelligible work, of a mind something like his own in the universe, because the universe does after all work: it is not all higgledy piggledy. The conversation was perhaps not worth saving, but he has great merits as a talker: he has many gaps in his thinking, but it is all absolutely his own – he never takes anything over. If he covers familiar ground he still uses maps of his own making.

I found him a wonderful antidote to the P'daytabird: the latter was made happily miserable by a Salvation Army band which played the Dead March from Saul up and down the streets – why I don't know. When we got back to our hotel we sat for a time in the dark hall on a very comfortable sort of benching, and the O.A.B. offered us drinks.

Uncle H. wd have some beer and so would I. O.A.B. (in his 'desperate' voice): 'I'll have a bottle of soda water. Here! Waitress: two half pints of bitter beer and a bottle of soda water – (pause) – and if you'd just put a little Scotch whiskey in it.' (The waitress goes and returns.) 'Here you are Gussie. Is that my soda water?' Waitress: 'Yes sir – with the whiskey in it.' O.A.B.: 'Hm'h.' (Roars of laughter from Uncle H.) This was truly in our best manner, wasn't it?

The next morning I was early astir, after an excellent night and a bath, to buy some aspirin surreptitiously at the nearest chemist's, having had a headache the night before but I never used it again. What is pleasanter than a hotel breakfast in a strange town – porridge, crisp fried fish, and an ample plinth? I have never outgrown the child's belief that food grows better with every mile further from our usual table (except tea, which I can never get good outside my Oxford residentiary).

On this second day I had a typed itinerary to keep me right: the Oxford journey, being unrehearsed, was not on it. In our seats at about ten. We drove through a hilly country, the weather being a little cooler, by Bath, Farrington Gurney and Chewton Mendip to Wells. The landscape has everything, tho' on a small scale: rocks, hills, woods and water. Chiefly you run along the sides of winding valleys. The villages and their churches are very pleasant.

At Wells I distinguished myself in a way to make you laugh: (should I remind you that it is the Cathedral city of the diocese of Bath and Wells?) We were not quite certain of our whereabouts, and seeing a military looking old gentleman standing on the pavement, I lean out and shout 'What's this place, sir?' M.O.G. (in a tone of thunder) 'The City of

Wells!' A minute later an irreverent little boy jerked a finger at the M.O.G. and informed us 'E's the Mayor'.

The whole street seemed to be in laughter. As Uncle H. said, it must have been the word 'place' which stuck in his gorge: we should have asked 'What great city are we now approaching?' I profited however by this lesson, and after Uncle H. had given me an itinerary and a look at the maps he had I steered our course very satisfactorily. The P'daytabird only advanced so far as to get hold of the Michelin every day and look up hotels: usually he looked up some place HE thought suitable to lie at: very often it was wrong – once or twice it was a place we had stopped at the night before.

We lunched at Wells after seeing the Cathedral. I do not know whether such things come into your horizon: I at any rate am no architect and not much more of an antiquarian. Strangely enough it was Uncle H. with his engineering more than the O.A.B. with his churchmanship that helped me to appreciate them: he taught me to look at the single endless line of the aisle, with every pillar showing at once the strain and the meeting of the strain (like a ships frame work inverted): it certainly is wonderfully SATISFYING to look at. The pleasure one gets is like that from rhyme – a need, and the answer of it following so quickly, that they make a single sensation. So now I understand the old law in architecture 'No weight without a support, and no support without an adequate weight'. For the rest, Wells is particularly rich in a wilderness of cloisters all round the Cathedral where one can cut the cold and quiet with a knife. There is a fine castle with the only real drawbridge I ever saw, just across the Close.[108]

We lunched pretty well in this city (I daren't call it a town) and were on the road by two. Henceforward the P'daytabird nearly always took the front seat since this seemed to please him. We ran through Westbury, Cheddar ('Are we in Cheshire, Gussie?' asked the Balloon), Axbridge, Highbridge, Bridgewater etc., into Somerset. All this was country I knew (towards the end), having stayed twice in the village of Old Cleeve: for this reason I had been able to name Dunster to Uncle H. as a likely stopping place. I had at first been rather troubled lest my apparent knowledge of the place should lead to long and tedious questioning from the

---

108 He means the Bishop's Palace, separated from the Cathedral by a moat. He refers to it again in his letter of 21 October 1925.

P'daytabird: but I found him advancing from his own resources that I had got to know it while stationed at Plymouth ('They're both in Devonshire aren't they?') – and did not pursue the subject.

Here it begins to be very beautiful. Through the village of Nether Stowey we climbed up through the Quantocks: they are a tremendous barrier of moor, with the most wonderful valleys, called 'combes', running up them. From the high ground we looked down into the last valley in Somerset – a little piece of ground that I love as well as any I have ever walked in. On your right is the Bristol Channel with the faint line of the Welsh coast beyond it. Ahead are the enormous hills of [the] Devonshire border, the beginnings of Exmoor, with Minehead just this side of them where they go down to the water. On the left are the lower moors, known as the Black Hills, and all between the pleasantest green country with no end of red iron streams, orchards, thatched villages and buried lanes that wind up the hills in leafy cuttings.

I pointed the Welsh coast out to the O.A.B. He replied, 'Ah, the thing's got twisted. It ought to be round to our left.' How I should like to draw a P'daytamap of England! It was a curious sensation for me to scoot down the Quantocks into Williton and on through Washford, passing at forty miles an hour through country that I had often walked.

We made Dunster at about 4 o'clock, and had our first engine trouble just as we drew up at the Luttrell Arms: my ignorance reduces me to saying that it 'was the gear jammed somehow'. Later on you may be able to gather what was really the matter. Uncle H. treated the business with admirable sang froid: his faculty of never being ruffled is a great virtue in a companion, and if life was confined to this kind of intercourse I really think it would cover all his other sins. The O.A.B. insisted on standing by with an expression like a pirate flag, making irritating suggestions: I made one or two attempts to remove him, in sympathy with our uncle, but of course they were unsuccessful. Later on he discussed the situation with me in private. I remarked that Uncle Gussie took it very well. O.A.B.: 'Ah Jacks, you don't know the fellow as I do. Making a mess of things like this just hits him on his sore point: he's as vain as a peacock. He's just fuming under the surface. That's why I waited: just to smooth things over'. Why by the way is any misfortune that happens to anyone but himself always described in P'daytesque as the sufferer's 'having made a mess of something'? It was finally arranged to have the car towed into Minehead, about two miles further on, where there is a well appointed garage: Uncle Hamilton was afraid that he would have to get a new part from Birmingham: the P'daytabird was strongly in favour of taking a 'day of rest tomorrow'.

For the present, however, we could do nothing but wait: and it was fortunately in the most delightful place. One of the many mountain valleys that I mentioned before ends in a small wooded hill attached to the main mountain by a sort of isthmus. The little hill is crowned by Dunster Castle: the village of Dunster winds up the isthmus, consisting chiefly of a very broad lazy street with old houses. The Luttrell Arms itself is a sixteenth-century building with embrasures for musketry fire on either side of the porch. Just opposite its door is a curious octagonal erection with a tiled roof, used I suppose for market purposes in wet weather. It was 'pierced by a ball' from the Castle during the Civil Wars. I remarked that this gave one a visible specimen of the trajectory of the old cannon: to which Uncle Hamilton very shrewdly replied that unless one knew whether it was AIMED at the thing or not, it told one nothing.

I am afraid that from my description this may sound a typical guide book village: as a matter of fact there is nothing really curious enough in it to attract the tourist, and it is more completely tucked away than anywhere. Wherever you look, through every V left by two meeting gables, you see the hills, so close that they seem to go straight up and the rare paths in the heather look perpendicular: it gives one a great sense of snugness. Only from the little garden at the back of the hotel do you get an unexpected view across to the cliffs by Watchet and the Bristol Channel. Nobody talks loud, nobody walks fast, rooms are deep and shady, chairs have their backs well broken so that you can't sit down without an 'Ah!', hotels are never crowded at Dunster. It has a personality as definite as, though antithetical to, Doagh. It has changed hands only once; from the De Mohuns to the Luttrells in almost mediaeval times. It's off the main road: nobody goes there: when I saw the car towed off to Minehead I had a notion that nobody ever leaves it either. Oh what a place for a soak – but not for a 'day of rest' with the P'daytabird. After an excellent dinner we strolled: Aunt Annie and I both climbed the nearest ridge – a very stiff scramble – and left the uncles behind, being rewarded with a fine view over Exmoor and the Channel: then, after the evening beer in the little garden, to bed.

Next morning was very warm again: the male section of the party – one of them most unwillingly, to wit myself – walked to Minehead to see if the car was done: the mechanic thought it would be quite alright. We drove it back and decided to take the road after lunch. The P'daytabird was now quite in love with Dunster (which he called 'Dernster', 'Deemster' and other wierd names) and was still talking of a day of rest. I noticed that he was usually in love with somewhere we had left: after anything good he could hardly be brought to admit merits anywhere else, and when he was, the whole process began over again. Thus for the first days, if you ventured to praise anything, you were told it was not to be compared with the Welsh mountains: after that it was Dunster that blotted every other halt than Land's End: when I left him he had settled down to the view that 'none of these places come up to' Salisbury.

But to proceed, we ran very comfortably through Minehead and immediately began to climb, tho' still on tolerable surfaces. We passed one barrier and saw the first real Exmoor ahead – tremendous mountains and awful gradients: but we weren't there yet and dropped into Porlock, a very pleasant town at the bottom of the moors. All through Devon and Cornwall a valley and a town are synonymous: 'they all live in holes' as Uncle Gussie said. At Porlock we had [a] choice of two roads: one the 'old' road and the other a private venture which the local lord of the soil supports by a shilling toll.

We paid our toll and Uncle G. was just changing gear in preparation for the next appalling hill when it stuck again. Telephoned back to Minehead for the same mechanic. More buttoning up of coats and stiffening of upper lips as per previous night. Aunt Annie and I went and looked at the Church – we found it cooler both psychologically and physically – for the sun was terrific (none of your traveller's advice here!). Apparently there is a bar that fits into a hollow cylinder where the gear works: and the Wolseley people 'have a catch of' making everything a perfect fit: which means that everything is just a little too tight when the metal gets hot. The bar was reduced by sand paper when the relief car came, and we had no more trouble with it. We were held up there for some three-quarters of an hour, greatly to the annoyance of the other traffic: and the heat as we stood still made us very glad to be in motion again.

Our objective was now Lynmouth, a very short run which would be occupied entirely in climbing up and down over the next shoulder of Exmoor into the next hole. Let me here solemnly warn you against ever attempting this ride on the Dawdle. The toll road is generally detestable in surface and hardly anywhere – after the first hundred yards – broad enough for two cars to pass: it ascends at a gradient which is habitually worse than Broadway hill and which seems all but impossible, especially at the inner corners of the twenty odd hairpin bends by which it reaches the top. The humourist who owns it has also left it without any kind of barrier at the outside, and everywhere the banking is all wrong.

I must confess that mountain scenery is often seen most impressively when I for one wd be least ready to enjoy it. To look back as you attack an almost perpendicular corner, down an enormous cliff: to see other hills piled up on the far side of the gorge and, in their unusual perspective from such a position, giving the whole scene a gauchmaresque appearance: to look forward at the same moment and see the road getting even worse ahead to the next bend: to remember that the cheery man from the garage told us that a car backed over into the sea further along this road a few days ago: to wonder what exactly you'd do if one of those char-a-banc came down – on my life I had the wind up. We did reach the top some-how, where nature played another practical joke by plunging us into a cold winter's day with a misting rain. It was fine here all the same: an enormous stretch of moor all round you, and a car going all out over a single road, which was now straight if it was rough. It reminded me of the opening chapter of Meriman's 'Sowers'. The descent from this into the next hole was even worse than the ascent. You just wind down the cliff edge on a road about seven ft wide, which touches, at times, the pleasant gradient of 1/4½. That's not my own conjecture, it's from some guide book of Uncle H. The view over the sea below you wd be very fine – on foot.

We were exceedingly glad to drop into Lynmouth, a little town wedged into this next wooded gorge round the edge of a broad, brown, stony river: the heights all round are perhaps too beetling, and to live there permanently would be like living at the bottom of a well. Our hotel had a veranda above the river, where we sat very pleasantly after the four o'clock and watched a water rat manoeuvring from stone to stone.

I had to share a room with Excellency here, and I am not likely to for-get the fact that it was the scene of a typical episode. We all walked out after dinner and up the road which we were to follow next day. Uncle Hamilton and I outstripped the others. It was a fine evening, delightfully cool and dewy. The road was good: it wound up the sides of big gorges that kept opening out of one and other into mysterious and chaotic landscape – 'forest on forest piled'. Looking back you saw the sea in the V shaped opening between the hills. Whenever you were still the sound of that stream under the trees many feet below and the EEe-ee of bats worked a kind of counterpoint on the general theme of silence. We walked faster: we talked most entertainingly. Finally we reached the top where these valleys, getting shallower and shallower, at last come out on the surface of the moor. We sat under a haystack enjoying the smell and the air of a good starless, moonless English country night.

We arrived back at the Hotel about eleven, and, incredible to relate, our Uncle gave me a drink. But when I reached my room, 'twas to be greeted by the O.A.B. in shirt and 'drawers' with the apostrophe 'Jacks, why did you do it?' How much real nervousness, how much pique and desire for drama went, and in what proportions, to making up a scene at once ridiculous and unpleasant, I cannot say. But the sound of the stream under our window drowned the puffings and blowings of the O.A.B. In fairness I should record how earlier that day, P'daytism had blossomed into something like grandeur: which it reaches at times, because of rather than in spite of its absurdity. After arriving there had been some discussion as to which hotel we should lie in. Aunt Annie suggested that the one we finally chose was rather too big. O.A.B.: 'IT'S NO BIGGER THAN WE ARE.' If only he had the right, no one could quarrel with his power to assume the grand manner.

I find that I have very few distinct images left of the next day's run, but I know that it was wild and beautiful. From this [point] onwards all the roads are bad. We ate Mittagessen at Clovelly. It carried the West Country tradition of living in holes to its logical conclusion, consisting simply of a stairway some 250 yards long with whitewashed houses on each side, ending in a cove and a jetty. The local tramway consists of a dozen well cared for donkeys on which lazy people travel up and down: goods are carried or trailed in a kind of wooden sledge. The bump bump from step to step is one of the most characteristic sounds of the place. Commercial enterprise has made the place convenient as a halt, for there are several eating places varying from the trimly modest and artificially rural where you can get galantines, salad and wines, to the frankly 'vulgar, easy, and therefore disgusting' where you can get – I suppose – mutton pies and brandy balls.

The O.A.B. strongly disapproved of going down to the cove before lunch, or indeed afterward over that infinite staircase: and it certainly was a very slippery and tedious journey of which you could say in Miltonic phrase

'Each stair mysteriously was meant, *nor stood*
There always'[109] *– where one's foot expected it.*

Arrived at the beach, he sternly refused the unanimous advice of his companions to facilitate his ascent by mounting one of the donkeys. Doubtless because he thought it unbecoming to his dignity: we continued to press him, for precisely the same reason: but he would not. After a hearty lunch, we proceeded.

This day we passed into Cornwall. I have always imagined Cornwall a place of rocky heights and gulfs. At first I was very disappointed: for, to be candid, it is so like County Down or parts of Antrim that it felt uncanny. The same absence of bright colours, the same cottages, the same sloping, somewhat bare hills, grey rather than green. The only thing that disturbs the illusion is the continual engine houses of the tin and copper mines: they are like this,[110] some in use and more half decayed. I can hardly remember a landscape which had not a dozen of these silhouetted on the horizon: they rather increase the general celtic dreariness and 'oddness' (you know what I mean) which bring it so close at times to our own country – a thing by the by far more insidious than the sensuous idleness of richer scenery. Are any 'flower coloured fingers' of the tropics half so numbing as the tepid morsels of putty that such places 'put down into your brain'?

The hills never rise into mountains, but are heaped together like eggs as far as the eye can reach, and the road winds on and on between them. The gates are coming off their hinges: the loose stones that divide the fields are all getting scattered. 'They'll do rightly – ach, never bother your head.' Then every little while you drop on one of the mining settlements: a valley probably, not unlike the back areas in France, splashed with great dirty pools and ringed round with enormous conical piles of shingle: and narrow gauge railways threading in and out like fussing insects among the debris. Why does a metal mine have such a glamour and a coal mine not?

The show parts of Cornwall – the parts one has read about – are all on the coast. We lay this night at Tintagel, storied name. There is a generally diffused belief that this place is connected with King Arthur: so far

---

109 Milton, *Paradise Lost*, III, 516–17.
110 He included an illustration in the original letter.

as I know from Malory, Layamon and Geoffrey of Monmouth, it is not:[111] it is really the seat of King Mark and the Tristram story. This has not however deterred some wretch, hated by the muse, from erecting an enormous hotel on the very edge of the cliff, built in toy Gothic, and calling it the King Arthur's Hotel. The interior walls are made of cement with lines stamped on them to represent stone. They are profusely illustrated with toy armour from Birmingham: a Highland target, suitable for Macbeth, jostles a reproduction of late Tudor steel plate and is lucky to escape a Cromwellian helmet for its next door neighbour. In the centre of the lounge, with the *Sketch* and *Tatler* lying on it, is – of course – THE Round Table. Ye Gods!! Even the names of the Knights are written on it. Then there are antique chairs – on which very naturally we find the monogram K. A. stamped.

I have not yet exhausted the horrors of the place: I was glad to see a book case in the lounge. All the books were uniformly bound, and I was surprised to see such unlikely titbits as the Ethics of Aristotle and the works of the Persian epic poet Firdausi. I solved the mystery by finding out that they were a uniform series of Lubbock's HUNDRED BEST BOOKS!!![112] How I abominate such culture for the many, such tastes ready made, such standardization of the brain. To substitute for the infinite wandering of the true reader thro' the byways of the country he discovers, a char-a-banc tour. This whole place infuriated me.

But the coast was wonderful: very like the Antrim coast only better: foreland after foreland stretching away on each side, and just in front of us, joined by a narrow ridge of rock and grass the huge Tintagel rock. There is a little sandy bay between it and the mainland. There are some remains of fortification on it, but not very old: nature has however so marked it for a stronghold that I could imagine its having been a fort almost immemorially. In the evening I extracted honey even from the hundred best books by reading an excellent play of Molière's. I cannot remember the title but it is the one from which the famous phrase 'Tu

---

111 Lewis is wrong here. Tintagel is given in Malory, Layamon and Geoffrey of Monmouth as the castle where King Uther Pendragon was wedded to Igraine, and where their son Arthur was born. It was subsequently the home of King Mark of Cornwall.

112 The choice of the hundred best books was made by the critic and biographer, Sir Percy Lubbock (1879–1965).

l'as voulu, Georges Dandin'[113] comes. Do you know him at all? We left Tintagel after breakfast. By the way it is of course pronounced Tingtagj-le: which was a sufficient reason for the P'daytabird's insisting on calling it TIntagEL, with a hard G. I find (like Bozzy) that 'I have preserved no record of the O.A.B.'s conversation during this period'.

We passed through a perfectly abominable town, Redruth. It was about here that a stinging rain, that might equally be described as a fast moving fog, attacked us. At Penzance we put up our side screens and excluded the view, but nothing would deter Uncle Hamilton from going on to Land's End: I indeed thoroughly agreed, but I was his only supporter. Of the last bit of England I saw nothing. Hot clothes began to steam under the screen and hood: outside there was only a genuinely celtic greyness: the road winds abominably and has no surface. My chief recollection is of Aunt Annie shouting 'Gus, don't run into that post!' We began to pass several hotels, nearly every one of which announced that it was the 'last hotel in England'. Some of them looked as if this was perfectly true. Our Uncle scorned them all and drove ahead till we reached the real end of the world where the road stops on a cliff outside the really last hotel.

It was pouring with rain and blowing a terrific gale. It is a place well worth seeing. The cliffs go down sheer, and one is so to speak in a salient. The same driving mist continued all the time we were there, clearing up for ten minute intervals with extraordinary suddenness every now and then. When this happens the blue suddenly leaps out of the grey and you see the clouds packing all along the cliff for miles, while a light house or some rocks about three and a half miles out turns up from nowhere. Indeed the appearance and disappearance of this place is what I most remembered. It has almost the regular phases of a revolving light: first the blank mist – then the outlines rather ghostly in it – then golden – then quite clear with hard outlines and waves breaking on it – then blurred again and so back into the fog. Watching it from behind the thick plate windows of the very snug hotel, I found there was something curiously soporific about it – this most 'debatable land' that comes and goes, as if it winked at you with confiding solemnity. Whenever the rain thinned we went out and climbed as near the cliffs as was safe and watched the enormous breakers.

---

113 *George Dandin, or le Mari Confonda*, is a 'comédie-ballet' by Molière first performed in 1667. Dandin, the hero of the comedy, is a tradesman who marries a nobleman's daughter and suffers many humiliations. His bitter refrain is, 'Vous l'avez voulu, George Dandin' ('You've got what you wanted, George Dandin').

We had – A big lacuna occurs here: some pages of journeying have been lost and you will perhaps be relieved to hear that I do not propose to rewrite them. Dartmoor and New Forest must remain unsung. Three more vignettes I give and then I will leave the tour.

The first is simply to record our monster run in one day from Lynd-hurst in the New Forest, thro' Camberley, Maidenhead and Oxford to Warwick, including our only headlight voyage.

The second is a good P'daytism – or shall I report as Minister of Experimental Philology a new word for an old thing – shall a P'daytism be a Balloon play or Ballonenspeil? – which occurred at Warwick. Uncle Hamilton could get no cover for the car which had to spend the night – a threatening night, in an open yard. When I lamented this fact, the O.A.B. replied 'Ah well, the holiday's nearly over now'. This remark contains so many distinct trains of thought and pure P'dayta ethics that you may spend a wet afternoon in disentangling them.

My third – as the Acrostics say – is connected with a certain Cathedral city in the North Midlands where I found the masterpiece of comic or satiric statuary. It represents a little eighteenth-century gentleman with a toy sword. I cannot explain how cunningly a kind of simpering modesty is combined with a certain profound vanity in this figure. Perhaps the eyes looking down the nose and the smug smile have something to do with it – perhaps it is the stomach thrust forward or the conventionally statuesque pose of the feet, as if to support a figure of heroic propor-tions, and then at once belied by the stiff little doll to which they really belong. Or, on second thoughts, perhaps it owes something to the colos-sal figure on the other pedestal, older and less ingenious work, obviously meant to be the centre and obviously made into the fool of the piece by its compulsory second. At any rate the effect is too funny for laughter: real genius went to make it. Need I add that the town was Lichfield and that the statue bore the mystic name – BOSWELL.

From Lichfield I returned to Oxford by train:[114] I am going home in a few days, but you had better send your next as usual to Univ. I was

---

114 In a letter to Warnie of September 1921 Mr Lewis wrote of the conclusion of his holiday: 'At Lichfield I parted company with Jacks very sorrowfully. He returned to Oxford and we pursued our journey. We lunched that day at Shrewsbury, another nice old town, with one of the very best hotels I have been in. From there we headed north. We had tea at Llangollen whose attraction is a very fine river. We were back in Capel Curig [Wales] that night...We spent two nights at Capel Curig – descended from there on Birkenhead "and so home"' (LP VII: 87).

delighted with your letter and have much to say in answer which must at present wait. I liked particularly your description of the rains – I can see that. Just one word about Paradise Regained – surely the real reason for the shrinkage of Satan is the very proper one that since the great days of P. Lost, he has spent sixty centuries in the Miltonic Hell? It comes out in his great speech beginning 'Tis true – I am that spirit unfortunate.'[115] Thanks for the photo. I hope the various delights of the season have left you in peace. I enclose my essay.

yours,
Jack

TO HIS FATHER (LP VII: 74–5):

Oxford Union Society
[Oxford]
Aug. 22nd [1921]

My dear Papy,

I hope that by this time you have begun to recover from your holiday and that the exhaustion of resting has left you. I am glad that you had at last the opportunity to return again to your favourite tit bit of the Welsh mountains. Certainly we had a famous tour: it deserves to be commemorated as Johnson's was to the Hebrides, but I am unfit for the job and find my recollections already in confusion. The elements of enjoyment and hazardous adventure were so well mixed that I do not know whether we should be more thankful to have gone or safely to have returned. I at any rate have felt much the better for it.

I have been pretty busy since I came back; and unless I were to tell you of the Roman Emperors I have murdered or the antinomies of pure reason that I have digested, I do not know that I have any news – except of bills! ominous item for all parents. Several worthy men whose services I unavoidably used seem all to have remembered the fact at once. There was a dentist who stopped a tooth: some one else obliged with a new pair of shoes and repairs: there was also a pair of flannel trousers. I regret two white shirts, as I should have had them but I found I had only one from Leeborough and it was indelibly stained. I also have had to get some new socks: those made by poor Annie's husband went to holes at once. As the conclusion of the whole matter I hope you will not think it extravagant

---

115 Milton, *Paradise Regained*, I, 358.

if I ask you for £7.18.6. Clothes and such are not usually a heavy item of my expenditure.

I have not forgotten the Magdalen inscription and am making you out a facsimile: but think again of my 'Laus fortius irritare' – the praise of brave men is their irritation – ask Barton about that. I have no news from Warnie since I got back, nor from anyone else. The drought has finally broken up, and we are now enjoying cool and rain.

I wish you could hear all the nonsense that is talked here about politics. In the meantime, thanks once again, very heartily for our capital jaunt.

your loving son,
Jack

TO HIS FATHER (LP VII: 80–1):

Oxford.
Aug. 31st, 1921

My dear Papy,

'For this relief much thanks'[116] says Bernardo when he is bitter cold and not a mouse is stirring. Thanks very much indeed for the generous enclosure.

As you say, the change from society for which 'lively' would at times have been too mild an epithet, and from the constant variety of our moving seats to the routine of ordinary work, is one that we are rather acutely conscious of at first. I still feel that the real value of such a holiday is still to come – in the images and ideas which we have put down to mature in the cellarage of our brains, thence to come up with a continually improving banquet. Already the hills are getting higher, the grass greener, and the sea bluer than they really were: and, thanks to the deceptive working of happy memory, our poorest stopping places will become haunts of impossible pleasure and Epicurean repast.

As for myself, I do not propose, as you may be sure, to spend the whole vac. here. I will do what I can: but I must 'sit to my book' for a little while yet. The fault of our course here is that we get so little guidance and can never be sure that our efforts are directed exactly to the right points and in the right proportions. I suppose that is part of the education – part at any rate of the game.

---

116 Shakespeare, *Hamlet*, I, i, 8.

I expect you have heard from Warnie before this. I had a letter since my return, the first for a considerable time. I am sorry to hear that he has had a bad attack of boils, followed by prickly heat: but he seems better now and is in excellent spirits and reading Dante. The revolutions which Africa has produced in his literary polity are really amazing. I am still working whenever I have half an hour to spare, at my account for him of our journey. It would be amusing and WILL no doubt be amusing for him to compare the two versions. We shall differ in selection and (so confused does one get) even on matter of fact, where a map will often show both authorities equally wrong. Uncle Hamilton on the other hand would be able to give exact information about every stage and distance – but totally incapable of describing anything at all.

I have had a touch of neuralgia, occasioned as I believe, by getting some water into my ear when washing and failing to get it out again. People tell me this is impossible and even suggest that the pains could not be of the types and in the places where I described them. I am rather disposed to take the view 'D–am it Cole, she ought to know. She's sitting on it.' Otherwise, I am in excellent form and acquiring new energy and spirits, as I always do, from the first nip of cold which is already beginning to steal into the air.

I keep on hearing of 'battle, murder and sudden death'[117] in the streets of Belfast. How long is this to continue I wonder? To me peace is so obviously the good and the condition of all other goods that perhaps I do not sufficiently appreciate the motives of those, in any party, who wish to settle everything by shooting. I hope you are keeping well, and that you already wear your shrapnel helmet when traveling on a tram.

your loving son,
Jack

TO HIS FATHER (LP VII: 92–3):

[University College,
Oxford]
Sunday
Postmark: 25 October 1921

My dear Papy,

I must first acknowledge with many thanks the needful, of whose appearance a letter from Cox informs me. Beyond a rather difficult

---

117 *Book of Common Prayer*, the Litany.

thesis from Aunt Suffern that is all that has reached me from the outside world since my return. The change from summer into severe Oxford winter increases the sharp contrast of the two worlds. I find certain home figures, some of those who habit on the edges of our world, like Bob and John, very phantasmal after I have crossed the Irish Sea.[118] W. owes me a letter, but it does not come. I really have no news.

Days here pass in a kind of hurricane. I am at lectures all morning: none of them yet shows signs of being bad enough to drop. One steals hours from work to talk to ones friends, hurries to meet and hurries to go away. The 'adorable dreamer' as some cove once called this city is less like dreaming than anything I know. Perhaps it is the cold that gives people the extra speed I observe in the streets – or is it only the contrast with the infinite leisure of the Circular Road. I find that considerable interest attaches to the great adventure of having been in such a place as Belfast. It is a curious paradox that Other Irishmen report such complete quiet from Dublin. By the by I mentioned that yarn about a certain public figure and his double role (the one I heard on the boat) to an Irishman yesterday, and he said he had already heard it. So the rumour, however ridiculous, is wide spread.

My journey here, though not unpleasant, deserves to be remembered for the continual misinformation. They seem to work with half a dozen different time tables in England now. Indeed the disorganization of all the ordinary conveniences of life, the general thorough badness of everything from a Gold Flake[119] upwards, is what impressed me most in this year of grace.

I hope you are keeping well and that your Uncle Hamilton has taken you for another of his nice rides.

your loving son,
Jack

TO HIS FATHER (LP VII: 93–4):

Union Society,
Oxford
30th
Postmark: 30 November 1921

---

118 Jack had just returned from several weeks with his father at Little Lea.
119 Jack's favourite brand of cigarettes.

My dear Papy,

Very many thanks for your kind note of good wishes and for the enclosure. It's a dreadful age, isn't it? By next year however I hope you will be finished at long last with my education and that I shall be unloading for the benefit of an astonished world the cargo that I have been so long in taking aboard.

I have had a touch of flu'. At least I suppose it may be called flu' since anything of the cough and cold variety now goes by that name. Although it has not been severe it has taken some time to shake off – this must be my defence for not having written before. I have also been warned by Aunt Kitty[120] that I am soon to be invited to London to assist at the wedding of some cousin infinitely remote. Her name appears to be 'Fireryee' or something of that sort. (Aunt Kitty's writing is awful). Of course I shall not go – can't you see me. You will be glad to hear however that 'dear old Bob' has been with them to Tonbridge and 'has been SUCH a help in making arrangements and in ENTERTAINING THE YOUNG COUPLE'. Truly an excellent air at Tonbridge that can do such things with our Bob.

I am afraid that my weakness in yielding to the Colonel's request for a copy of Optimism has reduced the poor man to permanent silence. I must try to get some sort of letter off to him before Christmas. A dread portent has arisen above our horizon here – an immoralist, nihilist, determinist, fatalist. What are you to do with a man who denies absolutely everything? The joke is that he's an army officer on a course. He talks you blind and deaf. The more I see of him the clearer does my mental picture become of his brother officers en masse – imploring him to take advantage of a two years course at Oxford – or Cathay or the Moon.

It is very cold here, but that is alright once you are used to it. I hope you keep well. The alarums and excursions of which I read daily in the paper are coming unpleasantly near places which you cannot choose but frequent.

Always reflect that the man who omits any possible and reasonable caution is simply a fool. But 'Lord knows what disorders we shall fall into'. With many thanks again.

your loving son,
Jack

---

120 This is Mrs Kitty Robbins mentioned in note 87 to the letter of 27 May 1917.

1922

— ❦ —

Warnie arrived at Little Lea on 7 April 1922, having been awarded a leave of six months.

TO HIS FATHER (LP VII: 129–30):

[University College]
May Day [1 May 1922]

My dear Papy,

Many thanks for your letter and also for the allowance which Cox have duly acknowledged. Also convey to the Maga Endoricana (that's scholarship) the thanks of the humblest of her servants: the rain of satisfaction has descended on the desert of appetite and the palate of enjoyment has signed the contract of marriage with the incarnation of perfect plumcakes, and the adamantine strength of sugar has been the Cadi. In the name of Allah (the compassionate, the all powerful) – 'thus far into the bowels of the cake have we dug down without impediment'. It has been praised of many and eaten of not a few, so if your unexpired portion is less than a ton, put it in your trench mortar and igniting the fuse, take cover and poop it in the direction of Oxford. With examinations in my head this at once leads to suggestions – curious the way the mind works – 'Trace the probable path of a plum cake projected from Strandtown to Oxford, noting any archeological or other etc.'

The news of Warnie's return is good and surprising. The news of his irreduced tissues is neither good nor surprising. But here is a good story for a tropical veteran. Coming the other day to a stream bridged by a single plank, I was just going to cross when, Lo, a khaki and black snake as long as my arm and as thick as the handle of a cricket bat. Yah! Where are the tropics now? It's my belief that this Sierra Leone business has been greatly exaggerated. As a matter of fact my snake was dead: it can't have been naturally as fat as that, but it would be accounted for by mortification. The colonel will tell you about dead 'balloon' horses in France.

I hope you will both believe my snake story and thereby show your originality, for no one else has. The popular theory is that it was a toy one, put there by little boys, and that the little boys were watching behind a hedge while I threw stones at it (à la Willie Jaffé) to see if it was dead.

In a country pub the other day I had a wonderful conversation with an old ranker who got a commission during the war and was at Drumshambo, Co. Leitrim: though sentenced to death twice by the I.R.A.,[1] he thinks the Irish 'very nice people' and rather inclines to the view that the English are to blame for most of the trouble. These old soldiers of fortune who have been everywhere are surely a unique and pleasing feature of our time? And does not his view – whether right or wrong – of the Irish question, illustrate the extraordinary fairness of the English masses. I should like to hear a French or a German Tommy after being in a similar situation.

It keeps very cold here, and mocks one with spring sunshine without heat. I am very busy, but very fit. I hope you have been reading about the Royal Commission on Oxford in the papers, and that the pundits are 'satisfied' with it. What the papers don't mention is that the Commission is composed entirely OF OXFORD MEN. However, Geddism is beginning to be felt in other ways. People who are trying for the Home Civil tell me there is not one vacancy this year and probably none next. Yet in the lower ranks it is full of conscientious objectors who got there during the war. The 'Grand Guignol' has been here, but I did not go. I hope you are well and in good form.

your loving son,
Jack

TO HIS FATHER (LP VII: 140–1):

[University College]
May 18th [1922]

My dear Papy,

Many thanks for your letter. Your news of a post at our back gate was, I must admit, rather a shock to the imagination when I first read it. I hope it will not 'draw the enemy's fire'. You will be in a position of the front area people in France, when they used to put up a notice for the benefit of Warnie's friends ET HOC GENUS OMNE, 'Don't raise a dust:

---

1 Irish Republican Army.

we live here, you don't'! Are you searched every morning on your way into town?

And now I want to talk about my plans. You will remember a talk we had when I was last at home. On that occasion I repeated to you a conversation which had taken place some time before between one of my tutors and myself. I had asked him for a testimonial, preparatory to giving my name to the employment agency. Instead of giving me one he advised me very earnestly not to take any job in a hurry: he said that if there was nothing for me in Oxford immediately after Greats, he was sure that there would be something later: that College would almost certainly continue my scholarship for another year if I chose to stay up and take another school, and that 'if I could possibly afford it' this was the course which he would like me to take. He ended with some complimentary remarks.

I was not particularly keen at the time about doing so: partly on your account, partly because I did not care to survive most of my contemporaries. At that time there seemed to be one or two things in view – a vacant fellowship at Lincoln, another at Magdalen. Soon however it 'transpired' (I know you love the word) that one of these was to lapse and the other be filled from its own college without open election. I thought of the Civil Service: but as my tutor says, 'There is no Civil Service now'. Thanks to the Geddes axe there will be none next.[2]

The advice of my first tutor was repeated by my other one: and with new points. The actual subjects of my own Greats school are a doubtful quantity at the moment: for no one quite knows what place classics and philosophy will hold in the educational world in a year's time. On the other hand the prestige of the Greats school is still enormous: so that what is wanted everywhere is a man who combines the general qualification which Greats is supposed to give, with the special qualifications of any other subjects. And English Literature is a 'rising' subject. Thus if I cd. take a First or even a Second in Greats, AND a first next year in English Literature, I should be in a very strong position indeed: and during the extra year I might reasonably hope to strengthen it further by adding some other University prize to my 'Optimism'.

2 Sir Eric Geddes (1875–1937) was from August 1921 to March 1922 chairman of the committee appointed by the Chancellor of the Exchequer to advise on all questions of national expenditure. In his report, published in *The Times* (10 May 1922), p. 18, he mentions the need to economize in education.

'While I yet pondered' came the news of a substantial alteration in the English Schools. That course had formerly included a great deal of philology and linguistic history and theory: these are now being thrown over and formed into a separate school, while what remains is simply literature in the ordinary sense – with the exception of learning to read a very few selected passages in Anglo-Saxon, which anyone can do in a month. In such a course, I should start knowing more on the subject than some do at the end: it ought to be a very easy proposition compared with Greats. All these considerations have tended to confirm what my tutor advised in the first place.

You may probably feel that a subject of this sort ought to be left for discussion by word of mouth: but, while I do not want to hurry you, my decision must be taken in the near future, as, if I stay up, I must apply to College for permission to do so and for the continuation of my scholarship; if not, I must beat up the agency at once. And after all, I do not know what discussion can do beyond repeating the same points over again. The facts – I hope my account is intelligible – naturally suggest all the pros and cons. I ought, in fairness, to say that I am pretty certain I can get a job of some sort as I am: but if it comes to schoolmastering, my inability to play games will count against me. Above all, I hope it is clear that in no case will Greats be wasted.

The point on which I naturally like to lean is that the pundits at Univ. apparently don't want me to leave Oxford. That is rather a loathsome remark for any man to make about himself – but no one overhears us, and it really is relevant. Now if, on all this, you feel that the scheme is rather a tall order and that my education has already taken long enough, you must frankly tell me so, and I shall quite appreciate your position. If you think that the chance thus offered can and ought to be taken, I shall be grateful if you will let me know as soon as may be. It is just possible that I might be able to help towards this extra year by getting a thing called the John Locke scholarship, but I have not yet discussed this with my tutor, and, as it is quite in the air, it can hardly be taken into account in what military men call 'appreciating the situation'.

My only bit of news is the adventure, if so you can call it, of seeing the Asquiths.[3] It happened while I was waiting in a queue to see a ballet to

---

3 These were Herbert Henry Asquith (later Earl of Oxford and Asquith, 1852–1928), who was Prime Minister 1908–16, and his second wife, Margot, whose magnetic personality proved to be something of a liability to her husband. Volume II of *The Autobiography of Margot Asquith* had just been published.

which I went because several of my friends were performing. She – Mrs Asquith – is much, much worse than even the memoirs or the photographs have made me believe. But the joke of the thing – for which I mentioned it – was the buzz of the crowd 'Mrs Asquith – Mrs Asquith' and the total indifference of everyone to poor old Asquith himself, flopping heavily out of the car behind her. How are the mighty fallen!

I enclose some old papers from the History Schools on which the Colonel may test how much knowledge of his period he has gained from these years of memoir reading.[4] I have got a poem accepted by a periodical called the Beacon – but I don't know when you'll see it. The usual plan is to wait one month for a reply, three more for the proofs, two more for its appearance, and Lord-knows-how-many-more for payment.[5]

your loving son,
Jack[6]

Lewis took his examination for Literae Humaniores *or 'Greats' during 8 to 14 June, and he was now waiting to hear the results.*

TO HIS FATHER (LP VII: 163):

University College,
Oxford
Wednesday [21 June 1922]

My dear Papy,

I have waited for some days to try and get a bird's eye view from a distance before telling you anything – only to find how difficult it is to form or keep any opinion of what I've done. With the history papers where I can look up facts and see how near or far I was, it is easier: and on these I think I have done pretty fairly – in one case, very much better than I expected. But my long suit is the philosophy and here it is like trying to criticize an essay you wrote a week ago and have never seen again, nor ever read over. Sometimes I feel I have done badly, sometimes that I have done brilliantly. Last night however I got a little light from my tutor who repeated the following conversation he had had with one of the

---

4 Memoirs of those in and around the court of Louis XIV.
5 It took longer than he thought. The poem, 'Joy', was published in *The Beacon*, III, No. 31 (May 1924). It is reprinted in *Collected Poems* (1994).
6 Mr Lewis sent a telegram at once saying, 'Stay on.'

examiners. 'One of your young men seems to think that Plato is always wrong' – 'Oh! Is it Simpson?' 'No.' 'Blunt? Hastings?'[7] 'No, man called Lewis: seems an able fellow anyway.' So that is good as far as it goes.

On the whole I may sum up: I don't at all know whether I have got a first or not, but at least I know that there was nothing in the nature of a debacle. Of course the VIVA[8] is still ahead, and there the family ability to bluff on paper will be no use. The Runic Salda will never do across the viva table. Luckily we had a spell of cool weather for the exam, which for six hours writing a day for six days is a great blessing. I hope you are keeping well.

your loving son,

Jack

TO HIS FATHER (LP XI: 263–4):

Univ. Coll.

July 20th [1922]

My dear Papy,

I am now close to my viva and of course on that subject I have nothing new to tell you. The details of the examination for the Magdalen Fellowship have however been published at last. The subjects are, as was expected, identical with those of Greats: but it is also notified that candidates may send in a dissertation on any relevant subject in addition to competing on the papers. I felt at once that this gave me a great pull. To choose your topic at your ease, to strike out your own line and display a modicum of originality – these, for men of our ilk, are more promising roads to victory than mere answering of questions. Indeed this condition is a rare bit of luck and of course I am all agog to begin. Naturally I shall not sit seriously to the work until my viva is over.

Under these circumstances you will understand that I cannot promise an early return home. I must see how I get on. No doubt this is disappointing for us all: but apart from that – on the score of health – you need have no misgiving. I am in excellent form at the moment and I shall not play the fool: midnight oil and ten hours a day were never my passion, and I am careful about the daily walk. Being confident on that

---

7 Philip Overend Simpson, Henry Pyot Blunt, and John Maurice Hastings – all of University College.

8 *Viva voce* ('by or with the living voice') or oral examination.

score I feel it would be folly to throw away any chance for the sake of an immediate holiday. Also – odious factor – in my present position it is advisable to be on the spot, to be seen, to let people remember that there's a young genius on the look out for a job. In the meantime I find the financial water a trifle low. I have had examination fees and a few odd wardrobe repairs to pay and I look forward to more expenses, including tipping, when I take my degree. The dates of terms naturally make a long interval between my spring and autumn allowances, but it has not been worth bothering you about before, and last year the Chancellors Prize helped to fill up. I had hoped to combine a little light tutoring with my own work – which would have been useful experience apart from the shekels – but I was too late and the possible jobs in Oxford were filled up.[9] Could you then let me have £25? I am sorry to 'cut and come again' but you will understand the reasons.

I thought I had got hold of a temporary job for next year the other day. It was before I knew full details of the Magdalen fellowship, and consisted of a classical lectureship at University College, Reading. For geographical reasons I had hoped that this would combine – by means of a season ticket – the diplomatic or 'advertisement' advantages of keeping in touch with Oxford with the advantages of a salaried post. This however turned out impossible. As well, pure classics is not my line. I told them quite frankly and they gave the job to some one else. Perhaps also I was too young. My pupils would nearly all have been girls. The funny thing was that the head of their classical department and one of the committee who interviewed me was Eric Dods. I had lunch with him in Reading and some talk. He is a clever fellow, but I didn't greatly take to him somehow.[10]

Arthur has been staying in Oxford.[11] He was painting and I was working, but we saw a good deal of one another. He is enormously improved

---

9 Lewis meant he could not get any tutoring with University College. He was feeling the
   financial pinch badly, and he had decided to strike out on his own and look for
   students. He ran the following advertisement in *The Oxford Times* on 23 June, 30 June
   and 7 July 1922: 'Undergraduate, Classical Scholar, First-class in Honour Moderations,
   University Prizeman will give TUITION, Philosophy, Classics, to Schoolboy or
   Undergraduate in Oxford, August, September. Highest references – Write D3, 183,
   "Times' Office, Oxford."'

10 This is E.R. Dodds, first mentioned in note 28 to the letter of 30 September 1914.
    Dodds was a lecturer in classics at University College, Reading, 1919–24, and Lewis's
    interview with him on 24 June is described in his diary (*AMR*), pp. 54–5.

11 Arthur's visit is described in *AMR*. While in Oxford he stayed with Lewis and the
    Moores at 28 Warneford Road.

and I didn't feel the qualms which I once should have about introducing him to people. He is not a brilliant talker and he seldom sees a joke but his years in London are brightening him up amazingly. His painting is getting on and he did one landscape here which I thought really good.

I hope you all do well. Belfast now figures less in the Daily Mail and silence, I suppose, is now best news.

your loving son,
Jack

TO ARTHUR GREEVES (W):

28 Warneford Rd.,
Oxford
[25 July 1922]

My dear Arthur,

We were all glad to get your letter and not only for the enclosure as you might maliciously say! Although we may seem to you at times ribald spectators we really feel the greatest sympathy for your present restoration to the paternal roof tree.

We all miss you very much and so, no doubt, do our neighbours. Veronica[12] is so heart broken that she has not sent us any word since. We duly delivered your message to Miss Wibelin[13] who has her exam. to morrow and is in an awful state of nerves. Baker is rehearsing for his play but is out nearly every day: it is going to be perfectly absurd and we are trying to arrange for Miss W., Maureen and me to go to it together.[14] The Doc is not very well and is going to Brittany in a few weeks.[15] Baker, by

---

12 Veronica FitzGerald Hinkley was a native of Oxford and a member of Lady Margaret Hall. She had just finished Schools and she took her BA in 1922.

13 Vida Mary Wiblin (1895–1937) was born in Oxford and matriculated at the Society of Oxford Home-Students (later to become St Anne's College) in 1920. She received her Bachelor of Music in 1924. She went on to read for a degree in Latin and Greek and took her BA in 1926. From 1926 to 1937 she was musical director at Magdalen College School, where she was a well-known and loved figure. Vida Mary was a close friend of the 'family', and in return for giving Maureen violin lessons, Lewis tutored her in Latin.

14 Leo Baker was admitted to hospital, suffering from nervous exhaustion, after finishing Schools. Mrs Moore arranged for him to come and convalesce at 28 Warneford Road, where he was to remain for some weeks. The play, *Glorious England* (1922), was by Baker's friend Bernice de Bergerac. It was performed in the priory gardens of Christ Church on 31 July.

15 'The Doc' was Mrs Moore's brother, Dr John Hawkins Askins (1877–1923). He was born in County Louth and educated at Trinity College, Dublin, where he obtained a

the bye, met an American woman in London who has devoted the last twenty years of her life to astrology. Without the least knowledge of his intended career she told him that he was going on the stage and prophesied early success.[16] I fancy this is telepathy and that the 'astrology' is all rot. I don't and won't see what stars have to do with it.

Ever since you left, it has been beastly weather, but to day was beautiful. We have the french window open in the dining room and a glorious night outside – there was a fine sunset awhile ago over the church tower.

Such a tragedy! On Friday we found the poor 'dam' Vee' lying dead in the hall, poisoned apparently. Before we were out of mourning for him a tiny fluffy black kitten from across the way began to visit us – and we really believe it is his son, for Vee led the devil of a life.

Do you remember my mentioning the Chanson de Roland in the old days? It is the Norman epic about Charlemagne etc, written in the eleventh century: I have been reading a copy with the Norman on one page and the French translation opposite.[17] It is exceedingly fine.

You have made a mistake about the cheque which should have been only £4-10s., and Minto remembers she owed you 2/1 so I enclose the balance of 12/2 with many thanks. Minto was most distressed at forgetting the 2/1 when you were going & we both hope you were not short for the journey.

Everyone sends best love (except Tibbie who is in a bad temper because of the intrusions of 'Vee's' son who ate all her supper and you should have seen her face). Minto specially asks me to say how much we enjoyed your being here & to add both our hopes that you will soon repeat your visit.

Bachelor of Medicine in 1904. He was commissioned a lieutenant in the Royal Army Medical Corps in 1915, and was promoted to captain in 1916. He was wounded in January 1917. Following his marriage to Mary Emmet Goldsborough, of Washington, DC, they lived in Clevedon, where their daughter Peony was born. Dr Askins' heath seems to have been broken by the war, and after his discharge he devoted much of his time to psychoanalysis. Shortly before 1922 he and his family moved to Iffley, just outside Oxford, to be near his sister. His wife's sister, Frances, was married to William Force Stead. See note 35 to the letter of 14 March 1921.

16 For some time it had been Leo Baker's intention to go on the stage. In his diary (AMR) for 28 August 1922 Lewis describes his visit to London to see Baker in his first professional role.

17 He was reading this 12th century poem in Léon Gautier's edition, Le Chanson de Roland: Texte critique, accompagné d'une traduction nouvelle, et précédé d'une introduction historique par L. Gautier (Tours, 1872).

Yrs. ever

Jack

P.S. Miss Wibelin says she's going to write to you. Lucky Choseph! Maureen has finally decided to leave school & devote her time entirely to music.

TO HIS FATHER (LP VII: 184–5):

University College,
Oxford.
July 26th [1922]

My dear Papy,

Very many thanks for the enclosure.[18] 'There's a power of wash-boards in that' as Meehawl Macmurrachu said when he found the crock of gold.[19] It is very kind of you to tell me to possess my soul in patience, when the patience has rather to be practised on your side. But let us hope that my unique merits will soon be appreciated and that I shall be able to rely on the inexhaustible patience of the tax payer and the sainted generosity of dead benefactors. In the meantime thank you and again thank you.

I have wondered, as you suggest in your letter, whether I unduly decried my own wares before the Readingites. I think, on the whole, that I behaved wisely: I am, after all, nothing remarkable as a pure scholar, and there is no good hiding what is so easily in their power to find out. As well one produces only misery for oneself don't you think, by taking on jobs one is not up to. Biting off more than you can chew is about the most poisonous sensation I know. As for the girls, if one considers only their faculties, it might seem an easy task. But then they would be reading for the same exams as the men: and that being so, the 'weakness of the sex' (assuming that they are dunces) would make the proposition all the tougher. It is a strange irony that Dodds who is a born pure scholar, spends his time lecturing on philosophy. As you say, however, the loss is hardly to be regretted: but there is a mean spirit somewhere in most of us that strives under all circumstances to explain away the success of the other fellow. The other jobs I hear of are mostly in America. In the wild

---

18 Mr Lewis sent his son £30.
19 Stephens, *The Crock of Gold*, ch. III.

west they seem to have a passion for young classical and other lecturers from English Universities, and offer what seem good salaries too: but of course that would be a counsel of desperation.

A curious little case was brought to my notice by a man the other day. A large asylum has sold some ground to Magdalen College. On the ground stand some cottages inhabited by tenants of whom the asylum wishes to be rid, but can't. The only access to these cottages is a path running through the ground bought by Magdalen. The Asylum, in selling, mentioned no right of way. Neither buyer or seller will allow the cottagers to go across, and they are in a desperate state. The interesting point is that a story goes that any road by which a body has once been carried out to burial becomes a legal entry to the house from which it was carried out. This is 'the custom of the country'. Have you ever heard it? It sounds pretty good rot, but such things usually have an origin, and England's full of quaint old survivals.

This is certainly the most miserable attempt at summer that I remember. I don't know if it's the same with you, but here we have perfectly autumnal mornings with mist and that indescribable thin smell that you get in October.

The storm centre seems now thoroughly shifted to Dublin. Long may it continue so! – a wish not so malevolent as it may sound. I hope you are keeping in the pink.

your loving son,

Jack

On 28 July Lewis had his viva for 'Greats'. On 1 August he and the Moores moved into a house they came to know well over the years – 'Hillsboro', at 14 Western Road, Headington, which road has since been renamed Holyoake Road. They remained there until 5 September when they returned to 28 Warneford Road. On 4 August Jack learned that he had taken a First in Greats, and he straight away wired his father this good news.

Warnie arrived in Oxford for a visit on 3 August and took a room at the Roebuck Hotel in Cornmarket. Jack had begun keeping a diary (AMR) on 1 April 1922 and we are able to follow in detail Warnie's main purpose in coming to Oxford – an attempt to persuade his brother to visit Little Lea in September. At the same time, Warnie refused to go out and meet Jack's 'family'. He later changed his mind, and he met Mrs Moore and Maureen for the first time on 5 August. The next day he moved into 'Hillsboro' where he remained until 26 August.

In October Lewis began reading for the English School. On 13 October he had his first meeting with his English tutor, F.P. Wilson,[20] *and on the day following he had his first tutorial in Anglo-Saxon with Edith Elizabeth Wardale*[21] *of St Hugh's College.*

TO HIS FATHER (LP VII: 263–5):

[University College,
Oxford]
28th [October 1922]

My dear Papy,

Your letter and wire both deserved an earlier answer, but you know when one is busy how easily tomorrow becomes the day after and that, the next week end. I judged that you would see my fate in the Times.[22] This needs little comment. I am sorry for both our sakes that the 'hasting days fly on with full career and my late spring no bud nor blossom showeth'.[23] But there's no good crying over spilt milk and one must not repine at being fairly beaten by a better man. I do not think I have done myself any harm, for I have had some compliments on my work. One

---

20 Frank Percy Wilson (1889–1963), Lewis's tutor in English, took a BA in English from Birmingham, and then a B.Litt. from Lincoln College, Oxford. While serving in the Warwickshire Regiment during World War I he was badly wounded on the Somme. He returned to Oxford in 1920 as a University lecturer, and was appointed Reader in 1927. He was Professor of English at the University of Leeds 1929–36, and Merton Professor of English Literature at Oxford 1947–57. He was one of the editors of the *Oxford History of English Literature*, and it was who invited Lewis to contribute *English Literature in the Sixteenth Century* (1954) to that series.

21 Edith Elizabeth Wardale (1863–1943) entered Lady Margaret Hall, Oxford, in 1887, and moved a year later to the recently opened St Hugh's Hall (now College). After obtaining a First in Modern Languages she became Vice-Principal and Tutor at St Hugh's and Tutor to the Association for the High Education of Women. She was Tutor in English at St Hugh's until 1923. Her publications include *An Old English Grammar* (1922) and *An Introduction to Middle English* (1937).

22 It was announced in *The Times* of 12 October 1922 that the Fellowship in Philosophy at Magdalen College, which Lewis had applied for in July, went to Henry Habberly Price (1899–1984). In 1935 he became Wykeham Professor of Logic and a Fellow of New College. He and Lewis were to debate a number of times at the Socratic Club.

23 John Milton, sonnet, 'On Being Arrived at Twenty-Three Years of Age', ll. 3–4: 'My hasting days fly on with full career, / But my late spring no bud or blossom shew'th.'

examiner, at any rate, said I was 'probably the ablest man in for it', but added that my fault was a certain excess of caution or 'timidity in letting myself go'. I fancy this means that I do not sufficiently use the kind of answer which is typified in the 'RUNIC SALDA', and that should be easy to alter. For the rest, except for the extra drain on you, I should be glad enough of the opportunity or rather the necessity of taking another School. The English may turn out to be my real line, and, in any case, will be a second string to my bow.

I very much appreciate your enquiries about the adequacy of my allowance, and hasten to assure you that it leads to no such privations as you imagine. I will be quite frank with you. It is below the average, but that is balanced by the longer period of time over which it has been spread. It leaves no margin for superfluities, but I am lucky in having found cheap digs and, as my tastes are simple and my friends neither rich nor very numerous, I can manage alright – specially as you have been always very ready to meet any extraordinary charges. I am very grateful for the slow period of incubation which you have made possible – and have no mental reservations on the subject. On the contrary, I very often regret having chosen a career which makes me so slow in paying my way: and, on your account, would be glad of a more lucrative line. But I think I know my own limitations and am quite sure that an academic or literary career is the only one in which I can hope ever to go beyond the meanest mediocrity. The Bar is a gamble which would probably cost more in the long run, and in business, of course, I should be bankrupt or in jail very soon. In short, you may make your mind easy on this subject.

As to looking run down – I suppose I am turning from a very chubby boy into a somewhat thinner man: it is, at all events, not the result of a bun diet. Your letter explains the wire (for which, thanks). I don't know whether my ear is getting very dull, but I must confess I did not notice the high lyrical strain until it was pointed out to me. Consequently I was completely baffled by the word 'copyright' and weighed the rival theories of a clerical error or a mental derangement on your part, with some interest. But now I catch the swing of it – oh that septennial spring!

I am drumming ahead like anything with my Anglo-Saxon, and it is great fun. One begins it in a Reader constructed on the admirable system of having nearly all the text in one dialect and nearly all the glossary in another.[24] You can imagine what happy hours this gives the young student – for example, you will read a word like 'WADO' in the text: in the glossary this may appear as WEDO, WAEDO, WEODO, WAEDU, or WIEDU. Clever bloke, ain't he? The language in general, gives the impression of parodied English badly spelled. Thus the word 'CWIC' may baffle you till you remember the 'quick and the dead' and suddenly realize that it means 'Alive'. Or again TINGUL for a star, until you think of 'Twinkle, twinkle little star'.

By the way I was quite wrong about Miss Waddell: it turns out to be Miss Wardale – an amazing old lady who is very keen on phonetics and pronunciation. I spend most of my hours with her trying to reproduce the various clucking, growling and grunted noises which are apparently an essential to the pure accent of Alfred – or Aelfred as we must now call him: as in that immortal work of Cornelius Jagenal's 'The upheaving of Aelfred' – 'Brother, what would you do if you felt a sudden etc., etc.' There does not seem to be very much excitement here about the election. As a B.A., I shall have a vote for the University, which is rather comic. And, by the same token, when you're next addressing a letter to me – and there is a propriety, a decency, an idoneity – Very cold these days!

I went to the Martlets the other night: now that I am doing English, I shall have to go regularly and take it seriously. We had a paper on Burns, read – of course – by a Scotsman: with libera-r-r-r-al quotations. I doubt if the Englishmen followed much of it. Of Burns I'm afraid I must say with Kirk 'Ach, I'm no good at that sort of thing'.

This is bad business about McGrigor's – I hope the Colonel had not much in it – I fancy not.[25] You remember the yarn about the officer who, being known to have a balance of £100, was tried for 'conduct unbecoming an officer and a gentleman'.[26]

I hope you are flourishing. Any more Artesian wells?

your loving son,

Jack

---

24 He is referring to Henry Sweet's *Anglo-Saxon Reader* (1876).

25 Warnie, who on 4 October became the assistant to the office in charge of the RASC at Colchester, had about £25 in McGrigor's Bank when it failed.

26 *Articles of War* (1872), 'Disgraceful Conduct' Article 79: 'Any officer who shall behave in a scandalous manner, unbecoming the character of an officer and a gentleman shall...be cashiered.'

On 23 December, Jack met Warnie in London and they visited their father in Belfast for Christmas. Jack remained at Little Lea until 12 January 1923, when he returned to Oxford and his work in the English School. His holiday in Ireland is covered in AMR, pp. 156–78.

1923

—— ❧ ——

TO A.K. HAMILTON JENKIN (B):

28 Warneford Road,
Oxford
April 21st [1923]

My dear Jenkin,[1]

I'm afraid this is almost unpardonable. I have outraged all decency towards you and every one else lately. My excuses are poor enough. Your card arrived on the day on which I had to go down to Bristol to the funeral of the poor old Doc. After all his troubles, after all our efforts against the nerve trouble, he died quite suddenly of heart failure – bloody business.[2] Since then there have been no end of minor bothers – a move to a new house with all its attendant labours and infuriating difficulties and incidental money worries.[3]

Also I have got myself thoroughly rattled about the future. I also absolutely forgot your card as if it had never been for the first few days. Afterwards it joined that huge mass of postponed correspondance which all this time has lain like a cloud at the back of my mind and driven me crazy. As to the answer (if its any use now) I can only say *don't count me in any arrangement.* If I get a pupil in the long Vac and make some money I may be able to come down for a time *late* in the long Vac. But as far as I see now it is long odds I shan't be able to. Can you accept the apology? I know that the fact one is plagued and depressed and tired is

---

1 Jenkin had taken his BA in 1922, written a thesis on Richard Carew, and had now returned to his native Cornwall.

2 The harrowing story of Dr John Askins' madness while staying with Mrs Moore and Lewis at 28 Warneford Road is told in *AMR*, pp. 201–18. He died on 5 April and his funeral was on 10 April.

3 Lewis and the Moores had been decorating 'Hillsboro' at 14 Holyoake Road, preparatory to returning there on 30 April.

not really an excuse for being uncivil. I can only 'cry your mercy' – I am like the first chapter of the Return[4] –

Yrs ever

C. S. Lewis

P.S. Your Chaucer Primer is in my desk & will be returned at request.

TO ARTHUR GREEVES (W):

28 Warneford Rd.

April 22nd [1923]

My dear Arthur,

Your letter was very welcome. We have been through very deep waters. Mrs Moore's brother – the Doc – came here and had a sudden attack of war neurasthenia. He was here for nearly three weeks,[5] and endured awful mental tortures. Anyone who didn't know would have mistaken it for lunacy – we did at first: he had horrible maniacal fits – had to be held down. We were up two whole nights at the beginning and two, three or four times a night afterwards, all the time. You have no idea what it is like. He had the delusion that he was going to Hell. Can you imagine what he went through and what we went through?

Arthur, whatever you do never allow yourself to get a neurosis. You and I are both qualified for it, because we both were afraid of our fathers as children. The Doctor who came to see the poor Doc (a psychoanalyst and neurological specialist) said that every neurotic case went back to the childish fear of the father. But it can be avoided. Keep clear of introspection, of brooding, of spiritualism, of everything eccentric. Keep to work and sanity and open air – to the cheerful & the matter of fact side of things. We hold our mental health by a thread: & nothing is worth risking it for. Above all beware of excessive day dreaming, of seeing yourself in the centre of a drama, of self pity, and, as far as possible, of fears.

After three weeks of Hell the Doc. was admitted to a pensions hospital at Richmond: and at first we had hopeful accounts of him. But the poor man had worn his body out with these horrors. Quite suddenly heart failure set in and he died – unconscious at the end, thank God. Of course I cannot pretend to have the same share in it as poor Minto, but I

---

4 Thomas Hardy, *The Return of the Native* (1878).

5 Between 23 February and 12 March.

am very, very sorry – tho to me the horrors he suffered here were much more heartrending than his death could ever be.[6] As you will understand we are all rather run down and dead tired, in mind at any rate. Isn't it a damned world – and we once thought we could be happy with books and music! We are at present engaged in moving to another house.

Your letter is rather cryptic. I gather you objected to your Irish visit more than ever – and so we shall every time till the bitter end. One thing in your letter however is excellent – I mean what you say you feel about your work. Thats the stuff! As you say, work is the only thing (except people of course, the very few people one cares about) that is worth caring about. I find it hard to imagine your way of thinking in painting – the technical side counts for so much more with you than with poets. One thing I take it is sure for all the arts – that the 'noble thoughts' and 'beautiful ideas' and 'vision' and all the other rot that appeals to amateurs is just what does *NOT* count for twopence: its the man who sees how to do something, that matters. I am glad you read Strachey's Victoria[7] – a capital book. In the intervals of packing etc I am working away at routine work for exams – chiefly the dull mechanical parts for wh. alone I am fit just at present. If you can make your visit to Oxford later than May you will be more likely to see something of us, for we're in the devil of a muddle at present. With love and good wishes from all the family.

Yrs ever
Jack

TO HIS FATHER (LP VIII: 119–20):

Univ. Coll.
May 27th [28] [1923]

My dear Papy,

I do not care to think how long it is since I last wrote to you. I have made some attempts to do so before this, but they have all collapsed under the pressure of work, or of the mere trifling and lassitude which is the reaction to work. You wrote to me that a disinclination to write

---

6 It would be difficult to exaggerate the effect of this experience on Lewis. He does not reveal Dr Askins' name in his autobiography, but it is the 'Doc' he has in mind when he cites a friend's madness as one reason for 'a retreat, almost a panic-stricken flight, from all that sort of romanticism which had hitherto been the chief concern of my life' (*SBJ* XIII).

7 Lytton Strachey, *Queen Victoria* (1921).

letters was 'one of the marks of approaching old age' which you felt or thought you felt. If that were true, what a premature senility is mine! It is a very ridiculous and a very wretched confession that I can hardly remember any period since I was a child at which I have not had a crowd of unanswered letters nagging at the back of my mind: things which would have been no trouble if answered by return but which hang on for weeks or months, getting always harder to write in the end, and contributing their share to the minor worries that lay hold of us when we have the blues or lie awake. That anyone should let himself maintain such a standing army of pinpricks would be incredible if it were not fairly common. Perhaps you will plead guilty yourself to a homefelt recognition of the state I am describing: if not, you are one of the proud minority. Our Colonel, on the principle of 'diamond cut diamond' knows how to defeat this laziness in another because he is so familiar with it himself. At Whitsun he wrote to me saying he would arrive for the week end unless he heard to the contrary: that at any rate means that no one can keep him waiting for a reply!

He came from Friday evening to Monday.[8] He is at present deep in Gibbon[9] and is very enthusiastic about it. I envy him his routine work – in itself apparently not uninteresting and finished definitely at four o'clock with the rest of the day free for general reading, with no uncertainties or anxieties. Despite the frittering away of time over drinks and gossip in the mess and the low mental level of the society, I cannot help feeling that for him the military life has solved the problem of existance very well.

The result of the Exeter fellowship has not yet been announced: but I have heard it said that it is one of those elections in which no electing is done: that they have had some pet candidate of their own in view from the beginning and are in fact merely delaying in order to 'give an air of artistic verisimilitude'. The rumour of course is unofficial but it came from a donnish source and is only too likely to be true. When I first heard it, it completely knocked me over: it was one of the biggest disappointments I have had in recent years. While ready enough to take my chance in an open field, I was disposed to question the candour or even the honesty of a College that set everyone's wits and hopes to work and

---

8 Warnie was there from 29 March to 2 April. See *AMR*, pp. 225–7.
9 Gibbon, *The History of the Decline and Fall of the Roman Empire.*

perhaps induced some to change their plans in order to give the false appearance of an election to what was in fact a kind of co-option.

I have since dismounted from my high horse of indignation and admit that this is the way in which the world is run and that a man may as well get used to it. Your own view of the Exeter project was quite right as far as fact goes: it WOULD be a small thing, about £200 a year and would be very rightly rejected on that account – if I had a supply of more lucrative and equally congenial openings at my feet or if you were a plutocrat who could, without feeling the strain, keep me indefinitely in my present position while I waited for the ideal job.

These however are 'IF'S and ANDS' according to the proverb. In the concrete situation I felt that the Exeter pittance was the shadow of a great rock in a thirsty land.[10] It would have given me exactly what I wanted: a means of subsistence during five years in which I could have gone on with my work, frequented the senior philosophical and literary societies, made myself known to all the important people, and produced a learned thesis after which it would go hard but I found a place here easily enough.

Your other argument about 'changing horses' is one that naturally occurs. Partly, one's conclusion on that depends on weighing chances and risks, not between a bird on the hand and one in the bush, but between two in the bush – which no two people will ever do quite alike. Partly – well I have taken the English school in such a very short time that a little interruption cannot make matters much worse. If I pull through it will be thanks to knowing most of the work before, and to a lucky faculty (which has always helped me till now) of being in spate at the right moment.

Our summer here consists of sleet, frost and east winds: tho' the summer invasion of Americans has come punctually enough. I mention this because they introduce a good American story which you may not have heard. In the old days of primitive sheriff rule in the western states a man was hanged and shortly afterwards his innocence was proved. The local authorities assembled and deliberated on the best method of conveying the news to the inconsolable widow. It was felt that a too sudden statement would be a little 'brutal' and the Sheriff himself, as the man of

---

10 Isaiah 32:2: 'As rivers of water in a dry place, as the shadow of a great rock in a weary land.'

greatest refinement, was finally deputed to wait upon the lady. After a few suitable remarks on the figs and the maize, he began with the following, 'Say Ma'am, I guess you've got the laugh of us this time!'

After my eloquent analysis of the state of the mind of the man who doesn't answer letters it would perhaps be incongruous to expect an early reply from you: but I shall hope for the best. I am very sorry not to have answered you before and thanked you for the enclosure, which I do now – if that did come after the gap, for indeed I am not sure. I hope you are in good health in spite of the vile weather: I, of course, have a cold.

your loving son,
Jack

TO HIS FATHER (LP VIII: 132–3):

[University College]
July 1st [1923]

My dear Papy,

Your letter came through unusually quickly and I am answering it after having slept on it. Before everything else let me thank you heartily for what it contains. I hope some day to repay these long years of education in the only way in which they can be repaid – by success and distinction in the kind of life which they aim at. But that is partly in the power of fortune and in the meantime I can only record that I am not foolish enough to take these things for granted and that the thought of how much you are doing for me is often, even insistently, before my mind.

The Exeter Fellowship, as you may have read in the Times, has been awarded – but not to the youth whom the rumour pointed out: what is more, not even to an Exeter man. The winner is a Balliol man and I am told is engaged in some archaeological work in Athens: this fact – that he already had some concrete job on hand which involved residence abroad and which needed money – must naturally and on the whole justly, have weighed very strongly in his favour and made him an almost deadly rival for the rest of us. The upshot, then, is that the rumour was false, and this fellowship at any rate, was awarded on its merits. While the realisation of the rumour might have been more flattering to our vanity, the actual result, as you will see, is – as far as it goes – an answer to the misgivings about influence which you mention in the first part of your letter and which, of course, I have felt quite as strongly as you. I will now turn to your next point.

I should not be a son of yours if the prospect of being adrift and unemployed at thirty had not been very often present to my mind: for of course the worrying temperament of the family did not end in your generation, and to quote Jeremy Taylor[11] 'we were born with this sadness upon us'. But, shaking off all that is temperamental and due to momentary fits of optimism and pessimism, I can only put the situation thus. I have, and of course shall have, qualifications that should, by all ordinary probability, make a tolerable schoolmastering job practically certain whenever we decide to give up Oxford as hopeless.

The same qualifications also put me fairly high in the rank of candidates for academic jobs here. The Magdalen people told my tutor quite recently that they thought my work for their fellowship quite on a level with that of the man who won it, except that it was 'more mature'. But of course the number of other hungry suitors with qualifications equal to mine, tho' not very large, is large enough to put up a well filled 'field' for every event: and the number of vacancies depends, as in other spheres, on all sorts of accidents. What it comes to is that there is a pretty healthy chance here which would, on the whole, be increased by a few years more residence in which I should have time to make myself more known and to take some research degree such as B.Litt or Doc. Phil. and which would be, perhaps, indefinitely or permanently lost if I now left. On the other hand, even apart from the financial point of view, I very keenly realise the dangers of hanging on too long for what might not come in the end.

Speaking, for the moment, purely for myself, I should be inclined to put three years as a suitable term for waiting before beating a retreat. We would hope of course that something would come along sooner than that, but I should take three years as a fair trail of the chances. I think too that there may possibly be a vacancy in Univ. by that time. It is unfortunate – or I feel it so – that even while we are on this subject, I have to ask you for some present money for expenses which I have had to meet. Some of them are rather old and have been paid. The items are, book bill £6-15, new shoes and repairs to old £2-7, grey flannel trousers £1-2-6, fees for examinations £5, two terms fees for Miss Wardale £8-15-1. I am afraid they loom rather big, but I do not think there is anything that could have been avoided.

---

11 Jeremy Taylor (1613–67), the Anglican bishop and writer.

The English School is come and gone, tho' I still have my viva to face. I was of course rather hampered by the shortened time in which I took the school and it is in many ways so different from the other exams that I have done that I should be sorry to prophesy. I have the chance of a little job examining for the 'Oxford Local' some time next month. It will mean very little money and a good deal of rather disagreeable work, but I shall take it because it will remind people of me and may lead to more lucrative work of the same kind some other time.

I am sorry to hear about the Goodman.[12] Although there is a good deal about him which I don't care for, he is such a familiar figure and has been a subject for 'wheezes' so long, that I can't help feeling what Macaulay calls 'a kindness for him' – and he has always been pleasant in his quaint way whenever I met him. I am afraid poor Mrs Greeves must be having a bad and anxious time.

The weather here is now warm and quite different from what you described at home. Once more with many thanks and hopes that all this business will solve itself soon,

your loving son,

Jack

On 16 July the University announced the examination results of the English School, and the following morning Jack wired his father the good news: 'A First in English.' Some time later, when compiling the Lewis Papers, Warnie made the following observation on his brother's achievement:

> *When we reflect on the circumstances of Clive's life during the time he was reading this School – the shortness of the period at his disposal, his ill health, the constant anxiety inseparable from supporting a family out of an undergraduate's allowance, his fears for the future, the unceasing domestic drudgery, the hideous episode of Dr John Askins' final illness, and the move to Hillsboro – we are*

---

12 Proverbs 6:19: 'The goodman is not at home, he is gone a long journey.' The 'goodman' (i.e. good man) or head of the house referred to here is Arthur's father, Joseph Greeves. He was very ill and had gone into the nursing home where he died on 20 February 1925.

> astounded at the extent of an achievement which must rank as
> easily the most brilliant of his academic career. (LP VIII: 140)

Arthur Greeves, who was still a pupil at the Slade School of Art in London, arrived in Oxford on 11 July and spent a fortnight with Lewis. There seems to have been a temporary 'cooling-off' between them, possibly owing to the fact that each was surrounded by new friends and new ideas. Arthur was comfortable with Lewis, but not with his Oxford friends. In his diary, Lewis said that when Arthur arrived on 11 July 'we renewed our earlier youths and laughed together like two schoolgirls' (AMR, p. 256). However, a few days later he wrote with disappointment that Arthur

> is changed...Someone has put into his head the ideal of 'being him-
> self' and 'following nature'. I tried on one occasion to point out to
> him the ambiguity of that kind of maxim: but he seems to attach a
> very clear meaning to it – namely that the whole duty of man is to
> swim with the tide and obey his desires...He has taken over from
> psychoanalysis the doctrine that repression in the technical sense is
> something quite different from self-control. (AMR, p. 257)

As he mentioned to his father, Lewis needed money badly, and no sooner had Arthur Greeves left Oxford, than he began correcting English essays for the School Certificate. These Certificates have disappeared, but they were a kind of miniature 'Schools' introduced by the Board of Education in 1905. Every boy and girl who had reached the age of 16, and who had not left school at the age of 14, was allowed to sit these examinations. The universities of Oxford and Cambridge had a large say in what went into them. To obtain a Certificate one was required to pass a minimum of five subjects of which English, Maths and Latin were mandatory. Upon completing the Certificate to the satisfaction of the Oxford and Cambridge Schools Examination Board one could, if one hoped to enter Oxford or Cambridge, take either the Board of Education's Higher School Certificate or Responsions – the 'entrance examination' administered by the two universities.

TO A.K. HAMILTON JENKIN (B):

Hillsboro,
Western Rd.,
Headington.
12th August [1923]

My dear Jenkin,

I'm so sorry your letter was not answered before – I've been having the hell of a job correcting the English Essays for the Higher Certificate, blue pencil in hand, twelve hours a day. You've no idea what its like. Fancy reading essay after illiterate essay on 'The Conquest of the Air' every single one telling you about Montgolfier[13] and his little fire balloons and ending up with a forward glance at the possibilities of the Helicopter. Now what might a helicopter be?

As to the important business – I'm afraid it looks like a dud. Our P.G.[14] (an atrocious little blackguard of a French nouveau riche boy with negro blood in him and the manners of a swine) does not go till after the first fortnight of September and then I'm afraid I shall have to go to Ireland for a bit. If the Blackguard shd. go a bit earlier (wh. I think is just possible) I will let you know at once and try to come – that would be early in Sept.

Yours, hot, hustled & fed up
C. S. Lewis

TO HIS FATHER (LP VIII: 161–3):

[University College]
22nd Nov. [1923]

My dear Papy,[15]

You wrote your first (and last) few lines before my letter reached you and I have been continually expecting an answer to mine. This,

---

13 Joseph Michael Montgolfier (1740–1810), the French aeronautic inventor. He and his brother Jacques (1745–99) built and went up in the first practical air-balloon (1783).

14 Paying guest.

15 Jack spent the period 22 September to 10 October with his father at Little Lea. Mr Lewis wrote in his diary on 11 October: 'While Jacks was at home I repeated my promise to provide for him at Oxford if I possibly could, for a maximum of three years from this summer. I again pointed out to him the difficulty of getting anything to do at 28 if he had ultimately to leave Oxford' (LP VII: 156).

combined with the usual reasons of a dilatory man, has eked out my silence to its present length.

I have a certain amount of news to give you, all of an inconclusive character. To get the least agreeable item over first, I am afraid old Poynton has proved a broken reed in the matter of pupils: I believe, because he put off the job too long. He is an oldish man and habitually overworked so I do not judge him hardly, tho' I was rather disappointed.

I had a really cheery conversation with my old history tutor, Stevenson – honest fellow, whom nature intended for a farmer: by which I mean no depreciation of his scholarship but an appreciation of his character. He told me that my name was much mentioned in connection with the vacant fellowship and suddenly exclaimed 'And I don't mind telling you, in my opinion it will be a scandal if you don't get a fellowship at this College or some College soon.' He also spoke of me to the new Master in the hope that the latter's wide acquaintance with journalism might give me a temporary lift by getting me some reviewing to do. Not to make the story too exciting I will tell you at once that this came to nothing.

It led however to an interview with the new Master – Sir Michael Sadler,[16] the education expert. I was very favourably impressed: he is much younger and more interesting than his predecessor and I fancy there is less of the 'to be sure the Bursar does that' business about him. He congratulated me on my past successes and added 'We will do whatever we can for you'. He gave me a new book on Wordsworth to review in a given number of words, which I found as difficult a job as I have ever done. He was however pleased with my effort which he pronounced 'Very much to the point' and wrote to six editors, including your friend Strachey, on my behalf. None of them could find room for me, but he tells me that there is still some hope for the future: and tho' I place very little confidence in it, it is as well to have established personal relations with the rising sun.

---

16 Sir Michael Ernest Sadler (1861–1943), educational pioneer and patron of the arts, was educated at Rugby and Trinity College, Oxford, where he took a First in *Literae Humaniores* in 1884. He served with the Education Department 1895–1903, after which he was Professor of Education at the University of Manchester 1903–11, and Vice-chancellor of the University of Leeds 1911–23. He was Master of University College, Oxford, 1923–34.

I have got quite recently ONE pupil, tho' not through Poynton. He is a youth of eighteen who is trying to get a Classical scholarship. I am to coach him in essay writing and English for the essay paper and general papers which these exams always include. I fear we shall win no laurels by him. I questioned him about his classical reading: our dialogue was something like this: –

> SELF: 'Well Sandeman, what Greek authors have you been reading?'
>
> SAND (cheerfully): 'I never can remember. Try a few names and I'll see if I can get on to any.'
>
> SELF (a little damped:) 'Have you read any Euripides?'
>
> SAND: 'No.'
>
> SELF: 'Any Sophocles?'
>
> SAND: 'Oh yes.'
>
> SELF: 'What plays of his have you read?'
>
> SAND (after a pause): 'Well – the Alcestis.'
>
> SELF (apologetically): 'But isn't that by Euripides?'
>
> SAND (with the genial surprise of a man who finds £1 where he thought there was a 10/- note): 'Really. Is it now? By Jove, then I HAVE read some Euripides.'

My next is even better. I asked him if he were familiar with the distinction that critics draw between a NATURAL and a LITERARY epic. He was not: you may not be either, but it makes no difference. I then explained to him that when a lot of old war songs about some mythological hero were handed down by aural tradition and gradually welded into one whole by successive minstrels (as in the case of 'Homer') the result was called a natural epic: but when an individual poet sat down with pen in hand to write Paradise Lost, that was a literary epic. He listened with great attention and then observed 'I suppose Grey's Elegy is the natural kind.' What idiots can have sent him in for a Scholarship? However, he is one of the cheeriest, healthiest, and most perfectly contented creations I have ever met with.

I am still weighing alternative schemes for my thesis in an unproductive but I hope not unprofitable indecision. I hope to get it straightened out before I come down. Whatever I fix on I see a good deal of work ahead. I hope you have got over the bad turn I left you in and are as well as anyone can be in this suffocating cold. Getting up and going to bed are two evil moments these days.

your loving son,

Jack

1924

— ≈ —

TO HIS FATHER (LP VIII: 180–2):[1]

[University College]
Monday [4 February 1924]

My dear Papy,

You will explain your long silence as an answer to mine – at least I hope there is no more serious reason for it than that and the desultoriness in correspondence which you claim as one of the penalties, if it is not rather one of the privileges, of the years beyond fifty. I, like the judge, have other reasons.

As soon as I had met people here I heard of a new will-of-the-wisp, a poor Fellowship at St John's now vacant and calling out for candidates. The warning that preference would be given to 'founder's kin and persons born in the County of Stafford' did not seem sufficient to deter me from trying my luck. At first I thought of sending them my old dissertation which I had written for Magdalen: but no man cares greatly for his own things when once the bloom is off them, and I decided in the end to write a new one. I was in pretty good form, but I was pressed for time: and of course there is a waste of time when one flings oneself back into work which one has abandoned for a few months – the old harness will not at once sit easily. It was only after I had sent this in that I discovered how small my chances must necessarily be. I had supposed – and who would not – that the preference for natives of Staffordshire etc. meant only a preference, others things being equal.

I find however that if any candidate appears who claims such preference and who has in addition either a SECOND in Greats or a FIRST in any other final school, he must be elected. I do not of course know in fact whether there is such a candidate in the field, but Stafford is a large

---

1 Warnie was still stationed at Colchester, and he and Jack travelled together to Little Lea where they were with their father from 9 to 28 December 1923.

county, and we may be sure that the founder was some philoprogenitive old fellow who, like Charles II in Dryden, 'scattered his Maker's image through the land'.[2] In short we may expect a defeat with almost complete certainty. I suppose that a privileged class of 'persons born in Staffordshire and founder's kin' is in the nature of things no more absurd than any other privileged class, though at first it struck me oddly. But in this long quest for a job I have determined to suppress all questionings about the justice of things and the comparative value of my own and other people's qualifications. Such feelings, once admitted, would be fatal.

I was particularly pleased, in a testimonial which my philosophy tutor gave me on this occasion, to read the following passage: – 'He has not only real enthusiasm for knowledge, as distinct from its emoluments, but an unusual originality in pursuing it on his own lines. He seems to me the sort of man who is most likely to do something that would justify endowment, though there are some who have directed their studies more immediately to its attainment.' I am afraid I inherit from you abilities that make it easier to produce than to advertise the goods.

This then occupied my first weeks. And I had hardly looked about me when a most irritating thing happened: I got chicken pox and am only now out of quarantine. I have of course been quite well enough to write for some time but I don't know whether you have had this complaint and thought it better not to chance infecting you: I am told that the older you are the less likely it will be to 'take', but the worse if it does. I had a pretty high temperature at the beginning and some very uncomfortable nights of intense perspiration, but it soon passed off. The danger of cutting any of the spots on my face of course made shaving impossible till this very day and I had a fine beard. I have left the moustache which would excite 'poor Warren's' envy, but I shall probably get tired of it in a few weeks. It is very stiff, and all the hairs grow in different directions and it is thicker on one side than on the other.

The greatest annoyance was of course that I could not get any light literature except what I happened to have in my hands. Here however comes 'the soul of virtue in things evil'. I have been converted to Thackeray. Somebody lent me a copy of Vanity Fair and as it was that or counting the cracks in the ceiling, I read that – almost at once with toleration

---

2 John Dryden, *Absalom and Achitophel* (1681), l. 10.

and soon with respect and enjoyment.[3] I think of course that it *is* a little jaundiced: the meanness of nearly all the characters is too much, and, what is worse, the author doesn't always know, I'm afraid, quite HOW mean they are. But this is amply made up for by its life, its pathos, and above all, its humour. Minerva House, Jos Sedley both at home in Vauxall and in Brussels, the Crawley ménage, the old aunt at Brighton, old Osborne saying, 'Jane, turn the cook out of the house tomorrow' and the Pumpernickel scenes at the end – all these simply beat Bannagher![4] The Waterloo scenes are splendid. How wise of him to avoid the temptation of a battle chapter – and how he gives you the feeling of war by those two slight references to the firing, heard far off the first day and a little nearer the second day!

Rawdon is I think one of the best characters in the book – he *Grows* so – begins as a comic figure sketched from the outside, and then gradually grows more and more human. But I must stop: I felt that I owed Thackeray a recantation in full. It's rather funny that I have since read 'Lady rose's daughter' by Mrs H. Ward[5] which opens with a situation taken consciously or unconsciously from Vanity Fair.

And now I am afraid I must fulfill friend Staples'[6] suggestion, 'Sons bleeding you?' You know of course that my Scholarship is at an end. It was nominally a scholarship of £80 a year. What I actually got out of it was about £11 a term. Sometimes it would be a little more or a little less, but it generally averaged out to £33 a year. My 'battells' or accounts for the last term from College show me that this time I am £3.4.3 to the bad instead of £11 to the good. (The items are not very enlightening – 'Domus Fund', 'Establishment Charges' and 'Service' which means I suppose that the porter says 'good morning' to me.) This amount will I think vary from term to term but will hardly go above £3.10. You will see that this leaves me with an annual reduction of income of £43.10s. I had

3 See the reference to *Vanity Fair* in the letter to Arthur Greeves of 20 February 1917.

4 In Ireland there is the phrase 'It beats Banagher!' or, in the local dialect, 'It bates Banagher!' which means that Banagher is the benchmark of excellence. Banagher, in County Londonderry, is a small town south of Dungiven, with a church founded by Muriedach O'Henry in the 12th century. I owe this reference to the Rt. Hon. David Bleakley, CBE.

5 Mrs Humphrey Ward, *Lady Rose's Daughter* (1903).

6 Robert Ponsonby Staples, who was distantly related to Jack and Warnie through the Hamiltons, was described by Warnie as 'one of the most remarkable and scandalous characters of his time in the North of Ireland' (LP III: 128).

hopes of being able to make up that in other ways – pupils and the like – but they have not been realised and I am afraid I must ask for help. I do not like increasing your charges – but as Kirk said, 'All this has been said before'.

I have lost Sandeman. He got good marks in his English in the Scholarship he tried for near Christmas and his mother and his other coach said the nicest things of me, when dash it if the fool doesn't go and break his leg. Then of course his mother, seeing a long interruption ahead and knowing that his chances depended on hard cramming, wrote to ask me what I thought. What chance had he? Was it worth going on? You may imagine that I chewed up many a pen and drew many a face on my blotting paper before I answered that letter, but of course, in common honesty, I had to say that his chances were not big. Perhaps I said it rather more plainly because I hear that they are poor – the father is bad or dead or something. At any rate Mrs Sandeman has decided to give the game up, thanking me for all the trouble I have taken with Austin – I have been SO helpful etc., etc. Poor Woman! – she says of her own son, 'I have tried every means I can think of to rouse some intellectual interest'.

I hope I shall hear from you soon – indeed, according to precedent, this will probably cross a letter of yours. It is miserably cold here and I am rather tired of four walls. I don't know that I have any other news. I have been reading the debates very conscientiously since the new government came in. Did you see Chamberlain's amusing speech?

your loving son,
Jack

TO HIS FATHER (LP VIII: 193–5):

[University College]
March 6th [1924]

My dear Papy,

I am sorry to hear about the 'flu'. You may remember that I had it about this time a year or two ago: and I well remember the black lethargy and depression which succeeds it. It is a period during which all seems 'weary, stale, unprofitable, flat': when all the thoughts which each one of us (I suppose) keeps at arms length, come in and take possession of the mind, till one is amazed at one's own ingenuity in finding out new sources of regret for the past and anxiety for the future. It is always rather 'shocking' – in the original literal sense of the word – to find how closely our states of mind depend on the states of our bodies. One reads now and then in the paper of people who have committed suicide through 'depression after flu' and one always thinks it rather absurd until one's own turn comes. However, it is unhealthy to chew the cud of these bad things. It is a horrible time, to be forgotten as soon as may be: and I suppose we should consider ourselves fortunate if it does not lead to pneumonia or any of the other complications which sometimes follow it.

After having said this, I trust I shall not be thought unsympathetic if I confess that the episode of the boiler, coming where it did in your letter, really had its funny side. Though it is very far from funny at the time, there is something absurd in the sudden descent to such a very prosaic incident – from the solemn world despair that we get after flu'. I do indeed remember the last time it burst. I remember your coming up in the twilight of a winter's morning to wake Warnie with the tragic announcement 'The boiler's burst': and the exquisitely unconcerned 'Is it?' with which 'as a door on its hinges so he on his bed etc.' I always regard that dance as one of the Hamilton's masterpieces. You and I certainly neither desired nor enjoyed it. The colonel may have had some pleasure of it: but I think the lion's share fell to Our Uncle and Aunt and their friends.

And now to business. The Univ. Fellowship has not been filled up. You may have read in the papers that a new 'Chaplain Fellow' has been elected, but that of course is a different job. If I don't mention it, it is because there is nothing new to say about it. Just at present a new and very good vacancy at Trinity (I mean Trinity, Oxford of course) has appeared, for which an election is to be held in the summer, and I shall certainly go in for it.

As to money: I had rather you had explained in detail what you 'don't follow' in my arithmetic, but I trust there is nothing seriously wrong with the figures I gave you and will proceed accordingly. What is more serious is your reference to £30 extras last year. The only part of this which I can at present identify are the extra tuition and the book bill. The former of course was purely abnormal and will not occur again. The book bill was naturally increased by my turning to a new subject. I try to use the libraries as much as possible: but when one is reading for a particular exam there are over a hundred other people taking the same books out of the libraries – and of course there are some things one must have at command. My expenditure on books will be less in future. I have a book bill due to be paid some time soon which is under five pounds: if you will pay that I think I can undertake to find myself for books in the future – tho' since you tell me to be frank, I will say that this may not always be easy. The rest of the £30 you mention is, I suppose, made up by items of clothing. I presume it does not include my two suits? As to clothing, I'm afraid that even if you increase my allowance as you suggest, I cannot undertake to find myself. I mean that my loss of the scholarship and my outlay on clothes would not be balanced by an addition of £40 or £50.

I cannot see how to cut down my expenses on clothing. You know I think that it does not go to fancy waistcoats or kid gloves. And I have some ties that date from before the war! Flannel trousers are an item that I have to repeat pretty often: they ARE ill wearing things, but if I didn't wear them I should need suits more often than I do. On shoes I admit that I am hard and have to get a good deal of 'soling' done: but I am afraid this reads rather as if I were defending myself against a charge of extravagance, which you will justly reply you never made: but you must not think that. I am only trying to put down the facts of the question as they actually occur to me from day to day in order to make my conclusion more reasonable and intelligible to you. And the conclusion is this. You ask me where £85 a term to 'cover everything' would be sufficient. If by 'covering everything' you mean covering my books, shoes, shirts, socks and other items that I have hitherto sent you, I am afraid it would not. As I said, if you wish it, I will try to undertake my own books in the future, and, at any rate to cut them down. I will also abandon the new dinner jacket suit that was mooted, and you must not imagine that I would feel that sort of curtailment as any hardship. As for a new over-coat, the one you gave me when I left home suits and fits me so well that the question need not be considered. But I do not think that I can manage to keep myself in minor articles of clothing.

I'm afraid this may seem to you but a charter of indefinite expenses for the future. Well then, to say all, if it is too much, you must tell me so. You have done all and more than all I can expect of you, and if you tell me that these extra years are too heavy, I assure you that I shall never, even in my secret thought, criticise such a decision. If on the other hand, you see fit to lodge £85 a year and to pay for such extras in the way of clothing, etc. as may occur, I will try to make them as little as I can.

I must point out however that it is much easier to save on the big items I have mentioned – the dress suit and overcoat – than on those necessary articles which have so often to be replaced. If you will give me a dress suit when I get a job, I ought to be able to tide over these years without any more 'suitings' from you at all. If, till they are over, you can lodge £85 a term and make it retrospective for the present year, while paying for my smaller articles of clothing, I think I can manage. And whether you can do this or not, I have nothing but deepest gratitude for the past.

I am not fretting against enforced idleness, for I am not idle, though I have made a change in my work. I started work experimentally on Dr Henry More[7] – a 17th Century theologian – with the idea of 'doing' him for a D.Phil. And I had a great deal of fun out of him before I stopped. He told me a great many curious 'facts' in natural history. You never knew that the leader of a flock of cranes carried a large stone in his mouth when in flight: the reason being, that when they alight, all the others go to sleep, but the leader, as soon as he does, is awakened by the sound of the stone falling. Or who would have thought that elephants had a religion and performed purificatory rites to the new moon? He was a very holy man, this More: his contemporary biographer tells us that his body 'at the putting off of his cloathes, exhaled sweet herbaceous smells, and his urine had the natural savour of violets'.[8]

---

7 Henry More (1614–87), Cambridge Platonist, was educated at Christ's College, Cambridge, became a Fellow of the College in 1639, and remained there for the rest of his life. Those works of his which Lewis was reading included *An Antidote Against Atheism* (1653), *An Explanation of the Grand Mystery of Godliness* (1660) and *The Immortality of the Soul* (1659). In them More sought to vindicate theism against the materialism represented by Thomas Hobbes. He did this particularly by emphasizing the instinctive reasonableness of divine truth. If it seems odd that Lewis should be interested in More, it is not because he believed in God, but because he believed in the importance of morals and ethics. During 1924 he was to write a number of papers on ethics, including 'The Hegemony of Moral Values' mentioned in note 9 to the letter of 9? March 1924.

8 Richard Ward, *The Life of the Learned and Pious Dr Henry More, Late Fellow of Christ's College in Cambridge* (1710), pp. 123–4: 'He hath told us...That not only his own Urine, had naturally the Flavour of Violets in it, but that his Breast and Body, especially when very Young, would of themselves, in like manner, send forth flowry and Aromatic Odours from them; and such as he daily almost was sensible of, when he came to put off his Clothes, and go to bed. And even afterwards, when he was Older, about the end of Winter, or beginning of Spring, he did frequently perceive certain sweet and herbacious Smells about him; when yet there were no such external Objects near, from whence they could proceed.'

I had not however gone very far in this naïf wonderland without deciding that I was on a fool's errand. The D.Phil. would add very little to my Firsts in the way of qualification: and in the mean time I should be letting my knowledge of philosophy and above all my Greek rust. I have determined instead to go on vigorously improving my philosophy and classics and also to learn some history – history being the gate to an All Souls fellowship, at which I must have my try. If to the consciousness of the long burden I am imposing on you and to the obstinate fears and despondences of the unemployed I added idleness, I should, I think, be mad. Work is our drug and we run to it as others do to drink.

The chicken pox has left no marks. Since your verdict on the moustache, tho' you had not seen it, agreed with that of everyone who had seen it, it has come off and I no longer front a stranger in the mirror. I think you were wrong about Warnie having had chicken pox 'as a little fellow'. I am almost sure he had it at Malvern. Uncle Bill, who was passing, came and looked at him through the window of the San. I was at Wynyard at the time.

Just two words more about Vanity Fair. I think an example of Thackeray's Waterloo art even better than that end of the chapter, is the passage where Dobbin pulls Osbourne out from Becky's and says, 'The enemy have crossed the Sambre and our left is already engaged'. That's the stuff! My second point is 'It was a damned unfriendly act?' Was Rawdon right? Is it a man's duty in the circumstances to shove his oar in?

your loving son,
Jack

TO HIS FATHER (LP VIII: 198):

[University College
9? March 1924]

My dear Papy,

'This won't do'. You really must not take so to heart my budget of expenses and economics, which was written, I can assure you, with no intention of producing such an effect on you. 'Cheese paring shifts and devices' has a bleak sound. But let us not be the dupes of words. It is natural for young men who have not yet made their way in the world to 'live close': you have had your share and I daresay a lion's share of this in your young days. I have everything to be pleased about and to be grateful for so long as I can peruse the goal I wish – how many have been forced into uncongenial drudgery before they had time to look round?

This is only a line to thank you and to answer your letter – but I must just mention a pleasant little success I had the other day when I read a philosophical paper to a rather unpleasant society who had brought the Professor of Moral Philosophy there to reply to me without telling me beforehand.[9] This worthy Professor said a lot of nice things which I discounted as 'manners': but what really mattered was that he said my idea was 'quite NEW' to him and 'very attractive' and advised me to publish it in 'Mind'. And as I heard him repeating the word 'new' to people in another group when we had broken up, I believe he really meant it.

your loving son,

Jack

TO HIS FATHER (LP VIII: 217–18):

[University College]
April 27th [1924]

My dear Papy,

Your letter with 'advertisement' as they say of doings with Cox's, is better than your word. We have now talked of this subject so much that I can say no more than that I thank you very heartily. I must also acknowledge your cheque for a dividend. 'The blessings that surround my path...'!

I have been exercised in the slightly unpleasant duty of getting all things in readiness for my application for the Trinity Fellowship – getting testimonials and talking to one or two people who will write unofficially for me. I also went to a dinner where I met the present philosophy man from Trinity[10] whose successor I should become if I were elected. This was done no doubt to give me an opportunity of impressing him with my unique social and intellectual qualifications. Unhappily the whole conversation was dominated by a bore who wanted to talk (and

---

9 In his diary of 6 March Lewis gives an account of how he read a paper on 'Hegemony of Moral Values' to the Oxford University Philosophical Society in Manchester College. The Professor of Moral Philosophy who commented on his paper was William Ross David (1877–1971) of Oriel College.

10 The Fellow of Philosophy at Trinity was Harold Arthur Pritchard (1871–1947). He was White's Professor of Moral Philosophy 1928–37 and the author of *Kant's Theory of Knowledge* (1909).

DID talk) about the state of India, and I suppose I hardly exchanged ten words with the Trinity man. However, it may have been just as well. A man who knows he is on show can hardly be at his best: and I was told that this Trinity man is a very shy, retiring, moody old man and difficult to talk to. In the meantime I send in my application and wait – reminding myself that the best cure for disappointment is the moderation of hopes.

I have just come across a book which I think you would find very much in your line. It is the diary of one William Allingham[11] (whom I never heard of before) a minor poet born at Ballyshannon, who lived in London in the very hey-day of the great Victorians. He was on intimate terms with Tennyson, Browning, Ruskin, Carlyle, Thackeray and the pre-Raphaelites, and the book consists chiefly of their conversations with him. Tennyson and Carlyle are the protagonists and there is any amount of good crack. One cannot help noticing however that none of the lot comes out of it half so well as old Johnson with his Boswell. They are not so savage of course: but what they gain on him in manners they lose in snap or 'pep'. But you ought to get hold of this book.

One never reads a printed diary without wishing to be a diarist one-self. What would I not give for a diary of my days in France – or better still a diary of Bookham recorded from day to day. One can imagine it – 'This morning at breakfast Kirk continues our argument on the date of the Old Testament. Asks have I read Puffendorf – Schliemann – Webster.[12] Argument closed. Mrs X, Y, and Z to tea. Bridge was intended. Kirk, driven in by rain, talked to them about physiological anthropology instead. All left early. Mrs K very snappy at supper time'.

I can't remember if I told you about my last visit to Aunt Lily.[13] I went out by bus. The conductor did not at once understand where I wanted to stop, and a white bearded old farmer chipped in, 'You know, Jarge – where that old gal lives along of all them cats'. I explained that this was exactly where I did want to go. My informant remarked, 'You'll 'ave a job to get in when you DO get there.' He was as good as his word, for when I reached the cottage I found the fence supporting a wire structure about

---

11 William Allingham, *A Diary* (1907).

12 The men Lewis heard Mr Kirkpatrick mention frequently were probably: Samuel Pufendorf (1632–94), the first German professor of natural and international law; Friedrich Daniel Ernst Schleiermacher (1768–1834), a German theologian; and Max Weber (1864–1920), the German pioneer of the analytical method of sociology.

13 A fuller description of this visit is found in Lewis's diary, *AMR*, pp. 302–3.

nine feet high which was continued even over the gate. She does it to prevent her cats escaping into the main road. On this occasion she presented me with a print of an old picture, 'St Francis preaching before Pope Honorious' because, she said, the Pope was a portrait of me. It is not one of her fads, for I do really see the likeness myself. I suppose nature has only a limited number of faces to use after all.[14]

The weather cleared up for Easter here, but it is still rather cold. I hope you have quite got rid of the last traces of flu' by now. With many thanks again,

your loving son,
Jack

TO HIS FATHER (LP VIII: 225–6):

[University College]
Sunday [11 May 1924]

My dear Papy,

I have a bit of good – or fairly good – news. Some nights ago I was summoned to call on the new Master after dinner, there to meet Farquharson[15] and my old philosophy tutor Carritt,[16] and when I arrived the following 'transpired'. Carritt it appears is going for a year to teach philosophy in the University of Ann Arbor, Michigan, and it was suggested that I should undertake his tutorial duties here during his absence and also give lectures. As soon as I heard the proposal I said that I was already a candidate for the vacancy at Trinity. To this they replied that they had no intention of asking me to sacrifice the possibility of a

---

14 The picture of 'St Francis preaching before Honorius III' is Number XVII in the 'Legend of St Francis' which Giotto painted around the walls of the upper basilica of St Francis in Assisi. It is reproduced in Elvio Lunghi, *The Basilica of St Francis at Assisi* (1996), pp. 84–5.

15 Arthur Spenser Loat Farquharson (1871–1942) went to University College, Oxford, in 1890 and took a First in Greats. After a short time as a schoolmaster he returned to University College in 1899 as a Fellow and remained there for the rest of his life. From 1900 until the outbreak of the First World War he held the office of Dean. During the war, when he was chief postal censor, he took missions to France, Belgium and Italy, and he was twice mentioned in despatches. He became a lieutenant-colonel in the Territorial Army in 1918, and was made a CBE in 1919. He taught philosophy to the men reading Greats, and later to those reading the new school of Philosophy, Politics and Economics. He was a keen student of military history, and a great admirer of Marcus Aurelius, the soldier-philosopher.

16 For information about Mr Carritt see note 33 to the letter of 1 May 1920.

permanent job: it would be understood that if I were elected to Trinity I should be released from my engagement to Univ. – unless indeed Trinity were willing to let me do both tasks and I felt able to do so.

This being settled, I of course accepted their offer. I was a little disappointed that they only offered me £200 – specially as I anticipate that when living in and dining at high table I shall hardly be able to economise as much as I do now. I am afraid that I shall still need some assistance from you. Of course Carritt's job must be worth more than that: I imagine he is keeping his *fellowship* and I am getting his *tutorial* emoluments and of these, Farquharson, who is 'taking a few of the senior men' is getting a share. Being under Farquharson's suprintendance will be in some ways troublesome: and indeed I have already had a specimen of his fussy futility. I sent in to the Master as the title of my proposed lectures for next term 'The Moral Good – its place among the values.' Within an hour I had a notice brought out to my digs by special messenger 'Farquharson suggests "position" instead of "place". Please let me know your views at once.' There's glory for you,[17] as Humpty Dumpty said! Well, it is poorly paid and temporary and under the shadow of Farquharson, but it is better to be inside than out, and is always a beginning. The experience will be valuable.

You may imagine that I am now pretty busy. I must try to get through most of the Greats reading before next term and do it more thoroughly than ever I did when I was a candidate myself. I must be ready for all comers and hunt out the bye ways which I considered it safe to neglect in my own case. There can be no throwing dust in the examiner's eyes this time. Preparing my lectures will however be the biggest job of all. I am to lecture twice a week next term, which comes to fourteen hours talking in all. You who have been so much on your legs, can tell better than I what a lot of talking a man can do in one hour. I rather fancy I could really tell the world everything I think about everything in five hours – and, Lord, you hear curates grumbling because they have to preach for twenty minutes a week. However, as Keats remarks somewhere, 'Demme, who's afraid?': we must learn that slow deliberate method dear to the true lecturer. As Farquharson remarked (without the ghost of a smile) 'Of course your first lecture would be INTRODUCTORY'. I felt like replying, 'Of course: that's why I always skipped YOUR first lectures'!

---

17 Lewis Carroll, *Through the Looking-Glass* (1872), ch. 6.

As a prospective candidate I dined at Trinity the other night. I found out afterwards that this is a better sign than I thought, for Ewing[18] ('the rabbit' you remember) is also a candidate, remarked to me 'Price of Magdalen is a very dangerous man – he has been asked to dinner'.[19] 'But', said I with unfeigned surprise, 'surely they will ask all the candidates?' 'Oh dear me, no' said Ewing, 'only those who are in the running.' I held my tongue of course, while feeling, as I have often done lately, that this whole struggle for jobs is very degrading. It puts you in unpleasant relations with other people, and although one is perfectly innocent, one feels ashamed. This however is not what I meant to say. The interesting thing is that the President of Trinity[20] turns out to have been a bosom friend of Smugy's. He's quite a nice old man, but shy and a poor talker and I couldn't get him to talk about Smugy as I should have liked. I was very favourably impressed with the Trinity people.

In the smoking room after dinner we were just of a number for conversation to be general and I had one of the best evenings imaginable, the 'crack' ranging over all things. A burlesque element was supplied by their Senior Tutor, a disreputable old man in Holy Orders and in liquor, who, finding that I came from Univ., regaled us with some stories of Farquharson. So if Trinity don't give me a Fellowship, at least they gave me a very good time. All the same Ewing is right, 'Price of Magdalen' is 'a dangerous man' and I clip my hopes accordingly.[21]

'Mr Rogers'[22] is a name that I can remember almost as far back as I can remember anything. I am very sorry to hear of his death and even

---

18 Alfred Cecil Ewing (1899–1973), also of University College, took a First in Greats in 1920, and a D.Phil. in Philosophy in 1923. He was a Lecturer in Moral Science in the University of Cambridge from 1931 until 1954 and Reader in Philosophy at Cambridge from 1954 until 1966.

19 H.H. Price who, in 1922, had been awarded the Fellowship at Magdalen that Lewis applied for. See note 22 to the letter of 28 October 1922.

20 The Rev. Herbert Edward Douglas Blakiston (1862–1942) was President of Trinity College from 1907 until 1938.

21 He was right to do so. On 7 June Lewis had a letter from the President of Trinity College informing him they had made their decision. They elected H.H. Price to the Fellowship.

22 Edgar Rogers (1863–1924) of County Down was educated at the Royal Academical Institution, Belfast, and the Queen's College. In 1882 he joined the tobacco manufacturing firm of Murray, Sons and Co., of which he became the managing director. He was a friend of Albert's of long standing, and he was a frequent visitor to Little Lea.

sorrier that he should have fallen on evil days before the end. The roll of casualties in your letter reminds me of one of the little trap doors in the Vision of Mirzah.[23] Young men are supposed to think themselves immortal, but the subject is not very often out of my mind for a long time together. It is however a subject that will keep, God knows.

It has rained for a week here.

your loving son,

Jack

TO HIS FATHER (LP VIII: 256–7):

[University College]
Sunday [10? August 1924]

My dear Papy,

I should have answered your last generous letter earlier but for the last three weeks I have been busy from morning to night examining.[24] To examine is like censoring letters in the army or (I fancy) like hearing confessions if you are a priest. Beforehand it seems interesting – a curious vantage point from which to look into the minds of a whole crowd of people 'as if we were God's spies':[25] but it turns out to be cruelly dull. As the censoring subaltern finds that every man in his platoon says the same things in his letters home, and as the priest, no doubt, finds that all his penitents confess the same sins, so the examiner finds that out of hundreds of girls and boys of all social classes from all parts of England, scarcely a dozen make themselves memorable either for original ideas or amusing mistakes.

The paper which I corrected most of was on David Copperfield and Kinglake's Eothen:[26] and the first question was 'Contrast the characters of Uriah Heep and Mr Micawber'. So one takes up ones first sheet of answers and reads 'Uriah Heep is the finished type of a rogue: Mr Micawber on the other hand is the portrait of a happy go lucky debtor'.

---

23 In Joseph Addison's *Vision of Mirzah* (1711) Mirzah has a vision of human life as a bridge. As the multitudes pass over, some drop through concealed trap-doors into the flood beneath.

24 Lewis was working, except for a short lunch break, from 8 a.m. to 7 p.m. correcting examinations for the Higher School Certificate.

25 Shakespeare, *King Lear*, V, iii, 17.

26 Alexander William Kinglake, *Eóthen: or traces of travel brought home from the East* (1844).

Then one plods on to the same question answered by the next candidate and reads 'Mr Micawber is the finished portrait of a happy go lucky debtor, while Uriah Heep is a typical (or perhaps 'typicle') rogue'. And so it goes on through all the weary hours of the day till ones brain reels with Uriah Heep and Mr Micawber and one would willingly thrash the editor or whoever it is who has supplied them with that maddening jargon about the 'finished portrait of a rogue'.

I must set down on the credit side the fact of having been thus forced to read Eothen. I know of course that it has stood in red cloth, skied near the ceiling in the bookcase nearest the study door, since I can remember – unmoved by twenty spring cleanings, the Russian Revolution, and the fall of the German Monarchy. I don't know whether this is one of the books you have advised me to read or not. It is even possible (such things have been known) that Eothen has lived there all these years in the study bookcase undisturbed not only by the Russian Revolution, but equally by the hand of its owner. (It was Sir Otto[27] was it not, who observed 'But this isn't cut Mr Lewis'?) At any rate I most strongly advise you to give yourself a very pleasant evening by taking down Kinglake. If you don't feel a stomach for the whole thing at least read the interview between the Pasha and the 'possible policeman of Bedfordshire' in the first chapter and the Surprise Sataleih in the last, for humour: and for ornate prose I should recommend the opening of the chapter on Constantinople, the part beginning 'the stormy bridge of the Doge is the bowing slave of the Sultan'. The Colonel was over here shortly before my durance began and I have converted him to my new idol: so you must by all means 'come in' and share the spoil – unless of course you really have read it already.

I have seen enough of the papers to imagine that Ulster must be pretty well humming with politics just at present: and indeed I suppose

---

27 Sir Otto Jaffé (1846–1929) was first mentioned in note 84 to the letter of 24 July 1915. He was a Jewish general merchant and linen manufacturer who was born in Hamburg and who became a resident of Belfast in 1848. He was twice Lord Mayor of Belfast (1899–1900 and 1904–5) and was knighted in 1900. He was an LL.D. of the Royal University of Ireland, and President of the Belfast Natural History and Philosophical Society 1906–8. In 1879 he married Paula Hertz, and they had two sons, Arthur (b. 1880) and William (b. 1883), who was a friend of Albert's. Warnie said that 'On the outbreak of the Great War the family was subjected to a cruel and stupid social persecution on account of its German origin, as a result of which Sir Otto and Lady Jaffé left Belfast and settled in London' (LP III: 124).

the situation is as serious now as it ever has been since the trouble started. Clap on top of this comes Macdonald's rushing through the treaty with Russia without the King's name on it.[28] What did you think of that? Is there any force in the legal defence put forward in the Times? It seemed to my lay eye to be great nonsense.

You must excuse me for a shortish letter. After my long spell with the blue pencil I am in an indolent mood which would be very pleasant if I could give it its head: but I must start and tackle my lectures tomorrow. I have ordered a dinner jacket suit at the same tailors: for that and for all else that your letter contained, many thanks.

I had almost forgotten to say that on the occasion of W's last visit I went over to Colchester for the night in order to come back with him in the sidecar.[29] The new byke is a noble machine and we stopped to eat our lunch at a railway bridge near Watford which used to be the regular goal of our walks when we were at Wynyard. Here we sat on the slope of the cutting looking down on the L.N.W.R. main line on which we used to gaze in the old days when it was the only object of interest in the landscape. It was strange to find that the said landscape was quite an ordinary, even pleasant English countryside: and it was almost impossible to realise the appalling blankness and hostility which it once wore. In those days we had not grown used to the English colouring (so different from Ulster): our interests and appreciation of nature were limited to the familiar: rivers might wind and trees bloom in vain – one saw it all only as an abominable mass of earth dividing one by hundreds of miles from home and the hills and the sea and ships and everything a reasonable man could care for.

We were puzzled for some time as to why the line was invisible from a fence on which we used to sit to watch it: until W. hit on the simple truth that some trees which had been little trees in 1909 had become big trees in 1924. That's the sort of moment that makes the youngest of us feel old. We also passed a large park in Hertfordshire whose famous name I know very well at the moment but it won't come into my

---

28 James Ramsay MacDonald, the Labour Prime Minister, was trying to get his Anglo-Soviet treaty passed. A draft of the proposed treaty, dealing with commerce and navigation between Great Britain and Northern Ireland and the Soviet Union, appeared in *The Times* of 8 August.

29 For an account of this outing with Warnie on 3 July see *AMR*, pp. 341–2.

head.[30] W. tells me that it is one of the places where you spoke on the Irish question in your young days. I don't know if he is right.

your loving son,

Jack

TO HIS FATHER (LP VIII: 260-1):

[University College]

Postmark: 28 August 1924

My dear Papy,

As you say, it becomes uncanny. Whenever I 'remember me of my sins' I know that this will happen, and usually, as in the present case, I fear I clinch the matter by forgetting for a day or so to post my letter. Thanks for the dividend.

When I came to the part in your letter where you speak of how God does temper the wind to the shorn lamb I fairly laid it down and laughed. A joke by letter seldom has this effect: it usually arrives but the ghost of a spoken joke – it reaches the intellect without disturbing the face. But the image of Warnie as a shorn lamb, and of the expression with which he would say 'What d'you mean?' if you tried to explain to him WHY he was funny as a shorn lamb, was too much for me. But though you didn't mention it, I know very well WHO tempered the wind in the present case.

I am plodding on with my fourteen lectures – I am at number five, or rather have just finished it. I think I said before that I am not writing them IN EXTENSO, only notes. The extemporary element thus introduced is dangerous for a beginner, but READ lectures send people to sleep and I think I must make the plunge from the very beginning and learn to TALK, not to recite. I practise continually, expanding my notes to imaginary audiences, but of course it is difficult to be quite sure what will fill an hour. Perhaps I will experiment on you when I come home! The laborious part is the continual verifying of references and QUOTING. As Johnson says 'a man can write pretty quickly when he writes from his own mind: but he will turn over one half a library to make one book.'[31]

---

30 Warnie appended a footnote to this letter in LP VIII: 257 suggesting that the place is probably Hatfield, the seat of Lord Salisbury.

31 *Boswell's Life of Johnson*, op. cit., vol. II, 6 April 1775, p. 344 (slightly misquoted).

And of course when one is trying to TEACH one can take nothing for granted. Hitherto I have always talked or read to people to whom I could say 'You remember Bradley's stunt about judgement' or 'The sort of business you get at the beginning of Kant'. But of course that won't do now – and the deuce of it is that when you actually look the passage up you always find that they either say more or less than you want. Consequently I spend my days running from library to library, or hunting things from the index of one book to another. By the way, in ORAL instruction, how many times do you have to say the same thing before people tumble to it? You should be able to answer that.

While it comes into my head – a propos of the photo of Warnie bathing – I take it it is the one of his FLOATING which he showed me: telling me at the same time that one of his colleagues had remarked 'It is one of the sights of the summer to see Lewis ANCHORED off the coast'. This should have come with my first paragraph, but I hadn't found your letter at that stage.

I was very much impressed by what you tell me about affairs at home. I know you must have often thought that W. and I treated the Irish question very lightly: indeed you once told me that my views were 'like those of every other Englishman'. This I think was natural: our trip to France had naturally altered the proportion of things and both views are explicable. The latest developments however have brought me much nearer to your way of looking at it. If there is a bust up now, the consequences will by no means end in Ireland. I cannot see how in the long run it could avoid leading to a repetition of the Curragh incident: and what that would mean with the present government is a nasty problem.[32]

---

32 In 1913 some 500 delegates of the Ulster Unionist Council, which had been formed in 1905 to bring together unionists' associations, nominated a provincial government which would take office if the Home Rule bill was passed. This group, which planned to resist Home Rule, called itself the Ulster Volunteer Force. It numbered over 84,000 men and it imported many thousands of rifles and other arms which were distributed all over Ulster. In March 1914 it was decided that a military force must be ready in the Curragh – the chief military training camp 32 miles south-west of Dublin. However, when the commander-in-chief of the army in Ireland demanded that any officer who was unwilling to invade Ulster must be dismissed from the forces, Sir Hubert Gough (1870–1963), the brigadier-general commanding the 3rd Cavalry Brigade at the Curragh, prepared to resign rather than initiate military operations against Ulster. This became known as the 'Curragh incident' or the 'Curragh mutiny'.

There has hardly been a day's sunshine here for months and most of the harvest is being lost. A propos, I had a little communication today asking me to contribute to the Salvation Army harvest thanksgiving! I can't understand why so many religious people keep up this dishonesty. For surely it is pure humbug to return thanks for what you haven't got?

I don't know that I have any news except that I was caught by Aunt Lily in the street the other day: that I am meeting her to lunch in some restaurant tomorrow: that I have had my hair cut: and am to have my dinner jacket tried on this week. I hope you keep well.

your loving son,
Jack

TO HIS FATHER (LP VIII: 263):

Univ. Coll.
Wednesday.
Postmark: 15 October 1924

My dear Papy,

My maiden lecture yesterday went off alright in a sense – the only difficulty was the audience.[33] They put me down for the same time at which a much more important lecture by an established man was being held elsewhere.[34] They also, by a misprint, put me down as lecturing at Pembroke, not at Univ. In these conditions it is not to be wondered at if no one came at all. As a matter of fact FOUR people turned up! This of course is not very encouraging. But I shall not let it come between me and my rest. Better men than I have begun in the same way and one must be patient. As long as Mr Pritchard's highly essential lectures are held at the same time as mine, I can hardly expect anyone to come to me. Don't be worried about it.

Otherwise everything goes well. All my new colleagues are kindness itself and everyone does his best to make me feel at home – especially dear old Poynton. I find the actual tutoring easy at the time (tho' I am curiously tired at the end of the day) and have already struck some quite good men among my pupils. I have seen only one real dud so far – a man

---

33 Lewis's first lecture in the University of Oxford, on 'The Good, its position among values', was delivered at 10 a.m. on Tuesday 14 October.

34 Harold Arthur Prichard, Fellow of Philosophy at Trinity College, was lecturing at this same time on 'History of the Theory of Knowledge (Descartes, Locke, Berkeley, Hume)'.

who celebrated his first hour with me by telling me as many obvious lies as I have heard in a short space.

I have paid the bill for my dress suit – ten guineas, less 10/6 discount so that it was actually £9.19.6.

I have both the parcel of books and the handkerchiefs, for wh. many thanks. I have the College football captain among my pupils and am busy making up THAT subject also in order to be able to talk to him.

your loving son,
Jack

Warnie arrived in Oxford on his motorbike and sidecar on 20 December, and he and Jack set off for home the next morning. They drove to Liverpool on the motorbike, crossed the Irish Sea by ferry, and arrived at Little Lea on the morning of 23 December. They remained with their father until 10 January.

1925

— ∾ —

TO HIS FATHER (LP VIII: 274–5):

[University] College
Thursday
Postmark: 11 February 1925

My dear Papy,

You should have heard from me before, but I have hardly been in a position to write. I spent the first fortnight of the term in bed with flu. I am very much afraid my organism is acquiring the HABIT of getting this troublesome complaint every time it becomes prevalent. As you have had it yourself and as you doubtless remember the curious psychological results it produces in the convalescent stage – the depression and dead alive feeling – I need not describe them. In my own case the spirits are not greatly improved by the necessity of having a tooth drawn as soon as I was fit for it. However it came out yesterday with gas, and the relief of having that off my chest has so cheered me that I think it has chased away the last dregs of the flu depression. So now 'my bosom's lord sits lightly on the throne'.[1] It has actually not rained today – and all is for the best.

W. and I had a magnificent ride back and I was sorry he had not his camera with him. From Shrewsbury to Oxford was all perfect: an orgy of woods, hills, broad rivers, grey castles, Norman abbeys and towns that have always been asleep. I wish I could describe Ledbury to you. It consists of about four broad streets in which every second house is of the Elizabethan type, timbered and white, with gables to the front. It is set in the middle of delightful rolling country and the end of Malvern hills comes down to the town end. Best of all, no one has yet 'discovered' it: it has not become a show place and the inhabitants are quite unaware that there is anything remarkable about it. Ludlow too I would like you to

---

1 Shakespeare, *Romeo and Juliet*, V, i, 3.

see: with its castle, former seat of the Earl of the Marches, where Comus was first performed. But after all, where can you go in the South and West of England without meeting beauty?

I don't think I have much news. All goes on as usual here – that is to say very pleasantly on the whole though with some sense of strain and little leisure. My lectures have gone off rather better this term though it's still very much a case of 'fit audience though few'.[2] My most persevering auditor is an aged parson[3] (I can't image where he comes from) who takes very copious notes and darts dagger glances at me every now and then. Some one suggests that he is a spy sent out by the board of faculties to detect young lecturers in heresy – and that he keeps on coming with the idea that if he gives me enough rope I shall hang myself in the end. There is also a girl who draws pictures half the time – alas, I have done so myself!

I hope you are keeping pretty well. This is the most trying time of the year I think. Even here far inland we have such gales that I thought the house was coming down. I say 'house' because the part of College which I am in is an old sixteenth century house which somehow got incorporated. Nevertheless the primroses are out in the College gardens. How are the corns? – mine are rather better.

your loving son,

Jack

TO HIS FATHER (LP VIII: 287–9):

[University College
April 1925]

My dear Papy,

Many thanks for your letter. I am sorry to hear of your 'rotten Easter': mine was redeemed by the glorious two days trip with Warnie.[4] Otherwise I was pretty well hustled during the vacation, working against time to prepare for this term, which, to tell the truth, I began in rather a tired state. As you once said to me, 'Talking is the most exhausting of all occupations'.

---

2 Milton, *Paradise Lost*, VII, 31: 'Fit audience find, though few.'

3 This was the Rev. Frank Nightingale who had gone to the University of London after being a clergyman in the Church of England since 1894, and who had now retired to Oxford.

4 This was another trip by motorbike and sidecar, on 6–8 April.

The trip was delightful. I was pleased to revisit Salisbury and see it more thoroughly. I well remember my former visit. 'It was a Sunday' and NOT very early in the morning, as you doubtless recollect, when we stopped for a few minutes in Uncle Hamilton's headlong career and heard morning prayer going on in the Cathedral. At that time I did not agree with you and cared for it less than Wells or Winchester.

This time as we came into sight of Salisbury, where, on those big rolling downs that spire can be seen from fifteen miles away, I began to have my doubts. Later, when we had had tea and strolled into the Close I decided that it was very good in its own way but not in my favourite way. But when we came out again and saw it by moonlight after supper, I was completely conquered. It was a perfect spring night with the moon nearly full, and not a breath of wind stirring nor a sound from the streets. The half light enhanced its size, and the sharp masses of shadow falling in three great patches from the three main faces of one side emphasized the extraordinary simplicity in which it differs so from say, Wells.

That is the real difference I think, and what repelled me at first: the others, mixed of a dozen styles, have grown from century to century like organic things and the slow history of secular change has been built into them. One feels the PEOPLE behind them more: the nameless craftsmen in this or that gargoyle which is different from every other.

Salisbury, on the other hand, is the idea of a master mind, struck out at once for ever. Barring mechanical difficulties it might have been built in a day. Doesn't Kipling talk of the Taj-Mahal as 'a sigh made marble'? On the same metaphor one might say that Wells is an age made into stone and Salisbury a petrified moment. But what a moment! The more one looks the more it satisfies. What impressed me most – the same thought has come into everyone's head in such places – was the force of Mind: the thousands of tons of masonry held in place by an idea, a religion: buttress, window, acres of carving, the very lifeblood of men's work, all piled up there and gloriously USELESS from the side of the base utility for which alone we build now. It really is typical of a change – the medieval town where the shops and houses huddle at the foot of the cathedral, and the modern city where the churches huddle between the sky scraping offices and the appalling 'stores'. We had another good look at it in the morning light after breakfast – when the plump and confident members of the feathered chapter cooing in the very porch added a new charm. W. says that Salisbury is Barset: if so, we must be standing near where the Warden said 'I'm afraid I shall never like Mrs Proudie' and the Archdeacon took off his hat to 'let a cloud of steam escape'.[5]

On our run that day we stopped at Stonehenge – a very fine morning and intensely quiet except for a battery practising over the next ridge. It was the first time I had heard a gun fired since I left France, and I cannot tell you how odd the sensation was. For one thing it seemed much louder and more sinister and generally unpleasant than I had expected: as was perhaps natural from the general tendency of memory to minimize, and also from the solitude and quiet of the place. I thought (as I had thought when we revisited Watford) how merciful it would be if we could sometimes foresee the future: how it would have carried me through many a long working night in the trenches if I could have seen myself 'seven years on' smoking my pipe in the oldest place in the old, safe, comfortable English fields where guns fire only at targets. But on the whole, however, it would not be a comfortable privilege: though I have no doubt at all that it is accorded to some – but like all these mysterious leaks through of Something Else into our experience it seems to come without rhyme or reason, indifferently chosen for the trivial or the tragic occasion. I don't know why I have blundered into this subject, which may not interest you: you must put it down as a momentary eruption of that sense of irremediable ignorance and bewilderment which is becoming every year more certainly my permanent reaction to things. Whatever else the human race was made for, it at least was not made to know.

This is my last term 'in the bond' at Univ. and there is still no word of the Fellowship. I begin to be afraid that it is not coming at all. A Fellowship in English is announced at Magdalen and of course I am applying for it, but without any serious hopes as I believe much senior people including my own old English tutor[6] are in for it. If he gets it I may get some of the 'good will of the business': I mean some of the pupils at Univ., Exeter and elsewhere whom he will have to abandon. These continued hopes deferred are trying, and I'm afraid trying for you too. About money, if you will put in £40 – if you think this is reasonable – I shall be on the pig's back.

---

5 Trollope, *Barchester Towers*, ch. VI.
6 F.P. Wilson.

My best pupil[7] is in great trouble. He went down in the middle of last term to attend his father's deathbed. He came up late at the beginning of this term, having been detained at home while his mother was operated on for cancer. To make matters worse this poor fellow has been left very badly off by his father's death, and it was even doubted last term whether he would be able to go on with his course. It is really extraordinary how long troubles are in letting go when they have once fastened on an individual or a house. If only he had a decent chance he would almost certainly get a first: he is in addition a very modest decent chap. One feels very helpless in coming continually into contact with such a case. If I were an older man, or again if I were his contemporary, I might be able to convey some sense of sympathy: but the slight difference in age, or some defect in myself, makes an insurmountable barrier and I can only feel how trivial or external and even impertinent my 'philosophy' must seem to him at such a moment.

I am sorry if this is rather a scrappy letter – and likewise rather smudged and meanly written. I have been writing in pauses between pupils, and odd moments. You must not think that I am forgetful in my long silences. I have often things to say to you day by day, but in the absence of VIVA VOCE conversation they die away and the time and mood for a set letter do not come so easily.

I have been into Hall and common room afterwards and heard an interesting thing. Do you remember Mrs Asquith's saying in that detestable autobiography that she once asked Jowett if he had ever been in love? He replied 'Yes' and being asked what the lady was like, replied 'Violent – very violent.' Apparently the lady was really Florence Nightingale. Poynton and Farquharson both knew of it. For her 'violence' see Strachey in 'Eminent Victorians'. The story – a strange tragi-comedy – seems to have been common property. Both the parties were irascible and opinionated and quarreled nearly as often as they met: and yet the affair hung on for a long time.

I hope you are fairly well and going along comfortably.

your loving son,

Jack

---

7 This pupil's name was Harold Henry Cox (1901–74). He matriculated at University College in 1919, and despite the troubles Lewis mentions, he succeeded in taking a First in Greats in 1927. He went on to become Tutor of Philosophy at Lincoln College, Oxford.

In his diary of 20 May Albert Lewis wrote: 'While I was waiting for dinner Mary came into the study and said "The Post Office is on the phone". I went to it. "A telegram for you." "Read it." "Elected Fellow Magdalen. Jack." "Thank you." I went up to his room and burst into tears of joy. I knelt down and thanked God with a full heart. My prayers had been heard and answered.'

Preserved with Mr Lewis's papers was this cutting from The Times *of 22 May 1925:*

> *NEW FELLOW OF MAGDALEN COLLEGE. The President and Fellows of Magdalen College have elected to an official Fellowship in the College as Tutor in English Language and Literature, for five years as from next June 15, Mr Clive Staples Lewis M.A. (University College). Mr Lewis was educated first at Malvern College. He won a scholarship in classics at University College in 1916, and, (after war service) a first class in Classical Moderations in 1920, the Chancellor's prize for an English essay in 1921, a first class in Literae Humaniores in 1922, and a first class in the Honour School of English Language and Literature in 1925.* (LP VIII: 290)

TO HIS FATHER (LP VIII: 291–2):

Univ. Coll.
26th May 1925

My dear Papy,

First, let me thank you from the bottom of my heart for the generous support, extended over six years, which alone has enabled me to hang on till this. In the long course I have seen men at least my equals in ability and qualifications fall out for the lack of it. 'How long can I afford to wait' was everybody's question: and few had those at their back who were both able and willing to keep them in the field so long. You have waited, not only without complaint but full of encouragement, while chance after chance slipped away and when the goal receded furthest from sight. Thank you again and again. It has been a nerve racking business, and I have hardly yet had time to taste my good fortune with a deliberate home felt relish.

First of all, as I told you, I thought that I had my own tutor Wilson as a rival, which would have made the thing hopeless. But that I found to be a false rumour. Then I wrote to Wilson and Gordon (the Professor of

English Literature)[8] for testimonials, relying on them as my strongest supports. Within twenty four hours I had the same answer from both. They were very sorry. If only they had known I was going in for it...they thought I had definitely abandoned English for philosophy. As it was, they had already given their support to my friend Coghill of Exeter.[9] Once more, they were exceedingly sorry, and remained mine sincerely etc.

This was enough to make anyone despair: but mark how the stars sometimes fight for us. Two days later came news that Coghill had been offered a fellowship by his own College and had withdrawn from the field. Wilson's testimonial – a very good one – came by the next post. Gordon said he wouldn't write anything as he was going to be consulted personally by the Magdalen people, but he would BACK me. This of course was much better than the testimonial. Still, I hardly allowed myself to hope. Then came a letter from Gordon – 'CONFIDENTIAL'. 'I was asked my opinion about the candidates yesterday and I put my money on you. I think your chances good, but of course one never knows what the spin of the coin may do in such things.' This, I said to myself, is at least nearer than I've ever got before: but don't hope, don't build on it.

Then came an invitation to dine at Magdalen on Sunday a fortnight ago. This showed only that I was one of the possibles. Then came the LITTLE problems that seem so big at the time. Was Magdalen one of the Colleges where they wore white ties and tails, or did they wear dinner jackets and black ties? I asked the Farq. and he advised white tie and tails: and of course when I got there I found everyone in black ties and dinner jackets. These dinners for inspection are not exactly the pleasantest way of spending one's evening – as you may imagine. You can hardly say 'He'll enjoy it when he gets there'. But I must say they carried off as well

---

8 George Stuart Gordon (1881–1942) became Magdalen College's first Fellow of English in 1907. He was Professor of English at Leeds University 1913–22, after which he returned to Oxford as the Merton Professor of English. Sir Walter Raleigh had inaugurated a discussion class for those reading English Literature, and Gordon continued this practice when he became Merton Professor. Lewis was a member of the discussion class and he wrote about it in *AMR*. He was to see a good deal of Gordon when he was President of Magdalen College from 1928–42.

9 Nevill Henry Kendall Coghill (1899–1980) matriculated at Exeter College, Oxford, in 1919. He and Lewis read English together. See **Nevill Coghill** in the Biographical Appendix.

as could be asked a situation which must be irksome to the hosts as well as to the guest. So far so good.

Then came a spell of thundery weather of the sort that makes a man nervous and irritable even if he has nothing on his mind: and the news that Bryson[10] and I were the two real candidates. Bryson comes from home and knows Arthur: but of course I mention his name in the strictest possible secrecy. One afternoon, in that week, I saw the said Bryson emerging from Magdalen: and ('so full of shapes is fancy')[11] felt an unanswerable inner conviction that he had won and made up my mind on it.

On the Saturday Warren[12] (1) met me in the street and had a vague tho' kindly conversation with me. On Monday I had a very abrupt note from him asking me to see him on Tuesday morning, with the curious addition, 'It is most important'. I didn't like it at all: it suggested some horrible hitch. Was I going to be viva-d on Anglo-Saxon verbs or asked my views on the Thirty Nine Articles?[13] We had thunder that night, but a poor storm and not enough to clear the air: and Tuesday rose up a grey clammy morning when one sweats every time one moves and the big blue bottles settle on your hands. This sounds like writing it up to an exciting conclusion: but it WAS a nasty morning and it WAS quite exciting enough for me at the time.

---

10 John Norman Bryson (1896–1976) was educated at the Queen's University, Belfast and Merton College. He was a lecturer at Balliol, Merton and Oriel Colleges 1923–40, when he became Fellow of English at Balliol College. He retired in 1963.

11 Shakespeare, *Twelfth Night*, I, i, 14.

12 Sir Thomas Herbert Warren (1953–1930) made his mark at Clifton College where he was head of the school and scholar-elect of Balliol College. When he came up to Balliol in 1872 Benjamin Jowett was Master and the college was at the height of its reputation. Warren took Firsts in Classical Moderations (1873) and *Literae Humaniores* (1876). In 1877 he was elected to a prize fellowship at Magdalen. Besides being a brilliant scholar and able to stimulate his pupils, he came to know them as personal friends. In 1885, at the age of 32, he was elected President of Magdalen, an office which he held until 1928, a period of 43 years. He threw himself into developing the college, and it was a marked tribute to the position he held in the University and outside it that in 1912 King George V chose it for the Prince of Wales. His contribution to classical scholarship was an edition of the first five books of Plato's *Republic* (1888). The two great literary enthusiasms of his life were Virgil and Tennyson, and there are reflections of both in his two volumes of verse, *By Severn Seas* (1897) and *The Death of Virgil* (1907).

13 The set of doctrinal formulae proposed by the Church of England in the 16th century as a method of defining its dogmatic position. See note 69 to the letter of 29 May 1921.

I got to Magdalen, and, would you believe it, he kept me waiting for HALF AN HOUR before he saw me. The choir boys were practising in the tower close by. When he did see me it turned out to be all formalities. They were electing tomorrow and thought me the 'strongest and most acceptable candidate'. Now IF I were elected would I agree to this, and would I be prepared to do that, and did I understand that the terms of the fellowship implied so and so. The only thing of the slightest importance was 'would I be prepared, in addition to the English pupils, to help with the philosophy.' (This, I imagine, stood me in good stead: probably no other candidate had done English as well as philosophy.) I need hardly say that I would have agreed to coach a troupe of performing bagbirds in the quadrangle: but I looked very wise and thought over all his points and I hope let no subservience appear. He then gave me a long talk about the special needs of Magdalen undergraduates – as if they were different from any others! – all as if I had been elected, but without saying I had been. During the whole interview he was cold and dry and not nearly so agreeable as he had been on the Saturday. He finally dismissed me with a request that I would hang about Univ. the following afternoon in case I were called for.

And then next day – about 2.30 – they telephoned for me and I went down. Warren saw me, told me I had been elected and shook hands: since he has written me a very nice letter of congratulations saying that he believes they may congratulate themselves. It is a fine job as our standards go: starting at £500 a year with 'provision made for rooms, a PENSION, and dining allowance'. The election for five years only in the first case of course means only that in five years they have the chance of getting rid of you if you turn out 'hardly one of our successes'. One hopes, in the ordinary course of events, to be re-elected.

A cat 'met me in the day of my success'[14] and bit me deeply in the right thumb while I was trying to prevent it from attacking a small dog. In fact, to go on with the Shakesperian allusion, I came 'between the fell incensed points of mighty opposites'.[15] By dint of poultices I have now reduced the inflammation, and this is the first day I have been able to write with ease. It would have been better sooner if I had not been forced daily to answer as best I could the kind congratulations which have

---

14 Shakespeare, *Macbeth*, I, v, 1 (slightly misquoted).
15 Shakespeare, *Hamlet*, V, ii, 60–1.

reached me. I must cut it short now. It has been an egotistical letter, but you asked for it. Once more, with very hearty thanks and best love,

your loving son,

Jack

(1) I mean the President of Magdalen of course, not Big Brother.

TO HIS FATHER (LP VIII: 297–9):

[University College]

Aug. 14th [1925]

My dear Papy,

Since our last interchange of letters I have been almost continuously employed in my usual summer task of examining. This year I had been promoted from the post of examiner to that of awarder. An awarder is one who besides examining himself revises the marks of the other examiners and so produces a final verdict: the principle being that if Mr A gives six marks where I should have given eight, then 85 should count for a pass in the candidates I have looked over, while his will get through on 75 or 80. In each department there are two awarders, one from Oxford and one from Cambridge, and the work is done alternately year by year in either university. This year it was at Cambridge and about forty Oxford people went over.

We were all put up in Queens College where I must say they did us like fighting cocks. It is all paid for by the 'Board' which I take it means the taxpayer, through the ministry of education. As I knew many of the Oxford people I had quite a good time. Cambridge is beautiful beyond description: more so, in many ways, than Oxford. My rooms looked out over the river. Unfortunately our work took from 9 a.m. till 7 p.m. and so I had little time to see the town. My Cambridge colleague was a man of no breeding – the sort of person who referred to the candidates as 'kiddies' – but quite a pleasant fellow and we got on comfortably together.

We were a good deal delayed by the carelessness of the examiners whose work we had to use: some of them were erratic and a great deal of the marking had to be completely revised. We also had to deal with the difficult problem of papers which seemed to have been tampered with by a schoolmaster after they had left the boys' hands. We came to the conclusion that the evidence was not strong enough to justify us in making such a serious accusation – but I still feel rather uncomfortable about it.

By an arrangement previously made, W. biked over from Colchester to take me there for the week end on the Saturday. We got away by five o'clock and after a journey through pleasant but tame country, we made Colchester at nine. The authorities have again taken advantage of our Colonel's good nature. The mess has broken up and every one has gone on maneuvers: W. has had to sacrifice the hope of long days in the saddle and short nights in the open air, forced marches and alarms and excursions under the suns of Salisbury plain, and content himself as best may with a suburban lodging house, short hours, books, and sea bathing. He bears up very well.

On Sunday he took me to the sea where we had a capital swim: it is the first time for several years that I have been in salt water. We saw a good deal of the country on Monday. As I said before, Essex and Suffolk are tame: but what nature lacks is compensated by the works of men and I have never seen a countryside so thickly studded with fine buildings. Every second village has a parish church that might be an abbey, a Tudor manor house, a ruined Norman keep, a full blown castle, or at least a venerable inn. I left him on Tuesday.

The only other event of importance since I last wrote has been my formal 'admission' at Magdalen. It is a formidable ceremony and not entirely to my taste. Without any warning of what was in store for me, the Vice-President (a young fellow called Wrong[16] whom I have since got to know on the Cambridge jaunt) ushered me into a room where I found the whole household – it is large at Magdalen. Warren was standing and when Wrong laid a red cushion at his feet I realized with some displeasure that this was going to be a kneeling affair. Warren then addressed me for some five minutes in Latin. I was able to follow some three quarters of what he said: but no one had told me what response I ought to make and it was with some hesitation that I hasarded DO FIDEM as a reply – copying the formula for taking your M.A. This

16 Edward Murray Wrong (1889–1928), a Canadian, was educated in Toronto and at Balliol College, Oxford, where he took a First in Modern History in 1913. He was elected a Fellow of Magdalen College in 1914. He was vice-principal of Manchester College of Technology 1916–19, after which he returned to Magdalen. His publications include *The British Empire* [1916], *Charles Butler and Responsible Government* (1926) and *History of England, 1688–1815* [1927]. E.M. Wrong was a man of enormous grace and charm, and his early death was the cause of grief to all who knew him. See his obituary in *The Times* (16 February 1928), p. 14.

appeared to fill the bill. I was then told (in English) to kneel. When I had done so Warren took me by the hand and raised me with the words 'I wish you joy'. It sounds well enough on paper but it was hardly impressive in fact: and I tripped over my gown in rising. I now thought my ordeal at an end: but I was never more mistaken in my life. I was sent all round the table and every single member in turn shook my hand and repeated the words 'I wish you joy'. You can hardly imagine how odd it sounded by the twenty fifth repetition. English people have not the talent for graceful ceremonial. They go through it lumpishly and with a certain mixture of defiance and embarrassment as if everyone felt he was being rather silly and was at the same time ready to shoot the first man who said so. In a French or Italian university now, this might have gone off nobly.

I had also forgotten to tell you – or did I tell you before – that previous to the examining I had a few days in London with a married friend of mine called Barfield, and met Arthur by accident in a theatre. But I have a feeling that I have written this to you already. The mind – or at any rate MY mind – plays tricks in these things. In a way I share your regret that when the opening came it did not come at Univ. I shall never find a common room that I did not like better: and every break in the continuity of one's associations is in some degree unpleasant. No one likes, even at my age, to see any slice of life being finally turned over to the past.

As to the other change – from Philosophy to English – I share your feeling less. I think you are mistaken in supposing that the field is less crowded in Philosophy: it seems so to you only because you have more chance of seeing the literary crowd. If you read 'Mind' and one or two other periodicals of the sort as regularly as you read the Literary Supplement, you would probably change your view. I think things are about equal in that way. On other grounds I am rather glad of the change. I have come to think that if I had the mind, I have not the brain and nerves for a life of pure philosophy. A continued search among the abstract roots of things, a perpetual questioning of all that plain men take for granted, a chewing the cud for fifty years over inevitable ignorance and a constant frontier watch on the little tidy lighted conventional world of science and daily life – is this the best life for temperaments such as ours? Is it the way of health or even of sanity? There is a certain type of man, bull necked and self satisfied in his 'pot bellied equanimity' who urgently needs that bleak and questioning atmosphere. But what is a tonic to the Saxon may be a debauch to us Celts. And it certainly is to the Hindoos.

I am not condemning philosophy. Indeed in turning from it to literary history and criticism, I am conscious of a descent: and if the air on the heights did not suit me, still I have brought back something of value. It will be a comfort to me all my life to know that the scientist and the materialist have not the last word: that Darwin and Spencer[17] undermining ancestral beliefs stand themselves on a foundation of sand; of gigantic assumptions and irreconcilable contradictions an inch below the surface. It leaves the whole thing rich in possibilities: and if it dashes the shallow optimisms it does the same for the shallow pessimisms. But having once seen all this 'darkness', a darkness full of promise, it is perhaps best to shut the trap door and come back to ordinary life: unless you are one of the really great who can see into it a little way – and I was not.

At any rate I escape with joy from one definite drawback of philosophy – its solitude. I was beginning to feel that your first year carries you out of the reach of all save other professionals. No one sympathises with your adventures in that subject because no one understands them: and if you struck treasure trove no one would be able to use it. But perhaps this is enough on the subject. I hope you are well and free from corns, sore gums and all other 'crosses'.

your loving son,

Jack

Jack visited his father in September, and this time they got on very well. His having a job, and no longer being dependent upon his father, removed the tension between them, and both seemed at ease. In his diary for 13 September, Mr Lewis said: 'Jacks arrived for holidays. Looking very well and in great spirits' (LP IX: 7). On 1 October he wrote: 'Jacks returned. A fortnight and a few days with me. Very pleasant, not a cloud. Went to the boat with

---

17 Herbert Spencer (1820–1903), philosophical and scientific thinker whose publications include *First Principles* (1862), *Principles of Biology* (1867) and *Principles of Ethics* (1893). He was the chief exponent of agnosticism in 19th century England. He divided the whole of reality into the knowable (the principles of science) and the unknowable (the principles of religion). He affirmed that progress was the supreme law of the universe.

him. The first time I did not pay his passage money. I offered, but he did not want it' (LP IX: 29).

Following his return to Oxford, Lewis divided his time between Magdalen and 'Hillsboro' which he shared with the Moores. During term he slept in his college rooms – Staircase III, Number 3, of New Buildings – and visited the 'family' at 'Hillsboro' in the afternoons. When term ended the routine was reversed, and he lived at 'Hillsboro' and came into Magdalen whenever there was a need to do so. However, from the time he moved into Magdalen he was to have two homes until his retirement many years later.

TO HIS FATHER (LP IX: 37–8):

Magdalen College
Oct. 21st 1925

My dear Papy,

When we discussed the question of furnishing my rooms before I left, I thought it a very remote contingency. It was rather a crushing blow to find that I had to get everything – and for three spacious rooms: the extent of College's bounty being some linoleum in the smaller sitting room and a washstand in the bedroom. It is hard to say on what principle fellows are provided with washstands but left to provide their own beds: unless it is a symbol of the combined VIGILANCE and purity which is so characteristic of their corporate life. Carpets, tables, curtains, chairs, fenders, fire irons, coal boxes, table covers – everything – had to be bought in haste. It has cost me over £90, although I was able to pick up some things second hand. It sounds an alarming total, but I do not think I have been extravagant; the rooms certainly do not look as if they had been furnished by a plutocrat.

My external surroundings are beautiful beyond expectation and beyond hope. To live in the Bishop's Palace at Wells would be good but could hardly be better than this. My big sitting room looks north and from it I see nothing, not even a gable or spire, to remind me that I am in a town. I look down on a stretch of level grass which passes into a grove of immemorial forest trees, at present coloured with autumn red. Over this stray the deer. They are erratic in their habits. Some mornings when I look out there will be half a dozen chewing the cud just underneath me, and on others there will be none in sight – or one little stag (not much bigger than a calf and looking too slender for the weight of its own antlers) standing still and sending through the fog that queer little bark or hoot which is these beasts' 'moo'. It is a sound that will soon be as familiar to me as the cough of the cows in the field at home, for I hear it day and night. On my right hand as I look from these windows is 'his favourite walk'.[18] My smaller sitting room and bedroom look out south-ward across a broad lawn to the main buildings of Magdalen with the tower beyond it. It beats Bannaher!

As to the 'College' in the other sense – as a human society – I can say little yet. One's first impressions of a new set are changed many times in the first month. They are all very nice to me. The general tone of the place strikes as a rather slack and flippant – I mean among the Dons – but I may very well be mistaken. Sambo[19] hardly ever appears. The most surprising thing is that they are much less formal than Univ. They don't dress for dinner except when the President dines, on which occasion a warning notice is sent round to our rooms. Again, there are an enor-mous number of us compared with Univ., and we meet much more often. Thus we breakfast and lunch in Common Room; meals in your own rooms (which I had thought universal at Oxford) being unknown here either for Dons or undergraduates. The latter are a little aloof from the rest of Oxford: not entirely thro' affectation but because as a matter of geography we are 'at the town's end': or, as someone said, we are the beginning of suburbia. I have very few pupils at present, wh. of course is helping me to improve my reading. They are quite nice fellows.

I had a most amusing journey with Arthur. When we got to the stew-ard's office nothing was known of the berth which he professed to have booked and for a time it looked as if we should have to sit up all night. He really took the prospect much better than I had expected, but not so well as to deprive me of considerable enjoyment.

We are having real autumnal weather here: some pleasant bright days of frost but mostly damp and fog. I hope you have not yet succumbed to the seasonable cold in the head.

---

18 The favourite walk of Joseph Addison (1672–1719), the essayist and poet known for his contribution to *The Spectator*. When he was a Fellow of Magdalen he lived in New Buildings and greatly enjoyed the walk which runs northward from the College build-ings and which has been known since the 19th century as 'Addison's Walk'. Lewis would have been surprised to know that on 13 May 1998 a C.S. Lewis Centenary Stone was erected in Addison's Walk on which is inscribed his poem about Addison's Walk – 'What the Bird Said Early in the Year' – found in *Poems* (1964) and *Collected Poems* (1994).

19 Nickname of the President of Magdalen.

your loving son,
Jack

TO A.K. HAMILTON JENKIN (B):

Magdalen College,
Oxford.
Nov. 4th [1925]

My dear Jenkin,

Your letter speaks of a possible meeting in the flesh. If I looked up from my study in New Buildings & saw you coming across the lawn I would fling a book in my pupils face and outstrip the winds in getting downstairs.

I cannot at present ask you to Hillsboro where Mrs Moore, alas, lies in bed sick of the varicose veins: but if you care for a night or two in College (preferable a Monday and Tuesday, not a week end), and if you were prepared to amuse yourself in the afternoons when I am out at Headington – why, then, we might look forward to two long evening talks and I can hardly express in temperate language how much the prospect pleases me.

Have you ever lived among deer? The windows of my Northern room look into the grove. There is a flat stretch of grass receding into big forest trees (all day long at present the leaves are eddying up the sky from them and the wind among them at night is magnificent). There is nothing in sight, not even a gable, to remind me that I am in a town: and over this grass the 'little dappled fools'[20] come right up to beneath my window. One morning there will be seven there chewing the cud in close squadron: next day not one in sight, till I go down to the bathroom. The window there is level with the ground and on these autumn mornings one gets a delicious earthy freshness and a horizontal view of dew and cobwebs along the turf: and perhaps one tiny solitary stag nibbling quite close to the sill as if he were the first animal in the world. But best of all is to hear them at night. They don't moo and they don't neigh, but they have two sounds. The one is a thin little hooting, rather like a faint cough, and most unearthly. The other (mark the catholicity of these beasts) the other is absolutely indistinguishable from the grunting of old fat pigs. And this last being most unpoetical and an anticlimax in the

---

20 Shakespeare, *As You Like It*, II, i, 22: 'the poor dappled fools'.

eyes of the universe, is really the best. If only to hear this you should come.

You shd. come if only to enter Magdalen after dark across the grove by my master key – on a moonlight night. With such a key at such an hour of night under such massy archways, through the length of such blind walks that sudden opened out into the freckled moonshine of tall groves, so secret and so wrapped Medea went by stealth to gather the enchanted herbs that did renew old Aeson.[21]

In plain prose there are two or three moments in that night entry by these successive posterns that I do it for the love of it when I might just as well go in past the porter's lodge. And if there is no moon (dazzlingly white among the trees after a long dark cobbled passage) perhaps instead there will be thick darkness and drumming rain and the hoofs of the deer (invisible) scampering away – and ahead the long lighted line of the cloisters in New Buildings. I wish there was anyone here childish enough (or *permanent* enough, not the slave of his particular and outward age) to share it with me. Now, it is that I am unfortunately in my meetings, or that I am growing a shell 'unprofitably travelling towards the crab', or is it that no man makes real friends after he has passed the undergraduate age? Because I get no forr'arder since the old days.

I go to Barfield for sheer wisdom and a sort of richness of spirit. I go to you for some smaller and yet more intimate connection with the feel of things, for a certain gusto and complete *rightness* of palate: to Harwood for 'humours' and the appreciation of them. I speak now of the points in which you severally excel, tho' of course your functions change and cross: and in a certain juncture of the planets each may play the other's part. Indeed I have expressed all the parts inadequately – specially Harwood's. But the question I am asking is why I meet no such men now. Is it that *I* am blind?

Some of the older men here are delightful: the younger fellows are none of them men of understanding. Oh for the people who speak one's own language: men and women in their different ways. A man can spread his legs out with them and talk: he can get something new from them. It is odd that only old friends bring *new* talk. With the others

---

21 Lewis is here remembering his poem on 'Medea' as mentioned in his letter to Arthur Greeves of 18 September 1919.

(those of our generation or a year or so older) 'whereso'er I turn my view / All is strange but nothing new.'

But a fig for them. If I wasn't worried to death about Mrs Moore's illness I should be on the pig's back. I have hardly any pupils at present and so am learning a little in my leisure. I am easy financially for the first time in my life: the material beauty of my surroundings is beyond all that I can desire – in its own style of course.

Thanks for your letter. The shooting star & the ninth wave must have been the thrill at second hand. I read Mrs G's Bronte years ago and don't remember it well, but I know what you mean (tho' not in connection with that book). Do try and come up. Regards and salutations from all here.

Yrs,

C. S. Lewis

TO HIS FATHER (LP IX: 42–3):

Magdalen College
Dec. 4th [1925]

My dear Papy,

It is strange if I forgot to acknowledge the cheque in a letter which I wrote primarily for that purpose. It is like going upstairs for a handkerchief and coming down with a book – a kind of adventure which overtakes even the wise. Let me hasten to cry MEA CULPA and also acknowledge with many thanks the two enclosures of your last.

I have had a nasty blow – don't be alarmed, it concerns neither life, limb or reputation. I was already worried about the difficulty of preparing an English lecture in the time at my disposal, but by dint of choosing a short subject which I know well (XVIII century precursors of the Romantic movement) I hoped to be able to acquit myself well enough. What was my displeasure on finding, when the rough draft of next term's lecture list was sent me, that my old tutor Wilson was lecturing on 'English Poetry from Thompson to Cowper'.[22] Now of course my 'precursors', with the exception of some critics and other prose writers, are just the poets from Thompson and Cowper. It is in fact the same subject under a different name. This means that, being neither able nor willing to rival Wilson, I am driven to concentrate on the prose people of whom

---

22 James Thomson (1700–48) and William Cowper (1731–1800).

at present I know very little. I have as hard a spell cut out for me between now and next term as I have ever had. Of course all the more easy and obvious subjects which will leap to your mind are long since occupied by the bigwigs.

The immediate consequence is that I am afraid I shall scarcely be able to take more than a week at home at Christmas. To compensate for this I shall try to get across at Easter. I am sorry to disappoint you (and myself): but it is only one of the many evils which I see following from this bad hunch about the lecture. At the very best it means working much harder for a much poorer result. Of course no one, least of all Wilson himself, is to blame.

I have very nearly had flu but by dint of keeping my rooms and fireside for two days, have succeeded in turning the corner without going to bed.

I dined at Balliol the other night for the first time. 'We were not amused'. Although it was supposed to be a guest night par excellence and I was one of a crowd of guests, more than half the Balliol Dons did not turn up. They were (heaven help us) at a boxing match and of those who did appear many slipped away to the spectacle as soon as we left the table. The dinner was cold. Worst of all we had our wine afterwards in a common room which is next door to a Laboratory and (there is no other word) stinks. The Master of Balliol is a very bad host: what is euphemistically called a 'shy' man and what one suspects to be either conceited, lazy, or a dull man.[23] But come, come: this is not the way to return hospitality. 'Nor to offer it' one might add.

This is the hardest winter I have known for a long time. For many weeks the earth has been as iron under my feet and the heaven, not as brass, but as grey steel or ground glass above me. But for the pressure of these lectures I would give myself up to some days skating. A little snow fell over a fortnight ago, and every flake has remained unthawed to decorate the trees and to make the telegraph wires like old fashioned woolly bell ropes.

I have only been back to Univ. once – to a Martlet's dinner. It is strange how soon the places we leave assume the charm of the past. I could almost sentimentalize over the Farq. – or well ALMOST!

---

23 Alexander Dunlop Lindsay, Baron Lindsay of Birker (1879–1952), read Greats at University College. After teaching for a few years in Scotland, he returned to Oxford in 1906 as Fellow of Classics at Balliol College. He was Master of Balliol from 1924 to 1949.

I cannot help being glad for the moment about W's change of prospect. Is there no chance that this dilly dallying may go on indefinitely until he retired without sight of India?

I hope you are well and standing the cold.

your loving son,

Jack

P.S. How does one get a copy of one's birth certificate? Can you let me have one or shall I write myself to Somerset House or the Tower of London or the National Gallery or wherever they keep these things? They want it for some sort of Insurance Scheme by which I contribute to my own pension.

1926

— ∾ —

TO HIS FATHER (LP XI: 265–6):

[Magdalen College]
Monday Dec. [January] 5th [1926]

My dear Papy,

I hope the cold has now gone. At best, I am afraid it will leave you weakened and shaken. It is the first week or two after one has got about again that is the dangerous part of such things: I hope you are taking all possible precautions.

Warnie and I had a rather interesting journey back.[1] First there was the episode of the friendly and intoxicated stranger in the smoking room of the Liverpool boat: but I feel that the Colonel's pen will do that story more justice than mine. Secondly there was the amazingly erudite fellow traveller in the train. I suppose he had gathered from our conversation – W. was reading Evelyn's diaries – that we were bookish people, but he let several hours pass before he quite suddenly chipped in, in a rather apologetic manner. I surmise that he lives among people who do not share his tastes and it is a relief to him to talk about them. He did not speak with the voice of an educated man, but his reading was curious: Pepys, Evelyn, Burnet, Boswell, Macaulay, Trollope, Thackeray, Ruskin, Morris and 'The Golden Bough'.[2] He seemed to be some kind of architect or decorator.

Now this is the sort of thing I like. To have a literary conversation in the study at Leeborough or the common room at Magdalen is (by comparison) nothing, because one remains in the charmed circle of one's own set and caste: there is nothing to refute the accusation of being out of the world, of playing with things that perhaps derive a fictitious value from the chatter of specially formed groups. But to talk over the same

---

1 Jack and Warnie were with their father at Little Lea from 20 until 28 December.
2 Sir James George Frazer, *The Golden Bough* (1890).

things with a man whose aitches are uncertain in a third class carriage – this restores one's faith in the value of the written word and makes one feel suddenly at home in one's country. It is the difference between grapes in a greenhouse and a hillside of vines.

The other interesting thing in our journey was the new scenery produced by the floods. Round about Warwick (you remember Warwick) for miles at a time there was nothing but water between one hedgerow and the next – and then the little hills made into islands. A village on a rise with 'the decent church that fronts (or is it *crowns*) the neighbouring hill'[3] has a very fine effect. You probably spotted the enclosed picture in today's Times, but I send it in case you have not. The long building to the right of the tower is 'New Building' which Gibbon,[4] who lived in it, called 'a stately pile'. The arrow points to the line whose windows belong to (1) Brightman[5] (the mechanical toy man) at the top. (2) 'J.A.'[6] ('nothing to

---

3 Oliver Goldsmith, *The Deserted Village* (1770), 12: 'The decent church that topt the neighbouring hill.'

4 Edward Gibbon (1737–94), author of *The History of the Decline and Fall of the Roman Empire*, lived in New Buildings 1752–3.

5 Frank Edward Brightman (1856–1932), liturgist of the Church of England, had been an undergraduate at University College, Oxford. He took a First in Mathematical Moderations (1877), a First in *Literae Humaniores* (1879) and a First in Theology (1880). He was ordained in 1885, having been made in 1884 an original librarian of Pusey House. He held that post until he was elected a fellow of Magdalen in 1902. There he remained until his death in 1932. He was one of the most learned scholars who flourished at the turn of the century. Amongst his publications is his monumental work, *The English Rite*, 2 vols. (1915), in which he set out the sources of the Book of Common Prayer and the changes from 1549 to 1662. See H.N. Bate's 'Frank Edward Brightman' in *Proceedings of the British Academy*, vol. XIX (1933). With reference to Lewis's verse 'We were Talking of dragons, Tolkien and I' in the essay on 'The Alliterative Metre' in *Selected Literary Essays* (1969), I asked Professor Tolkien the source. In his reply of 20 February 1968, he said: 'I remember Jack telling me the story of Brightman, the distinguished ecclesiastical scholar, who used to sit quietly in Common Room saying nothing except on rare occasions. Jack said there was a discussion on dragons one night and at the end Brightman's voice was heard to say, "I have seen a dragon." Silence. "Where was that?" he was asked. "On the Mount of Olives," he said. He relapsed into silence and never before his death explained what he meant.' *The Letters of J.R.R. Tolkien*, ed. Humphrey Carpenter (1981), p. 389.

6 John Alexander Smith (1863–1939), philosopher and classical scholar, was educated at Edinburgh and Balliol College where he took a First in *Literae Humaniores* in 1887. He became a fellow of Balliol in 1891 after which he was the Waynflete Professor of Moral and Metaphysical Philosophy and Fellow of Magdalen 1910–36. He was a distinguished scholar of Aristotle, and his translation of *De Anima* appeared in 1931. For the intellectual influence of J.A. Smith and other Oxford philosophers see James Patrick, *The Magdalen Metaphysicals: Idealism and Orthodoxy at Oxford, 1901–1945* (1985).

be gained by stammering over the word consciousness'). (3) Myself. (4) Ground Floor, and undergraduate rooms. You can imagine from the picture what a magnificent view I now have when the park has been converted into a lake. On a fine day when the sky makes the water blue and the wind fills it with ripples, one might almost take it for an arm of the sea. Of course I am not forgetting the serious side of the floods: but after all, what would you? I can't save the life of Dutch peasants or the pockets of Warwickshire peasants by refusing to enjoy the beauty of the thing as it appears from my window.

I am getting on nicely, or at least enjoying myself, over the lectures. New facts and new connections between old facts turn up every day. Do you remember an essay of Arthur Benson's about travelling by rail through a countryside where one has walked as a child?[7] He describes how he saw all sorts of things which he had known all his life 'linking up' in new ways. The big field with the stile, when one used to look out into the unknown world, turned out to be only *the other side* of the field with the duck pond which one passed on another walk. The *two* big *woods* turned out to be one little plantation dividing two familiar walks. He goes on to describe the peculiar pleasure which these discoveries gave him. That is the kind of pleasure I am enjoying at present. For instance if you have known long ago that the Wartons[8] wrote a certain kind of romantic poem full of phrases from Milton, and that Collins[9] did the same sort of thing: and if you have hitherto regarded these as two isolated facts: how delightful to find out suddenly that the Wartons and Collins were at school together and made a sort of poetry club there as boys and had evolved it together. This is only one example. Something like it turns up every day. Coincidences, accidents, isolated phenomena,

---

7 Benson, *Upton Letters*, letter of 4 August 1904, pp. 177–82.

8 Joseph Warton (1722–1800), one-time headmaster of Winchester College, published poems and odes. But he is best known as a critic of wide knowledge and good judgement. His *Essay on the Writings and Genius of Pope* (1756, 1782), distinguishes between the poets of 'the sublime and pathetic' and the 'men of wit and sense' such as Shakespeare, Spenser and Milton. His brother Thomas Warton (1728–90) was Professor of Poetry at Oxford 1757–67 and became Poet Laureate in 1785. He edited the works of Milton, but is best known for his celebrated *History of English Poetry*, 3 vols. (1774–81).

9 William Collins (1721–59) was educated at Winchester College (where he met Joseph Warton), and then Oxford. Later when he moved to London he became a friend of Dr Johnson, and he is mentioned in Dr Johnson's *Lives of the English Poets*. Collins's *Odes on Several Descriptive and Allegoric Subjects* (1746) has had considerable influence.

are disappearing all the time and being replaced by intelligible connections. 'Linking up' in fact. It is a most satisfying process. Let me have a line soon to say how you are, even if you can't manage a letter.

your loving son,
Jack

TO HIS FATHER (LP IX: 70–2):

Magdalen College.
Sunday
Postmark: 25 January 1926

My dear Papy,

There was no need for any apologies about the affair of the cheque. I was of course puzzled for the request for the return of an unknown cheque and wondered why you had not taken the more obvious step of 'stopping' it. In any case however I am so often guilty of dilatoriness in such matters that I can hardly complain if I am sometimes suspected in error.

As to the German measles – will you think me affected if I number a small illness among the minor pleasures of life? The early stages are unpleasant but at least they bring you to a point at which the mere giving up and going to bed is a relief. Then after twenty four hours the really high temperature and the headache are gone: one is not well enough to get up, but then one is ill enough not to want to get up. Best of all, work is impossible and one can read all day for mere pleasure with a clear conscience.

I re-read some of my favourite Jane Austens and read for the first time that jolly, unexacting tale, Quentin Durward.[10] I even took the chance of going on with my neglected Italian and got through several cantos of Boiardo:[11] an interminable fairy-tale kind of a poem, full of dragons and distressed damsels, without the slightest moral or intellectual significance. It is suited to the atmosphere of a day in bed with the snow falling outside: the drift, the holiday from all sublunary cares. Then one returns to a primitive and natural life as regards sleeping and waking. One dozes when the doze comes unsought and if one lies castle building at night one does not mind because there is no getting up in the

---

10 Scott, *Quentin Durward*. See note 175 to letter of 25 October 1916.
11 Matteomaria Boiardo, *Orlando Innamorato* (1487).

morning.[12] But of course all these delights have to be paid for: the first few days back to work when legs still ache and hours are long, are an unwelcome shock of earth – and that, I think, is the really bad part of it. I hope you are now past that stage.

I read with pleasure your account of how you had dealt with John.[13] It is a miserable business. But while nothing can alter one's contempt for John, my sympathy for the girl is modified by my settled conviction that John was certain to cause unhappiness sooner or later to any decent woman who had the bad luck to care about him. The real misfortune came long ago when they got engaged: something of this sort could then be foreseen, and it is better that it should have come in the form of a jilt than later, through the divorce courts, after years of unhappy marriage. That any process could have made John different, I don't believe. He is as perverted in heart as he is feeble in head. He has no natural goodness of feeling to supply his lack of any kind of principles, and no inherited tradition of decent behaviour to act as a curb on his selfishness. None of that family has any notion of self control. In the case of Lily and Arthur you see this illustrated over small things and merely leading to bad manners: greediness at table, pettish discontent over trifling inconveniences, the perpetual 'I want'. In John's case the circumstances only are different. If one has no notion of restraint I suppose it is largely a matter of accident whether one commits great or small faults. But Lord! how my tendency to preach is running away with me. Better say simply that John is a rotter and leave it at that. And perhaps I ought to put in a word for Arthur who, after all, is an old friend of mine. At least he knows what is wrong with him and, I think, makes some effort to overcome it. As to Lily – what would she NOT do if she really wanted to?

I have given my first lecture.[14] I suppose my various friends in the English Schools have been telling their pupils to come to it: at any rate it was a pleasant change from talking to empty rooms in Greats. I modestly

---

12 Lewis was later to write in the last chapter of *The Allegory of Love* (1936): 'Johnson once described the ideal happiness which he would choose if he were regardless of futurity. My own choice, with the same reservation, would be to read the Italian epic – to be always convalescent from some small illness and always seated in a window that overlooked the sea, there to read these poems eight hours of each happy day.'

13 This is Arthur Greeves's elder brother, John Greeves (1892–1969), of whom there is a description in LP III: 305.

14 At noon on Saturday, 23 January, Lewis gave the first of his eight weekly lectures on 'Some Eighteenth Century Precursors of the Romantic Movement'.

selected the smallest lecture room in College. As I approached, half wondering if anyone would turn up, I noticed a crowd of undergraduates
coming into Magdalen, but it was no mock modesty to assume that they
were coming to hear someone else. When however I actually reached my
own room it was crowded out and I had to sally forth with the audience
at my heels to find another. The porter directed me to one which we
have in another building across the street. So we all surged over the High
in a disorderly mass, suspending the traffic. It was a most exhilarating
scene. Of course their coming to the first lecture, the men to see what *it*
is like, the girls to see what *I* am like, really means nothing: curiosity is
now satisfied – I have been weighed, with results as yet unknown – and
next week I may have an audience of five or none. Still it is something to
be given a chance.

We have been as heavily snowed up here as I ever remember to have
been since that winter long ago at home when you had to walk along the
bank by the roadside to reach the tram. It was fine, dry, powdery snow
while it lasted and the College looked very beautiful under it. The slush
and dirt of the thaw is now over. I hope to have a letter from you soon,

your loving son,

Jack

TO NEVILL COGHILL (B):

Magdalen College,
Oxford.
[3 February 1926]

Dear Coghill

I am in hopes that this, whatever its literary merits, will at least
help to make clear what I was trying to express last night: and last night's
conversation in its turn may make cantos VII & VIII more intelligible. If
you are disposed to any *detailed* criticism (a task I nowise impose on
you) please put it in pencil on the margin.[15]

---

15 Lewis had been working on his narrative poem, *Dymer*, since 1922, and Nevill Coghill
was one of the first ones he showed it to, asking for his criticism. Recalling this in his
'Approach to English', Coghill said: 'He showed me [*Dymer*] during the early days of
our acquaintance, towards 1924. He told me he had been visited many years before by
a dream or myth that had remained completely mysterious to him, and yet compelling.
It held his imagination though he could not explain its significance. He had made a
poem of it, he said. I asked him to let me see it, and presently it arrived, a thickish
folder of typewritten cantos in rhyme-royal. It was the first time that I had been

Can you come & dine to day week (the 10th) at 7.15. I want to get down to it about some of the very difficult things we raised last night: but you needn't have read Dymer by then – you shan't be viva'd! I was delighted with de la Mare: its the real thing all thro' and like cool water after Yeats and — fill in to taste,

yrs

C. S. Lewis

By the bye the MS. is confidential: I don't want it known that I am writing 'pomes'.

TO NEVILL COGHILL (B):

Magdalen College,
Oxford.
Feb. 4th 1926

My dear Coghill

It is as if you had given me a bottle of champagne – a dangerous moment and difficult to reply to. For any one of my temperament there is always a certain difficulty in quite believing praise, especially from a new reader. It is not exactly modesty – more a sort of fear that we must be leaving something out of account. Yours, however, is of the best sort. Waiving any application to myself your remark about 'the delight of giving admiration in exchange' is quite a new light to me and enables me to understand better a great deal of my own experience as a reader.

Your remarks on the Masefieldian lines go to the root of the matter – I should say the *bad* Masefieldian lines, for, in some points, one wd. not be in the least ashamed to have learned from him. The 'pretense of carrying more weight of beautiful meaning' is absolutely true. I shall be very glad to have any passages where that happens pointed out to me: the thing has gone on so long now that it is hard to spot them for myself. As to 'slickness', I am sure I have often deluded myself and tried to delude the reader that way. All the same, it is not quite plain sailing here. The early parts *must* have a certain neat, shallow speed – they must appear rather cheap compared with the later because that phase of the journey *was* cheap, wasn't it. Of course I know we are here up against the devil of

---

entrusted with an original work of such weight and I read it with all the excitement natural in one who is first privileged to see new work by a new poet.'

a problem: how to present bores without being a bore, or second-rateness without being second rate: complicated by the fact that the reader must be made to share that stage with Dymer and feel the spell himself.

As to the other side – it pleases me more than I can tell that you *recognize* the spiritual experiences. I was afraid that they might be private or not of this age. Also you relieve me of my two greatest anxieties *a.* Whether Canto III was mere vulgar nonsense *b.* Whether the 'redemption by parricide' myth in general wd. seem simply preposterous & shocking.

Dymer hardly felt mediocrity *after* waking (my dear Sir, how uncannily well you have understood it!) because he died i.e. the special problem of adolescence worked itself out to a finish. We feel it because we are in a different problem now: all Dymer's problems are past history to us and we live where he never came. At least I think that is true.

With many thanks, & hoping to see you Wednesday

yrs

C. S. Lewis

P.S. Of course *I'm* not Dymer: I am about to him as he to his son. At any rate he has done his best to kill me these three years!

TO HIS FATHER (LP IX: 102–4):

Saturday 5th June 1926
Magdalen

My dear Papy,

While not disposed to question the strictly mathematical parts of the reasons submitted in your letter, I suggest that you omit the real question. Did you reply to my last letter? Was the move with you or with me? However, let the move be where it will, I was wrong to leave it for such a length of time. As often before, I can only plead that what has no special date and may be done tomorrow as well as today, is hard to do at all.

I hear with delight from Warnie that you propose to visit England this summer. Let us determine that no light reason shall be allowed to upset this plan, and no difficulty be made into an impossibility. My idea is that I should cross to Ireland for part of my usual time and that we shd. then return to Oxford and you spend some days with me in College. There is a set of guest rooms on this very staircase, so we should be very snug and able to hob nob a'nights without going out of doors. We could dine in Common Room (not dressed) or go to an ordinary in the town as we preferred, and you would have an opportunity of sauntering about the city and its fields with more leisure than Uncle Hamilton's peremptory programme allowed us. Then, if possible, W. would come up for a week end and we might proceed to London or elsewhere. Do make every effort to realise the plan. Now that I am in College we have a pied à terre in England which seems to have all the advantages and none of the drawbacks of a hotel, and which certainly ought to make visits more possible than they have ever been before. It is rather important to try and fix a date, and I should be glad to know when you think you could get away.

But I know what I do in raising the point of 'date'. At least I presume it is from you that I inherit a peculiar tendency by which a chill comes over the happiest designs as soon as a definite detail of time or place is raised. At first all is attractive and like a floating island, detached from the actual world: at the mention of a date, obstructions crowd upon the mind: arrangements to be made, difficulties to be overcome, and all the repellent lumber of packings, boats, time tables and interrupted habits rush in and 'quench the smoking flax'.[16] The odds are that the whole scheme, if injudiciously pressed at that moment becomes a sort of bug-bear. Is this a true bill? It is of me, I know only too well. The only remedy seems to be to remember that every happiness we have attained in the past depended on the lucky moments when we were not cowed by the 'lumber'. (Lord! Was there ever such a young fellow for preaching at his elders? He cannot take up his pen but a steady flow of doctrine begins. Perhaps it comes from taking pupils.)

A heavy responsibility rests on those who forage through a dead man's correspondence and publish it indiscriminately. In those books of Raleigh's[17] we find, as you say, letters like 'a glass of good champagne' side by side with mere squibs thrown off in high spirits or mere grumbles written when he was liverish. Notice how Liverpool, India and Oxford all come up for castigation in turn. Much of this should never have seen

---

16 Isaiah 42:3.

17 *The Letters of Sir Walter Raleigh (1879–1922)*, ed. Lady Raleigh, with a Preface by D.N. Smith, 2 vols. (1926). In 1904 Sir Walter Raleigh (1861–1922) became the first holder of the new chair of English Literature at Oxford, and in 1914 he was elected Merton Professor of English Literature.

print. The anti-religious passages are odd. Something must be allowed for the mere turn of his language which was always violent and dogmatic – like Johnson. When he says 'Jesus Christ made a mess of it'[18] I doubt if he really *means* much more than another might mean by saying 'Even the teaching of the Gospel seems to involve fundamental difficulties'. But I am speaking without book and of course it all depends on the context. In so far however as his remarks show a real ignorance of the importance of Christianity as (*at least* and on my view) one of the biggest and most venerable things in the history of the mind – in so far as they refuse to allow to it even that reverent consideration which any educated person must allow, say, to Greek Philosophy, or the Renaissance, or Buddhism – to that extent they are merely silly and unenlightened. On the other hand, so far as they are merely using terms of expression which are offensive to religious feeling in order to express legitimate, tho' may be very erroneous, views about Christianity, I think they are covered by the fact that they occur in private letters. On the whole I must confess that the reading of the letters, much as I enjoyed them, did not raise my opinion of Raleigh. When all allowance has been made for the haphazard nature of casual letter writing, it remains true that there must be some flaw in a man who is always blessing or damning something or other. There are *too many ecstasies* and the opposite. The funny thing is that his own view on the things of the spirit, in a large sense – I mean about what is really valuable and what is not, and about the position of mind in the world – are not really in opposition to the atmosphere of Christianity. Whatever he thought about the historical side of it, he must have known perfectly well (everyone seems to be getting to know now) that the religious view, whether literally true or not, was at any rate much more *like* the reality than the views of the scientists and rationalists.[19] I daresay the whole thing springs from some prejudice contracted in early boyhood. You speak of '*comfort* to tens of millions of men and women' and this

---

18 ibid., vol. II, p. 287, letter to John Sampson of 2 December 1905: 'Jesus Christ didn't fetch it off.'

19 ibid., vol. I, p. 19, letter to his sister Alice of 4 March 1885: 'I am a good deal depressed at the way people mix up their beliefs with unessentials. The probability of a future life, the existence of God, the case for miracles, the validity of conscience are all hopelessly muddled so that if I say that my conscience is not justly called the voice of Christ I am excommunicated from the sympathy of people with whom I am in the deepest accord on essentials.' Vol. II, p. 324, letter to John Sampson of 26 December 1907: 'Give me Christ and morals – not Christianity and moralists.'

just reminds me to quote a sentence from Raleigh's 'Wordsworth' to show him at his best. 'The vision shown to the pure in heart does not fulfill, it corrects their desires'.[20] I do this to adjust the balance, lest I should seem to have forgotten that 'with all his faults etc., etc.'

I have been bothered into the last job I ever expected to do this term: taking a class of girls once a week at one of the women's Colleges.[21] However, I am not engaged to be married yet, and there are always seven of them there together, and the pretty ones are stupid and the interesting ones are ugly, so it is alright. I say this because as a general rule women marry their tutors. I suppose if a girl is determined to marry and has a man alone once a week to whom she can play the rapt disciple (most fatal of all poses to male vanity) her task is done.

Otherwise things go on as usual. Nearly all my pupils went off during the strike to unload boats or swing batons or drive engines.[22] The best strike story I have heard was about engines. A train (with amateur driver) set out from Paddington to Bristol, first stop Bath. When it reached Bath *half an hour* earlier than normal express time, every single passenger got out of that train and refused to enter it again. Apparently the genius in the engine had just opened the throttle full, said to the stoker 'Carry on', and left the rest to fate.

A boy I knew at Merton drove an engine for twenty seven hours. At the end he never could remember whether the last light he had seen was green or red. Sometimes he painfully shunted back to see: but he found that if he did that once, he wanted to do it again. There were surprisingly few accidents. Warnie had some ugly adventures in London but if he has not told you, perhaps they are not to be committed to the *written* word.

---

20 Walter Raleigh, *Wordsworth* (1928).

21 Lewis's diary, *AMR*, contains details of the class he gave to the young ladies of Lady Margaret Hall.

22 Lewis is writing about the General Strike. It began as a result of the Samuel Committee recommending cuts in the wages of miners. The owners of the mines, however, while accepting a cut in wages, argued for longer hours, and at the end of April they locked the miners out of the pits. The Trades Union Congress called a meeting and agreed a 'national strike'. They hoped that such a threat would force the Government to settle. But Stanley Baldwin, the Prime Minister, called off talks with the Trades Union Congress because printers refused to print an anti-union article in the *Daily Mail*. Beginning on 3 May workers in transport, iron and steel, electricity, gas, building and newspaper printing all stopped work. Every town had its own strike committee which tried to keep essential supplies moving. While the miners refused to give in, the TUC called off the strike.

We of course had to stay on as long as any pupils were left, and it had just got to the point of our having got to go when the thing ended. I don't mind telling you I was in a funk about it. Docking was filled up and I would sooner have gone to the war again than been a constable. The necessity for either moral or physical courage is bad enough, but the two together are 'a bit thick'. I could make some shift to stand and have things thrown at me: I could make such shift to lift up my voice in an angry crowd. But to have the spiritual ordeal first and then the physical! As well, I haven't got the right voice or face for 'moving on' people. The first time I spoke they wouldn't hear me: the second time they'd say 'F— off!: the third time I'm afraid they'd simply laugh. In fact I had come down to thinking of inglorious canteen work when the whole nightmare came to an end.

Well, I must go to bed. I think I am beginning, as you say, to feel my feet under me. Every one is very pleasant. I am examining in a fellowship examination in the autumn – rather a sudden reversal of positions. You diddle me over Falstaff: it certainly is surprising when taken out of context.

your loving son,
Jack

TO A.K. HAMILTON JENKIN (B):

Magdalen
Sept. 8th [1926]

My dear Jenkin,

When your hymeneal epistle[23] reached me I was spending my days in correcting exam papers and my nights chiefly in thinking about toothache – nature having then favoured me with particular opportunity for a first hand study of that phenomenon. With the immense superiority of a miserable man who was startled at the shallowness of character shown by people who married and were given in marriage while my tooth ached: I reflected that so they had done in the days of Noe until the flood came and swept them all away.[24] Since then, as leisure

---

23 A few months earlier Hamilton Jenkin married Luned Jacob, the daughter of the writer, W.W. Jacob.

24 Reflecting on the marriage of his friend Rodney Pasley in 1922, Lewis said in his diary of 9 July 1922, 'A friend dead is to be mourned: a friend married is to be guarded against, both being equally lost' (*AMR*, p. 66).

and ease have gradually returned, I confess that my judgement of your exploit has progressively softened. From scorning it as impertinent, I tolerated it as pardonable: from toleration (it was even at that moment when the fumes of the gas began to leave my brain and I heard a voice say, Rinse your mouth out with this)[25] I proceeded to approval. The thing was innocent: even laudable: nay profitable, comfortable, and a cause of gratulation. You see that at no earlier moment could I properly have taken in hand to offer you (as I now do) the heartiest congratulations and the very best wishes (even to a Shandëan particularity of curious beatitude) of Mrs Moore and myself.

Indeed there was something in your manner of announcing it – with the parenthetical ease of a man borrowing a box of matches – which hardly invited a formal reply. 'It was not unpremeditated'. Egad, was it not? Well, the lady is fortunate: I am sure you are too. You have as much of the gift of happiness as any man I know, barring donkeys, and I am sure you will taste domesticity (the Augustans wd. have said 'vertuous love') with the same fine palate you have applied to mines, birds, woods, wind, rain, fires, crime, letters and ghosts.

Authors ought to marry author's daughters (a notable tongue twister) as they may be supposed to be already inured to living with genius. It must be a wonderful experience. (1) Please recommend me to your wife and, even in my absence, remit the friendship with her new seal, which as Lamb says, you know, is needful.

I have had an infernally busy summer, writing lectures, and have nothing to tell you: except that I grow daily more and more doubtful in all subjects. Once more heartiest congratulations and best wishes to you both,

Yrs

C. S. Lewis

(1) I mean marriage, not 'living with genius'.

---

25 Addressing the subject of Purgatory, Lewis said in *Letters to Malcolm* (1964), ch. 20: My favourite image on this matter comes from the dentist's chair. I hope that when the tooth of life is drawn and I am "coming round", a voice will say, "Rinse your mouth out with this." *This* will be Purgatory.'

Jack was unable to persuade his father to travel to Oxford for a visit. He did, however, manage a visit to Little Lea from 11 to 20 September. He was with his father when the narrative poem he had been working on since 1922, Dymer, *was published by J.M. Dent on 18 September. As with* Spirits in Bondage, Dymer *was published under the pseudonym 'Clive Hamilton'.*

TO CECIL HARWOOD (B):

Magdalen College,
Oxford.
Postmark: 28 October 1926

My dear Harwood,

Thanks for your letter. I can think of a thousand replies to what you say about Cantos I and II, but you must be right, as Barfield, the reviewer in the New Leader (my best so far), and the only don who is in my confidence, all think the same.[26] Securus judicat.[27] That is one of the many quotations of which my knowledge is purely functional: one knows where it applies, but what the de'il it was about I never discovered.

About powers other than reason – I would be sorry if you mistook my position.[28] No one is more convinced than I that reason is utterly inadequate to the richness and spirituality of real things: indeed this is itself a deliverance of reason. Nor do I doubt the presence, even in us, of faculties embryonic or atrophied, that lie in an indefinite margin around

---

26 *The New Leader*, Vol. XIII, No. 53 (15 October 1926). In this periodical of the Labour Party, C. Henry Hamilton said of *Dymer*: 'In a lucid and dramatic Tale we follow the adventures of Dymer revolting from the standardized society in which he was born, he fled into the Wood of the World; and there, one by one, and through bitter experience, he sloughed off those unreal selves that life in the Perfect City had endowed him with. It is an allegory, at once so live and satisfying that we could well accept it as a Tale and leave it at that. But when the excitement of the drama slackens in memory the significance of the poem strikes home, and we know that Dymer is Everyman, his heritage the heritage of us all to-day – though not, alas! to all of us comes his unfolding. A fine poem, indeed, marred only by an opening canto that is commonplace in comparison with the rest of the work' (p. 15).

27 Lewis was thinking of the phrase 'Securus judicat orbis terrarum' – 'The world is a safe judge' – which he came across in John Henry Newman's *Apologia Pro Vita Sua* (1864), ch. III. It comes from St Augustine's *Contra Epistolam Parmeniani*, iii, 3.

28 He means as regards Anthroposophy. Cecil Harwood and Owen Barfield had become believers in Rudolf Steiner's Anthroposophy in 1923, and Lewis was totally opposed to it. What follows is an explanation of why he cannot accept Anthroposophy.

the little finite bit of focus which is intelligence – faculties anticipating or remembering the possession of huge tracts of reality that slip through the meshes of the intellect. And, to be sure, I believe that the symbols presented by imagination at its height are the workings of that fringe and present to us as much of the super-intelligible reality as we can get while we retain our present form of consciousness.

My scepticism begins when people offer me explicit accounts of the super-intelligible and in so doing use all the categories of the intellect. If the higher worlds have to be represented in terms of number, subject-and-attribute, time, space, causation etc (and thus they nearly always are represented by occultists and illuminati), the fact that knowledge of them had to come through the fringe remains inexplicable. It is more natural to suppose in such cases that the illuminati have done what all of us are tempted to do: – allowed their intellect to fasten on those hints that come from the fringe, and squeezing them, has made a hint (that was full of truth) into a mere false hard statement. Seeking to know (in the only way we can know) more, we know less. I, at any rate, am at present inclined to believe that we must be content to feel the highest truths 'in our bones': if we try to make them explicit, we really make them untruth.

At all events if more knowledge is to come, it must be the wordless & thoughtless knowledge of the mystic: not the celestial statistics of Swedenborg,[29] the Lemurian history of Steiner,[30] or the demonology of the Platonists. All this seems to me merely an attempt to know the super-intelligible *as if it were a new slice of the intelligible*: as though a man with a bad cold tried to get back smells with a microscope. Unless I greatly misunderstand you, you are (in a way) more rationalist than I, for you would reject as mere ideology my 'truths felt in the bones'. All this, by the bye, is meant for exposition, not argument.

---

29 The Swedish scientist and mystical thinker, Emanuel Swedenborg (1688–1772).

30 Rudolf Steiner (1861–1925), founder of Anthroposophy. He was educated at Vienna University and worked for several years on an edition of Goethe. In 1902 he became the leader of the German section of the Theosophical Society. He later rejected the eastern associations of the society and in 1913 founded the Anthroposophical Society as an independent association. His aim was to develop the faculty of spirit cognition inherent in ordinary people and to put them in touch with the spiritual world from which materialism had caused them to be estranged. His works include *The Bible and Wisdom* (1923), *Anthroposophy and the Social Question* [1933] and *Cosmic Christianity and the Impulse of Michael: Karma in the Life of Individuals and in the Evolution of the World* (1953). Anthroposophy was condemned by the Catholic Church in 1919.

I should dearly like a visit. Term ends on Dec. 11th, but I am not quite certain whether I shall be able to interpose a weekend between that and the beginning of a scholarship examination. But I will do my best. But seriously, are you certain that I shall not be a bother? I know that even an intimate friend cannot come to a house without disturbing to some extent the even tenor of its way – and there's the *parvus puer*.[31] Please make quite sure about this: and above all don't let Daphne persuade herself that it won't be a bother, because she thinks you'd enjoy having me. The fact that you have inflicted the whole of Dymer on her

> *(Unhappy fate the poet's wife attends*
> *– He reads his own stuff, and he reads his friends')*

has given me such large idea of her altruism, that I am afraid.

Barfield spent a night with me in college last week and we had a golden evening. With best wishes to all of you,

yrs

C. S. Lewis

TO MRS LILY SUFFERN (P):

Magdalen College,
Oxford
[November? 1926]

My dear Aunt Lily

A copy of this[32] has been set aside for you ever since publication, but I lost your address many months ago and so it has stood over. You gave me a bad fright in your letter – it was a relief to get to the doctor's revised verdict. Do let me know if there is anything more to know. Both you and I have had dealings with pain and death: I hope we can talk to each other with soldierly freedom. You will tell me everything, won't you?[33]

I am sure your attitude is the right one: half the people who die are killed off by fright at the names of diseases – often falsely diagnosed! But quite apart from this present trouble, is it really wise to live so entirely

---

31 'little boy'.
32 i.e. *Dymer*.
33 Lewis's Aunt Lily had cancer.

alone? You know you nearly fell into your well out at Thame...of course there are difficulties and a stupid housemate is a cross: but perhaps a fairly wholesome kind of cross.

Harley[34] is priceless. The incurable vulgarity of mind in our Holywood relations is a thing I shudder at: incurable, because it is accompanied by conceit.

What luck having the £250 to publish with – but surely it hasn't got down to publishing at your own expense. Surely even in this country there must be someone sufficiently alive to be interested in what you are saying. I long to see it as I still have only some idea of it in its earlier forms.

I am well, except for a cough, and live in the midst of (probably) too much beauty and too much comfort for soul's good: the only corrective is – well, not real overwork, but a continued succession of jobs, social and academic, which fritter away one's time.

As to Dymer – I always rely on you for plain honest criticism. The first four Cantos you have seen already: the last four are the best, I think, and certainly the most in your line. It has had one or two good reviews and is promised another, but I am still in Harley's position about sales.

I shall be very anxious to hear from you again as soon as possible. As regards all practical advice, you are much better informed than I am: I only beg you not be foolish and undertake more than you can manage. Can't you have even a girl in to help? It is dreadful to think of you in a cottage alone, falling thro' ceilings etc. I wish I could do anything that might be of help to you. Is there anything I possibly can do? Is there anything I can send you – you must be out of reach of most of the resources of civilisation. In the mean time, I can only assure you of my deepest sympathy in all the bothers you have had and my intense admiration of your courage. I saw the following dedication in a book the other day, and it made me think of you 'To —, —, and —, who had nothing in common except that they were not governed by fear and desire and you cd. believe what they said.' That is simple and sound, isn't it? With best love and best wishes in every way,

your affectionate nephew
Clive

---

34 Harley Hamilton was the daughter of Gussie and Annie Hamilton.

TO ARTHUR GREEVES (W):

[Magdalen College
December 1926]

My dear Arthur,

I was on the point of writing to find out where you were, when your letter arrived.[35] Of course I am sorry that we shall not meet at Christmas, but I quite understand that after your long spell of home you are not eager to return.

About the play[36] – of course I ought not really to speak without knowing more details of your new ideas than I do: but I can not help thinking that the introduction of incest is a mistake. I think it is quite legitimate for a man to take incest as his main theme, if he is really interested in a tragedy of it or the various moral and psychological problems which it raises. And in that case I shd. regard any moral objection to his work as invalid. But it is a very different thing for him simply to throw it in as the makeweight in a play whose real purpose and interest lie elsewhere. *That*, I think, might be legitimately objected to. At any rate it would irritate the best kind of spectator by diverting his attention from your real theme into the realm of mere pathology, and attract the wrong kind who will always find sexuality (specially abnormal sexuality) more interesting than anything else. Besides, you bring it in only to make things 'more so'. Wasn't it just that desire for the 'more so' which spoiled so many Elizabethan plays – piling horror on horror and death on death till the thing turns ridiculous? It's quality not quantity that counts. If you can't make tragedy out of the story as it was, you won't be any the more able to do so by the help of the unnatural. I think, myself, the whole feeling about incest is very obscure – almost a savage taboo, and not really moral at all: that makes it, to me, rather external and superficial. Again, won't it force you to load your play with improbabilities & long explanatory dialogues? I don't know if Gribbon is in your confidence about the play. If he is, you should discuss my view with him and try to reach a conclusion. The Banshee may be a good idea enough – it all depends, as you know, on the way it is introduced.

Minto and Maureen are well and send their love. I have had rather a nasty term with a cough wh. has kept me awake at nights and a good

---

35 From Paris, where Arthur Greeves had gone for a visit.
36 Arthur's play 'Trees', which was never published.

deal of work. I don't know how Dymer is selling, if at all. One thing is most annoying: you remember that the T.L.S. reviewer wrote a very kind letter, promising a good review.[37] It has not yet appeared. No doubt it will in time, but it is too late now to give a lead to other papers – wh. wd. have been its chief value. I am learning Old Norse and thus beginning to read in the original things I have dreamed of since before I really knew you. Dreams come true in unexpected ways.

yrs
Jack

P.S. I don't know the French for C/O. Is it 'chez' or 'au son soin de'?

37 Hugh l'Anson Fausset (1895–1965) wrote to Lewis on 29 September saying: 'I have just read and reviewed your Dymer for the Times Literary Supplement, but as some weeks will probably elapse before the review gets printed, I wish to send you a line to say what a remarkable achievement I consider your poem to be. I have not read any poem recently which has so impressed me by its inevitability of expression and by the profundity of its metaphysic. I use the word "metaphysic", unpleasant as it is, because it is by its metaphysical reach that your poem stands head and shoulders above most modern verse. But it is a metaphysic which is wholly and quite incalculably translated into terms of image and symbolism, and this seems to me the final test of greatness in poetry' (LP IX: 130–1). Fausset's review appeared in *The Times Literary Supplement* (13 January 1927), p. 27. See note 8 to letter of 30 March 1927.

1927

—— ≈ ——

*O*n 19 September Warnie learned that he had been selected to attend a
six-month course in economics at London University beginning on
4 October. He was able to travel with Jack to Belfast on 21 December to be
with their father for Christmas. On 18 January 1927 Mr Lewis wrote in his
diary: 'Warnie and Jacks returned tonight by Fleetwood. As the boat did not
sail until 11 o'c. they stayed with me to 9.30. So ended a very pleasant
holiday. Roses all the way' (LP IX: 139).

TO HIS FATHER (LP IX: 165–8):

Magdalen
March 30th 1927

My dear Papy,

I was sorry both to hear of the eclipse of the visit scheme and of
your disappointing state of health. As to the former, if it stood by itself, I
would reply (adapting Falstaff) 'Are there not trains? Are there not
motor buses? Are there not men of war in side cars?'[1] Why should your
movements depend on the erratic and extremely hazardous aurigations
of a boiler maker?[2] On the score of economy, trains have it every time.
On the score of safety I can think of no method of travelling which is not
superior to a seat in Uncle Gussie's car.

Of course, if you are not well enough to move at present, that is a different matter. Your account of the swelling on the right knee elicited the
word 'gout' from the only knowledgeable person I mentioned it to. I
know there is a sort of semi-jocular attitude adopted by everyone
towards the suggestion that he himself is suffering from gout. The connection between gout and port wine is so strong in our minds that we

---

1 William Shakespeare, *Henry IV, Part 2* (1600), I, ii, 84–7: 'Is there not wars? Is there not
employment? Doth not the king lack subjects? Do not the rebels want soldiers?'
2 i.e. Uncle Gussie Hamilton.

forget how flimsy it is in physiology. Did Grandfather or Grandmother suffer from it? I don't really see what you *can* do in the long run except go to some doctor who will really diagnose the complaint and really prescribe the proper treatment. I am quite sure you *will* do this in the end, and I cannot see what you will gain by postponing it. If you propose to offer up several months of pain as a sacrifice on the altar of old acquaintance, I reply that such an offering will not have the least effect. If Squeaky is going to be offended, he will be just as offended a month or an year hence as he would be tomorrow.

Of course on this question in general – the question of patronizing or dealing with the people you have always dealt with, even if they are not the best – I am entirely of your mind. I have never regretted Gillespie and his hexagonal wheel,[3] and if I lived at home would continue to use Gillespie all my life. But there must come a limit – a point at which the inefficiency of the man and the importance of the service in question absolutely demand a change. Hang it all, even you wouldn't suggest that because I've known Warnie a long time I ought to trust him as an interpreter on a holiday in Spain.

The scene of Squeaky in the office is a masterpiece and made me roar with laughter. One is re-assured to find that the comic spirit remains undefeated in the 'vile body'.[4] 'Fiat mixtura'[5] is the real titbit – to prevent Mopsi from sending you up the *aqua pura* in a separate bottle, as he would so naturally have done if left to himself. It reminds me of the President's latest exploit, when we met to elect a Proctor (it falls to each College in turn to choose one of its own Fellows as Proctor). When the election had been made the President said that a formal notice had to be sent to the Vice-Chancellor at once 'so perhaps Mr Benecke' (Benecke is about sixty years of age) 'you wouldn't mind going round: and then you must ring at the door and hand it to the maid'. As some one said, it only needed the additional injunctions 'and remember to wipe your feet and take a clean handkerchief' to make it really complete.

While I'm on this, I must tell you another. We are putting up a new building. In the committee that met to discuss it, someone suggested an

---

3 Mr Gillespie was a taxi driver.

4 Philippians 3:21.

5 'Let them be mixed.' Presumably Squeaky (i.e. Dr Richard Leslie) imagines Mopsi (the chemist) will not mix the aqua pura with the other unidentified substance unless Squeaky gives clear directions to the contrary.

architect's name, adding by way of explanation, 'that's the man who built Liverpool Cathedral'. To which the President at once retorted with an air of closing the matter, 'Oh, I don't think we want anything quite so large as that'.

He has at last announced his intention of retiring, so I suppose we shall live in the excitement of an election for the next year. He has certainly had a wonderful run for his money, and tho' a very laughable, is also a very lovable old fellow. He has the ludicrous, without the odious side of snobbery. He may have reverenced a Prince or a Duke too much, but never in his life did he despise or snub a poor scholar from a grammar school. When snobbery consists *only* of the admiring look upward and *not* of the contemptuous look downward, one need not be hard on it. A laugh – no unfriendly laugh – is the worst it deserves. After all, this kind of snobbery is half of it mere romance. A man may like Kings and Lords not so much because they have patronage to bestow as because he connects them (unconsciously no doubt) with stories and histories read at school. There is what is supposed to be a portrait of Sambo in 'Rough Justice' by C.E. Montague,[6] which just misses what I have been describing and represents him as a snob of the *un*pardonable type. It might interest you all the same, and the book is worth reading on other grounds. But don't believe him about Sambo.

I have had a pretty busy term, but good on the whole. I had been suffering a good deal before I went home at Christmas from sleeplessness, and from depression and nervousness (including nightmares) at nights. At first the change didn't seem to have done me much good and I was rather worried about myself, but after the first few weeks of this term the devils departed and I am now in excellent fettle. Nightmares are rather delightful things *afterwards*. As remembered (not heaven help us, as endured) they often have a sublimity and strangeness which one couldn't reach with the waking mind. It is dangerous to tell them – they sometimes sound flat to everyone except the dreamer. But here is one so good (it seems to me) that I must hand it on. I dreamed that I was walking among the valleys of the moon – a world of pure white rock, all deep chasms and spidery crags, with a perfectly black sky overhead. Of course there was nothing living there, not even a bit of moss: pure mineral solitude. Then I saw, very far off, coming to meet me down a narrow ravine,

6 Charles Edward Montague, *Rough Justice* [1926].

a straight, tall figure, draped in black, face and all covered. One knew it would be nicer not to meet that person: but one never has any choice in a dream, and for what seemed about an hour I went on till this stranger was right beside me. Then he held out an arm as if to shake hands, and of course I had to give him my hand: when suddenly I saw that instead of a hand he had a sort of metal ring which he closed round my wrist. It was sharp on the inside and hurt abominably. Then, without a word, drawing this thing together till it cut right to the bone, he turned and began to lead me off down the same long valley he had come from. It was the sense of being on the moon you know, the complete desolateness, which gave the extraordinary effect.

This Vac., besides the usual 'College Meetings', 'Tutorial Boards' etc., is involved in an Entrance Examination for which I have been nabbed. It is pleasant not to have pupils appearing at regular hours, but otherwise I am as busy nearly as in term, and if I can get away for two or three nights to do a walk somewhere, shall consider that I have done very well.

I never realised the proper question to ask oneself about reviews until it was put to me the other day by a friend who has published, and therefore been through the mill himself. It is of course 'What kind of a review *would* really satisfy you?' If honestly answered the question will lead one to demand for oneself a sort of *succès fou*[7] with large headlines – a degree in fact of recognition which could never be won now-a-days by any book of the sort one tries to write. Fausset's review really says as big things as I could, with any reason, wish for.[8] The question 'Is epic now possible?' has

---

7 'A huge success'.

8 In his review of *Dymer*, found in *The Times Literary Supplement* (13 January 1927), p. 27, Hugh l'Anson Fausset said: 'Mr Hamilton's poem is notable because it is in the epic tradition and yet is modern in idiom and reflects a profoundly personal intuition. The hero of the old epic kills monsters, giants, and dragons and these are rather symbols of the malign forces of nature with which the primitive man lives in constant conflict, than images of those forces as they war against the spiritual possibilities in the nature of man. As the epic ceases to be a primitive expression it ceases also to be symbolical and becomes allegorical. Its giants and dragons remain and its heroes contend against them with more and more knightly circumstance. But his adventures are only a pictorial tapestry woven for its own sake, to which a moral interpretation is somewhat arbitrarily attached. And doubtless the prejudice which exists against the epic as a modern art form is due to a belief that in civilized hands it must prove an impure form, a form in which substance and form are not necessarily related. Mr Hamilton has disproved that belief by showing that, in modern epic, the spiritual may be translated into terms of the physical, as inevitably in the primitive epic the physical was translated into terms of the imaginative. He has shown this more convincingly than Mr Masefield in Dauber, with

been a stock question for years. Taking the word 'epic' to mean his sense, there is no candidate between Milton and our own times. He puts up Masefield as a possible, and prefers me. He says I have brought back under modern conditions something that has seemed impossible since the days of myth – for I think he includes the Miltonic along with the Spenserian in his sentence about 'allegory' and 'knightly circumstance'. I don't mean of course that he thinks I am better than Milton and Spenser, but that I have brought back something lost before (and during) their time. If what he said were true, it wd. mean that I was a very considerable turning point. Of course he is wrong: whatever merits Dymer has are not really of the epic kind. But that is another question. He may be going in a direction which I think wrong but I certainly cannot demand that he should go further.

We live in the most absurd age. I met a girl the other day who had been teaching in an infant school (boys and girls up to the age of six) where the infants are taught the theory of Evolution. Or rather the Headmistress's version of it. Simple people like ourselves had an idea that Darwin said that life developed from simple organisms up to the higher plants and animals, finally to the monkey group, and from the monkey group to man. The infants however seem to be taught that 'in the beginning was the Ape' from whom all other life developed – including such dainties as the Brontosaurus and the Iguanodon. Whether the plants were supposed to be descendants of the ape I didn't gather. And then people talk about the credulity of the middle ages! A propos of this can you tell me who said 'Before you begin these studies, I should warn you that you need much more *faith* in science than in theology'. It was Huxley or Clifford or one of the nineteenth century scientists, I think. Another good remark I read long ago in one of E. Nesbitt's fairy tales – 'Grown ups know that children can believe almost anything: that's why they tell you that the earth is round and smooth like an orange when you can see perfectly well for yourself that it's flat and lumpy.'[9]

---

which his poem may be usefully compared, because Dymer's experience is throughout metaphysical. His ordeal is not on the high seas, but in swamps and places of his own soul's making...'

9 'Grown-up people find it very difficult to believe really wonderful things, unless they have what they call proof. But children will believe almost anything, and grown-ups know this. This is why they tell you that the earth is round like an orange, when you see perfectly well that it is flat and lumpy.' E. Nesbit, *Five Children and It* (1902), ch. I.

Almost the only interesting thing that has happened to me lately was a visit from a young German. He called to see me because he is a friend of a friend of mine in London. The friend had written asking me to be civil to him. He turned out to be more like a comic picture of a German in a war time Punch than you would have thought it possible for a living man to be. I mean, his neck went up quite straight from the back of his collar into his head, and he had hardly any hair. But this was nothing to the joys of his conversation. I asked if he had served in the war. He replied after deep thought (he is a high falutin sort of a fellow, philosophical, theosophical, very spiritual – *geistlic* I think he'd call it) 'Ach...I could not bring to my mind the reality of that life...I could not connect myself systematically with this war, this soldat...so I became very ill'. I wish I'd known that tip in 1919. I refrained from asking him the German for 'to swing the lead'.

His next was almost as delicious. He was already engaged to dine at Christ Church, and I was going out to lunch, so the best that I could do (by way of fulfilling the requests of our mutual friend) was to ask him if he could come in and have a talk and a drink that evening after dinner. He said he would if he could. Next day a postcard arrived saying that tho' our engagement had been of a vague kind, still he thought he would write and apologise for not coming as 'his consciousness not was quite pure'. By the by, while everyone can see the joke, how many can correct him here? I mean make absolutely clear to a foreigner the difference between 'consciousness' and 'conscience', within the limits of a postcard? I gave up the attempt: it really turned out too difficult. Of course it is easy enough if there is a German word for 'conscience' as opposed to 'consciousness' – but I don't know whether there is. I think French uses 'la conscience' for both, while on the other hand the Latin 'conscientia' is hardly ever used for 'consciousness'.

I dined the other night at an Italian Professor's, who is a Fellow of Magdalen,[10] and sat next to a Frenchwoman who has met Mussolini. She says he is a rhetorician, and escapes from questions he doesn't want to answer into a cloud of eloquence. I asked if she thought him a charlatan. She said no: he quite believes all his own gas, like a school boy, and is

---

10 Cesare Carolo Foligno (1878–1963), Italian scholar, was Taylorian Lecturer in Italian at Oxford University 1909–15, and Serena Professor of Italian and Fellow of Magdalen 1919–40. He was Professor of English at the University of Naples 1940–53.

carried away by it himself. It interested me very much as being true to type – Cicero must have been just that sort of man. She also claimed to have said to him 'Yes, I have heard all the rhetoric, now I want the real answer', which I took leave (silently) to disbelieve. But my host told me that it is almost certainly true, for she appears to be a sort of Aunt Lily on the grand scale, who meets the biggest lions by accident and tells them their own business. A good remark about lions was made the same evening (by a lady). 'When I meet that sort of person I am always divided between two fears: one that he will speak to me: the other that he won't.'

This letter has grown to an intolerable length. I have discovered the real secret of letter writing. (I mean the secret of quantity of course. Quality is another matter.) It is to write a letter when you have another task you ought to be doing. For instance I proposed this morning to finish a few notes on English sound laws (which are not gay), badly needed for next term. Then when you get to the really nasty part of course as usual one's thoughts begin to stray. 'Why not write that letter' comes as a seduction rather than an admonition. Hinc illae.[11] You ought to try it. I hope I shall profit by it to the extent of many pages the next time you decide to spend an evening with your accounts – if the rheumatics allow you.

I quite see that the hotel in Donegal is in some way unattractive. But temperance and plain diet are to be had everywhere. May I suggest that nothing hinders – indeed the Lenten season encourages, – you and the Colonel to make Leeborough during the coming week into a *temperance hotel* with *plain but plentiful food*. Dumb bells and 'Instant Postum' you know.

your loving son,
Jack

P.S. Did I tell you that I was asked to tea by a pupil not long ago and noticed a copy of Dymer in his bookcase? That is fame.

---

11 'Flitting from this to that'.

TO HIS BROTHER (LP IX: 224–31):[12]

[Hillsboro,
Western Avenue,
Headington,
Oxford]

Easter Monday [18 April 1927]

My dear W.,

I had both your communications and remain about as wise as before. We, or at any rate Minto, will scan the papers daily: but in what *part* of the press will the information be given? In the shipping? Or the Gazette? We will do our best, but I doubt very much whether this will be posted till we have had word from you?

Mr Papworth[13] continued to manifest his disapproval of the proceedings until we were out of Oxford and almost starting the ascent of Cuckoo Lane: in fact he showed every flattering degree of attention compatible with his 'beastly kind' (wh. sounds more beefy and affecting somehow than our modern 'animal nature'). He is still frequently struck by a resemblance to you in some grocer or roadmender of portly habit and springs to investigate. You will be surprised to hear that while I write this, Minto is out to dinner. This results from the chief event since you left – the arrival of 'un ami' of Florence de Forest – not staying here, thank heavens. He is a little Swiss commercial traveller, 'Villie Goût', as smart as a bandbox, and very polite. Beyond making horrible noises in clearing his 'pipes' (a la Sir Roger)[14] and being intensely ugly, he is really quite harmless, tho' of course very vulgar. He and Florence absolutely insisted on Minto's dining with them at the Eastgate tonight, and won the day. They know how to move their monde, as you will see from this fact and also when I tell you that they made me take them up Magdalen Tower this morning – as well as round the College. When I showed them

---

12 On 11 April 1927 Warnie set sail on the troopship *Derbyshire* for Shanghai where he would remain for almost three years.

13 Mr Papworth, or Baron Papworth, was Lewis's and Mrs Moore's dog. They had many dogs and cats over the years, but Baron Papworth, who died in 1937, was always their favourite.

14 Sir Roger de Coverley, a delightful character in *The Spectator*, the periodical conducted by Sir Richard Steele and Joseph Addison. *The Spectator* ran from 1 March 1711 to 6 December 1712, and part of 1714. In issue No. 269 (by Addison) of 8 January 1712 Sir Roger de Coverley could be heard 'upon the Terrace hemming twice or thrice to himself with great Vigour, for he loves to clear his Pipes in good Air'.

the deer he made one of those extremely simple French jokes with which Maurice and M. Zée have familiarised us.[15] I had explained that these deer were descendants of a herd wh. had been there before the College was founded (that is quite true by the by, or as true as a College tradition need be), and I added 'So you may say they are the oldest members of the College'. 'And ze most intelligent?' returned M. Goût.

I was really glad they made me go up the Tower. I think I only tried to take you up but I didn't then know where the key was to be had. It was superb on top. There was a magnificent sky of blue and white, and the whole cluster of roofs and towers simply blazed in sun light. One also gets the effect of the town in its frame – it is just small enough for there to be a margin of green hill beyond the roofs on every side, except north-ward, where trees play the same role. Then the lawn in the cloister quad-rangle below – it is far enough away to look more perfect than any grass could be. 'Velvet' and 'shaven' were no longer poetical metaphors applied to *it*. It gave me a good idea of the peculiar kinds of beauty one must get from a low flying aeroplane.

We have a visitor at present, a Miss Whitty,[16] a music teacher of Maureen's at Bristol, who is one of Minto's lame ducks. 'Sir, he is poor, he is miserable, and that is recommendation enough to Johnson'. But while ill health, poverty and overwork may justify her presence in Hillsboro, they can hardly justify her appearance in this letter. I cite her because she clears up a problem. You must have wondered very often for *what* public illuminated texts of Kipling's 'If',[17] calendars with a thought for every day, mottoes in crackers, Easter cards, etc., etc., etc. were produced. Now I know. To Miss W. these are food and drink. It is most embarrassing. She is really struck by a 'Thought for the week' in the Sunday Pictorial and will *read it out*. You know how those things are, even when you glance at them in turning over the pages of the paper. But you can have no conception what they *sound* like if actually pronounced during a pause at the breakfast table. There are things extant in print which, one took it for granted, had never, would never reach the viva voce level of

---

15 The Frenchmen, Maurice Delangues and Monsieur Zée, had been paying guests at one time. See *AMR*, 1 August–9 September 1923, for the period Maurice Delangues was with them.

16 Kathleen Whitty, who had been Maureen's music teacher in Bristol, often visited the Moores in Oxford.

17 Rudyard Kipling, 'If–' (1910).

existance. I will inflict one only on you – and am rather chary about it even on paper, well impounded in inverted commas. 'No one is utterly useless in this world who helps to lighten another's burden'. We needn't bother about 'in this world': they all take care to tell you that they refer to 'this world' or 'this life'. It gives a sort of atmosphere. But just look at the rest. To lighten someone's burden can only mean to do him a service, which again can only mean to be useful to him. So that the gem precisely informs us that if you're any use you can't be useless. The length of the oscillation my mind performs – from the extreme of subtlety, reading Coleridge's Biographia Literaria till the lunch bell goes – to the extreme of platitude when I reach the table!

I forget if you know the Biographia. A good deal of it is too philo-sophical to interest you, but the earlier chapters on Christ's Hospital under Bowyer are an interesting supplement to Lamb's account, and there is lots of good literary criticism. As an attempt at a book (as opposed to mere Coleridgean talk) it is preposterous. Indeed it contains, nay *consists of*, the best unconscious bit of literary joke that was ever played. In about the 2nd or 3rd chapter Coleridge makes his famous dis-tinction between imagination and fancy,[18] and decides that he must explain what imagination really is. In the Coleridgean style (it must be exactly like his conversation) this very naturally involves a preliminary sketch of the history of the theory of the association of ideas from Aris-totle down to his own time, which leaves one more or less ready to begin a flanking movement on the main subject, via Kant, Fichte, Schelling, Spinoza, the Neo-Platonists, and the mystics. Somewhere half way through the book, after a suggested theory of knowledge in general and a development of Cartesianism along new lines (with a few mild ten page

---

18 Coleridge, *Biographia Literaria*, ch. XIII: 'The imagination then I consider either as primary, or secondary. The primary imagination I hold to be the living power and prime agent of all human perception, and as a repetition in the finite mind of the external act of creation in the infinite I AM. The secondary I consider as an echo of the former, co-existing with the conscious will, yet still as identical with the primary in the kind of its operation. It dissolves, diffuses, dissipates, in order to re-create; or where this process is rendered impossible, yet still, at all event, it struggles to idealize and to unify. It is essentially *vital*, even as all objects (as objects) are essentially fixed and dead. Fancy, on the contrary, has no other counters to play with but fixities and definites. The fancy is indeed no other than a mode of memory emancipated from the order of time and space; and blended with, and modified by that empirical phenomenon of the will which we express by the word *choice*. But equally with the ordinary memory it must receive all its materials ready made from the law of association.'

episodes of the anecdotal, critical and religious type) we actually get into touch with the enemy's outpost line. We see 'Imagination' as a chapter heading. We beat to quarters (or whatever it is) and are all ready when suddenly our author quotes a letter from 'a friend' advising him after all *not* to give an account of imagination. While you are still wondering what this is put in for, Coleridge, remarking 'that this judicious letter produced *immediate conviction* in his mind'[19] has quietly closed the chapter – and the fixture is off. 'And what good came of it at last, quoth little Peterkin'.[20] The answer is *nothing* – nothing whatsoever.

It reminds me of my friend Barfield who recently wrote me a letter full of plans for our Easter walking tour and added in the last line 'Wash out, Beckett[21] has just rung up to say he couldn't manage such a day' – but solemnly posted and sent it all the same. We start on this walk tomorrow, assembling at Goring station at 2.30 – a loathsome hour to begin at, but it couldn't be helped. We shall lie our first night at East Ilsey. We propose to walk through Lambourn on the downs and Savernake Forest to Marlborough: thence on to the Plain, and Salisbury itself is not beyond our ambitions. We had originally planned a more adventurous tour over Exmoor, but it proved too long for the short holidays of some and the purses of others.

April 26th

I arrived back from my travels at lunch time yesterday and found your letter, posted at Gib.,[22] awaiting me. It had come in fact the day after I left. It left me with a fine impression of boundless leisure and sea air, that is particularly tantalizing in view of the recollection that term begins on Friday. The arrival of income tax forms this morning drives home my irritation with this hanky-panky which keeps a few hundreds of self-indulgent fellows like you fooling about in the Mediterranean on my money in order to fill the pockets of the 'China Merchants'. However, you may be in less pleasant circumstances by the time this reaches you, so I must suppress the note of envy. Still, provided that you don't meet

---

19 ibid.
20 Robert Southey, 'The Battle of Blenheim' (1800), ll. 12–13.
21 (Sir) Eric Beckett (1896–1966), who often walked with Barfield, Lewis and the others, took a First in Jurisprudence from Wadham College in 1921. He was a Fellow of All Souls College 1921–8. He was called to the Bar in 1922 and was assistant legal adviser to the Foreign Office 1925–45 and legal adviser 1955–8.
22 i.e. Gibraltar.

with a war in China, every ordinary boredom and discomfort which may await you is a price almost worth paying for a free trip half round the world, well fed, unworked, and in tolerably congenial society. (You must be putting on flesh at a desperate rate.)

I thought we had mentioned Squire Western's choice of table talk before.[23] It goes to the root of the matter, doesnt it? By the way I have never been able to share that popular feeling about Western as a fine type of bluff, honest, genial Englishman: he seems to me one of the four or five most intolerable people in fiction (I mean to meet: of course he is excellent in a book). *Tom Jones* goes far to explain why Johnson and his set didn't like the country. I can quite imagine that a countryside of highwaymen and the rural jokes of the period, inhabited by Westerns and Blifils would have led him to 'abstract his mind and think of Tom Thumb':[24] for one can hardly imagine him knocking them down with folios. At least, if he had made the attempt, he would have liked the country even less after it than before it. He would have dismissed Mr Square as an infidel dog, and I dont feel that he would have got on with Thwackum. Sophia is good. She comes during that lucid interval when good heroines were possible in novels written by men, when the restoration tradition by which a heroine must be a whore was dead, and the Victorian tradition by which she must be a fool had not been born.

Now for my own adventures. I was joined [on 19 April] at Oxford station by two others and we proceeded together to Goring.[25] One of them was new to the game and turned up carrying a Tommies pack filled square like a tommy's pack, for inspection. On the way we extracted from it a large overcoat, a sponge, four shirts, a heavy tin mug holding about a pint, two strong metal cigarette cases of pudaita proportions, and a number of those insane engines which some people associate with holidays. You know – the adaptable clasp knife which secrets a fork at

---

23 In Henry Fielding's *The History of Tom Jones* (1749).

24 Percival Merritt, *The True Story of the so-called Love Letters of Mrs Piozzi* (1927), p. 70.

25 The friends who met Lewis in Oxford for a walk on the Berkshire Downs were Owen Barfield and Cecil Harwood. They were joined at Goring by Walter Ogilvie 'Wof' Field (1893–1957). Field came up to Trinity College, Oxford, from Marlborough College in 1912. He left to join the Warwickshire Rifle Regiment in 1914, and in 1916, having continued his studies, he took a war degree from Trinity College. He was promoted to captain in 1916, and after seeing action in France and Italy he was wounded and forced to retire in 1919. In 1926 he became a teacher at the Rudolf Steiner School in Forest Row, East Sussex.

one end and a spoon at the other, but in such a way that you could never really use the fork and the spoon together – and all those sort of things. Having recovered from our delighted laughter and explained that we were going to walk in an English county and not in Alaska, we made up the condemned articles into a parcel wh. we compelled him to post home from Goring. It weighed about seven pounds. Our fourth met us at Goring station.

After tea in the garden of the lock keeper at Goring lock – we ate it sitting just beside the weir, dipping our hands into the water and enjoying the rush and the noise – we set out N.N.W. In half an hour the suburbanity of Goring was out of sight. We soaked for a long time in a winding valley with all the bigness of downs opening behind and the richer Chiltern country towards Henley rising in the distance. We were on the broad grass track of the Icknield Way, the grass very short and fine and perfectly dry, as it is nearly all the year round in these chalk hills. It was an afternoon of lovely sunshine with a pleasant light wind, and a lark overhead displayed all its accomplishments. That night we slept at East llsley which (I think) you and I went through on our way to Salisbury.

We spent nearly the whole of Wednesday [20 April] following the Icknield Way along the northern edge of the downs, overlooking the Wantage valley on our right. Around us, and to our left, the country had all the same character: close smooth grass, very pale in colour, deliciously springy to the foot: chalk showing through here and there and making the few ploughed pieces almost cream colour: and, about three to a mile, clumps of fir, whose darkness made them stand out very strikingly from the low tones of the ground. The extent of prospect was (or seemed to be) larger than any I have seen, even from the highest hills I have been on – just wave after wave of down, and then more of them, for ever. The air is very clear here and one sometimes sees a hay stack or a farm on a ridge, so distinct and at the same time so remote that it is like something seen through the wrong end of a telescope. We had tea at Lambourn and slept at Aldbourne.

Thursday [21 April] opened with discussions. A survey of the maps showed a lamentable discrepancy between the route we wanted to follow and the possible places for lunch. Then emerged the dark and hideous prospect of 'taking' lunch. Perfectly simple you know. Buy some bread and cheese before we start and have lunch where we like. Makes you independant you know. Drinks? Oh, get a few oranges if you don't feel inclined to carry a bottle of beer in your pack for the first ten miles. I need hardly say that our novice – the Knight of the Adaptable Jack Knife – was entirely in favour of a scheme which promised to restore his original conception. I of course, who had seen days spoiled this way before, was the head of the opposition. The wrong party won. We stuffed our packs with bread, butter, cheese and oranges. The only thing I look back on with satisfaction was that the butter, at any rate, was not in my pack. Then we set off.

The first mile made us thoroughly aware of the fact that the wind (wh. had been in our faces since Goring) had risen to a gale. The next three miles left no one in any doubt of the fact that when a strong wind blows in your face all day, it parches your throat and chaps your lips without cooling your body. We were now in sight of 'Barberry Castle', a Roman Camp, for the sake of seeing which all this folly had started. The exponents of the 'carry your lunch' school had now reached the stage of indulging in a quite unusual degree of praise of the scenery and the pleasures of walking tours, on the 'this is fine' lines. But long before we had reached the top of that disastrous camp they slunk in silence, and only the malcontents (Barfield and myself) felt inclined to talk. In fact we talked quite a lot.

When we reached the top we found ourselves in one of those places where you can neither speak for the hurricane nor open your eyes for the sun. Beyond the suggestion (mine) of performing on the wind (and the Romans) a certain physiological operation disallowed by English law and by polite conversation, we were silent here. Turning up our collars and pulling our hats down hard on our heads, we couched under a scrannel gorse bush wherever prickles and sheep dung left a space, and produced our scanty and squalid meal. The appearance of the butter faintly cheered us (all of us except the man among whose socks and pyjamas it had travelled), but it was a sight that moved mirth, not appetite. The last straw was the oranges, wh. proved to be of the tough, acrid, unjuicy type, which is useless for thirst and revolting to taste.

The midday siesta (that great essential of a day's walking) was out of the question in that abominable camp, and we set off gloomily S.W. Barfield and I dropped behind and began composing in Pope-ian couplets a satire on the people who arrange walking tours. Nothing cd have been happier. At a stroke every source of irritation was magically changed into a precious fragment of 'copy'. By the time we had walked three miles we were once more in a position to enjoy the glorious country all round us. Five o'clock found us descending a slope full of druidical stones, where we started three hares successively so close that we had nearly trodden on them, into the village of Avebury.

Avebury overwhelmed me and put me into that dreamlike state which is sometimes the reward of being very tired. Imagine a green ancient earthwork with four openings to the four points of the compass, almost perfectly circular, the wall of a British city, large enough to contain broad fields and spinneys inside its circuit, and, in the middle of them, dwarfed by its context, a modern village. Obviously here was the capital of a great king before the Roman times. We had been passing British things all day – stones, mounds, camps etc. But it was extraordinary to find a Berkshire village inside one. Here we had tea gloriously, in the orchard of an inn: and took off our shoes, and ordered a fresh pot and more hot water, and fair copied the satire and lay on our backs and talked Oxford reminiscences and smoked pipes.

Then Wof – he's the jack knife man – did a sensible thing by returning after a moment's absence and saying 'If you're not very keen on *walking* to Marlborough there's a man here with a milk cart who will take us in'. So we sat among milk cans (which are just the right angle to lean against) and bumped and rattled along the Bath road (of Pickwickian and coaching memories) into Marlborough. Field is an old Marlburian but we were too tired to let him show us the sights. He told us however (what will interest you) that the fine old Georgian building which faces you as you enter the school precincts was an inn on the Bath road in the old days. Pleasant days they must have been.

Next day [22 April] we walked about four miles into Savernake Forest. It is not to be compared with the Forest of Dean, but well worth an hour or so. It is the typically English kind of wood – nearly all big oaks with broad mossy spaces between them and deer flitting about in the distance. Leaving the forest we struck westward into the vale of Pewsey, and were threading about little woods and fieldpaths for an hour or so. After our windy days on the Downs this was a pleasant change: the richness of the colours, the soft burring of the wind (now harmless) in the little trees, and the flowers everywhere were specially delightful by contrast. We crossed a fine rise called Hansell Hill: a thing rising so abruptly on both sides that it was like a gigantic tumulus. From the top of this we had one of the finest views in England. Northward, the Berkshire Downs, huge even in their apparent extent, and huger to our minds because we had spent two whole days walking on them. Southward, across the valley, rose the edge of the Salisbury plain.

We came down the side of that hill over a big spur called the Giant's Grave and lunched admirably in the village of Ocue – beer and bread and cheese followed by a pot of tea, and then a game of darts: you know the apparatus for that game which one finds in pubs. Shortly after lunch we had the best 'soak'[26] I've ever had in a walk, by turning out of a little grassy lane into a wood where the grass grew soft and mossy, and there were solid clumps of primroses the size of dinner plates: not to mention a powdering of those little white flowers – wood anemones. We laid ourselves flat on our back with packs under our head for pillows (for it is in the beauty of a pack that it can thus convert into a regular bed a flat ground otherwise useless for soaking): some rash attempts at conversation were ignored and we spent an hour with half shut eyes listening to the burring of the wind in the branches, and an occasional early bumble bee. The remainder of the day brought forth a bad bit of wrong map reading: but this also is among the delights of a journey: for it found us ambling into our tea stopping place along the grassy tow-path of an all but obsolete canal, where we had never meant to go and which was all the better for that. We lay at Devizes: a poor inn.

Next day [23 April] we struck south across the vale of Pewsey. We expected to be bored in this low ground which divides the Berkshire Downs from Salisbury Plain: but it turned out a pleasant morning's tramp through roads with very fine beech trees and a tangle of footpaths. Even if it had been dull, who would not make sacrifices to pass through a place called Cuckold's Green. (We passed Shapley Bottom two days before.) I myself was for tossing a pot of beer at Cuckold's Green, which we might have done by going two hundred yards out of our course, but the other two being both married, ruled that this was no place to rest a moment longer than we need. So did literary associations render possible a joke that the illiterate would hardly venture on. (In passing, if one had lived in the 17th century, what a horrible fate it

---

26 The reader should remember the definition of a 'soaking machine' in the letter to Arthur Greeves of 11 May 1915: 'The word "soak" means to sit idly or sleepily doing nothing, and a S'ing machine is [a] place for this operation.'

would have been to live at Cuckold's Green. 'Your servant sir. Your wife tells me that you are carrying her to the country in a few days. Pray sir where do you live?' 'Cuckold's Green.' By the age of forty one wd be quite definitely tired of the joke.)

We lunched this side of the climb on to the Plain, and crawled up on to that old favourite afterwards. It pleased me as much as ever: more than all, after being given tea by a postmistress, with boiled eggs and bread and jam at lib., for which she wanted to take only 6d. Oddly enough, up there in the chalk of the plain, that village was almost completely under water. Our evening walk, up and down mile after mile of unfenced chalk road with smooth grey grass all round and sheep and young lambs (so numerous that in places they were deafening), and a mild setting sun in our faces, was heavenly.

But what no one can describe is the delight of coming (as we came) to a sudden drop and looking down into a rich wooded valley where you see the roofs of a place where you're going to have supper and bed: specially if the sunset lies on the ridge beyond the valley. There is so much mixed in it: the mere physical anticipations as of a horse nearing its stable, the sense of accomplishment and the feeling of 'one more town', one further away into the country you don't know, and the old never hackneyed romance of travelling (not of 'travel' wh. is what you are doing and wh. no doubt has its own different pains and pleasures). It always seems to sum up the whole day that is behind you – give it a sort of climax and then stow it away with the faintly melancholy (but not unpleasant) feeling of things going past. This town I am gassing about was Warminster. Here we had the ill luck to come into a fair: so that half an hour after that quiet moment on the edge of the Plain (with the first stars just coming out) we were treading our way through the noisy and sweaty crowds of a narrow street, lit up by naked gas flares and bellowing with the steam organs of roundabouts and the voices of cocoa-nut-shy people. We even had confetti on us. And alas! all the hotels were in that street. Luckily it was a Saturday so they had to stop at midnight. (Let us here bless that much abused Puritan Sunday of ours which gives rest to the labouring classes and peace to ours.) So after ham and eggs, cider, bread, cheese, marmalade and tea, we had a philosophical discussion (or so it seemed at the time) till twelve o'clock, and so to bed, all three of us in a room: where as long as I lay awake I heard the showmen (v. tired poor fellows) taking down their shows. Their conversation was of a purely military kind. 'Wot the f—g 'ell are you doin Jarge?' 'Where's that bl—dy f—g hammer?' 'I 'ant got yet bleedin' 'ammer. Go and f—g well b—r yerself' etc. etc.

Next day [24 April] we walked all morning through the estates of the Marquis of Bath, in a very old and fine forest on a hillside. About a mile and a half below us on the hillside we saw the house – a rather tiresome place on the lines of Blenheim, with three lakes – and we emerged at one o'clock into a village just outside one of the park gates. The atmosphere here is feudal, for the hostess of our mittagessen pub would talk about nothing but His Lordship, who apparently lives here all the year round and knows everyone in the village. We asked how old he was. 'O, we don't think 'im old', she replied, which stumped me. The rest of that day was so intensively complex in route and so varied in scenery (also we were so embroiled in conversation) that I give no account of it. Suffice it that 8 o'clock found me in a hot bath at Shepton Mallett which is just under the eastern end of the Mendips and half a day's march from Wells. So that if you take Goring in the right way (really a suburb of London) and if you take Wells as being just outside Bristol, we might say (the P'daitabird undoubtedly *would* say) that we had walked across England. At any rate, another day and a half and we could have dipped our hands in the Bristol Channel. 'There's glory for you' as Humpty Dumpty said! Next day we all returned home by train.

I have spent so long (to my entertainment more perhaps than yours) on my tour that I must huddle up everything else. I had your letters from Gib. and from Aden and also the long letter forwarded by the P'daita Bird, wh. I read with very great interest and enjoyment. The description of the Red Sea coast (how differently one imagines it when Milton says 'The red sea coast whose waves ov'erthrew / Busiris and his Memphian chivalry')[27] particularly took my fancy and has really enriched me with a new conception.

I sympathise with you in your uncongenial society and above all in your P.T. I suppose there are two points of view for a trooper in the tropics, (1) 'Well you can't possibly take exercise *here*'. (2) 'Well, a man must do something to keep himself sweet in a place like this'. I need hardly say that the one point of view as compared with the other seems to me as light to darkness. It is most chilling to reflect how long you must wait

---

27 Milton, *Paradise Lost*, I, 306–7.

before you get this: but it has really been impossible to get it finished any sooner.

And now for Lamb's final division of a letter – 'puns'. I think I have only two. (1). The story of a man[28] who was up with me, and who was the only genuine maker of malapropisms I ever met: but this one I never heard till the other day. It appears that while having tea with the 'dear Master of University' he conducted a long conversation with the ladies, chiefly re places to stay for one's holidays, under the impression that the word 'salacious' meant 'salubrious'. You can imagine the result. But what you can't imagine is that when the Mugger himself, whose brow had been steadily darkening for some minutes (during which he had heard his daughters told that they wouldn't like Devonshire very much because it wasn't very salacious) finally decided to cut it short and broke in with 'Well Mr Robson-Scott, how do you like Oxford?' Robson-Scott turned to him with imperturbable good humour and said 'Well to tell you the truth sir, it isn't so salacious as I had hoped.'

This fellow Robson indulged also – as I well remember – in a kind of complicated misfire of meaning: rather like a rarefied or quintessential p'daitaism. Two I can vouch for. When arriving with me late somewhere he observed panting, 'We might have known that it wd. take us longer than it did.' Another time, in a debate, he said, 'I quite agree with Mr So-and-So's point *as far as it goes* – but it goes much too far.' You will see how easily this sort of thing wd. pass for sense in the heat of the moment.

(2). I don't know if this can rank as a pun, but I'll put it down. When S.P.B. Mais (whose Diary of a Schoolmaster we have both read) got a 3rd in English here, the examiners told him they were very sorry, but added by way of consolation that he 'was the very best Third they had ever examined'. On which Raleigh[29] remarked 'It is bad enough for a man to get a Third: but to be pointed out as the most brilliant Third of your year is damnable.'

(3). I've just remembered another – rather more suitable. An old pupil of mine who is now a master at Stowe came to see me the other day. Among other things, he told me that the moral tone there was very

---

28 William Douglas Robson-Scott (1900–80), who matriculated at University College in 1919, and in 1923 took a First in English Literature. He became Professor of German Language and Literature at Birkbeck College, University of London.

29 i.e. Sir Walter Raleigh, the first Professor of English at Oxford.

high. I told this to a cynical colleague whose reply was, 'From what I saw of Stowe, the grounds are so large and so well wooded that the moral tone couldn't help being high'. By the by, the moral tone at Stowe seems to be really insane. What are boys thinking of? This master (my pupil) said 'Damn' in a game of rugger. Whereupon, if you please, a deputation of prefects waits upon the Headmaster to complain. They have just succeeded in stopping bad language in their houses: and what are they to do if master etc., etc. I must say if I were the Headmaster I should be tempted to the P'daita policy of thrashing the lot. Or better still 'I'd teach them to say damn if I had to lie under their beds all night' (Perhaps no bad expedient for the purpose!).

Well, I must stop. I have taken pupils, and walked Mr Papworth, and played bowls and it is near twelve o'clock. I look forward to your next letter. The family all send their good wishes to which I add my own – the sum total being a speedy return.

yrs.

J.

Warnie arrived in Singapore on 10 May, and from there his ship made its way to Kowloon on mainland China, a few miles from the island of Hong Kong, arriving there about 15 May. Writing to Jack on 7 June, he said:

> *I am second in command of the Base Supply Depot, with [Captain J.E.] Drysdale as my O.C., which naturally is as pleasant an arrangement as could have happened...Broadly speaking I am a cross between a ship's officer and a wharf manager. A steady succession of store ships arrive at our wharf with supplies from home or Australia and it is my duty to receive and check them and stack them in the 'godown' as they call it, which is the local name for a warehouse. (LP IX: 237)*

He went on in the same letter to describe their commanding officer, Colonel G.E. Badcock, 'who is really,' he said,

> *I believe the most excessively unpleasant man I have ever met in the whole of my life. To describe him properly would need a letter in itself, but briefly he is a pompous bully with a thoroughly common*

mind. He has some ability, but his real talent is that of a showman. His advertising is really admirable, and he has what amounts to a genius for assimilating the ideas of other men, and text books, and later on reproducing them as his own. (Ibid.)

Warnie mentioned Colonel Badcock in a letter to his father of 14 June:

This fellow is, with one solitary war time exception, the most objectionable man I have ever served under in my life. I personally have not fallen foul of him yet, but I fear it is only a matter of time till I do so...Short of some maddened soldier putting a bullet in him, I see no prospect of escape, for he is one of those great oxes of men whom no climate appears to affect...In the mean time he is determined to get something for himself out of this show if he kills every officer and man under him in doing it. (LP IX: 241)[30]

Colonel Badcock was to make the first five months in China almost intoler-able for Warnie.

---

30 In fact, Colonel Gerald Eliot Badcock (1883–1966) was a distinguished soldier. He was born in Murree, India, on 26 August 1883, the son of General Sir Alexander Robert Badcock (1844–1907), and was educated at Wellington College and Pembroke College, Cambridge. He was commissioned a 2nd lieutenant in the Army Service Corps in 1904, promoted to captain in 1912, adjutant in 1914, major and then brevet lt.-colonel in 1918, and colonel in 1931. From 1915–19 he was Assistant Director of Transport for the Middle East Force and the Egyptian Expeditionary Force. He became Commanding Officer of the Royal Army Service Corps in China in 1927, but returned to England in 1929 to serve as Chief Instructor at the Royal Army Service Corps Training College at Aldershot, 1929–31. From there he went on to become an instructor at the Senior Officers' School at Sheerness, 1931–3. He was Assistant Quartermaster General for the War Office from 1934 until his retirement in 1936. Colonel Badcock served as Bursar of Clifton College, Bristol, 1936–9, after which he was re-employed by the War Office as Director of Salvage, 1940–44. On his retirement he moved to Dorchester where he died 13 January 1966. He is the author of *A History of the Transport Services of the Egyptian Expeditionary Force, 1916–1917–1918* (1925), and an autobiographical work (which contains his photograph), *Two Generations: General Sir A.R. Badcock, Colonel G.E. Badcock* [1933].

TO HIS FATHER (LP IX: 234–6):

Magdalen College,
Oxford.
Saturday.
[28 May 1927]

My dear Papy,

Your wire, which arrived this morning, contributed more to my grandeur than to my peace of mind. It contributed to my grandeur because it happened to be the third communication of an urgent nature which I had received during that hour, and the pupil who was with me, seeing me inundated with these messages and telegrams, must doubtless have supposed that I was the hub of some mighty academical, or even national intrigue. I am sorry you were bothered. I had not thought my silence had been long enough to give you serious anxiety, though it was longer than I wished. If I had written before I could only have given you a line, for the summer term is always the busiest and my days are very full.

Many thanks for the 'Wandering Scholars'.[31] I have so far been able to read it only bit by bit, a quarter of an hour daily, between being called at 7.30 and getting out of my bed at 7.45. It is difficult to judge such a book, for the matter is so extremely interesting to me and my appetite of ignorance so sharp set, that I have paid little attention to the style and disposition. And of course there is always an impossibility in forming a real judgement of a work of scholarship unless you have independent knowledge of the author's raw material. I cannot say how she has *handled* the stuff when I depend on her for knowing the stuff at all. I think, on the whole, that it is a delightful book, tho' rather over-written (all the things she mentions can't really be as good as she claims) and too emotional. But, after all, it tells me much that it is very hard to find elsewhere and will be very useful to me: one cannot ask for much more.

Now for a more important matter. W. and I both agreed that heaven and earth must be moved to get you out of Ireland this summer – preferably to some place where rheumatics are cured. The Colonel's parting instructions were given with characteristic emphasis 'Take him to Droitwich and just get him *boiled in mud* or whatever it is they do to people there.' And I agreed, and promised to do my best. I don't insist on

---

31 See note 8 to letter of 16 February 1921.

the boiling and the mud: but I do frankly think that it would be absurd for a man who has otherwise a very tolerable constitution to sit down with 'close lipped patience, sister of despair' under rheumatism while all the natural cures (muds, waters etc.) and all the modern electrical cures remain untried. Confess that the man who could be induced to wearing zinc in his boots and drinking (what was it you were advised to drink – an onion soaked in gin, or port or mustard?) but who could not be induced to try what has cured hundreds, is in an indefensible position.

I therefore propose that part or all of my annual holiday should be spent in some such places as I have suggested with perhaps a few days here in Oxford – as our jam after our powder. I know there are difficulties. What have you ever done in which there was not? A man of your age and in your position cannot really be the slave of business engagements. I know too that the thought of an hotel in a 'spa' does not fill you with rapture: but even a troglodyte can't find the presence of strangers as painful as sciatica. And after all, once the plunge is made, would there not be a sort of holiday spirit that would descend on us in such a place and make us no unpleased spectators of the 'stir'. The change of diet alone, and of hours and of way of life is I think a pick-me-up. I know I have always found it so. Monotony is no better for the body than for the mind. Now the first essential of this scheme is to concert our movements. August would be impossible for me. That leaves September and the early part of October. Whether you have time or inclination to write me a long letter or not, please let me have a line soon giving me at least the outline of a scheme possible for you. I have really set my heart on the plan and very earnestly hope that an indulgence of my wishes and a reasonable care for yourself will combine to persuade you to the effort (it cannot really be a very great one) of making arrangements and removing obstacles. If you will fix a time for getting away I will start finding out details at once (I wish W. were here, he'd do it far better and serve you up five alternative operation orders worked out to a half minute at every station, while you waited. But alas – !)

Yes. There is no good balking the fact that this China journey is a bad business, a piece of rotten luck. I confess that when he sailed I was horribly uneasy. By this time (if I can judge at all from the papers) the chance of a war in China is greatly lessened and I am more cheerful. If the trouble clears up I don't see why he might not be home again in eighteen months or so. Of course there is the danger that, once he is out there, he may be put into some peacetime Eastern station for ordinary duty. But I am not really very much afraid of that. It is certainly what would seem reasonable and economic to you and me if we ran the British army. But one hasn't observed that *they* act that way. Even if they designed him for ordinary duty in China soon, they wd. be quite likely to bring him home again first, and we should gain while the tax payer lost.

His letters are of the greatest interest and very good. How the travels of anyone we know suddenly light up the waste places of the Atlas. I suppose the Red Sea coast is described in hundreds of books: but we had to wait till Warnie went East before we ever heard about it.[32] (I always imagined it flat and sandy myself.)

There is no need to bother about my health, and, even when busiest, I usually get my daily walk. I work as a rule from 9 till 1, from 5 till 7.15 (when we dine) and then after dinner till about 11 or 12. This you see gives me time for a good long tramp every afternoon. Nightmares I am afraid are hereditary in more senses than the one you meant. The thing, or what it stands [for] is in the blood of not one family but of the creature called Man.

I had to see Sambo about something this morning and he asked me if I were writing anything. I said I hoped to in a few years (I am hoping to write a book about Sir Thomas More and Erasmus and the people of that time. But my ordinary work gives me v. little time for the necessary reading and it will be a slow, slow business). He then said 'Oh. I was told that you had just published a considerable poem anonymously.' So I had to own up. He wouldn't say who his informant was, but asked if he might see the work: so of course I am presenting him with a copy, and will let you know his comments if he makes any. I foresee that all conversation with him henceforth must run on the lines of 'We authors, Ma'am.'[33]

One never knows what one will run across in the course of one's reading. You will be interested in the following extract from an essay by

---

32 In a letter to his father of 25 April 1927, Warnie described the area around the Red Sea thus: 'Sullen grey white rocks and cliffs, soaring up into fantastic peaks and towers of rock, baking away eternally at a temperature of perhaps 130, in utter desolation – no sign of any living thing, no blade of grass nor tree – just nothing. I imagine that the mountains of the moon, if one could visit them, would give the same horrid impression of the end of all things' (LP IX: 198).

33 Benjamin Disraeli to Queen Victoria following the publication of her *Leaves from a Journal of Our Life in the Highlands 1848–61*(1869).

Sir William Temple written in 1690, just after William and Mary had come to the Throne. 'I shall conclude with a saying of Alphonsus, sur-named the Wise, King of Aragon – that among so many things as are by men possessed or pursued in the course of their lives, all the rest are baubles, besides old wood to burn, old wine to drink, old friends to con-verse with, and old books to read.'[34] There! I'll bet a hundred pounds to a ha'penny you didn't guess how that quotation was going to end when you began to read it. 'Alphonsus the Wise' seems to have lived in the fourteenth century. I know nothing else about him. But perhaps this is enough and tells one all one wants to know.

Well, I must to bed. 'So to bed' as Pepys says. I am sorry you were worried. Be sure and let me have an answer to my main question and in the meantime, good night.

your loving son,
Jack

TO ARTHUR GREEVES (W):

[Magdalen College
26 June 1927]

My dear Arthur,

Knowing the state of your finances I couldn't find it in my con-science to keep the whole of your extremely kind and unexpected pres-ent, and herewith return £1. The other I retain with very many thanks, and shall devote it to a pleasant edition of Thomas Browne in three vol-umes which I saw lately: or perhaps I shall get Dryden's plays in a folio wh. I think sells for about that amount. De la Mare's poems I have had for a long time and I read them more often than any other book. I put him above Yeats and all the other moderns, and in spite of his fantasy find him nearer than any one else to the essential truth of life.

I was sorry to hear such a poor account of my father from you. Of course three weeks in an English hotel with him would for me have all the disadvantages of my usual spell at home without any of the advan-tages: but I feel bound not only to make the suggestion but to try and bring it to reality. This by itself would give me unhappy anticipations of this summer, but I am much more bothered by the possibility of Minto's

---

34 'On Ancient and Modern Learning', in *Essays of Sir William Temple*, vol. II (1822), pp. 93–4.

having to have an operation – not, thank heavens, a very serious one, but her bad veins make even a slight one unpleasant. At present things seem more hopeful than they did a few weeks ago, and it may not be necessary: but you can imagine that we are all pretty uneasy.

I am glad to hear that you are still working on the play, and think that the new idea you have of the Trees is a great advance. I haven't read the essay of Clutton Brock's[35] which you mention, but the theory – that out of the deep reservoirs of nature (the caverns of Erda) we draw power and inspiration which *we* make good or evil – is a familiar and favourite one of my own. If you will re-read what I make the girl say in Canto VIII of Dymer you will get my view on that subject better expressed than I can hope to put it in a letter, and summed up in the line 'With incorruptibles the mortal Will corrupts itself.'[36] But I will read the Clutton Brock as soon as I come across it and see what he says. I like and agree with most of his work.

I am realising a number of very old dreams in the way of books – reading Sir Gawain in the original[37] (you remember my translation of it in a companion volume to my translation of Beowulf) and, above all, learning Old Icelandic. We have a little Icelandic Club in Oxford called the 'Kólbitar':[38] which means (literally) 'coal-biters', i.e. an Icelandic word for old cronies who sit round the fire so close that they look as if they were biting the coals. We have so far read the Younger Edda and the Volsung Saga: next term we shall read the Laxdale Saga. *You* will be able to imagine what a delight this is to me, and how, even in turning over the pages of my Icelandic Dictionary, the mere name of god or giant catching my eye will sometimes throw me back fifteen years into a wild dream of northern skies and Valkyrie music: only they are now even more

---

35 Arthur probably mentioned Arthur Clutton-Brock's 'The Adoration of the Magi' in *Essays on Art* (1919), pp. 1–2.

36 *Dymer*, VIII, xv, 5–6.

37 He had recently acquired *Sir Gawain and the Green Knight*, ed. J.R.R. Tolkien and E.V. Gordon (1925).

38 See **J.R.R. Tolkien** in the Biographical Appendix. J.R.R. Tolkien became Professor of Anglo-Saxon at Oxford in 1925, and in *AMR*, pp. 392–3, Lewis mentions their first meeting on 11 May 1926. Tolkien began at Oxford the study of Old Icelandic texts. At the same time he founded a society called the Kolbítar or 'Coalbiters' for the purpose of reading the Icelandic sagas and myths in the original Old Icelandic or Old Norse. It was through this society, which Lewis joined in 1926 or 1927, that Lewis and Tolkien became friends.

beautiful seen thro' a haze of memory – you know that awfully *poignant* effect there is about impression *recovered* from ones past.

I feel great sympathy with your situation at home and can just imagine it this wet Sunday morning on which I write – with St Mark's bell ringing in the distance and 'the O'Mulligan'[39] trotting off to Church. Talking about home, have you seen Helen Wadell's book. I am sure Tchanie is never tired of talking of it. It is specially interesting to us because when you have read it you see what an enormous influence H.W. has had on Tchanie: the book is full of passages that Tchanie wd. have written herself if she could. I know now where Tchanie's dreadful serious moments (when she recites!) come from. Alas poor Tchanie! 'I was chust saying to Chanie.' So Gundred is married.[40] Tout change! I hope you will keep me informed as to what my father is *really* thinking of doing. As I said before, I shall press the English trip: but I have a secret conviction that it will not come off, and we shall probably meet this summer as usual. With many thanks again, and with love from all here.

Yours
Jack

TO HIS BROTHER (LP IX: 252–8):

Hillsboro
July 9/27

My dear W.,

This particularly unpleasant paper is a direct result of the great war, for I went to the door today and met an ex-service man selling writing pads. This was 1/3. It happens about twice a week and as Minto's excellent principles never allow her to send the poor devil empty away, we have an enormous supply of expensive paper of the worst quality. However it has jogged me into starting a fresh letter to you.

The Term has now been over some weeks, for which I am not sorry. It produced one public event of good omen – the carrying in Congregation

---

39 Miss Lizzie Mulligan and her sister who lived on Glenfarlough Road, about 200 yards from Little Lea, had been friends of Lewis's mother. Albert and his sons referred to her affectionately as 'the O'Mulligan' as she passed Little Lea and Bernagh on her way to St Mark's.

40 On 15 June 1927 Gundreda Ewart married Colonel John Forrest, formerly of the Royal Army Medical Corps, who had just become the secretary of the Royal Victoria Hospital in Belfast.

of a Statute limiting the number of wimmen at Oxford.[41] The appalling danger of our degenerating into a woman's university (nay worse still, into *the* women's university, in contradistinction to Cambridge, *the* men's university) has thus been staved off. There was fierce Opposition of course, our female antagonists being much more expert than we in the practice of 'whipping' in the parliamentary sense.

Since the victory the papers have been full of comment from such people as Sybil Thorndike, Lady Astor, Daisy Devoteau, Fanny Adams and other such notable educational authorities. They mostly deplore (especially in the Daily Mirror and the Little Ha'penny Sketch) one more instance of the unprogressiveness of those 'aged Professors'. The word 'academic' is also worked hard: tho' how the politics of an academy could, or why they should, cease to be 'academic', 'might admit of a wide conjecture'.

But the question of the age of the anti-feminists is an interesting one: and the voting (we have no secret franchise) revealed very consolatory facts. First came the very old guard, the octogenarians and the centurions, the full fed patriarchs of Corpus, the last survivors of the days when 'women's rights' were still new fangled crankery. They were against the women. Then came the very-nearly-as-old who date from the palmy days of J.S. Mill, when feminism was the new, exciting, enlightened thing: people representing as someone said, 'the progressiveness of the 'eighties'. They voted for the women. Then came the young and the postwar (I need not say I trust that I did my duty) who voted solid *against*. The arrangement is quite natural when you think it out. The first belong to the age of innocence when women had not yet been noticed: the second, to the age when they had been noticed but not yet found out: the third to us. Ignorance, romance, realism. The queer thing was that one solitary woman voted against her sex. She has since married and given up her job. *Una de multis face nuptial digna*: your Horation apprenticeship will carry you as far as that.[42]

But what irritated me beyond bearing during the whole thing was the re-iterated statement made even by people on our side, that, if we ought

---

41 The principle that 'the university has a right to remain predominantly a men's university' was asserted in a statute passed in the University on 14 June 1927. For more on this issue see the chapter on 'Women' in *The Twentieth Century* (ed. Brian Harrison), volume VIII of *The History of the University of Oxford* (1994).
42 Horace, *Odes*, Book 3, poem 11, ll. 33–4: 'One of the many worthy of the bridal torch'.

on principle to put up a show, it was really no good, because 'it was bound to come'. If I remember rightly your friend Drysdale,[43] on the only occasion I met him, indulged in the same fatalism. It is a very remarkable thing, this kind of view. Because the 18th century was fond of personifying abstractions ('Corruption has seized the provinces' etc.) and because Carlyle carried that further and gave us a tinge of poetry in his French Revolution,[44] whence it passed into every writer who wants to write impressively on poetical and historical subjects, we have now reached a stage at which causes, movements, tendencies etc. are talked of as if they were real things who did things: as if it were Bolshevism, not Bolsheviks, who fomented revolutions, and the revolutionary spirit, instead of the revolutionary spirits, which made men drunk. The natural corollary is that the world is managed by beings such as 'Woman' or 'The Locarne spirit' and real human beings are pawns in their hands. Now a days you can resist a given spirit or tendency only by hitching yourself to its equally spirituous or tendentious opponent – much like an ancient Egyptian who, helpless himself against the name of a god, can put it across it by means of the name of an higher god. I was just going to describe this as the return to polytheism. But the polytheists were more sensible for they accepted their positions as pawns because they believed in their gods. And if the wiseacre really believed in the beings to whom he attributes all public events (as I wd. be quite prepared to do with certain reservations) I cd. forgive him. But he is the first man to denounce you for a mystic if you hint that there might really be an entity such as the 'spirit of the age' over and above the human beings acting in that age. He is thus in the remarkable position of suspending everything on a peg which (he believes) isn't there, and preaching the uselessness of human endeavor because we are helpless in the hands of – Nobody. However, the subject seems to be carrying me further than I foresaw.

Much more important in the term's history was a private event in Magdalen common Room which lasted only a minute – but that minute should have recalled Lamb from the dead. The hero is Brightman,[45] that very old prebendary, whom some call Lob: for 'he looked elvish by his countenance' (he is less than five feet high, clean shaven, bald, and round

---

43 Captain J.E. Drysdale was Warnie's officer in command in China.
44 Thomas Carlyle, *History of the French Revolution* (1837).
45 Frank Edward Brightman. See note 5 to letter of 5 January 1926.

as a barrel). A former fellow who had returned to dine, rallied him in the words, 'Well, Brightman, I suppose you're as ready to bur'rn me at the stake as ever?' referring I suppose to some old theological dispute. Mark the answer: Lob, ignoring the main question as too obvious, waited a moment and then reflectively added the rider, 'You're a Scotchman amongst other things'.

I haven't yet made up my mind as to whether this is a pudaita story or not. Sometimes I think it is just in his line (being closely parallel to 'but there are other reasons') at others I am desperately afraid of some such complex reply as 'Why, is this fellow Bunkman a Scotchman himself?' Indeed perhaps its resemblance to 'there are other reasons' is an additional danger and may lead to the familiar (yet ever new) infuriating beginning 'Sure this is only the old wheeze of so-and-so' with the net result that having ventured on a story yourself you are forced to laugh at a very old story of some one else's.

The rest of the term was mainly occupied by the nonsense connected with Commem. Magdalen gave a ball which you would not suppose could have concerned me: but it did, for they put up a huge marquee between the cloisters and New Building, which not only spoiled all the beautiful spaciousness but on windy nights groaned and creaked like a ship under sail and kept me awake.

Sailing boats reminds me – I have just read Smollet's *Roderick Random*[46] which, as you probably know, is our chief literary document for the life of the navy in the 18th century. It is there that Captain Whiffle orders the officer out of the cabin because he cannot stand the stink of him. His picture as a whole is much what I expected – infernal. The resigned but bottomless contempt of all ranks for their senior officers, the certainty that everything is being mismanaged, and that the staff are fools and cowards is especially interesting: I suppose it is the normal state in all armies and navies. The book as a whole belongs to a type whose disappearance I do not much regret: the autobiographical novel in the form of memories of one who relates his misfortunes (for he is very unfortunate): that is, a string of frauds, oppressions and accidents piled on the hero in such a way as to give him the opportunity of fluctuating rapidly through all social strata, now 'a fine gentleman', now in a sponging house, pressed, imprisoned, etc. At one time he becomes a foot

---

46 Tobias George Smollett, *The Adventures of Roderick Random* (1748).

soldier in a French regiment. It is all very lively and will hold your attention wherever you open it: but the author's determination to ring the changes and show every side of the life of his times, by making it certain that whatever the hero is doing at the moment, some accident will completely reverse the position in the next ten pages, prevents the development of any continuous interest. Like Tom Jones, it uses the device of a story in a story and Roderick is constantly meeting people who at once tell him their story. (You will remember one instance of this in Tom Jones). This, together with the rambling episodes, recalls the structure (tho' not of course the atmosphere) of the Faerie Queene. In fact in reading this, Tom Jones, and Evelina[47] (which I have also read recently for the first time) I was struck by the real identity of method between the mediaeval romance and the early novel, and also by the wonderful reform that Scott and Jane Austen effected in reaching the modern complex but unified plot.

By the way, can you suggest why it is that when you read Boswell, Walpole's letters, or Fanny Burney's diary you find the 18th century a very delightful period, differing from ours chiefly by a greater formality and 'elegance' of manners whereas when you turn to the novel (including Evelina), you suddenly step into a world full of full-blooded, bawdy, brutal, strident, pull-away-the-chair barbarity? The sea captain in Evelina who supplies the comic element does so by playing a series of tricks on an elderly French lady, whom he addresses as 'Madam Frog', throws into ditches, and trips up in the mud. What is the common denominator between this and Johnson's circle? And which is true? Perhaps both are and one sees what the Doctor meant when he said that in a jail the society was commonly better than at sea.

But I mustn't spend too long on books for I have the ludicrous adventure of my own to tell. Unfortunately it needs a good deal of introduction to render it intelligible, but I think it is worth it. Mme Studer is the widow of M. Studer[48] who died recently under distressing circumstances. She had been temporarily insane once during his lifetime: and tho' there was no serious fear of a relapse, her state of mind after his death, together with some traces of hysteria and more depression than even the

---

47 Fanny Burney, *Evelina, or a Young Lady's Entrance into the World* (1778).
48 Mrs Studer was the wife of Paul Studer (1879–1927), Taylorian Professor of the Romance Languages in the University of Oxford, who died 23 January 1927. They were both Swiss, and had three children.

death of a husband seemed to justify, led most of her friends to keep an eye on her. Minto went to see her pretty regularly. So did (the heroine of my story) a Mrs Wilbraham. She is what is called 'a brave little woman' (tho' it is not known what dangers she ever had to encounter) and is never idle. She brings up her daughter in the light of lectures on child psychology delivered by professors whose own children never get born at all or are notable puppies. She is a spiritualist: a psychoanalyst, but does not believe in the theories of Freud because they are so horrid: she weighs the babies of poor women: her business in fact is universal benevolence. 'If only one feels that one can be of some use in the world …' as she often says.

Well, the other night I was just settling down to translate a chapter of the Edda, when suddenly Minto called me out of the dining room and said 'Mrs Wilbraham is here. She says Mrs Studer has twice tried to commit suicide today. She's got a taxi here and wants me to go and see the doctor at the Warneford.[49] We shall have to get a nurse for Mrs Studer.' I said I'd come along, because Minto has been rather poorly and I didn't know what she might be let in for. So Mrs W., Minto and I drove off to the Warneford. I remained in the taxi while the two ladies went in to see the Doctor. It was about half past nine, dusk and raining. At an unlighted window just opposite stood a very pale man with a long beard who fixed his eyes on the taxi with insane steadiness for half an hour without ever blinking or moving as far as I could see: to complete the picture (you'll hardly believe it) a large black cat sat on the window sill beneath him. (I always imagined they kept the patients in back rooms or something or at any rate had bars on the window.) I liked this so little that in desperation I tried to start a conversation with Griffin the taxi-man (also your garager when you are at Headington). 'This is an unpleasant place, Griffin', said I. He replied promptly 'You know sir you can't put her in without a doctor and a magistrate'. I then realized that he thought we were there for the purpose of 'putting in' either Minto or Mrs W. In my dismay, not quite decided what I meant, I blurted out 'Oh I hope that won't be necessary' – and when he replied 'Well it was the last time I got one put in 'ere' I realized that I had hardly improved matters.

49 The Warneford Hospital opened in 1826 as the Oxford Lunatic Asylum, and in 1843 it took the name Warneford Asylum. The asylum was purpose-built, and it recreated the atmosphere of a country gentleman's house, with a chapel and landscaped grounds.

The others emerged at last with a Nurse Jones and we started off for the Studer's. But now the question was what to do? Madame would certainly refuse to have a strange young woman thrust upon her for the night for no apparent reason: as her husband was dead and her relatives abroad, no one had any authority over her. And even if we wished, no doctor would certify her as insane on the evidence of a child – the only person who ever claimed to have seen the attempt at suicide. Mrs Wilbraham said it was all perfectly simple. She would stay hidden in Mme Studer's garden all night. Nurse would be put up in the bungalow of a stranger opposite Madame's house. She must herself stay in the garden. It was no good arguing. It was her duty. If only her nephew was here! If only she could have a man with her, she confessed, she would feel less nervous about it. I began to wish I'd stayed at home: but in the end of course I had to offer.

No one raised the question as to why the Nurse had been prevented from going to bed at the Warneford in order to be carried half a mile in a taxi and immediately put to bed in another house totally unconnected with the scene of action, where she could not possibly be of the slightest use. The girl herself, who was possibly in some doubt as to who the supposed lunatic might be, remained in a stupefied silence.

I now suggested as a last line of defence that nothing wd be more likely to upset Mme Studer than to find dim figures walking about her garden all night: to which Mrs W. replied brightly that we must keep out of sight and go very quietly. 'We could put our stockings on outside our boots you know.' At that moment (we were all whispering just outside a house further down in the same street as Madame's, and it was now about eleven o'clock) a window opened overhead and someone asked me rather curtly whether we wanted anything, and if not, would we kindly go away. This restored me to some of the sanity I was rapidly losing, and I determined that whatever else happened, four o'clock should not find me 'with my stockings over my boots' explaining to the police that I was (v. naturally) spending the night in some one else's garden for fear the owner might commit suicide.

I therefore ruled that we must keep our watch in the road, where, if we sat down, we wd be hidden from the window by the paling (and, I added mentally, wd be open to arrest for vagabondage, not for burglary). Several neighbours had now turned up (all women, and nearly all vulgar) to revel in excitement, and Mrs W. (while insisting on the absolute necessity of letting no one know – 'it would be dreadful if it got about poor thing') gave each newcomer, including the total strangers, a full account of the situation. I came home with Minto, drank a cup of tea, put on my great coat, took some biscuits, smokes, a couple [of] apples, a rug, a waterproof sheet and two cushions, and returned to the fatal road. It was now twelve o'clock. The crowd of neighbours had now melted away: but one (neither vulgar nor a stranger) had had the rare good sense to leave some sandwiches and three thermos flasks. I found the brave little woman actually eating and drinking when I arrived. Hastily deciding that if I were to lie under the obligations of a *man* I wd assume his authority, I explained that we should be really hungry and cold later on and authoritatively put a stop to that nonsense. My next step was to provide for my calls of nature (no unimportant matter in an all night tête-à-tête with a fool of an elderly woman who has had nothing to do with men since her husband had the good fortune to die several years ago) by observing that the striking of a match in that stillness wd easily be heard in the Studer's house and that I wd tiptoe to the other end of the road to light my pipe.

Having thus established my right to disappear into the darkness as often as I chose – she conceded it with some reluctance – I settled down. There had been some attempt at moonlight earlier, but it had clouded over and a fine rain began to fall. Mrs Wilbraham's feminine and civilian vision of night watches had apparently not included this. She was really surprised at it. She was also surprised at its getting really cold: and most surprised of all to find that she became sleepy, for she (after the first ten minutes) had answered to my warning on that score with a scornful 'I don't think there's much danger of that!' However all these hardships gave her the opportunity of being 'bright' and 'plucky' as far as one can be in sibilant whispers.

If I could have been quit of her society I wd have found my watch just tolerable – despite the misfortune of finding my greatcoat pockets stuffed with camphor balls (Minto is very careful about moths) which I flung out angrily on the road, and then some hours later forgetting this and trying to eat one of the apples that had lain in those pockets. The taste of camphor is exactly like the smell. During the course of the night my companion showed signs of becoming rather windy and I insisted on playing with her the old guessing game called 'Animal, Vegetable, or Mineral'. (Incidentally I thought I would find it more interesting than her conversation.) After assuring me that she was thinking of an animal, a live animal, an animal we had seen that night, she had the impudence to announce in the end that 'it' was the 'voice of an owl we had heard' – which shows the working of her mind. However my story is over now, and when I have added that the crows had been 'tuning up their unseasonable matins' a full half hour before any other bird squeaked (a fact of natural history which I never knew before) I may dismiss Mrs-Ruddy-Wilbraham from my mind.

The whole affair has suggested to me the idea of an admirable short story for wh. we have all the characters ready. Let Mrs W. suspect the P'daytabird of insanity on the Witch of Endor's information: and then have your story told in the first person by him. He finds himself receiving visits from crowds of strangers on the flimsiest pretexts, who relieve one another from eight till twelve (because it's dangerous to leave him alone): he finds, or learns from the Witch of Endor, of the gradual but steady disappearance of all *cutlery*: the denouement might come when on one of his rare nights alone he suddenly finds the study plunged in total darkness and after calling 'Mary' repeatedly at the study door, blunders down into the lower regions where by the light of a match he discovers a brave little woman (with her stockings over her boots) who says soothingly 'Its alright Mr Lewis, I just came in to turn the gas off at the metre' – and a moment later his 'What on earth...' coinciding with her signal whistle to those without, he might find himself overpowered by a miscellaneous collection of people (mostly 'cattle') who had been spending the night in the wash house.

I was agreeably surprised yesterday morning by your letter from Hong Kong – or the mainland opposite, which gives me a lively impression of your present predicament.[50] You will not be able to appreciate the

---

50 'As regards our friends the Chinese,' Warnie wrote on 7 June 1927, 'the West African is a curious person with many odd habits but you never lose the sense of a common humanity shared with him, and the same is of course true of the Indian. But it is impossible to visualize these disgusting creatures as human beings at all or even as animals. One somehow has a freakish feeling that some extraordinary accident blew them off another planet into China. To take the few illustrations I have so far encountered, what are you to make of a race who nod their heads when they mean "no" and shake them when they mean "yes" – where the corpse is the only person who does not attend his own funeral – where a group of friends are chatting at a street corner and on one being knocked down by a lorry and fatally injured, the others, after bursting into a peal of laughter, stroll on and leave him to die in the road – where the

point of William James'[51] remark that the great presumptive argument against personal immortality was 'What are you going to do with the Chinese?' One can't help feeling that when people are so very different as all that, one has no business to be connected with them at all. The society of things human (or roughly human) in form but in nothing else must be v. injurious. The only things I have ever read or heard about their culture exactly agree with your account: not that one can place much reliance on your friend Ahmed Din, if he is a Moslem, as I presume by the name: you remember Mackail's description of Islam as being 'polygamous methodism' – I mean they have the name of looking on all other cultures much as a Plymouth Brother looks on the ungodly. Surely A. Din's primary grudge against the Chinks is that they are *idolaters* – and the rest follows. However, I expect that in this case he is quite right. Their national vanity is confirmed by everything that one hears of them. Didn't we both read somewhere that the typical Chinese reaction to any new invention is an elaborate historical research ending with the statement 'Sure this is only the old so-and-so business that we invented in the nth Dynasty'. I am alarmed by the great philologist Jesperson[52] who argues (v. cogently) that the English language is rapidly moving towards a structure and syntax of wh. the Chinese is the only other example.

I have no difficulty in imagining a day grey and drizzling as an English November 'seeing as how' we have lived under such days for a week or so, relieved by the mutterings of a chronic thunderstorm. The popular theory is that the weather is all 'caused by the eclipse', the eclipse which has been 'news' in the papers long before and after its occurrence: or as

---

language is such that a Chinaman from two hundred miles away would not understand what a Hong Kong Chinaman is saying?...This detachment from the human family is difficult to explain but I honestly believe that if I saw a dozen Chinamen hit by an H.E. shell I should feel nothing but a mild disgust at the mess. Another of their characteristics is I am told an immense conceit and a self satisfaction with their own civilization which appears to me quite unwarranted. My informant is one Ahmed Din, an Indian tailor, and a very clever man, with whom I had a most interesting chat the other day. He knows Chinese and has read a lot of their literature, from which he contemptuously denies them any claim to a culture' (LP IX: 239).

51 William James (1842–1910), American philosopher. He was Professor successively of Psychology (1887–97) and Philosophy (1897–1907) at Harvard University. In his *Varieties of Religious Experience* (1902), he distinguished between 'once-born' and 'twice-born' religious types, and made a scientific analysis of conversion.

52 Otto Jesperson, *Language, its Nature, Development and Origin* (1922), ch. XVIII, xix–3, 'Structure of Chinese', pp. 369ff.

Rose Macaulay wd. say, it produced 'amazing crowds' and in them were 'many well dressed women'. Unfortunately it was not visible from Headington. What I can't understand is why, if the moon is constantly revolving round the earth, it gets directly in the light of the sun only once in a century or so: I shd. have imagined that it would happen about twice a year. None of the elaborate explanations in the papers touch this point, so I suppose it must just be given up.

I wrote to the OAB shortly after your departure professing my eagerness to take an English holiday with him in some health resort this year, and putting the case for it as strongly as I could: my letter has had the usual result of reducing him to several weeks of complete silence. If you ever want to make sure of *not* hearing from him, the infallible method is to ask him some question which requires a definite decision of his to answer it. I've never known it fail: and I must confess that I react in precisely the same way myself. How easy to answer an important letter: how impossible to answer any of those inexcusable epistles which insolently *demand* an answer.

Joynson Hicks[53] (did you know that he was the leading light of the survivors of English Evangelicalism and as such has been a centre of opposition to the Papistical tendencies of the new Prayer Book?[54] Now, continue to be a Tory if you dare) – well this Joynson Hicks said yesterday that troops were being rapidly recalled from China. I suppose that is too good to be true, and wouldn't have been said if it were true.

Well, examining begins tomorrow and this letter, with all other rational activities, must end. Write when you can. All here send their affectionate compliments.

yours,

J.

---

53 Sir William Joynson Hicks (1865–1932), statesman, was Home Secretary 1924–9, and prominent in the defeat of the Prayer Book revision of 1927–8.

54 Early in 1927 the bishops of the Church of England completed a revision of the Book of Common Prayer. It was different in many ways from all previous Prayer Books, and it was rejected by the House of Commons on 15 December 1927. *The Book of Common Prayer with the Additions and Deviations Proposed in 1928*, as it is known, was published in 1928. While it does not have official approval, it is used by some parishes. For Albert Lewis on the 1928 Prayer Book see note 19 to the letter of 13 April 1929.

TO HIS FATHER (LP IX: 260–2):

[Magdalen College]
July 29th. [1927]

My dear Papy,

I was glad to hear from you. A letter from Arthur some time ago had let me know that you were still suffering from the old complaint and I was therefore more pleased to hear that there was at least some relief than disappointed to hear it was not greater.[55] I am a little surprised at your response to the programme of being 'boiled in mud'. Neither of us of course would choose Harrogate or any similar place for pleasure: that may be taken as a starting point to any discussion on the subject – tho', I repeat, the unpleasantness must not be exaggerated. (Damme Sir, are we to be frightened of some retired colonels and rich old maids?) I suggested it purely and simply on medical grounds and your reply strikes me rather as if I had said to a man with toothache 'Why not go to a dentist?' and he had answered 'You're quite right – I will go out. But I won't go to a dentist. I'll go and get fitted for a new pair of boots.' However, I am so pleased at your agreement on the main issue, that of going away, that I must not press the other too hard. It would be only reasonable to be guided by Joey in this matter. If he has any faith in mud baths etc., surely we can manage to combine the business with pleasure, even on the site of the mud baths. I am delighted to hear that you have changed your Doctor at last.[56]

As for Joey – after all I may as well be frank. As a matter of cool judgement, no doubt, I do disapprove his behaviour during the war: on the other hand, like all us Celts, I am a born rhetorician, one who finds pleasure in the forcible emotions independently of their grounds and even to the extent to which they are felt at any time save the moment of speaking. Like the obscure poet whom I saw mentioned in the local newspaper at Caerleon, I love to 'ride like a cork on the ocean of eloquence': and

---

55 Mr Lewis had been seized by lumbago during the night of 17 June, and for a fortnight he was completely prostrated by it.

56 He had exchanged Dr Leslie for his nephew Dr Joseph 'Joey' Lewis (1898–1969). 'Joey' was the son of Albert's eldest brother, Joseph. His career at Campbell College, Belfast, and medical schools had been brilliant. In 1928 he was appointed bacteriologist to the Belfast Infirmary, and he became one of the leading blood specialists in Northern Ireland. It annoyed Jack, however, that he had not served during the war. See **The Lewis Family** in the Biographical Appendix.

whenever you hear me inveighling in 'Ercles vein' you must take this into account. A tirade against war shirkers is an exhilarating after dinner exercise: but while not wholly unreal it implies no such heartfelt animosity as would jibb at Joey's attendance even on myself. Certainly if the choice is between Squeaky and Joey one can't hesitate. I hope you will commit yourself to the 'blood specialist's' hands from this day forth and profit by it.

I am just in the few days lull between my two 'fittes' of summer examining. I have finished reading the boys' answers in Oxford, and next week I go to Cambridge for the pleasanter (and more profitable) business of awarding. I had rather a heavy dose of it this time, and the strain took the form of giving me neuralgia. At least my dentist, after striking probes into me, punching me in the face, and knocking my teeth with small hammers – accompanied with the blatantly impertinent question 'Does that hurt?' (to which the proper reply seems to be a sharp return blow at *his* jaw with the words 'Yes, just like that') – my dentist I say, assured me that there was nothing wrong with my teeth and therefore it must be neuralgia. I managed in spite of it to sleep pretty well by dint of soaking my feet in water as hot as I could stand, immediately before going to bed. This is an excellent plan if you have to work right up to bedtime and your head is in a whirl, as it draws the blood away to the extremities and makes you stop thinking.

My labours were rewarded by some good things from the candidates (who are school boys under sixteen). The definition of a *Genie* as 'an oriental spirit inhabiting bottles and buttons and rings' is a rather rare example of a correct answer which is funny. 'A *Censer* is one who incenses people' is more of the familiar type. In answer to a question from a paper on *Guy Mannering* 'Would you have liked Colonel Mannering as a father? Support your answer by an account of his behaviour to Julia', one youth sagely replied that he would. It is true that Mannering was cold, suspicious, autocratic etc., 'but he was very rich and I think he would have made an excellent father'. That boy should be sent to the City at once: he has the single eye. But the best of all came from a paper (set by me) on Macbeth.

> Question: *Give the context of, 'Throw physic to the dogs, I'll none of it.'* [57]

---

57 Shakespeare, *Macbeth*, V, iii, 47.

Answer: *'Macbeth said these words near the end of the play. He was feeling uneasy before the battle and Seyton told him he ought to take some medicine.'*

It is very interesting to speculate what would have happened if Seyton *had* done this. Would the line have run 'Throw Seyton to the dogs, I'll none of him.' Yet, incredible as the mistake may seem, it was repeated (of course with small variations) in some fifteen or twenty papers. In one, Seyton suggested the dose not only for Macbeth but for his soldiers as well.

As I have spent ten days or so glued to my table at this task I have naturally not much news. Sambo, after asking for Dymer and being sent a copy, has made neither comment on it or acknowledgment of the gift. I suppose he is waiting to read it in his holidays, or else has forgotten all about [it]. The other hypothesis – that his feelings about it were 'too deep for words' is rendered improbable because I have dined with the Warrens since: so at least he has decided not to cut the acquaintance over the head of it.

Now let me see if anything else has a curious, but quite independant parallel to your 'but there are other reasons' story. A Scotchman, formerly a Fellow of this College, came to dine, and rallied old Brightman (with whom I suppose he had had theological arguments in the old days) by saying 'Well Brightman, I suppose ye're still as ready to bur-r-rn me as ye always were'. To which Brightman, ignoring the main question as too obvious for an explicit answer, replied meditatively 'You're a Scotchman amongst other things'.

My only other recent adventure was a purely literary one – that of quite accidentally picking up *The Woman in White*[58] and reading it: a book of course now practically unknown to anyone under forty. I thought it extremely good of its kind, and not a bad kind. But what spacious days those were! The characters, or at least all the wicked ones, flame in jewels and the hero is so poor in one place that he actually travels *second class* on the railway. I have decided to model my behaviour for the future (socially I mean, not morally) on that of Count Fosco, but without the canaries and the white mice.

---

58 Wilkie Collins, *The Woman in White* (1860).

Another curious thing is the elaborate descriptions of male beauty, which I hardly remember to have seen since Elizabethan poetry: or do the 'noble brow, the silky beard' and the 'Manly beauty' still flourish in fiction which I don't happen to have read? Of course only third rate people write that kind of novel now, whereas Wilkie Collins was clearly a man of genius: and there is a good deal to be said for his point of view (expressed in the preface) that the first business of a novel is to tell a story, and that characters etc. come second. Aristotle thought the same about tragedy.

Warnie seems to be having a rotten time.[59] The only consolation seems to be that (as far as one can judge from the papers) things look like clearing up in China and he may be sent back sooner than we expected. I shall be pretty busy all August, but will get across as soon as I can in September. I hope we shall have a famous jaunt. I am going bald at a prodigious rate and in a few years time you will have a better head of hair than either of your sons. What sort of a wig would you recommend?

your loving son,

Jack

TO HIS FATHER (LP IX: 264–5):

Magdalen.
Aug. 12th [1927]

My dear P.,

So sorry – I find I forgot to send the enclosed with my last letter. I am back from Cambridge, where I had the usual unwholesome combination of high living (we are fed splendidly, both food and drink being free) and sedentary occupation.

I heard a rather impressive thing while I was there. While we were at work one morning, some one came in and informed my Cambridge colleague of the death of a common friend. When the other had gone, my friend told me the story. Mr — (I forget the name) was a Fellow of a Cambridge College. Shortly before the war his pancreas went badly out of order, and finally ceased to work at all. The ordinary doctors could do little for him: but as he was a rather distinguished bio-chemist, and lived among bio-chemists, he managed to get along somehow on the

---

59 Things were worse than Jack and his father thought. On 12 July Warnie went into the 3rd British General Hospital with a fever and an outbreak of boils over his entire body.

experiments that he and his circle tried on him: but he was subject to frequent attacks and (what worried him the most) could never do more than about two hours work a day. Three weeks ago one of his bad turns came on. Whereupon he said to his doctor, 'Look here doctor, would it make any difference to you professionally if a patient of yours chose to die of starvation?' The Doctor (who must have been an unusual man) said it would not. The patient immediately put his plan into action and from that moment no food passed his lips. He was constantly visited by his friends and refused to discuss his own situation, while indulging with all his former spirit in science, politics, and banter – banter of the rather schoolboyish quite unintellectual type which is so common in England. My colleague's informant had been to see him a few days ago: and the last words of the patient (now almost a skeleton) had been 'Well bye bye – thank the Lord I shall never have to be your partner at Bridge again!' There is a story in Pliny's letters of a Roman[60] who chose exactly the same plan in similar circumstances: but he seems to have spent his last hours in rhetorical 'last words' and Stoic platitudes about contempt of death. Perhaps I shouldn't say 'platitudes': the Roman was probably quite sincere. But the difference of temperament strikes one.

The other story I heard at Cambridge was very funny tho' very blasphemous. However, as it was told to me in the presence of an Archdeacon by a B.D., two laymen may be excused for enjoying it. It is told of Phelps the Provost of Oriel,[61] but will do equally well for anyone who 'has a good conceit of himself'. Phelps dreamed that he had died and reached the gate of heaven. Here a resplendent being, bowing obsequiously, said 'Very pleased to see you, Mr Provost I'm sure. Right straight on up the stairs.' At the top of the stairs a much more resplendent being, respectful rather than obsequious, met him. 'Ah, Provost, delighted to see you. Just turn to your right.' Following these directions he suddenly found himself in front of a throne in a blaze of light. 'Why my dear Phelps' exclaimed the Occupant. 'This is delightful', then rising 'Why – bless me – I beg your pardon – I'm afraid I've got your chair!'

Have you any views as to *where* you and I shd. go, if we don't get boiled in mud? I had thought of N.Wales, some of the mountainous

---

60 Pliny, *Letters*, Bk. I, letter to Calestrius Tiro.
61 Lancelot Ridley Phelps (1853–1936), Provost of Oriel College, Oxford 1914–29.

places. But possibly that wd. be too relaxing, and too wet in September.

your loving son,

Jack

P.S. The blots on this page are not my tears – it rained on to my table while I was away at lunch.

TO ARTHUR GREEVES (W):

The Folly,
Perranporth,
Cornwall.
Aug 24th [1927]

My dear Arthur,

A thousand apologies. We have come down here for a bit to set us all up, specially Minto, and you can imagine that the almost nomadic grandeur of family packing and family travelling, combined with the pleasant, yet crowding, picnic life we are now leading, has left me little leisure for writing. Still, I certainly ought to have let you have a line if only to acknowledge the cheque, and am very sorry that I did not. Very many thanks: but I still protest that it is an excessive gift from poor you to me. However, if you are going to challenge me to a duel in case I return it again, I will see what I can do towards spending it. Again, many many thanks.

As to showing my father the play. I think his criticism, tho' formal, is valuable on questions of *style* for a speech or essay or the narrative parts of a novel. Whether it wd. be much use for *dialogue*, I am hardly prepared to say. The general philosophy and meaning and all that, would not, I think, interest him, nor would he take very much trouble to understand it. He would assure you that he knew exactly what you meant and then substitute something of his own: probably identifying your view with some very superficially similar view expressed in some book he had read, in the words 'Sure this is the old business of so-and-so.' I fancy, however, he wd. have a pretty good eye for theatrical effect, specially on the humorous side. I am afraid I cannot be much more conclusive, and you must decide for yourself. After all you know his literary conversation nearly as well as I do. One thing you must be warned of. If he thinks the whole thing bosh he will be much too kind to tell you so: and at the same time he is habitually *rather* contemptuous of local literary endeavours. It would be hard for you to excite his admiration, and yet he will be determined not to hurt you.

I expect to be home on the 5th of September – leaving the others here. The doctor thought Minto ought to get away – she is much better and really (but touch wood!) has made a remarkable escape from the trouble that threatened her. We are having a delightful time and the best surf bathing I've had since our old days at Portsalon. As I write I look out on a deep blue sea and a golden sand, divided by twenty yards of pure white foam. *Of course you won't mention at home that I am not in Oxford.*

I am busy all morning at rather dull and mechanical work, and fit in more at odd times when I can. Looking forward to seeing you again, & with many thanks.

Yrs

Jack

In his letter of 7 July 1927 (LP IX: 248–52) Warnie told his brother that since he'd been in China Colonel Badcock had

> succeeded in 'breaking' two Majors, a Captain, and a Subaltern: when I say 'breaking' I do not mean that they have been cashiered, but that they are being sent home with reports that they are inefficient...This reign of terror under which we live does not make existence in the tropics any pleasanter. I personally am sufficiently convinced of the reality of our danger to intend warning the O.A.B. that I do not think I can last out the year and that I expect to be home and workless by December.

Jack and Mr Lewis did not know it yet, but Warnie left the hospital in Kowloon on 1 September after being transferred to the convalescent camp at Wei-Hei-Wei in northern China. He and other patients sailed to Shanghai, arriving there on 4 September and from there they travelled on to Wei-Hei-Wei which they reached on 7 September.

A serious consideration for Warnie was that if he remained and did foreign service for three years he would not have to go abroad for another six years. On the other hand, if he returned home now his stay in China would not count as part of the necessary period abroad, and it would all have to be done again some other time. Before he went to Wei-Hei-Wei, Colonel Badcock told him of a vacancy coming up in the Army Service Corps in Hong Kong. Offered the post, Warnie accepted it, to discover later that while he was convalescing in the north, the 15th Infantry Brigade broke up and Colonel Badcock and one of the regiments returned to England.

TO HIS BROTHER (LP IX: 270–6):

[Perranporth,
Cornwall]
3 September [1927]

My dear W.,

Many thanks for your letter describing the beastliness of the Colonel and the missionary's wife, the beauty of bathing, and the demonology of the Chinese.[62] I think it is always very difficult to 'evaluate' these superstitions – I mean to gauge the amount of barbarism and stupidity which they imply in those who believe in them. What exactly does the fact that English dinner parties have been ruined by having thirteen at table prove about English civilization? The idea however of running

---

62 'It is the incredible, cruel evil beastliness of the fellow [Colonel Badcock],' Warnie wrote to Jack on 7 July 1927, 'which makes me wonder whether there was not after all something to be said for the ancient personal existence theory of the Devil. However I have no right to use you as a safety value for blowing off this festering hate with which we go to bed at night and get up in the morning...Speaking of devils, these appear to play a very big part in the life of the Chinese – another proof I think that they are not the "perfectly polite" people of popular legend, but distinctly on the low level of humanity...When a Chinese house is being built, the tops of the scaffolding poles have large bunches of grass tied to them: the explanation is simple – with no roof on the house it would be an obvious temptation to any out of work devil to drop into the interior, wait till the place was inhabited, and then annoy its tenants...Last year, during the Hong Kong strike, there was an enormous number of deaths by motor car accidents in the streets of Hong Kong, which the authorities not unnaturally attributed to suicide owing to trade depression: but it turned out to be nothing of the sort. The prevalent scarcity of work was attributed by every intelligent Chinese to the malignancy of that personal devil who stalks at most men's heels...We landed at about nine o'clock at the end of a narrow wooden jetty at the bathing beach, and, walking up the smooth perfectly white sand to the bamboo and wattle bathing club, secured two cubicles against our afternoon dip. As we watched the blue water rippling round the spur of sponge cake looking rock which guards the beach and the waves breaking on the sand, I said to [Drysdale] that one of the most comforting things in life is that wherever you may be sent, a wave breaking on a beach looks the same and sounds the same: if you are serving on a coast you can never be entirely cut off from the old familiar life' (LP IX: 248–50).

across in front of a car in order to get your follower squashed, is certainly immense: I cannot decide whether it argues a great sense of humour or a great absence of humour. The colonel nuisance has all my sympathy: that sort of thing, or the more or less constant danger of it, is the snag which wd. make a military life intolerable to me, and it is chiefly for the escape from that that I congratulate myself on having ceased to be a boy.

I confess I can't look at the prospect you suggest (I hope not very seriously) without complete dismay. A recrudescence in middle life of the 'What are you going to be' menace, continued through months of residence at Leeborough – a continual urgence of the desirability of 'going into' anything that would remove you to that undiscovered country 'the colonies' – this would be extremely unpleasant. Still, with your 'little bit of savings' to spend on luxuries, you could always hope to grow a Leeborough skin (as we did in the old days) wh. would render you insensible to diatribes. The old expedient of just sitting there with 'that wooden face' and going on with your books would have to come into play again: and perhaps the new expedient of replying (to the dear old question) 'a pudaita' might now be actually put into practice. One pictures the problem of a career ceasing to be a practical problem at all and becoming merely a periodical outlet for the OAB's spleen – a storm at whose appearance one philosophically buttoned up the collar and raised the umbrella. (Another possible repartee that occurs is 'What are you going to be?' – 'A blue gentleman').

Or perhaps it would be better for you to put the whole thing on a different footing from the start and take up the position of the dominant and adult son to the oppressed 'Pa' and always to anticipate the storm by taking your place on the hearthrug with legs astride and hands in pockets and bellowing 'Pa! You and I had better understand one another'.

It is true that the financial framework of the scene does not at once adapt itself to such treatment: but as Johnson says of Pastoral Poetry, the artist must use his skill in keeping out of sight those parts of his subject which are mean and disgusting.[63] However I had better beware as you say

---

63 Johnson, *Lives of the English Poets*, op. cit., vol. III, Life of William Shenstone: 'The four parts of his *Pastoral Ballad* demand particular notice. I cannot but regret that it is pastoral; an intelligent reader acquainted with the scenes of real life sickens at the mention of the *crook*, the *pipe*, the *sheep*, and the *kids*, which it is not necessary to bring forward to notice, for the poet's art is selection, and he ought to shew the beauties without the grimness of the country life' (p. 356).

of the 'selection of two presents' and not joke too long about a subject which may (tho' I trust the possibility is very remote) have become more serious by the time this letter reaches you.

Now for my own history. My period of examining passed over with its usual accompaniment of neuralgia and oaths, relieved by the one excellent boy who defined 'a genie' correctly, yet more than correctly, as 'an eastern spirit inhabiting bottles and buttons and rings'. Pretty good for a boy. I was also pleased with a youth who, being asked to write a letter to a friend recommending Guy Mannering, wrote to his brother recommending it and saying 'I think you wd. be interested in the character of Colonel Mannering, he is so like our father': and then later in a paper *on* Guy Mannering in which I had set the question 'Would you have liked Colonel Mannering as a father?' – illustrate your answer etc. – began decisively 'I would not have liked Colonel Mannering as a father in the least'.

Then came my usual week at Cambridge, where, despite long hours I revisited King's College Chapel, sauntered round the Backs, and bathed in the Cam, under a pearl-coloured sky simmering with summer river haze from morning till twilight. Even the hours of work passed not disagreeably in the company of my very vulgar and uneducated but not unpleasant and amusing Cambridge colleague. You shd. have heard us going over the work of a female examiner called Helen Laybourne who was v. bad and gave us a lot of trouble, chanting with one voice full of meaning 'I would I were where Helen lies'.[64]

I returned from Cambridge and almost immediately set out with Minto, Maureen, Florence de Forest and Baron Papworth, for Perranporth (Cornwall) where I am now writing. On Sunday (it is now Friday) I set out for P'daitaheim: whether to spend my days interminably strolling in the cemetery-like walks of a hydro garden or drinking two o'clock buckets of sherry in the study, I don't yet know: for of course it is still quite uncertain whether he can be got to move or not.

In the mean time I sit looking out on a tawny strip of sand (four miles of it in length but I can't see all from here) and the bluest shiningest sea that a home dweller like me has ever seen – the one divided from the other by about twenty yards of Chinese white varied with something like champagne – row after row of full Atlantic rollers. Beyond them the

---

64 Ballads (anonymous), 'I wish I were where Helen lies.'

sea is unstained with a single fleck of foam, except on the point (about three miles half right from where I sit) and there one sees the white go perpendicularly up the rocks. Except the fishing fleet which comes and goes in the offing every three days there is hardly a boat to be seen from this place: once or twice from the highest cliffs I have seen a steamer, usually at sunset, sitting apparently immovable against the end of the world.

Of course there is a drawback to Cornwall. All along this coast the bathing is a death trap except at full tide, which means that we are reduced to one bathe a day (for who, in real life, can bathe at 6 a.m. and 6.20 p.m.) when, for the excellence of it, one would willing (like Wordsworth) 'make one long bathing of a summer's day'.[65] I have never had such surf bathing in my life: not so much here as at St. Agnes' Cove, a few miles S.W., where we go nearly every day. When you have got in up to your belly you get the waves already broken – a solid wall of foam about a foot and a half high (above the level water this side) and about ten feet broad. Then when you have put down your head with a smack, and spluttered through this, you get to business. They come in at places, where you're in your depth between the waves, far higher than a man. They are kindly creatures if taken the right way, and I daily slide up into hollowing breakers which, at first, I would have thought dangerous. The excitement is to guess when they will break. You see the bright bottle green mass of water before you and you bob over it like a floating gull and it keeps its thunders till it is behind you. Usually it crashes just before you reach the top and then you go hurtling back, kicking and spitting, and stand up finally far inland with spent water swimming round your ankles. But when you actually get it in the break, anything may happen. Usually you go far under and if you try to swim your arms are worked rapidly round and round – the movements in the root of a wave being apparently circular. The other day however, turning my back rapidly to the breaking wave, I had the rather remarkable experience of having my head actually in the hollow cave under the curl (which has been seen so often from the outside): so that I saw a second of shining water before my still *unwetted* face, much like a tourist passing between rock and water under Niagara.

My pen has run away with me thus far before I recall that you also have been bathing, and that you even take the wind out of my sails in

---

65 Wordsworth, *The Prelude*, I, 290.

advance by observing that a falling wave is the same all the world over. We have therefore studiously described to each other the *one* element in our experiences which is common to us both. However I think the interest of any description is great in proportion to the extent to wh. (Lord – what a sentence) one already knows the thing described: i.e. the less it is needed the more one is prepared to listen to it.

Baron Papworth by the sea has removed for ever the reproach of cowardice. As long as only the girls and I are in he contents himself with galloping to and fro in the inch of water where the waves have retreated, barking at the top of his voice. Then when Minto goes in a moment later, he is to be seen steadily swimming after her, ploughing *through* every wave like a tramp, his hair all back from his nose, showing how thin and rapier muzzled he is and indeed making him look rather like a torpedo or an ocean going ant eater. Nothing will stop him, tho' swamped and scuttled times without number. This heroic practice makes him much sweeter than your nose will remember him: except when its beneficial effects are frustrated by the fact that he finds sea water acts on him as a violent purgative. The only other things I have to say about the sea proper are (1) That I quite agree that to lose the *sound* of a sea bathe wd. be to lose a great deal of the delight, (b) that Florence, in her bathing things, is an almost perfect figure of the plumper type.

As to Cornwall itself: the basic formula is 'The County Down country plus the Antrim Coast'. The resemblance of the interior to Co. Down is quite remarkable: the same white cottages, the crumbling dry stone walls, the patchy fields, small and rather oddly shaped, and the bleak colouring. But when you have got this well into your mind's eye you must proceed to moderate it a bit. First of all, magnify the hills to about the Antrim size, while keeping them in the main strictly to the Co. Down quality. That is, tho' big, they are not long gaunt bluish hogbacks, but all criss cross, rounded, and higgledypiggildy. If Co. Down was described (Kelsie says it was) as 'eggs in a basket', this is turkey's eggs in a basket. Then you must add (what is rare in Down) masses of heather and gorse, not crowning the hills which would give them the mountain look, but most often on the sides of valleys where they are steep: and when you reach the valleys themselves, specially the narrower ones, you may give up the Co. Down idea altogether.

Here an utterly different country meets you, a richness like the Devonshire combes, a hot labyrinth of lanes beside streams that flow glass clear over red and yellow stones, lanes very deep sunken and full of ferns, with occasional sub-tropical things (I have not seen a palm but they grow here) lanes that go through absolute tunnels of vegetation, dank and green, buzzing with bees and darted through by huge dragon flies. The grasshoppers are noisier than I ever heard them, and sing long after sunset. If you can picture these winding valley-strips of a more luxurious and exotic world inconsequently trickling (each with a lovely stream) though the bottom of a Co. Down landscape you will get some idea of this wonderful place.

Yet the most characteristic feature is still untold – and one wh. I am afraid will go far to render the rest unpicturable. I have been speaking of the narrower valleys – those shaped like the human anal cavity. But now suppose you have just come to the brink of a broader, more saucer like depression. Here you are almost sure to find heathery sides sloping down to a floor of flat grey stones and clay (just what one imagines lava ground like) with here and there a very old slag heap: a sort of great raw gash of abandoned industrialism with the engine house of a mine (*always* like this but of course in very various stages of decay) brooding over an odd litter of miscellaneous buildings that have long been quarries to the neighborhood, of things like mill wheels idly suspended, of artificial oblong pools with a last green stagnant trickle on the floor of – Lord knows what! You can't walk a mile without coming to a mine: there are rather more in the valleys than on the hills: but every hill-horizon too, shows three to six variations of the engine house theme, the high tower like building and the slightly higher stumpy chimney. Silhouetted against the sky far off, as I see it every night, it has the exact appearance of a giant's armchair. The deserted mines outnumber those at work almost as the dead outnumber the living. Of course it is only the comparatively modern ones that are marked by engine house, or still unvegetated slag.

One comes across other relics that may be Elizabethan, Saxon, Roman, or even British: sometimes a shaggy low lintelled doorway opening inconsequently into the side of a hill, where only one man cd. enter at a time, and, frankly, nothing would induce me to be that one: often, miles from anywhere, one finds a reddish stream coming out of such a doorway and perhaps very old timbers still making the door posts. Or else, you are plodding along on the heathery slope of a valley and suddenly see a place, about the size of Hillsboro's drawing room, fenced (or stone walled) about. Go nearer and you see a plain round hole: its sides, of green or red and usually dripping rock, are visible for twenty feet or so and then disappear into darkness. If you throw a fair sized stone down you hear it go '*BANG-BANG*-BANG-BANG-bang-bang' with decreasing noise from side to side on its journey down: but you never hear any *final* noise to that journey. The 'bangs' just get less and less and fade insensibly to nothing. Few ideas give me (as the 18th century wd. have said) such 'pleasing horror' as that of the bottom of the shaft in a mine abandoned, say, about the year the Armada was defeated. A working mine would be bad enough.

By the bye there is *one* more modification in the original 'Down-and-Antrim' scheme – namely that, owing to mineral wealth the sea cliffs are nearly all red: solid rock of course and beaten into every spire and arch of ruinous architecture, but red as garden clay. If you take all this that I have tried to describe and put over it a bluer sky, and round it a bluer 'poster' sea than Ireland ever dreamt of, you will have the best I can do for you about Cornwall: but nothing can describe the feeling with which, from brooding over the deserted mine shaft and throwing your stone down it, you suddenly *return* (as if you yourself had been in a deadly place) to the riot of sunshine and gorse and birds and wind about you. I think even the Baron feels those holes in the ground to be rather awful.

The only Cornish city I have been to is Truro. The town is an ordinary little market town, much less pleasing than any in the 'homely' counties between Morlockheim and the West Country: in fact so true is the Co. Down element in my Cornish recipe that Truro has more than a flavour of Newtownards about it. The Cathedral is the poorest, almost, that I have ever seen. This is a rough idea of it: a very tall square central tower supporting a spire, and four narrow towers or pinnacles of the same sort at the four corners, but all so thin in proportion to their height that it gives the impression of one of those buildings that figure on the lid of a child's box of bricks and for the construction of wh., no sensible child has ever used the bricks.

The history of this abortion is a painful mystery to me. The West Front is adorned with statues of Edward VII and of obviously Victorian and Edwardian prelates, and it appears to be of exactly the same date as the rest – the whole thing being of one texture, a rather ugly and very new looking pale stone, cut small, and the joinings between the blocks aggressively black and staring. On the other hand the interior contains a 16th century monument (none earlier so far as I could see). Do you suppose the monument is the sole survivor of a small old cathedral which was replaced wholesale by a contractor in the reign of the late King? Anyway, the whole thing is a deplorable business (except the height of the interior which has a fine effect) and it is made worse by the fact that *one* of the cupolas is bright green copper coloured – the rest all pale stone.

The main object of my visit was to get a book, having finished Martin Chuzzlewit which I brought down. And here let me digress for a moment to advise you v. strongly to make one more effort with Dickens and make it on Martin Chuzzlewit if only for the sake of an account of 19th century America. In loathing for America you will at last find what you and Dickens have in common. For sheer cruelty and uproarious farce with a horrid essential truth (every American without exception whom Martin meets is first introduced to him as 'one of the most remarkable men in our country, sir')[66] it beats everything. Of course to enjoy it, or any other Dickens, you must get rid of all idea of realism – as much as in approaching William Morris or the music hall. In fact I should say he is the good thing of which the grand Xmas panto. is the degeneration and abuse: broadly typical sentiment, only rarely intolerable if taken in a jolly after dinner pantomime mood, and broadly effective 'comics': only all done by a genius, so that they become mythological. Just try Mr Tigg, the blue gentleman in Martin Chuzzlewit. You will never meet a blue gentleman like him: and certainly Turner's *mot* 'Don't you wish you could?' wd. here be answered by a very decided 'No'. But he is what every blue gentlemen is trying to be – a sort of eternal Platonic form of blue gentleman. But this is all by the way.

I had assumed that as Truro was a cathedral city, it must have at least a clerical intelligentsia: and if that, a decent bookshop. It appeared to have only a Smith's and a faded looking place that seemed half a news agents. At the door of this I stopped an elderly parson and asked him whether this and Smith were the only two booksellers. He said they were: then a few moments later came back walking on tip toes as some parsons do, and buzzed softly in my ear (he had a beard) 'There is an S.P.C.K. depot further down this street'. This almost adds a new character to my

---

66 Dickens, *Martin Chuzzlewit*, ch. XVI: "'Jefferson Brick,' he observed after a short silence, in commendation of his correspondent, "is one of the most remarkable men in our country, sir.'"

world: henceforth among my terms of abuse none shall rank lower than 'he's the sort of man who'd call an S.P.C.K. depot a bookshop'.

I discovered however that my unpromising bookshop had a second hand quarter upstairs. This at first was depressing as it appeared to consist entirely of two sections: one labeled 'books on Cornwall', the other 'Second hand rewards'. That also is a valuable new idea. I suppose a Truro child, after having spent a sufficient number of year's study of the S.P.C.K. depot, may be examined by a beard-buzzing clergyman on tiptoe and then, if successful, receive a 'second hand reward' (the second hand rewards ranged from Paley's evidences[67] to the 'Queen of the upper Fourth', so he has no need to complain). However in the end I discovered an upper garret where there were at last some *books*. I had v. little money and the selection was poor. I got inter alia the poetical work of 'Armstrong, Dyer, and Green' with lives and prefaces to all three by the Rev. Gilfillan.[68] He lived in the early 19th century and wrote lives and prefaces to everyone in the 'British Poets'[69] – those long thin greyish backed volumes ('Of which I have an hondred in my celle') with fine large type of the period when they still had generosity and elegance and were only just beginning to lose beauty. Gilfillan is incredible. Here is a little passage from his preface to Dyer. 'The painter himself too, becomes one of the finest objects in the landscapes of earth as seen sitting motionless under the rainbow, and perchance in his reverie dropping his pencil into the bubbling stream, or copying with severe sympathy the cataract with a rain of bright berries and green leaves descending on him...thus at the young Dyer etc.'[70]

As for my poets, Dyer you will remember as the author of 'The Fleece',[71] perhaps the best example of that curious 18th century growth, the commercial epic – cf. Also 'Cyder'[72] and 'The Sugar Cane'.[73] Armstrong

---

67 William Paley, *A View of the Evidences of Christianity* (1794).

68 *The Poetical Works of Armstrong, Dyer and Green*, with memoirs and critical dissertations by the Rev. George Gilfillan (1858).

69 George Gilfillan (1813–78), a Scottish dissenting minister, literary critic and editor, was a champion of 'Spasmodic' poetry – poetry which described interior psychological drama, and which was violent and verbose. His *Gallery of Literary Portraits* ran to three series published in 1845, 1850 and 1854.

70 *The Poetical Works of Armstrong, Dyer and Green*, p. 102.

71 The biography of John Dyer (1700–57) is found on pp. 101–14 of *The Poetical Works of Armstrong, Dyer and Green*. *The Fleece*, included in this volume, was originally published in 1757.

72 John Philips, *Cyder* (1708).

73 James Grainger, *Sugar-Cane* (1764).

wrote a similar poem in Miltonic blank verse on 'The Art of preserving Health'.[74] I have read it with huge enjoyment. It is beyond all parody as the specimen of the noble art of making poetry by *translating* ordinary sentences into 'Miltonic' diction. Thus 'some people can't eat eggs' is rendered,

> *Some even the generous nutriment detest*
> *Which, in the shell, the sleeping embryo rears.*[75]

(Where 'rears' I suspect is a misprint for 'bears.') If one eats too much fat,

> *The irresoluable oil*
> *So gentle late and blandishing, in floods*
> *Of rancid bile o'erflows: what tumults hence*
> *What horrors rise, were nauseous to relate.*[76]

One is surprised to learn that even then some people took cold baths,

> *To fortify their bodies, some frequent*
> *The gelid cistern: and, where nought forbids*
> *I praise their dauntless heart.*[77]

Is 'cistern' merely poetical for a bathtub? – or did they really bathe in cisterns? If so, I agree about their dauntless hearts. I can't imagine anything nastier than a dip in the cistern off the Leeborough attic. Green, I confess, I had never heard of. He wrote a poem on 'The Spleen'.[78]

While I am on this subject I should mention the even stranger bookshop at Newquay. It bore the legend 'New and Second Hand Bookseller'. But when I went in, the following dialogue occurred. 'Where are your

74 The biography of John Armstrong (1709–79) is found on pp. v–xxii of *The Poetical Works of Armstrong, Dyer and Green*. *The Art of Preserving Health*, included in this volume, was originally published in 1744.
75 *The Poetical Works of Armstrong, Dyer and Green*, p. 16, *The Art of Preserving Health*, Bk. II, 111–12.
76 ibid., pp. 15–16, Bk. II, 83-6.
77 ibid., p. 15, Bk. III, 292–4.
78 The biography of Matthew Green (1696–1737) is found on pp. 233–8 of *The Poetical Works of Armstrong, Dyer and Green*. His poem, *The Spleen*, included in this volume, was originally published in 1747.

second hand books?' 'They're all in private rooms'. 'Well can I see them?' 'No. They're all locked up.' 'Aren't they for sale?' 'No.' What do you make of that? The other great disadvantage of Cornwall is the beer. It costs 4d a half pint and (though draught) tastes like Bass – the lowest level surely that beer can attain. Draught cider seems to be unknown. I wonder what the miners drink – 'metheglin'[79] or 'majogony' do you suppose?

I hope you will continue your admirable letters on the same scale as long as you are abroad: they also deserve Johnson's praise – but we must not degenerate into admiration of each other's epistolary style or the thing will become self conscious. My next will be sodden and stuffy with the fumes of Leeborough: and can hope, at best, for a fine P'dayta-crop. I enclose some photos and good wishes from all.

Yours,

Jack

TO HIS BROTHER (LP IX: 290–1):[80]

Belfast Steamship Company Limited
S.S. Patriotic.
Oct. 5th 1927

My dear W.,

Tho' I am uncertain when my next proper letter to you will be written, I should be unpardonable if I failed to salute you on an occasion over which your spirit so emphatically presides. (You will perceive that at the moment of writing I am not absolutely sober). The cry of 'Any more for the shore' has gone round. Arthur, who saw me off and drank with me (nay! at *his* expense) has just gone. The 'flip, flip' of the boots of Belfastians on the rubber floor of the saloon deck is heard on all sides. In a moment we shall shove off. I gave the P'daytabird *four* solid weeks and a day: tomorrow I shall be in Oxford.

Of course it proved impossible to get him away. He had just put himself under the injection treatment of our cousin the 'blood specialist': and his first line of defence thus turned on the necessity of 'giving this serum business a fair trial'. He couldn't go away and break it for a few

---

79 Metheglin is a spiced or medicated form of mead peculiar to Wales.

80 Lewis was with his father at Little Lea from 6 September until 5 October. This portion of a letter, written aboard the SS *Patriotic* as it was about to leave Belfast, was enclosed with the bulky instalment dated 'Dec. 12th' and the whole was posted to Warnie on 16 December.

weeks. ('These serums are a funny business Jacks. You know there're made of – ' 'Yes, yes, I remember you told me the other night.' 'Well, you know it's really very funny. They take a swab of your throat – ' 'Yes, I know, very funny.' 'Aye, but that's not the cream of the joke. The other two ingredients are your own urine and your own excrement.') These details I have heard at least twice a week for the last month.

His second defence was a pure windfall. A letter from Uncle Dick gave it him. Eileen was coming over to stay at Sandycroft.[81] That provided his second defence. 'Well you know, I *couldn't* go away now. Uncle Dick will expect me to [do] my little bit of manners – I'll have to have that girl up to dinner and all that sort of thing' – a suggestion wh. was converted in a few days to 'I tell you what I'll do. I'll ask her to *tea* some day.' So the attempt to get him boiled in mud, which I made sincerely and even importunately, was a complete failure. A usual Leeborough holiday took its place, with an inordinate number of P'dayta Days. It is cruelest of all when he comes home on Monday at 11.30. To be given just enough time to decant the brisk liquour of Monday morning and then to have the cup dashed from your hand.

It was specially annoying this time because I wanted to be very busy putting into action my project of an Encyclopedia Boxoniana. I have worked through the texts down to The Locked Door[82] and at Christmas hope to be able to begin the actual encyclopedia. Big 4 (the one you know best) will be by far the largest article and B the longest letter (Bob, Bar, Bradley, Bradshaw, Bublish, Bumregis, Brus (vin de), Bears, Benjamin I, Benjamin VI, Benjamin VII, Boj, Bojaren, Borata, Boys, the, Big I, Big II, Big III, Big IV – all lengthy). I find the work fascinating: the consistency between the very early texts and the ones we usually read is much greater than I dared to hope for: and an odd sentence in the Locked Door or the Life of Big will fit into a narrative written in Wynyard or pre-Wynyard days in the most startling way. I suppose it is only accident, but it is hard to resist the conviction that one is dealing with a

---

81 'Uncle Dick' was Richard Lewis (b. 1861), one of Albert Lewis's four brothers and two sisters. See **The Lewis Family** in the Biographical Appendix.

At the time this letter was written, Jack and Warnie seem never to have met Richard Lewis nor any of his family. 'Sandycroft' was the home of C.S. Lewis's great-grandfather, Joseph Lewis (1803–90), in Saltney, Flintshire. Richard and his daughter Eileen were going to visit members of the Lewis family still living there.

82 'The Locked Door' is one of the many histories and stories of Boxen that Lewis wrote as a boy. See note 10 to letter of c. 1906 to Warnie Lewis.

sort of reality. At least so it seems to me, alone in the little end room. How it will appear tomorrow in Magdalen Common Room or a month hence to you in How Kow is another matter.

We're off. The screw turns. I had stewed steak for lunch today and boiled mutton for supper dinner. I am going to eat some supper. Can you forget the flavour of one's first non-P'dayta meal. (I was mistaken. The screw has stopped again.)

TO HIS FATHER (LP XI: 266–8):

> [Magdalen College,
> Oxford
> 29? November 1927]

My dear Papy,

Many thanks for your letter.[83] My own long silence has the cause (I wish it were also the excuse) which you suggest. I have got my evenings nearly full up this term. On Monday nights I entertain as many of my own pupils and other undergraduates as care to come and join in the reading of an Elizabethan play: I was driven to institute this because I saw no other way of persuading them to get through the enormous number of plays they are supposed to read (I am often tempted to curse the fertility of our Elizabethans). On Wednesdays some of the junior pupils come to read Anglo-Saxon with me.[84] The actual work is usually done by half past ten: but they are comfortably by the fire and like to sit on and talk – and after all, it is part of ones job to get to know them – so that evening is usually full up till midnight. Then there are functions which occur fortnightly: the Kolbitar or Icelandic Society, and a fortnightly philosophical supper with Hardie[85] and some others.

None of these engagements is onerous in itself, indeed they are all agreeable: but when you add to them the inevitable interchange of invitations to dinner, an occasional visit, and an odd night when one is tired and goes to bed early, it leaves few evenings free in term time. My mornings are

---

83 Mr Lewis's letter of 23 November is found in LP IX: 306–7.
84 These became known as Lewis's 'Beer and Beowulf Evenings'. During these sessions he introduced his pupils to mnemonic devices he invented for learning Old English, they chanted *Beowulf* aloud, and the beer-jug was passed around.
85 William Francis Ross Hardie (1902–90), educated at Balliol College, became a Fellow of Philosophy at Magdalen in 1925. He was Fellow and Tutor in Philosophy at Corpus Christi College, Oxford 1926–50, and President of Corpus Christi 1950–69.

of course occupied with tutoring or preparation for it: and even my afternoons are sometimes invaded by a college meeting. a meeting of the Tutorial Board, or a meeting of the English Faculty. This is not to say that I am overworked: a labourer or a tram driver might justly describe all that I have enumerated as a round of strenuous idleness. But if I am as free as any man can hope to be from 'work' in the original and proper sense of drudgery (the curse of Adam), in revenge, I have as little leisure, in the sense of vacant time, as I can well have.

I do not think the accounts of Hogarth in the newspapers were exaggerated – except in so far as a natural feeling about the newly dead, a wish to do the best you can for a man, affects all obituary notices and funeral orations whatsoever.[86] Most of his work lay rather outside my own sphere: though I read the 'Ancient History of the Near East'[87] when I was doing Greats (a work of immense learning which includes much of the best results of Assyriology, Egyptology, and Babylonian, Greek and Hittite archaeology, while remaining fairly short and almost popular). I also read his 'Wanderer in the Levant'[88] which is purely popular and gives you a sort of essay like account of his experiences in the Near East, not as a scholar, but as a traveller.

He did not dine in very often and I seldom talked to him – only once had a real conversation with him and that was about Doughty's poetry.[89] He was a very fine looking soldier like man: straight as a ramrod: but there was something which I at least found a little uninviting in his face – a tinge of that haughtiness, almost cruelty, which you see so often in the faces of people who have got into the habit of lording it among coloured races east of Suez. (You can trace the thing I am referring to in many of the episodes and reflections, even in the style, of Kinglake's

---

86 David George Hogarth (1862–1927), scholar and traveller, took his degree from Magdalen in 1885. He travelled and excavated in Asia Minor, Cyprus, Egypt and Knossos, many of which places are discussed in his books. In 1908 he became Keeper of the Ashmolean Museum, Oxford. According to a note Lewis wrote on the presidential elections (LP IX: 307–9), most of the Fellows of Magdalen were hoping to elect Hogarth as their next President when he died suddenly on 6 November 1927. An obituary appeared in *The Times* (7 November 1927), p. 14.

87 Hogarth did not write a book with that title. Lewis was probably thinking of Harry Reginald Hall's *The Ancient History of the Near East: from the earliest times to the Battle of Salamis* (1914).

88 David George Hogarth, *A Wandering Scholar in the Levant* (1896).

89 The poetry of Charles Montagu Doughty, which Lewis mentioned in his letter to Arthur Greeves of 14 February 1920.

Eothen).[90] Still it is no doubt easier to wear kid gloves and think of the brotherhood of man when we are in Little Lea or Oxford than it would be in Arabia. That is the excuse which W. would certainly urge for all those Anglo-Indian officers, sea captains, and others in whom I find this disturbing element. And I allow it. But wouldn't you agree (tho' I find it constantly forgotten) that there is all the difference in the world between saying that a thing is excusable and saying that it needs no excuse? As if 'the driver couldn't prevent the train leaving the rails' means the same as 'the train is still on the rails'.

They had great fun at the Union last week. Birkenhead came to speak.[91] The first thing that worried him was the private business in which two gentlemen got up and discussed the library list – additions to the library of the Union being a subject which naturally comes up in private business. On this occasion the merits of *Smith in Journalism*[92] by P. G. Wodehouse, *That Ass Smith*[93] by the same author, and *The Wreck of the Birkenhead*[94] were hotly canvassed. The noble lord was understood to make some observations to those around him in which the word 'schoolboys' figured.

Then the debate began. The first speaker produced the good old ancient Wadham story of how Smith and Simon[95] had decided what parties they were to follow in their political careers by the toss of a coin the night before they took schools. You will hardly believe me when I tell you that Smith jumped up: 'baseless fabrication' – 'silly, stale story' – 'hoped that even the home of lost causes had abandoned that chestnut, etc. etc.' – and allowed himself to be sidetracked and leg pulled to such an extent that he never reached his real subject at all. It seems to me impossible that a man of his experience could fall to such frivolous tactics: unless we accept the accompanying story that he was drunk at the time, or the even subtler explanation that he was *not*.

Many thanks for the birthday wishes and the birthday present. I will select the latter in the next few days and let you know. I am not sure that

90 For Kinglake's *Eóthen* see note 26 to letter of 10? August 1924.
91 Lord Birkenhead, or F.E. Smith (1872–1930), read Law at Wadham College, and was Lord Chancellor of England from 1919 until 1922.
92 P.G. Wodehouse, *Psmith, Journalist* (1915).
93 *That Ass Smith* is not a Wodehouse title.
94 William Gilly, *The Wreck of the Birkenhead* (1873).
95 John Allsebrook Simon, first Viscount Simon (1873–1954), statesman, was, like Lord Birkenhead, educated at Wadham College. He was Lord Chancellor between 1940 and 1945.

I shall not get a picture instead of the books. I am sorry to hear that the electrical treatment is not more permanent in its results: but I still stick to my original theory that a change of air and diet must be at least the *first* step towards a cure. The weather of course is very much against you at present: at least if ours is at all like yours. We have had no sight of the sun now for these four days, and fogs more dense and more frequent than I ever remember. Most of these mornings it has been so damp that the door handles are wet to the touch.

    your loving son,

    Jack

Warnie left the convalescent camp at Wei-Hei-Wei at the end of September and travelled to Shanghai en route to Hong Kong to rejoin his unit. While awaiting passage headquarters decided to leave him in Shanghai for the next 18 months in command of the Shanghai Supply Depot. This was much to his liking because he was told that his foreign service would be completed in 18 months, after which he could return home. However, there was a sudden change of plans and on 18 October he was posted to Hong Kong. Upon his arrival there on 21 October, Colonel Badcock ordered him straight back to Shanghai. Apart from his delight in returning to Shanghai, Warnie soon had the pleasure of learning that he was finally free of Colonel Badcock who on 14 November returned to England to become training instructor at the Royal Army Service Corps Training College at Aldershot.

TO HIS BROTHER (LP IX: 320–5):

[Magdalen College]

Dec. 12th. [1927]

    I enclose a fragment written when and how, you will see. I had hoped to continue it in reasonable time: but the monthly letter has proved an impossibility during the term. My evenings for the fortnight in term run thus. *Mon.* Play reading with undergraduates (till Midnight). *Tue.* Mermaid club.[96] *Wedn.* Anglo-Saxon with undergraduates. *Thurs. – Frid. – Sat. – Sunday.* Common room till late. *Mon.* Play reading.

---

96 The Mermaid Club was founded in 1902 'to promote the reading and study of the Elizabethan and post-Elizabethan drama'. Lewis was President of the Mermaid Club in Michaelmas Term 1927.

Tue. Icelandic Society. *Wedn.* Anglo-Saxon. *Thurs.* Philosophical supper. *Fri. – Sat. – Sunday.*

As you will see this gives at the very best only three free evenings in the even weeks, and two in the odd. And into these two everything in the way of casual entertaining, correspondence and what we used to call 'A-h-h-h!' has to be crammed. Without increasing the Ah-h-h to any tolerable proportions I can well find myself at the end of eight such weeks with my letter still unwritten. Even if this fails to convince you, you will be satisfied with the ironical vengeance which now falls upon me – when I find myself sending off to you that note from the Liverpool boat within a few days of my revisiting the same boat again, this time with a nasty error in the direction of her bows.[97] How loathsome now are all those details with which I tried to create the atmosphere for you! The smells and sounds will all be there again next week: but the one fatal error of direction dashes them all. Before leaving this now ancient subject, perhaps I should give you some account of my stay in P'daytaheim.

I have already mentioned your father's refusal to move and his frivolous reasons. For the rest, he suffered a good deal from his complaint while I was there. It is always difficult with him to estimate the exact amount: but it was I think fairly bad, tho' a little improved. I cannot understand what his doctors are up to. In England one always hears drastic dieting prescribed for rheumatic complaints – with a special reduction (or complete prohibition) of animal foods. I asked him if they had said nothing on that subject: to which he very characteristically replied 'No. I asked Joey if I ought to give up my little drop of whiskey and he said it didn't matter.' It was quite useless to point out that diet (even his) did not consist exclusively of whiskey. As regards his 'parts' he was often agreeable and cheerful. The chief change I notice in him with advancing years is a very rapidly 'increased rate of increase' in the coarseness of his conversation. With some such prelude as 'It's not a nice subject but – ' or, more ominous still, 'You're a man now and we can talk – ' night after night he launches forth on what for its blueness and its salacity may well be called an *ocean* of stories. There was one about a man who had to empty his bowels in a Co. Down Railway carriage: and when I had been told (with illustrative gestures) how 'these fellows'

---

97 He is referring to the fact that he was returning to Little Lea for Christmas. Lewis was with his father from 21 December until 11 January 1928.

spread a newspaper on the floor and how 'this chap got down' on his hunkers and 'did the best he could', I discovered that *that* – the mere fact – was the whole point of the story.

There were also occasions on which he appeared in his earlier manner. One morning I had gone down to the hall early to get a morning cigarette (that will conjure up in your mind the whole quality of a day in mid-holidays when you have let yourself run out of non-P'dayta cigarettes). I saw a letter from Barfield for me: but didn't take it, knowing that it would be a long piece of argument not suited for reading in bed. I returned to bed and in due course was summoned to the bath room. Before I had locked the door I heard him shouting up from the hall, 'Here's a letter for you.' I shouted 'Thanks' and banged the door. In an incredibly short time he was rattling at the door (he must have wolfed his breakfast abominably). Admitted to wash his teeth, he repeated in an aggrieved voice 'You've got a letter waiting for you. D'you not want it?' I continued drying myself as soon as he was gone and after dressing came down stairs. As I reached the lowest step a voice from the cloakroom boomed out 'You'll find that letter on the hall table.' As I was perfectly easy in my mind about this particular letter, I could not refrain from leaving it where it lay while I went to ring the dining room bell. In a moment he was after me (now hatted and coated) with the letter in his hand. That episode was pure fun: this that follows was of the kind that is funny in memory but was insufferable at the time.

One afternoon Arthur and I went for a long walk over the hills round Divis. I said 'I don't know when we shall be back.' He said 'That's all right, my son, I'll wait dinner till you come.' I explained 'very loud and clear' that he was not to wait: if I didn't turn up at the right time, would he please go on and I would have some cold supper with tea whenever I got back. To my surprise he actually consented: the arrangement was most distinct and I set off with my mind at ease. At 8.30, after a glorious afternoon I came in: my feet sore, my cheeks cool, my mind full of heather and sky, with not a care in the world. That mood does not live long after you have crossed the threshold of Leeborough. I found him in the hall. 'I waited as long as I could,' he said, 'I'm sorry.' I explained with some heat that I thought we had arranged he was not to wait. To which he returned in a low voice, 'Well get your boots off and take your bit of dinner' – then, opening the glass door, 'Mary! Master Jacks is in now.' I was then brought to the dining room and given a disgusting meal of soup, joint, vegetables and pudding, which had been kept hot for me. The O.A.B. *standing* in the room in various attitudes of resignation until I had finished. I resolved that night that once and for all I would put an end to this tomfoolery and repeated a few days later the experiment of saying I would be late for dinner and should prefer a cold meal when I came in. His preference for a grievance was apparently not proof against a second night's abstinence and this time the scheme worked to admiration. I had cold supper with tea, alone, in almost non-Leeburian comfort.

Emboldened by this I actually took the unprecedented step of dining in town with Arthur and an Oxford man called Bryson[98] one night! No objection was raised: indeed he entered into the project so keenly and discussed how we should 'handle the thing' so often that I was heartily sick of the affair long before it came off. It became such an *affair*. The whole point was an evening's escape into the haphazardness and absence of fussiness which one longs for so at home. But (he always has an unsuspected trump card) he contrived, without raising a finger in objection, to banish all that. Where would we go? Would we dress? How would we arrange about meeting? It would be a bad business *if* – and here a thousand perverse hypotheses which he contrived to make real for the moment. Still – to be seated in a hotel, eating an ordinary dinner and drinking your wine, indulging in ordinary chat, and then to reflect that Belfast is outside the window, is a marvellous sensation. I discovered to my surprise that Bryson (whom I always regarded as an imposing junior Don) was in just the same state at home as Arthur and myself.

During my month in Ireland I had the most glorious jaunts. You can walk nearly all the way from Craigantlet to Helen's tower through thick woods, crossing the road only once. You can drive out to Hannah's Town (at the Western extremity of Divis range) and then spend all afternoon coming over the mountains to Ligoniel. We did it on an afternoon when there were some moving clouds overhead, but all the more distant sky towards the horizon was a pale transparent blue: and the distant objects very clear. At our first halt we could see, (1) *Half left* – a rolling blue green plain stretching out to the Mournes: the Mournes, as you know, jagged like mountains in a romance, and of such a pure blue colour that you felt, if a bird flew behind them, you could have seen it *through* them. (2) *Straight ahead* – the heather sloping down in big folds to the road we

---

98 i.e. John Bryson. See the letter of 26 May 1925.

had left: beyond that a deep narrow valley filled with woods. Beyond the valley the ground rose, studded with white cottages and crossed with hedges, to a well peaked conical hill – one side wooded with steeply perpendicular pines. (3) *Half right* – the expanse of Lough Neagh, shining like the roof of a greenhouse, and more mountains beyond it. (4) *Full right*: like this, over the shoulder of our own slope a very remote rocky looking slice of Antrim for the first time – where I think you have preceded me. That valley with the rock rampart on one side and the woods below and the open spaces on the high moors at the head of the valley, with their glimpses of the Scotch coast, are among the best things I have seen.

At the moment of writing I have forgotten the order of places and distances: I remember working out at the time that a walking tour in those parts, starting from Larne or perhaps from Belfast would be quite possible. Shall we make a resolution to do it together when we are next both at home? My dinner in town has proved that the pleasant things of life can be carried out during a P'daytaholiday. Do not let us put off all these projects for amelioration of the Irish visit which we have so often discussed. By the way the O.A.B. was with us on our ride to the Glens: and said, 'The last time I was in Cushendun was on a Boxing day – bitterly cold, and I had to set off for here and leave you boys: a miserable business it was.' It is odd that the memory of that occasion has entirely faded from my mind. Yet it must have been epic. The house to ourselves all day in the Wynyard period and Christmas food! Possibly we should date there the memorable artillery engagement with mince pies.

It comes into my head for no reason at this point to tell you that I have read Coningsby: having been informed that his grandfather (drawn by the way from the same original as Thackeray's Lord Steyne[99]) has found a very suitable seat in the house for him, he objects that his principles will not allow him to support the ministry: and receives from the old man the reply 'You'll go with your family, boy, like a gentleman, and not start talking about principles as if you were an adventurer.' But apart from this you, who have always been a Tory, and yet felt some uneasiness at finding yourself in the same boat as all the canting and comfortable exploiters of sweated labour, will find just what you want in Dizzy: Toryism at its extreme of opposition to the 'Manchester School' and anxious

99 In *Vanity Fair*.

to restore (as he calls it) '*the estate* of the peasantry' in the place of the Whig created '*class* of the poor'.[100]

And while we are on 'estates', you will probably be surprised to hear (as I was to read) that King Alfred, translating Boethius and interpolating a passage of his own, says that a king must have as tools for his work 'the three estates' (tha threo gerferscipu), prayer men, money men and work men'. (A moment later he comfortingly mentions *beer* as another essential.) This seems to show that the conception goes back pretty far in mediaeval theory: Alfred came to the throne in 871. But possibly to you – more acquainted than I with European history – this may be stale news.

I also (while at home) bought a capital Montaigne in three very large quartos with magnificent type: printed (oddly enough) in London cum privilegio regis in the early XVIII century – 1712 I think.[101] I found the French more difficult than I expected: also the matter at once more seriously valuable as thought (in some parts) and more deliciously absurd (in others) than I had ventured to hope. Some of his 'facts' go beyond anything in Burton.[102] Do you remember the story of the man who could break wind in time with a tune, and the other who broke wind continuously for forty years and then died? The only thing one gets rather bored with is the endless succession of stories from Plutarch – 'Agesilaus being besieged by the Epirotes –' 'Scruma Nonius, being made aedile etc.' Plutarch is one of those unhappy authors whom we are bored with years before we read him. Shakespeare is almost another: and you may add Blake, Pascal and Montaigne himself. It is curious the boredom which broods over certain things. Why is 'The Empire' such a dull subject?

I have done very little reading outside my work these last months. In Oman's 'Dark Ages'[103] I have come up against a thing I had almost forgotten since my school days – the boundless self assurance of the pure text book. 'The four brothers were all worthy sons of their wicked father – destitute of natural affection, cruel, lustful, and treacherous.' Lewis the Pious was 'a man of blameless and virtuous habits' – tho' every other sentence in the chapter makes it plain that he was a sh-t. 'Charles had

---

100 Disraeli, *Coningsby*, bk. III, ch. 3.
101 *Les Essais de Michel seigneur de Montaigne, avec des notes etc. pas Pierre Coste*, 3 vols. (1724).
102 Robert Burton's *Anatomy of Melancholy*.
103 Sir Charles Oman, *The Dark Ages 476–918* (1893).

one lamentable failing – he was too careless of the teaching of Christianity about the relations of the sexes.' It is so nice too, to be told without a hint of doubt who was in the right and who was in the wrong in every controversy, and exactly why every one did what he did. Yet Oman is quite right: that is the way – I suppose – to write an *introduction* to a subject. Indeed I have confessed this in turning to him because Gibbon, however delightful to read, simply won't do, if, starting from scratch, you want to get a clear skeleton outline which you can afterwards colour in at leisure. There is also this advantage in Oman, that you can see when he is being silly: with Gibbon one is up against a really clever man and I expect that much besides 'infidelity' is 'artfully intermixed'.

I am almost coming to the conclusion that all histories are bad. Whenever one turns from the historian to the writings of the people he deals with there is always such a difference. What is in my mind at present is (on the one hand) Beowulf and Alfred and the Sagas, and (on the other) Gibbon and Oman about 'the barbarians'. What common measure is there between 'Odoacer had alienated the sympathies of his Italian subjects by seizing a third of the land to reward his veterans' and 'Oft Scyld Scefing overthrew the mead benches of many a kindred. The dwellers round had to obey him across the whale's way. That was a good king...So shall a young hero *do good* and give lordly gifts, that his retainers may repay him when war comes.'[104] The implication (always present) in the first version that Odoacer oughtn't to have given the land to his men, or that any choice in the matter could have occurred to him, as against the perfectly untroubled sincerity with which the other describes the hero as 'doing good' in scattering the 'lordly gifts' (acquired no doubt at the cost of 'alienating the sympathy' of someone) makes one despair. Then 'his veterans' – memories of Chelsea Hospital! Of course one can see in some sense that the two passages refer to the same sort of fact. But what is left of the 'fact' if you take away both its two 'appearances'? And if you plump for *one* of them, is that historical truth? I wish there was a good translation of Beowulf. Isn't this good? (The funeral of Scyld Scefing). 'They bore him down to the brim of the sea: there rode in harbour – with rings at her bows – ice-hung, eager, the atheling galley. They laid in her their beloved lord, their giver of rings, in the galley's

---

104 *Beowulf*, ll. 4–24.

waist... They let the sea carry him away. No one knew who took in that cargo.'[105]

I hear with pleasure of your separation from the unpleasant Colonel, of your sea voyagings, and that you think to spend on 18 months in 'furrin parts'. The Shanghai news looms very formidable in the papers at this distance: but I comfort myself by the reflection that the state of Belfast when we have been there, would often have read much the same.

I was delighted with your account of the American. You remember Carritt's mot concerning them – 'they lisp in numbers for the numbers come'.[106] If you cast back your mind, when we were at Wynyard we were in exactly that phase: it gave us a pleasure at which I still blush to din into peoples ears the fact that Belfast had the largest gantry in the British isles or had launched the largest ship afloat. But we have outgrown it: it would now give me no appreciable thrill to convince the fellows of Magdalen that my father was the largest batata in Europe. If the analogy between peoples and individuals were sound, I suppose we should have to forgive the Americans for being in a state which we once passed through ourselves. But the analogy is nonsense. I never can see why a fat middle aged American whose ancestry (in the purely biological sense of course) must stretch back as far as any one else's, and whose nation started with all the history of European culture as a jumping off point, should be excused any of his vulgarity on the score of youth. Incidentally they didn't start the business about being 'young' and shouting, hallooing, and indulging in horseplay until the earlier stages of their career were well over.

There is none of the breezy and laborious rawness of Whitman[107] in Hawthorne[108] or Lowell – of whom I have received from the O.A.B. the handsome complete set that has languished in 'my' dressing room for so many years.[109] I read most of the essays before crossing back to England.

---

105 ibid., ll. 28–52.

106 Alexander Pope, *An Epistle from Mr Pope to Dr Arbuthnot* (1734–5), 125: 'I lisp'd in Numbers, for the Numbers came.'

107 The American poet, Walt Whitman (1819–92), whose *Leaves of Grass* (1855) Lewis had read.

108 Lewis mentioned Nathaniel Hawthorne's *The House of Seven Gables*, *The Marble Faun* and *The Scarlet Letter* in his letters of 22 November 1916 and 28? October 1917.

109 *The Writings of James Russell Lowell*, Riverside Edition, 10 vols. (1890).

His hatred of his fellow countrymen is far from being the only endearing characteristic about him. In addition to the literary essays – always worth reading – there is one on winter which need not be ashamed to show its face in any collection. Lowell, sir, is a book that a man may be proud to have stand on his shelves. And Hawthorn I admire beyond words: and 'I have a sneaking affection' for Longfellow. But in none of these is there the faintest trace of this abominable 'youth'. Longfellow is never happy unless he is in the dark ages: Hawthorne takes some old building dating from the New England times and weaves out of the very few centuries at his disposal an air of antiquity which is not often attained even in Europe where we have so much *arithmetically* greater a past to conjure with. (By the by, what a wonderful conceit of Thomas Browne's referring to the age of the long lived antediluvians – 'an age when living men might be antiquities'.[110] Query: *Would* a living man a thousand years old give you the same feeling that an old building does? I think there is a good deal to be said for Alice Meynell's theory that one's idea of antiquity and the standard one measures it by, is derived entirely from one's own life.[111] Certainly 'Balbec and Tadmor'[112] (whoever they may be) could hardly give one a more weird sense of 'ages and ages ago' than some early relic discovered in the drawers of the little end room often does.

One has one's own 'dark ages'. But I daresay this is not so for everyone: it may be that you and I have a specially historical sense of our own lives. Are you often struck, when you become sufficiently intimate with other people to know something of their development, how *late* their lives begin so to speak? I mean these men you meet who seem to have

---

110 Sir Thomas Browne, *Religio Medici* (1642), Pt. I, sect. 42.

111 Alice Meynell, *The Colour of Life* (1896), 'The Illusion of Historic Time': 'When a child begins to know there is a past, he has a most noble rod to measure it by – he has his own ten years. He attributes an overwhelming majesty to all recorded time. He confers distance. He, and he alone, bestows mystery. Remoteness is his. He creates more than mortal centuries. He sends armies fighting into the extremities of the past. He assigns the Parthenon to a hill of ages, and the temples of Upper Egypt to sidereal time. If there were no child, there would be nothing old. He, having conceived old time, communicates a remembrance at least of the mystery to the mind of man' (pp. 89–90).

112 Baalbek or Balbec is the ancient city of Coele-Syria, forming part of modern Lebanon. It was a centre of the worship of Baal. The ancient city of Tadmor is better known by its Roman name, Palmyra. It stood in an oasis of the Syrian desert, and its remains include a huge temple of Bel.

read everything, done everything, and yet they were pure barbarians until they left school, and had turned twenty perhaps before they began to be interested in the things that interest them now?

When I was at home I committed the unpardonable folly of telling your father that a man called Hogarth was one of the 'possibles' for our new President. Two results follow. (a) That his election was henceforth treated as absolutely certain. (b) His powers as infinite. (c) His name became Hogg-arth (to rime with 'Sogarth' in 'Sogarth Aroon'). By the end of the month I was pretty tired of 'Well is this new President of yours, this Hogg-arth, an able chap?' and 'Well, I suppose Hogg-arth will put a stop to all that'. But since then Hogarth has died. I have already had a letter observing 'So Hogarth is not going to be the new President at all.' Can't you already see the career of 'poor Hogarth' as one of the stock figures of Leeborough conversation henceforth – forever linked with 'John Burnett' and 'Prendergast'.[113] The crop of P'daytaisms was poor: all his energies have now been thrown into pronunciation and philology. This time, in answer to his 'his – to use a word I hate – mentality' I ventured to tell him that he used the word mentality more often than anyone I knew.

You will be seriously alarmed to hear that so far this winter I have followed my hot bath every morning by a cold shower. I mention it, not because I think the fact can give you any pleasure, but because of the happy turn given to it by my friend Harwood who visited me for a few days this term. 'Ah yes' he said, 'the hardening treatment. I used to do it too. Then I realised that one ought to be hardened to all extremes of temperature: so I harden myself now by living in overheated rooms.'

Well, there is no good in prolonging the agony. I must send off by this post a letter to Coast Lines for a berth. Unless your life at present is much nastier than I suppose it to be, I have a claim on your sympathies.

yrs,
Jack

---

113 John Burnett, who lived in Watford, was at Wynyard School with Warnie and Jack and was their closest friend there. He paid a visit to Little Lea in the summer of 1909. He is mentioned in the letter of 28 February 1909, and several times in the diary Jack kept in 1909. See LP III: 158–61. Prendergast is probably another school friend.

1928

— ≈ —

TO HIS FATHER (LP IX: 329–31):

Magdalen.
Feb. 25th. 1928

My dear Papy,

I am afraid I have been a sad defaulter. The truth is that one finds oneself in the middle of term before there is time to look round, and this particular term has not been a very good one with me. First of all, I walked out through the College garden one fine Sunday morning and slammed the door of it on my finger. I wrapped a handkerchief round it to stop the bleeding and gave utterance to a few 'blasphemies', but until I had set out to a place where I could get it dressed and had very nearly fainted on route, I hardly realised what a nasty knock it was. Luckily it was the left hand, but I had some pain and great inconvenience with it. Then I developed a series of colds and a troublesome cough which kept me for some weeks in that border line condition wherein one manages to stumble through the daily round but slinks to bed very soon after dinner (when this is possible) and wakes muddy and unrefreshed. In the end it would not be denied. In spite of my coyness I found that I would have to keep my annual assignation with our lady influenza. A few days in bed soon settled that (this comes rather unfortunately after the assignation metaphor – a consequence not foreseen by the writer) and I am now on my legs again and indeed much better than I have been for many weeks.

The chief event has been the death of one of our fellows, Wrong,[1] which you may have seen in the papers. He was Vice President when I first joined: and had invited me to become Pro-Proctor with him as a junior Proctor – which could not be done as I was just a term too little from my matriculation to be eligible. He was always extremely friendly

---

1 See note 16 to letter of 14 August [1925].

745

to me, and I liked him as well as any one in College. He was that very rare and very delightful thing, a colonial aristocrat – being of an old Canadian family. His grandfather was one of the last people to fight a political duel; to which he was challenged on whatever corresponds to the floor of the 'House' in Canada. The blend is curious. It is odd to find a man who has canoed in Hudson bay and knows all about trapping and skunks and Indians, and yet who has distinction in the lines of his face and tradition in his outlook. No doubt, like other good things, it is disappearing: the influx of commercial democracy and the rule of the Bosses from the States will soon put an end to that element in Canada, just as (I am told) it has always swamped some things in their own vaunted southern states. He had (as Johnson would have said) 'a great deal of literature', though his own subject was history, and I have had much good crack with him about books. He was even responsible himself for a thin volume of poetry – whose merit it would be unkind now to discuss. He was one of the most brilliant of our men, and we shall have trouble in filling his place. Our 'Mods' tutor is also leaving us: so with his place, Wrong's, and the President to fill, we shall live this summer in a riot of elections. The great consolation is that Sambo cannot take part in the choosing of his own successor: if he could, heaven knows what Homeric length of meetings, speeches, committees, memoranda, and what not might await us!

I have had one letter from Warnie since I left, but it largely duplicated his last to you. I cannot help envying him the richness of his subject matter. My own life is hard to turn into matters for letters. You make the same complaint I know of yours: but at least you have the advantage, that you can write trifles to me because I know the people and places concerned. If you tell me you had a very jolly evening's chat with John Greeves or went and had a slap-up dinner with excellent champagne at Uncle Hamilton's, that is of interest because I know who John Greeves and Uncle Hamilton are. If I, on the other hand, were to tell you how I enjoyed Bircham's[2] brilliant and original views on Hamlet last night, or what a pleasant talk I had the other day with Nicholl Smith[3] (statements

---

2 Arthur Christopher Halsey Bircham (1908–) was one of Lewis's least promising pupils. He took his BA in 1926 and his MA in 1929.

3 David Nichol Smith (1875–1962) was a senior man in the University. He was Fellow of English at Merton College from 1921 until he became Merton Professor of English Literature in 1929.

by the way as probable as those I have put in your mouth), it would convey nothing.

However, I see that the main thing is to go on talking: for this wheeze brings into my head the fact that I did really have a very good evening the night before last when I exercised for the first time my newly acquired right of dining at Univ. – an exercise which must be rare because it is so damned expensive. Poynton, the Fark, Carritt and Stevenson, as luck would have it, were all in that evening and it was delightful to revisit the whimsical stateliness of that particular common room. There's no getting away from the fact that we at Magdalen are terribly 'ordinary' beside it. We are just like anyone else: there, every single one of them is a character part that could be found nowhere outside their own walls.

I wonder is there some influence abroad now-a-days that prevents the growth of rich, strongly marked personal peculiarities. Are any of our contemporaries 'characters' as Queen Victoria or Dizzy or Carlyle were 'characters'? I am not asking the ordinary question whether we produce greater or smaller men. 'To be a character' in this sense is not the same thing as 'to have character'. For instance, I suppose Abraham 'had character', but no one ever thought of calling him 'a character': your friend in the Rocket, on the contrary, was lacking in character, but he distinctly was 'a character'. There seems to be no doubt that the thing is growing rarer. Or is it that you need to be at least elderly to be a character? In that case, each generation, seeing the characters all among its elders, would naturally conclude that the phenomenon was passing away. Or perhaps it goes further yet. Perhaps the secret of being a character in the very highest degree is to be dead, for then the anecdotes cluster and improve unchecked.

But all this is from the purpose. What I began on was the difficulties of letter writing. I fear

> '*The fault, dear Brutus, is not in our stars*
> *But in ourselves.*'[4]

for the born letter writer is quite independent of material.

Have you ever read the letters of the poet Cowper?[5] He had nothing –

---

4 Shakespeare, *Julius Caesar*, I, ii, 139–40.
5 *The Letters and Prose Writings of William Cowper*, ed. James King and Charles Ryskamp, 5 vols. (1979–96).

literally nothing – to tell any one about: private life in a sleepy country town where Evangelical distrust of 'the world' denied him even such miserable society as the place would have afforded. And yet one reads a whole volume of his correspondence with unfailing interest. How his tooth came loose at dinner,[6] how he made a hutch for a tame hare,[7] what he is doing about his cucumbers[8] – all this he makes one follow as if the fate of empires hung on it.

Some authors, on the other hand, are far below themselves in their letters. Notably Charlotte Brontë and Mrs Gaskell whose life I re-read again while I was laid up. I had forgotten one of the best unintentionally funny things in literature until I saw it again. It comes where a letter written by Charlotte immediately after her profligate brother's death has been quoted. The situation is genuine tragedy. After giving the letter, Mrs Gaskell proceeds 'The dear friend to whom these affecting lines were written was unfailing in her sympathy for the poor worn mind and harassed frame and shortly afterwards sent her a present of a shower bath.'[9] (I cannot resist thinking of the idea of giving presents of this sort instead of letters of condolence. 'Poor so and so, I must send his wife a vacuum cleaner tomorrow'. It would be 'brutal' to work it out in detail: but undeniably a good idea.

I find that when I left home I came away without (1) a cardigan jumper, (2) a mackintosh. If you can conveniently lay your hands on these and direct the Witch of Endor to send them to me, I shall be much obliged. Try to let me have a letter in the near future – I hope it will contain a favourable account of your health and doings.

your loving son,
Jack

TO HIS FATHER (LP X: 2–3):

Magdalen.
March 31st.[1928]

My dear Papy,

Many thanks for the parcel which arrived safely. I should have acknowledged it earlier but I was in hope that I would have heard from

---

6 ibid., letter to Lady Hesketh of 17 December 1787, vol. III, p. 73.

7 ibid., letter to *The Gentleman's Magazine* of 28 May 1784, vol. V, pp. 40–1.

8 ibid., letter to William Unwin of 3 July 1782, vol. II, pp. 63–4.

9 Gaskell, *The Life of Charlotte Brontë*, ch. XVIII: 'The kind friend, to whom she thus wrote, saw how the poor over-taxed system needed bracing, and accordingly sent her a shower-bath.'

you before now. I hope that your continued silence has no worse cause than 'a truant disposition'[10] and the enticements of forty winks of a Sunday afternoon. Try to let me have a line – if no more – in the course of the next week or so to let me know how you are getting on. I have had no word from the Colonel either for a great while.

I have succeeded, at last, in shaking off the ailments of one of the most troublesome terms I have yet had. I forget whether I told you that after the squashed finger and the flu, I developed a swollen gland under my tongue. A doctor soon put my mind at rest about it, but of course before consulting him I had plenty of opportunity of listening – specially at night – to all the grim suggestions which the selfishness and cowardice of one's uncorrected 'natural man' pours into ones ear on such occasions. The nail, by the by, *is* going to come off and at present hangs by a thread, looking very black and ugly and catching in everything. It reminds me of the far off days when one used to get a shilling for pulling out one's own tooth. I await with much philosophical interest to see how a new nail grows.

My studies in the XVIth Century – you will remember my idea of a book about Erasmus – has carried me much further back than I anticipated. Indeed it is the curse and the fascination of literary history that there are no real beginnings. Take what point you will for the start of some new chapter in the mind and imagination of man, and you will invariably find that it has always begun a bit earlier: or rather, it branches so imperceptibly out of something else that you are forced to go back to the something else. The only satisfactory opening for any study is the first chapter of Genesis.

The upshot of all this is that the book will be a very different one from what I imagined, and I hope to try a preliminary canter in a course of lectures sometime next year. In the mean time I spend all my mornings in the Bodleian:[11] and the evenings in trying, for the hundredth time, to get a real working knowledge of the German language, since in my present occupation I find my ignorance of it up against me at every turn. For example, the only history of mediaeval Latin literature is in

---

10 Shakespeare, *Hamlet*, I, ii, 169.
11 The Bodleian, one of the oldest libraries in the world, is the library of the University of Oxford. Those parts of it, including the 'Duke Humfrey Library', that Lewis used to work in, were built in the 15th and 16th centuries and are some of the most beautiful buildings in Oxford.

German. The authoritative edition of an old French poem I shall have to read is in German. And so on. But I am making progress.

If only you could smoke, and if only there were upholstered chairs, the Bodleian would be one of the most delightful places in the world. I sit in 'Duke Humphrey's Library', the oldest part, a Fifteenth-Century building with a very beautiful painted wooden ceiling above me and a little mullioned window at my left hand through which I look down on the garden of Exeter where, these mornings, I see the sudden squall of wind and rain driving the first blossoms off the fruit trees and snowing the lawn with them – At the bottom of the room the gilt bust of Charles I presented by Laud, faces the gilt bust of Strafford – poor Strafford.[12]

The library itself – I mean the books – is mostly in a labyrinth of cellars under the neighbouring squares. This room however is full of books (duplicate copies I suppose, or overflows) which stand in little cases at right angles to the wall, so that between each pair there is a kind of little 'box' – in the public house sense of the word – and in these boxes one sits and reads. By a merciful provision, however many books you may send for, they will all be left on your chosen table at night for you to resume work next morning: so that one gradually accumulates a pile as comfortably as in ones own room. There is not, as in modern libraries, a forbidding framed notice to shriek 'Silence': on the contrary a more moderate request 'Talk little and tread lightly'. There is indeed always a faint murmur going on of semi-whispered conversations in neighbouring boxes. It disturbs no one. I rather like to hear the hum of the hive, and it is pleasant when someone steps into your box and says 'Hello, are *you* here?'

As you may imagine one sees many oddities among one's fellow readers – people whom I have never met elsewhere and who look as if they were shut up with the other properties every night. Positively the only drawback to the place is that beauty, antiquity and over-heating weave a spell very much more suited to dreaming than to working. But I resist to the best of my abilities and trust in time to become innoculated. (The

---

12 William Laud (1573–1645) became prominent in the Church of England under King Charles I, and in 1633 he was made Archbishop of Canterbury. He defended the Anglican Church as a national institution, and supported the King in his struggle against the Commons. As Archbishop of Canterbury he enforced uniformity in the Church. In 1640 Parliament impeached him of high treason, and he was beheaded in 1645. The Earl of Strafford (1593–1641), chief adviser to Charles I from 1639, was impeached by the Commons in 1640. He was executed, with the King's assent, in 1641.

practice of opening the window in one's box is not, I need hardly say, encouraged.) In such a life as this, what news should there be?

By the time this reaches you, you will probably have heard the result of the boat race – with the same very moderated grief as myself. Perhaps you will also have heard that there is a religious revival going on among our undergraduates. Which is true. It is run by a German-American called Dr Buchman.[13] He gets a number of young men together (some reports say women too, but I believe not) and they confess their sins to one another. Jolly, ain't it? But what can one do? If you try to suppress it (I am assuming that you agree with me that the thing is unhealthy) you only make martyrs.

The rumour that Big Bill Thompson[14] is to be the new President of Magdalen is untrue, and should be contradicted.

your loving son,

Jack

TO HIS BROTHER (LP X: 37–43):

[Hillsboro]
All Fool's Day, 1928
Postmark: 24 April 1928

My dear W.,

Once again I have found it impossible to keep up my letters to you during the term. This will be a chronic complaint and I am afraid you will have to accept it as a law of nature.

My last letter, if I remember rightly, was ironically begun on the return from the summer visit to P'daytaheim and finished only on the eve of the Christmas visit. I have thus a new 'holiday' period to record, which is almost barren in events. The P'dayta crop was singularly poor. The only item worth remembering was his curious contribution to the problem of venereal disease, to the effect that obviously it must have

---

13 Frank Buchman (1878–1961), the American founder and director of the Oxford Group, was a pupil at Mount Airy Seminary, Philadelphia, and entered the Lutheran ministry. On a visit to England in 1908 he was converted by a sermon he heard on the Atonement. He took up evangelistic work among the students of Pennsylvania State College, and from 1915 on he travelled widely preaching to student congregations, including some at Cambridge and Oxford. In 1938 he began his work of Moral Re-Armament, which stressed the role of individuals in transforming society.

14 Big Bill Thompson (1869–1930) was mayor of Chicago.

begun with women and spread thence to men. Being asked why, he replied 'Sure how could a man have given it to a woman if he hadn't got it from a woman herself?' This is unanswerable.

Another illuminating remark was made in answer to some casual remark of mine as to the control of one's imagination – I was talking, I think, about not letting one's mind brood on grievances or fears. He replied 'What on earth do you mean by controlling the imagination? One controls ones appetites.' That is the whole psychology of his generation in a nutshell, isn't it? A man sits thinking of negus and making 'iron rules' not to drink any, with much contortion of the face and muttered 'oh Lords' until the inevitable moment when he finds some excellent reason for breaking the iron rules. The idea of a simpler method – that of applying his mind to something else and using a little concentration – would never occur. The discussion ended (of course) with the infuriating statement that we were not 'ad idem' on the 'connotation' of the word control.

Which reminds me of the splendid definition of an egoist which he read to me out of Punch in happy unconsciousness of its application. 'An egoist is a man who thinks that all the words he doesn't understand are misprints.' He said I ought to write it down. I told him I should certainly remember it. He said, 'Well I bet you if I ask you tomorrow you won't know.' Next evening just as he was about to leave the study, he suddenly whipped round (in the 'I'll tell you another thing' style) and bellowed out in a voice that made me jump out of my skin, 'Jacks!! What's an *optimist*?'

We had indeed a good deal about words, because I had given him Fowler's 'Modern English Usage', a kind of prig's dictionary which contains such entries as 'METICULOUS, see vogue words,' and 'CACHIN-NATION, see Humour, polysyllabic', and which agrees with him about nearly everything. I really lacked the courage to give him another picture. I added to Fowler the new Nineteenth Century volume of the Dictionary of National Biography. Both these proved to be the most successful jumping jacks we have ever struck on, without exception. Both were intolerable nuisances also, lending themselves fatally well to the 'Now there's a very funny thing' style of conversation. My third and last was Max Beerbohm's 'Zuleika Dobson'[15] which was much less

---

15 Max Beerbohm, *Zuleika Dobson* (1911). In this novel a beautiful young lady comes to Oxford to visit her uncle, who is Warden of Judas College. It is Eights Week, and all the young men fall madly in love with Zuleika. When she rejects them, they throw themselves in the Isis and drown.

successful because he insisted on trying to find a hidden meaning in it. 'I wonder what this fellow's driving at...' 'AH, he's got some meaning in all this you know.' Apart from these there is little to record.

We had the usual regrets that you were in the army and the usual astonishment that you didn't appear to be nearly as unhappy as a man of your income ought by all reason to be. We had the usual discussions on theology, drifting off into something else as soon as one had cleared one's ground to begin. His health was tolerable, I thought. But there will be no more calculable days or weeks of non-p'dayta time at home. That is a problem that you and I will have to have a very serious talk about one of these days.

The little end room and all it stands for is rapidly becoming uninhabited territory. My Encyclopedia Boxoniana made hardly any progress at all. And I have not yet done going through the texts, let alone making the actual entries.[16] And even when he does go to town, he may return any time between eleven and three. By the way, what is the explanation of the fact that even if he returns at one o'clock when the lunch ought to be already cooking, the domestic staff immediately goes into p'dayta hours and puts the meal back to two or two thirty? He tells us that it is by no order of his, but I strongly suspect that he's hiding something from us. I find the bucket of sherry a very poor consolation for the disturbance of my day. Talking of sherry you will be surprised to hear that I have been at last moved on to the whiskey roster. I have even overshot you to such an extent that lemon, hot water, and sugar bowl now appear nightly together with the whiskey. The new regimen is accompanied of course with many ponderous jocosities of look, word, and wink, and a frequent use of that very offensive word 'boozing'. This can hardly fail to redound to your advantage. You being now the old guard and I the novice, no doubt the jokes and insinuations (and also the suggested alternative of 'your' Burgundy and soda) will hence forward be transferred to my lot. But I hope there will be no nonsense about continuing in the medium of whiskey the good old theme of the large and the small suitcase. (With what resignation will he explain to visitors, nay with what viciousness 'They each have their whiskey now'. Or more pointedly, 'Yes, when I take my little drop they each have a tumbler of whiskey.')

---

16 Lewis did not complete his Encyclopedia Boxoniana. However, what he did write is contained, with most of his Boxen stories, in *Boxen*, op. cit.

One of the misfortunes of my position is that my reading contains less and less that I can share with my non-professional friends. Except Pickwick[17] (a *very* overrated work) I have read hardly anything this term which you would care to hear of. At present I am deep in medieval things.[18] I find I shall have to try to 'get' some Old French. Don't you think this is rather jolly. In one of those gardens in a dream, which mediaeval love poetry is full of, we find the tomb of a knight, dead for love, covered with flowers. Then: –

> '*Oysiaus i ot: por l'ame del signor*
> *Qui la gisoit, cantent de vrai amor.*
> *Quant il unt fain, cascuns baise une flor,*
> *Ja puis n'arunt ne faim ne soif le jor.*'[19]

I am still so ignorant that I don't know what 'i ot' (1) or 'Ja' mean, but I suppose it can be v. roughly Englished,

> '*And birds that for the soul of that signor*
> *Who lay beneath, songs of true love did pour:*
> *Being hungered, each from off the flowers bore*
> *A kiss, and felt that day no hunger more.*'

The odd thing is that one would expect the same rime going all through to be monotonous and ugly: but to my ear it produces a beautiful lulling like the sound of the sea. I fancy one pronounces the N's less nasal than the modern French N, and almost certainly makes a real syllable out of the mute E's. In quite a different vein I like the mere baldness of this address to ladies,

> '*Toutes estes, seres, ou futes,*
> *De fait ou de volonte, putes.*'[20]

---

17 Charles Dickens, *The Pickwick Papers* (1837).

18 As Lewis mentions in his letter to Owen Barfield of 27 May 1928, he was 'starting a book on...the Romance of the Rose and its school'. This is the first reference to what would become Lewis's first, and perhaps greatest, work of literary history, *The Allegory of Love: A Study of Medieval Tradition* (1936).

19 *Li Fablel dou Dieu d'Amours*, ed. Achille Jubinal (Paris: 1834), stanza 112, p. 31. This was the first publication of this 13th century poem.

20 Guillaume de Lorris and Jean de Meun, *Le Roman de la Rose*, ll. 9155–6. Lewis was using *Le Roman de la Rose*, ed. Ernest Langlois (Paris: Société des Anciens Textes Français,

where you can easily guess the meaning of *putes* if you don't know it already – and also understand the insolence of Swift in calling his flying island 'La Puta'.[21] Which leads to another question. The only modern editions of 'The Romans de la Rose' are old fashioned enough to print asterisks for certain words. So you get,

> '*Car volontiers, non pas enirs*
> *Mist Diex en C****** et en v***
> *Force generacion.*'[22]

We all see what c...... and v.. are. Do you know the words? And is c...... the same as its modern English equivalent? I think you and I ought to do a little old French together, where your superior knowledge of the modern language and my wider experience of language in general would put us at the same point. We might begin with Aucassin and Nicolette,[23] to which, if I remember rightly, you first introduced me. Also, sooner or later, you will be bound to look back at the mediaeval roots out of which your France grew.

1914), and either he or Warnie made some errors in transcribing these lines. They are: 'Toutes estes, sereiz e fustes / De fait ou de volenté putes.' ('All women are, will be, or were – either de facto or by intent – whores.') The best modern edition of *Le Roman de la Rose* is that of Félix Lecoy (Paris, Les Classiques Français Du Moyen Age, 1965–70). In his edition the same lines are numbered 9125–6 and are given as: 'Toutes estes, serez et fustes, / de fet ou de volenté, pustes.' The *Romance of the Rose* is a 13th century French allegorical romance in octosyllabic couplets. It is cast as an allegorical dream-vision, and describes a young man's initiation into love and his efforts to possess the rosebud of which he is enamoured. The first 4,058 lines were written c. 1230 by Guillaume de Lorris (d. 1237) and the remaining 17,622 lines of the poem were written c. 1275 by Jean de Meun. About a third of the whole was translated into the Middle English *The Romaunt of the Rose*, the first part of which may be by Chaucer. The poem, discussed in *The Allegory of Love*, ch. III, is central to Lewis's understanding of courtly love. On courtly love see note 72 to the letter of 3 November 1928.

21 In Jonathan Swift's *Gulliver's Travels* (1726).

22 *Le Roman de la Rose*, ed. Langlois, ll. 6965–6: 'Car volentiers, non pas enviz, / Mist Deus en coilles e en viz.' *Le Roman de la Rose*, ed. Lecoy, ll. 6935–6: 'car volentiers, non pas enviz / mist Dex en coillons et en viz *force de generacion.*' (*The Romance of the Rose*, translated by Frances Horgan (1994): 'For it was by his own will rather than against it that God in his wonderful purpose put the generative power into the testicles and penis, in order that the race would live forever, renewed by new births.'

23 *Aucassin and Nicolette* is a 13th century courtly story in French. It is composed in alternating prose and songs, and believed to be a pastiche of the excesses of courtly love. The story tells of how Aucassin, the son of Count Garins of Beaucaire, loves Nicolette, a Saracen captive. The Count opposes their love and imprisons them. They escape, and after many adventures, they are married.

(1) On second thoughts 'ot' must be an old preterit of avoir, and i ot equals il ya avait.'

April 15th

Last week end I was away on my Easter walking tour, and as Sundays are the only days I can spare for these 'loose undigested pieces' this has had to lie fallow for a fortnight. You should take a box of English maps away with you whenever you go abroad: recalling old jaunts and planning new ones would be a great solace to you and you would also be able to follow any itineraries I write. And, by the same token, don't you approve of the suggestion made by a friend of mine that there shd. be a set of new conventional signs to put on one's map: e.g. [24]means here we bathed our feet in a cool stream. [25]Here we drank beer: [26]bad beer: [27]fleas in beds here, and so forth.

My own Oxford sheet at least shows the right tendency in bearing crossed swords, the sign of a battle, at the point of N.W. of Chipping Norton where you and I contended with that puncture in the teeth of a gale. As I presume that you haven't your maps with you, I shall not give you a detailed account of our journey. It was the inexhaustible Cotswolds again, as all of us this year happened to be too straitened for time and money to attempt a longer walk. I say 'inexhaustible' advisedly. This year, within a mile or so of country we had walked before, we found valley after valley and wood after wood as beautiful as ever, and whole days of country different totally in character from what we had already seen. The Bathurst estate beyond Cirencester is a place we must revisit when you come home. You can take the whole breakfast to lunch walk in the glorious woods and then emerge into the open in time to lunch at the most glorious village on the edge of the Stroud valley, which winds away as far as you can see, delightfully wooded and watered. (The first Lord Bathhurst, I am told, was raised to the peerage for inventing a new kind of toilet paper for Queen Anne. I have often heard of honours won by getting up the ....[28] of one's superiors. Perhaps this is the origin of the expression. Now there is an idea quite silly enough to write to *Notes and*

---

24 Here there is a drawing of a pipe.
25 Here there is a drawing of a beer mug.
26 Here there is a drawing of a beer mug with a slash through it.
27 Here there is a drawing of a flea.
28 Warnie deleted a word here.

Queries or the *Spectator* about – if only public prejudice didn't render it impossible on other grounds.)

Shortly after this one passes the western mouth of the (now disused) canal tunnel that runs under the Chilterns. It is very awe inspiring and suggests the mouth of the Styx. It seems in the nature of things that one real blunder should be produced by each walking tour. This time we committed the folly of selecting a billeting *area* for the night instead of one good town: i.e. we said 'Well here are four villages within a mile of one another and the map marks an inn in each, so we shall be sure to get in somewhere.' Your imagination can suggest what this results in by about eight o'clock of an evening, after twenty miles of walking, when one is just turning away from the first unsuccessful attempt and a thin cold rain is beginning to fall. Yet these hardships had their compensations: thin at the time, but very rich in memory. One never knows the snugness and beauty of an English village twilight so well as in the homelessness of such a moment: when the lights are just beginning to show up in the cottage windows and one sees the natives clumping past to the pub – clouds meanwhile piling up 'to weather'.

Our particular village was in a deep narrow valley with woods all round it and a rushing stream that grew louder as the night came on. Then comes the time when you have to strike a light (with difficulties) in order to read the maps: and when the match fizzles out, you realise for the first time how dark it really is: and as you go away, the village fixes itself in your mind – for enjoyment ten, twenty, or thirty years hence – as a place of impossible peace and dreaminess. Failure to find lodging brings to my mind the excellent story of the Golden Opportunity which I heard for the first time the other day. I hope it is new to you.

'They say and they sing and relate' that a young man on a walking tour found himself benighted once in Scotland with only a tiny farm house in sight. Knocking at the door, he was greeted by a gaunt God-fearing man who told him to get out of that: when suddenly the voice of the farmer's young wife from behind said, no, let the laddie in. So the farmer reluctantly admitted him. At supper an excellent meat pie was produced. The young man was very hungry, but when the hostess offered him a second helping, the God-fearing man said 'Na. Na. The rest of yon pie's for ma breikfast': so it was put away. Upstairs was only a single bed. The guest got in first: then the God-fearing man: then the wife. They had hardly had time to close their eyes when a voice from

without bellowed up 'Jock! Jock! Come down man, the grey coo's goin'
to calve.' Unwillingly for many reasons did that God-fearing man arise,
and bundling his long white nightshirt into his trousers, shuffle away.
Then 'Young man' said the hostess softly, 'He maun be oot there twa
hours at the least. It's a golden opportunity.' 'By Gad, maam, you're right.
It *is* a golden opportunity' replied the guest fervently, as he leapt from
the bed: and going downstairs swiftly, finished to the last morsel that
very excellent meat pie.

I sincerely hope this is a really modern story, for it would show that
the mind of the nation was not yet spoiled. But it has a suspiciously
Chaucerian flavour, and I expect we shall meet [it] in the middle ages
again some day. What pleases me so much is the idea of the breakfast
party next morning, on one side 'Hell hath no fury like a woman
scorned':[29] on the other the G.F.M., up most of the night and breakfast-
less.

Our own adventures in the inhospitable billeting area ended by the
miserable expedient of walking on five miles of main road into that most
loathsome city, Cheltenham: in the outskirts of wh. – you will find this
hard to believe – we found a brilliantly lighted hotel, echoing with
music, in the midst of a garden, and *no gate* into it anywhere so far as we
could discover. The wind blew and the rain poured. We walked on until
we had clearly passed the hotel grounds: then we walked back. But we
found no gate and I am still divided as to whether it was merely a
Christina dream[30] or an extension of the view taken up in that hotel
where you and I were asked whether we'd be wanting anything more
after our tea and where (if you remember) we concluded that the propri-
etors regarded us as a nuisance. You may imagine how glad we were to
get down to it when we did finally reach an hotel in the middle of Cheltenham. Though I have decided not to be topographical (in your lack of

---

29 William Congreve, *The Mourning Bride* (1697), III, viii: 'Heaven has no rage, like love
   to hatred turned, / Nor Hell a fury, like a woman scorned.'
30 In the Preface he wrote for the second impression of *Dymer* (1950) Lewis explained
   that: 'In those days the new psychology was just beginning to make itself felt in the
   circles I most frequented at Oxford. This joined forces with the fact that we felt
   ourselves (as young men always do) to be escaping from the illusions of adolescence,
   and as a result we were much exercised about the problem of fantasy or wishful
   thinking. The "Christina Dream", as we called it (after Christina Pontifex in Butler's
   novel), was the hidden enemy whom we were all determined to unmask and defeat.'

maps), I must just put on record the delightful valley in which Temple Guiting stands – a place we ought certainly to visit.

I had almost forgotten to tell you of another snatch of holiday – only a week end – which I had immediately after term when a colleague motored me down to his bungalow at Rhossilli in the Gower peninsula. This, as you probably know, lies on the south coast of Wales, near the mouth of the channel. The bottle neck is closed by the formidable city of Swansea. The tide of people of leisure and taste (who, by the by with their cars, villas and bungalows, really spoil sport for us far more than the bluecoat and the burley) having looked at Swansea, very naturally go further. But once past that detestable town (I once v. nearly tried for a job there) you find yourself in a solitude of bare hills, limestone cliffs and crags, coves well wooded, and more Norman castles than I ever believed possible. As the peninsula is a dead end leading to nowhere but a harbourless sea, nothing comes down its road: even tramps have long since decided not to walk down and have to walk back. There is nothing spectacular: no real mountains and no *great* cliffs – rather the sort of cliffs that is sheep bitten grass half the way up and then breaks into grey spires. (Limestone is the pale grey rock that tends to go pointy. How useful these sciences are after all!). The whole of the western end of Gower is owned by an old lady who, because she will not sell any of her land for building – in other words will not raise her income by rendering her home uninhabitable – is described as eccentric. Blessings on her.

My visit would have been pleasanter if my host had not discovered in himself elements of the Burnetto-Desmond[31] which I had no previous means of discovering. I could have pardoned his firm adherence to the Take-Lunch-With-You school on our daily expeditions – being a malady specially incident to married men – but his fixed idea about picking up any bit of odd timber on the way home for firewood was what really annoyed me. His account of the thing was 'If I see a nice bit of firewood when we're in sight of home, I sometimes bring it along with me.' The *fact* was that any time after lunch on an all day walk, not he, but *we*, began to burden ourselves with every lump and spar of timber we could find. In my simplicity I had joined in planning a walk that would bring us home along four miles of sand (A wonderful bathing beach it would

---

31 This is private language between the Lewis brothers, and it seems to mean the artificial, the contrived, the opposite of what was to them comfortable and natural.

be in summer, and not a human habitation). Little did I realise that his praises of a beach walk were inspired by something very much more lively than aesthetic appreciation and that the word which flashed across his mind was 'Driftwood'. I had indeed wondered whether it might not be tiring to walk so far on sand. It was. By six o'clock I was feverishly engaged in keeping his attention fixed on the horizon for fear he would notice the foreparts of a wrecked rowing boat which we were passing. By half past six I heard, to my inexpressible horror, that even *metal* objects came in very useful, and saw him stop to look longingly at an old anchor which four men could not have lifted. Whether he smelts them or chemically produces one of those heats in which iron will burn I stayed not to inquire. However, I had a very pleasant week end on the whole: and how few people has one followed into their native haunts without finding some such drawback.

The only disadvantage in the place was the ever present danger of his latrine: whereof he only appraised me as my hand was on the latch after breakfast the first morning, by remarking casually that I'd better not drop a match down it as he de-odorised it with a highly inflammable chemical. To throw a cigarette end or a match down the rears is an action so natural that I was always in terror of the place. It reminds me of what someone told me about his school where a continuous channel underneath united a row of rears, and it passed for an excellent witticism to set fire to a mass of toilet paper and launch it burning on the stream – thus, according to naval traditions, introducing as it were a fire ship under the bottoms of a man's acquaintances.

It is a long time since I've heard from you, and I am not even clear when exactly your oriental spell comes to an end. All here are pretty fit. I re-read The Man of Property[32] in the mornings in bed last week. I didn't change my views at all about the general merits of it, but was surprised not to have noticed before [that these] who are meant (I suppose) to be sympathetic are really v. like the rest. If anyone contended that Irene herself is a typical Forsyte it wd. be quite easy to make out a case for him. Do you observe that no disinterested action is anywhere recorded of her? One also discovers that Soames is much more broadly drawn in the early parts of the Man of Property than anywhere else in the saga – much more a figure of satire. He is described as 'mousing' along the street. I

---

32 John Galsworthy, *The Man of Property* (1906), the first of his Forsyte novels.

don't think Galsworthy would have used the word later on. Indeed I wish he'd kept more to the original level: I want more of the glorious Forsytism, the soup and port and saddle of mutton and family gatherings and less of the ordinary novelistic 'pash' – less about young Jolyon's feelings and Irene's hips. I don't think I like Galsworthy in his tender vein. A man so sensual ought not to be so serious about it. All those scents and sunsets – we all know it's bosh really. But a great book, whenever he stops writing a novel and just tells us about the Forsytes.

yrs,
Jack

TO OWEN BARFIELD (W):

[Hillsboro]
Whitsunday [27 May 1928]

My dear Barfield,

After an unconscionable delay for which no excuse was offered, Messrs. Brooks have been out to view the 'property' at Crendon.[33] They sent me a letter saying that the matter seemed rather difficult and would I come to call on them. I replied that I would if they wished: but added that I had already said all I had authority to say, and that if it were a question of interpretation, my interpretation would have no more warrant than theirs and they had better write to you direct. I hope you won't attribute this to mere laziness. It is quite clear that I can't really move an inch without again referring to you, and, that being so, it seems absurd for the resulting correspondence to go round from you to me and me to Brooks. What is the train to do at my station beyond having the doors opened and slammed again and the wheels tapped? So I hope you are now in communication with them.

I have just got a copy of Poetic Diction – having just learned of its appearance from a marvelously absurd review in the T.L.S.,[34] where the critic fiddles about for a paragraph with the main argument, obviously

---

33 Owen Barfield and his wife, Maud, loved the country and it was their wish to return to the small village of Long Crendon where they had lived for a while. Long Crendon is about 14 miles from Oxford. See **Owen Barfield** in the Biographical Appendix.

34 *Poetic Diction: A study in Meaning* began as Owen Barfield's B.Litt. thesis at Oxford, and it had just been published. It was reviewed in *The Times Literary Supplement* (17 May 1928), p. 375.

unable to make anything of it and very much afraid of giving himself away, and then with almost audible relief grasps at some parenthetical remark of yours about Lamb, and having at last got something he can understand, begins eagerly 'But surely Mr Barfield is wrong in calling Lamb a minor poet' – But you must not be angry with him: the poor man was having a very bad time and this was the shadow of a great rock in a thirsty land. I spent ten minutes after breakfast this morning trying to lend the book to J.A.[35] but like the two girls in Sense and Sensibility he 'resolutely and fervently' declined the invitation.[36] People will never borrow the books you want to lend, but always the others. I haven't yet re-read it, but am rather astonished at what I have seen so far. In Appendix IV iii you quote with approval a passage from Steiner where he seems to be saying just what I always say and you always deny.[37] That the subject is a product of thought and not its author is almost my ἀρχή.[38] I think in general that I am going to agree with the whole book more than we thought I did. We are really at one about imagination as the source of meanings i.e. almost of *objects*. We both agree that it is the *prius* of truth. But I can't write about it now.

When are you coming home? I must see someone sane again soon. Just by the bye – and you must not repeat it to anyone, even myself – this college is a cesspool, a stinking puddle, faex Romuli,[39] inhabited by

---

35 i.e. J.A. Smith who is mentioned in note 6 to the letter of 5 January 1926.

36 Austen, *Sense and Sensibility*, ch. 20: 'eagerly and resolutely'.

37 Barfield quotes the following passage from Rudolf Steiner's *Philosophy of Spiritual Activity*, pp. 51–2: 'Thinking must never be regarded as a merely subjective activity. Thinking transcends the distinction of subject and object. It produces these two concepts just as it produces all others. When, therefore, I, as thinking subject, refer a concept to an object, we must not regard this reference as something purely subjective. It is not the subject, but thought, which makes the reference. The subject does not think because it is a subject, rather it conceives itself to be a subject because it can think. The activity of consciousness, in so far as it thinks, is thus not merely subjective. Rather it is neither subjective nor objective; it transcends both these concepts. I ought never to say that I, as individual subject, think, but rather that I, as subject, exist myself by the grace of thought.'

38 'Origin' or 'First Cause'.

39 Lewis believed there to be some truth in the accusations he was making, but he was primarily having fun with a friend who he knew would understand the exaggeration. There is an instance of *Faex Romuli* – dregs of Romulus – in Cicero's *Letters to Atticus*, 21.8: '[Cato] speaks in the Senate as though he were living in Plato's Republic instead of Romulus's cesspool [*Romuli faece*].'

Fals-Semblant,[40] Favel,[41] Mal-Bouche[42] and Losengeres:[43] things in men's shapes climbing over one another and biting one another in the back: ignorant of all things except their own subjects and often even of those: caring for nothing less than for learning: cunning, desperately ambitious, false friends, nodders in corners, tippers of the wink: setters of traps and solicitors of confidence: vain as women: self-important: fie upon them – excepting always the aged who have lived down to us from a purer epoch. Don't you think it dammed unfair to have resisted all youthful temptations to cynicism and then to have ones lines cast in a sewer where all that the cynic asserts in general happens for the nonce to be true?

I forgot. We have *one* honest man. He preaches what he practices: tells you openly that anyone who believes another is a fool, and holds that Hobbs alone saw the truth: tells me I am an incurable romantic and is insolent by rule to old men and servants. He is very pale, this man, good-looking, and drinks a great deal without getting drunk. I think he is best of our younger fellows and I would sign his death warrant to-morrow, or he mine, without turning a hair.[44] Don't conclude that all Oxford colleges are like this: I've seen a good deal of them, and I know.

---

40 Fals-Semblant – false appearing – is found in John Gower's *Confessio Amantis* (1390), II, 1879–8: 'Of Falssemblant if I schal telle, / Above alle othre it is the welle / Out of the which deceipte flowethe.'

41 Favel is the hero of Gervais du Bus's *Roman de Fauvel* (1310–14). In this story Fauvel is an anthropomorphic horse, the ultimate hypocrite, and one who turns everyone else into hypocrites too. The expression 'curry favour' comes from him. Another example of Favel as insincerity is found in William Langland, *Piers Plowman* (written about 1367–70), II, 22–3: 'To-morewe worth the marriage made of Mede and of Fals; / Favel, with fair speche, had forgid them togidere.' 'Tomorrow would be the marriage of Reward and Deceit, / Favel with fair speech, had given them to one another.'

42 Mal-Bouche means evil mouth, as in Sir Richard Ros, *La Belle Dame* (c. 1460), 741: 'Male-bouche in courte hath great commaundement.'

43 Losengeres are the traitors who turn up in almost every courtly romance, spy on lovers and betray them, as in Chaucer, *The Legend of Good Women*, 352: 'For in youre court ys many a losengeour.'

44 Lewis was almost certainly describing Thomas Dewar Weldon (1896–1958). He took a BA from Magdalen in 1921 and was Fellow and Tutor of Philosophy there 1923–58. There is a good deal about Weldon in Lewis's *AMR*. Weldon is also one of the subjects of the nine 'portraits' Lewis wrote about his colleagues in about 1927 and which are found in *AMR*, pp. 482–3. It seems likely that Weldon is the man Lewis was writing about in *SBJ* XIV in which he said: 'Early in 1926 the hardest boiled of all the atheists I ever knew sat in my room on the other side of the fire and remarked that the evidence for the historicity of the Gospels was really surprisingly good. "Rum thing," he went on. "All that stuff of Frazer's about the Dying God. Rum thing. It almost looks as if it had really happened once."' This may have occurred on the night of 27 April 1926,

I have written no poetry since. Last Vac. I spent mostly in Bodley starting a book on – what do you think? – the Romance of the Rose and its school. I'll explain the choice when we meet, till when roll on the time. Love to both of you.

yrs.,

C. S. Lewis

I've no right to ask for a letter after my endless silences: but if you had a wet afternoon or so it would be a very meritorious act.

TO OWEN BARFIELD (W):

[Magdalen College
7? June 1928]

My dear Barfield,

When I asked you I forgot that that evening wd. find me in the middle of examining in B6. Can you both take Wednesday June 13th instead, and will Mrs Barfield lie at Headington & you lie at Magdalen that night? I hope this presents no difficulties. I enclose a scrap of paper to pull the controversy together: I have been trying very hard to see whether I could find my trace of consciousness of *thinking pure* and am concluding definitely *Wal – I don't believe it.* Let me have a line.

Yrs.,

C. S. Lewis

TO OWEN BARFIELD (W):

[Magdalen College
8? June 1928]

Come on Tuesday next and let your lady wife come and lie at Headington while you stay in College, for both will be very welcome. I haven't read Aeschylus this long time but I don't mind having a shot. The Prometheus is a bit easier than the Agamemnon.[45] You cd hardly expect

---

about which Lewis says in *AMR*: 'In the evening...Weldon came in. This meant whiskey and talk till 12.30...We somehow got on the historical truth of the Gospels, and agreed that there was a lot that could not be explained away.' See Martin Moynihan's 'C.S. Lewis and T.D. Weldon', *Seven: An Anglo-American Literary Review*, vol. 5 (1984), pp. 101–5.

45 Aeschylus (525–456 BC) was a Greek tragic poet, two of whose plays are *Prometheus Vinctus* and *Agamemnon*. Lewis and Barfield often met for the purpose of reading Greek plays or other works of literature. Lewis mentions their reading *Prometheus* together on 25 January 1927 (*AMR*, p. 436).

the man in the T.L.S. to know the esoteric doctrine of myths. By the bye, we now need a new word for the 'science of the nature of myths' since 'mythology' has been appropriated to the myths themselves. Would 'mythonomy' do? I am quite serious. If your views are not a complete error this subject will become more important and it's worth while trying to get a good word before they invent a beastly one. 'Mytho-logic' (noun) wouldn't be bad, but people wd read it as an adjective. I have also thought of 'mythopoeics' (cf. 'Metaphysics') but that leads to 'a mythopoeician' wh. is frightful: whereas 'a mythonomer' (better still 'The Mythonomer Royal') is nice. Or shall we just invent a new word – like 'gas'. (Nay Sir, I meant nothing.)

I am writing a great new poem – also a Mnemonic rime on English sound changes in octosyllabic verse

> (*Thus Æ to Ĕ they soon were fetchin',*
> *Cf. such forms as ÞÆC and ÞECCEAN.*)

which will be about as long as the Cursor Mundi, & great fun.

Arrive about 3 o'clock on Tuesday, if that suits you. P.S. Wd 'Mytho-logics' do?

C.S.L.

TO HIS FATHER (LP X: 73–5):

July 10th [1928]
Magdalen.

My dear Papy,

It is so long now since I have heard either from you or from Warnie that I begin to wonder whether I am one of the men who came out of the earth full grown in a Greek story and had neither kith nor kin. Try to let me have a few lines soon if you can possibly manage it.

Since I last wrote to you I have had a visit from Uncle Dick and Aunt Agnes.[46] I had them to lunch and they had me to dinner and we met once or twice in between: after my first suggestion of taking Uncle Dick to the top of Magdalen Tower had been refused, they showed no desire to solicit, or even to tolerate my services as a showman. It was the oddest

---

46 This is Albert's brother, Richard Lewis, and his wife Agnes. See **The Lewis Family** in the Biographical Appendix.

sensation to see him again and brought a great many submerged memories to life. After the first embarrassment, which I always feel in meeting that queer mixture of the intimate and the stranger – a rarely seen relation – I liked them both extremely. I found that my picture of him had got rather badly mixed up with Uncle Bill,[47] greatly to its disadvantage. That was all swept away in the first ten minutes. But what surprised me most of all was that, apart from his parrot nose and grey hair, his appearance reminded me strongly of you: and not only his appearance but his turns of expression and even something of his voice that kept on becoming audible even through the top dressing of Scotch. This set me thinking on the strange persistence of a family type and how it breaks through differences of environment. I could not help wondering whether the same voice was really present beneath *my* southern English as it was beneath his Scotch. That the appearance is there, we have all heard *ad nauseam*: and there are certainly traits of a common character both welcome and unwelcome, which I am sometimes startled to observe in myself. As I said to him 'We're a cantankerous lot' to which Aunt Agnes replied 'Indeed you are', but he 'Speak for yourself.' Of course he hardly came up to my childhood's memories of the 'funny' Uncle Dick. But he has certainly a great sense of humour, and to watch him enjoying the joke is almost as good as the joke itself. His stories are not as good as yours and are drawn from a narrower field, but they have gusto. To an irreverent member of the younger generation, of course the best fun of all was the attitude of not unkindly pity – on the 'Poor Warren' lines – which he adopted throughout when speaking of you or Uncle Bill. Aunt Agnes is a dear. In fact if they liked me anything like so well as I liked them, the meeting may be pronounced a brilliant success.

I have actually begun the first chapter of my book.[48] This perhaps sounds rather odd since I was working on it all last vac., but you will understand that in a thing of this sort the collection of the material is three quarters of the battle. Of course, like a child who wants to get to the painting before it has really finished drawing the outline, I have been itching to do some actual *writing* for a long time. Indeed – you can imagine it as well as I – the most delightful sentences would come into

---

47 Uncle Bill or 'Limpopo' was William Lewis. See **The Lewis Family** in the Biographical Appendix.
48 i.e. *The Allegory of Love*.

one's head: and now half of them can't be used because, knowing a little more about the subject, I find they aren't true. That's the worst of facts – they do cramp a fellow's style. If I can get it – the first chapter – to the stage of being typed, I shall bring a copy home for your amusement.

I should warn you, by the by, that Erasmus and all that has had to be postponed to a later book. The actual book is going to be about mediae-val love poetry and the mediaeval idea of love which is a very paradoxi-cal business indeed when you go into it: for on the one hand it is extremely super-sensual and refined and on the other it is an absolute point of honour that the lady should be some one else's wife, as Dante and Beatrice, Lancelot and Guinevere etc. The best introduction is the passage in Burke about 'the unbought grace of life'.[49]

I am intending by the way to pay you my summer visit in *August* this year instead of at the usual time. This is because the whole of the later part of the Long[50] will be occupied with the preliminary stages of the Presidential election, specially the informal conversations which matter most. I am particularly anxious to be there, with one or two others, at the early parts and see what is going on: for – I am almost ashamed to tell you – I am beginning to be rather disillusioned about my colleagues. There is a good deal more intrigue and mutual back-scratching and even direct lying than I ever supposed possible: and what worries me most of all, I have good reason to believe that it is not the same in other colleges.

---

49 Edmund Burke, *Reflections on the Revolution in France* (1790), ed. Conor Cruise O'Brien (Penguin Classics: 1986), p. 170: 'The age of chivalry is gone. – That of sophisters, oeconomists, and calculators, has succeeded, and the glory of Europe is extinguished for ever. Never, never more, shall we behold that generous loyalty to rank and sex, that proud submission, that dignified obedience, that subordination of the heart, which kept alive, even in servitude itself, the spirit of an exalted freedom. The unbought grace of life, the cheap defence of nations, the nurse of manly sentiment and heroic enterprize is gone! It is gone, that sensibility of principle, that charity of honour, which felt a stain like a wound, which inspired courage, whilst it mitigated ferocity, which ennobled whatever it touched, and under which vice itself lost half its evil, by losing all its grossness.'

50 i.e. Long Vacation. Oxford's academic year is divided into three terms and three vacations. Each Oxford term consists of a period of eight weeks, beginning on a Sunday. In each of these terms there is a period of eight weeks known as Full Term. (1) Michaelmas Term is the first of the academic year and it begins on and includes 1 October and ends on and includes 17 December; (2) Hilary Term begins on and includes 7 January and ends on and includes 25 March or the Saturday before Palm Sunday; (3) Trinity Term begins on and includes 20 April or the Wednesday after Easter, whichever is the later, and ends on and includes 6 July. Long Vacation runs from the end of Trinity Term to the start of Michaelmas Term.

Of course it may simply be that, being rather an innocent in practical matters myself, and having been deceived once or twice, I have rushed too hastily to conclusions: as they say a simple man becomes too knowing by half when he once becomes knowing at all. Let us hope so. But the bad thing is that the decent men seem to me to be all the old ones (who will die) and the rotters seem to be all the young ones (who will last my time).

I have a bad cold, I think from sleeping in a damp bed at the cottage of a friend (whose wife was away) last week. Is it of any use to ask how you are? I mean will one get an answer? I earnestly hope that your long silence means nothing bad.

your loving son,
Jack

TO HIS BROTHER (LP X: 75–81):

Hillsboro.
Begun Aug. 2nd. [1928]

My dear W.,

Your letter of the 23rd June reached me yesterday and just gave me the mental pick-up required after my annual week's penance as an examiner. It has even stimulated me to begin an early reply, for though I had not said in my wrath that I'd see you farther if I wrote until I heard from you again, still I was certainly allowing your silence to act as a sort of makeweight with my own idleness. At the moment I can't clearly recollect when I last wrote to you or how much has happened since.

To start with something I am certain of, I have recently made the acquaintance of Uncle Dick and Aunt Agnes, who came for a few days to Oxford towards the end of last term. I think I remember you once wishing that we had been old enough to appreciate the spectacle of the three P'daytas together when that conjunction (good idea – in the astronomy of our island there would be a P'dayta constellation so that you would have 'The Greater P'dayta in Negus' or something of that sort) – when that conjunction occurred at Helensburgh. Failing that, the next most interesting thing was to see one of the other P'daytas alone, and I profited by it.

The result that emerges clearly is the overwhelming steadiness of the type: there are differences between the Pomum Terrestre Albertense and the Pomum Terrestre Ricardense, but they are a mere nothing compared to the resemblances. (What ghastly speculations this raises about myself, you may easily imagine). To begin with, the faces are very much alike: and so are the voices. But it's the style of conversation which simply hits you in the chest. You know what I mean...the indefinable allusiveness, knowingness, the tipping the wink, the pantomime. The language in which 'They raised a subscription' becomes 'So these Johnnies (jerk of the head towards the imaginary Johnnies) had to take the hat round (wide opened eyes and head suddenly lowered, with expression suggesting the worst come to the worst) and then of course we had to put our hands in our pockets (imitative gesture) and see what could be done' etc. Under the heading of *manner* I should perhaps record how – after I had given them a posh lunch *with wine* in College – having asked me to dinner in the Clarendon, he suddenly beamed into that expression of hospitality to the Nth with a touch of roguery and one-of-the-boys-ness known only to P'daytas and said 'Well Jacksie, as this is a special occasion I think I may order two *pints*, eh?'

So much for manner. As for matter, it consisted entirely of wheezes: not only like the P'dayta wheezes but often the identical wheezes. Of course he is a man of far less erudition than your father, and the wheezes were drawn from a narrower field: nothing of the literary or legal element came in. Rather what we may call the McGlusgie element – stories about men getting their heads broken and then being arrested for making a disturbance – what makes only a part of the P'dayta's repertory made Uncle Dick's whole stock in trade. It is quite a sound sort of humour of course, and we all appreciate it – indeed I submit that an intensive appreciation of it is one of the few genuinely P'dayta traits which has descended to you in fuller measure than to me. However, Uncle Dick doesn't tell his stories nearly so well as the P'daytabird, and indeed recalls him less vividly in the humour of the thing than in the intolerable quantity and in the merciless determination to extract from you the last guffaw – you know: repeating the denouement and saying 'Eh? What?' when your jaws are already aching. I hate a joke used as a thumbscrew. Indeed it just occurs to me at the moment of writing that the proper answer to the P'daytesque 'Well it was very funny' is 'Yes – it *was*! Half an hour ago.'

In one way he is above the P'daytabird – he doesn't whine. He described, in answer to my enquiries, the difficulties of his business etc. (Of course you know he's 'ruined') with the same humour he applied to everything else and without a touch of the Limpopo or P'daytesque self-pity. That is all to the good. On the other hand he descends to conversational depths which the P'daytabird knows not, such as carrying in his pocket case a joke (of the McGlusgie type) which he has cut from a comic paper and producing it suddenly for your delectation. Now that is the sort of thing which I thought was only done by people in trains.

You must not imagine from all this that I didn't like him. We got on admirable, and if when I first saw him from my window stumping towards new buildings with his large block hat and respectable umbrella, I felt a moment's qualm, it was checked by the memory of Sir Willoughby when he saw his naval relative walking up the drive with his carpet bag.[51]

One great subject of conversation which we had in common was the P'daytabird himself. Of all the jokes, Uncle Dick enjoys his brother James the best. Your father's faculty of getting stung financially in every undertaking was referred to again and again with gusto. He also said that both the O.A.B. and Uncle Limpopo were born old. And the moral of that is, Master Pigibuddie, that you and I needn't imagine that we are necessarily outside the orbit of P'datism when we laugh at it – perhaps we are then fullest inside, for they all find each other ridiculous.

Of course the alternative is to say that Uncle Dick is not a P'dayta. Sometimes I almost think not: specially when having written home and said 'he referred to you and Uncle Bill with a vaguely humorous tone on the "poor Warren" lines' – wh. I thought would amuse him – I got a reply 'I know very well the tone you refer to. Anyone who is not up to concert pitch all the time is only shamming and needs to pull himself together and be shaken up. It is, I confess, an attitude that I am sometimes very tired of.' There certainly is a wide rift there. But all it comes to is that Uncle Dick's unpardonable offence in the eyes of his brothers is courage. He will not join the Crying Club. He has all the typical P'dayta troubles – suffers from lumbago and his business is going to the dogs – but he will *not* take them in the right way. He makes jokes of them. Still, they are P'dayta jokes. He has the P'dayta dislike of animals. He has the P'dayta habit of drifting away from a subject the moment it becomes interesting – the movement of his mind is from story to story by association of words, not from topic to topic by association of ideas. I think we must

---

51 Sir Willoughby Patterne is the egoist in George Meredith's novel *The Egoist*.

call him a P'dayta – say, a 'P'dayta with courage' – a sweet P'dayta – a clam.

As for Aunt Agnes, she is one of those very reliable, solid, affectionate, dull wives and mothers who are so profitable and comfortable to their own menfolk, but not very interesting to anyone else: a walking justification for that mixture of Northern respect and Oriental suppression which is the essentially P'daytesque answer to the female sex – and not a bad answer either. While hunting for a definition to fit Uncle Dick my mind threw up a phrase, I think, of yours 'a *new* P'dayta'. Do you remember who you coined it for?

And talking of memory ('dear me, it's a funny thing the way the human mind works') I can tell you about Pongee.[52] We did get it from print, but not from the book about Tibet. A person called the 'Crown Prince of Pongee' was referred to in a children's story in a magazine long ago, and the word passed into our stock much as 'Lord Bugabu' passed into it from the P'dayta conversation – you remember of course that Bugabu is a name for a lord whenever the O.A.B. is in his democratic mood. Could anyone say whether he hates or loves a lord most? (Did I tell you his good remark when I was last at home, and had told him that Lord Chelmsford[53] was a possible new President of Magdalen, and he observed 'Ah he wouldn't be a suitable man' – admitting a little later that he confessed he didn't know *who* this fellow Chelmsford might be. But that of course was done with an air which made it an additional argument against Chelmsford.)

It was odd your mentioning Dr Thorne, as I had just re-read the book. He, you remember, 'hated a lord and would have died in defence of the House of Lords.'[54] What do you think of Thorne as a character? I felt he would have been nicer if the author hadn't been so determined to make him so nice. He's just a little bit too manly with his basins of tea and his suppressed emotions. I am afraid, brother, he gulped. As in the

---

52 Pongee is a place in the geography of Animal-Land or Boxen. See 'History of Animal-Land' in *Boxen*, op. cit., p. 43.

53 Viscount Chelmsford, or Frederick John Napier Thesiger (1868–1933) had been educated at Winchester College and Magdalen College. He was trained in jurisprudence and was Viceroy of India 1916–21, and First Lord of the Admiralty in 1924. In 1929 he was re-elected a Fellow of All Souls, Oxford.

54 Trollope, *Doctor Thorne*, ch. III: 'It is hardly too much to say that he naturally hated a lord at first sight; but, nevertheless, he would have expended his means, his blood, and spirit, in fighting for the upper house of Parliament.'

only extant chapter of your father's public school novel 'A swallowing sound was heard'. But this is really rather rot I suppose, and all books need an allowance for the emotional code of their times. Yes – the dinner given by the Duke of Omnium is almost incredible and suggests Roman society more than anything else. I am so ignorant that for all I know things may be very much the same still. If you or I became celebrities of some sort and were asked to a crush at some great house tomorrow, I wonder how exactly we would be treated?

At any rate, after reading Jane Austen, Trollope, and Thackeray a man must give up the pleasure of talking about the coarse snobberies of the nouveaux riches. *All* the evidence shows that as far as that goes, the aristocracy was not a bit better than the plutocracy which has replaced it. They may have differed in other ways: but for downright crudity in throwing their weight about, can one really see a pin to choose between the modern millionaire and say Lady de Bourgh, the de Courcys, Lord Chesterfield?[55] I know that we are told that they did all with the grace of unconsciousness, but it doesn't sound at all as if they did.

I am glad you like the Lives of the Poets.[56] There is no subject on which more nonsense has been talked than the style of Johnson. For me his best sentences in writing have the same feeling as his best conversation – 'pop! it was so sudden'. I don't know anyone who can settle a thing so well in half a dozen words. I have read a good deal of the Rambler[57] last term, which is supposed to be more Johnsonian than the Lives. But he does the dagger business – or no, it's more like a mace, but a mace properly used is not a cumbersome weapon – what is there clumsy about choosing an infinitesimal point of time in which quietly to break a man's head with a perfectly directed tap of a sledge hammer? – he does it again and again.

You know that the Rambler is a mass of moral platitudes – and infuriates the French critics who say that they haven't come to their time of life to be told that life is short and that wasted time can never be recovered. Johnson, anticipating that kind of objection, simply remarks

---

55 Lady Catherine de Bourgh is a character in *Pride and Prejudice*; the De Courcy family are characters in *Doctor Thorne*; Lord Chesterfield (1694–1773) was a distinguished statesman who is remembered in connection with Dr Johnson's *Dictionary*.
56 Johnson, *Lives of the English Poets*, 3 vols., ed. George Birkbeck Hill (1905).
57 *The Rambler* was a twice-weekly periodical in 208 numbers issued by Dr Johnson between 20 March 1750 and 14 March 1752.

'People more frequently require to be reminded, than to be instructed'.[58] What more is there to say? or again 'The natural process of the mind is not from enjoyment to enjoyment but from hope to hope'.[59] That would be a page of whining and snivelling in Thackery – ah, which of us, dear reader, has his hearts desire etc., etc.

Better still, this on marriage: 'Marriage is not otherwise unhappy than as life is unhappy.'[60] I can't say that would be a whole novel with the moderns because the whole novel would not get as far as that. The author would make a great fuss about how Pamela got on Alan's nerves and how in the end they decided that life was a failure, and would be praised for his fearless criticism of the institution of marriage, without ever getting one glimpse of the fact that he was merely describing the *general* irritatingness of daily life, as it happens in the case of married people. Johnson just knocks a whole silly literature aside. He has been through all that (Ibsen and Wells and such) before it was written. But the Lives are the best – specially Savage, Dryden and Pope. I can imagine that the atmosphere, the Englishness, is specially delightful to you in 'furrin parts'. To me, the queerest thing about Johnson is that he is by no means an enthusiastic critic and yet he always makes me want to read the people he talks of even when I know that I shall dislike them.

I remember your precious account of Wei-Hei-Wei and rather envy you. Except for my twenty one days Field Punishment[61] we shan't be able to manage a holiday this year, and we are having one of our rare really hot summers – when a lane by a brickyard is not to be thought of – the first since that terrific one when you were in Sierra Leone. Its first sweets are long over. The flowers wither on their stalks in the garden, the pea pods are shriveled and yellow, the soil is mere dust, red roses are bleached white, and white are also brown. There is no dew either morning or evening. Wasps are very plentiful and to go for a walk is to make yourself the leader of a column of flies. In fact it is rich man's weather, pleasant only on a sea shore with flannels and long long drinks.

---

58 *The Rambler*, No. 2, 'On Looking into Futurity': 'Men more frequently require to be reminded than informed.'
59 ibid., No. 2: 'The natural flights of the human mind are not from pleasure to pleasure, but from hope to hope.'
60 ibid., No. 45, 'Causes of Marital Disagreement': 'Marriage is not commonly unhappy, otherwise than as life is unhappy.'
61 He means the three weeks he was to spend at Little Lea from mid-August until the second week in September.

I must allow that earlier in the year – just before term began – I had a delightful week end at a farm house in the Forest of Dean. As you know, I have walked in those parts before, but never stayed there. It is, I think, the most glorious *inland* place I know. Imagine two clumps of forest, one about the size of Island Magee, the other about the size of a quadrilateral whose corners are St Marks, Holywood, Helen's Tower and Canadian Villas. Both occupy very hilly, almost mountainous ground, and are divided by a couple of miles of fields. The smaller one is cut by the deep gorge of the Wye, a broad, brown, rattling river with islands in it. Though they are quickly being destroyed as forests – for the Crown fells far more quickly than it replants and indeed is quite a wanton forester – they are still almost untouched by trippers, and excellently solitary: almost uncannily so on an all day walk if one gets into the fir districts where birds don't sing and happens to be for a moment out of the sound of a stream (Mr Papworth by the way decided at once that the whole forest was a dangerous place, and always kept close to heel). Here and there in the wood you come on a little old farm house with a few acres of clearing, surrounded by a hedge and approached by a road so desolate that it is hardly different from the green 'rides' that pierce the wood in every direction. In these 'islands' of farms – in one of which we stayed – there is the most comfortable sense of being tucked away miles deep from the world, of being snugged down in a blanket, of having found a lee shore. We lived in a world of country butter and fresh eggs and boiled fowl, of early hours and hens lazily squawking (*not* crowing, just making that long drawling sound that they make). The nights were noisy with the sounds that keep no right thinking man awake – owls, a very good nightingale, and once the barking of a fox. 'A pleasant land of drowsyhead it was...'[62] But as a matter of fact it isn't the drowsiness that really counts, its the sense of being 'well away' – of having avoided the 'Crewe Train'.[63]

I read that admirable book some months ago and instantly thought of you. There are two passages in it which I shall always remember. (A) When the mother in law explains to the heroine that 'doing out a room' means taking all the furniture out and then putting it back again, and

---

62 Thomson, *The Castle of Indolence*, I, 6: 'A pleasing land of drowsyhead it was.'
63 Rose Macaulay, *Crewe Train* (1926). The book is dedicated to 'The Philistines, the Barbarians, the Unsociable, and those who do not care to take any trouble'.

she (i.e. the heroine) 'could not help wondering whether the same end might not be attained by leaving it where it was.'[64] (B) When she tells her husband that she thinks she is going to have a child, and keeps on saying 'Of course it may pass off' until he exclaims in exasperation 'I wish you wouldn't talk about it as if it were the measles.'[65] Another admirable passage is the first review of his novel. Have you noticed that in almost every one of Rose Macaulay's novels there is a character something like this – a person who just lives in some private world of her own (it is always a woman in these novels) and lets the whole life of the other characters slip by, anxious only not to be forced into adult, practical, moral, or immoral, social, or economic life? In *Orphan Island* there is the girl who is interested only in islands: in *Potterism* the girl who is always going away to see battleships launched and pretending to be a naval officer: and in the *Lee Shore* the same thing, treated more seriously and perhaps less sincerely, is the whole theme.

The *Crewe Train* goes far to answer that old question in natural philosophy whether there can be in nature such a thing as a female PB.[66] I take it the heroine is one: and so, in a less degree, the corresponding characters in the other books. Of course in Rose Macaulay they all have – and they are the *only* characters in the books who do have – a touch of poetry about them: an earthy poetry like that of Caliban: hence Denham's cave, and the other girl's islands. And perhaps that is foreign to the true nature of PBism. I am not absolutely certain about this, for there may be a kind of poetry about a brewing outfit. But I think not. The great ideal projection of PBism in Boxen is a world which has almost every charm *except* that of poetry. The only character who ever showed the slightest trace of an aesthetic side was Polonius Green,[67] who did enjoy the opera. I wonder how we could define the genuine PB spirit. *Idleness* won't do: any fool can be idle. Perhaps 'idleness raised to the dignity of a principle and pursued by at least two idlers in common, with the zest of a conspiracy'. I am sure there must be an element of conspiracy, of making common cause against a stubbornly un-idle world: and that, in its turn, necessitates at least two. *Quaere* in a perfectly idle world

---

64 ibid., pt. III, ch. VI, p. 298 (slightly misquoted).

65 ibid., pt. II, ch. VIII, pp. 155–6 (slightly misquoted).

66 i.e. a female piggiebottom. See note 1 to letter of 8 January 1917.

67 'Ah it's cod,' said Macgoullah despairing the opera in 'The Locked Door' (*Boxen*, op. cit., p. 80). '"Cod!?" cried the musical Green aghast, "I'd like to see you write it!"'

could there be such a thing as a Pigiebotie? Must he not be a pilgrim fly-ing from the City of Industry, a brand snatched from the fire of Energy? A door bolted on the inside against a crowd of Bernetto-Desmonds who would fain get in, not to share but to shatter what is inside, seems to be essential. Again, a Pigiebotie must be *conscious* of idling and approve of it. He must not merely like to sit still, but he must also like to think of himself sitting still, or even like to think of himself *liking* to sit still. He must be rewarded by the pleasures of a good conscience which applauds his own immobility. He must say 'A-h-h-h' not only with his lips, but in spirit. He is the only true 'Quietist'. He sitteth down like a giant and rejoiceth *not* to run his course. He eateth all things, neglecteth all things, moveth not himself, is not waked up.[68] Observe – no man is really a Pigiebotie when tired. Aching limbs and unconquerable yawns sink us all into a common mass: Burnetto-Desmonds and Pigibudda snore together. There is no merit in lying down when you can't stand up. The Pigiebotie slumber must come not by merit but by grace. It is, brother, a Mystery of Inactivity.

You know the only real disadvantage of poetry as against negus – since you make the comparison – is that there's less of it. It sounds astonishing but English poetry is one of the things that you can come to the end of. I don't mean of course that I shall ever have read everything worth reading that was ever said in verse in the English language. But I do mean that there is no longer any chance of discovering a new long poem in English which will turn out to be just what I want and which can be added to the Faerie Queene, The Prelude, Paradise Lost, The Ring and the Book, the Earthly Paradise, and a few others – because they aren't any more. I mean, in the case of poems one hasn't read, one knows now pretty well what they're like, and knows too that tho' they may be worth reading, they will not become part of ones permanent stock. In that sense I have come to the end of English poetry – as you may be said to have come to the end of a wood, not where you have actually walked every inch of it, but when you have walked about in it enough to know where all the boundaries are and to feel the end near even when you can't see it: when there is no longer any hope (as there was for the first few days) that the next turn of the path might bring you to an

---

68 A play on 1 Corinthians 13:7, in which Charity 'beareth all things, believeth all things, hopeth all things, endureth all things'.

unsuspected lake or cave or clearing on the edge of a new valley – when it can no longer conceal anything.

This reminds me by the way – I'm afraid I must be a P'dayta, for I made a P'daytism the other day: I began talking about the world and how it was well explored by now and, said I 'We know there are no undiscovered islands'. It was left for Maureen to point out the absurdity.

Well, as the Tommies say, 'no more now' (and by the way, *all* the writers of the Paston letters[69] – XV Century you know – end up just in the same way). I go to Ireland at the end of the week. I think the Everyman volume of Fletcher[70] is the best form for you to read the Faithful Shepherdess in, and will have it sent. I don't think you can get Chatterton in any cheap edition but I will make enquiries. I shan't go more than 10/- without further instructions. They are mostly bosh to my mind.

yrs,
Jack

TO HIS FATHER (LP X: 94–6):

[Magdalen College
3 November 1928]
Saturday.

My dear Papy,

Thank heavens our electioneering troubles are nearly over. This day fortnight we shall all be locked into chapel like so many Cardinals and proceed to make a President and then goodbye to the endless talk and agreements and disagreements and personalities that I have lived in since term began. A subject of this sort hanging in the air manifests itself chiefly by a plethora of informal meetings which naturally spring up on those few hours and days when the ordinary routine has left one a little freedom. As I have anyway a rather heavy time table this term – chiefly, alas, those philosophy pupils whom I share with Weldon and whom he regards as his if they turn out well and mine if they turn out ill – I am now heartily sick of the whole business.

At the same time I have added to my occupations in other and I hope more hopeful ways. Two or three of us who are agreed as to what a

---

69 This is a collection of letters preserved by three generations of the Paston family of Norfolk, written between c. 1420 and 1504.

70 Francis Beaumont and John Fletcher, *Select Plays*, with an Introduction by G.P. Baker, Everyman's Library (1911).

College ought to be, have been endeavouring to stimulate the under-graduates into forming some sort of literary society. In any other Col-leges the idea that undergraduates should require, or endure, stimulus in that direction from the dons, would be laughable. But this is a very curi-ous place. All College societies whatever were forbidden early in the reign of the late President – an act which was then necessitated by the savagely exclusive clubs of rich dipsomaniacs which really dominated the whole life of the place. This prohibition succeeded in producing decency, but at the cost of all intellectual life. When I came I found that any Magdalen undergraduate who had interests beyond rowing, drinking, motoring and fornication, sought his friends outside the College, and indeed kept out of the place as much as he could. They certainly seldom discovered one another, and never collaborated so as to resist the pre-vailing tone. This is what we wish to remedy: but it had to be done with endless delicacy, which means, as you know, endless waste of time.

First of all we had to make sure that our colleagues would agree to the relaxation of the rule against societies. Then we had to pick our men amongst the undergraduates very carefully. Luckily I had been endeav-ouring already for a term or two to get a few intelligent men to meet one another in my rooms under the pretext of play reading or what not, and that gave us a lead. Then we had to try to push those chosen men v. gen-tly so that the scheme should not appear too obviously to be managed by the dons. At present we are at the stage of holding a preparatory meeting 'at which to discuss the foundation of a society' next Monday – so the whole show may yet be a dismal failure.[71] I hope not: for I am quite sure that this College will never be anything more than a country club for all the idlest 'bloods' of Eton and Charterhouse as long as undergraduates retain the schoolboy's idea that it would be bad form to discuss among themselves the sort of subjects on which they write essays for their tutors. Ours at present are all absolute babies and terrific men of the world – the two characters I think nearly always go together. Old hearts and young heads, as Henry James says: the cynicism of forty and the mental crudeness and confusion of fourteen.

I sometimes wonder if this country will kill the public schools before they kill it. My experience goes on confirming the ideas about them

---

71 This society, named the Michaelmas Club, was founded by Lewis and his Magdalen colleague, Kenneth Bruce McFarlane (1903–66), a distinguished medieval historian who was Tutor in Modern History.

which were first suggested to me by Malvern long ago. The best scholars, the best men, and (properly understood) the best gentlemen, seem now to come from places like Dulwich, or to be wafted up on country scholarships from secondary schools. Except for pure classics (and that only at Winchester, and only a few boys even there) I really don't know what gifts the public schools bestow on their nurslings, beyond the mere surface of good manners: unless contempt of the things of the intellect, extravagance, insolence, self-sufficiency, and sexual perversion are to be called gifts.

Arthur came and went and I think enjoyed his visit. He was a little alarmed at the idea of rising at 7.30, but did not mind it when it came to the point – indeed decided that a long morning was so valuable that he wd. stick to 7.30 rising when he got back to Bernagh. Good resolutions! I piloted him away from unsuitable people and those whom he met he got on with admirably. It was very pleasant to have him – but I could not help reflecting on another guest who has a nearer claim on my best arm chair and reading lamp and whose visit has been already very long delayed. But it needs Uncle Dick to talk to you on a subject like that!

The first chapter of my book is finished and typed and the only two people who have seen it approve. The unfortunate thing is that nobody in Oxford really knows anything about the subject I have chosen. I may have made some elementary blunder which the French people – who have so far mainly studied the matter – would pounce on in a moment.[72] However, my translation of some Old French into contemporary English

---

72 In the letter to his father of 10 July Jack had mentioned the 'mediaeval idea of love' he was writing about in *The Allegory of Love*. The technical name for this idea is 'courtly love', and the definition which Lewis provides in the first chapter of his book will help the reader understand it. 'Everyone has heard of courtly love, and every one knows that it appears quite suddenly at the end of the eleventh century in Languedoc...The sentiment, of course, is love, but love of a highly specialized sort, whose characteristics may be enumerated as Humility, Courtesy, Adultery, and the Religion of Love. The lover is always abject. Obedience to his lady's slightest wish, however whimsical, and the silent acquiescence in her rebukes, however unjust, are the only virtues he dares to claim. There is a service of love closely modelled on the service which a feudal vassal owes to his lord...The whole attitude has been rightly described as a "feudalization of love".'

(forgery is great fun)[73] has passed Onions[74] who knows more than any-one else about the English of that period.

I am afraid this has been an egotistical letter. But it is dull work asking questions which you can't (at any rate for the moment) give a reply to. You do not need to be told that I hope you are keeping fairly well and that I shall be glad to hear if this is the case. For myself – if you came into the room now you would certainly say that I had a cold and that my hair needed cutting: what is more remarkable: you would (this time) be right in both judgements.

your loving son,
Jack

Mr Lewis had been following the presidential election at Magdalen College with great interest, and when he opened The Times *on 19 November he learned that Magdalen had elected Professor George Gordon. He remembered that Gordon had supported Jack for his election to a Fellowship (see letter to A.J. Lewis of 26 May 1925), and when he wrote to Jack on 25 November he said: 'I hope his election is acceptable to you. I am heartily glad the thing is over' (LP X: 96). Jack replied with this brief but clear account of the whole process.*

TO HIS FATHER (LP X: 97):

Magdalen
[27? November 1928]

My dear Papy,

Many thanks for your letter and kind offer. I think I shall take the liberty of rolling Christmas and birthday into one and get myself another picture.

---

73 What, in the end, Lewis attempted was much harder than translating Old French into modern English. He was translating into what he hoped would pass as Middle English for he felt this would carry the 'flavour' of the period more nearly. His translations are considered one of the great successes of his book.

74 Charles Talbut Onions (1873–1965) was a distinguished lexicographer and grammarian. He joined the staff of the Oxford English Dictionary in 1895. He was appointed a Fellow of Magdalen College in 1923 and was a lecturer in English at Oxford 1920–27 and Reader in English Philology 1927–49.

I am not dissatisfied with the election. The history of the thing was this. *Stage 1. Hogarth* put forward with almost universal approval. Hogarth dies. *Stage 2. Chelmsford* put forward by all the Winchester interest and *Craig*[75] put forward by Weldon and his friends – to be their puppet. *Stage 3. Benecke* put forward by party including myself who dislike both *Chelmsford* and *Craig. Stage 4.* Absolute determination of the *Craig*-ites not to have *Chelmsford* – absolute determination of the *Beneck*-ites not to have *Chelmsford* or *Craig. Stage 5. Benecke* leading by a long way. *Stage 6.* Proposal of *Gordon.* Satisfies *Craig*-ites as being at any rate better than *Chelmsford*: satisfies *Beneck*-ites as better than *Chelmsford* or *Craig. Stage 7. Benecke* v. *Gordon. Stage 8.* No clear majority for Benecke possible. Fear of letting in *Chelmsford* if the *Craig*-ites and *Beneck*-ites quarrel about *Benecke* and *Gordon. Stage 9.* Agreement of the two parties on *Gordon*, which then out-votes the remnant of the *Chelmsford* and *Craig* people. So, as you say, it is more or less of a compromise.

I hope to come down on Friday next (i.e. crossing Friday night) and shall have to leave home on 5th January.

your loving son,

Jack

---

75 Edwin Stewart Craig (1865–1939) was a demonstrator in the electrical laboratory of the University of Oxford 1905–13 and a Fellow of Magdalen 1918–30. See Lewis's 'portrait' of him in the Magdalen College Appendix, *AMR*, pp. 476–7.

1929

— ∽ —

TO HIS FATHER (LP X: 100–1):

Magdalen.

Sunday.[3 February 1929]

My dear Papy,

What an unhappy career this group photograph has had! Before visiting the shop again I should be glad to know more exactly what condition it was in when it arrived and whether I am justified in making a fuss about it.

As I expected, my return to England plunged me into a winter compared with which our little cold snap at home was positively balmy. The fields were covered with snow all the way on my train journey south, there has been some skating, indoor temperatures in rooms without fires have fallen below freezing point, and I have woken more than once to find a tumbler partially full of ice on the table beside my bed. In fact – to make a confession – I have so far bowed to the rigours of the season as to start using a hot water bottle, a luxury which I had hitherto regarded as an indulgence for holiday times at Leeborough. I told Hatton[1] apologetically that I thought it was the beginning of middle age: to which he replied 'Oh don't say that sir' in the same voice of unconvincing gravity with which he might have made the same answer if I had said I thought I was getting delirium tremens. Can you remember the first occasion on which you habitually had about you a servant younger than yourself? It gives one a feeling of antiquity I find, because servants, from the early days when one watched them at work in the kitchen, have always belonged so essentially to the grown up world.

I look in vain for any item of news fit to be extracted from the uneventful routine. Let me see. Brightman – your friend Toys – has had

---

1 W.K. Hatton, who joined the staff of Magdalen College in 1923, was Lewis's 'scout' or college servant.

influenza but has happily got over it. The new President and his family have not yet moved into the Lodgings, where the work of putting in bathrooms which is now going forwards, throws a new light on the venerable domestic economy of the previous regime.

My current lecture (on Elyot,[2] Ascham,[3] Hooker[4] and Bacon[5]) has attracted as a distinguished member of its audience the Mother Superior of the local hostel for papish undergraduettes – I suppose because I fired off by an attack on Calvin. If you hear indirectly that the Church of Rome is hoping for a distinguished convert among the young Oxford dons you will know how to interpret it.

---

2 Sir Thomas Elyot (c. 1490–1546) is the author of the *Boke of the Governour* (1541), a treatise on education and politics which displays the particular influence of the classics and Plato in particular. It illustrates as well the evolution of English prose. As a result of it Elyot was appointed ambassador to Charles V. His other works include *The Image of Governance* (1540) and *The Castel of Helth* (c. 1536). His translations did much to popularize the classics in England. Lewis's fullest treatment of Elyot is found in bk. II, ch. 3 of *English Literature in the Sixteenth Century* (1954), where he says 'Elyot is a well informed man, not a scholar; a sensible man (for the most part), not a deep thinker. As a stylist he has perhaps higher claims.'

3 Roger Ascham (1515/16–68) distinguished himself at St John's College, Cambridge, and became the college reader in Greek in 1540. His *Toxophilus* (1545) is a delightful treatise on archery. It is set in the form of a dialogue between Toxophilus (lover of shooting) and Philologus (lover of books). In 1554 he became Latin secretary to Queen Mary, but he was allowed to continue being a Protestant. In his last years he wrote *The Scholemaster* (1570), of great value to education, which was published posthumously. Lewis's fullest treatment of him is in *English Literature in the Sixteenth Century*, bk. II, ch. 3, where he says Ascham 'is everyone's friend...His delightful, and delighted, temperament has flowed into his writing.'

4 Richard Hooker (?1554–1600), theologian, was a Fellow of Hebrew at Corpus Christi College, Oxford, 1577–84. He was the greatest of all apologists of the Elizabethan Settlement of 1539, and the finest advocate that Anglicanism has ever had. He developed his doctrines in his massive treatise, *The Laws of Ecclesiastical Polity* (1593, 1597). Lewis delighted in Hooker, and wrote at length about him in *English Literature in the Sixteenth Century*, bk. III, ch. 2, where he speaks of the *Polity* as a 'work of prudence, of art, of moral virtue, and...of Grace'.

5 Francis Bacon (1561–1626), a barrister, was elected to Parliament in 1584. He became Lord Chancellor in 1618. His writings are of various kinds. His best-known works are *The Advancement of Learning* (1605) and *Essays* (1597). Writing about Bacon's *Essays* in *English Literature in the Sixteenth Century*, Epilogue: New Tendencies, Lewis said: 'If Bacon took his title from Montaigne, he took nothing else. His earliest essays resemble essays by Montaigne about as much as a metallic-looking cactus raised on the edge of the desert resembles a whole country-side of forest, filled with light and shade, well stocked with game, and hard to get out of.'

The undergraduates have just brought off a good rag by getting a copy of the university seal and circularizing all the garages in Oxford with a notice purporting to come from the Vice Chancellor and Proctors and rescinding an order made last term by which all these places were compelled to shut for undergraduate use at eleven. Unfortunately this excellent joke was disclosed before it had had any time to run its course.

Oh – I had nearly forgotten my exploits as a printer. I am attending a lecture for postgraduates on Bibliography this term, and we were all taken to the Clarendon Press last Thursday to examine a hand press, to set up our own names, and to print them on a broadsheet. The episode was rendered more amusing by the fact that J.A. happened to meet me on my way to the Press and insisted on attaching himself to the party, greatly to the surprise of the instructor, who, I could see, all the time was trying to puzzle out who or what he was. The venerable philosopher delayed us by asking the printers a number of questions, none of which they could understand and lecturing them in return on a variety of subjects from cookery to bookbinding, and ended up by printing his own name upside down – which however we corrected in proof, so it does not appear in the enclose 'lelult'. I hope you notice the grace and feeling – the creative touch – of my own rendition of our name!

Well, as I say, I have nothing to say, and this is only a word of chat, 'hoping it finds you as it leaves me' – or rather not, as I have a vile cold. I hope you are keeping tolerably well.

your loving son,

Jack.

P.S. I find I have been carrying this in my pocket for a day or so. This however gives me the chance of opening it again to insert two things which I had forgotten.

(1) Two of my reviews from the Oxford Magazine.[6]

---

6 The first of these items was Lewis's review (unsigned) of Evelyn Waugh's *Rossetti: His Life and Works* which appeared in *The Oxford Magazine*, XLVII (25 October 1928), pp. 66, 69. The second was a review of Hugh Kingsmill's *Matthew Arnold* in *The Oxford Magazine*, XLVII (15 November 1928), p. 177, signed 'C.S.L.'

(2) My best thanks for my birthday picture which is both beautiful in itself and suited to its place, so that it makes a great change in my room. It has been much admired.

J.

TO ARTHUR GREEVES (W):

[Magdalen College
March 1929]

My dear Arthur

I am very sorry your message has been so long delayed. If you remember my way of life, you will know that I am kept in by pupils all morning, that I then have to go out to Headington, that I then return to pupils again after tea – after which the shops are shut. It really is with the greatest difficulty that I ever get free in the streets of Oxford to visit shops. I ought, I confess, to have *made* the occasion, but I want to plead in my defence that it is not, as you, forgetting, probably suppose, a question of just walking out any old day and doing it. Term ends soon (don't say so at Leeboro) and I will really try to get it done.

I admit freely that I was in the wrong and apologise. I wish you could avoid writing things like <'Am I so soon forgotten.'> You had a right to be annoyed: but you certainly did not really think that my failure to do an errand for you betokened any change in a friendship that has now lasted the greater part of our lives: and if you had thought so, this was hardly a manly or a sensible way of opening the subject <(If I had left the letter lying about anyone wd. have supposed it was from a girl whom I had deserted and who was just going to have a baby!)> I am sorry to have inconvenienced you, but hope the matter is not mortal.

Yrs

Jack.

TO HIS BROTHER (LP X: 118–23):[7]

[Hillsboro]
Postmark: 13 April 1929

My dear W.,

I am ashamed of my long idleness, though indeed the gap between my last and your last was almost as long as the gap between your last and this. I must admit too, that I am moved to write at this moment by the selfish consideration that I heard last night a thing which you of all people ought to hear – you know how one classifies jokes according to the people one wants to tell them to – and am therefore uneasy till I have unloaded it.

The other night an undergraduate, presumably drunk, at dinner in the George covered the face of his neighbour with potatoes, his neighbour being a total stranger. Whether this means simply that he flung the contents of the potato dish at him or (as I prefer to think) that he seized him firmly by the short hairs and systematically lathered him with warm mash, my informant could not say. But that is not the point of the story. The point is, that being haled before the Proctors and asked why he had done so, the culprit, very gravely and with many expressions of regret, pleaded in so many words 'I couldn't think of anything else to do!'

I am sure you will share my delight at this transference of the outrage from the class of *positive* to that of *negative* faults: as though it proceeds entirely from a failure of the inventive faculty or a mere poverty of the imagination. One ought to be careful of sitting near one of these *unimaginative* men. The novel idea can be worked equally well from either end: whether one thinks of the mohawk bashing your hat over your eyes with the words 'Sorry old chap, I know its a bit hackneyed, but I can't think of anything better' – or of some elderly P'dayta exclaiming testily 'Ah what all these young men lack now-a-days is initiative' as he springs into the air from the hindward pressure of a pin.

With *the* P'daytabird I had quite a good three weeks at Christmas. The arrangement about the jumping jack at your sole charges (for I accepted your offer and you will have had the account by now) had this

---

7 Writing to his father on 11 February 1929 Warnie said, 'Unless something very unexpected happens, I should leave Shanghai early in November and will be with you shortly after Christmas. This means that I shall complete a foreign tour with a total of two years and say eight months abroad' (LP X: 103–4).

inconvenience, which we should have foreseen, that no effort on my part seemed to make him understand that the present was from you as well as from me. If you have said nothing implying responsibility in any of your letters, I am afraid you have had no credit: if you *have*, I must by now (with shoulder shrugs and upward jerks of the head) stand suspected of 'a very shabby business'. I hope, by the way, that besides getting the bill for the jumping jacks, you have also got Chatterton[8] and The Faithfull Shepherdess.[9] Of the former, as you know, I have a very poor opinion – the dirge 'Sing unto my roundelay' being to my mind the only item in his tremendous fake which has real merit. But the Faithfull Shepherdess I love. Ones pupils, trained in 'just opinions' tell one it is artificial: not that the criticism would worry you with your penchant for Versailles shepherds and shepherdesses. But what is the really interesting thing about it is the way it manages to keep the homely L'allegro-and-Il Penseroso-[10] English-village-and-country feeling going along with the pastoral conventions. The priest of Pan is exactly like a country parson.

By the by, I thoroughly agree with you about Scott: in fact I think that even his most fanatical admirers have 'given up' his heroines (with the exception of Die Vernon and Jeanie Deans)[11] and his love scenes. But then one gives that up in all XIX Century novels: certainly in Dickens and Thackeray. And when you have ruled that out, what remains is pure delight. Isn't it nice to find a person who knows history almost entirely by tradition? History to Scott means *the stories remembered in the old families*, or sometimes the stories remembered by sects and villages. I should say he was almost the last person in modern Europe who did know it that way: and that, don't you think, is at the back of all his best work. Claverhouse,[12] say, was to Scott not 'a character' out of Macaulay (or Hume or Robertson) but the man about whom old Lady so and so tells one story and about whom some antediluvian local minister's father

---

8 Thomas Chatterton, *Poems*, ed. Sidney Lee, 2 vols. (1905).

9 See note 56 to letter of 6 March 1917.

10 John Milton, *L'Allegro* and *Il Penseroso* are companion poems published in 1645.

11 Die Vernon is the heroine of *Rob Roy*, and Jeanie Deans the heroine of *The Heart of Midlothian*.

12 John Graham of Claverhouse (?1649–89) was a royalist officer employed by the Scottish Privy Council in executing the severities of the government in Scotland during the reigns of Charles II and James II. He was determined to raise the Highlands for James, and was killed at the battle of Killiecrankie. He figures prominently in Scott's *Old Mortality*.

told another. Printed and documented history probably kills a lot of this traditional local history and what is finally left over is put in guide books (When nothing else can be said about an old church you can always say that Cromwell stabled his horses in it.)

Scott was only just in time to catch it still living. This (so historians tell me) has had one unforeseen result, that Scotch history has ever since been more neglected than that of any other civilized country: the tradition, once stamped by Scott's imagination, has so satisfied curiosity that science has hardly ventured to show its head. It is a pity that no one similarly caught the tradition in England – tho' probably there was less to catch.

I suppose the Scotch were a people unusually tenacious of old memories, as for example Mr Oldbuck. I am not sure that The Antiquary is not the best. Do you remember his efforts to get the hero to write an epic on the battle of ? in order to work in his excursus on castramentation?[13] On the other hand it has perhaps the worst heroine of all. Of heroines, there is something to be said for Julia Mannering ('Yes sir. And is my future friend red headed?' 'I am sure we all thank Mr. Sampson for the extraordinary countenance he has shown us'.) The beginning of Guy Mannering is excellent. What an admirable P'dayta the old Laird is: and what an admirable description of P'daytism the jumble of thoughts in his conversation. But of all the Scott characters I know, I give the palm to three above all the others – the Baron of Bredwardine, Cuddy Headrigg, and Baillie Mickle (sic) Jarvie.[14] I am very fond of Dandie Dinmont[15] too. By the way – it is very unfair – but did you too like me hate the name of Dandie Dinmont long before you knew who he was?

And that brings me to the very curious fact that nothing militates so much against Scott as his popularity in Scotland. The Scotch have a curious way of rendering wearisome to the outside world whatever they admire. I daresay Burns is quite a good poet – really: if only he could ever escape from the stench of that unmerciful haggis and the

---

13 Sir Walter Scott, *The Antiquary* (1816), vol. I, ch. 14. Lewis was referring to the battle of Mount Graupius between the Roman general, Agricola, and the Caledonians in 82 or 83 AD as recounted by Tacitus. Mr Oldbuck maintained that the battle took place on the site of his house, Kaim of Kinprunes (an imaginary name). Castramentation is the art of laying out a military camp.

14 The Baron of Bredwardine is a character in *Waverley*; Cuddie Headrigg a character in *Old Mortality*; and Bailie Nichol Jarvie a character in *Rob Roy*.

15 Dandie Dinmont is a character in *Guy Mannering*.

lugubrious jollities of *Auld Lang Syne*. What a world it opens upon – the 'kail yard' school – beside the bonny briar bush – Mansie Wauch.

I have just suddenly (as I write) seen what is the trouble about all this Scotchness. When you want to be typically English you pretend to be very hospitable and honest and hearty. When you want to be typically Irish you try to be very witty and dashing and fanciful. That is to say, the typical English or Irish mode consists in the assumption of certain qualities which are in themselves quite pleasant. But the typically Scotch consists not in being loud or quiet, or merry or sad, or in any recognizable quality, but just in being *Scotch*. You make roast beef the English dish because it is nice (or fairly nice), and the rose is a pleasant flower. But the haggis and the thistle never could have any merit beyond their sheer, unredeemed, monumental Scotchness. I notice that the nicest Scotch people claim to be Picts. This theory of Scotchness probably comes to me from some excellent remarks of Hazlitt's on respectability which I read in the summer. A good many people have tried to find out why respectability is contemptible, but I think only Hazlitt has got it right.[16] He points out that if you are describing a person, and there is any quality in him which is at all pleasing, you mention *that*. You say 'He is an amusing man' or 'He is a good shot' or even that 'He is very good looking'. It is only when there is nothing whatsoever to say in his favour that you come down to 'He is a very respectable man': i.e. the 'respectable' is that which we have agreed to respect although there is nothing respectable in it. ('Scotch' things similarly are those which even a Scot can find no reason for liking other than their Scotchness).

---

16 William Hazlitt, *The Plain Speaker: Opinions on Books, Men and Things* (1826), Essay XXXI 'On Respectable People': 'There is not any term that is oftener misapplied, or that is a stronger instance of the abuse of language, than this word *respectable*. By a *respectable* man is generally meant a person whom there is no reason for respecting, or none that we choose to name; for if there is any good reason for the opinion we wish to express, we naturally assign it as the ground of his respectability. If the person whom you are desirous to characterize favourably, is distinguished for his good nature, you say that he is a good-natured man; if by his zeal to serve his friends, you call him a friendly man, if by his wit or sense, you say that he is witty or sensible; if by his honesty or learning, you say so at once; but if he is none of these, and there is no one quality which you can bring forward to justify the high opinion you would be thought to entertain of him, you then take the question for granted, and jump at a conclusion, by observing gravely, that "he is a very respectable man." It is clear, indeed, that where we have any striking and generally admitted reasons for respecting a man, the most obvious way to ensure the respect of others, will be to mention his estimable qualities.'

What a very Conradian adventure with your engineer![17] As to have, you may be quite sure that some scotch people do say 'has' for 'hae' as the consequence of have. The proper verb is 'have' as we pronounce it. Have is a lengthening of this which occurred originally in sentences where the emphasis fell on the word *have*, but afterwards became stereotyped in certain parts of the country and at certain periods. 'Have' and 'Have' are both good English in certain parts of the country and in [the] XVII Century: so that when Milton writes (Comus – the lady's song.)

> *'if thou have*
> *Hid them in thine airy cave.'*[18]

it is not, as we are apt to suppose, a bad rime: he probably pronounced it like that. Have lasted longer in Scotland than in England: but a whole nation, depend upon it Sir, does not carry about a word like *have* without often (i.e. in some districts) dropping the end and thus giving *hae* (hay).

As to the doctrine that to profess no philosophy is to *have* a bad philosophy, I am not conscious of having borrowed it from anywhere and could not tell where to look for it in a book, but of course I may have done. On the other hand the idea is one obvious enough to strike a good many people independently. Your engineer sounds a very typical Scotch philosopher, judged by his library. I would warn you that a 'Scotch philosopher' means something much more than a philosopher who happens also to be a Scotchman: almost as much more as a Welsh Rabbit or

---

17 In his letter of 23 October 1928 Warnie wrote of a sea voyage to Hong Kong. 'The most interesting person on board,' he said, 'was the Chief Engineer who was a character straight out of Kipling – such a man as I had always believed never existed outside novels...I first came across him one night after dinner when a few of us collected in the saloon for a mouthful of the port, and McAndrew's Hymn being mentioned, he expressed his warmest approval of it...This and some more chat led to an invitation to adjourn to his room and inspect "ma buiks". It was a severe shock after a discussion on Kipling to arrive at his room and come bolt under a withering collection of philosophy – Spencer, Comte, and similar books. I had to mumble something about having no philosophy, which was met with "When ye say ye haaaave no pheelawsophy, Cap'n, ye only mean ye haaave a bad pheelawsophy." Is this remark a philosophical cliché or is it pure coincidence that you should have made exactly the same remark to me some years ago? By the way it is only apparently in funny stories that Scotchmen say "hae" for "have" – actually they say "haaaave" with a very broad vowel sound as I have tried to describe it above' (LP X: 92).

18 Milton, *Comus*, 237–8: 'Hid them in some flowery cave'.

a Prairie Oyster. The Scotch School represents all that is most negative, analytic, and dry: in fact what you think of all metaphysics is true of the Scotch type. Now I give you my word that when I started to write this I had no intention of talking about the Scotch at all: and yet my two attempts to break away from the subject have proved entire failures. Let us throw off the incubus – .

The P'daytabird was in pretty good form while I was at home. The P'daita crop was poor. The only goodish one was as follows. 'Lord Hugh Cecil is a fine chap. You know he took a very moderate line over the prayer book: he didn't object to this reservation business – '[19] (I'm sorry but now that I come to write it down I find that I have forgotten the ins-and-outs of this one, and after some attempt to puzzle it out, I think I had better give it up. This looks as if it were deliberately done to tantalise you, but it isn't.)

I think you asked in your last letter whether Uncle Dick perpetrated genuine P'daitisms. I must confess that during our rather short time together I did not succeed in collecting a single unambiguous example. The nearest he got to it was his complete indifference to the remoter consequences of his own views, as I described before: but I am afraid that hardly amounts to P'daitism. In a way it would be disappointing if we found that our own P'daita was the only perfect specimen in the family. I have just seen that that leaves open to you a very silly and obvious retort.

I had a glorious day of walking in Antrim with Arthur while I was at home. We reached the top of Glengariff by car at about 11 o'clock, and walked till dark, not in the glens, but on the moors above the northern wall of the valley. There was hoar frost on the heather and ice on most of

---

19 During 1927–28 Lord Hugh Cecil (1869–1956) was active in the Church Assembly which brought forth the Revised Prayer Book of 1928. It was, greatly to his disappointment, rejected by the House of Commons. One of their reasons for rejecting the 1928 Prayer Book was its recommendation of 'Reservation', the practice of keeping the consecrated Host enshrined in a tabernacle for the purpose of Holy Communion and for communion of the sick. Jack Lewis later recalled what his father said about the matter, for he recorded the incident in 'Pudaita Pie' as follows: 'He remarked "Lord Hugh Cecil is a fine chap. Though he is a high churchman, he is a *sane* high churchman over this prayer book business." "Indeed," replied his interlocutor, "what line does he take?" – "Well, I confess I don't remember, but I expect you'd find it was very much what I take myself. You know, *I've* no objection to reservation." – "I see. But that would hardly prove his moderation as a high Churchman, for surely it was just the high Church party that wanted reservation?" "I can't quote you chapter and verse, but that's my impression of the man."' On the 1928 Book of Common Prayer see note 52 to the letter of 9 July 1927.

the streams, looking startlingly white wherever the peat water emerged at a break. The sun was trying to break through all day, but hardly succeeded further than to make clouds scatter and gleam and smoulder along the big peaks inland, with a series of wonderful apocalyptic end-of-the-world effects, or occasionally to send a watery gleam across the slopes. Up there it is more solitary than Exmoor, and I don't think I ever passed a day in grander desolation. We had a magnificent tea in what looked like a pigsty but was really a Post Office: seated one on each side of a wood fire (the only light in the room) and eating new soda bread under the directions of the post mistress who charged us 6d. each.

I often wonder, specially lately, whether you are right (if you still hold the opinion) in thinking Ireland the right country to live in, with all its drawbacks. Certainly the actual country appeals to me more every time I go home. In fact I am coming round by a long circuit to a position not unlike that of our Wynyard days: a different position, because I find more and more a something in almost every Irish scene which you can't get elsewhere, and which, though not better in itself, is better *for us*. I think 'roughness without severity' is the nearest one can get to it. It is grand and desolate and yet somehow one feels at home. We really must manage that Irish walking tour when we are next at Leeborough together. I amused myself while at home by working out an itinerary which of course I have since lost, and found that a reasonable walk could be arranged through Ballynahinch, Newcastle and Rostrevor. The first day would have to cover about twenty five miles, which is of course more than one wants: but it is better that a big journey shd. fall on the first than on the second day, and after that it panned out pretty well. As for your ridiculous contention that you will be out of condition when you arrive in England, I understand that there are admirable facilities for exercise on a modern liner, and what between dumb bells, the gymnasium, quoits, and deck tennis, you ought to arrive lean and bronzed.

Someone called A. Tilley has just published a book called The Decline of the Age of Louis XIV[20] (Cambridge University Press 25/-) which has been very well recieved, so you had better make a note of it. I have had a week in bed with 'flu since I began this letter, during which I re-read *The Antiquary*, *Sense and Sensibility*, and *Pickwick*. The latter I shall not read

---

20 Arthur Tilley, *The Decline of the Age of Louis XIV: or, French Literature 1687–1715* (1929).

again. I thought I had won my freedom of it last year, but a second reading brought back my old invincible distaste. The language and conception seem to me exactly those of the crudest comic passages in our own Boxoniana, and without the charm of old associations I can't swallow it.

My week in bed gave me the pleasure of emerging into a world quite different from the one I had left – all the hedges out, the daffodils under the trees, and birds singing. We have started keeping hens at Hillsboro who provide us with from three to four fresh eggs a day (that's rather a silly remark – they cd. hardly lay stale ones) and make the most beautifully rural and leisurely noises while one is lying between sleeping and waking in the morning. On Friday I set off on my annual walking tour: this time we start from Salisbury and hope to end up on the coast of Lyme Regis. I look forward to renewing my acquaintance with that cathedral; you remember our excellent Daudelspiel.[21]

I was much interested to hear of the new phase of your musical history. I, as you know, have long been a great admirer of Beethoven, though I probably know much less of him than you. I put him about on a level with Milton and in very much the same kind – taking Puccini to be the same as Swinburne, Mozart as Shelly, Verdi as Tom Moore. It is curious how one finds oneself all along the line coming to like the *drier* flavours as ones palate grows older – or rather, the really tip top people like Milton and Beethoven have the richness and sweetness *as well as* the staying power of the dry.

I find I am 'bringing in gabble' and had better make an end on't. Is it next Christmas that I may look to see you? You have been an infernal time away.

yrs,
Jack

TO ARTHUR GREEVES (W):

[Magdalen College
22 April 1929]

My dear Arthur,
I have had ten days in bed with flu', four days walking tour from

---

21 On 6–8 April 1925 Warnie and Jack had taken a trip on Warnie's 'Dawdle' or 'Daudel', a motorcycle with sidecar. They had gone to Salisbury during that 'Daudelspiel' or 'Daudel-play'.

Salisbury to Lyme Regis and a week with Minto and family in a Sussex farmhouse – of which items only the walking tour had better be communicated to the P'daitabird – but before all this I visited Blackwells and looked up their Lamb. After investigating such copies as I could lay my hands on (viz. two) in private and finding that neither of them contained the missing letters I consulted the man who thought they might have some second hand old sets in stock, but thought wrongly. I am sorry if it has been my dilatoriness that led to this negative result, but trust that even when you have learned by heart all the remaining letters (and, dear me, what a convenience that will be to *me*!) the lack of those ten will not drive you to desperation (Of course, perhaps, the most sensible thing would be for both of us to blow our brains out).

I am also, and more seriously sorry that I wrote you rather a snarky[22] letter when we last communicated, and tried to turn an apology into an accusation, which was a very unhandsome thing to do. I hope you will allow for end of term feeling and frayed nerves.

We arrived back from Sussex to day and travelled within a couple of miles of Bookham, all up the Dorking valley which I know so well. It very nearly made me weep, I got such a rich poignant whiff of memory from the old days – Phantastes, Bleheris, Dymer, Papillon, T. Edens Osborne all jumbled up. But as you know, one has the secret of these memories now and knows how to extract the spiritual sweet without falling into mere desire and regret.

While ill, I re-read both *Sense & Sensibility* and *The Antiquary* and most strongly advise you to read the latter again, and specially notice the effect of Elspeth in her earlier scenes.

Yrs
Jack

TO HIS FATHER (LP X: 125–6):

Magdalen.
Sunday.[19 May 1929]

My dear Papy,

I hope your recovery from the winter 'flu has been permanent. My own prolonged cold, having lasted out the term, worked up into a sore

---

22 Lewis Carroll, *The Hunting of the Snark* (1876), Fit IV, ll. 33–4: 'For the Snark's a peculiar creature, that won't / Be caught in a commonplace way'.

throat and temperature and a few days in bed about Easter time. This finally got rid of the trouble and was not unpleasant. It gave me the excuse to be idle and the chance to re-read some old favourites – including *The Antiquary*. Read the Antiquary. I think it contains the cream of Scott's humour and very nearly the cream of his tragedy.

I also re-read Pickwick, but this, as you know, I can hardly call an old favourite. Indeed I have only read it once before. This time I hoped I had at last got the secret and become a real convert: but my second reading has broken the spell, I am a relapsed heretic. It won't do. I like the Wellers, both father and son, and I like the trial: but Eatanswill and Mrs Leo Hunter and Bill Stumps, his Mark, seem to me laboured and artificial, and I can't forgive him for showing us poor Jingle in prison and repentance. The whole spirit in which we enjoy a comic rogue depends on leaving out the consideration of the consequences which his character would have in real life: bring that in, and every such character (say Falstaff) becomes tragic. To invite us to treat Jingle as a comic character and then spring the tragic side on us, is a mere act of bad faith. No doubt that is how Jingle wd. end in real life. But then in real life it would have been our fault if we had originally treated him as a comic character. In the book you are forced to do so and are therefore unjustly punished when the tragedy comes.

I had four days away from Oxford and spent them walking with my usual party – friends from my undergraduate days – from Salisbury to Lyme Regis. Luckily I need not describe Salisbury to you. It will be enough to say that I have now seen it three times and each time with increasing admiration. But I made the mistake of attending a week day evensong. (We assembled at Salisbury in the afternoon, starting our walk on the following morning.) There was no music, and the psalms were read. Four fat and spongy clergymen, two on each side, in a little week day chapel at the back of the main altar, scampered and simpered through the job in a way that really disgusted me. It is perhaps too much to expect any intense spiritual quality in the reading of men who have to do it every day (and yet why are they in the church if the thing means so little to them as that?). But I think one is entitled to expect the decency of clear and unaffected pronunciation and such a general appreciation of the mere literary qualities of the service as ought to belong to any educated men. I know I should be ashamed to read out a recipe as abominably as they read out the psalms. Then one looked round at the

Cathedral and the contrast between those who built it and those who now officiate in it was pretty steep.

Our walk was delightful but I can't sit down to describe all the pleasant villages and windy hills that we walked, or all the shady rookeries and old towns that we rested in: it is a wonderful country and we had wonderful talk and forgot our various professions and discontents and got through the serious arguments in the ten miles before lunch and came down to mere fooling and school-boy jokes as the shadows lengthened. I came back quite set up in body and mind.

I have done most of the second chapter of the book but can't get it ready for typing before the end of this term. You may have noticed that I have recently been enlightening the literary world through the correspondence columns of the Times Literary Supplement.[23] I missed the copy in which my letter appears, so I don't know whether the world shaking truths have been conveyed to the public with that accuracy – that *meticulous* accuracy – which they deserve. I am now waiting for a reply letter which will begin 'Your correspondant seems to be unaware...'

I have a capital story which is quite new to me. The hero is a certain Professor Alexander, a philosopher, at Leeds, but I have no doubt that the story is older than he. He is said to have entered a railway carriage with a large perforated cardboard box which he placed on his knees. The only other occupant was an inquisitive woman. She stood it as long as she could, and at last, having forced him into conversation and worked the talk round (you can fill in that part of the story yourself) ventured to ask him directly what was in the box. 'A mongoose madam.' The poor woman counted the telegraph posts going past for a while and again could bear her curiosity no further. 'And what are you going to do with the mongoose?' she asked. 'I am taking it to a friend who is unfortunately suffering from delirium tremens.' 'And what use will a mongoose be to him?' 'Why, Madam, as you know, the people who suffer from that disease find themselves surrounded with snakes: and of course a mongoose eats snakes.' 'Good Heavens!' cried the lady, 'but you don't mean

---

23 His letter on 'The Kingis Quair' appeared in *The Times Literary Supplement* (18 April 1929), p. 315. 'The Kingis Quair', which means 'The King's Book', is a poem of 379 lines of rhyme-royal used by King James I of Scotland while he was a prisoner in England and at about the time of his marriage to Lady Jane Beaufort. In his letter Lewis attempts to explain the connection between the 'apparently rambling' introduction and 'the poem which follows'.

that the snakes are real?' 'Oh dear me, no said the Professor with imperturbable gravity. 'But then *neither is the mongoose!*'

I hope this is not an old chestnut.

your loving son,

Jack

'Why are they in the church,' Lewis asked about the clergymen in Salisbury Cathedral, 'if the thing means so little to them as that?' This concern with sincerity is perhaps the first indication of a huge change in Lewis's spiritual life. For it was about this time – we don't know the exact date – that Lewis came to believe in God, though not yet in Christ. Speaking of his conversion to Theism, he said in Surprised by Joy:

> *You must picture me alone in that room in Magdalen, night after night, feeling, whenever my mind lifted even for a second from my work, the steady, unrelenting approach of Him whom I so earnestly desired not to meet. That which I greatly feared had at last come upon me. In the Trinity Term of 1929 I gave in, and admitted that God was God, and knelt and prayed: perhaps, that night, the most dejected and reluctant convert in all England. I did not then see what is now the most shining and obvious thing; the Divine humility which will accept a convert even on such terms. The Prodigal Son at least walked home on his own feet. But who can duly adore that Love which will open the high gates to a prodigal who is brought in kicking, struggling, resentful, and darting his eyes in every direction for a chance of escape? The words* compelle intrare,[24] *compel them to come in, have been so abused by wicked men that we shudder at them; but, properly understood, they plumb the depth of the Divine mercy. The hardness of God is kinder than the softness of men, and His compulsion is our liberation.* (SBJ *XIV*)

---

24 Luke 14:23 (Vulgate): 'Et aid dominus servo: Exi in vias, et sepes: et compelle intrare, un impleatur domus vea.' 'And the lord said unto the servant, Go out into the highways and hedges, and compel them to come in, that my house may be filled.'

TO ARTHUR GREEVES (W):

Magdalen College,
Oxford.
May 19th [1929]

My dear Arthur,

I enclose a letter wh. I have been waiting to send you for ages.[25] Of course I am delighted to hear of your coming to Oxford to-morrow, but hope that you will stay in College with me. You will remember that last time you found the hardships of Collegiate life worse in anticipation than in experience. If you insist on going to a Hotel try the Eastgate which is cheap & quiet & just beside Magdalen. Let me have a line or wire at once. I am looking forward tremendously to meeting again

Yrs
Jack

TO HIS FATHER (LP X: 127):

Magdalen College,
Oxford
Monday 18th [17 June 1929]

My dear Papy,

I was hoping to have elicited a letter from you before now. I have heard neither from you nor from the Colonel for a long time – not that I'm much better myself, but I think I am one up on both of you at the moment.

I am thinking of taking my summer holiday earlier than usual this year – from three to four weeks from the 12th or 13th of August. We ought to have the hottest part of the year then, and I hope you will be able to take most of your time off. But I have been burdened with a job – a friend wants me to look after his dog while he is in Switzerland. I am certainly of all his friends the best acquainted with the beast, and I have agreed. Can you tell me whether there is any difficulty – e.g. quarantine etc. – about bringing him into Northern Ireland and out of it again. Perhaps I ought also to ask whether there is any difficulty about bringing him into Leeborough? I can vouch for his cleanliness, courtesy, and other canine virtues. I think you will rather like him.

---

25 Presumably the letter of 22 April.

I have just finished a week of examining for the Pass Degree here, which of course means examining the extreme dullards. I got one delightful sentence in a paper on *Paradise Lost*, about Adam and Eve praying 'before they *turned in*' at night.

Hoping you are tolerably well and also hoping for an early answer (after you have 'taken legal advice' about the dog question!).

your loving son,
Jack

TO HIS FATHER (LP X: 140–2):

[Magdalen College]
Sunday [7 July 1929]

My dear Papy,

Many thanks for your letter on 'this dog business'. I begin to see, in the uncertainty of my friend's plans, a faint gleam of hope that the whole question is going to solve itself, and I shall arrive home blessedly dogless. As to your cautions about the looking after another man's dog – depend upon it I did not consent until every decent subterfuge had been tried. If, as I hope, the scheme falls through, how cheaply I have earned my credit. And then people say that virtue isn't rewarded.

I am sorry to hear of your poor health. Ought we not to think of spending part of my time away from Leeborough? I will go any where you wish – even to Moorgate.[26] Think of this, but don't pin yourself to a date without consulting me again. I am still undecided (it depends largely on when I finished Chapter II of the book) whether August 12 or something like August 25th or 24th would be best for me. I expect that a change of air, scene, and diet would do you more good than many nostrums. (I wonder what precisely a *nostrum* is and why it is so called?)

I am busy at the book at present, and next week shall start examining. This year, by all accounts, I have an ugly row to hoe. As I have probably told you before, every group of Awarders consists of one Oxford and one Cambridge man, and they shift them about from year to year. This time I have lost my Cambridge colleague with whom I have worked very pleasantly for the last four years, and getting instead a man whom everyone has warned me against. (How I hate, except in the most formal

---

26 The home of William Lewis in Glasgow. Albert's brothers in Scotland were pressing him to visit them.

composition, that 'against whom' instead of the more natural form.) He has quarreled with every previous colleague he has had and it remains to see whether I shall fare better. He is old too, which makes the matter worse: it is easier to stand ones rights to contemporaries without the appearance of insolence. Can you suggest any spiritual exercises – perhaps our old friend 'Calvinistic exercises' would do – suitable as a prophylactic against loss of temper in trying circumstances? There ought to be somewhere a Collect for the Use of Examiners.

I don't think I have much news to tell you. My days – like the man in the poem – 'are passed among the dead', that is in the Bodleian, which I have already described to you; and as to these said dead themselves you may have heard more of them than you wish in August, for I shall certainly bring you a chapter to read. It remains however a very pleasant way of spending one's time, tho' I shall be glad to get out of this windless hollow and see the sea again.

I am in good health and form, except for a kind of summer rash which gives me occasionally the sensation of being covered with fleas. I shall be glad when it is gone. I haven't much time for general reading but I have been amusing myself in the 'Sweet o' the night' – the odd half hour before going to bed – with an anthropological book of Andrew Lang's called 'Myth, Ritual and Religion'.[27] Among other things it gives the Zulu deluge story – a story which in some or other form as you know turns up in every mythology. Apparently at one time all the animals and men were like to die of thirst. The reason was that a huge frog had swallowed all the water: after which of course he was larger than ever. The remaining inhabitants of the world laid their heads together and decided that their only chance was to force the frog to disgorge by inducing him to laugh. They therefore assembled and each of them did the funniest thing he could think of. The frog, for a long time, like Queen Victoria, was not amused: but at last the eel stood on the tip of its tail and this was too much for him and he laughed so that he fairly split himself and all the water ran out and made a huge ocean in which most of the world was drowned. But the story is, to my mind, less funny than what follows. Lang quotes it from the record of some missionary, who, after listening for several days to stories of this kind, began in turn to produce for the enlightenment of the poor heathen his own account of the world,

---

27 Andrew Lang, *Myth, Ritual and Religion* (1887).

starting off with the story of creation as it is told in Genesis. The result was disappointing. 'The savages' we are told 'laughed consumedly and replied that he could expect no one but old women to believe such a story as that'. A missionary goes I suppose prepared for hardships and danger: but its a bit hard to be ridiculed for pulling the long bow by an audience who believed the story about the frog and twenty others of the same kind. This is the altar-cloth and the door-mat with a vengeance.

We have been suffering for weeks here from the most shocking drought – flowers withering on their stalks, our bowling pitch in the quadrangle yellow as straw, and the earth cracking everywhere. It has now broken up in the most terrific hailstorms – I got wetter in fifteen minutes yesterday than I have often got during a whole wet afternoon on the hills at home. Luckily the hay is all in, but corn will be in a bad way.

Oh – I had nearly forgotten my best bit of news. Weldon[28] is going to be away for two terms. I can hardly tell you with what glee I look forward to seeing the place even temporarily rid of that sinister presence.

your loving son,

Jack

TO ARTHUR GREEVES (W):

Magdalen College,
Oxford.
[16 July 1929]

My dear Arthur

It is only to-day that we have made up our minds about our arrangements for the summer. As far as I can see, I shall be in Ireland from the 12th of August onward, for three to four weeks. I very much hope that this will fit in with your plans, as it will be impossible for me to fit it in either later or earlier. I will make a note of the *Rebel Passion*.[29]

Bryson told me you were going to visit these parts? Is that untrue? And, by the way, could you let me know whether there is any difficulty about bringing dogs into Northern Ireland? Can you let me have an answer.

Yrs

Jack

---

28 For information on Thomas Dewar Weldon see note 44 to letter of 27 May 1928.
29 Katharine Burdekin, *The Rebel Passion* (1929).

TO HIS FATHER (LP X: 142–3):

Magdalen.

July 17th.[1929]

My dear Papy,

Well – the dog business is finally settled and I shall not have to burden myself (or you) with the animal. And I propose to come home on August 24th. All this being made plain you can now go ahead with any plans you came to make about this joint holiday. I, as I have said, am ready to agree with anything, in fact – like another travelling companion of yours –'I'm a mere parcel.'[30] Whether you prefer to seek out some quiet place on our own, or whether domestic comforts and long standing invitation recommend Helensburgh,[31] is all one to me. I must say I should like to do that journey up the Kyles of Bute once again. These however are points of detail. On the main issue (like Kirk's farewell) everything has been said before.

This week a curious thing has happened. I have had a letter from Malvern stating that 'Malvern College Ltd' has been wound up and the school has now been put under a board of governors, and asking me to allow my name to be put up for election as one of them. As they are to number over a hundred the honour is not so overwhelming as at first appears. In my first heat I composed a very fine letter declining on the ground of my 'limited knowledge of public school life and, still more, my imperfect sympathy with the aims and ideals of public schools'. This I enjoyed doing: but then alas 'the native hue of resolution was sickled o'er with the pale cast of thought'.[32] I reflected that this would get about and that the great junta of masters and old boys of various schools

---

30 Jack was quoting his mother's father, Grandfather Thomas Hamilton. In a little biography Warnie provided of him in the Lewis Papers he said: 'Albert's attachment of Florence ("Flora") Hamilton, had begun about the year 1890, when the Revd. Thomas was 64 years old. The Rector, with considerable astuteness realized at an early stage in the proceedings that the attachment could be made to serve his own purposes; he was a man much addicted to short jaunts or holidays...In the unfortunate Albert, he was to find not only a courier, but also on many occasions, a disbursing officer... "I'm a mere parcel" he would say genially, leaving Albert to make all the arrangements. But at any hitch, especially at any overcharge, the geniality gave place to loud, bitter, and worse still, public complaints, which shamed the sensitive Albert to the soul' (LP I: 4–5). See **The Hamilton Family** in the Biographical Appendix.

31 The little town near Glasgow where Albert's brother, Richard Lewis, lived.

32 Shakespeare, *Hamlet*, III, i, 84–5.

would pass from one to the other the word – 'If you have a boy going to Oxford, I shouldn't recommend Magdalen. Lot of queer fish there now. Cranks etc. etc.' So I funked it, tore up my first letter, and wrote an acceptance. I hope I should have been able to hold out against the purely prudential considerations ('funk' is the simpler word) if I had not been supported by the feeling, as soon as I had cooled, that membership of such a huge board would be purely nominal, except for the ring of 'insiders', and that therefore if I refused I should be only making a storm in a teacup. But won't Warnie be tickled? – if I remember, you and I discussed this situation purely as a joke when I was last at home.

Try to let me have a line when you feel like it. Don't be put off writing altogether because you feel unequal to an essay – just a note to say that you have made up your mind where we are going. I should also be glad to hear some news of the Colonel and of when he is coming back. He is badly in my epistolatory debt.

your loving son,
Jack

TO ARTHUR GREEVES (W):

[Magdalen College
18? July 1929]

My dear Arthur,

Good man. I shall book for the 12th and look forward to our journey together as a very bright spot.[33] I had of course thought of the possibility of my father & you and I going away together, but don't want to raise false hopes in you or me in case it doesn't come off. It would be just as good for him & of course infinitely better for me.

If you are wondering where to go for a few days out of London, I shall be at Cambridge from the 8th to the 10th.[34] I shall be working all day till 6 p.m., so it wd. be absurd for you to come to *see me*: but if on other grounds you cared to visit that ancient city we might have a couple of evenings together. I shall have a sitting room to myself in Queens. However, that's as it may be.

---

33 Greeves was residing in London and, as his time was very much his own, Lewis hoped he would accompany him to Belfast on 12 August.

34 August 8–10 when he would be examining in English Literature at Cambridge.

Thanks again & again for coming home – my faithful Arthur! I'm dead tired examining all day.

Yours

Jack

When Albert's brother, Dick, visited him during the first week of July he thought he looked very unwell. After that, Uncles Dick and Bill began urging him to see a doctor. Then come some ominous entries in Albert's diary. Saturday 20 July: 'The old pain began,' he said. 'Never so violent before. I spent a wretched night.' Sunday 21: 'Mary rang up Leslie at 10 o'c. Leslie in England attending a medical conference and wd. not be home till Thursday or Friday. Mary rang up Joey. He was in Newcastle for the weekend but wd. be home at 7 o'c. I decided I must endure until the morning.' Tuesday 23 July: 'Irwin and Joey here before 10 o'c. Irwin...did not think any operation wd. be necessary, but I must go into a nursing home and be washed out and next morning Xrayed.' Friday 26: 'Went from home to Dr Beath. Xrayed. Result rather disquieting. Joey drove me out to Little Lea' (LP X: 143–4). Not long after this Albert wrote to Jack about his illness, and Jack also had a letter from Uncle Dick expressing concern.

TO ARTHUR GREEVES (W):

Hillsboro,
Western Rd.,
Headington
July 25th [1929]

My dear Arthur,

I have had bad news from home. First a letter from my Scotch uncle commenting on my father's poor state of health, saying that he is losing wait and that they suspect 'something internal', and urging me to get him away for a holiday. Second, a letter from my cousin Joey to say that they are putting him into a nursing home for inspection to-day (the 25th) but, thank goodness, saying that they don't suspect any growth, though they do suspect some inflammation.

The way in which this concerns you and me in common is this (a) I shall have to spend a good deal longer with him this summer than usual (b) I shall have to do my best to get him away for part of that time and as long a part as possible, and it will probably have to be to our relations in Scotland. As far as my selfish wishes go this, of course, is the last thing on earth: but you will easily see that I've got to try and bring it about. I shall go home on the 11th or 12th of August. Now it is extremely likely that with all my efforts *either* I shall not be able to get him away at all *or* I shall be able to do so only after hammering away at persuasion for some considerable time. In the first event I need hardly say how glad I should be if you and I cd. both have together in Ireland this longer-than-usual spell. In the second event (which is more probable and which, probable or not, it is my duty to try to bring about) I hope I shall not have the chagrin of being at home *alone* for a fortnight or so and then setting off for the loathsome Scotch relations just as *you* arrive in Ireland and thus missing our time together for the year.

Poor Arthur, I have so B-g—red you about that you will hardly know whether you are on your head or your heels! I only lay this before you because you suggested in your last letter that you wd. have been coming home earlier if *I* had not proposed coming later. You will not feel hardly if you remember from your own experience how horrible one feels when the people whom one ought to love, but doesn't very much, are ill and in need of your help & sympathy;[35] when you have to *behave* as love wd. dictate and yet feel all the time as if you were doing nothing – because you can't give what's really wanted. Among other things I have to face the prospect that it may be my duty to get him permanently over here – with God knows what upsets & difficulties for everyone I care about – you, Minto, Warnie, myself, everyone.

Do let me have a line as soon as you possibly can: at best, to say you will come home (with me) on the 12th: at worst a word of good cheer. Isn't it all beastly. Poor, poor, old Pdaitabird, I cd. cry over the whole thing

Yrs

Jack

TO HIS FATHER (LP X: 152–3):

[Magdalen College]
Postmark: 5 August 1929

My dear, dear Papy,

I am very glad you have written. I had heard the news and was anxious to write, but hardly knew how to do so. I will, of course, come

---

35 Arthur's father, Joseph Greeves, had died on 19 February 1925.

home at the first moment. Unfortunately I have to go to Cambridge on the 8th for this examining, but will cross to Ireland on the 12th. Don't bother to write yourself if you are not up to it, but see that I am informed.

I gather from what I heard that there is much that is hopeful in the first photo. It would be silly to pretend that this can set worries at rest for either of us; there is surer ground – at least for you – in the wonderful spirit, as shown in your letter, with which you are taking it. I wish I could convey to you one tithe of the respect and affection which I felt in reading it. For the rest, what can I say to you that is not already understood? What can any of us do for one another except give a handshake and a good wish, and hope to do as well when our own time comes to be under fire. It has been a bit of a strain this last week to keep my mind on examination papers for nine hours a day, and I am specially glad that you have written. I was told everything in confidence, I didn't know that you knew I knew, and I could do nothing. I wish I could come straight away but I can hardly get out of Cambridge now. I know what hospitals and nursing homes are like – there at any rate I can sympathize with some experience.

Whatever the next few days brings forth I hope you will make no decision about your treatment without letting me know. I don't of course mean to postpone such decision (necessarily) till next week: but see that I am told. Of course if there is serious trouble, you will have other advice than that of the Belfast crowd.

With all my love and my best wishes – I wish there was anything more useful I could offer – your loving son,

Jack

TO HIS BROTHER (LP X: 182–3):

Leeborough.
Sunday, Aug. 25th. 1929.
In the study, 8.30. p.m.

My dear W.,

This is a line to let you know that P. is rather seriously ill. The first I heard of it was from Uncle Dick about a month ago when I was still in Oxford, and then, in answer to my inquiry, from Joey who is attending him. The trouble is abdominal. The first fear was of course cancer. Xray photos cannot apparently disprove this with certainty, but their evidence, I'm glad to say, is all against it and according to Joey the other features of the case render it very improbable. We must not of course kid ourselves by saying impossible. The present diagnosis is that he is suffering from a narrowing of the passage in one of the bowels. The ordinary cure for this is the operation known as short circuiting: but they had hoped that if he would go on a light diet he would manage to get along, not in perfect health but in tolerable comfort, without being operated upon – or at any rate that the operation would be indefinitely postponed.

I came home immediately after my Cambridge examining and found things at this point. He was up and pretty well. About a week ago however he had an attack in the night of a sort of convulsion and shivering – they call it *rigor* – of which I only learnt next morning. This was not regarded as a very serious symptom by either Joey or Squeaky, but they kept him in bed. Next night when I took his temperature about nine I found it 103 and got the surgeon McConnell (a colleague of Joey's in the case from the start) out to see him about midnight. He was light headed but the temperature fell in the morning. Since then he has been monkeying up and down and of course he has been in bed. This evening they have told him that it is pretty certain that he will have to have the operation. They are to consult again in a few days and we shall then know for sure. He is taking it extraordinarily well. I shall of course stay until the operation is over, unless they postpone it till Christmas. AS FOR YOU, I suppose it would be (a) Impossible, (b) Useless for you to get special leave as the affair is pretty sure to be settled before you could get home.

I have a great many things on other subjects to say – on Liverpool Cathedral and the new Liverpool boat and so forth – but this is only a note for necessity. I have been up the most of a good many nights with the P'daitabird and can't leave the house long enough to get decent walks, so am rather tired and do not feel in form for a letter. This is from the little end room at about 10. p.m. What a pity you're not here. In spite of the worrying situation we should find redeeming features about Leeborough under the present regime. When one is alone it is by no means so pleasant. Thanks for your last letter and excuse me for this scrawl. Remember I have the Leeborough demoralization on me as well as the cures of a patient. And by Gum, both ones *morals* and ones morale are hard put to it.

Of course the present emergency does not cancel immemorial rules. If your letter arrives P. may be – lets hope to goodness he will be – up again, and you must write therefore only what can be shown. When I am creeping about at night at present, or looking at his fire, I often derive a sort of whimsical pleasure from thinking of the long training in stealth for quite different purposes of which he is now the object in a new sense. I'm sorry that you have had an envelope in my handwriting, of which the contents will disappoint you so much as this.

I am just going to creep on tiptoe to the cellar – the key being very sensibly in my charge – to get a mouthful of the whiskey.

yours,

Jack[36]

TO HIS BROTHER (LP X: 183–90):

[Little Lea]
Aug. 29th. 1929[37]

My dear APB.,

To be frank, you owe this second letter to a typically Leeburian situation. I had mentioned to the P'daitabird that I was writing to you, and this has provoked such a hailstorm of advice and warning – I must write on the thinnest paper and I must go to Condlin[38] to get the right sort of envelope – and of questions – how am I getting on with my letter to the Colonel – that there is nothing for it. Sooner or later I must satisfy him with the touch and sight of a letter that by its size will not [be] too obviously a notification of his illness and therefore a cause of alarm to him. And I think it would be really too unkind to send you a wad of toilet paper.

---

36 To this letter Warnie appended a note in the Lewis Papers: 'It is perhaps as well that the reader should be reminded at this point of the "time lag" in the whole of the Belfast–Shanghai correspondence. The above letter for instance, dated Aug. 25th, was posted in Belfast on Aug. 27th. It was not endorsed "via Canada" and would therefore have been despatched by the long sea route via Suez: i.e. it could not have reached Shanghai, at the earliest, until 43 days later, or the 9th October. Warren's letters to Belfast, being written to catch a particular steamer running on the short sea route (i.e. via Canada or the U.S.A.) would be reaching Belfast some 32 or 33 days after they were written' (LP X: 183).

37 This letter, which was endorsed 'via Canada', reached the army post office in Shanghai on 11 October.

38 J.W.A. Condlin had been Albert's managing clerk since 1917.

Things are no better since I last wrote, and I am really very despondent about him. Yet it would be an offence against Pigiebotian ethics to seal ourselves up therefore in perpetual solemnity: and, however you may feel in China, I on the spot can only get through my days and nights by allowing myself an enjoyment of the old humours, which, needless to say, show through even this situation. If only it did not always raise anxiety, the daily visit of the Doctor would be irresistibly funny. The patient's utter refusal to answer to the point, his hazy accounts (on the familiar 'mouthful' principle) of what he has eaten, and his habit of replying to some such question as 'Have you noticed any change in yourself?' with a sudden 'Doctor! I'm perfectly satisfied in my own mind that the root of all this trouble etc. etc.' and his subsequent belief that the doctor has propounded to him the grossly improbable theory which he had in fact propounded to the doctor – all this you will be able to imagine on the slightest of hints from me. It was very alarming the night he was a little delirious. But (I cannot refrain from telling you) do you know the form it took? The watercloset element in his conversation rose from its usual 30% to something nearly like 100%.

And though, thank heavens, he has never been lightheaded since, this percentage has not been much reduced. Indeed I may be said to live at present in a dominantly excretory world: for you must add to his merry tales all the serious conversation on such subjects which his condition entails, and all the reminiscences of family illness to which this leads...The funniest event was the borrowing of a commode from Bernagh. The moment Arthur had left me, promising to return with this humble piece of apparatus, of course Janie[39] turned up to make kind enquiries. You know the difficulty she finds in getting out of a room; and when that is conquered, the further difficulty of getting off a doorstep. Picture me standing with her at the hall door, keeping one eye on her and doing my little bit of conversation while with the other I watched the corner for the appearance of Arthur followed by the Bernagh chauffeur trundling a commode in a wheelbarrow.

However, perhaps all this water closet world is appropriate to me at the moment as I have just finished the formidable task of reading the whole of the works of Rabelais. The original 17th century translation can now be had uncut in a single fat volume at 6/- with very good print

---

39 i.e. Janie McNeill. See note 41 to letter of 4 May 1915.

and paper.[40] I had to read him for the light he throws on the Renaissance in general and his particular influence on our own Elizabethans. Would I advise you to do the same? I hardly know. He is very long, very incoherent, and very, very stercoraceous. But you must base no opinion of him on what you hear from uneducated people who have never read any other comic book written before the reign of Queen Victoria and are therefore so blinded by a few familiar words when they first see them in print that they never go on seeing the drift of a page, much less a chapter, as a whole.

The first surprise is that about a quarter of the book is perfectly serious propaganda in favour of humanist education. The comic parts are mostly satires on the papacy, monasticism, and scholastic learning. The free farce of the Miller's Tale[41]-cum-Decameron[42] type is really only about a third of the whole. There is a great deal of quite sincere piety and humanity of a pleasant Shandeyian,[43] Montaignesque type. Some of the aphorisms must be added to our stock at once. 'The greatest loss of time that I know is to count the hours' – 'Drunkards live longer than physicians'. Some of the preposterous humour is excellent. I like the scene where in visiting a certain island they are taken to witness 'the ceremony of a bursting', and while they are on the way hear 'a loud report like the cleaving of a tree' by which they gathered that the man had burst already. I like the gentleman 'whose life was a perpetual dinner' and the abbot, who, being asked on his deathbed to allow his successor to take over, replied that 'the last f—- he should utter would be the f—- of an abbot'. The word 'utter' is here specially pleasing and in indexing Rabelais – without which, in the case of so shapeless a work, to have read it is the same as not to have read it – I enjoyed making the entry 'ABBOT, last utterance of'.

Some of the satire – tho' satire tends always to bore me – is very 'sly', to use a good old word which we moderns have dropped or degraded

---

40 François Rabelais, *Gargantua & Pantagruel*, prefaced by Life of Rabelais by Henri Clouzot, illustrated by 525 vignettes by Joseph Hémard (London: Joseph Hamilton, 1927).

41 In Chaucer's *Canterbury Tales*.

42 A collection of tales from many sources by the Italian author Giovanni Boccaccio, and assembled in their definitive form between 1349 and 1351.

43 After Laurence Sterne's character in *Tristram Shandy*. See letter to Arthur Greeves of 25 October 1916.

without finding a better to fill its place. The 'clergyhawks' (clergy of course) were shown to Pantaguel in their cage. It was explained to him that they were originally men who came over from a neighbouring country called Want o'Bread ('a cruel country where the days are of a weary length') and were turned into birds. Pantaguel remarks that he quite believed this, for they looked very *like* men: in fact if he hadn't been told, he would never have known that they *had* been turned into birds at all. You must have a look at this author and see if he is for you. At the least one is always pleased to have turned a name into a memory. I shall write no more tonight. By an unpardonable folly I have forgotten to secure the cellar key this evening and am fain to experiment on that curious Victorian drink, sherry and soda. This is from the little end room at 11.15 of a chilly August night. Don't try sherry and soda. I have just had my first sip. It tastes just like sherry only less so.

Next day. [30 August]
    Leeboro is a curious place. My sherry and soda, tho' mawkish to the taste, made me quite drunk last night. Today is in our worst manner. I am just going out to buy him a new bottle of ink. I have assured him there is a bottle in the little end room with which I am writing daily: but he does not think this will be sufficient for a dozen cheques which he has to endorse, and there is no arguing with a sick man so I must waste my short time out in a journey to Strandtown: and lucky at that – for his idea was a journey to Condlin who would direct me to a suitable station-ers, and it was only with difficulty he was brought to admit that Strand-town might supply some writing fluid that would do at a pinch until tomorrow, when of course I must go into town and get some of 'the proper' ink. As this sort of thing happens every hour of every day you will understand that I need an outlet of frankly heartless laughter if I am to keep my temper. How the servants put up with his glaring injustice to them I don't know. Almost every day he decides on his lunch at about 1 and then is furious because he does not get it before two.

    But in spite of this I have a growing respect for him. He faces the major issue very pluckily, and from his reminiscences, in which he is at present indulging very freely, I get a more acute impression of the abominable rock from which he was hewn. One should rather be sur-prised that he has gone so far than annoyed that he has gone no further. Some glimpses I have had lately of old Ty-isa show it as a positive sink.[44] His own going to Lurgan, happily as it turned out, appears to have been originally a penal measure – in fact 'a serious quarrel ending in his going to a Boardingschool'. He had a scrap with Limpopo in their bedroom and Uncle Dick at once went and shouted downstairs to the Grandpadaita to come up for 'they couldn't stand this fellow James any longer'. (Of course there may be a Richardian version of this story too, but even if untrue it is significant).

The next is worse. You may have forgotten that we had on the P'daita side an Aunt Jenny KIONE (is that the spelling?) who by the by was 'a really *lovely* girl – big black lustrous eyes and fuzzy hair and all the rest of it'. She had a female friend who came and lived with her at Ty-isa for eleven years. And the P'daitas, who so far seem wonderfully patient, didn't like the friend. Then Jenny married Kione and arranged with the consent of her husband that her friend was to come and live with them in their new home.[45] 'We all' – that is the Grand-pudaita and all his pouting, puffing, black-as-a-thundercloud hobble-de-hors – 'We all said if the Kiones had that woman to live with them all connection between the two households was at an end'. And she *did* have her to live with her and her husband: and all connection *was* at an end. I ventured to suggest that

---

44 'Ty-isa' in Lower Sydenham, Belfast, was the home of Albert's parents, Richard Lewis (1832–1908) and Martha Gee Lewis (1831–1903). The Lewis family moved there in 1870, and it was their home until Martha Lewis's death in 1903. After the sale of Ty-isa in 1903, Richard Lewis lived with each of his sons in turn until he moved into Little Lea in 1907. See David Bleakley, *C.S. Lewis – At Home in Ireland* (1998) for a photo of Ty-isa.

45 Although Albert Lewis was ill when he was talking to Jack about his sister, Sarah Jane 'Jeannie' (1856?–1901), it helps explain why the relations between Jeannie and her family were strained. Jeannie's friend, Miss McConnell, was living with the Lewis family at Ty-isa when, in 1882, Jeannie became engaged to Thomas Heron Keown. They were married the following year and Miss McConnell accompanied them to their home in Duncairn Gardens, Belfast. Jeannie and her husband had four children, Sarah, Thomas, Richard and Henry. Mr Keown owned Dundela Villas (where Warnie and Jack were born) and he rented this to Albert Lewis after the latter had married Flora Hamilton. Following the Lewis family's move to Little Lea, Thomas Keown and his family moved into Dundela Villas. Despite the fact they lived so close together, Jeannie rarely saw any of the Lewis family, and when she was dying, Flora wrote to Albert on 27 June 1901 saying, 'I am very sorry to hear of Mrs Keown on your mother's account. Does she know about it? I wonder would Mrs Keown like to see any of you? You know I have always had the feeling that she would have liked to be friends with us, she always, on the few occasions I met her, seemed glad to talk to me and to hear about the children. It seems dreadful to think of her dying like that, away from you all' (LP II: 321).

her husband was perhaps the person to decide whom he would allow to stay in his own house. The reply was delightful – 'Ah he was a weak creature.' It is part of my duty as a nurse to redouble my hypocrisy and to refrain from all vexatious argument, but such an unheard of violation of personal liberty put my self control to the pin of its collar. Can't you see them all? And what on earth would one do if one was married and a crowd of one's relations in law (including that colossus of rancid butter, Bill – plumbago Bill) suddenly turned up and said 'If you have a friend of your wife's to stay with you, we'll cut you and her'. I know what line I'd take.

I crossed this time by the new Liverpool boat. I had not heard of her until my porter on the landing stage volunteered the information that I'd be crossing by the, it sounded like 'Ulstermanic'. I thought it an odd name but nothing like so bad as the name they have actually given her[46] – a pleasure boat name as you rightly say in a letter which reached us three or four days ago. Now as regards comfort below decks, this is the very best boat I have ever been on. The extraordinary width of the berths is the most striking feature. Though I had a cabin without a porthole the ventilator was so efficient that I had to put my head under the clothes: and there is hot and cold in the basin in your stateroom. But as a ship she is disgusting. The deck hamper is piled up almost to the top of the funnels – the squat oval toy funnels of the motor boat. There is no place at all for open air walking except the boat deck. She sails an appalling height out of the water. The internal decorations are the worst example of fake taste I have ever seen. As the ship sails to *Ireland*, some brute has had the idea of doing her up internally in what he would probably call 'the olde Irishe cottage style'. The ceiling of the chapter house is covered with faked beams: the walls are adorned with targets and spears: and (would you believe it) their walls are painted to represent the rough stone work of a cottage. What should be done with the man whose idea of decorating a ship is to try and make you think that she is built throughout of undressed stones and mortar? But let us give honour where honour is due. In this chapter house the chairs are comfortable, the open floors are spacious: and it opens on to a verandah (also in 'olde Irishe cottage' style) looking aft where you can sit and enjoy the air under cover. But tis a bad business on the whole. It only remains to

---

46 *Ulster Monarch.*

disguise the engines as spinning wheels and dress the officers in plush breeches and cutaway coats with shillelaghs,[47] to make the stewardesses into colleens,[48] and to substitute a huge electrically twanged harp on each funnel for the horn, and then the crowd of annual English visitors for this infernal motor race will feel really comfortable.

I must take my mouthful of the negus and go to bed. I have had a trying day. I would give a pint of blood – nay, what's more a tooth (stipulating for a general anesthetic) if you would throw a pebble at the window and announce your unexpected return. The little end room as I write shows all the traces of occupation by a solitary and disgruntled Pigibudda. You know – the extraordinary litter of a dozen P'daita books which one is still trying to read concurrently and the dozen more which one has abandoned but not returned to their places: the two or three dusty volumes, neither P'daitesque or Pigiboetean which one has fished out from among the flies and gurglings of the attic with the vague idea that they might be interesting: the packets of Gold Flake deplorably empty and the tins of P'daita cigarettes deplorably full. I have reached the stage of looking long and fixedly at the photo of the Oldish. Its simply frightful at present because one never gets a real solid hour to work without interruption, and one can never get a decent jaunt into Down or Antrim: the two great mainstays against sheer undiluted Leeburianism (a dreadful thing when taken alone) are thus removed.

[31 August] This is the next day at 12.30. I have been continuously on the run since I got up – going to the McNeills to fetch the various jellies and confections with which they daily supply us – their decency to the O.A.B. all along has been extraordinary – helped your father to shave, giving him cheques to sign and endorse. If I start to work now I shall be interrupted by the doctor before I have well got my head into it, so I may as well put in ten minutes conversation with you.

After finishing your letter-portion last night and wiping up the deluge occasioned by opening one of those remarkable soda water bottles, I read a few pages of Macaulay's letters. My reading them pleased the patient and as I have to do them some time or other I may as well do it now when it provides a common topic for our conversations. They are not uninteresting. Do you know that Macaulay developed his full

---

47 An Irish cudgel of blackthorn or oak.
48 An Anglo-Irish name for a girl.

manner as a schoolboy and wrote letters home from school which read exactly like pages out of the Essays? This is very illuminating. He was talking about the nature of government, the principles of human prosperity, the force of the domestic affections and all that (you know the junk) at the age of fourteen. He could not at that age have *known* anything about them: least of all could he have known enough for the flowing generalizations which he makes. One can see quite clearly that having so early acquired the *talk* he found he could go on quite comfortably for the rest of his life without bothering to notice the *things*. He was from the first clever enough to produce a readable and convincing slab of claptrap on any subject whether he understood it or not, and hence he never to his dying day discovered that there was such a thing as understanding. Don't you think the last word on him is Southey's statement – 'Macaulay's a clever lad, and a clever lad he'll remain' – ?[49]

The most interesting thing in the book so far is the picture of the remains of the real old Whig aristocracy (Toryism you know is incurably vulgar in England, whatever it may have been in France or the Highlands: illiterate squires, place hunters in Parliament, and farmer Georges in long succession on the throne) at Holland house. The account of old Lady Holland's conversation is very pleasing. 'Mr Macaulay, ring the bell. Allen there is not enough turtle soup for you, you must be content with gravy soup. Mr Craddock, take that candle into the next room and show Mr Smith the portraits. Lord Russell, put down that screen: you will spoil it.'[50] This is all verbatim. The parts which excite my contempt for the author most are the letters from India. He is not, of course, an oppressor, a mere Collector of Bogley Wallah. He is conscientious and even tolerant. But it's impossible to conceive any man walking through an ancient civilisation more completely cased in the armour of Holland House, Manchester, nineteenth century 'progress', and general cocksureness that spinning jennies and spelling books are the ultimate secret of life, and that anything other than these exists simply to be first ridiculed, then patronized, and finally 'improved'.

49 Sir George Otto Trevelyan, *The Life and Letters of Lord Macaulay* (1876), vol. I, ch. 3, p. 138. The remark was not made by Robert Southey (1774–1843), but by John Wilson ('Christopher North') in response to an attack by Macaulay on Southey.
50 ibid., vol. I, ch. 4, pp. 209, 235. These comments by Lady Holland were made on several occasions, and are recorded in Macaulay's letters to his sister, Hannah More Macaulay, of 30 May and 25 July 1831. Lewis misquoted the command given Mr Craddock, for it is 'Mr Allen, take a candle and show Mr Craddock the picture of Buonaparte.'

It is Grandfather Hamilton over again, with Liberalism instead of Evangelicalism. He laughed consumedly at the first native he saw, not for anything the man said or did, but simply and solely because he was 'black'.[51] (Damn it, master Pigiebotie, I should have had time to do some work after all!) I don't say this is a crime: but doesn't it just reveal in a flash the provincial and the urchin under the veneer of general culture? He was also apparently responsible for one of the greatest absurdities in the Empire – I mean the fact that I as a Lower Certificate examiner get papers by little Mohammedan girls in Purdah on, say, *Ivanhoe*: a story which rests at every turn on what the Germans call *Frauendienst* – the mediaeval knight and lady romantic ideal, *place aux dames*, breaking of lances, and 'all that'. What on earth it can mean to them I have often wondered. Well when Macaulay arrived in India, the Company was just agitating the question of native education, and had fixed up the only scheme by which any real education was possible: an education of Indians in their own classics, Sanskrit and Persian, conducted on European lines – i.e. according to the standards demanded by European scholarship.

Macaulay (who of course could hardly speak a syllable of even the vernacular, let alone any classical Oriental language) wrote a minute which is a real masterpiece of Philistinism and P'daitism.[52] First of all you have the familiar device of the false parallel. To teach native scholarship would be as if Europe at the Renaissance, instead of studying Latin, and Greek, had gone back to Norman French or Anglo-Saxon. Notice the delicious implication that English (an alien contemporary language)

---

51 ibid., vol. I, ch. 6, p. 334: In 1833 Macaulay was appointed to the Supreme Council of India, and on 10 June 1834 he arrived at Madras. 'On the 10th June the vessel lay to off Madras; and Macaulay had his first introduction to the people for whom he was appointed to legislate in the person of a boatman who pulled through the surf on his raft. "He came on board with nothing on him but a painted yellow cap, and walked among us with a self-possession and civility which, coupled with his colour and his nakedness, nearly made me die of laughing." '

52 ibid., vol. I, ch. 6, pp. 370–2: 'On the 2nd February [1834], Macaulay ... produced a minute in which he adopted and defended the view of the English section in the Committee..."We have to educate a people who cannot at present be educated by means of their mother-tongue. We must teach them some foreign language. The claims of our language it is hardly necessary to recapitulate. It stands pre-eminent even among the languages of the West. It abounds with works of imagination not inferior to the noblest which Greece has bequeathed to us...What the Greek and Latin were to the contemporaries of More and Ascham, our tongue is to the people of India." '

is to India as Greek, Latin (ancient native languages) are to Europe. Don't forget that even inside the parallel Macaulay knows exactly nothing of Norman French or Anglo-Saxon, but he is quite sure that there is nothing in them. How should there be – he never learned them.

Then comes the master stroke. He 'suspects' that Sanskrit is little superior to Anglo-Saxon, 'in some departments, such as history, certainly inferior'.[53] That is, while the reader is still being amused by the false parallel, he is bowled over by a 'how much the less, therefore' argument based on a comparison of two literatures *both* absolutely unknown to the writer and the reader! It is worth remarking that the clever lad, as he wrote the minute, was really creating the Babu.[54] For what is a Babu but a man sufficiently servile to take pride in having imperfectly acquired the jargon of a culture which he cannot assimilate and which he would never have attempted to master but for purely financial reasons? 'Muddlejee-All-Buggard-Up, Failed Calcutta Entrance' is the natural epitaph of Macaulay's education policy in India. You remember Raleigh: 'Macaulay – God's ape. He stinks in my nostrils'.[55] And mine. Yours too I trust.

This is Saturday night. The patient is rather better...Another thing almost too good to be true is that someone in town advised him, as a cure for rheumatism, to carry a pudaita in each pocket – which he actually tried. Oh, and another interesting thing. He was talking, as often, about the insolence of Uncle Hamilton and said 'You know, what I don't like about Gussie is that he never says these desperately insolent things when we're alone. It's always to raise a laugh from you boys at my expense.' I wonder does he regard 'that fellow Gussie' as the origin of the whole anti-Pudaita tradition. If so, a certain remark overheard on the stairs that eventful night so many years ago must have gone deep.

The great consolation about Leeborough at present is my control of the meals. As soon as I came home and found P. on light diet I said I would make things easier for him by giving up my own meat for lunch.

---

53 ibid., vol. I, ch. 6, p. 372: 'The literature of England is now more valuable than that of classical antiquity. I doubt whether the Sanscrit literature be as valuable as that of our Saxon and Norman progenitors. In some departments – in history, for example – I am certain that it is much less so." '

54 A native of India who has acquired some superficial education in English.

55 *The Letters of Sir Walter Raleigh*, op. cit., vol. II, p. 278, letter to David Nichol Smith of 3 July 1908: 'Macaulay – God's Ape – he stinks in my nostrils. Cheap, vain, poor, noisy, blind.'

I substituted bread and cheese, cream crackers and butter, and fruit. This may not appeal to you: but the glory is that I can have it when I choose. There has not been a day for the last fortnight on which one o'clock has not seen me sitting down to my cheese, fruit and wine in a dining room with the windows open. A little effort of imagination will enable you to realize what a comfort this is. I maintain the same arrangement during the week end. Fancy a Leeboro *Saturday* with light lunch at *one* instead of a gorge at half past two, and then high tea (cold roast chicken and ham tonight) at seven! Again, during the first bad nights when I had to sit up I got 'the old woman' to give me a cup of tea before she went to bed. This excellent practice has been continued ever since, so that between tea at 10.30 and negus at 11.30 I get through my evenings very well. If only I wasn't constantly bothered about the P'daitabird (for one never knows really what the next temperature may bring forth), if only I could get decent walks, and if only I could get some more work done, it wouldn't be a bad life. A formidable list of exceptions! It's like the poacher in Punch 'If I get three more after the one I'm after now, I shall have caught four'...[I] break off here and drink my drop of spirits.

By the way we had tonight the old stunt about whiskey being an unpalatable drink. Incidentally all the doctors without exception say that he has done and is doing himself harm with it. Joey says that when he mentions this to the patient, the patient simply laughs at him – and has ruled that there's no good trying to stop it as the good which cd. now be done by cessation would be less than the psychological irritation. He gave me a real fright as I was going out of the gate the other day, having left him as comfortably settled up for the afternoon as I could. He suddenly appeared at his window shouted at me in a voice that made me think some terrible crisis had come I...[went] tearing upstairs to find the real tragedy: he had suddenly discovered that I was going out with the cellar key in my pocket – and apparently the 'odd dregs' in the *two* bottles which he keeps in the wardrobe were not enough to last him the afternoon. There is a very serious side to all this, but I agree with Joey: and I'd go a long way before I'd be leagued with the doctors to deprive the poor old chap of what is about his only pleasure. Let us hope Rabelais is right. Well now for the negus. Stand by for the intolerable moment of opening a P'daita soda water bottle. (If I die of alcohol some day, how ironically this last sentence will jostle the parenthesis before it.)

Sept. 3rd.

The surgeon and Squeaky and Joey have all consulted today and decided on an operation. He is taking it like a hero. By the time this reaches you all will be settled for good or ill. It has been the devil of a day as you may imagine, infernally nerve racking and painful and I'm dead sleepy. I shall post this tomorrow. I had meant to write more, but I'm too tired. As to *facts*, theres nothing more to add. Anyway this can't reach you in time to give any information.

yrs,
Jack

By the by, tho 'special leave' is clearly out of the question, I think, if all goes fairly well at the operation, you would have a real claim to preferential treatment as regards the first boat instead of the second, on grounds of U.P.A.[56] Whether there is any chance of its being regarded, you know better than I.

TO OWEN BARFIELD (W):

Little Lea,
Strandtown,
Belfast
Sept. 9th 1929

My dear Barfield,

Many thanks for your letter. I am not sure that the distinction between 'intimacy' and 'familiarity' is really very profound. It seems to be largely a matter of accident that you know so little of my previous history. I know more of yours because we meet in England: if we had met in Ireland the position would be reversed. Again, we do not much narrate our past lives, but this is because we have so much else to talk about. Any day might have started a topic to which such narrative would have been relevant, and out it would have come. Consider how many bores whose history you know well after a short acquaintance, not because familiarity has in their case replaced intimacy but because they had nothing to say and would not be silent.

I am not saying that there is nothing in the distinction. When the parties are of different sexes it may be more important. I suppose a good

---

56 Uniformed Personnel Allowance.

Greek was familiar with his wife and intimate with his εταιρα.[57] But between men I suspect that intimacy includes familiarity potentially. Now with a woman, of course, no degree of intimacy includes any familiarity at all; for that there must be στοργη[58] or ερωσ[59] or both.

The test really is this. When you have talked to a man about his soul, you will be able, whenever the necessity arises, say, to assist him in using a catheter or nurse him through an attack of dysentery, or help him (if it should so happen) in a domestic problem. This is not so in the case of a woman.[60]

As for my present situation, it frightens me for what it implies. I argue thus: 1. I am attending at the almost painless sickbed of one for whom I have little affection and whose society has for many years given me much discomfort and no pleasure. 2. Nevertheless I find it almost unendurable. 3. Then what in heavens name must it be like to fill the same place at the sickbed, perhaps agonised, of someone really loved, and someone whose loss will be irreparable? A formidable argument *a fortiori*. No doubt under 1. it is proper to include the fact that if lack of real affection spares some pains, it introduces others. Where every kind word and forbearance is the result of calculated duty, and where all we do leaves us still rather ashamed, there is, I suppose, a particular *kind* of strain which would be absent from the other situation. There is also, in this present case, though no spiritual sympathy, a deep and terrible physiological sympathy. My father and I are physical counterparts: and during these days more than ever I notice his resemblance to me. If I were nursing you I should look forward to your possible death as a loss lifelong and irremediable: but I don't think I should shrink from the knife with the sub-rational sym-pathy (in the etymological sense) that I feel at present.

Having said all this I must proceed to correct the exaggeration which seems to be inherent in the mere act of writing. Who was it said that disease has its own pleasures of which health knows nothing? I have my good moments to which I look forward, and perhaps, though the whole

---

57 'Friend'.
58 'Affection'.
59 'Love', as that between a man and woman.
60 We find here Lewis defining those loves which later became the subject of his book *The Four Loves* (1960).

tone of the picture is lowered, there is as much chiaroscuro as ever. When my patient is settled up for the night I go out and walk in the garden. I enjoy enormously the cool air after the atmosphere of the sick room. I also enjoy the frogs in the field at the bottom of the garden, and the mountains and the moon. I often get an afternoon walk when things are going well, and my friend Arthur Greeves – the 'friend' of It[61] you know, who mentioned the beech tree in his letter – sees me every day, and often twice a day. Some of my consolations are very childish and may seem brutal. When Arthur and I talk late into the night there is, even now, a magical feeling of successful conspiracy: it is such a breach, not of course of the formal rules, but of the immemorial custom of a house where I have hardly ever known freedom. There is pleasure of the same kind in sitting with open windows in rooms where I have suffocated ever since childhood: and in substituting a few biscuits and fruit for the Gargantuan mid-day meal which was hitherto compulsory, I hope this is not so uncharitable as it sounds. I do not suppose I look after him the worse for it.

At any rate, I have never been able to resist the retrogressive influence of this house which always plunges me back into the pleasures and pains of a boy. That, by the bye, is one of the worst things about my present life. Every room is soaked with the bogeys of childhood, the awful 'rows' with my father, the awful returnings to school: and also with the old pleasures of an unusually ignoble adolescence By the way, that is just the point about intimacy *containing* familiarity. If it ever became really relevant to some truth that we were exploring in common I could and would expand the last sentence into detail: on the other hand I have not the slightest inclination to do so. i.e. what would be an *end* for familiars is only an instrument for intimates. I enclose a few epigrams on which I would like your opinion. With many thanks,

yours

C. S. Lewis

Jack had been nursing his father at home for over a month when, in the second week of September, Mr Lewis was admitted to a nursing home at

---

61 'It' was Lewis's early name for what he later defined as 'Joy' in his autobiography, *Surprised by Joy.*

7 *Upper Crescent, Belfast. An operation discovered carcinoma of the colon, and for a while he seemed to rally. The doctors thought he might live for some time and, following their advice, Jack returned to Oxford on 22 September. On Tuesday 24 September he received word that his father was worse, and he left for Belfast immediately. He was too late to see him: his father died of cardiac arrest on Wednesday 25 September. His funeral was in St Mark's, Dundela, on Friday 27 September, after which he was buried beside his wife Flora in the city cemetery. The day before, the* Belfast News-Letter *and the* Belfast Telegraph *published long obituaries. 'The death of Mr Lewis,' said the* Telegraph, *'removed from our midst a strong upright man, a faithful friend, a keen and able advocate, a cultured and educated gentleman, and by his death the city in which his brilliant professional career was spent is appreciably the poorer.'*

Warnie had not yet received the two letters from Jack about his father's illness when on 27 September he wrote in his diary:

> *I got down to the office at quarter to nine [and] Lee handed me a cable: it was from J., handed in at Belfast at 4.20 p.m. yesterday – 'Sorry report father died painless twenty fifth September. Jack.' In a dull nagging way it is hurting me more than I should ever have imagined it would have done...All day I have been seeing pictures of him at his best, jumbled up in no chronological sequence – Saturday evening tram rides and visits to the Hippodrome with late supper afterwards in Malvern days...I am glad that the last time we spent together was also one of the happiest we ever had – the first week of April 1927 – unclouded by the emotionalism with which he would have spoilt it had he known that I would be half way to China before the month was out. I suppose it is cowardly to be glad that I was not at home for the final scene: saying goodbye is a thing which I shirk whenever possible, but the final goodbye is almost unendurable: at times Mammy's is still a horribly vivid memory...Mixed, perhaps rather callously, with my feelings about P., is the wrench of losing Leeborough, the Leeborough of the little end room and the attics, and of our room, and rare warm summer afternoons in the garden with the gramophone. And worst of all, being pulled up by the roots...The thought that there will never be any 'going home' for me, is hard to bear. I'd give a lot at this minute for a talk with J. (LP X: 192)*

TO HIS BROTHER (LP X: 194–5):

Hillsboro

Sept. 29th. 29.

My dear APB,

By this [time] you will have had my cable and the two letters written from Leeboro. As there is a good deal of business I will only give you the bare facts. The operation, in spite of what they prophesied, discovered cancer. They said he might live a few years. I remained at home, visiting him in the Nursing Home, for ten days. There were ups and downs and some bad spasms of pain from flatulence (apparently the usual sequence to abdominal operations) going over the wound: but nothing really dreadful. Quite often he was himself and telling wheezes, tho' of course he was often wandering from the dopes.

By this time I had been at home since Aug. 11th and my work for next term was getting really desperate, and, as Joey said, I might easily wait several weeks more and still be in the same position – i.e. not really making the progress he should, but not likely to take a sudden turn for the worse. I therefore crossed to Oxford on Saturday Sept. 22. On Tuesday 24 I got a wire saying that he was worse, caught the train an hour later, and arrived to find that he had died on Tuesday afternoon.[62] The immediate cause seems to have been some blood moving on to the brain: at least that is how they interpreted it. The facts were that he never woke on Tuesday, and remained all that day in a state of unconsciousness with a rising temperature. Now for business.

1. *The business in the office is being carried on under the name of Mr Hayes, solicitor, of Belfast.* (The reason is as follows. The moment the news got about there would be applications by other solicitors for the work of the big permanent clients, such as the Corporation, and the Railways, and therefore, before we could sell the business, there would be no business to sell.[63] It is therefore necessary to tell these clients 'Business

---

62 Jack is confused about the dates. He crossed to Oxford on Saturday, 21 September, and received a wire about his father on Wednesday, 25 September. Albert Lewis died on 25 September.

63 The *Belfast News-Letter* of 26 September 1929, citing Mr Lewis's many clients, said that besides being Prosecutor for the Belfast Corporation 'he acted in the Police Courts for the Belfast Harbour Commissioners (since 1924); and for the Belfast Water Commissioners; the Belfast branch of the National Society for the Prevention of Cruelty to Children; the Belfast & Co. Down Railway Co.; the Great Northern Railway; the Post Office, and the Ministry of Labour'.

as usual.' but tho' Condlin *in fact* does all the work, it cannot legally be done except under the auspices of a qualified solicitor. Mr Hayes receives no payment for lending his name, but any *new* business which accrues during his nominal reign goes to him. I gave authority for this step to be taken, on the advice of Condlin, seconded by Limpopo (I wish I had time to tell you my adult impression of *him*!)

2. *Condlin is sending you a copy of the Will and as soon as possible, an estimate of the Estate.* (In the will, we are given equal shares. Before the operation however the P'daitabird said that, having regard to the insecurity of your career and the comparative security of mine, he would like to leave you more than me: in fact to divide the whole in the proportion of 3 to $2^1/2$: it being understood however that if Magdalen failed to re-elect me, or any other such contingency made me as insecure as you, you would restore equality. This statement I have made known to Condlin. It has of course no *legal* status).

3. *There are two methods of disposing of the business.* a. *Sale outright for a lump sum.* b. *The Drage method.* – i.e. the purchaser to make us a fixed annual payment for a given term of years (I mean fixed in amount of course – *not* a fixed percentage of his takings).

Condlin would advise accepting (b) if the purchaser who on other grounds is most desirable insists on having it so: i.e. not to turn down a good offer solely because the payment is to be deferred.

4. *I have postponed the sale of Leeborough until your return, retaining the Witch of Endor as a housekeeper.* This, I am afraid will sound very uneconomic. But,

a   In the state of my work I cannot spend the fortnight or three weeks more in Ireland which would be necessary for cleaning the house out and dividing what we wanted to keep from what we wanted to sell.

b   My decisions as to what we wanted to keep might not agree with yours.

c   Frankly Pigibuddie it would really be too bloody to sit down and do it alone in that house now.

d   I can't let anyone like the Hamiltons do it at *their* discretion because – well you know *two* good reasons for that.

e   I can't shut it up and leave it empty because damp and rats would render it unsaleable in a few weeks.

f   Also, I confess I should be sorry to give up the idea of you and I having one more stay there together before it goes. (I have of course got
rid of the gardener and house maid, ordered all papers to cease –
except a 'Tally' for the Witch – and impressed upon her that it is no
longer a rich house.)

5. Nearly all the silver – i.e. all except a few knives and forks for you
and me at Xmas – including much that has been locked up in a trunk in
the attics since Mamy's death – has been packed and sent to the bank.
I think that is all. Please if you possibly can let me have a line by
return to say whether you agree with these steps: and also if there is any
further certainty when you are coming back. I have lots more to say but,
as you may imagine, what between the last few days and piles of my own
work and replying to letters of condolence, I am pretty well cooked. You
have still every right to work the U.P.A. as regards the date of sailing if it
is likely to be any good,

yours,
Jack

P.S. Limpopo is *much worse* than I remembered (h'm – wha'?)
P.P.S. He drinks too – *our* whiskey – and ordered a taxi on his own bat
on Thursday in which he kept me driving about all day. Old associations
are so strong that it was only afterwards that I realised that *we* were paying for it. (h'm – wha'?)

TO HIS BROTHER (LP X: 197–9):

Hillsboro.
Oct. 17th 1929

My dear W.,
I got your letter of Sept. 27th yesterday and am more disappointed
than I can say to hear that you will not be home till April. My pleasant
fancy of a last stay at Leeborough together must, among other things, be
abandoned.
Perhaps after all the reality would have turned out to be a gloomy,
or at any rate an uneasy one. In the meantime someone is already
approaching Condlin about the purchase. I am waiting to hear from
Condlin the price we can reasonably or without flagrant unreason,
demand. The trouble is that this man wants possession by Dec. 1st, and

the term doesn't end till Dec. 7th., and the week end, which is all the absence I could take in term, would be utterly useless towards clearing it out. I shall of course attempt to get the purchaser to be content with possession a little later: but if he won't he won't: and if I can't get the house cleared in time for him, I can't. So don't blame me if I let him slip – you see I am in a cleft stick.

Now as to this terrible clearing out itself. To be absolutely safe from selling anything you want to keep my right line would be to store the whole contents of the house until your return: but the price of storage and deterioration wd. eat up or even reduce to a minus quantity the product of the sale. I think therefore I must sell all the furniture except the Chippendale bookcase in the drawing room, the bureau in the study, a bookcase or so, the grandfather clock, the two hall chairs from great grandfather's Welsh farmhouse, and some such oddments. All silver, jewelry and crockery I shall bring to Oxford and keep for your consideration.

As to books, the situation is difficult and I think I can only go on the principle of selling nothing but absolute rubbish. E. g. I don't *suppose* you want to keep the Dumas but you just *may*, so it can't be sold. The picture of Grandp'daita I propose to give to Joey. There may be first editions among the novels and so forth. Pictures are even worse. The P'daita portraits of course can't be sold. We owe Joey a very handsome present for his really very assiduous attendance unpaid, at all hours of the day and night: he is the only member of the family who is propagating: it is not a good picture: and he can't refuse it.[64] Medici prints will be kept: the other pictures (except of course photos) I suppose can be knocked down. 'Relics', MSS or both, of all three generations I shall of course strictly preserve.

As regards money, £1200 is the best offer for the business, and the law library may sell for £500. The list of investments you will understand better than I. The funeral expenses were £55.10.0. Doctors, surgeons, and nursing home have not yet come in. £100, by his directions, (with my v. hearty approval) are to be given to the Witch of Endor.

---

64 The 'P'daita portraits' are probably the oil portraits of Albert Lewis, Grandfather Richard Lewis and Grandfather Hamilton painted by A.R. Baker. As explained in note 186 of Lewis's letter to his father of 27 October 1916, all three P'daita portraits went with Lewis to Oxford. Baker's portrait of Albert Lewis is still in Magdalen College.

What you say in your letter is v. much what I am finding myself. I always before condemned as sentimentalists and hypocrites the people whose view of the dead was so different from the view they held of the same people living. Now one finds out that it is a natural process. Of course, on the spot, ones feelings were in some ways different. I think the mere pity for the poor old chap and for the life he had led really surmounted everything else. It was also (in the midst of home surroundings) almost impossible to believe. A dozen times while I was making the funeral arrangements I found myself mentally jotting down some episode or other to tell him: and what simply got me between wind and water was going into Robinson and Cleaver's to get a black tie and suddenly realising 'You can never put anything down to his account again.' By the way, a great deal of his jollities and wheezes remained to the end. One of the best things he ever said was the day before I left – four days before his death. As I came in the day nurse said 'I've been telling Mr Lewis that he's exactly like my father.' P. 'And how am I like your father?' N. 'Why, he's a pessimist.' P. (after a pause) 'I suppose he has several daughters.'

As time goes on the thing that emerges is that, whatever else he was, he was a terrific *personality*. You remember 'Johnson is dead. Let us go to the next. There is none. No man can be said to put you in mind of Johnson.'[65] How he filled a room! How hard it was to realise that physically he was not a very big man. Our whole world, the whole Pigiebotian world, is either direct or indirect testimony to the same effect. Take away from our conversation all that is imitation or parody (sincerest witness in the world) of his, and how little is left. The way we enjoyed going to Leeborough and the way we hated it, and the way we enjoyed hating it: as you say, one can't grasp that *that* is over. And now you could do anything on earth you cared to in the study at midday or on Sunday, and it is beastly.

I sympathise with you in the strange experience of returning to a British Isles which no longer contains a P'daitaheim. I hope that when all your books are set up (presumably in the non-glassed little end room bookcase) in Magdalen, where you can always have an empty sitting

---

65 'Johnson is dead. – Let us go to the next best: – there is nobody; – no man can be said to put you in mind of Johnson.' The words are those of William Gerard Hamilton and are quoted by James Boswell in his *Life of Johnson*, op cit., vol. IV, p. 42.

room to which you can repair at all hours, I hope that a leave at Hillsboro will be able to pass not unpalatably. Its no good pretending that its the old thing, but there you are.[66]

You may be grateful for your absence at present in one way. Two nights out of three I sit down at 10 o'clock after my own work to do an hour's business correspondance with Condlin. Hardly my long suit! By the by about the *proportion* between your share and mine, I think you ought to know that I have mentioned and shall mention it to no one alive except Condlin: so you need not feel that you are facing a public opinion that cd. misunderstand or criticise.[67] Write when you can.

yours,

J.

TO ARTHUR GREEVES (W):

Magdalen College,
Oxford.
Monday [28 October 1929]

My dear Arthur,

A straggling letter in diary form is in process of composition and will be posted in due course:[68] the present is written for practical purposes and contains a proposal wh. I make with some diffidence. However I must take my courage in both hands: here goes.

Warnie is not coming home till April. Therefore the proposed visit by him and me to Leeborough to clear it out at Christmas will not take place. But unless a purchaser turns up I am disposed to leave the house as it stands until his return. The danger is that if I do not do something this vac. a purchaser may suddenly spring on me next term wanting immediate possession, when I could only run across for a week end at

---

66 A letter from Mrs Moore of 27 October was placed in the envelope with Jack's. In it she wrote: 'I do hope you will always look on Hillsboro as a home and that you will come straight to us on your return in April...We hope some day to get a larger house, when things would be more comfortable for you, so please do think of our home as your home, and be assured always of a very hearty welcome' (LP X: 197).

67 As soon as he received this letter on 2 November, Warnie sent a telegram to Jack saying, 'Equal shares, otherwise agree proposals including retention Leeborough. Home early April. Warnie' (LP X: 199).

68 Portions of the 'letter in diary form' which he writes about here were composed before this and the next two letters, but all are given in the order in which the individual items were received by Greeves.

the most, and it wd. be almost impossible to do the whole job in the time. I have therefore decided at least to make a start at the end of the present term. I want to have Minto with me and she v. much wants to come: partly that she may have a look at household things of whose value W. and I are ignorant, partly because we shd. both like her to have seen my old home before it goes. But I cannot (and she agrees) take her to Leeborough. There are ghosts there who wd. not be happy to see her nor anxious to make her happy. Also, it wd. look like the traditional insolence of an heir, trampling on the old king's laws before the crown is warm on his head. But I could take her to Bernagh as a mutual friend of yours and mine.

So what I want to know is could you possibly put the pair of us up (only us two – no Maureen, no cats & no dogs) for a week from Dec. 7th to Dec. 15th. This is the cheekiest proposal I have ever made to any one in my life: but – well, my want is urgent, you are my oldest friend, and I think I can count your mother such too. If it is inconvenient, don't be afraid to say so. I wait for an answer v. eagerly.

Yrs
Jack

TO ARTHUR GREEVES (W):

Magdalen College,
Oxford.
[4? November 1929]

My dear Arthur,

A thousand thanks! I was 'all in a flutter of spirits' when I got your letter for my proposal seemed to me & still seems extraordinarily cool. I am now trying to prevent my anticipations from running so high as to ensure their own disappointment. Lovely sunrise through tall elms twinkling over the frosty grass this morning.

Yours
Jack

TO ARTHUR GREEVES (W):

Magdalen College,
Oxford.
[11? November 1929]

My dear Arthur,

Yes, it is *Sunday*[69] morning we shall arrive on, all being well. If you arrive by 9.30 I expect we shall have breakfasted on board, being then hungry, wh. will be no harm as we can then be washing and changing etc while you are at breakfast. I *have* primed Minto. I presume you have primed your mother. Provided they don't hurt one another their cross purposes & misunderstandings will be very funny. Selah!

Yours
Jack

TO ARTHUR GREEVES (W):

[Hillsboro]
Thursday Oct 3rd [1929][70]

My dear Arthur,

I have decided to write a snippet to you every odd time when I have a moment and thus gradually to fill up a letter. This is the first snippet. I am feeling better. Oh how delicious the gradual recovery from a time of horror is. There is a good description in *The Ring & the Book* of this: where a man speaks of beginning to feel again 'the comfortable feel of clothes And taste of food'.[71] Remember also Herbert's poem – *The Flower* I think – 'I once more feel the sun and rain And relish versing.'[72]

It is much colder here and from my window I see the lawn covered with yellow leaves: the long drought had shrivelled them so that they drop early this year at the first touch of cold. I am sleeping solid and it is a delight to wake up each morning with the sense of peace and safety and home. Then I sing in my bath & take Mr Papworth for a run before

---

69 Sunday 8 December – when Lewis and Mrs Moore arrived in Belfast and where they remained until 20 December.

70 This is the first portion of the 'letter in diary form' mentioned in the letter of 28 October 1929.

71 Robert Browning, *The Ring and the Book* (1868–9), X, 1710: 'The healthy taste of food and feel of clothes'.

72 George Herbert, 'The Flower' (1633), 38–9: 'I once more smell the dew and rain / And relish versing...'

breakfast, eating my apple the while. Unfortunately the morning has to be given to uninteresting work done as fast as I can manage to get through it – a process which would rob even voluntary work of its interest. How thankful you should be that you never have tasks which are not chosen by yourself. And yet I don't know. So many things have now become interesting to me because at first I had to do them whether I liked them or not, and thus one is kicked into conquering new countries where one is afterwards at home.

Oct. 4th

Yesterday Barfield came to lunch and afterwards took me out for a drive-and-walk – you see you are not the only friend I sponge on. We walked in the flat fields by the Thames near Iffley. I wonder if you remember Iffley, where the Norman church is. I sat on the bridge at Iffley lock with you and Minto's doctor brother, Johnnie, (the one who died) and we talked about sailing up the Amazon.[73] It was a luminous grey day yesterday with a fresh wind that curled the river into crisp waves. A fleet of ducks that passed us were going up and down about as much (in proportion to their size) as fishing smacks in a real swell. We also saw two swans and their cygnets. As often happens with the best of friends we were not in a very good talking mood – only that pleasant sense of security that comes from being with those who understand you.

Last night I told Minto about your nursery rime book, and we went all through 'The dog began to bite the pig' together, and then the House that Jack built. She said she so wished to be a grandmother so as to tell them to her grand-children. I said that now that she has big spectacles and her eyes look very big through them she could do it most impressively.

To day I worked in the morning and afternoon and walked into town by Cuckoo Lane and Mesopotamia[74] after tea. The real autumn tang in the air had begun. There was one of those almost white skies with a touch of frosty red over the town, and the beginnings of lovely colouring in the college garden. I love the big kitchen garden there. There is something very attractive about rows of pots – and an old man potting – and

---

73 On 18 July 1922, Lewis wrote in his diary, 'The Doc. gave us a vivid description of his sail 1500 miles up the Amazon. Speaking of exploring central Brazil, Arthur said "That's the sort of thing I'd like to do!!"' *AMR*, p. 73.

74 See note 73 of letter to Arthur Greeves of 13 May 1917.

greenhouses and celery trenches. I suspect that 'trench' was a delicious earthy word (like 'ditch') before it was spoiled by the war associations. I saw both a squirrel and a fat old rat in Addison's walk, and had glimpses of 'it'.

I think almost more every year in autumn I get the sense, just as the mere nature and voluptuous life of the world is dying, of something else coming awake. You know the feeling, of course, as well as I do. I wonder is it significant – in stories nymphs slip out of the tree just as the ordinary life of the wood is settling down for the night. Does the death of the natural always mean the birth of the spiritual? Does one thing never sleep except to let something else wake. Milton found that his genius was never in full tide except in autumn and winter.

We have our first fire to night. Mr Papworth is asleep in his basket and Minto is listening-in[75] and mending on the sofa.

Oct. 6th

I have nothing to tell you about books these days. The mornings and afternoons are occupied with making notes on *Loves Labour's Lost*,[76] the last of those four plays which I have been making up all this summer & which will also be associated with this time in my mind. The evenings so far have been nearly always occupied in answering letters of condolence or business correspondence from Condlin. Last night was an exception and I read a short new book, Foligno's *Latin Thought in the Middle Ages*,[77] which I strongly suspect of being Fascist propaganda. When a man is very anxious to emphasise (what everyone admitted before), the greatness and influence of Rome, and to suggest that even yet we have not fully appreciated it, my suspicions are awakened – perhaps unjustly. I also glanced through A. E. Houseman's *Shropshire Lad*[78] for the hundredth time. What a terrible little book it is – perfect and deadly, the beauty of the gorgon. I think you know it.

I have not yet started meditation again. The difficulty is to find a suitable time. These are not suitable days for sitting out of doors: indoor times are occupied with work or conversation. In bed at night – well

---

75 i.e. to the radio.

76 William Shakespeare, *Love's Labour's Lost* (1598).

77 Cesare Carolo Foligno, *Latin Thought During the Middle Ages* (1929).

78 A.E. Housman, *A Shropshire Lad* (1896).

work and Headington make me so sleepy that I have never yet mustered the resolution to tackle such a difficult job when the pillow and the sheet and the rain on the window are wooing me to glide away into drowsiness. (By the way I don't ever remember a time when the coming of sleep was such a positive pleasure to me as it has been since I left Ireland: and by the way there is a fine passage on that subject in Barfield's novel.)[79] Then in bed in the morning, at early-tea time, I am still sleepier. When I go back into College perhaps I shall be able to fit in five minutes after breakfast. (Memo: can meditation be combined with emptying of the bowels? What a saving of time, specially for a constipated man like you.)

To-day, Sunday, I worked till lunch. After lunch, dug up the hen-run and worked again till tea. All this time it was raining hard. After tea it cleared and I sallied forth for a v. good walk. There was a very high wind, the trees were waving, and a lot of tattered rain clouds were scudding across the sky, unusually low. I walked down Cuckoo Lane and into the Private Road[80] where I had a magnificent view of Oxford below me all gleaming in a sudden dazzling gold break in the cloud. I came home through the fields to old Headington, where the colouring in the hedgerows was rich. But these winds are bringing the leaves down too quickly.

Oct. 10th

We haven't been having a very nice time for the last day or so as Mr Papworth has been seriously ill, which bothers me not only for the poor beast's sake, but also for Minto's, who takes it so to heart and gives herself so much extra work about it. I am also very busy getting ready for term. You can well imagine how I dislike all these preparations because they are always associated with leaving my homely timeless days at Hillsboro and going back to the solitude of my college bedroom and the routine of a time-table. Of course college and ones own rooms & books have their charm: but you know what I mean – especially late at night when people go away and you find that you have let the fire [go] out.

---

79 The novel 'English People', which has never been published.
80 Pullens Lane.

I am slowly reading a book that we have known about, but not known, for many a long day – Macdonald's *Diary of an Old Soul*.[81] How I would have scorned it once! I strongly advise you to try it. He seems to know everything and I find my own experience in it constantly: as regards the literary quality, I am coming to like even his clumsiness. There is a delicious home-spun, earthy flavour about it, as in George Herbert. Indeed *for me* he is better than Herbert.

Oct. 15th?

I have been back in College for about a week and find I can't go on with this very well. I may try to start another on a more purely diary model. The return to College and its regular routine has done me good: the lag ends of recent horrors have begun to fade in my mind. I am very busy this term, but the beautiful weather over-rides everything.

Yrs

Jack

TO ARTHUR GREEVES (W):

[Magdalen College]
Thursday Oct. 17th [1929]

Altho I had not gone to bed till one and had then been kept awake by the brilliant moonlight in my room (after walking a half hour in the same moonlight thro' the grove with Griffiths[82]) I woke perfectly refreshed after one of those sleeps deeper than usual which sometimes comes to us in a short night. Went round the walks with Griffiths after breakfast and both enjoyed the bright yellow leaves floating on the water. He packed off and set out to bicycle home to Newbury at 10.

---

81 Though it may not have been the copy he was reading at the time, Lewis owned the 'New Edition' of *The Diary of an Old Soul* (1885) which contains the inscription in MacDonald's hand, 'Charlotte Kölle with kindest regards from George & Louisa MacDonald. April 27, 1885.' It contains, as well, an inscription in Lewis's hand, 'Later: from C.S. Lewis to Joy Davidman, Christmas 1952.'

82 Alan Richard Griffiths (1906–93) matriculated at Magdalen in 1925 and read English under Lewis. In *SBJ* XV, Lewis speaks of him as his 'chief companion' on the road to Christianity. In 1931 Griffiths was received into the Catholic Church, and in 1936 he took his solemn vows as a Benedictine monk, at which time he took the name Dom Bede Griffiths. In 1955 he was sent to India, and he remained there for the rest of his life. The story of his joint pilgrimage to the Faith with Lewis is found in *The Golden String* (1954).

From 10 to 1 pupils. Out home for lunch. Dug the hen run, dug worms for the hens, and took Tykes[83] for the short walk which is all he can manage at present: then at 3.30 walked v. quickly up Shotover getting back about 4.15 for tea. Left home at 5 and got back for pupil at 5.30.

My new book on Marlow[84] had come which I read after dinner. It is chiefly concerned with the appalling career of Poole,[85] who was one of those present when Marlow was murdered: an incredible person who was receiving pay from the Papists for carrying letters to Mary Queen of Scots and also from the govt. for spying on the Papists and Mary: at the same time engaged in litigation with the husband of a woman who visited him while in prison for debt.

Dropped in on Christie[86] for half an hour and was in bed by 11.15 after reading my daily verse from *The Diary of an Old Soul.*

Mon. Nov. 4th – After breakfast returned to College from home where I had been spending the week end in the hope of getting rid of my flu'ey cold. I had foolishly taken last week end out there in bed, had to get up too soon, and consequently felt v. poorly all week. No pupils on Monday morning. Spent the whole time till lunch answering letters and setting examination papers. A dull job, rewarded by those sudden gleams of fugitive association that have the habit of starting up only when the intellect is fully engaged on something else.

Home for lunch. Dug the hen run and dug for worms. Worms are a case in which the extension of a name has altered a physical feeling for me. From reading Beowulf and the Edda the word 'Worm' in the sense of 'dragon' has become so familiar to me that I always think of these humble twisters as poor relations of Fafner and Jormungander; their kinship with the monstrous has taken from them the merely disgusting and I can now lift them in my fingers without a shudder. Even if I could not, earth is such a lovely thing that it reconciles one to all its contents. As Minto always says 'There's comfort in the clay.' Took Mr Papworth for his walk.

---

83 Another name for Mr Papworth, Lewis's dog.

84 Frederick Samuel Boas, *Marlowe and His Circle* (1929).

85 Robert Poley or Robert Poole was a government agent so deeply involved in plots and counterplots that no one knew whose side he was on. Boas devotes ch. 2 of his book to him.

86 John Traill Christie (1899–1980) was Fellow and Classical Tutor at Magdalen from 1928 to 1932; headmaster of Repton School, 1932–7; headmaster of Westminster School, 1937–49; and principal of Jesus College, Oxford, 1950–67.

The leaves on the ground are now very thick in Cuckoo Lane. A white liquid sky with horizontal bands of darker grey and a white sun behind them. Not a breath of wind. I had hoped to go and see old Foord-Kelcie[87] after the walk but I am still rather groggy and was tired & sweating when I came back so I did not.

Into college after tea. I intended to write a page or so for you before dinner, but answering letters to Condlin filled up the whole time. After dinner the Michaelmas Club met in my rooms. (An undergraduate society wh. McFarlane and I were instrumental in founding a year ago.) Acton,[88] a funny little chap with a cockney accent but the best philosopher as well as the most earnest and *real* thinker in College – nothing blasé about him – read an excellent paper on *Pessimism*. It had the touch of reality about it – quite unlike most young men's pessimism. A fairly good discussion afterwards till about 11.45 when the Club broke up. McFarlane stayed with me till 12.30 talking by the fire, to the accompaniment of the stags grunting in the grove outside. V. tired.

Tue. Nov. 5th – One of *our* days. Woke to a great roaring wind that kept the trees in the grove rising and falling with the motion and noise of seas all morning while the leaves fell in showers. Work all morning and home at 1 o'clock, where the Barfields, a pleasant surprise, turned up after lunch. Mrs B.[89] stayed with Minto while he and I took a short walk. Talked chiefly about his novel (this seems to be a practice of my friends!). He said among other things that he thought the idea of the spiritual world as *home* – the discovery of homeliness in that wh. is otherwise so remote – the feeling that you are coming *back* tho' to a place you have never yet reached – was peculiar to the British, and thought that Macdonald, Chesterton, and I, had this more than anyone else. He doesn't know you of course[90] – who, with Minto, have taught me so much in that way <(in *that* way? No, no.).>

---

87 The Rev. Edward Foord-Kelcey (1859–1934), a retired clergyman who entered Pembroke College, Oxford, in 1884 and whose last preferment before moving to Oxford was Great Kimble in Buckinghamshire. There is a short biography of him by Lewis in LP XI: 24–5.

88 Harry Burrows Acton (1908–) matriculated in 1927 and took a First in PPE (Philosophy, Politics and Economics) in 1930. In 1931 he became an assistant lecturer in philosophy at University College, Swansea.

89 Owen Barfield had married Matilda 'Maud' Douie (1885–1980), a professional dancer and producer, in 1923. See **Owen Barfield** in the Biographical Appendix.

90 He means they didn't know one another well. They met for the first time at 28 Warneford Road on 7 July 1922, on which occasion Greeves drew a sketch of Barfield. See *AMR*, p. 65.

Had to be back in Oxford by 5 to attend Simpson's[91] class on Textual Criticism (no, no, Arthur – *T*extual) which I am learning this year in order to teach next. After dinner read with Ker[92] (a pupil) some of the fragments of Anglo-Saxon poetry. Immensely fine. There's one begins with a man going to the window & looking out and saying 'No. This light is not the day breaking, nor a fiery dragon, nor is the house on fire. Take your shields & swords.'[93] Ker shares to the full my enthusiasm for the saga world & we had a pleasant evening – with the wind still roaring outside.

Wed. Nov. 6. – A nasty day. Work all morning. Then lunch in college, which I hate, as there was a college meeting at 2: at which everything went the way I didn't want it to go. I had just time to rush out home, take Mr Papworth for a run and have tea, returning to give my lecture at 5, take a pupil at 6, dine at 7.15 and receive a visit from a pupil with a terrible stutter at 8.30. Fortunately McFarlane came in at about ten wh. encouraged this poor fellow – to his own relief as much as mine – to take himself off. We then made cocoa and chatted till eleven. V. tired and – the old phraze – v. much 'entangled in the world' & v. far in spirit from where I would be.

Thurs. Nov. 7th. – Got an unexpected free evening off owing to a pupil's having another engagement and like a fool wasted it lounging about in the smoking room till after 10 talking to various people whom I don't greatly care for of subjects I'm not greatly interested in. Such fools we are.

---

91 Percy Simpson (1865–1962) was educated at Selwyn College, Cambridge. After taking a degree in 1887 he taught at Denstone School until 1895. In 1888 he embarked on what was to be his life's work: the annotation of Ben Jonson's plays. Over many years, Simpson, his wife Evelyn M. Simpson and C.H. Herford edited the 11 volumes of Jonson's *Works* (1925–52). In 1913 he arrived in Oxford to work for the Clarendon Press, and was almost at once invited to help as a lecturer in the English Faculty. In 1914 he was appointed first librarian of the new English faculty library, a post which he held until 1934. Simpson also lectured on textual criticism for students reading for the B.Litt. degree. Lewis, who had learned textual criticism from Simpson, began teaching his own class for B.Litt. students in the Trinity Term of 1930 when his subject was 'The Text of Milton's *Comus*'.

92 Neil Ripley Ker (1908–82) matriculated in 1928, and was a Fellow of Magdalen and Reader in Paleography from 1946 to 1968. He brought to the study acute powers of observation, and included among his distinguished works are the *Catalogue of Manuscripts containing Anglo-Saxon* (1957) and *Medieval Manuscripts of Great Britain* (1969 onwards).

93 The opening lines of *Finnsburg*, ed. George Hickes (1705).

Dec. 3rd. – I tried hard to keep this up but it wouldn't do. Awful business correspondence with Condlin filled up any spare hours I had of an evening. I have also got rather into a whirl as I always do in the latter part of the term. I have too many irons in the fire – the Michaelmas Club, the Linguistic Society, the Icelandic Society, and this and that. One week I was up till 2.30 on Monday (talking to the Anglo Saxon professor Tolkien[94] who came back with me to College from a society and sat discoursing of the gods & giants & Asgard for three hours, then departing in the wind & rain – who cd. turn him out, for the fire was bright and the talk good?), next night till 1 talking to someone else, & on Wednesday till 12 with the Icelandics. It is very hard to keep ones feet in this sea of engagements and very bad for me spiritually.

I am trying not to look forward too much to next week. How odd it will be to sleep in Bernagh – and to walk into Leeborough with Minto. I wonder does the future hold for us things as strange to our present point of view as *this* is to our old one? Barfield's novel[95] is finished and already refused by one publisher. To day there is a fog, and all the trees quite bare now.

In spite of the failure so far I intend to keep up the effort of continuing a journal letter to you. In the Vac. it shd. be easier than in the term, and perhaps habit will at last teach me to fit a portion however small into my day's routine. But you must do the same. Think how we shall enjoy the product when we are old.

Yrs
Jack

P.S. Give my love to your mother and v. many thanks for having us.

TO HIS BROTHER (LP X: 211-18):

Hillsboro.
Dec. 21st 29

My dear APB,

Thank you for your letter of the 2nd Nov. and specially for your generous decision about the money – though it would be mere

---

94 J.R.R. Tolkien is mentioned in note 38 to the letter of 26 June 1927. See also **J.R.R. Tolkien** in the Biographical Appendix.
95 i.e. 'English People'.

hypocrisy to pretend it was unexpected. When you say that we have lived long on a communal basis, I am afraid I cannot help reflecting that it has largely been a communism in which I have played the receiving proletarian to your bleeding capitalist: that however is a form justified by the best models. As to the proportions of the money – P's decision was based on the belief that I was safely and amply provided for while you, despite the surprising quantity of 'music' you got out of life, were very poor at the moment and liable to be axed in the near future. I feel justified in taking half because he was of course ignorant that more than one shared my income, and also much too sanguine about the safety of my job. But I want it to be clearly understood that if you get axed (*absit omen*),[96] and I still have a job, we shall then revert to unequal portions.

This all sounds as if I were in hourly expectation of being turned out of my fellowship, but that is not exactly what I mean. I am simply taking into account the fact that re-election – for which I come up next summer – though very usual is not inevitable or merely formal and depends on far reaching wangles. I do not think it at all probable that the Tutorial board would care to set the ominous precedent of refusing to recommend one of its own members for re-election (too many can play at that game once it is started), but there are anti-English Schools and anti-SPB and the thing is conceivable. All this must sound very strange to you, but you must try to realise what a real democracy like a College means. Suppose Sir, that your continued employment depended on the votes of the other officers in your unit, and that some one (who also rather disliked you personally) wanted your place for an officer of a different type e.g. wanted a horse transport bloke *instead*, it being impossible to increase the strength...you see the sort of situation which results. There is no reason to be seriously worried about it, and I have already spent longer on the subject than I intended.

Now as to other business. I think I told you in my last letter that a purchaser was nibbling at Leeborough. After inspection he decided not to buy. The episode however gave me rather a fright. If another purchaser turned up next term, what was I to do? He would probably want immediate possession: and, much as you might want to spend another fortnight there in April, I take it you would not wish to do so at the cost of three thousand odd pounds – that would be a curious commentary on our old slogan 'it's a

---

96 'May this omen be absent' or in this instance, 'Heaven forbid!'

very *cheap* hotel'. Again, the house is so unsaleable that if you turned down one purchaser you might never get another: and pleasant as it may be now to reflect that 'we still have Leeborough', the same reflection will rather pall if we are making it fifteen years hence. On the other hand I could not get over for more than a couple of nights in term: so that if such a situation arose, I should probably have to let the place be turned out and a sale held with very little supervision. This alternative was clearly quite out of the question. I accordingly decided to go over at the end of last term and sort things into such an order that if I had to give sudden authority for a sale, no great prying or larceny could go on. I decided to take Minto with me, partly to give her a change, and partly to have her advice about china and linen, and as I felt it wd. be a breach of decorum to take her to Leeborough, we both billeted ourselves at Bernagh for about ten days, arriving back in Oxford today. The following is a record of what I have done.

(1) *All keeps* in the way of books I have put in the study: i.e. all your books, all my books which I wish to keep, all P'daita books which I know that I want or suspect that you want. The *Cambridge Modern History*[97] and the big translation of Dumas are the inclusions that I felt most doubtful about: but if we finally condemn them they will sell as well a year hence as now.

(2) All Boxonian and pellesmonic documents (after one last unsuccessful search for that *ignis fatuus* Zoe Pasquali)[98] I have carefully collected into the playbox and placed in the study.

(3) *Other papers.* These are all in the study in the other playbox and the big chest from the cistern attic. 1. Family letters. Of Grandfather and Grandmother Lewis and Granduncle Thomas Lewis (neither of whom could spell), I have kept all. Of Mammy's and P's letters I have kept all except bills, receipts, invitations and the like. Of Uncle Bill and Uncle Dick I have kept a selection (These are such utter rubbish that it was kind to keep any considering the enormous bulk of papers I dealt with). Hamilton letters there were hardly any, but I kept all I could find. All letters of yours (i.e. to and from you) I kept. I took the liberty of removing the envelopes towards the end, as space was by this time becoming a serious question.

---

97 *The Cambridge Modern History*, planned by the late Lord Acton, edited by Alphonsus William Ward, George Walter Prothero, Sir Stanley Leathes and Ernest Alfred Benians, 13 vols. (1902–12).

98 That 'deceiving flame', Zoe Pasquali, was presumably a character in a Boxen story that has not come to light.

2. *Diaries*. Grandfather's (Hamilton), yours and fragments of diary by
P. 3. Documents relating to Mammy's academic career, your Mention
etc., all of course kept. In the time at my disposal it was quite impossible
to arrange these three classes of papers in any sort of order, so I am
afraid that both chest and playbox will have to be turned out to find any
given piece. What I can say for sure is that I have destroyed nothing of
yours that I could find. I would have assembled them if I had found
them even remotely assembled – but you know what it is like in Leeborough. It had to be simply a case of taking drawer after drawer, as you
came to them, and going on doggedly, often for hours at a stretch.

(4) *Pictures*. (a) All *photographs* of yours are either in the drawers of
P's study desk, or with the papers in the chest and playbox. (This means
of course that at first I began putting photos in with the letters but later
found them too big an item). Family photos e.g. of Mammy, P., ourselves
etc, are all in the drawers in the study desk. Various endless photos of
our cousins at various ages, or of utterly unknown people, I destroyed.
Malvern and Army groups and other large framed photos are all in the
study. (b) the two grandfather portraits, the 3 P'daita portraits, the 2
Medicis, the pictures from the little end room, the drawings from the
hall, are in the study.

(5) Forrest Reid (a novelist and friend of Arthur's)[99] and Arthur, with
the aid of the leading booksellers catalogues, picked out for me the
cream of the novels by which I mean the cream, not from the reading,
but from the collector's standpoint. Here I had to make a decision of
my own. I decided, I hope not wrongly, that you would as soon read
your *Man of Property* in a contemporary edition as in a first, listed by
booksellers at £17.10.0. I have therefore brought back with me a packing case full of the most valuable of these: a trunk follows containing
the less valuable, but still too good to be knocked down at an auction.
I shall have about twenty copies of the list typed and send it to several
booksellers and take the best offers I get. I ventured to act without
authority because the Galsworthys are now about as high as they are
likely to go.

---

99 Forrest Reid (1875–1947), the novelist, was living in Belfast at this time. His story is
   told in his two autobiographies, *Apostate* (1926) and *Private Road* (1940). There are
   several references to Arthur Greeves and J.N. Bryson in Russell Burlingham's *Forrest
   Reid: A Portrait and a Study* (1953). A portrait of Reid, painted by Greeves, is in the
   possession of the Royal Academical Institution, Belfast.

(6) *The Dud books* I have collected altogether on the floor of the landing and some bedrooms. Arthur and Reid have promised to bring a librarian to see them as lending libraries often offer more for ordinary novels in decent condition than a bookseller buying by weight.

(7) *Clothes.* 1. All clothes of yours except obviously antediluvian dress softs and infantile shirts have been kept, including a great deal which I am pretty sure is useless. 2. All P's clothes that are in reasonable condition have been kept to provide knockabouts for us. 3. Mammy's clothes were a very difficult problem. a. some things are in cardboard boxes in the study. I suppose we had better give them as presents to people like Aunt Annie. These are ones in which the material has intrinsic value. b. some small intimate things I burned. c. some things which had no intrinsic value I gave to the Witch of Endor to dispose of among poor people as she chose. All clothes of P's and yours are in the wardrobe in his dressing room. Condemned clothing (i.e. hopelessly small, torn, or moth eaten) I have partly given to the Witch, partly brought back to give to the very frequent people who ask for clothes at our door. I hope this was a right disposal. You can't sell such things and to destroy it all (incidentally, how would you set about it?) in a country where dozens of people have no coats, seems rather harsh.

(8) *Archpigiebotian miscellanies.* The heavy canvas parcel (damnably heavy) in P's dressing room, the topees, the horrid rubble of spurs, and iron spikes in the same room, the maps, the steel box, the African spear, and everything unintelligible which looked like being yours, I have conveyed to the study.

(9) *Silver and jewelry* all packed and in the bank except a few things too large, like lamps, and a few things of small value overlooked, which I gathered up and put in the study: besides a modicum for our own table use in the spring if (as I still hope) we are there together again.

(10) *China and glass.* Minto thought very little of this was good, and what was good was often cracked and defective. A small selection at her advice I put in a special place in one of the pantries and notified the Witch – who agreed about the small value of this item as a whole. (She has served in several big houses and is also a *very* loyal Leeburian, so I think her opinion good.).

(11) The piano I have sold for £18.0.0 to one French, who came out to value the contents of the house for death duties. Condlin, Arthur, and Minto all advised my acceptance of this figure and indeed were surprised

that we got it. (Such payments are made to the account of C. S. Lewis Exctr. of A. J. Lewis decd., at the Bank of Ireland so that there is no danger of their getting mixed up with my private account at Barclay's Bank in Headington. I should have preferred to have cheques made out to us both, but this is much too simple for the Law who prefer that the present executor (for of course I act qua executor and not as one of the heirs) should act entirely on his own, so that the other executors can have a chance to sue him as and when they turn up).

(12) *Mammy's collection of stamps.* P. frequently mentioned this to me and intended it to be sold. In fact he left in the album a note dated 1929 saying 'Some of these may be worth money' – a note which I have of course preserved as one of the best and least P'daita-ish actions of his life. The best stamps in the album were forgeries, so that I was glad to sell it for four pounds.

(13) I have also sold (a) to Reid: *The Graphics*[100] and the 'famous trials' for £3.2.6. As the *Graphics* can be bought for 6d a volume, we have no reason to be dissatisfied. (b) To Arthur: *the Smaller Temple Shakespeare*[101] and some oddments for £4.6.6.

(14) *Furniture.* I have placed in the study (or left there) the desk, the sofa, the tables, the two screens, grandfather's chair from the little end room, the soft study chair, one of the drawing room arm chairs, the little end room armchair, four upright armchairs from the drawing room. I have labeled *not for sale* the two hall chairs, the glazed drawing room bookcase, Mammy's desk in drawing room (which I can find no key to unlock), the cloak room settle, the two little end room bookcases, and the grandfather clock. (Gramophone, telescope, and microscope also in the study).

Having got thus far, I begin to fear that the impression produced on you will be much as if I had written 'I have moved all the study furniture into our bedroom and carefully placed all our bedroom stuff in the hall: I have had the water closet seats pulled out and refixed in the little end room at a very moderate cost: I have sunk a swimming bath in the croquet lawn and been fortunate to dispose of a bushel of parsley to Bob

---

100 *The Graphic* was a periodical which ran from 1869 to 1932, after which it was continued as *The National Graphic.*

101 He was probably referring to *The Temple Shakespeare for Schools*, 8 vols. (1902), which had been preceded by *The Temple Shakespeare*, ed. Israel Gollancz, 40 vols. (1894–97) and *The Larger Temple Shakespeare*, ed. Israel Gollancz, 12 vols. (1899, 1900).

Ewart for 9¹/2d. The collection of bowler hats I am bringing to England to distribute among the dealers who offer the best figures...'

But what my proceedings really boil down to is this: All real treasures and relics are now in the study. All *valuables* are either in the Bank of Ireland or (like the first editions) in Magdalen. Therefore, if a good purchaser appears suddenly this term wanting immediate possession, I can sell the house and hold a sale of effects at Leeborough, carefully excepting from the sale the whole study and certain things outside the study which I have labeled. I have made the division and can give orders to carry it into effect at a moments notice. In making it I have no doubt committed several errors of judgement and still more of negligence – it is very hard to avoid mistakes in going through thousands of articles. I feel pretty confident that you will not blame me for having made the divide on my own. The only alternatives were to risk the loss of a very considerable sum of money or to leave the division to make itself during a two days visit from me surrounded by auctioneers and relations. The only thing I have left wholly out is the trunk of 'characters' in the attic. If you are home before the house is sold, we can act together: if not, it can go to storage with the things in the study.

Of course it is very likely that no one will buy before April – and you may add 'Or after': and it is one of the disadvantages of what I have done that in that case you will return to a Leeborough hideously changed by my conversion of the study into a store. But I can say quite honestly from my experience of the last ten days that I believe it will be a damned sight pleasanter to get it all at once like that than to watch it gradually assume that aspect. I certainly had the idea that we could still have a few days of the old type, but as soon as you get there you see that it's quite impossible. As there are no silences in the Arctic circle, because there's no noise, so there can be no nonp'daita days when there's no P'daita. If we are there together in April the only thing to do is to give up from the start any idea that it is the real thing again. If we start on that basis we may get along quite well: on any other you'll find that it gives you the blues like the devil.

As to the points in your letter. Re *List of Securities*. Of course in the question of dividing this I shall do nothing till you come home. Like you, I can make very little of it: indeed I cannot sometimes resist a smile at the idea that he keeps the secret of 'his little bit of savings' as tenaciously as ever. But there are certainly a good many steam tramways. As to *what Condlin means* – for the Lord's sake don't ask me. A very short interview with Condlin invariably reduces me to the state of wondering which of us is mad. As for gratuities: to the Witch of Endor £100 by P's own request. To Condlin – I should like to be decent to him, but have no idea what one can do. His social and financial status are so very indeterminate that I am not sure whether he falls in the class to whom one gives money or the class to whom one gives keepsakes. I am rather afraid he falls in that class to whom one gives money, but only in enormous quantities. We must talk this over when we meet.

Window – I am greatly attracted by this idea, but have no idea what the cost would be.[102] I suggest as a preliminary that the sum realised by the sale of Mammy's jewelry* should be set aside as the basis of a fund for this purpose. *Silver*. The whole question of valuables kept by me, for of course I shall keep more than you (furniture etc.) is rather a problem. Everything has been valued for probate, so that I suppose we had better add up the values of all articles kept by either of us: and the man with the heavier list (i.e. SPB) hands over the difference. The other way is to auction everything and let us appear as bidders, but I don't fancy that. I think the best thing would be to hand over our several keeps (excluding communal keeps) for re-evaluation by some competent person – the value for probate being a little lower than real market value. We should then get a sum like this.

Realised by the sale.	*£x.*
W's share of this	*£$x/2$*
J's share of this	*£$x/2$*
But W. keeps	*£30*
J. keeps	*£150*
J. pays W. £150 – 30	*£120*
W. now has	*$x/2$ plus 120 (plus 30's worth)*
i.e. $x/2$ plus 150	
J. now has $x/2$ plus 150's worth	
i.e. $x/2$ plus 150	

---

102 In 1935 Jack and Warnie gave a stained glass window to St Mark's, Dundela, in memory of their parents.

This is no doubt a cumbersome way of representing a simple operation but you know that these things are not my long suit.

One of the pities of the present state of affairs seems to be that it is impossible for either of us to write the other a real letter. I will try to break the spell by giving you some account of my adventures since you last heard from me before the great divide. The chief adventure is the quite new light thrown on P. by a closer knowledge of his two brothers. One of his failings – his fussily directed manner 'Have you got your keys etc.' – takes on a new air when one discovers that in his generation the brothers all habitually treated one another in exactly the same way.

On the morning of the funeral Uncle Dick arrived before breakfast and came to Uncle Bill who was sleeping in the spare room. I drifted in. After a few greetings, it was with a shock of mild surprise that I heard Limpopo suddenly cut short a remark of Uncle Dick's with the words 'Now Dick, you'd better go and take off your collar, huh, (gesture) and wash yourself and that sort of thing, eh, and have a bit of a shave.' To which his brother, with perfect seriousness replied 'Now how had we better handle the thing, eh Jacks? You'd better go to the bathroom first and I'll go downstairs and get a cup of tea. Bill, you'd better lie down (gesture) and cover yourself up and I'll come and tell you...' Limpopo (cutting in) 'Well Dick, get along downstairs, huh, and Jacks will go and tell you, wouldn't that be best, eh?'

Later in the day we had a session of the wardrobe committee quite in the old manner: and in the afternoon I was told 'Jacks, show Mrs Hamilton that coat you found. Isn't it a splendid fit, huh, might have been made for him, wha'?'

Another light came to me during the visit to the undertakers: the whole scene had such an insane air of diabolical farce that I cannot help recording it. After a man with a dusty face had approached me with the assurance that he had buried my grandfather, my mother, and my uncle, a superior person led us into an inner room and inquired if we wanted 'a suite of coffins'. Before I had recovered from this – and it sounded like the offer of some scaly booking clerk at an hotel in hell – the brute suddenly jerked out of the wall a series of enormous vertical doors, each one of which when lowered revealed on its inner side a specimen coffin. We were quite surrounded by them. Slapping one of them like a drum with his resonant hand he remarked 'That's a coffin I'm always very fond of' and it was then that the 'light' came.

Limpopo – and even Limpopo came as a relief in such an atmosphere – put an end to this vulgarity by saying in his deepest bass 'What's been used before, huh? There must be some tradition about the thing. What has the custom been in the family, eh?' And then I suddenly saw, what I'd never seen before: that to them family traditions – the square sheet, the two thirty dinner, the gigantic overcoat – were what school traditions and college traditions are, I don't say to me, but to most of our genera- tion. It is so simple once you know it. How could it be otherwise in those large Victorian families with their intense vitality, when they had not been to public schools and when the family was actually the solidest institution they experienced? It puts a great many things in a more sym- pathetic light than I ever saw them in before.

But apart from these two lights, what I carried away from those few days was the feeling (perhaps I mentioned it before) that all the other members of that family were only fragments of our own P'daitabird. Uncle Dick has the wheezes, but only the crudest of them and none of the culture. In Joey you see the wheeze side of the character gone to seed – the man whose con- versation is nothing but giggles. In Limpopo, of course you see simply all the bad points without any of the good: with the additional property of being an outrageous bore, which is the one thing P. never was at any time.

His idea of conversation is almost unbelievable. On the evening of the day of his arrival, after dinner, having been supplied with whiskey, he drew up the little wooden seated study chair to the fire, and having placed his little tubby body in it and crossed his flaccid hands on his belly, proceeded to enunciate the following propositions. 'I usually leave town about quarter to six, huh, and then I get out to Helensburgh about quarter past and walk up to me house, eh, and then I (Jacks I'll have another drop of that whiskey) put on an old coat, huh, then I come down and have something to drink and a bit of a chat with your Aunt Minnie, huh, and then...' Without any exaggeration, he kept me up till 1.30 with this drivel. The last night, when the Hamiltonians were there, was much better. Limpopo explained that he had given up dealing with Hogg. 'The last suit he sent me...the trousers came up to my chin (ges- ture)...I was very nearly going to law with him.' *Uncle Gussie*: 'I think you should. You should have gone into court wearing that suit.' *Limpopo* (with profound gravity) 'Oh, I wouldn't like to have done that, huh.'

While in Ireland we had two days off from work. On one the Greeves's motored us up the coast road and up the glens of Antrim: on the other Uncle Gussie and Aunt Annie took us down to Cloghy to their cottage at the end of the Ards. The beauty of both drives you know without need of description. Which reminds me, come what may, you and I must have that walk to the Mournes: after a fortnight or so of breaking up and other horrors at Leeborough, it would be just the thing to get the taste out of our mouths. I don't know that I have any other news. I seem to have read nothing except for work – indeed to have had no normal life or leisure – for ages. One scrap worth quoting comes to my mind from a Wynyard letter of yours which I read before putting it into the box. It began 'Mrs Capron died today and we are all very sorry about it. Mr Capron is in a very bad temper over it.' *Ex ore infantium*[103] – could that be bettered? One book I did read during P's illness was 'All quiet on the Western front':[104] but perhaps I mentioned that to you before.

I suppose I shall hear from you again before April – let me have exact dates of arrival as soon as you can. By the way, do they schedule troopships to arrive at a certain day – or week – or month? I feel more bored at present than I ever remember feeling.

yrs,
Jack

* If any. Jewelry is not v. easy to sell at present I hear.

P.S. If we had both volumes of the 1st Editn. of the Jungle Book[105] we could probably get £40 or £50 for it: but after hunting high and low I can find only one.

---

103 Matthew 21:16 (Vulgate): 'Out of the mouths of babes and sucklings [thou has perfected praise].'
104 The German author Erich Maria Remarque (1898–1970) published his great novel of the First World War under the title *Im Westen Nichts Neues* (1929). Arthur Wesley Wheen's English translation, *All Quiet on the Western Front*, was published the same year.
105 Kipling, *The Jungle Book*. They had a 1897 reprint of *The Jungle Book*, first published in 1894, but a first edition of *The Second Jungle Book* (1895) and they retained both of them.

TO ARTHUR GREEVES (W):

Hillsborough,
Headington,
Oxford.
[27 December 1929]

My dear Arthur,

The perfect guest again! An awful thing has happened: I find that I have not got with me my three most valuable keys. I have wired to the Ulster Monarch[106] & had an answer to say that they cannot be found. My last hope is that they are in the study. Will you please look and then let me know, but do *not* send them till further notice. There are three tied together with string, two ordinary looking keys and one very short & shiny one. They may be in the key hole of my father's desk – i.e. the small one in the key hole & the other two hanging from it – or on the top of the same desk. As one of the keys is my college key which will cost me £100 if I lose it, I am rather in a stew & shall be glad to have a line as soon as possible. Just like me, you will say.

Many thanks & much love from us both. Minto is writing in a few days.

Yrs

Jack

P.S. Of course have a look elsewhere, but if they're not in the study I expect they're a gonner. If you get them please take them home with you (after making sure that the desk is locked) & guard them carefully till further notice. Shall write as soon as I can.[107]

[Hillsboro
1929]
Dec. 21st

Although if I had had my choice I should have preferred some real talk between you and me alone, still I think it worth while to say that I felt something very pleasant in our final chat with John[108] and our drinking on board the Ulster Monarch. On occasions that are rather melancholy a plunge into the cheery and homely world of 'good fellows' and women has something of the same wholesome effect as a romp with

---

106 The cross-channel boat on which Lewis and Mrs Moore returned from Ireland on 20 December.
107 Greeves wired on 28 December to say he had found the keys.
108 Arthur's brother, John Greeves.

dogs or children; it was specially appropriate to this visit too, since the main thing that I bring away with me is a new view of John. Besides, as Barfield said when Christie interrupted us one night that he was staying in College, it is rather important that friends should occasionally share together their experience of a third person.

Dec. 22nd

I think the L.N.W.R. mainline must run through the dullest country in the British Isles – tho' of course no country is without some charm. I read *Grace Abounding* in Everyman, having (you remember) read *Mr Badman* in the same volume on the way over. *Grace Abounding* is incomparably the better of the two. Some of the sentences in it reach right down. 'But the milk and honey is beyond this wilderness'[109] – 'I thought I could have spoken of his love and his mercy even to the very crows that sat upon the ploughed lands before me'[110] – 'I could not find that with all my soul I did *desire* deliverance.'[111] Of course a great part of it paints the horrors of religion and sometimes almost of insanity. What do you make of the curious temptation that assailed him just after he had been converted and felt himself united to Christ; when a voice kept saying 'Sell Him, sell Him': sometimes for hours at a stretch, until in mere weariness Bunyan blurted out 'Let Him go if he will'[112] – which afterwards led him into despair, believing he had committed the unpardonable sin?

I suppose this is the same mental disease of which you and I have felt a trace in the impulse to throw ones new book in the fire – some strange twist that impels you to do a thing because it is precisely the one thing of all others that you *don't* want to do.

I should like to know, too, in general, what you think of all the darker side of religion as we find it in old books. Formerly I regarded it as mere devil worship based on horrible superstitions. Now that I have found, and am still finding more and more, the element of truth in the old beliefs, I feel I cannot dismiss even their dreadful side so cavalierly. There must be something in it: only what?

---

109 John Bunyan, *Grace Abounding and The Life and Death of Mr Badman*, with an
    Introduction by G.M. Harrison, Everyman's Library [1928], preface, p. 6.
110 ibid., para. 92, p. 31.
111 ibid., para. 194, p. 34.
112 ibid., para. 139, p. 44.

Dec. 23rd

Delighted to get back to my books again and did a good morning's work on Chaucer, mostly textual problems. Too wet for anything but a short walk after lunch. In the evening wrote part of a long letter to Warnie. I find I am (so far) surprisingly little upset about the affair of my keys.

Dec. 24th

Into town in the morning to get my hair cut, and then, before lunch, began indexing my Bunyan. I had a lovely walk in the afternoon – a perfect winter day with mellow sunlight slanting through a half frosty mist on the grey fields, the cosy farms, and the tall leafless elms, absolutely unmoving in the air. On my way back the sun was down and it was cold. I passed two men engaged in penning sheep and walked just by the baa-ing crowd, whose breath looked like smoke.

At seven in to College to dine, which I didn't much enjoy as I got an awful bore called Parker[113] on my left and on my right the Italian professor[114] whose English is so bad that I can't understand *him*, and who is so deaf that he can't understand *me*.

At 9 o'clock we went up into hall for the Christmas Eve revels, which of course I have never seen before. The hall looks very noble with its green branches, and a roaring fire and the centre cleared, and a Christmas tree. Female guests, including, of course Minto and Maureen, were in the musicians gallery. From 9 to 10 the choir gave us the first part of the *Messiah*: a great mistake, I thought, with only a piano at our disposal for accompaniment. Then came an interval during which those who had no guests remained in hall for supper and to watch the choir boys having *their* Christmas supper, which is the best sight of all: I, and others in the same plight, went down to common room to feed our ladies on sandwiches and hot negus and talk small talk. We returned to hall to find lights out and candles lit on the tree and to hear carols: all the really good ones like the Coventry Carol and *In dulci jubilo* and one by Byrd that I never heard before. This last comes just on the stroke of midnight

---

113 Henry Michael Denne Parker (1894–1972), Fellow and Tutor in Ancient History at Magdalen College. Lewis usually referred to him as the 'Wounded Buffalo' or 'Wounded Bison'. See his portrait of him in *AMR*, 'Magdalen College Appendix', pp. 480–1.

114 Professor Cesare Foligno. See note 10 to the letter of 30 March 1927.

after the Vice President has sent a message to the ringers to begin the peals. I had been rather bored with the proceedings earlier in the evening but at this moment the glorious windy noise of the bells overhead, the firelight & candlelight, and the beautiful music of unaccompanied boys voices, really carried me out of myself. We then have sack passed round in a loving cup and pledge one another and so break up: home by taxi at about 12.30.

Taking it all in all, with the walk and the evening, and the blessed sense of charity, so rare in me, – the feeling, natural at such a moment that even my worst enemies in college were really funny and odd rather than detestable, while my friends were 'the many men so beautiful'[115] – this was as good a day as I could wish to have. If only it wasn't for those damned keys!

Dec. 25th

A slack day. All up very late after our debauch of the night before. Went for several short strolls with Mr Papworth, but no real walk. My afternoon one, about five o'clock was the best: an evening of bitter wind with the trees lashing one another across a steel coloured sunset. Afterwards – as a Christmas treat! – I read a modern novel, H. G. Wells' *Meanwhile*[116] which deals chiefly with the General Strike, and contains very good comic elements. You and I ought to read, think and talk of these things more than we do.

Dec. 26th

Another lazy day. Went in to College at about 10.30, by arrangement to go for a walk with McFarlane. We were on the road by about eleven. Neither of us was at first disposed for more than desultory chat. The trudge out of Oxford was tedious (as always) and I did not really begin to enjoy myself till we had climbed Cumnor Hill. Once through the beautiful grey and mossy village of Cumnor, I became extremely pleased with everything. Walking on unfrequented paths, we hardly met a soul: the sky was palest blue, without a cloud or a breeze, and the weak sun laid a lovely unity of pale colour over the ploughed fields, the haystacks and the church towers in each village. 'Unity of colour' is not just a phrase – I mean that everything, except the woods (which of course were brownish-black) and the crows, was almost the same colour of chilly greenish grey.

---

115 Coleridge, *The Rime of the Ancient Mariner*, Part IV, 236.
116 H.G. Wells, *Meanwhile* (1927).

As we dropped down the far side of the hill the floods began to spread themselves out wider and wider below us. Where the Thames should have been there was a sheet of water about a mile broad, intersected with the tops of hedges and polled willows. We began to wonder whether we could reach the ferry at Bablock Hythe. I was in favour of taking off shoes & stockings, not, of course, to wade the river, but to wade the shallow flood to the real river bank where the ferry begins. McFarlane however couldn't as one of his feet was bandaged under the sock as the result of wearing a tight shoe yesterday. However, when we got there, and called, the man at the pub brought a punt not only across the river but across the floods to where we stood. Once over, we feasted in the pub on bread & cheese, beer, and a following cup of tea – my invariable walking lunch. It left us in that delightful state which (I remember) Harwood once described – 'One is neither full nor hungry and goes on like a ship.' As it was boxing day, no one was working in the fields, and all was so still that the wheeling starlings made quite a noticeable noise.

You know how it sometimes is when you are out for a day's jaunt – as it has so often happened to you and me – that there comes a period when things are getting better and better every moment till suddenly one says 'Oh!' or 'By God!' and that is IT – the centre of the whole day, the thing one will remember it by. Such was the moment when the old man came over the gate in the frost-mist up by our wood: or when we saw the fire that night near the house of the sinister old man who sold lemonade: or when we were shown into the postmistress's cottage above the glens of Antrim. To day was of course totally different from all these. It happened by luck that two things came at the same moment.

We came round a turn into the village of Stanton Harcourt and suddenly got a view of the towered manor house and the church, across a farmyard, where a very fine old horse with a white star on his forehead was looking at us across a half gate. That was the first thing. And at the very same moment – this is the second thing – the ringers in the church began practicing their peal. It sounds poor on paper, but the thing about it was the sense of absolute peace and safety: the utter homeliness, the Englishness, the Christendom of it. And then I thought of Antrim only a week or so ago, and what you said (in the rainbow and sleet scene on Divis – itelf another instance of this *apex* in the day's outing) about the 'broad-mindedness' of the infinite – Antrim that's desolate and keen in July, Stanton Harcourt and all the sleepy Cumnor country (isn't the very name Cumnor good) which is snug and dreamy and like cotton wool even in winter.

Perhaps it is less strange that the Absolute should make both than that we should be able to love both. Bacon says 'The whole world cannot fill, much less distend the mind of man.'[117] (By the way, that is the answer to those who argue that the universe cannot be spiritual because it is so vast and inhuman and alarming. On the contrary, nothing less would do for us. At our best, we can stand it, and could not stand anything smaller or snugger. Anything less than the terrifyingly big would, at some moments, be cramping and 'homely' in the bad sense – as one speaks of a 'homely' face. You can't have elbow room for things like men except in endless time and space and staggering multiplicity.)[118]

A few miles beyond Stanton Harcourt – in the tower of that manor house, by the way, Mr Pope translated 'his Iliads'[119] – the peace of the afternoon was broken by brutes in the distance firing guns. The only good result of this was that it started a pair of white owls to blunder across our road, stupid with the daylight, poor chaps, and very grotesque to see. We had tea at Eynsham, and sitting over the fire in the pub there we fell (at last) into serious conversation – about the rival claims of reason and instinct. We continued this on the homeward journey – a long stretch of road (we dared not try the tow-path in the floods) which would have been dull by daylight. Now that the stars were out it was good enough. The remains of the sunset was before us, and all between us and it seemed to be water. McFarlane observed that it was one of the rare occasions on which night seemed a tangible thing: and looking back I saw what he meant, for the darkness and stars did seem to come up at our backs and then stop just over our heads, while in front was twilight.

We got back to Oxford, very happy but very footsore and tired, at about 6.30, and I was home (by bus) at about 7. Finished *Meanwhile*

---

117 A conflation of several lines of Francis Bacon's *The Advancement of Learning* (1605), First Book, I, 3.

118 Cf. 'Dogma and the Universe', in Lewis's *God in the Dock: Essays on Theology*, ed. Walter Hooper (London: Fount Paperbacks, 1979); *God in the Dock: Essays on Theology and Ethics*, ed. Walter Hooper (Grand Rapids: Eerdmans, 1970). 'What sort of universe do we demand? If it is small enough to be cosy, it would not be big enough to be sublime. If it is large enough for us to stretch our spiritual limbs in, it must be large enough to baffle us...It is to be expected that His creation should be, in the main, unintelligible to us.'

119 Alexander Pope, *The Iliad*, 6 vols. (1715–20).

after supper and took a hot bath to cure my stiffness – this being the first real exercise I have had for ages. It only needed a more perfectly receptive companion – such as you – to have made it one of the really great days: not that McFarlane is half bad, and one ought to learn to like more, and more different, people.

Dec 27th

Worked at Chaucer all morning. After lunch as I was carrying a plate into the scullery I suddenly got one of those vivid mental pictures that memory sometimes throws up for no apparent reason – a picture of the deep stony and brambly vallies on the side of Scrabo, wet and grey as they were one day when you and I came down that way. 'Jesus, the times this knight and I have had!'[120] (That's from Henry IV. Read it all, but specially the scene where Falstaff meets his old acquaintance Shallow in the country – one of the best 'Do you remember' conversations in any book that I know.)

After lunch Maureen took Mr Papworth for a walk, which always gives me a blessed liberation to go where I choose: for much as I like Mr P., his presence is a considerable restraint. You can't go *that* way because there is a dog that fights: and you can't go *that* way because there are sheep and you have to keep him on the lead. In fact it is rather like Dick Swiveller's walks in London.[121] I bussed into College, took out the second chapter of my book[122] & left it at the house of a Professor in Marston who had promised to give me his views on it. Thence home up the hill under grey and windy skies with a little rain. I tried my practice of keeping myself free from thought – a mere sponge to sense impressions – for a certain part of the way. Later I hope to resume the higher stage of meditation proper. Went on with Chaucer before supper: afterwards wrote to Condlin, Aunt Annie, Uncle Bill, Uncle Dick and you.

Dec. 28th

Went to Barfield's to day for my stay. Thanks awfully about the keys – your wire was a great relief. When will *your* big letter arrive? –

Yours

J

---

120 A conflation of lines 228–9 and lines 236–7 in Shakespeare's *Henry IV, Part 2*, III, ii.
121 A character in Charles Dickens' *The Old Curiosity Shop* (1841).
122 i.e. *The Allegory of Love.*

1930

___ ❦ ___

TO ARTHUR GREEVES (W):

[Hillsboro]
3rd Jan 1930

My dear Arthur,

By now I hope you have my long letter and are well advanced with your long reply. You shall have another gripping instalment, D.V., in the course of the next ten days. We both enjoyed your description of your visit to the witches den,[1] most of which I read aloud to Minto. I am now, as you will already have guessed, going to give you the opportunity of paying her another one! This time it is my cheque book (Bank of Ireland) – which is unlikely to be in my Father's desk – tho' it may be, my dear fellow, it may be – and may be in the study or at Bernagh. If found it could be sent by post: and any odd collars or handkerchiefs left at Bernagh would be convenient packing. Don't hate me for ever!

Yours
Jack

TO ARTHUR GREEVES (W):

[Hillsboro
13? January 1930]

My dear Arthur:

Thurs Jan 2

Got home to day from four day's stay with Barfield. For the first two days his wife and adopted baby[2] were away, so we had the house to ourselves – alas that you and I never have such an uninterrupted feast of each other's society.

---

1 i.e. 'The Witch of Endor' (Mary Cullen), the cook-housekeeper at Little Lea.
2 Alexander Barfield (b. 1928).

We had promised ourselves some solid reading together, and in spite of the temptations of conversation and walking, we stuck to it: Aristotle's *Ethics* all morning, walk after lunch, and then Dante's *Paradiso* for the rest of the day.

The latter has really opened a new world to me. I don't know whether it is really very different from the *Inferno* (B. says its as different as chalk from cheese – heaven from hell, would be more appropriate!) or whether I was specially receptive, but it certainly seemed to me that I had never seen at all what Dante was like before. Unfortunately the impression is one so unlike anything else that I can hardly describe it for your benefit – a sort of mixture of intense, even crabbed, complexity in language and thought with (what seems impossible) *at the very same time* a feeling of spacious gliding movement, like a slow dance, or like flying. It is like the stars – endless mathematical subtility of orb, cycle, epicycle and ecliptic, unthinkable & unpicturable, & yet at the same time the freedom and liquidity of empty space and the triumphant certainty of movement. I should describe it as feeling more *important* than any poetry I have ever read. Whether it has the things you specially like is another question. It is seldom homely: perhaps not *holy* in our sense – it is too Catholic for that: and of course its blend of complexity and beauty is very like Catholic theology – wheel within wheel, but wheels of glory, and the One radiated through the Many.

One night we sat up till four, and heard the cock's crowing as we went to bed: a very good moment, and who shall I ever find to share it with me fully? For *you* would be too sleepy, and Barfield doesn't really taste a thing like that as keenly as you and I. They have a most delightful house, an ex-farmhouse with many outbuildings and an orchard: in one of the most beautiful villages I know. We had one very good walk among the floods, and one very good sky.

Frid. Jan 3

In the Bodleian all morning. Back after lunch, arriving there at 3 o'clock to find it shutting! Bought the new book on Malory by Vinaver[3] at 15/-, which is necessary for work, but not worth the price.

---

3 Eugène Vinaver, *Malory* (1929).

Sunday Jan 5th

I spent the morning finishing a long letter on philosophical subjects which I had carried about with me all the time in Ireland, to my
friend and former pupil, Griffiths. It was owing to this that you have no
Saturday's instalment from me: and if you knew how long Griffiths had
waited for an answer you would not grudge it to him.

In the afternoon I had a most delicious walk, in that rarified afternoon sunlight which I have tried to describe so often. It is the peculiar
glory of the English winter. Apart from a period of meditation – mind-
emptying, I mean – which was fairly successful, I was on the whole
as free from thought and fancies as I have been for a long time. Two
moments are worth preserving.

One, when I suddenly paused, as we do for no reason known to consciousness, and gazed down into a little ditch beneath a grey hedge,
where there was a pleasant mixture of ivies and low plants and mosses,
and thought of herbalists and their art, and what a private, retired wisdom it would be to go groping along such hedges and the eaves of woods
for some herb of virtuous powers, insignificant to the ordinary observer,
but well known to the trained eye – and having at the same time a
stronger sense of the mysteries of living stuff than usual, specially the
mysteries twining at our feet, where homeliness and magic embrace one
another.

The second was a stiffish five minutes up-hill towards a hedge of
small trees and bushes, behind wh. the sun was setting. A keen frosty
wind in my face: all beyond me flaming yellow, and on that yellow, in
perfect black, the rich and varied pattern of the hedge, looking quite flat,
so that the whole had a Chinese or Japanese appearance.

In the evening I started to read the Everyman volume of Jacob
Boehme[4] which I had ordered sometime ago. The Dialogue at the end,
called the Supersensual Life, was fairly easy going, and I should advise
you to get and read it at once. Then I turned back and began the longer
work, the Signatura Rerum. I could see at once that I was reading the
most serious attempt I had ever met to describe (not to explain, for he
speaks as one who has seen and his description *is* his explanation) – to
describe the very mystery of creation and to show you the differences

---

4 Jacob Boehme, *The Signature of all Things, with Other Writings* [translated by John
Ellistone], Introduction by Clifford Bax, Everyman's Library [1912].

actually coming into being out of the original One and making a world and souls and good and evil. Almost at the same time, I saw, alas, that it was hopelessly beyond me: yet tantalising for I could just grasp enough to be quite sure that he was talking about something tremendously real, and not merely mystifying you.

I had two quite distinct experiences in reading it. (a) Certain sentences moved and excited me although I couldn't understand them – as the mysterious words in the Crock of Gold, which Aengus told the Philosopher. In case they may have the same effect on you I quote two of them: 'That the nothing is become an eternal life and has found itself, which cannot be, in the Stillness.'[5] – 'The wrath extinguishes and the turning orb stands still, and instead of the turning a sound is caused in the essence.'[6] (b) At certain points a feeling of distress, and even of horror. I had always assumed, in my way, that if I could reach the things Boehme is here talking about, I should *like* them! There is something really very dreadful in this second chapter of the Signatura. (You'll think I'm putting this on *just a little bit*. Honestly, I'm not.) I intend to try and get hold of some good commentator on this book, if there is one, and worrey out the meaning.

In the meantime, I wish to record that it has been about the biggest shaking up I've got from a book, since I first read *Phantastes*. It is not such a pleasant experience as Phantastes, and if it continues to give me the same feeling when I understand more I shall give it up. No fooling about for me: and I keep one hand firmly gripped round the homely & simple things. But it is a real book: i.e. it's not like a book at all, but like a thunderclap. Heaven defend us – what things there are knocking about the world!

Monday [Jan. 6]

Morning's work in town as usual and to the station at 1.30 to see the Harwoods whose train was stopping there for ten minutes. I shall always think of you in connection with him, as through your imitations of his manner, he has become one of our stock characters. It was a silly and useless tryst – nothing can be less like conversation than chatter at a carriage door with a man in the presence of his wife and two babies –

---

5 ibid., ch. II, para. 18, p. 16.
6 ibid., ch. II, para. 19, p. 16.

and I only kept it to return a pair of skates wh. he left in my rooms last winter.

I walked as usual after lunch, dropping in on the way to see if old Foord-Kelsie would accompany me. I think I have mentioned him to you – a retired country parson of 80, who drives his own car, carpenters, and mends everyone's wireless. He is an irreplaceable character – a great reader, specially of *Tristram Shandy*, Boswell, & *Pickwick* – and as redolent of English country life as an old apple in a barn. He is deliciously limited: cares for no poetry but Shakespeare, distrusts all mysticism and imagination, and all overstrained moods. Yet you could not wish him to be otherwise: and inside this almost defiantly human and mundane framework there is such tenderness of heart that one never feels it bleak. He was in his workshop when I arrived, with shavings all about his ankles, making a cover for the font of old Headington Church. He would not come out, and I stayed to shout conversation for fifteen minutes above the thudding and singing of his circular saw. We had a bit of everything: an outburst against Shaw, a broad story, and then, as always, onto Tristram Shandy. 'Wonderful book – oh a wonderful book. You feel *snug* when you read that – you get in among them all in that little parlour. And my uncle Toby – ah (a *very* parsonical, long-drawn, almost devotional *a-a-ah*) ah, a beautiful character. And the jokes – I'm sure I don't know how the rascal thought of it all – the rascal!' I wish you could have seen him saying all this, bending down as he shoved a beam of wood against the saw, with one dear old wrinkled eye screwed up and held close to the work. You must hurry up and come and see me before he dies, for he of all people should be added to our stock characters.

Wed. January 8th

I have just got your excellent letter. I find I am getting great pleasure out of this correspondence – both the writing and the reading. It recalls old times. I quite agree with what you say about letters being haphazard and informal – in their choice of subject. Things ought to come up just as they do in conversation. The actual expression is a different matter. There is such a thing as being unnaturally natural – I mean it doesn't really come naturally to most of us to write exactly as we speak. I say this in self defence, lest you should think I am sometimes trying to be literary. (There's a good example. I should never say *lest* in conversation, but it comes naturally to me in writing perhaps because *lest* is four letters and *for fear* is seven.) My only attempt is to get across the picture in my mind: and in order to do that one *has* to choose ones words, because there is no chance of correcting a wrong impression as we shd. in conversation. As for the diary form, that is not much more than a framework, to keep one going from evening to evening.

I agree about the not looking forward to the time when we shall re-read them. But one's between the devil and the deep sea. That pleasure in the future is the chief spur to diary-writing: and yet to think of it makes the thing artificial. Still, I suppose one can play hide and seek with ones own mind in that way: e.g. in playing a game. You've got to hoodwink yourself into thinking that winning is important, or else it is no fun: and at the same time you've got to remember that it is not important, or else it ceases to be a game.

I liked your description of your second visit to Leeborough – like Arthur at Orgoglio's castle. And I'm glad you have the Smaller Temple. That smell will always carry you back to the old days. Chevasse[7] really has a *talent* for evil, hasn't he? I've had a very busy day, and lots more to do, so good-night. (Tidying up I came across the old prose Dymer the other day. Emotions and comments can be supplied to taste!)

Thurs 9th

Another day all on Chaucer. What I am actually doing is going thro the parts of the Canterbury Tales which I know least with the aid of several commentators, making copious notes and trying to get really 'sound' on them. You see there has been a new edition since my undergraduate days, so that most of my knowledge – it was never very exact – on Chaucer, is out of date. This sounds dull, but as a matter of fact I take great pleasure in it.

What a glory-hole is the commentary of an old author. One minute you are puzzling out a quotation from a French medieval romance: the next, you are being carried back to Plato: then a scrap of medieval law: then something about geomancy: and manuscripts, and the signs of the

---

7 The Rev. Claude Lionel Chavasse (1897–1983), of an Anglo-Irish family, was educated at Haileybury College and Exeter College, Oxford. Following his ordination he was curate of St Mark's, Dundela, 1928–31. He served a number of parishes in County Cork, and was vicar of Kiddington, Oxon, 1947–57. For information about his early life see his essay 'An Irish Setting' in *To Nevill Coghill from Friends*, collected by John Lawlor and W.H. Auden (1966).

Zodiac, and a modern proverb 'reported by Mr Snooks to be common in Derbyshire', and the precession of the equinoxes, and an Arabian optician (born at Balk in 1030), five smoking room stories, the origins of the doctrine of immaculate conception, and why St Cecilia is the patroness of organists. So one is swept from East to West, and from century to century, equally immersed in each oddity as it comes up, and equally sudden in ones flight to the next: like the glimpses (oh how I hate the word *vignette*) that you get from an express train, when the cart going under the bridge seems to be a little world in itself, until it is replaced – instantaneously – by the horses running away from the line in the next field.

About Bunyan – I had forgotten the passage you mention in which a share in judging the damned is held out as one of the pleasures of the saint. I quite agree that it is horrid. As to whether it is contrary to the spirit of Christ – it is certainly not contrary to the letter: for he himself in the Gospels (if I remember rightly) does hold out that very reward to the disciples – 'And ye shall sit on twelve thrones judging the twelve tribes of Israel.'[8] In spite of all my recent changes of view, I am still inclined to think that you can only get what *you* call 'Christ' out of the Gospels by picking & choosing, & slurring over a good deal. However that's as may be. Of course in Bunyan's case, one must remember the persecution he had undergone – which makes his vindictiveness more pardonable than the intolerance of those you speak of who have never suffered anything at the hands of the 'ungodly'.

To day has been a day of howling wind and low, fast-driving clouds, but no rain. On my afternoon walk my 'NO THINKING' period was rather more successful than usual. I find as I go on that one becomes more conscious of ones thought by trying to stop. After shoving out the obvious loud thought, one listens to the whispered thought underneath. When one has checked that, I suppose there will be another layer underneath! Perhaps it is thought all the way down. Anyway, it is not a bad thing to get even this far: to step out of the thinking and listen to it going on. Perhaps it will teach you to control it better when you step back into the stream. Of course the trouble of writing about it is that the words inevitably mean more than one intends: as these, for instance, sound as if I'd got far further than I really have – wh. wasn't

---

8 Luke 22:30: 'That ye may eat and drink at my table in my kingdom, and sit on thrones judging the twelve tribes of Israel'.

the effect I wanted to produce. Oh! my hand is tired. I've been writing on and off nearly all day.

Frid 10th

It will probably be short commons to night for I have been pretty hard at work all day, except for walk, and I feel rather tired. My life tends to go in spurts. When I am interested in a subject, my interest drives me like a daemon, and for a few days the time at meals (or the time spent in digging the hen run and rinsing plates and talking) seems as if it would never be done and let me back to work. And for the first few days I feel as if I could never be tired. Then suddenly, one evening, (tho the interest remains) virtue has gone out of me, and my legs ache and I feel as if I could do nothing. So I shall do slightly different work to morrow. Another lovely day. I think January, when it is fine, is one of the most exquisite months in the year. I love these skies with level alternate bars of pale yellow and of grey, exactly the grey of a grey horse. Also one seems to hear almost as many birds as in spring.

The others were out for tea, and I had another go at Boehme. Much the same effect. I must try him again in different circumstances and at a different time of the year, to see if it is some trick of my health or of the weather that makes this book have such an astonishing effect on me. On the whole, this time there was a little less of the sinking feeling, and a little more understanding. But there is no question that it is full of the most lovely sentences: 'That many a twig withers on the tree is not the tree's fault, for it withdraws its sap from no twig, only the twig gives forth itself too eagerly with the desire: it runs on in self will, it is taken by the inflammation of the sun and the fire, before it can draw sap again in its mother and refresh itself'[9] – 'He breaks self-hood as a vessel wherein he lies captive, and buds forth continually in God's will-spirit, with his desire regained in God, as a fair blossom springs out of the earth'[10] – 'If the soul did but truly know that all beings were its mothers, which brought it forth, and did not hold the mother's substance for its own, but for common.'[11]

---

9 Boehme, *The Signature of all Things*, ch. XVI, para. 36, p. 219.
10 ibid., ch. XV, para. 31, p. 203.
11 ibid., ch. XV, para. 8, p. 198.

I suppose by now you are at, or finished, Henry IV. Isn't Hotspur a wonderful picture of the kind of hearty public school 'no nonsense' type?

I am afraid this correspondence is sure to languish on my side after the end of next week when term begins: it will be your turn then to put your back into it. A letter a day keeps the apples away. (Why not a new slogan – 'Daily castration Prevents Master Bation' – 'Who goes daily to Wadham, he Need have no fear of sodomy' – 'Decapitation each night Teaches you to spell right' – 'Tchanie each afternoon Cures heresy soon.') By the way, I am saddened about the McNeills.[12]

Sunday [Jan. 12]

I have had a letter from Warnie, in which he says that he particularly wants to keep *Mother Goose's Fairy Tales* 'the first book of my own which I ever had – this is written in the front of it'.[13] I find something very pathetic in this sudden streak of sentiment in so unsentimental a character, and I expect you will feel the same, and therefore will not mind facing the Witch again and transferring this book (it is probably on the landing or the room opposite my father's) to the study. At the same time would you (wu-u-u-d) you please send me the MS. book catalogue that Minto made. It is shoved in on top of the books in one of the shelves of the big bookcase on the north wall of the study – i.e. it is probably now behind one of the grandfathers' portraits. I am sorry to keep on sending you on these errands. You must feel rather like Crusoe rowing out to the wreck every few days to bring off a bag of tools or a tin of biskets (That is, by the way, an old and good way of spelling *biscuits*) I expect a good long letter from you any day now –

Yours

Jack

---

12 It is not clear what this means. While neither Janie McNeill nor her mother were ill, they were deeply saddened over the death of Mr Lewis. Janie visited Albert daily during his last illness, and upon his death Mrs McNeill offered Warnie their spare room when he was in Belfast. See their letters to Warnie of 7 January 1930 in LP X: 224–5.

13 The actual title is *Mother Goose's Nursery Rhymes, Tales and Jingles* (London: Frederick Warne and Co. [1890]). Inscribed in it is a note from Albert to Warnie: 'Badgie, his first book from his Papy. Novr. '96.'

TO HIS BROTHER (LP X: 228–32):

Hillsboro,
Western Rd.
Headington,
Oxford.
Jan. 12th. 1930.

My dear W.,

I was very glad to see your handwriting yesterday, tho' a little disappointed at the thinness of the envelope. However, perhaps it would be artificial to try to keep up an ordinary correspondence at present: and even if one starts with the idea 'I'll polish off the business in the first page or so and then go on to a real letter' as I did in my last – the first few pages seem to exhaust all one's desire for writing.

Do you find that the present state of affairs produces a permanent condition of – so to speak – comfortless excitement? Every thing is unsettled: all the old *structure* of things has collapsed and the complete liberty of making plans exactly as we choose, which one would once have sighed for, turns out to be in practice merely a bewildering impossibility of envisaging the future at all.

For the moment however, you will be most anxious to hear about the present, or, as it will be for you, the past. Well up to date Leeboro has not been sold. I will become very anxious as the time draws nearer your return. If a really good offer, *plus* a demand for immediate possession turns up, say, a fortnight before you are due at Liverpool, I really think I shall go out of my mind. And I am afraid, whatever happens, you are bound to be in the pretty b——y situation of setting your foot on shore in complete uncertainty as to whether we can go to Leeboro or not. I think however there is nothing for it but to leave the place (as it is at present) on the houseagent's books, with fires still burning and the Witch still in possession, and to accept the first good offer we get, while secretly hoping that no such offer will come till after April. It is not at all (as one passage of your letter seems to suggest) a question of the cost of upkeep. It is not 'Can we afford to keep it three – or ten – months longer before selling it?' but 'Can we afford to refuse any good offer for a thing that may turn out to be unsaleable?' Can we afford to gamble on the off chance of there being a second good offer *at all*? (Remember, there hasn't been *one* yet.) That is, we are not in the position of an impoverished Victorian Colonel wondering whether he can afford to go on hunting for one season more, but rather in that of a middle aged Victorian spinster wondering if she can safely refuse *any* proposal.

This infernal 'two presents' system – which began by being a joke and has ended by being an incubus – has naturally reduced most of your logical divisions and subdivisions of alternative possibilities to matchwood. To take the points that survive:

As to book keeps. I had already placed in the study as keeps, *The Bab Ballads*,[14] *Out of the Hurley Burley*,[15] *Through the forbidden land*, and Ludwig's *Kaiser Wilhelm*.[16] I am very sorry that I did not know about *Mother Goose*: but I have just finished a letter to Arthur (which will go by next post) asking him to look out for it and, if he can find it, to put it in the study. I cannot say that I distinctly remember having handled it in my recent labours, but I know the book you mean.

The trunk in the attic.[17] I entirely agree with you. Our only model for dealing with our world is the heavenly P'daita's method of dealing with this: and as he has long since announced his intention of ending the universe with a general conflagration, we will follow suit. If you and I are together for it, I should even propose – 'I am serious sir' – that we reduce all the characters to their original lead and bury the solid pig that will result. Rolling stock can of course only be buried as you can't melt tin except in a furnace. I should not like to make an exception even in favour of Benjamin. After all these characters (like all others) can, in the long run, live only in 'the literature of the period': and I fancy that when we look at the actual *toys* again (a process from which I anticipate no pleasure at all), we shall find the discrepancy between the symbol (remember the outwards and visible form of *Hedges, the Beetle* – or *Bar* – or even *Hawki*) and the character, rather acute. No, Brother. The toys in the trunk are quite plainly corpses. We will resolve them into their elements, as nature will do to us. As to *stage sets*: I can't remember whether I did come across some and put them in the chest of paper keeps in the study, or whether I merely decided that if I did come across any I would do so. The solid bits – houses, banks etc – I think should be

---

14 W.S. Gilbert, *The Bab Ballads* (1925).
15 Charles Heber Clark, *Out of the Hurly-Burly, or, Life in an Odd Corner, by Max Adeler* [1874].
16 Emil Ludwig, *Kaiser Wilhelm II* [1926].
17 i.e. the trunk containing the Boxen toys.

burned: but a few side and back sheets should be preserved in *Leeboro Studies*.[18]

The New little end room The most jarring comment on this proposal reached me before the proposal itself, in the form of a rather offensive letter from that old harridan Aunt Mary,[19] to the following effect – that she had heard that Little Lea was going to be sold: that she supposed I knew about the two book cases of Uncle Joe's that P. has 'stored' for him: that she very much wanted to have them: could she send and have them taken away at once: she had expected to see me at Christmas etc. etc. The minute I read it I knew in my bones that it was our little end room bookcases. I replied: that I should certainly not hold a sale without giving my relations the chance of mentioning to me any articles which did not belong to you and me: that I had never heard of the articles she mentioned, but if she would describe them I would order them to be set aside, so that she need have no fear of their being confused with other things: (I very nearly wrote 'of our own things' but decided to make no *admission* of her claim until I was forced): that if she really required them for immediate use, of course we must make some other arrangement: but that I should very much prefer not to start dismembering the house before you returned.

By the same post I forwarded to Condlin an abstract of both letters and asked his advice, which I expect in a day or two. Of course if they are really hers (as I suspect) they will have to be given to her: but I don't choose to be jostled into settling these sort of things single handed the moment a greedy and possibly mendacious old woman tackles me. Well that is the first and great comment on your plan of a new little end room.

The second is that to my mind the question largely turns on another: if we can succeed in getting another and larger house than Hillsboro, and you (as I hope – but this comes in a later paragraph) are with us, should such a room be there or in College. Thirdly, apart from these questions, your proposal is one that I partly agree with and partly disagree with. It

---

18 'Leeborough Studies' or 'Leeboro Studies' is described in the 'Encyclopedia Boxoniana' (*Boxen*, op. cit., p. 201) as: 'A series of drawings of all period collection in two exercise books with limp yellow covers'. The 'Studies' are now in the Wade Center, Wheaton College, Wheaton, Illinois.

19 This was Mrs Mary Tagert Lewis (1868–1941), the widow of Albert's brother, Joseph. See **The Lewis Family** in the Biographical Appendix.

runs in your letter 'A place where we can always meet on the common ground of the past and *ipso facto* a museum of the Leeborough we want to preserve'.

Now my view would run 'A place where we can always meet on the common ground of the past and present and *ipso facto* a continuation and development of the Leeborough etc.' You see, Pigiebuddie, a *museum* is preciously like a *mausoleum*. An attempt at exact reconstruction (supposing it could succeed – wh. it can't in a room of quite different size and shape –) would fix the externals of a certain period for ever. But if you and I had gone home and lived at Leeborough, that is precisely what wouldn't have happened. Sooner or later we should have substituted good prints for the groups. As our library grew, new bookcases would have come. In the mere course of time the long thin table would have finished the process which it had already made a good start on, of falling to pieces. A thing fixed in imitation of the little end room as it is, can only be a perpetual reminder that that whole life is not *going on*. If it were going on, it would gradually change. The mere act of setting up your present French library introduces a new element. The unavoidable presence of my books (I have about twice as many there now as there were in the Little End Room) introduces another.

I want to give full weight to two considerations (1) That distance, and a long fast, makes the little end room even more poignant a picture to you than to me. (2) That the general trend of our lives, you having never had any real kind of *chez toi* except it, has some effect. Whether I ought to set against this the fact that by temperament – as opposed to circumstances – I am probably the more sentimental bloke of the two, is doubtful. I don't think I am really being influenced by considerations of my own convenience – because in any case I should *have* to keep a great many non-Pigiebotian books in that room: and I can quite honestly say that I am, to the best of my knowledge, not influenced at all by any Forsytian desire to 'call my rooms my own' or nonsense of that sort. On the contrary I had already proposed to myself that some room – whether in a house or in College – (College has certain advantages) should become in the fullest sense '*our room*' and in that way be a 'new little end room'. And of course such a room would naturally contain most of the Leeboro relics that we shall keep. And further, you and I would tackle the problem of fitting up this room together just as if we had bought a house and were tackling it there. In all this we are in full agreement.

What I [am] thinking [is] that an attempt to imitate the little end room in detail would be a mistake. A mistake in sentiment, for it could only mean that we were embalming the corpse of something that isn't really dead, and needn't die at all. An aesthetic mistake – because we don't really want to have the taste of our schooldays established as a boundary for our whole lives: and also, you can't really fit up a room with complete neglect of its actual shape and size. A utilitarian mistake because you'll find in practice that the draughts and lights of *this* room and the habits of *this* life demand their own treatment. But perhaps all this argument is unnecessary: firstly because we shall probably not have the bookcases, and secondly because, once you get here, with things round you, and the actual room in front of you, you will probably develop ideas about our arrangements quite as quickly – and quite as independently of mere imitation – as I shall. No doubt we shall have differences: well, we must quarrel about them and settle in the old way.

What I am chiefly talking against in all this is the faint implication that the *past* is the only 'common ground' on which we can meet. I think, perhaps this is an occasion for frankness – a virtue which should be very sparingly used, but not never. I have no doubt that there have been times when you have felt that, shall we call it, Pigiebotianism was in danger of being swallowed up by, shall we say, Hillsborovianism: at such moments you may even have felt that the past was the only common ground – that wearing the national costume had become, as in Wales, an archaic revival. I am very sorry to have been the cause of such a period (this is not an apology but a statement) – but isn't that period itself passed? We have both changed since the real old days, but, on the whole, we have changed in the same direction. We are really much nearer together now than in the days when I was writing ridiculous epic poems at Cherbourg and you were wearing scarcely less ridiculous patent leathers at the Coll.

Now, as to your own plans. If you decide to become a full and permanent member of the household, you will be very welcome to all of us: and I must confess that it doesn't seem good enough that the two Piggiebudda should spend so much of their life divided by the whole breadth of the planet. Having laid this down as a starting point, you won't I hope think that I am trying to dissuade you if I put up certain signposts. e.g. I Suppose you do realize that to exchange an institutional for a domestic life is a pretty big change. (I take it for granted obviously that as a permanent member you neither could nor would wish to have, even remotely, the guest status.) Both kinds of life have their discomforts: and *all* discomforts are in a sense intolerable. The great thing is to choose with one's eyes open. Can you stand as a permanency our cuisine – Maureen's practising – Maureen's sulks – Minto's burnetto-desmondism – Minto's mare's nests – the perpetual interruptions of family life – the partial loss of liberty? This sounds as if I were either sick of it myself or else trying to make you sick of it: but neither is the case. I have definitely chosen and don't regret the choice. What I hope – very much hope – is that you, after consideration, may make the same choice, and not regret it: what I can't risk is your just floating in on the swell of a mood and then feeling trapped and fed up. Of course to weigh it fairly one must compare the best of this sort of life with the best of the other, and the worst of this with the worst of the other. What one is tempted to do is just the opposite – when one is exasperated in a home, to compare it with one of those splendid evenings one had in a mess or common room. Of course what one ought to do is to weigh it against the evening with the mess bore. On the whole my judgement would be that domestic life denies me a great many pleasures and saves me a great many pains.

There is also this further point. I spoke above of Pigiebotianism and Hillsborovianism. I presume that if you join us you are prepared for a certain amount of compromise in this matter. I shall never be prepared to abandon Pigiebotianism to Hillsborovianism. On the other hand there are the others to whom I have given the right to expect that I shall not abandon Hillsborovianism to Pigiebotianism. Whether I was right or wrong, wise or foolish, to have done so originally, is now only an historical question: once having created expectations, one naturally fulfills them. All this I am sure you see: I am sure you did not entertain the idea that you and I could set up a purely Pigiebotian household with the others simple as 'staff' or 'chorus'. One hopes of course that we should live in a 'blend': but pure, unadulterated, orthodox, high flying Pigiebotianism would naturally appear only from time to time when we were off on our own. But then again, it wouldn't be fair on the others if I allowed the 'blend' to become merely the background and our neat Pigiebotian moments to become definitely *my life*. (Of course really *my life* is my own, just as your's is your own, but I'm looking at it as it would appear to the others.) All this is very disagreeable stuff: also, once it gets on paper, it sounds terrible poetical and forbidding. I don't think really that the problems are specially difficult – quite stupid people solve them every day – but I think they had to be set out. I don't want you either to buy or sell a pig in a poke.

Of course I'm not forgetting that for you the question turns on the larger question of retirement: but that seems to be one on which I can say nothing. Not that I can't think of a great many PRO's and CON'S, but after all its your show. Anyway it clearly can't be decided at once. It all comes back to the old tragedy of our civilization: that no one has the decency to give us a good sinecure apiece. (*One sinecure per pigiebudda* would be a good party slogan)! As for spending your leaves here, that of course goes without saying.

And now it is really time to make some immediate arrangements. Will you please reply *instanter* to the next question – do you know the exact date and port of your arrival? If not, will you be able to inform me of same, say by posting at Marseilles? If not, by cable from some port on the way? The present idea is that Minto and Maureen should go to Rostrevor or Cushendall at Easter. If Leeboro is still there, you and I will of course go there. In these circumstances it is highly desirable that we should meet you at Liverpool, if that is your port, so as to save you from travelling to Oxford and back. I also suggest that if the others are still at Rostrevor when we have finished at Leeboro we might go on foot and thus get in our long contemplated walking tour. The chief reason for their going there is to look for some suitable place as a summer resort for us all.

Minto is quite in love with Ulster since her visit (she got on famously with the Witch of Endor). Maureen is dying to see the sea, qua sea, and you and I of course need no persuasion to revisit these counties. One suggestion was that we should permanently rent a house from the Hamiltons at Cloghy. It is next door to the Hamiltons own. However the rent is £15 per annum – i.e. from our point of view £15 for a few weeks every year. True they will 'do it up', but I have my own idea about that. Also I rather doubt whether the younger generation of Hamiltons (and their friends) as next door neighbours, and Uncle Hamilton as a landlord would be a great success. On the other hand there are great attractions: a solitary place, and the elder Hamiltons as neighbours, both of whom we like. I said I would write and consult you about it. One of the things Minto hopes to find out is whether cottages on the Down coast for the summer months can be got at better cheap. Don't forget to reply at once to the questions in the past paragraph.

yours,

J.

TO ARTHUR GREEVES (W):

[Hillsboro]
Jan 26th Sunday [1930]

My dear Arthur,

Thanks very much for sending on the lists: but I was genuinely disappointed not to find a letter inside. Now that term is upon us I shall not be able to keep up letters of my vacation size, but I had certainly hoped that we might manage a short weekly letter as we did in the Bookham days and I think we both had a good deal of pleasure from them.

Of course there is one possibility that must be frankly taken into account – i.e. that my present letters, dealing necessarily so much with a life you don't share and only rarely touching on common reading – may be, if not tedious to you, (note the vanity of the 'if not'), at any rate too little interesting to repay you for the labour of keeping up your side. I shan't be in the least offended if this is so: tho' even then I would like a line occasionally. However, one good result of growing up is that one learns how small accidents everyone's conduct depends on. I do not assume that you have foresworn my acquaintance forever, nor will I 'fly into a passion'.

This you will notice is a very dignified, magnanimous letter on my part: it will look very well to posterity! (As a matter of fact, to write private letters with an eye on posterity is a lovable fault, springing from honest vanity: to try to forestall criticism by parodying ones own mood, as I did in the last sentence, is a beastly modern sophisticated kind of vanity)

And now, for my first week of term. All private reading has ceased, except for 20 minutes before bed (if alone) when I drink a cup of cocoa and try to wash the day off with Macdonalds Diary of an Old Soul. I shall soon have finished it and must look round for another book. Luckily the world is full of books of that general type: that is another of the beauties of coming, I won't say, to religion but to an attempt at religion – one finds oneself on the main road with all humanity, and can compare notes with an endless succession of previous travellers. It is emphatically coming home: as Chaucer says 'Returneth *home* from worldly vanitee.'[20]

I am called at 7.30 (as you remember to your cost) and rise about 8. Monday morning I have no pupils and can devote to my own work or to preparation. Out home at 12, lunch, dig the hen run, walk (on Mondays with Foord-Kelsie) back to home for tea, then into college for a pupil at 5.30. After dinner a meeting of a society. Tuesday, pupils from 10 to 1 then again at 5: and similarly on Wednesday. Thursday differs by pupils beginning at 9, and by an Anglo Saxon class after dinner, which usually develops into informal talk till midnight. Friday and Saturday are like the other days except that there is no pupil after tea. So far, until things close in on me as they presently will, I have five evenings free a week after dinner. For the first week they have mostly been occupied in correcting what we call 'Collection papers' – i.e. exams one sets the young men on what they have done or neglected to do in the Vac.

On Friday Christie came in from about 11 till 12.45: mostly stood on the fender eating biscuits, and talked on a variety of subjects. I never can make up my mind whether I most like or dislike this man. Perhaps his hard, insistant voice is really what prevents him from being nicer. He is genuinely religious: he has a real love of poetry and nature, – real enthusiasm, quite different from the usual blasé, côterie, critical, twaddle wh. is in fashion here: he even likes Macdonald – a bit. But then suddenly a whiff of the schoolmaster comes reeking out of him: you know he is not thinking whether your view is *true*, but what it signifies in relation to your character: he's not thinking what will be true for him to reply, but what will be best for you, what will rouse least opposition and yet do you most good. All this, damn him!, *very* charitably & making full allowances, internally, for all your antecedents and previous history. It is a habit schoolmasters have got from 'understanding' boys. In fact you might say Christie is so taken up with 'understanding' me, that he has no time to understand what I say. 'Yes' he will say 'I quite understand how you can come to think that, and I quite sympathise: but – ' and all the time he hasn't really taken in what I said. But on the whole I think his good points out-number his bad: and as you are always rightly telling me one mustn't demand to[o] much. (So is he, by the way. He is particularly strong on charity. Now what follows isn't a sneer, for I am really

---

20 Chaucer, *Troilus and Criseyde*, V, 1837.

trying to become more charitable, and I think I can at least admire charity in another. But I don't think Christie's is of the right brand. He always seems to select the really evil people to defend: and the next moment you find him being extraordinarily hard on some harmless old man because he is a bore. I suppose there is such a thing as imagining you have got beyond the stage of hating bad men, when in reality you haven't got *as far* as hating them. Divine charity must be very different from human *truckling* to bullies, or human indulgence for rotters because they are amusing: I doubt if Christie knows this difference.)

Just before term began I had to go and call on Farquharson[21] in Univ. He is the senior tutor there, and of course I have known him since my undergraduate days. On the strength of having done some office work at Whitehall during the war, and having been in the Territorials before, he has called himself Lieutenant Colonel ever since. He lives in a tall, narrow house, cheek by jowl with Univ. Library which itself is like a mortuary chapel. The space between them is about six feet across; into the Fark's house daylight never comes. I have never been beyond the ground floor: here in broad low rooms, lined with books, he works by artificial light most of the day. Somewhere upstairs, is a wife one never meets. He came gliding towards me in the dusk, about five feet four inches high, his face exactly like an egg in shape, with sandy-hair fringing a bald patch, a little military moustache, and eyebrows so far up his forehead that it gives him a perpetual air of astonishment. On this occasion, as on every other on which I have met him, he came towards me with an air (not a gesture, an air) that would have suggested an embrace rather than a handshake: then, laying one hand on my shoulder, he wrung my hand with the other, cooing in refined military voice 'My *dear* fellow, this is very good of you.' (He knew perfectly well that I had come on business and hadn't any choice but to come.) No underlining can convey the emphasis on the word *dear*: it was as if he had said 'darling'. At the same time, however, the eyebrows moved a good deal higher up the forehead and while his voice gave the *darling* effect, his face gave the effect of 'Well what a pair of fools we are, to be sure.'

Waiving the matter in hand, he began to consult me on an incredibly obscure point of Greek – he is one of the people producing the new Lexicon. He knows perfectly well that he knows twenty times more Greek

---

21 See note 15 to the letter of 11 May 1924.

than I do, but every word and tone suggested that I was the one man in Oxford, if not in Europe, who could help him out of his scrape: but every *look* said just as plainly, 'Isn't this fun? Or course you don't know anything about it, and nobody really knows much about this question, and it doesn't really matter anyway, but you won't mind my pulling your leg a bit, will you?' And I didn't. Then every now and then, his manner would become if possible a little more serious, and a little more insanely deferential, and out would come some extremely indecent story: without a tremor of his gravity: but perhaps a minute later the egg would suddenly crack and he would go off into great solid chunks of laughter – the sort of 'Ha – Ha – Ha' with long intervals between which one imagines Johnson laughing. When I left he told me how much I'd helped him. I said I hadn't known anything at all about the points he'd raised. He said 'It was the stimulus of my presence' (same contradictory effect of voice & face) and left me wondering whether he went back to chuckle at me, or to forget the whole visit as instantly and irrevocably as we sometimes forget a dream. Either seems equally probable. It is an old subject of controversy just how mad the Fark is. (He has put himself down on the list as lecturing on Heraclitus every summer term for years. I am the only person who ever volunteered to go, and he said it was off *that* year: also the surviving fragments of Heraclitus occupy about two pages!)

Well, I have made a big hole in my Sunday time for reading, and I'm glad I have. Tho' you don't reply, I have a friendly feeling from writing and a sort of homeliness: and I enjoy and like the Fark better for having tried to describe him. Try this recipe yourself, and after writing the letter you will go to bed happier.

Minto sends her love to all, & thanks for your mother's letter. A dead still night.

Yours
Jack

TO ARTHUR GREEVES (W):

[Magdalen College]
Jan 30th 1930

My dear Arthur,

Yesterday I was not out to home at all, since morning tutoring ended at one only to be succeeded by a College meeting at 2, which lasted till 5: then evening pupil from 5.30 to 6.30, and a dinner engagement at 7.

Consequently I did not get your letter till to-day. Not even to-day did I read it at once, as I had orange cutting for marmalade with Minto to do after lunch – (this sounds a nice homely job, but is as a matter of fact rather unpleasant as the bitter juice always find little cracks in ones skin and smarts like the devil) which lasted till 3 when I sallied forth taking your unopened letter with me.

I cannot remember that I ever took your letters to read on a walk at Bookham – indeed, funnily enough, I can't remember at what time of day they used to arrive and be read. I wonder did they come at breakfast – and did I read them on my little after breakfast walk? Anyhow, whatever the cause, taking it out to read as I walked like that gave me a remeniscent feeling. I'm afraid (almost) to say much for fear after all we can't keep it up – but at the moment I feel like asking 'Why have we missed this pleasure all these years?' I enjoyed your letter extremely: specially your sight of the

> Hebrid isles
> Set far amid the melancholy main[22]

or at least of their light. I quite agree about the value of the word Hebrides. What you can hardly feel as I do is the value of such words as 'Causeway' and (even) 'Portrush'. Not that I care or know about the places: but they are places to which people in my Irish life have always 'gone' – they call up the feeling of antedeluvian holiday arrangements and put me back for the moment in a world where Castlerock & Newcastle seemed as far away as Edinburgh and Paris do now.

It was in the Italian that we read Dante and I have been wondering rather hard whether it would be a good thing for you to try in Cary. If you do, I think the great point is to *give up any idea* of reading it in long stretches (with one's feet on the fender) for the general atmosphere and conduct of the story, and, instead, read a small daily portion, in rather a liturgical manner, letting the *images* and the purely intellectual conceptions sink well into the mind. i.e. I think what is important (or most important) here is to remember say 'The figures stand in these positions, coloured thus, and he is explaining about free will' – rather as if one was remembering a philosophical ceremony. It is not really like any of the things we know.

---

22 Thomson, *The Castle of Indolence*, XXX, 1–2.

I quite agree that the new Everyman backs are a great improvement. There, by the way, is the plague of these letters. *That*, in conversation would be a perfectly natural thing not only for me to say to you, but for any booky man to say to another: but in a letter I can't help feeling 'How like our old letters', and thus it has the air of a *revival*. The cure, clearly, is to go boldly on. Let us look forward to the time when instead of feeling 'We have started the old letters again', we shall feel 'Ah yes' – and remember before this long period of correspondence there was that early two years at Bookham that one always forgets. Yet that can never be, perhaps. *Two years* at that age was so enormous. And one can't regret it, for it means that I cannot think of you without thinking of all that so that you have the aroma of the magical past.

Now I come to a more serious problem. What I feel like saying, if I am to give you my news, is 'Things are going very, very well with me (spiritually).' On the other hand, one knows from bitter experience that he who standeth should take heed lest he fall, and that anything remotely like pride is certain to bring an awful crash. The old doctrine is quite true you know – that one must attribute everything to the grace of God, and nothing to oneself. Yet as long as one *is* a conceited ass, there is no good pretending not to be. My self satisfaction cannot be hidden from God, whether I express it to you or not: rather the little bit of self-satisfaction which I (probably wrongly) beleive myself to be fighting against, is probably merely a drop in the bottomless ocean of vanity and self-approval which the Great Eye (or Great I) sees in me. So I will say it after all: that I seem to have been supported in respect to chastity and anger more continuously, and with less struggle, for the last ten days or so than I often remember to have been: and have had the most delicious moments of It. Indeed to day – another of those days which I seem to have described so often lately, the same winter sunshine, the same gilt and grey skies shining thro bare shock-headed bushes, the same restful pale ploughland and grass, and more than usual of the birds darting out their sudden, almost cruelly poignant songs – to-day I got such a sudden intense feeling of delight that it sort of stopped me in my walk and spun me round. Indeed the sweetness was so great, & seemed so to affect the whole body as well as the mind, that it gave me pause – it was so very like sex.

One knows what a psychoanalyst would say – it is sublimated lust, a kind of defeated masturbation which fancy gives one to compensate for external chastity. Yet after all, why should that be the right way of look-ing at it? If he can say that It is sublimated sex, why is it not open to me to say that sex is undeveloped *It*? – as Plato would have said.[23] And if as Plato thought, the material world is a copy or mirror of the spiritual, then the central feature of the material life (=sex), must be a copy of something in the Spirit: and when you get a faint glimpse of the latter, of course you find it like the former: an Original *is* like its copy: a man *is* like his portrait. It occurs to me one might have a myth about the psy-choanalyst – the story of a man who was always insisting that real people were only fanciful substitutions for the *real* things (as he thought them) in the mirror. However, one cannot be too careful: one must try to hold fast to ones duties (I wish I did) which are the prose of the spiritual life and not learn to depend too much on these delightful moments.

What worries me much more is *Pride* – my besetting sin, as yours is *indolence*. During my afternoon 'meditations', – which I at least *attempt* quite regularly now – I have found out ludicrous and terrible things about my own character. Sitting by, watching the rising thoughts to break their necks as they pop up, one learns to know the sort of thoughts that do come. And, will you believe it, one out of every three is a thought of self-admiration: when everything else fails, having had its neck bro-ken, up comes the thought 'What an admirable fellow I am to have broken their necks!' I catch myself posturing before the mirror, so to speak, all day long. I pretend I am carefully thinking out what to say to the next pupil (for *his* good, of course) and then suddenly realise I am really thinking how frightfully clever I'm going to be and how he will admire me. I pretend I am remembering an evening of good fellowship in a really friendly and charitable spirit – and all the time I'm really remembering how good a fellow I am and how well I talked. And then when you force yourself to stop it, you admire yourself for doing *that*. Its like fighting the hydra (you remember, when you cut off one head another grew). There seems to be no end to it. Depth under depth of self-love and self admiration. Closely connected with this is the difficulty

---

23 Speaking of friendship, Plato said in the *Symposium*, 192c: 'They may be hard put to it to say what they really want with one another, and indeed, the purely sexual pleasures of their friendship could hardly account for the huge delight they take in one another's company. The fact is that both their souls are longing for a something else – a something to which they can neither of them put a name, and which they can only give an inkling of in cryptic sayings and prophetic riddles.' (Translation by Michael Joyce.)

I find in making even the faintest approach to giving up my own will: which as everyone has told us is the only thing to do.

As to my outer news for the past week or so, let me see. On Monday last but one I had to read a paper before the *Junior Linguistic* Society, which led me into strange haunts very typical of one side of Oxford: for the *Junior Linguistic* has hired the rooms belonging to the *Oxford Broadsheet Club*. These are situated in a very small alley on whose right stands the door into the cheap seats at a Cinema, and on whose left – with its lights gleaming out on to the wet cobbles – stood the sinister public house in which the notorious *Shove Halfpenny* Club meets, or used to meet until it was broken up by the interference of the Proctors.[24]

Beyond this after three flights of narrow stairs I found myself at my destination, in a crowd of about thirty young men packed into a tiny room whose furniture seemed all to have been specially made for it by people with 'stunt' ideas of furniture. As soon as my eyes had grown accustomed to the sea of tobacco smoke so as to allow me to take in the decorations etc I discovered that the *Broadside* Club might with much more propriety have been called the Oxford Pornographical Society. The walls were adorned with drawings of singularly powerfully-built female nudes whose bellies and genital organs showed a remarkable degree of development, while, in compensation they usually lacked both head and feet. I speculated on the artistic pretext of this omission, until one of the Junior Linguists suggested to me the very obvious consideration that feet and faces are hard to draw: and the bad execution of the hands led to the conclusion that this was the real reason. On the table were several brochures advertising the work of various private presses, of which they themselves were specimens. I must confess that the printing was in most really beautiful: the works advertised were largely translations of the more indecent classical authors. It really does seem a pity that the cause of good printing should have got itself thus intangled with the cause of obscenity – specially as the catalogue betrayed their real ignorance of the classics. One specimen page offered a translation from Catullus – the poem beginning *Vivamus mea Lesbia*[25] – Come, my Lesbia, let us love.

---

24 Lewis read a paper entitled 'Some Problems of Metaphor' to the Oxford University Junior Linguistic Society on Monday 27 January. The meeting was held in the rooms of the Broadside (not 'Broadsheet') Club at No. 19 Friars Entry. The house was destroyed some years ago and is replaced by a pub named the Fuggle & Firkin which stands across the alley from the Gloucester Arms public house.

25 Catullus, *Poems*, no. 5.

Lesbia, of course, is simply the girl's name, or rather pseudonym. The blockheads, however, with the idea of Lesbianism snivelling round their muddy little minds, had jumped to the wrong conclusion and decorated the poem with a woodcut representing two more of the same beefy female nudes sprawling on a bed.

But what really completed the piquancy of the whole scene was the contrast between the Junior Linguists themselves and the surroundings which they had borrowed: for the Junior Linguists is a society consisting entirely of undergraduates of just the Opposite type – hardworking eccentrics of all ages and social classes as far removed from the conventional games playing mob in one direction as the Broadsheet decadents are in the opposite direction. It gave me a pleasant sense of the real variety of the society in which I live. Later on at about ten, when my paper had been read I got into a long philosophical discussion with a total stranger who appeared to be a lunatic.

By the way, one of the results of my having left my keys at home is that I can't let myself into College and therefore always have to be back by 12 which didn't matter on Monday but did matter at the Icelandic Society (the Kolbítar) (pronounced Coal-béet-are) when I had to leave Tolkien, Bryson, Dawkins[26] just as we were getting comfortable. However, I hope to reap the benefits of the earlier hours I am thus forced to keep. Bryson you know: Tolkien is the man I spoke of when we were last together – the author of the voluminous unpublished metrical romances and of the maps, companions to them, showing the mountains of Dread and Nargothrond the city of the Orcs.[27] In fact he *is*, in one part of him, what we were.

Monday 10th [February]

I had intended to give you a sketch of Dawkins, the fourth Kólbíti (and very well worth describing) but am carried away once more to nature by the heavenly walk I had yesterday. I had gone out to home

26 Richard MacGillivray Dawkins (1871–1955) was educated at Emmanuel College, Cambridge, where he read Classics. He was Director of the British School of Archaeology, Athens, 1906–14, and Bywater and Southby Professor of Byzantine and Modern Greek Language and Literature at Oxford University 1922–39.

27 He is referring to Professor Tolkien's vast, invented world of Middle-earth which we can now read about in *The Hobbit* (1937), *The Lord of the Rings* (1954–5) and *The Silmarillion* (1977).

after breakfast and had to spend the whole day till tea time working on textual criticism – a beastly job involving no interest & continual minute attention, & abominably tiring to the eyes. After tea I went out, thro' old Headington and over the fields towards Forest Hill – i.e. to that spot where (on your last visit to Oxford) you and I saw the low blue bit of distance framed between the two trees which you always say you remember. The evening was wildly cold. Mark what I say: not *intensely* cold, but wildly: i.e. tho there was little movement in the air the cold gave the feeling of *wildness* to the world – a raging silence. I walked out over the big fields and behind me there was the flaming orange colour that you often get at frosty sunset, but only a thin strip, and above that – green: then above that silver: above my head – at the zenith – stars: before me the moon, at present dead & lightless tho' white, a little above the horizon. I walked faster and faster as one does in sympathy with such 'wildness' until – when I had come out of the big fields and was going up among the pines to where you and I sat, rather a funny experience happened. I had not noticed any change in the light: moon rising and sun setting had so evenly divided the sky that there was no break, and I still attributed the light in which I walked to the sunset behind me. Imagine then what it was like when with a quiet shock I saw my shadow *following* me over the turf and thus *in the shadow* first perceived how bright the moonlight must be. I'm afraid I can hardly express it in [a] letter. At any rate the whole walk was wonderful, and that bit in particular ghostly – ghostly in the good sense, not in the spookikal.

Barfield came and had a walk with me on Saturday with tea en route in a pub at Stanton St. John. Splendid talk and splendid evening. I also had Griffiths to stay with me for a night last week. Griffiths was a pupil of mine. He was all mucked up with naturalism, D. H. Lawrence, and so on, but has come right and is I do believe really one of 'us' now: and is even tending on the rebound to a high degree of asceticism. Tobacco and meat he never used <more than he could help>: he now half humorously suggests that hot baths must go the same way, as voluptuous, enervating, and leading to an effeminate love of the clean. He is a magnificent looking creature – a dark Celt, but very big.

I think this is enough now.

Yrs

Jack

P.S. When I said that your besetting sin was Indolence and mine Pride I was thinking of the old classification of the seven deadly sins: They are *Gula* (Gluttony), *Luxuria* (Unchastity), *Accidia* (Indolence), *Ira* (Anger), *Superbia* (Pride), *Invidia* (Envy), *Avaricia* (Avarice). *Accidia*, which is sometimes called *Tristicia* (despondence) is the kind of indolence which comes from indifference to the good – the mood in which though it tries to play on us we have no string to respond. *Pride*, on the other hand, is the mother of *all* sins, and the original sin of Lucifer – so you are rather better off than I am. You at your worst are an instrument unstrung: I am an instrument strung but preferring to play itself because it thinks it knows the tune better than the Musician.

GULA J.A.G.
LUXURIA J.A.G., C.S.L.
ACCIDIA J.A.G.
IRA C.S.L.
SUPERBIA C.S.L.
INVIDIA C.S.L.
AVARICIA (neither, I hope)

TO OWEN BARFIELD (W):

[Magdalen College
3? February 1930]

My dear Barfield,
Domestic strain is, I hope, now over. On Wednesday, however, we have College meeting in the afternoon.

> *There, an hour from noon,*
> *Men work by lamplight in the month of June.*[28]

Either Saturday, or (better still) next Monday wd. be my best day.
I have been up in that balloon or one of similar pattern – what a pity we never met. But the sky is pretty large.
Terrible things are happening to me. The 'Spirit' or 'Real I' is showing an alarming tendency to become much more personal and is taking the

---

28 'Here, an hour from noon, / Men work by lamplight in the month of June.' The lines are from Lewis's 'The Queen of Drum', V, 3–4, found in his *Narrative Poems* (1969).

offensive, and behaving just like God. You'd better come on Monday at the latest or I may have entered a monastery.[29]

– Interrupted by Wyld!![30]

yrs,

C. S. Lewis

TO ARTHUR GREEVES (W):

Magdalen College,
Oxford.
Feb 24th 1930.

My dear Arthur,

I also have been ill but, more fortunate than you, have contrived to enjoy my illness on the whole – re-reading among other things *Middlemarch*, & reading Pascal (who seems to me pretty poor stuff). I hope to start another real letter to you soon.

In the meantime can you please let us have the following information. (1) Was it Cushendall or Cushendun[31] that we lunched at on the day of our last drive together? (2) What was the name of the hotel? (3) Do you know anything of De Largy's Hotel either at Cushendall or Cushendun?

Lucky devil to come on a deposit of Geo. Macdonalds. I will buy any you don't like – at any rate don't let any go till I've seen them.

Yrs.

C. S. Lewis

---

29 Lewis appeared to be having the very experience he later described in *SBJ* XIV: 'As the dry bones shook and came together in that dreadful valley of Ezekiel's [Ezekiel 37:7], so now a philosophical theorem, cerebrally entertained, began to stir and heave and throw off its gravecloths, and stood upright and became a living presence. I was to be allowed to play at philosophy no longer. It might, as I say, still be true that my "Spirit" differed in some way from "the God of popular religion". My Adversary waived the point. It sank into utter unimportance. He would not argue about it. He only said, "I am the Lord"; "I am that I am"; "I am".'

30 Henry Cecil Kennedy Wyld (1870–1945), English philologist and lexicographer, was a Fellow of Merton College and Merton Professor of English Literature from 1920 to 1945. One of the books used at this time for the study of English was Wyld's *A Short History of English* (1921). Lewis found it a muddled piece of writing, and he may here mean that he was trying to unravel some part of it for use in teaching Anglo-Saxon.

31 Both are in Co. Antrim.

TO ARTHUR GREEVES (W):

Magdalen College,
Oxford.
[26 February 1930]

My dear A

In great haste – the ending up C. S. Lewis must have been due to the fact that I had just written *nine* letters all ending in that way. Other things, reply later

Yours
Jack

TO ARTHUR GREEVES (W):

[Magdalen College]
Feb. 27th [1930]

My dear Arthur,

I am sorry for my mistake about the signature of my last letter but one, but I hope this has now been set right by my note – was it legible? – yesterday. The overwhelming majority of the letters I write (and I seldom get through a day in term without writing a letter) are naturally signed with my surname and initials, so that to add these at the end is almost as mechanical as to turn the envelope over and lick the flap. On this particular occasion, as I said, your letter was the last of nine which I had had to write, and so I inadvertently followed on – or so I now learn, for, of course, until I heard from you I was quite unaware of what I had done. It is the sort of slip [of] the pen that must, I imagine, be not very uncommon with writers in haste – so be prepared for it happening again!

Now as to our plans. My request to you for information was not so much the result of any decision as an attempt to get data for deciding on. I thought you knew that I, at any rate, would be at home in the Easter Vac? For the rest we are in a state of great indecision. The *basic facts* (as the Newspapers say: and by the way, isn't this new party 'The prosperity Party' a portent and a sign: commercialism more *naked* that it has yet dared to show itself in politics. Just imagine the sort of people who are joining it!) the basic facts are as follows. My term ends on March 15th. Maureen's term ends on March 29th. Warnie is expected to be home about April 10th. The idea was that we should all go to stay somewhere in Northern Ireland for about four weeks beginning from March 29th:

but that after W's return he and I should spend a week or so together at Leeboro' for the last time and 'break it up'. I was surprised to hear of your proposed trip as I don't think you had mentioned it. I need hardly say that I had looked forward to seeing you both while W. and I were at home, & also I thought you might run down & see us occasionally while we were at the other place – whether Rostrevor, Cushendall, or elsewhere finally proves best (By the way can you recommend *cheap rooms* at any nice place where you are catered for? If you cd., you wd. do us a *very great service.*) But if you are coming to England, *do* try & arrange it so that you can come & spend a few nights with me in College before I leave it on the 15th. The week 9th–15th March is free: next week is pretty full. Do consider this: I have the pleasantest memories of our joint collegiate life on your last visit.

I am sorry if I failed to make clear to you when we last met that I shd. be in Ireland at Easter – I certainly thought I had done so, but I may not, & confess I am in the habit of forgetting what I have said & what I have merely thought. As to the other matter – the signature (not *Of All Things*, but of my last letter) I hope you now realise that it was quite unintentional and also see how the accident happened.

I can't possibly manage a letter for some days. By the way I said that I couldn't understand Boehme in my first letter on the subject. As for Macdonalds, no need to urge me to read any I can get hold of. The faults are obvious but somehow they don't seem to matter. I hope you are better, now.

Yours
Jack (I v. nearly did it again!!)

TO ARTHUR GREEVES (W):

Magdalen College,
Oxford.
March 5th [1930]

My dear Arthur,

Just a line to tell you that the stay (*en famille*) at Rostrevor or elsewhere is off. This of course does not affect W's and my visit to Leeborough – still less the proposal of your coming to Magdalen next week, which I do hope can be managed.

yrs
Jack

TO ARTHUR GREEVES (W):

Magdalen College,
Oxford.
March 15th 1930

My dear Arthur

(1) Our plans are now fairly settled. We shall be at Oxford till about the 4th of April when the others will go to Southbourne (Hampshire) and I for a four days walking tour after which I shall rejoin them where they are. Any time between the 10th & the 14th I expect to hear of W's arrival upon which he and I will instantly go to Ireland. I leave College to day.

(2) It is a great bore your not being able to come and see me before, as now that Maureen has a separate room instead of the little annex off Mintos we have no spare bedroom when I am at Headington & I therefore can't offer to put you up. If in spite of this inhospitality you still care to come & put up elsewhere I needn't say what a delight it would be. I always lay in a store of real tranquil receptivity for the country when I'm with you, and it is now beginning to wear thin again & needs reviving.

(3) When you leave Bernagh please leave the keys with Mrs Greeves so that I can get 'em when I come home

(4) Now that term is over I hope to begin a proper letter to you again & finish it in the course of a week. Till then good bye

Yours
Jack

P.S. I am very sorry to hear that you have to think of seeing a specialist & hope the result will be good. After that do try to stick to one doctor's advice – don't you think you have been rather blown about between different doctors' views. Yet what is one to do. Best of luck!

TO A.K. HAMILTON JENKIN (B):

Hillsboro,
Western Rd.,
Headington.
March 21st 1930

My dear Jenkin,

How extremely disappointing! Almost as disappointing as when I was in Cornwall a few summers ago and you were in Herts. All the more so, as I don't see my way to sparing a day for a visit to London. And now, what is to be done about it all? I can't become a regular correspondent: and I can't take trips to St Ives.

Is there no chance of your ever being able to do as I suggested and coming to spend a couple of nights with me in College in term? Come and hear the click-click of the antlers of fencing deer in the park: come and dine at Univ. again and see the Fark: come and see the Alpine glow on St. Mary's spire of a fine June evening. You have a place in my mental world – you are a gap in my inner bookshelf – a drawn tooth in my psychic jaw – a *hiatus valde deflendusi*[32] in the manuscript of my mind – a broken lace in my spiritual boots – which no one else supplies. It seems hard that we should never meet. I honestly can't go to you, so you must come to me. Could you run down from London for a day now & visit me (Hillsboro, Western Rd., Headington?): or better still come for a couple of nights next term so that we can really have our feet on the fender together.

There will be many changes to take stock of. I can hardly imagine you as a married man of several years standing. Please lay my compliments at the feet of the family.

On my side there are changes perhaps bigger: you will be surprised to hear that my outlook is now definitely religious. It is not precisely Christianity, tho' it may turn out that way in the end. I can't express the change better than by saying that whereas once I would have said 'Shall I adopt Christianity', I now wait to see whether it will adopt me: i.e. I now know there is another Party in the affair – that I'm playing poker, not Patience, as I once supposed. Let me have a line,

yours
C. S. Lewis
Love from all here.

TO ARTHUR GREEVES (W):

Hillsboro.
April 3rd [1930]

My dear Arthur,
I am very sorry that our correspondence has languished so of late. My plans now are as follows. (1) Leave to morrow for a walking tour

---

32 'a yawning gap, very much to be lamented'.

on Exmoor, with Barfield and Co. (2) Rejoin the others at The Rest, Hengestbury Rd., Southbourne, Hants on the 8th. (3) Cross to Ireland with W. on the 12th or 14th. (4) Return to Oxford on the 25th. There's glory for you.

As for a visit from you at Southbourne, I hope you will believe me when I say that there are no times or places at which I should not like a walk and talk with you. But there are other factors in the case. Minto has very generously invited W. to make his home with us henceforward when he is on leave. They like one another and I hope, as W. gets broken in to domestic life, they may come to do so still more – but in the interval there is a ticklish time ahead and in any case it is a big sacrifice of our

[Greeves, in a pencilled note at the top of this letter, states that it is 'very private' and 'to be burnt'. What he did, however, before passing the letters on was to destroy half the first page and the whole of pages 2 and 3. What follows is page 4.]

...have fallen so far below – MYSELF!!! Which is rather like a man repenting of being drunk because it was unworthy of his career as a forger.

I hadn't meant to give you such a dose of myself – but there is hardly any of it that I can say to any one but you and it is a relief to let it out. Don't imagine that I'm always like this. I was, on the whole, glad to hear that all your disorders have been traced to the bowels (what a glorious sentence!) Does that mean that the heart is now judged to be alright? As you know, I think there is a great danger of your being buffeted to & fro between the opinions of varying doctors: but heaven knows it is easier to say that than to see how you can avoid it. Does your silence about Harrogate mean that the surrounding country and the people are unworthy of notice or only that you weren't in the mood for a long letter?

I have been nailed down ever since term ended to a very hard, tho' quite interesting, task: a study of the different versions of *Comus*.[33] You know that Milton's MS is extant & we can trace all his corrections. I am sure you, as an author, will be interested to learn that he often crossed out a phrase, put something else, crossed that out, & then returned to the original phrase. Just like ourselves in fact! Or like our

---

33 The result of this study was his essay, 'A Note on Comus', in *The Review of English Studies*, vol. VIII, no. 30 (1932), reprinted in Lewis's *Studies in Medieval and Renaissance Literature*, ed. Walter Hooper (1966).

brother in law Mr Suckling.[34] (By the way I read her unfinished novel 'The Watsons'[35] the other night & wished there was more of it – a splendid beginning.)

I have had v. little time for general reading. I began *Moby Dick*[36] on the week end when term ended, and thought, despite its obvious defects of rhetoric & un-dramatic dialogue, that I liked it: but somehow I feel no inclination to go on. Have you ever tried it? I have had a few notable walks. Shall I be seeing you in Ireland. At any rate write.

You are my only real Father Confessor so you owe me a line

Yours

Jack

TO ARTHUR GREEVES (W):

> [The Rest,
> Hengestbury Road,
> Southbourne
> 13? April 1930]

My dear Arthur,

Many thanks for both your letters. You mustn't think of mucking up your arrangements on my account. Of course it would make my impending time in Ireland v. much nicer if you were there, but it would be quite monstrous to expect you to come back from London – especially as the latest news is that W. will not reach Liverpool until Wednesday, so that I shall have only a week at home. ('At home' – an awful feeling comes over me at those words. It is impossible to get accustomed to change.) So don't think of altering your arrangements on my account: accept instead my hearty thanks for your second letter, which was one of the nicest I have ever had, and set out on your trip with a clear conscience. You are doing perfectly right and I should be a most exacting & selfish person to demand for a moment that you should do otherwise. I hope you will do yourself and your Pole good.

Beware of holidays, though. The old puritans were wrong but they had something real at the back of their minds when they denied pleasures

---

34 A character in Jane Austen's *Emma*.

35 A fragment of a novel by Jane Austen, written about 1805 and appended by J.E. Austen-Leigh to his *Memoir of Jane Austen* (1871).

36 Herman Melville, *Moby Dick* (1851).

because 'it would only unsettle the boy'. I speak feelingly, for, having felt it my duty to drop work here and devote myself entirely to holidaying with the others (heavens knows I did it for the best) I am at present suffering from all the spiritual consequences of idleness.

I am reading Virginia Wolfe's Orlando[37] to Minto at present. Have you read it? And if so what do you make of it? I think there is a quite astonishing power of rendering the feel both of landscapes and moods, rising sometimes to real loveliness, and a total absence of any matter on which to use the power. Also the usual stale cynicism – the nineteenth century guyed as usual – in fact all the tricks of the clevers. I note what you say about your George Macdonalds and will certainly borrow one for my stay. Think of me at your bookcase a few days hence. Ah Arthur – aren't things odd? Many thanks & good bye

Yours
Jack

Warnie arrived in Liverpool on 16 April after being away, as he recorded in his diary, 'three years and five days, and after a journey of fifty days from Shanghai' (LP X: 309). He met Jack in London and after a night in Oxford they joined Mrs Moore and Maureen in Southbourne. Jack and Warnie left for Belfast on 22 April, arriving there on the 23rd. That evening Warnie wrote in his diary:

> *The sight of P's grave with its fresh turned earth, and a handful of withered daffodils at its head, alongside Mammy's, was perfectly beastly...And so out through the dingy familiarity of Ballymacarret and a much altered Strandtown to Little Lea. There was a chill about the rank untended garden, but inside, at first, the house seemed much less strange than I had expected it to be, in spite of J's labours – superficially it was as if a spring cleaning was in progress: but soon I noticed the intense stillness, and as I went from room to room, its utter lifelessness: silent it has of course been for many years during most of the day, but this was something new and horrible. It brought home to me as nothing else could have done, the tremendous personality of the Pudaitabird – the whole*

---

37 Virginia Woolf, *Orlando* (1928).

place is as blank as a frame from which a picture has been stripped...We took turn about in digging a hole in the vegetable garden in which we put our toys...and then carried the old attic trunk down and buried them: what struck us most was the scantiness of the material out of which that remarkable imaginary world was constructed: by tacit mutual consent the boxes of characters were buried unopened. (LP XI: 5)

They returned to Oxford the next day, where Warnie stayed at Hillsboro until he was posted to Bulford, Wiltshire, as assistant to the officer in charge of supplies.

TO ARTHUR GREEVES (W):

[Magdalen College]
April 29th [1930]

My dear Arthur,

I will write to Mary about the commode. Meanwhile I am tearing my hair and dancing with rage so that the books are rattling on my table and the eyes of the undergraduate in the room beneath have dropped out, and all because in the collection of your letters which I have looked over I cannot find the one in which you went to the door on the evening when you were first read[ing] *Phantastes*. It will be maddening if any are lost. Have you got any of them? Did you bring them all back at the end of that time? Be sure to reply to this.

And by the way how that time has already become a remote memory. During my recent flying visit I saw the summer seat out in the middle of the lawn and had such a vivid recollection of sitting there with you and watching that strange illusion of shadowy people creeping up to the hall door and always vanishing just as we set eyes on them – and avoiding Chevasse. I met him for a moment, with W., just outside our back gate, showing his teeth as ever.

The two days and one night were very queer. I found that even with W. there the memory of *our* Ireland was stronger than the memory of his and mine. At least I don't know that 'stronger' is the right word: 'larger' wd. be better. The Ireland I shared with him seemed to be a strictly limited and rather thirsty land: yours was like dewy hills and woods fading into a mist where I felt that one could wander forever. This is not flattery, nor contempt of him. If I have so lived with him as to call forth mainly the sensual, the trivial, & the conspiratorial part of my nature in his society, then *I* have done *him* as great an injury as one man can do to another, but he has done me none, poor chap. I also feel very strongly – as I fancy you do with John – that so many things are innocent in him when the very same things are wrong in me.

Mary was an old dear as ever. I spent the night, no doubt my last in that house, appropriately enough, lying awake with a stomach ache. About three o'clock, getting up to drink water & eat aspirin, I looked out of the window. A thick white mist gleaming from the lamps in the road, and a dripping from the leaves. How many miserable nights have I looked from that window – terror of rows, terror of ghosts, worrey about Minto, toothache, quarrels with W. away back in early boyhood when he was my only home so to speak. V. odd that at such a moment it was entirely that side of Leeborough that came back to me: pain, fear, loneliness. I suppose it is steeped in my father's long years of loneliness – and pain & fear too, for all I know. Shall we add to the advertisement (boards are ordered to be put up) 'This house has been well suffered in'? Really I think Leeboro' looks best to me seen from Bernagh.

As to what you say in your letter about introspection & scruples, I think you are right in general: but you must remember how much bigger than itself a thing becomes by being put in writing. A very small dose of self-examination, so small as to be quite wholesome, looks a positive jorum in a letter. You must not imagine that I spend all or most of my time thinking the sort of things I have lately written to you: but in the act of writing to you those things naturally come uppermost which I can only imperfectly share with anyone else.

I wish you could have been with me on my walking tour.[38] We motored from Oxford to Dunster, three of us leaving the car about five miles before it & the fourth driving on. It was about six when we did so and we therefore had a delightful evening 'prologue' to the whole walk over moors with a ragged sunset ahead of us lighting up the pools: very like an illustration to Scott: then down into a steep valley, over a swift stream as broad as Connswater but only an inch or so deep above its rattling pebbles and so into the broad, empty, practically dark street of Dunster wh. stretches up to the castle.

---

38 His companions on the walking tour, from 4 to 8 April, were Owen Barfield, Cecil Harwood and Walter Field. These are the same three friends who had taken a walking tour in April 1927 and are mentioned in note 24 to the letter of 26 April 1927.

Next morning there was a thick fog. Some of the others were inclined to swear at it, but I (and I soon converted Barfield) rejoiced to meet the moor at its grimmest. Imagine a wonderful morning following a narrow path along the side of a steep hill with gaunt fir trees looming up suddenly out of the greyness: and sometimes a thinning of the mist that revealed perhaps a corner of a field with drystone wall unexpectedly far beneath us or a rushing brook, or a horse grazing. Then down into greener country and hedges for lunch at the village of Luccombe. In the afternoon the fog thickened but we continued in spite of it to ascend Dunkery Beacon as we had originally intended. There was of course not a particle of view to be seen, and we knew when we had reached the top only by the fact that we could find nothing higher and by the cairn of stones over which the wind was hurrying the fog like smoke from a chimney on a stormy day. The descent, largely guided by compass, was even more exciting: specially the suddenness with which a valley broke upon us – one moment nothing but moor and fog: then ghosts of trees all round us: then a roaring of invisible water beneath, and next moment the sight of the stream itself, the blackness of its pools and the whiteness of its rapids seeming to tear holes (as it were) in the neutral grey of the mist. We drank tea at the tiny hamlet of Stoke Pero where there is a little grey church without a tower that holds only about twenty people. Here, according to an excellent custom of our walks, one of the party read us a chapter of Scripture from the lectern while the rest of us sat heavily in the pews and spread out our mackintoshes to let the linings steam off. Then after a leisurely walk through woods we reached Wilmersham Farm where we found our car parked in the farmyard and Field looking out of a window to assure us that there were beds and suppers for all. We had a little parlour with a wood stove to ourselves, an excellent hot meal, and the bedrooms, – two in a room – were beautifully clean. We had only made about 16 miles but were tired enough as it had been v. rough country.

Next morning when I woke I was delighted to find the sun streaming through the window. Looking out I found a blue sky: the farmyard, with hens scratching and a cat padding stealthily among them, was bright with sunlight: beyond the long blue-grey horizons of the moor rolled up to the sky in every direction. This day we made about ten miles by paths across the open moor to a place where we met a road & there Field met us in the car with lunch. A cold wind was blowing by that time so we had our meal (as you and I have often done) in the closed car with all windows up and had the sensation of snugness. About $2^1/2$ hours after lunch, having done a very tricky walk across heather by pure map reading (no paths) we were relieved to strike the valley of a river called Badgworthy Water (pronounced Badgerry). A glorious comb[e], deepening of course as it proceeds, steep sided, with many rocks in it, and soon with dotted trees that thicken later into woods: not of fir but of stunted oaks, so gnarled that they give the impression of being in a subterranean forest of sea weed, & the branches often coated with moss to the top. We had to ford the Badgworthy: not v. easy as (like all mountain streams) it will be 6 inches deep in one place and 5 feet the next: ice cold and the bottom slippery.

Barfield created great amusement by putting his socks in his boots and trying to throw them across a narrow place so that he shd. not have that encumbrance while wading: instead they lit in the middle and, after sailing a few yards like high-pooped galleons, lit on the top of a fall where they stuck, rocking with the current and threatening every second to go sailing down into a whirlpool beneath. I, who was already safe on the farther shore, ran down in my bare feet and hoiked them to land with a stick. We sat down for about half an hour with our backs against a little cliff of rock, in the sun and out of the wind, to eat chocolate and dry & warm our numbed legs. The first bumble bee buzzed by us. The colours of the stream, broken by a series of falls above us, and floored with green, brown, golden, & red stones, were indescribable. When we were dry we worked our way down the valley to Cloud Farm where billets had been secured by Field. Minto, Maureen and I had stayed here about five years before, so I had a great welcome from the farm people. This evening all four of us had a kind of formal philosophical discussion on The Good. I shared a room with Barfield. Lay awake a little while, listening to the noise of the stream which is only about twenty feet from the farm house: and under that noise a profound silence. These Exmoor farms are the loveliest habitations you can imagine.

Next day we walked down the valley of the Lynn and lunched at Lynmouth. The valley is very deep – about 800 ft. – and the woods on the sides almost deserve to be called forest. The river – which again we had to wade – is much bigger than the Badgworthy and so agonisingly cold that at the first shock it is almost the same feeling as stepping into a bath much too hot for you. Lynmouth you know. After lunch our route lay along the cliffs and through the Valley of Rocks which I had not greatly admired: a place of enormous crags *without water* is a little bit horrible: one needs a stream to give these huge carcases a soul, don't you think? Best of all was after tea when we struck inland again over the moor in one of those golden evening lights that pours a dreamlike *mildness* over the world: light seemed to be a liquid that you could drink, and the surrounding peace was, if anything, deepened by the noise and bustle of a fussy little narrow gauge railway, the only living thing, which had a train puffing slowly along it, all its windows turned to gold in the light of the sunset. We saw several herons this day. That night we slept at Challacombe and composed ex-tempore poetry: telling the story of the Fall between us in the metre of Hiawatha.[39] We had done well over twenty miles and felt immortal.

The next day was grey with occasional rain. We got badly lost on some rather forbidding hills & failed to meet Field for lunch: got a lift along a dull stretch of road in a lorry: had tea at South Molton and motored to Exeter. Here, seeing the cathedral all lit up and notices outside it about a performance of the Messiah, we had supper in great haste and rushed off only to find that the Messiah was next week and that the lights were on for an ordinary evening service. It was horrid to be in a city again. As Field said 'After training ourselves for the last few days to notice *everything* we have now to train ourselves to notice nothing.' Next morning the party broke up, Barfield & Harwood motoring back North, while Field and I trained to Bournemouth where I rejoined Minto & Maureen at Southbourne. I will describe Field, whom you don't yet know, in another letter. I shall post this as soon as I hear your address, when I hope also to hear your news. You must have plenty to write of. I enclose my latest: I think you understand the experience – when we fall not because That is so attractive but because it makes everything else seem so drab.

Yours

J.

> *When Lilith means to draw me*
> *Within her hungry bower*
> *She does not overawe me*
> *With beauty's pomp and power,*

---

39 Henry Wadsworth Longfellow, *The Song of Hiawatha* (1858).

Nor with angelic grace
Of courtesy and the pace
Of gliding ship comes veil'd at evening hour.

Eager, unmasked, she lingers,
Heart shaken and heartsore: –
With hot, dry, jewelled fingers
Outstretched, beside her door,
Offers, with gnawing haste,
Her cup, whereof who taste
(She promises no better) thirst far more.

What moves, you ask, to drink it?
Her charms, that all around
So change the world, we think it
A great waste, where a sound
Of wind like tales twice-told
Blusters, and cloud is rolled
Always above, yet no rain falls to ground.

Across drab iteration
Of gaunt hills line on line
The dull road's sinuation
Creeps: and the witche's wine
Tho' promising nothing, seems,
In that land of no streams,
To promise best – the unrelish'd anodyne.[40]

During his stay at Hillsboro Warnie was considering his brother's and Mrs Moore's invitation to make his home with them when he retired. Meanwhile, he recorded in his diary of 10 May his plan for 'drawing up a scheme for the editing and arrangement of our family papers' (BF, pp. 45–6). On 15 May he took up his post at the army base at Bulford, on Salisbury Plain. On 25 May he arrived at a decision about the invitation to make his home with Jack and Mrs Moore:

---

40 The poem, considerably revised, was later to appear in Lewis's *The Pilgrim's Regress* (1933), and it has subsequently been included in his *Poems* (1964) and *Collected Poems* (1994).

> *The answer seems to be that just as the discomforts of my 'lone wolf' existence are inseparable from its luxuries, so that one cannot expect to have the good of domesticity without the bad. Finally there is the consideration of the assets of Hillsboro life to which the army can show not only no corresponding assets but actual debits – a closer intimacy with J., and a correspondingly fuller intellectual life: a healthier life too, by the cutting out of those hours spent in social and ceremonial drinking...I came home more than ever convinced that I have made a wise decision and should throw in my fortunes with Hillsboro as soon as it becomes economically possible. (BF, p. 52)*

On 31 May Warnie went to Belfast to go through Little Lea one last time before it was sold. He stayed in Little Lea for the last time during 1 to 4 June. Little Lea was sold in January 1931 for £2300.

TO ARTHUR GREEVES (W):

[Magdalen College]
June 1st 1930

My dear Arthur,

I have decided to return to the old regulation four page letter once a week as in Bookham days. The long screeds I have been sending you lately will certainly languish some time or other and then there will be an end of the correspondence: but this I think I shall be able to keep up. I hope to get your first letter on Tuesday at latest.

And now let me see (it already seems so long ago since you were here). On the day you left I went our usual walk, through Old Headington, past that little isolated house wh. you admired, across the brook, and then over two fields to our soaking machine. It was just such another glorious summer day with a kind of mist that made the grass and buttercups look watery. I felt that sort of melancholy (you probably know it) wh. comes from going through the same scenes through which you walked with a friend a few hours ago, when he has gone. Now that I come to think of it, you must have had this experience much more often than I: so often in your old letters do I find you describing how you went this or that old walk just after my return to Bookham. Mixed with this melancholy, however, (you will not be offended) there was the freshness of solitude which itself, on such occasions, feels like a friend revisited,

and what between the two I fell into an extremely receptive state of mind
– a sort of impersonal tenderness, which is the reason why I am mentioning this walk, as one of my good ones wh. was valuable in itself and
will, I hope, become even more so in memory.

Just to give you the other side of the picture (I shall not often tell you
these things) – I have 'fallen' <twice> since you left after a long period of
quite untroubled peace in that respect. Serves me right, for I was beginning to pat myself on the back and even (idiotically) beginning to fancy
that I had really escaped, if not for good, at any rate for an indefinite
time. The interesting thing was that on both occasions the temptation
arose <when I was almost asleep,> quite suddenly, and carried me by
storm <before I really had my waking mind fully about me.> I don't
mean to disclaim responsibility on this account: but I feel grateful that
the enemy has been driven to resort to *stratagems* (not by me, but by
God) whereas he used to walk boldly up to me for a frontal attack in the
face of all my guns. I hope I don't delude myself in thinking that this is
an improvement.

My rooms are quite settled down now and having worked in them for
a week I find the novelty falling into the background. The slow business
of transferring Headington books to Headington[41] – a little brief-bag full
a day – is going regularly forward. Last night I began the business of
going through the records, and sorting out those which are such rotten
things or so badly worn that I will give them away. I lay on the sofa and
played through *The People that Walked,*[42] *Overture & Intermezzo from
Carmen,*[43] *Fire Music from the Valkyrie,*[44] *The Laughing Song from the
Starlight Express.*[45]

Lying on the study sofa and hearing these old favourites I had sensations which you can imagine. And at once (here is the advantage of
growing older) I knew that the enemy would take advantage of the vague
longings and tendernesses to try & make me believe later on that *he* had
the fulfilment which I really wanted: so I baulked him by letting the
longings go even deeper and turning my mind to the One, the real object

---

41 He was unpacking the books and phonograph records from Little Lea, keeping some in
   his Magdalen College rooms and transferring others to Hillsboro.
42 'The People that Walked in Darkness' from Handel's *Messiah*.
43 Georges Bizet's *Carmen*.
44 From Richard Wagner's *Valkyrie*. See note 38 to letter of 4 May 1915.
45 Edward Elgar, *The Starlight Express*. See note 47 to letter of 16 May 1916.

of all desire, which (you know my view) is what we are *really* wanting in all wants.

At this point it occurred to me that the noise might be disturbing J.A.[46] above and went up to ask him: rather to my disappointment he was so far from being disturbed that he volunteered to come down with me and listen. Still there was something nice and even homely about having the old man there. We went through the *March of the Dwarfs*[47] & *Danse Macabre*[48] (which I thought rubbish) & Delibes *Cortège de Bacchus* from the *Aprez-midi d'un Faune*.[49] How on earth can we ever have liked this latter? It seemed to me the merest music hall patriotic song rhetoric on the brass pretending to be something better. Then, as I had anticipated, J.A. became talkative and we drank together and drifted into philosophical conversation.

In reading I have of course little to record, and never shall have much in term time. I read in two evenings a little book that came from Leeborough called *The Practice of the Presence of God*[50] which I picked up & put in the study when I was there last because it seemed to me a promising title. It is by a Seventeenth century monk. It is full of truth but somehow I didn't like it: it seemed to me a little unctuous. That sort of stuff, when it is not splendid beyond words, is terribly repulsive, or can be, can't it? No doubt it depends v. largely on ones mood. I had just finished the fourth Gospel in Greek (as I think you know) before you came, and after that most other things are a come down. Not that I liked *that* in all respects either. I have also read an essay on Death, in typescript, which Barfield sent me, which is to my mind one of the finest things there is. He handles death as you would expect it to be handled by a pupil & lover of *Lilith & Phantastes*.

Talking of which, I hope you will not be disagreeably surprised to find with this letter the first instalment of a new romance.[51] I don't know

---

46 John Alexander Smith, whose rooms were on the floor above.
47 From Edvard Grieg's *Lyriske Stykker* (1898).
48 By Camille Saint-Saëns (1875).
49 The *Cortège de Bacchus* is from Léo Délibes' *Sylvia* (1875). The *Prélude à l'après-midi d'un Faune* is the work of Debussy.
50 Brother Lawrence (c. 1614–91), *The Practice of the Presence of God*.
51 Nothing is known about this 'romance' Lewis was writing nor about the instalments he sent Arthur. In his letter of 22 June Lewis calls the story 'The Moving Image' and describes it as 'almost a Platonic dialogue in a fantastic setting wth story intermixed. If you take *The Symposium*, *Phantastes*, *Tristram Shandy* and stir them up all together you will about have the recipe.' The only unpublished writing which Lewis may have shown Arthur about this time is the fragment of his 'Ulster Novel' found in LP IX: 291–300, but it does not seem possible that 'The Moving Image' and the 'Ulster Novel' can be the same.

how long I shall keep it up, but it occurred to me that I could fit in four pages most weeks and that if I persevered I should thus get quite a lot written. Please criticize freely as it goes on. Of course if I get no answers I shall drop it: on the ground that if you are so changed that you can't write to me, you may also be so changed that you can't be trusted not to use my story for spills. When it is done (if ever) I shall ask you to get it typed in Belfast & sent to me. Is it possible that when you get the novel off your chest you might think of doing *your* next work in instalments? I think there are distinct advantages in that method of writing. But, whatever you do, let me have your weekly letter.

Yours
Jack

TO ARTHUR GREEVES (W):

[Magdalen College]
June 7th 1930

My dear Arthur,

I was delighted to get your prompt letter. Don't you enjoy the feeling of getting back into our old rhythm again? To me there is another pleasure which you, without a regular routine of work to distinguish the days from one another, will hardly feel: I mean the pleasure of adding another *pivotal* point to my week – so that in addition to Wednesday (interesting pupil) Thursday (Times Literary Supplement) etc I shall now have your letter. I enjoyed the description of your walk through our woods with Gribbon, and wish I could see them again.

As to what you say about instalments & the difficulty of seeing the story as a whole: (1) If you mean the *author's* difficulty, then I reply that I have so little time for writing that this is the only way to get a story done: and that benefit compensates for the disadvantages (Benefit to whom, you may ask!) (2) If you mean the *reader's* difficulty, then you may easily remedy that by *not* reading them until you have about ten (or better still, not reading them at all! As I wrote this I had such a vivid imagination of your voice as you might have said that). As regards your criticism, I was conscious of the fault you refer to while I was writing: specially in the sentence ending 'anxiety for the future'. It is not that I am trying to be complex, but a habit that sticks to my pen from years of writing on subjects that almost inevitably lure one into a rather unsimple style. I am glad you noticed it and will try to simplify: though I should say from the outset that the matters this story deals with *can't* beyond a certain point be put into the absolutely plain narrative style.

I have managed to get a few evenings free this week and have read two new books. The first was Kingsley's *Water Babies*.[52] It was one of the books belonging to my mother which my father had locked up at her death and I only recovered at the recent clearance. It was strange – after the first few pages the most incredibly faint memories began to come about me: she must have read it, or started to read it, to me when I was very small indeed. I had even a curious sense of bringing my mother to life – as if she were reading it through me. The feeling was impressive, but not entirely pleasant. (I don't mean that it was at all unpleasant in the commonplace ghostie sense.) The book itself seems to me not very good. There is some fancy, and I don't object to the preaching: but after Macdonald it is tasteless. Put the two side by side and see how imagination differs from mere fancy, and holiness from mere morality. Have you ever read it? As I say it is not *very* good: but well worth reading.

The other was Coventry Patmore's *Angel in the House*. As you know, it is a long poem in a very strict & even monotonous metre, describing a very simple story of love & marriage, interspersed with half philosophic, half religious odes on the author's theory of marriage as a mystical image of & approach to divine love. The story parts are deliberately prosaic & hum-drum, & would be very easy to parody: e.g. such lines as the following (put in the mouth of the housemaid)

> 'The Dean
> Is out, Sir, but Miss Honor's in'[53]

though it is surprising how one feels less and less inclined to sneer as you go on. But the bits in between are really often sublime. Isn't this good, of Love (=God on his view)

> To praise the thing whose praise it is
> That all which can be praised is it.[54]

---

52 Charles Kingsley, *The Water-Babies* (1863).

53 Coventry Patmore, *The Angel in the House* (1863), book II, canto I, 'Accepted', stanza 2, ll. 12–14.

54 ibid., book I, canto VIII, 'The Praise of Love', stanza 5, ll. 3–4.

He is extremely down on people who take the ascetic view. These will be shut without the fold as 'too good' for God. The whole poem has raised a lot of difficulties in my mind. Even if it were true that marriage is what he says, what help does this give as regards the sexual problem for the innumerable people who can't marry? Surely for them asceticism remains the only path? And if, as he suggests, marriage & romantic love is the real ascent to Spirit, how are we to account for a world in which it is inaccessible to so many, and are we to regard the old saints as simply deluded in thinking it specially denied to them? As a matter of fact he does seem to suggest in one passage that romantic love is *one* ascent, and imagination the other – At all events the book has left me with an extraordinary renewal of my appetite for poetry.

I had an interesting & humiliating experience to-day (Saturday). I had to go out to tea on Boars' Hill and a man I had been lunching with, Lawson,[55] offered to drive me. I used to know him at Univ. and I lunch wth him & Keir[56] once a week for old sakes sake, though Lawson is a most terrible bore. As soon as he got me in the car he decided that we had a good deal of spare time & said he wd. drive me first to see his old father, recently widowed, whom he has just set up in a little house at the neighbouring village of Holton. On the way I bitterly regretted having been let in for this. Lawson is a tiny little man with puffed out cheeks, a pursed in mouth, and a bristly moustache: v. bright staring eyes: and rolls the eyes, jerking his head this way & that, like a ventriloquists dummy, while he talks, talks, talks, all about himself: or else talks big of university politics, retailing opinions which I know not to be his own and wh. in any case I despise. I thought 'Now he is going to show me over this house and tell me how he arranged this and why he did that – reams of it.'

When we arrived we found a lovely wild garden with a little red cottage in it. We met an old man speaking wth a broad Yorkshire accent &

---

55 Frederick Henry Lawson (1897–1983), academic lawyer, was Lecturer in Law at University College 1924–5, at Christ Church 1925–6, Junior Research Fellow of Merton College 1925–30 and official Fellow and Tutor in Law 1930–48. He was Professor of Comparative Law and a Fellow of Brasenose College from 1948 until his retirement in 1964. See *Essays in Memory of Professor F.H. Lawson*, ed. P. Wallington and R.M. Merkin (1986).

56 David Lindsay Keir (1895–1973) was a Fellow of New College 1921–39, President and Vice-Chancellor of Queen's College, Belfast 1939–49, and Master of Balliol College from 1949 until his retirement in 1965.

plainly in the technical sense 'not a gentleman'. Point No. 1 in favour of Lawson – he is not ashamed of his origins: he rose enormously in my eyes. Then Lawson shut up completely and let the old man talk, which he did, describing all he was doing in the garden. He was just like Lawson, only in an old man it was different: and the courage of him setting to work to build up a new life here in his old age was impressive. When we had been round the whole place and into the house, & when I saw so many things out of Lawson's rooms in Merton brought out here, and saw the affection between them, and realised how Lawson had busied himself about the whole – and then remembered how abominably I had treated *my* father – and worst of all how I had dared to despise Lawson, I was, as I said, humiliated. Yet I wouldn't have missed it for anything. It does one good to see the fine side of people we've always seen the worst of. It reminded me v. much of the clerk in *Bleak Ho.* (or is it *Great Expectations*) who takes the hero out to see his father & has a cannon on the roof.[57] Do you remember?

I am glad to hear that Gribbon was really appreciative on your walk: I always feel he may become much nicer yet in time – at present, for me, he is spoiled by that cynical & coarse-grained side to his character.

Yrs

J.

TO OWEN BARFIELD (W):

Magdalen College,
Oxford.
June 19th 1930

(1) Write short critical notes on the following:

They tell me, Sir, that when I seem
To be in talk with you,
Since you make no replies, it is but dream
– One talker aping two.

And so it is, but not as they
Interpret it. For I
Seek in myself the things I thought to say,
And lo, the wells are dry.

---

57 It is in Dickens' *Great Expectations* that Wemmick takes Pip to meet 'the aged P'.

Then seeing me empty, you forsake
Your listening part, and through
My dumb lips breathe and into utterance shake
The thoughts I never knew.

Therefore you neither need reply
Nor can; thus, where we seem
Two talking, thou art One forever, and I
No dreamer, but the dream.[58]

(2) I have just finished the *Angel in the House*. Amazing poet! How all of a piece it is – how the rivetted metre both expresses and illustrates his almost fanatical love of incarnation. What particularly impressed me was his taking – what one expects to find mentioned only in anti-feminists – the Lilithian desire to be admired and making it his chief point – the lover as primarily the mechanism by wh. the woman's beauty apprehends itself.[59]

I see now why Janet saw female breasts on the dog collars, and have at last brought into consciousness the important truth: Venus is a female deity, *not* 'because men invented the mythology' but because she is. The idea of female beauty is the erotic stimulus for women as well as men. (You are v. good on this, in Margaret in the novel)[60] i.e. a lascivious man thinks about women's bodies, a lascivious woman thinks about her own. *What* a world we live in! By the way the poem beginning 'When'er I come where ladies are' is delicious.

(3) I hope my walking stick continues to give satisfaction. Do not hesitate to bring it back if you find it disappointing.

---

58 This is perhaps the first version of a poem Lewis was to publish 'anonymously' and in a slightly different version in *Letters to Malcolm: Chiefly on Prayer* (1964), ch. 13, where he says, 'I've just found in an old note book a poem, with no author's name attached, which is rather relevant to something we were talking about a few weeks ago – I mean, the haunting fear that there is no-one listening, and that what we call prayer is soliloquy: someone talking to himself. This writer takes the bull by the horns and says in effect: "Very well, suppose it is", and gets a surprising result.' It is reprinted in Lewis's *Collected Poems* (1994).

59 In Hebrew folklore Lilith is the first wife of Adam, and she stands in contrast to Eve. Lewis was later to point up the difference between them in *That Hideous Strength* (1945), ch. III, pt iii: 'To desire the desiring of her own beauty is the vanity of Lilith, but to desire the enjoying of her own beauty is the obedience of Eve.'

60 Barfield's novel, 'English People'.

(4) When shall I next see you?

Yours,

C.S.L.

TO ARTHUR GREEVES (W):

My dear Arthur,

I spoke too soon about the pleasures of adding Tuesday to my list of regular bright spots in the week! My disappointment was aggravated by the fact that for the rest of the week whenever the post came in and I thought 'Ah! This will be it' I actually got (on five several occasions) a beastly business letter from Condlin involving hours of tedious work. I had already mentally resolved (a) Not to write again (b) To write a letter full of such cutting sarcasms as wd make you die of mortification (c) To write a letter in such a strain of solemn, manly pathos that you would expire in an ecstasy of repentance (d) To show my magnanimity by writing as if I hadn't noticed the omission – when on getting back to college at 10 o'clock last night I was delighted to find your letter.

I fully appreciate what you say about the Clandeboye woods and think that I too notice smaller things much more than I did: which is a great advantage since, in what we ordinarily call dull country, a flower or the turn of a stream can now make up for the lack of mountains and woods. As for your other point – any comparison between Spring & Autumn – as between youth & age or man and woman – is, I think, hopeless. One becomes less & less inclined to pick & choose, or to pit one part of reality against another. It is all the one thing working itself out in orderly rhythms & branchings which could not be better or other than they are.

'Sentimental stodge' is exactly what one would think of Coventry Patmore, or certain parts of him, if you read them in the wrong mood – though even then, I think, there is a kind of scholarly keenness and cleanness in language and metre which makes stodge hardly the right word. (I don't know if you get my meaning. Can you imagine a picture in which the subject is extremely sentimental, and even the colouring rather bad, but in wh. the *fine firm* lines reveal that it is a master after all?)

I envy you your shelf of Macdonalds and long to look over them wth your guidance. I have read both *The Princess the Goblins* & *The Princess*

*& Curdie.*⁶¹ In fact I read the former (the other is a sequel to it) for about the third time when I was ill this spring. Read it at once if you have it, it is the better of the two. There is the fine part about the princess discovering her godmother in the attic spinning. (This reminds me at once of Mrs McNeill, wh. reminds me I recently discovered a letter written by her to my mother at the time of old McNeill's death in wh. she said 'He always said you were his best pupil and when you came to call I always sent to tell him because I knew he loved to see you' – a fact wh. she has told me a hundred times, with solemn shake of the head, and wh. I can hear her saying at this moment.⁶² Never omit to say that I have asked for them, when you meet, and that I send my love: and plead my cause when you can. I don't want it to be by any fault of mine if that old link is broken). Another fine thing in *The Pr. & the Goblin* is where Curdie, in a dream, keeps on dreaming that he has waked up and then finding that he is still in bed. This means the same as the passage where Adam says to Lilith 'Unless you unclose your hand you will never die & therefore never wake. *You may think you have died and even that you have risen again*: but both will be a dream.'⁶³

This has a terrible meaning, specially for imaginative people. We read of spiritual efforts, and our imagination makes us believe that, because we enjoy the idea of doing them, we have done them. I am appalled to see how much of the change wh. I thought I had undergone lately was only imaginary. The real work seems still to be done. It is so fatally easy to confuse an aesthetic appreciation of the spiritual life with the life itself – to dream that you have waked, washed, and dressed, & then to find yourself still in bed.

I was glad to hear that you had had a long talk with Reid, because I argue from this that the anger wh. Bryson attributed to him has turned out to be all a mare's nest, or at least has blown over. Give him my compliments. As I write I have a vivid memory of that day with you and him in the woods beyond Hannah's Town⁶⁴ – what wd. I not give to see them this minute. Tho' I believe that longing for them is as good, for if I were there what could they (or any other beautiful object) give me but more longing.

---

61 George MacDonald, *The Princess and the Goblin* (1871); *The Princess and Curdie* (1882).
62 Mrs Margaret McNeill's husband, James Adam McNeill (1853–1907) had been the mathematics master at the Methodist College, Belfast, when Flora Lewis was a pupil there at various sessions between 1881 and 1885. Mrs McNeill's letter to Flora of 3 October 1907, quoted above, is found in LP III: 84–5.
63 George MacDonald, *Lilith* (1895), ch. XL, p. 302.
64 i.e. Hannahstown, Co. Antrim.

The period of bright green meadows golden wth buttercups is over here and they are mowing the hay. One hardly *walks*, it is too hot – in spite of a temporary cooling yesterday after a magnificent thunderstorm the night before; but I have had some delightful 'soaks' amid the smell (almost *maddeningly* remeniscent) of the mowing and the sound of the mowers.

This afternoon I have lounged in the garden & began Mary Webb's *Precious Bane*.[65] I can't remember whether you recommended it to me or not. If it goes on as well as it has begun I shall put it very high indeed. In fact I hardly know a book which has given me such a delicious feeling of *country* – homely yet full of eeriness, as in real life. I have it in the *Travellers' Library* edition. The language – tho some people will call it 'pastiche' – seems to me delicious. Why after all should one always write the speech of ones own time & class?

Isn't it an exciting moment when the whole of a work is typed? Be sure to report further progress.

Yrs

Jack

TO ARTHUR GREEVES (W):

Hillsboro,
Western Rd.,
Headington,
Oxford
June 22nd 1930

My dear Arthur,

Your last letter is mysterious. What is the meaning of the cryptic word 'Pharoh' (sic) added to the sentence 'I think I told you this before'? After cudgelling my brains I can make neither head nor tail of it. Again, why should my leaving a margin shorten your weekly allowance? I'm afraid I must be getting very dense. Then why the last page of your letter should be called 'the Jacobean MS of 1930' I cannot remotely conjecture. If your jokes continue to be [as] profound as this you will probably find me in an asylum when you next visit England.

By the way, please note that I moved out to Headington last night and am now to be addressed there. It is delightful to have term over and I can feel it so though to-day has been a most exasperating one. It is terrible to

---

65 Mary Webb, *Precious Bane* (1924; Travellers' Library, 1928).

find how little progress ones philosophy and charity have made when they are brought to the test of domestic life. However I think I got over most of my fusses fairly quickly and (I hope) without letting them hurt anyone else.

Did I tell you in my last that a former pupil of mine, Griffiths, had been to spend a night with me? I mention him now because his name deserves to be honoured. I happened to tell him that Barfield (he has only met him once but then he has read *Poetic Diction* so often that he knows him well) was hoping to edit the unpublished works of Coleridge if an American university, which was at present toying with the idea, made up its mind to finance him: but that if they did not he would go into his father's business. A few days later a letter came from Griffiths to say that he and the two friends he lived with had £800 a year between the three of them: that it was impossible morally to spend this on themselves, and that the surplus, on any right view, was not justly their own: did I therefore think that Barfield could be prevailed on to accept £100 a year for the next few years. This is the sort of thing that really makes one feel fit. Of course I hope he will not accept it, but that doesn't alter the merit of the proposers – specially the other two who don't even know him. They must be a remarkable trio.

They have pooled their money – Griffiths by the way had none – and live together in a Cotswold cottage doing their own work and pursuing their studies.[66] Their aim is, as far as possible, to use nothing which is a product of the factory system or of modern industry in general: for they think these things so iniquitous that every one is more or less party to a crime in using them. I can't help wondering where their own income comes from, and suspect an inconsistency here. Indeed whether the whole thing is folly or not I haven't made up my mind. What do you think? There is certainly something attractive about the idea of living as far as may be on the produce of the land about you: to see in every walk the pastures where your mutton grazed when it was sheep, the gardens where your vegetables grew, the mill where your flour was ground, and the workshop where your chairs were sawn – and to feel that bit of country actually and literally in your veins.

---

66 The two friends, with whom Alan Griffiths (later Dom Bede Griffiths) lived in a commune, were his friends from Magdalen College, Hugh Waterman and Martyn Skinner. The story of the commune and Griffiths' story afterwards is told in Griffiths' *The Golden String*, ch. 4. The correspondence between the three men is found in the Bodleian Library.

Tolkien once remarked to me that the feeling about home must have been quite different in the days when a family had fed on the produce of the same few miles of country for six generations, and that perhaps this was why they saw nymphs in the fountains and dryads in the wood – they were not mistaken for there was in a sense a *real* (not metaphorical) connection between them and the countryside. What had been earth and air & later corn, and later still bread, really was in them. We of course who live on a standardised international diet (you may have had Canadian flour, English meat, Scotch oatmeal, African oranges, & Australian wine to day) are really artificial beings and have no connection (save in sentiment) with any place on earth. We are synthetic men, uprooted. The strength of the hills is not ours.[67] My pen has run away with me on this subject.

I am delighted to hear that you have taken to Johnson. Yes, isn't it a magnificent style – the very essence of manliness and condensation – I find Johnson very *bracing* when I am in my slack, self pitying mood. The amazing thing is his power of stating platitudes – or what in anyone else wd. be platitudes – so that we really believe them at last and realise their importance. Doesn't it remind you a bit of Handel? As to his critical judgement I think he is always sensible and nearly always wrong. He has no ear for metre and little imagination. I personally get more pleasure from the *Rambler* than from anything else of his & at one time I used to read a Rambler every evening as a nightcap. They are so *quieting* in their brave, sensible dignity.

I know the feeling you describe – of talking far into the night wth one friend while the rest of the house sleeps. (I notice it is a feeling you have never given me occasion to indulge in *your* society) By the way, about the 'Moving Image' I should warn you that there is going to be a great deal of conversation: in fact it is to be almost a Platonic dialogue in a fantastic setting wth story intermixed. If you take *The Symposium, Phantastes, Tristram Shandy* and stir them up all together you will about have the recipe. So now you are prepared for the worst!

I am reading the *Politics* of Aristotle[68] which contains one of the few reasoned defences of slavery in ancient literature – most of th. ancients

---

67 Psalm 95:4: 'In his hand are all the corners of the earth: and the strength of the hills is his also.'

68 *The Politics of Aristotle*, from the text of Immanel Bekker, with English notes by J.R.T. Eaton (1885).

taking it for granted and therefore feeling no need to defend it. Very subtle, but I think I see his weak point. I have finished *Precious Bane* and think I have enjoyed it more than any novel since the Brontë's. Why do women write such good novels. Men's novels, except Scott, seem to me on the same level as womens' poetry.

Yours

J.

TO ARTHUR GREEVES (W):

[Long Crendon,
Bucks.]
June 31st 1930
[1 July 1930]

My dear Arthur,

As your letter did not reach me till yesterday (that is Monday) – and I had before then passed through all the stages of disappointment, you can hardly complain if this comes late. My excuse is that Warnie came up on Saturday and was with me the whole of Sunday, and on Monday I journeyed to Long Crendon to stay wth Barfield where I now am – amid thatched roofs and the crooning of hens, with a pony & a donkey in the orchard and honeysuckle over the door.

The great event of the last week, in one sense, has been in my library. I have effected the exchange of my Bombay Kipling[69] for the big Morris,[70] with the pleasant surprise that they allowed me £50 for the Kipling and charged only 18 guineas for the Morris so that I have a credit balance of £30 odd at Blackwells. Oh what a feast this would have been in the old days! Have you any advice as to the best way of using it? In the meantime I am delighted with the Morris, tho it seems to be rather carelessly printed – i.e. I have already found readings in it wh. must be mistakes. However this is only a trifle.

The real point is that it has made me read *Love is Enough*[71] wh. I never did before, and I most strongly advise you to do so at the first opportunity. You know that it is a play – you will find a very illuminating account of it in Mackail's life. The story is *in one way* a typical Morris

---

69 The Bombay Edition of the Works of Rudyard Kipling, 31 vols. (1913–38).

70 *The Collected Works of William Morris*, ed. Mary Morris, 24 vols. (1910–15).

71 William Morris, *Love is Enough* (1872).

story, that of a King who dreams of a fair woman in a distant land and finally abandons his kingdom to go and find her. He does so. Returns and finds his kingdom taken by another, but departs again without bitterness because 'love is enough'. But although this sounds so typical it is extremely different from the usual Morris.

In the first place, his long wanderings, such as you found too long drawn out in the *Well at the Worlds End*, instead of being given in full, are just hinted at in the dialogue, and for this reason gain enormously in suggestiveness. In the second place – I hardly know how to put it. You know I always thought Morris the most essentially *pagan* of all poets. The beauty of the actual world, the vague longings wh. it excites, the inevitable failure to satisfy these longings, and over all the haunting sense of time & change making the world heart breakingly beautiful just because it slips away ('Oh death that makest life so sweet' as he says) all this, I thought, he gave to perfection: but of what this longing really pointed to, of the reason why beauty made us homesick, of the reality *behind*, I thought he had no inkling. And for that reason his poetry always seemed to me dangerous and apt to lead to sensuality – for it is the frustrated longing that drives us to the *pis aller*, and as we lose hope of our real immortal mistress we turn to harlots.

Now in *Love is Enough* he raises himself right out of his own world. He suddenly shows that he is at bottom aware of the real symbolical import of all the longing and even of earthly love itself. In the speeches of Love (who is the most important character) there is clear statement of eternal values (coupled with a refusal to offer you crudely personal immortality) and also, best of all, a full understanding that there is something beyond pleasure & pain. For the first (and last?) time the light of *holiness* shines through Morris' romanticism, not destroying but perfecting it. Reading this has been a great experience to me: and coming on top of the *Angel in the House* has shown me that in my fear of the sensual cheat wh. lurked at the back of my old romantic days (see Dymer VII) I have aimed at too much austerity and even dishonoured love altogether. I have become a dry prig. I do hope I am not being mocked – that this is not merely the masked vanguard of a new sensuality. But I verily believe not. In this light I shall come back to Morris and all that world. I have the key now and perhaps can stand the sweetness safely. For this too is a feature of life that becomes gradually clearer: namely that the road is always turning round and going back to places we seemed to have left –

but they are different (yet in a way the same) when you come to them the second time.

I don't remember your *Lives of the Poets*[72] – what is the new Johnson like?

As to the business about being 'rooted' or 'at home everywhere', I wonder are they really the opposite, or are they the same thing. I mean, don't you enjoy the Alps more precisely because you began by first learning to love in an intimate and homely way our own hills and woods? While the mere globe-trotter, starting not from a home feeling but from guide books & aesthetic chatter, feels *equally* at home everywhere only in the sense that he is really at home nowhere? It is just like the difference between vague general philanthropy (wh. is all balls) and learning first to love your own friends and neighbours wh. makes you *more*, not less, able to love the next stranger who comes along. If a man loveth not his brother whom he hath seen – etc.[73] In other words doesn't one get to the universal (either in people or in inanimate nature) *thro'* the individual – not by going off into a mere generalised mash. I don't know if I make myself clear.

Your description of the empty rooms at home gave me a terrible thought – supposing my father had died when I was sixteen and all that had been lost before I found anything else – and you and I wd. probably never have met again. This week's instalment has been written alright but I forgot to bring it here with me, so you will probably have two next week.

The Barfields have been making wine from the vine that grows on their cottage and next year when it is ready to drink we think of having a Bacchic festival.[74] The adopted baby is to be the infant Bacchus. Harwood with his fat shiny face, on the donkey, will be Silenus. B. and I

---

72 On Johnson's *Lives of the English Poets* see note 56 to letter of 2 August 1928.

73 1 John 4:20: 'If a man say, I love God, and hateth his brother, he is a liar: for he that loveth not his brother whom he hath seen, how can he love God whom he hath not seen?'

74 In Greek mythology Bacchus or Dionysus is the god of wine and merriment whose rites are celebrated with music and dancing. In his entourage are the tipsy satyr, Silenus, and frenzied women followers called maenads. The sedate Corybantes are priests. Of course the real Greek cult of Bacchus was very serious and sometimes frightening, but Lewis had in mind something as lighthearted as he was later to make the Bacchic festival in chapter 11 of the Narnian story, *Prince Caspian* (1951): 'The crowd and dance round Aslan...grew so thick and rapid that Lucy was confused...One was a youth, dressed only in a fawn-skin, with vine-leaves wreathed in his curly hair.

Corybantes. Mrs B. a Maenad. B. and I will write the poetry & she will compose a dance. You ought to come.

Yrs

J.

TO ARTHUR GREEVES (W):

[Hillsboro]
July 8th 1930

My dear Arthur,

Your letters get later and later every week. If you write on Monday the first week, on Tuesday the second week, and so on, then in seven weeks you will be writing on Monday again: but you will have written one letter less than you should. In a year you will have written eight letters less, that is thirty six pages. Assuming that we both live thirty years more you will in that time have cheated me out of one thousand and eighty pages. *Why*, oh why, do you do these things?

My examining begins on the 17th and for about ten days I shall be at it from morning till night, so that you must look for no instalments or letters during that time: but I hope you will continue to write to me – as your letters, if they arrive, will be about the only pleasure that remains.

I am interested to hear that you have a new friend. Is he really one of us? – not that I don't think dozens of people v. well worth having as friends without their sharing the things we specially like – indeed in *some* ways better worth having on that account.

You have I think misunderstood what I said about the return from austerity. I never meant for a moment that I was beginning to doubt whether absolute chastity was the true goal – of that I am certain. What I meant was that I began to think that I was mistaken in aiming at this goal by the means of a stern repression and even a contemptuous distrust of all that emotional & imaginative experience wh. seems to border on the voluptuous: whether it was well to see in certain romances and

---

His face would have been almost too pretty for a boy's, if it had not looked so extremely wild...There were a lot of girls with him, as wild as he. There was even, unexpectedly, someone on a donkey. The man on the donkey, who was old and enormously fat, began calling out at once, "Refreshments! Time for refreshments," and falling off his donkey and being bundled on to it again by the others, while the donkey was under the impression that the whole thing was a circus and tried to give a display of walking on its hind legs.'

certain music nothing but one more wile of the enemy: whether perhaps the right way was not to keep always alive in ones soul a certain tenderness & luxuriousness always reaching out to *that of which* (on my view) sex must be the copy. In other words, whether, while I was right in seeing that a copy must be different from an original, I ought not to have remembered that it must also be *like* it – else how wd. it be a copy? In the second place, what I feared was *not* lest this mood should be temporary but lest it should turn out to be another wile. What I also ought to have said in my last letter but didn't is that the whole thing has made me feel that I have never given half enough importance to love in the sense of the *affections*.

One passage in your letter – in which you corrected *bare* to *bear* amused me v. much, as the original wd. have read 'I find it more difficult to *bare* myself lovingly towards my neighbours & my relations.' The picture of you *baring* yourself 'lovingly' to a long row of neighbours (the O'Mulligan etc) & relations – so remeniscent of a notorious passage in Rousseau – is not easily surpassed!

Almost ever since the Vac. began I have been reading a little every evening in Traherne's *Centuries of Meditations* (Dobell. About 7/-. Lovely paper). I forget whether we have talked of it or not. I think he suffers by making out everything much too easy and really shirking the problem of evil in all its forms: at least, as far as I have got, for it is unfair to say this of a book not yet finished. But apart from this he has extraordinary merits. What do you think of the following; – 'The world…is the beautiful frontispiece to Eternity'[75] – 'You never enjoy the world aright till the sea itself floweth in your veins, till you are clothed with the heavens and crowned with the stars…till you can sing and rejoice and delight in God as misers do in gold'[76] – 'I must lead you out of this into another world to *learn your wants*. For till you find them you will never be happy'[77] – 'They (i.e. Souls) were made to love and are dark and vain and comfortless till they do it. Till they love they are idle or misemployed. Till they love they are desolate.'[78] But I could go on quoting from this book forever.

A complete Coventry Patmore[79] wh. I ordered shortly after reading

75 Thomas Traherne, *Centuries of Meditations*, ed. Bertram Dobell (1927), 'The First Century', no. 20, p. 13.

76 ibid., no. 29, p. 19.

77 ibid., no. 43, p. 28.

78 ibid., 'The Second Century', no. 48, p. 112.

79 *Poems by Coventry Patmore*, with an Introduction by Basil Champneys (G. Bell & Sons, 1906).

the *Angel in the House* has arrived – Bell & Sons, 7/6, quite a pleasant volume – and I have just dipped into it. I don't remember for many years to have felt so disposed for new reading as I do now, and specially poetry. Everything seems – you know the feeling – to be beginning again and one has the sense of immortality.

Barfield and I finished the *Paradiso* when I was with him. I think it reaches heights of poetry which you get nowhere else: an ether almost too fine to breathe. It is a pity that I can give you no notion what it is like. Can you imagine Shelley at his most ecstatic combined with Milton at his most solemn & rigid? It sounds impossible I know, but that is what Dante has done.

We also read some Beowulf with a very remarkable young woman. She was a farmer's daughter who got a county scholarship and went up to London getting a good degree in English. Then – and here's the marvel – she settled down at home again and divides her time between milking the cows & taking occasional pupils, apparently contented in both. Thats what we want, isn't it? *Emigration* from the uneducated class into ours only swells the intellectual unemployed: but to have education transforming people & yet leaving them wth their roots in the earth (which *then* they will be able to appreciate) is the way to make class disappear altogether. She is 'remarkable' only in this: otherwise the adjective does her gross injustice for she is exquisitely ordinary – and not at all pretty except with the bonny open air plumpness of her age & class.

I also had some lovely bathes wth Barfield in a reach of the little river Thame. Picture us lounging naked under the pollards on a flat field: mowers in the next field: and tiny young dragon flies – too small to be frightful yet – darting among the lilies. Here I learned to dive wh. is a great change in my life & has important (religious) connections. I'll explain that later. They are still v. ungraceful dives but I do get in head first.[80]

This is the last letter you'll get till the infernal (but profitable) examining is over – but like a good chap (!) (old man!) do keep on writing to me. So glad you approve of precious bane. Isn't Wizard Beguildy a lovely character: also the scene of Prue Sarn alone in the attic.

Yrs

J.

---

80 C.S. Lewis, *The Pilgrim's Regress* (1933), bk. ix, ch. 4: ' "Alas," said [John], "I have never learned to dive." "There is nothing to learn," said [Mother Kirk]. "The art of diving is not to do anything new but simply to cease doing something. You have only to let yourself go." '

TO ARTHUR GREEVES (W):

[Hillsboro]
July 29th 1930

My dear Arthur,

Harrah! Examining is over. As to your question why I dislike it, it is not the jaunt to Cambridge (by the bye I am not going this year) wh. I dislike but the fortnight or so of actually marking the papers that precedes it. I had fewer than usual this time, but even so it means working absolutely solidly from after breakfast till supper: often it means going on after supper as well. As the work has no interest whatever & yet demands unsleeping attention, one gets very tired.

Thank you for writing – I enjoyed your two letters enormously. Do stop apologising for them and wondering archly (à la Tchanie!) how I can read them. Surely it needs no great imagination for you to realise that every mention of things at home now comes to me with the sweetness that belongs only to what is irrevocable. Secondly, there are a great many subjects on which you are the only person whom I can write to or be written to by with full understanding. Thirdly our common ground represents what is really (I think) the deepest stratum in my life, the thing in me that, if there should be another personal life, is most likely to survive the dissolution of my brain. Certainly when I come to die I am more likely to remember certain things that you and I have explored or suffered or enjoyed together than anything else.

It is an interesting and rather grim enquiry – how much of our present selves we cd. hope to take with us if there were another life. I take it that whatever is *merely* intellectual, *mere* theory, must go, since we probably hold it only by memory habit, wh. may depend on the matter of the brain. Only what has gone far deeper, what has been incorporated into the unconscious depths, can hope to survive. This often comes over me when I think of religion: and it is a shock to realise that the mere *thinking* it may be nothing, and that only the tiny bit which we really practice is likely to be ours in any sense of which death can not make hay.

I think you must be mistaken about having shown me Traherne. Surely it is much more likely that *you* are talking balls. Anyway I am glad you like him. Your question about the difference of writing between my instalments and my letters I don't understand. If you mean handwriting, of course the answer is that in the letters I just scribble as hard as I can lick, while in the instalments[81] I stop to think. If you mean language, the answer is (I shd. have thought) obvious.

Oh you can't imagine the poignancy with wh. your account of the sunny windy day near the dry tree fell across a dreary, dusty afternoon of those sordid papers, when my head was aching and the boys' horrid handwriting seemed to jump on the page.

I don't know quite what I feel about your assistance at the accouchement of our sister the cow. I know what I ought to feel – simply the same thrill that I feel at the first coming up of a flower. Physical disgust is a sensation wh. I have very often and of which I am always ashamed. If one lets it grow upon one it will in the end cut one out from all delighted participation in the life of nature. For God is gross and never heard of decency and cares nothing for refinement: nor do children, nor most women, nor any of the beasts, nor men either except in certain sophisticated classes. And yet its hard to feel that the faculty of disgust is a sheer evil from beginning to end. I don't know what to make of it. (Perhaps in one way it is, in another, it isn't!) At any rate there can be no two opinions about the delightfulness of seeing the other cows coming round to inspect the infant. Did they show any signs of congratulating the mother? for I notice that when one of our hens lays an egg, *all* join in the noise – whether that is congratulation or simply that they regard themselves as a single individual and announce '*We* have laid an egg.'

Talking about hens, have you read the Nonne Prestes Tale in Chaucer – its *delicious*: homely & ridiculous in the best possible way. Which reminds me, did you ever in your 'pink book' stage read any version of Reynard the Fox? It is one of the great medieval creations, and I want someday to get it: the English version is by Caxton,[82] I am afraid from a rather late French version, but probably quite good.

Since writing the last sentence I have come into College to entertain two people to dinner & spend the night. As they did not leave till 3 o'clock (it is now 10) I am feeling rather morning-after-ish! One of them is a man called Dyson[83] who teaches English at Reading. He is only in

---

81 This was to be his last reference to 'The Moving Image'.

82 *Reynart the Foxe* (Caxton, 1481).

83 Henry Victor Dyson 'Hugo' Dyson (1896–1975) was an undergraduate at Exeter College, Oxford, taking his BA in 1921. He was a lecturer and tutor in the University of Reading 1921–45, and Fellow and Tutor in English Literature at Merton College 1945–63. For details of their friendship, and the part he played in the Inklings, see *SBJ*, *CG* and Humphrey Carpenter's *The Inklings* (1978). See **Henry Victor Dyson 'Hugo' Dyson** in the Biographical Appendix.

Oxford for a few weeks and having met him once I liked him so well that I determined to get to know him better. My feeling was apparently reciprocated and I think we sat up so late with the feeling that heaven knew when we might meet again and the new friendship had to be freed past its youth and into maturity in a single evening. Although my head aches this morning I do not regret it. Such things come rarely and are worth a higher price than this. He is a man who really loves truth: a philosopher and a religious man: who makes his critical & literary activities depend on the former – none of your damned dilettante. In appearance he is like a plumper edition of Uncle Gussie & has something the same vivacity & quickness of speech, but a much more honestly merry laugh. Have you observed that it is the most serious conversations which produce in their course the best laughter? How we roared and fooled at times in the silence of last night – but always in a few minutes buckled to again with renewed seriousness. Then, as always here, the close of the whole thing is the journey through pitch black cloisters to let them out by the little gate with my key, where after the dark one suddenly sees the tower far above, in the light cast up from the street lamps. How I shall remember all this some day!

The other man was Coghill of Exeter, a friend of Chevasse, who talks v. like Chevasse (in voice I mean) but is a far better fellow. I am looking forward to reading *Desert Islands*[84] & am glad to have your judgment of it. Oh, by the way, I forgot to thank you for your offer of the Macdonalds. *Pro tanto quid retribuamus*? as the tramcars say – what can I give you in return? About Johnson & Milton – wasn't it M's politics that made J. so unfair?[85] The old die-hard Tory could never forgive the puritan, republican & regicide.

Yrs.

Jack

---

84 Walter de la Mare, *Desert Islands* (1930).

85 Johnson, *Lives of the English Poets*, op. cit., vol. I, p. 157: 'Milton's republicanism was, I am afraid, founded in an envious hatred of greatness, and a sullen desire of independence; in petulance impatient of controul, and pride disdainful of superiority. He hated monarchs in the state and prelates in the church; for he hated all whom he was required to obey. It is to be suspected that his predominant desire was to destroy rather than establish, and that he felt not so much the love of liberty as repugnance to authority.'

TO ARTHUR GREEVES (W):

[Hillsboro]
Aug. 3rd 1930

My dear Arthur,

Your account of your novel is certainly v. obscure. I thought the whole was already typed – or was that only a draught? I am sorry that I cannot be present at the accouchement, however 'painful and disgusting'.

I have been wondering why these days of rain & wind in the summer have such a charm for me. Is it simply an offshoot of my general love of winter, and these days please me as a foretaste of winter – as if the wind shook Summer and he buttoned his coat and said 'Dear me. I'm beginning to get old.' I walked in the fields beyond Barton after tea to day and sat under a hedge – the sort of hedge that is nearly all trees. The wind tossed it and tumbled it: and from the field – which was full of stacks of corn – straws kept on blowing up to me. Endless rain clouds went overhead. Somehow I was very happy in it – snug, you know. And yet one ought to feel snugger in a warm ditch in winter. Or is it that such days fall outside ones conventional categories of the seasons, being neither typical summer days nor typical autumn days, nor typical anything, and therefore, thwarting ones *derivative* reactions and all that has been already stereotyped by literature and painting, they force one to wake up and see the thing as it really is? Or is it part of the same general law which makes the landscape look more exciting upside down? However a fool can ask more questions in an hour than a wise man can answer in a life time.

The other thing I was thinking on my walk was this: I had just begun M. Arnold's *Studies In Celtic Literature*[86] and looking on to the end I saw that he said that German Romanticism (he particularly mentioned Novalis[87]) was a kind of clumsy attempt at the 'natural magic' of the Celts. Now I was perfectly certain that whatever else was true, that was not: but this set me puzzling as to what the real difference between the two was. I found that when I tried to get the spirit of German romance I got the idea of smiths, gold, dwarfs, forests, mountains, cottages and castles: while the other gave me the idea of water and rushes and clouds.

---

86 Matthew Arnold, *On the Study of Celtic Literature* (1867).
87 Novalis was the pseudonym of the German romantic poet and novelist, Friedrich Leopold von Hardenberg (1772–1801).

Then I noted that the Celtic was much more sensuous; also less *homely*: also, entirely lacking in *reverence*, of which the Germanic was full. Then again that the Germanic *glowed* in a sense with rich sombre colours, while the Celtic was all transparent and full of nuances – evanescent – but very bright. One sees that Celtic is essentially Pagan, not merely in the sense of being heathen (not-Christian), as the Germanic may be, but in the sense of being irredeemably Pagan, frivolous under all its melancholy, incapable of growing into religion, and – I think – a little heartless. In fact, add Roman civilisation to it and you get – France. I'm not running it down: before it gets Romanised it is delicious and refreshing. I don't want to give up either: they are almost ones male and female soul. Do you feel at all in sympathy with what I have been saying? And do you agree that the Germanic – gold & smiths – runs peculiarly to mineral images, i.e. the Earth – while Celtic runs to the elements. I think in the *Tempest* Caliban Is – almost a picture of the Germanic at its lowest, and Ariel the Celtic: but look at the lovely earthy poetry put into Caliban's mouth on two occasions.

To be frank I was rather prepared for *Desert Islands* turning out a disappointment, tho' my hopes had been temporarily resurrected by what you said of it. De La Mare has fallen infinitely below himself. I was looking at the *Connoisseur*[88] again not long ago. Of course it is good – he can't write anything that isn't that. But isn't there just a touch of the dilettante about it? – certainly a lack of the real spirituality one finds in the *Veil*? My idea is that he really bade good bye to the best part of himself in the lovely poem 'Be not too wildly amorous of the far'.[89] The peculiar kind of vision he had was of a strangely piercing quality and probably almost unbearable to the possessor: only a man of great solidity, of real character, sound at the bases of his mind & braced with philosophy, could have carried it safely. But De La Mare was not such a man. It was quite likely really leading him to madness, & he knew it. Hardly knowing what he did, and yet just knowing, he *sent* it away. I am told he lives in the midst of the silly London literary sets. His real day is over. Do you think this a possible theory?

Yes. The Witch is gone. Do you ever go into Leeborough garden? How strange it would be for you to sit on that summer seat now: it almost

---

88 Walter de la Mare, *The Connoisseur* (1926).

89 The opening line of 'The Imagination's Pride' from de la Mare's *The Veil and Other Poems* (1921).

makes me shudder. Do you know it sometimes comes to me as a shock to realise that all the *rest* of Strandtown is going on just the same.

As to when we shall meet: we are moving house in September (I'm going to tell you nothing about this so that it will be a surprise when you see it) so I am afraid I shall not be able to come to Ireland this summer. As to your coming here, it wd. be obviously a bad time to choose the move! (I hear[d] your views on this after your last experience!) I think October would be the best, and will keep you informed. Of course if you *are* in England at the end of August let me know. How I long for one of our walks & talks together: and how I would like to see you peering into the pages of my Ellis' *Metrical Romances*[90] wh. at last I have got: not to mention the Morris. A propos of which (& this is what my whole letter *should* have been about) what with Morris & other things I really seem to have had youth given back to me lately. But I must try to describe this another time, as I am spoiling the margin wh. you demand!

Yrs

J.

TO ARTHUR GREEVES (W):

[Hillsboro]
Aug 13. 1930

My dear Arthur,

I wonder what has happened. Are you ill – or away – or simply lazy? However, as you wrote to me so perseveringly during *my* silence (tho' you must allow that mine was foretold and unavoidable) I will continue to write during yours: and also to prevent a bad habit of silence setting in on both sides.

It is a curious thing that as I look back I can remember no breaks in the regular course of letters during the Bookham period. Breaks I suppose there must have been and my failure to recollect them is part of the same delusion (but not all delusion either) of memory, wh. makes the past summers always fine and the past winters always frosty. Yet on the whole I do really think that we were very regular, and am very anxious to keep it up now without a break – at least until the habit is so fully formed that it is sure to survive a short intermission. This is becoming rather prosy!

---

90 George Ellis, *Specimens of Early English Metrical Romances* (1805).

Talking about the breaking of resolutions – you see how skilfully I glide away from my prosing to something really gay and brilliant and witty and novel – in fact 'much more rational but much less like a ball'[91] – talking then of resolutions (but we weren't talking. Yes, but we are now!) – talking of resolutions, one of the worst things about a moral relapse – to me – is that it throws such a shadow back on the time before during which you thought you were getting on quite well. Having found oneself – for the hundredth time – back where one started, it seems so obvious that one has never really moved at all: and that what seemed progress was only [a] dream, or even the irrelevant result of circumstances or physical condition.

I have again begun my German and do half an hour every morning before beginning my other work. I am still at Novalis – you will wonder how I have not finished it long ago, and even to myself I seem to have been reading it almost all my life. As I go at about the pace of a school-boy translating Caesar I expect it will last me for the rest of my days. (I am like the man in the story. 'Why not buy a book?' 'Oh I have one already.') This certainly leads to economy. It has better results too. As you know, 'Heinrich Von Ofterdingen'[92] wh. I am reading is a very Macdon-aldy book – indeed Novalis is perhaps the greatest single influence on Macdonald – full of 'holiness', gloriously German-romantic (i.e. a delicious mingling of earthy homeliness and magic, also of a sort of spiritual voluptuousness with innocence) and to be compelled to spell out such stuff word by word instead of galloping greedily thro' it as I certainly should if I could find a translation really forces me to get the most out of it. There is *no* translation either into French or English: so you will have to rely on what I tell you. However I have probably said all this before.

Last night I slept very little owing to a pain I sometimes have wh. Joey says is the kidneys: so I have gone a walk longer than usual to day in the hope of tiring myself out. In spite of the heavy green August foliage it really might be October: the wailing wind and the clouds are sheer Autumn. How unfortunate it is that you cannot follow my walks as I can yours. It would convey nothing to you if I said that I went thro' the Eatons (Wood Eaton and Water Eaton). The first half of the walk is all in

---

91 Austen, *Pride and Prejudice*, ch. 11.
92 Friedrich Leopold von Hardenberg (or Novalis), *Heinrich von Ofterdingen* (1802).

a road, absolutely flat, with a clear stream behind it: through every break in the high hedges you get specimens of that sort of beauty that flat country has: i.e. that you never see further than across the first field, and beyond its further hedge the big elms – tho really scattered – look like a continuous forest. Nearer, of course, are the wild flowers and the cows whisking their tails. Wood Eaton itself is an almost ideal village. There is a great house (Georgian),[93] severe in outline, but mellowed with yellow moss, in a park where there are some fine cedars: about sixteen cottages round a pond and green, all of grey stone and nearly all thatched: a church: and in every direction very high walls of flat stones without mortar, and inside them the invariable rows of huge elms – greatly improved this afternoon by the wind.

Thence my walk led out into open fields, where the flatness made the sky enormous and the cows seemed to go on forever and ever. Do you know the strange sort of contrast there is in such a place on such a day between the utter placidity of the landscape and the hurry and scurry of the clouds – at least of the clouds immediately overhead, far away on the horizon, with the absent sun shining on *them*, one always sees remote, clear, shining clouds that look almost calmer than anything else in the world. The only adventure on the ground was the sudden discovery of a field almost black with crows, which, of course dashed up cawing into the air as I approached them and then were blown about. 'The untidy crows' as Sackville West says in *The Land*[94] (a poem you should read) speaking of their flight on a windy day.

Did I tell you I have been reading a lot of Matthew Arnold's prose (I've got to for tutorial purposes). Oh, I remember, I talked about him in my last letter. I don't know that I recommend him. How do you get on with your Johnson? And how does your accouchement proceed. Perhaps it is that which has hindered you from writing.

I had a most horrible dream the other night, which I retail in case you would like to make use of it. Mrs Lovell was a poor old woman whom Minto used to give odd jobs to: she has now disappeared. I dreamed that I went to a cupboard in the kitchen to look for something. A heavy thing in brown paper dropped out at my feet. Picking it up and unwinding it I found – Mrs Lovel's HEAD! (I think it might be worked in along with

---

93 Wood Eaton Hall.
94 Vita Sackville-West, *The Land* (1926): 'Autumn', l. 94.

the hairy gums, 'Your grandmother etc etc' into the super-shocker that so often flits about our minds.)

There will, I think, be no shortage of hedgehogs in our new garden.

Do write

Yours

Jack

TO ARTHUR GREEVES (W):

[Hillsboro]
Aug. 18, 1930

My dear Arthur,

The first thing, when one is being worried as to whether one will have to have an operation or whether one is a literary failure, is *to assume absolutely mercilessly that the worst is true*, and to ask *What Then?* If it turns out in the end that the worst is not true, so much the better: but for the meantime the question must be resolutely put out of mind. Otherwise your thoughts merely go round and round a wearisome circle, now hopeful, now despondent, then hopeful again – that way madness lies. Having settled then that the worst is true, one can proceed to consider the situation: and I will talk to you as one in that situation.

Now the worst of all the things we usually say to a man who is suffering is that they inevitably provoke him to retort, in feeling, if not in words, 'Yes. It's all very well for *you*. It isn't *your* tooth that is aching.' So as soon as I read your letter I bethought me of myself on the evening when the MS of *Dymer* came back from Heinemanns rejected without a word of criticism or encouragement: and I remembered that after a very miserable night I sat down to assume the worst, as I advise you to do, and *on that basis* to come to terms with the situation. Only I did it in writing. I have been in to College this morning and found the document wh. I enclose. It is perfectly genuine and unaltered except for the marginal notes wh. I have now added in explanation of one or two expressions you might not have come across. I don't know whether it will be any help to you: it was of the greatest to me. You will be tempted to say that my situation was quite different from yours: for I succeeded in the end. To this I answer (1) That when I wrote this document I did not know I should succeed in publishing. (2) That when I did finally publish, the book was a complete failure.

To you, no doubt, at the moment it seems that to read your own book in print and to have it liked by a few friends would be ample bliss, whether any one bought it or not. Believe me, Arthur, this is an *absolute delusion*. It might satisfy you for a moment: but very soon, if it didn't sell, you would find yourself just as disappointed as you are now. So that in this sense I am *still* as disappointed an author as you. From the age of sixteen onwards I had one single ambition, from which I never wavered, in the prosecution of which I spent every ounce I could, on wh. I really & deliberately staked my whole contentment: and I recognise myself as having unmistakably failed in it. So that not only in my enclosed document, but now, in this letter, I feel that I have some right to talk to you as a man in the same boat.

Suffering of the sort that you are now feeling is my special subject, my profession, my long suit, the thing I claim to be an expert in: and if I were not writing to a man still smarting under the novelty of the blow I should point out at length how absurd it is to dignify such disappointment with the name of suffering in a world like this. (There is a woman lives in our road who is sinking into creeping paralysis and going blind: and for the last three nights she has been awake, and crying, all night, with neuritis. She says 'I feel as if my blood was boiling in my arms.') This side of the question you cannot yet be ready to feel: it wd. be more than human if you did. I only mention it because otherwise I wd. be ashamed, in speaking of myself, to use the noble word 'suffering'. However, whether you call it 'suffering' or not, I claim to be a dab at it.

The worst of it is that all the mental habits contracted during the work, go on after hope is dead. You see a tree waving in the wind and you think 'I'll put that in.' You notice some psychological fact in yourself and think 'By Jove! I'll use that in such a scene.' You read in some review a statement about contemporary literature and think 'I wonder if his opinion will be modified when he reads—, and then *bang*! it comes back again: ALL THAT IS OVER. And yet one has to go through with it: and little by little the real consolations come. Read what Bunyan says about the valley of humiliation.[95] Read about Anodos at the low island where the old woman lived.

---

95 Bunyan, *The Pilgrim's Progress*, op. cit., pt. II, p. 252: 'When we went...down the Hill, into the Valley of Humiliation, [Mr Fearing] went down as well as ever I saw man in my Life, for he cared not how mean he was, so he might be happy at last. Yes, I think there was a kind of Sympathy betwixt that Valley and him. For I never saw him better in all his Pilgrimage, than when he was in that Valley.'

For its quite true what my document says. The side of me which longs, not to write, for no one can stop us doing that, but to be approved as a writer, is not the side of us that is really worth much. And depend upon it, unless God has abandoned us, he will find means to cauterise that side somehow or other. If we can take the pain well and truly now and by it *forever* get over the wish to be distinguished beyond our fellows, well: if not we shall get it again in some other form. And honestly, the being cured, with all the pain, has pleasure too: one creeps home, tired and bruised, into a state of mind that is really restful, when all ones ambitions have been given up. Then one can really for the first time say 'Thy Kingdom come': for in that Kingdom there will be no pre-eminences and a man must have reached the stage of not caring two straws about his own status before he can enter it.

Think how difficult that would be if one *succeeded* as a writer: how bitter this necessary purgation at the age of sixty, when literary success had made your whole life and you had *then* got to begin to go through the stage of seeing it all as dust and ashes. Perhaps God has been specially kind to us in forcing us to get over it at the beginning. At all events, whether we like it or not, we have got to take the shock. As you know so well, we have got to *die*. Cry, kick, swear, we may: only like Lilith to come in the end and die far more painfully and later. Does it sound like priggery if I say 'I implore you'? Heaven knows I do it as a friend not as a preacher: do it only because you stand very high among the half-dozen people whom I love. I implore you, then, seriously, to regard your present trouble as an opportunity for carrying the dying process a stage further. If necessary, go back to the Puritan language you were brought up in and think of your literary ambitions as an 'idol' you have to give up, as a sacrifice demanded. I 'implore' because such disappointments, if *accepted* as death, and therefore the beginning of new life, are infinitely valuable: but if not, are terrible dangers. Once let self-pity come uppermost and you know where you are sure to turn for consolation. In other words they are bound to leave a man (permanently perhaps) very much better or very much worse than they found him.

So far I have said nothing about Reid's judgement, nor about your going on with the attempt. I am afraid, human nature being what it is, you must have glanced eagerly thro' this letter for some word on those very subjects: even have wondered dismally when I wd. have done moralising and get to business. Perhaps even when you so strongly urged me to write, you had always the hope that my letter would restore your confidence in yourself as a literary man. Perhaps all this time what you are asking yourself is 'Does this letter mean that Jack thinks Reid is probably right and doesn't like to say so?' Poor Arthur! You must – it is only nature – be simply starving for some word of *literary* encouragement instead of all this moral encouragement. But don't you also see that I mustn't give it? For as long as you are still thinking about *that*, still wondering whether Reid is right, you haven't taken the *first step*. Whether you are going to be a writer or not, *in either case*, you must so far die as to get over putting that question first. The other thing is so very much more important. For be sure, until we learn better, we shall get this kind of suffering again and again. Better take it now: better learn the trick that makes you free for the future. It sounds merely brutal I expect: but do remember I'm in the same boat. I would have given almost *anything* – I shudder to think what I would have given if I had been allowed – to be a successful writer. So don't think I am writing this in order to avoid giving my own opinion about your possibilities of success. I couldn't give an opinion in any case without seeing the book: but I am writing as I do simply & solely because I think the only thing for you to do is absolutely to *kill* the part of you that wants success. It's like in Phantastes where the voice said 'Ride at him or be a slave *forever*.'[96]

At present (1) Maureen is away (2) Minto is bad with indigestion (3) We are going to move on Sept. 25th (4) There is a possible visitor in the next three weeks.* In these distressing conditions I can neither go to you nor ask you to come to me. But I could (I am pretty sure) get you quite nice rooms in Old Headington and we cd. meet every day. I am *dying* to show you the new place & to have a walk & talk with you. Wd. you think of this while your mother is away. Do. It wd. honestly give me more pleasure than any (possible) thing at the moment. I am sorry to seem so inhospitable – and I would *love* to come to you for a week if I could.

Write soon. If you eat this you will grow into a unicorn. I hope you won't loathe this letter

Yours
Jack

*which unspecified!

---

96 MacDonald, *Phantastes*, ch. 22.

[The 'document' referred to in the letter above, with notes added 18 August 1930]

Saturday March 6th 1926

Last night Heinemann's returned the MS. of Dymer on which I have been at work for several years. Though I intend to try all the publishers, it seems good, in the event of a complete failure, to find out by the analysis of my present disappointment what exactly it is I hope to gain by poetical success: and what the abandonment of the hope would mean. To understand is the safest resource.

1. A certain part of my disappointment is clearly special to the present case. Heinemann's had treated me well before. I had allowed myself to think of them as οικειους (1) and flattered myself on being admitted to the rank of the number of good poets whose work they publish. I had also hoped that rejection, if it came, wd. come signed by Evans with some personal expression of regret or kindness. This is an element in my feelings at the moment wh. cannot occur when another house returns it. It may therefore be eliminated.

2. I may clearly also eliminate the desire for money, as I never seriously hoped that Dymer would pay. Or if, in more sanguine moods, I sometimes dreamed of having a few pounds of extra pocket money by it, this is something that counts for a negligible quantity in my disappointment.

3. I can also rule out, tho' not entirely, the desire for Fame, if this means the desire to be known as the author of an approved poem, the *monstrari digito*. (2) It is true that I should like and like greatly to be known (and praised) by one or two friends and good judges: but I hold this as a refinement of pleasure easily foregone. If it went by another's name, so long as it was read and liked, I should be quite content.

4. But I cannot say simply that I desire not my fame but that of the poem. In the impossible case of an exactly similar poem written by someone else and winning success I should be very far from content. Though no one else need know that the approved poem is mine, I at least must know it. The feeling is not, therefore, a disinterested love for Dymer simply as a poem I happen to like.

5. It is then a desire that something which I recognize as my own should be publicly found good: whether it is known by others to be mine is of comparatively little importance. Is it then what Aristotle says? I

desire public praise as a proof that it really is good: i.e. I wish to be able to think that I am a good poet and desire applause (tho not paid to my name) as a means to that end.

6. This is the most probable account yet suggested. One objection occurs. If an archangel or a mystical intuition admitting of no doubt, assured me that Dymer was the greatest poem ever written by man, but added that it would never be read, I should be hardly more contented than I am now. The supposition, however, raises many difficulties. (a) Is the reason of my dissatisfaction that a poem unread is not a poem at all, and that there is therefore no sense in calling it great? (b) Does the disinterested wish that, if it were great, humanity should enjoy it, count for anything? (c) Is my acquiescence in not being known (or thought) great by others, not quite what it seemed to be in Para. 3?

7. (b) is very attractive but I cannot find that it is what I feel. No poem is indispensible. In my worst moods I never supposed that the 'spirit of man' would be the worse for not having Dymer. Let it be as good as you like: they will get the same thing out of other books sooner or later. For in a larger sense and in the long run we do get the same thing out of different books.

8. (a) certainly seems to be true. The greatness of a poem can mean only the good that particular readers do actually get from it. And it is certain that no acknowledgement, however public, of my claims as a poet would make up for Dymer's not being read and enjoyed. If my archangel promised that the human race wd. go about ever after lamenting a great lost work of mine, and pay me the highest honours: no doubt this wd. give me some kind of pleasure, but not the kind I am really concerned about at present.

9. (c) This seems to have some truth in it. I shall be forced to admit that tho I do not want public praise for 'someone called Lewis' I do want it for 'the author of Dymer'. In fact the suggestion in Para. 5 is not true. I do not desire the praise *simply* as a proof. I desire that my value as a poet should be acknowledged by others as well as myself, even if they do not know where to find 'this great poet' or what he looks like etc. Perhaps some dream of being sooner or later discovered mixes still with my acquiescence in such anonymous success. I honestly don't know: tho' I might know if I cd. be perfectly honest. *That* problem I leave open for the present.

10. My desire then contains two elements. (a) The desire for some proof to myself that I am a poet. (b) The desire that my poet-hood

should be acknowledged even if no one knows that it is mine. (b) is a means to (a) but it is not valued only as a means.

11. As far as I can see both these are manifestations of the single desire for what may be called mental or spiritual rank. I have flattered myself with the idea of being among my own people when I was reading the poets and it is unpleasing to have to stand down and take my place in the crowd. Such a desire is contrary to my own settled principles: the very principles which I expressed in Dymer. It is fair to say that I had already gone some way towards repressing it – the writing of Dymer was a purgation – when the completion of the poem, Coghill's praise of it, and the sending off to a publishers (after so many years) threw me back into a tumult of self-love that I thought I had escaped. This must be recognised as pure retrogression. The desire will not bear examination. To stand above ὁ τυχῶν (3) is a wish that cannot be universalised. (4) Worst of all I have used the belief in such secret pre-eminence as a compensation for things that wearied or humiliated me in real life: Thomas Browne's insidious nonsense about 'they that look upon my outside etc.'(5).

12. The cure of this disease is not easy to find – except the sort of violent, surgical cure which Reality itself may be preparing for me. I was free from it at times when writing Dymer. Then I was interested in the object, not in my own privileged position of seer of the object. But whenever I stopped writing or thought of publication or showed the MS. to friends I contemplated not that of which I had been writing, but my writing about it: I passed from looking at the macrocosm (6) to looking at a little historical event inside the 'Me'.

The only healthy or happy or eternal life is to look so steadily on the World that the representation 'Me' fades away. Its appearance at all in the field of consciousness is a mark of inferiority in the state where it appears. Its claiming a central position is disease.

13. Is self-consciousness, the possibility of contemplating the object Me, a pure mistake? It may be, rather, that this power of objectifying myself has its value as a necessary preliminary to being rid of it.

(1) 'My ain folk'.
(2) Being pointed at with the finger (i.e. pointed out as the 'great man' in the streets).
(3) The ordinary man.

(4) Kant says that you should desire nothing wh. you can't 'universalise', i.e. desire for every one else as well as for yourself. Now clearly I can't desire that every one shd. be pre-eminent above the ordinary run of people, for there wd. then be no ordinary run, & therefore no pre-eminence.

(5) i.e. used it to console myself by saying 'Ah! I mayn't cut a great figure externally: but if only you knew what a poet I was!'

(6) The great world.

TO ARTHUR GREEVES (W):

[Hillsboro]
Aug 28th 1930

My dear Arthur,

I was delighted to get your cheering letter. Do not thank me, much less admire me. The splendid *talking* has, as usual, fallen to my share: what had to be done and lived fell to yours. All men can give excellent advice!

I quite agree by the bye with your rejection of Forrest's consolatory remark that you may write as a hobby. It reminds me of that romantic saying of R. L. Stevenson's 'It is better to travel hopefully than to arrive':[97] against whose abuse Barfield is always protesting. For as he says, how can you travel hopefully except in the hope of arriving? And if a person, having taken away your hope of arriving, still tells you to travel hopefully, he is talking nonsense. (It's like saying 'What a bore. I see we shant be able to go to the opera after all. However we can still enjoy *looking forward* to going!' or 'It's true that I am going to get nothing to eat. But then what a splendid appetite I have!') If this sort of thing is consolatory, certainly no human evil can lack consolation.

As for the real motives for writing after one has 'got over' the desire for acknowledgement: – in the first place, I found and find, that precisely at the moment when you have really put all that out of your mind and decided not to write again – or if you do, to do it with the clear consciousness that you are only playing yourself – precisely then the ideas –

---

97 Robert Louis Stevenson, *Virginibus Puerisque* (1881), 'El Dorado': 'O toiling hands of mortals! O unwearied feet, travelling ye know not whither! Soon, soon, it seems to you, you must come forth on some conspicuous hill-top, and but a little way farther, against the setting sun, descry the spires of El Dorado. Little do ye know your own blessedness; for to travel hopefully is a better thing than to arrive, and the true success is to labour.'

which came so rarely in the days when you regarded yourself officially as an author – begin to bubble and simmer, and sooner or later you will *have* to write: and the question *why* won't really enter your mind. In my own case it is a very remarkable thing that in the few religious lyrics which I have written during the last year, in which I had no idea of publication & at first very little idea even of showing them to friends, I have found myself impelled to take infinitely more pains, less ready to be contented with the fairly good and more determined to reach the best attainable, than ever I was in the days when I never wrote without the ardent hope of successful publication.[98]

The truth is, I think, that 'our deeds are ours: their ends none of our own'. Who knows – why should we know? – what will in the end reach the ear of humanity? The successes of our own age may be speedily forgotten: some poem scribbled in pencil on the fly leaf of a schoolbook may survive and be read and be an influence when English is a dead language. Who knows, even, whether to reach the ears of other men is the purpose for which this impulse is really implanted in us? Perhaps in the eyes of the gods the true use of a book lies in its effects upon the author. You remember what Ibsen said, that every play he wrote had been written for the purgation of his own heart. And in my own humbler way I feel quite certain that I could not have certain good things now if I had not gone through the writing of Dymer. Or if a book has an audience of one – surely we must not assume that this may not be, from some superhuman point of view, as much justification as an audience of thousands. I am sure that some are born to write as trees are born to bear leaves: for these, writing is a necessary mode of their own development. If the impulse to write survives the hope of success, then one is among these. If not, then the impulse was at best only pardonable vanity, and it will certainly disappear when the hope is withdrawn. So that whether the necessity and duty of writing is laid on a man or not can soon be discovered by his own feelings. With remote consequences we have no concern. We never know enough.

I think the thing is to obey the ordinary rules of morality: subject to them, to be guided by those impulses which *feel* the most serious and innocent as opposed to those that *feel* trivial and shamefaced: but for

---

98 Those religious lyrics were later to appear in Lewis's *The Pilgrim's Regress* (1933), and they have subsequently been included in his *Poems* (1964) and *Collected Poems* (1994).

ultimate justifications & results to trust to God. The bee builds its cell and the bird its nest, probably with no knowledge of what purpose they will serve: another sees to that. Nobody knows what the result of your writing, or mine, (or Masefield's) will be. But I think we may depend upon it that endless and devoted work on an object to which a man feels seriously impelled will *tell* somewhere or other: himself or others, in this world or others, will reap a harvest exactly proportional to the output. The accounts of this universe are probably very well kept: everything finds its place in the long run. As Von Hügel (an author you shd. read – remind me about him some other time) says 'No effort will ever be as if it had not been'. The situation may be just the reverse of the nightingale in *Endymion*, who

> '*Sings but to her mate, nor e'er conceives*
> *How tiptoe night holds back her dark grey hood.*' [99]

Unsuccessful writers like us thought that night would stand tiptoe to hear us: perhaps we really are singing to some mysterious mate within. Remember too what Traherne says that our appreciation of this world – and *this* becomes fully conscious only as we express it in art – is a real link in the universal chain. Beauty descends from God into nature: but there it would perish and does except when a Man appreciates it with worship and thus as it were *sends it back* to God: so that through his consciousness what descended ascends again and the perfect circle is made.

Dear oh dear! I never meant to fill this whole letter with the subject: and my pen has been running away with me. I suppose it is natural on a subject that touches both of us so near. In fact my experience at this moment is not a bad example in little of my whole argument. For I started aiming at you and thinking that the value of my words lay in the effect they might have on *you*: but now I have drawn out of my own letter so much unexpected matter for my own needs that if it should be lost in the post, I at least will remain a gainer.

Unfortunately it has crowded out a lot of other things. I wanted to tell you about De Quincey's *Autobiography* [100] which I have just finished the first volume of. Not the *Opium Eater* [101] – tho it covers some of the same

---

99 Keats, *Endymion*, I, 830–1.
100 Thomas De Quincey, *Autobiographical Sketches*, 2 vols. (1853–4).
101 See note 30 to letter of 21? March 1915.

ground. It is really splendid reading, but I'm too tired to try and explain why. I wanted to tell you all about the bonfire I spent most of yesterday in stoking – and so on. By next week perhaps I shall be finding room for other things. It has been a most terribly hot day here to day and I am *dripping*! I'm glad to hear that *Desert Islands* has bucked up again & shall certainly try it at the first opportunity. Good night

Yours

Jack

TO ARTHUR GREEVES (W):

[Hillsboro]
Aug 31st 1930

My dear Arthur,

I have had two delightful moments since I last wrote. The first was the arrival of the Macdonalds. Thank you over and over again! Perhaps the best way I can thank you at the moment is by trying to give you a share in my delight.

Imagine me, then, seated in a shady, but even so sweltering, corner of the garden with a shade temperature of 88°, in the middle of the afternoon. Imagine the sound of Mr Papworth barking and my rising wearily, as at the 100th interruption, to investigate. I took in the bulky parcel carelessly enough and looked at it without hope of interest, till suddenly your handwriting transformed the whole situation and in a minute I had it opened. Three distinguishable waves of pleasure went over me. The first was a welling up of all that Macdonald himself stands for: the second an added delight as this present, coming so appropriately from you, linked itself up with all our joint life and old times (I begin to see that it is not all rot – tho' it often is – when people say they will value a gift more for the sake of the giver): the third a pleased surprise at finding three, at least, of the books respectably bound, and clean pages of decent type and paper within – for I had always taken it for granted that they would be hideous.

If I followed my inclinations I would have read them all by now: but fortunately work forbids me such a dangerous orgy. I have however finished *Wilfrid Cumbermede*[102] – I took it down with me after tea that same afternoon to Parson's Pleasure and read naked under the willows. I shall

---

102 George MacDonald, *Wilfrid Cumbermede* (1872).

not venture on my next Macdonald, tho' tempted, for some time, for fear of spoiling my own delights.

As you said in one of your letters, his novels have great and almost intolerable faults. His only real form is the symbolical fantasy like *Phantastes* or *Lilith*. This is what he always writes: but unfortunately for financial reasons, he sometimes has to *disguise* it as ordinary Victorian fiction. Hence what you get is a certain amount of the real Macdonald linked (as Mezentius linked live men to corpses)[103] – linked onto a mass of quite worthless plot: and as his *real* parts have to involve strange happenings, the plot is usually improbable, obscure, and melodramatic. Thus Wilfrid's dream of Athanasia, his waking to find Mary (transfigured) by his side, and the sword between them, is pure vision. It is in fact closely connected in *that* world with the sword-divided sleep of Sigurd and Brynhild, and also with Dymer's adventure (For we don't individually invent these things, perhaps. Look how the 'empty castle' theme is present in *Phantastes, Wilfrid,* & *Dymer.* No doubt it passed into *Dymer* from *Phantastes*: but then, from it, in Dymer, I passed on to the mysterious bedfellow without any guidance from Macdonald – and only *now* find that he has got that bit of the story too, only in another book. Don't you get the feeling of something waiting there and slowly being recovered in fragments by different human minds according to their abilities, and partially spoiled in each writer by the admixture of his own mere individual invention?) This is pure vision, as I say: unfortunately, in order to keep up the pretence that he is writing a novel, he has to explain it all away – hence all the impossible rigmarole about Clara's putting the sword there and Mary's getting into the wrong bed. Yet the gold is so good that it carries off the dross and I hope to read this book many times again. Things that particularly affected me were the grass plain round the old farm (I don't know why this gives such a magical air), the storm raised by the pendulum and the sudden appearance of the horseman, the chapter called '*On the Leads*', the scene of Wilfrid lost on the Alps, and the dream of Charley (*what* a name!) and Wilfrid dead, and perching on the bushes. I don't think as a whole it is so good as *Sir Gibbie* which seems of all G.M.'s novels so far as I've read to avoid best the mere deadweight of 'plot' that I have complained of. Thanks, Arthur,

---

103 Mezentius was a mythical Etruscan king who bound living men to corpses and left them to die of starvation. See Virgil, *Aeneid,* VIII, 485–8.

again and again. I know nothing that gives me such a feeling of spiritual healing, of being washed, as to read G. Macdonald.

My second delightful moment was of a different kind, and takes a little arrangement to describe. Imagine first a pure rosy pink sunset: in the extreme distance a sky covered with thin 'mackerel' as delicate as the veins in a shell, & all pink: in the foreground, blackly outlined against this, huge crags and castles and Valkyrie-shapes of cloud. Got that? Now; – imagine that all this existed only for a fraction of [a] second, the pink light being in fact no sunset but a vast flood of summer lightening: so that all those beetling cliffs and tottering cities of the gods, together with the rosy flush behind which made them visible, had leaped out of pure star-set darkness an instant before, and vanished into it instantaneously again – and so times without number. Later in the night it developed into a real thunderstorm: but for a long while it was very distant and I heard thunder at a greater distance (it seemed) than I had ever heard it before. It was *tinkly* – like the crushing of very delicate tumblers by a giant millions of miles away. The comparison is not very good: at any rate it had the most extreme beauty, and the most unlike the grandeur of ordinary thunder, that you can imagine.

I have also had some splendid bathes in the last few days and have suffered, along with the exhaustion of extreme heat, something of a trance-like condition that exhaustion sometimes brings.

We have an old maid, Miss Walsh, staying with us, who, on a very small income, seems to have travelled nearly everywhere. She talks too much of her travels, but there is an old-maidish torrent of details about trunks and trains and an American I met in Corsica (quite *un*like Kelsie – no attempt at humour) which somehow I rather like. A little pinched face with pince-nez. She surprised me by having read the *Crock of Gold* and saying she loved fairy tales: so I have lent her *Phantastes* and await results.

I am now in the second volume of de Quincy's *Autobiography* which continues excellent. We expect to move on Sept. 29th. I suppose I shd. end up 'again thanking you v. much' as we used to do in replying to Christmas boxes! –

Yrs
Jack

TO ARTHUR GREEVES (W):

[Hillsboro]
Sept. 15th 1930

P.S. This is a very mortuary letter, be prepared for the worst!

My dear Arthur,

Apologies for delay! I was feeling rather seedy on Sunday besides having a weary right arm, whether this was neuritis or writer's cramp from making notes all day long: as I am v. busy making notes for an extremely dull subject wh. I have to take next term.

I was glad to get your letter from Cushendun. Did you visit our old friend at the Post-Office? And how did the new friend turn out on closer acquaintance?

Miss Walsh, by the way, did *not* get through *Phantastes* and I now strongly suspect that her alleged love of fantasy was merely a bye-product of her fanatical love of everything Irish. This, wh. in any case cd. only be a respectable weakness took in her case the degraded form of endless chit-chat about all the famous Irish literary people she had met. She referred to Yeats as 'W.B.' – 'for short' – until I asked her how four syllables could be a shortened form of one. The last five minutes of her, while I was seeing her off at the bus, led to the horrible discovery that I was learning Icelandic, and not learning Irish: for which I was soundly scolded. In fact she behaved about Ireland as Americans behave about America, and finally went off with her head in the air as who shd. say Hoity-Toity!

The most interesting thing since I last wrote is a dream I had about my father. As a rule dreams about the dead fall into two distinct classes. (a) Those in wh. one simply forgets that the person has died (b) Those in which the dead appears as a bogey. My dream belonged to neither. I was in the dining room in Little Lea, with all the gasses lit and talking to my father. I knew perfectly well that he had died, and presently put out my hand and touched him. He felt warm and solid. I said 'But of course this body must be only an appearance. You can't really have a body now.' He explained that it *was* only an appearance, and our conversation which was cheerful and friendly, but not solemn or emotional, drifted off onto other topics. I then went over to fetch you and we came across together in a closed car. As we drove I told you of his return in order to prepare you for meeting him: and I think (tho' this may be a waking invention) that at that point I was looking forward to seeing him come to the door and say 'Well, Arthur' and offer you your drink. We were exactly at that place where an increased crushing under the wheels tells you that you have passed off the cinders onto the gravel at the study corner: when you, in a voice of suppressed anxiety, said 'Oh no, Jack. Its just that you've been thinking about him and you've *imagined* he's there.' Till that moment everything had been pleasant and homely: but suddenly, as your words made me see the whole adventure *from outside*, as I realised how it would sound if repeated that I had been TALKING TO A DEAD MAN, the thing wh. had been SO normal in the experiencing it, rose up with such retrospective horror that the nightmare feeling flared up and I woke in terror. The dream seems to me a good idea of what might v. probably happen if one really met a ghost. At least I sometimes hope so.

Have I propounded before to you my theory that the *corpse* and the *ghost* each owe all their terrors to the other? The corpse, tho so horribly different, is yet so like a man that you can't help thinking it has a life of its own – i.e. you put a ghost in it. But for the idea that this un-man may still live, it wd. not be horrible. Conversely, when you think of the spirit, tho you know it to be unpicturable, you can't help picturing it, and yet you feel you must make it different from the man as he was: then in comes the horrible association of the corpse. In each case you are trying to think of a thing as living and dead at the same time, and from the impossible conception comes the horror.

Certainly ones own death wd. be a much pleasanter idea if one cd. be quite rid of the lingering idea that the corpse is alive. I thought I had got over this years ago: but every now and then some old stain of savage materialism starts up and tries to make me believe that it is *me* they will nail in a box and bury. The same sort of confusion explains why the idea of being buried alive, with a hearse & a coffin etc, is so much worse than the idea of being smothered, say, in a landslip, or by getting on your face in sleep, – wh. latter of course are just the same mode of death really. The secret is that what one fears is *not* smothering – wh, tho' bad enough, is probably much nicer than the 'natural' deaths which most of us are going to die.* It is that the funeral accompaniments give you the idea of entering alive into the normal and regular *status* of a corpse – i.e. of being alive and dead at the same time. It can't really be worse than drowning. So the next time you're buried alive, Arthur, be sure and remember that its no worse than drowning. Trust an old hand, my boy.

It pays! Heigh-ho! If we were talking instead of writing letters I shd. begin to fool now ('Beshrew me, the knight's in excellent fooling')

What put you onto the Priestly novel? It may be excellent, but it somehow never occurred to me to try. Perhaps I will after your recommendation.

I think you must have misunderstood me about the Macdonald. I never meant the novels wd. be better without a *story*, nor that the good parts consisted of anything other than story. All I meant was that a really valuable story of the Phantastes kind was constantly being interrupted by a story of a quite inferior kind, and even an inferior specimen of that kind. Also, I agree that the first few chapters of *S. Gibbie* are nothing like as good as the first few chapters of *W. Cumbermede*. But by now you will have got to the good parts. Don't you love 'sleep was scattered all over the world'[104] – and the lovely homeliness of the farm kitchen – and the apparition of Sir Gibbie when the old woman mistakes him for Christ. I hope for your views on it on Saturday – also for a final account of your time at Cushendun.

Yours

Jack

*One might almost leave directions in ones will that one was to be buried alive.

TO ARTHUR GREEVES (W):

[Hillsboro]
Oct. 6th 1930

My dear Arthur,

I had hoped to get off not a letter (that was out of the question) but a line of apology on Sunday: but Sunday when it came was wholly occupied with packing jam. You will excuse my silence when you hear that I am (all at the same time) (a) Having a perfectly stupifying cold, almost 'flu. (b) Packing for a move on Saturday. (c) Preparing for term on Saturday. (d) Finishing a course of lectures. (e) Setting papers for next summers Exams.

Oh Arthur – do you know how lucky you are to be able to say any evening 'I may take a day in bed to-morrow' – the luck of one in a million.

---

104 MacDonald, *Sir Gibbie*, vol. I, ch. ix, p. 138.

This is just to explain my silence.

Yours

Jack

Lewis had at last acquired the house he had been hinting at. This was The Kilns, at Headington Quarry, which lies about two miles further from the centre of Oxford than Hillsboro. On Sunday 6 July Jack and Warnie saw it for the first time, and the next day Warnie wrote an enthusiastic account in his diary:

> *We did not go inside, but the eight acre garden is such stuff as dreams are made of. I never imagined that for us any such garden would ever come within the sphere of discussion. The house... stands at the entrance to its own grounds at the northern foot of Shotover at the end of a narrow lane, which in turns opens off a very bad and little used road, giving as great privacy as can reasonably be looked for near a large town: to the left of the house are the two brick kilns from which it takes its name – in front, a lawn and hard tennis court – then a large bathing pool, beautifully wooded, and with a delightful circular brick seat overlooking it: after that a steep wilderness broken with ravines and nooks of all kinds runs up to a little cliff topped by a thistly meadow, and then the property ends in a thick belt of fir trees, almost a wood: the view from the cliff over the dim blue distance of the plain is simply glorious. (BF, p. 58)*

Jack, Mrs Moore and Warnie bought the house together for £3300 and they moved in on 10 October.

TO ARTHUR GREEVES (W):

Magdalen College,
Oxford.
Oct. 29th 1930

My dear Arthur,

Things are no better and I don't know when I shall have time to write to you properly again. I really am at it from morning till night at present, Sundays included. Thanks so much for your letter. Try to give me another as soon as may be and don't abandon me to my fate. You mustn't think that I am having a specially *nasty* time – in some ways quite a good one, in every respect except leisure. My days are filled with pupils in college and settling in in the new house at Headington: and I am enjoying both. I have made a vow not to tell you anything about our new residence, because if I do you will certainly be disappointed when you actually see it. But oh – ! I never hoped for the like.

About Geo. Macdonald, I am afraid we must agree to a real difference. The exciting story in Wilfrid Cumbermede seems to me a pure drag and Sir Gibbie seems to me much better because the excitement in it is of the *real* sort and not interrupted by the mere machinery of the old melodramatic 3-vol novel. I bought two others in London, *Adela Cathcart* & *What's Mine's Mine*[105] just before term began (By the way the bookseller told me that there was a small but steady demand for Macdonalds – wh. is interesting and encouraging) *Adela* I'm afraid I think definitely bad, tho it begins well: and *The Seaboard Parish*[106] the same. The real holiness is, in them both, degenerating into mere flat moralising and sometimes it is hard to feel that you're reading the author of *Phantastes*.

Have you been having lovely autumn? We have. Woods all speckled with yellow, drifts of leaves at the roadside, and the most exquisite pale skies. The other morning on some gorse bushes I saw a wonderful display of cobwebs – like a thick bridal veil, unbroken, extending for many yards. The smells are delicious. I also had the experience lately of walking under an avenue of trees after a shower, and saw that tho all the rest was still, a kind of wave-motion was passing over the branches on one side, followed by a patter of drops. Coming nearer I found it was a squirrel leaping from branch to branch and sending a wake of tiny showers to earth as they bent under him.

Had tea the other day with the Provost of Worcester[107] who is a wonderful old man and has a huge garden which he has converted into a real country farm in the middle of Oxford. He introduced me to two

---

105 George MacDonald, *Adela Cathcart* (1864); *What's Mine's Mine* (1886).
106 George MacDonald, *The Seaboard Parish* (1868).
107 The Rev. Francis John Lys (1863–1947) took his degree from Worcester College, Oxford, in 1886, and was an assistant master at Radley College from 1887 to 1888. He returned to Oxford as a lecturer at Worcester in 1889, and was Fellow, Tutor, Senior Tutor, Bursar and Provost of Worcester from 1919 to 1946.

alderneys – lovely creatures, as delicately made as deer: you wd. hardly believe that cows cd. be so dainty – and their sweet breath.

I have started going to morning Chapel at 8, wh. means going to bed earlier: and indeed I live such vigorous days that I am usually glad to go. My moral history of late has been deplorable. More and more clearly one sees how much of one's philosophy & religion is mere talk: the boldest hope is that concealed somewhere within it there is some seed however small of the real thing

Yrs

J.

TO ARTHUR GREEVES (W):

This is the only paper I can find!

[The Kilns,
Kiln Lane,
Headington Quarry,
Oxford]
Dec 24th 1930

My dear Arthur,

I take no blame for the long silence. In the latter half of term writing became quite impossible and then when term was over I had to waste the first fortnight of my Vac. examining – which, as you know, means work from morning till night. I am now free at last – hungry to get back to my *real* work, and ordinary life: in which I include the resumption of my correspondence with you.

By this time you should have a book which I sent you[108] (a) Because I have been asked to help the author by drawing peoples attention to it – he is a friend of mine. (b) Because he is the same man who wrote *Harvest in Poland*,[109] that v. dubious book lent me by the sinister Chevasse. (c) Because I have myself enjoyed it and think – tho' with some doubts – that you will enjoy it too. The get-up is rather what we should once have liked than what we like now: but the Dürer on the wrapper is worth having for its own sake.

I envy you your stay at Ballycastle: even the name gives me a faint pleasant twinge. But there is one odd thing I have been noticing since we

---

108 Geoffrey Dennis, *The End of the World* (1930).
109 Geoffrey Dennis, *Harvest in Poland* [1925].

came to our new house, which is much more in the country, and it is this. Hitherto there has always been something not so much in the landscape as in every single visual impression (say a cloud, a robbin, or a ditch) in Ireland, which I lacked in England: something for which homeliness is an inadequate word. This something I find I am now getting in England – the feeling of connectedness, of being part of it. I suppose I have been growing into the soil here much more since the move.

You would be surprised how few walks I have taken. My afternoon hours of exercise have been almost wholly occupied with sawing and axing for firewood, or cleaning the lines of future paths with shears, with feeding birds, and messing about in an old punt on a small lake or large pond which is a stone's throw from our house. You have no idea what horrid work sawing is for the first week, and how delightful after that when your muscles have got used to it and your hands are hardened. Almost every afternoon as I stand at my sawing block looking as I work at the sun going down beyond a line of bare pollards. Nearly always a red cannon ball sun, for we have had gloriously winter weather. I also love the sound of the saw and the flying of the sawdust. Then after sawing the log into lengths comes the splitting of each of these with an axe.

It is absurd how remote all simple human activities have been from me all my life: so much so that when I heave up my axe I still always see myself as an illustration in Robinson Crusoe. There is something in country work of this sort which you can't get out of walks. Silently clipping (silent except for the noise of the clipping itself) among thick brambles in the depth of winter afternoon – when the day takes on its *Grendel* hue – I am continually watched by bright-eyed robbins which come surprisingly close. More than once I have seen a pair of squirrels among the fir trees, and rabbits in our own garden: and up at the top (for our bit runs up the side of a hill) there is a burrow too big for rabbits which Foord-Kelsie (the old booky carpenting parson – you remember) avers to be that of a badger. Now to meet a badger on your own land, if such chance ever befell me – would be almost the crown of one kind of earthly bliss!

At night owls are very plentiful: and one thing I have noticed since the very first night I slept here, is that this house has a good night atmosphere about it: in the sense that I have never been in a place where one was *less* likely to get the creeps: a place less sinister. Good life must have been lived here before us. If it is haunted, it is haunted by good spirits.

Perhaps such things are the result of fantasy: yet the feelings are real. Even if they signify nothing more than the state of ones organs, yet are not ones organs real, and is not their state also a fact of spiritual significance? For if anything is spiritual, everything is.

I have of course read very little apart from work. One more Macdonald 'Annals of a Quiet Neighbourhood',[110] which went far to restore my faith in him: badly shaken by an unsuccessful attempt to read the *Seaboard Parish*. Yesterday I picked up for 4/6 *Alec Forbes*[111] in three half leather volumes. Do you know it? One reason I enjoyed the Quiet Neighbourhood so much was that I read it immediately after Trollope's *Belton Estate*:[112] quite a good book, but all the time one was making excuses for the author on the moral side: saying that this bit of uncharitableness and that bit of unconscious cynicism, and, throughout, the bottomless *worldliness* (not knowing itself for such) belonged to the period. Then you turned to Macdonald, also a Victorian, and after a few pages were ashamed to have spent even an hour in a world so inferior as that of Trollope's.

Have you had glorious fogs – frost-fogs? We have had some of the finest I have ever seen. In fact we have had all sorts of beauty – outside. Inside myself the situation has been quite the reverse. I seem to go steadily downhill and backwards. I am certainly further from self control and charity and light than I was last spring. Now that W. is with us I don't get enough solitude: or so I say to myself in excuse, knowing all the time that what God demands is our solution of the problem set, not of some other problem which we think he ought to have set: and that what we call *hindrances* are really the raw material of spiritual life. As if the fire should call the coal a hindrance! (One can imagine a little young fire, which had been getting on nicely with the sticks and paper, regarding it as a mere cruelty when the big lumps were put on: never dreaming what a huge steady glow, how far surpassing its present crackling infancy, the Tender of the Fire designed when he stoked it).

I think the trouble with me is *lack of faith*. I have no *rational* ground for going back on the arguments that convinced me of God's existence: but the irrational deadweight of my old sceptical habits, and the spirit of this age, and the cares of the day, steal away all my lively feeling of the

---

110 George MacDonald, *Annals of a Quiet Neighbourhood* (1867).
111 George MacDonald, *Alec Forbes of Howglen* (1865).
112 Anthony Trollope, *The Belton Estate* (1865–6).

truth, and often when I pray I wonder if I am not posting letters to a non-existent address. Mind you I don't *think* so – the whole of my reasonable mind is convinced: but I often *feel* so. However, there is nothing to do but to peg away. One falls so often that it hardly seems worth while picking oneself up and going through the farce of starting over again as if you could ever hope to walk. Still, this seeming absurdity is the only sensible thing I do, so I must continue it. And all the time, on the other side, the imaginative side, (the fairy angel) I get such glimpses and vanishing memories as often take my breath away: as if they said 'Look what you're losing' – as if they were there just to deprive one of all excuse.

How well I *talk* about it: how little else I do. I wonder would it be better not to speak to one another of these things at all? Is the talking a substitute for the doing?

Yrs

Jack

1931

— ~ —

TO ARTHUR GREEVES (W):

The Kilns,
Headington Quarry,
Oxford
Jan 10th 1931

My dear Arthur,

I am writing this in the principle sitting room of the new house, which we call the common room, at my Mother's desk which you remember in the drawing room at Little Lea. I wonder when last it was written at? The others are all out: I have come in from my walk – a beautiful pearl grey winter sky – and it is now half past three.

I was delighted to get your letter. Next term, which begins next week, promises to be not quite so hectic as last, so I will do my very level best to get back to our weekly interchange: but you know what my difficulties are in term time and you will not be surprised if I have to give up.

As regards my giving all the reasons but the right one for sending a book – I suppose the right one is friendship. But that can only be a reason for gifts in general: what I was explaining was my reasons for sending *this particular* book at *this particular* time. As regards the latter, I gave special reasons because I did not want it to be a Christmas present since you and I don't give them. Your complaint therefore, my dear Sir, is as if a man said 'We'd better lunch here, because it will be too late when we get to London, and they give you an excellent meal here for 2/6' and you had replied 'Ah but those are not the right reasons for eating lunch. The right reason is that the vital processes are attended by a wastage of the tissues and certain organic substances if introduced into the stomach have the power of repairing this wastage.' In other words, for any action there is usually *a*. A general reason for doing it *at all*. *b*. A particular reason for selecting to do it at such and such a time and place and in such and such a way. We usually take *a*. for granted, and explain *b*. You are the sort of man who would try to persuade a girl to marry you by reading her all the general reasons for marriage out of the prayer book ('procreation of children & prevention of sin' etc) Again, the actual presence of a W.-C. cd. never to you be a reason for emptying your bladder: for you deal only in generalities: and as the general reason for this operation (i.e. the fact that the bladder is finite in size) always holds good, you on your principles, I suppose, think it a matter of indifference where and when it is performed. But come – my pen runs away with me (I am afraid I can never resist a ludicrous piece of logic) and I shall have wasted my whole letter on foolery.

The most important thing since I last wrote is a three days walking tour wh. Warnie and I took.[1] We trained to Chepstow, breaking our journey at Gloucester for a couple of hours to see the cathedral. Got to Chepstow that evening & went out for a stroll after dinner. It was brilliant moonlight and freezing hard. Having reached a bridge over the Wye – the cliffs of the far bank shining in front of us and the little huddled town behind – we looked back and saw on our left, rising above a grassy sweep of hill, the ruins of a big castle.[2] We came back with only a very faint hope of getting near it, when as if by magic a lane led us out of the main street into fields and up without hindrance to the great gate of the castle itself. The doors were shut, but through the chinks and under them a bright light seemed to be streaming 'What is this?' said I. 'A witches' Sabbath' said he. We looked through the key hole and saw nothing but moonlight. The whole thing was an optical delusion: we had been in the shadow of the castle as we came up and the moonlight within, thro the cracks had somehow looked exactly like artificial light. We then walked all round it. The space is empty for a long way from the walls – just grass and a few seats – and you can walk in the bottom of the former moat wh. is very deep. I never saw so huge a castle. The circuit is not much smaller than the town hall at home: tower after tower, and battlements with ivy falling over them like a cascade, and even little wild bushes growing out of crannies, and above them all the roofless gables of what must have been the great hall, not much smaller than a cathedral. Imagine all this under a cloudless moon and the grass, stiff with frost, crunching under our feet.

---

1 The walking tour began on New Year's Day, Lewis and his brother returning home on 4 January.
2 The ruins of this 11th century castle are washed by the River Wye.

Next day we walked to Monmouth, passing Tintern about eleven A.M. Have you seen it? It is an abbey practically intact except that the roof is gone, and the glass out of the windows, and the floor, instead of a pavement is a trim green lawn. Anything like the *sweetness* & peace of the long shafts of sunlight falling through the windows on this grass cannot be imagined. All churches should be roofless. A holier place I never saw.[3] We lunched at St Briavels where there is another castle inhabited by the Aunt of a pupil of mine who is 'worreyed' by 'the ghosts', but won't 'do anything' about them because she doesnt like 'to be unkind'[4] (This is the pupils account. A *very* queer fellow indeed: it was he who put me onto the *End of the World*). That night to Monmouth, after a lovely walk: not on *roads* more than half an hour all day. Next day to Ross, and then next to Hereford I can't describe it all. We had two days of pure winter sunlight, and one of mist: the latter luckily was spent almost entirely in woods whose delicious feeling of confusion it served only to increase.

This was W's first experience of a walking tour. I had been a little nervous as to whether he would really care for it, & whether his selfish habits wd. really accomodate themselves to the inevitable occasional difficulties. My fears however were quite unfounded. He has been with us all the month here and everyone says how greatly he is improved. He and I even went together to Church twice: and – will you believe it – he said to me in conversation that he was beginning to think the religious view of things was after all true. Mind you (like me, at first) he didn't *want* it to be, nor like it: but his intellect is beginning to revolt from the semi-scientific assumptions we all grew up in, and the other explanation of the world seems to him daily more probable. Of course I have not had and probably never shall have any *real* talks on the heart of the subject with him. But it is delightful to feel the whole lot of us gradually beginning to move in that direction. It has done me good to be with him: because while his idea of the good is much lower than mine, he is in so many ways better than I

---

3 This is the ruined abbey immortalized in William Wordsworth's *Lines Composed a Few Miles Above Tintern Abbey* (1798) in which he reflects that 'we are laid asleep / In body, and become a living soul: / While with an eye made quiet by the power / Of harmony, and the deep power of joy, / We see into the life of things' (ll. 45–9).

4 St Briavels Castle, which was built during the reign of Henry I (1100–35), was inhabited at this time by the Hon. Mrs Ronald Campbell. Her nephew, Lewis's pupil, was John Colquhoun Campbell (1907–) who received his BA from Magdalen in 1930. He worked with the Anglo-Iranian Oil Co. Ltd 1930–52, after which he was in HM Diplomatic Service 1952–67.

am. I keep on crawling up to the heights & slipping back to the depths: he seems to do neither. There always have been these two types.

About Dennis:[5] I doubt whether the kind of effects he aims at could be attained by a simpler style, tho' an effect you and I prefer probably could be. Still, one mustn't be dogmatic about simplicity. It may be our favourite style – but the pomps and sonorities are good in their different way none the less.

I have read Alec Forbes – good things in it, but not by any means a good book. The more I read his novels the more I rage at the tragedy of his being forced to write for money and thus diverted from his true sphere, so that we get only as much of the real Macdonald as he can smuggle in *by the way*. It is, I really think, a loss as irreparable as the early death of Keats.

Glad to hear you are at *Tristram Shandy*. What good company! Isn't Uncle Toby, seriously and morally, one of the loveliest characters ever created.

Must stop now. When are you coming to see me? I have no chance of visiting you till the summer at earliest.

Yours
Jack

At present reading the Autobiography of Keat's friend the painter Haydon[6] – quite good. W. has finished Lockhart's *Scott*[7] & pronounces it excellent.

TO ARTHUR GREEVES (W):

[The Kilns]
Jan 17, 1931

My dear Arthur,

I am much divided in my mind as to whether I should devote this after tea hour – the first free one of the day – to starting a new book or to writing you a letter. The fact that you are in my debt is strong for the first alternative: on the other hand when I hear from you during the week (as I

---

5 i.e. Geoffrey Dennis.

6 *The Life of Benjamin Robert Haydon from his Autobiography and Journals*, ed. Tom Taylor (1853).

7 John Gibson Lockhart's *Memoirs of the Life of Sir Walter Scott*. See note 174 to letter of 25 October 1916.

hope I shall) I shall probably be too busy to reply. Then again I have been in a bad temper to day over trifles: and it is too much to face bedtime with the added knowledge of having neglected you as well – so here goes. Perhaps this sounds unflattering, and you may retort that you wd. rather not have a letter on these terms. However, I am sure you understand how a momentary disinclination to begin is quite compatible with a real interest in going on.

I have read a new Macdonald since I last wrote, which I think the very best of the novels. I would put it immediately below Phantastes, Lilith, the Fairy Tales, & the Diary of an Old Soul. It is called *What's Mine's Mine*.[8] It has very little of the bad plot interest, and quite frankly subordinates story to doctrine. But such doctrine. Some of the conversations in this book I hope to re-read many times. The scene and the characters are Highland Celtic, as opposed to the Lowland Scots of most of the novels: highly idealised. Yet somehow they convince me. Or if they don't quite convince me as real people, they differ from most ideal characters in this, that I wish they *were* real. A young chief of a decaying clan is the hero: and the chief contrast is between the clansmen and a vulgar rich Glasgow family who have come to live in the neighbourhood. These are, like most of Macdonald's worshippers of Mammon, over-drawn. I venture to think that there was some *moral*, as well as some literary, weakness in this. I mean in characters like the baronet in *Sir Gibbie* etc. I observe that M. is constantly praying against anger

Keep me from wrath, let it seem never so right.

I wonder did he indulge (day-dreamily) an otherwise repressed fund of indignation by putting up in his novels bogeys to whom his heroes could make the stunning retorts and deliver the stunning blows which he himself neither could nor would deliver in real life. I am certain that this is morally as well as artistically dangerous and I'll tell you why. The *pleasure* of anger – the gnawing attraction which makes one return again and again to its theme – lies, I believe, in the fact that one feels entirely righteous oneself only when one is angry. *Then* the other person is pure black, and you are pure white. But in real life sanity always returns to break the dream. In fiction you can put absolutely *all* the right, with no

---

8 See note 104 to letter of 29 October 1930.

snags or reservations, on the side of the hero (with whom you identify yourself) and all the wrong on the side of the villain. You thus revel in unearned self-righteousness, which wd. be vicious even if it were earned.

Haven't you noticed how people with a fixed hatred, say, of Germans or Bolshevists, *resent* anything wh. is pleaded in extenuation, however small, of their supposed crimes. The enemy must be unredeemed black. While all the time one *does* nothing and enjoys the feeling of perfect superiority over the faults one is never tempted to commit:

> 'Compound for sins we are inclined to
> By damning those we have no mind to.'[9]

I suppose that when one hears a tale of hideous cruelty anger is quite the wrong reaction, and merely wastes the energy that ought to go in a different direction: perhaps merely dulls the conscience wh., if it were awake, would ask us 'Well? What are you *doing* about it? How much of your life have you spent in really combatting this? In helping to produce social conditions in which these sort of things will not occur!?

Term began yesterday. Yesterday afternoon & evening and this morning I spent in correcting papers: not only a hard but a depressing job, for ones pupils always seem to do worse than you expect. That, by the way, is the angle from which to understand (instead of being self-righteous about) the cruelty of schoolmasters. One can't gauge the temptation to cruelty for a man who is trying to keep his wife and family on the profits of a decaying private school, and who sees the boys getting fewer & fewer scholarships each year and can never, even if honest, be quite sure that it is not the boys fault. 'God help everyone' as you say.

The night before last (my last night of Vac) we had the most glorious storm: trees plunging like terrified but tethered horses, leaves eddying, chimneys howling, and under all the lesser and lighter noises a great solid roar above the house. I lay in bed and revelled in it – tho' it is partly spoiled for me by the fact that Minto hates it and hears in it only a sound of death and desolation. Odd, what different notes we different souls draw from the organ of nature. Some people hate the cry of an owl at night: I love it.

---

9 Samuel Butler, *Hudibras* (1663–78), part I, canto I, i, 213.

Oh, by the bye, our new maid says she has been kept awake at night this week by the squirrels! Asked what kind of noise they make she replied 'I don't know' – wh. I think is her way of saying 'I can't describe it.' But what a lovely idea. And what a lovely sentence for the Witch of Endor – 'Please, Mr Lewis, the squirrels – '

You say Reid is reading his new book[10] to 'some of us'. Who are the others? Give him my kind regards.

I find this cold weather desperately trying to the bladder.

Yrs

Jack

TO ARTHUR GREEVES (W):

[The Kilns]
Feb 1st 1931

My dear Arthur,

This will probably be a short, and certainly a dull letter, for I am tired. Minto has been in bed all week with flu' which means a good deal of bustle and extra work: I am recovering from a baddish cold myself and have had a pretty tough week. I was glad to get your letter.

I haven't read Jeans' book[11] and it is unlikely I will – there are so many things I want to read more. One of the blessings of your life is that you ought to be able to read fairly well nearly everything that interests you. As a matter of fact – apart from time – I am not now greatly attracted to that kind of book: though you will remember that astronomy, fed on H. G. Wells' romances, was almost my earliest love. I don't know why it has not lasted, nor why it now interests me much less than I should expect. Partly I think, because one knows that all the really interesting things about other planets and systems can't be found out: partly, too, I suspect that philosophy and religion (in a person of my limited range) rather take the shine out of curiosity about the material universe. It seems like having new bits of a curtain described to one, when one is all agog for hints of what lies behind the curtain. Now that I come to think of it, it is not quite true to say that I don't feel any interest in these things now: rather they rouse a very intense, impatient interest for a very short time, which quite suddenly leaves one at once sated & dissatisfied. Mind I am not *recomending* this state of mind – only recording it.

---

10 Probably Forrest Reid's *Uncle Stephen* which was published in October 1931.
11 Sir James Jeans, *The Mysterious Universe* (1930).

I liked very much your account of the party who meet to hear Reid's novel. It reminded me of Tristram Shandy – just such an ideally inappropriate conjunction of minds as he delights to bring together. Don't you think the great beauty of that book is its picture of affection existing across unbridgeable gulfs of intellect? My Father & Uncle Toby never understand one another at all, and always love one another. It is the true picture of home life: far better than the modern nonsense in wh. affection (friendship is a different thing) is made to depend on mental affinities.

I am almost shocked to find from more than one passage that Geo. Macdonald hated Sterne. The coarseness apparently revolted him: but I cannot understand how he was not attracted by the overflowing goodness at the heart of the book. One must remember that the wayward Highland temperament, with its reserve and delicacy, may find coarseness a greater trial than our rougher Saxon grain.

I had a lovely ten minutes the afternoon before last in a wood of fir trees in the snow. The wood comes down to within a few yards of the top of a small cliff, from which direction the snow was coming. Just as the flakes got near this edge, some current of air caught them and whirled them upwards so that in the wood they were flying skywards as if the earth was snowing. I am often in this bit of wood, and have seen a great many fine winter sunsets – very pale, you know – through (first) the tall straight firs and then some twisted beechtrees which form the border of the wood. I have also had some fine hours of storm in it when all the trees were groaning and swaying.

I hope you won't be disappointed by What's Mine's Mine. Of course it has not the fantastic charm of Phantastes: nor the plot excitement of Wilfrid Cumbermede. It is just the spiritual quality with some beautiful landscape – nothing more.

I wonder how your tea with the McNeils went off. Give them my love when next you meet.

The O.U.D.S.[12] are doing *Hassan*[13] this term and I think I shall go to it.

---

12 Oxford University Dramatic Society.
13 James Elroy Flecker, *Hassan: The Story of Hassan of Bagdad and How he Came to Make the Golden Journey to Samarkand: A Play in Five Acts* (1922). James Elroy Flecker (1884–1915) was educated at Trinity College, Oxford. He spent some time in the East with the Consular service and wrote several volumes of lyric verse. He is best remembered for this poetic Eastern drama which he wrote in 1914. Following his death it was adapted for the stage by Basil Dean, with music by Frederick Delius, and first performed in 1923.

I can't remember whether we have talked of this play or not, but I imagine you know it. However badly the O.U.D.S. do it, at least they will not turn it into a Chu Chin Chow[14] as (I am told) the London actors did. Which reminds me of Kismet[15] (one of my early thrills) which reminds me of lying on the beech at Donaghadee reading to each other out of the Arabian Nights.

Do or die for it – I *must* manage to get over to Ireland in the summer and revisit some of the old haunts with you. Once more to spend one of our delightful banjo evenings with Jimmy Thompson – to have another of our old rousing evenings at the Hippodrome – once more to dance the Black Bottom at midnight with Sir Robert Ewart & the Witch of Endor – whether-her-mother-will-let-her-or-no – I'm too tired for anything but foolery. Bryson is to marry the Princess Elizabeth: poor chap, it is a pity he was castrated by the Vice Chancellor and Proctors last week for riding a bicycle in St Mary's. I suppose you have heard about Warnie's peerage – for gallantry during the recent manoeuvres. I have grown a beard – Good night

Yrs
Jack

P.S. In that fir wood I suddenly got a terrific return the other day of my earliest Wagner mood – the purely Nibelung, Mime, mood before the Valkyries rose on my horizon. You know – very earthy, and smith-y, and Teutonic. How *inexhaustible* these things are. You think you have done with a thing and – whoop! – it's all back again, strong as ever.

TO ARTHUR GREEVES (W):

[The Kilns]
Feb 23rd 1931

My dear Arthur,

I was glad to hear from you again, despite the fact that your letter, specially towards the end, appears to have been written in a state of intoxication.

---

14 *Chu Chin Chow: A Musical Tale of the East* (1931) was an enormously popular musical play by Oscar Ashe, with music by Frederick Norton. It was first performed in 1916, and created a record with its 2,238 performances. See *Oscar Asche, by Himself* (1924).

15 Edward Knoblock's *Kismet: An 'Arabian Night' in Three Acts* (1912) was an 'oriental spectacular' first performed in 1911 and which was very popular.

I was almost relieved to hear that you shared my views of *What's Mine's Mine*. Yes, you are right in saying that it is good not despite, but because of, its preaching – or rather (preaching is a bad word) its spiritual knowledge. So many cleverer writers strike one as quite *childish* after Macdonald: they seem not even to have begun to understand so many things.

On Saturday I went to the matinee of Flecker's *Hassan* done by the O.U.D.S. I can't remember whether you saw it in London, but I suppose you read it. It was not very well done, but well enough for me: indeed to see it really well acted would be too much for me. In reading it the cruelty is just about balanced by the extreme beauty of the lyrics and much of the dialogue, so that the total effect, tho' sinister, like a too-bright dream which is sure to turn into nightmare before the end, yet is bearable. On the stage, where one has less time to dwell on the cadence or suggestion of the individual words, the cruelty is unendurable. Warnie went out half way through. I felt quite sick but thought it almost a duty <for one afflicted in my way to remain, saying to myself 'Oh you like cruelty do you? Well now stew in it!'> – the same principle on which one trains a puppy to be clean – 'rub their noses in it'. It has haunted me ever since.

On its merits as a work of art I am very undecided. The intense effect which it produces is not, in itself, proof of greatness, for it is easy to produce an effect by the suggestion of physical pain: and such an effect, reaching the spectator through his nerves rather than his imagination, is perhaps as much outside art in one direction, as pornography is in another. On the other hand, the whole of the ending seems to me almost great. You remember how Ishak finds Hassan fainting after being compelled to witness the torture of the lovers, and how, when Hassan begins to stammer out some of the horrible details, Ishak says 'You are still full of devils. Wake up! STOP DREAMING!!'[16] – and that, flashing ones mind back to what Pervaneh says in the Diwan scene about this world's being an illusion,[17] and leading straight on to the caravan for Samarkand – the broad moonlit desert stretching away and swallowing up the nightmare city in its clean solitude – all that does give one the true tragic

---

16 Flecker, *Hassan*, V, i: 'Be silent. You are full of devils. I tell you, it is not true. Stop dreaming: look into my eyes: listen!'

17 ibid., III, iii: 'We have heard the Trumpets of Reality that drown the vain din of the Thing that Seems.'

feeling of having been brought, thro horrors, right out of the ordinary illusion of life into some higher world. Another thing that is good is the scene in which all the adventures begin – where they are taken up in the basket into the house with no doors whence they heard the sounds of dancing. This is the only place which strikes the note of the real Arabian nights – the midnight possibilities of an Eastern city full of magicians. It is a pity he didn't work it out on those lines. As it stands it is too morbid: and one sees Flecker in places not feeling it as tragic at all but licking his lips (you remember his horrible face – it is the frontispiece of the *Poems*)[18] and gloating. Still, his powers were extraordinary and one is sorry that he didn't live to grow out of consumption and Parnassianism and decadence: he would have been a great writer in the end I believe.

As a contrast to my nightmare afternoon at the theatre I spent most of Sunday with W. and Dorothea Vaughan[19] (did you meet her?) digging holes for planting trees for what W. calls 'the Kilns Afforestation Scheme'. A lovely afternoon of early spring sunlight – the distance very pale blue, primroses out, and birds trilling and chuckling in abundance. All the better for the contrast with Hassan.

Did I tell you I was reading Ruskin's *Praeterita*[20] i.e. his autobiography? Contains an account of his boyhood which wd. particularly interest you, R's mother having had a great deal in common with your father. The good thing about it is that while not disguising the narrowness & pride at all, the final impression he leaves with you is one of peace & homeliness: the dateless, timeless peace of childhood in a really regular household. Later on there is some of the best description of travel wh. I have ever read.

I have had a baddish cold but am otherwise well. Any sign of the new people moving into Little Lea? How strange it will be to you. Try to reply in less time than last!

Yours

Jack

I was just going to put

C. S. Lewis again

---

18 James Elroy Flecker, *Forty-Two Poems* (1911).

19 Dorothea Vaughan, who had been a day pupil at Headington School with Maureen, was a frequent visitor at Hillsboro and The Kilns.

20 John Ruskin, *Praeterita*, 28 parts (1885–9).

TO ARTHUR GREEVES (W):

The Kilns,
Kiln Road,
Headington Quarry,
Headington, Oxford
Sunday, March 29th 1931

My dear Arthur,

I am afraid I am badly behind hand with this letter. I am afraid I cannot honestly plead that I have been too busy to write. The trouble is rather that when once the end of term has set me free from my compulsory work, I am so hungry for my real, private work,[21] that I grudge every moment from my books. This is a bad, selfish reason for not writing and I only give it because it happens to be true.

By the bye – I spoke some time ago about coming to visit you for a week in the summer, and you suggested fixing a date. If you still want to have me, how would the second or third week in August do? I should like it because I shall have finished my examining then wh. usually leaves me rather knocked up, and a holiday with you would be just the right tonic. Let me know how it would suit you. If this won't do, I should then – as a second choice – take my week with you as a *preparation* for examining instead of a cure, and come about the second week of July. But of course it is nicer to take the medicine first and the sweet after, than vice-versa. I try not to spoil this visit by thinking too much about it, but every now and then it comes over me with a delicious whiff of anticipation.

The most interesting thing that has happened to me since I last wrote is reading *War and Peace*[22] – at least I am now in the middle of the 4th and last volume so I think, bar accidents, I am pretty sure to finish it. It has completely changed my view of novels.

Hitherto I had always looked on them as rather a *dangerous* form – I mean dangerous to the health of literature as a whole. I thought that the strong 'narrative lust' – the passionate itch to 'see what happened in the end' – which novels aroused, necessarily injured the taste for other, better, but less irresistible, forms of literary pleasure: and that the growth of novel reading largely explained the deplorable division of readers into

21 i.e. the writing of *The Allegory of Love.*
22 Leo Tolstoy, *War and Peace* (1865–72).

low-brow and high-brow – the low being simply those who had learned to expect from books this 'narrative lust', from the time they began to read, and who had thus destroyed in advance their possible taste for better things. I also thought that the intense desire which novels rouse in us for the 'happiness' of the chief characters (no one feels that way about Hamlet or Othello) and the selfishness with which this happiness is concerned, were thoroughly bad (I mean, if the hero and heroine marry, that is felt to be a happy ending, tho every one else in the story is left miserable: if they don't that is an unhappy ending, tho it may mean a much greater good in some other way). Of course I knew there were tragic novels like Hardy's – but somehow they were quite on a different plane from real tragedies.

Tolstoy, in this book, has changed all that. I have felt everywhere – in a sense – you will know what I mean – that sublime *indifference* to the life or death, success or failure, of the chief characters, which is not a *blank* indifference at all, but almost like submission to the will of God. Then the variety of it. The war parts are just the best descriptions of war ever written: all the modern war books are milk and water to this: then the rural parts – lovely pictures of village life and of religious festivals in wh. the relations between the peasants and the nobles almost make you forgive feudalism: the society parts, in which I was astonished to find so much humour – there is a great hostess who always separates two guests when she sees them getting really interested in conversation, who is almost a Jane Austen character. There are love-passages that have the same sort of intoxicating quality you get in Meredith: and passages about soldiers chatting over fires which remind one of Patsy Macan: and a drive in a sledge by moonlight which is better than Hans Andersen. And behind all these, and uniting them, is the profound, religious conception of life and history wh. is beyond J. Stephens and Andersen, and beside which Meredith's worldly wisdom – well just *stinks*, there's no other word.

I go on writing all this because my pen runs away with me: meanwhile perhaps you have read the book long ago and even advised *me* to read it! If you have not, I strongly advise you to try it. Its length, which deters some people, will not frighten you: you will only rejoice, when the right time comes, – say after tea some day next autumn when fires are still a novelty – at that old, delicious feeling of *embarkation* on a long voyage, which one seldom gets now. For it takes a book nearly as long as *War and Peace* to *seem* as long now as a Scott did in boyhood.

And talking of boyhood – I recently re-read (being out-of-sorts) both *She* and the sequel *Ayesha*,[23] and found the story good in both: what troubles one is the v. silly talk put into She's mouth, which is meant to be profound. You feel that she has made very ill use of her opportunities. In re-reading them I re-visited one of the very few parts of my past which is not associated with you – tho' if I remember rightly we once discussed together the pictures in my editn. of Ayesha.

About Flecker's face – I don't think it is just sensuality that's the trouble. There is a sort of slyness and knowingness, tipping-the-wink-ness with it. Some sensuality one pities: other kinds one admires – full, Pagan magnificence. But there is a kind at once furtive and self-satisfied, at once secret and defiant that seems peculiar to very highly educated people in very big cities, which makes me shudder. You know – the atmosphere of the whispered confidence and the leer – one eye always watching to see how you take it and the whole face ready, at a moment's notice, *either* to take you into full conspiratorial confidence (if the man sees you like it) *or else* to turn up his nose and sneer at you (if you don't). In Barfield's long poem it is well described: the man who tells stories

> *Purring with female, strutting in the puddle*
> *Of his great naughtiness.*[24]

We had a fine burst of spring last week and I have sat and worked in the garden: one morning I saw a rabbit come out and wash its face not fifteen yards away from me. To-day I was only just warm enough while sawing wood in the shed in a gale that sent the sawdust whirling round me and covered Mr Papworth like snow.

You wd. have been so amused if you'd been here last week end. Mrs Armitage is a sort of blend of Kelsie and Tchanie and often comes to call. I had had a pupil to tea and took him out for a walk after. Coming back at 7 I found Mrs A. *still there*, seated on the same sofa with Warnie, and

---

23 Sir Henry Rider Haggard, *She* (1887); *Ayesha, or the Return of She* (1905).

24 Owen Barfield, 'The Tower', stanza II, ll. 36–7. This 'long poem' of Owen Barfield's, written between 1922 and 1928, has never been published. Writing about it in his diary of 21 June 1922, Lewis said: 'The "Tower" is full of magnificent material and never a dead phrase...The story is (to me) as hard to follow as *Sordello*. But what genius! The metre *too* eccentric for me, but on that subject Barfield has probably forgotten more than I ever knew' (*AMR*, p. 53). *Sordello* (1840) is by Robert Browning.

conducting a feverish conversation with him about married life, women, and kindred subjects, and under the impression (she is a widow) that she was making great headway. I wish she cd. have seen W., a few minutes later when she had left (for of course my return broke up the party), coming out of the front door into the twilit garden, drawing his hand across his brow, and remarking with great solemnity 'I'm going down to "the Checkers" to have a LARGE whisky and soda.'

Perhaps this doesn't sound funny as I tell it: at the time it reminded me so of the lady and the man (both of whose names I've forgotten) in your '*Trees*'. Let me hear soon. How delightful our old hills will be in a week or two now.

Yrs

Jack

TO ARTHUR GREEVES (W):

The Kilns,
Kiln Rd.,
Headington Quarry,
Oxford. [26? April 1931]

My dear Arthur,

No time for a proper letter. Minto is laid up with pleurisy. She is past the worst and I hope all is now on the right path: but tho' our anxiety is less, of course we are still very busy and tired. I had hoped to be giving you an account of my usual spring walking tour, but of course that's off.

I don't think I shall be able to come for more than a week in the summer – and in a way, wouldn't it be rather a waste to spend any time of our precious holiday except in the old haunts? You can hardly imagine how I pine for our wood, and our new wood, and the shepherds hut, and Divis. I can hardly look forward to it without dancing.

I don't think Barton[25] is insincere – at any rate as far as you are concerned. Maureen met him last summer while staying with her uncle[26] in Cavan and said 'He seemed to think a great deal of Arthur.' The worst of

---

25 Arthur William Barton, rector of St Mark's, Dundela, 1914–25. See note 47 to letter of 13 May 1915.

26 Mrs Moore's brother, the Very Rev. William James Askins (1879–1955), was Dean of Kilmore Cathedral.

a Parson's life is that the duty of being pleasant to people is bound to give a certain taint of insincerity to the *manner*.

I see this is too late for your address.[27] If they don't forward it, let me know at once.

Yrs

Jack

P.S. I *do* hope you will come and see us on your way back. I'm dying to show you some of my new haunts.

TO ARTHUR GREEVES (W):

> The Kilns,
> Kiln Rd.,
> Headington Quarry,
> Oxford.
> May 18th (Monday) [1931]

My dear A,

Come on the day you suggest rather than not coming at all – a thousand times rather, but this week is a bad one. I am staying out here recovering from flu: therefore I can't have you in College. We are threatened with two week end visitors: therefore I can't have you here. So there is hardly any week when I should miss so much of your society – specially those odd evening hours which are good for talking. What I should like would be for you to come on *Monday* next – if you can amuse yourself in London till then. In that case we could be in college together.

I shall not book the room without hearing from you again.

I am longing to see you. Reply at once.

Yours

Jack

P.S. Yes I have read Wm. Law[28] – a v. severe but wholesome draught! It may save *trouble* if you bring a dinner jacket, but not absolutely essential. (But a razor and clean handkerchief you *must* bring)

---

27 Arthur had just left for a holiday in London.
28 He is referring to William Law's *A Serious Call to a Devout and Holy Life* (1728).

TO ARTHUR GREEVES (W):

The Kilns,
Kiln Rd.,
Headington Quarry,
Oxford.
Wednesday. [20 May 1931]

My dear Arthur,

I have just got your letter and am rather disappointed. Do you mean that you may possibly not come *at all*? I should be very sorry if that were so. At the same time I am acutely conscious that I have not much to offer in my busy life and chaotic days to such a lover of tranquility as you: and I certainly don't wish to press a visit on you as a duty. All the same – (I don't think this is making a duty of it) I would remind you that there is a good case for coming to see me even at the cost of some discomfort; because it is important to the continuance of a friendship that each should have some experience of the other's life. I have always specially prized those few pleasant walks we had last time you were here, on that ground. Our sitting in the little thicket by that stream is an important addition to our stock of memories shared. And now that I am in quite new surroundings I shall never feel at ease till you have shared them with me. How can I write to you about places you have never seen?

As to your doubt whether you can stay in London till Monday – I quite realise that it is a bore to you just to mark time there for my convenience, when your mind is beginning to turn pleasantly towards books and home. You will admit that I (on whom your letter fell without warning very late in the day) could hardly have made plans to avoid this. And then, is there not perhaps a special reasonableness in asking *you* to do this? I mean being one of the very, very few who can live without a profession and having therefore so few demands on your time, ought you not to yield the more readily to such rare demands as do turn up?

As to staying in College, I take it the real objection is the early rising. I can offer you breakfast at 8.45; not later, for I have a pupil at 9 most mornings. But you will remember that last time, after trying it, you became a complete convert and swore always to be an early bird in future – so little terrible did it prove in actual practice. Of course you must please yourself: but I feel v. strongly that to spend our evenings hanging about in public rooms or in a bedroom at a hotel will be as it always has been, a miserable makeshift. Surely last time was much the most successful time we've had? Surely our snug evenings together (you can go to bed as early as you like) are worth having. The other arrangement is not only inconvenient, but (I find) rather depressing. Conversation does not flow in those conditions, and neither of us is himself.

Well, I have trotted out all my arguments. I wish I could believe they wd. all seem as strong to you as to me: but, as I say, I haven't much to offer. I can only moralise and plead the claims of friendship: but perhaps these will weigh as heavily with you as the more solid claims of comfort and convenience wd. weigh with a more selfish man. I await your reply eagerly

Yrs
Jack

TO ARTHUR GREEVES (W):

[Swiss Cottage,
16 Buckland Crescent,
London]
26th(?) June 1931

My dear Arthur,

My conscience accuses me of laziness. I have done *nothing* since term ended but sit in deck chairs in the shade, bathe twice a day in the pond, and talk. A little pottering about with Donne and Beowulf which I have done hardly deserves the name of work. The truth is that I am not only lazy but tired. I still can't walk a mile without aching legs. Whether I can write a page without aching hand is an experiment now to be tried. I am writing this in London where I am spending a day or two with Barfield – splendid talks and reading of Dante, but of course our nights tend to be late so that perhaps it is not a very judicious kind of holiday. However, it is short.

During this spell of hot weather the Kilns has been delightful. I know the pond looks dirty, but as a matter of fact one comes out perfectly clean. I wish you could join me as I board the punt in the before-breakfast solitude and push out from under the dark shadow of the trees onto the full glare of the open water, usually sending the moor hens and their chicks scudding away into the reeds, half flying and half swimming, with a delicious flurry of silver drops. Then I tie up to the projecting stump in the middle and dive off the stern of the punt. There is one thing in which fresh water bathing surpasses the sea – the beauty of broken ground and trees and flowers seen from an unfamiliar angle as you swim.

Thanks for your account of the fox. I don't see why a fox shouldn't be as happy as a dog in captivity if he is properly treated – but I certainly shudder for one whose owners contemplate such drastic dental treatment!

No – I didn't feel the earthquake and am rather sorry to have missed what must have been (and what we hope will *remain*) so rare a sensation.

You cannot have enjoyed your time in Oxford more than I did – it seemed to me quite one of the best times we have ever had together. Our stroll on the roof, our window seat at the bonfire, our good long talks on one or two evenings, are still in my mind – though of course memory has not yet done its real work in transfiguring them.

It is a long time since I read Peacock:[29] I remember him as having something of the whimsical charm of Lewis Carroll's minor works, and have always meant to go back to him.

Warton's *History of Poetry*[30] marks the beginning of our modern interest in mediaeval literature. Being pioneer work, it is quite unreliable and some of the theories he develops are grotesque: but what it lacks in accuracy it amply makes up in enthusiasm. He is discovering all the charm of the old writers for the first time, and infects you with his feeling, and sends you back to the feelings you had yourself as a boy. In fact, though not a great authority, it is a great book: and its very plentiful quotations will supply you with thousands of lines of old poetry which you will probably never meet elsewhere. If it is a nice edition it would make a really sound purchase for your library: and, besides being a great, it is an eminently 'dippable' book.

I am reading Inge's 'Personal Religion and the Life of Devotion'[31] (Longmans) – one of the best books of the kind I have yet struck.

I am at Hampstead which gives me quite a new idea of the suburbs of London. There is a little quiet court of Georgian houses here which might come out of any beautiful English country town – besides immense views from the Heath. Distant 'townscapes' have a peculiar *dreamy* beauty of their own which makes one feel it ungrateful to blame them for not being landscapes.

---

29 Thomas Love Peacock (1785–1866). See note 112 to letter of 11 November 1915.
30 Thomas Warton, *The History of English Poetry from the Eleventh to the Eighteenth Century*, 3 vols. (1774–81).
31 William Ralph Inge, *Personal Religion and the Life of Devotion* (1924).

Forgive me for a short letter – even this much has been done with some effort. I hope I shall wake up properly in a week or so.

Yours
Jack

TO ARTHUR GREEVES (W):

> The Kilns,
> Headington Quarry,
> Oxford.
> 26th [July 1931]

My dear Arthur,

I am in the midst of the annual examining. I propose to cross to Ireland on Saturday night August the 8th and stay with you till Saturday morning August 15th when I will join W. for breakfast on the Liverpool boat. If I can possibly get away from Cambridge on the Friday I will do so, but it is not likely. If any of these arrangements don't suit please let me have a line *at once*. I am looking forward to it almost *unbearably*!

Yours
Jack

P.S. In the event of a hitch about W's times can I come the following week instead? i.e. *from* the 15th.

TO ARTHUR GREEVES (W):

> [The Kilns
> 30? July 1931]

My dear Arthur,

Why do you do (or rather leave undone) these things? Owing to a variety of circumstances I now choose the *second* of the two periods you offer in your wire – i.e. from the 18th. That will be Tuesday and I shall come to you in the evening at about 9. The advantage of the second period is that I can give you a full week (Perhaps this may not seem advantageous to you?)

I shall turn up (D.V) on that evening unless I hear to the contrary – unless you'd like to come in and fetch me from the Liverpool boat where I shall be seeing W. off.

Yours
Jack

TO ARTHUR GREEVES (W):

Queen's College,
Cambridge.
Aug 6th [1931]

My dear Arthur,

I have your letter of the second August. I don't quite understand, as in my wire I said the 2nd period – 19th–26th was preferred (or didn't I?) At any rate I now intend to come to Bernagh on the evening of the 20th (Thursday) and stay till the 27 (following Thursday). If you cared to come in and meet me at the Liverpool boat (where I shall be seeing W. off) at about 8 and bring me out, that would be admirable. Have you and I ever brought off a scheme without these intense complications. However I have some excuse. I now *shall* arrive on the 20th *whatever* you say, so there's no good trying to prevent me!

I am here examining but having quite a good time – a lot of nice people, and I think this College the most beautiful in either University

Yours
C.S.L.

TO ARTHUR GREEVES (W):

Golf Hotel,
Castlerock,
Co. Derry.[32]
Aug. 19th [1931]

My dear Arthur,

Thanks for letter. W. says he would love to come and dine on Thursday night. We want, for sentimental reasons, to make the railway journey from town to Sydenham, so if you wd. meet us at Sydenham that would be capital. As I don't know the exact times of the rail motors I will ring you up from the Co. Down Ry. station at about 6.45 to 7. Isn't this going to be great! I still feel a great fear of something happening to prevent it: perhaps the world will end before to-morrow night!

Yours
Jack

---

32 i.e., Co. Londonderry. Jack and Warnie had spent a few days in Belfast with their relatives before going to Castlerock on 17 August. Castlerock was particularly precious to them because their mother had taken them there for a holiday in 1901.

TO ARTHUR GREEVES (W):

[The Kilns]
Sept 5th 1931

My dear Arthur,

How long ago it seems since I left you. I had a delightful evening, though tinged with melancholy, on the Liverpool boat, watching first the gantries and then the Down coast slipping past and picking out, more by imagination than sight, our favourite woods. I did not go to bed till we were off the Copelands. I felt and still feel that I was returning from one of the very best holidays I have ever had. Please thank your Mother (who was in one sense my hostess) and tell her how I enjoyed myself. I probably enjoyed the time more than you did, for the hills cannot have quite the same feeling for you who have never left them. What sticks in my mind most of all is the walk on which we visited Mrs McNeil. We were both in exactly the right mood. In another kind I have very fine memories of Croob and our session on top of it: as also of our homely and familiar evenings.

Meanwhile, as tangible mementoes of your almost excessive hospitality I have Hooker[33] and Taylor.[34] I did not thank you nearly enough for them at the time. The Taylor has been to the binders and returned very neatly mended yesterday. I started him after church this morning. He is severe and has little of the joyous side of religion in him: and some of his incentives (e.g. where he reminds you that there will be different degrees of glory in Heaven and would have you aim at getting as high a degree as possible) seem to me unspiritual or at least highly dangerous. But his painstaking, practical attitude has the charm of an old family doctor: beautifully homely and sincere. I have dipped into Hooker again and re-read some of my favourite passages.

On Thursday W. motored me over to Bulford (his station) on Salisbury plain, where he wanted to get some of his things, and we visited the village of Boscombe where Hooker was vicar and saw (from without) the parsonage in which he wrote most of his book. The church is the smallest one I have ever been in and contains some of the old square pews. It is very primitive and lit by oil lamps and candles. It has not

---

33 Richard Hooker, the theologian mentioned in note 4 to the letter of 3 February 1929.
34 Jeremy Taylor (1613–67), Anglican bishop best known for his *Rule and Exercise of Holy Living* (1650) and *Rule and Exercise of Holy Dying* (1651), which Greeves had given Lewis in one volume.

much real architectural beauty, but being honestly and unaffectedly built and now having the charm of antiquity it is very pleasant. I love these little old parish churches more and more: even the stuffiness delights me, and a sort of cosiness and friendliness in which the dead under their brasses seem to share. It all speaks of a life in which everyone knew every one else, and of real neighbourliness. What a nice word neighbour is – don't you like 'Well, neighbour So-and-So' in Bunyan.[35] I forget whether you know Salisbury plain or not? I love it – all chalky downs and little beech woods and fir woods: a most excellent air.

As for reading – in the train I bought and read Yeats-Brown's 'Bengal Lancer'.[36] Unless you remember the reviews of it (which were what made me buy it) you will wonder at my opening a book with such a title. It is the autobiography of a man who began as an ordinary Cavalry officer in the Indian army and ended up by becoming a Yogi – a mystic on the Hindu pattern. A strange story and in its latter stages told with real beauty. One can't help feeling that if he had been more educated he could have found what he wanted in traditions more hereditary to him than that of the Yogis – but judge not.

I have also been studying the Winters Tale. You remember the last scene – where Hermione is introduced as a statue and then comes to life.[37] Hitherto I had thought it rather silly: this time, seeing that the absurdity of the plot doesn't matter, and is merely the scaffolding whereby Shakespeare (probably unconsciously) is able to give us an image of the whole idea of resurrection, I was simply overwhelmed. You will say that I am here doing to Shakespeare just what I did to Macdonald over Wilfrid Cumbermede. Perhaps I am. I must confess that more and more the value of plays and novels becomes for me dependent on the moments when, by whatever artifice, they succeed in expressing the great *myths*.

This afternoon W. and I have been at work in the wood clipping the undergrowth, he with shears and I with a sickle. I hope you can see the whole scene – the light slanting through the fir trees, the long elder branches swaying and then swooping down with a rustle of leaves, the click-click of the shears, and the heavy odour of crushed vegetation.

---

35 John Bunyan, *The Pilgrim's Progress*, op. cit., part I, pp. 12–13: 'Come Neighbour Pliable, how do you do?...Well Neighbour Obstinate...Come Neighbour Christian.'
36 Francis Yeats-Brown, *Bengal Lancer* (1930).
37 Shakespeare, *The Winter's Tale*, V, iii.

What pleasures there are in the world. I seem to have more than anyone could deserve – a fortnight ago with you on our own hills, and now woodcutting on a fine autumn day in this delightful place.

Minto is well and sends her love. I met Baxter, the professor of English at Belfast,[38] last night. The only common acquaintance we discovered was – Dr Leslie!!

Yours

Jack

Jack had given the smaller of his rooms at Magdalen to Warnie, who had now turned it into a kind of new 'little end room'. The family papers were there, and Warnie was putting them in order, and typing them out, with editorial notes, on his little Royal typewriter. 'It is one of the most engrossing tasks I have ever undertaken,' he wrote in his diary of 9 January 1931, 'and I look forward with more eagerness than ever to my days of retirement in order to finish it' (BF, p. 75). This massive task, undertaken over a number of years, would result in the 11 volumes of 'Lewis Papers: Memoirs of the Lewis Family 1850–1930'. About the middle of the year Warnie re-enlisted for a second tour of duty in China so he could retire earlier than originally planned. He went on embarkation leave on 26 August, and sailed for China on 9 October, not to return home until 14 December 1932.

TO ARTHUR GREEVES (W):

[The Kilns]
Sept 22nd /31

My dear Arthur,

Thanks for your letter of the 11th. I couldn't write to you last Sunday because I had a week end guest – a man called Dyson[39] who teaches English at Reading University. I meet him I suppose about four or five times a year and am beginning to regard him as one of my friends of the 2nd class – i.e. not in the same rank as yourself or Barfield, but on a level with Tolkien or Macfarlane.

---

38 Frederick William Baxter (1897–1980) was Professor of English Literature at the Queen's University, Belfast, 1930–49, and Professor of English Language and Literature at the same university 1949–58.

39 See **Henry Victor Dyson 'Hugo' Dyson** in the Biographical Appendix.

He stayed the night with me in College – I sleeping in in order to be able to talk far into the night as one cd. hardly do out here. Tolkien came too, and did not leave till 3 in the morning: and after seeing him out by the little postern on Magdalen bridge Dyson and I found still more to say to one another, strolling up and down the cloister of New Building, so that we did not get to bed till 4. It was really a memorable talk. We began (in Addison's walk just after dinner) on metaphor and myth – interrupted by a rush of wind which came so suddenly on the still, warm evening and sent so many leaves pattering down that we thought it was raining. We all held our breath, the other two appreciating the ecstasy of such a thing almost as you would. We continued (in my room) on Christianity: a good long satisfying talk in which I learned a lot: then discussed the difference between love and friendship – then finally drifted back to poetry and books.[40]

On Sunday he came out here for lunch and Maureen and Minto and I (and Tykes) all motored him to Reading – a very delightful drive with some lovely villages, and the autumn colours are here now.

I am so glad you have really enjoyed a Morris again. I had the same feeling about it as you, in a way, with this proviso – that I don't think Morris was conscious of the meaning either here or in any of his works, except *Love is Enough* where the flame actually breaks through the smoke so to speak. I feel more and more that Morris has taught me things he did not understand himself. These hauntingly beautiful lands which somehow never satisfy, – this passion to escape from death plus the certainty that life owes all its charm to mortality – these push you on to the real thing because they fill you with desire and yet prove absolutely clearly that in Morris's world that desire cannot be satisfied.

The Macdonald conception of death[41] – or, to speak more correctly, St Paul's[42] – is really the answer to Morris: but I don't think I should have understood it without going through Morris. He is an unwilling witness to the truth. He shows you just *how far* you can go without knowing God, and that is far enough to force you (tho' not poor Morris himself) to go further. If ever you feel inclined to relapse into the mundane point

---

40 Further important details of this 'memorable talk' with Dyson and Tolkien on Saturday 19 September are found in the next two letters to Greeves.

41 There are many good examples in Lewis's *George MacDonald: An Anthology* (1946). Extract number 146 reads: 'All that is not God is death.'

42 e.g. Romans 5:12–21, 6:5–23; 1 Corinthians 15:12–58.

of view – to feel that your book and pipe and chair are enough for happiness – it only needs a page or two of Morris to sting you wide awake into uncontrollable longing and to make you feel that everything is worthless except the hope of finding one of his countries. But if you read any of his romances through you will find the country dull before the end. All he has done is to rouse the desire: but so strongly that you *must* find the real satisfaction. And then you realise that *death* is at the root of the whole matter, and why he chose the subject of the Earthly Paradise, and how the true solution is one he never saw.

I have finished the Taylor, and enjoyed it much from the purely literary point of view. As a religious writer I put him low and still think as I did when I last wrote.

I have been studying Hamlet very intensively, and never enjoyed it more. I have been reading all the innumerable theories about him, and don't despise that sort of thing in the least: but each time I turn back to the play itself I am more delighted than ever with the mere atmosphere of it – an atmosphere hard to describe and made up equally of the prevalent sense of death, solitude, & horror and of the extraordinary graciousness and lovableness of H. himself.[43] Have you read it at all lately? If not, do: and just surrender yourself to the magic, regarding it as a poem or a romance.

I don't *think* I left any pyjamas at Bernagh, but I'm afraid I want you to send me something else, W. is editing (i.e. arranging and typing) all the letters we brought from home (*don't* mention this to any one) so as to give a continuous history of the family.[44] We have just got to 1915 and it is maddening to have all my Bookham letters to my father (wh. tell nothing) and to know that all my Bookham letters to you are eating their heads off at Bernagh. Also, once I had them in type, I could renew those glorious years whenever I read them. Would it be a great bother to you to let me have the lot. If you want, you can have them back when they have been edited: and I promise faithfully that he will see nothing wh. gives you away in any respect, for I will go through them all first by myself. If you wd. let me have them *as soon as possible* and tell me what I owe you for registered postage, I shd. be very much obliged.

---

43 These are some of the ideas that went into Lewis's essay, 'Hamlet: The Prince or the Poem?' found in *Selected Literary Essays*.
44 The result of which was the Lewis Papers.

It is perfect autumn here – splashes of yellow on every other tree and delicious smells. We have been up in the wood clipping all afternoon.

I think I know the walk at the back of Stormont and may have done it oftener than you. This is a bad business about the rum. Give my love to your Mother. Tell Forrest I ask every one I meet about the human tendency to represent oneself as a daring sinner (untruly) and have met no one yet who doesn't regard it as being too obvious to be worth talking about

Yrs

Jack

About a week after the above letter was written, Monday 28 September, Warnie took Jack to Whipsnade Zoo in the sidecar of his motorbike, and it was during this outing that Jack took the final step in his conversion. 'As I drew near the conclusion,' he wrote in the last chapter of SBJ,

> *I felt a resistance almost as strong as my previous resistance to Theism. As strong, but short-lived, for I understood it better. Every step I had taken, from the Absolute to 'Spirit' to 'God', had been a step towards the more concrete, the more imminent, the more compulsive...I know very well when, but hardly how, the final step was taken. I was driven to Whipsnade one sunny morning. When we set out I did not believe that Jesus Christ is the Son of God, and when we reached the zoo I did. Yet I had not exactly spent the journey in thought. Nor in great emotion. 'Emotional' is perhaps the last word we can apply to some of the most important events. It was more like when a man, after long sleep, still lying motionless in bed, becomes aware that he is now awake.*

TO ARTHUR GREEVES (W):

[The Kilns]
Oct. 1st /31

My dear Arthur,

Very many thanks for the letter and enclosure that arrived this morning. Now, as to their return. I confess that I had not supposed you often read them, and had in view merely an *ultimate* return when W. had finished his editing, that is, in about 4 years' time. If however you want them at once, they are of course your property and will be returned by registered post whenever you wish. I shall follow absolutely your directions. In the meantime you can feel quite confident about their safe keeping. I have spent this morning on them and established a pretty good order for all except about eight. (How maddening my habit of not dating them now becomes! And how ridiculous the arguments by wh. I defended it!)

All the ones that deal with what we used to call 'It' I am suppressing and will return to you in a day or two. I am surprised to find what a very large percentage of the whole they are. I am now inclined to agree with you in *not* regretting that we confided in each other even on this subject, because it has done no harm in the long run – and how could young adolescents really be friends without it? At the same time, the letters give away some of your secrets as well as mine: and I do not wish to recall things of that sort to W's mind, so that in every way they had better be kept out of the final collection. I am also sending back some others in which my replies to you imply that you have said foolish things – you will see what I mean when I return them. Finally, I am suppressing (i.e. sending back at once and keeping from W. – that is what the word 'suppressing' means throughout) all letters that refer to my pretended assignation with the Belgian.[45] I am not at all sure that if J. Taylor were at my elbow he would not tell me that my repentance for that folly was incomplete if I did not submit to the 'mortification' of having them typed and laid open to posterity. I hope, however, this is not really necessary in the case of a sin so old and (I hope) so fully abandoned.

Thanks for all you say about the letters in general. You see mine with too friendly eyes. To me, as I re-read them, the most striking thing is their egotism: sometimes in the form of priggery, intellectual and even social: often in the form of downright affectation (I seem to be posturing and showing off in every letter): and always in the form of complete absorption in ourselves. I have you to thank that it was at least 'ourselves' and not wholly 'myself'. I can now honestly say that I envy you the much more artless letters you were writing me in those days: they all had at least the grace of humility and of affection. How ironical that the very things wh. I was proud of in my letters then should make the reading of them a humiliation to me now!

---

45 See the letter of 2 February 1915 *et seq.*

Don't suppose from this that I have not enjoyed the other aspect of them – the glorious memories they call up. I think I have got over *wishing* for the past back again. I look at it this way. The delights of those days were given to lure us into the world of the Spirit, as sexual rapture is there to lead to offspring and family life. They were nuptial ardours. To ask that they should return, or should remain is like wishing to prolong the honeymoon at an age when a man should rather be interested in the careers of his growing sons. They have done their work, those days and led on to better things. All the 'homeliness' (wh. was your chief lesson to me) was the introduction to the Christian virtue of charity or love. I sometimes manage now to get into a state in wh. I think of all my enemies and can honestly say that I find something lovable (even if it is only an oddity) in them all: and your conception of 'homeliness' is largely the route by wh. I have reached this. On the other hand, all the 'strangeness' (wh. was my lesson to you) has turned out to be only the first step in far deeper mysteries.

How deep I am just now beginning to see: for I have just passed on from believing in God to definitely believing in Christ – in Christianity. I will try to explain this another time. My long night talk with Dyson and Tolkien had a good deal to do with it.

I am so glad you liked the *Seasons*.[46] I agree with you that some parts are frankly boring, and some (e.g. the bathing episode in *Summer*) are in a false taste. I don't myself think that any of it is as good as the opening of *The Castle of Indolence*: the second canto everyone gives up as hopeless. It is delightful to hear of your thinking of having another try at Spenser. I have read nothing that would interest you since my last letter and am engaged on the Poetical Works of Skelton[47] (XVIth century) – a very bad poet except for the half dozen good things I knew already.

W. and I are busy still clearing the undergrowth in the top wood. This place gets more beautiful every day at present, with yellow leaves and crimson leaves and a more and more autumnal smell. I do hope you will some time make an opportunity of visiting it in winter.

---

46 James Thomson, *The Seasons* (1730).
47 John Skelton, *Poetical Works*, ed. Alexander Dyce, 2 vols. (1843). Lewis's fullest treatment of Skelton is found in *English Literature in the Sixteenth Century*, bk. I, ch. 2, pp. 133–43.

Did it strike you in reading those letters how completely *both* of us were wrong in most of our controversies, or rather in the great standing controversy about 'sentiment' wh. was the root of most of our quarrels? If anyone had said 'There is good feeling and bad: you can't have too much of the first, and you can't have too little of the second' it wd. have blown the gaff on the whole argument. But we blundered along – my indiscriminate hardness only provoking you into a more profound self pity (wh. is the root of all bad sentiment) and that bad sentiment in return making me harder and more willing to hurt.

Term begins next Friday.

Yours

Jack

P.S. I have just finished *The Epistle to the Romans*, the first Pauline epistle I have ever seriously read through. It contains many difficult and some horrible things, but the essential idea of Death (the Macdonald idea) is there alright. What I meant about the Earthly Paradise was simply that the whole story turns on a number of people setting out to look for a country where you don't die.

TO ARTHUR GREEVES (W):

[The Kilns]
Oct. 18th 1931

My dear Arthur,

I must have expressed myself rather confusedly about the letters. When I asked you for them I did not think that you would want them back except 'ultimately' – that is, the question of *time* was not seriously in my mind at all. Besides this, as people usually do in such circumstances, I was half consciously fooling myself about the length of time W. had still here. You know how 'He's not going just yet' leads one to plan and feel as if there was a month more when there is really 10 days. Then came your letter, showing your wish (a very flattering one to me) to have the letters back quite soon: and on top of that the *fact* (now unconcealable) that W. was actually packing and wd. be off in a day to two. It was therefore impossible that he should finish his editing of the family letters and get them all typed before he went: if I had known that you wanted them back soon, and if I had faced the real date of his departure, I would not have raised the question of the letters with you till after his return, 3 years hence. That indeed is what I ought to have done.

As things are, the four years I mentioned consist of 1 year's editing preceded by 3 years during wh. W. will be in China and the letters will be lying neatly in a drawer – safe, but idle. You see what a fool I have made of myself! The matter is now entirely in your hands, for of course they are your property not mine. If you want them seriously I will send them back: if you don't, they will be perfectly safe where they are, and safer indeed without the risk of a second postal journey. Still, the next move is to you and I will obey any orders you give.

This has filled up nearly a page so that I don't know whether I should now start to try and explain what I meant about Christianity. For one thing, reading your reply, I began to feel that perhaps I had said too much in my previous letter, that perhaps I was not nearly as clear on the subject as I had led you to think. But I certainly have moved *a bit*, even if it turns out to be a less bit than I thought.

What has been holding me back (at any rate for the last year or so) has not been so much a difficulty in believing as a difficulty in knowing what the doctrine *meant*: you can't believe a thing while you are ignorant *what* the thing is. My puzzle was the whole doctrine of Redemption: in what sense the life and death of Christ 'saved' or 'opened salvation to' the world. I could see how miraculous salvation might be necessary: one could see from ordinary experience how sin (e.g. the case of a drunkard) could get a man to such a point that he was bound to reach Hell (i.e. complete degradation and misery) in this life unless something quite beyond mere natural help or effort stepped in. And I could well imagine a whole world being in the same state and similarly in need of miracle. What I couldn't see was how the life and death of Someone Else (whoever he was) 2000 years ago could help us here and now – except in so far as his *example* helped us. And the example business, tho' true and important, is not Christianity: right in the centre of Christianity, in the Gospels and St Paul, you keep on getting something quite different and very mysterious expressed in those phrases I have so often ridiculed ('propitiation' – 'sacrifice' – 'the blood of the Lamb') – expressions wh. I cd. only interpret in senses that seemed to me either silly or shocking.

Now what Dyson and Tolkien showed me was this: that if I met the idea of sacrifice in a Pagan story I didn't mind it at all: again, that if I met the idea of a god sacrificing himself to himself (cf. the quotation opposite the title page of *Dymer*)[48] I liked it very much and was mysteriously moved by it: again, that the idea of the dying and reviving god (Balder, Adonis, Bacchus) similarly moved me provided I met it anywhere *except* in the Gospels. The reason was that in Pagan stories I was prepared to feel the myth as profound and suggestive of meanings beyond my grasp even tho' I could not say in cold prose 'what it meant'.

Now the story of Christ is simply a true myth: a myth working on us in the same way as the others, but with this tremendous difference that *it really happened*: and one must be content to accept it in the same way, remembering that it is God's myth where the others are men's myths: i.e. the Pagan stories are God expressing Himself through the minds of poets, using such images as He found there, while Christianity is God expressing Himself through what we call 'real things'. Therefore it is *true*, not in the sense of being a 'description' of God (that no finite mind could take in) but in the sense of being the way in which God chooses to (or can) appear to our faculties. The 'doctrines' we get *out* of the true myth are of course *less* true: they are translations into our *concepts* and *ideas* of that wh. God has already expressed in a language more adequate, namely the actual incarnation, crucifixion, and resurrection. Does this amount to a belief in Christianity? At any rate I am now certain (a) That this Christian story is to be approached, in a sense, as I approach the other myths. (b) That it is the most important and full of meaning. I am also *nearly* certain that it really happened.

No time for more now. I hope to have some literary chat in my next letter.

Yours
Jack

---

48 *The Hávamál*, no. 138: 'Nine nights I hung upon the Tree, wounded with the spear as an offering to Odin, myself sacrificed to myself'. *The Hávamál*, which means 'Sayings of the High One' (i.e. Odin, the chief god of Norse mythology), is a ninth century composite poem of 164 maxims or strophes in Old Norse. It is one of the poems collectively known as the Elder Edda.

BIOGRAPHICAL APPENDIX

BAKER, Leo Kingsley (1898–1986), was born in London on 14 August 1898, the son of Laura Jane Baker and James Leopold Hawes. He was educated at St George's School, Harpenden, from 1909 to 1917 where he was a school prefect, captain of rugby and of cricket. After matriculating at Wadham College, Oxford, in June 1917 he enlisted in the Royal Flying Corps. He was commissioned a 2nd lieutenant in November 1917, and a 1st lieutenant in April 1918. In May 1918 he went to France as a pilot with the 80th Squadron of the Royal Air Force. After being severely wounded in August 1918, he was awarded the Distinguished Flying Cross.

Baker returned to Oxford in 1919 and read Modern History. He and Lewis, who met soon after Baker arrived in Oxford, were drawn together by a love of poetry, and Lewis's letters to Baker contain some of his most interesting observations on poetry. He was a frequent visitor at Lewis's and Mrs Janie Moore's* home, and there are many references to him in *AMR*. It was Leo Baker who introduced Owen Barfield*, also of Wadham, to Lewis.

After taking his BA in 1922, he was from 1922 to 1925 an actor with the Old Vic Company under Lilian Baylis. His experience included parts in 30 Shakespeare plays, some old comedy, and two years of stage management. In 1925 he married Eileen Brookes and they had three daughters, Susan Mary (b. 1930), Elizabeth Margaret (b. 1933), and Rachel Mary Rosalind (b. 1939). Baker gave up the theatre owing to troubles resulting from his war wounds, and he and his wife set up a handloom weaving business in Chipping Campden, known as the Kingsley Weavers. It was dissolved on the outbreak of the Second World War. He was an Anthroposophist, and in 1933 he became a priest with the Anthroposophical 'Christian Community'. After the war broke out he took the family out of London to Gloucester, where he taught at a Rudolf Steiner school. He left the school in 1942 to become drama adviser for Gloucestershire, and in 1946 he became national drama adviser for the Carnegie United Kingdom Trust.

Upon his retirement at 65 he became head of acting for the Rose Bruford College of Speech and Drama in Sidcup, having been the chairman of governors when it was founded. His final retirement was at the age of 72. His wife suffered a severe stroke in 1976 and for five and a half years he devotedly visited her in hospital every day. She was paralysed and unable to speak. Leo Baker died on 5 September 1986 at the age of 88, his intellectual faculties as bright as ever.

BARFIELD, Owen (1898–1997) was born in Muswell Hill, North London on 9 November 1898, the youngest of four children, two sons and two daughters, born to Arthur Edward Barfield and Elizabeth (Shoults) Barfield. His father was a solicitor and his mother an ardent feminist. Both of his parents had been born Congregationalists, but the family observed no religion. When he was eight, Owen Barfield joined his brother Harry at Highgate School, and it was there he met one of his greatest friends, Cecil Harwood.* During the First World War he served mainly in Belgium as a wireless officer in the signal service of the Royal Engineers – now the Royal Corps of Signals. The wireless (or radio) was at that time in its infancy, and still using the Morse code.

In October 1919 he went up to Wadham College, Oxford, on a Classical scholarship. However, because of his growing interest in English literature, it was not Greats he read, but English Literature. During his first term he met Lewis and they were friends from then on. 'Barfield towers above us all', Lewis wrote in his diary of 9 July 1922. Lewis's diary (*AMR*), which covers the years 1922 to 1927, contains much about their shared interests.

After taking his BA with first class honours in 1921, Barfield began writing a B.Litt. thesis on 'Poetic Diction'. In 1923 he became a follower of Anthroposophy, the religious system evolved by Rudolf Steiner whom Barfield heard lecture on 24 August 1924. He was to be involved with the Anthroposophical Society for the rest of his life. Barfield's beliefs about poetic diction had led him to the Romantic poets and their doctrines of imagination, and then to the conclusion that Romanticism had never fulfilled itself, never been philosophically 'justified'. Now, on reading Steiner, he found that Steiner had understood all this before him. In the Introduction to *Romanticism Comes of Age* (1944), which contains his debt to Steiner, he said: 'Anthroposophy included and transcended not only my own poor stammering theory of poetry as knowledge, but the whole Romantic philosophy. It was nothing less than Romanticism grown up.' Lewis was not in sympathy with Anthroposophy and he and Barfield engaged in a 'Great War' argument through the post. It is recounted in Lionel Adey's *C. S. Lewis's 'Great War' with Owen Barfield* (1978).

During their second year at Oxford, Barfield and Cecil Harwood joined the English Folk Dancing Society, and it was through this society that Barfield met Matilda ('Maud') Douie, a professional dancer and producer who had worked with Gordon Craig. They married on 11 April 1923, and lived for a while in Long Crendon, where Lewis often visited them. In 1925 they moved to London to help with Barfield's literary career. He worked for the magazine *Truth*, and during this time he wrote a fairy tale of the Hans Andersen kind, *The Silver Trumpet* (1925). This was followed by *History in English Words* (1926) which is not merely about the changes in the meanings of words over time but what he called 'evolution of consciousness'. In 1928 he published a revised version of his B. Litt. thesis, *Poetic Diction: A Study in Meaning*, which contains many of his leading philosophic ideas.

Unfortunately, Barfield was forced to abandon his literary career. His father lost the services of a brother in their London firm of Barfield and Barfield, and in 1929 Owen joined the firm in order to help. He received a BCL from Oxford in 1930, and spent the next 28 years as a solicitor in London. One of the most pleasant things to come out of what he called these 'colourless' years was a charming *jeu d'esprit* called *This Ever Diverse Pair* (1950), published under the name G.A.L. Burgeon. In the story 'Burgeon' is the idealistic alter ego or 'sleeping partner' of the practical-minded solicitor named 'Burden'. They represent the tension between the demands of the legal profession and the need to live in the larger world of thought and letters. 'Burden is eating me up,' complains Burgeon in Chapter I,

> *my time, my wit, my memory, my 'shaping spirit of imagination', my whole me. Take poetry, for instance. The other evening he was so exhausted and spiritless and devoid of hope that he asked me to write a poem about his feelings. That's the sort of thing he does – calls on me to exert the very abilities he is destroying. I produced the following quatrain for him: –*

> > *'How I hate this bloody business,*
> > *Peddling property and strife*
> > *While the pulse of Europe falters –*
> > *How I hate this bloody life!'*

In the 1940s Lewis asked Barfield to set up a charitable trust into which he could direct most of his royalties, which trust was administered by Barfield. Chapter VI of *This Ever Diverse Pair* is about a client named 'Ramsden' who is based on Lewis, and it deals in a humorous way with the charitable trust which Lewis and Barfield referred to as the 'Agapargyry' (love + money).

But there was colour in his private life. Over the years the Barfields adopted three children, Alexander (b. 30 January 1928), Lucy (b. 2 November 1935) who is Lewis's godchild and to whom he dedicated *The Lion, the Witch and the Wardrobe*, and Jeffrey (b. 6 June 1940) to whom Lewis dedicated *The Voyage of the 'Dawn Treader'*. Barfield was baptized in the Church of England in 1949. Meanwhile, the friendship between Barfield and Lewis afforded them many happy times, and of Lewis's numerous tributes to Barfield the most memorable comes from *SBJ* XIII:

> *There is a sense in which Arthur [Greeves*] and Barfield are the types of every man's First Friend and Second Friend. The First is the* alter ego, *the man who first reveals to you that you are not alone in the world by turning out (beyond hope) to share all your most secret delights. There is nothing to be overcome in making him your friend; he and you join like raindrops on a window. But the Second Friend is the man who disagrees with you about everything. He is not so much the* alter ego *as the antiself. Of course he shares your interests; otherwise he would not become your friend at all. But he has approached them all at a different angle. He has read all the right books but has got the wrong thing out of every one. It is as if he spoke your language but mispronounced it. How can he be so nearly right and yet, invariably, just not right? He is as fascinating (and infuriating) as a woman. When you set out to correct his heresies, you find he forsooth has decided to correct yours! And then you go at it, hammer and tongs, far into the night, night after night, or walking through fine country that neither gives a glance to, each learning the weight of the other's punches, and often more like mutually respectful enemies than friends. Actually (though it never seems so at the time) you modify one another's thought; out of this perpetual dogfight a community of mind and a deep affection emerge. But I think he changed me a good deal more than I him. Much of the thought which he afterward put into* Poetic Diction *had already become mine before that important little book appeared. It would be strange if it had not. He was of course not so learned then as he has since become; but the genius was already there.*

A revolution in his life came about when he was 60. About the time of his retirement in 1959 he at last found time to write many of his best books. They include his own favourite – *Saving the Appearances* (1957) – as well as *Worlds Apart* (1963), *Unancestral Voice* (1965), *Speaker's Meaning* (1967), *What Coleridge Thought* (1971), *The Rediscovery of Meaning, and Other Essays* (1977), and *History, Guilt, and Habit* (1979). Chapter VI of *This Ever Diverse Pair* is reprinted in a work containing nearly everything Barfield has written about Lewis, *Owen Barfield on C. S. Lewis*, ed. G.B. Tennyson (1990).

For the first two decades of this second part of his life he was a visiting scholar in many American colleges and universities. There was always a welcome for his numerous American friends at his home 'Orchard View' in Dartford, Kent. His wife died there on 13 February 1980. In 1986 Barfield moved to Forest Row, Sussex, and he died there on 14 December 1997, a month into his centenary.

For information about him, see *Evolution of Consciousness: Studies in Polarity*, ed. Shirley Sugerman (1976), a volume of essays offered to him. A very good biography is G.B. Tennyson's 'Owen Barfield: A Life in Thought' in *A Barfield Reader: Selections from the Writings of Owen Barfield*, ed. G.B. Tennyson (1999). Another good work of biography is the introduction to *A Barfield Sampler: Poetry and Fiction by Owen Barfield* (1993) by the editors, Jeanne Clayton Hunter and Thomas Kranidas. Of the many studies of his writings the one he thought best is Gareth Knight's *The Magical World of the Inklings: J.R.R. Tolkien, C. S. Lewis, Charles Williams, Owen Barfield* (1990).

CAPRON, Robert ('Oldy' or 'Oldie') (1851–1911), headmaster of Wynyard School, called 'Belsen' in *SBJ* II. Capron was born in Brampton, Devon, on 29 October 1851 and received a BA and a BSc from the University of London in 1873 and 1875 respectively. From 1873 to 1878 he was a teacher at Bowdon College in Altrincham, Cheshire. He was ordained an Anglican clergyman in 1878, and was curate of Wordsley, Staffordshire. In 1881 he moved to 99 Langley Road, Watford, where he founded Wynyard School.

The school was just beginning when, in 1882, he married Ellen Barnes (1849–1909). They had three daughters, Norah, Dorothy and Eva, and a son, John Wynyard (1883–1959) who was educated at King's College, Cambridge. The entire family helped with the school which, for a while, was successful. At its height it could accommodate 30 boarders and as many day-boys. During those early days Robert Capron was considered very successful for his teaching of the classics, and some of his boys gained scholarships to Charterhouse, Malvern, Uppingham and Rugby.

In 1896 a local boy, Ernest Benskin, enrolled at Wynyard. In an unpublished autobiography he revealed that he was there when Capron, who had already shown evidence of cruelty, went into an extreme rage, battering a pupil named 'Punch' Hickmott so unmercifully that the boy's parents took legal proceedings against him in the High Court. The school began to decline from this point.

Albert Lewis* knew nothing about all this when he enrolled his elder son at Wynyard. 'It is difficult to understand how this came about,' wrote Warnie Lewis,* 'having in view the careful and exhaustive enquiries which had culminated in the narrowing of the choice to three or four schools, of which Wynyard was not one' (LP III: 33). In any event, Warnie arrived there with Mrs Lewis on 11 May 1905. In his reminiscences of his years there (LP III: 33–41) Warnie describes Capron:

> A fine forehead surmounted a pair of piercing eyes of the shade of brown which is nearly black. He wore a short grey beard and moustaches, and his hair, which was plentiful, was of the same colour; his complexion was ruddy, healthy, and weather beaten. The face was marred by the nose, which was small, had the appearance of being varnished, and from which the lobe of the right nostril had at some time been removed. He was, I imagine, above middle height, and was a well built and extremely powerful man physically; I have seen him lift a boy of twelve or so from the floor by the back of his collar, and, holding him at arms length as one might a dog, proceed to refresh the unfortunate youth's memory by applying his cane to his calves.

By the time C. S. Lewis entered Wynyard on 18 September 1908, Capron had been examined in 1906 by a brain specialist who found him mad. By this time the school had dwindled to eight boarders and about as many day-boys. Capron's only assistants at this time were his daughters and John Wynyard Capron who was ordained in 1909. It was not long before Jack was as appalled by Capron's cruelty as Warnie, and he wrote of this in *SBJ* II.

When a blast of Capron's temper fell upon Warnie on 19 September 1908 both boys wrote to their father. Warnie said: 'I have stood this sort of thing for three years and I cannot stand it any longer. Please let us leave at once' (LP III: 147). Jack, in his letter of 29 September, urged his father to allow them to come home: 'We simply *cannot* wait in this hole till the end of term.' Mr Lewis, trying to be helpful, replied on 20 September 1908: 'All schools – whether for boys or the larger school of life for men – press hardly and sorely at times. Otherwise they would not be schools. But I am sure you will face the good and the bad like a brave Christian boy, for dear, dear Mammy's sake' (LP III: 140).

They did not have to hold on much longer. Mrs Capron died on 1 March 1909, and Warren left to go to Malvern in July 1909. Reduced to a handful of pupils, the school began to sink. Capron wrote to Albert Lewis on 27 April 1910 to say he was 'giving up school work' (LP III: 206). The school closed in July 1910, Capron having been inducted into the living at Radwell on 13 June of that year. There he began flogging the choirboys and, when they tried to stop it, the churchwardens as well. He was put under restraint, certified insane, and he resigned his living in June 1911. He died of pneumonia in Camberwell House Asylum, Peckham, Kent, on 18 November 1911. His body lies with that of his wife in Watford Cemetery.

COGHILL, Nevill (1899–1980). This friend and colleague was born on 19 April 1899 at Castle Townshend, Skibbereen, County Cork, the son of Anglo-Irish Protestant gentry. Nevill's parents were Sir Egerton Bushe Coghill, 5th Baronet, a noted amateur landscape painter, and Elizabeth Hildegarde Augusta Somerville – sister of the writer Edith Anna Oenone Somerville. He was educated at Bilton Grange and Haileybury College, after which he was commissioned a 2nd lieutenant in the trench mortar division of the Royal Artillery. He served as a gunner on the Salonika front in 1918. He went up to Exeter College, Oxford, in 1919 and read History and then English. He gained a First in English in 1923.

Coghill and Lewis began reading English together in 1922 and the first mention of Coghill occurs in Lewis's diary (*AMR*) of 2 February 1923 after they had attended George Gordon's 'Discussion Class': 'He seems an enthusiastic sensible man, without nonsense, and a gentleman, much more attractive than the majority.' It was the practice of the discussion class to keep the minutes of the meetings in verse. After Lewis read a paper about Spenser on 9 February 1923 Coghill wrote the minutes in some of the same Chaucerian verse for which he was to become famous. Describing Lewis's paper on Spenser, he said:

> Sir Lewis *was ther; a good philosópher*
> *He hade a noblé paper for to offer.*

Well couthe he speken in the Greeké tongue;
And yet, his countenance was swythé yong.

Lewis was an unbeliever when he met Coghill and in *SBJ* XIV he explained the 'disturbing factors in Coghill' which threatened his atheism:

> *I soon had the shock of discovering that he – clearly the most intelligent and best-informed man in that class – was a Christian and a thoroughgoing supernaturalist. There were other traits that I liked but found...oddly archaic; chivalry, honour, courtesy, 'freedom', and 'gentilesse'. One could imagine him fighting a duel. He spoke much 'ribaldry' but never 'villeinye'.*

After teaching for a while in the Royal Naval College at Dartmouth, Coghill was elected a research fellow at Exeter in 1924. He became an official fellow and librarian in 1925. In 1927 he married Elspeth Nora Harley and they had a daughter, Carol. The marriage was dissolved in 1933. Over the years he developed his very considerable talents as a dramatic producer. After his production of *Samson Agonistes* at Exeter College in 1930, he went on to produce plays for the OUDS (Oxford University Dramatic Society). When he was casting *Measure for Measure* in 1944 he chose a talented young man from his own college to play the part of Angelo. Although baptized Richard Jenkins, he later took the name Richard Burton. He and Coghill became and remained good friends. A detailed account of Coghill's contributions to OUDS, with a photo of him rehearsing *Dr Faustus* with Richard Burton, is found in Humphrey Carpenter's *O.U.D.S.: A Centenary History of the Oxford University Dramatic Society* (1985).

John Wain left a delightful portrait of the Nevill Coghill in *Dear Shadows* (1986):

> *He was a big man, with a tallness that would not be remarkable now that so many people are tall, but also built on generous lines, broadshouldered and deep-chested. His head was large, and brown hair, greying in middle life, curled and clustered on it as wiry as heather. He smiled easily, revealing somewhat battered teeth, and indeed his whole face had a slightly rough, knocked-about quality, like a chipped statue. I had one friend who used to say that he looked like one of the emperors' heads outside the Sheldonian...But if his head was*

statue-like, it was a noble statue, generous in expression and bearing. His voice was deep and strong, his speech soft and gentle; and this contrast was carried through everything. He was totally courteous, a gentleman by instinct as well as by tradition...In fact, he was more endowed with grace of manner and of mind than anyone I ever met. (p. 13)

In 1957 Coghill was elected Merton Professor of English Literature. He was a scholar of Middle English literature and his translation into contemporary English of Chaucer's *The Canterbury Tales* (1951) has enjoyed a wide audience. Lewis thought highly of it and he was pleased that Coghill had succeeded in making Chaucer understandable to many who would have never been able to read him. Coghill's translation of Langland's *Piers Plowman* was published as *Visions from Piers Plowman* in 1949, and his translation of Chaucer's *Troilus and Criseyde* in 1971.

Lewis and Coghill saw one another often, and Coghill attended a good many meetings of the Inklings, through which he got to know Warnie Lewis. In his essay 'Approach to English', in *Light on C. S. Lewis*, ed. Jocelyn Gibb (1965), Coghill wrote of those years when he and Lewis were reading English together as undergraduates.

In 1966, the year of his retirement, Coghill directed his former pupil Richard Burton and Elizabeth Taylor in *Dr Faustus* at the Oxford Playhouse. The following year the film, with almost the same cast, was shot in Rome, with Coghill and Burton co-directing. In 1968 he mounted a very successful musical version of *The Canterbury Tales* which ran for five years at the Phoenix Theatre in London. In the late 1960s Coghill went to live with his brother Sir Jocelyn Coghill at Aylburton, Gloucester. He died in Cheltenham on 6 November 1980. See *To Nevill Coghill from Friends*, Collected by John Lawlor and W.H. Auden (1966), John Carey's biography in the *Dictionary of National Biography*, and the biography in *CG*.

DUNBAR OF HEMPRIGGS, Dame Maureen Daisy Helen, Baronetess (1906–97). She was born Maureen Moore in Delgany, County Wicklow, Ireland, on 19 August 1906, the daughter of Courtenay Edward Moore and Jane King Askins Moore,* and the sister of Edward Francis Courtenay 'Paddy' Moore*. Following her parents' separation, her mother moved with Maureen and Paddy to Bristol in 1908. In June 1917 she and her mother took rooms in Wellington Square, Oxford, so they could be near Paddy while he was training with the Officers' Training Corps in Keble College. She met Lewis soon after his arrival there on 7 June. He was sharing a room in Keble with her brother, and over the next few months she and her mother came to know him well. He visited their home in Bristol several times. On one of these visits she heard Lewis and Paddy promise that if one of them survived the war he would look after Lewis's father and Paddy's mother. They went to France soon after this. Paddy was killed in action in March 1918 and was awarded the Military Cross. Lewis wished to keep his side of the bargain, and after he came home from France and returned to Oxford they moved there to be near him.

Maureen was educated at Headington School, with Lewis providing tutorials in Greek and Latin to help her get her School Certificate. Lewis's diary, *All My Road Before Me*, contains much about his life with the Moores, and the various places they lived. Maureen loved music, and had taken lessons in Bristol. After moving to Oxford, her mother did much to encourage her. On leaving Headington School she went to the Royal College of Music where she obtained her Licentiate of the Royal Academy of Music in 1928. She taught music at Monmouth School for Girls from 1930 to 1933; Oxford High School from 1935 to 1940; and at Malvern College from 1957 to 1968. It was appropriate that she should marry someone as musical as she was, and on 27 August 1940 she married Leonard Blake (b. 7 October 1907) who had been Director of Music at Worksop College since 1935, and who in 1945 became Director of Music at Malvern College. They had two children, Richard Francis Blake, Lewis's godson, born on 8 January 1945; and Eleanor Margaret Blake born on 16 November 1949.

Even after she married she did all she could to help her mother. She and her family would often change houses with Jack and Warnie Lewis, so she could look after Mrs Moore and they could have a holiday in Malvern. When Joy Lewis was very ill and in hospital during 1957, Maureen invited her two sons to spend their school holidays in Malvern.

On 4 February 1963 a distant relative, Sir George Cospatrick Duff-Sutherland-Dunbar, died. He was unmarried and Maureen Blake discovered that she was next in line, through her father's side of the family, to a baronetcy and an estate in Caithness, Scotland. She became the 8th Baronet. She had not seen Lewis since this happened when, in July 1963, she visited him in hospital. He had not recognized others that day, and she said: 'Jack, it is Maureen.' 'No,' he replied, 'It's Lady Dunbar of Hempriggs.' 'Oh, Jack,' she said, 'how could you remember that?' 'On the contrary,' he replied, 'How could *I* forget a fairy tale?'

Her inheritance of a baronetcy was more complicated than it first looked, because no one was sure a woman could inherit one. However, it came right in the end. In August 1965 Maureen was proved to be the rightful successor by the Lord Lyon, Chief of Heralds in Edinburgh. The Hempriggs Baronetcy, a 'Nova Scotia' one, was created in 1706 'to heirs whomsoever, whether male or female'. On 6 August 1965 *The Times* carried an article headlined 'Woman Wins Claim to Title – Baroness of Scotland Recognized'. 'The court, in a judgement issued today,' it said, 'granted a petition brought by Mrs Maureen Daisy Helen Moore or Blake, of The Lees, Malvern, Worcestershire, and recognized her as Dame Maureen Daisy Helen Dunbar of Hempriggs, Baronetess.'

Lady Dunbar and her family spent a month each summer at Ackergill Tower, near Wick, Caithness – in the far north of Scotland. The inheritance did not bring her wealth. Indeed, it brought many responsibilities which she handled with skill and feeling. Her Scottish home also furnished her and her husband with a great deal of interest and they managed to go up north every summer. When they retired from teaching at Malvern, they moved to the small village of Winchcombe in Gloucestershire. Leonard Blake died on 1 August 1989 and Lady Dunbar died on 15 February 1997. At her death, her son became the 9th Baronet, Sir Richard Dunbar of Hempriggs.

DYSON, Henry Victor Dyson, 'Hugo' (1896–1975), was born on 7 April 1896 in Hove, Sussex, the son of Philip Dyson and his wife Henrietta. He was educated at Brighton College. On leaving there in 1911 he went to the Royal Military College at Sandhurst. In December 1915 he was commissioned a 1st lieutenant in the Queen's Own Royal West Kent Regiment and sent to France where he took part in the Battle of the Somme during July–August 1916, and the Battle of Arras during April 1917. It was in the Battle of Passchendaele at Ypres during October–November 1918 that Dyson was seriously wounded.

He came up to Exeter College, Oxford, in October 1919 and read English, taking a BA in 1921. He remained to write a thesis on John Ford and took a B.Litt. degree in 1924, and his MA in 1925. On completing his thesis, Dyson was offered a post as Lecturer and Tutor in English at Reading University where he taught from 1914 until 1945. During this time he was an Oxford Extension Lecturer and an Oxford examiner for St Andrew's and Durham University. In 1925 he married Margaret Mary Bosworth Robinson (b. 26 December 1903) of Wantage. The next year Reading University achieved independence from the University of London and became the University of Reading.

Dyson was introduced to Lewis in 1930 through their mutual friend Nevill Coghill.* Lewis described their second meeting in a letter to Arthur Greeves* of 29–30 July 1930. Dyson and Coghill had dined with Lewis in Magdalen College on 29 July and remained until three o'clock in the morning: 'Having met him once I liked him so well that I determined to get to know him better...He is a man who really loves truth: a philosopher and a religious man: who makes his critical & literary activities depend on the former – none of your damned dilettante.'

When Lewis next wrote to Greeves about Dyson it was about an even more important evening at Magdalen – 19 September 1931 – this time with J.R.R. Tolkien.* The 'memorable talk' between the three of them went on until four in the morning, and when Lewis wrote to Greeves on 1 October 1931 he said: 'I have just passed on from believing in God to definitely believing in Christ – in Christianity...Dyson and Tolkien had a good deal to do with it.' The final letter in this book, that of 18 October 1931, describes in detail what happened to Lewis as a result of the long and important conversation with Dyson and Tolkien. From this time on Dyson was a valued member of the Inklings.

Lewis and the others were to see much more of this charming man when Dyson became a Fellow and Tutor of Merton College in 1945 and moved to Oxford. Warnie Lewis* had met him in 1933 and his diary provides the best description of Dyson's wit and vivacious spirits. He is, he wrote on 18 February 1933, 'a man who gives the impression of being made of quick silver: he pours himself into a room on a cataract of words and gestures, and you are caught up in the stream – but after the first plunge, it is exhilarating' (*BF*). There is much evidence of this 'cataract of words' in the book he wrote with J.E. Butt, *Augustans and Romantics 1689–1830* (1940). Jack wrote to Warnie on 3 March 1940 about reading the book in proof. 'It is, as one would expect,' he said, 'almost too bright, but some of the sparks are admirable.'

Dyson shared Warnie's disappointment in Jack's choice of Mrs Janie Moore* as his companion. On 8 August 1946 Warnie dined with Hugo Dyson in Merton, and that night he wrote in his diary: 'He was in high spirits when I met him, and his spirits rose steadily for the rest of the evening. I was more than ever struck with his amazing knowing of Shakespeare; I don't suppose there is a man in Oxford – with the possible exception of [C.T.] Onions – who can quote so happily, e.g. tonight, apropos of J[ack]: "O cursed spite that gave thee to the Moor": poor [Jack's] whole catastrophe epitomised in nine words!'

Dyson retired from Merton in 1963 and he and his wife moved to a house in Sandfield Road, Headington. His works include *Pope* (1933), '"The Old Cumberland Beggar" and the Wordsworthian Unities' in *Essays on the Eighteenth Century Presented to David Nichol Smith* (1945), and *The Emergence of Shakespeare's Tragedy* (1950). Patrick Garland, the producer, had been one of his pupils, and at his instigation Dyson gave several television talks on Shakespeare for the BBC as well as introducing Garland's television series *Famous Gossips*. In 1965 he made an appearance in John Schlesinger's film *Darling*, which starred Julie Christie and Dirk Bogarde. He died on 6 June 1975, and his beloved Margaret died 27 May 1993. They are buried in a single grave in the cemetery of St Cross Church, Oxford. See Humphrey Carpenter's *The Inklings* (1978).

The Ewart Family. The head of this Belfast family was Sir William Quartus Ewart (1844–1919) who was born on 14 June 1844, the eldest son of Sir William Ewart, MP, the 1st Baronet. After taking a degree from Trinity College, Dublin, he went to work in the family firm of Wm. Ewart & Son Ltd., Flax Spinners and Linen Manufacturers. In 1876 he married Mary Heard (1849–1929), the eldest daughter of Robert Heard JP of Pallastown, Kinsdale, Co. Cork. Mary Heard was the niece of C. S. Lewis's maternal grandmother, Mrs Mary Warren Hamilton (see The Hamilton Family*). Sir William and Lady Ewart were the first cousins of Flora Lewis,* and they are the relatives Lewis refers to as 'Cousin Quartus' and 'Cousin Mary' in *SBJ* III.

The Ewart family lived in Strandtown, very near the Lewises, in a house called 'Glenmachan' – it is referred to in *Surprised by Joy* as 'Mountbracken'. Lewis wrote in *SBJ* III:

> *Lady E. was my mother's first cousin and perhaps my mother's dearest friend, and it was no doubt for my mother's sake that she took upon herself the heroic work of civilizing my brother and me...Sir W. ('Cousin Quartus') was...gracious, childlike, deeply and religiously humble, and abounding in charity. No man could feel more fully his responsibility to descendants. He had a good deal of boyish gaiety about him; at the same time I always felt that the conception of duty dominated his life. His stately figure, his grey beard, and his strikingly handsome profile make up one of the most venerable images of my memory.*

Warnie Lewis also wrote of the Ewarts, and in LP III: 252 he said of Sir William:

> *My father once summed up his character in four words – 'A great Christian Gentleman'. He had the Christian ideal that wealth is a trust, and his disbursements were never the mere largess of a rich man who chooses to avoid the momentary discomfort which the refusal of alms entails...Children loved him, and he was at his best in their company. His love of children knew no restriction of race, class or creed...He found his chief conversation in simple tales of his own town and countryside, and in stories of other lands gathered from the accounts of various missionaries; he had a keen relish for any story illustrative of the shrewd pawky humour of Ulster.*

Of Lady Ewart he wrote (LP III: 253):

> *Tranquillity was her outstanding characteristic, and this quality, engrafted on the easy gracious good breeding of the old fashioned southern Irish aristocrat, made her in her middle and later years a perfect mistress of her table and drawing room, and a very loveable old lady. Her mere presence in a room diffused something of the quiet charm of a still day in autumn.*

The Ewarts had five children: (1) Robert Heard Ewart (1879–1939), who succeeded to the baronetcy after his father; (2) Charles Gordon Ewart (1885–1936), who married Lily Greeves, the sister of Arthur Greeves;* (3) Hope Ewart (1882–1934) who in 1911 married George Harding and moved to Dublin; (4) Kelso 'Kelsie' Ewart (1886–1966), who lived near Glenmachan all her life; (5) Gundreda 'Gunny' Ewart (1888–1978) who married John Forrest in 1927.

Describing the Ewart sisters in *SBJ* III, Lewis said:

> *It was the three daughters whom we knew best. All three were 'grown-up' but in fact much nearer to us in age than any other grown-ups we knew, and all three were strikingly handsome. H., the eldest and the gravest, was a Juno, a dark queen who at certain moments looked like a Jewess. K. was more like a Valkyrie (though all, I think, were good horsewomen) with her father's profile. There was in her face something of the delicate fierceness of a thoroughbred horse, an indignant fineness of nostril, the possibility of an excellent disdain. She had what*

the vanity of my own sex calls a 'masculine' honesty; no man ever was a truer friend. As for the youngest, G., I can only say that she was the most beautiful woman I have ever seen, perfect in shape and colour and voice and every movement – but who can describe beauty?

Warnie added to their portraits as well. Of Hope he said:

She was a handsome woman of a dark, almost Italian type, with an air of dignity which she acquired early in life...She was very near to the Edwardian ideal of the beautiful woman...It was she who gave to Glenmachan an infusion of the larger world which lay outside Belfast and Ireland. She inherited and combined in herself that thoughtfulness and charm which she found in each of her parents...She was the best of good company, even tempered and radiating a cheerful common sense serenity in whatever company she found herself. Her marriage began the break-up of Glenmachan which was never quite the same house again after she left it. (LP III: 256)

Of Kelsie he wrote:

Kelsie was the least intelligent and most energetic member of the household...She had less pretensions to beauty than her sisters, but there was an open air freshness about her which supplied its place. The war was the great event of her life: at the first opportunity she joined the corps of women car drivers known as the 'Fannys', and went to Aldershot where she so enjoyed her experiences that for ever afterwards her conversation was liberally sprinkled with anecdotes of her army days. (LP III: 256–7)

And of Gundreda he said:

Gundreda was the most beautiful woman I ever saw: she had masses of red gold hair, and the glinting brown eyes and perfect complexion which so often goes with such a colouring...She had a radiant and infectious almost childlike gaiety which was always bubbling over into delighted and delightful laughter. She possessed in a supreme degree the Ulster capacity for extracting amusement from the dialect and idiom of her own countryside, and to hear her frequent imitations of the broad Co. Down accent was a joy. (LP III: 257)

GREEVES, Joseph Arthur (1895–1966), was born in Belfast on 27 August 1895, the youngest of five children born to Joseph Malcomson Greeves (1858–1925) and Mary Margretta Gribbon (1861–1949) of Brooklyn, New York. Their home, 'Bernagh', was directly across the road from 'Little Lea', where the Lewis family lived. Arthur's father was the director of J. & T.M. Greeves, Ltd., flax spinners. The family had traditionally been members of the Society of Friends, but had converted to the Plymouth Brethren in 1830. Arthur's only formal education came from his years at Campbell College, Belfast, between 1906 and 1912. He enrolled at the Slade School of Fine Art in London in 1921 and left with a Certificate in 1923. For years he had tried to get to know Jack and Warnie Lewis, but without success. Then came their first real meeting in April 1914. 'I had been so far from thinking such a friend possible,' Lewis wrote in *SBJ* VIII, 'that I had never even longed for one; no more than I longed to be King of England.'

Their correspondence, which began in 1914, lasted half a century. There seems to be almost nothing that Lewis felt unable to mention to Arthur. When Albert Lewis* died in 1929 Jack found a home at 'Bernagh' or wherever Arthur was living. It was during a summer holiday at 'Bernagh' in 1932 that he wrote *The Pilgrim's Regress*. Lewis seems not to have preserved many of Arthur's letters; but Arthur saved nearly all of Lewis's and they were published as *They Stand Together* (1979). During the compilation of the Lewis Papers in 1933–5 Warnie Lewis contributed a portrait of Arthur (IV: 181–2) in which he said:

> *His circumstances have been such that he has never been compelled to face the issues of life, to know it as it is, to gauge the degree of toleration which the community owes to the individual and the individual to the community. I do not here refer to the fact that he has never had to earn his living, but mean that with a child's liking for being liked he has the child's distress at the obtuseness of the grown ups who cannot see that if only everyone would always do as he wants them to do, the world would be a very delightful place to live in.*

Jack 'felt obliged to supplement' this portrait with something from his own pen (LP X: 218–20), and he said of his friend:

> *Arthur was the youngest son of a doting mother and a harsh father, two evils whereof each increased the other. The mother soothed him the more, to compensate for the father's harshness, and the father became harsher to counteract the ill effects of the mother's indulgence.*

Both thus conspired to aggravate a tendency...towards self pity...It can easily be imagined how such a child grew up: but who could have foretold that he would be neither a liar nor a tale bearer, neither a coward nor a misanthrope?

He was the frankest of men. Many of the most ludicrous episodes which could be told against him, turn on his failure to acquire that 'visor to the human face' which such a training usually teaches a man to wear. He was the most faithful of friends, and carried the innumerable secrets of my own furtive and ignoble adolescence locked in a silence which is not commonly thought effeminate. Under illness or inconvenience he was impatient – a loud and violent, but not a lengthy grumbler: but danger left him unmoved...

Until I met him, and during my frequent absences, his position was much the same as that of an imaginative boy in one of our public schools. Yet he never showed any inclination to revenge himself after the fashion so familiar among our modern intelligentsia. *He continued to feel – indeed he taught me to endeavour to feel with him – at once a human affection and a rich aesthetic relish for his antediluvian aunts, his mill-owning uncles, his mother's servants, the postman on our roads, and the cottagers whom we met in our walks. What he called the 'Homely' was the natural food both of his heart and his imagination. A bright hearth seen through an open door as we passed, a train of ducks following a brawny farmer's wife, a drill of cabbages in a suburban garden – these were things that never failed to move him, even to an ecstasy, and he never found them incompatible with his admiration for Proust, or Wyndham Lewis, or Picasso. He was completely unworldly. He never in his life read an 'advanced' book or imitated a 'modern' painter because he felt that he could thus become a superior being. The motive was always either his genuine pleasure in them, or else the advice of ill-chosen friends. For Arthur was both humble and unstable. He could be persuaded to read, or at least begin, any book: to adopt (for a time) any canons of taste. The last speaker was always right to him. But all these fluctuations went on over a fundamental constancy: to the charm of the 'homely' he was never untrue, and if he was easily drawn into the follies of any and every coterie, he could not, by any process, be infected with its pride.*

During the earlier years of our acquaintance he was (as always) a Christian, and I was an atheist. But though (God forgive me) I bombarded him with all the thin artillery of a seventeen year old rationalist, I never made any impression on his faith – a faith both vague and confused, and in some ways too indulgent to our common weaknesses, but inexpugnable. He remains victor in that debate. It is I who have come round. The thing is symbolical of much in our joint history. He was not a clever boy, he was even a dull boy; I was a scholar. He had no 'ideas.' I bubbled over with them. It might seem that I had much to give him, and that he had nothing to give me. But this is not the truth. I could give concepts, logic, facts, arguments, but he had feelings to offer, feelings which most mysteriously – for he was always very inarticulate – he taught me to share. Hence, in our commerce, I dealt in superficies, but he in solids. I learned charity from him and failed, for all my efforts, to teach him arrogance in return...If I had to write his epitaph, I should say of him what I could say of no one else known to me – 'He despised nothing'. Contempt – if not the worst, surely the most ludicrously inappropriate of the sins that men commit – was, I believe, unknown to him. He fulfilled the Gospel precept: he 'judged not'.

Arthur was deemed unable to work because of a bad heart and he lived on an income from the family business. He nevertheless won some recognition as a landscape painter, and was exhibited in 1936. He was a member of the Royal Hibernian Academy. His painting of his friend, Forrest Reid, the novelist, is in the possession of the Royal Academical Institution, Belfast. Much of his time was spent painting in and around his beloved County Down where he spent the whole of his life. After his mother's death in 1949 he moved to a cottage, 'Silver Hill', in Crawfordsburn, Co. Down, where Lewis often stayed. It was here that Arthur entertained Jack and his wife, Joy, during the summers of 1958 and 1959.

It is ironic that, while Lewis's acceptance of thoroughgoing supernatural Christianity was due in part to Arthur's influence, Arthur himself vacillated between religious beliefs. The original damage may have been caused by his Plymouth Brethren parents, but other forces were soon at work. He vacillated between the Church of Ireland and the Baha'i faith. Near the end of his life he settled down to what had always suited him best, Quaker services with about five elderly friends in a small meeting house in Bangor, close to 'Silver Hill'. There he seems to have found the peace he was looking for all his life.

The last time Jack and Arthur were together was a weekend spent at The Kilns in June 1961. Jack was making plans to visit Arthur in Ireland during the summer of 1963, but a heart attack prevented this. 'It looks as if you and I shall never meet again in this life,' he wrote on 11 September 1963, 'Oh, Arthur, never to see you again!' (*TST*).

Among Arthur's closest friends was Lisbeth Greeves, wife of his cousin, Ronald. A fortnight before he died he asked her to lunch with him, after which she recalls that he sensed that he would die soon. He asked her to pray with him that when his time came he would die in his sleep. On 27 August 1966 he celebrated his 71st birthday. Two days later, his cousin Lisbeth recalled, 'he died in his sleep – just like a happy child sleeping peacefully – with a linen handkerchief over his eyes, to shade them from the early morning sun.'

The Hamilton Family. C. S. Lewis's mother's family can be traced back many generations. The Irish branch of her family was descended from (A) Sir James Hamilton of Finnart (d. 1540),[1] who married Helen Cunningham. Their son (B) Hugh Hamilton (d. 1671) settled at Lisbane, Co. Down, in the time of King James I. His second son was (C) Alexander Hamilton (d. 1676) of Killyleath, Co. Down, who married Jean Hamilton of Belfast. Their son was (D) Alexander Hamilton (d. 1768), MP of Knock in the County of Dublin and Newtown Hamilton in the County of Armagh. He married Isabella Maxwell (b. 1729). Their eldest son was (E) the Right Reverend Hugh Hamilton (1729–1805), who was successively a Fellow of Trinity College, Dublin, Dean of Armagh, Bishop of Clonfert, and finally, Bishop of Ossory, which see he occupied from the time of his translation in 1799 until his death on 1 December 1805. He is buried in St Canice's (or St Kenny's) Cathedral in Kilkenny. He married Isabella Wood, and they had two daughters and five sons.[2] (F) Their son, the Reverend Hugh Hamilton (1790–1865) of Inishmacsaint, Co. Fermanagh, married Elizabeth Staples, daughter of the Right Honourable John Staples M.P. of Lissan, Co. Tyrone.[3] (The other daughter, Grace Louise Staples, married the 2nd Marquis of Ormonde.)

---

1 There is an entry for him in the *Dictionary of National Biography*.
2 Lewis may have inherited some of the talents of his great-great-grandfather, Bishop Hugh Hamilton (1729–1805) who wrote a number of books: *De Sectionibus Conicis Tractatus (A Geometrical Treatise of the Conic Sections)* (1758); *Philosophical Essays* (1766); *On the Duty of Obedience to the Laws and of Submission to Magistrates* (1772); *An Attempt to Probe the Existence and Absolute Perfection of the Supreme Unoriginal Being, in a Demonstrative Manner* (1784). See *The Works of the Right Rev. Hugh Hamilton, D.D., Late Bishop of Ossory*, Collected and Published, With some Alterations and Additions from his Manuscripts, by Alexander Hamilton, Esq., his Eldest Son, 2 vols. (1809). There is an entry on him in the *Dictionary of National Biography*.
3 Clive Staples Lewis derived his second Christian name from this grandfather.

Hugh Hamilton's son was (G) the Rev. Thomas Robert Hamilton (1826–1905) who was born on 28 June 1826. He took his BA degree from Trinity College, Dublin, in 1848, and in 1849 he was ordained a deacon in the Church of Ireland. In October 1850 he set off with his father and mother on the Grand Tour of Europe. Thomas kept his first diary during this tour, and it was reproduced by Warnie Lewis in LP I: 5–30. Because of ill health he undertook a voyage to India between 9 November 1852 and 6 April 1853 (this diary is reproduced in LP I: 32–64). He was ordained a priest in 1853 and during the years 1854–70 he was a chaplain in the Royal Navy, serving with the Baltic squadron of the fleet throughout the Crimean War. Mr Hamilton kept a very detailed diary during much of his period as a chaplain. It covers the periods 21 January to 20 December 1854; 19 February to 10 December 1855; 20 January to 26 June 1856; and about a month between 28 May and the end of June 1868, and it is all reproduced in LP I: 66–207.

In 1859 Thomas married Mary Warren[4] (1826–1916), who was the fifth child and second daughter of Sir John Borlase Warren (1800–63). Mary's sister, Charlotte Warren, married Robert Heard, and their daughter, Mary, married Sir William Ewart (see The Ewart Family*). Thomas and Mary Hamilton had four children: (1) Lilian Hamilton (1860–1934) who married William Suffern (d. 1913) but who never had any children. She was very fond of her nephew, Clive, and there are a number of references to her in *All My Road Before Me*.[5] (2) Florence Augusta 'Flora' Hamilton (1862–1908)* who married Albert James Lewis.* (3) Hugh Cecil Waldegrave Hamilton (1864–1900) was born on 17 November 1864. After an unsuccessful attempt to obtain a regular commission in the Royal Artillery, he emigrated to Australia where he became a sheep farmer in Queensland. He became a captain in the Queensland Artillery and saw active service in the South African war. He died on 12 July 1900, and is buried at Marandellas, South Africa. Finally, there is (4) Augustus Warren Hamilton (1866–1945) who was Albert Lewis's best friend. He was found to have an extraordinary genius for mathematics, but unfortunately his mother would not allow him to go to the university. So after leaving school he went to sea, but returned to Belfast and founded the firm of Hamilton & McMaster, marine boiler makers and engineers. In 1897 he married Anne Sargent Harley (1866–1930). They had four children,

---

4 It is from this grandmother that Warren Hamilton Lewis takes his name.
5 See the letter to Mrs Lilian Suffern dated [November? 1926].

Molly (d. 1904); Ruth (b. 1900) who married Desmond Parker; Harley; and John Borlase Hamilton (b. 1905).

HARWOOD, Alfred Cecil (1898–1975) was born on 5 January 1898 in Eckington, Derbyshire, where his father, the Rev. William Hardy Harwood, was a Nonconformist minister. He was educated at Highgate School, London, and it was there he met Owen Barfield* in 1910. On leaving school Harwood joined the Royal Warwickshires and served with the infantry as a 2nd lieutenant. He saw some active service in France. He went up to Christ Church, Oxford in Hilary Term 1919, and Barfield followed him there shortly afterwards. Harwood met Lewis through Barfield and thus began a lifelong friendship.

After taking his BA in 1921 Harwood returned with Barfield to Oxford for postgraduate studies. They lived for a time in 'Bee Cottage' in Beckley, where Lewis was a frequent visitor. Their great mutual interest was poetry, and Lewis valued Harwood's criticism highly. Many of the poems Harwood wrote during these years, and which Lewis found 'original, quaint and catchy', are found in *The Voice of Cecil Harwood*, ed. Owen Barfield (1979). Another of their shared interests was the walking tour, and such was his enthusiasm for these that Lewis dubbed him 'Lord of the Walks'.

After leaving Oxford he had a temporary job with the British Empire Exhibition in London, after which he went into publishing. Writing about this period in his life in the Anthroposophical Society's *Supplement to Members' News Sheet* (Feb. 1976), Barfield said: 'He was at that time making a rather half-hearted attempt to turn himself into what used to be called a "young man about town," and even the Bloomsbury set were not wholly outside his orbit. I don't think the experiment could ever have succeeded. But there was another reason why it did not last long.'

The other 'reason' is related to his future wife. During his second year in Oxford, Harwood followed Owen Barfield into the English Folk Dance Society. In the summer of 1922 they joined an amateur concert party touring some Cornish towns and villages. A friend of the organizers, the Honourable Daphne Olivier, was invited and this was Harwood's first meeting with the woman he was to marry. Daphne Olivier was the daughter of Sydney Haldane Olivier (Lord Olivier), Governor of Jamaica from 1907 to 1913. She read the Medieval and Modern Languages Tripos at Newnham College, Cambridge, and after taking her BA in 1913, she became a teacher. In August 1922 she attended a conference on 'Spiritual Values in Education and Social Life' held at Manchester College, Oxford, and it was here that she first heard Rudolf Steiner lecture. She became a convinced and devoted follower, and went to hear him lecture on other occasions. It was during a conference at Ilkley that a group of teachers, including Daphne Olivier, expressed their desire to found a co-educational day school in England on the basis of Dr Steiner's educational principles and along the lines of the Waldorf school in Germany. Steiner approved the formation of a Founders' Committee, whose job it was to find a way of bringing about such a school.

It was through Daphne Olivier that Harwood heard of Anthroposophy. He accompanied Miss Olivier to the second International Summer School held at Torquay from 9 to 23 August 1924 where Rudolf Steiner gave a course of lectures. During this conference Steiner met with the four women who wanted to found a Steiner school in London, and recommended that they would do well to have some male assistance. Pointing to Harwood, he said, 'What about him?'

From that point Harwood was committed to Anthroposophy for the rest of his life, and he was to have a very large part to play in its dissemination in England. 'The New School', as it was called, was founded in January 1925 at 40 Leigham Court Road, Streatham, London, with Harwood and Miss Olivier as two of its original five teachers. On 14 August 1925 Harwood and Daphne married, and moved into a house at 51 Angles Road. Very little was known about Steiner in the country as a whole, and Harwood, who had a talent for lecturing, did much during the early years to spread the knowledge of Anthroposophy throughout the English-speaking world.

The Harwoods' first child, John (who had Lewis as his tutor at Magdalen College), was born 31 May 1926. They were to have four more children: Lois (b. 1929); Laurence (b. 1933) who was Lewis's godson; Mark (b. 1934); and Sylvia (b. 1937). Lewis was often a visitor to their house, and in 1947 he dedicated *Miracles* to Cecil and Daphne. One of the highlights of Lewis's life was the annual walking tour with Harwood and Barfield. The best known of his tributes to Harwood is found in *SBJ* XIII:

> *Closely linked with Barfield of Wadham was his friend (and soon mine) A.C. Harwood of The House, later a pillar of Michael Hall, the Steinerite school at Kidbrooke. He was different from either of us; a wholly imperturbable man. Though poor (like most of us) and wholly without 'prospects', he wore the expression of a nineteenth-century gentleman with something in the funds. On a walking tour when the last light of a wet evening had just revealed some ghastly error in*

map-reading (probably his own) and the best hope was 'five miles to Mudham (if we could find it) and we might get beds there', he still wore that expression. In the heat of argument he wore it still. You would think that he, if anyone, would have been told to 'take that look off his face'. But I don't believe he ever was. It was no mask and came from no stupidity. He has been tried since by all the usual sorrows and anxieties. He is the sole Horatio known to me in this age of Hamlets; no 'stop for Fortune's finger.'[6]

Harwood was grieved when his beloved Daphne died in 1950. He nevertheless continued his teaching, lecturing and writing. On 1 November 1954 he married Marguerite Lundgren, the founder of the London School of Eurythmy. After his retirement Harwood remained in Forest Row, Sussex. Even during his last years, when he was afflicted with diabetes, he did not lose that remarkable imperturbability Lewis admired so much. He died on 22 December 1975. Many of his poems, stories and essays are collected in *The Voice of Cecil Harwood*. His other works include *The Way of a Child, an Introduction to the Work of Rudolf Steiner for Children* (1940), *The Recovery of Man in Childhood* (1958), and *Shakespeare's Prophetic Mind* (1964).

JENKIN, Alfred Kenneth Hamilton (1900–80), friend from undergraduate days. He was born on 29 October 1900 at 378 Green Lane, Redruth, Cornwall, the son of Alfred Hamilton Jenkin and Amy Louisa (Keep) Jenkin. His family had lived in Redruth since the 18th century. Jenkin matriculated at University College, Oxford, in 1919 where he began reading English. This was to be an unhappy year for him. While out on a bicycle ride with his father, the latter suffered a heart attack, and Kenneth had to leave him dying at the roadside while he sought help. He nevertheless took his BA in 1922, and then stayed on to write a thesis for a B.Litt. on Richard Carew.

Lewis and Jenkin met soon after each arrived at University College in 1919. Both were members of the Martlets Society, a literary society of University College, and Lewis's diary (*AMR*) is filled with details of their walks, their bicycle rides and their talk. Jenkin became a frequent visitor at the house Lewis shared with Mrs Moore, and in his diary of 25 June 1922, Lewis observed that he and Mrs Moore 'were amused to notice again how in his conversation all roads lead to Cornwall'.

---

6 Shakespeare, *Hamlet*, III, ii, 75–6: 'They are not a pipe for fortune's finger / To sound what stop she please.'

There was no keeping Jenkin from his native county. After leaving Oxford and returning to Cornwall, where he lived at St Ives, he worked as a journalist and broadcaster. Then came his many books. His first major work was *The Cornish Miner: An account of his life above and underground from early times* (1927), the standard work on the subject and one which established him as a historian. This was followed in the next decade by *Cornish Seafarers* (1932), *Cornwall and the Cornish* (1933), *Cornish Homes and Customs* (1934), and *The Story of Cornwall* (1934). In the 1960s he brought out his vast 16-part series on *Mines and Miners of Cornwall* (1961–78), running to nearly a thousand pages and embodying the results of 16 years' research involving visits to some 2,000 Cornish mines.

Lewis met Jenkin infrequently after Cornwall had reclaimed him, but he remained indebted to Jenkin for teaching him to enjoy 'the very quiddity of each thing'. 'The first lifelong friend I made at Oxford,' Lewis wrote in *SBJ* XIII, 'was A.K. Hamilton Jenkin, since known for his books on Cornwall':

> *He continued (what Arthur [Greeves*] had begun) my education as a seeing, listening, smelling, receptive creature. Arthur had had his preference for the Homely. But Jenkin seemed to be able to enjoy everything; even ugliness. I learned from him that we should attempt a total surrender to whatever atmosphere was offering itself at the moment; in a squalid town to seek out those very places where its squalor rose to grimness and almost grandeur, on a dismal day to find the most dismal and dripping wood, on a windy day to seek the windiest ridge. There was no Betjemannic irony about it; only a serious, yet gleeful, determination to rub one's nose in the very quiddity of each thing, to rejoice in its being (so magnificently) what it was.*

In 1926 Jenkin married Luned Jacobs, the daughter of the novelist W.W. Jacobs. They had two daughters, Jennifer Hamilton Heseltine (b. 1929) and Honor Bronwen Goldsmid (b. 1930). The marriage was dissolved about 1934. During the Second World War Jenkin met Elizabeth Lenton (née Le Sueur) at Mullion Cove Hotel, where she was managing director. They married in 1948, and together managed the Poldu Hotel, Mullion, whilst Jenkin also continued his research into *News from Cornwall* (1951). In 1954 they went to live in the family home in Redruth, 'Trewirgie House', where his family had been since 1770. One of the early occupants of this house had been his great-great-grandfather, William Jenkin, who became in later life steward to the Lanhydrock family estates. Elizabeth died in 1977.

Jenkin assisted in the formation of Old Cornwall societies, and he was elected President of the Federation of Old Cornwall Societies in 1959–60. In 1962 he became the Federation's first Life Vice-President. At the Gorsedd of Cornwall in 1978 he was presented with a medal, most appropriately struck in tin, which commemorated the fact that he was one of only two living Bards who had been initiated by Henry Jenner at the first Gorsedd in 1928. He took the bardic name of Lef Stenoryon – 'Voice of the Tinners'. That same year he was awarded a D.Litt. by Exeter University.

Jenkin was largely responsible for setting up the Cornwall County Record Office in Truro, one of the finest in the country. When he died on 20 August 1980 he left his printed books and pamphlets to the Redruth public library and his historical notes, documents, photos, maps and MSS to the County Record Office in Truro.

KIRKPATRICK, William Thompson 'The Great Knock' (1848–1921), was headmaster of Lurgan College, County Armagh, Northern Ireland, 1876–99. Albert Lewis* had been his pupil at Lurgan between 1877 and 1879, and W. H. Lewis* and C. S. Lewis were tutored by him. Chapter IX of *SBJ* is devoted to this extraordinary man, and he is the model for MacPhee in *The Dark Tower* and *That Hideous Strength*. He was born in the little townland of Carrickmaddyroe, Boardmills, Co. Down, on 10 January 1848, the second child of James Kirkpatrick and his wife Sarah Thompson. He was baptized in Boardmills' First Presbyterian Church on 24 February 1848. His sister, Anne Mussen Kirkpatrick, was born on 8 December 1845. Carrickmaddyroe is located approximately 20 miles south of Belfast, between Carryduff and Dromara. William Thompson Kirkpatrick was named after his grandfather, William Kirkpatrick (1766–1848) who is buried with his wife Mary Blackley (1766–1849) in Boardmills First Presbyterian Graveyard.

The family was living at 21 Eliza Street, Belfast, when Kirkpatrick matriculated at the Royal Belfast Academical Institute, a liberal Presbyterian boys' school, in 1862. From there he went to Queen's College, Belfast (now Queen's University) where he graduated in July 1868 with first class honours in English, History and Metaphysics. He wrote the English Prize essay under the nom-de-plume 'Tamberlaine'. That same year he was awarded a Double Gold Medal by the Royal University of Ireland. He took his MA from Queen's College in 1870.

Kirkpatrick became assistant master in the English department of the Royal Belfast Academical Institution in 1868, and he remained there for eight years. The same year, 1868, Kirkpatrick entered the Assembly's College (the Presbyterian seminary in Belfast) and spent the normal three years in theological studies for ordination in the Irish Presbyterian Church. He took classes in Christian Ethics, Oriental Languages, Biblical Criticism, Ecclesiastical History and Rhetoric. Mr Kirkpatrick became a licentiate – i.e. he fulfilled the Church's academic and other demands for ordinands. But he was never ordained and appears in the records of the General Assembly as a licentiate under the care of the Belfast Presbytery for ten years from 1871 to 1880.

Mr Kirkpatrick excelled as a teacher. The Lewises were not the only ones to be impressed by him. Robert Millar Jones, who was Mr Kirkpatrick's student from 1876–9, wrote:

> No boy and no man could be in his company for even a very short time without being impressed by the fact that he was in the presence of a man of unusual mental power and grasp, of an overmastering influence on the mind, and of an intellectual honesty and vigour before which pretence and make-believe were dissipated like smoke before a strong wind. None who knew him could be surprised that it was he who subsequently made Lurgan College for many years one of the most remarkable and successful schools in Ireland. He became an almost incomparable teacher, and under him the boys swept on to victory over their work and to mastery of their subjects and of themselves. His pistol never missed fire; but he gave you the impression that, if it did, as Goldsmith said of Johnson, you would be knocked down by the butt-end.[7]

In 1876 Kirkpatrick became headmaster of Lurgan College, Co. Armagh, where he remained until his retirement in 1899. Lurgan College was founded in 1873 on the endowment of Samuel Watts who had extensive interests in brewing and tobacco. When he died in 1850 he left almost £10,000 to endow an 'English, Classical and Agricultural School of boys' in Lurgan. Watts's will is remarkable in that it laid down that no clergyman, or person in holy orders, could have any part in the teaching or the management of the school. Besides this, it prohibited any religious

---

7 Quoted in Robert M. Jones, *Royal Belfast Academical Institution: Centenary Volume 1810–1910* (Belfast, 1913), pp. 122–3.

instruction during the hours normally laid down for school lessons. These provisions have always been seen as controversial. It is suggested, however, that it was Watts's intention to establish a school for older boys that would be on the same foundation as those National Schools envisaged by the Government in the 1830s, and which combined secular and separate religious instruction. Mr Kirkpatrick had applied for the position as headmaster of Lurgan College in 1873, but the position was given to Edward Vaughan Boulger. When Boulger left Lurgan in December 1875, Mr Kirkpatrick succeeded him. Whatever Mr Kirkpatrick's beliefs were by this time, and he seems to have become an agnostic, this second time he applied he took pains to prove that he was *not* 'in holy orders'. Believer or not, Mr Kirkpatrick insisted that religious instruction be given to the boarders at Lurgan College, and he attended the local Presbyterian church every Sunday with the Presbyterian boarders. Mr Kirkpatrick had brought his sister Anne with him to Lurgan and she helped with the management of the boarders.

Mr Kirkpatrick was a very successful headmaster of Lurgan College. There were 16 pupils when he arrived in 1876, and when Albert Lewis was there he would have witnessed a considerable expansion because in only four years Mr Kirkpatrick had built it up to over 60. Besides expanding the college, high academic records also marked Mr Kirkpatrick's tenure of office. By the late 1880s Lurgan College was one of the top schools in Ireland.

On 15 July 1881 Mr Kirkpatrick married Louisa Ashmore Smyth of 81 Pembroke Road, Dublin, in St Bartholomew's Church, Dublin. Louisa was the daughter of George Smyth, a stockbroker. Two days earlier, on 13 July, Anne Kirkpatrick had married a former assistant at Lurgan, Alexander Stewart Mitchell, in St Anne's Church, Belfast. W.T. Kirkpatrick's only child, George Louis, was born on 23 May 1882 and educated at Charterhouse from 1896 to 1899.

Lewis said of Mr Kirkpatrick in *SBJ* IX: 'He had been a Presbyterian and was now an Atheist...I hasten to add that he was a "Rationalist" of the old, high and dry nineteenth-century type. For Atheism has come down in the world since those days, and mixed itself with politics and learned to dabble in dirt.' As a licentiate of the Presbyterian Church, who preached on a number of occasions, Mr Kirkpatrick almost certainly entertained the ambition of becoming a minister. What led to his loss of faith? The Royal Belfast Academical Institution was a haven of liberalism when he was there, and it may be that caught, as it were, between the liberalism of the Institution and the dogmatism of the Presbyterian Church as a whole, he lost his faith.

Following his retirement in 1899 Mr and Mrs Kirkpatrick went to live in 'Sharston House', Northenden, so they could be near their son Louis who was articled to the electrical engineers Browett, Lindley & Co., Engine Makers of Patricroft, Manchester. Later, while Louis was in Berlin gaining experience with electric tramways, the Kirkpatricks moved to 'Gastons', Great Bookham, Surrey, where Mr Kirkpatrick took private pupils and where they spent the rest of their lives.

Albert Lewis had been acting as Mr Kirkpatrick's solicitor since he qualified, and it was natural that he ask him to tutor Warnie and Jack. This turned out to be yet another great success for Mr Kirkpatrick because, not only did he like them very much, but they benefited greatly from being taught by him. A few weeks after Jack arrived at Bookham, Mr Kirkpatrick wrote to Albert on 2 October 1914 saying:

> First, I should say, he has the literary temperament in a very marked degree. I look upon this as in the main an inherited quality, and I am the more convinced of this view from the very obvious fact of his physical resemblance to you. When I first saw him at the station I had no hesitation in addressing him. It was as though I was looking at yourself once more in the old days at Lurgan. He has also your good temper and vivacity. These are valuable qualities, and they mean much, both intellectually and morally. (LP IV: 223)

A little later (25 November 1914) he said:

> Clive is altogether an exceptional boy. The maturity of his literary judgements is remarkable, he follows his own instinct and is not to be imposed upon by the mere weight of authority. In literary power he is outside the range of ordinary schoolboys altogether, and it would be unfair to herd him with 'Narrow foreheads vacant of his glorious gains'. (LP IV: 250).

Mr Kirkpatrick had imagined that his best years were behind him when he retired from Lurgan. From another point of view, and in terms of all the good that came from it, one could say his best years began in 1913 with the arrival of Warnie, and then Jack. Besides learning from this wonderful old man, the whole family loved him dearly, and they were grieved when they learned of his death on 22 March 1921.

Mrs Kirkpatrick lived until 1933. Louis, who was married but had no children, was general manager of Bruce Peebles & Co. (Engineers) in

Edinburgh from 1932 until his death in 1943. On Mr Kirkpatrick's years at Lurgan College, see 'A History of Lurgan College, Part II – Consolidation 1876–1899' by J.I. Wilson in *Ulula* (*Lurgan College School Magazine*) (1977), pp. 67–74.

LEWIS, Albert James (1863–1929), father of C. S. Lewis and W. H. Lewis*, was born on 23 August 1863 in Cork. He was one of six children born to Richard Lewis (see The Lewis Family*) and his wife Martha Gee who had emigrated to Ireland from Wales. In 1868 the family moved to Belfast, where his father became a partner in MacIlwaine and Lewis, Boiler Makers, Engineers, and Iron Ship Builders.

Albert attended the District Model National School, after which he spent the years 1877 to 1879 at Lurgan College, in Lurgan, County Armagh. The headmaster was W.T. Kirkpatrick,* who was to become a lifelong friend. On 9 August 1880 Albert was articled to the law firm of Maclean, Boyle and Maclean in Dublin. His first love was always the law, but he was devoted as well to English literature and the liturgy of the Church of Ireland. In 1881 he was elected a member of the Belmont Literary Society.

After qualifying as a solicitor on 10 June 1885 he set up a practice of his own at 83 Royal Avenue, Belfast. Over the years he held a number of important legal appointments in connection with various companies and public bodies, the most important of which was the position of police court prosecuting solicitor for the Belfast Corporation. He was as well solicitor for the Belfast City Council, the Belfast and County Down Railway, the Belfast Harbour Commissioners, the Post Office, the Ministry of Labour, and the National Society for Prevention of Cruelty to Children. Albert was a political speaker of considerable importance for the Conservative Party.

The battle which seemed hardest for him was that of winning the love of Florence Augusta 'Flora' Hamilton,* daughter of the Rev. Thomas Robert Hamilton (1826–1905), rector of his parish church. The Lewis family had been parishioners of St Mark's, Dundela, since Thomas Hamilton arrived there and assisted with its founding in 1874. Albert tried to get to know Flora in 1885, but she was cool towards him. He nevertheless persisted and proposed in September 1886. She replied that she 'had nothing but friendship to give' (LP II: 152). Albert turned to corresponding about literary subjects, and in the end they became engaged in 1893 and were married in St Mark's on 29 August 1894.

It was an exceptionally happy marriage, Flora's cheerful and tranquil affection being exactly the right complement to Albert's sentimental, passionate and rhetorical nature. Their first home was one of two semi-detached houses named Dundela Villas, now covered by Dundela Flats, 47 Dundela Avenue, Belfast. Their first son, Warren Hamilton 'Warnie' Lewis* was born at Dundela Villas in 1895, and Clive Staples 'Jack' Lewis on 29 November 1898. As he became more prosperous Albert had a new house built for his family, 'Little Lea', 76 Circular Road, where they moved in 1905. Theirs was a very happy home until the winter of 1907–8 when Flora was discovered to have cancer. Albert never recovered from her death on 23 August 1908.

With the loss of their mother, Warnie and Jack felt smothered by Albert's love, and Little Lea was never a very happy home to them thereafter. Albert nevertheless did the best he knew, and he never stopped trying. Not having Flora to protect him from excess, he spent most of his time in his law office. When he did relax it was usually with Flora's brother, Augustus ('Gussie'), who was his best friend. He read widely and he was three times churchwarden at St Mark's as well as the church's legal adviser.

In his portrait of his father, Warnie said:

> *He preserved throughout his life a high and scrupulous standard of honour. I have heard his managing clerk relate that not once, but many times, he has seen Albert throw open the door of the inner office and hustle out a would be client with the words, 'In fact, you want to make use of my legal knowledge to help you to commit a swindle! Get out of this!' And I speak from personal knowledge of the man when I say that the latter sentence, delivered with all the force of his formidable personality, had the effect of a kick from a heavy boot...In appearance he was of middle height, well built, and of a commanding presence: his hair, which was black and naturally lustrous, he wore parted at the side: a fine forehead and heavy brows covered a pair of penetrating dark brown eyes: the mouth was concealed by a strong moustache; the chin was firm. In his whole bearing there was an air of authority, heightened by the timbre of his voice, which was strong and resonant. Both women and men considered him good looking. As the years mellowed him, his appearance was improved by the elimination of a sullen, almost sulky air which he had in middle life. He was proud of his appearance, and as sensitive on the score of his age, which he would never disclose, as any fading spinster. Amongst his idiosyncrasies was an almost childish resentment of bodily pain: a corn loomed larger in his horizon than bankruptcy, and a headache was a*

family disaster: but when the end came, he died bravely and without murmuring. (LP II: 66–7)

Albert was not a wealthy man, but he nevertheless provided for all his younger son's undergraduate years at Oxford and until he had a job of his own. His interest in his parish church never flagged, but his greatest natural consolation came from his work as a solicitor. He continued at his practice until his death on 25 September 1929.

There is a short contemporary biography (and photograph) of him in Robert M. Young's *Belfast and the Province of Ulster in the 20th Century* (Brighton, 1909), p. 520. His vast correspondence with his sons and Mr Kirkpatrick is found in the Lewis Papers. Over the years Lewis and Warren preserved 100 of their father's dicta which they copied into a notebook entitled 'Pudaita Pie' after Albert's 'low' Irish pronunciation of 'potato'. Many of the sayings later went into *Surprised by Joy*. The manuscript of 'Pudaita Pie' is in Wheaton College. A photograph of the portrait of Albert painted by A.R. Baker in 1917 is found in Walter Hooper's 'The Lewis That Stayed Behind', in the *Magdalen College Record* (1995). A longer biography is found in *CG*.

LEWIS, Florence Augusta 'Flora' (1862–1908), mother of Warren Hamilton Lewis* and C. S. Lewis, was one of two daughters and two sons born to the Rev. Thomas Robert Hamilton and Mary Warren Hamilton. At the time of her birth on 18 May 1862 in Queenstown, County Cork, her father was a chaplain with the Royal Navy. During 1870 to 1874 the family lived in Rome where Thomas Hamilton was chaplain of Holy Trinity Church.

From Rome the Hamiltons moved to Belfast where Flora's father was rector of St Mark's, Dundela, from 1874 until 1900. Flora attended classes at the Methodist College, Belfast, in the sessions 1881–2, 1883–4 and 1884–5. At the same time that she was going to the Methodist College she was attending Queen's University, Belfast (then the Royal University of Ireland), where she performed brilliantly. She took a first degree in 1880, and in her second examinations in 1881 she passed with first class honours in Geometry and Algebra. In 1885 she passed the second university examination with first class honours in Logic and second class honours in Mathematics, and took a BA in 1886.

Flora had known Albert Lewis* and his family since the Hamiltons arrived in Belfast, but it was years before anything approaching intimacy came about. Albert may have thought it best to save serious matters until he had qualified as a solicitor in 1885. When he proposed to her in 1886 she had already turned down his brother, William, and he seems to have understood this as increasing his own chance. However, in her reply of 21 September 1886 Flora said 'I always thought you knew that I had nothing but friendship to give you' (LP II: 152). She really did want Albert as a friend, and, indeed, seemed to value all friendships highly.

Their first shared interest was literature. Flora had a story, 'The Princess Rosetta', published in *The Household Journal* of London. Albert said at once that he hoped that 'to the collegiate honours' Strandtown had already gained through Flora, 'will be added the higher distinction of producing a great novelist'. Flora presented him with the manuscript of the story, but for whatever reason it has not survived, and no copies of *The Household Journal* containing Flora's story, nor any of the other stories she wrote, can be traced. Flora and Albert exchanged many letters, but only Flora's have survived.

What has, however, survived in the Lewis Papers is a burlesque sermon she wrote sometime before she was married. Her father had a curate, Mr Palmer, in 1892, and this cheerful piece may be a parody of his style of preaching – or that of her father! Flora's 'Modern Sermon' as she called it, begins:

> *Brethren, the words of the text are:*
>
>> *'Old Mother Hubbard, she went to the cupboard*
>> *To get her poor dog a bone.*
>> *But when she got there, the cupboard was bare,*
>> *And so the poor dog got none.'*
>
> *Mother Hubbard, you see, was old; there being no mention of others, we may presume she was lone, a widow – a friendless, old, solitary widow. Yet did she despair? Did she sit down and weep, or read a novel, or wring her hands? No. She went to the cupboard, and here observe, she WENT to the cupboard, she did not hop or skip or run or jump, or use any other peripatetic artifice; she solely and merely WENT to the cupboard.*
>
> *We have seen that she was old and lonely, and we now see that she was poor. For, mark, the words, THE cupboard; not 'one of the cupboards', or the 'right hand cupboard' or the 'left hand cupboard' or the one above or the one below, but just THE cupboard. The one humble little cupboard the poor widow possessed. And why did she go to the*

cupboard? Was it to bring forth golden goblets or glittering precious stones, or costly apparel, or feast on any other attributes of wealth? IT WAS TO GET HER POOR DOG A BONE. Not only was the widow poor, but the dog, the sole prop of her age, was poor too. We can imagine the scene. The poor dog, crouching in the corner, looking wistfully at the solitary cupboard, and the widow going to the cupboard in hope, in expectation... (LP II: 213)

Comparing the Lewises and the Hamiltons, C. S. Lewis described his father's people as 'sentimental, passionate, and rhetorical', while the Hamiltons were 'cooler', with minds 'critical and ironic' (*SBJ* I). The 30 letters Flora wrote to Albert before they were married and the 48 she wrote afterwards (preserved in the Lewis Papers) provide evidence of this. They supply as well a clue as to where Lewis got his own clarity of thought. 'I am not quite sure that I would like it if you *only* talk to me on "sensible subjects",' Flora wrote to Albert on 5 July 1893:

Why should it bore me to hear about your love for me? You know it does not. I like you to love me, and if your love bored me, your society would, still more, so there would be no use in your talking to me on any subject at all...Gussie [her brother] is right about our not being a demonstrative family. I don't think we are, but do you know I really think it is better than being too demonstrative; men soon get tired of that sort of thing. (LP II: 251–2)

Albert and Flora became engaged in June 1893, and were married in St Mark's on 29 August 1894. Following a honeymoon in North Wales, they moved into Dundela Villas, Dundela, Belfast. Warren Hamilton 'Warnie' Lewis* was born in 1895 and named after the two sides of Flora's family; Clive Staples 'Jack' Lewis was born in 1898. Because Albert loathed going on holiday, the responsibility of taking the boys on holidays thus fell on Flora, and Warnie and Jack often recalled what happy occasions these holidays were. But Albert was not forgotten. No matter how short the distance from home, Flora wrote to him daily. In the holiday at Castlerock in 1901 she learned that he was fussing over life insurance. 'I wish I could make you feel more satisfied about things of this sort,' she wrote, 'but I am afraid it is your nature to take a gloomy view of life' (LP II: 316).

In 1905 the family moved into 'Little Lea' on the outskirts of Belfast, which Albert had specially built for Flora. Warnie went to Wynyard School in England soon afterwards, while Jack's education began at home, with Flora teaching him French and Latin, and Annie Harper, his governess, teaching him everything else. Flora's last holiday with the boys was in Berneval in the summer of 1907. In the little diary Jack wrote the following Christmas – 'My life During the Exmas Holadys of 1907' – we glimpse the contentment of the happy Lewis family. He described his father as 'very sensible' and 'nice when not in a temper' while his mother is 'like most middle-aged ladys, stout, brown hair, spectaciles, kniting her chief industry'. As Christmas draws near we learn how Warnie comes home from school, of the various Lewis and Hamilton relations who drop in, how 'Mamy stoned raisins for the Xmas pudding', of how Jack and Warnie take to 'rushing about the house' and of the play which Jack is writing to perform for the family on Christmas Day. The diary ends: 'The old year out and the new year in' (LP III: 88–92).

Not long afterwards Flora became ill. On 7 February 1908 she was operated on at home. The doctor found cancer. She rallied for a while, but a few months later she had another operation. The trouble had returned, and Flora was confined to bed. Her faithful husband attended her with touching devotion, rarely leaving her bedside. She died on 23 August 1908, deeply lamented by a devoted family. For a longer biography see *CG*.

LEWIS, Warren Hamilton ('Warnie') (1895–1973): brother of C. S. Lewis. He was born at Dundela Villas, Dundela, Belfast on 16 June 1895, the son of Albert James Lewis* and Florence Hamilton Lewis*. The family was still in Dundela Villas when his brother, Clive Staples 'Jack', was born in 1898. They were to be the best of friends all their lives. The family had only just moved to Little Lea when in May 1905 he was sent to Wynyard School in Watford, Hertfordshire, where he passed four miserable years. His recollections of the school and Robert Capron*, the headmaster, are found in LP III: 33–42.

Warnie entered Malvern College at Malvern, Worcestershire, in September 1909 and here he was very happy. He was made a prefect in May 1913 when he also began considering a career in the Army Service Corps (ASC). He left Malvern in July 1913 and on 10 September 1913 he presented himself to Albert Lewis's old headmaster, W.T. Kirkpatrick* in Great Bookham, Surrey, to be prepared for the Sandhurst entrance examination. It was a very successful move. Reflecting on his time with Mr Kirkpatrick afterwards, Warnie said:

*When I went to Bookham I had what would now be called 'an inferi-
ority complex,' partly the result of Wynyard, partly of my own idleness, and partly of the laissez faire methods of Malvern. A few weeks of
Kirk's generous but sparing praise of my efforts, and of his pungent
criticisms of the Malvern masters restored my long lost self confidence:
I saw that whilst I was not brilliant or even clever, I had in the past
been unsuccessful because I was lazy, and not lazy because I was
unsuccessful.* (LP IV: 62)

In 1914 Warnie won a Price Cadetship to Sandhurst after being placed
21st out of 201 successful candidates.

Due to wartime needs his officer's training was accelerated to nine
months instead of two years, and on 4 November 1914 he went to France
with the 4th Company 7th Divisional Train, British Expeditionary Force.
During the First World War he was an officer with the Army Service
Corps, and he served in France. It was there he met his first love – the
Grand Siècle, the splendid century dominated by Louis XIV. 'One day in
1919 in St Omer,' he said, 'I saw in a shop window an abridgement of St
Simon's Memoirs, bought it as a change from French novels, and became
a life-addict to the period.' Following the Armistice in 1919 he was reas-
signed to service in England. On 9 March 1921 he left to serve in Sierra
Leone, West Africa, where he remained for over a year, arriving home on
7 April 1922. After six months' leave he reported to his new assignment in
Colchester. On 11 April 1927 he sailed for China where he was in command of the supply depot at Shanghai for much of the time he was there.
He learned of his father's death in October 1929.

On 4 March 1930 when he was standing before the Great Buddha of
Kamakura he became convinced of the truth of Christianity. He said in
his diary of 13 May 1931: 'I started to say my prayers again after having
discontinued doing so for more years than I care to remember: this was
no sudden impulse but the result of a conviction of the truth of Christianity which has been growing on me for a considerable time...I intend
to go to Communion once again...The wheel has now made the full revolution – indifference, scepticism, atheism, agnosticism, and back again
to Christianity' (*BF*, pp. 79–80). He returned home in April 1930 and was
assigned to Bulford. During Christmas 1931 at The Kilns he began the
mammoth task of editing the Lewis Papers. On 9 October 1931 he left for
his second tour of duty in China, and was in Shanghai when the Japanese
attacked on 29 January 1932.

He returned home on 14 December 1932, retired from the ASC, and moved into The Kilns with his brother. During 1933 to 1935 he completed his editing of the Lewis Papers, 11 volumes of family papers. On 4 September 1939 he was recalled to active service and was sent to Le Havre. Following his evacuation in May 1940 he was transferred to the Reserve of Officers and sent to Oxford where he served as a private soldier with the 6th Oxford City Home Guard Battalion.

In 1943 he began acting as his brother's secretary, typing many letters for him. He became as well an active member of the Inklings. Warnie was a remarkable diarist, and that portion of it which has been published as *Brothers and Friends* (1982) is a chief source of information about the Inklings. He later regretted that he did not write more about his brother. 'Oh if only I could have known in time that he was to die first,' he wrote on 8 April 1966, 'how I would have Boswellised him!' (*BF*, p. 256). He inspired love in nearly everyone who knew him. John Wain, describing his presence at the Inklings' meetings, said of him in *Sprightly Running: Part of an Autobiography* (1962), ch. V:

> *There was no fixed etiquette, but the rudimentary honours would be done partly by Lewis and partly by his brother, W.H. Lewis, a man who stays in my memory as the most courteous I have ever met – not with mere politeness, but with a genial, self-forgetful considerateness that was as instinctive to him as breathing.*

Over the years he published: *The Splendid Century: Some Aspects of French Life in the Reign of Louis XIV* (1953); *The Sunset of the Splendid Century: The Life and Times of Louis Auguste de Bourbon, Duc de Maine, 1670–1736* (1955); *Assault on Olympus: The Rise of the House of Gramont between 1604 and 1678* (1958); *Louis XIV: An Informal Portrait* (1959); *The Scandalous Regent: A Life of Philippe, Duc d'Orleans, 1674–1723* (1961), and *Levantine Adventurer: The Travels and Missions of the Chevalier d'Arvieux, 1653–1697* (1962). He also published an edition of the *Memoirs of the Duc de Saint-Simon* (1964). Like his brother, he preferred his enjoyment of places to come through books. When asked if he would like to visit Versailles he said 'Oh no! That would ruin it!'

He had a problem with drink that became serious in the 1940s. During a holiday in Ireland in June 1947 he collapsed and was hospitalized in Our Lady of Lourdes Hospital, Drogheda, run by the Medical Missionaries of Mary. With their help he struggled to overcome the problem. Although the reasons for his alcoholism were numerous and complex, one of them was his shyness. In their youth he had been gregarious and Jack something of a recluse. As time went on they seemed to exchange positions. While Jack's fame as a Christian apologist drove him to mingle with all sorts of people, most of whom he came to like, Warnie withdrew more and more into the company of books and fewer friends. With alcohol he regained, briefly, the gregariousness he had known as a young man.

He was devastated by his brother's death. For the first few years he retreated more and more to Ireland. Eventually Our Lady of Lourdes Hospital was unable to accommodate him, and this forced him to remain in Oxford. It was, however, during these lonely years that he edited the *Letters of C. S. Lewis* (1966), to which he attached a touching 'Memoir'. During the summer of 1972 he became seriously ill while on holiday in Drogheda. The Medical Missionaries of Mary took him in and nursed him for the next nine months. He left the hospital at the beginning of April 1973, and died at The Kilns on 9 April 1973. He is buried in the same grave as his brother at Holy Trinity Church, Headington Quarry.

The Lewis Family. C. S. Lewis's family can be traced back four generations to (A) Richard Lewis (c. 1775–1845), a farmer who lived in the small village of Caergwrle situated between the borders of Flint and Denbigh in Wales. Almost nothing is known of him except that he had six sons and one daughter. His fourth son, (B) Joseph Lewis (1803?–90) was also a farmer who moved first to Saltney, Cheshire, and later to Sandycroft, Flint. Although Joseph was brought up in the Church of England, this simple, pious, uneducated man did not feel he was given the prominence he deserved, and he seceded and became a Primitive Methodist minister. In about 1825 he married Jane Ellis and they had five sons and three daughters: Frances, Thomas, Mary, (C) Richard, Jane, John, Joseph, and Samuel.

It was Joseph's and Jane's second son, (C) Richard Lewis (1832–1908) who was the father of Albert James Lewis* and the grandfather of C. S. Lewis. In 1853 he married Martha Gee (1831–1903) of Liverpool. He and his brothers John and Joseph emigrated to Cork in Ireland where they were employed by the Cork Steamship Company. Richard was a master boiler maker, and there is evidence that he was part of the working-class intelligentsia in the forefront of that artisan renaissance which gave birth to the trades union and Co-operative movements. Richard returned to the Church of England, and those interested in tracing C. S. Lewis's theological and writing gifts may wish to look at the two theological essays he read to the Cork Steamship Company's Workmen's Library and Reading Room, an 'Essay on a Special Providence' and an 'Essay on Jonah's Mission to Ninevah', preserved in the Lewis Papers (LP I: 236–46). The Lewis Papers contain as well two papers delivered to the Library and Reading Room dated 18 January 1860 (LP I: 248–72), and an essay, 'Self Denial', which Richard Lewis read to the Cork Steamship Company's Workmen's Library and Reading Room on 15 October 1860 (LP I: 276–84). It was while he was working with the Cork Steamship Company that Richard's children were born.

In July 1864 Richard Lewis left the Cork Steamship Company and went to Dublin where he hoped to better himself as a boiler maker and iron ship builder. This does not seem to have benefited him, and in 1865 he moved to Belfast where he worked with the Abercorn Iron Works. On 1 January 1868 he and John H. MacIlwaine, a draughtsman in the Dublin shipyard, entered into a business which they called 'MacIlwaine and Lewis, Boiler Makers, Engineers, and Iron Ship Builders'. The family settled at 'Ty-isa' in Strandtown. John MacIlwaine was seduced into signing a contract which all but obliterated the firm of MacIlwaine and Lewis. The business was dissolved in August 1887, and Richard went to work for the Belfast Harbour Commission. Martha Lewis died on 19 January 1903, and on 1 April 1907 Richard moved to Little Lea to live with Albert and Flora. However, because of Flora Lewis's illness, he moved out, and he died on 2 April 1908.

The children of Richard and Martha Lewis were: (D) (1) Martha Lewis (1854–60) and (2) Sarah Jane 'Jeannie' Lewis (1856?–1901) who in 1883 married Thomas Heron Keown (1860–1935) and was for most of her life estranged from the rest of the family (see letter of 30 August 1929).

(3) Joseph Lewis (1856–1908) who settled in Belfast at 'Sandycroft', Bloomfield. He was a marine consulting engineer with an office at 19 Donegal Quay and whose work involved a good deal of travelling around the seaports of Great Britain. In his sketch of this uncle, Warnie Lewis said:

> Though not an educated man, he had a natural shrewdness, and was an interested spectator of men and manners. In spite of, or perhaps on account of his peripatetic mode of life, he always struck me as being the most domesticated of the four brothers; he had married and founded a branch of his own before the middle classes had felt the first stirrings of that disruptive tendency which, coming to full maturity in

our own times, has practically obliterated the collective family – the clan – as the unity of national life; this fact, coupled with a complete absence of any element of snobbery in his character, made him pre-eminently the champion of the family in the larger sense of the term...With his Celtic blood he inherited little of the national tendency to violent oscillation between the heights of optimism and the extremes of depression, which had been a marked feature of his father's character, and in consequence, lacking the spasmodic generosity of Albert, the irascibility and prodigality of Richard, and William's morose ostentation, he was the most balanced and most uniformly kindly of the four brothers. He was not without wit; he was not a well read man, though he greatly enjoyed the works of Dickens which formed his ordinary, and indeed his sole reading. His favourite recreations were gardening and the collection of pictures and china, on which he spent money lavishly, but unfortunately neither with knowledge or taste...In appearance he was below middle height, and sturdily built; had blue eyes which generally held a twinkle, and was the only one of the brothers to wear a beard. (LP II: 57–8)

In 1882 Joseph married Mary Tegart (b. 1868) and they had five children, Martha (b. 1884), May (b. 1887), Sarah Elizabeth, Richard (b. 1890), and Joseph Tegart (1898–1969).

(4) William Lewis 'Limpopo' (1859–1946), the second son of Richard Lewis, obtained a certificate from the National School in 1871. He served an apprenticeship of five years to James Moore the printer and stationer. He lost his job as secretary of the Belfast Ropeworks in 1882 and in 1883 he and his brother Richard went to Glasgow where they entered into a partnership called 'W. & R. Lewis, Rope and Twine Manufacturers'. In 1890 he married Wilhelmina Duncanson and they had three children, Norman (b. 1891), Claire (b. 1895) and William Desmond (b. 1897). In 1903 they moved into a new home, 'Moorgate' near Glasgow. In his sketch of him, Warnie said:

He was distinguished from the rest of the family by a nattiness in his dress, which he retained all his life...He was the least amiable of the brothers – the most easily depressed and the most rarely elated. He had less of the boisterous joviality, sometimes rising to wit, less of the inquisitive interest in the pageant of provincial life, than had the others. His mind was heavy, common place, and self centred. With him, sententiousness took the place of sentiment. Albert's children, with the acuteness of childhood, bestowed on him the nick-name of 'Limpopo', and if the word be pronounced in three heavy, distinct syllables, it is itself a felicitous character sketch. Neither family tradition nor papers record of him a single witty saying or amusing tale...In person he was a small man, who became fat in later life. His eyes were deep sunk in fleshy cheeks. His hair, which was scanty, was brushed diagonally across his head in the manner which had come into fashion in the English Public Schools about 1912. He wore a small moustache. Even in old age, his appearance was noticeably soigné; in his tie, he often wore a pearl pin. He enjoyed the pleasures of the table, and, though not intemperate, was fond of the bottle. Albert was the brother who most nearly resembled him. (LP II: 59)

(5) Richard Lewis (b. 1861), third son of Richard Lewis, obtained a Certificate of Merit from the National School in 1871. He began his working life as a traveller for the tea firm, Richard Twining & Co. of Belfast. On leaving this firm in 1882, he went with his brother William to Glasgow where in 1883 they became partners in the firm W. & R. Lewis, Rope and Twine Manufacturers. In 1890 he married Agnes Young and they had two children, Eileen (b. 1892) and Leonard (b. 1896). 'He was the most transparent of the brothers,' wrote Warnie,

at once the simplest and the most zestful. He shared their mercurial temperament, with the difference that in his case short lived irascibility was substituted for sulkiness. He possessed such a fund of animal spirits, such a gusto in observing and narrating the most homely incidents of life's comedy, such an infectious enjoyment of life that, though neither clever nor genuinely witty, there was something of a tonic effect about his company...He was the perfect 'man in the street', the ideal 'stroller'. To him a crowd was an unfailing lure, to know what 'the stir was about' an imperious necessity. It may safely be premised that the appeal on a blank hoarding, 'Watch this space', was never made to him in vain. He keenly enjoyed comic stories and jokes; the simpler the story, the more he enjoyed it...In his domestic life he was, I think, happy. Children loved him. At the annual family reunions which were held until his father's death, he was the axis round which young and old revolved...In appearance, he was of middle height, stoutly built, with large eyes, extraordinarily sensitive in expressing the mood of the moment: a curved sharp bridge nose surmounted a drooping moustache, which gave a faint but unmistakable suggestion of a seal. (LP II: 60–1)

(6) Albert James Lewis* (1863–1929) who was the father of C. S. Lewis.

MOORE, Edward Francis Courtenay 'Paddy' (1898–1918), was born at 8 Windsor Terrace, Kingstown, County Dublin, Ireland on 17 November 1898, the son of Courtenay Edward Moore and Janie King (Askins) Moore.* When his parents separated, he moved with his mother and his sister Maureen (see Dunbar of Hempriggs, Dame Maureen*), to Bristol where his mother's brother, Dr Robert Askins, was a government medical officer. Paddy was a pupil at Clifton College, Bristol, from 1908 to 1917.

After joining the Officers' Training Corps, he was sent to Keble College, Oxford, for training. Wishing to be with him as long as they could, Mrs Moore and Maureen came to Oxford with him and found rooms in Wellington Square. On reporting to Keble College on 7 June 1917 Paddy found himself sharing a room with C. S. Lewis. They liked one another from the beginning, and Paddy soon introduced Lewis to his mother and sister. In a letter to his father of 10 June 1917 Lewis said, 'Moore of Clifton, my room companion, is a little too childish for real companionship, but I will forgive him much for his appreciation of Newbolt.'

As time went on he began writing about the whole Moore family to his father. 'Moore, my room mate, comes from Clifton and is a very decent sort of man,' he said on 18 June, 'His mother, an Irish lady,' mentioning her for the first time, 'is staying up here and I have met her once or twice.' On 27 August 1917 he wrote to his father about a week of manoeuvres in Warwick. 'The following week,' he said, 'I spent with Moore at the digs of his mother who, as I mentioned, is staying at Oxford. I like her very much and thoroughly enjoyed myself.' From Paddy's point of view, he too had found a friend he liked very much. Lewis invited Paddy to his room in University College (Staircase XII, Room 5). Two photographs of this period, probably taken with Paddy's camera, and reproduced in *All My Road Before Me* show Lewis and Paddy with other OTC cadets on bivouac, and punting on the Cherwell. When all is said, those months of preparing for France were very happy.

On 26 September 1917 they were commissioned 2nd lieutenants and given a month's leave. Rather than go directly home, Lewis went to the Moores' home at 56 Ravenswood Road, Redland, Bristol, where he spent the first three weeks of his leave. Besides his love of the poetry of Sir Henry Newbolt – like himself, an Old Cliftonian – Paddy loved Clifton College, and on Sunday 30 September he took Lewis to see it. It was during these weeks that the young men made a solemn promise to one another. So many officers were being killed at the front – most Oxford colleges lost a quarter of their members in the war – that it was natural for Jack and Paddy to want to make some provision against this. Maureen remembered them promise that if one survived the war he would look after Paddy's mother and Lewis's father.

Jack arrived home on 12 October. On 16 October he was gazetted into the Somerset Light Infantry, and he had to leave his father on 18 October to join his regiment at Crownhill, South Devon. Paddy, meanwhile, had been placed in the 5th Battalion of the Rifle Brigade and he crossed to France in October. Jack was on training in Devon when he wrote to his father on 5 November 1917 saying: 'I have really been very lucky in getting here...Paddy Moore, in the Rifle Brigade, seems to have got in with a most terrible lot of outsiders, so after all our separation was a blessing in disguise. He also seems to be much harder worked than I.'

Paddy, who had been transferred to the 2nd Battalion of the Rifle Brigade, took part in the great German attack which began in the early hours of the morning of 21 March 1918 when General Ludendorff launched the offensive that was intended to bring victory to the German forces on the Western Front. By the end of that day 21,000 British soldiers were taken prisoner, and whole villages had been destroyed. It became worse every minute, and on 24 March the Germans crossed the Somme. The May 1918 issue of *The Cliftonian*, the magazine of Clifton College, contains a letter from the adjutant of Paddy's battalion to Mrs Moore in which he said:

> *Your very gallant son was reported missing on the 24th of last month. He was last seen on the morning of that day with a few men defending a position on a river bank against infinitely superior numbers of the enemy. All the other officers and most of the men of his company have become casualties, and I fear it is impossible to obtain more definite information. He did really fine work on the previous night in beating off a party of Germans who had succeeded in rushing a bridgehead in our lines. We all feel his loss very deeply, and I cannot express too strongly our sympathy with you.*

It was extremely painful for Paddy's family because he was missing for over a month. Then they learned that he had died in battle at Pargny. 'Of all my own particular set at Keble he has been the first to go,' Lewis wrote to his father on 14 May 1918, 'and it is pathetic to remember that he at least was always certain that he would come through.'

William W. Seymour's *History of the Rifle Brigade in the War of 1914–1918*, vol. II (1936) gives a full account of the 2nd Battalion of the Rifle Brigade during the battle in which Paddy played an heroic part and was reported missing.

On 2 December 1918 Paddy was awarded the Military Cross for 'conspicuous gallantry and initiative'. In the *List of Officers and Other Ranks of The Rifle Brigade Awarded Decorations, or Mentioned in Despatches, for Services During the Great War*, compiled by T.R. Eastwood and H.G. Parkyn (1936), the citation (pp. 64–5) reads:

> *Moore, 2nd Lieut. E.F.C. (2nd Bn.) M.C. 2.12.18. For conspicuous gallantry and initiative. When a party of the enemy succeeded in rushing a bridgehead in the dark, their officer, whose company was in support, immediately led forward, under heavy machine-gun fire, a small party to get in touch with the enemy. He did so, and having killed two or three of them returned with information which led to the destruction of them all and the recapture of the bridge. He rendered excellent service.*

Paddy Moore's name is one of the 600 inscribed on the Memorial Gateway of Clifton College, and boys are urged to offer gratitude to these brave men as they pass through. It would have pleased Paddy to see over their names the following lines by Sir Henry Newbolt:

> *From the great Marshal to the last recruit,*
> *These, Clifton, were thy Self, thy Spirit in Deed,*
> *Thy flower of Chivalry, thy fallen fruit,*
> *And thine immortal seed.*

MOORE, Janie King 'Minto' (1872–1951) was born in Pomeroy, County Tyrone, Northern Ireland, on 28 March 1872. She was the eldest of three daughters and two sons of the Rev. William James Askins (1842–95) and Jane King Askins (1846–90) daughter of the Ven. Francis King. The family moved to Dunany, County Louth, Ireland, in 1872 when Mr Askins was Vicar of Dunany and Dunleer from 1872 to 1895. It was at Dunany that Janie grew up. Her brothers and sisters were: Edith 'Edie' Askins (1873–1936), John Hawkins Askins (1877–1923), William James Askins (1879–1955), Robert Askins (1880–1935), and Sarah Askins. Following the death of her mother in 1890 Janie, the eldest of the children, found herself with the task of bringing up the others. Her parents are buried at Dunleer.

On 1 August 1897 she married Courtenay Edward Moore (b. 26 June 1870). He, too, was from a clerical family, his father being Canon Courtenay Moore (1840–1922), rector of Michaelstown in County Cork. Courtenay Edward Moore had taken a BA from Trinity College, Dublin in 1893 and at the time of their marriage he was a civil engineer in Dublin. They had two children, Edward Francis Courtenay 'Paddy'* (b. 1898) and Maureen* (b. 1906). It was an unhappy marriage, and Janie left her husband and moved with the children to Bristol in 1907. Her brother, Robert Askins, a doctor, had his practice there and Paddy became a pupil at Clifton College. Mrs Moore and her husband were never divorced.

In the spring of 1917 Paddy joined the Officers' Training Corps, and in June of that year he was sent to Keble College, Oxford, for training. Mrs Moore and Maureen, wishing to be near him, moved to Oxford and took rooms in Wellington Square. It was probably during the second week of June 1917 that she and Lewis first met. 'I like her immensely,' Lewis wrote to his father on 27 August 1917. It was not long before Lewis came to prefer the company of the Moores to that of his father. After Lewis and Paddy were given a month's leave before embarking overseas, Lewis spent three weeks of it with the Moores at their home in Bristol, and only a week in Belfast with his father. It was during this visit to Bristol that Paddy and Lewis promised that if one or other were spared, the survivor would look after Paddy's mother and Lewis's father.

The young men did not see one another again. In October Paddy was sent to France with the Rifle Brigade, and Lewis followed him over in November with the Somerset Light Infantry. Paddy took part in the great German attack around Pargny which began on 21 March 1918. He fought gallantly and was reported missing on 24 March. His death was confirmed in April, and in December 1918 he was awarded the Military Cross. 'I just lived all my life for my son,' Mrs Moore wrote to Albert Lewis on 1 October 1918, 'and it is hard to go on now. I had built such hopes on my only son, and they are buried with so many others in that wretched Somme...Jack has been so good to me. My poor son asked him to look after me if he did not come back' (LP VI: 44–5).

Before going to France, Lewis had told Arthur Greeves* of his feelings for Mrs Moore, and he later said to him in the letter of 2 February 1918, 'There is room for other things besides love in a man's life.' After Lewis came back from the war and returned to Oxford in January 1919 Mrs Moore took a place there to be near him. From this time onwards they shared a house for the rest of her life. We learn much about their day-today life from Lewis's diary, *All My Road Before Me*, which covers the years 1922–7.

It is not improbable that there was a sexual element to the relationship between Lewis and Mrs Moore before he became a Christian. Be that as it may, what is absolutely certain is that Lewis spent the next 20 years devotedly caring for this ageing and ailing woman.

In her declining years Mrs Moore was often in much pain, and in April 1950 she went into a nursing home in Oxford. She died on 12 January 1951 and is buried in the churchyard of Holy Trinity Church, Headington Quarry. Mr Moore, with whom she was never reconciled, died in Dublin on 9 June 1951.

TOLKIEN, John Ronald Reuel CBE (1892–1973) was born in Bloemfontein, South Africa, to English parents on 3 January 1892. His father, Arthur Reuel Tolkien, who had married Mabel Suffield in 1891, was the manager of the Bank of Africa in Bloemfontein. His brother Hilary Arthur Reuel Tolkien was born on 17 February 1894. Because the intense heat was harming Ronald, Mrs Tolkien returned to England with the boys in 1895 and moved into 5 Gracewell, Sarehole, near Birmingham. Before they could rejoin him in South Africa, Arthur Tolkien died in 1896.

In 1900 Mabel Tolkien, despite family opposition, became a Roman Catholic and began to instruct her sons in the Catholic faith. That same year Ronald went to King Edward's School, Birmingham, where his love of languages blossomed. In 1902 the family moved to 26 Oliver Road, Edgbaston, so that Ronald and his brother could be educated by the priests of Birmingham Oratory at St Philip's School. However, after winning a scholarship, Ronald returned to King Edward's School in 1903.

After her long struggles, Mabel Tolkien died on 14 November 1904. The sacrifice she made to raise her children as Catholics was not lost on Ronald, who later wrote: 'My own mother was a martyr indeed, and it is not to everybody that God grants so easy a way to his great gifts as he did to Hilary and myself, giving us a mother who killed herself with labour and trouble to ensure us keeping the faith.' The boys went to live with their aunt, Beatrice Suffield, in Birmingham.

Tolkien came up to Exeter College, Oxford, in 1911 and read Honour Moderations. For his special subject he chose Comparative Philology and was taught by Joseph Wright. He then read English Language and Literature, taking a First in 1915. It was during these undergraduate years that he developed his interest in painting and drawing. Tolkien was a lieutenant with the Lancashire Fusiliers from 1915 to 1918 and took part in the

Battle of the Somme. While convalescing from an illness he began writing *The Silmarillion*, the myths and legends of what later became known as 'the First Age of the World'.

On 22 March 1916 he married Edith Mary Bratt (1889–1971) and they had four children: John (b. 16 November 1917), Michael (b. 22 October 1920), Christopher (b. 21 November 1924), and Priscilla (b. 18 June 1929). After demobilization from the army in November 1918 Tolkien moved to Oxford where he worked for a while on the Oxford Dictionary. He became a Reader in English Language at the University of Leeds in 1920, and Professor of English Language at Leeds in 1924. In 1925 he returned to Oxford as Rawlinson and Bosworth Professor of Anglo-Saxon. He was elected Merton Professor of English Language and Literature in 1945.

They may have seen one another before, but the first time he and Lewis spoke was at a faculty meeting on 11 May 1926 (*AMR*). The next year Tolkien enrolled Lewis in his Kolbítar or Coalbiters, a society he founded in 1926 for the purposes of reading the Icelandic sagas and myths in the original Old Icelandic or Old Norse. Soon they were meeting regularly, usually on Monday mornings, and this could be taken as the beginnings of The Inklings.

Lewis was converted to Christianity in 1931, and in a letter to Dom Bede Griffiths of 21 December 1941, he spoke of Hugo Dyson* and Tolkien as 'the immediate human carriers' of his conversion. The part these men played in this is explained in detail in the letter to Arthur Greeves* of 18 October 1931, the last letter in this book. Further light is shed on Lewis's conversion and Tolkien's understanding of myth by Tolkien's poem, *Mythopoeia*, found in his *Tree and Leaf*, ed. Christopher Tolkien, (2nd edition: 1988).

Although *The Silmarillion* was in draft form during the 1920s, Tolkien turned from it to *The Hobbit* (1937) which he began in about 1930 to amuse his children. The next work to emerge from the huge mythological world of *The Silmarillion* was *The Lord of the Rings* which he began in 1937. Much of what the Inklings called 'the new Hobbit' was read aloud to them while it was being written. This most famous of all Tolkien's works appeared in three volumes. The first, *The Fellowship of the Ring* came out in 1954, and the other two volumes, *The Two Towers* and *The Return of the King* in 1955. Few works of literature had ever meant so much to Lewis, and Tolkien often mentioned the help he received from Lewis's encouragement.

Tolkien retired in 1959. Mrs Tolkien was by now quite lame from arthritis, and increasingly Tolkien withdrew from the active life of the university to spend more time with her. While the publication of *The*

Lord of the Rings brought fame and wealth, it also brought visitors and an enormous number of fan letters. Still he continued work on *The Silmarillion*, and his publications over the next few years included *The Adventures of Tom Bombadil and other verses from The Red Book* (1962), *Tree and Leaf* (1963), and *Smith of Wootton Major* (1967).

When Lewis died suddenly in November 1963 no one could have been more generous with praise. In a letter to his daughter, Priscilla, of 26 November 1963, he compared the death of Lewis to 'an axe-blow near the roots. Very sad that we should have been so separated in the last years; but our time of close communion endured in memory for both of us. I had a mass said this morning, and was there, and served'.[8] In the letter he wrote to his son Michael, he said: 'We owed a great debt to the other, and that tie with the deep affection that it begot, remains. He was a great man of whom the cold-blooded official obituaries only scraped the surface.'[9]

In 1965 Tolkien learned that an American publisher planned on issuing an unauthorized paperback edition of *The Lord of the Rings*. To remedy the situation Tolkien had to make a number of textual changes in his book so that it would be reprinted as the 'authorized' paperback. In the end he revised both *The Hobbit* and *The Lord of the Rings* and the new editions were published in 1966. In 1968 Tolkien and his wife moved into a bungalow at 19 Lakeside Road, Branksome Park, Poole, which was only a short taxi-ride from the Catholic church and the Miramar, a residential hotel where they often stayed. They were thus able to divide their time between their home and the hotel.

Mrs Tolkien died on 29 November 1971. Following her burial in Oxford, Merton College invited Tolkien to become a resident honorary Fellow, and they gave him a set of rooms in 21 Merton Street. In June 1972 he went to Buckingham Palace to be presented with a CBE by the Queen. Amongst the many honorary degrees conferred on him was an honorary Doctorate of Letters from his own university on 4 June 1972. While in Bournemouth in August 1973 he became ill and he died on 2 September 1973. He and his wife are buried in the Wolvercote Cemetery. For information and photos see Humphrey Carpenter's *J.R.R. Tolkien: A Biography* (1977), and *The Inklings* (1978); *The Tolkien Family Album* (1992) by John and Priscilla Tolkien, and the entry on Christopher Tolkien in *CG* which contains a list of the many works of Tolkien edited by his son.

---

8 *The Letters of J.R.R. Tolkien*, ed. Humphrey Carpenter (1981), p. 341.
9 ibid.

INDEX

INDEX

James, Rev. Sydney Rhodes:
21, 25, 32, 33, 37, 48, 51, 56,
147, 208; *Seventy Years*, 21n
James, William: 440, 711;
*Varieties of Religious
Experience*, 711n
J. and T.M. Greeves, Ltd.: 993
Järnefelt, Armas: *Praeludium*,
38
Jason: 192, 201, 209, 249, 269,
277, 282, 293
Jean de Meun: see Guillaume
de Lorris
Jeans, Sir James: *Mysterious
Universe*, 952
Jeffrey, John: 474n, 477, 483
Jeffrey, Mrs John: 474n, 476,
477, 483
Jekyll, W.: 406n
Jenkin, Alfred Hamilton: 1000
Jenkin, Alfred Kenneth
Hamilton: biography,
1000–2; letters to, 604–5,
613, 652–4, 668–9, 886–7;
men. 525–6, 545–6; *Cornish
Homes and Customs*, 101;
Cornish Miner, 1001;
Cornish Seafarers, 1001;
*Mines and Miners of
Cornwall* 1001; *News from
Cornwall*, 1001; *Story of
Cornwall*, 1000
Jenkin, Amy Louisa: 1000
Jenkin, Elizabeth Lenton:
1001–2
Jenkin, Honor Bronwen
Goldsmid: 1001
Jenkin, Jennifer Hamilton
Heseltine: 1001
Jenkin, Luned Jacob: 668–9,
887, 1001
Jenkin, William: 1001–2
Jenner, Henry: 1002
Jerome, St: 434
Jervis, Edwin Cyril: 32–3
Jesperson, Otto: *Language*,
711
Jesus Christ: 8, 17, 231, 234–5,
242, 271, 309, 397n, 548,
666, 796, 862, 939, 972, 974,
976–7, 989
Jesus College (Cambridge):
512n
Jesus College (Oxford): 32n,
835n
Job, Book of: 333
Joel, Book of: 60
John, St: First Epistle of, 912;

Gospel of, 899; Revelation
of, 121
Johnson, Laurence Bertrand:
341, 365, 388
Johnson, Sergeant-Major R.:
357n
Johnson, Dr Samuel: 185, 262,
320, 327, 353, 454, 464–5,
467, 492, 524, 532, 565, 583,
626, 633, 661n, 666, 687,
706, 730, 827, 875, 909, 923,
1003; *Dictionary*, 772; *Lives
of the English Poets*, 223n,
659n, 721, 772, 773, 912,
918; *Rambler*, 772–3, 909
Jones, Robert Millar: *Royal
Belfast Academical Institu-
tion*, 1003
Jonson, Ben: *Works*, 837n
Jordan (the postman): 27–8
Jormungander: 835
Joseph, Horace William
Brindley: *Introduction to
Logic*, 518
Jowett, Benjamin: 329, 430,
641, 644; 'Interpretation of
Scripture', 329n
Joy ('It'): 821n, 832, 877, 906,
911–12, 971
Joyce, Michael: 878n
Jubinal, Achille: 754

Kalevala: 222, 228, 232, 235,
476
Kant, Immanuel: 625n, 634,
685, 931
Keats, John: 98, 171, 288, 290,
303, 310, 628, 949;
Endymion, 220, 499, 933; *Eve
of St Agnes*, 220, 466; *Fall of
Hyperion*, 544; 'To one who
has been long', 385
Keble College (Oxford):
letters from, 316–22, 325–7,
329–30, 334–6; men. 315,
369, 416, 436, 986, 1018,
1021
Keefe, Carolyn: (ed.) *C. S.
Lewis: Speaker and Teacher*,
430n, 511n
Keir, David Lindsay: 902
Kelmscott (Oxfordshire): 559
Kelmscott Press: 287, 384,
386, 559
Keown, Henry: 812n
Keown, Richard: 812n
Keown, Sarah: 812n

Keown, Sarah Jane Lewis
('Jeannie'): 812–13, 1015
Keown, Thomas: 812n
Keown, Thomas Heron:
812–13, 1015
Ker, Neil Ripley: 837;
*Catalogue of Manuscripts
containing Anglo-Saxon*,
837n; *Medieval Manuscripts*,
837n
Ker, William Paton: 554,
556–7
Keyes, Sir Roger: 553–4
Kidlington (Oxfordshire):
861n
Kildare (Co. Kildare): 34n
Kilkenny (Co. Kilkenny): 996
Killyleath (Co. Down): 996
Kilmore (Co. Cavan): 120n
Kilmore Cathedral
(Co. Cavan): 960n
Kilns, The: letters from,
942–63, 965, 967–77; men.
921, 927, 936, 940, 941,
963–4, 995, 1012–14
King, Ven. Francis: 1020
King, James: 747n
King Arthur Hotel (Tintagel):
581–2
King Edward VI School
(Birmingham): 1022
King Edward VII School
(Sheffield): 448n
Kinglake, Alexander William:
Eóthen, 630, 631, 733–4
King's College (Cambridge):
317, 318n, 319, 512, 722
Kingsley, Charles:
Water-Babies, 901; *Westward
Ho!*, 184
Kings 2, Book of: 214, 498
Kingsmill, Hugh: *Matthew
Arnold*, 784n
King's Own Scottish
Borderers: 328
King's School (Taunton): 19n
Kingstown (Co. Dublin): 1018
Kinsdale (Co. Cork): 990
Kinver (Staffordshire): 19n
Kipling, Rudyard: 26, 149–50,
413, 414, 432, 639; *Barrack-
Room Ballads*, 149, 233, 237;
'British Roman Song', 130;
'Brushwood Boy', 149; *Day's
Work*, 149; Dedication Poem
to Wolcott Balestier, 233,
237; 'First Chantey', 149; 'For
All We Have and Are', 149;

INDEX

INDEX

INDEX

INDEX

INDEX